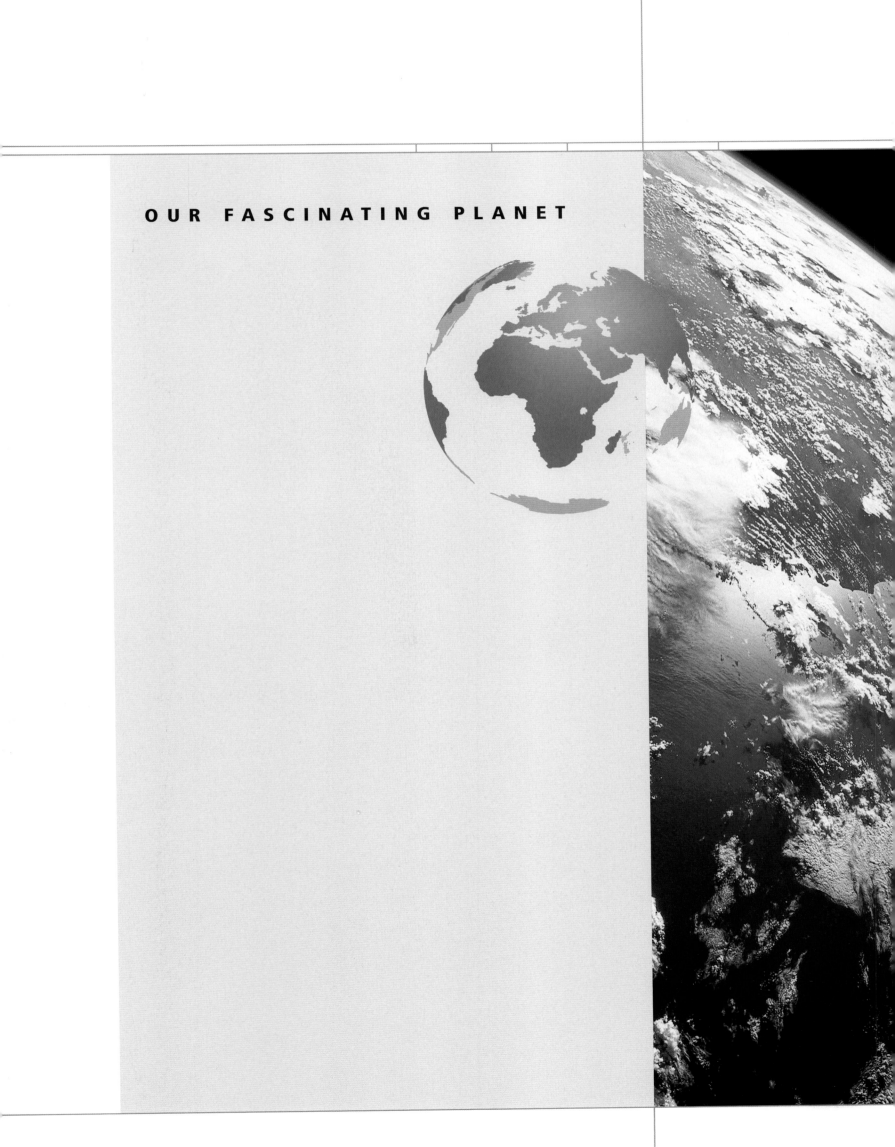

OUR FASCINATING PLANET

The power of wind and water erosion shaped the beautiful landscapes of the Colorado Plateau – including the sandstone arches in Arches National Park.

FAMILY WORLD ATLAS

"I wish to be a citizen of the world, at home everywhere...and everywhere a traveller."

This thoroughly modern idea was actually expressed in the early 16th century by humanist, thinker and theologian Erasmus of Rotterdam, in an age when the world was "opening up": an age of discoveries and conquests, of truly great adventures.

In recent centuries, scientists and explorers have discovered every "terra incognita" and now use satellites to survey and photograph the Earth with incredible accuracy. Our planet, however, still offers countless surprises, adventures and exotic wonders: the vastness of Asia, the isolated islands of the Pacific, the dense rain forests of Africa, Alaska's wilderness, ancient villages in Europe and the summits of the Andes. Presenting all of these, and the many other fascinating places on our planet, is a difficult but rewarding task.

"A journey of a thousand miles begins with the very first step" – Lao-tzu (Chinese philosopher, 4th century BC).

And now we can begin our journey with the new Family World Atlas. The ground-breaking concept of this atlas serves several functions: the first is to offer basic geographical knowledge of our planet with detailed and clear cartography. It also functions as a comprehensive travel guide in which more than 17,000 fascinating attractions are highlighted – including landscapes, national parks, cities, cultural attractions, monuments, holiday destinations and travel routes. These sites are presented through a new system of pictograms, developed specifically for this book. The atlas cartography is complemented by an extensive and richly illustrated country encyclopedia which provides key geographical, political and economic facts and figures.

It is our hope that the Family World Atlas will inspire in our readers the feeling that they are "citizens of the world" and serve as a "first step" on a fascinating journey of discovery to the countless wonders of the planet we call home. This atlas should deepen our understanding of our Earth and its multifaceted splendour, and awaken our curiosity, tolerance and feelings of responsibility towards one another as inhabitants of this planet.

In the words of the famed Indian poet Rabindranath Tagore: "We live in this world as long as we love it".

The Publisher

Table of Contents

Islamic heritage in southern Spain: La Mezquita cathedral, once the Great Mosque of Córdoba, is a beautiful example of Moorish architecture with large chambers and splendid facades.

Beautiful landscapes on the Li River: The green, craggy mountains around the city of Guilin are located in one of China's most scenic regions.

Table of Contents

Marrakech (Morocco): Djemâa el-Fna square, located near the Koutoubia mosque, is a lively meeting place for vendors, street artists, traditional storytellers, and tourists.

Wet Tropics National Park in northeastern Australia features fascinating flora and fauna as well as beautiful landscapes such as Milla Falls.

Map locator

Europe

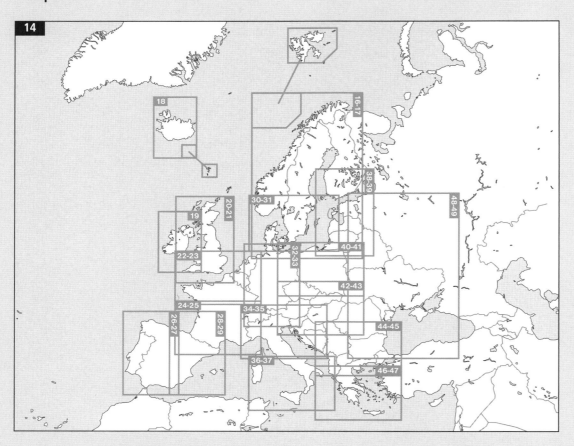

Southeastern Asia, Australia/Oceania

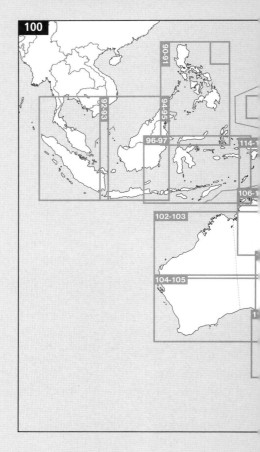

Near and Middle East, Northern Asia, Central Asia, Southern Asia

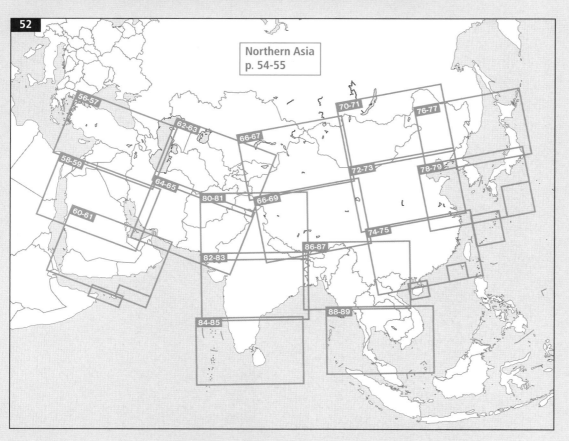

Africa

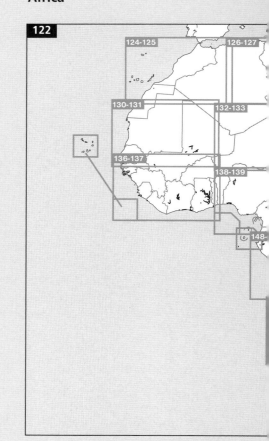

The impressive modern skyline of Chicago, along the shores of Lake Michigan. The city is a leading commercial and financial center.

Easter Island was once home to an advanced civilization. The more than 300 stone sculptures (moai) scattered around the island are the most important remnants of this culture.

North and Central America

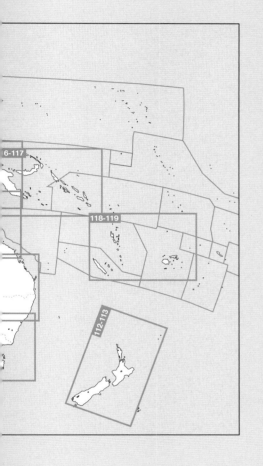

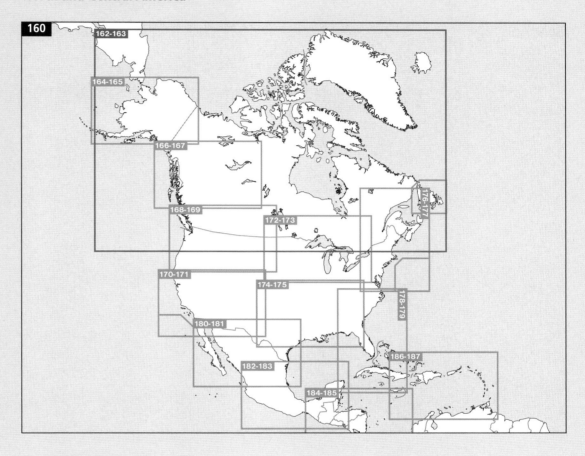

South America

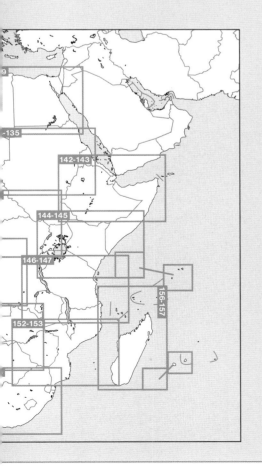

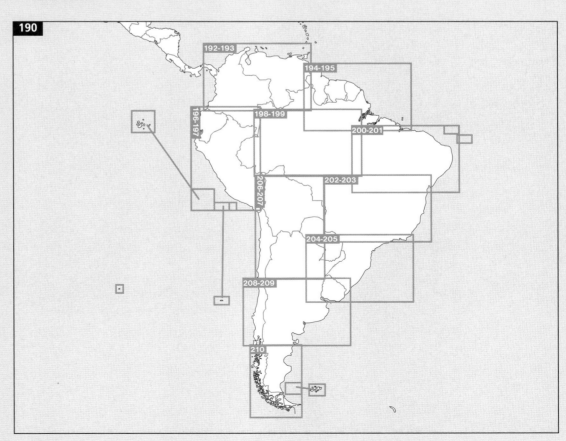

Legend · Natural geographical features

The Polynesian island of Moorea is the remnant of a massive volcano. The island, like so many in the Pacific Ocean, is surrounded by coral reefs.

The Scottish Highlands in the United Kingdom feature a variety of romantic and beautiful landscapes, including craggy mountains, pristine lakes, and rugged valleys.

Bodies of Water

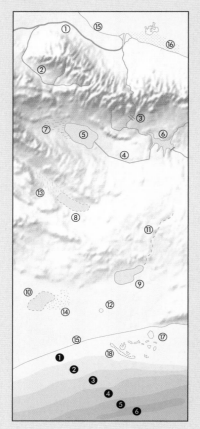

1. Stream, river
2. Tributary with headstreams
3. Waterfall, rapids
4. Canal
5. Lake
6. Reservoir with dam
7. Marsh, moor
8. Intermittent lake
9. Salt lake
10. Intermittent salt lake
11. Intermittent river (wadi)
12. Well, spring
13. Salt swamp
14. Salt pan
15. Shoreline
16. Mud flats
17. Island, archipelago
18. Coral reef

Depth tints

1. 0 – 200 meters
2. 200 – 2000 meters
3. 2000 – 4000 meters
4. 4000 – 6000 meters
5. 6000 – 8000 meters
6. below 8000 meters

Topography

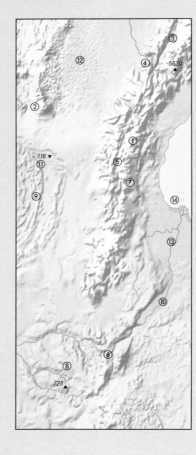

1. High mountain region
2. Volcano
3. V-shaped valley
4. Gorge
5. U-shaped valley
6. Canyon
7. Glacier
8. Highland with valleys
9. Escarpment
10. Rift Valley
11. Depression
12. High dunes in arid areas
13. Lowland
14. Delta

Color tints of climate and vegetation zones

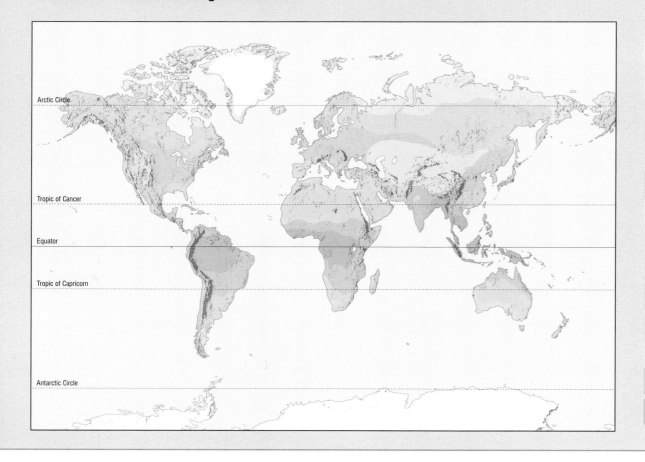

Polar and subpolar zone

Perpetual frost, all months below 0° C (32° F)

Arctic flora and Tundra (lichens, mosses, grasses, dwarf shrubs)

Boreal zone

Taiga, northern coniferous trees; pines, firs, larches, spruces

Temperate zones

Rainy climates with mild winters; deciduous broadleaf forests, mixed forests

Winter-cold desert and semidesert climates; steppe, prairie, grasslands, semideserts

Subtropics

Mediterranean climate with dry summers and moist winters; broadleaved evergreen forests

Warm, summer-humid moist climate; subtropical forests

Desert and semidesert climates; open shrub lands

Tropics

Humid and dry savannahs with dry seasons; woody savannahs

Tropical rainforest, rainy climate with no winter; high temperatures

Manmade geographical features · **Legend**

Beijing's historic Forbidden City was the main residence of China's monarchs and the great imperial court for many centuries.

A full moon above the skyline of San Francisco in northern California. The city's beautiful Golden Gate Bridge is one of the world's longest suspension bridges.

Settlements and transportation routes

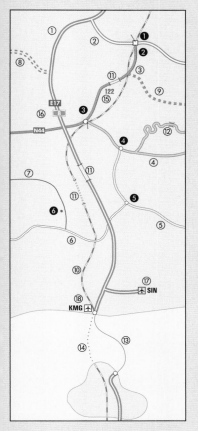

Transportation routes

① Interstate highway/motorway
② Multilane divided highway
③ Primary highway
④ Secondary highway
⑤ Main road
⑥ Secondary road
⑦ Unimproved road
⑧ Interstate highway/motorway under construction
⑨ Primary highway under construction
⑩ Railroad
⑪ Tunnel
⑫ Pass with elevation in meters
⑬ Ferry, shipping route
⑭ Railroad ferry
⑮ Distances in kilometers (in miles within USA and UK)
⑯ Road numbers
⑰ International Airport with IATA-code
⑱ Airport with IATA-code

Settlements

❶ Urban area
❷ City, over 1 million inhabitants
❸ City, 100,000 – 1 million inhabitants
❹ Town, 10,000 – 100,000 inhabitants
❺ Town, under 10,000 inhabitants
❻ Hamlet, research station

Political and other boundaries

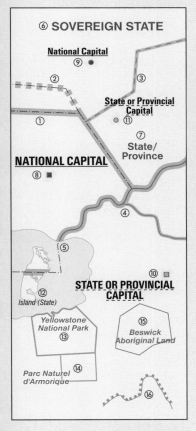

① International boundary
② Disputed international boundary
③ Administrative boundary
④ Boundary on rivers
⑤ Boundary in lake or sea
⑥ Country name
⑦ Administrative name
⑧ Capital with more than 1 million inhabitants
⑨ Capital below 1 million inhabitants
⑩ Administrative capital with more than 1 million inhabitants
⑪ Administrative capital with less than 1 million inhabitants
⑫ Dependent territory with administering country
⑬ National parks and biosphere reserves
⑭ Nature parks and other protected areas
⑮ Reservation
⑯ Walls (Great Wall of China, Hadrian's Wall)

Typefaces of cities and towns

① □ **NEW YORK**
② ○ **Stuttgart**
③ ○ Narvik
④ ○ Porta Westfalica
⑤ ○ Storuman
⑥ ○ White Owl
⑦ • Glenayle
⑧ □ **BEIJING (PEKING)**
⑨ ○ **Firenze (Florence)**
⑩ Tikal
⑪ Grand Canyon du Verdon

① City, over 1 million inhabitants
② City, 100,000 – 1 million inhabitants
③ Significant city, 10,000 – 100,000 inhabitants
④ City, 10,000 – 100,000 inhabitants
⑤ Significant town, under 10,000 inhabitants
⑥ Town, under 10,000 inhabitants
⑦ Hamlet, research station
⑧ City, over 1 million inhabitants with translation
⑨ Town 100,000 – 1 million inhabitants with translation
⑩ Point of cultural interest
⑪ Point of natural interest

Typefaces of topographic features

① *PACIFIC OCEAN*
② *GULF OF MEXICO*
   Gulf of Thailand
③ *Antalya Körfezi*
④ *Elbe   Rio Grande   Murray*
⑤ *White Nile   Suez Canal*
⑥ *HIMALAYA*
⑦ *Great Plains*
⑧ Mt. Olympus ▲ 2424
⑨ – 116 ▼ *Danakil Depression*
⑩ *Tahiti*
⑪ *Cape of Good Hope*
⑫ <u>325</u>
⑬ 5425
⑭ *Mexican Basin*
⑮ *Mariana Trench*

① Ocean
② Gulf, bay
③ Small bay, strait
④ River, lake, canal
⑤ River, lake, canal (translated)
⑥ Mountain name
⑦ Area name, landscape name
⑧ Mountain name with elevation above sea level in meters
⑨ Depression with depth below sea level in meters
⑩ Island name
⑪ Cape name
⑫ Elevation of lake above sea level
⑬ Depth in oceans and lakes
⑭ Undersea landscapes, mountains and trenches
⑮ Deepsea trench

Text labels within the political boundaries map: ⑥ SOVEREIGN STATE, National Capital, State or Provincial Capital, State/Province, NATIONAL CAPITAL, STATE OR PROVINCIAL CAPITAL, Island (State), Yellowstone National Park, Beswick Aboriginal Land, Parc Naturel d'Armorique

Explanation of symbols

Principal travel routes

Remarkable landscapes and natural monuments

Beautiful natural landscapes, fascinating wildlife, historic architecture, and vibrant cities – our world is rich in wonders. The modern cartography and layout of the Family World Travel Atlas highlight many of the world's attractions – unspoiled wilderness areas, the most famous and significant historic sites, culturally diverse urban areas, holiday resorts, and sporting venues. The system of pictograms developed specifically for this atlas gives the reader a clear impression of the diverse attractions in the world's regions. All of the pictograms featured on each map are listed and labeled in a legend at the bottom of the respective page.

The following pages offer brief characterizations of the various pictograms used in the atlas. The pictograms are divided by color into two groups: green and blue pictograms represent natural attractions, while yellow pictograms represent cultural attractions and other manmade sites. The names of significant towns and cities are highlighted in yellow throughout the atlas. Blue pictograms represent sporting and recreational facilities. Important and well-known transportation routes, including highways and shipping routes, are also featured in the atlas. These routes are not only highlighted by pictograms but also by distinctly colored lines that identify each type of route.

Auto route
The maps display many of the world's most famous and historically significant roads and routes, such as the ancient Silk Road in Asia and historic Route 66 in the United States, The maps also feature important modern highways, including the Pan-American Highway that stretches through the Americas from Alaska to Tierra del Fuego, the highway stretching between Bangkok in Thailand and Singapore, and the Stuart Highway, which traverses the fascinating landscapes in Australia's sparsely populated interior.

Railroad
The age of the railroads started in 1804 when the world's first steam locomotive began operation in Wales. By the end of the 19th century it was possible to travel through most regions of Europe and North America and much of Asia and South America by train. The Orient Express, Europe's first long-distance luxury passenger line, began operation in 1883 and traveled between Paris. Bucharest, and Istanbul. The Trans-Siberian line was constructed between 1891 and 1916 with the goal of connecting Siberia to European Russia. The Trans-Siberian still runs between Moscow and Vladivostok on the Pacific Ocean almost 100 years after construction ended.

High speed train
The Eurostar trains travel at speeds up to 300 kilometers an hour and transport passengers between London and Brussels or Paris in less than three hours. Japan's Shinkansen line, also known as the "bullet train", connects several of the country's major cities. In Europe, France and Germany maintain the most extensive networks of high speed trains.

Shipping route
Millions of passengers travel on cruise ships every year and experience one of the most leisurely and comfortable forms of long-distance travel. Thousands of cruise ships traverse the oceans, seas, and rivers of the world. The Caribbean Sea, Mediterranean Sea, Scandinavia, and Alaska are among the most popular locations for cruises on the open seas. Modern cruise ships offer an astounding variety of attractions including casinos, entertainment, fine restaurants, and shops.

UNESCO World (Natural) Heritage
Since 1972, UNESCO, a body of the United Nations, has compiled a growing list of specially designated natural attractions and wonders that are deemed to be of outstanding importance and "universal" significance.

Mountain landscape
Mountain ranges are among the most scenic areas in the world. Many of the world's ancient low-mountain ranges, including the Appalachians and the Central Massif, feature heavily eroded and rounded peaks. Other, younger mountain ranges feature jagged and high peaks that are often covered by snow and glaciers.

Rock landscape
Many of the world's most interesting stone formations were shaped by wind and water erosion, including the natural attractions of Monument Valley National Park in the USA.

Ravine/canyon
Canyons and gorges are narrow and often deep valleys created by river and wind erosion. The Grand Canyon, in the American state of Arizona, is the most famous and one of the most spectacular canyons on the planet.

Extinct volcano
Volcanoes are formed when solid, liquid, or gas-like materials from the Earth's interior rise to the planet's surface. Magma passes through the structure of a volcano and leaves its crater as lava, often accompanied by plumes of hot ash. An extinct volcano is a volcano that has not experienced an eruption in the last 10,000 years.

Active volcano
Geologists consider any volcano that has erupted in the last 10,000 years to be an active volcano. Most of the world's active volcanoes are concentrated in geologically active regions, such as areas near the boundaries of the world's tectonic plates or mid-ocean ridges. The Pacific Ring of Fire is an area of relatively frequent volcanic activity.

Geyser
Active geysers are hot springs that occasionally release plumes of water into the air. Geysers are located in volcanically active regions.

Cave
Caves are formed during the creation of stone formations (mountains, underground layers of stone, etc.) or emerge later due to the eroding effects of water that seeps into stone and often carves out entire networks of large caves containing lakes and rivers.

Glacier
Glaciers are large fields or rivers of ice that often migrate through mountain valleys. Glaciers are formed above the snow line in mountainous areas such as the Alps or in regions with cold climates such as Alaska, northern Canada, and Greenland.

River landscape
The eroding power of flowing water formed many of the world's valleys and canyons. Many of the world's early civilizations emerged in fertile river valleys such as Mesopotamia or the Indus Valley. Many rivers in lowland areas have large branching deltas containing delicate ecosystems.

Waterfall/rapids
Waterfalls are formed when rivers flow over an area with a sudden drop in elevation. They come in a variety of heights and lengths. Waterfalls are among the most stunning natural attractions on the planet.

Lake country
Most of the world's major lakes were created by glaciers during the ice ages. Several regions have a large number of lakes, often interconnected and located near one another. In addition to glacial lakes, many lakes were created as a result of tectonic and geological activity.

Desert
Vast landscapes covered by sand dunes, sand fields, or stone with sparse rainfall, deserts are the most arid regions on the earth and only a few types of plants and animals can survive in these harsh environments. Most deserts have major differences between night and daytime temperatures. Most of the world's deserts remain sparsely populated.

Oasis
Oases are fertile islands surrounded by barren, arid deserts or steppes. They are supplied with water by rivers, springs or subterranean ground-water repositories.

Depression
Depressions are small basins located on land but at significant depths below sea level. Many depressions – including the Dead Sea – were created through tectonic activity.

Explanation of symbols

Remarkable cities and cultural monuments

Fossil site
Fossils are the ancient remnants and traces of animals and plants that have inhabited our planet during its long history.

Nature park
Conservation areas have been created to protect local flora and fauna. Most designated nature parks tend to be relatively small in size.

National park (landscape)
These large conservation areas protect areas of natural beauty and significant national or international importance. Development and industry are forbidden or heavily restricted in such area. Yellowstone National Park, in the US-State of Wyoming, is the world's oldest national park.

National park (flora)
This symbol designates national parks with interesting local flora.

National park (fauna)
This symbol designates national parks with unique local wildlife.

National park (culture)
National park with cultural attractions such as Native American historic sites.

Biosphere reserve
This symbol points out undeveloped conservation areas with pristine examples of distinct climate or vegetation zones. Many biosphere reserves exhibit high levels of biodiversity.

Wildlife reserve
These conservation areas have been created for the protection of endangered animals. Selous Game Reserve in Tanzania is home to herds of African elephants.

Whale watching
Boat tours providing the chance to observe whales or dolphins in their natural habitats.

Turtle conservation area
Several countries in the world have specially designated coastal areas where endangered sea turtle species live or lay their eggs.

Protected area for sea lions/seals
Some countries have coastal areas that have designated conservation sites to preserve the natural habitats of endangered seals and sea lions.

Protected area for penguins
These protected areas were created to preserve threatened penguin colonies and to observe these creatures in their habitats.

Zoo/safari park
Zoos are park-like areas that feature collections of animals, mostly from a variety of regions. Safari parks are large properties open to tourists that feature wildlife in open wilderness.

Crocodile farm
Most crocodile farms are commercial operations where the animals are bred. Many are open to the public.

Coastal landscape
Coastal areas often feature diverse landscapes including beaches, cliffs, tidal flats, and marshlands. Some coastal areas are flat with sand dunes, while others are lined by rock formations, stony beaches, and high cliffs. The beautiful fjords of Scandinavia are among the most stunning coastal areas in the world.

Beach
Beaches often offer diverse recreational activities. Sand beaches are common in flat areas. Many of the world's beaches are now heavily developed.

Coral reef
Coral reefs are formed by small animals called coral in warm saltwater. Many of the world's large coral reefs exhibit astonishing biodiversity and are accessible to divers. The world's largest coral reef is the Great Barrier Reef off the coast of Australia.

Island
Islands are land masses surrounded by water. Most islands are part of island groups. The islands on our planet have a combined land area of 10.5 million km². Many of the world's islands have become popular tourist destinations.

Underwater reserve
Underwater conservation areas have been created to protect local marine flora and fauna.

UNESCO World (Cultural) Heritage
Since 1972, UNESCO has compiled a list of specially designated cultural sites that are deemed to be of outstanding importance. The list now includes hundreds of cultural and historic sites around the world.

Remarkable city
Large and small cities of global importance or with an abundance of tourist attractions are highlighted in yellow on our maps.

Pre- and early history
Sites related to ancient human cultures and their ways of life during times before the emergence of written records. The most grandiose pre-historic sites include large megaliths created by different cultures, such as the circle of stone pillars at Stonehenge in the United Kingdom.

Prehistoric rockscape
Prehistoric paintings, carvings and reliefs created by nomadic peoples during ancient times. Such sites have been found on all of the world's inhabited continents and often provide scientists with valuable information about life in the times before the first civilizations emerged on our planet.

The Ancient Orient
Sites related to the ancient cultures that developed in the region comprising modern Anatolia (Asia Minor), Syria, Iraq, Israel, Lebanon, Iran, and in some cases Egypt, during the period between 7000 BC and the time of Alexander the Great (400 BC). The Sumerians developed one of the first urban civilizations on the planet. They also developed one of the first number systems. After 2000 BC, the first large empires emerged in the region including the kingdoms of the Babylonians, Assyrians, and Hittites. The region features temples, ziggurats, and palaces from ancient times.

Ancient Egypt
One of the greatest ancient civilizations developed on the banks of the Nile River in Egypt. Around 3000 BC, Egypt was unified under the reign of one ruler for the first time. Between this time and the period of Alexander the Great's conquests, Egypt was ruled by more than 31 dynasties. The all-powerful pharaohs were considered living gods in Ancient Egypt. The ancient Egyptians developed a writing system, a calendar, and eventually advanced building techniques. The greatest legacy of this fascinating culture is the spectacular pyramids. The arts of the ancient Egyptians were devoted primarily to religion and mythology.

Ancient Egyptian pyramids
The monumental pyramid tombs of Egyptian pharaohs were constructed during the Old Kingdom. The largest and most impressive pyramid is the 137-meter-high Great (Cheops) Pyramid at Giza.

Minoan culture
The advanced Bronze-Age culture of the Minoans flourished on the island Crete during ancient times. Minoan civilization first emerged during the 3rd millennium BC, after which the Minoans rapidly became the dominant power in the eastern Mediterranean. Modern Crete features the remnants of Minoan villas with impressive frescoes and interior design.

Phoenician culture
During ancient times the area encompassing modern Israel, Lebanon, and Palestine was once the center of Phoenician culture. The Phoenicians were the dominant trading power in the Mediterranean for several centuries and founded many colonies.

Early African culture
Ancient African civilizations include the cultures of the Kingdom of Ghana, Axum (Ethiopia), the Great Zimbabwe culture, and Kush, a complex and advanced society that developed south of Egypt.

Etruscan culture
The Etruscans probably originated in central Italy. During the 10th century BC, they conquered large sections of the Italian Peninsula before they were conquered by the Romans. Italy has numerous archeological and historic sites related to the culture of the ancient Etruscans.

Greek antiquity
No other civilization has had a greater influence on European culture than that of Ancient Greece. The city-state of Athens was one of the first basic democracies in history. The art, philosophy and architecture of Ancient Greece continue to inspire and shape our modern world. Ancient Greece was divided into city-states, many of which founded distant colonies in Southern Europe, the Middle East, and North Africa. Ancient Greek art dealt mostly with subjects related to Greek mythology. The Greek city-states constructed many great structures including impressive temples and amphitheaters. During the Hellenistic period – after the death of Alexander the Great – Greek-speaking cities outside the mainland, including Alexandria in Egypt, replaced the city-states as the centers of Greek civilization.

Explanation of symbols

Sunset above the Pyramids of Giza: the enormous pyramids were constructed as monumental tombs during the reign of ancient Egypt's pharaohs.

Borobudur: the Buddhist complex in Indonesia features numerous sculptures and reliefs. The site was buried beneath volcanic ash for centuries until it was rediscovered in the 19th century.

Remarkable cities and cultural monuments

Roman antiquity
Over a period of centuries the once small city of Rome emerged as the center of a powerful empire. The Roman Empire was at its largest under the reign of the Emperor Trajan (98–117 BC); during this period its borders extended from North Africa to Scotland and from Iberia to Mesopotamia. The Roman state that existed between 509 and 27 BC is referred to as the Roman Republic. The Roman state that was created after the reforms of Caesar Augustus is known as the Roman Empire. Roman art and culture was greatly influenced by Ancient Greek and other Mediterranean cultures. The Romans constructed impressive structures including amphitheaters, temples, and aqueducts.

Nabatean culture
The ancient city of Petra (in modern Jordan) was first settled by the Nabateans in the fifth century BC. By the 1st century BC, the Nabateans ruled a powerful trading empire. The monumental ruins of Petra are the greatest remnant of this ancient culture.

Vikings
Between the 9th and 11th centuries, Scandinavian Vikings conquered territories throughout Europe. During their centuries of conquest, the Vikings founded numerous settlements and trading posts in Russia, Western Europe, and in the British Isles.

Ancient India
India has a wealth of cultural and historic attractions. The Indus Valley civilization (2600–1400 BC) was one of the first urbanized civilizations to emerge on the planet. Indian culture reached one of its high points during the period between the 7th and 13th centuries. Many of India's greatest Buddhist and Hindu architectural masterpieces, as well as artworks, were created during these centuries. During the Mogul era (16th and 17th century), many impressive works of Islamic architecture were created throughout the country, including modern India's most famous structure, the Taj Mahal.

Ancient China
The oldest remnants of early Chinese culture date from the era between 5000–2000 BC. The Shang dynasty (1600–1000 BC) was the most influential and advanced bronze-age culture in China. Daoism and Confucian philosophy were both developed in China during the 5th century BC. The first great unified Chinese Empire was forged around 220 BC by Ying Zheng, the king of Qin. After the emergence of the first Chinese Empire, China was ruled by various dynasties and experienced many periods of cultural and technological advancement. The country's most impressive historic sites include the Great Wall of China, the tomb of Emperor Qin with its army of terracotta warriors in Xi'an, and the Forbidden City in the capital city Beijing.

Ancient Japan
The Yamato period of Japanese history began around AD 400. During this period, the country was ruled by an imperial court in Nara. During the 5th century the Japanese adopted the Chinese writing system and in the 6th century Buddhism arrived in Japan. The Fujiwara clan dominated the country for more than 500 years starting in the 7th century. During this period the country's imperial capital was moved from Nara to Kyoto. Between 1192 and 1868, Japan was ruled by a series of shoguns (military rulers). The Meiji Era (1868–1912) saw the restoration of imperial power and the emergence of modern Japan.

Mayan culture
The Maya are an Amerindian people in southern Mexico and Central America. During pre-Colombian times, the Maya developed an advanced and powerful civilization that ruled over a vast territory. Mayan civilization reached its cultural and technological peak around AD 300 and was eventually devastated by the arrival of the Spanish in the 16th century. Central America and Mexico have many impressive Mayan ruins.

Inca culture
The Inca culture emerged around Cusco during the 12th century. By the 15th century, the Inca ruled a vast empire that encompassed parts of modern Peru, Bolivia, Ecuador, Chile, and Argentina. Although their empire was shortlived, the Inca left behind impressive stone monuments and structures throughout western South America. The Inca city of Machu Picchu in Peru is one of the most impressive historic sites in South America.

Aztec culture
At some point during the second millennium BC, the Aztec people migrated into Mexico, where they eventually established a powerful empire. The Aztec capital, Tenochtitlan (modern Mexico City), was founded in 1325 and was once one of the world's largest cities. The Aztecs constructed many grand temples and pyramids throughout their empire and made important cultural advances, including the creation of a writing system and calendar. Central Mexico has numerous Aztec cultural sites.

Other ancient American cultures
Advanced Amerindian cultures appeared in both North America and the Andean regions of South America. Countless Amerindian historic sites, including the remnants of ancient settlements, can be found throughout the Americas.

Places of Jewish cultural interest
Judaism is the oldest of the world's major monotheist religions. The Jerusalem temple was a great achievement of early Jewish culture – now only a section of its walls remain (the Western Wall). Historic synagogues can be found throughout the world, a legacy of the Jewish Diaspora.

Places of Christian cultural interest
Christianity is the world's most practiced and widespread religion. Christianity is based on the teachings in the old and new testaments of the Bible, and emerged in western Asia during the first century AD. Christian religious sites, including churches, cathedrals, and monasteries, can be found in most regions of the world.

Places of Islamic cultural interest
Islam, one of the world's major religions, was founded by Mohammed (AD 570–632). The teachings of the Quran (Koran) are its basis. Muslims around the world pray in the direction of Mecca in Saudi Arabia, Islam's holiest city.

Places of Buddhist cultural interest
Buddhism is based on the teachings of Siddhartha Gautama (around 560–480 BC), also known as the Buddha. Most of the world's Buddhists live in East Asia. Important Buddhist sites include temples, pagodas, stupas, and monasteries.

Places of Hindu cultural interest
Most of the at least one billion followers of Hinduism, one of the world's most practiced religions, live on the Indian subcontinent. Hinduism encompasses a variety of beliefs and practices, many of which are thousands of years old.

Places of Jainist cultural interest
Most followers of Jainism live in India. It is based on the teachings of Mahavira, who lived in the 5th century BC. Jainist sites include temples and monasteries.

Places of Sikh cultural interest
The Sikh religious philosophy emerged in 16th-century northern India, as an attempt to merge the teachings of Islam and Hinduism. The "Golden Temple" in Amritsar is the most important Sikh religious center.

Places of Shinto cultural interest
Shinto, the indigenous religion of Japan, is based on the reverence of kami (nature spirits) and ancestral spirits. Historic Shinto shrines can be seen throughout Japan.

Sites of interest to other religions
Sites related to other religious and spiritual communities.

Places of cultural interest to indigenous peoples (native peoples)
Sites related to the culture or history of indigenous peoples around the world.

Aborigine land reserves
The almost 500,000 Aborigines form only a small portion of Australia's population. Many Aborigine communities administer large land reserves.

Places of Aboriginal cultural interest
Cultural sites of the Aborigines, including rock paintings, are among the interesting attractions in Australia.

Native American reservation
Most of the Native American reservations in North America were founded during the 19th century. Despite the history of low living standards on some reservations, many Native American communities have successfully protected their traditions.

Pueblo Indian culture
The Pueblo Indians are a group of Native American communities who have lived in the southwestern United States for centuries. Their traditional settlements – known as pueblos – consist of adobe buildings.

Places of Amerindian cultural interest
The different regions of North America feature hundreds of sites related to the history and cultures of Native Americans.

Amazonian Amerindians/ protected area
Land reserves have been created to protect the Amerindian cultures in the Amazon basin in South America.

Explanation of symbols

Spanish settlers built Nuestra Senora church in Cholula, Mexico atop a series of ancient Amerindian pyramids. The historic church lies close to the snow-capped volcano Popocatepetl.

Las Vegas, the largest city in the American state of Nevada, is a popular tourist destination with numerous casinos, theme hotels, and amusement parks.

Sport and leisure destinations

Cultural landscape
Areas with landscapes that have been shaped by human settlement or cultivation.

Historical cities and towns
Historic cities and towns with well-preserved architectural attractions.

Impressive skyline
Cities featuring modern skylines, such as New York City, Chicago, and Hong Kong.

Castle/fortress/fort
Europe features the greatest concentration of these structures.

Caravansary
Historic inns along the ancient caravan routes of the Middle East, Central Asia, and North Africa.

Palace
Grand castles and palaces that once housed nobility and royalty can be found in many different regions.

Technical/industrial monument
Man-made attractions related to the achievements of industrialization and modern times.

Dam
The largest and most important dams and retaining walls on the planet.

Remarkable lighthouse
Many coastal areas feature beautiful or historic lighthouses.

Remarkable bridge
Many of the world's great bridges are considered engineering marvels.

Tomb/grave
Mausoleums, monuments, burial mounds, and other grave sites.

Theater of war/battlefield
Site where important battles occurred, including Waterloo in Belgium.

Monument
Sites dedicated to historic figures and important historical events.

Memorial
Site dedicated to the victims of wars and genocides.

Space mission launch site
Landing and launch sites of manned and unmanned space missions.

Space telescope
Radio, X-ray, and gamma-ray telescopes are important tools of modern astronomy.

Market
Important markets where people gather to trade and purchase goods.

Festivals
Large celebrations of music and culture including Rio de Janeiro's Carnaval.

Museum
Important collections of man-made works (art, technology, anthropology) and natural relics.

Theater
Famous theaters presenting opera, musicals, and other productions.

World exhibition
Cities that have hosted world expositions, including London in the United Kingdom.

Olympics
Cities and towns that have hosted the modern summer or winter Olympic Games.

Arena/stadium
The largest and most famous sporting venues in the world – including stadiums for football (soccer), baseball, rugby, hockey, and other popular sports.

Race track
Auto and motorbike racing are popular sports in many of the world's regions. The atlas highlights many of the most famous autoracing venues, including Formula 1 and NASCAR race tracks in Indianapolis, Melbourne, and numerous other cities.

Golf
Golf has become an increasingly popular sport around the world in recent years. The atlas highlights several of the most famous and beautiful golf courses as well as areas that host important golf tournaments.

Horse racing
Horse racing has a long history in many regions. Several well-known race tracks and events are highlighted in the book, including the Ascot racecourse in England, a major event for Britain's high society. The Kentucky Derby remains one of the most popular annual sporting events in the United States, while Hong Kong's Happy Valley draws thousands of visitors every week.

Skiing
The maps in the atlas point out the most important ski areas in the world, including Chamonix in the French Alps, St. Moritz in Switzerland, Aspen in the Rocky Mountains of Colorado, and Whistler in Canada. Many of these areas also offer facilities for other winter sports, including snowboarding.

Sailing
Once a sport for the wealthy, sailing is now enjoyed by millions of people. The atlas highlights areas with good conditions for recreational sailing.

Diving
Beautiful, colorful coral reefs, fascinating shipwrecks, and close encounters with wonderful marine life – this atlas presents popular and famous dive sites around the world.

Wind surfing
A mix of surfing and sailing, windsurfing is a popular aquatic sport. The atlas points out coastal areas well suited to the sport.

Surfing
Popular coastal areas with adequate waves for surfing are highlighted – including well-known beaches in Australia, California, Europe, and in Hawaii, the birthplace of surfing.

Canoeing/rafting
Travelers can enjoy both adventurous and relaxing journeys along many of the world's rivers and lakes in canoes or rafts.

Seaport
The largest and busiest harbors in the world are highlighted.

Deep-sea fishing
The atlas highlights several of the best and most well known locations on the world's seas and oceans for recreational fishing.

Waterskiing
Popular beaches, coastal areas, and lakes with ideal conditions for waterskiing.

Beach resort
Many of the world's beachside communities feature a laid-back atmosphere and excellent tourist facilities. The atlas highlights popular beaches and resorts.

Mineral/thermal spa
The atlas locates several historic and beautiful towns with spas that have attracted visitors for centuries.

Amusement/theme park
Modern amusement parks offer diverse attractions. The parks highlighted in the atlas include Walt Disney World in Orlando, Sea World in California, Disneyland Paris, and Tivoli in Copenhagen.

Casino
Well known casinos, including the historic casino of Monte Carlo and the resort-hotels of Las Vegas.

Hill resort
Exclusive resorts located in temperate highland areas. Mostly in Asia, hill resorts were once very popular destinations, especially for European colonial officials.

Lodge
Comfortable and luxurious camps or inns in pristine wilderness areas, mostly in Africa and North America.

Light and water are the sources of all life on Earth.

The crater of Mount St. Helens, an active vulcano that last erupted in 1980

THE WORLD

THE BLUE PLANET

The total surface area of the Earth covers 510 million km², 71 % of which is covered by water and 29 % by land. Most of the world's water is contained in the four vast oceans: Pacific, Atlantic, Indian, and the relatively small Arctic Ocean. The world's land area is divided between the seven continents: North America, South America, Europe, Asia, Africa, Australia, and Antarctica. While the surface of the planet's southern hemisphere is dominated by the oceans, the northern hemisphere is almost equally covered by land and water. The shape of the Earth's surface and the creation of the continents are the result of tectonic plate movements, a process that began billions of years ago.

Catastrophic volcanic eruptions and powerful earthquakes are not uncommon along the edges of the various tectonic plates. Compared to the total diameter of the Earth (12,700 km) the height variations on our planet's surface are small. Mount Everest, the world's tallest mountain, rises 8,850 meters, while the deepest point in the ocean, the Mariana Trench in the Pacific, extends 11,034 meters beneath the planet's surface. Including Mount Everest there are 14 mountains rising above 8,000 meters; all of them are located in Asia.

Most of the world's highest mountains are part of massive mountain chains, several of which cover large sections of the continents. The Pyrenees in Europe are the westernmost chain in an almost continuous belt of mountain systems stretching to Southeast Asia. The world's largest body of water, the Pacific Ocean, is surrounded by the circumglobal mountain belt and East Africa has a long mountain belt. Mountain chains are the source of many rivers. The longest rivers on Earth are the Nile (6,671 km) in Africa, the Amazon (6,400 km) in South America, and the Yangtze (Chang Jiang) in East Asia (6,300 km).

The vast Sahara Desert covers most of North Africa.

The location of the world's various climate and vegetation zones depends on the Earth's rotation, the tilt of its axis, and ocean currents, among other factors. In equatorial regions constant heavy rainfall leads to the growth of thick vegetation coverage. Many tropical and subtropical regions border large arid regions; the Sahara in Africa is the world's largest desert (9 million km²).

The world - physical map

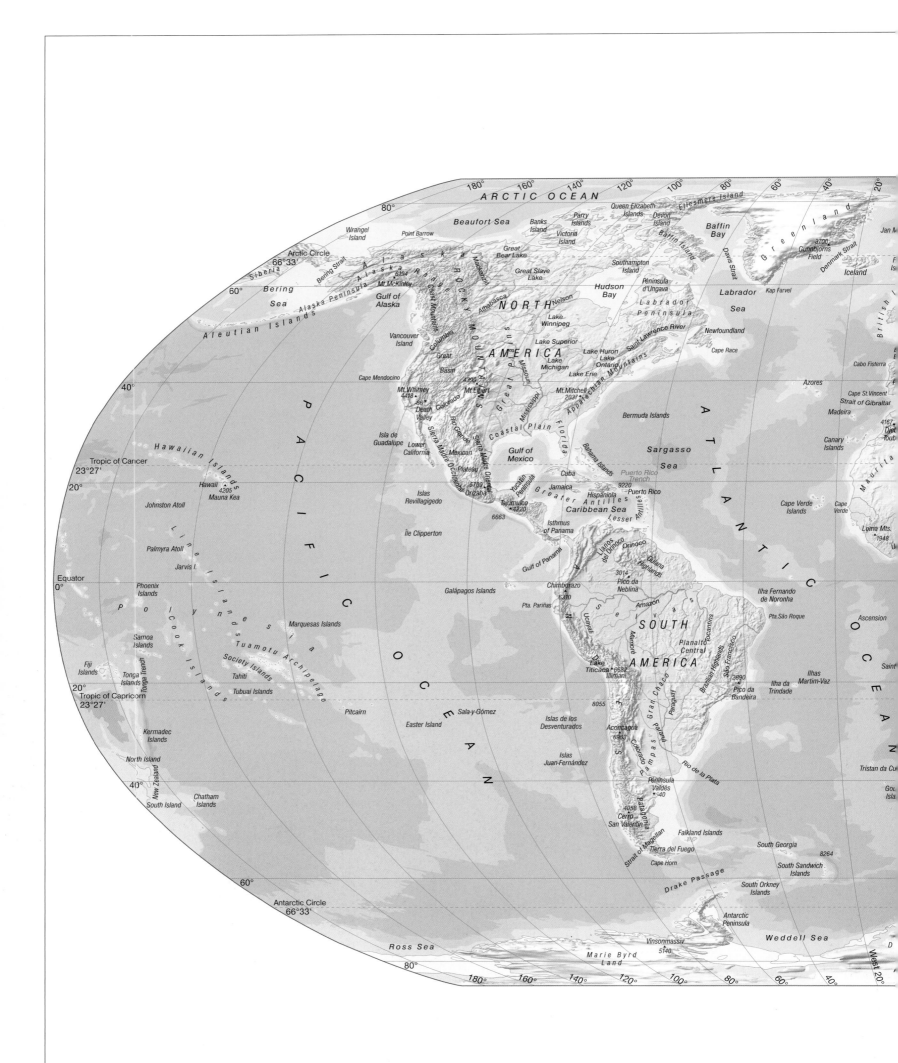

Scale 1:80,000,000

0   1000   2000   3000 Kilometers

0   1000   2000 Miles

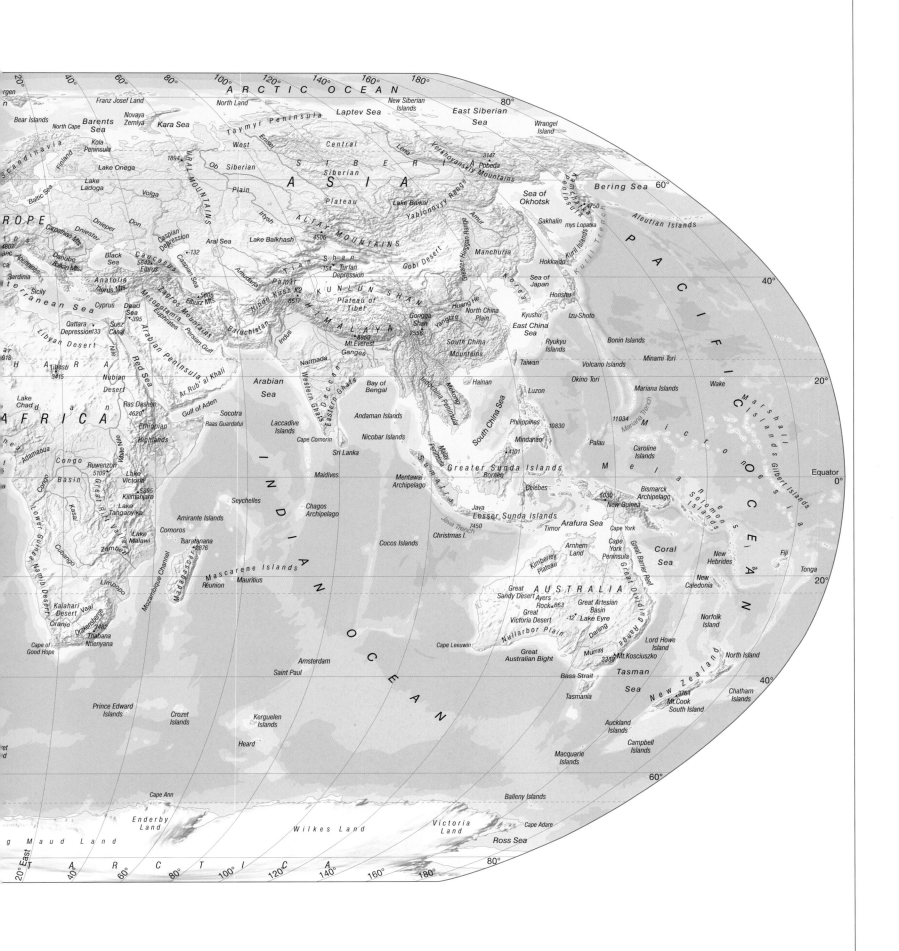

ARCTIC OCEAN

20° 40° 60° 80° 100° 120° 140° 160° 180°

rgen
n

Bear Islands   North Cape   Franz Josef Land   North Land   New Siberian Islands   East Siberian Sea   80°
Scandinavia   Barents Sea   Novaya Zemlya   Kara Sea   Laptev Sea   Wrangel Island
North Cape   Kola Peninsula   Finland   West   Taymyr Peninsula   Central Siberian   Lena   Verkhoyansk Range   mys Lopatka   Bering Sea   60°
Lake Onega   1894   Ob   Ob   Siberian   Plateau   Yablonovyy Range   Amur   4750   Aleutian Islands
ROPE   Lake Ladoga   Volga   URAL MOUNTAINS   Irtysh   SIBERIA   ASIA   Lake Baikal   Sea of Okhotsk   Sakhalin   Kamchatka Peninsula   Kuril Trench
Dnieper   Caspian Depression   Aral Sea   Lake Balkhash   ALTAY MOUNTAINS   4506   Yablonovyy Range   Greater Hingan Range   Hokkaido   Kuril Islands   PACIFIC   40°
Carpathian Mts.   Dniester   Don   132   Caspian Sea   Tian Shan   154   Turfan Depression   Manchuria   Korea   Sea of Japan   Honshu
Black Sea   5642 Elbrus   Caucasus   Pamir   KUNLUN SHAN   Gobi Desert   Huang He   North China   Sea of Japan   Kyushu
Danube   Balkan Mts.   Anatolia   Taurus Mts.   5605   Hindu Kush   K2 8611   Plateau of Tibet   Gongga Shan   Yangtze   North China Plain   East China Sea   Ryukyu Islands   Bonin Islands   Minami Tori
Sicily   Cyprus   Dead Sea   Elburz Mts.   Mesopotamia   Baluchistan   HIMALAYA   7556   South China   Taiwan   Volcano Islands   Okino Tori
Mediterranean Sea   Qattara Depression   395   Suez Canal   Euphrates   Persian Gulf   Indus   8850 Mt.Everest   Ganges   Mountains   Izu-Shoto   20°
Libyan Desert   Red Sea   Arabian Peninsula   Narmada   Deccan   Western Ghats   Bay of Bengal   Indochina Peninsula   Hainan   Luzon   Mariana Islands   Wake
Tibesti   3415   Nubian Desert   Ar Rub' al Khali   Arabian Sea   Eastern Ghats   Andaman Islands   Malay Peninsula   South China Sea   Philippines   10830   11034   Mariana Trench   Micronesia   Marshall Islands   Equator   0°
AFRICA   Lake Chad   Ethiopian Highlands   Gulf of Aden   Socotra   Ras Dashon   4620   Laccadive Islands   Cape Comorin   Nicobar Islands   Mindanao   4101   Palau   Caroline Islands   Gilbert Islands
Adamaoua   Congo   Ruwenzori   5109   Lake Victoria   Sri Lanka   Maldives   Mentawai Archipelago   Greater Sunda Islands   Borneo   Celebes   5030   Bismarck Archipelago   New Guinea   Solomon Islands
Congo Basin   Kasai   Kilimanjaro   5895   Lake Tanganyika   INDIAN   Seychelles   Chagos Archipelago   Java   7450 Java Trench   Lesser Sunda Islands   Arafura Sea   Cape York   Coral Sea   New Hebrides   Fiji   20°
Lower Guinea   Zambezi   Lake Malawi   Amirante Islands   Comoros   Tsaratanana   2876   Cocos Islands   Christmas I.   Timor   Arnhem Land   Cape York Peninsula   Great Barrier Reef   New Caledonia   Tonga
Namib Desert   Cubango   Limpopo   Mozambique Channel   Madagascar   Mascarene Islands   Réunion   Mauritius   OCEAN   Kimberley Plateau   Great Sandy Desert   Ayers Rock 863   Great Artesian Basin   Norfolk Island
Kalahari Desert   Vaal   Drakensberg   3482   Amsterdam   AUSTRALIA   Great Victoria Desert   12 Lake Eyre   Darling   Lord Howe Island   North Island
Oranje   Thabana Ntlenyana   Saint Paul   Nullarbor Plain   Murray   3330 Mt.Kosciuszko   Great Dividing Range   40°
Cape of Good Hope   Great Australian Bight   Cape Leeuwin   Bass Strait   Tasman Sea   New Zealand   Chatham Islands
Prince Edward Islands   Crozet Islands   Kerguelen Islands   Heard   Tasmania   3764 Mt.Cook   South Island   Auckland Islands   Campbell Islands   60°
ret
d   Cape Ann   Balleny Islands   Macquarie Islands
Enderby Land   Wilkes Land   Victoria Land   Cape Adare
g Maud Land   ANTARCTICA   Ross Sea   80°
East   20°   40°   60°   80°   100°   120°   140°   160°   180°

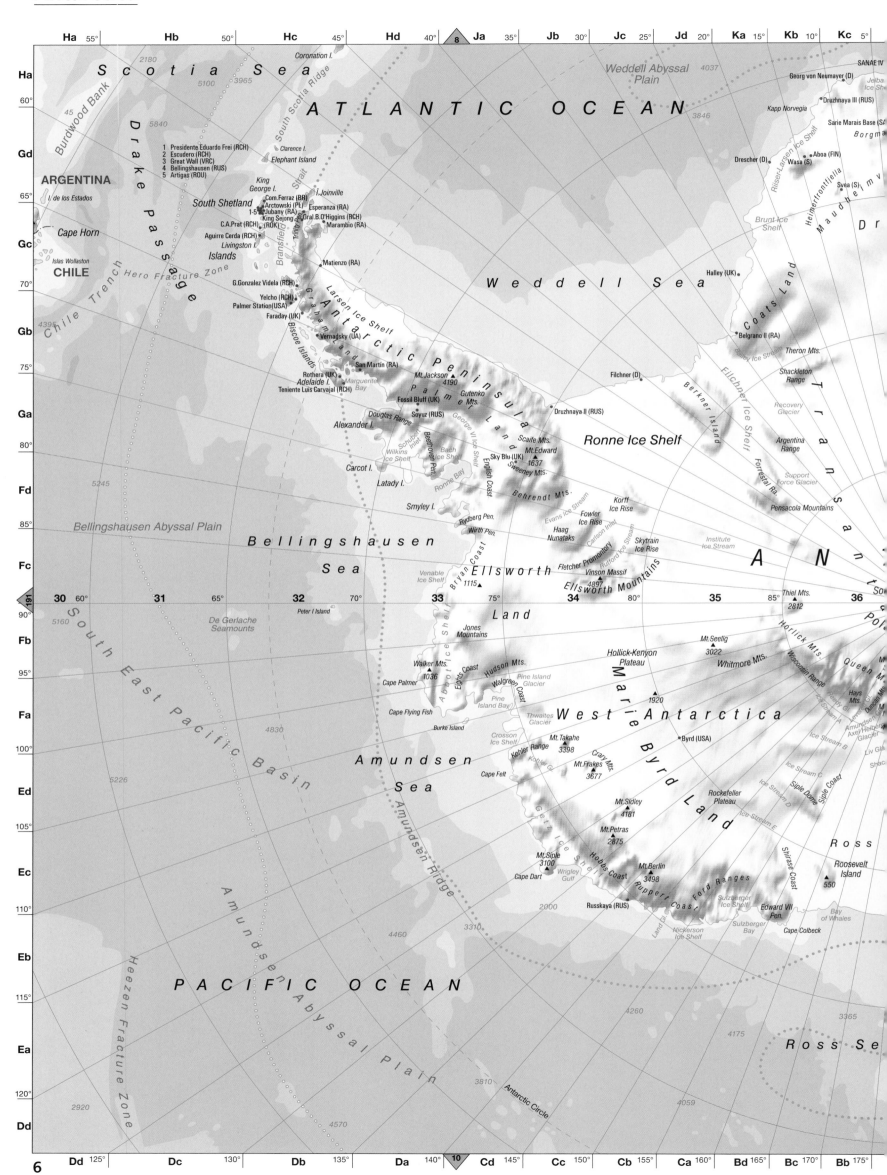

Antarctica

Scotia Sea

Coronation I.

Weddell Abyssal Plain

4037

SANAE IV

Georg von Neumayer (D)

Jelba Ice She

5100 3965

ATLANTIC OCEAN

3846

Druzhnaya III (RUS)

Kapp Norvegia

Sarie Marais Base (SA

Burdwood Bank

Drake Passage

South Scotia Ridge

Clarence I.

Elephant Island

45

5840

Borgma

Riiser-Larsen Ice Shelf

Heimefrontfjella

Maudheim

ARGENTINA

1 Presidente Eduardo Frei (RCH)
2 Escudero (RCH)
3 Great Wall (VRC)
4 Bellingshausen (RUS)
5 Artigas (ROU)

King George I.

I.Joinville

Drescher (D)

Wasa (S)

Aboa (FIN)

Svea (S)

Dr

I. de los Estados

South Shetland

Com.Ferraz (BR)
Arctowski (PL)
1-5 Jubany (RA)
King Sejong (ROK)

Esperanza (RA)

Gral.B.O'Higgins (RCH)

Svea (S)+

Cape Horn

C.A.Prat (RCH)

Marambio (RA)

CHILE

Aguirre Cerda (RCH)

Bransfield Strait

Trinity Pen.

Islas Wollaston

Livingston I.

Islands

Matienzo (RA)

Weddell Sea

Halley (UK)

Coats Land

G.Gonzalez Videla (RCH)

Larsen Ice Shelf

Belgrano II (RA)

Emily Ice Stream

Theron Mts.

T

Yelcho (RCH)

Palmer Station(USA)

Graham Land

Shackleton Range

Faraday (UK)

Antarctic Peninsula

Filchner (D)

Berkner Island

Recovery Glacier

Filchner Ice Shelf

Vernadsky (UA)

Bscoe Islands

San Martín (RA)

Mt.Jackson

Palmer Land

4190

Rothera (UK)

Gutenko Mts.

Druzhnaya II (RUS)

Ronne Ice Shelf

Argentina Range

Adelaide I.

Marguerite Bay

Fossil Bluff (UK)

Teniente Luis Carvajal (RCH)

Soyuz (RUS)

Scaife Mts.

George VI Ice Shelf

Alexander I.

Douglas Range

English Coast

Mt.Edward
1637

Support Force Glacier

Pensacola Mountains

Schubert Inlet

Beethoven Pen.

Bach Ice Shelf

Sky Blu (UK)

Sweeney Mts.

Wilkins Ice Shelf

Ronne Bay

Carcot I.

Behrendt Mts.

Forrestal Ra.

Latady I.

Smyley I.

Rydberg Pen.

Korff Ice Rise

A   N

Bellingshausen Abyssal Plain

Wirth Pen.

Evans Ice Stream

Fowler Ice Rise

Haag Nunataks

Carlson Inlet

Rutford Ice Stream

Skytrain Ice Rise

Institute Ice Stream

Bellingshausen Sea

Bryan Coast

Venable Ice Shelf

Ellsworth

Fletcher Promontory

Vinson Massif
4897

Thiel Mts.
2812

1115

Land

Ellsworth Mountains

So

5160

Peter I Island

Jones Mountains

Pol

De Gerlache Seamounts

Hollick-Kenyon Plateau

Mt.Seelig
3022

Horlick Mts.

Queen M

Walker Mts.
1036

Hudson Mts.

Whitmore Mts.

Wisconsin Range

South East Pacific Basin

Cape Palmer

Abbott Ice Shelf

Eights Coast

Walgreen Coast

Pine Island Glacier

Marie

Byrd

Land

Hays Mts.

Cape Flying Fish

Pine Island Bay

Ice Stream A

4830

Burke Island

Thwaites Glacier

Byrd (USA)

Amundsen Axel Heiberg Glacier

West   Antarctica

Ice Stream B

5226

Crosson Ice Shelf

Mt.Takahe
3398

Kohler Range

Liv Gl

Amundsen

Kohler Gl.

Mt.Frakes
3677

Crary Mts.

Rockefeller Plateau

Ice Stream C

Siple Coast

Sea

Cape Felt

Mt.Sidley
4181

Ice Stream D

Siple Dome

Ross

Getz Ice Shelf

Mt.Petras
2875

Shirase Coast

Roosevelt Island
550

Mt.Siple
3100

Cape Dart

Wrigley Gulf

Hobbs Coast

Mt.Berlin
3498

Ford Ranges

Sulzberger Ice Shelf

Edward VII Pen.

Russkaya (RUS)

Ruppert Coast

2000

Nickerson Ice Shelf

Sulzberger Bay

Cape Colbeck

Land Gl.

4460

3310

PACIFIC OCEAN

Amundsen Ridge

Amundsen Abyssal Plain

Bay of Wholes

Heezen Fracture Zone

4260

4175

3365

Antarctic Circle

3810

4059

Ross Se

2920

4570

Chile Trench

Hero Fracture Zone

4395

5245

Atlantic Ocean

Scale 1:50,000,000

8

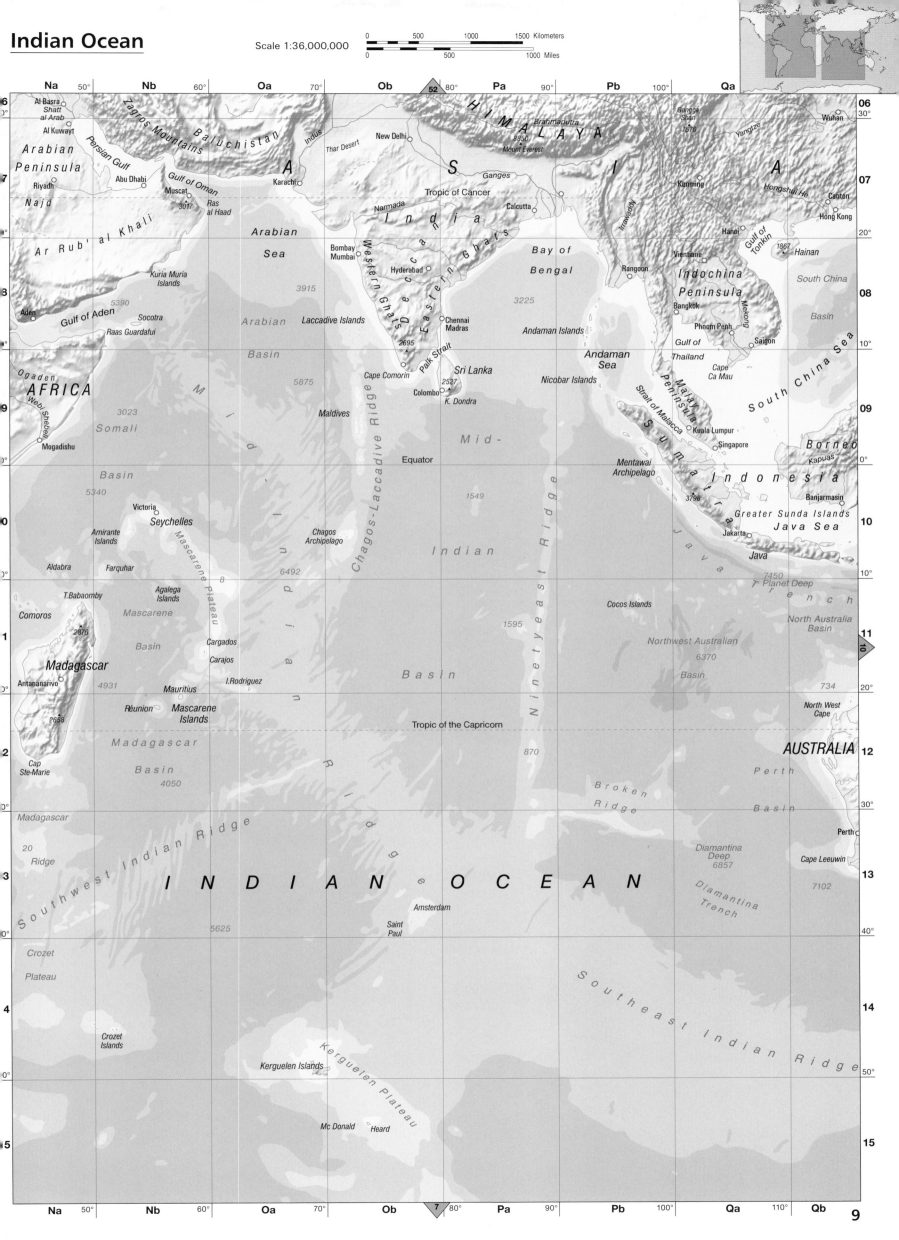

Indian Ocean

Scale 1:36,000,000

500   1000   1500 Kilometers
0
0   500   1000 Miles

Na 50°   **Nb** 60°   **Oa** 70°   **Ob** 80°   **Pa** 90°   **Pb** 100°   **Qa**

Al Basra
Shatt
al Arab
Al Kuwayt

Zagros Mountains
Baluchistan
Indus
New Delhi
HIMALAYA
Brahmaputra
8850
Mount Everest
Gongga
Shan
7576
Wuhan
Yangtze

Arabian
Peninsula
Riyadh
Najd
Persian Gulf
Abu Dhabi
Gulf of Oman
Muscat
3017
Ras
al Haad
Karachi
Thar Desert
A
S
Ganges
Tropic of Cancer
I
A
Kunming
Hongshui He
Canton
Hong Kong
Hanoi
Gulf of
Tonkin
1867
Hainan

Ar Rub' al Khali
Arabian
Sea
Narmada
Calcutta
Indochina
Peninsula
South China

Aden
Gulf of Aden
Socotra
Raas Guardafui
Kuria Muria
Islands
5390
3915
Bombay
Mumbai
Hyderabad
Western Ghats
Deccan
Eastern Ghats
Bay of
Bengal
Vientiane
Rangoon
Bangkok
Basin

OGaden
Webi Shebeli
AFRICA
Arabian
Basin
5875
Laccadive Islands
2695
Chennai
Madras
Palk Strait
Andaman Islands
Andaman
Sea
Malay Peninsula
Gulf of
Thailand
Phnom Penh
Cape
Ca Mau
South China Sea

Mogadishu
Somali
3023
Maldives
Cape Comorin
Sri Lanka
2527
Colombo
K. Dondra
Nicobar Islands
Mid-
Strait of Malacca
Sumatra
Kuala Lumpur
Singapore
Borneo
Kapuas

Basin
5340
Equator
1549
Indian
3798
Jakarta
Java
Banjarmasin
Greater Sunda Islands
Java Sea

Victoria
Seychelles
Amirante
Islands
Aldabra   Farquhar
Chagos-Laccadive Ridge
Chagos
Archipelago
6492
Ninetyeast Ridge
Cocos Islands
Northwest Australian
Basin
6370
North Australia
Basin
734

T.Babaomby
Comoros
2876
Mascarene Plateau
Agalega
Islands
Mascarene
Basin
Cargados
Carajos
I.Rodriguez
8
Basin
1595
Mentawai
Archipelago
Indonesia
7450
Planet Deep
North West
Cape

Madagascar
Antananarivo
4931
Mauritius
Réunion
Mascarene
Islands
Tropic of the Capricorn
870
Perth
Basin
AUSTRALIA

Cap
Ste-Marie
2658
Madagascar
Basin
4050
Ridge
Broken
Ridge
Perth

Madagascar
20
Ridge
Southwest Indian Ridge
INDIAN OCEAN
Ridge
Amsterdam
Saint
Paul
Diamantina
Deep
6857
Diamantina
Trench
7102
Perth
Cape Leeuwin

Crozet
Plateau
5625

Crozet
Islands
Kerguelen Plateau
Southeast Indian Ridge

Kerguelen Islands
Mc Donald   Heard

Na 50°   **Nb** 60°   **Oa** 70°   **Ob** 80°   **Pa** 90°   **Pb** 100°   **Qa** 110°   **Qb**

9

Pacific Ocean

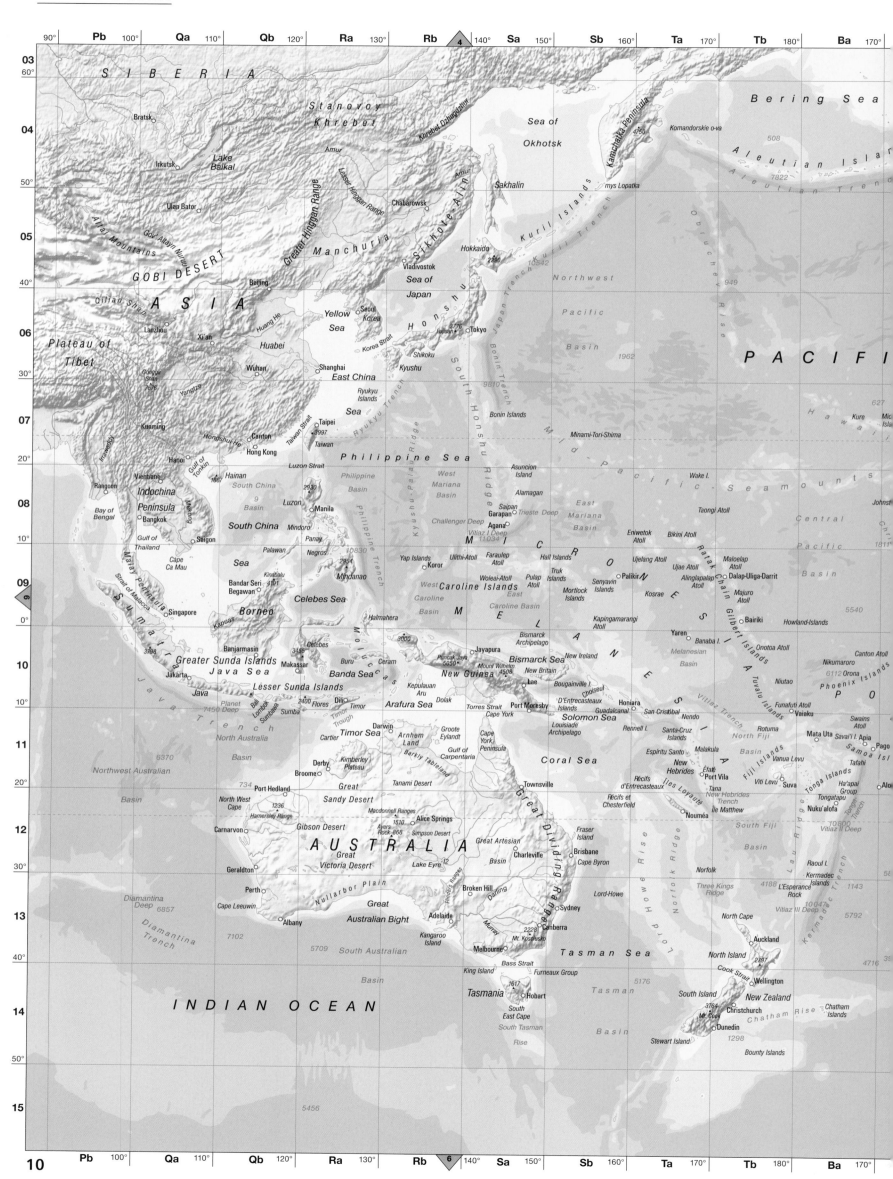

Scale 1:50,000,000

0 500 1000 1500 2000 Kilometers
0   500   1000   1500 Miles

Ca 150° **Cb** 140° **Da** 130° **Db** 120° **Ea** 110° 5 **Eb** 100° **Fa** 90° **Fb** 80° **Ga**

03 60°
04
05 50°

Gulf of Alaska
Peace
Hudson Bay
Labrador Peninsula
Coast of Labrador

ROCKY MOUNTAINS
Edmonton
Calgary
Churchill
Nelson
Lake Winnipeg
Winnipeg
Îles Laurentides

Mt. Waddington 4016
Vancouver Island
Vancouver
Columbia
Great Plains
Duluth
Lake Superior
Lake Michigan
Lake Huron
Ottawa
Québec
Halifax
Nova Scotia

Northeast
Mt. Rainier 4392
Grand Teton 4198
NORTH AMERICA
Lake Ontario
St. Lawrence River
Chicago
Lake Erie
Cape Cod

4343
Coast Mountains
Great Basin
Great Salt Lake
Denver
4399
St. Louis
Missouri
New York
Washington D.C.
Appalachian Mountains
Norfolk
Cape Hatteras

Mendocino Fracture Zone
San Francisco
Mt. Whitney 4418
4399
Mt. Elbert
Colorado
Arkansas
Ohio
2037
ATLANTIC
North American

O C E A N
Murray Fracture Zone
Pacific
-86 Mojave Desert
Baldy Peak 3476
Phoenix
Los Angeles
San Diego
Ciudad Juárez
El Paso
Rio Grande
Mexican Plateau
Dallas
Mississippi
Houston
New Orleans
Florida
Jacksonville
Cape Canaveral
Miami
O C E A N
Basin

Isla de Guadalupe
Lower California
Gulf of California
Monterrey
Gulf of Mexico
Straits of Florida
Havana
Bahama Islands

Tropic of Cancer
4465
La Paz
Cuba
Hispaniola
Puerto Rico Trench
9219
Milwaukee Deep

Cabo San Lucas
Guadalajara
Mérida
Yucatán Peninsula
Cayman Trench
Jamaica
Puerto Rico
Guadeloupe

Kauai
Oahu
Maui
Mauna Kea 4205
Hawaii
Clarion Fracture Zone
Islas Revillagigedo
Popocatépetl 5464
Mexico City
Middle America Trench
Greater Antilles
Caribbean Sea
Lesser Antilles

4425
Basin
4663
Guatemala Basin
Tajumulco 4220
Guatemala
San Salvador
Managua
Lago de Nicaragua
Punta Gallinas
Maracaibo
Caracas
Trinidad

Île Clipperton
San José 3820
Chirripó
Panamá
P. Colón
5775
Orinoco

4371
Teraina
Tabuaeran
Kiritimati Atoll
226
Clipperton Fracture Zone
4114
Cocos Island
Cocos Ridge
Gulf of Panama
Isla de Malpelo
Bogotá
Nev. del Huila 5750
Llanos de Orinoco
Guiana Highlands
Mt. Roraima 2810
Pico da Neblina 3014
Rio Negro

Jarvis I.
Malden Island
Starbuck I.
5065
Equator
Galápagos Fracture Zone
4060
Galápagos Islands
Quito
Chimborazo 6310
Selvas
Manaus
Amazon
Iquitos
Amazon Lowland

Manihiki Atoll
Pernhyn Atoll
Caroline Atoll
Hiva Oa
Marquesas Islands
3694
Punta Aguja
6768 Huascarán
6601
Rio Branco

451
Flint Atoll
4755
Tuamotu Archipelago
Îles du Désappointement
Lima
Peru
SOUTH AMERICA

Motu One Atoll
Rangiroa Atoll
Île Raiatea
Fakarava Atoll
Makemo Atoll
4385
La Paz
6520 Sajama
Aitutaki-Atoll
Society Islands
Papeete
Tahiti
Hao Atoll
Reao Atoll
Basin
6867
8055

Manuae-Atoll
Maria Atoll
4572
3429
Tureia Atoll

Avarua
Rarotonga Atoll
4845
Tubuai Islands
Mururoa
Gambier
Oeno
Ducie
Adamstown
Tropic of Capricorn
4124
6887 Nev. Ojos del Salado
Gran Chaco

Tematangi Atoll
Raevavae
4645
Tuamotu Ridge
Pitcairn Island
Sala-y-Gómez
Islas de los Desventuradas
Aconcagua 6963
Córdoba
Pampas

Rapa
Bass
Easter Island
Sala-y-Gomez-Fracture Zone
Santiago
Islas Juan-Fernández

P A C I F I C   O C E A N
2836
3884
Chile Basin
Puerto Montt
Chiloé

Southwest Pacific Basin
5121
4248
Chile Rise
4058
Co.S.Valentín
Comodoro Rivadavia
I. Wellington
Patagonia

Falkland Islands
Punta Arenas
Strait of Magellan
Tierra del Fuego
Cape Horn
Drake Passage

Ca 150° **Cb** 140° **Da** 130° **Db** 120° **Ea** 110° 7 **Eb** 100° **Fa** 90° **Fb** 80° **Ga** 70° **Gb**

06 40° 30°
07 20°
08 10°
09 0°
10 10°
11 20°
12 30°
13 40°
14 50°
15

11

Italy: The beautiful rolling hills of Tuscany.

Budapest: The Parliament on the bank of the Danube River.

EUROPE

THE OLD CONTINENT

With an area of 10.5 million km², Europe is the second smallest continent in size. Separated in the east from Asia by the Ural Mountains, Europe extends more than 5,000 kilometers to the western coast of Ireland and more than 4,000 kilometers from the North Cape to Crete in the Mediterranean north to south. The Atlantic Ocean marks the western borders of Europe, the Mediterranean and Black Sea border the continent in the south and the Arctic Ocean lies to the north.

The topography of Southern and Central Europe is dominated by a bow-shaped series of mountain chains. The mountain system extends from the Sierra Nevada, to the Pyrenees, the Alps, and the Carpathian Mountains. North of this mountain belt lies a series of medium elevation ranges – including the French Massif Central, the Harz Mountains, and the Tatras – that gives way to the plains of northern and Central Europe. One of the most striking features of Europe's geography is the large number of peninsulas (Scandinavia, Iberia, Greece, etc.) on the continent. The European mainland is also surrounded by many islands, including Great Britain and Iceland.

With a population of 740 million, Europe is the third most populous continent. Several European states have populations exceeding 50 million – including Italy, France, the United Kingdom, Russia, and Germany. Immigrants from outside Europe have changed the faces of many once homogenous European nations since the second half of the 20th century.

The Alps: Matterhorn (4,478 m).

With the relatively recent political development in Eastern Europe – the collapse of the Soviet Union for example – many new states have emerged on the continent. The migration of people from eastern to western Europe and between southern and northern Europe continues to bring the continent's diverse cultures and nations closer together.

Europe

Greenland

Kong Frederik VIII Land

G r e e n l a n d
S e a

Nordaustlandet

1717

Svalbard

Edgøya

380

Novaya Zemlya

Kara Sea

Gydanskiy
P-ov

1547

W e s t

Kong Christian X Land

Greenland
Basin

3069

Bear Islands

B a r e n t s   S e a

Yamal P-ov

S i b e r i a n

Kong Christian IX Land

Arctic Circle

03

Denmark Strait

Jan Mayen

832

Iceland
Basin

ATLANTIC

Reykjavik

Grimsvötn
1719

Iceland

Norwegian
Sea

3188

Lofoten Basin

Norwegian

Basin

North Cape

Pečorskoe
more

1894

P l a i n

Ob

U
R
A
L

Murmansk

Kola
Peninsula

2117
Kebnekaise

Oulu

White Sea

Syktyvkar

Timanskiy Kryazh

Severnye Uraly

1569

YEKATERINBURG

PERM'

04

465

Rockall Plateau

Faroe Islands

Shetland Islands

Jotunheimen
2472

Bergen

Umeå

Gulf of Bothnia

Helsinki
Helsingfors

Lake Onega

Lake Ladoga

ST. PETERSBURG

UFA

KAZAN'

Hebrides

Rockall Trough

Ireland

OCEAN

Dublin

Cork

BIRMINGHAM

Orkney Islands

Ben Nevis
1343

Edinburgh

Pennines

North Sea

Great Britain

240

Oslo

Stockholm

Vänern

Göteborg

459

Gotland

Vänern

Lake Peipus

Riga

MINSK

MOSCOW

NIŽNIJ
NOVGOROD

Orel

Volga Upland

SAMARA

Oral

E

P

50°

Celtic Sea

LONDON

Amsterdam

Copenhagen

Jutland

Baltic Sea

Bornholm

Gdańsk

WARSAW

Vistula

KIEV

Dnieper

Don

VOLGOGRAD

Caspian Depression

Caspian

Land's End

English Channel

BRUSSELS

COLOGNE

Elbe

HAMBURG

BERLIN

Sudetes

PRAGUE

Cracow

L'viv

Dniester

DNIPROPETROVS'K

ROSTOV-
NA-DONU

Manych Depression

Sea

8

Brittany

Normandie

PARIS

Rhine

Burgundy

MUNICH

VIENNA

BUDAPEST

Béskid Mts.

Carpathian Mts.

ODESSA

C A U C A S U S

g.Elbrus
5642

TBILISI

05

5465

E

Massif
1885
Central

Lyon

Loire

Rhône

Mt.Blanc
4807

A
L
P
S

U

Berne

MILAN

Po

3797

Zagreb

Alföld

2100

Transylvanian Alps
2544

BELGRADE

Danube

BUCHAREST

Crimea

Black Sea

2180

YEREVAN

Ararat
5137

La Coruña

Cabo Fisterra

Gijón

Bordeaux

Pyrénées

3404
Pico d'Aneto

Marseille

Provence

Apennines

Dinaric Alps

Dalmatia

Adriatic Sea

Balkan Mts.

SOFIA

Varna

İSTANBUL

Pontic Mountains

Trabzon

Van Gölü

Van

40°

Porto

Cantabria Mountains

Cordillera Central

MADRID

Tagus

Sistema Ibérico

Ebro

BARCELONA

València

Corsica

2622

ROME

Sardinia

2914

Tirané

Rhodope Mts.

Olymp
2917

Pindhos Mts.

Aegean
Sea

ANKARA

İZMİR

A n a t o l i a

Taurus Mts.
3524

A

AL-MAWSIL

ALEPPO

LISBON

Sierra Morena

Cordillera Bética

Sevilla

Granada
3491

Palma de M.

Balearic Islands

2784

1834

NAPLES

Vesúvio 1281

Palermo

Etna
3323

Tyrrhenian
Sea

1955

Ionian
Sea

Peloponnesus

ATHENS

Rhodes

5054

Tuz Gölü

ADANA

Cyprus

BEIRUT

DAMASCUS

Euphrate

Al Widyan

06

Tangier

RABAT

CASABLANCA

MARRAKECH

AR-RIF

Fès

Oran

2305

ALGIERS

Constantine

TUNIS

Sicily

Sfax

Île de Jerba

2456

Crete

2427

M E D I T E R R A N E A N   S E A

Levantine
Basin

AMMAN

Jerusalem

Port Said

An Nafud

H

30°

Haut Atlas

A T L A S   M T S.

Atlas Tellien

Atlas Saharien

Hamada du Drâa

Béchar

Great Western Erg

El Ménia

Great Eastern Erg

TRIPOLI

Tripolitania

Gulf of Sirte

Benghazi

Cyrenaica

882

Sahra Surt

Tubruq

ALEXANDRIA

CAIRO

Qattara Depression

134

Sinai
2285

1207

El Aqaba

Eastern Desert

e
j
a
z

Red

2300

Erg Iguidi

S

A

Erg
Chech

Taoudenni

Tropic of Cancer

Tanezrouft

Plateau du Tademaït

F

Asedjrad

Hamada de Tinrhert

R

Tassili n'Ajjer

Adrar
2158

Awbari Sahra

Al Jufra
Oasis

Fezzan

I

Ramlat Rabyanah

C

Libyan Desert

Great Sand Sea

El Kufrah
Oasis

Western Desert

A

Nile

Luxor

Aswân

Lake Nasser

Djebel
Musbih
1445

Sea

Ras Banas

07

20°

Djebel Timétrine

S

Tahat
2918

A

H o g g a r

H

Tassili du Hoggar

Ténéré du
Tafassasset

A

Pic Touside 3376

Tibesti

Tarso Emissi
3315

Sarir Tibesti

R

Erdi

A

1893
Djebel Al Awaynat

Nubian Desert

Nubia

Nile

Port Sudan

08

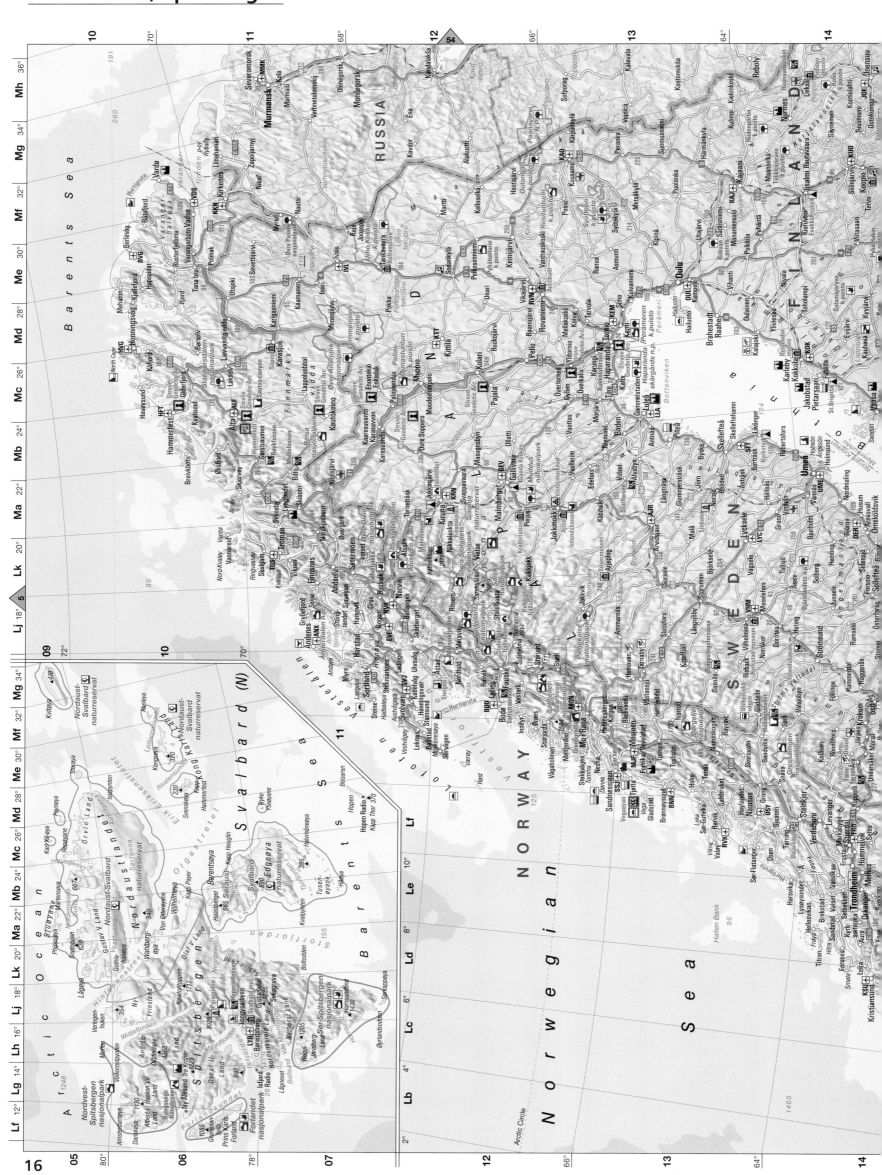

Iceland/Ireland

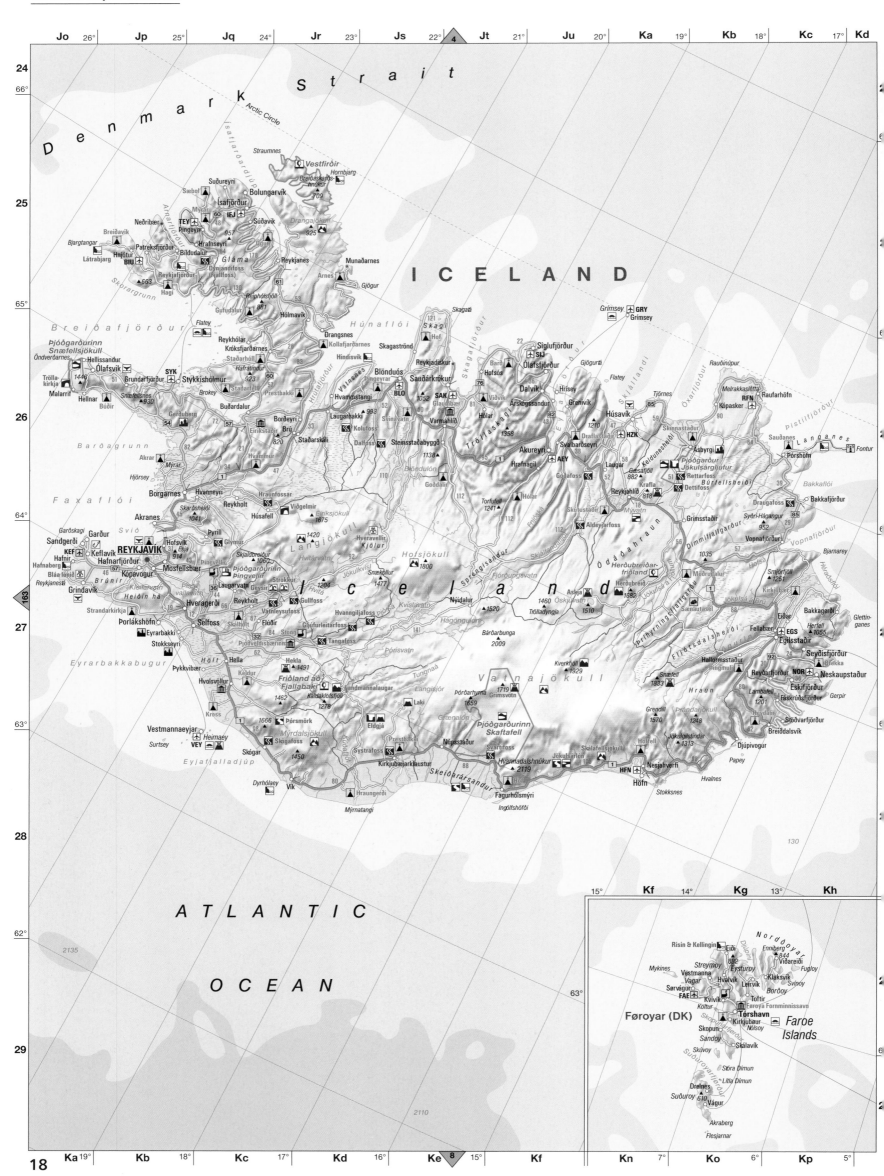

0   25   50   75 Kilometers
0   25   50 Miles

Kg 13°   Kh 12°   Kj 11°   Kk 10°   Kl 9°   Km 8°   Kn 7°

Rockall Trough

ATLANTIC

OCEAN

Sea of the Hebrides

Stanton Bank 33

Inner Hebrides

Eigg
Muck
Coll
Arinagour
Kilchoan
Mallaig
Arisaig
Strontian
Tiree
Scarinish
Tobermory
Glengorm Castle
Portnacroish
Stalker Castle
TRE
Isle of Mull
Ben More 966
Craignure
Lismore
Connel
Iona
Fionnphort
Duart Castle
Oban

Colonsay
Scalasaig

Jura
Lochgilphead

Islay
Port Askaig
Tarbert
Kennacraig
Port Ellen
Portnahaven
Bowmore
Rinns Point
ILY
Gigha
Claonaig
Tayinloan

Kintyre
Lochranza
Goat Fell 874
Arran
Brodick

North Channel
CAL
Campbeltown
Mull of Kintyre

Tory Island
Bloody Foreland
Brinlack
Inishtrahull Sound
Inishtrahull
Malin Head

Aran Island
CFN
Dunfanaghy
Portsalon
Carndonagh
Giant's Causeway
Rathlin Island
Fair Head
Dunglow
Glenveagh N.P.
Errigal 752
Buncrana
Grianan of Aileach
Portrush
Ballycastle
Coleraine
Folk Village Museum
Letterkenny
Bridge End
LDY
Limavady
Dunluce Castle
Ballymoney
Antrim Mts.
Glenariff
Rossan Point
Fintown
Londonderry (Derry)
Dungiven
Maghera
Glenarm
Glencolumbkille
Slieve League
Glenties
Blue Stack Mts. 676
Donegal
Ballybofey
Strabane
Sperrin Mts. 678
Newtownstewart
Moneymore
Randalstown
Larne
Killybegs
Lifford
Omagh
Cookstown
Ballymena
Island Magee

Donegal Bay
Bundoran
Ballyshannon
Kesh
Enniskillen
Ballygawley
Dungannon
Ballyclare
Carrickfergus

Sligo
L. Melvin
Drumcliff
Manorhamilton
Belcoo
Irvinestown
Magheresbridge
Aughnacloy
Armagh
Newtownabbey
Belfast
Holywood
Bangor
Newtownards
SXL
L. Gill
Ballysadare
Dowra
Clones
Monaghan
Portadown
Lisburn
BHD
Ards Peninsula
Carryduff
Tobercurry
Charlestown
Boyle
Carrick-on-Shannon
Belturbet
Cootehill
Castleblayney
Lurgan
Banbridge
Dromore
Downpatrick
Strangford
Foxford
Ballaghaderreen
L. Allen
L. Oughter
Cavan
Clogher Head
NOC
Swinford
Tulsk
Rathfriland
Newry
Newcastle
Portaferry

Westport
Castlebar
Ballyhaunis
Castlerea
Roscommon
L. Gowna
Granard
Virginia
Ardee
Dundalk
Mourne Mts.
Kilkeel
Point of Ayre
Ramsey

Leenane
Claremorris
Longford
L. Sheelin
Kells
Slane
Drogheda
Isle of Man (UK)
Snaefell 621
Clifden
Maam Cross
Kilmaine
Tuam
Ballymahon
Edgeworthstown
Castlepollard
Navan
Gormanston
Balbriggan
Spanish Head
Calf of Man
Port Erin
Douglas
Isle of Man
IOM
Castletown

Recess
Oughterard
Bellew
Mount
Ballinasloe
Athlone
Mullingar
Delvin
Trim
Dunshaughlin
Skerries
Lambay Island

Connemara
Galway
GWY
Oranmore
Loughrea
Moate
L. Ennel
Kinnegad
Fairyhouse Racetrack
Malahide Castle
DUB

Black Head
Kilcolgan
Gort
Portumna
Tullamore
Edenderry
Innfield
Maynooth
Celbridge
Curragh Racetrack
Dublin/Baile Atha Cliath
Howth

Lisdoonvarna
Kinvarra
Clonmacnoise
Birr
Slieve Bloom Mts.
Portlaoise
Kildare
Naas
Dublin Bay
Dun Laoghaire

Burren N.P.
Lahinch
Ennistimon N.P.
Loughrea
Cloghan
Mountmellick
Port Laoise
Newbridge
Enniskerry
Bray

Ennis
Scarriff
Borrisokane
Roscrea
Athy
Hollywood
Greystones

Kilkee
Kilbaha
Kilrush
Killimer
Shannon
SNN
Nenagh
Thurles
Abbeyleix
Glendalough
Wicklow Mts. N.P.
Laragh
Rathdrum
Rathnew
Wicklow

Loop Head
Tarbert
Foynes
Limerick
Bunratty Castle
King John's Castle
Templemore
Silvermine Mts. 693
Durrow
Carlow
Tullow
Wicklow Head

Mouth of the Shannon
Kerry Head
Ballybunion
Listowel
Askeaton
Adare
Patrickswell
Milestone
Horse & Jockey
Urlingford
Bagenalstown
Mt. Leinster 793
Carnew
Arklow

Brandon Head
Brandon 950
Tralee Bay
Newcastle West
Abbeyfeale
Knocklong
Tipperary 919
Cashel
Kilkenny
Killenaule
Callan
Gowran Park
Bunclody
Gorey

Gallarus Oratory
Blasket Islands
Dingle
Camp
Castleisland
Charleville
Galty Mts.
Caher
Fethard
Clonmel
Graiguenamanagh
Cahore Point

Slea Head
Dunbeg Fort
Anascaul
Killarney
Kanturk
Mallow
Mitchelstown
Lismore
Carrick-on-Suir
New Ross
Enniscorthy

Dingle Bay
Glenbeigh
Killorglin
KFF
Farranfore
Mallow
Blackwater
Fermoy
Suir
Wexford
Wexford Harbour

Valentia I.
Bray Head
Cahersiveen
Carrauntoohil 1038
Muckross
Rathmore
Blarney Castle
Midleton
Youghal
Mine Head
Rosslare
Rosslare Harbour

Waterville
Caherdaniel
Killarney N.P.
Kenmare
Macroom
Blarney
Cork/Corcaigh
Cork Harb.
QRK
Dungarvan
Tramore
WAT
Waterford
Arthurstown
Carnsore Point

Skellig Michael
Sneem
Ring of Kerry
Kenmare River
Glengarriff
Bandon
Bandon
Kinsale
Ringaskiddy
Youghal Bay
Hook Head
Kilmore Quay
Saltee Islands

Dursey Island
Castletownbere
Bear Island
Bantry
Ballydehob
Dunmanway
Fota Wildlife Park
Charles Fort
Old Head of Kinsale

Mizen Head
Crookhaven
Roaringwater Bay
Skibbereen
Clonakilty
Drombeg Circle
Galley Head

Cape Clear

IRELAND / ÉIRE

Irish Sea

Carmel Head
Amlwch
Holyhead
Anglesey
Gt. Ormes Head
Llandudno
Holy Island
Beaumaris Castle
Menai Bridge
Conwy
Colwyn Bay
Caernarfon
Bangor
Llanberis
Llanrwst
Betws-y-Coed
Caernarfon Castle
Snowdon 1085
Snowdonia
Portmeirion
Harlech Castle
Porthmadog
Ffestiniog
Abersoch
Pwllheli
Bardsey Island
Tremadog Bay
Bala
Barmouth
Dolgellau
Cadair Idris 893
Mallwyd

UNITED KINGDOM

Cardigan Bay
Aberystwyth
Machynlleth
Plynlimon 752
Caersws
Newtown
Llanidloes
Aberaeron

St. George's Channel

Pembrokeshire Coast National Park
St. David's Head
Cardigan
Fishguard
Lampeter
Llandovery
Builth Wells
Ramsey Island
St. David's
St. Bride's Bay
Haverfordwest
Narberth
Carmarthen
Llandeilo
Sennybridge
Brecon
Talgarth
Milford Haven
Pembroke Dock
Pembroke
Tenby
Cross Hands
Brecon Beacons N.P.
Crickhowell
Merthyr Tydfil
Blaenavon

St. Govan's Head
Carmarthen Bay
Llanelli
Mountain Ash
Rhondda
Cwmcarn Pontypool
Caerphilly

Celtic Sea

Swansea
The Mumbles
Neath
Port Talbot
Porthcawl
Bridgend
Newport
Cardiff
Barry
Penarth
Weston-super-Mare

Bristol Channel

Lundy Island
Ilfracombe
Lynton
Exmoor
Minehead
Burnham-on-Sea
Barnstaple
Braunton
Hartland Point

Kl 9°   Km 8°   Kn 7°   Ko 6°   Kp 5°   Kq 4°   Kr

19

British Isles

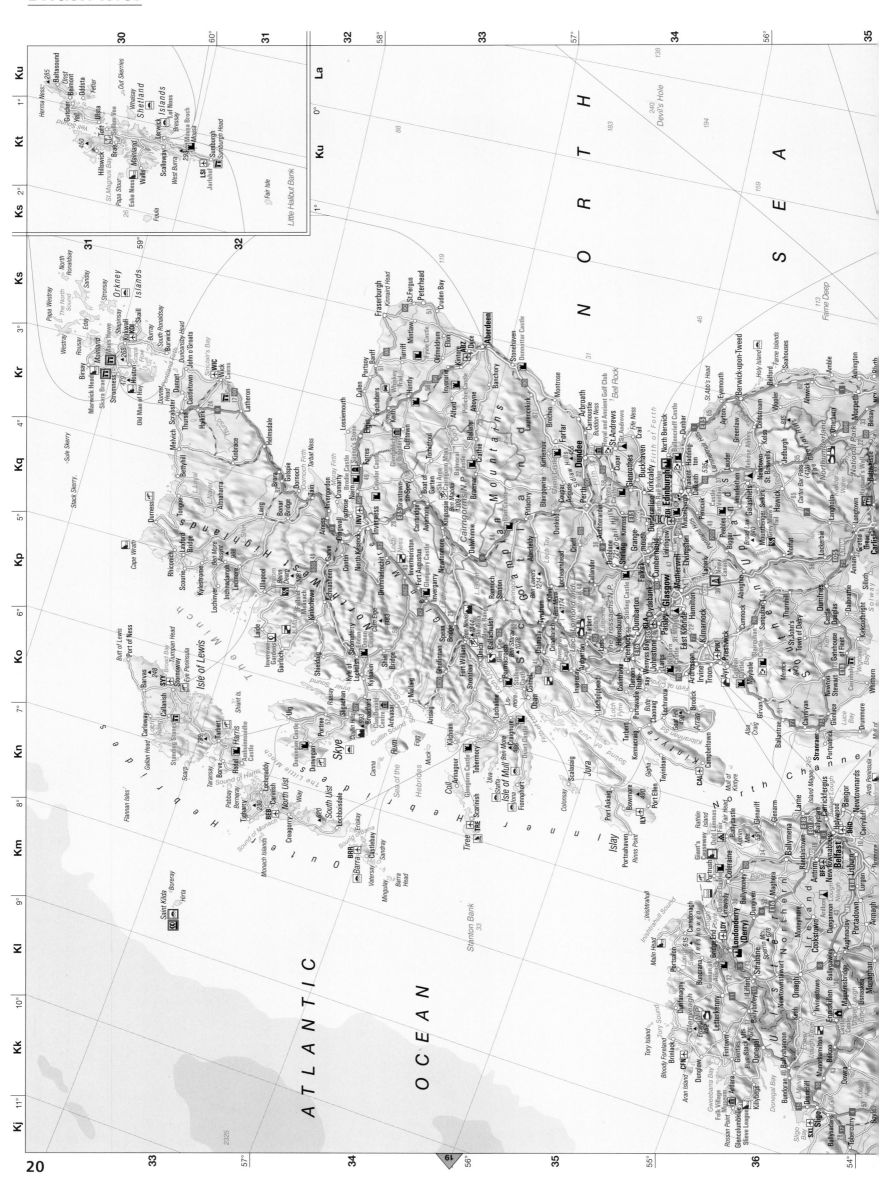

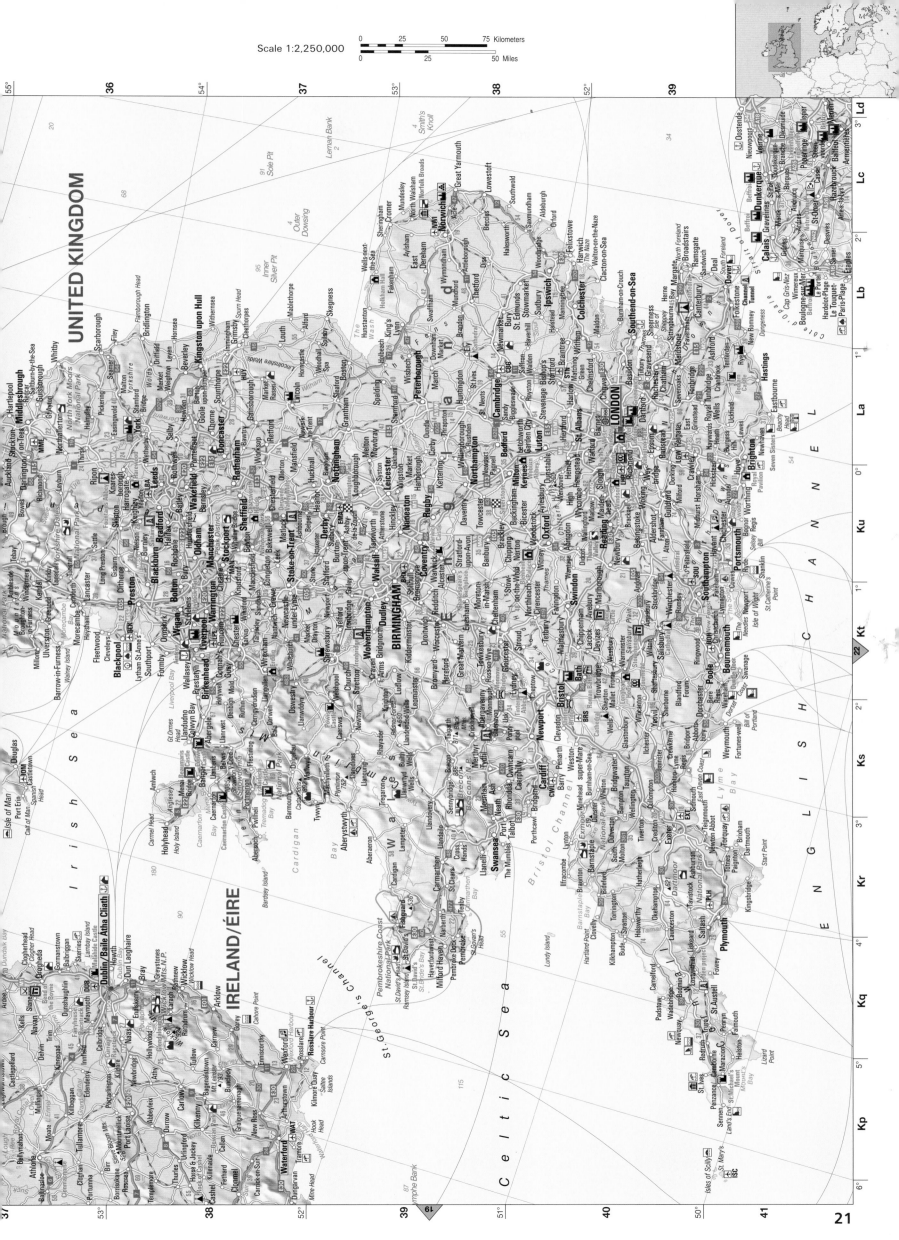

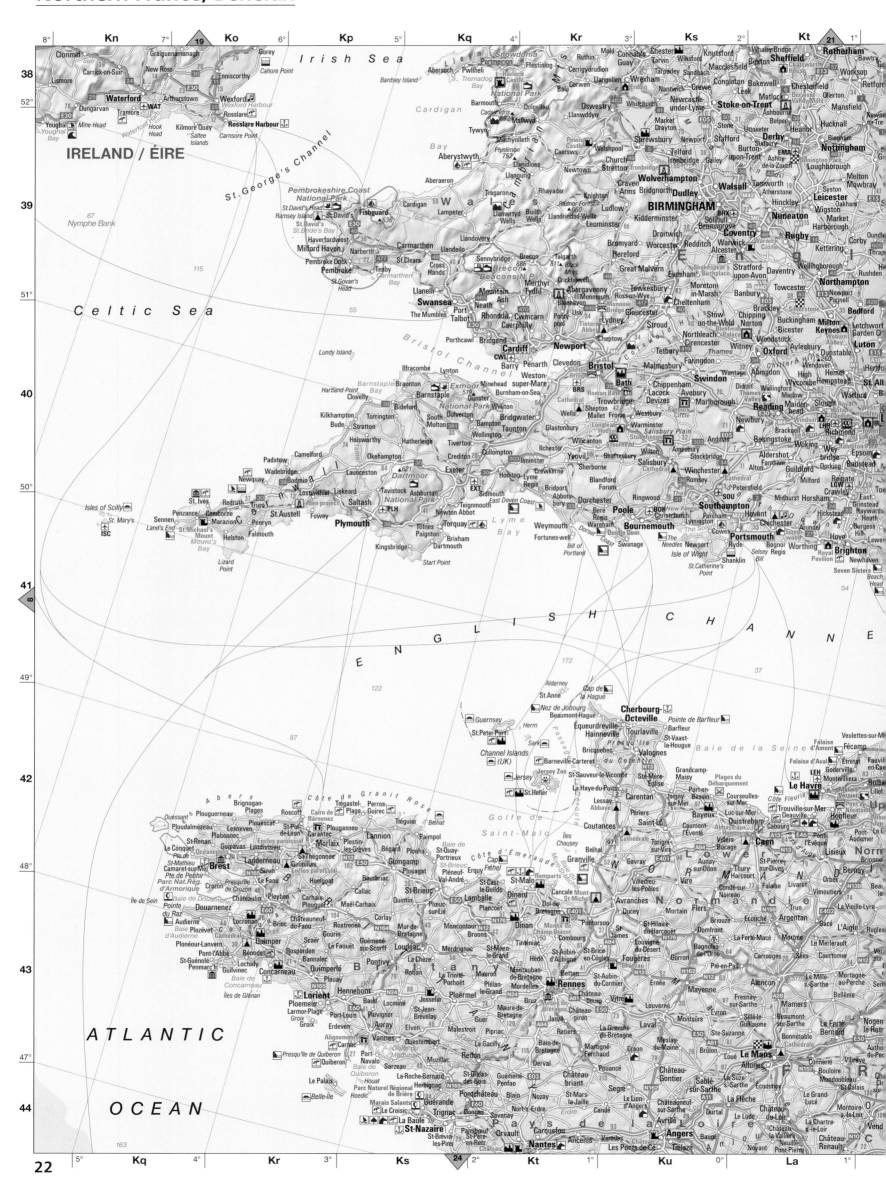

Scale 1:2,250,000

0   25   50   75 Kilometers
0   25   50 Miles

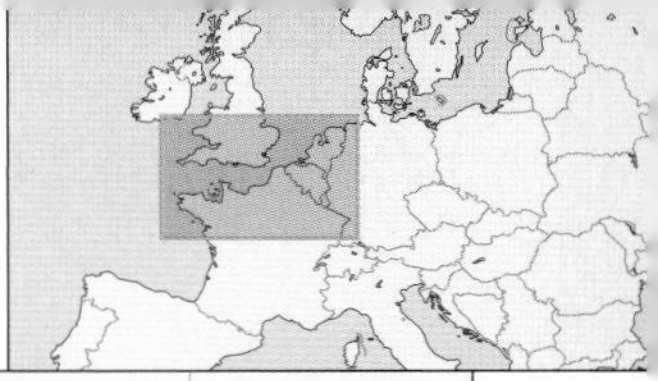

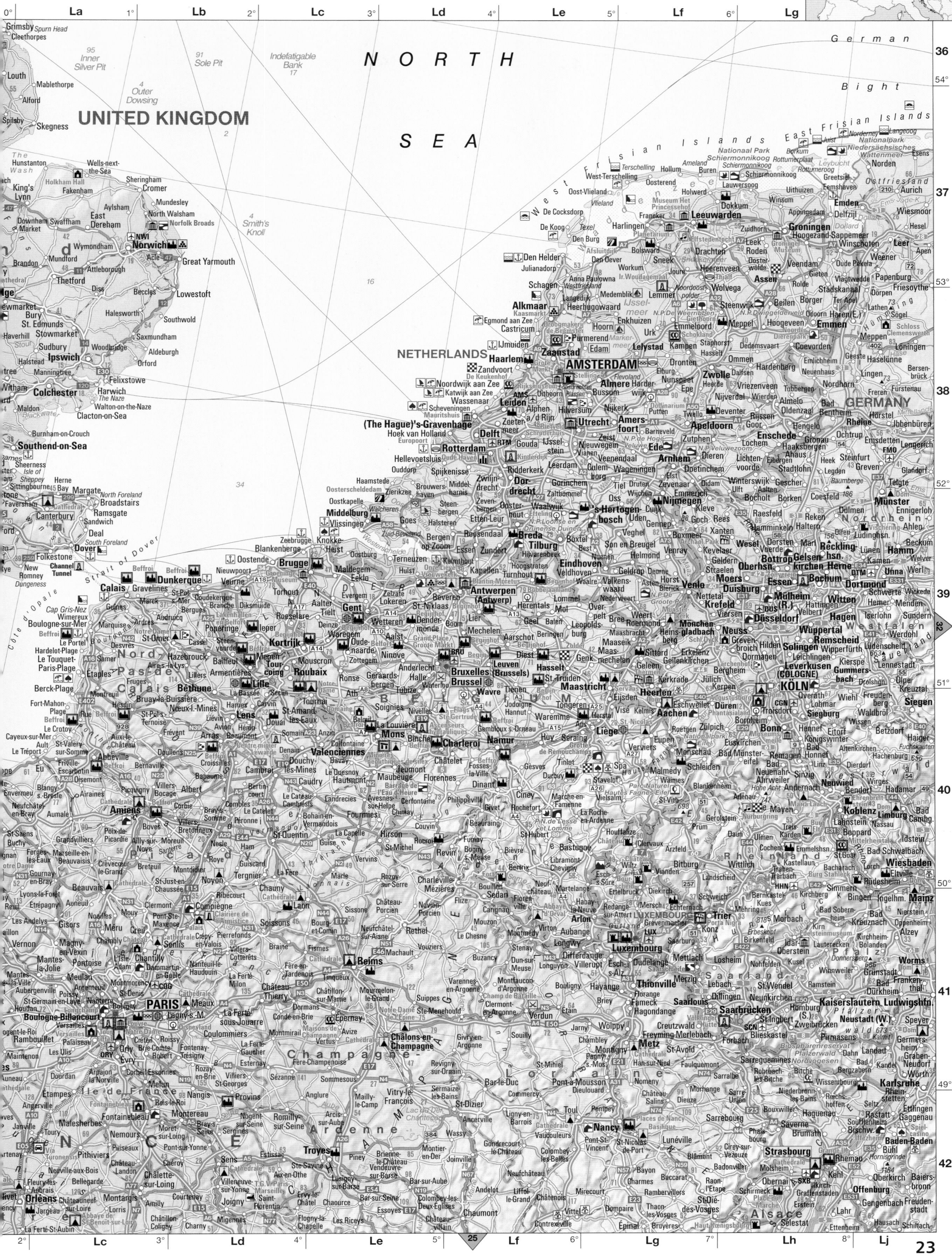

La   Lb   Lc   Ld   Le   Lf   Lg

NORTH
SEA

UNITED KINGDOM

NETHERLANDS

GERMANY

AMSTERDAM

(The Hague)'s-Gravenhage

Rotterdam

Utrecht

Arnhem

Nijmegen

Eindhoven

Antwerpen (Antwerp)

Gent

Bruxelles (Brussel)
Brussel

Liège

Namur

Charleroi

Mons

KÖLN

Düsseldorf

Dortmund

Essen

Bochum

Wuppertal

Bonn

Aachen

Koblenz

Wiesbaden

Mainz

Luxembourg

Trier

Saarbrücken

Metz

Nancy

Strasbourg

Karlsruhe

Baden-Baden

PARIS

Boulogne-Billancourt

Reims

Troyes

Orléans

Calais

Dunkerque

Lille

Amiens

Valenciennes

Arras

Châlons-en-Champagne

North Foreland

Strait of Dover

Channel Tunnel

German Bight

East Frisian Islands

West Frisian Islands

Groningen

Leeuwarden

Emden

Münster

Germersheim

2   1   3   4   5   6   7   8

36   54°   37   53°   38   52°   39   51°   40   50°   41   49°   42

23

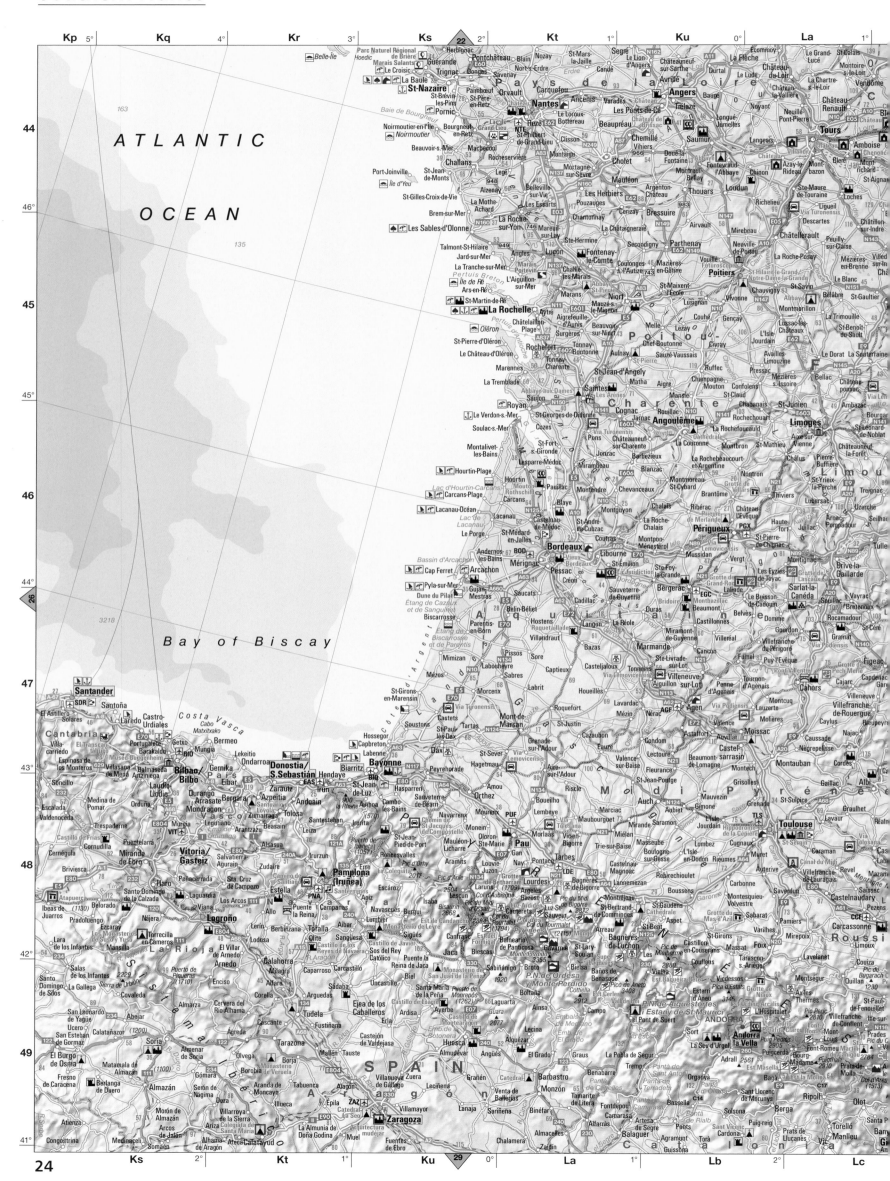

Scale 1:2,250,000

0 25 50 75 Kilometers
0 25 50 Miles

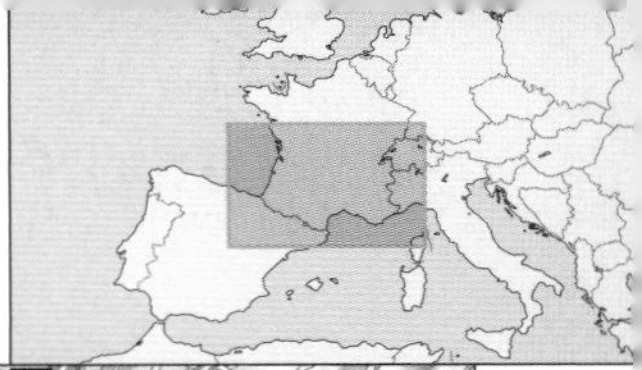

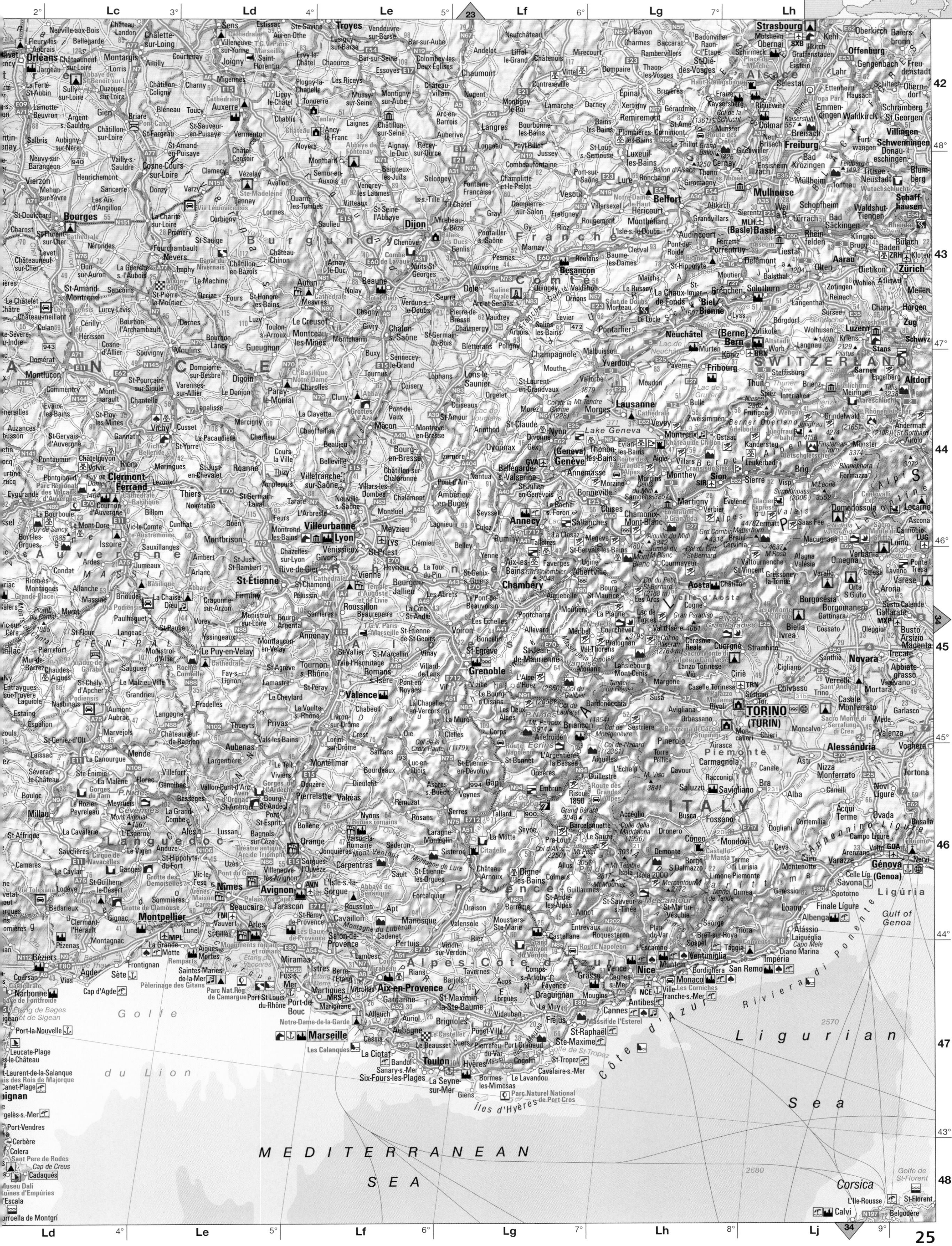

MEDITERRANEAN SEA

LIGURIAN Sea

Gulf of Genoa

Golfe du Lion

Golfe de St-Florent

FRANCE

Burgundy

Franche-Comté

Alsace

Auvergne

Languedoc

Provence

Alpes-Côte d'Azur

Côte d'Azur

Riviera di Ponente

SWITZERLAND

ITALY

Piemonte

Valle d'Aosta

Ligúria

Corsica

Berner Oberland

Massif Central

Major cities labelled include:
Orléans, Bourges, Troyes, Strasbourg, Dijon, Besançon, Belfort, Mulhouse, Basel, Zürich, Bern, Neuchâtel, Lausanne, Genève (Geneva), Lyon, Villeurbanne, St-Étienne, Clermont-Ferrand, Vichy, Valence, Grenoble, Chambéry, Annecy, Chamonix, Mont-Blanc, Aosta, Torino (Turin), Novara, Alessándria, Génova (Genoa), Nice, Monaco, Cannes, Antibes, St-Raphaël, Toulon, Marseille, Aix-en-Provence, Avignon, Nîmes, Montpellier, Béziers, Narbonne, Fribourg, Freiburg, Mâcon, Beaune, Chalon-s.-Saône, Montluçon, Moulins, Roanne, Le Puy-en-Velay, Mende, Privas, Gap, Digne-les-Bains, Menton, San Remo, Imperia, Savona

** france**

2° 3° 4° 5° 6° 7° 8° 9°

Lc Ld Le Lf Lg Lh Lj

42 43 44 45 46 47 48

48° 47° 46° 45° 44° 43°

34

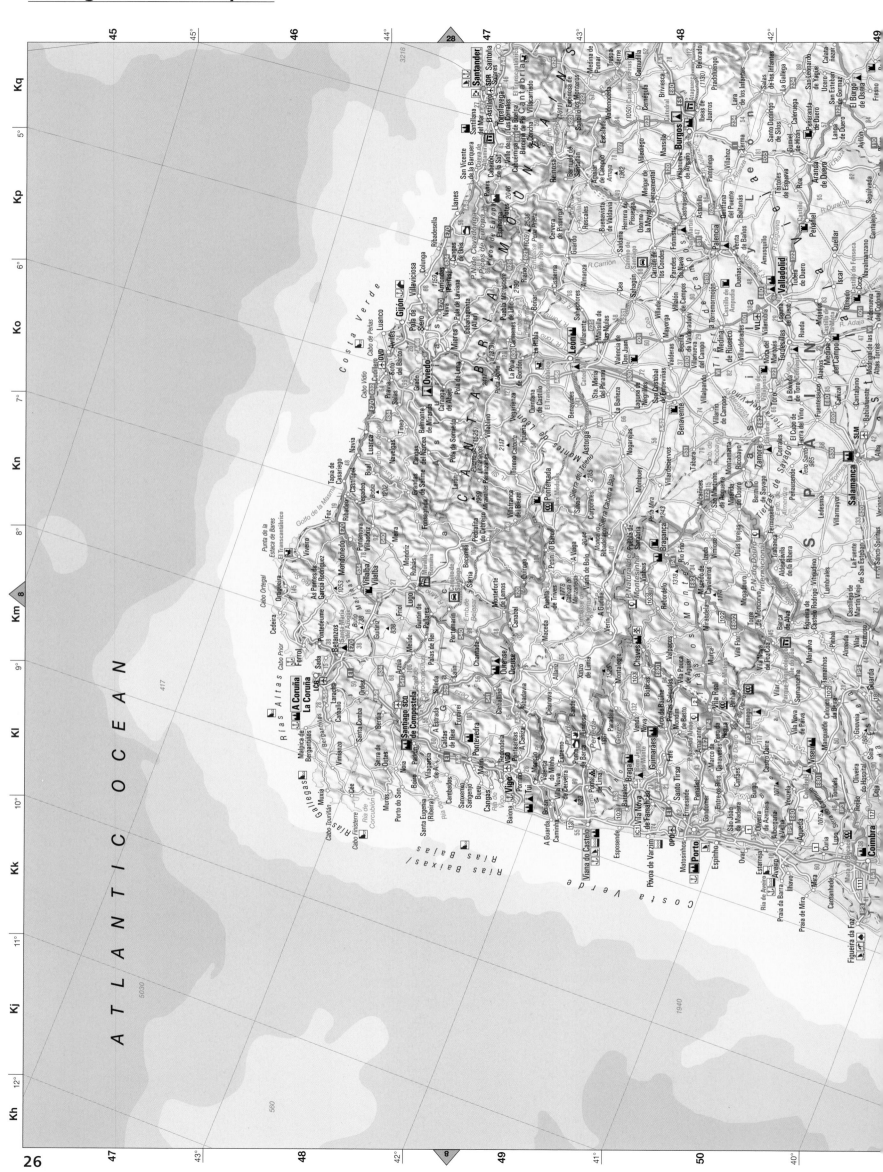

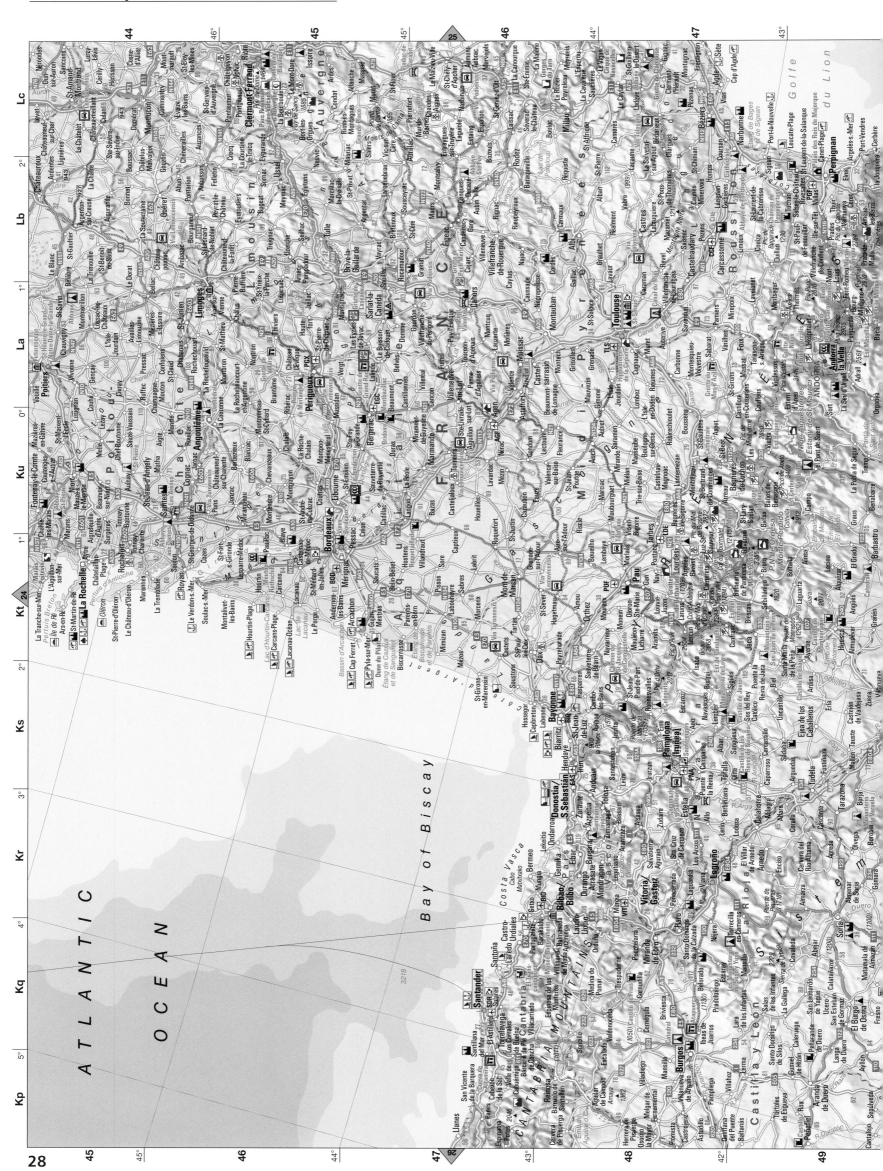

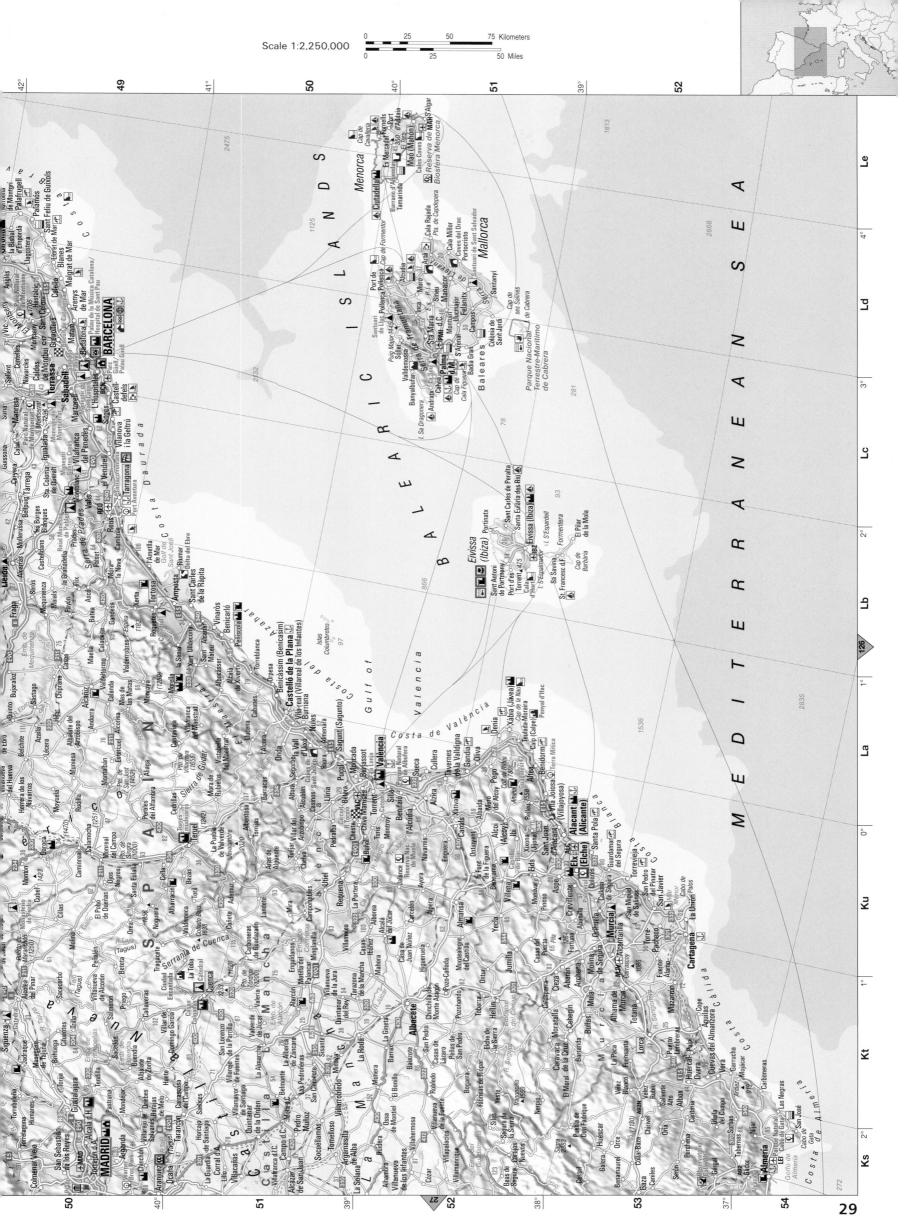

Scale 1:2,250,000

0 25 50 75 Kilometers
0 25 50 Miles

MEDITERRANEAN SEA

BALEARIC ISLANDS

Menorca
Ciutadella
Maó (Mahón)
Reserva de Biosfera Menorca

Mallorca
Port de Pollença
Alcúdia
Manacor
Felanitx
Palma
Santanyí
Parque Nacional Terrestre-Marítimo de Cabrera

Baleares

Eivissa (Ibiza)
Santa Eulària des Riu
Formentera

BARCELONA
Sabadell
Terrassa
L'Hospitalet

Lleida
Tortosa
Castelló de la Plana
Gulf of Valencia
Costa de Valencia
València
Alacant (Alicante)
Elx (Elche)
Murcia
Cartagena
Albacete
Almería

MADRID

29

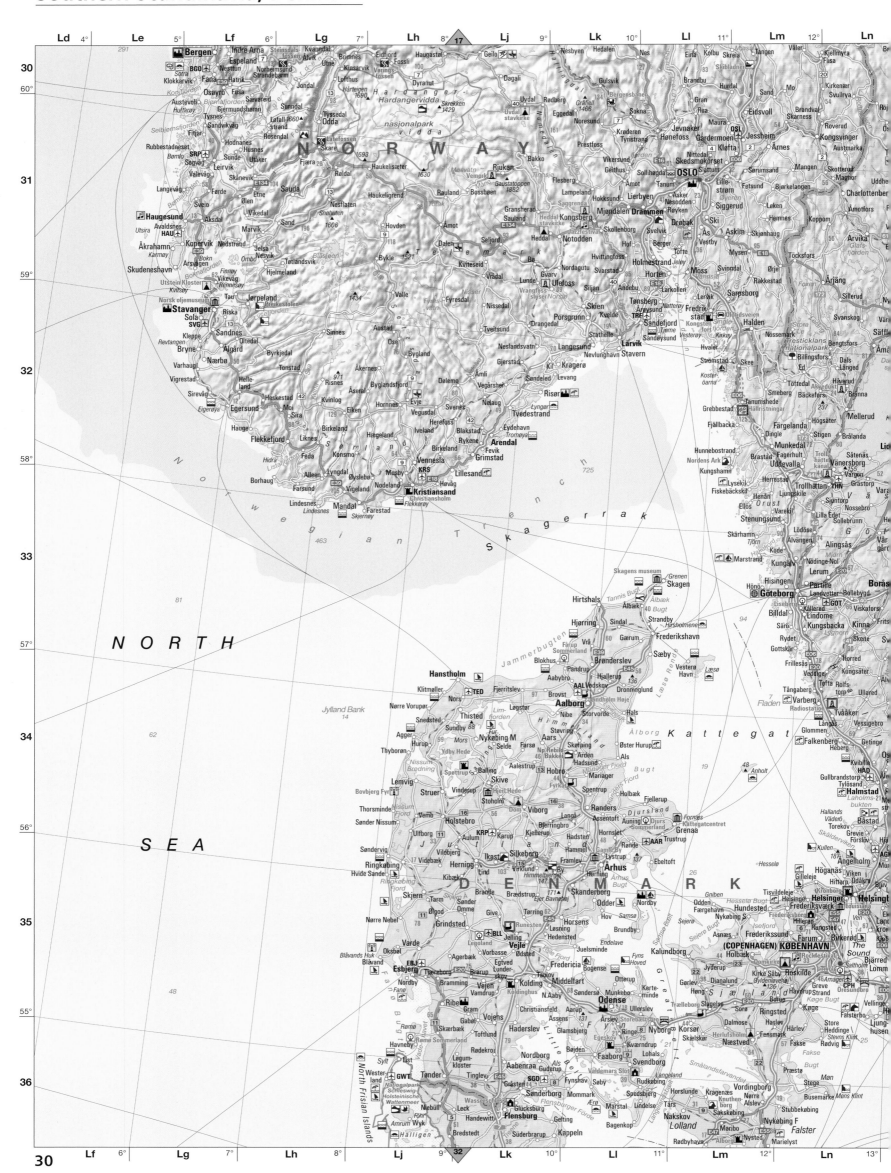

14° Lp 15° Lq 16° Lr 17° Ls 18° 17 Lt 19° Lu 20° Ma 21° Mb

FINLAND

SWEDEN

ESTONIA

LATVIA

LITHUANIA

POLAND

RUSSIA

B A L T I C   S E A

Gotland

Öland

Saaremaa

Hiiumaa

Bornholm (DK)

Courland Lagoon

Gulf of Gdansk

Åland/Ahvenanmaa

Södra Kvarken

Ålandshav

Gävle
Falun
Borlänge
Uppsala
Västerås
STOCKHOLM
Eskilstuna
Södertälje
Örebro
Norrköping
Linköping
Jönköping
Växjö
Kalmar
Karlskrona
Oskarshamn
Västervik
Visby
Turku/Åbo
Mariehamn/Maarianhamina
Klaipėda
Palanga
Liepāja
Ventspils
Kuldiga
Kaliningrad

14° Lp 15° Lq 16° Lr 17° Ls 40 Lt 19° Lu 20° Ma 21° Mb

60°
59°
58°
57°
56°
55°

30
31
32
33 39
34
35
36

31

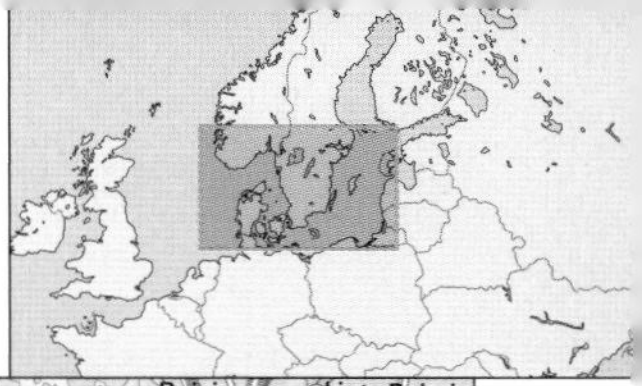

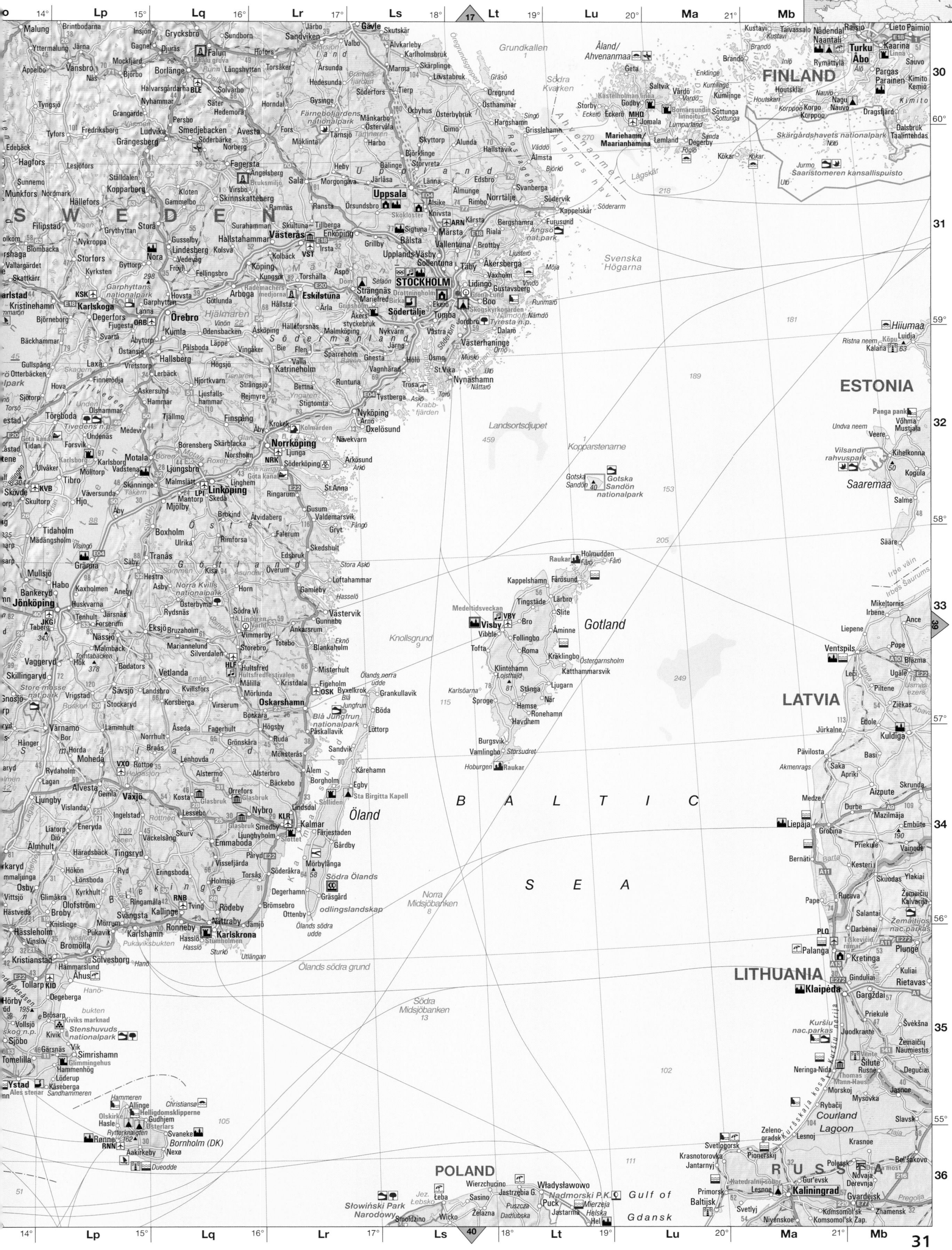

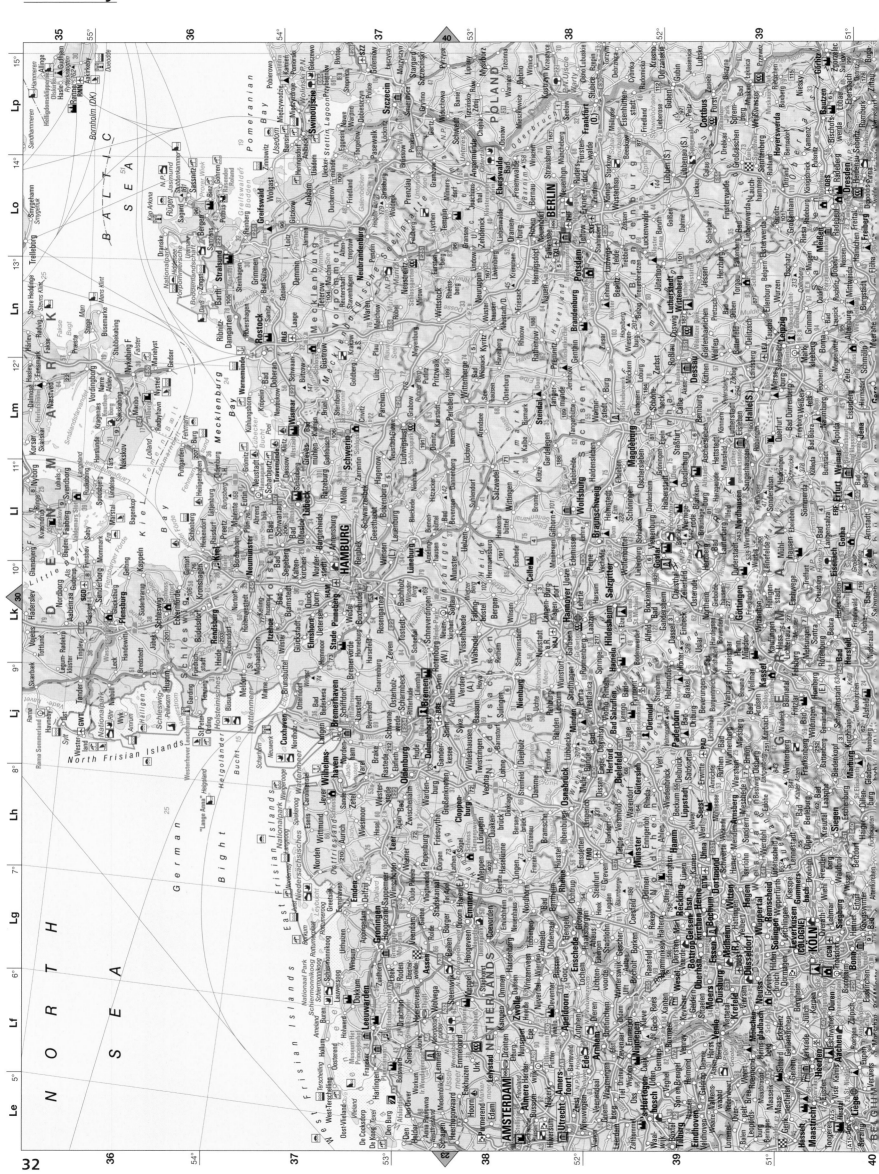

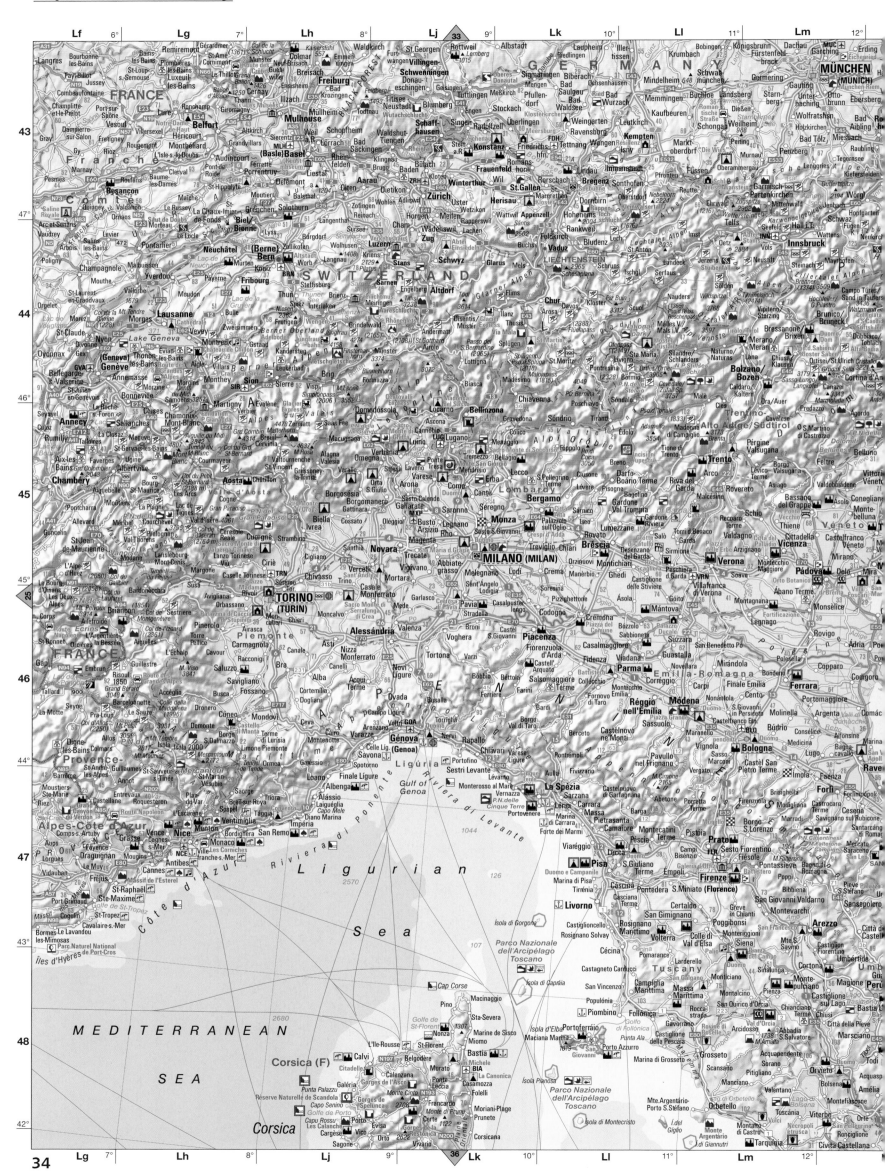

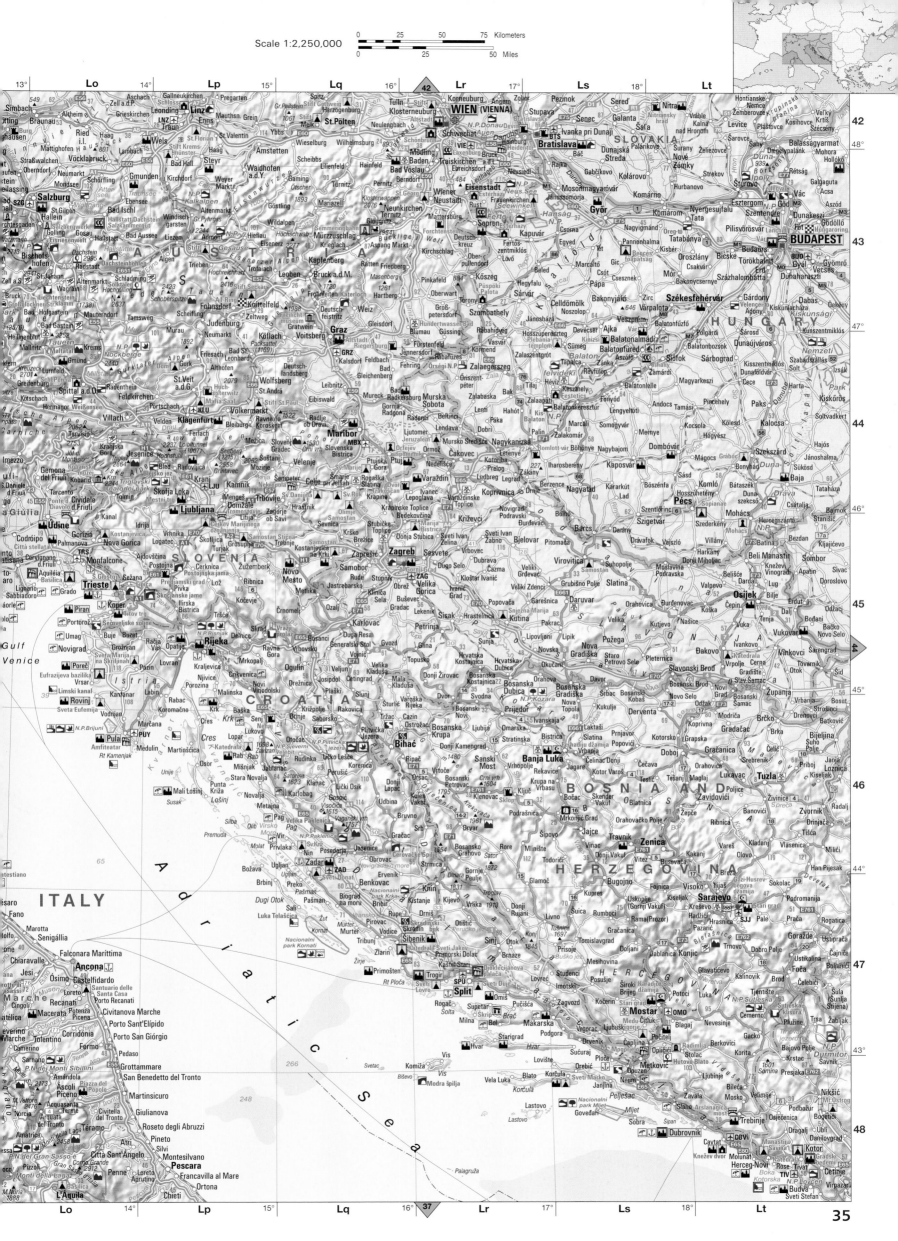

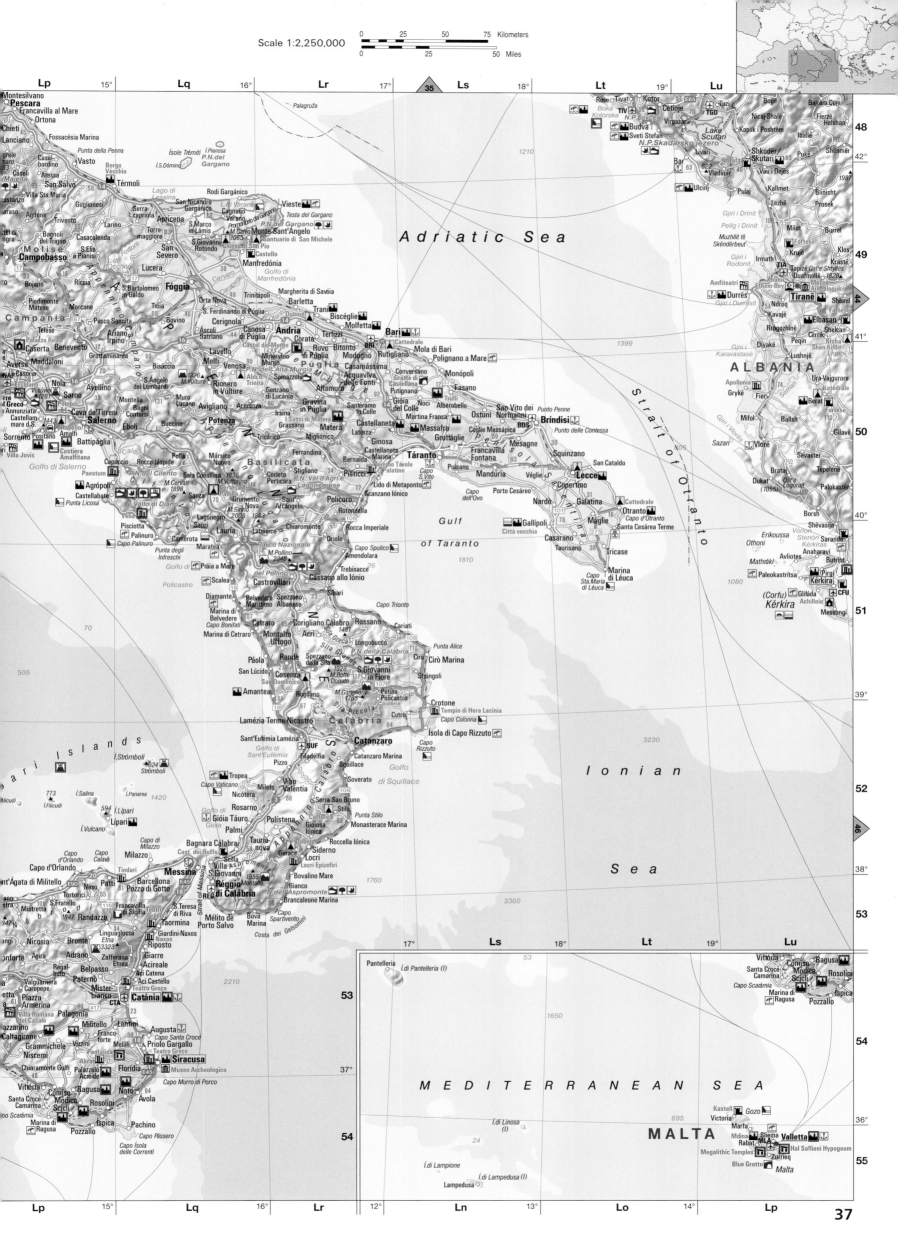

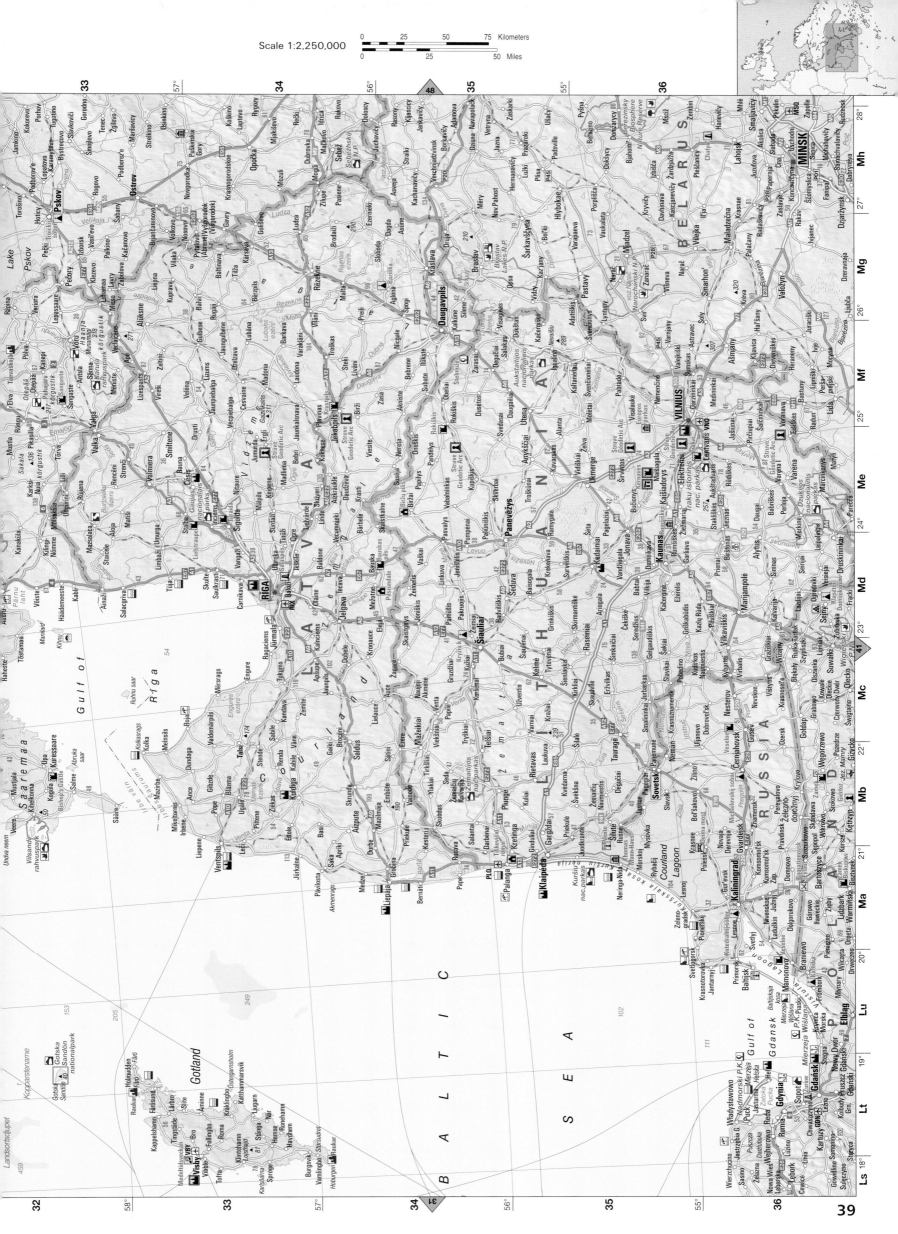

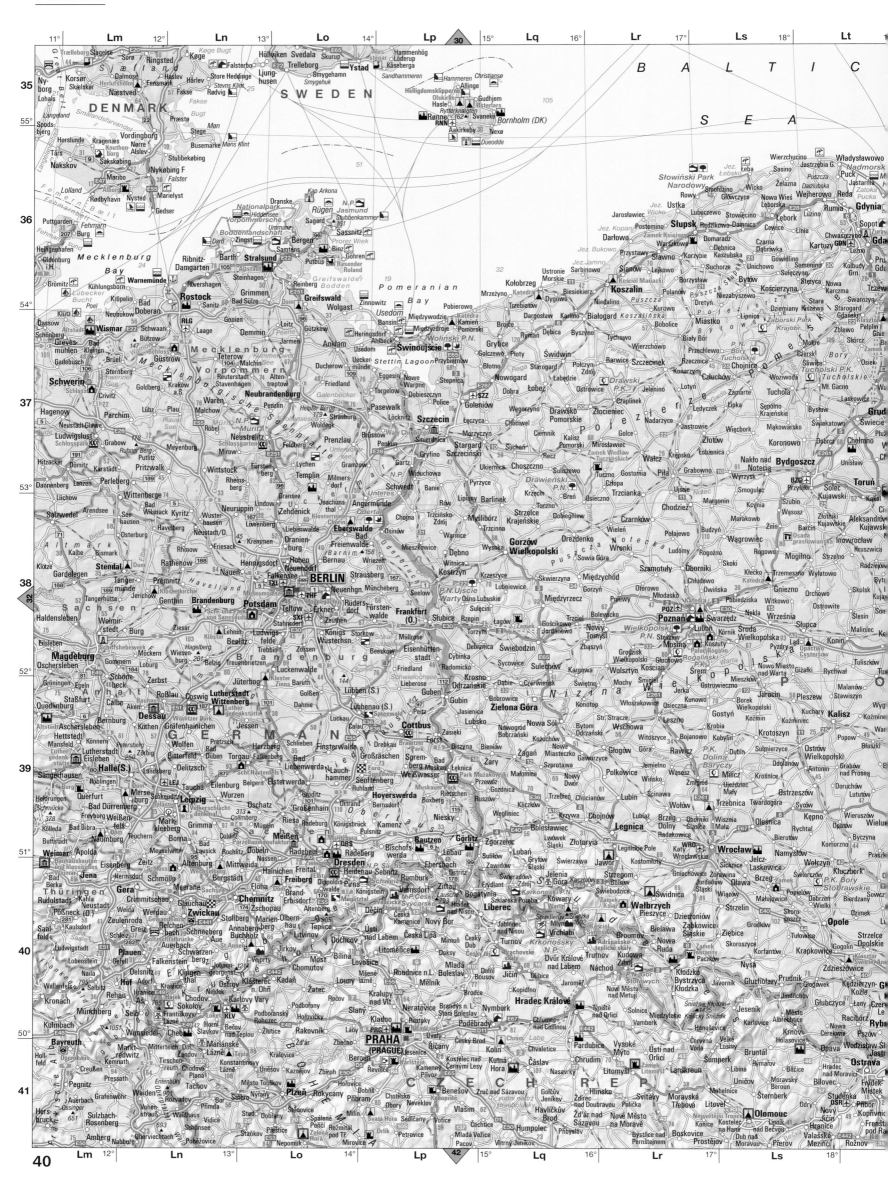

Poland

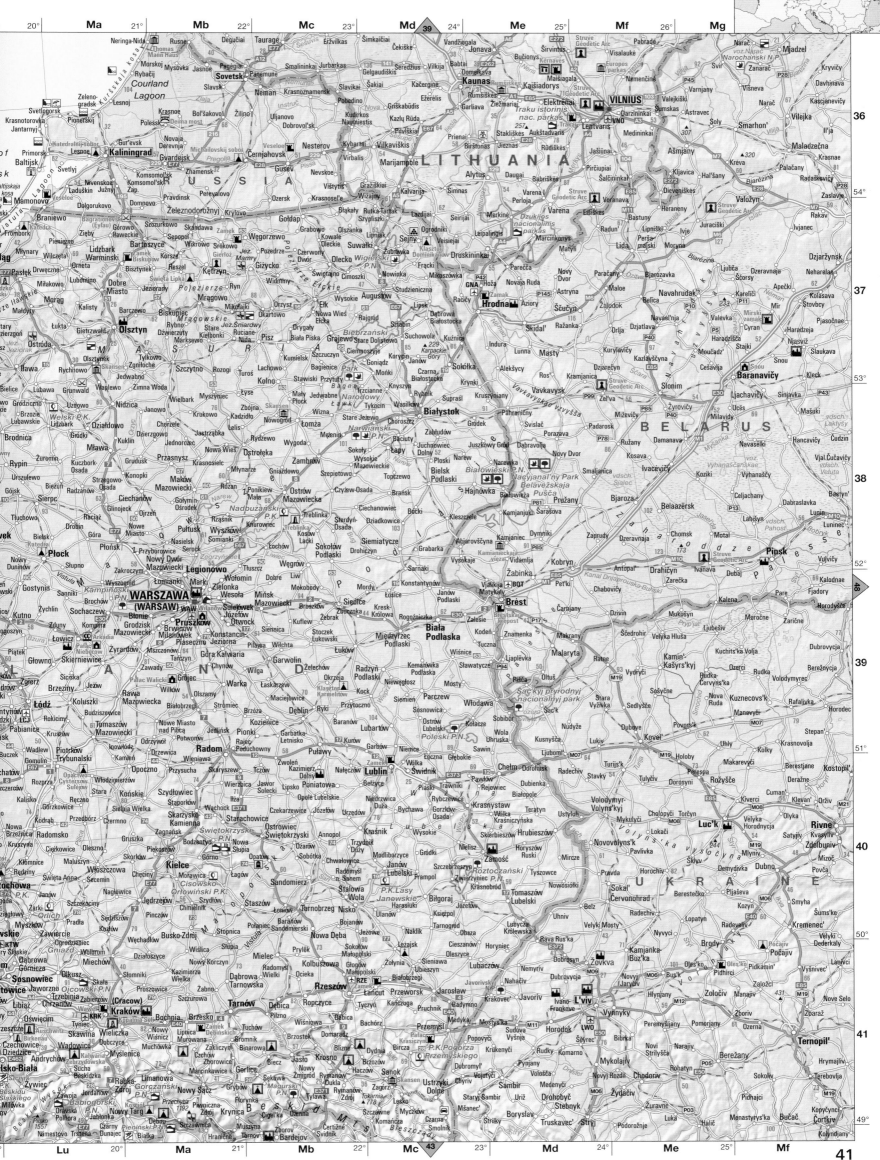

0 25 50 75 Kilometers
0 25 50 Miles

Ma 20° 21° Mb 22° Mc 23° Md 39 24° Me 25° Mf 26° Mg

Neringa-Nida · Rusne · Deguciai · Taurage · Eizvilkas · Simkaiciai · Cekiske · Vandziugala · Jonava Ga · Sirvintos · Pabrade · Narac · Mjadzel

Thomas Mann Haus · Mysovka · Pagegiai · Panemune · Jurbarkas · Seredzius · Vilkija · Babtai · Kernaves · Maisiagala · Europos parkas · Svir · Kryvicy

36

RUSSIA · Kaliningrad · Gvardejsk · Cernjahovsk · Gusev · LITHUANIA · KAUNAS · VILNIUS · IVNO

54°

37

BELARUS

53°

POLAND

WARSZAWA (WARSAW)

38

52°

39

Brest · Biala Podlaska

40

UKRAINE · L'viv · Ternopil'

41

Lu 20° Ma 21° Mb 22° Mc 43 23° Md 24° Me 25° Mf 49°

41

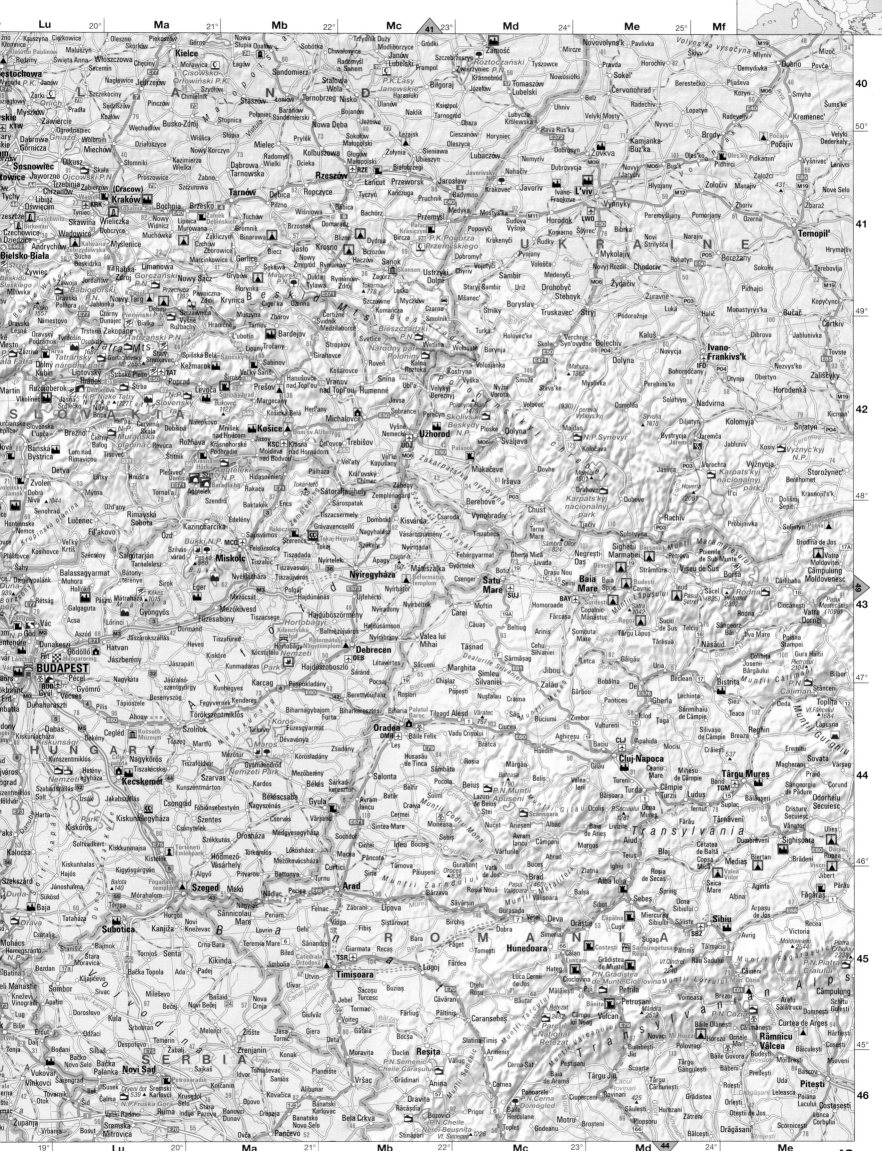

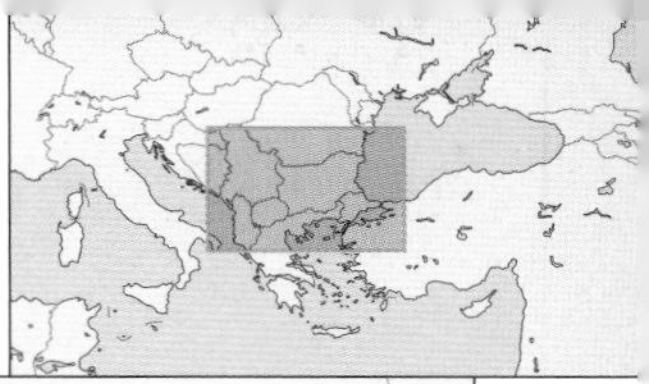

Scale 1:2,250,000

0 25 50 75 Kilometers
0 25 50 Miles

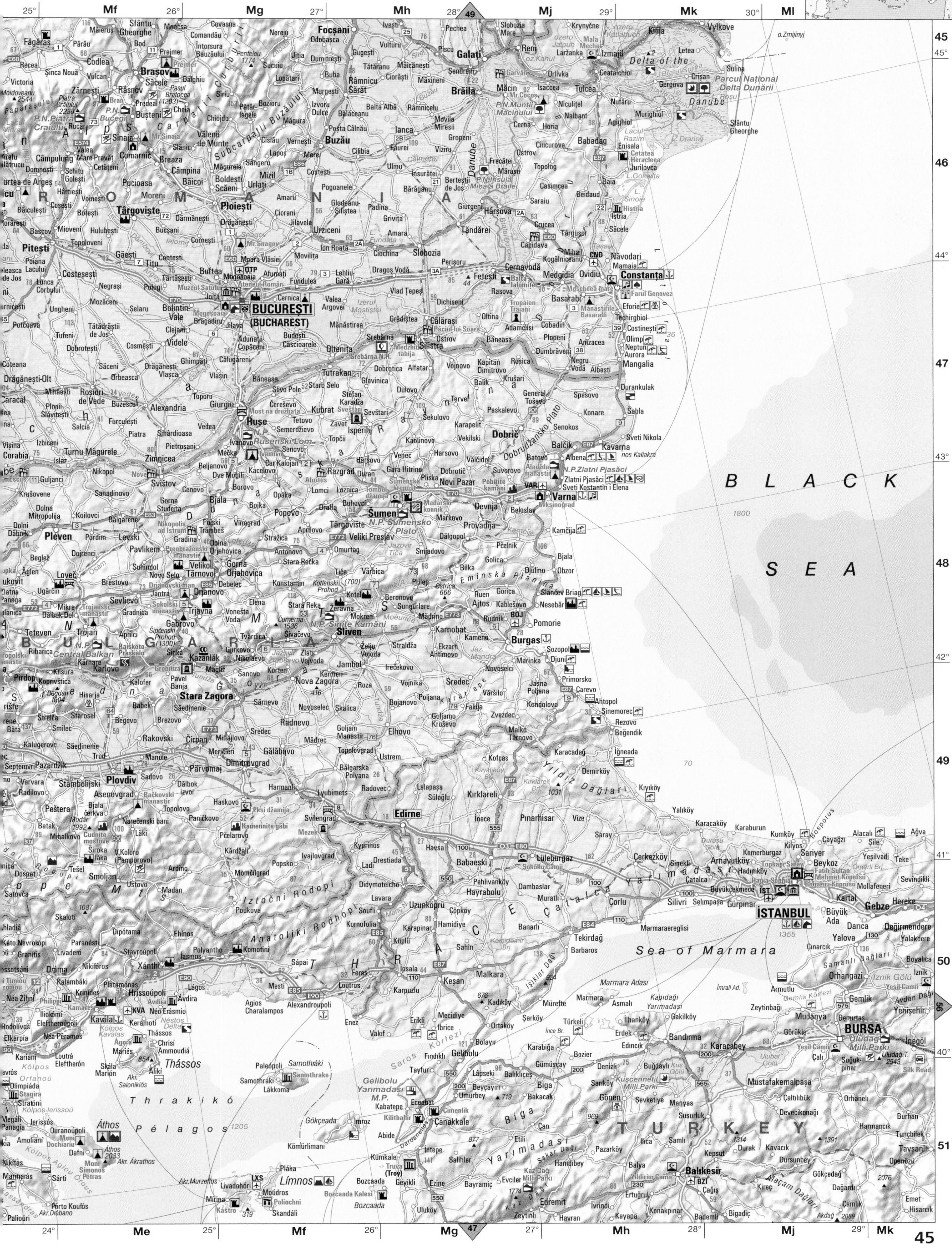

Mf 25° Mg 26° Mh 28° 49 Mj 29° Mk 30° Ml

45
45°
46°
44°
47
43°
48
42°
49
41°
50
40°
51

ROMANIA

BULGARIA

TURKEY

BLACK SEA

Sea of Marmara

Thrakikó Pélagos

Delta of the Danube
Parcul National Delta Dunării

BUCUREŞTI (BUCHAREST)

İSTANBUL

BURSA

Braşov
Galaţi
Brăila
Focşani
Buzău
Ploieşti
Târgovişte
Piteşti
Pleven
Veliko Tărnovo
Ruse
Varna
Šumen
Stara Zagora
Plovdiv
Burgas
Sliven
Edirne
Constanţa
Dobrič
Gebze
Balıkesir

Me 24° Mf 25° Mg 47 26° Mh 27° Mj 29° Mk

24° 25° 26° 27° 28° 29°

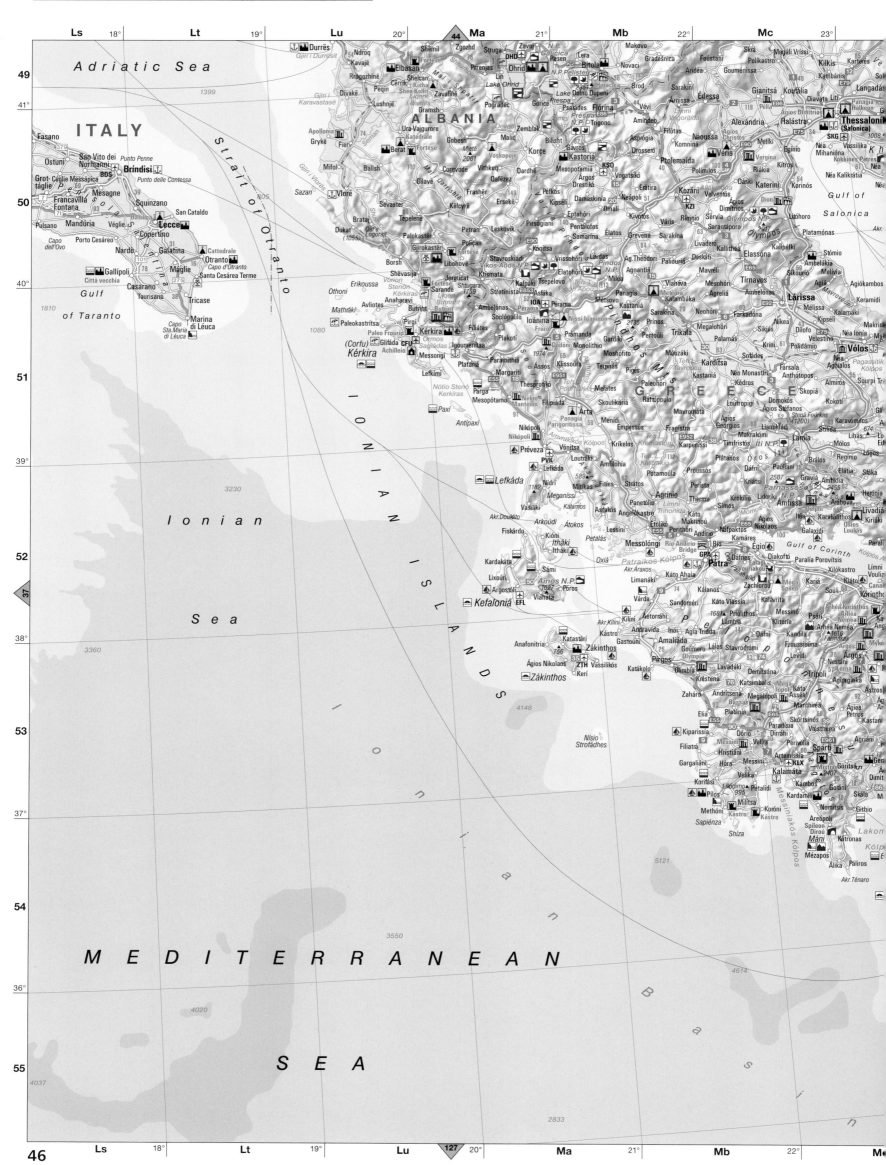

Ls 18°   Lt 19°   Lu 20°   Ma   21°   Mb 22°   Mc 23°

Adriatic Sea

Durrës
Gjiri i Durrësit

49

41°

ITALY

Fasano

Ostuni

San Vito dei Normanni

Brindisi

BDS

Punto Penne

Grot-táglie   Céglie Messápica

Mesagne

Francavílla Fontana

Squinzano

San Cataldo

Pulsano   Mandúria   Véglie

Copertino

Lecce

50

Capo dell'Ovo

Porto Cesáreo

Nardò

Galatina

Cattedrale

Otranto

Casarano

Maglie

Santa Cesárea Terme

Gallípoli

Città vecchia

Taurisano

Tricase

Gulf

of Taranto

1810

40°

Capo Sta.Maria di Léuca

Marina di Léuca

Strait of Otranto

Gjiri i Vlorës

Sazan

Vlorë

Apollonia

Grykë

Fier

Mifol

Ballsh

Berat
Fortesë

Bávros
2061

ALBANIA

Durrës   Ndroq

Kavajë

Rrogozhinë

Peqin

Lushnjë

Gramsh

Ura-Vajgurore

Katedrale

Shemil   Zgozhd

Forcësën

Elbasan

Shelcan

Cërrik
Shen Kollit

Zavalinë

Divakë

Gobesh

Malig

Struga   Zavoj

Prrenjas

Lin

Lake Ohrid

Pogradec

Gorice

Zemblak

Bilisht

Korçë

Voskopoje

Pëfkos

Frashër

Ersekë

Leskovik

Petran

Kipséli

Damaskinia

Neápoli

Korinós

Bitola

Novaci

Brod

Florína

Kastoría

Eptahóri

Kastaniá

Grevená

Deskáti

Elassóna

Tírnavos

Lárissa

Vólos

Ionian Sea

MEDITERRANEAN

SEA

46

Ls 18°   Lt 19°   Lu 20°   Ma 21°   Mb 22°   Mc

Scale 1:2,250,000

Kilometers 0 25 50 75
Miles 0 25 50

Thrakikó Pélagos

Aegean Sea

Northern Sporades

TURKEY

BURSA
İZMİR
Balıkesir
Manisa
Aydın
Denizli

ATHINA (ATHENS)
Pireás (Piraeus)

Mirtóon Sea

Southern Sporades

Dodecanese Sporades

Rhodes
Kárpathos

Sea of Crete

Crete
Iráklio
Hania (Khania)

Livikó Pélagos

Levantine Basin

47

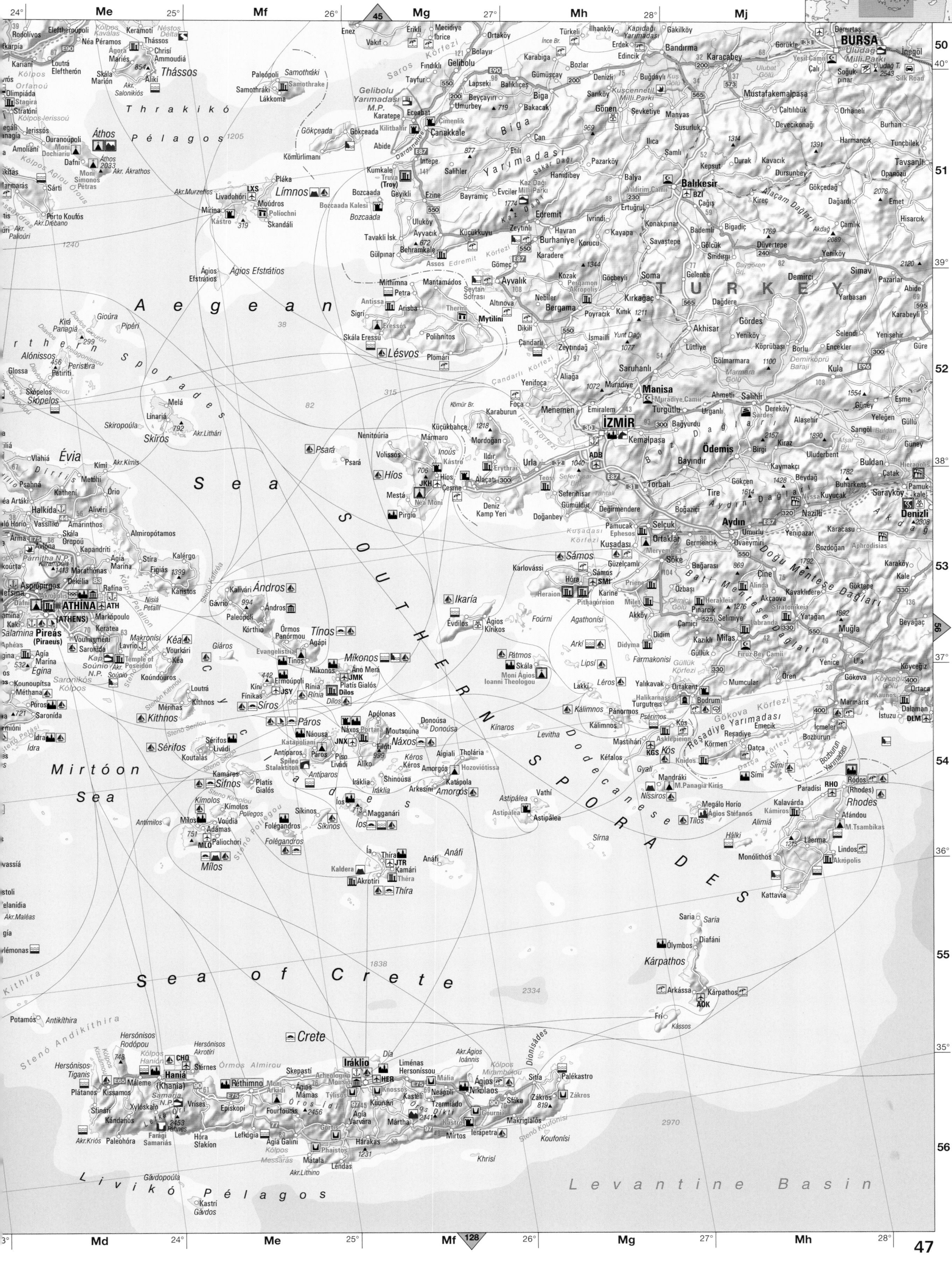

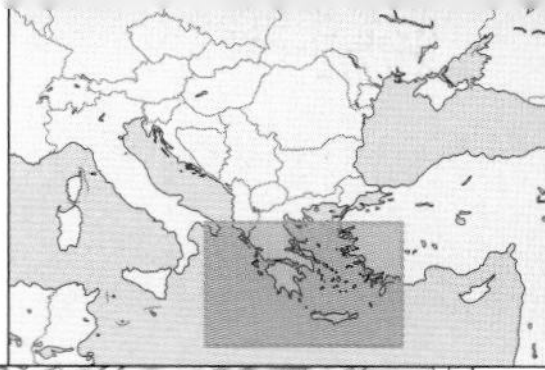

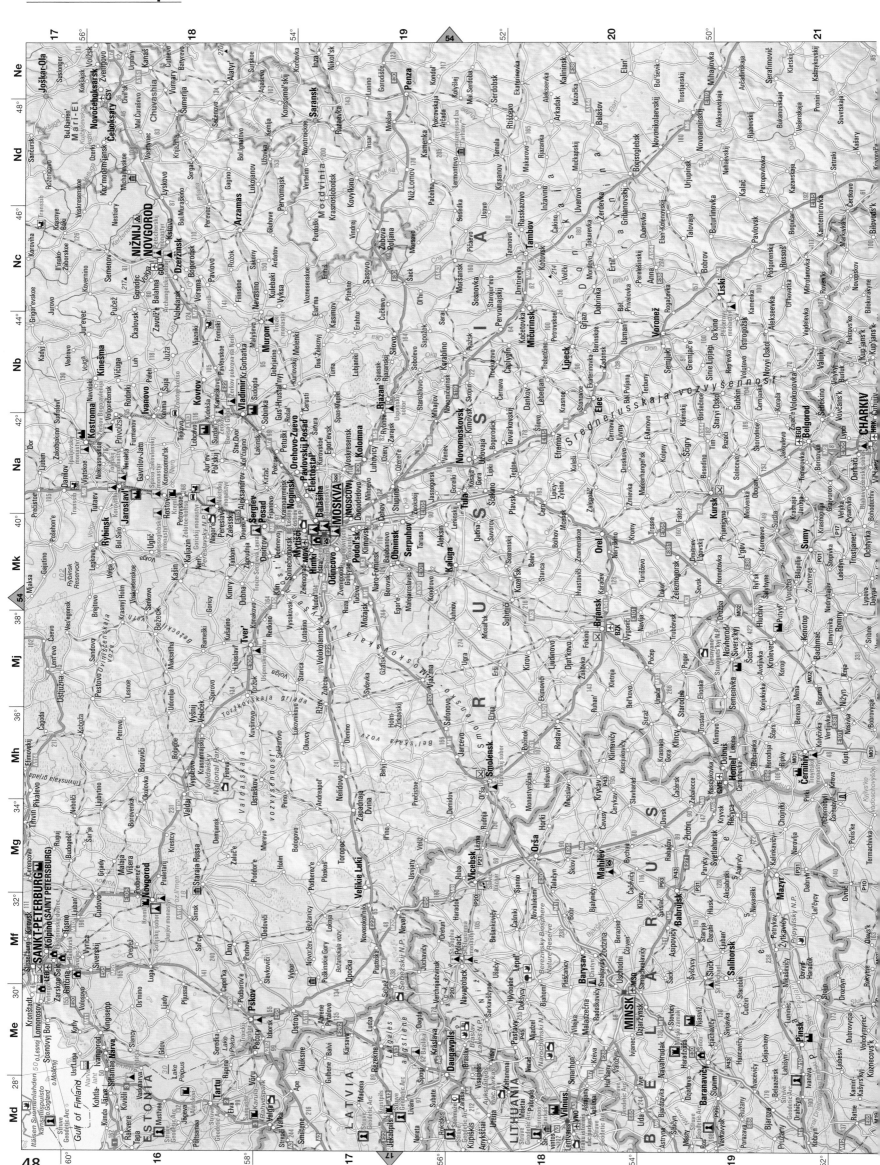

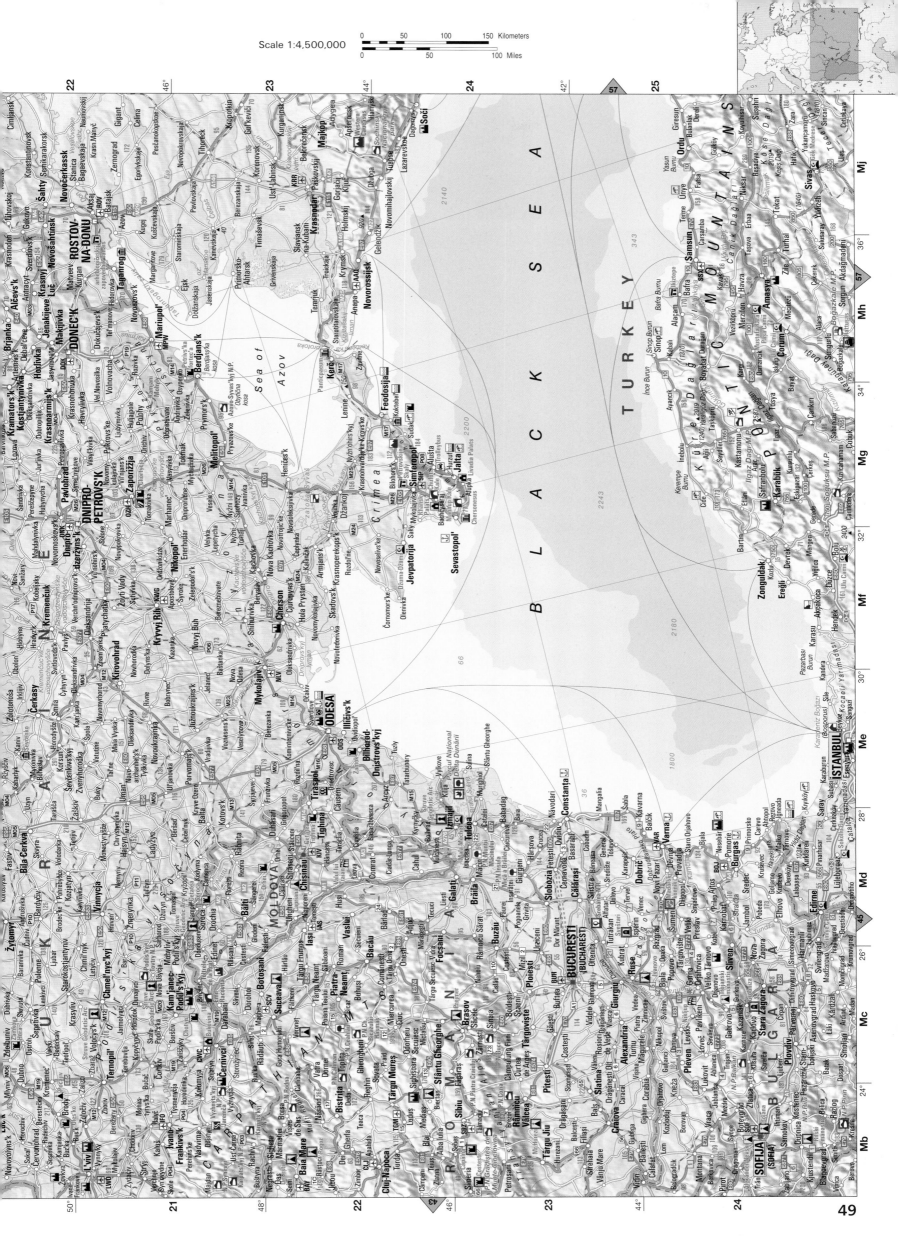

Caravans were once vital for travel through the Syrian desert.

Mount Everest (8,850 m), the world's tallest mountain.

ASIA

THE CRADLE OF CIVILIZATION

Asia has a total area of 44.4 million km^2 and encompasses around one-third of the world's land. The continent has a maximum length of 11,000 kilometers from east to west and a maximum of 8,500 kilometers from north to south. The vast majority of Asia's land area is above the equator in the northern hemisphere. Only a few areas in Southeast Asia and the Indian subcontinent are south of the equator. The continent borders the Arctic Ocean in the north, the Pacific Ocean in the east, and the Indian Ocean in the south. In the west, Asia borders Europe, the Mediterranean Sea, North Africa and the Red Sea. The Bering Sea, a section of the Pacific, separates Siberia in northern Asia from North America. The Arabian Peninsula, India, the Malay Peninsula, Korea, and Kamchatka are the largest and most significant of the many peninsulas on the continent. The Japanese Islands are located off the northeastern coast of mainland Asia. A large belt of mountain systems extends from the Caucasus (maximum height, 5,642 m) and the Pontic Mountains (3,937 m) in western Asia to the Himalayas and farther east into Southeast Asia.

Asia is by far the most populated of the world's seven continents and its more than 3.4 billion inhabitants are unequally distributed. Sparsely populated Mongolia has a population density of just two inhabitants per square kilometer. Bangladesh, one of the world's most crowded nations, has a population density in excess of 900 inhabitants per square kilometer. China and India, the world's most populous nations, are both home to more than one billion people.

Tokyo: Modern skyscrapers in Japan's capital and largest city (10 million inhabitants.).

Most of the world's major religions were founded in Asia many centuries ago. Judaism, Islam, and Christianity all originated in western Asia. India was the birthplace of Hinduism and Buddhism, while Taoism and Confucianism both originated in China.

Asia

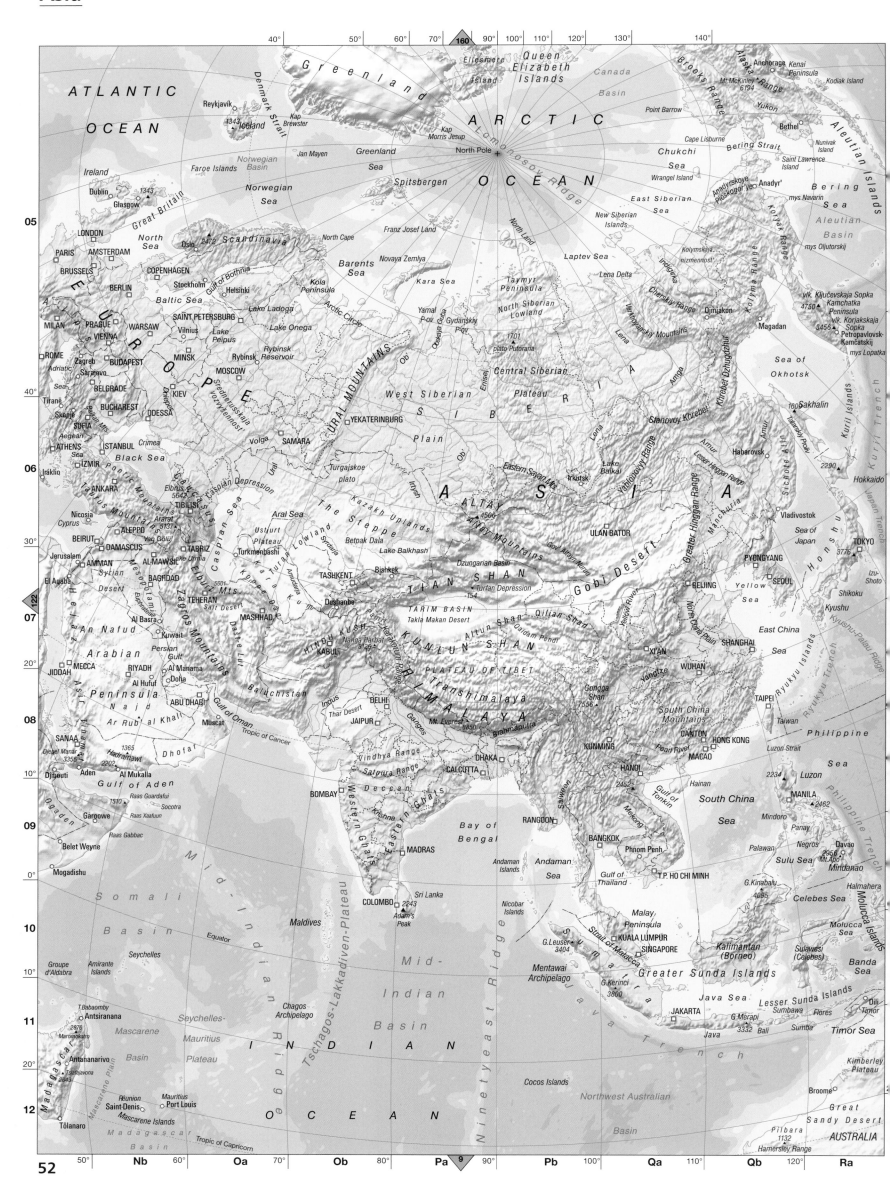

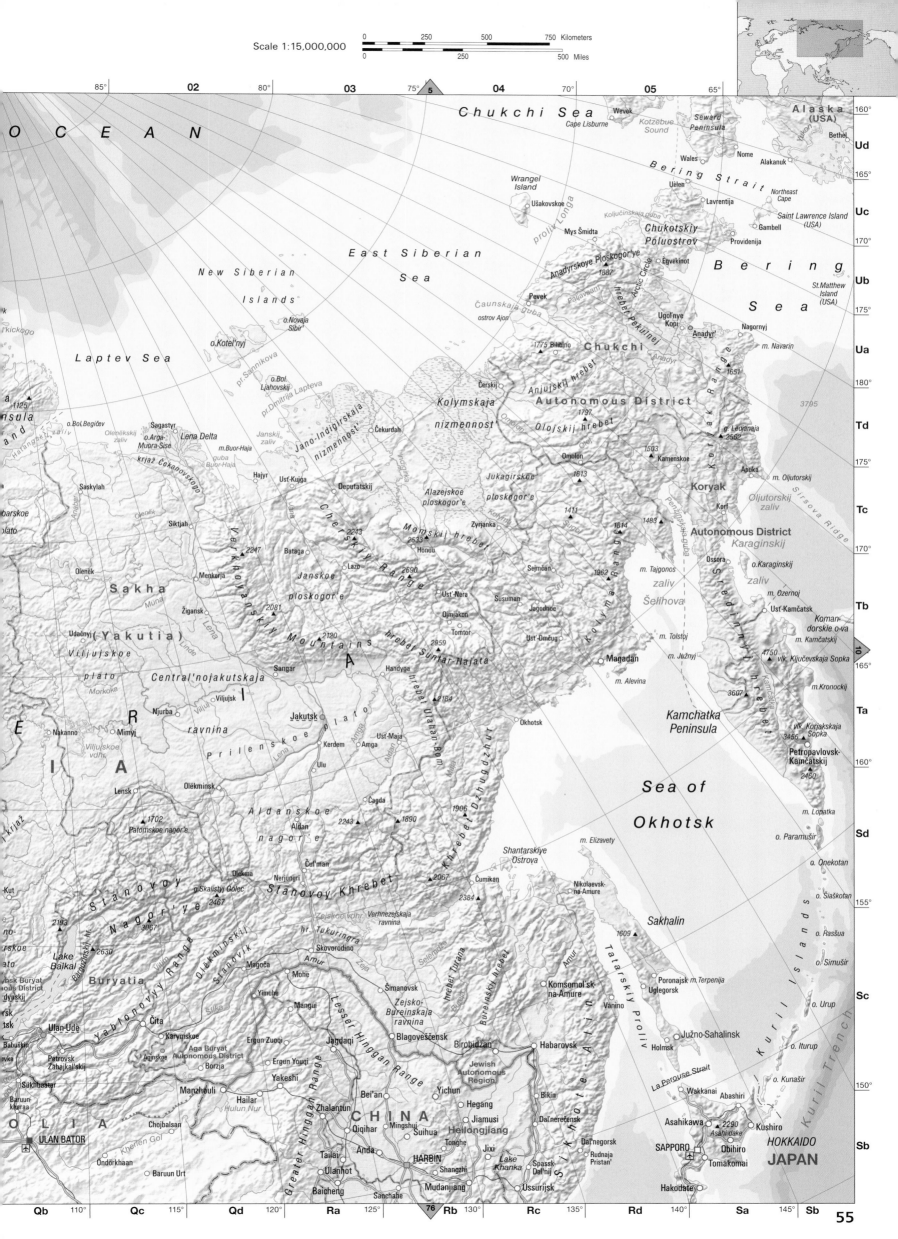

Scale 1:15,000,000

0 250 500 750 Kilometers
0 250 500 Miles

O C E A N

Chukchi Sea

Wevek
Cape Lisburne
Kotzebue Sound
Seward Peninsula
Alaska (USA)
Yukon
Bethel

Wrangel Island
Ušakovskoe
Mys Šmidta
Kotzebue
Wales
Nome
Alakanuk

Ud

East Siberian Sea

prolix Longa
Bering Strait

Uělen
Northeast Cape
Lavrentija
Saint Lawrence Island (USA)

Uc

New Siberian Islands

o.Novaja Sibir'
Koljučinskaja guba
Chukotskiy Poluostrov
Gambell
Providenija

Ub

o.Kotel'nyj
Čaunskaja guba
Anadyrskoye Ploskogor'ye 1887
Egvekinot
St.Matthew Island (USA)

Bering

Pevek
ostrov Ajon
hrebet Pekul'nej
Ugol'nye Kopi
Sea

Ua

Laptev Sea

o.Bol. Ljahovskij
pr.Sannikova
1775 Bilibino
Chukchi
Anadyr'
Nagornyj
m. Navarin

pr.Dmitrija Lapteva
Čerskij
Autonomous District
Anadyr
1651

Td

1125
Hatanga?
zaliv
o.Bol.Begičev
Olenëkskij zaliv
Sagastyr
Kolymskaja nizmennost'
Olojskij hrebet 1797
g.Ledjanaja 2562

o.Arga-Muora-Sise
Lena Delta
m.Buor-Haja
Janskij zaliv
Jano-Indigirskaja nizmennost'
Omolon
1503
Kamenskoe
Apuka
m. Oljutorskij

kraj Čekanovskogo
guba Buor-Haja
Čekurdah
Indigirka
Jukagirskoe ploskogor'e
1613
Oljutorskij zaliv
Sirsova Ridge

Saskylah
Hajyr
Ust'-Kujga
Deputatskij
Alazejskoe ploskogor'e
Zyrjanka
Kolyma
Koryak
Korf

Tc

Andylah
Olenëk
Olenëk
Siktjah
2247
Cherskiy Range 2243
Momskij hrebet 2533
Honuu
Sejmčan
1411
1814
1483
Autonomous District Karaginskij
Ossora
o.Karaginskij

Sakha
Menkerja
Bataga
Lazo
2690
Ust'-Nera
1962
m. Tajgonos
Šelihova
zaliv
m, Özernoj

Tb

Udačnyj
(Yakutia)
Žigansk
2081
Janskoe ploskogor'e
Ojmjakon
Susuman
Jagodnoe
Ust'-Kamčatsk
Koman- dorskie o-va
m. Kamčatskij

Viljujskoe plato
2120
Verhojanskiy Mountains
Sangar
hrebet Suntar-Hajata 2959
Tomtor
Ust'-Omčug
m. Tolstoj
m. Južnyj
4750
vlk. Ključevskaja Sopka

Muna
Lena
Linde
Central'nojakutskaja
A
Handyga
m. Alevina
3607
m.Kronockij

Nakanno
Viljuj
Viljuj
ravnina
Kerdem
Amga
Okhotsk
Kamchatka Peninsula
vlk. Korjakskaja Sopka 3456

Ta

Mimyj
Njurba
Jakutsk
Ust'-Maja
Petropavlovsk-Kamčatskij

Viljujskoe vdhr.
prilenskoe
plato
Lena
Aldan
2460

E
R
I
A
Lensk
Olëkminsk
Ulu
Aldanskoe nagor'e
Čagda
2243
1890
1906
Sea of Okhotsk
o. Paramušir

Sd

1702
Palomskoe nagor'e
Aldan
2067
Čumikan
m. Elizavety
o. Onekotan

Stanovoy
g.Skalistyj Golec
2467
Stanovoy Khrebet
2384
Nikolaevsk-na-Amure
1609
o. Šiaškotan

Sc

2193
Nagor'ye
3067
hr. Tukuringra
Verhnezejskaja ravnina
hrebet Turana
Sakhalin
o. Rassua

2630
Yablonovyy Range
Skovorodino
Zeja
hrebet Dzhugdzhur
Amur
Komsomol'sk-na-Amure
o. Simušir

Lake Baikal
Mogoča
Olëkminskij
Šimanovsk
Zejsko-Bureinskaja ravnina
Poronajsk m.Terpenija
Uglegorsk

Ulan-Udè
Čita
Karymskoe
Yimube
Mangui
Blagoveščensk
Birobidžan
Habarovsk
Vanino
Južno-Sahalinsk
Holmsk

Buryatia
Aginskoe
Šilka
Ergun Zuoqi
Jewish Autonomous Region
Bikin
La Perouse Strait
o. Kunašir

Petrovsk Zabajkal'skij
Borzja
Ergun Youqi
Hegang
Dal'nerečensk
Wakkanai
Abashiri

Sухbaatar
Ulan-Ude
Manzhouli
Yakeshi
Bei'an
Yichun
Spassk-Dal'nij
Pristan'
Rudnaja
Asahikawa
2290
Asahi dake
Kushiro

OLIA
ULAN BATOR
Hailar
Hulun Nur
Zhalantun
Jagdaqi
Heilongjiang
Tonghe
Jixi
HOKKAIDO

Chojbalsan
CHINA
Qiqihar
Mingshui
Suihua
HARBIN
Jiamusi
Lake Khanka
Dal'negorsk
SAPPORO
JAPAN

Baruun Urt
Kherlen Gol
Tailai
Anda
Shangzhi
Mudanjiang
Ussurijsk
Hakodate
Tomakomai

Ondörhaan
Uhanhot
Baicheng
Sanchagie

Sb

55

Scale 1:4,500,000

0 50 100 150 Kilometers
0 50 100 Miles

RUSSIA

KAZAKHSTAN

GEORGIA

ARMENIA

AZERBAIJAN

IRAN

IRAQ

C A S P I A N   S E A

C A U C A S U S

Mk Na Nb Nc Nd Ne

38° 40° 42° 44° 46° 48° 50°

23 44° 24 42° 25 40° 26 38° 27 36° 28 34° 29

Lazarevskoe · Psebaj · Čerkessk · Suvorovskaja · Zelenokumsk · Južno-Suhokumsk · Kulaly aral
Soči · AER · Adler · Kislovodsk · Pjatigorsk · Georgievsk · Mozdok · Kočubej · Fort-Shevchenko
Sokhumi · Nal'čik · Nazran · Groznyj · Mahačkala · MCX · Kaspijsk · Manghystau · Aktau
Kutaisi · Tbilisi (Tibilisi) · Vladikavkaz · Derbent
Batumi · Rustavi · Gori · Telavi · Quba
Trabzon · Artvin · Gyumri · Vanadzor · Gänžä · Mingeçevir · Xaçmaz
Erzurum · Kars · YEREVAN · Sumqayit · Baki (Baku)
Erzincan · Ağrı · Ararat · Xankendi (Stepanakert) · Şuşa
Van · Khoy · Naxçivan · Kapan
Diyarbakır · Batman · TABRIZ · Ardabil · Rasht
Al Mawsil · Orumiyeh · Maragheh · Zanjan · Qazvin · Karaj
Arbil · As Sulaymaniyah · Sanandaj · Hamadan · TEHRAN (TEHERAN)
Kirkuk · Kermanshah · Qom
Samarra · Baghdad · Borujerd · Arak · Kashan

57

Northern Arabian Peninsula

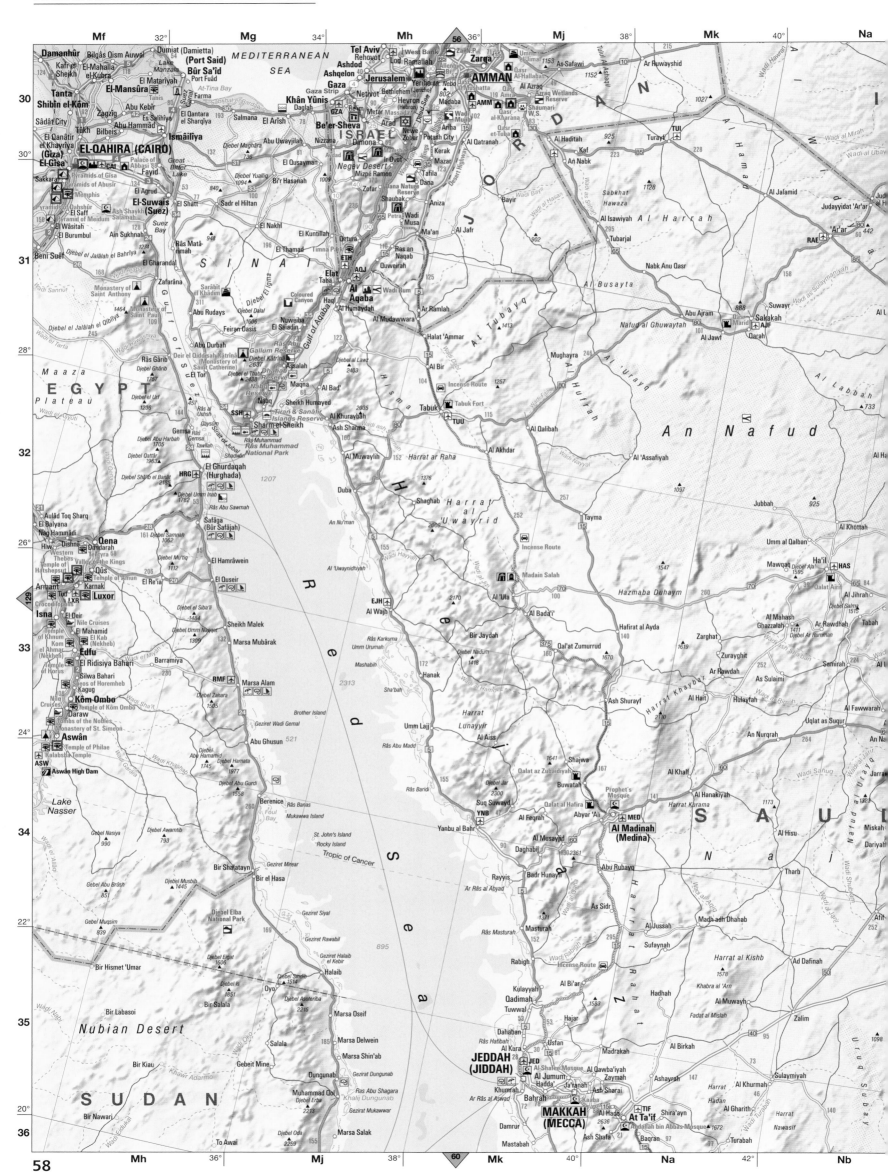

BAGHDAD

IRAQ

MESOPOTAMIA

ZAGROS MOUNTAINS

IRAN

Karbala · Al-Hillah · Babylon · Borsippa

An Najaf · Ad Diwaniyah · Al Kut · Khorramabad

Al Amara · An Nasiriyah · Ur · Eridu · Uruk

Dezful · Šuš · Shushtar · Ahvaz

ESFAHAN (ISFAHAN)

Najaf Abad · Natanz

AL BASRA · Abadan · Khorram Shar · Bandar-e-Emam Khomeyni

Umm Qasr · Al Faw · Shiraz · Pasargad

KUWAIT

Al Kuwayt (Kuwait) · Salmiya · Hawalli · Ahmadi · Fahaheel

Bandar-e-Busher

Hafar al Batin · Al Qaysumah · Ras al Khafji

Wafra · Mina Saud

A R A B I A

Buraydah · Az Zilfi · Unayzah

Persian Gulf

Jubail al Sinaiyah · Raihaimah · Tarut · Ad Dammam · Dhahran · Al Khobar

BAHRAIN · Al Manama

QATAR · **Ad Dawhah (Doha)** · Ar Rayyan · Al Wakrah · Umm Said

Al Hufuf · Abqaiq · Dukhan

AR RIYAD (RIYADH) · Ad Dir'iyah · Masmak Fort

Al Kharj · Harad

UNITED ARAB EMIRATES

Ruwais · Liwa Oasis

Layla · As Sayh

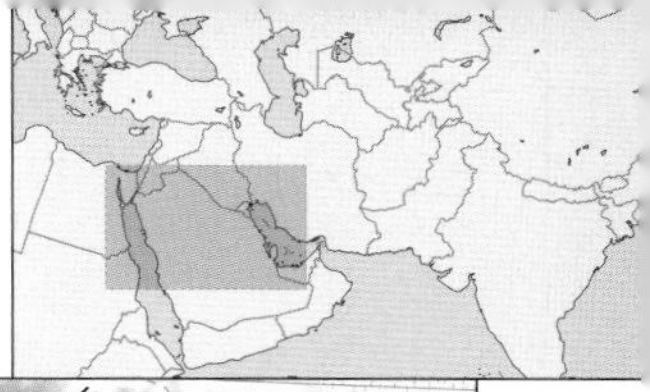

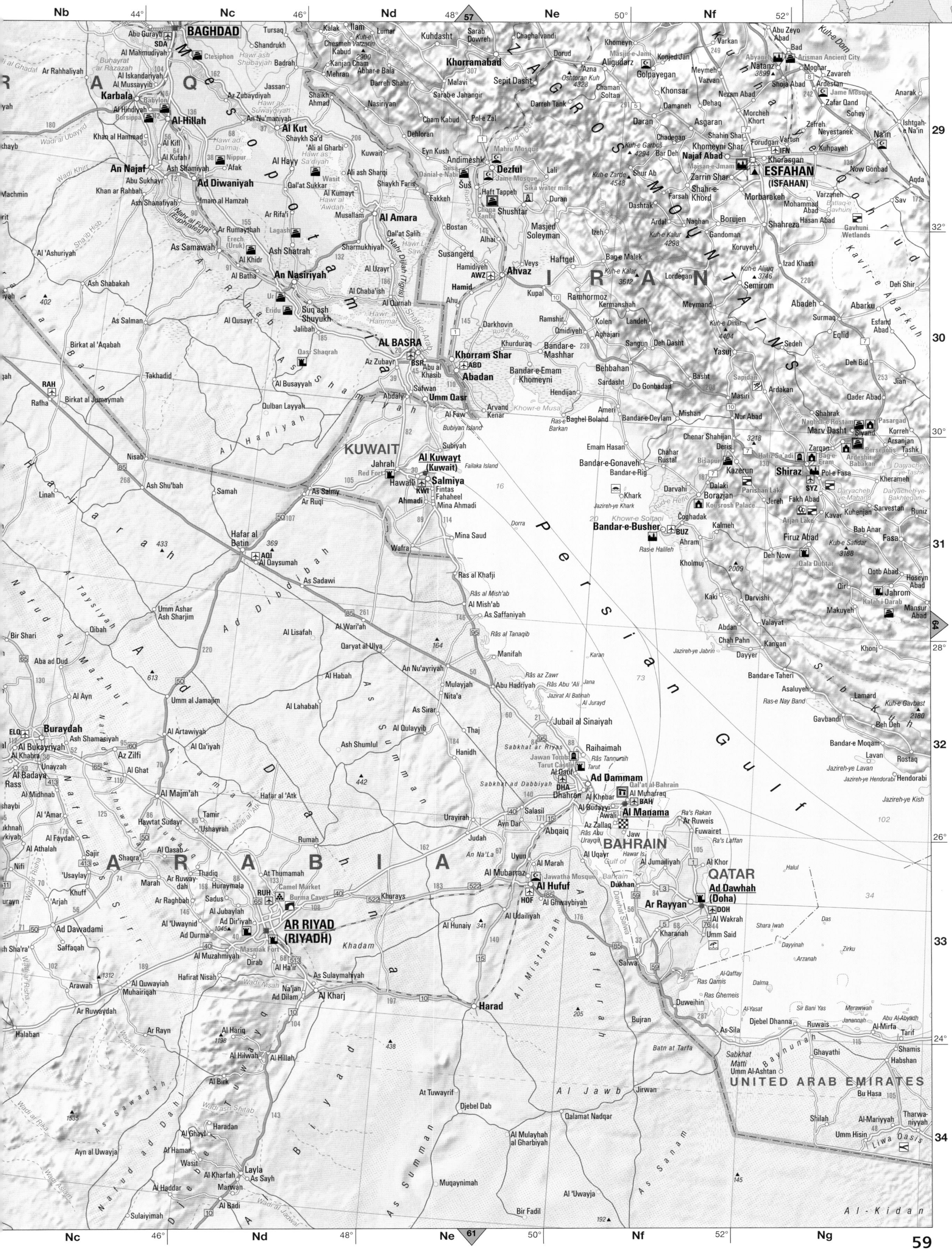

Southern Arabian Peninsula

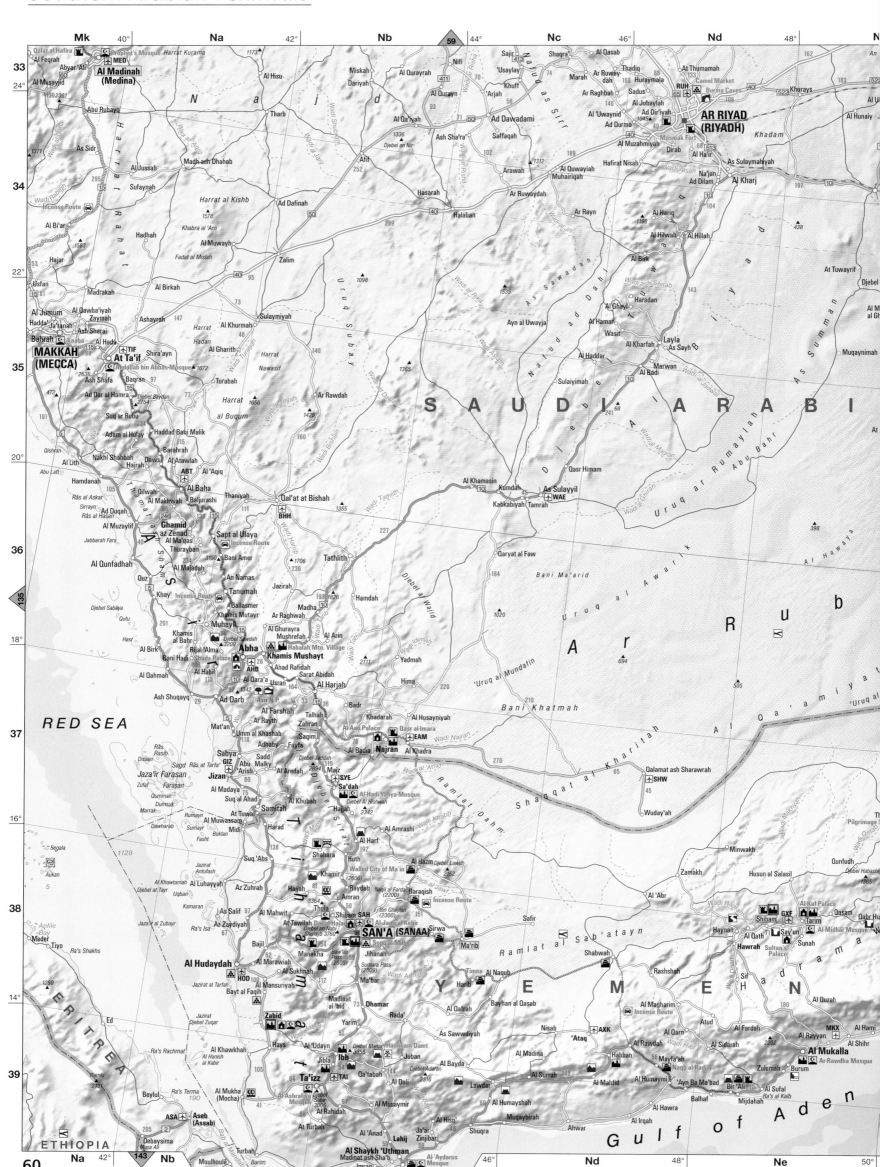

Central Asia

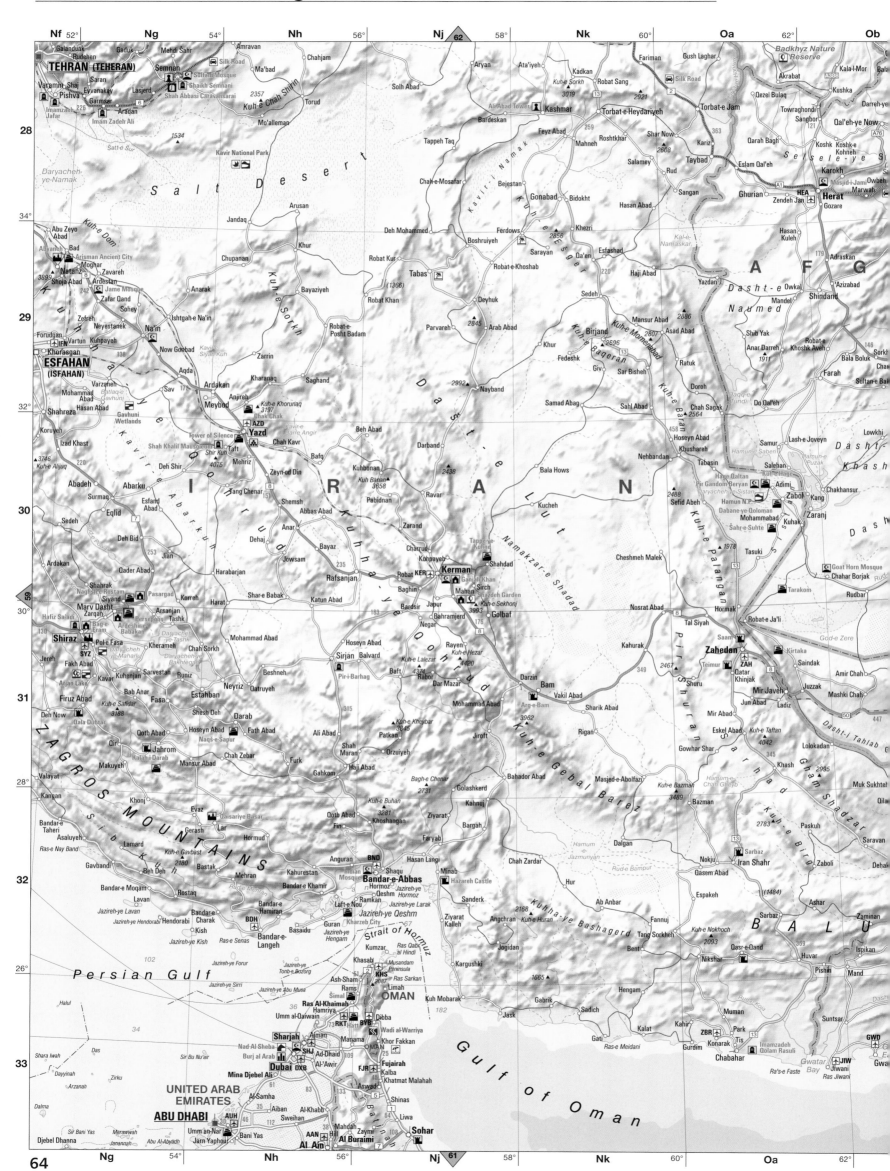

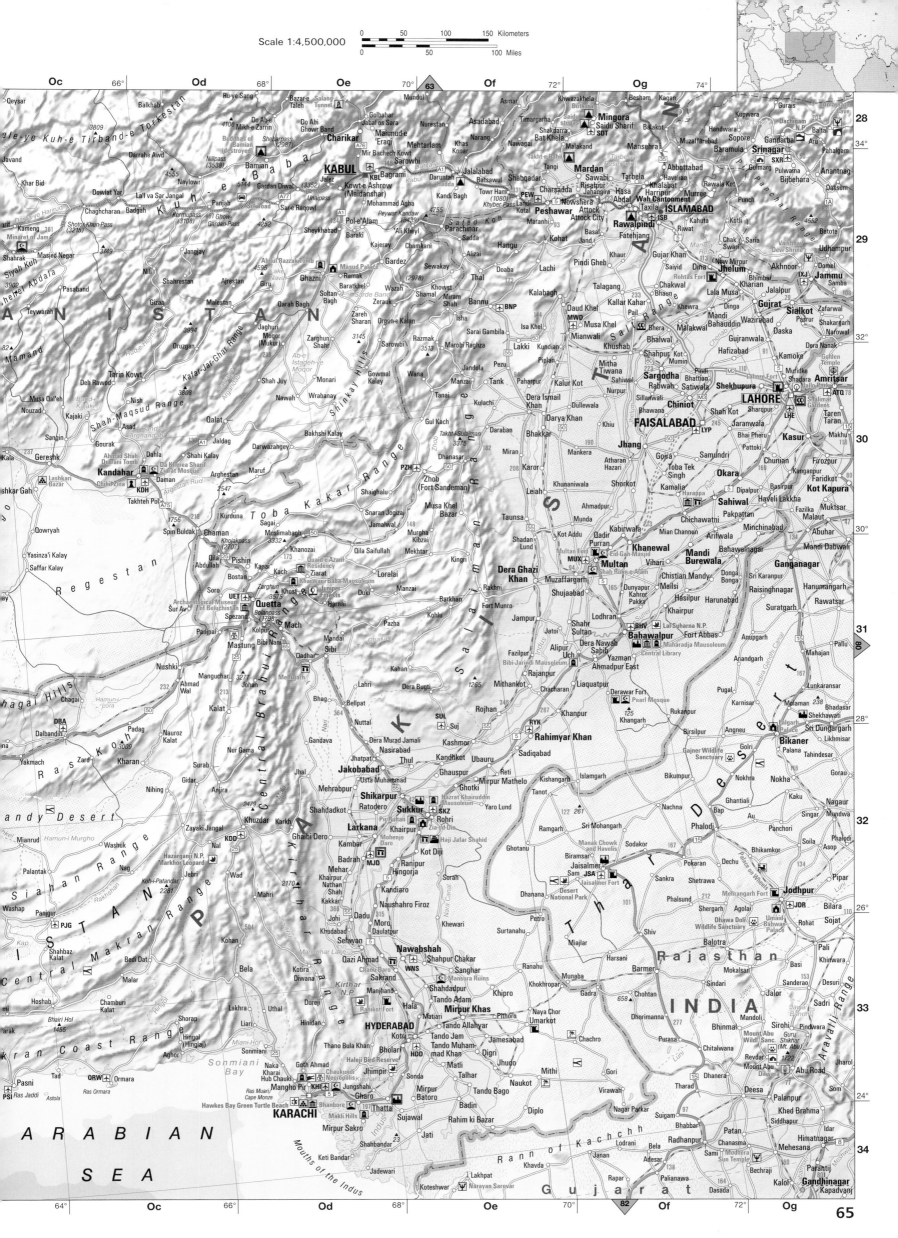

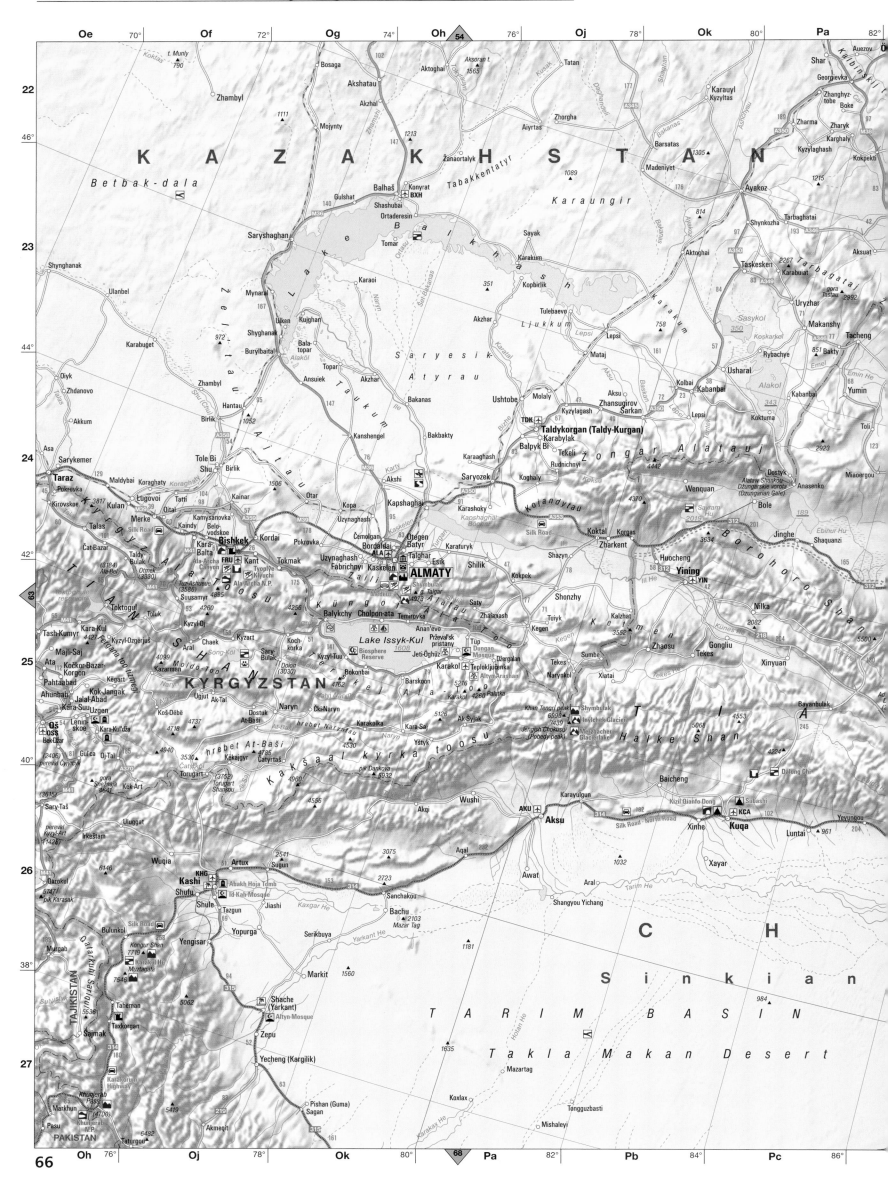

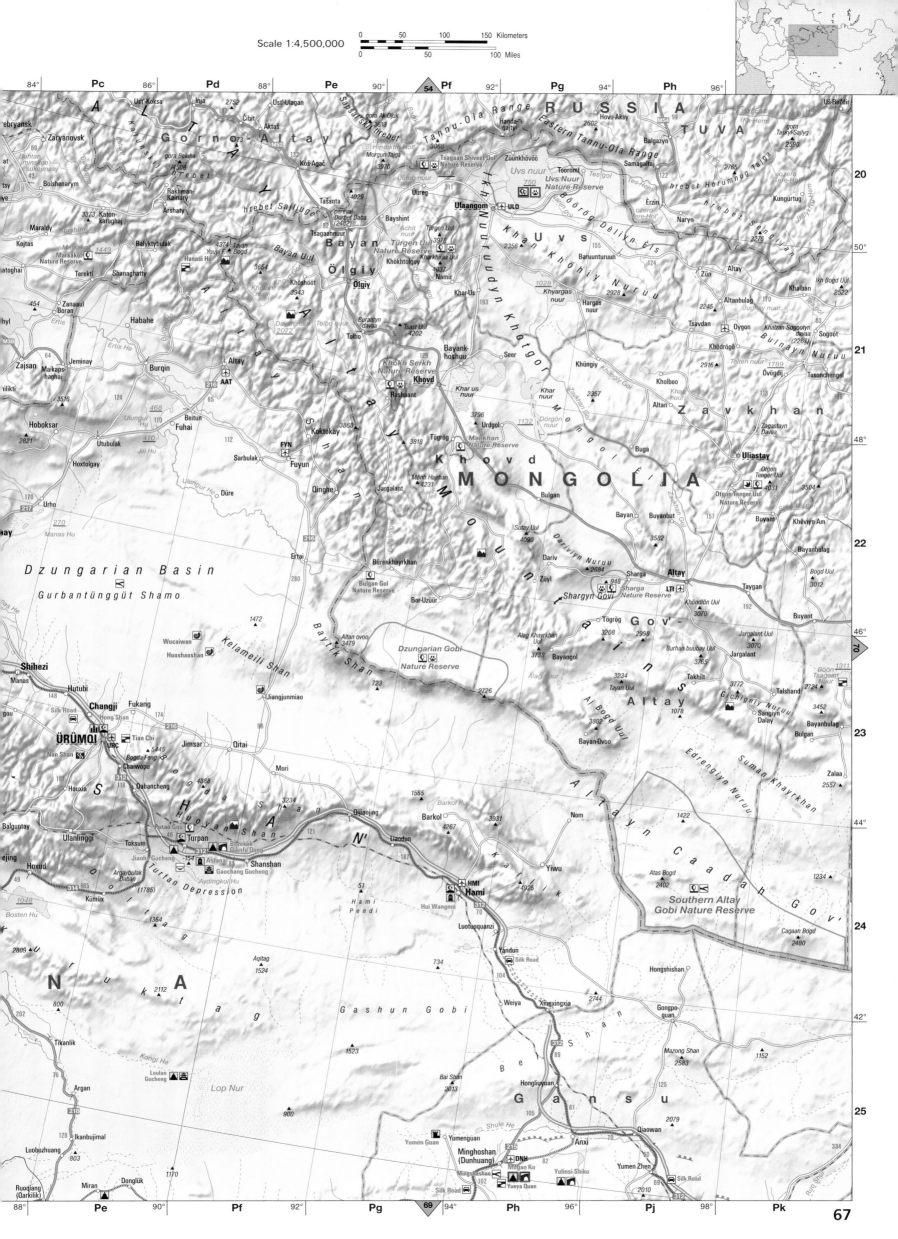

Tibet

Scale 1:4,500,000

0 50 100 150 Kilometers
0 50 100 Miles

SHAN

Gansu

QILIAN

Miran
Dongluk
Baxkorgan
Altun
Mangnai Zhen
Tomorlog Huatugou
Youdunzi
Gebituolatuo
Mangnai
Gansen
Urt Moron
Haya'er Da Juh
Boluntay
Bukadaban Feng 6860
Hoh Sai Hu
Huiten Nur
Elsen Nur
Xijr Ulan Hu
Ulan Ul Hu
Geladaindong 6559
Tanggula Shan 6241
Wequan
Kili Bulak
Tanggula Shankou (5160) 5776
Amdo
Monza
Dongqiao
Nyainrong
Namco
Horra
Damxung
Kyogche La (4900)
Atlas Gompa Lhari
Sera Monastery
Potala
Jokhang
Ganden
Lhasa
Maizhokunggar Jimda
Rito Gompar Gongbogyamda
Zhanang
Zêtang Samye Monastery
Qusum Nang Xian
Gyaca
Lhünzê
Tato Yiyu Shol
Mega Karko
Miling
INDIA

Altun Shan 5400 5798
Dangjin Shankou (3519)
Aksay Subei
Dingzikou
Lenghu
Tsagaan Chulunta
Huahaizi
Suhai Hu
Chalengkou
Yugia Iqe
Xi Taijnar Hu
Dong Taijnar Hu
Da Qaidam
Dabsan Hu
Qarhan
Golmud
GOQ
Xiaonanchuan
Naij Tal
Qagan Tahoi
Kunlun Shankou (4849) 6300
Qumar Heyan
Budongquan
Wuli
Tuotuo Heyan
Moron Us
Tukola Tolha
Kulanhor
Zhidoi
Qumarlêb
Qingshuihe
Zadoi
Nangqên
Xagquka
Boqên Sog Xian
Nagqu
Serca
Dênggên
Riwoqê
Banbar
Lhorong
Alamdo
Tangmai
Bayizhen Nyingchi 7755
Namjagbarwa
Sumzom
Rawu
Bruni
Bomi
Baxoi

Dang He
Silk Road
Yema Shan
Dalai Shan 5489
Yema Nanshan 4612
Shule Nanshan 4806
Har Hu
Bayan Shan 5030
Delhingha
Toson Hu 2680
Ga Hai
Bugt Shan 4601
Ulan
Caka
Heimahe
Nomhon
Balong
Dulan
Bacang
Gawa Obo
Donggi Conag
Huashixia
Madoi
Gyaring Hu
Ngoring Hu 4285
Yamatan
Bayan Har Shan 5267
Bayan Har Shankou (5100)
Horgorguinba
Xiwu
Yushu Chumda
Sêrxü
Toramarkog
Za Qu (Mekong)
Gushi
Enda
Qamdo Toba
Gyitang
Zogang
Mongotong
Bamda
Bomi
Zhowagoin
Cakalho
Guihua Temple

Yumen Zhen Silk Road
Yumen Jiayuguan Jiuquan Jinta
Qianfo Dong
Qingshui Gaotai
Hong-liuyuan
Jingtie Shan 5206 Qilian Shan 5547
Jingtieshan 5148
Kangz'gyai 5803
Zhangye Shandan
Sunan Matisi Shiku Minle
Qilian
Obo Muri
Cêtar
Gangca
Tianjun
Niao Dao
Qinghai Hu
Zakou Shankou
Haiyan
Huangyuan
Daotanghe
Gonghe
Daheba
Wenquan
Tongde
Zêkog
Magên Gangri 6282
Quamalung Magên
Cairiwa
Yiqikai
Bande
Shanh Gongma
Darlag
Qingqiang
Jiqzhi
Golog Shan 5369
Beima
Aba
Sêrtar
Gamda
Zogqên
Chola Shankou
Dêgê Chola Shan 6168
Lama Monastery
Gamtog Maniganggo
Baiyü
Jomda
Garzê Khor Gande Kasa
Rasha Luhuo
Changtai
Xinlong
Dawu
Bozi
Qianning
Kuqa Danba
Yidun
Litang
Xinduqiao
Yajiang
Kangding
Rilou
Zongza
Xiangcheng
Sumdo
Jijü
Tanggu

TIBET

TANGLHA SHAN

KUNLUN SHAN

Qinghai

Sichuan

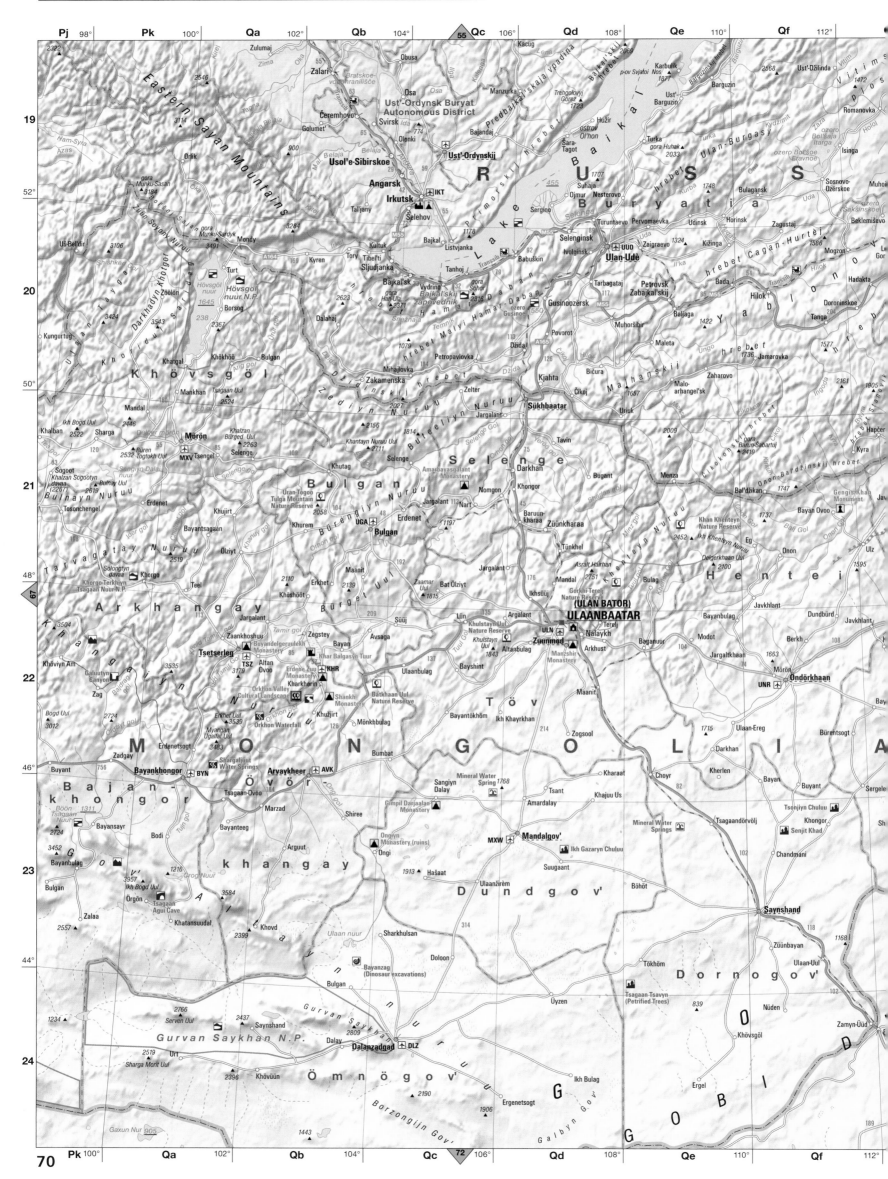

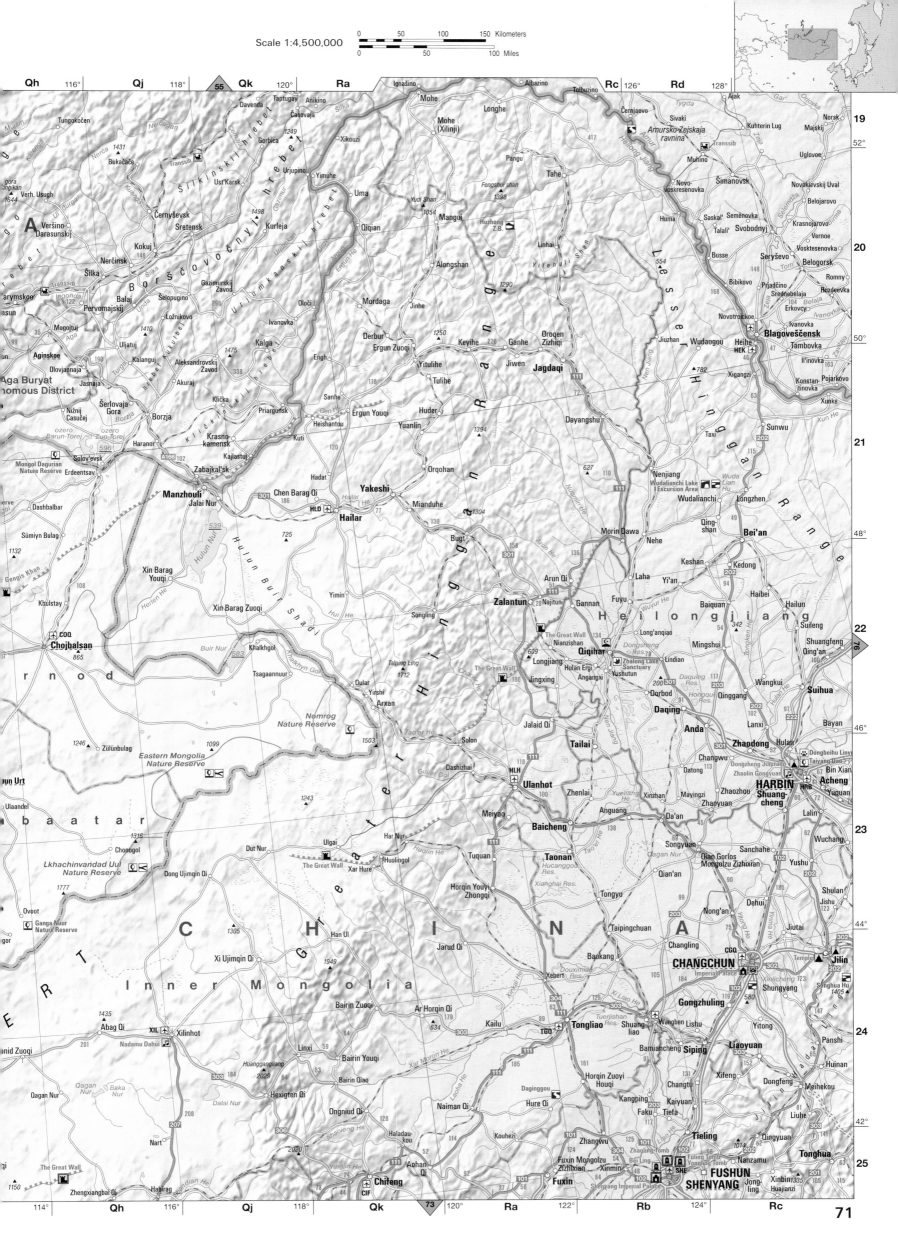

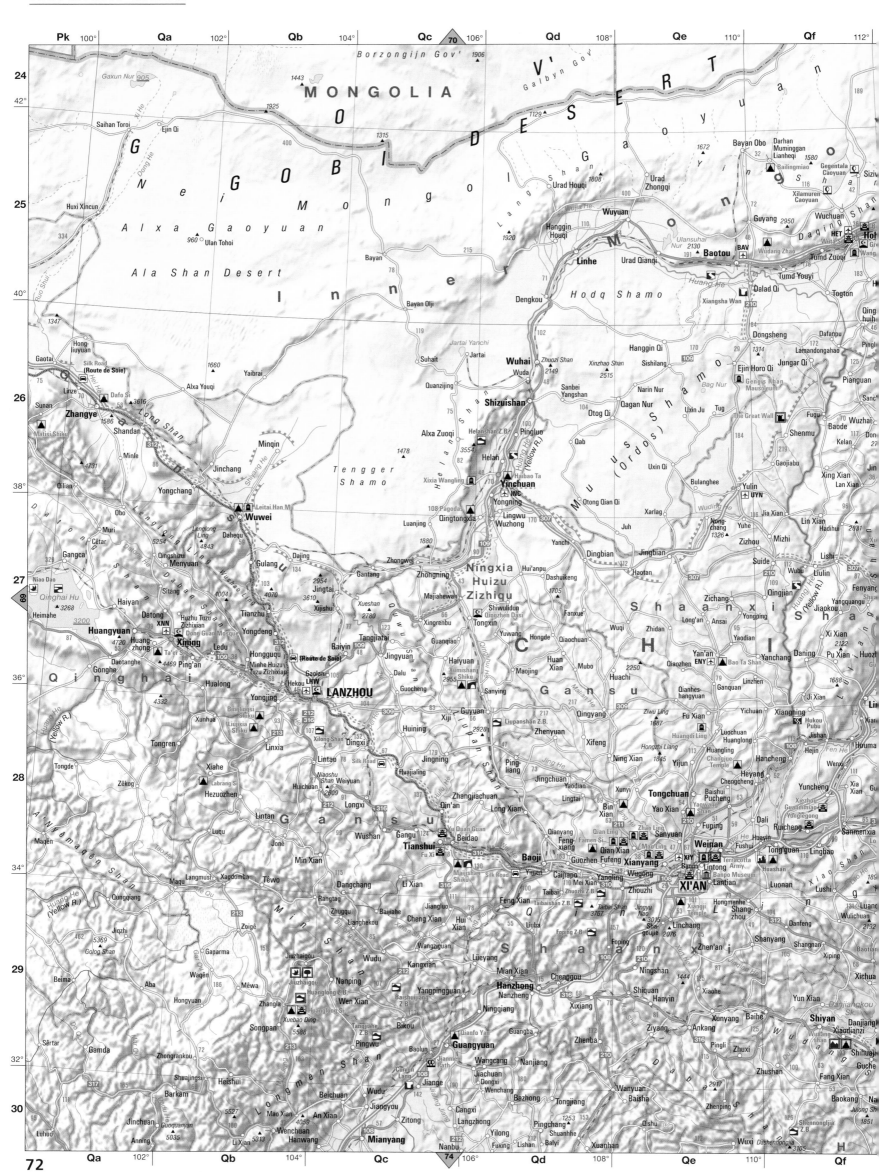

Southern China, Taiwan

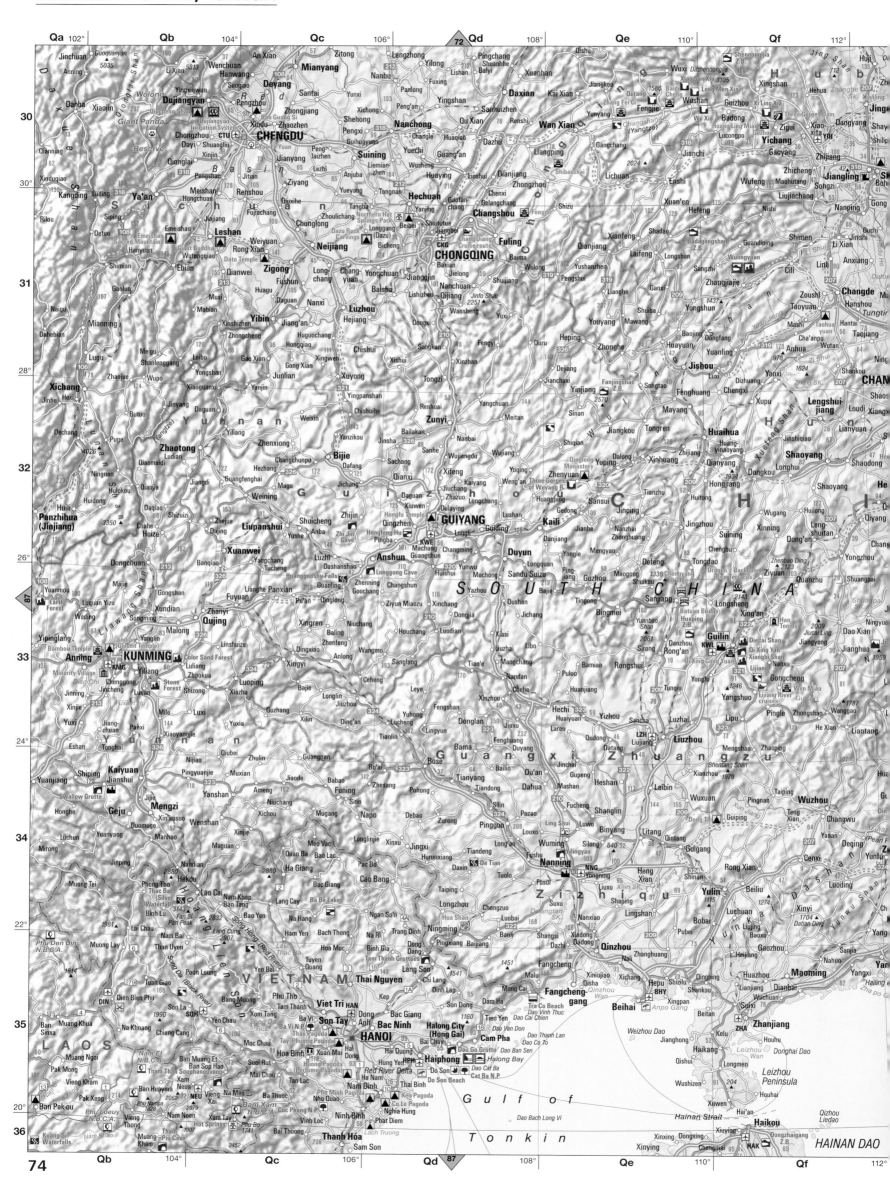

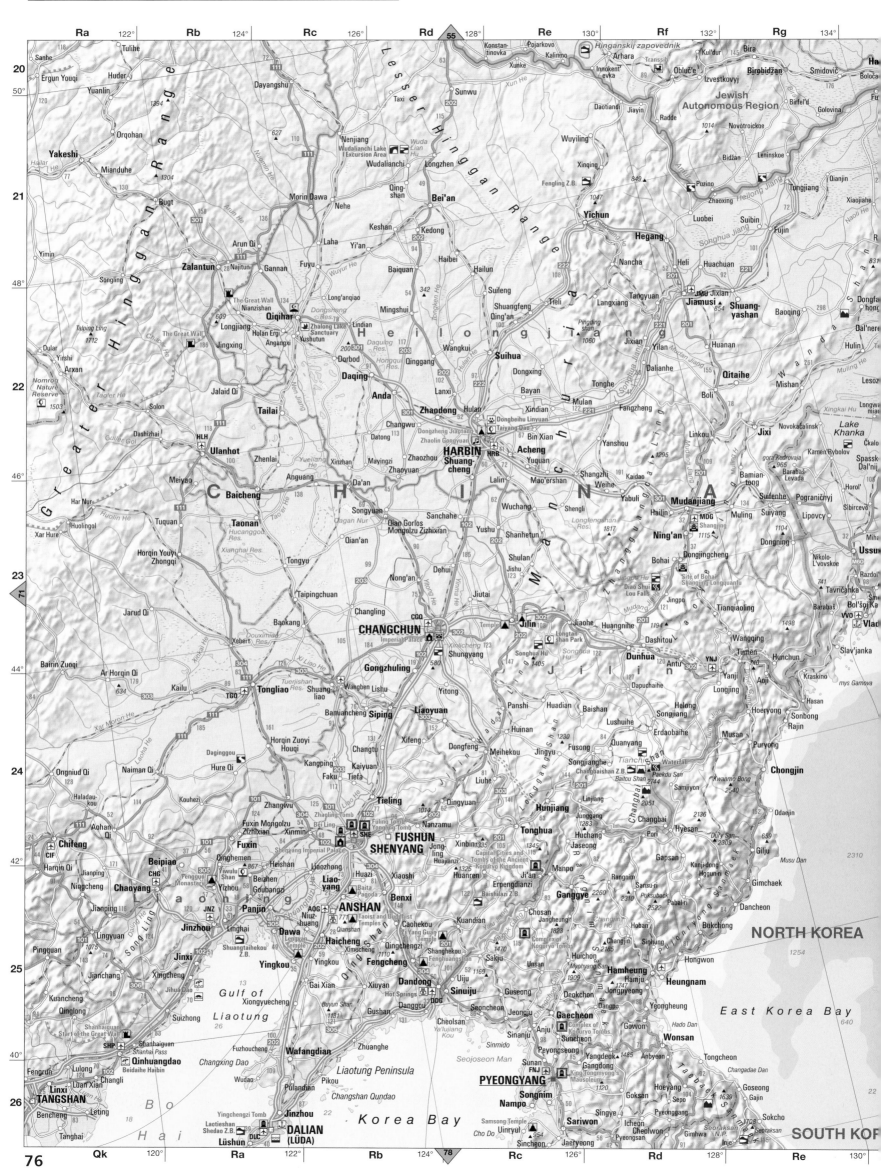

Scale 1:4,500,000

0 50 100 150 Kilometers
0 50 100 Miles

RUSSIA

Sakhalin

Južno-Sahalinsk
UUS
Holmsk
Ožidaevo
Dal'nee
Čaplanovo
Ohotskoe
Ozerskij
Jasnomorskij
Gornozavodsk
Nevel'sk
Šebunino
Brjanskoe
Korsakow
Novikovo
zaliv Aniva
Anivа
Hvostovo
Kuznecovo
Atlasovo
o. Moneron
mys Aniva
mys Kril'on

La Perouse Strait

Kuril Islands

gora Kamuj
Slavnoe
zaliv Prostor
Kuril'sk
Pioner
Rejdovo
gora Stokan
Burevestnik
Lesozavodskij
mys Lovcova
mys Rikorda
proliv Ekateriny

o. Iturup

Soya-misaki
Wakkanai
Sarufutsu
Hama-Tombetsu
Naku-Tombetsu
Esashi
Rebun-to
Funadomari
RBJ
WKJ
Rishirifuji
Rishiri
Rishiri-to
Rishiri-Rebun-Sarobetsu N.P.
Reburi
RIS
Toyotomi
Nakagawa
Otoineppu
Omu
Okoppe
Mombetsu
Nishi-Okoppe
Takinoue
Engaru
Shari
Abashiri
Shari-dake
SHB
Naka-Shibetsu
Shibetsu
Shiretoko-misaki
Shiretoko-hanto
Rausu-dake
Shiretoko N.P.
Nemuro-kaikyo
Serno-vodsk
Golovnino
ozero Kunašir
Južno-Kuril'sk
ozero Šikotan
ozero Zelenyj

Rumoi
Mashike
Fukagawa
Takikawa
Asahikawa
AKJ
Asahi-dake
Daisetsuzan
Bihoro
Kitami
Rubeshibe
Teshikaga
Akan N.P.
Akankoshan
Shibecha
Attoko
Kiritappu
Akkeshi
Kushiro-Shitsugen N.P.
Kushiro
KUH
Kushiro-cho
Nemuro-hanto
Nemuro
Noseppu-misaki

HOKKAIDO

Hamamasu
Atsuta
Ishikari
Ebetsu
Otaru
SPK/CTS
SAPPORO
Eniwa
Chitose
Hiroshima
Yubari
Hidaka
Shimizu
Obihiro
OBO
Ashoro
Hombetsu
Ikeda
Ashibetsu
Furano
Tokachi-dake
Kami-Shihoro
Shintoku
Hiroo
Hidaka sanmyaku
Urakawa
Erimo
Erimo-misaki

Niseko Shakotan Otaru-kaigan Q.N.P.
Furubira
Yoichi
Yubari-dake
Syakotan-hanto
Iwanai
O.N.P.
Rakonshi
Suttsu
Kuromatsunai
Abuta
Shikotsu-Toya N.P.
Tomakomai
Noboribetsu
Date
Shiraoi
Muroran
Onuma Q.N.P.
Oshamambe
Kunni
Yakumo
Mori
Shikabe
Minamikayabe
Nanae
Okushiri
Kumashi
OIR
Okushiri-to
Esashi
Kaminokuni
Hakodate
HKD
Esan
Kikonai

PACIFIC OCEAN

Erimo Seamount

Oma-saki
Oma
Sai
Shirya-saki
Mutsu
Shimokita-hanto
Kawauchi
Yokohama
Rokkasho
Shimokita Q.N.P.hanto
Mutsu-wan
Daisengendake
Fukushima
Matsumae
Seikan Tunnel
Tsugaru Q.N.P.
Kikonai
Minmaya
Kanita
Wakino-sawa
Hiranai
Nohei
Misawa
MSJ
Shiura
Nakasato
Goshogawara
Aomori
AOJ
Towada
Shichinohe
Namioka
Hachinohe
Hirosaki
Shirakami-Sanchi
Henasi-saki
Kyuroku-jima
Shirakami-dake
Odate
Towada-Hachimantai N.P.
Sannohe
Karumai
Noda
Genohe
Ninohe
Kuji
Kazuno
Kuzumaki
Iwaizumi
Takanosu
Kazuno
Iwate-san
Miyako
Noshiro
Morioka
Yamada
Rikuchu-Kaigan N.P.
Toda-saki
Fukusen-ko
Kamaishi
Nyudo-saki
Oga-hanto
Oga
Kakunodate
Hanamaki
Tono
Kitakami
Akita
AXT
Samurai Houses
Omagari
Yokote
Mizusawa
Ofunato
Kesennuma
Honjo
Yuzawa
Yakote
Ichinos
Tsugaru Strait

Sea of Japan

HONSHU

Chokai Q.N.P.
Chokai-san
Tobijima
Hasama
Furukawa
Ishinomaki
Sakata
Shinjo
Obanazawa
Izumi
Shiogama
Kinkasan-jima
Tsuruoka
Banda-Asahi N.P.
Yamagata
Tendo
Sendai
SDJ
Sendai-wan
JAPAN
Sanpoku
Zao-san
Iwanuma
Murakami
Nanyo
Shiroishi
Arakawa
Bandai-Asahi N.P.
Yonezawa
Soma
Azuma-san
Fukushima
Haramachi
Asahi N.P.
Ide-san
Namie
Awa-jima
Hajiki-saki

Yamato Rise

SDO
Ryotsu
Niigata
KLJ
Kitakata
Nihonmatsu
Koriyama
Iwaki
Aikawa
Niitsu
Aizu-Wakamatsu
Sanjo
Sukagawa
Sado-jima
Sado Yahiko Q.N.P.
Nagaoka
Echigo-Sanzan Tadami Q.N.P.
Shirakawa
Tajima
Yamatsun
Kashiwazaki
Ojiya
Nikko
Kitaibaraki
Tokamachi
Imaichi
Hitachi
Noto-hanto
Sozu
Wajima
Toyama-wan
Joetsu
Kubiki
Nikko N.P.
Utsunomiya
Katsuta
Itoigawa
Arai
Yaita
Moka
Mito
Noto-jima
Asahi
Shin
Nanao
Togi
Joshin Etsu Kogen N.P.
Shimodate
Ishioka
Noto-kongo Coast
Hakui
Himi
Nagano
Maebashi
Kiryu
Ashikaga
Oyama
Suzu-misaki
Takaoka
Ueda
Takasaki
Kumagaya
Tsuchiura
Toyama
TOY
Umachi
Sawara
Choshi
Tsubata
Tonami
Komoro
Tomioka
Saku
Chichibu
Kashiwa
Inubo-saki
Kanazawa
Matto
Chubu Sangaku N.P.
MMJ
Matsumoto
Tama N.P.
Kawagoe
TYO/NRT
Narita
Kujukuri-hama
TOKYO
Tokyo Disneyland
Chiba

Sea of Japan

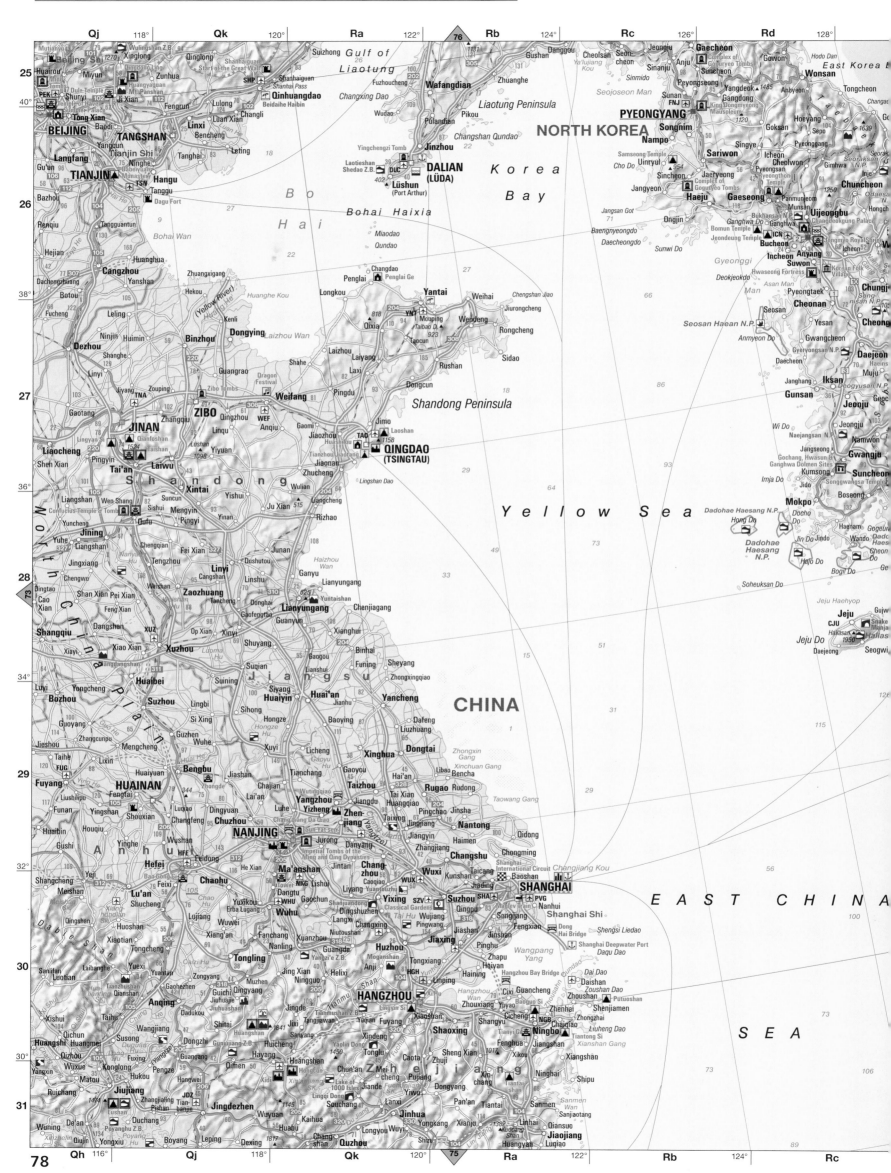

Scale 1:4,500,000

0 50 100 150 Kilometers
0 50 100 Miles

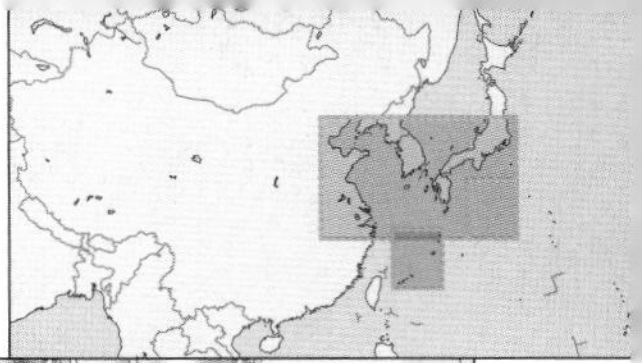

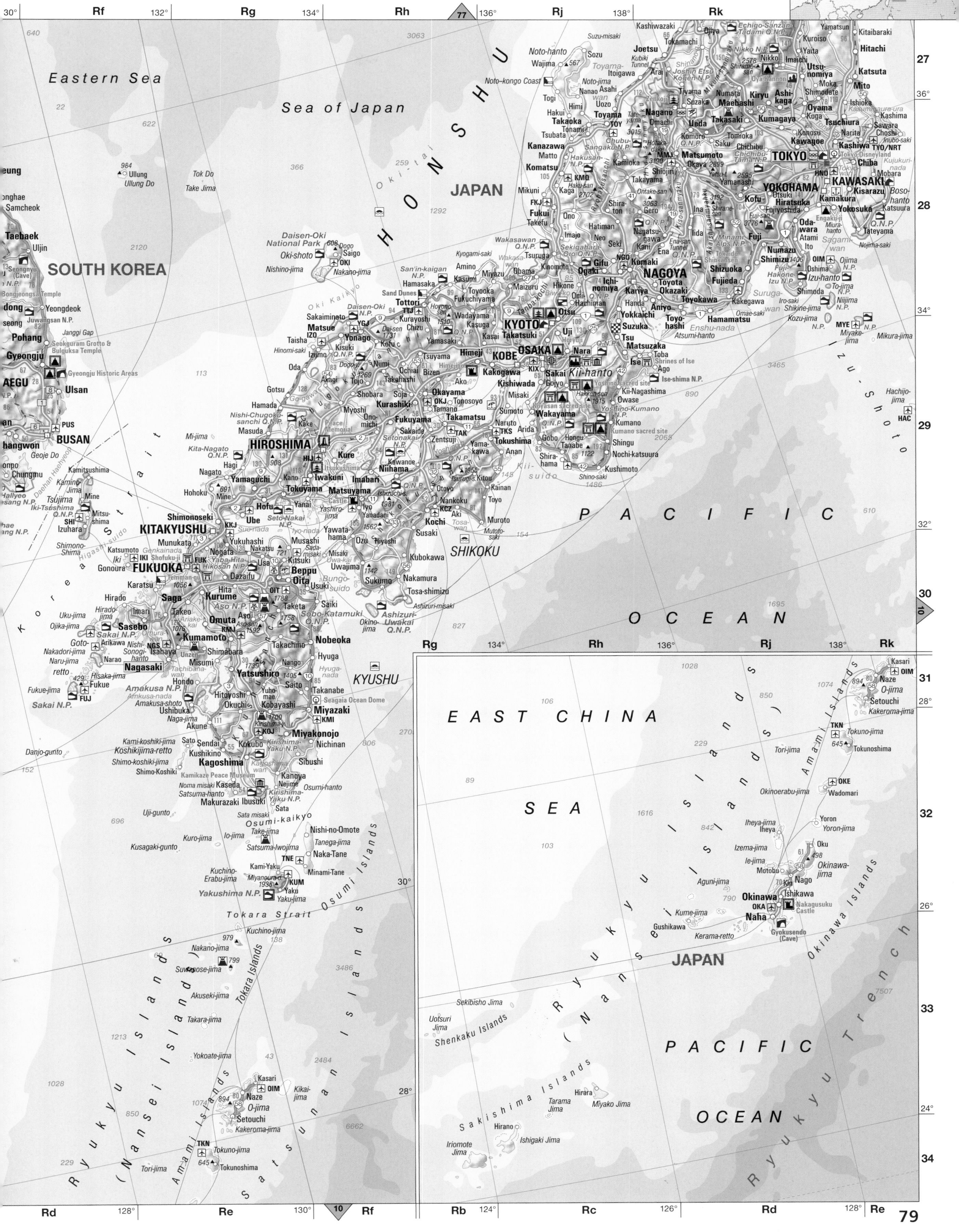

Eastern Sea

Sea of Japan

SOUTH KOREA

Taebaek
Uljin
Ullung
Ullung Do
Tok Do
Take Jima
Yeongdeok
Juwangsan N.P.
dong
seong
Gyeongju
Seokguram Grotto & Bulguksa Temple
Gyeongju Historic Areas
DAEGU
Ulsan
Pohang
BUSAN
PUS
Kamitsushima
Tsujima
Iki-Tsushima Q.N.P.
Kamino-shima
Mitsu-shima
Shimonoseki
Hohoku
Nagato
Hagi
Mine
KITAKYUSHU
Munakata
Genkainada
Nogata
Yukuhashi
Shofuku-ji
FUK
Dazaifu
FUKUOKA
Hita
Kurume
Saga
Karatsu
Takeo
Hirado
Imari
Sasebo
Omuta
Kumamoto
Nagasaki
Isahaya
Shimabara
Yatsushiro
Amakusa N.P.
Hondo
Kagoshima
Sendai
Kushikino
Makurazaki Ibusuki
Kaseda

HONSHU

JAPAN

Sea of Japan

Kashiwazaki
Joetsu
Nagano
Matsumoto
Takasaki
Kumagaya
Maebashi
Utsunomiya
Nikko
Mito
Hitachi
Katsuta
TOKYO
YOKOHAMA
KAWASAKI
Kamakura
Yokosuka
Chiba
Kanazawa
Komatsu
Toyama
Takaoka
Takayama
Gifu
NAGOYA
Toyota
Okazaki
Fukui
Shizuoka
Hamamatsu
Fujieda
Numazu
Odawara
Atami
KYOTO
OSAKA
KOBE
Nara
Himeji
Kakogawa
Sakai
Tsu
Matsuzaka
Ise
Wakayama
Tanabe
Shingu
Kumano

Fukuyama
Okayama
Kurashiki
Takamatsu
HIROSHIMA
Kure
Iwakuni
Matsuyama
Imabari
Niihama
Tokushima
Kochi
Nankoku
Yamaguchi
Tokuyama
Hofu
Ube
Yanai

SHIKOKU

PACIFIC OCEAN

KYUSHU

Beppu
Oita
Usuki
Saiki
Nobeoka
Hyuga
Takanabe
Miyazaki
Miyakonojo
Nichinan

EAST CHINA SEA

Amami Islands
Kasari
Naze
O-jima
Setouchi
Tokunoshima
Okinoerabu-jima
Wadomari
Yoron
Yoron-jima
Iheya-jima
Izena-jima
Ie-jima
Motobu
Nago
Okinawa-jima
Ishikawa
Okinawa
Naha
Kume-jima
Kerama-retto
Gushikawa

JAPAN

Ryukyu Islands (Nansei Islands)

Shenkaku Islands
Uotsuri Jima
Sekibisho Jima

Sakishima Islands
Iriomote Jima
Ishigaki Jima
Hirano
Tarama Jima
Miyako Jima
Hirara

PACIFIC OCEAN

Ryukyu Trench

Yakushima N.P.
Tanega-shima
Osumi-kaikyo
Tokara Islands
Nakano-jima
Suwanose-jima
Akuseki-jima
Takara-jima
Yokoate-jima
Kuchino-jima

Ryukyu Islands (Nansei Islands)

Satsunan Islands

Amami Islands
Kasari
Naze
O-jima
Setouchi
Tokuno-shima

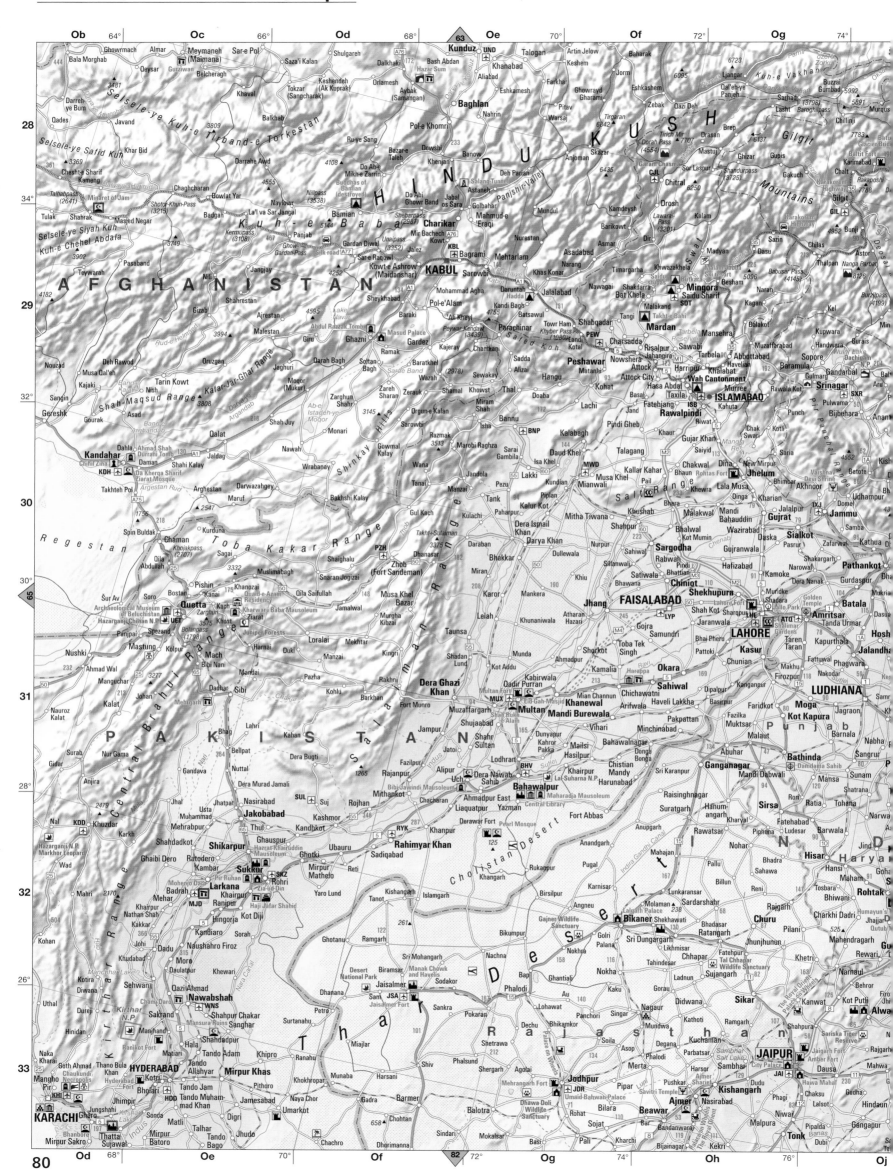

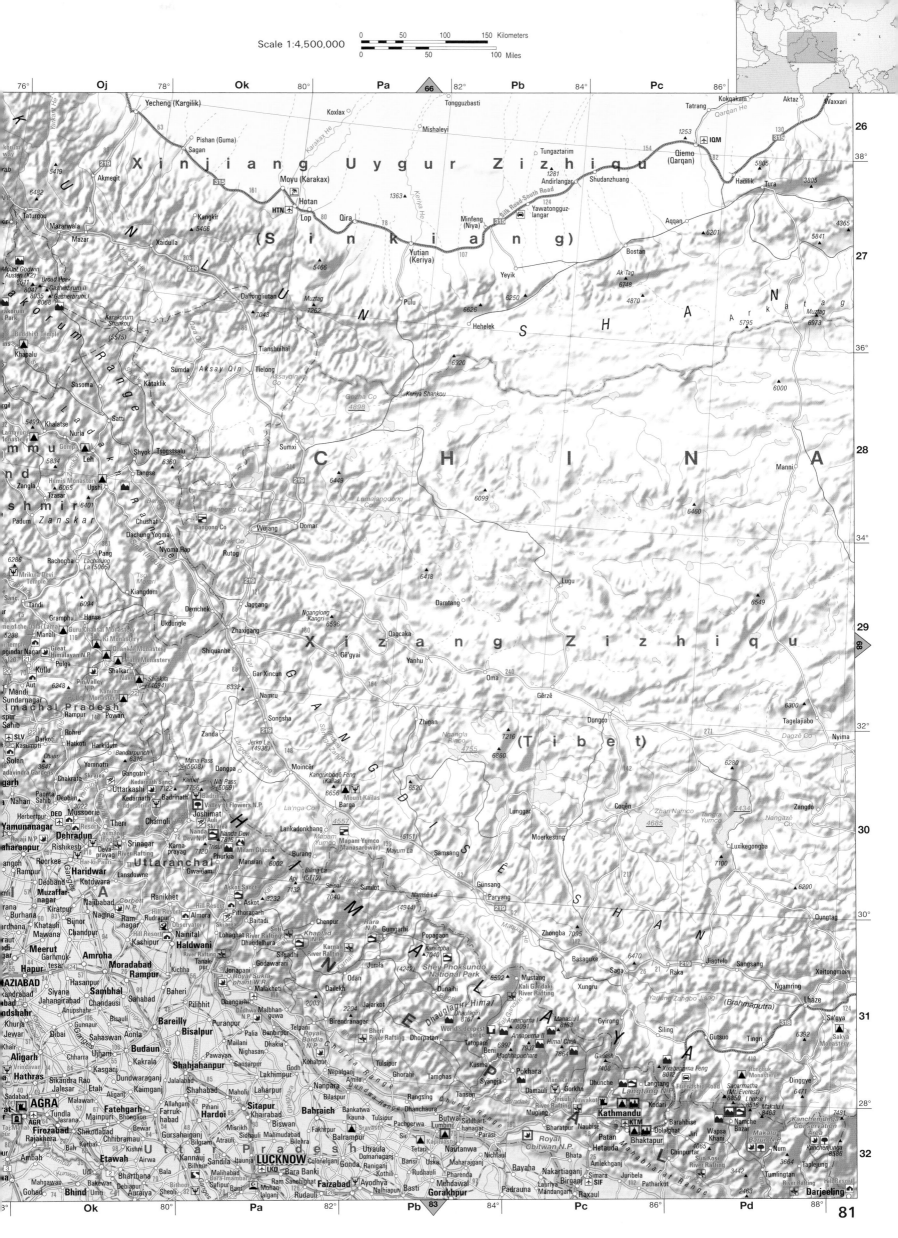

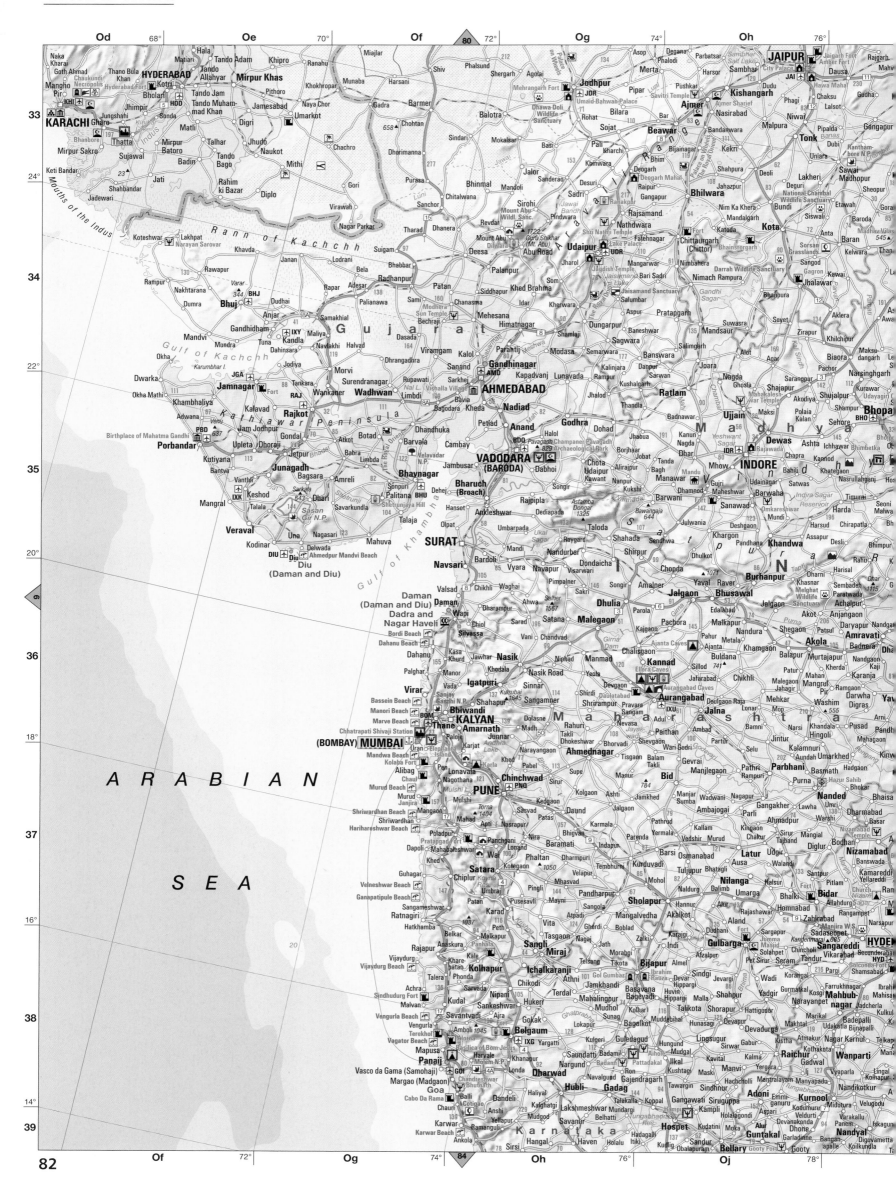

78°   Ok   80°   Pa   82°   Pb   81   84°   Pc   86°   Pd

AGRA

LUCKNOW

KANPUR

NEPAL

Kathmandu

Mt. Everest

Darjeeling

Biratnagar

U t t a r   P r a d e s h

Jhansi

Faizabad

Gorakhpur

Muzaffarpur

Darbhanga

Purnia

Katihar

VARANASI

Mirzapur

PATNA

B i h a r

Bihar Sharif

Bhagalpur

Ingraj Bazar

Rewa

Gaya

Satna

JABALPUR

Baghelkhand

Chota Nagpur Plateau

DHANBAD

Asansol

Durgapur

Ranchi

Jharkhand

Raniganj

West Bengal

Murwara

Bankura

C h h a t t i s g a r h

Bilaspur

Jamshedpur

Raurkela

Kharagpur

KOLKATA (CALCUTTA)

Durg

Bhilai

Raipur

Mahanadi Basin

Sambalpur

Cuttack

BHUBANESWAR

Nagpur

Raj Nandgaon

Gondia

O r i s s a

E   a   s   t   e   r   n   G   h   a   t   s

Puri

Berhampur

Chandrapur

Ballarpur

Bastar Hills

Jagdalpur

Karimnagar

Warangal

A n d h r a   P r a d e s h

Vizianagaram

VISHAKHAPATNAM

Khammam

Kottagudem

Vijayawada

Guntur

Eluru

Kakinada

Bhimavaram

Yanam (Pondicherry)

Ongole

Mouths of the Krishna

B a y   o f

B e n g a l

80°   Pa   82°   Pb   85   84°   Pc   86°   Pd   88°   Pe

83

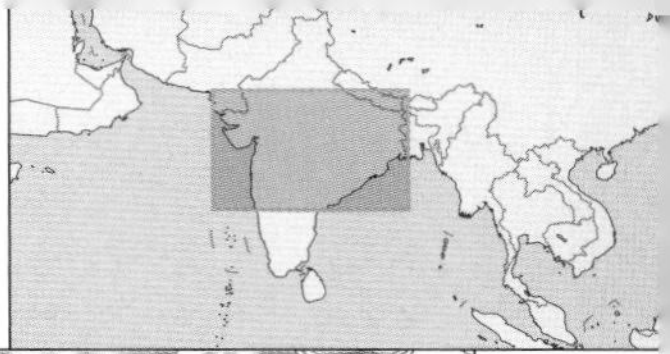

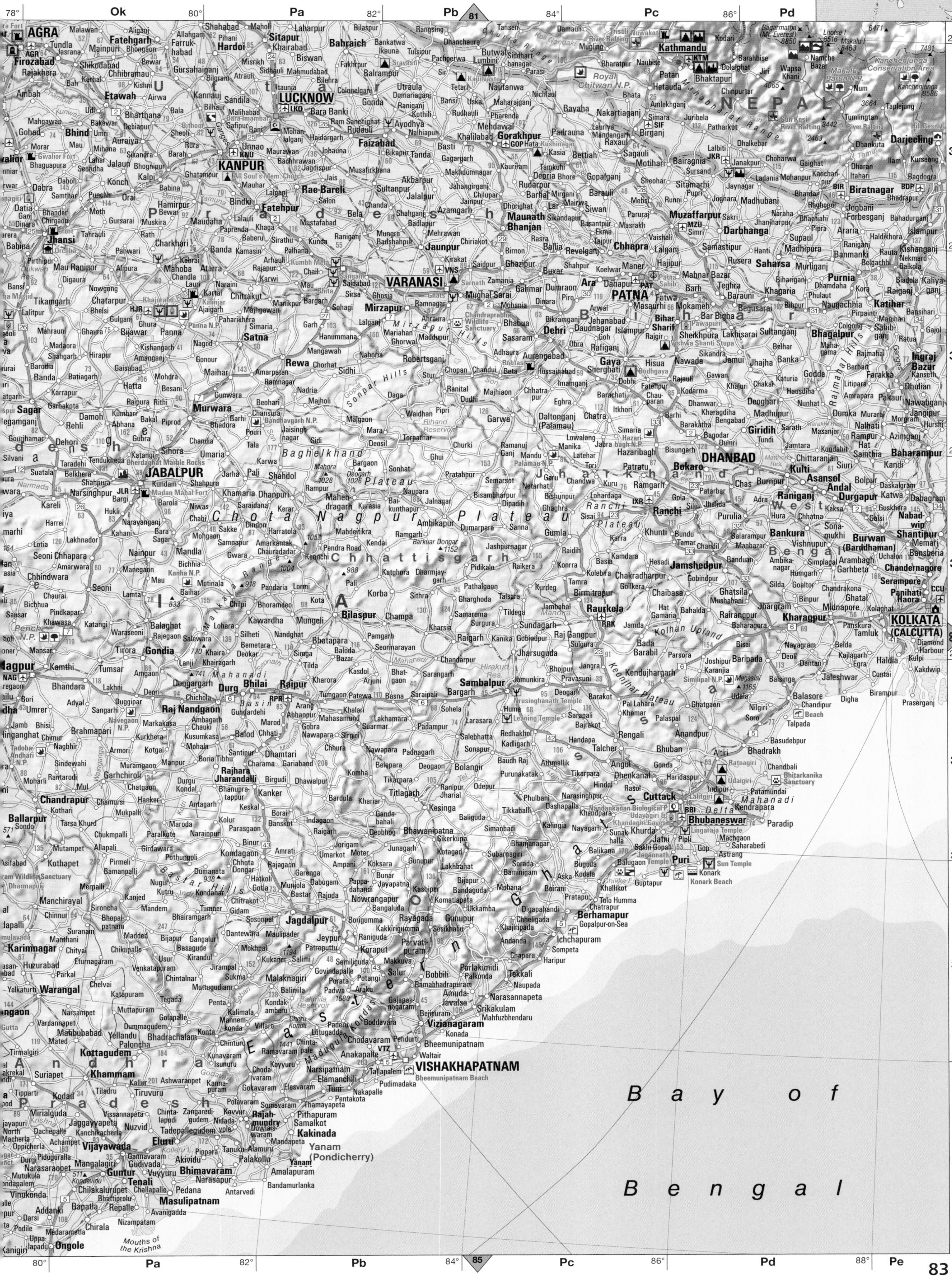

A R A B I A N

S E A

Laccadive Islands

Bitra I.
Chetlat I.
Amindivi Islands
Kiltan I.
Perulmar Par I.
Kadmath I.
Bangaram I.
AGX
Agatti I.
Amini I.
Kavaratti
Kavaratti I.
Andrott I.
Suhell I.

Cannanore Islands
Kalpeni I.

Lakshadweep

Nine Degree Channel

Minicoy I.

Eight Degree Channel

Lakshadweep

S e a

Haa-Alifu Atoll
(North Thiladhunmathee Atoll)

Gallandhoo Channel
Dhidhdhoo
Haa-Dhaalu Atoll
(South Thiladhunmathee Atoll)
Makunudu Atoll
Nolhivaranfaru

Shaviyani Atoll
(North Miladhunmadulu Atoll)
Farukolhu

Raa Atoll
(Maalhosmadulu North)
Noonu Atoll
(South Miladhunmadulu Atoll)
Ugoofaaru
Manadhoo

Pearl Island
Neifaru
Moresby Channel
Lhaviyani Atoll
Baa Atoll
(Maalhosmadulu South)
Eydhafushi
Kaashidhoo
Kardiva Channel

Gaafaru Channel

MALDIVES

Tohddoo Atoll
North Male Atoll
Rasdhoo Atoll

Arie Atoll
(Alifu Atoll)
Male MLE
Mahibadhoo
South Male Atoll

Beaches   Scuba diving
Felidhoo Channel

Ariadhoo Channel
Felidhoo Atoll
(Vaavu Atoll)
Faafu Atoll
(North Nilandhoo Atoll)
Vattaru Channel
Magoodhoo

Dhaalu Atoll
(South Nilandhoo Atoll)
Muli
Meemu Atoll
(Mulaku Atoll)
Kudahuvadhoo

Kudahuvadhoo Channel
Thaa Atoll
(Kolhumadulu Atoll)

Veymandhoo

Veymandhoo Channel
Laamu Atoll
(Hadhdhunmathee Atoll)
Hithadhoo

Southern India region (Karnataka, Kerala, Tamil Nadu)

Karwar
Karwar Beach
Ankola
Karnataka
Kumta
Honavar
Harihar
Bhatkal
Davangere
Ranibennur
Chitradurga
Shimoga
Bhadravati
Mangalore
Bantval
Udupi
Karkal
Mangalore
IXE
Kasaragod
Bekal Beach
Hosdrug
BANGALORE
Mandya
Mysore
Kannur (Cannanore)
Thalasseri (Tellicherry)
Mahé (Pondicherry)
Kozhikode (Calicut)
CCJ
Manjeri
Coonoor
Salem
Erode
Tiruppur
COIMBATORE
Pollachi
Palakkad (Palghat)
Kerala
Thrissur (Trichur)
Valparai
Dindigul
MADURAI
Irinjalakuda
Kodungallur (Cranganore)
Ernakulam
Fort Kochi
Jew Town
KOCHI (COCHIN)
COK
Alappuzha (Alleppey)
Alleppey Beach
Changanassery (Changanacherry)
Haripad
Kayankulam
Kollam (Quilon)
Papanasam Beach
Nedumangad
THIRUVANANTHAPURAM TRV
(TRIVANDRUM)
Kovalam Beach
Kovalam
Padmanabhapuram
Nagercoil
Kanniyakumari
Cape Comorin
Kumari Amman Temple

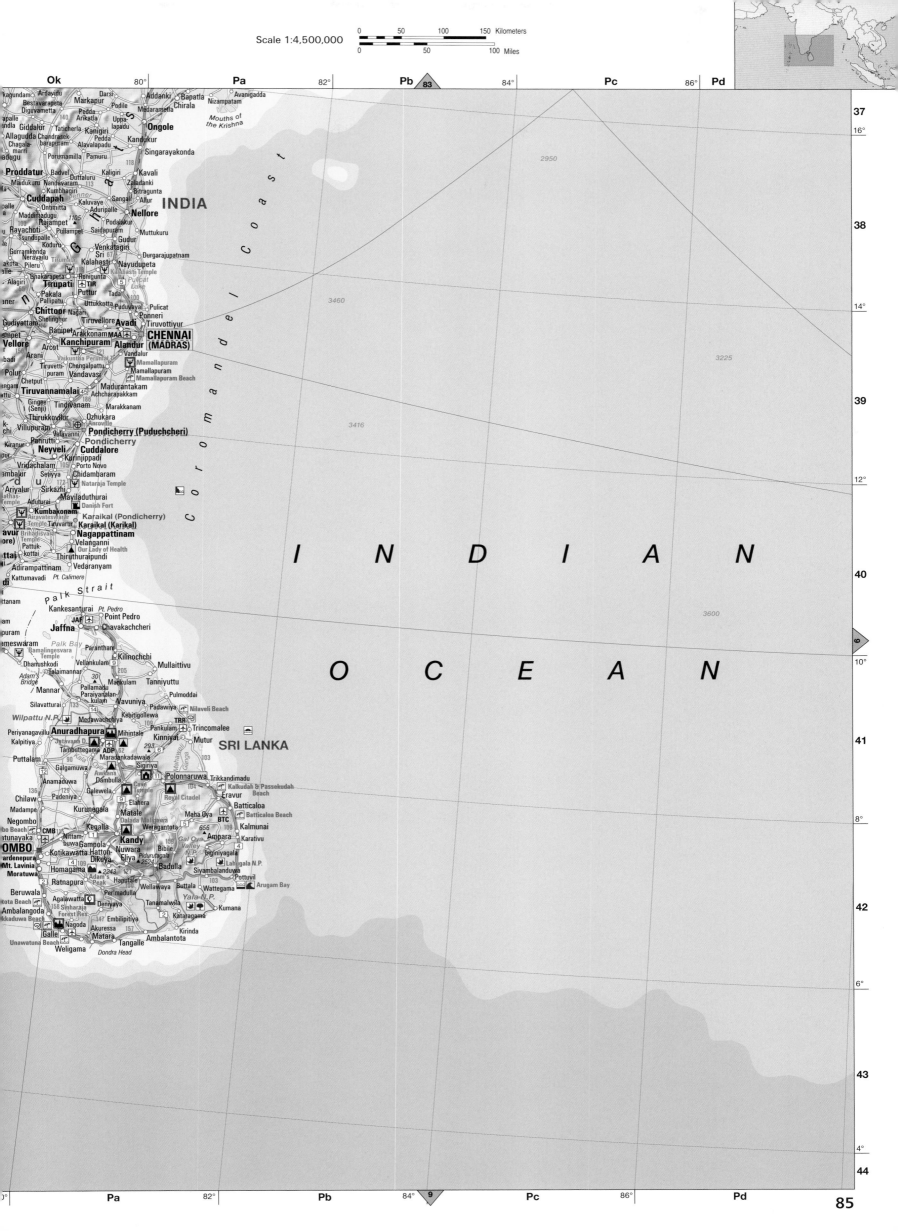

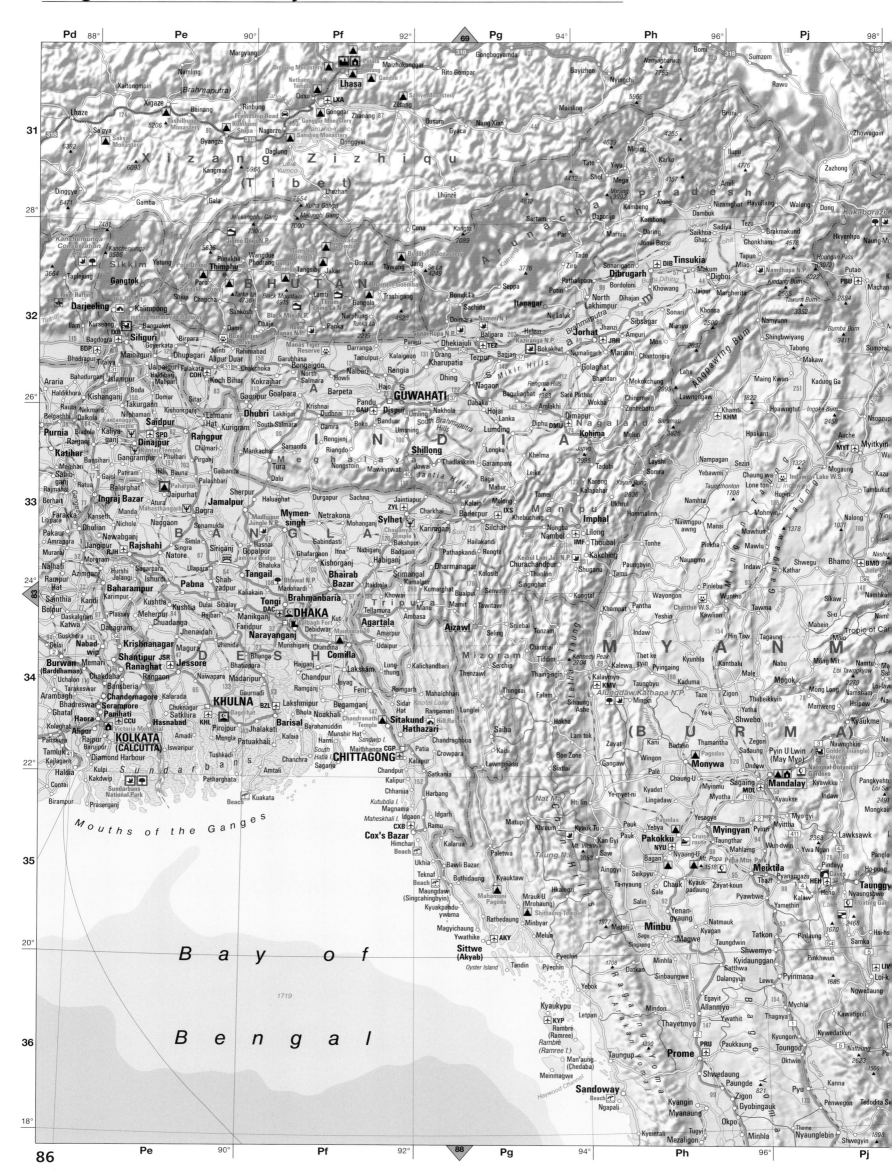

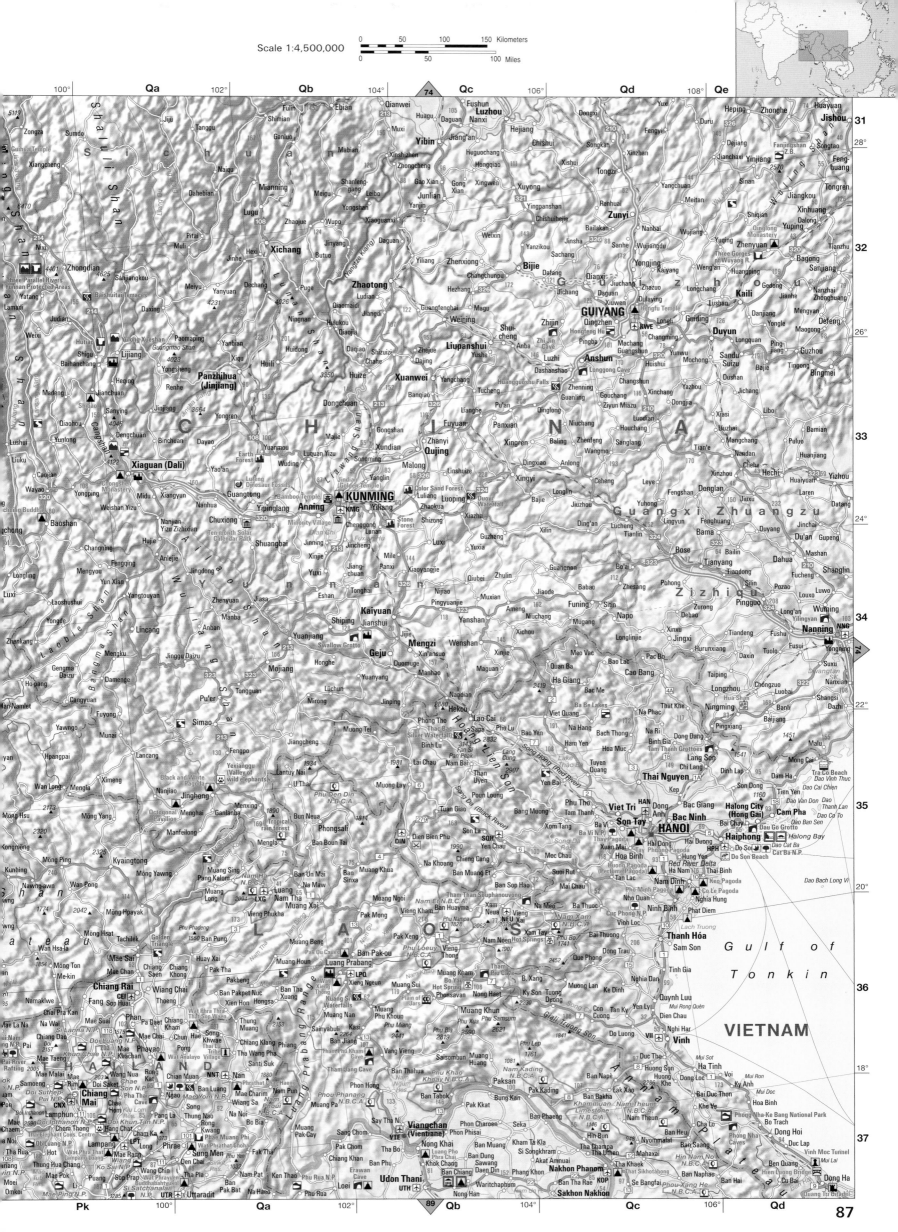

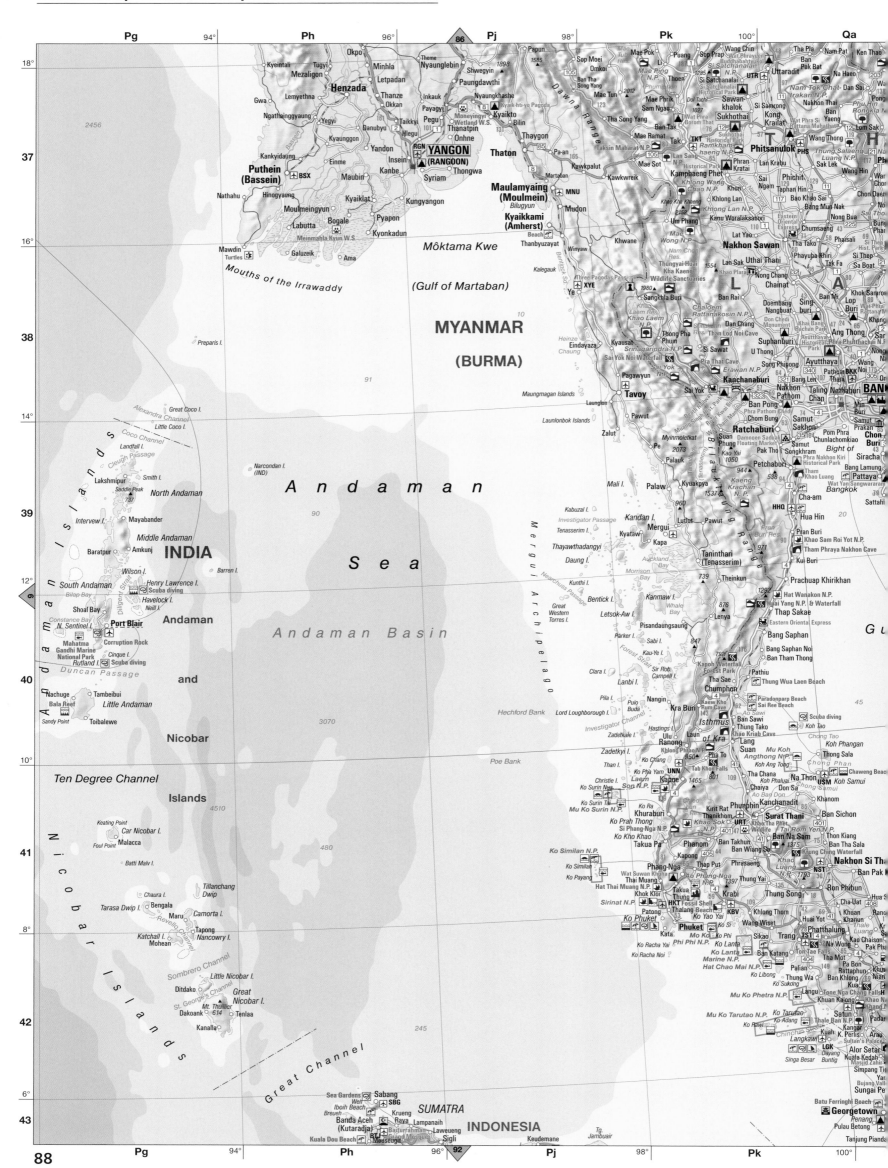

Philippines

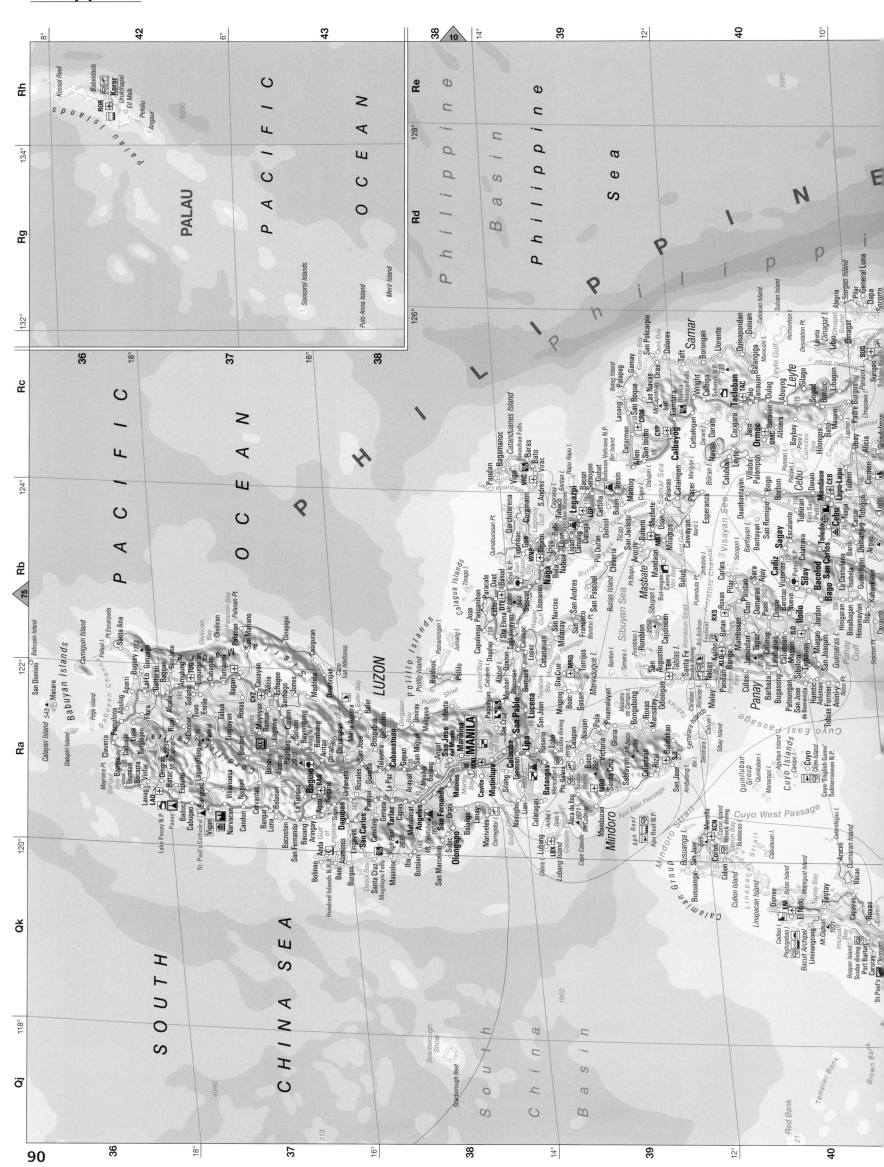

PACIFIC OCEAN

SOUTH CHINA SEA

PALAU

LUZON

MANILA

PHILIPPINE

Philippine Sea

Philippine Basin

South China Basin

Babuyan Islands

Samar

Leyte

Cebu

Panay

Mindoro

Masbate

Palau Islands

Visayan Sea

Sibuyan Sea

Sulu Sea

Baguio

Dagupan

Olongapo

Angeles

San Fernando

Legazpi

Naga

Calbayog

Tacloban

Bacolod

Iloilo

Cadiz

Ormoc

Koror

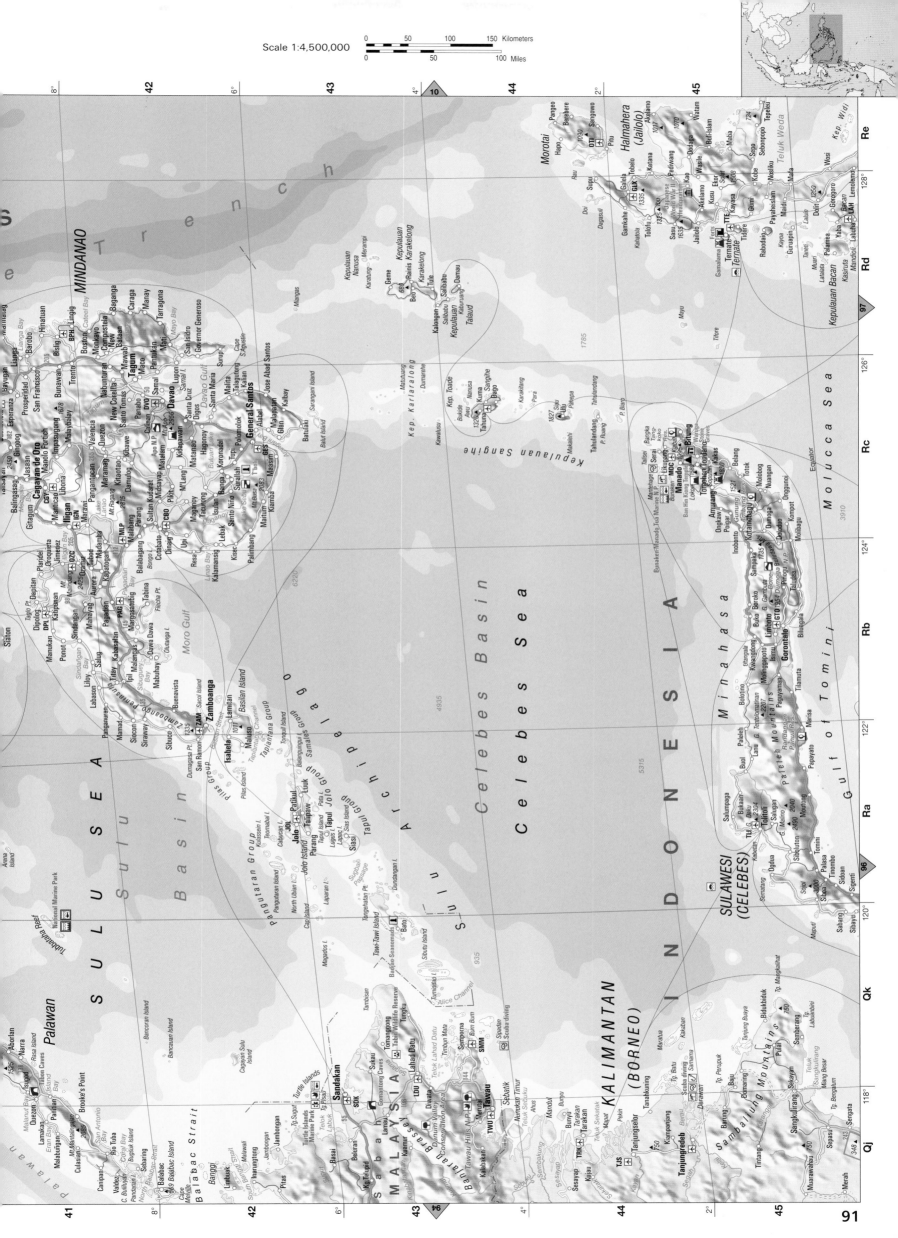

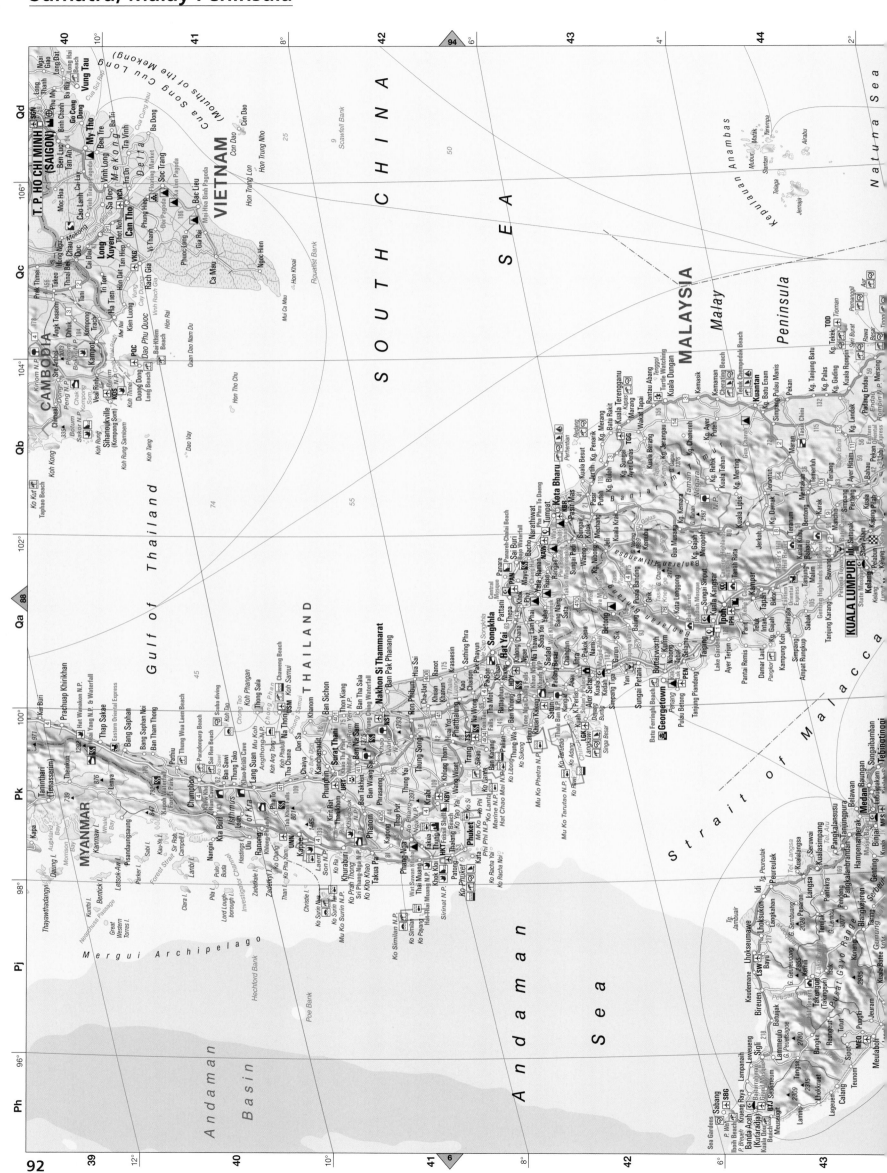

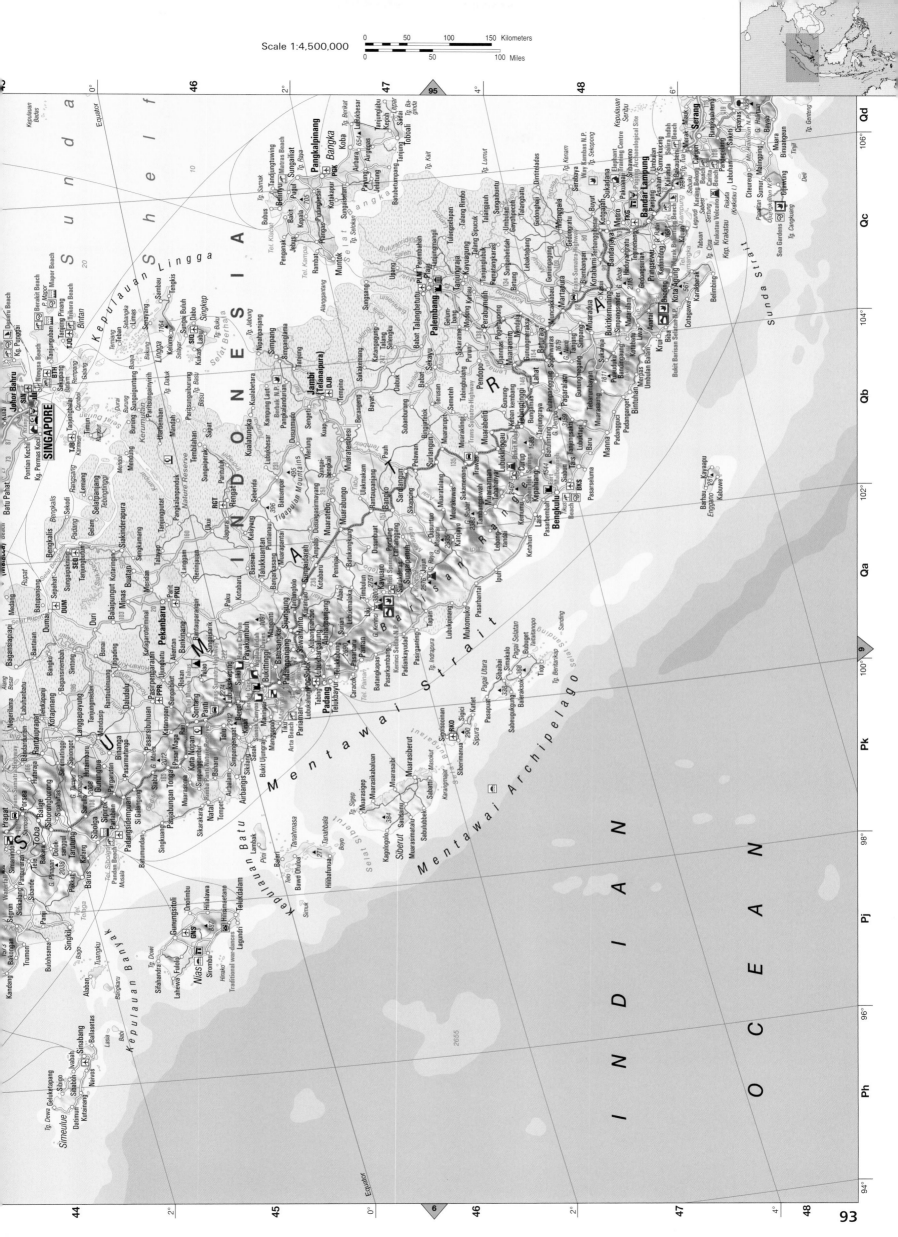

Kalimantan, Java, Bali

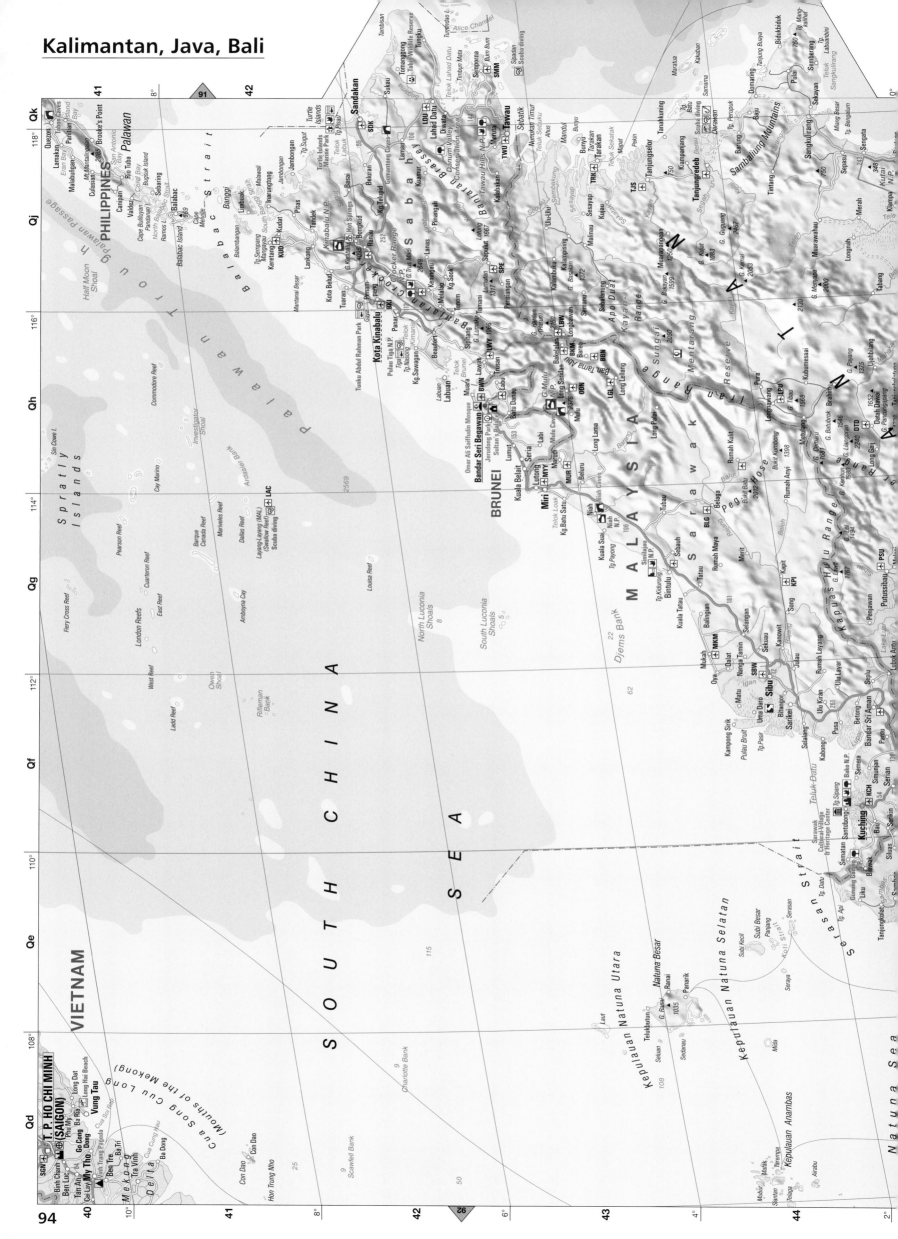

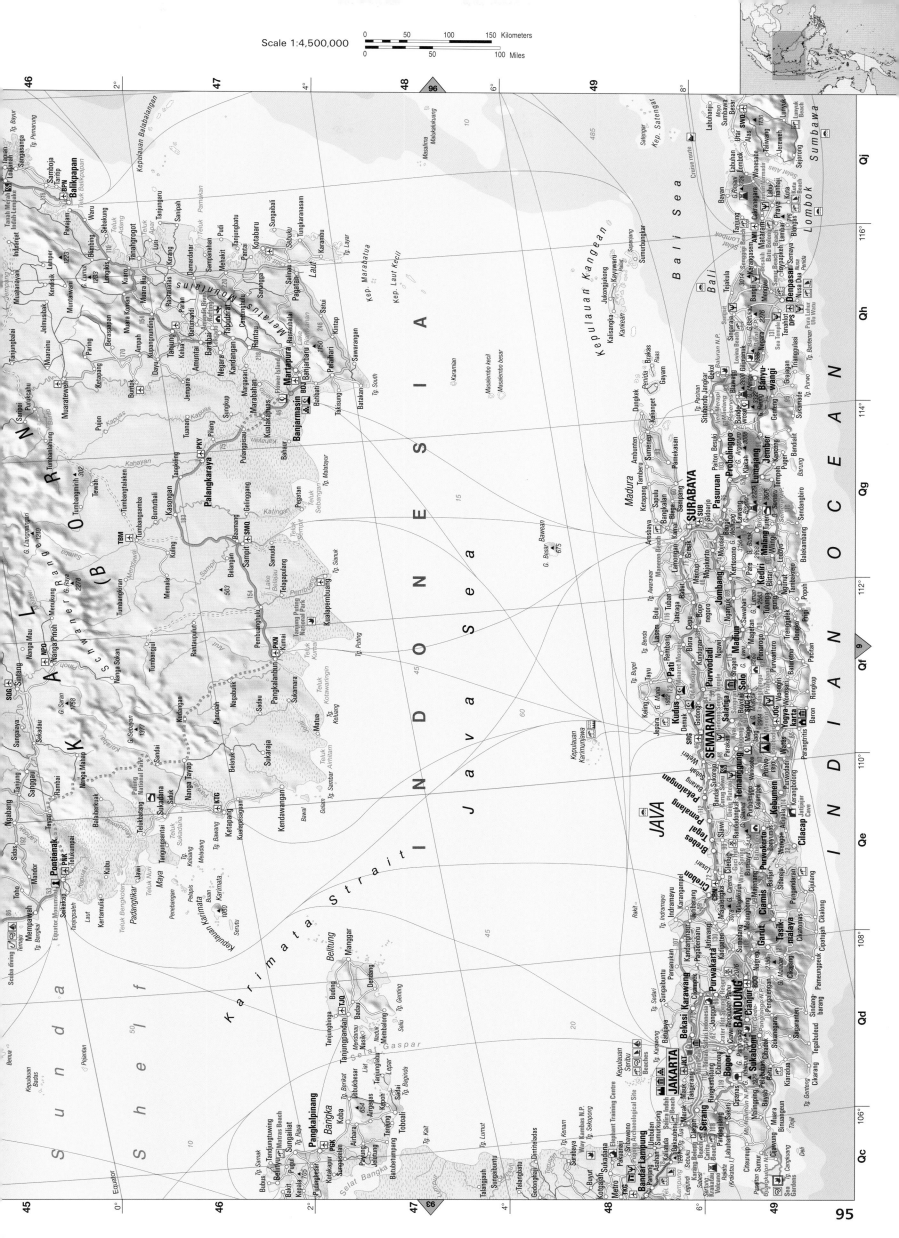

Sydney: The economic, industrial and cultural center of Australia.

The Pinnacles: a group of limestone formations in the desert near Perth.

AUSTRALIA/ OCEANIA

THE FIFTH CONTINENT AND THE ISLANDS OF THE PACIFIC

This region of the world is comprised of two unequal parts: the massive landmass of Australia and the countless scattered islands of the South Pacific. The region's islands range from the very smallest of islets to large islands such as New Guinea and New Zealand.

Australia is a continent of vast distances. Most of Central and Western Australia consist of deserts. Australia's largest desert, the Great Sandy Desert, covers 520,000 km². Ayers Rock, also known by its Aboriginal name Uluru, is located near the geographic center of Australia. Australia's highest mountains are in the Australian Alps, a section of the Great Dividing Range that stretches along the eastern coast. Mount Kosciuszko (2,228 m) is the highest mountain on the continent.

The Great Barrier Reef off the northeastern coast of Australia is the world's largest coral reef. It has a total length of more than 2,000 kilometers from north to south. The islands of Oceania are usually divided into three regions: Micronesia, Melanesia, and Polynesia. The thousands of islands in Oceania, scattered over 70 million km² in the Pacific Ocean, have a total land area around 1.3 million km².

Around 90 % of Australia's 19.7 million inhabitants occupy just 3 % of the continent's land concentrated in the Southeast with the majority of people living in a few large coastal cities. Aborigines, the continent's indigenous people, represent just 2.2 % of the population. Most Australians are the descendants of European immigrants. After the arrival of the first Europeans at the end of the 18th century, the Aboriginal population began to decline. Like the Aborigines, the Maori of New Zealand and the Papua of New Guinea were dramatically affected by the European colonization of their countries. These ethnic groups still struggle to preserve the most important aspects of their cultures, including their languages and traditional arts.

Sepik River: The region along New Guinea's longest river is home to many different tribes.

Australia/Oceania

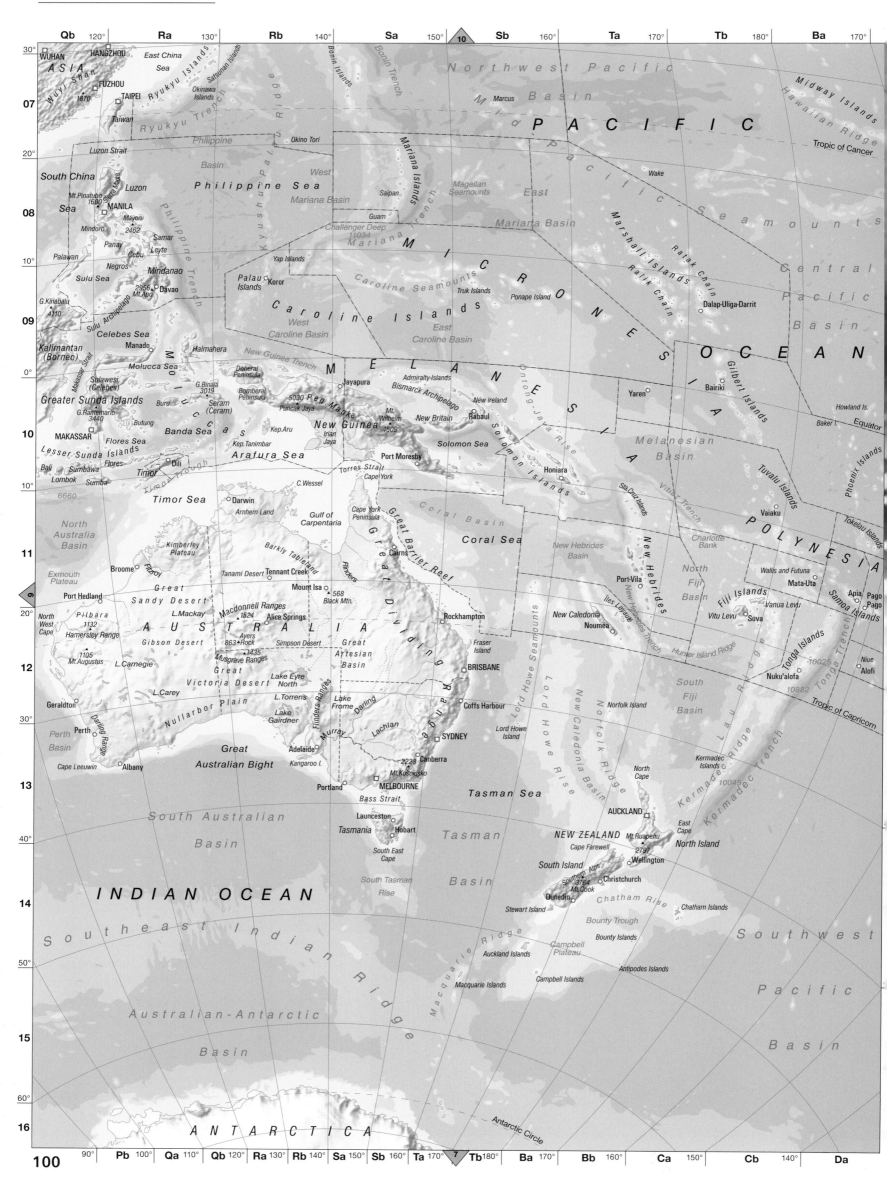

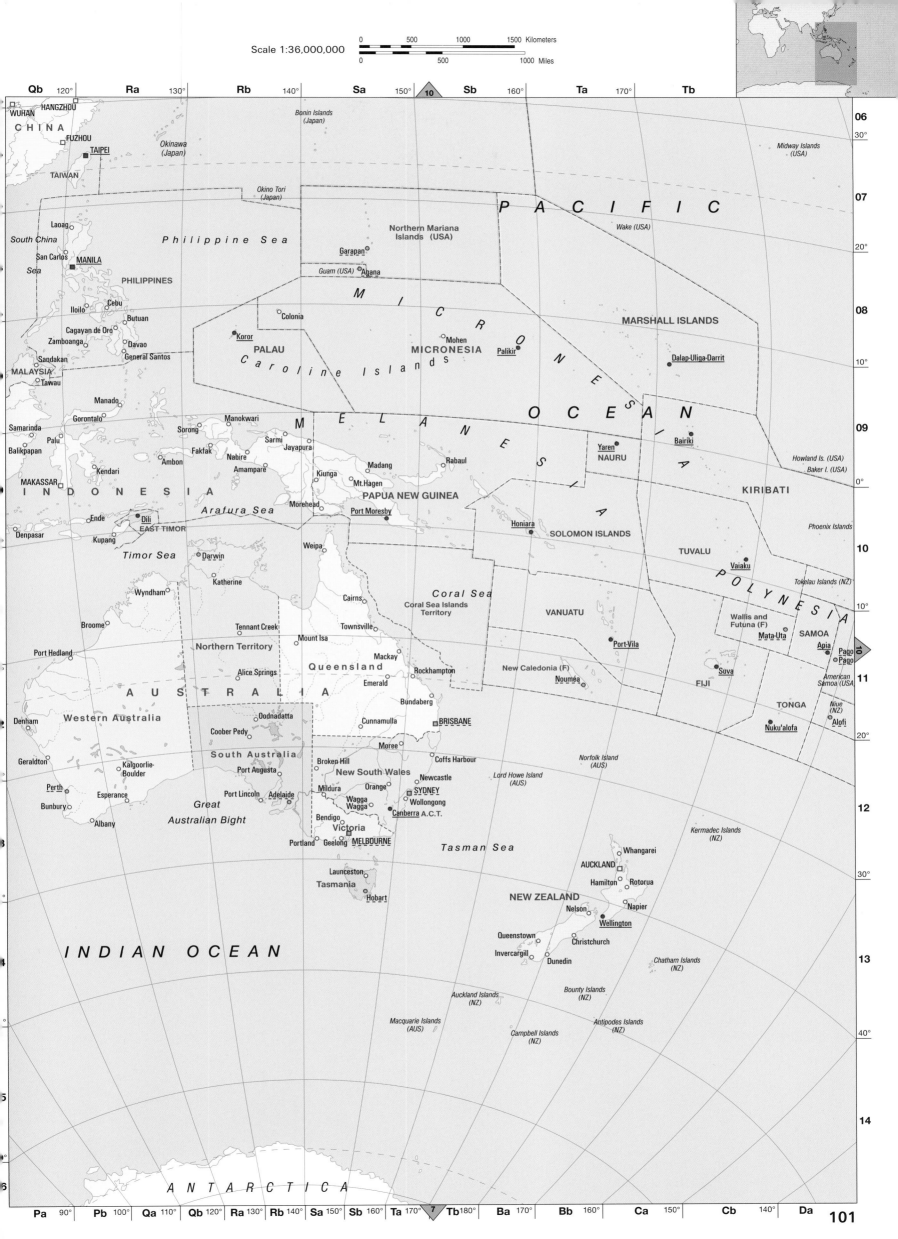

Scale 1:36,000,000

| 0 | 500 | 1000 | 1500 Kilometers |
| 0 | 500 | | 1000 Miles |

06
30°

C H I N A
WUHAN
HANGZHOU
FUZHOU
TAIPEI
TAIWAN

Bonin Islands
(Japan)

07

Okinawa
(Japan)

Midway Islands
(USA)

Laoag
South China
San Carlos
Sea
MANILA

Okino Tori
(Japan)

P A C I F I C

Wake (USA)

20°

PHILIPPINES

Northern Mariana
Islands (USA)

Garapan

08

Iloilo Cebu
Butuan
Cagayan de Oro
Zamboanga Davao
Sandakan General Santos
MALAYSIA
Tawau

Guam (USA) Agana

M I C R O

Colonia

Koror
PALAU

MICRONESIA

Mohen
Palikir

MARSHALL ISLANDS

Dalap-Uliga-Darrit

10°

Manado
Gorontalo
Samarinda
Palu
Balikpapan
Kendari
MAKASSAR
I N D O N E S I A

Manokwari
Sorong
Sarmi
Fakfak Jayapura
Nabire
Ambon Amampare
Kiunga
Morehead

Caroline Islands

M E L A
Madang
Mt.Hagen

N E

Rabaul

N E S I A

Yaren
NAURU

Bairiki

O C E A N

Howland Is. (USA)
Baker I. (USA)

09

0°

KIRIBATI

Ende Dili
EAST TIMOR
Denpasar Kupang

Arafura Sea

PAPUA NEW GUINEA
Port Moresby

S I A

Honiara
SOLOMON ISLANDS

Phoenix Islands

Timor Sea
Darwin

Weipa

Coral Sea

TUVALU
Vaiaku

P O L Y

Tokelau Islands (NZ)

10

10°

Wyndham
Katherine
Broome

Tennant Creek

Cairns
Townsville

Coral Sea Islands
Territory

VANUATU

Port-Vila

Wallis and
Futuna (F)
Mata-Uta

N E S I A

SAMOA
Apia
Pago
Pago

10°

Port Hedland

Northern Territory
Alice Springs

Mount Isa
Queensland
Mackay
Emerald
Rockhampton
Bundaberg

New Caledonia (F)
Nouméa

Suva
FIJI

American
Samoa (USA)

11

Denham

A U S T R A L I A
Western Australia

Oodnadatta
Coober Pedy

Cunnamulla
BRISBANE
Moree

Norfolk Island
(AUS)

TONGA
Nuku'alofa

Niue
(NZ)
Alofi

20°

Geraldton
Kalgoorlie-
Boulder
Perth
Esperance
Bunbury
Albany

Port Augusta
Port Lincoln Adelaide

South Australia

Broken Hill
Mildura
Orange
Wagga
Wagga
Bendigo
Geelong **MELBOURNE**
Victoria
Portland

New South Wales
Newcastle
SYDNEY
Wollongong
Canberra A.C.T.

Coffs Harbour

Lord Howe Island
(AUS)

Great
Australian Bight

12

Tasman Sea

Whangarei
AUCKLAND
Hamilton Rotorua

Kermadec Islands
(NZ)

30°

Launceston
Tasmania
Hobart

NEW ZEALAND
Nelson
Napier
Wellington

I N D I A N   O C E A N

Queenstown
Invercargill Dunedin
Christchurch

Chatham Islands
(NZ)

13

Auckland Islands
(NZ)

Bounty Islands
(NZ)

40°

Macquarie Islands
(AUS)

Campbell Islands
(NZ)

Antipodes Islands
(NZ)

14

A N T A R C T I C A

Southwestern Australia

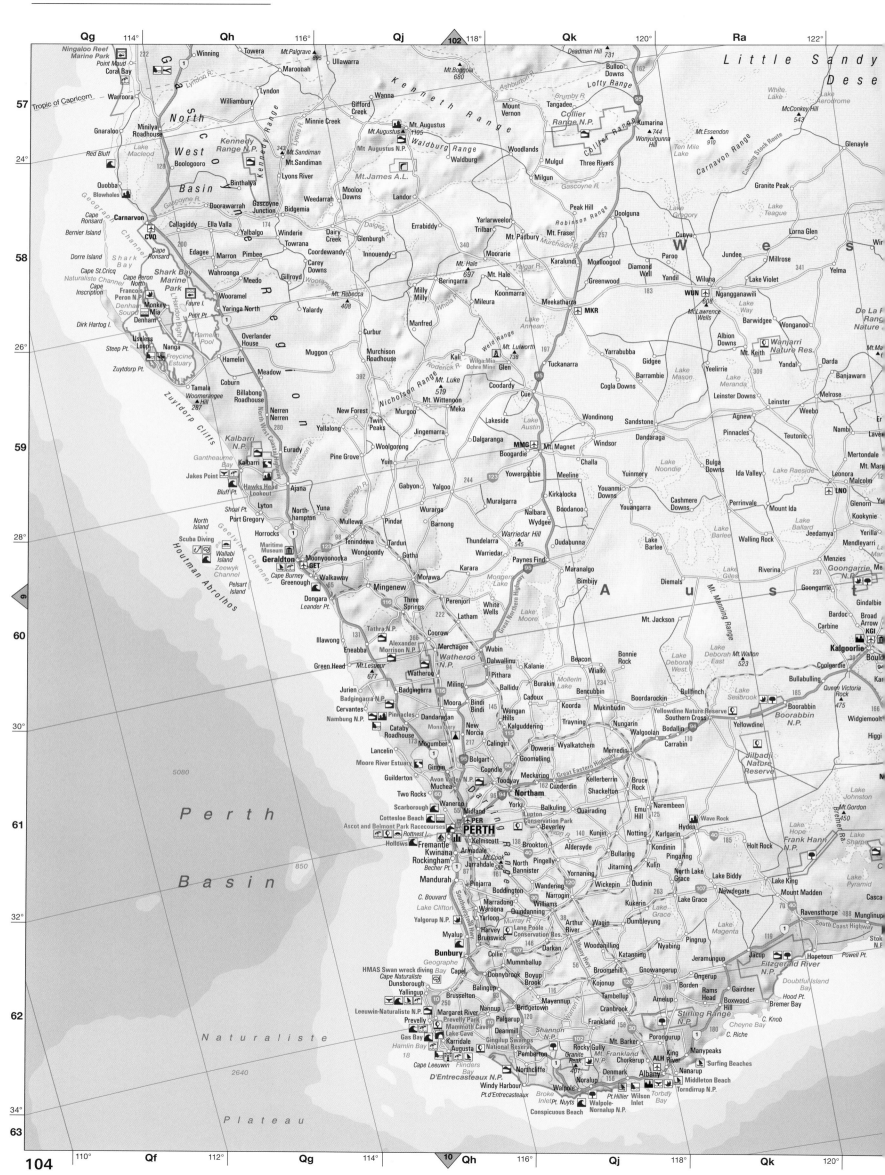

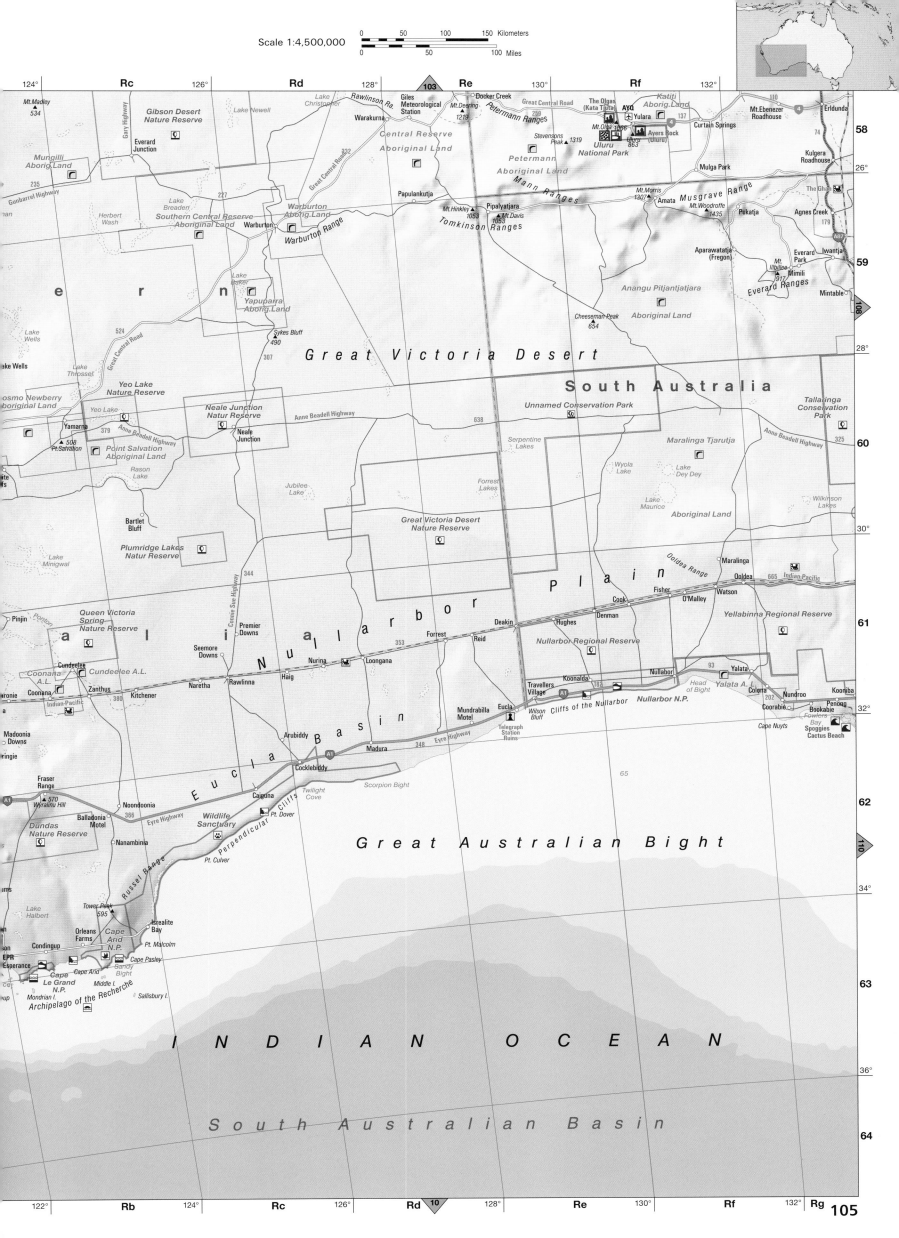

Northern Australia

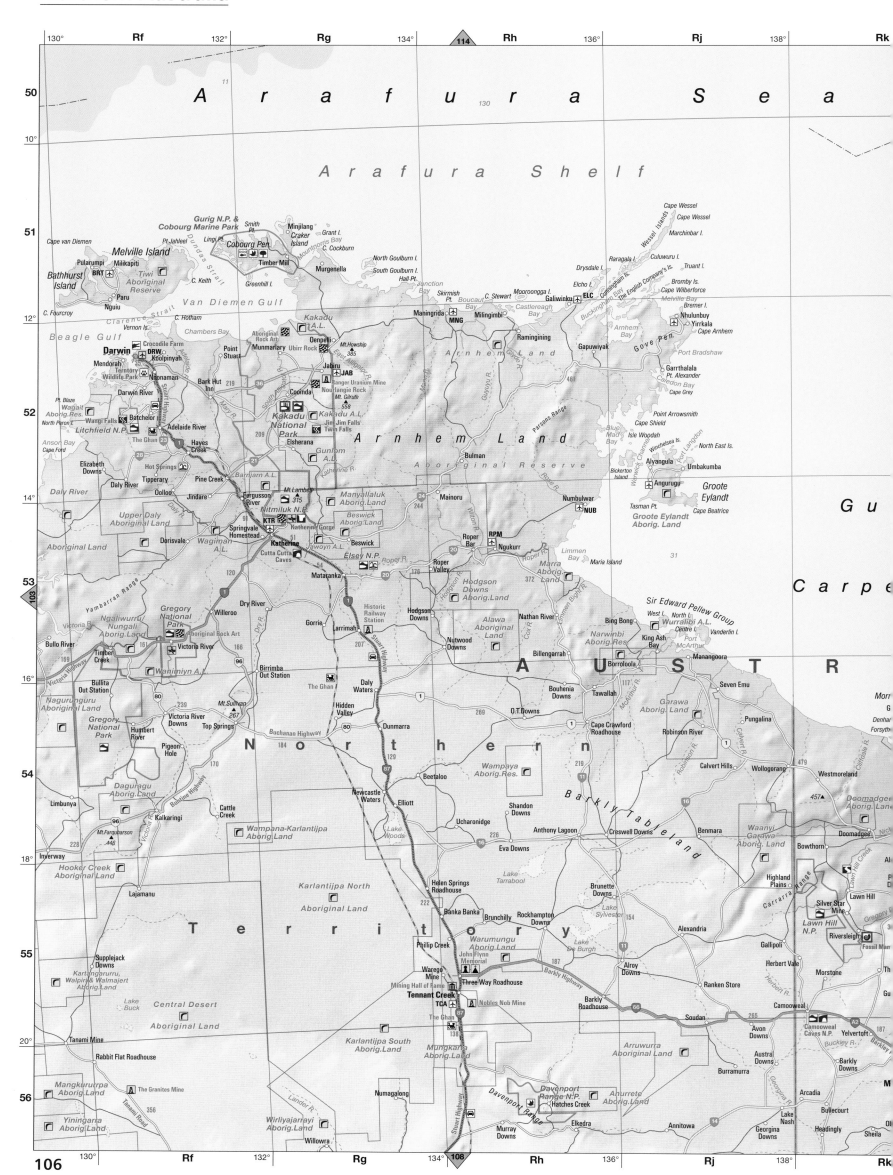

A r a f u r a   S e a

A r a f u r a   S h e l f

Gurig N.P. &
Cobourg Marine Park

Melville Island

Bathhurst
Island

Tiwi
Aboriginal
Reserve

Van Diemen Gulf

Beagle Gulf

Darwin

*Kakadu
A.L.*

Kakadu
National
Park

Kakadu A.L.

A r n h e m   L a n d

A r n h e m   L a n d

A b o r i g i n a l   R e s e r v e

Arnhem Land

Nitmiluk N.P.

Katherine

Elsey N.P.

Gove Pen.

Groote
Eylandt

Groote Eylandt
Aborig. Land

G u

C a r p e

Sir Edward Pellew Group

Barkly   Tableland

N o r t h e r n

Gregory
National
Park

Gregory
National
Park

T e r r i t o r y

Central Desert
Aboriginal Land

Lawn Hill
N.P.

A U S T R

Tennant Creek

Stuart Highway

The Ghan

Davenport Range N.P.

106

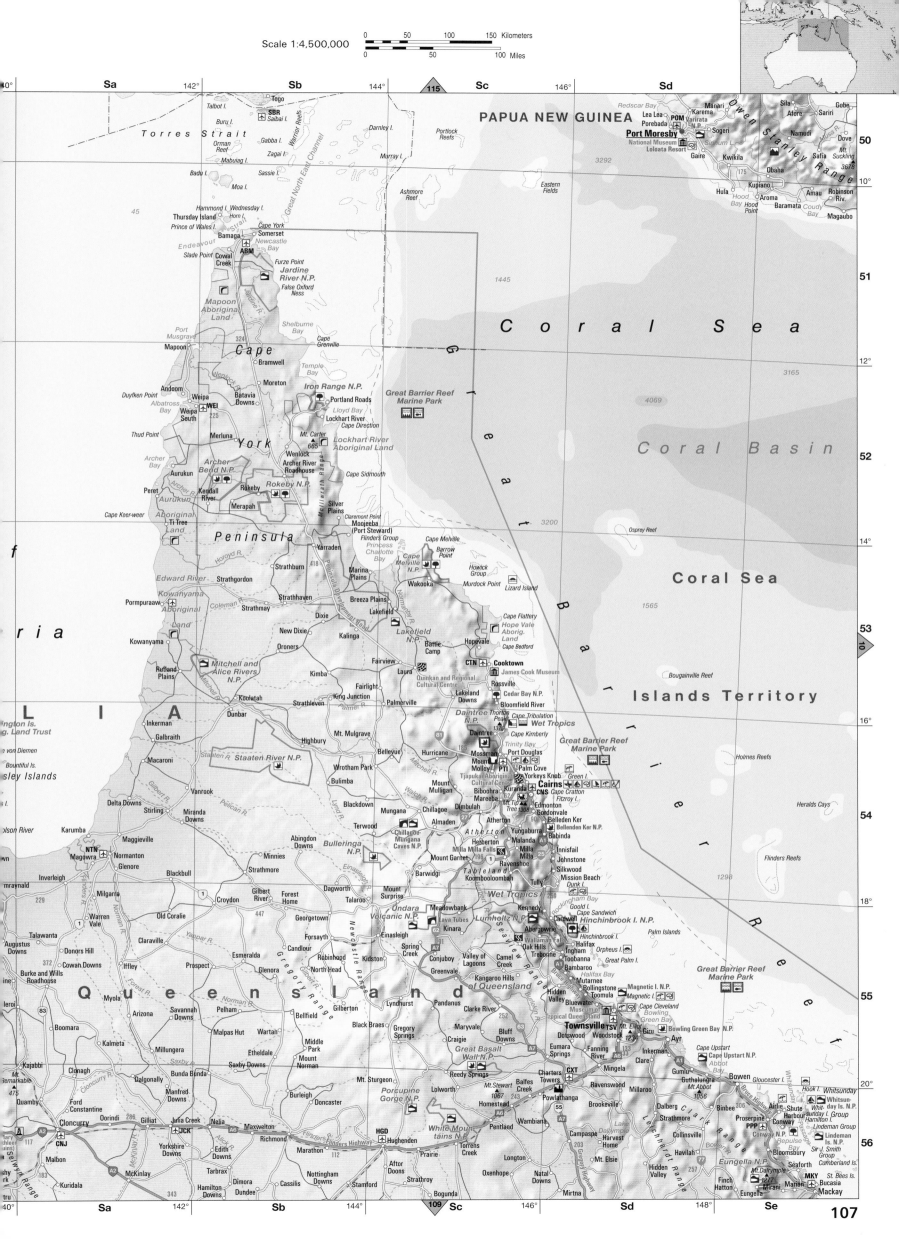

Sa   142°   Sb   144°   Sc   146°   Sd

PAPUA NEW GUINEA

Redscar Bay   Lea Lea   Manari   Sila   Afore   Gobe
Togo   Porebada   POM   Varirata   Karema   Namudi   Sariri
SBR   Saibai I.   Port Moresby   Sogeri   Sirium L.   Kwikila   Safia   Mt. Suckling   Dove
Talbot I.   Buru I.   Orman Reef   National Museum   Gaire   Obaha   Kupiano   3678
Darnley I.   Loloata Resort   Hula   Aroma   Amau   Robinson Riv.
Gabba I.   Zagai I.   Murray I.   3292   Hood   Baramata   Coudy
Mabuiag I.   Sassie I.   175   Bay   Magaubo

Torres   Strait   Ashmore   Eastern   Owen Stanley Range   50
Hammond I. Wednesday I.   Reef   Fields
Thursday Island   Horn I.   45
Prince of Wales I.   Moa I.   Badu I.
Endeavour   Bamaga   Cape York   10°
Slade Point   Somerset
Cowal   Newcastle   Coral   Sea
ABM   Creek   Bay   51
Furze Point
Jardine
River N.P.   1445   3165
Cape York   False Oxford
Mapoon   Ness   Coral   Basin
Aboriginal   Shelburne
Land   Bay   12°
Port   Cape
Musgrave   Bramwell   Grenville   4069
Mapoon   Cape   Temple
324   Bay
Andoom   Moreton   Iron Range N.P.   Great Barrier Reef
Duyfken Point   Batavia   Portland Roads   Marine Park
Weipa   Downs   Lloyd Bay   Osprey Reef   52
Albatross   WEI   Lockhart River
Bay   Weipa   225   Cape Direction   3200
South   Mt. Carter
Thud Point   Merluna   665   Lockhart River
Archer   York   Aboriginal Land   Coral   Sea   14°
Bay   Wenlock   Cape Sidmouth   1565
Archer   Archer River
Aurukun   Bend N.P.   Roadhouse   Silver
Peret   Kendall   Rokeby   Plains   Bougainville Reef   Islands Territory   16°
River   Rokeby N.P.   Claremont Point
Cape Keer-weer   Aurukun   Merapah   Moojeeba
Aboriginal   (Port Steward)   Holmes Reefs
Ti Tree   Flinders Group
Peninsula   Land   Princess   Cape Melville
Charlotte   Barrow
Yarraden   Bay   Point   Heralds Cays   18°
Horoyd R.   Cape Melville
Edward River   N.P.
Strathburn   418   Wakooka   Howick
Strathgordon   Group
Kowanyama   Marina   Murdock Point
Pormpuraaw   Strathhaven   Plains   Lizard Island
Aboriginal   Strathmay   Breeza Plains
Land   Dixie   Lakefield   Cape Flattery   20°
Kowanyama   New Dixie   Kalinga   Lakefield   Hope Vale Aborig.
Oronses   N.P.   Land   Flinders Reefs
Rutland   Fairview   Battle   Cape Bedford   1298
Plains   Camp
Mitchell and   Kimba   Laura   Hopevale   CTN   Cooktown
Alice Rivers   Fairlight   Quinkan and Regional   James Cook Museum
N.P.   King Junction   Cultural Centre   Rossville
Koolatah   Palmerville   Lakeland   Cedar Bay N.P.
Dunbar   Strathleven   Downs   Bloomfield River
Inkerman   Daintree Thorton   Cape Tribulation
Galbraith   Mt. Mulgrave   Peak   Cape Kimberley   Wet Tropics
Macaroni   Highbury   N.P.   Daintree   Great Barrier Reef
Staaten   Belleyue   Mossman   Trinity Bay   Marine Park
Vanrook   River N.P.   Hurricane   Mount   Port Douglas
Delta Downs   Wrotham Park   Molloy   PTI   Yorkeys Knob   Green I.
Stirling   Bulimba   Mount   Tjapukai Aboriginal   Cairns
Miranda   Mulligan   Cultural Centre   CNS   Cape Cratton
Maggieville   Downs   Blackdown   Biboohra   Kuranda   Fitzroy I.
Karumba   Mungana   Chillagoe   Mareeba   Mt. Tip   Edmonton
NTN   Minnies   Dimbulah   Tree 1306   Gordonvale   Herald Cays
Normanton   Magowra   Chillagoe   Almaden   Atherton   Belleden Ker
Glenore   Mungana   Hebberton   Belleden Ker N.P.
Inverleigh   Strathmore   Caves N.P.   Yungaburra   Babinda
Blackbull   Abingdon   Mount Garnet   Malanda
Downs   Bulleringa   Ravenshoe   Milla   Innisfail
N.P.   Barwidgi   Milla   Johnstone
Milgarra   Croydon   Mount Surprise   Tableland   Silkwood
Warren   Gilbert   Forest   Talaroo   Koombooloomba   Mission Beach   Flinders Reefs
Vale   River   Home   Undara   Wet Tropics   Dunk I.
Old Coralie   Volcanic N.P.   Tully
Talawanta   Meadowbank   Kennedy   Rockingham Bay
Donors Hill   Georgetown   Lava Tubes   Lumholtz N.P.   Cardwell   Goold I.
Augustus   Iffley   Forsayth   Einasleigh   Kinara   Abergowrie   Hinchinbrook I. N.P.   Cape Sandwich
Downs   Claraville   Candlour   Spring   Wallaman Falls   Hinchinbrook I.   Palm Islands
Prospect   Rubinhood   Creek   Oak Hills   Halifax   Orpheus I.
Cowan Downs   Esmeralda   North Head   Conjuboy   Valley of   Ingham   Great Palm I.
Burke and   Glenora   Greenvale   Lagoons   Trebonne
Wills   Gilberton   Camel   Toobanna   Great Barrier Reef
Roadhouse   Savannah   Lyndhurst   Creek   Mutarnee   Marine Park   55
Boomara   Downs   Pelham   Pandanus   Kangaroo Hills   Rollingstone   Magnetic I. N.P.
Myola   Arizona   Gilberton   of Queensland   Toomula   Magnetic I.
Kalmeta   Bellfield   Clarke River   Hidden   Bluewater   Cape Cleveland
Black Braes   Valley   Bowling
Millungera   Malpas Hut   Wartan   Maryvale   Rowes Museum   Townsville   Green Bay
Kajabbi   Gregory   Craigie   Bluff   Dotswood   TSV   Cape Upstart N.P.
Quamby   Middle   Springs   Downs   Woodstock   1234   Giru
Park   Mt. Stewart   Charters   Eumara   Mt. Elliot   Ayr   Cape Upstart
Dalgonally   Mount   Balfes   Towers   Springs   Fanning   Inkerman
Clonagh   Norman   Maryvale   1067   Creek   CXT   River   Clare   Abbot
Bunda Bunda   Mt. Sturgeon   Lolworth   243   Powlathanga   Mingela   Gumlu   Bay
Ford   Burleigh   Homestead   55   Guthalungra
Cloncurry   Constantine   Porcupine   Ravenswood   Hook I.   Whitsunday
Gorge N.P.   Millaroo   Whitsun-   I. Group
Julia Creek   Doncaster   Brookeville   Bowen   day Is. N.P.
CNJ   Gilliat   White Mountains   Mt. Abbot   1056
JCK   Nelia   N.P.   Collinsville   Dalberg   Strathmore   306   Binbee   Airlie
Maxwelton   203   Strathmore   Conway   Proserpine   Harbour   Conway
Oorindi   Richmond   HGD   Hughenden   Campaspe   Lindeman   Lindeman Group
Yorkshire   Marathon   Flinders Highway   112   Harvest   Whitsun-   Is. N.P.
McKinlay   Downs   Edith   Prairie   Home   Repulse   day I.
Tarbrax   Downs   Reedy   Shute   Bay   Group
Dimora   Aftor   Springs   Hamilton I.
Kuridala   Hamilton   Dundee   343   Doons   Longton   Dingo   St. Bees I.
Downs   Cassilis   Strathroy   Oxenhope   Natal   257   Eungella N.P.   MKY
Bogunda   Downs   Mirtna   Mt. Dalrymple   Seaforth
1277   Finch   Marian   Mackay
Hatton   Mirani

Q u e e n s l a n d

LIA

107

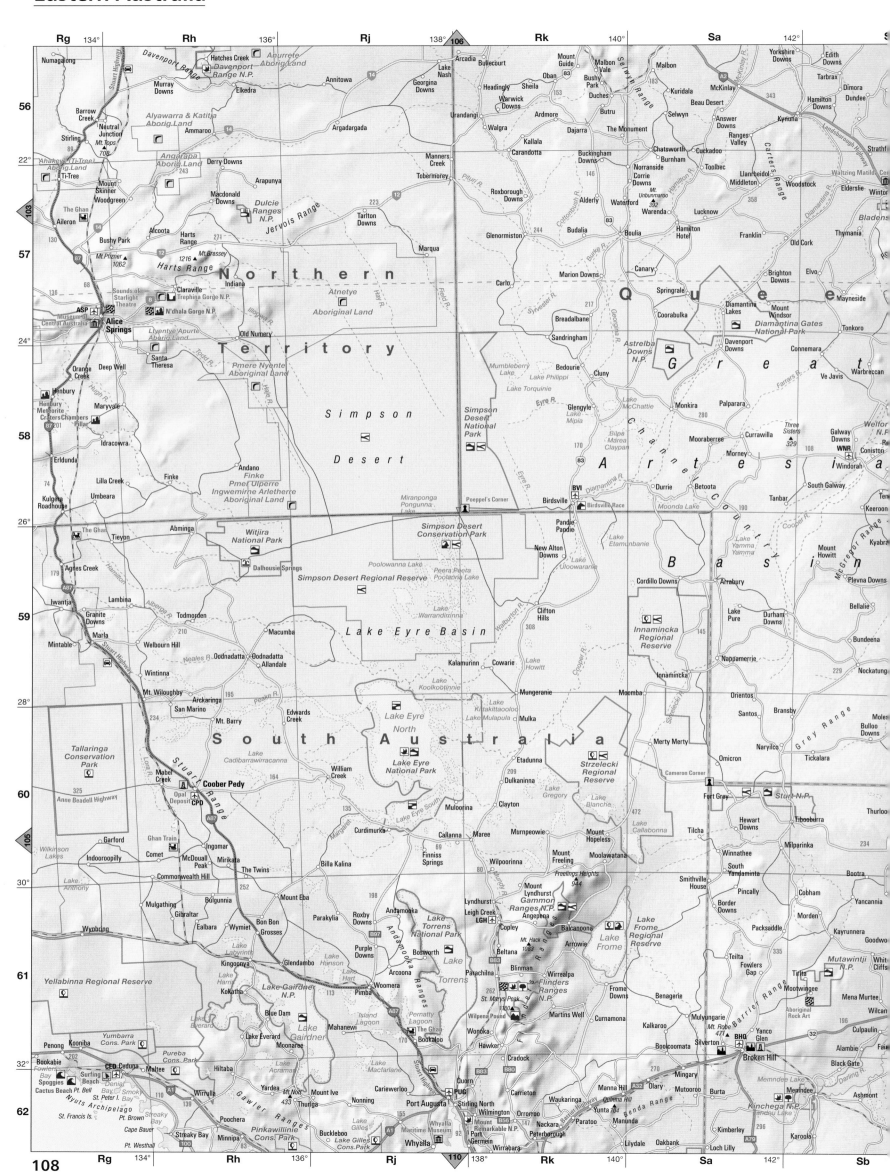

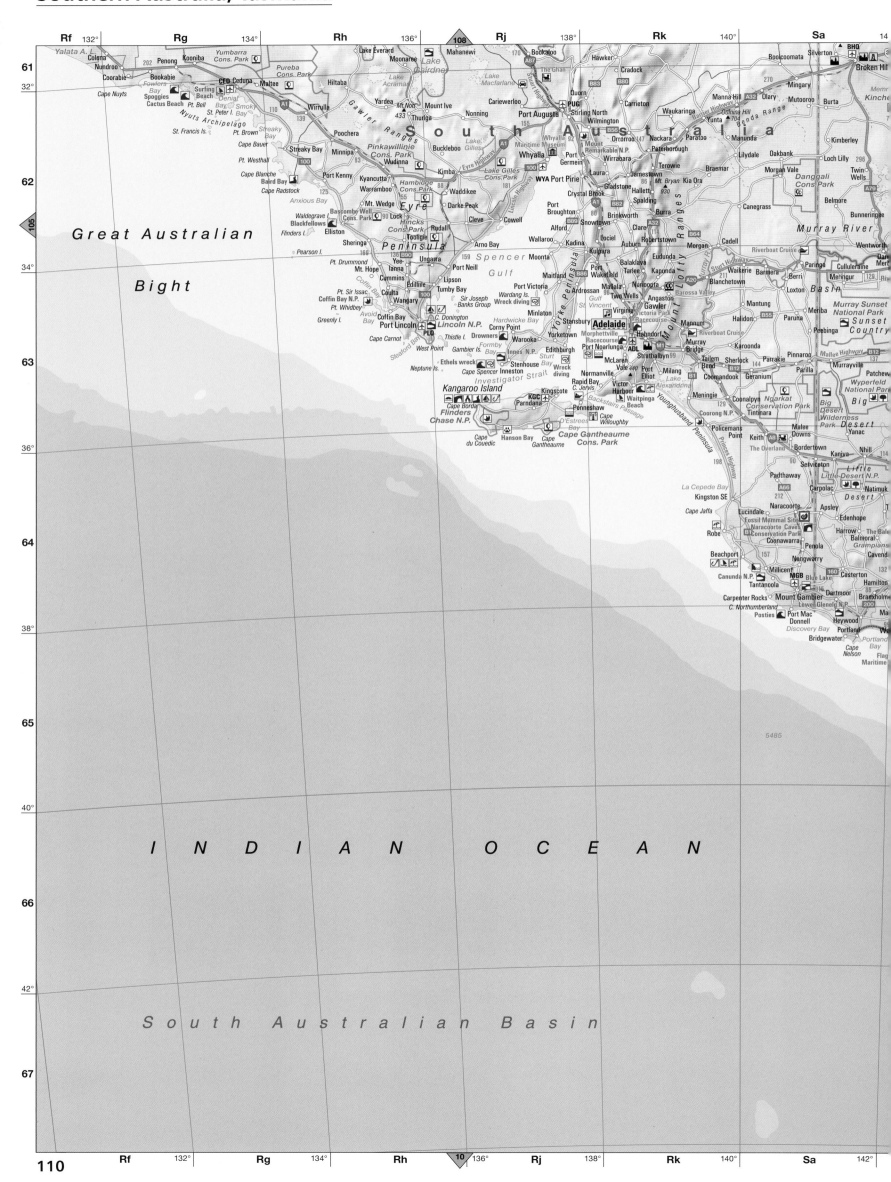

New Zealand

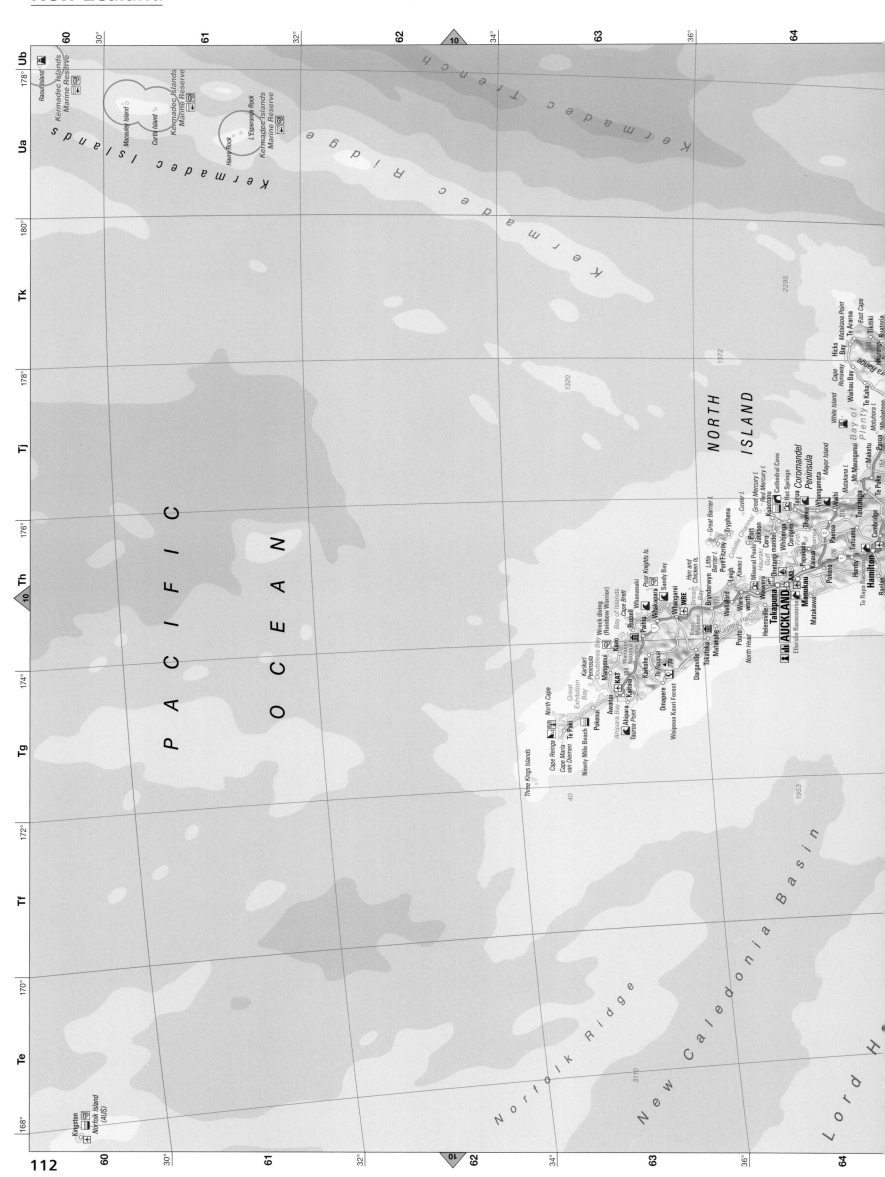

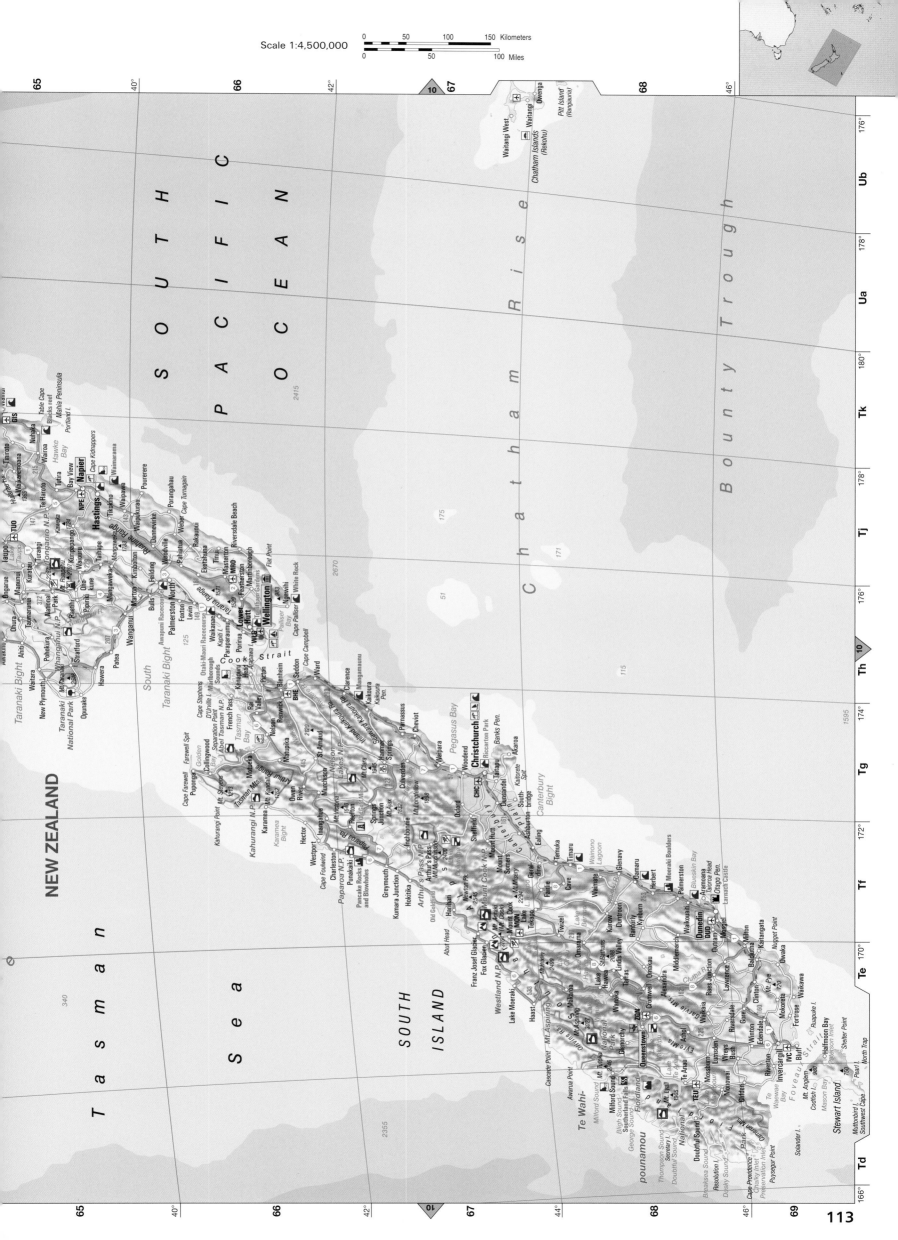

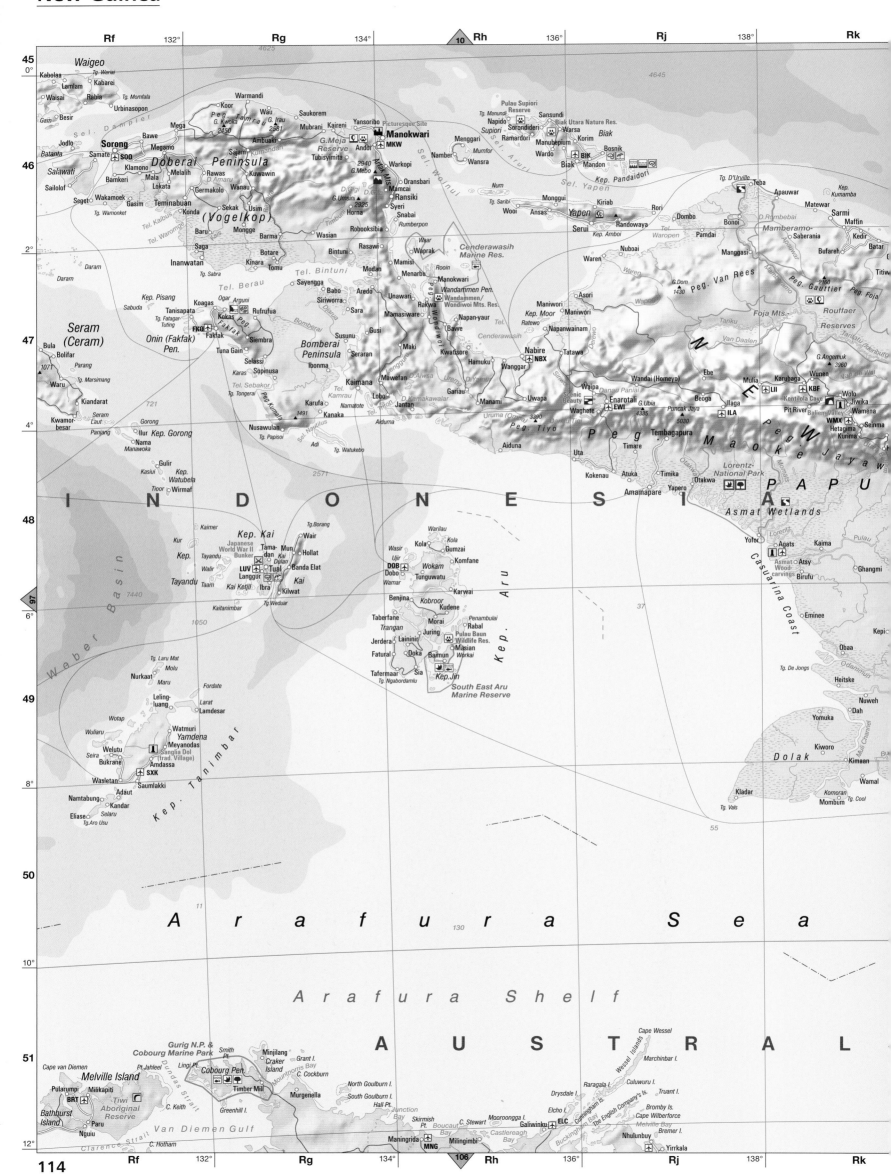

New Guinea

45
0°

Waigeo

Kabolaa
Tg. Wariai
Lamlam Kabareti
Waisai Rabia
Gain Besir Urbinasopon
Jodlo Bawe
Batanta Megamo
Samate SQQ
Salawati Klamono
Sailolof Wakamoek Gasim
Seget Konda
Wakamoek

Sorong
SOO

Mega
Koor
Warmandi
Wau
Saukorem
Mubrani Kaireni
Yansoribo Picturesque Site
Andor
Manokwari
MKW

Namber
Mumfor
Wansra

Pulau Supiori
Reserve
Tg. Manundi
Napido
Supiori Sorondideri
Menggari Ramardori
Warsa

Biak Utara Nature Res.
Sansundi

Manubepium
Wardo Korim
Biak
Bosnik
BIK
Biak Mandon

Kep. Pandaidori

46
1°

Doberai Peninsula

Melalih
Rawas
Germakolo Wanau
Mala
Lokata
Teminabuan Sekak Usim
Baru Mongge
Saga Barma

Kuwawin
DiGigi
G. Umsini
Horna

Ransiki
Syeri
Snabai
Rumberpon

Waar
Waprak

Num

Tg. Saribi
Monggui
Wooi Ansas

Yapen
Serui
Kep. Amboi

Randowaya
Dombo
Pamdai
Nuboai
Waren
Waropen

Rori
Kiriab

Tg. D'Urville Teba
Apauwar
Kep. Kumamba
Matewar
Sarmi
Maffin

Mamberamo
Saberania
Kedir
Batar
Bufareh
Titiw

2°

(Vogelkop)

Inanwatan
Botare
Kinara
Tomu

Kep. Pisang
Sabuda

Koagas
Ogar Arguni
Rufrufua

Sayengga
Siriworra
Sara

Bintuni
Rasawi
Modan
Menarbu

Mamisi
Rooin
Manokwari

*Cenderawasih
Marine Res.*

Asori
Maniwori
Kep. Moor
Maniwori
Napanwainam

G.Dom
1430

Peg. Van Rees

Tariku
Van Daalen

2160
Peg. Gauttier

*Rouffaer
Reserves*

Peg. Foja
Foja Mts.

47
Tarilatu/Idenburg

*Seram
(Ceram)*

Bula
Bolifar
1071
Parang
Waru
Tg. Marsimang

*Onin (Fakfak)
Pen.*

Kokas Peg.
Tanisapata
Tg. Fatagar-
Tuting
FKQ
Faktak
Siembra
Tuna Gain
Karas
Sopinusa

*Bomberai
Peninsula*

Susunu
Seraran
Ibonma

Gusi
Maki

Wanggar

Kwatisore
Hamuku
Manami

Nabire
NBX
Tatawa

Waipa
Uwapa
Waghete

Ebe

Mulia
Ilaga
Puncak Jaya
5030

G.Angemuk
3960
Wunen
Karubaga
KBF
Kontilola Cave
Wolo
Jiwika
WMX
Baliem Valley
Wamena

Kiandarat
Kwamor-
besar

Selassi
Karufa

Seram
Laut

Gorong
Panjang

Ilur Kep. Gorong
Nama Manawoka

Namatote
Kanaka
Aiduma

1491

Nusawulan
Tg. Papisoi
Adi

Lobo
Jantan

Gariau
D.Aiwea

Mawefan

Uruma (Oia)
3390

Uta

Peg. Tiyo
4335

Timare

Atuka
Timika
Tembagapura

Maoke

Peg.
Hetagima
Kurima
Seinma

Puncak Jaya

48

I N D O N E S I A

Gulir
Kasiui
Kep.
Watubela
Tioor Wirmaf

Kaimer
Kur
Kep.
Tayandu
Walir
Taam
Tayandu

Kep. Kai

Japanese
World War II
Bunker
LUV
Tual
Langgur
Ibra
Kilwat
Kai Ketjil

Tg.Borang
Wair
Mun
Tama-
dan Kai Dulan
Hollat
Banda Elat

Kai

Tg. Weduar

Warilau
Wasir
Ujir
Wokam
Kola
Kola
Gumzai
Komfane
Tunguwatu

DOB
Dobo

Kep. Aru

Kokenau
Amamapare
Yapero

Atuka

*Lorentz-
National Park*

Yofor

Asmat Wetlands

Agats
Asmat
Wood
carvings
Atsy
Birufu

Kaima
Pulau
Ghangmi

P A P U

97

*Weber
Basin*

7440

1050

Kaitanimbar

Benjina
Taberfane
Trangan
Jerdera
Fatural
Tafermaar

Kobroor
Morai
Juring
Laininir
Doka
Baimun
Sia

Kudene
Penambulai
Rabal
Pulau Baun
Wildlife Res.
Masian
Workai
Kep.Jin

*South East Aru
Marine Reserve*

37

Casuarina Coast

Eminee

Obaa
Heitske

Kepic

49

Nurkaat
Maru
Leling-
luang
Watmuri
Meyanodas
Sangla Dol
(trad. Village)
Amdassa
Wasletan
SXK

Molu
Fordate
Larat
Lamdesar
Yamdena

Kep. Tanimbar

Dolak

Nuweh
Dah
Yomuka
Kiworo
Kimaan
Wamal

8°

Namtabung
Kandar
Eliase Selaru
Tg.Aro Usu

Adaut
Saumlakki

Kladar
Komoran
Mombum
Tg. Cool

50

11

A r a f u r a   S e a

130

55

10°

A r a f u r a   S h e l f

51

Cape van Diemen
Melville Island
Pularumpi Milikapiti
BRT

*Gurig N.P. &
Cobourg Marine Park*

Smith
Pt.
Lingi Pt.
Cobourg Pen.
Timber Mill
Minjilang
Craker
Island
Grant I.
C. Cockburn

North Goulburn I.
South Goulburn I.
Hall Pt.

Cape Wessel
Wessel Islands
Marchinbar I.

Culuwuru I.
Truant I.

A U S T R A L

Bathhurst
Island
Paru
Nguiu
*Tiwi
Aboriginal
Reserve*

C. Keith
Greenhill I.

Murgenella

Junction
Bay
Skirmish
Pt.
Boucaut
Bay
C. Stewart
Mooroongga I.
Elcho I.
Galiwinku
ELC

Drysdale I.

Raragala I.
Bromby Is.
Cape Wilberforce
Melville Bay
Bremer I.

12°

Van Diemen Gulf
Clarence Strait
C. Hotham

Maningrida
MNG

Milingimbi
Castlereagh
Bay
Buckingham Bay
Cunningham Is.
The English Company's Is.
Nhulunbuy
Yirrkala

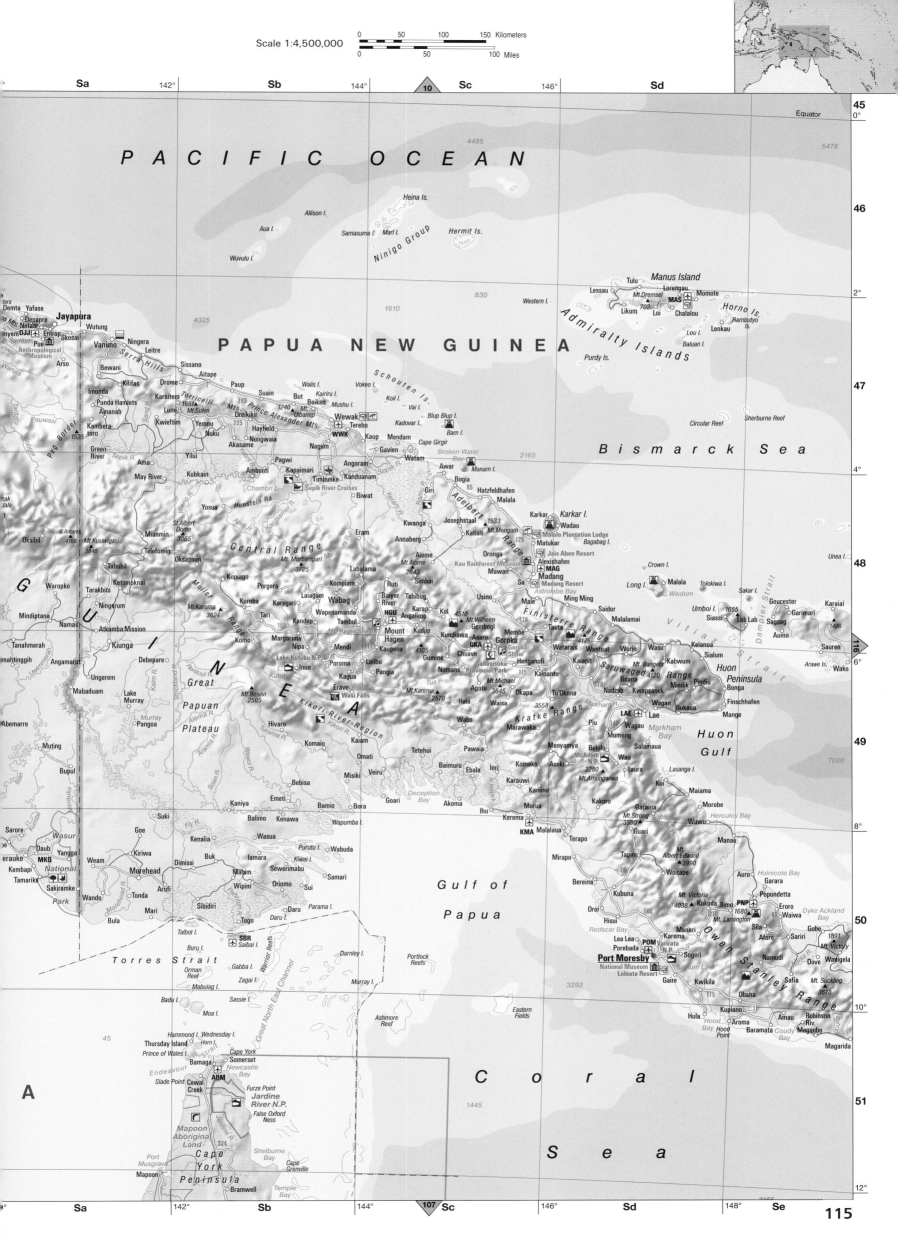

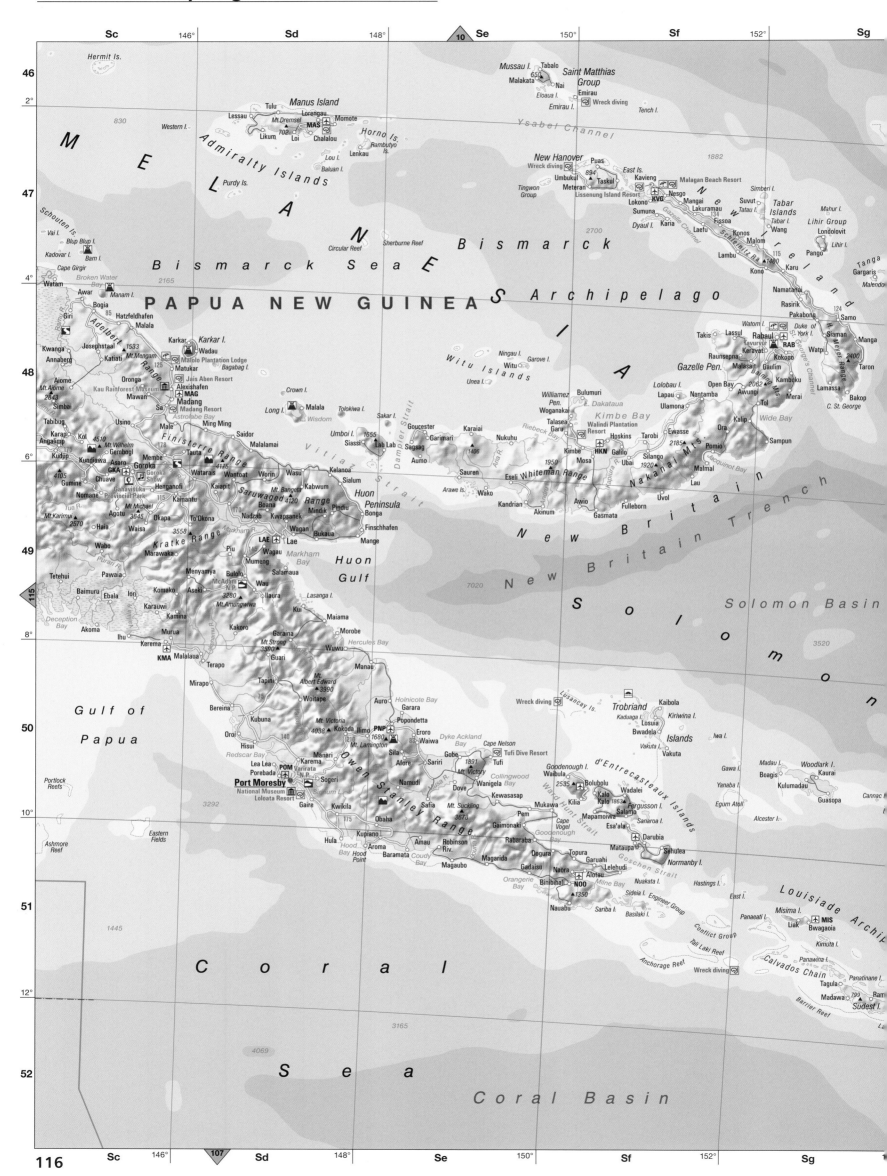

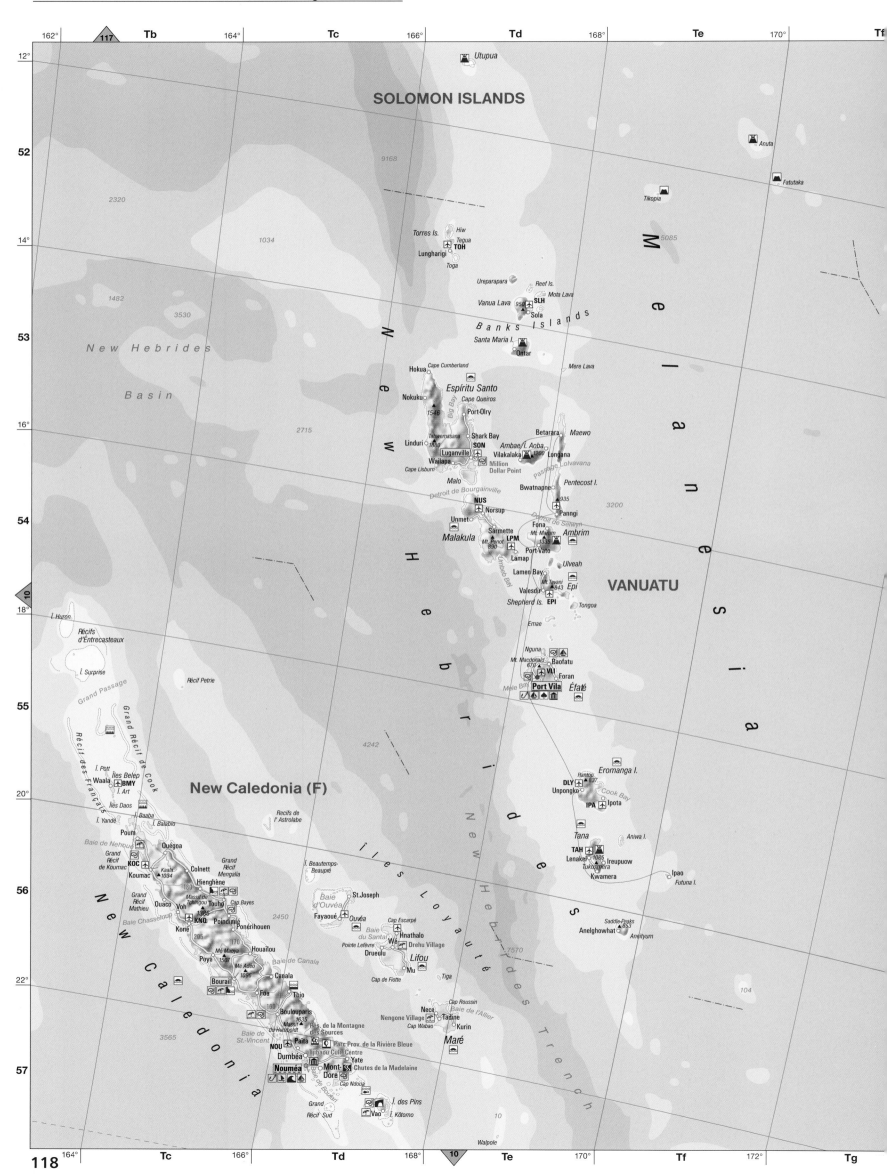

SOLOMON ISLANDS

Utupua

Anuta

Fatutaka

Tikopia

M e l a n e s i a

9168

2320

1034

Hiw
Tegua
Torres Is.
TOH
Lungharigi
Toga

Ureparapara
Reef Is.
Mota Lava
Vanua Lava
SLH
Sola
Banks Islands

5085

New Hebrides

Basin

Santa Maria I.
Ontar

Mere Lava

Hokua
Cape Cumberland
Espíritu Santo
Nokuku
Cape Queiros
Port-Olry
1546
Big Bay

1482

3530

2715

Tabwemasana
Linduri
1380
SON
Luganville
Wailapa
Cape Lisburn
Shark Bay
Betarara
Maewo
Ambae/Í. Aoba
Vilakalaka
1200
Longana

Million
Dollar Point
Malo
Bwatnapne
Pentecost I.

3200

N e w

Detroit de Bourgainville
NUS
Norsup
Panngi
935

Unmet
Sarmette
Fona
Mt. Marum
1335
Ambrim
Port-Vato
Malakula
Mt. Penor
890
LPM
Lamap
Ulveah

H e b

Lamen Bay
Mt. Tavani
843
Epi
VANUATU
Valesdir
Shepherd Is.
EPI
Tongoa

r i

Emae

Nguna
Baofatu
Mt. Macdonald
670
VLI
Foran
Mele Bay
Port Vila
Éfaté

d e s

4242

Eromanga I.
Rantop
837
DLY
Unpongko
Cook Bay
IPA
Ipota

N e w

T r e n c h

Aniwa I.

Tana
TAH
1085
Lenakel
Ireupuow
Tukosmera
Kwamera
Ipao
Futuna I.

Í. Huron
Récifs
d'Entrecasteaux
Í. Surprise
Récif Petrie

Grand Passage

Récif des Français
Grand Récif de Cook

Í. Pott
Îles Belep
Waala
BMY
Í. Art
Îles Daos
Í. Yandé
Baaba
Í. Balablo
Poum
Baie de Nehoué
Ouégoa
Grand
Récif
de Koumac
KOC
Koumac
Kaala
1034
Colnett
Hienghène
Grand
Récif
Mengalia

New Caledonia (F)

Recifs de
l'Astrolabe

Í. Beautemps-
Beaupré

St.Joseph

H e b r i d e s

Saddle-Peaks
653
Anelghowhat
Aneityum

N e w

Grand
Récif
Mathieu
Quaco
Voh
1386
Touho
Cap Bayes
KNQ
Poindimié
Koné
205
Ponérihouen
Mé Maoya
1508
Houaïlou
Mé Adeo
1098
Poya
Canala

2450

Baie
d'Ouvéa
Fayaoué
Ouvéa
Baie
du Santal
Wé
Hnathalo
Drehu Village
Pointe Lefèvre
Drueulu
Lifou
Mu
Tiga

L o y a u t é

7570

104

Í l e s

Cap Escarpé

Bourail
Foa
Thio
Boulouparis
1635
Massif
du Humboldt
Rés. de la Montagne
des Sources
Baie de
St-Vincent

Baie de Canala

Cap de Fiotte

Neca
Cap Roussin
Cap de l'Allier
Nengone Village
Tadine
Cap Wabao
Kurin
Maré

3565

NOU
Paita
Dumbéa
Tjibaou Cult.Centre
Parc Prov. de la Rivière Bleue
Yate
Nouméa
Mont
Dore
Chutes de la Madeleine
Cap Ndoua

N e w   C a l e d o n i a

Í. des Pins
Vao
Í. Kôtomo
Grand
Récif Sud

10

Walpole

Ethiopia: Traditional two-story dwellings with thatched roofs in Lalibela.

The Sahara Desert encompasses a variety of contrasting landscapes.

AFRICA

THE DEVELOPING CONTINENT

Africa has an area of approximately 30.4 million km². The world's second largest continent encompasses around 20 % of the Earth's total land area. From north to south, Africa stretches more than 8,000 kilometers. Africa is separated from Europe by the Mediterranean Sea, but at the Strait of Gibraltar the two continents are less than 14 kilometers apart. The Red Sea is located between northeastern Africa and the Arabian Peninsula. In the west, Africa is bordered by the Atlantic Ocean, while the Indian Ocean borders the continent to the east and southeast. The coasts of Africa are remarkably smooth, with few peninsulas and large natural harbors. Madagascar is situated near a series of smaller island groups including the Comoros and the Seychelles. Several small island groups – including the Cape Verde Islands – are located near Africa's western coast. The terrain of Africa is dominated by a series of basins, including the immense Sahara basin, the Niger-Chad-White Nile basin, and the Congo basin. The Great Rift Valley, an ancient fracture on the Earth's surface, stretches through East Africa. Many of Africa's tallest mountains – including Kilimanjaro and Mount Kenya – are located in or near the Great Rift Valley.

Africa is home to more than 700 million people. North Africa is inhabited by a variety of ethnicities, including Arabs, Berbers, and the Tuareg. The areas south of the Sahara are populated mostly by dark-skinned black African ethnicities. Most black Africans are categorized into one of two distinct groups: Bantu speaking and Sudanic ethnicities. Other major ethnic groups in Africa include the Somalis, Ethiopians, and the San.

Maasai: The semi-nomadic Maasai tribe lives in northeastern Tanzania and southern Kenya.

Africa has the highest birthrates of any continent. The rapid population growth is seen by many as a major obstacle to the continent's economic and social development. Despite widespread social problems, several African states have experienced positive economic and political developments in recent years.

Africa

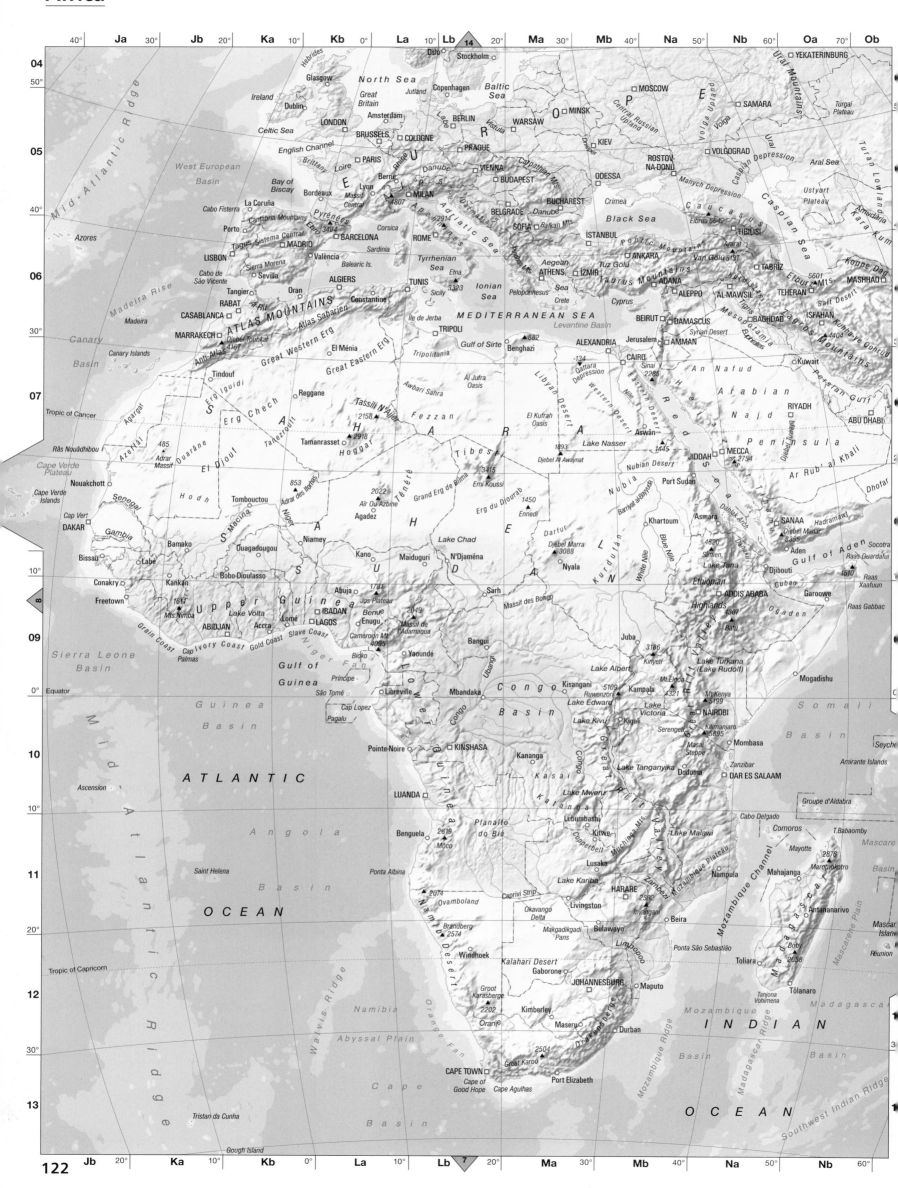

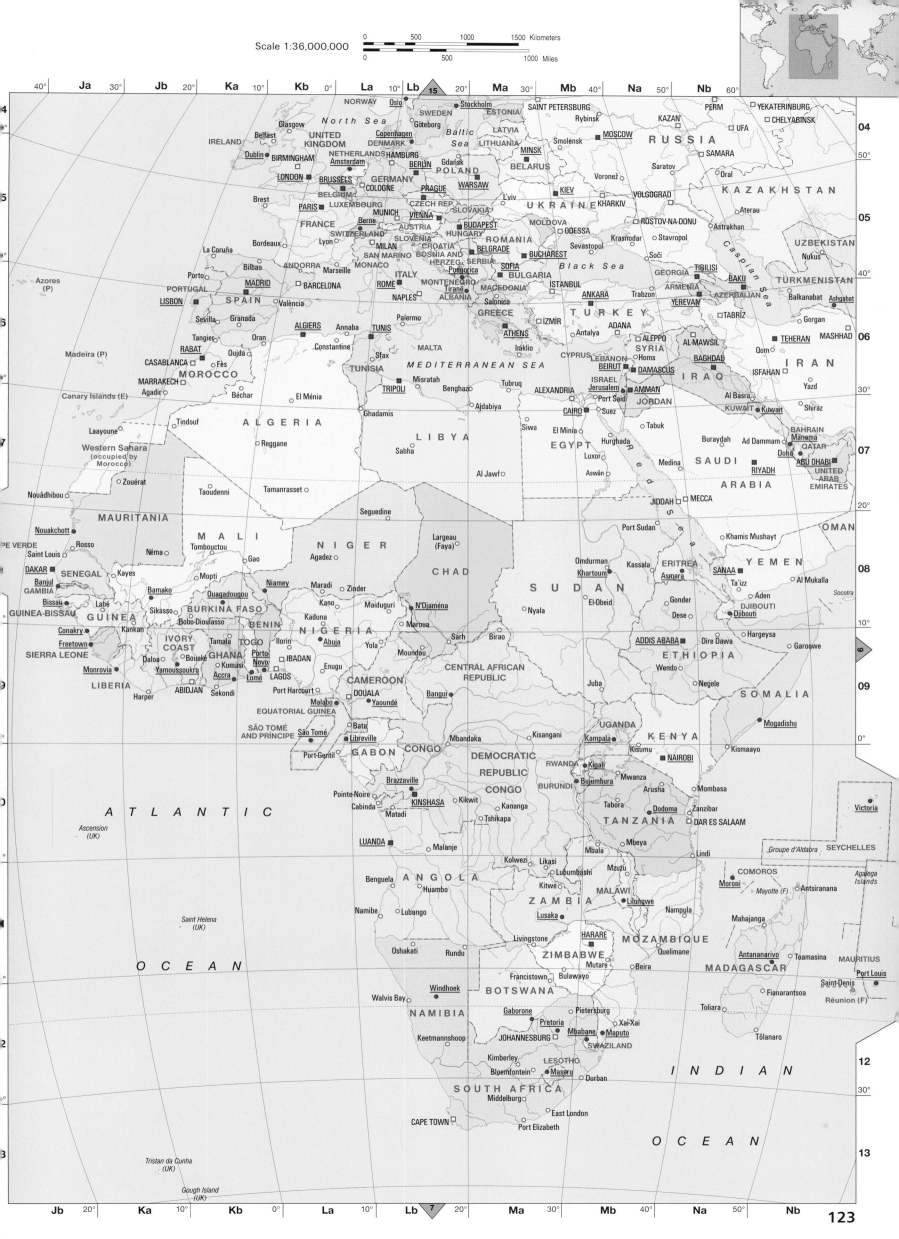

Scale 1:36,000,000

| 0 | 500 | 1000 | 1500 Kilometers |
| 0 | 500 | | 1000 Miles |

04

NORWAY Oslo Stockholm SAINT PETERSBURG PERM YEKATERINBURG
SWEDEN ESTONIA Rybinsk KAZAN UFA CHELYABINSK
Glasgow Göteborg LATVIA Smolensk MOSCOW
IRELAND Belfast North Sea Copenhagen Baltic LITHUANIA RUSSIA SAMARA
UNITED DENMARK Sea MINSK Voronež SARATOV Oral
Dublin BIRMINGHAM KINGDOM HAMBURG Gdańsk BELARUS KAZAKHSTAN
NETHERLANDS BERLIN POLAND VOLGOGRAD Aterau
LONDON BRUSSELS COLOGNE PRAGUE WARSAW KIEV KHARKIV
PARIS BELGIUM LUXEMBOURG GERMANY UKRAINE ROSTOV-NA-DONU UZBEKISTAN
Brest MUNICH VIENNA SLOVAKIA L'viv Astrakhan Nukus
FRANCE Berne AUSTRIA BUDAPEST MOLDOVA ODESSA Krasnodar Stavropol
SWITZERLAND SLOVENIA HUNGARY ROMANIA Sevastopol Soči TURKMENISTAN
Lyon MILAN CROATIA SERBIA Black Sea GEORGIA TBILISI BAKU
La Coruña Bordeaux SAN MARINO BOSNIA AND BELGRADE BUCHAREST İSTANBUL ARMENIA AZERBAIJAN Balkanabat Ashgabat
Bilbao HERZEG. Podgorica SOFIA BULGARIA ANKARA YEREVAN
Porto ANDORRA Marseille MONACO ITALY MONTENEGRO Tiranë MACEDONIA GREECE Trabzon TABRÎZ Gorgan
MADRID BARCELONA ROME NAPLES ALBANIA Salonica İZMİR TURKEY TEHERAN MASHHAD
PORTUGAL SPAIN València ATHENS Antalya ADANA SYRIA AL-MAWSIL Qom IRAN
LISBON ALGIERS TUNIS Palermo ALEPPO
Sevilla Granada Annaba MALTA İráklio CYPRUS LEBANON AL-MAWSIL BAGHDAD ISFAHAN
Tangier Oran Constantine HOMS BEIRUT DAMASCUS IRAQ Yazd
RABAT Oujda TUNISIA Sfax MEDITERRANEAN SEA ISRAEL Al Basra Shiraz
CASABLANCA Fès Misratah Jerusalem AMMAN KUWAIT Kuwait
MOROCCO Béchar TRIPOLI Benghazi Tubruq ALEXANDRIA Port Said Suez JORDAN Ad Dammam BAHRAIN
MARRAKECH Agadir El Ménia Ghadames CAIRO Tabuk Manama QATAR
Canary Islands (E) Siwa EGYPT Hurghada Bur.aydah Doha ABU DHABI UNITED
Laayoune Tindouf ALGERIA El Minia Medina RIYADH EMIRATES ARAB
Western Sahara Reggane LIBYA Luxor SAUDI
(occupied by Morocco) Sabha Al Jawf Aswân ARABIA OMAN
Nouâdhibou Zouérat Taoudenni Tamanrasset JIDDAH MECCA
Nouakchott Rosso Seguedine Port Sudan Khamis Mushayt
CAPE VERDE Néma MAURITANIA Largeau YEMEN
Saint Louis Tombouctou MALI (Faya) Omdurman Kassala ERITREA SANAA
DAKAR Kayes Gao NIGER Khartoum Asmara Ta'izz Al Mukalla
SENEGAL Mopti Agadez CHAD SUDAN Aden Socotra
Banjul BAMAKO Niamey Maradi Zinder El-Obeid Gonder DJIBOUTI
GAMBIA Sikasso OUAGADOUGOU Kano Nyala Dese Djibouti
Bissau Labé BURKINA FASO Kaduna Maiduguri N'Djaména Maroua Sarh Birao Wendo ADDIS ABABA Dire Dawa Hargeysa
GUINEA-BISSAU Bobo-Dioulasso BENIN NIGERIA Yola Moundou ETHIOPIA Garoowe
GUINEA Kankan IVORY Tamala Ilorin Abuja Enugu CENTRAL AFRICAN Negele SOMALIA
Conakry COAST GHANA IBADAN REPUBLIC Juba
Freetown Daloa Bouaké Kumasi Porto- LAGOS CAMEROON Bangui UGANDA Mogadishu
SIERRA LEONE Yamoussoukro Accra Novo Port Harcourt DOUALA Yaoundé Kampala Kisumu KENYA
Monrovia ABIDJAN Lomé Malabo Bata DEMOCRATIC Mbandaka Kisangani NAIROBI Kismaayo
LIBERIA Harper Sekondi EQUATORIAL GUINEA Libreville REPUBLIC RWANDA Kigali Mwanza
SÃO TOMÉ Port-Gentil GABON CONGO CONGO BURUNDI Bujumbura Arusha Mombasa
AND PRÍNCIPE São Tomé Brazzaville Kikwit Tabora Dodoma Zanzibar
ATLANTIC Pointe-Noire Cabinda Kananga TANZANIA DAR ES SALAAM Victoria
Ascension (UK) Matadi KINSHASA Tshikapa Mbeya Lindi Groupe d'Aldabra SEYCHELLES
LUANDA Malanje Mbala COMOROS Agalega Islands
Kolwezi Likasi Mzuzu Moroni Antsiranana
ANGOLA Lubumbashi MALAWI Mayotte (F)
Benguela Huambo Kitwe Lilongwe Nampula Mahajanga MAURITIUS
Namibe Lubango ZAMBIA Lusaka MOZAMBIQUE Antananarivo Toamasina
Saint Helena (UK) Livingstone HARARE Quelimane MADAGASCAR Port Louis
OCEAN Oshakati Rundu ZIMBABWE Mutare Beira Saint-Denis
Francistown Bulawayo Réunion (F)
Walvis Bay Windhoek BOTSWANA Fianarantsoa
NAMIBIA Gaborone Pietersburg Xai-Xai Toliara Tôlanaro
Keetmanshoop Pretoria Xai-Xai
JOHANNESBURG Mbabane Maputo INDIAN
Kimberley SWAZILAND
Bloemfontein LESOTHO OCEAN
SOUTH AFRICA Maseru Durban
Middelburg
CAPE TOWN East London
Tristan da Cunha (UK) Port Elizabeth OCEAN
Gough Island (UK)

Jk   20°   Ka   18°   Kb   ▲8   16°   Kc   14°   Kd   12°   Ke

35
Gettysburg
Seamount

28

5633

55
Ampére
Seamount

662

C a n a r y

4600

2450

Seine
Bank
170

B a s i n

29

Madeira
Islands

Ilha do Porto Santo

4686

Porto Moniz
1818   Santana
Machico
Funchal
Madeira (P)   Ilhas Desertas

A T L A N T I C

30

3950

Dacia
Bank
85

Cap Beddo
Le Jardin
(Safi) As
Dar el-Bal
Sebt-des-G
Dar-Caíd-Hadji
Talmest

Essaouira
ESU
Ounara
Tleta-
Henchane
84

Imi-n-Ta
Tamanar
N1

O C E A N

1572

Ilhas Selvagens (P)

161

2650

Dar-Caíd-
Ifal-bou-Fenzi
Tamri
Cap Rhir   Imouzzèr-des-
Ida-Outanane   Dj
1549▲   El
Taroudann

2725

Agadir
AGA
Inezgane
Ait-Mellout   Oulad-Teim
Inchaden   Biougra
Aït-Baha
P.N.Sous-Massa   130
N1   Réserve de Bio
Arganeraie
Djebel Lek
2359▲

31

4362

C a n a r y   I s l a n d s

Isla Alegranza

Isla Graciosa
Jameos del Agua
P.N.de
Timanfaya   Haría
Playa Blanca   **Lanzarote**
Corralejo   Arrecife
ACE

Tafraoute
Tleta-Akhssass
Chapeau
napoleon

Tiznit   Assaka
Jemaa-Ida
Oussernal
Ida-Oumrakt

La Palma
2426   San Andrés
Cal.de Taburiente   Santa Cruz de la Palma
Los Llanos de Aridane
P.N.de la
SPC
Fuencaliente
de la Palma

Tenerife
TFN
La Laguna
Garachico   **Santa Cruz de Tenerife**
Santiago del Teide   Puerto de la Cruz
3718   P.N.del Teide
Pico del Teide
TFS
Los Cristianos   La Aldea de
1949

Parque Natural de
las Dunas de Corralejo
Taca
Fuerteventura
Betancuria   Puerto del Rosario
Tuineje   FUE

Mirleft
Sidi Ifni
Bouizakarne

Guelmim
112
1194   Fask
Foum el-
Hassane
Ida-Oumarkt

1021   N
Gravures
rupestres

28

Sabinosa
Valverde
Taibique   **VDE**
Hierro

La Gomera
Vallehermoso
P.N.de Garajonay
Valle Gran Rey   San
GMZ   Sebastián
de la Gomera
San Bartolome
de Tir
3434

Agaete   Teror
Telde   **Las Palmas
de Gran Canaria**
San Nicolás   LPA
Maspalomas
Canary Islands (E)   *Gran Canaria*

Puerto
de la Cruz   Morro Jable

Plage Blanche   El Ouatia
Cap Drâa   N1
TTA   Tan-Tan
125
Djebel Guir
959   898
Djebel Rich   Tadalt
TTA   Tan-Tan   1064
Tilemsen   Oued Drâa   Teskalouine   Assa
Amon   Tisgui-Remz
Tiguguit

205   Cap Juby
Tarfaya   Sidi Akhfennir   Djebel   Zag
Sebkha   157
Tah
Khaoui N'am   101   As Sakn   671
El Hagounia   245

32

El Ouatia
1660   Cap Boujdour
Boujdour

Al-'Ayun
(Laâyoune)
Laâyoune-Port
EUN   99
Dchira   N1
Anakch   284
Jdiriya   El Farciya
Hawza   641
106

Al-Mahbas
68
TIN

26

Lemsid   188
Metmarfag   N5
Boukra
240   Smara
Oumcheggag   N14   Amgala   701
637

Tal at Damya   252

2414

Iraifia
N1   *Z e m m o u r*
153
Dhaym-
al-Khayl   90

Lemluia   756   Tfaritiy   Al Bîr Lahlou
Atonyia
Ain Ben Tili   423

33

Echtoucan
Skaymat   126
N1

Bîr Mogrein   671
Galtat Zemmour   Agmar   Bîr Bel Guerdâne
Iguetti   256

20

W e s t e r n

S a h a r a
(occupied by Morocco)

708
Iguetti

24

Kb   16°   Kc   14°   Kd   130   12°   Ke   10°   Kf   8°

Scale 1:4,500,000

0 50 100 150 Kilometers
0 50 100 Miles

MEDITERRANEAN SEA

SPAIN

MOROCCO

ALGERIA

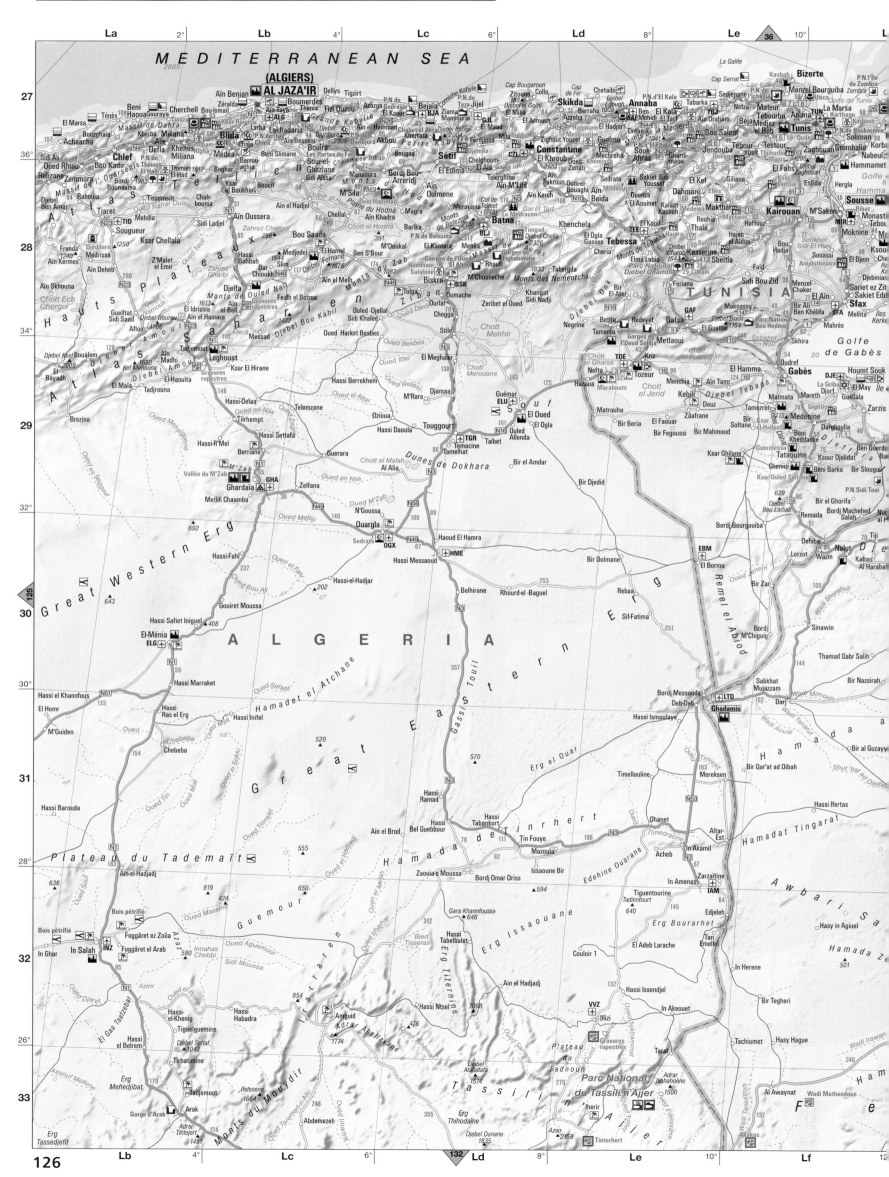

Scale 1:4,500,000

0   50   100   150 Kilometers
0   50   100 Miles

ITALY

Lg   14°   Lh   16°   Lj   37   18°   Lk   20°   Ma

Castelvetrano Lercara Nicosia Adrano Etna 3323 Teatro Greco
Menfi Friddi Calta- Paternò Acireale Golfo de
Mazara del Vallo Selinunte 1578 Castel- nissetta Enna Piazza Catania Catania
Sciacca termini Canicattì Armerina CTA Catania
Agrigento Villa Romana Caltagirone Lentini
Valle dei Templi del Casale Augusta
13 Licata 75 Ragusa 143 Siracusa
1650 Gela Vittoria Módica Teatro Greco
Ísola di Pantelleria (I) Noto Avola
1250 Pantelleria Ispica
Sicily Capo Ísola delle Correnti

GREECE Zákinthos Gastoúni Amaliáda Dafni
Zákinthos Keri ZTH Pírgos Olympia E55
Nísio Stroládhes Megalópoli E65
Kiparissía Messíni Dhírak
Sapienza Shiza Pílos Kalamáta KLX Sparti
Álika Koróni 2407 Geáki
Akrotírio Messiniakós Máni Githio
Ténaro Kólpos Areópoli Lakonikós Kólpos

I o n i a n   S e a 3410

I o n i a n 4116 5121
B a s i n 4300 5015

M E D I T E R R A N E A N   S E A

Gozo Megalithic Temples and
Victoria Hal Saflieni Hypogeum
Marfa Ísola di Linosa (I)
Rabat Valletta
Malta MLA 91
Ísola di Lampedusa (I) **MALTA**
Lampedusa

420 881 3400 3110 1800

36°
28°
34°
29°

(TRIPOLI)
TARABULUS Tajura'
urman Az Zawiyah Bin Ghashir Al Garabull
Al'Aziziyah TIP Al Qasabat Al Khums Hamamah Susah Apollonia
Bi'r al Suq al Khamis Labdah Al Bayda Shahhat Ra's al Hilal
hanam Mudakim Tarhunah Zliten (Leptis Magna) Al Libya LAQ Qaryat al Darnah
Gharyan Sidi as Sayd Al Faid Misratah Ptolemais Fa'idiyah
Yafran Majir Mahjub Fanar Qasr Ahmad Teuchira (Tocra) Suluntah Al Djebel al Akhdar
Abu Zayyan Al Kararim Bi'r Jimi Tansulukh Marawah Bi'r Tuhab
Wamis Bi'r Dhu'fan Tawurgha Daryanah Madinat At Taban
980 Tawurgha Al Marj al Abyar Zawiyat al Izziyat
Sabkhat Tawurgha Sidi Khalifah Banghazi Ar Rajmah Bi'r al Banakish
Faysal Bani Walid Sabkhat Umm al 'Izam Taykah (Benghazi) Qasr al Zawiyat Masus
Nasmah Qaryat Sabkhat al Hayshah Qaryat Jarrufah Jardinah Kharrubah C y r e n a i c a
Mizdah Al Qala'a Shumaykh Bu'ayrat Qaminis Suluq Bi'r Umar Bi'r Ben Ghimah Bi'r Tanjdar
Ras Attabil al Hasun Al Maqrun Sultan 82
assanu -120 Bi'r al 'Utaylah SRX As Sultan Ajdabiya Bi'r al Ghararah
Bi'r Bu Surt (Sidra) Madrasat Qaryat az Zuwaytinah 83
al Ghurab 127 Qasr Abu Hadi Barqah al Bayda Sawinnu
Al Qaryah Assdadah Bi'r Bin 'Isa Annofliyah Bin Jawwad Marsga al Burayqah Wadi al Farigh Bu Athlah
ash Sharqiyah 100 As Sidr Ras Lanuf Bishr LMQ Dur al Fawakhir
Al Qaryah al Qaryat Abu 182 Thimad al Al 'Uqaylah Hisn as Sahabi
Gharbiyah Nujaym 251 Fata'im Bi'r al Sabkhat
mrah Abyar ash Shuwayrit Mabruk 'Akkariyah Shunayn
Bi'r al Khawr Bi'r ar Rijl Bi'r Qaryas Dahra Oil Field 117
Bi'r al Bi'r al S a h r a Oil Gathering Station Sabkhat J a l u
'Alaqah Kammuniyan S u r t Ghuzayyil Jakharrah
Bi'r al Fatiyah Hun Thamad Bu Maradah
Waddan Maras 225 Awjilah Jalu
Sawkanah Wahat al Jufra Wadi al Awra Ar Raqubah O a s i s
HUQ Bi'r al Washkah Tarzah Abu Na'im 225
840 166 Bi'r al Zaltan Bi'r Zaltan
Djebel as Sawda' 180 Zillah Muwaylih
530 As Sawdayah Al Wahah
Uwaynat Thamad al Qattar Tlisan
Wannin 197 Bi'r al Qaf
Djebel al Hasawinah 190 Wadi al Ugayb
600 Thamad 320 Sarir
Qarat al Harah 130 al Hadh Kalanshiyú
Barqin Dabdab Qararat Al Fuqaha' Wadi Bu al Wali 356
Adiri 140 Al Mahruqah al Hayyirah Qarat as Wadi al Wali
ankurt Agar Birak 168 I B Sab'ah Y A
Wadi ash Shati 1200 Qarat Khalaf Allah 307
Samnu Al Hulayq al Kabir Al Hamudiyah Qararat 255
Bi'r Khalaf Allah SEB Tamanhint Al Haruj an Na'ikah
Ramlat Sabha al Aswad Wadi ar Ru'ays
Zallaf Qasr Khulayf Ghadduwah Al Khanabah 542 Thamad Bu Hashishah
Germa Mandara 133 Zawilah Tmassah Khashm al Jubayl
59 Bab al Es Sabah Qararat 110
Ghrayfah Maknusah Al Hufrah ash Sharqiya Waddan 750 Wadi al Bayadah
Qasr Larocu Umm al Aranib al Kalb
zuq Al Tsawah 155 T a z i r b u
Marzuq Taraghin 140 Wadi al Hadh Ad-Dhawah Tazirbu
arju 77 Ta'zirbu
Bi'r al Mastutah O a s i s
740 Waw al Kabir Zighan

30°
31°
28°
32°
26°
33°

Lg   14°   Lh   16°   Lj   133   18°   Lk   20°   Ma   22°

127

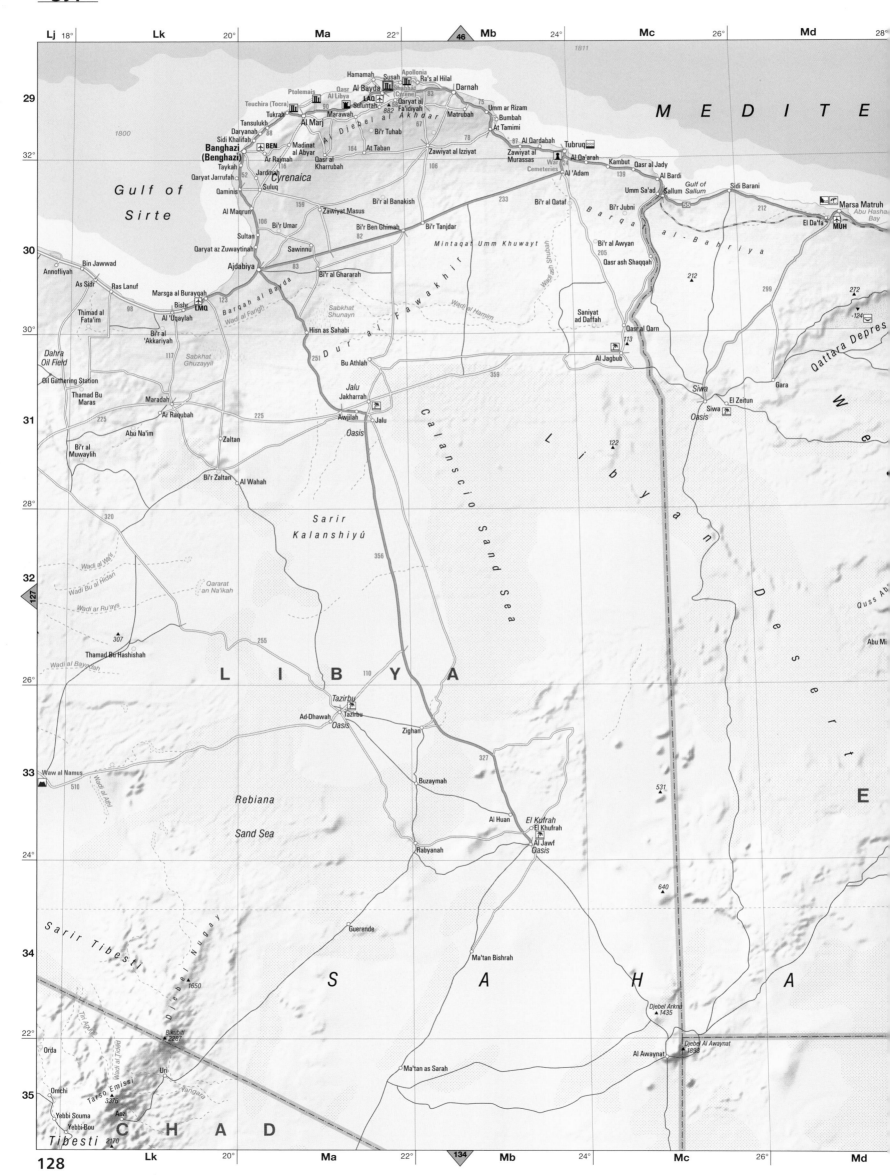

Lj 18°   Lk   20°   Ma   22°   Mb   24°   Mc   26°   Md   28°

M E D I T E

MEDITE

Gulf of Sirte

Cyrenaica

Banghazi (Benghazi)

Al Djebel al Akhdar

Barqal al-Bahriya

Barqah al Bayda

Dur al Fawakhir

Mintaqat Umm Khuwayt

Qattara Depres

Siwa Oasis

Ajdabiya

Calanscio Sand Sea

Libyan Desert

Sarir Kalanshiyú

Wadi al Welf

Dahra Oil Field

Sarir Tibesti

Rebiana Sand Sea

L I B Y A

Waw al Namus

El Kufrah
El Khufrah
Al Jawf Oasis

Tazirbu Oasis

Ad-Dhawah

S A H A R A

Djebel Nugay

C H A D

Tibesti

128

Lk   20°   Ma   22°   Mb   24°   Mc   26°   Md

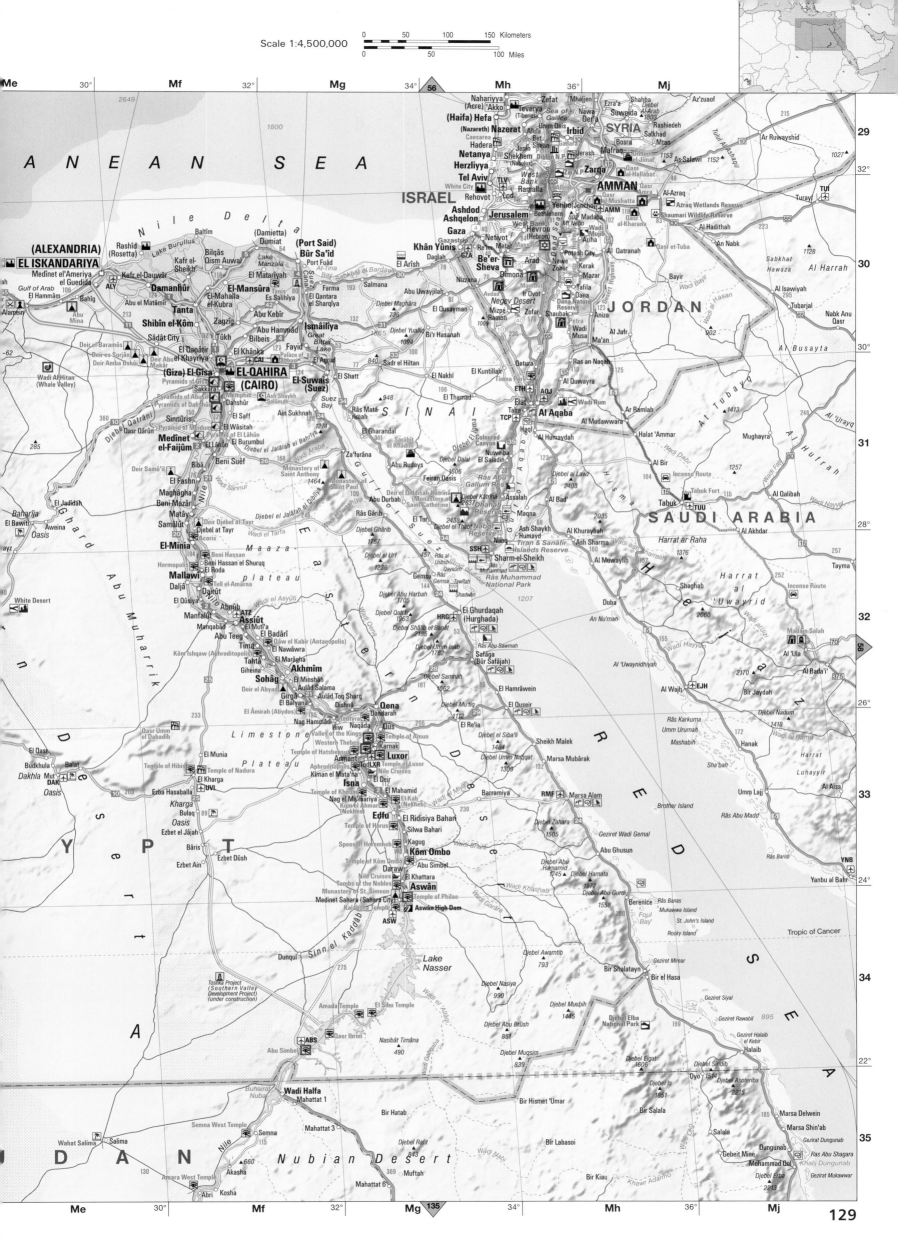

33

24°

Skaymat

Echtoucan

20

Tourassine

Sebkhet Oumm
ed Droûs Telli

126

N1

Bir Anzarane

Gleibat El Foula

711

Guelb Zednes
460

Dakhla
El' Argoub

VIL

31

Tropic of Cancer

Western

Sebkhet
Aghzoumal

1145

Imlili

N3   230

Sahara

Sebkhet Oumm
ed Droûs Guebli

34

306

G

ATLANTIC

Golfe de
Cintra

Sahara

(occupied by Morocco)

Mijek

574

Sebkhet
el Jill

Guelb El Rhein

Zouérat
OUZ

24

El Khatt

Sebkhet
Tidsit

Mijek

El   Hammâmi

OCEAN

Cap Barbas

327

Sebkhet
Grinnah

Aoussard

518

Sellâourich

Fdérik

Kediet ej Jill
915

Tenoûmer
370

22°

521

Aghoninit

Touríne

El Khatt

Adrâr   Souttouf

375

Train du Désert

180

Aghreïjit

Maqteir

Bir Gandouz

Tichla

Zoug

Char

647

El Beyyed

330

N1

Guerguarat

Choûm

Chreïrik

El Beyyed

El Gallâouiya El Gallôuiya

35

Boû Lanouâr

Train du Désert

Inâl

Tmeïmîchât

Aggui

120

Guelb
er Richât

485

Aghouedir

Massif

NDB   Nouâdhibou

40

Ben Amera

Ouadâne

de

La Gouira
Râs Nouâdhibou

Dakhlet
Nouâdhibou

Bir el Gâreb

Khatt Atoui

Ksar
Torchane

Passe d'Amogjâr

l' Adrâr

20°

Parc

National
du Banc

Râs Tafarît

Azougui
Atâr

ATR

N1

Chinguetti

57

Iouîk

Châmi

Aîn Attaya

605

Terjît

Aouelloul

Île Tîdra
Île Kijî

Ti-n-Brahim

Akjoujt

Irijî

Oujeft

Tifrirt

181

Far'aoun

Chig

Achegtim

Achguig el Adam

36

Râs Tîmirist
Nouâmghâr

Bennichchâb

Aguelt ez Zerga

Amazmaz

Neterguent

Zli

400

306

Khezmir

433

Chegge

El Mhaïjrât

Boû Guettâra

Ti-n-Medjouf

Bou Nâga

El Moïnâne

Tiouilît

Boû Rjeimât
Al Asma x

254

Boû Nâga

326

Bokh el Mâ

8

Sebkha
Ndrhamcha

Tamassoumît

Rachid

88

MAURITANIA

Tanit

Tâtîlt

Aguilâl Faï

Ksar El Barka

Lekhcheb

Gâneb

Dhar Tic

18°

Jreïda

Tigniré

El Melhes

Tidjikja

TIY

THI   Tich

Nawakshut
(Nouakchott)

NKC

Idini

Maugris

Khang
Acheft

Niemelane

En Tmadé

554

Ouâd Nâga

Boudbouda

El Tichilt

Matmata

433

Moudjéria

El Gheddiya

Aoudech

Ntatrat

Letfata

Gamra

Dakhla

Hâssei Mbârek

37

126

Nimjat

Zar

N3

Sangarafa

65

Boumdeit

Dimalla

Tiguent

Boutilimit

OTL

Magta Lahjar

140

Jreif

Louth

Aoudaghost

Togba

Tâmchekket

Nbâk

Aguila

111

N3

Oued el Abiod

203

Passe de Djoûk

Bir Taleb

45

Méderdra
Frede

Rkîz

El Goss

70

Djonâba

Âîn Boubat

Ekamour

Oumm
el Khezz

El Beyyed

161

Keur Massène

Lac de Mâl

Leqceiba

Dar el Barka

465

Barkéwol
el Abiod

Guérou

120

Montagnes
del'Affolé

600

Ejouj

AEO

H

Rosso
Richard Toll

Tékane

Podor

Bogué

Mônguel

La'oueïssi

Koûroudjel

Rioug

373

'Ayoûn el'Atro

P.N. du Diawling

Ross-
Bethio

G'nit

Dagana

Thillé
Boubakar

Gamadji
Saré

154

Bababé

Mbagne

Mbout

146

Sâni

95

Tintâné

Kiffa

KFA

N2

Te-n-Guemba

16°

Maka
Ndiago

XLS

Mbane

Haéré
Lao

Kaédi Leqcéia

MBR

Rioug

Kankossa

In-Farba

Saint Louis

Réserve de Faune
de Ndjael

Yaré Lao

Ngouye Pété

Gorgol

115

KED

Passe
de Soufa

Ouadou

158

P.N. de la Langue de Barbarie

Rao
Léona

Keur
Momar Sar

Lagbar

Thilogne

Loumbi

Boki

Matam

Sivé

Maghama

Hamoud

Kobenni

Gleibat
Boukel

Kobe

38

1410

Lombol

Louga

Yang-Yang

Dogji

Rewane

Réserve
de Faune
du Ferlo Nord

Sabudo

Ouro Sogui

108

Artemou

Ould Yénjé

El Gleita

Kiranè

Touil

Diandioumé
Kamara

Koré

Fas Boye

Ouarak

Dâra

43

Linguèr

69

Ranérou

Fourdou

Kanel

N3

Dendoudi

Bouli

Nagara

Kersiniané

NIX

N1

Béma

Mboro Ndeundekat

Kébémer

82

Khogué
Tobène

Sagata

N3

Vélingara

106

Orkadiéré

Diamounguér

150

Sagne

Sélibabi

SEY

Ambidédi

Sandaré

Gogui

Noto Gouye
Diama

Mékhé

N2

Afé

Barkédji

Vélingara

Réserve de Faune
du Ferlo Sud

Mâmari

Ouro Amat

Fêté
Bowé

76

Doundé
Bagué

Gouray
Khabou

Koussané

Marena

Diangounté

Ouakam
Kayar

DKR

Tivaouane

N2

Ndindi

Touba

Déali

Tiel

Ferlo

Dindouli
Séydi

Aourou

Baediam

Yélimané

Tambakara

Diakon

Lakamané

Cap Vert
Yof

Pikine

Thiès

Ndiago

Mbacké

Sindia

Bambay

Sadio

Gassane

Payar

Ndia

Senoudébou

Kidira

Samé

Kayes

N1

Ségala

Diakon

Sandaré

P.N.les de la Madeleine

Rufisque

DAKAR

Diourbel

Koloboné

SENEGAL

Ndioum
Guènt

Ribo Escale

Lofé

Goudiri

Naye

Fort
St-Pierre

KYS

Lontou Oussoubidiagna

Diallan

Lambidou

14°

Mbour

Nianing

Joal-Fadiout

Ndangane

Fatick

Gandiaye

Guinguinéo

Kabone

Bala

Toubéré Bafal

Koussanar

Kédougou

Koutia
Gaïdi

Koungheul

Koumpentoum

Daniédo

N1

Gorges
de Talari

Dalafi

KDA

Séféto

Parc National
de la Boucle
du Baoulé

Parc National du
Delta du Saloum

Sakone

Keur
Madiabel

Nioro
du Rip

Maka Gouye

Koussanar

Kotiari Naoudé

Tambacounda

Demba Koli

Sadiola

Falaise de Tambaoura

Sinkégni

130

Chutes
du Billy

Oualia

560

Bamanan

39

GAMBIA

Bakau

Niumi N.P.
Fort Bullen

Banjul

Abreda

Soma Su

Kangaba

Sikasso

Kaolack

Kaffrine

Wassu

Kuntaur

Georgetown

Maka

Pata

Nétéboulou

Missira

Diana

Boutougou Fara

Manantali

Barrage de Manantali

Badoumbé

485

417

560

R11

Fouladougou Rése

Djidian

Djibouti

0   50   100   150   Kilometers
0   50   100   Miles

Kf   8°   Kg   6°   Kh   4°   Kj   2°   Kk

125

ALGERIA

MALI

BURKINA FASO

NIGER

Erg Chech
Grizim
El Mzereb
370
333
El Mreiti
Ti-n-Bessaïs
250
Bîr 'Amrâne
Oued el Ma
Oued Khârroûb
Agâraktem
Taoudenni
El Guettara
Oglat el Khnâchîch   El Khnâchîch
El Khnâchîch
Bir Ounâne
Erg Atouila
Foum el 'Alba   282
324
343
I-n-Techerène
Tessounfat
Tessalit
Ancien   I-n-Akli
273   367
I-n-Échaï
Tamandouririt   I-n-Akhmed
Abanko
Timétrine (Ti-n-Kâr)   Tichet
Oued el Hajâr   Mabroûk   Aguelhok
Boû Nâga   El Mraïti
Djebel
Araouane   Guîr   El Mamouel
Sidi el Mokhtâr   Boû Djébéha   El Mâmoûn   Aslegh (Asselar)
Abelbod   Adrar Tachdaït
Tadânet Keyna   El Ma'mour-Ighichârene   Timétrine
Aghezzaf   Ammouk   Anéfis
Touerât   271   I-n-Milach
Douaya   I-n-Aleï   Tabankort
I-n-Abaléha   Oudeïka   Almoustarat
Kerchouél
Oualâta   Tigoumatene   Ti-n-Tehoun   Agamor
Tagoûrâret   El Basriyé   Ti-n-Aguelhaj (Tangoutranat)   Hâssi Karkabane   Karkarichinkat
Hâssi Fouîni   Ti-n-Tijot'   I-n-Amazzagh   Bintagoungou   265   Bamba   Téméra Bisane   Taoârdeï
Latik   Ourei   Zoûgh   Bourem   Bourem
Agoueïnît   Nema   Nkhaïlé   El Nbeïket el Ahouâch   Nbeïket Dlim   Tombouctou   Inali   Ber   Gourma-Rharous   Ouani   Tondibi   Teiskot
El Bouz   Houeïriye   Outeid Arkâs   Farache   Koriome   TOM   Mandiakoy   Obinardene   Amakouladji   Iménas
El Arhlaf   Râs el Ma   Danga   Karouassa   Tombeau des Askia   Djebok
Amourj   Dendâra   Hâssi Touïl   Goundam   GUD   Diré   Haibongo   Aglal   Bambou   Fintrou   Adiora   Gao   GAQ   Tacharane
Nioût   Kataouâne   Chet Korkora   Tondidarou   Tonka   Fati   Haribomo   Doro   Biliali Koyra   Ti-n-Azabo
Boû Gâdoûm   Bassikounou   Banikane   Saréyamou   Kanioume   Haoussa-Foulane   Gargouna
Koumbi Saleh   Fassala Néré   Niafounké   Koumaira   Gossi   Dorey   Tagarane Gabout
Mobdoua   Léré   Ambin   Ngorkou   I-n-Adiattafene   Léléhoy   Ansongo
Adel Bagrou   Koronga   Medd Allah   Gati-Loumo   Ngouma   I-n-Tillit   Tassiga   Bentia (Koukia)
Nara   NRM   Fatiba   Nampala   Youvarou   Tanal   Ndaki   Ouatagouna
Dilli   Goumbou   Boulel   Dogo   Nyiminiama   Boré   Hombori   Tessit   Figoun
267   Boundjiguiré   Oura-Ndia   Dialloubé   Konza   Dala   Boumboum   Ayorou   Toumkou
Mourdiah   Dogofri   Togué-Koumbé   Konna   Douentza   Mondoro   Douna   Oursi   Ouanzerbé
Doubabougou   Danfa   Diabali   Diondiori   Sévaré   Kani-Gogouna   Diankabou   Forage Christine   Ti-n-Akof   Markoy   Famalé
Boron   Niono   Ténenkou   Mopti   Sanga   Yoro   Sélba   Gorom-Gorom   Dolbel   Méhana
Wardé Séguéla   Ndébougou   Sossobé   Ouro-Modi   Bandiagara   Madougou   Barabouté   Timé   Aribinda   Sikire   Gaigou   Sara Koyra
Madina-Sako   Doura Togou   Massina   Diafarabé   Soma-Dougou   Koporokénité Na   So Tongo-mayél   Béléhédé   Gorel   Gomadji   Yatako   NIGER   Tillabéri
Sagala   Pogo   Say   Taga   Sofara   Bankass   Koro   Ban   Tibo   Solé   Djibo   Barabqulé   Fala-gountou   Dori   Katchirga   Dargol
Markala   Togo   Sarro   Si   Konio   Sokoura   Toroli   Diallassagou   Ouahigouya   Kagaré   Pobé Mengao   Namissiguima   Bani   Sampelga   Bangaré
Ségou   Dioro   Fatimé   Fangasso   Bay   Louta   Gomboro   Tangay   Zogoré   Séguénéga   Kongoussi   Ouenkoro   Koala   Tougouri   Sebba   Solna
Bénénikényi   Tori   Tominian   Konodimini   Bangas   spoko   Toeni   Lac de Bam   Barsalogo   Gouya   Bossey Bangou

Kg   6°   Kh   4°   Kj   2°   Kk   La   0°

137

131

Niger, Western Chad

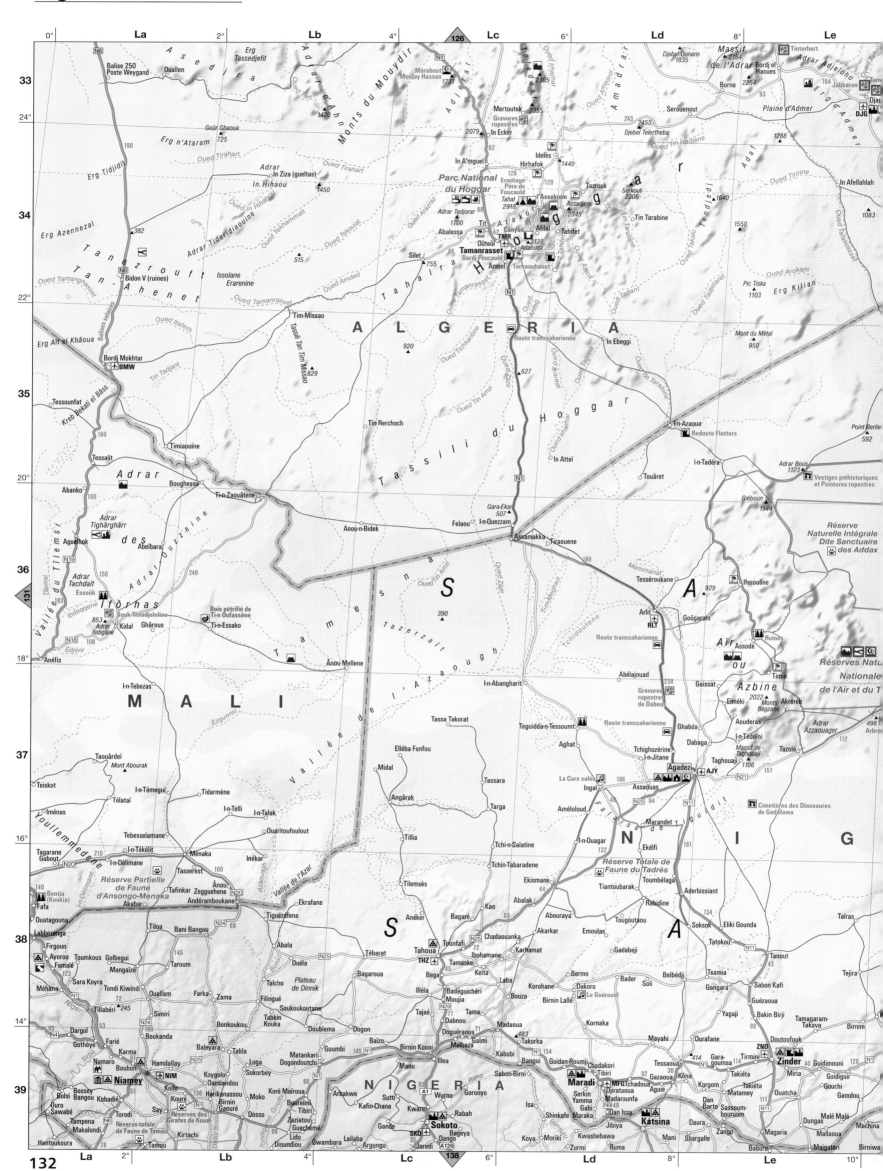

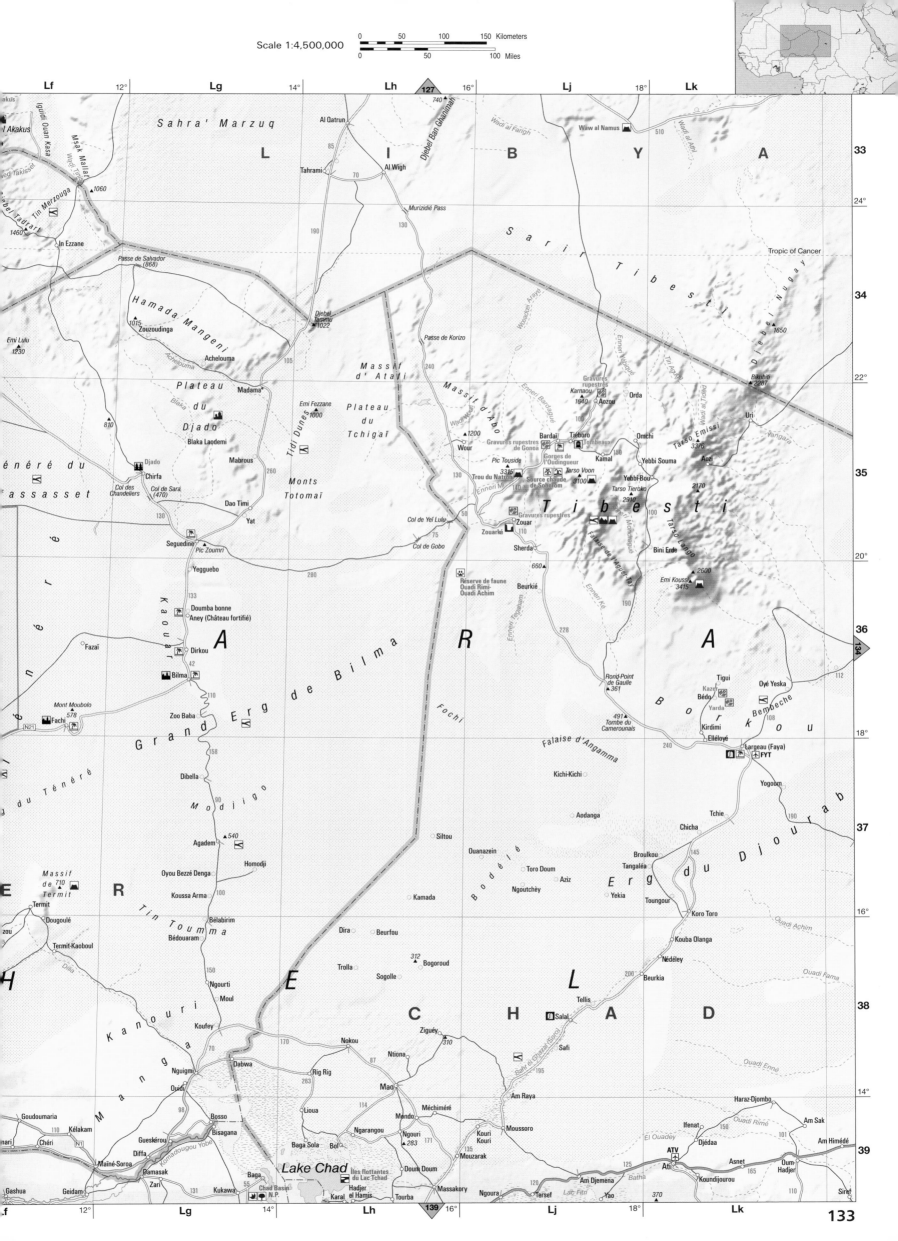

0   50   100   150 Kilometers
0   50   100 Miles

Lf 12° Lg 14° Lh 127 16° Lj 18° Lk

Sahra' Marzuq

740 Djebel Ban Gharbnah

L I B Y A

Al Qatrun
Al Wigh
Tahrami
85
70
Murizidié Pass
190
130
33
24°

S a r i r   T i b e s t i

Tropic of Cancer
34

Passe de Salvador
(868)

Djebel Nugay
1650
Biktibiti 2287

I n   E z z a n e
Hamada Mangeni
1015 Zouzoudinga
Achelouma
Passe de Korizo
Massif d'Atafi
Gravures rupestres
Karnaou Orda
1640 Aozou
Uri
22°

Plateau du Djado
Madama*
Emi Fezzane 1000
Plateau du Tchigaï
240
Massif d'Abo
1200 Wour
Bardaï Tieboro
Tombleaux
Kamal
Omchi
Tarso Emissi 3376
Aozi
35

Blaka Laodemi
Mabrous
Tidi Dunes
Gravures rupestres de Gonoa
Pic Touside 3315
Gorges de l'Oudingueur
Trou du Natron
Source chaude de Sohorom
Tarso Voon 3100
Yebbi Souma
Yebbi-Bou
Tarso Tieroko 2910
2170
35

Djado
Chirfa
Col des Chandeliers
Col de Sara (470)
Dao Timi
Yat
Monts Totomaï
Col de Yeï Lulu
Zouarké Zouar
Gravures rupestres
110
Sherda
T i b e s t i
Bini Erde
Emi Koussi 3415 2600
36
134

Seguedine
Pic Zoumri
Yegguebo
Col de Gobo
75
660
Réserve de faune Ouadi Rimi-Ouadi Achim
Beurkié
190
228

Kaouar
133
Doumba bonne
Aney (Château fortifié)
Dirkou
42
B O R K O U
Rond-Point de Gaulle 361
Tigui
Bédo
Oyé Yeska
Yarda
Bembeche
112
36

Fazaï
Bilma
Mont Moubolo 578
Fachi
N21
Zoo Baba
110
G r a n d   E r g   d e   B i l m a
Fochi
Falaise d'Angamma
491 Tombe du Camerounais
Kirdimi
Elléloyé
240
Largeau (Faya) FYT
18°

Dibella
90
Modjigo
158
Kichi-Kichi
Yogoum
Erg du Djourab
37

Massif de Termit 710
Agadem 540
Homodji
Siltou
Ouanazein
Bodélé
Toro Doum
Aodanga
Tchie
Chicha
Broulkou
Tangaléa
145
190
37

Termit
Dougoulé
Oyou Bezzé Denga
Koussa Arma
100
Aziz
Ngoutchèy
Yekia
Toungour
Koro Toro
Ouadi Achim
16°

Termit-Kaboul
Tin Toumma
Bélabirim
Bédouaram
Kamada
Dira
Beurfou
312 Bogoroud
Kouba Olanga
Nédéley
Beurkia
200
Ouadi Fama
38

150
Ngourti
Moul
Trolla
Sogolle
Tellis
38

Koufey
Kanouri
Nguigmi
Koundjourou
E C H A D
Salal
Ati ATV
39
14°

Goudoumaria
Kélakam
Chéri
N1
Ouidi
Dabwa
Rig Rig
263
Nokou
Ntiona
310
Ziguéy
Safi
Am Raya
Haraz-Djombo
Am Sak
14°

Gashua
Geidam
Diffa
Damasak
Zari
Kukawa
Baga
Bisagana
Gueskérou
Maïné-Soroa
98
Bosso
Komadougou Yobe
Iles flottantes du Lac Tchad
Lioua
87
Mendo
Ngarangou
Baga Sola
Bol
Ngouri 283
171
Mao
Méchiméré
Kouri Kouri
Mouzarak
Moussoro
Doum Doum
Massakory
El Ouadi
Ifenat
Djédaa
150
101
Asnet
Oum-Hadjer
39

Lake Chad
Chad Basin N.P.
Karal
Hadjer el Hamis
Tourba
Ngoura
Am Djemena
Tersef
Lac Fitri
Yao
370
Batha
Koundijourou
Siref
110

Lf 12° Lg 14° Lh 139 16° Lj 18° Lk

133

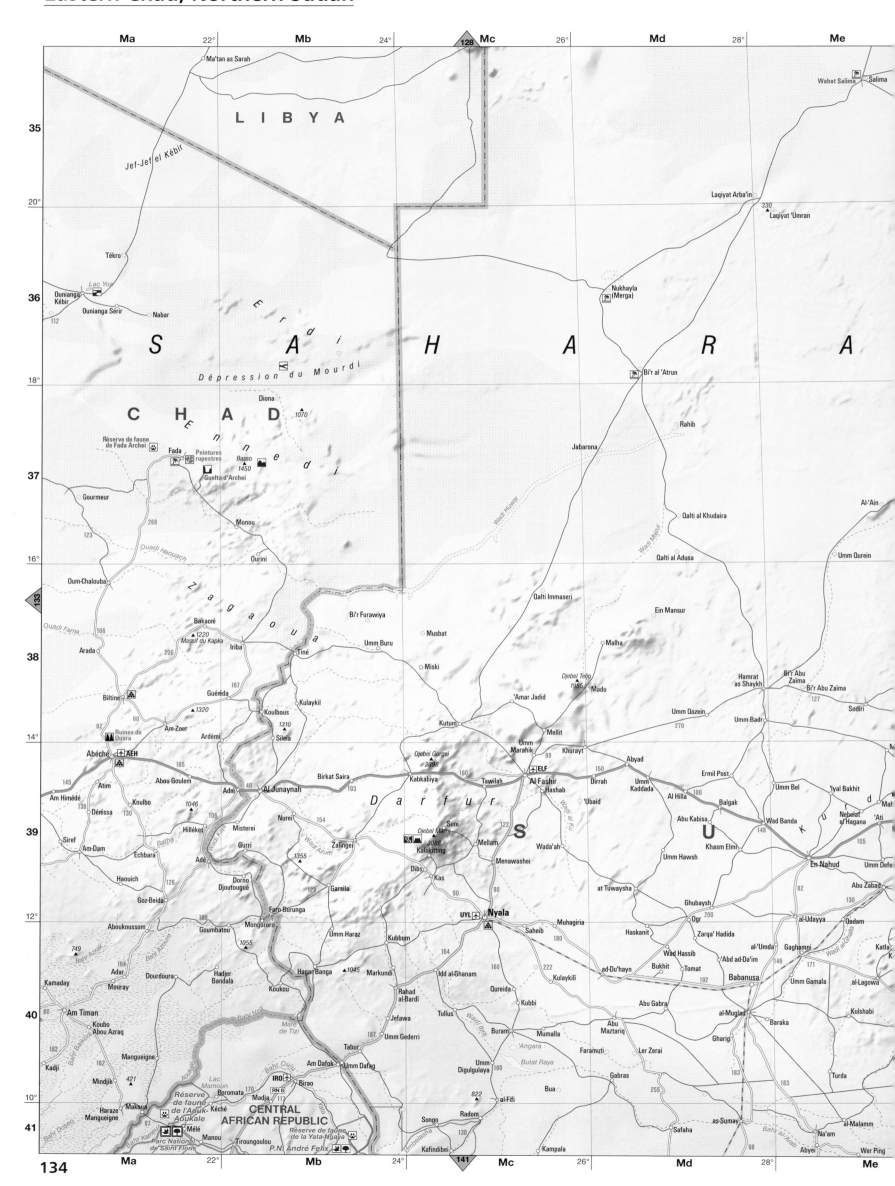

Ma 22° Mb 24° Mc 26° Md 28° Me

LIBYA

Ma'tan as Sarah

Wahat Salima 🏠 Salima

35°

Jef-Jef el Kébir

Laqiyat Arba'in
20° 330
Laqiyat 'Umran

Tékro

36° Ouanianga
Kébir 🏠
Ouanianga Sérir • Nabar
112 Nukhayla 🏠
(Merga)

E r d i

S A **H** A **R** A
Dépression du Mourdi 🏠 Bi'r al 'Atrun
18°

Diona

1070 Rahib

C H A D Réserve de faune Jabarona
de Fada Archei 🏠 Fada 🏠 Peintures
Basso rupestres Al-'Ain
37° ▲ 1450 🏠 Guelta d'Archei
Gourmeur Wadi Huwar Qalti al Khudaira

Monou Umm Qurein
123 Umm Burein
268 Ourini Qalti al Adusa
16°

Oum-Chalouba Qalti Immaseri
133 Ein Mansur

Quadi Fama Bakaoré Bi'r Furawiya
166 ▲ 1220 Musbat Malha
Massif du Kapka Djebel Teljo Madu Hamrat Bi'r Abu
Arada 200 Iriba Tiné 1985 as Shaykh Zaïma
38° Umm Buru Bi'r Abu Zaïma
Biltine 🏠 167 Guéréda Miski Umm Qozein 127
60 Koulbous 'Amar Jadid Umm Badr Sodiri
92 ▲ 1320 1310 Kulaykil Kutum 270
Ruines de Am-Zoer Silera Mellit
14° Ouara 🏠 Ardémi Umm Djebel Gurgei Marahik 89 Khurayt Abyad Ermil Post
Abéché 🏠 AEH ▲ 2398 Al Fashir ELF Dirrah Umm 'Iyal Bakhit
145 165 Birkat Saira Kabkabiya 160 Tawilah Hashab Kaddada 150 Umm Bel
Atim Abou Goulem Adré 40 Al Junaynah 193 'Ubaid Al Hilla 100 Balgak d
Am Himédé 138 Koulbo 106 1046 Nurei 154 122 Abu Kabisa Wad Banda
Déressa Hilléket Misterei Suni 3088 148 Khasm Elmi Nebelat
39° Siref Am-Dam Ade Gurri Zalingei Djebel Marra Mellam **S** Umm Hawsh el Hagana
Echbara 1355 Kalokitting Wada'ah U En Nahud
Haouich 126 Dorno Dibs Menawashei Umm Hawsh d 105
Goz-Beida Djoutougué Kas 80 at Tuwaysha Umm Defe
128 Garsila 90 Ghubaysh Abu Zabad
12° Fero-Burunga Umm Haraz Kubbum UYL Nyala Muhagiria 200 82 130
Aboukoussom Mongororo Saheib Haskanit Ogr al-Udayya
Goumbatou 1055 164 180 Zarqa' Hadida
749 Hadjer 180 Hagar Banga Markundi Kulaykili Wad Hassib al-'Umda Gaghamni
Adar Bandala 1045 160 ad-Du'hayn Bukhit 'Abd ad-Da'im 146 171 Katla
Kamaday Mouray Dourdoura Koukou Rahad 222 Tomat 192 Babanusa Umm Gamala al-Lagowa
164 al-Bardi 164 Qureida Abu Gabra
40° Am Timan Hadjer Jefawa Kubbi Abu Abu Qadam Kulshabi
182 Koubo 162 421 Madja Umm Gederri 187 Tullus Buram Mumalla Maztariq Gharig Baraka
Abou Azraq Boromata RN 8 Tabur Umm Dafag 100 al-Muglad Turda
Mangueigne Birao Am Dafok Umm Faramuti Ler Zerai 183 as-Sumay
Kadji Mindjik Makaoua IRO Digulgulaya Gabras 255 Na'am
Réserve de faune Madja 117 822 Butat Raya Kampala Safaha Abyei Wer Ping
Haraze 97 Mélé de l'Aouk- Radom al-Fifi 130 98
41° Mangueigne Manou **CENTRAL** Songo
Parc National Tiroungoulou **AFRICAN REPUBLIC**
de Saint Floris Réserve de faune
de la Yata-Ngaya 🏠
P.N. André Felix

Ma 22° Mb 24° Mc 26° Md 28° Me

Scale 1:4,500,000

50   100   150 Kilometers

50   100 Miles

Mf   32°   Mg   34°   Mh   129   36°   Mj   38°   Mk

Bir Hatab
Bir Salala
Bir Labasoi
Marsa Delwein
(JIDDAH) JEDDAH
Hadda
Khumrah
Bahrah
Kaaba
MAKKAH (MECCA)
Semna
Mahattat 3
Djebel Rafit 843
Bir Kiau
185 Marsa Shin'ab
Ar Rās al Aswad
72
Akasha
660
Kosha
Muftah
Mahattat 6
369
Bir Nawari
Salala
Dungunab
Gebeit Mine
Muhammad Dol
Gezirat Mukawwar
Damrur
Mastabah
472
SAUDI ARABIA
35

West Temple
Kudayn
Nile
115
Abu Sari
Delgo
285
Mahattat 8
To Awai
Djebel Erba 2213
Khalij Dungunab
191
Qishran
5
20°

ash-Shalal ath-Thalith 3rd Cataract
Necropolis Deffufa
Abu Hamed
Bir en Nugeim
Bir Fanoidiq
Djebel Oda 2259
Marsa Salak
2635
36

Arqu
Gharb Binna
al-Koin
Temple of Kawa
Keheili
Shemkhiya
Dagash
Djebel Eigrim 1257
Djebel Homor Tohadar 1754
Kamob Sanha
56
Bur Sudan (Port Sudan)
PZU
Sallom
3040
Urbi
Al Qulayd Bahri
Abu Ghirban
El Kab
Kabna
Abu Hashim
Shereiq
Nadi
Djebel Abadab 1596
Gebeit
Sinkat
Erkowit
152
Suakin
Old Suakin coral stone houses
Aqaba Pass
18°

Napata and Djebel Barkal Temples
Nuri Necropolis
Karima
Umm Rahaw
Birti
4th Cataract
El Aiadia
El Begeir
El Karabi
244
Rawai
Barameiya
Suakin Archipelago
Ras Asis
37

Marawi
al-Kurru
az-Zuma
Ghazali
Sanam
Hannik
Barriyat
5th Cataract
Gananita
Artoli
Togni
289
Er Rogel
Talguharai
Haya
Tohamiyam
Erheib
Herbagat
Aqiq
Ras Kasar

Amentego
Megauda
Old Dongola
Kanisa
Kurti
Abu Dom
258
Abu Saffay
Berber
Dugwaya
Gammams
Djebel Mismar 958
Imasa
Djebel Sabdana 1906
Mersa Teklay
Algena
Falkat
al-Ghaba
ad-Dabba
Abu Dom
Fagrinkotti
140
al-Bayyuda
Atbara
ATB
Duredeb
Djebel Hamoyet 2780
Karora
Mersa Teklay
18°

Burayqa
Umm Rumetla
Ed Damer
Saiyala
Gemmeiza
Adarama
Djebel Asoteriba 765
Eriba
1663
Djebel Hamoyet 2780
Nakfa
1736

Eilai
133
Mahmiya
Dawabi
Meroe Temple and pyramids
Umm Rumeila
357
Kerkebet
Reserve Hagar Nish Plateau
2599
Baden
2603
Anaghit
Nakfa Wildlife Reserve
Harat

al-Basabir
Sandi
Guwayr
Kabushiya
Taragma
El 'Uteishan
'Amm Adam
Mitatib
Said Abu Bakr al-Mirgani
Suara
Afabet
Kela Met
Anaghit
ERITREA
16°

Abu Dawn
6th Cataract
al-Huqna
Palace
Wad Ban Naqa
Temples of Musawwarat
Temples of Naqa
Daru
Bir el Fakama
Goz Regeb
Aroma
Akala
Barade
Keren
Mersa Gulbub
38

Qerri
al-Gayli
Sabaluka Game Reserve
Rugheiwa
Abu Deleiq
As Sharma
Amara Abu Sin
Kassala
KSL
Sebderat
Djebel Takka 1390
Bisha
Haykota
Akordat
Himbirti
ASMARA
ASM
(MASSAWA) Mitsiwa
142

(Omdurman) Umm Durman
al-Hartum Bahri (Khartoum North)
Camel Market
Mahdi's Tomb
Halfayat al-Muluk
New Halfa
Malawiya
Djebel Aderuba 1484
11
Teseny
Barentu
Dukambiya
Areza
Dekemhare
Adi Keyih
38°

AL-HARTUM (KHARTOUM)
KRT
Fattasha
Djebel Auliya
Wad Rawa
Husheib
Khashm el Girba
Moqatta
212
Gash Setit Wildlife Reserve
Sitona
Adi Da'iro
Chire Wildlife Reserve
Adi Ugri
Oheleiss royal city
Senafe
Matara
Adi Kwala

1120
Hamrat al-Wuzz
Umm Inderaba
193
Wad al-Magid
Rufa'a
al-Musallamiya
Udayd
Khashm el Girba Reservoir
Om Hajer
Himora
HUE
Debre Damo
Yeha
Temple of Yeha
AXU
Idaga Hamus
Adigrat
3293

Abu Tunaytin
Umm Sayyala
657
ad-Dubasi
al-Qutayna
Qurrasa
al-Uqda
Adrag
Wad Madani
Barakat
Thowak
Setit
Ayayei
Keftya
Adi Da'iro
Inda Silase
Aksum
Ruins of Aksum
Adwa
Hawzen
14°

Abu Tunaytin
Rudayba
Shabasha
ad-Duwayn
al-Maneqil
Ma'tuq
al-'Amara
Uhaymir
Hag Abdullah
Migre
227
Matna
Fargha
Tunaydiba
Adi Ramets
Adi Ark'ay
Mesfinto
Aiy Adi
Mek'ele
MQX
39

63
Umm Busha
Kabur
Dararisa
Sennar
Maiurno
Es Suki
Inderaba
Maya
ash-Shawal
Qala'en Nahl
Rasid
Doka
152
Rahad Game Reserve
Rumeila
Basunda
Wolkefit Pass (3150)
3599
3750
Simien Mountains National Park
Ras Dashen 4620
Debark
Adi Gudom
Abergele
Amba Alage 3941

id
Kusti
Rabak
Tandalti
Tamaso
Fariq at-Fil
al-Gabalayn
Abu Higar
Dindar
El Hawata
Shamman
Gallabat
Metema
Amba Giyogis
Wehni
Aykel
Dabat
Angereb
Simien Mts.
Sek'ot'a
39°

75
Umm Ruwaba
75
al-Ghabsha
Dali Sharafat
87
Djebel Bozi
Wad en Nail
Galegu
Galegu
Rahad
Gonder
Azezo
GDQ
Degoma
Safad 4620
Abune Yosef 4190

SUDAN
ar-Rahad
Semei
Geifil
At-Tayyara
Keri Kera
ar-Ru'at
Djebel Mazmun
215
Sheikh Hasan
Dangur
Dinder National Park
Debre Sina
Gorgora
114
T'ana Hayk (Lake Tana)
1830
Yifag
Adis Zemen
Lalibela
LU
Cave churches
12°

Djebel ad-Dair 1410
al-'Abbasiya
Tingal 1460
Mushayfat
al-Garef
Er Roseires
Ed Damazin
RSS
Almahel
Abu Mendi
Daga Istephanos Monastery
Wetora
Debre Tabor
DBT
Nefas Mewch'a

Dalami
Hayban
Djebel al-Haybau 1325
Rashad
ar-Rank
al-Barun
Roseires Reservoir
Kukur
Bobuk
Bau
Bikori
Bambudi
Guba
Dangali
Amedamit 3296
Injibara
Bahir Dar
BJR
Tis Isat Falls (Blue Nile Falls)
4231
Guna Torare
Adet
Bete Hor
Mekdela
40

Hitau
Djebel al-Liri 1095
Abu Gubayba
Girban
Tosi
Umm Barbit
Shaykh Gok
Keili
Gaysan
Amiri
Cula Sancai 2438
1849
Chagne
Finote Selam
Mota'
Nedrata
Mertule Maryan
Mekane Selam
Amba Farit 3975

Talwadi
Tekeim
55
Quayrd
Niaro
Tungaru
Belgo
Kurmuk
Belfodiyo
Koko
2384
Dembecha
Birhan
Debre Work
4154
Bichena

iangnom
Fagwir
246
Debalo
Malakal
Tonga
Taufikia
Kodok
Dawir
Akoke
Fama
Aboni
Wuntau
Kungila
104
Nejo
Mount Nasi 2975
Alibo
Gelila
Shambu
Gorch'an 3276
Muger Falls
Muke Turi
Kembolcha
41

Talawdi
Debalo
al-Ghazal
Chidu
Jarso
Mortesoro
Shali al-Fil
ETHIOPIAN HIGHLANDS
Finchaa Reservoir
Gebre Gurache
Fiche
3544
Debre Libanos
Denneba

Asosa
ASO
Mendi
NDM
Bambesi
Dabus Wenz
Blue Nile
Gebre Guracha

Mf   32°   Mg   34°   142   Mh   36°   Mj   38°   Mk   135

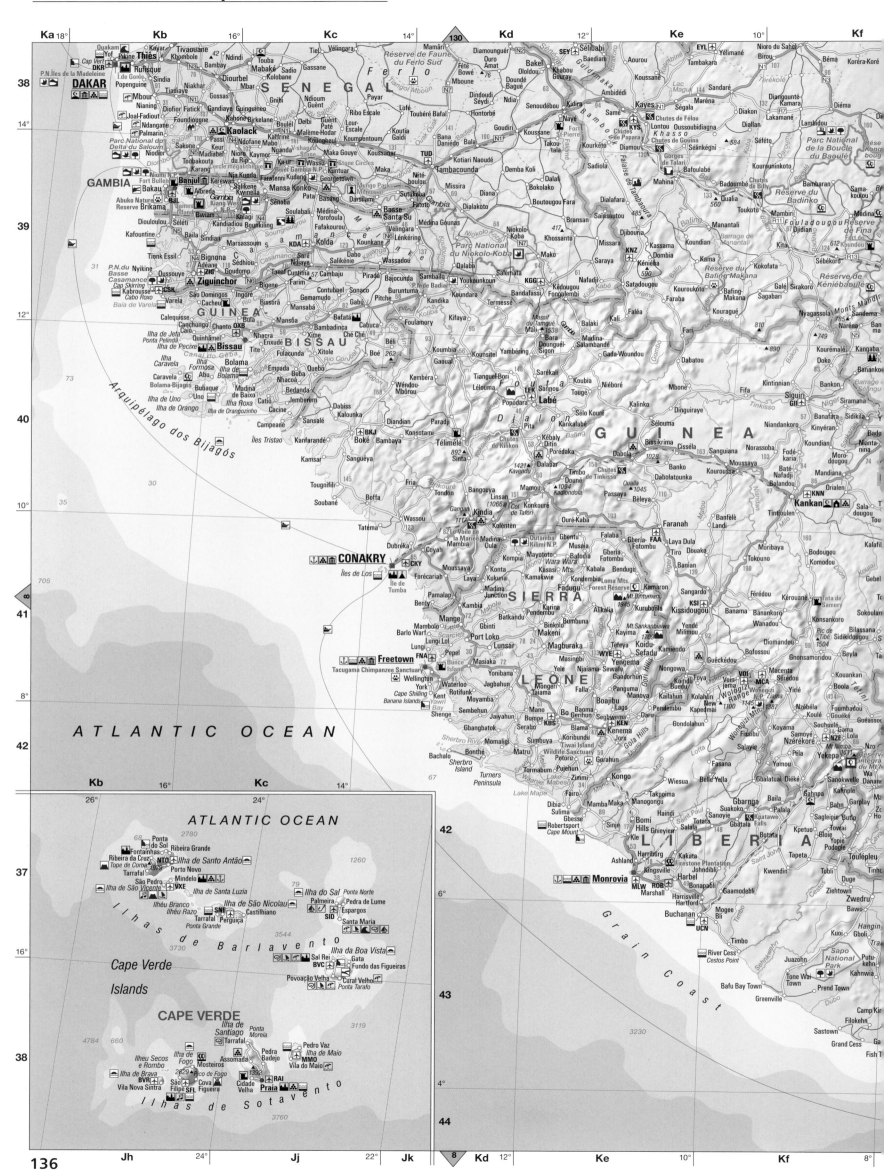

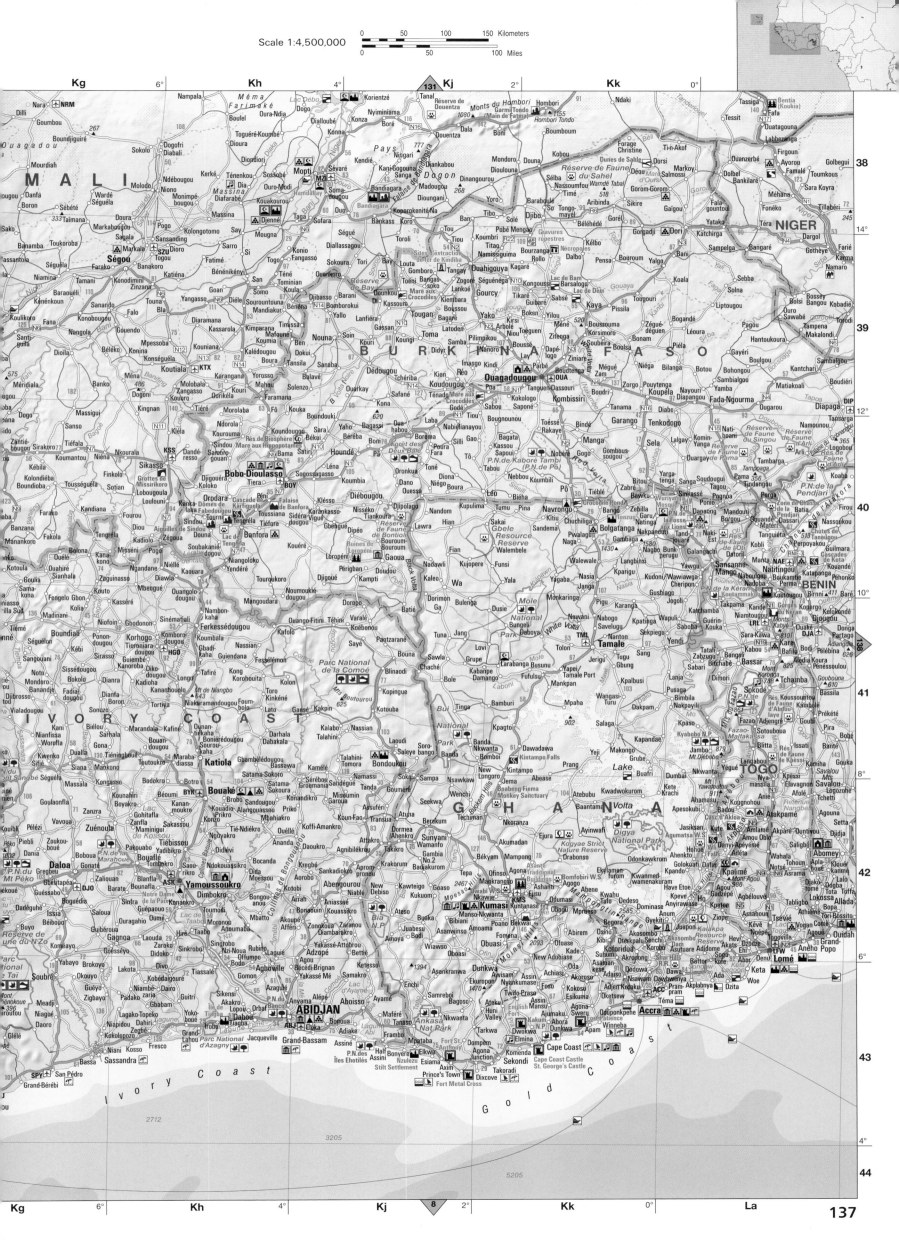

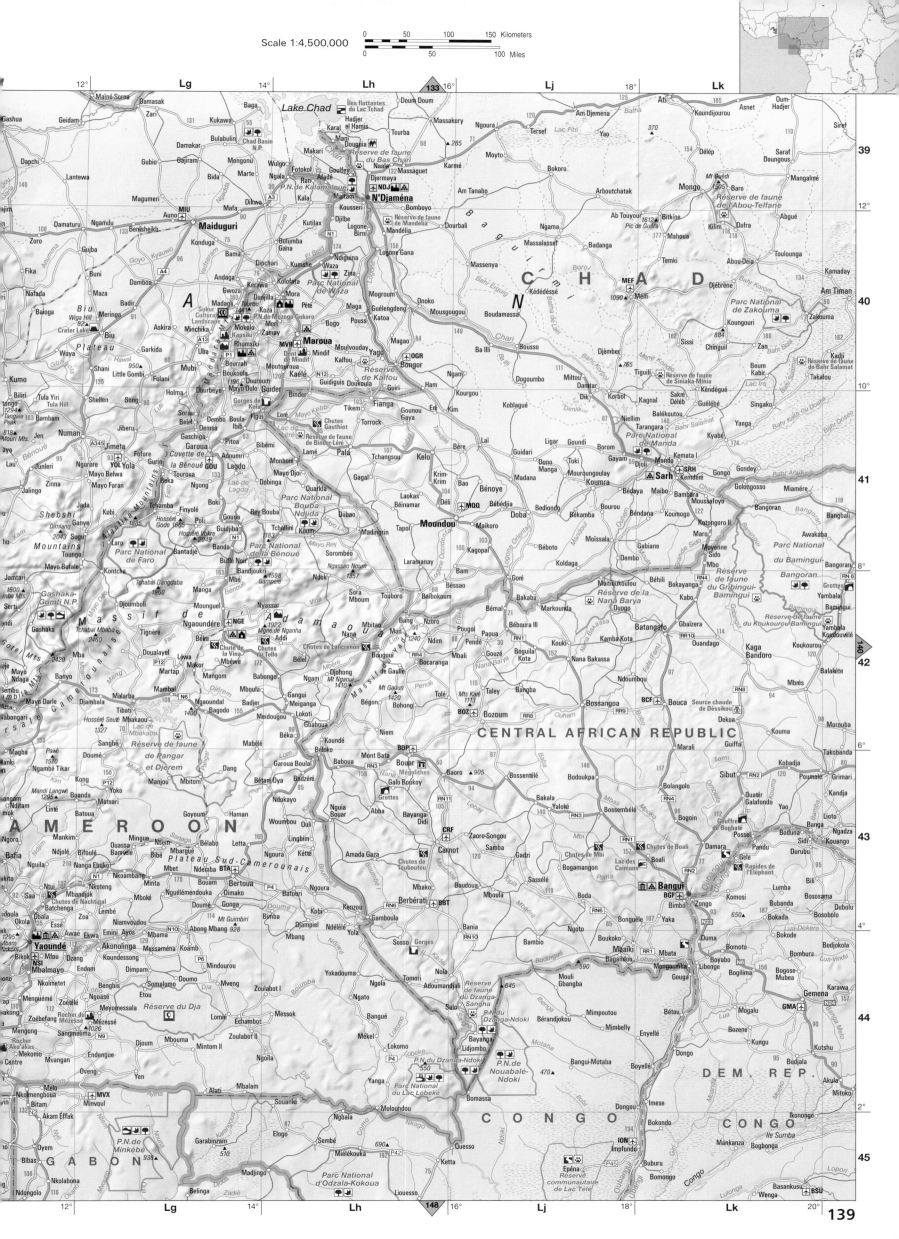

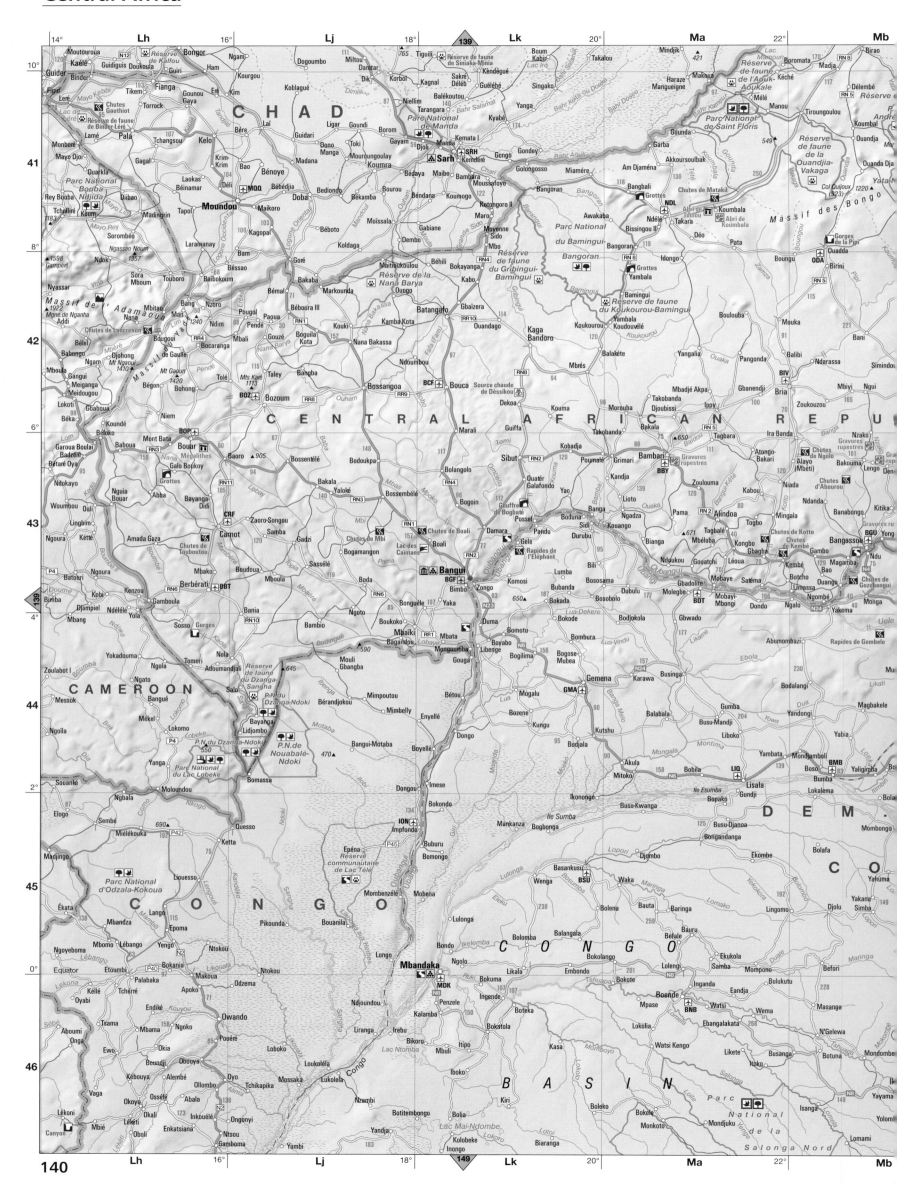

Central Africa

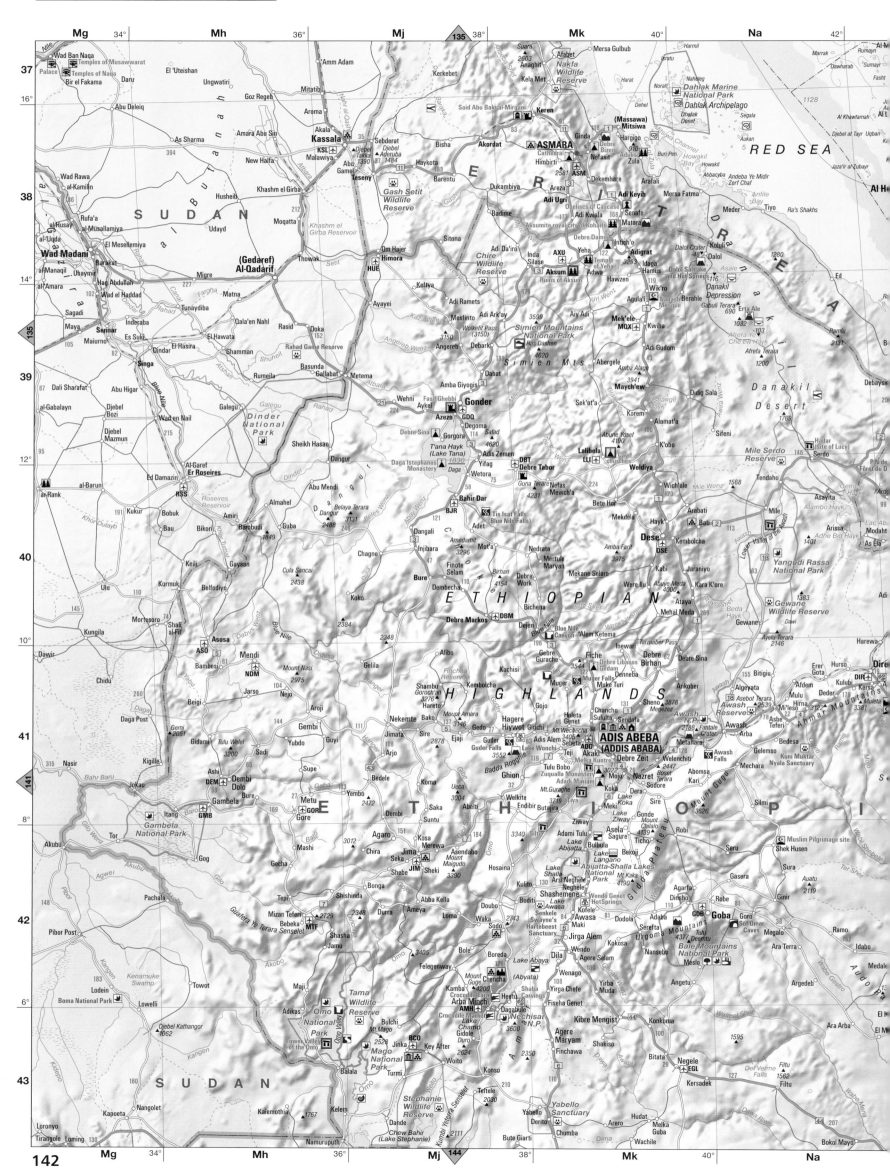

Scale 1:4,500,000

50 100 150 Kilometers

50 100 Miles

YEMEN

Al Harf • Shahara • Huth • Khamir • Al Hazm • Djebel Lawdh 2152 • Al 'Abr • Wadi Hadhramawt • Al-Kaf Palace • Qasam • Qabr Hud • Ghubbat al Qamar
'Abs • Raydah • Walled City of Ma'in (2600) • Nagil al Farda (2200) • Baraqish • Incense Route • Safir • Haynan • Shibam GXF • Tarim • Al-Midhar Mosque • Marakhayy • Magrat • Harut
Hajjah • Amran 3364 • Al-Jami' al-Kebir • Sirwa • Ma'rib • Ramlat as Sab'atayn • Shabwah • Al Qath • Say'un • Sultan's Palace • Sunah • Wadi al Masilah • Saqr • Ra's Fartak • Haswayn
Al Mahwit Shibam • Dar al Hajar • SAH • SAN'A (SANAA) • Souq al Milh • Jihanah • Al Naqub • Rashshah • Sif • Hawrah • Al Magharim • Atud • Al Quzah • Al Hami • Qusay'ir • Qalanah • Qishn • Ra's Sharwayn • Sayhut
At Tawilah • Manakhah • Baw'an Pass (2809) • Sumara Pass (2809) • Ma'bar • Harib • Ma'rib • Incense Route • Bayhan al Qasab • Al Qarn • Al Fardah • MKX • Al Shihr • Ghaydah • Thamun
Al Sukhnah • Madinat al 'bid • Dhamar • Rada' • Al Qafrah • Nisab • 'Ataq AXK • Al Madina • Al Rawdha • Mayfa'ah • Naqb al-Hadjar • Al Rayyan • Ar-Rawdha Mosque • Al Mukalla
Bayt al Faqih • Yarim • As Sawwdiyah • Habban • 'Ayn Ba Ma'bad • Balhaf • Bir 'Ali • Al Sufal • Zulumah
Zabid • At 'Udayn • Ibb • Djebel Manar 3355 • Juban • Al Bayda • Djebel Adaran 2516 • Lawdar • Al Surrah • Al Mahfid • Mijdahah • Ra's al Kalb
Hays • Jibla • Qa'tabah • Al Dali • Al Humayshah • Muqaybirah • Ahwar • Al Hawra • Al Irqah
Ta'izz • Al-Ashrafiya Mosque • Djebel Sabir 3006 • Al Rahidah • Al Musaymir • Ja'ar • Al Hisn' • Shuqra
Mukha (Mocha) • At Turbah • Al 'Anad • Zinjibar • Lahij • Madinat ash Sha'b • Al Ahaykh 'Uthman • Al-'Aydarus Mosque
Turba • Barim (Perim) • Ra's al Arah • Imran • 'Adan as Sughra (Little Aden) • 'Adan (Aden) ADE
Iles 7 Freres • Khor Anghar • Ra's Bir

Gulf of Aden

Obock • Golfe de Tadjoura • Ile Moucha • 'Abd al-Kuri
DJIBOUTI • DJIBOUTI JIB • Loyada
Saylac • Raas Maskan • Caluula • Raas Caluula • Bereeda • Raas Caseyr (C.Guardafui)
Silil • Gerisa • Geesaley • Bandar Murcaayo • Dhurbo • Tooxin
Sidhi • Abdul Qaadir • Lughaye • Maydh • Raas Surud • Laasqoray • Ceelayo • BSA Boosaaso • Qandala • Ceel Gaal • Bargaal
Ceel Baxay • Bullaxaar • Berbera BBO • Dubar • Raas Khansiir • Karin • Maydh • Xiis • Hadaaftimo • Karin • Criradhme • Ufeyn • Raas Binna
Tog • Mandheera • Darburruk • Sheekh • Sara Hahan • Shimbiris 2416 • Dayaxa • Cheerigaabo • Las Dawaco • Meeladeen • Jaceyl • Handha • Hurdiyo
Nabadeed • Hargeysa HGA • Cadaradey • Burco • Yufle • Buraan • Iskushuban • Ashira • Xaafuun (Dante) • Raas Xaafuun
Gadhyogol • Bander Wanaag • Oodweyne • Haro Shiikh • Garadag • Xingalool • Rako Raaxo • Weyla • Adinsoone • Qardho • Bender Beyla • Raas Macber
Kaha • Salahly • Ceek • Kirit • Ceel Dhaab • Caynabo • Ceel Afweyn • Xudun • Taleex • Xalin • Dan Gorayo • Dhuudo
Degeh Bur • Durukhsi • Daryaleh • Laas Caanood • Sinujiif • Rabaable • Garoowe • Kalis • Gabbac • Raas Gabbac
Aware • Darar • Buuhoodle • Gibaganle • Laas Cano • Eyl HCM • Raas Illig
Tukayel • Domo • Bur Tinle • Jirriban
Curale • Gafidda • Bacadweeyn • El Humurre • Garacad
Bircot • Welwel • Warder • Geladi • Berdale • Dhanane
El Fud • Warandab • Gedlegube • Agar Uen • Dudub • Beyra GLK • Galcaio (Gaalkacyo) • Gal Adhale • Af Barwaargo • Dabaro

SOMALIA

Gode (Melka Teko) GDE • Kebri Dehar • Yoube • Mererale • Dagaari • Xingod • Colguula • Iidaan
Denan • Hadaluma • K'orahe 40 • Shilabo • Gellinsoor • War Galon • Cadaado • Godinlabe • Mirsale
Kalafo • Busle • El Bioba • El Abred • Ceeldhere • Dhuusa Mareeb • Sinadogo • Bulacle • Wisil • Hobyo (Obbia) CMO
Ididole • Wabe Shebele Wenz • Mustahil • Ferfer • Habor Cirir • El Bur (Ceelbur) • Ceel Huur
El Mallaile • Ted • Hiiraan • Beledweyne (Belet Weyne) • Buqda Koosaar • Maxaas • Jacai • Gal Hareeri • Ceel Gaan

INDIAN OCEAN

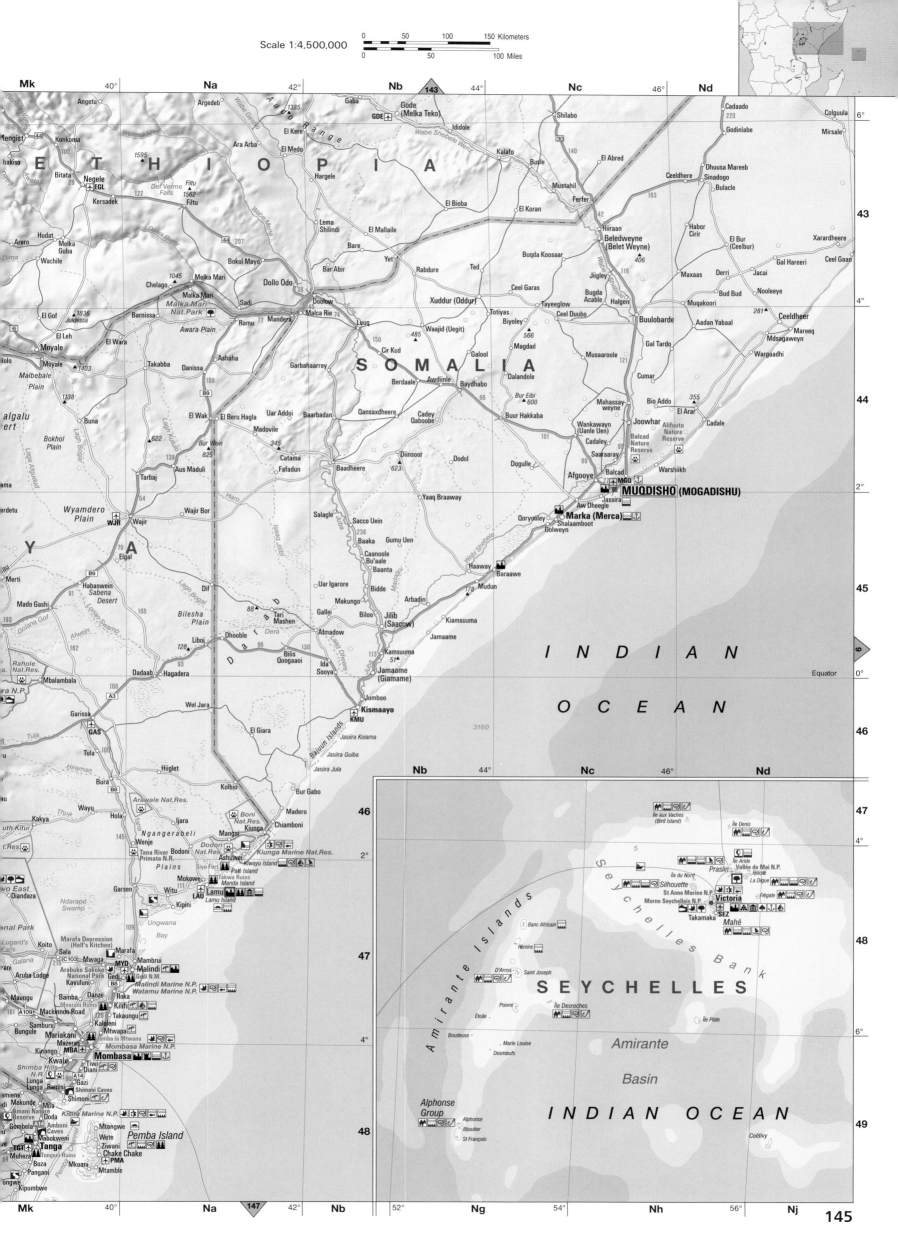

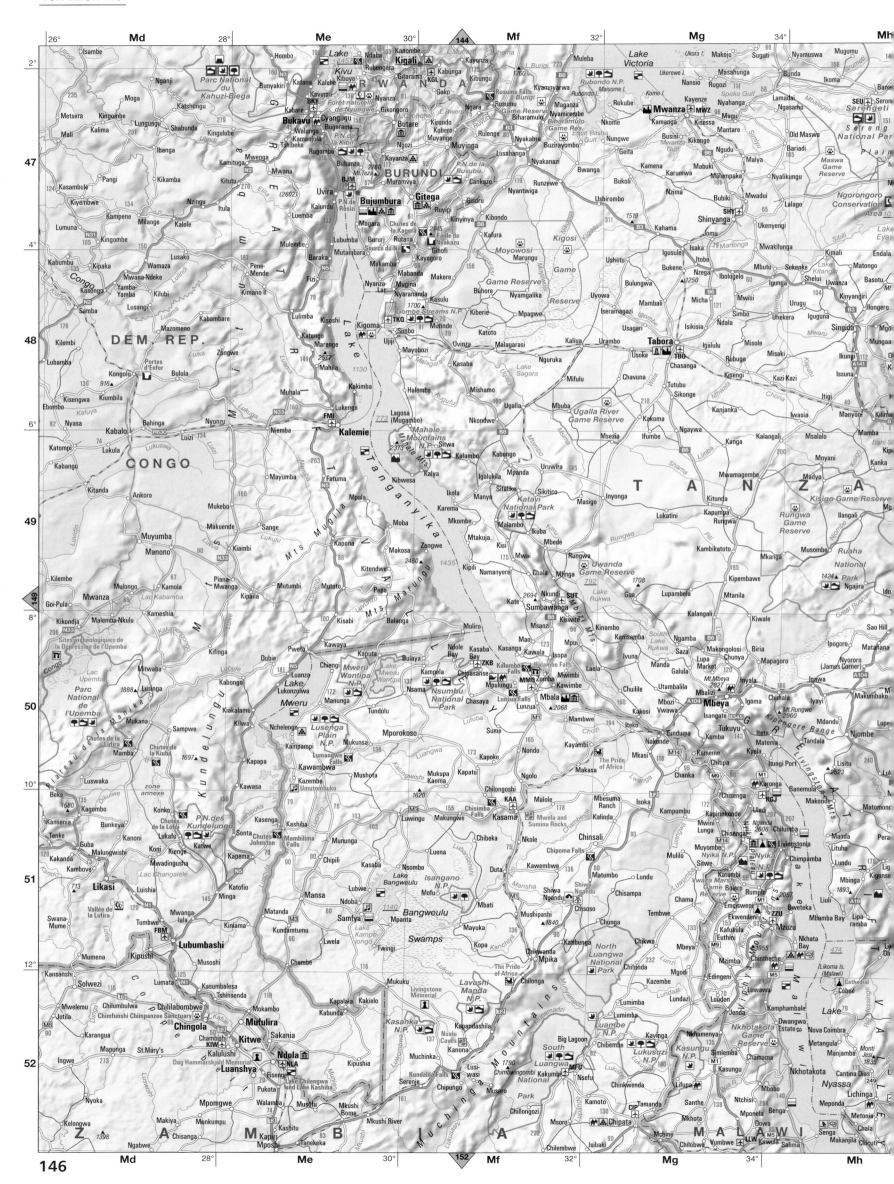

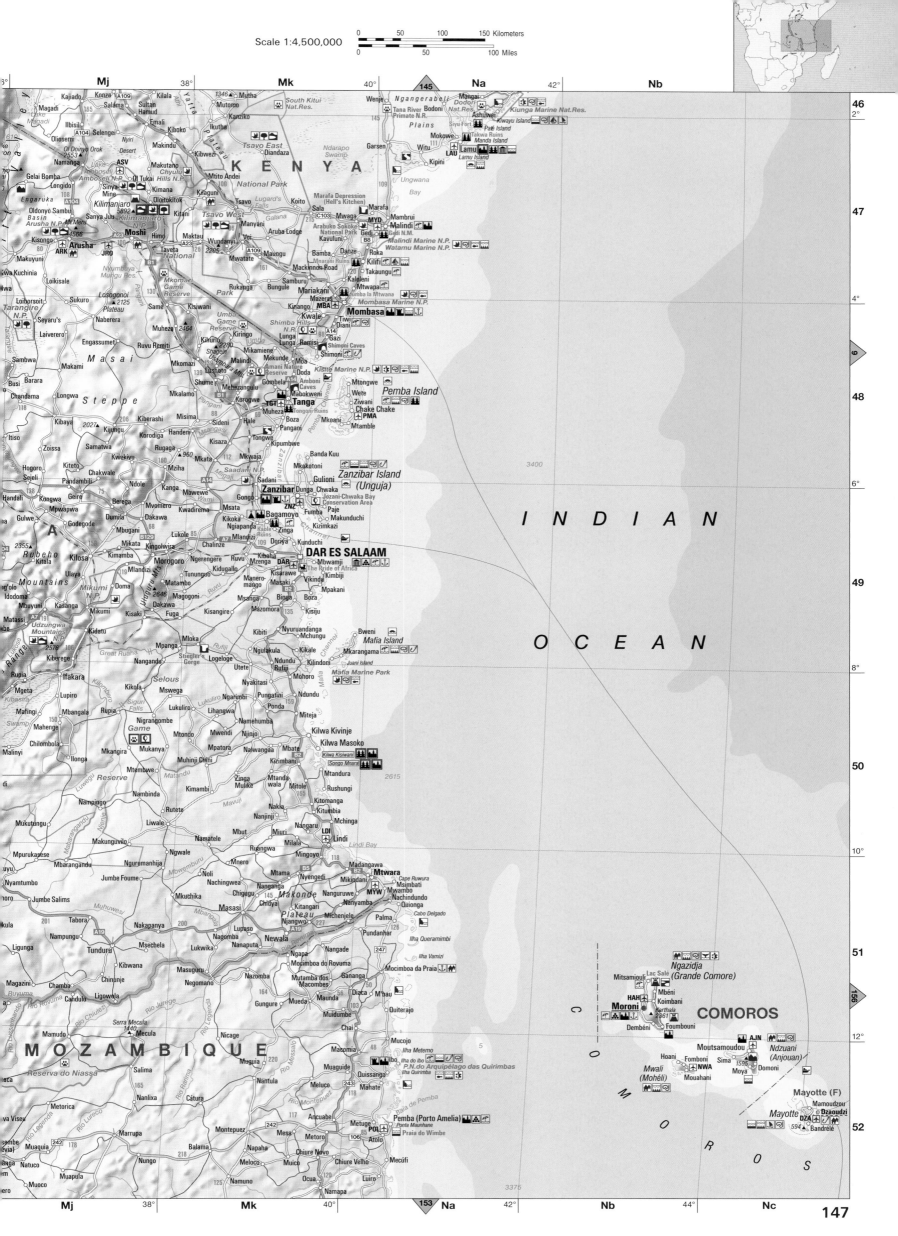

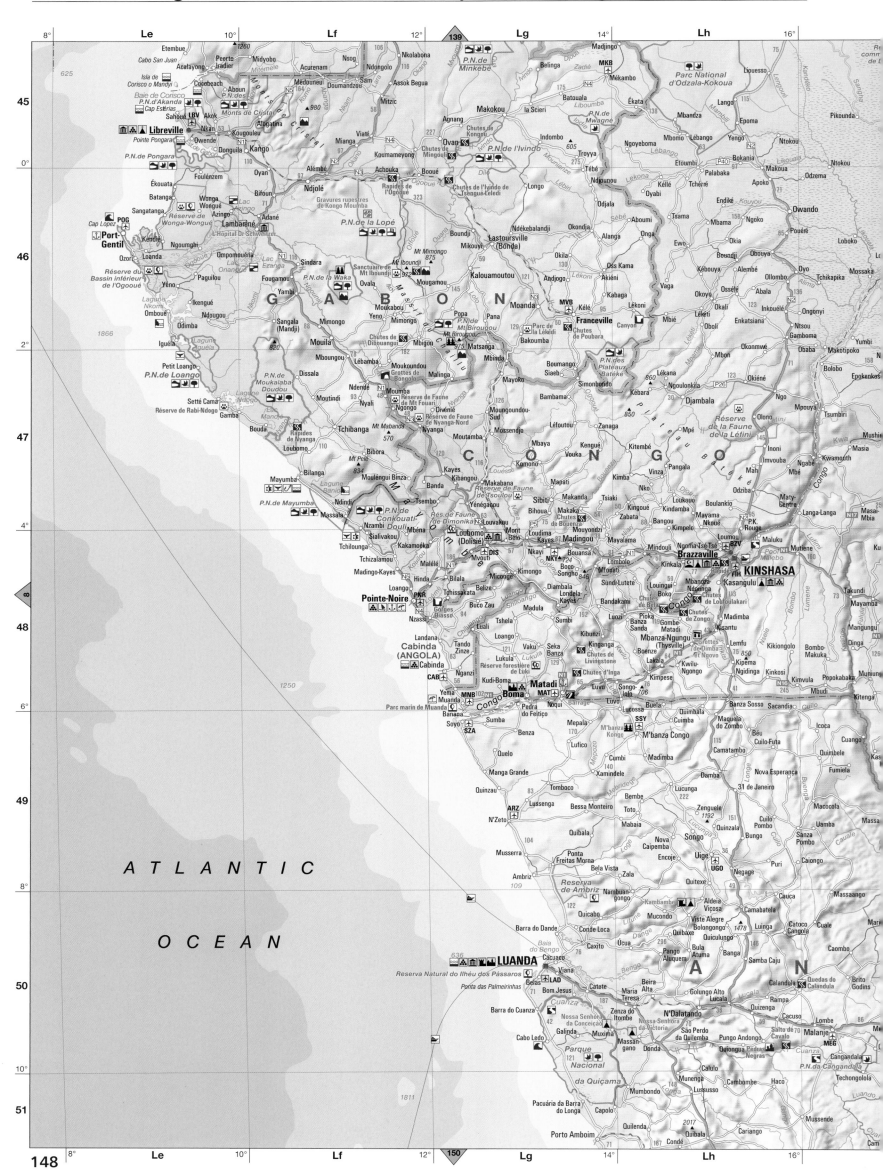

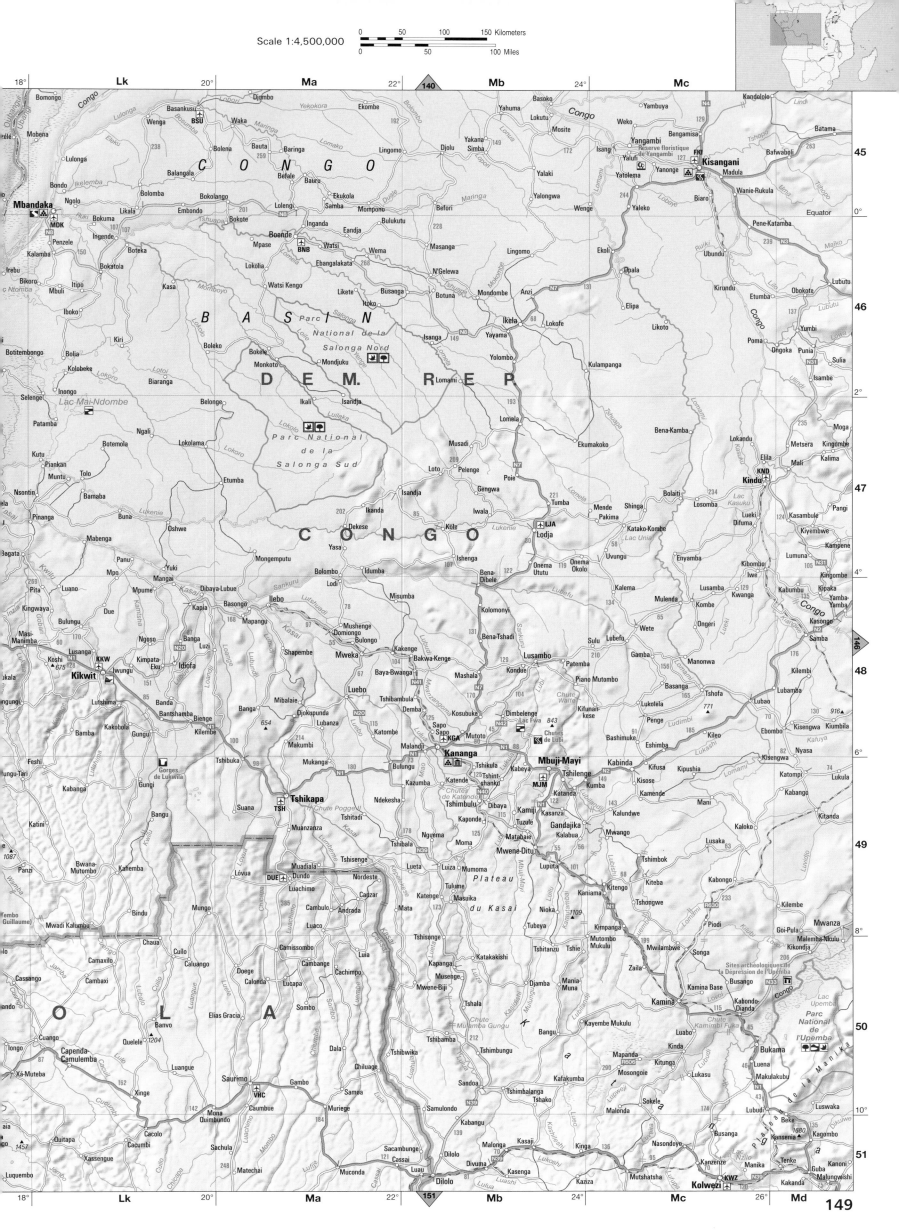

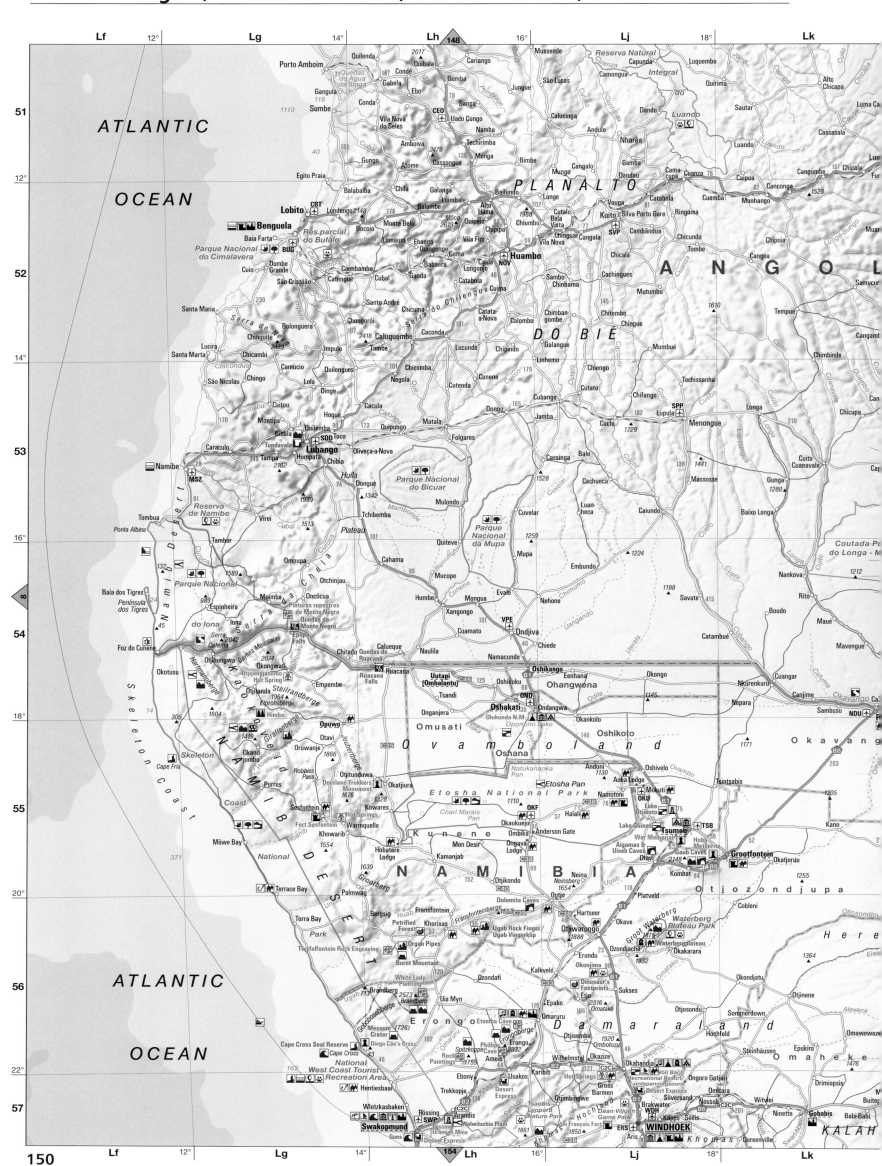

Scale 1:4,500,000

0 50 100 150 Kilometers

0 50 100 Miles

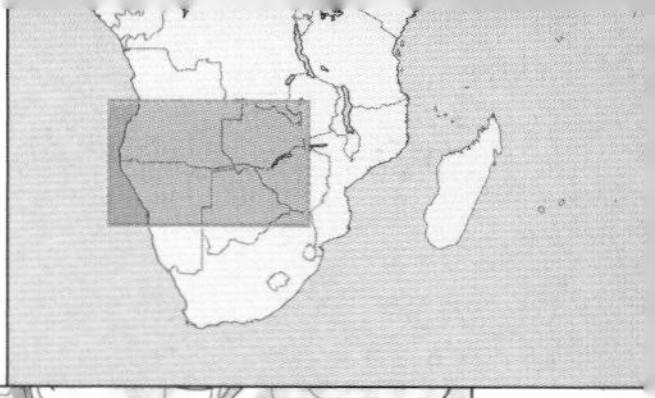

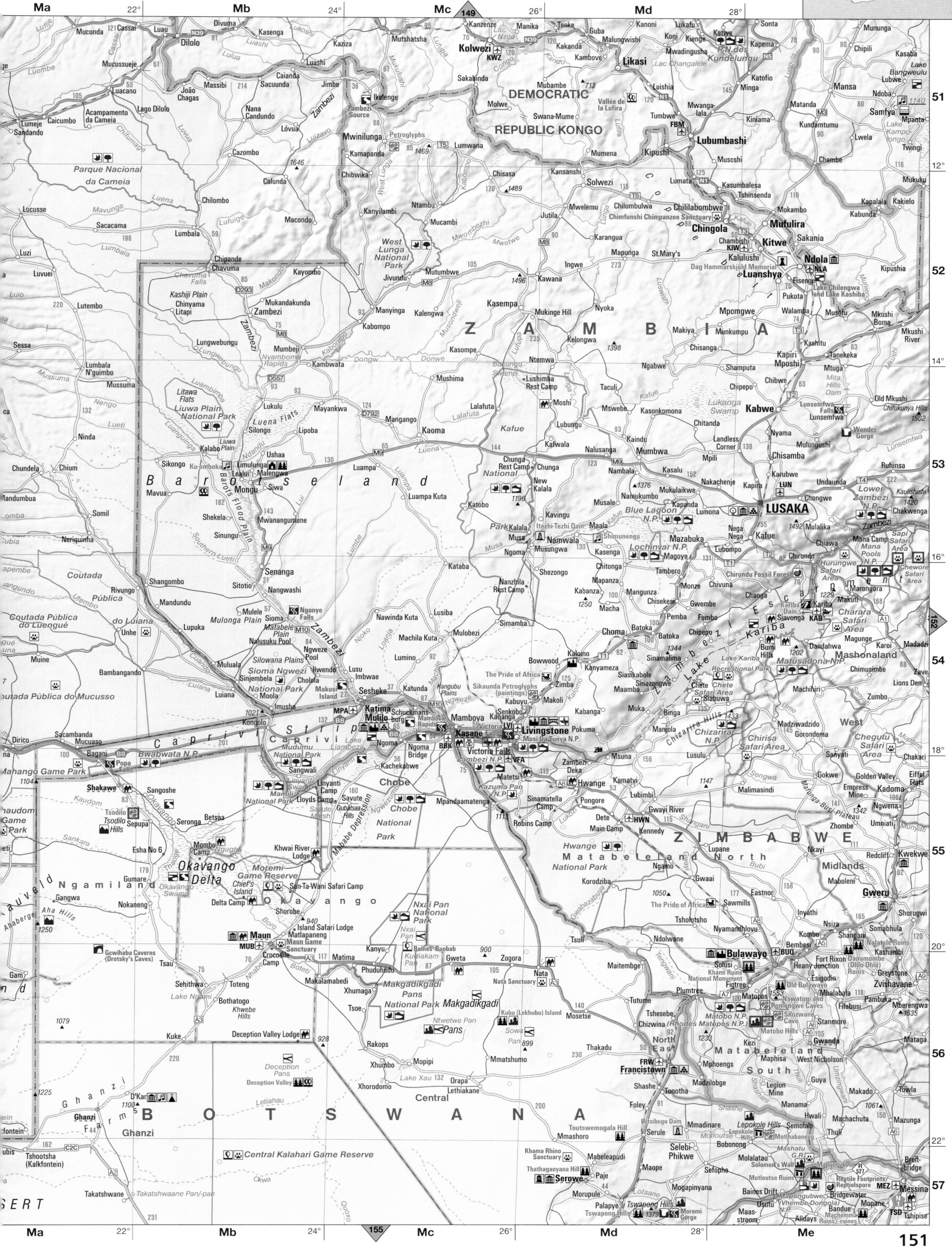

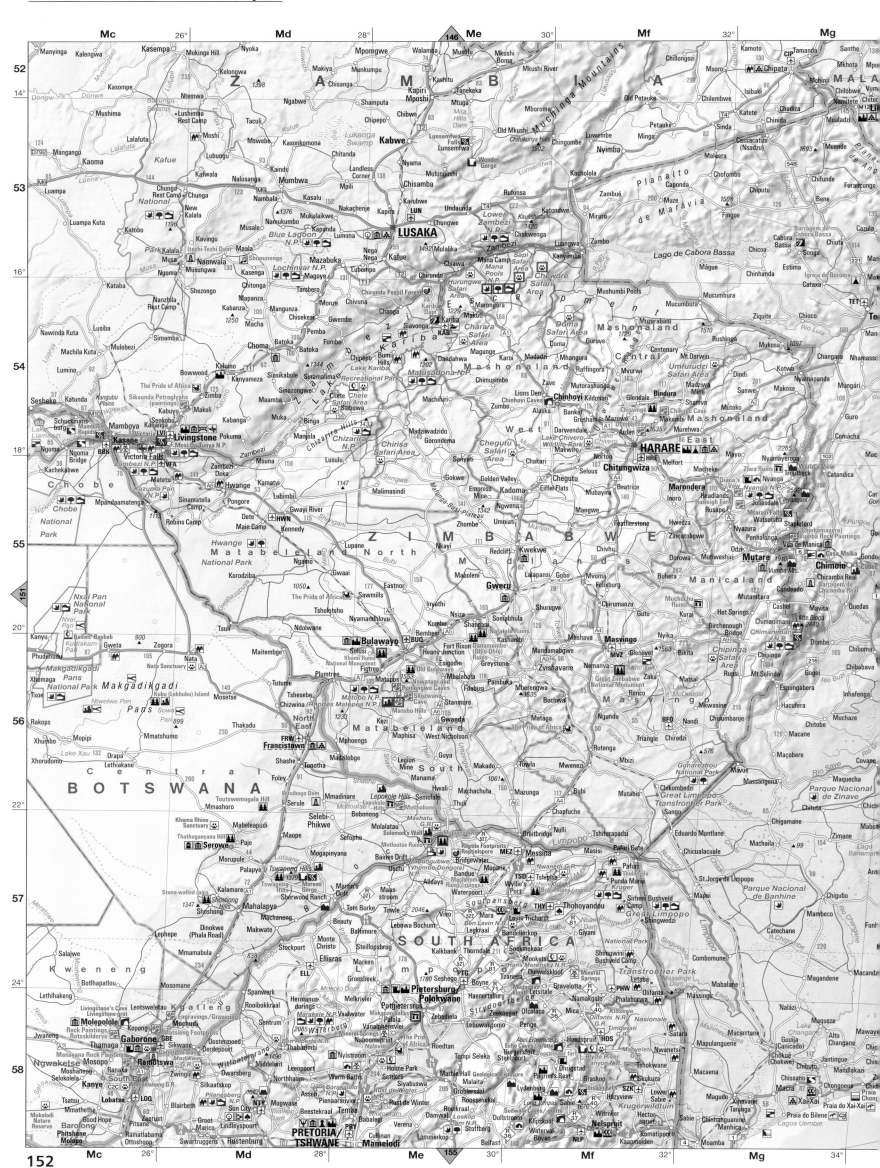

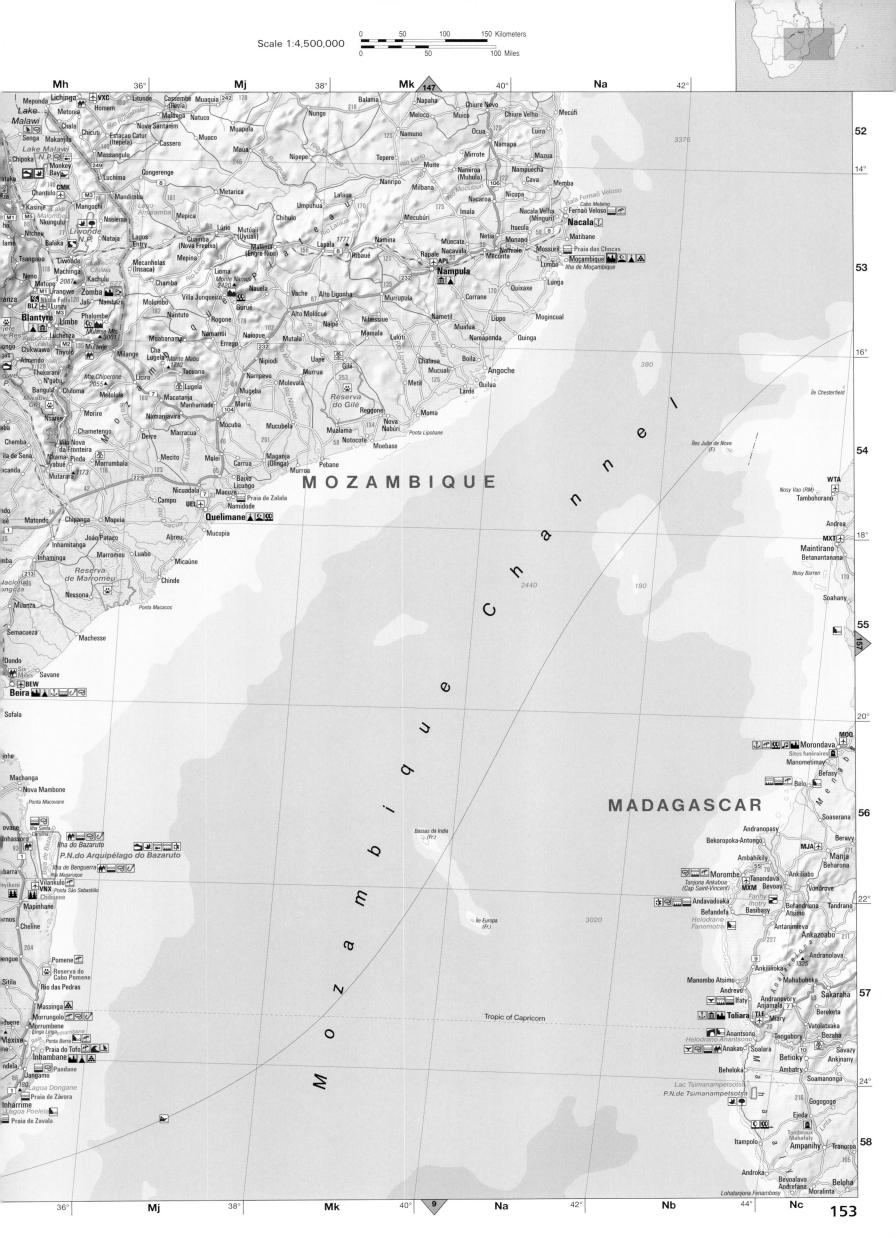

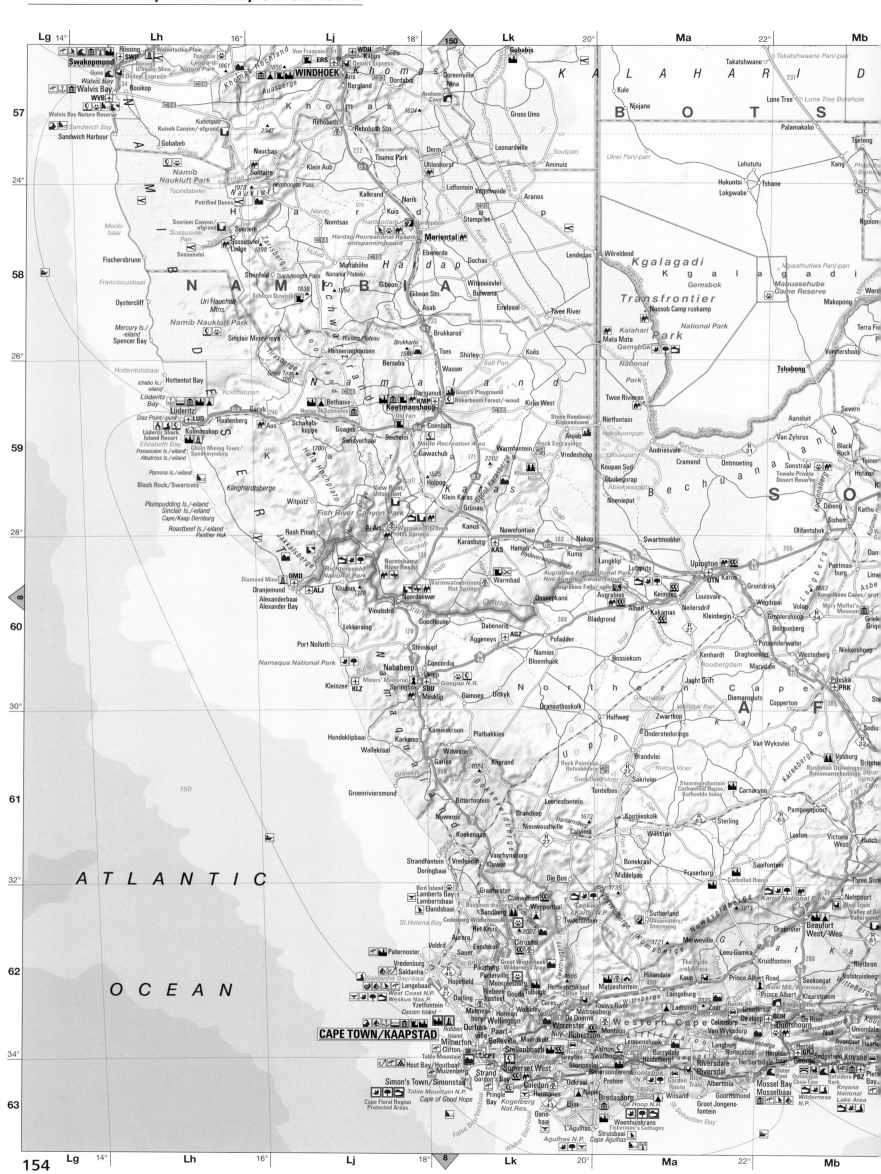

Scale 1:4,500,000
0 50 100 150 Kilometers
0 50 100 Miles
Mc 26° Md 28° 152 Me 30° Mf 32°
57
58
59
60
61
62
63
24°
26°
28°
30°
32°
34°
MOZAMBIQUE
Parque Nacional de Banhine
Tropic of Capricorn
Transfrontier Park
Great Limpopo
Soutpansberg
Limpopo
Pietersburg/Polokwane
Thohoyandou
Louis Trichardt
Phalaborwa
Waterberg
Gaborone
Molepolole
Kanye
Lobatse
Mochudi
Ramotswa
Mafikeng
Mmabatho
Rustenburg
PRETORIA/ TSHWANE
Roodepoort
Benoni
Springs
SOWETO JOHANNESBURG
Germiston
Vereeniging
Klerksdorp
Potchefstroom
Mpumalanga
Witbank
Middelburg
Nelspruit
Lydenburg
Barberton
Ermelo
MAPUTO
Baía de Maputo
Mbabane
Manzini
SWAZILAND
Piet Retief
Vryburg
Kimberley
Bloemfontein
Welkom
Kroonstad
Bethlehem
Harrismith
Ladysmith
Newcastle
Vryheid
Ulundi
Richards Bay/Richardsbaai
KwaZulu Natal
Pietermaritzburg
Durban
Kwa-Mashu
Umlazi
Maseru
LESOTHO
Drakensberg
Aliwal North
Queenstown
Umtata
Port St.Johns
Cradock
Graaff-Reinet
Middelburg
Colesberg
Grahamstown/Grahamstad
East London
Mdantsane
Bisho
King Williams Town
Port Alfred
Port Elizabeth
Uitenhage
Jeffrey's Bay
Algoa Bay
INDIAN
OCEAN
Mc 26° Md 28° Me 9 30° Mf 32° Mg 34° Mh

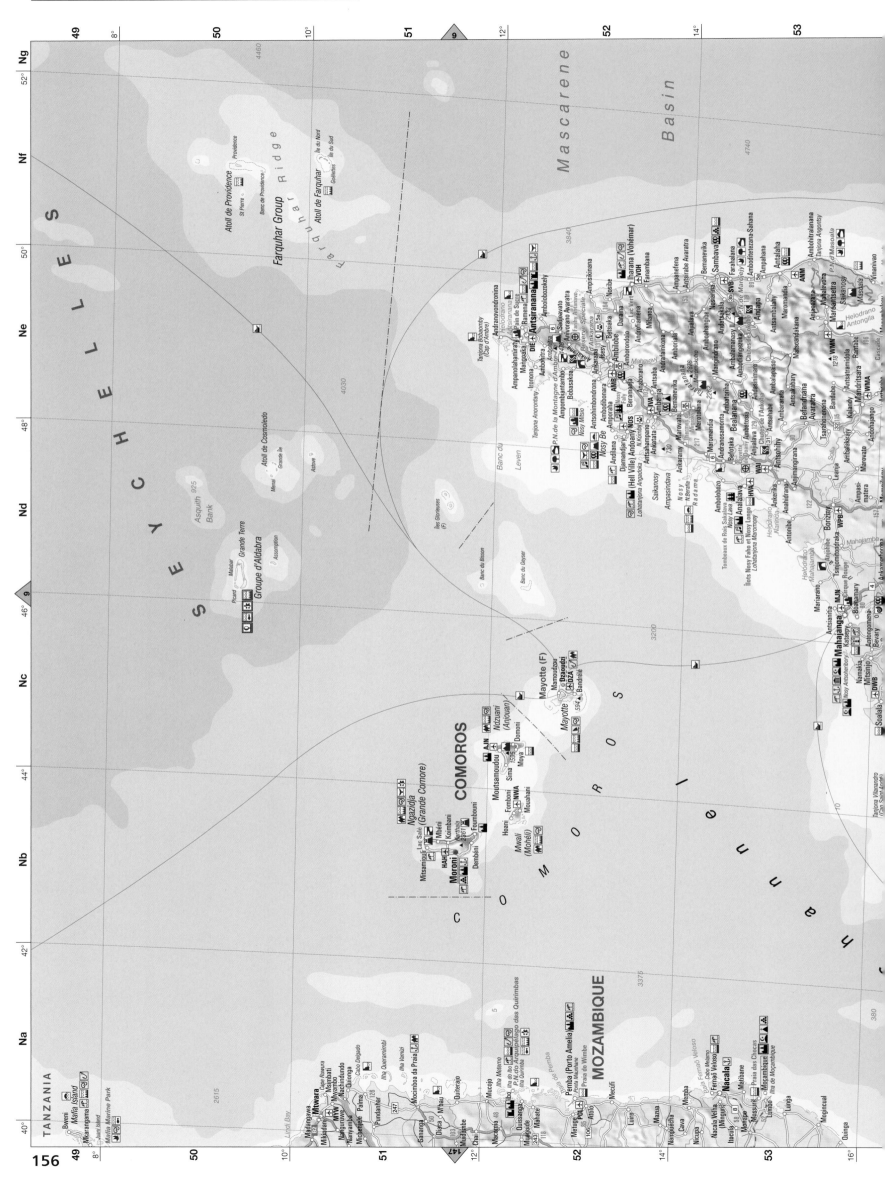

Scale 1:4,500,000

0 50 100 150 Kilometers
0 50 100 Miles

INDIAN OCEAN

INDIAN

OCEAN

Mascarene Plateau

MADAGASCAR

Mascarene Islands

MAURITIUS

Pamplemousses
Port Louis/Rose Hill
Beau-Bassin/Rose Hill
Curepipe
Rivière Sud-Est
Mahébourg
Souillac
MRU

Mauritius

Réunion (F)

Saint-Denis
Saint-André
Le Port
Saint-Benoît
Saint-Paul
Piton des Neiges
Piton de la Fournaise
Saint-Philippe
Saint-Leu
Saint-Joseph
Saint-Pierre

Réunion

Madagascar Basin

Mozambique

Tropic of Capricorn

The Virgin Islands are surrounded by beautiful tropical coasting.

Chicago: The modern skyline of the city glitters next to Lake Michigan.

NORTH AND CENTRAL AMERICA

THE NEW WORLD

The northern continent of the Western Hemisphere stretches from the Arctic Ocean to the Caribbean Sea. North America can be divided into three large geographic regions running from north to south. The western portion of the continent is dominated by the Cordilleras, a series of mountain ranges which contains Alaska's Mount McKinley (6,194 m), the continent's highest mountain. The Appalachian Mountains stretch through much of eastern North America. In between these two regions lie the vast Central Plains. One of the continent's most interesting geographic attractions is Death Valley, the lowest point on the planet's surface.

The Rocky Mountains, the largest mountain chain in North America, extend through the United States and Canada. In the American Southwest, the Rockies border the Sierra Madre mountain range, which extends through most of Mexico and into Central America. The Isthmus of Panama is only 50 kilometers wide. The islands of the Caribbean form a large chain running from Cuba to South America and are separated into two groups: the Lesser Antilles and the Greater Antilles.

In addition to the three large nations on the continent (Canada, Mexico, and the United States) there are numerous smaller North American nations. The indigenous people (Native Americans and Inuit) form only a small portion of the population in Canada and the United States, while most Mexicans and Central Americans are at least of partial indigenous descent.

Over the centuries millions of European immigrants settled in North America and most of the continent's population is of European descent. Millions of North Americans, mostly in the United States and the Caribbean, are of African descent. Canada and the USA attract a large number of immigrants every year, including many migrants from neighboring Mexico.

Hollow Water First Nation Land: Native reservation in Manitoba – on the southern shore of Lake Winnipeg.

North and Central America

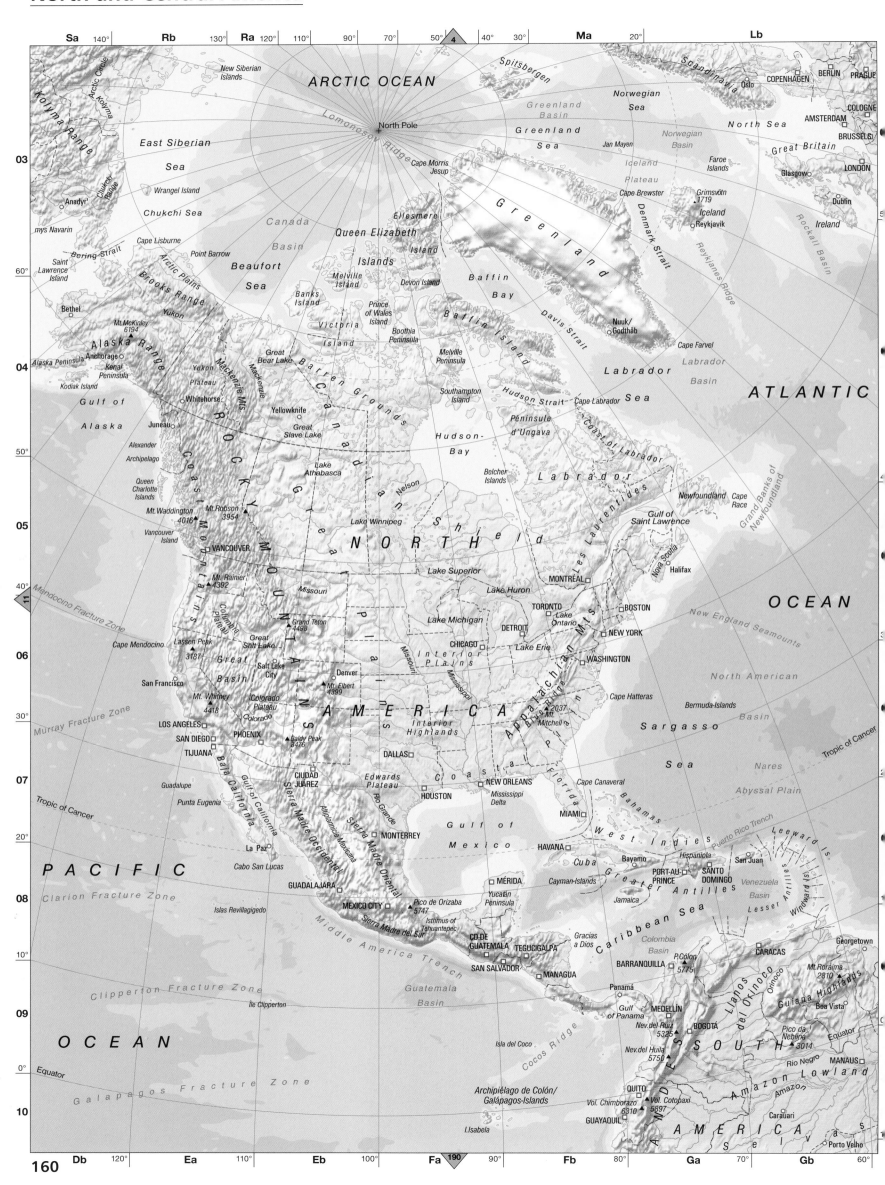

ARCTIC OCEAN

Kolyma Range
East Siberian Sea
Arctic Circle
New Siberian Islands
Spitsbergen
Scandinavia
Oslo COPENHAGEN BERLIN PRAGUE
Norwegian Sea
Greenland Basin
Greenland Sea
COLOGNE
AMSTERDAM
BRUSSELS
Jan Mayen
Norwegian Basin
North Sea
Great Britain
Glasgow LONDON
Dublin Ireland

03 Anadyr'
Chukchi Ridge
Wrangel Island
Chukchi Sea
Cape Lisburne
mys Navarin
Bering Strait
Point Barrow

Cape Morris Jesup
Lomonosov Ridge
North Pole
Canada Basin
Queen Elizabeth Islands
Ellesmere Island
Devon Island
Baffin Bay
Greenland

Iceland Plateau
Cape Brewster
Grímsvötn 1719
Iceland
Reykjavik
Faroe Islands

Denmark Strait
Reykjanes Ridge
Rockall Basin

60° Saint Lawrence Island
Bethel
Brooks Range
Arctic Plains
Beaufort Sea
Banks Island
Melville Island
Prince of Wales Island
Baffin Island
Davis Strait
Nuuk/ Godthåb
Cape Farvel
Labrador Sea
Labrador Basin

Mt.McKinley 6194
Anchorage
Alaska Range
Alaska Peninsula
Kenai Peninsula
Kodiak Island
Yukon
Whitehorse
Yukon Plateau
Mackenzie Mts.
Great Bear Lake
Victoria Island
Boothia Peninsula
Melville Peninsula
Southampton Island
Hudson Strait
Péninsule d'Ungava
Cape Labrador

04 Gulf of Alaska
Juneau
Yellowknife
Great Slave Lake
Barren Grounds
Hudson Bay
Belcher Islands
Labrador
Coast of Labrador
ATLANTIC

50° Alexander Archipelago
Queen Charlotte Islands
Mt.Waddington 4016
Mt.Robson 3954
Lake Athabasca
Lake Winnipeg
Canadian Shield
NORTH
Les Laurentides
Newfoundland
Gulf of Saint Lawrence
Cape Race
Grand Banks of Newfoundland

05 Vancouver Island
VANCOUVER
Coast Mountains
ROCKY
Nelson
Lake Superior
MONTRÉAL
Nova Scotia
Halifax

40° 11 Mendocino Fracture Zone
Mt. Rainier 4392
Missouri
MOUNTAINS
Lake Huron
Lake Michigan
TORONTO
DETROIT
Lake Ontario
BOSTON
NEW YORK
WASHINGTON
OCEAN
New England Seamounts

06 Cape Mendocino
Lassen Peak 3187
Great Salt Lake
Grand Teton 4498
Great Basin
Salt Lake City
Denver
Interior Plains
CHICAGO
Lake Erie
AMERICA
North American Basin

30° San Francisco
Mt. Whitney 4418
Colorado Plateau
Mt. Elbert 4399
Colorado
Missouri
Mississippi
Appalachian Mts.
2037
Mt. Mitchell
Cape Hatteras
Bermuda-Islands
Sargasso

LOS ANGELES
SAN DIEGO
TIJUANA
PHOENIX
Baldy Peak 3476
Interior Highlands
DALLAS
Sea
Tropic of Cancer

07 Tropic of Cancer
Murray Fracture Zone
Guadalupe
Punta Eugenia
Baja California
Gulf of California
CIUDAD JUÁREZ
Edwards Plateau
Rio Grande
NEW ORLEANS
HOUSTON
Mississippi Delta
Florida
Cape Canaveral
Bahamas
MIAMI
Nares
Abyssal Plain
Puerto Rico Trench

20° La Paz
Cabo San Lucas
Sierra Madre Occidental
Altiplanicie Mexicana
MONTERREY
Gulf of Mexico
HAVANA
Cuba
Bayamo
West Indies
Hispaniola
San Juan
Leeward Is.
PACIFIC
Clarion Fracture Zone
GUADALAJARA
Sierra Madre Oriental
MÉRIDA
Yucatán Peninsula
Cayman-Islands
Greater Antilles
PORT-AU-PRINCE
SANTO DOMINGO
Jamaica
Venezuela Basin
Lesser Antilles
Windward Is.

08 MEXICO CITY
Pico de Orizaba 5747
Isthmus of Tehuantepec
Caribbean Sea
Gracias a Dios
Panamá
BARRANQUILLA
P. Colón 5775
CARACAS
Georgetown
Islas Revillagigedo
Sierra Madre del Sur
CD.DE GUATEMALA
TEGUCIGALPA
SAN SALVADOR
MANAGUA
Colombia Basin
MEDELLÍN
Llanos del Orinoco
Mt.Roraima 2810
Guiana Highlands
Boa Vista

10° Middle America Trench
Guatemala Basin
Gulf of Panama
Nev.del Ruiz 5325
BOGOTÁ
Orinoco
Equator

09 OCEAN
Clipperton Fracture Zone
Île Clipperton
Cocos Ridge
Isla del Coco
Nev.del Huila 5750
Pico da Neblina 3014
MANAUS

0° Equator
Galapagos Fracture Zone
Archipiélago de Colón/ Galápagos-Islands
Vol. Chimborazo 6310
Vol. Cotopaxi 5897
QUITO
SOUTH
Rio Negro
Amazon Lowland
Amazon

10 I.Isabela
GUAYAQUIL
AMERICA
Carauari
Porto Velho

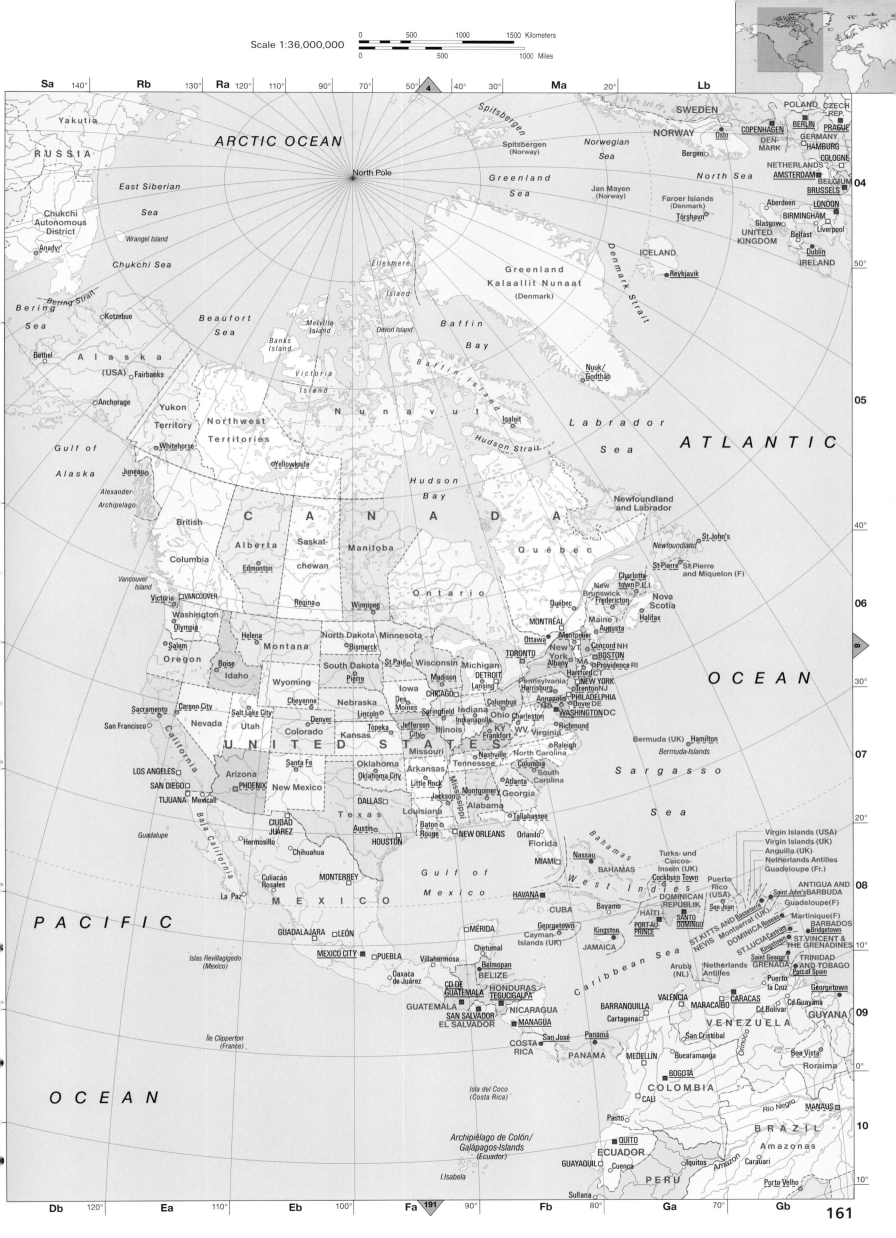

ARCTIC OCEAN

North Pole

RUSSIA

Yakutia

East Siberian
Sea

Chukchi
Autonomous
District

Anadyr

Wrangel Island

Bering Strait

Chukchi Sea

Bering
Sea

Kotzebue

Bethel

A l a s k a
(USA)

Fairbanks

Anchorage

Gulf of
Alaska

Juneau

Alexander-
Archipelago

Whitehorse

Yukon
Territory

Northwest
Territories

Yellowknife

Victoria
Island

Banks
Island

Melville
Island

Beaufort
Sea

Devon Island

Ellesmere
Island

Baffin
Bay

Baffin Island

Nuuk/
Godthåb

Iqaluit

Hudson Strait

Labrador
Sea

N u n a v u t

Hudson
Bay

Greenland
Kalaallit Nunaat
(Denmark)

Denmark Strait

ICELAND

Reykjavik

SWEDEN

NORWAY

Oslo

Bergen

Norwegian
Sea

Jan Mayen
(Norway)

Greenland
Sea

Spitsbergen
(Norway)

Spitsbergen

North Sea

Faroer Islands
(Denmark)

Tórshavn

Aberdeen

Glasgow

UNITED
KINGDOM

Belfast

IRELAND

Dublin

POLAND CZECH
REP.

BERLIN PRAGUE

COPENHAGEN GERMANY

DEN-
MARK HAMBURG

COLOGNE

NETHERLANDS

AMSTERDAM BELGIUM

BRUSSELS

LONDON

BIRMINGHAM

Liverpool

04

ATLANTIC

05

06

07

08

09

British
Columbia

Alberta

Saskat-
chewan

Manitoba

C A N A D A

Ontario

Québec

Newfoundland
and Labrador

St.John's

Newfoundland

St-Pierre St.Pierre
and Miquelon (F)

Edmonton

Vancouver
Island

Victoria VANCOUVER

Washington

Olympia

Salem

Oregon

Helena

Montana

Boise

Idaho

Regina

Winnipeg

North Dakota

Bismarck

Minnesota

South Dakota

Pierre

Wyoming

Cheyenne

Nebraska

Lincoln

Iowa

Des
Moines

Wisconsin

St.Paul

Madison

Michigan

Lansing

DETROIT

Québec

MONTRÉAL

Ottawa

TORONTO

New
York

Montpelier

Concord NH

Maine

Augusta

New
Brunswick

Fredericton

Charlotte-
town P.E.I.

Nova
Scotia

Halifax

BOSTON

VT

Albany

MA

Providence RI

Hartford CT

NEW YORK

Pennsylvania

Harrisburg

TrentonNJ

PHILADELPHIA

Dover DE

Annapolis

WASHINGTON DC

MD

OCEAN

Bermuda (UK) Hamilton

Bermuda-Islands

Sargasso

Sea

PACIFIC

Sacramento

San Francisco

California

Carson City

Nevada

Salt Lake City

Utah

Denver

Colorado

Topeka

Kansas

Jefferson
City

Lincoln

CHICAGO

Springfield

Illinois

Indianapolis

Indiana

Ohio

Columbus

Columbia

Charleston

KY

WV

Virginia

Richmond

Nashville

Tennessee

North Carolina

Raleigh

Missouri

U N I T E D S T A T E S

LOS ANGELES

SAN DIEGO

TIJUANA Mexicali

Guadalupe

Baja California

Arizona

PHOENIX

New Mexico

Santa Fe

Oklahoma

Oklahoma City

DALLAS

Texas

Austin

HOUSTON

CIUDAD
JUÁREZ

Hermosillo

Chihuahua

Arkansas

Little Rock

Jackson

Louisiana

Baton
Rouge

NEW ORLEANS

Mississippi

Montgomery

Alabama

Atlanta

Georgia

South
Carolina

Tallahassee

Orlando

Florida

MIAMI

Nassau

BAHAMAS

Bahamas

West Indies

Turks- und
Caicos-
Inseln (UK)

Cockburn Town

Virgin Islands (USA)
Virgin Islands (UK)
Anguilla (UK)
Netherlands Antilles
Guadeloupe (Fr.)

MÉXICO

Culiacán
Rosales

La Paz

MONTERREY

Gulf of
Mexico

HAVANA

CUBA

Bayamo

Georgetown

Cayman-
Islands (UK)

JAMAICA

Kingston

HAITI

PORT-AU-
PRINCE

DOMINICAN
REPUBLIC

SANTO
DOMINGO

Puerto
Rico
(USA)

San Juan

ANTIGUA AND
Saint John's BARBUDA

Guadeloupe(F)

Basseterre

ST.KITTS AND
NEVIS

Montserrat (UK)

DOMINICA Roseau

ST.LUCIA Castries

Saint George's

GRENADA

Martinique(F)

BARBADOS

Bridgetown

ST.VINCENT &
THE GRENADINES

Kingstown

TRINIDAD
AND TOBAGO

Port of Spain

GUADALAJARA

LEÓN

MÉRIDA

Chetumal

Villahermosa

Belmopan

BELIZE

Oaxaca
de Juárez

CD.DE
GUATEMALA

HONDURAS

TEGUCIGALPA

GUATEMALA

SAN SALVADOR

EL SALVADOR

NICARAGUA

MANAGUA

San José

COSTA
RICA

Panamá

PANAMA

Caribbean Sea

BARRANQUILLA

Cartagena

Aruba
(NL)

Netherlands
Antilles

MARACAIBO

VALENCIA

CARACAS

Puerto
la Cruz

Cd.Bolívar

Cd.Guayana

Georgetown

GUYANA

VENEZUELA

MEXICO CITY

PUEBLA

Islas Revillagigedo
(Mexico)

Île Clipperton
(France)

OCEAN

Isla del Coco
(Costa Rica)

MEDELLÍN

Bucaramanga

San Cristóbal

Boa Vista

Roraima

BOGOTÁ

COLOMBIA

CALI

Pasto

QUITO

ECUADOR

GUAYAQUIL

Cuenca

Iquitos

PERU

Rio Negro

MANAUS

B R A Z I L

Amazonas

Amazon

Carauari

10

Archipiélago de Colón/
Galápagos-Islands
(Ecuador)

I.Isabela

Sullana

Porto Velho

Alaska, Canada, Greenland

Koryak
Penžinskaja guba
Autonomous District
Kamenskoe
Bilibino
ostrov Ajon
Caunskaja guba
East
Siberian
Sea

R U S S I A
Koryak Range
Penžina
Pevek
proliv Longa
Komsomolskij
38
A R C T I C   O C E A N

06
2562
g. Ledjanaja
Krasneno
Chukchi
Ust-Belaja
Ušakovskoe
Mys Šmidta
Wrangel
Island
155
328
Chukchi Plateau
Movement of
North Magne...
200...

Hatyrka
Anadyr
Ugol'nye Kopi
Egvekinot
Iultin
C a n a d a
Que...
Eliza...
Isla...
P...

Autonomous District
Nagornyj
Gulf of Anadyr
1897
Mackenzie
King Island
Prince Patrick
Island

60°
mys Navarin
Chukchi
Anadyr
65
Providenija
Chukchi
Peninsula
Cape
Lisburne
Point Hope
Wevok
Ice
Cape
Point Barrow
3822
B a s i n
Mould Bay
Sabine
Pen.
Hazen Strait
Parry Isla...

B e r i n g
Gambell
Lavrentija
Uelen
Bering Strait
Wales
Barrow
B e a u f o r t
Cape Prince Albert
P a r r y   I s l a...
Melville
Island
Viscount
Melville Sour...

Saint Lawrence Island
Teller
Kotzebue Sound
Kotzebue
Selawik
Prudhoe Bay
914
S e a
Cape Kellet
Sachs
Harbour
B a n k s
Island
Stefansson
Island
Storkerson
Peninsula

07
St.Matthew
Island
Northeast
Cape
Nome
Seward
Peninsula
Norton Sound
Galena
Allakaket
Wiseman
B R O O K S   R A N G E
Arctic Plains
36
Cape Bathurst
Prince
Albert
Peninsula
V i c t o r i...
Island

Cape
Romanzof
Unalakleet
Mackenzie
Bay
Cape Parry
Franklin
Bay
Amundsen
Gulf
Holman
Island
Wollaston
Peninsula
N...

Cape
Mohican
Nunivak
Island
Bethel
38
Aniak
A l a s k a
Tanana
Kuskokwim Mountains (USA)
Stony River
Yukon
Fort Yukon
Flats
Old Crow
Tuktoyatuk
Inuvik
Paulatuk
Dease
Kent Pen...

Cape Newenham
65
Dillingham
Mt.McKinley
6194
Fairbanks
Fort
McPherson
B...

55°
Bristol
Cape Constantine
Bay
Kvichak Bay
King
Salmon
A L A S K A   R A N G E
Palmer
Glennallen
Tetlin
Junction
Y u k o n
Dawson
Y u k o n
Norman Wells
N o r t h w e s t
Fort Good Hope
Coronation Gulf
Kugluktuk
B a r r e n   G...

Cold
Bay
Port
Heiden
Homer
Kenai
Peninsula
Seward
Prince
William
Sound
P l a t e a u
Stewart
Crossing
Great
Bear Lake
Port
Radium
Bathurst Inlet

55
Chignik
257
Afognak
Island
Valdez
Carmacks
Territory
Ross River
R O C K Y
Contwoyto
Lake

Aleutian Islands
6137
Kodiak
Kodiak Island
Shelikof Strait
Cape
Yakataga
Mt.Logan
5959
Haines
Junction
Whitehorse
Watson Lake
Mackenzie Mts.
Fort
Simpson
Great
Slave Lake
Lutselk'e
Nonacho
Lake

08
G u l f   o f
Yakutat
3355
Skagway
718
A l a s k a
566
Haines
Atlin
Lake
Dease Lake
Summit
Lake
Fort Nelson
Fort Liard
Hay River
Fort Resolution
T e r r i t o r i e s
Yellowknife
Great
Slave Lake
Fort Smith

50°
1134
Chichagof
Island
Juneau
Alexander
Sitka
Baranof
Island
Petersburg
C O A S T   M O U N T A I N S
Ware
High Level
Fort
Vermillion
Fort Chipewyan
Uranium City
Lake
Athabasca
Stony
Rapids

Archipelago
Kupreanof I.
Wrangell
Prince of Wales I.
Ketchikan
Fort St.John
Dawson
Creek
Peace
River
Fort McMurray
La Loche
Reindeer...

09
P A C I F I C
4882
Queen
Charlotte
Islands
Graham
Island
Masset
Sandspit
Moresby
Island
Hecate Strait
Dixon Entrance
Prince
Rupert
Terrace
Kitimat
Williston
Lake
B r i t i s h
Vanderhoof
Prince
George
Grande
Prairie
Lesser
Slave Lake
Slave Lake
Cree Lake
Wollaston
Lake
Woll...
Southend
Saskatchewan
La Ronge
Lac la
Ronge

45°
Cape
St.James
Queen
Charlotte
Sound
Bella Coola
Queen Charlotte Strait
Quesnel
Mt.Waddington
4016
Williams
Lake
Mt.Robson
3954
C O L U M B I A
A l b e r t a
Jasper
Grand
Centre
Meadow
Lake
North
Battleford

295
Cape Scott
Port Hardy
Fraser
Columbia
Plateau
Edmonton
Fort
Saskatchewan
Camrose
Lloyd
minster
Saskatoon
Prince
Albert
Hudson Bay

10
3258
Vancouver
Island
4197
Campbell River
Powell
River
Port Alberni
Nanaimo
R A N G E
Revel
stoke
Vernon
Kamloops
Golden
M O U N T A I N S
Red Deer
Drumheller
Calgary
Banff
Kindersley
Brooks
Regina

O C E A N
4514
32
Juan de...
Cape Flattery
VANCOUVER
Surrey
Victoria
Olympic Peninsula
SEATTLE
Everett
Kelowna
Penticton
Cranbrook
Medicine Hat
Lethbridge
Swift
Current
Lake
Diefenbaker
Moose Jaw

40°
3258
Bremerton
Tacoma
Olympia
Mt.Rainier
4392
Washington
Spokane
Coeur
d'Alene
Kalispell
Great
Falls
Havre
Malta
Weyburn
Est...

11
Astoria
Portland
Salem
Mt.Hood
3426
Yakima
Kennewick
Walla
Walla
Pendleton
Moses Lake
U N I T E D   S T A...
Lewiston
Missoula
M o n t a n a
Helena
Fort Peck
Lake
Glendive
Dickins...

Alaska

RUSSIA

Sireniki
Providenija   Novoe   1158
Urelik   Caplino   Jandrakinot   Raupeljan   Lorino
mys Čukotskij   PVX   pr. Senjavina   Lavrentija
Čečen   Caplino   ostrov Arakamčečen   mys Nyglian   Inč

ostrov Rathmanova (Big Diomede I.)   Little Diomede
Inalik   St

Bering

Northwest Cape   Gambell   Wales   Lopp
Ningeehak   Cape Prince of Wales   Lost River   Brooks M 883
Powooiliak Camp   Savoonga   King I.   Point Spencer
673   Atuk Mtn.   Port Clarence   Teller
Saint Lawrence I.   Iveetok Camp

Niyrakpak Lagoon
Koozata Lagoon

58°   Sinuk   Pilgri Spring
Lietnik   555   Northeast Cape   Kigluaik Mts.   Sinuk R.
Southeast Cape   Kinipaghulghat Mts.

Hall I.   450
Alaska Maritime Wildlife Refuge   Saint Matthew I.   Cape Upright
67   Nome   OME   Iron C

Cape Nome

Norton   Sound
Bluff
White Mountain
18
95   Rocky Point   Golovnia   Cape Darby

Sea
20
Cape Mohican   Nash Harbor
Yukon   Delta
Waklarok   Alakanuk   Kwikpak
Emmonak   Stuart I.
C. Romanzof   Askinuk Mts.   Kotlik   Pastol Bay
Hooper Bay   714   Scammon Bay   New Knockhock   Akulurak   Hamilton   Stebbins
Chevak   New Hamilton   St. Michael
Nunavakanuk Lake   701   Unalakleet

17°   Mekoryuk   Cape Etolin   Hazen Bay   Mountain Village   MOU   Pitkas Pt.   Andreafsky R.   396
Yukon Delta Wildlife Refuge   283   Nunivak I.   C. Vancouver   Chakaktolik   Pilot Station
Tununak   451   Keyaluvik   Apropuk Lake   Kgun L.   Atchuelinguk R.   1402
Cape Mendenhall   Nelson I.   Cahwkwaktolik   Marshall
Cape Corwin   Nightmate   Chiftak   National   Stuyahok   Anvik
Kasigluk   Ohogamuit   Yukon River   Shageluk
Chefornak   Kegum   Takleskuk Lake   Wildli
Etolin Strait   Kagati Lake   Holy Cross
Kikegtek I.   Wildlife Refuge   Kalskag
Kinak Bay   Nunavacnak Lake   WhiteFish Lake   Flat
Pingurbek I.   Kipnuk   BET   Bethel   Aniak
Kwigillingok   Tuntutuliak   Napakiak   Akiachak   Tuluksak   ANI   Crooked Creek   George R.   Kuskokw

Pribilof Islands
St. Paul I.
Otter I.   SNP   Northeast Point
St. Paul   Walrus I.
55   St. George I.

56°   Kuskokwim   Bay   Eek   Eek R.   Kisaralik R.   Horn Mts. 1097
Quinhagak   Mt. Plummer 1463

Carter Spit
Explorer Mtn.   811
Cape Newenham   Platinum   Goodnews Bay   Mt. Oratia 1645   Chigmiornok   Holitna R.   Nogamut
Goodnews Mining Camp   Manvakak Lake   Kukaktlik R.   Taylor Mts. 1091
Calm Point   Togiak   National   Cairn Mts. 1158
Hagemeister Strait   544   Wildlife Refuge   Nuyakuk Lake   Stony R.   Henglimut R.
Hagemeister I.   Togiak   Togiak Bay   Ahklun   Mountains
High I.   Nerka Lake   Swift R.
Crooked I.   Lake Nunayugaluk
Walrus Is.

18°   Aleknagik   Alaganik Lake   Koliganek   Ketok Mtn.   Old Village
Nushagak   New Stuyahok   517   Mulchatna R.
Nushagak Peninsula   DLG   Dillingham   Telaquan Lake
Clarks Point   Nushagak R.

Bristol   Bay
Cape Constantine   Lake Clark National Park and Preserve
Etolin Point   Nondalton   Chigmit
Hallersville   Newhalen   Mountains   Redou 108
Cape Sarichef   Cape Mordvinof   Kvichak Bay   Igiugig   Iliamna Lake   Pile Bay Village   Iliamna Vol. 3084
Unimak I.   Anvak I.   Naknek   Williamsport
Unimak   Shishaldin Volcano 2862   Moffet Pt.   Kvichak R.   Chenik   Burr Pt. 1196
Kudiakof Is.   Izembek Wildlife Refuge   Lagoon Point   King Salmon 745   Katmai   Burr Cove   Chinitna Vol.
False Pass   CDB   Cold Bay   AKN   King Salmon   National Park and Preserve   Chinitna Pt.
Deer I.   Pavlof Vol. 2504   Walrus I.   Naknek Lake   Kukaklek Lake   HOM
King Cove   Pavlof Bay   Ilnik   Seal Is.   Strogonof Point   Pilot Point   Katmai   Mt. Douglas   English Bay
Sanak I. Sanak   Mt. Dana 1310   Port Moller   Becharof   Mt. Peulik 1500   C. Douglas   Pt. Adam   Seldovia
Fawn Pt.   Unga I.   Veniaminof Volcano 2507   Port Heiden   Becharof Lake   Mt. Katmai 2047   2153   Portlock
Dolgoi I.   Unga   Black Lake   Aniakchak   Ugashik Lakes   N.W.R.   Kenai
Pavlof Is.   Stepovak Bay   Aniakchak   Nat. Mon.   Dog Salmon R.   Kanatak   Pt. Banks
54°   Caton I.   Sand Point   Korovin I.   and Preserve   Ranges   Chugach Is.
Sanak Islands   Popof I.   Perryville   Chignik   Aleutian   Mt. Chiginagak 2143   Katmai N.W.R.   C. Nukshak   Augustine I.   Gore Pt.   Nuka Ba
Kupreanof Pt.   Chiach I.   C. Kumlik   C. Kekurnoi   C. Douglas   Tonki C.
Shumagin Islands   Mitrofania I.   Seal I.   C. Providence   C. Ilktugiak   690   Marmot C.
Nagai I.   Big Koniuji I.   Nakchamik I.   Sutvik I.   Wide Bay   Afognak I.
Chernabura I.   Little Koniuji I.   Castle C.   Foggy Cape   Alaska Marine Highway   Shelikof Strait   Raspberry I.   Black I.   Port William   Alaska Marine Highway
19°   Simeonof I.   Semidi Is.   Cape Ikolik   Karluk   Uganik I.   Port Vita   Shuyak I.   Gulf
Chowiet I.   Kodiak Island   Larsen Bay   Kodiak   Afognak Mtn.
Low Cape   National   Fort Abercrombie State Historic Park   Spruce I.   Marmot Bay   Gulf o
Akhiok   Wildlife Refuge   Port Loins   ADU   Kodiak   Alaska Marine Highway
Tugidak I.   C. Alitak   Old Harbor   Chiniak Bay
Alaktalik I.   Sitkinak Strait   Pasagshak S.R.S.   C. Chiniak   Alask

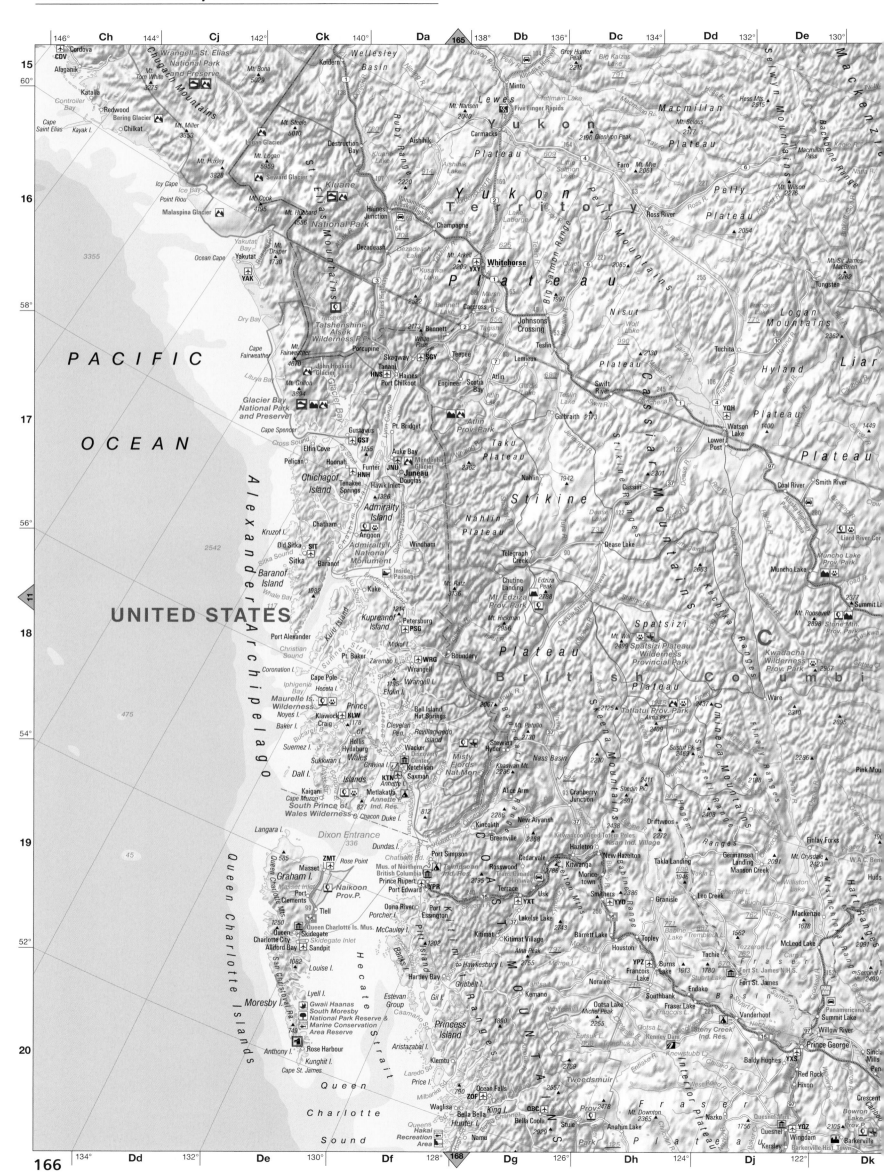

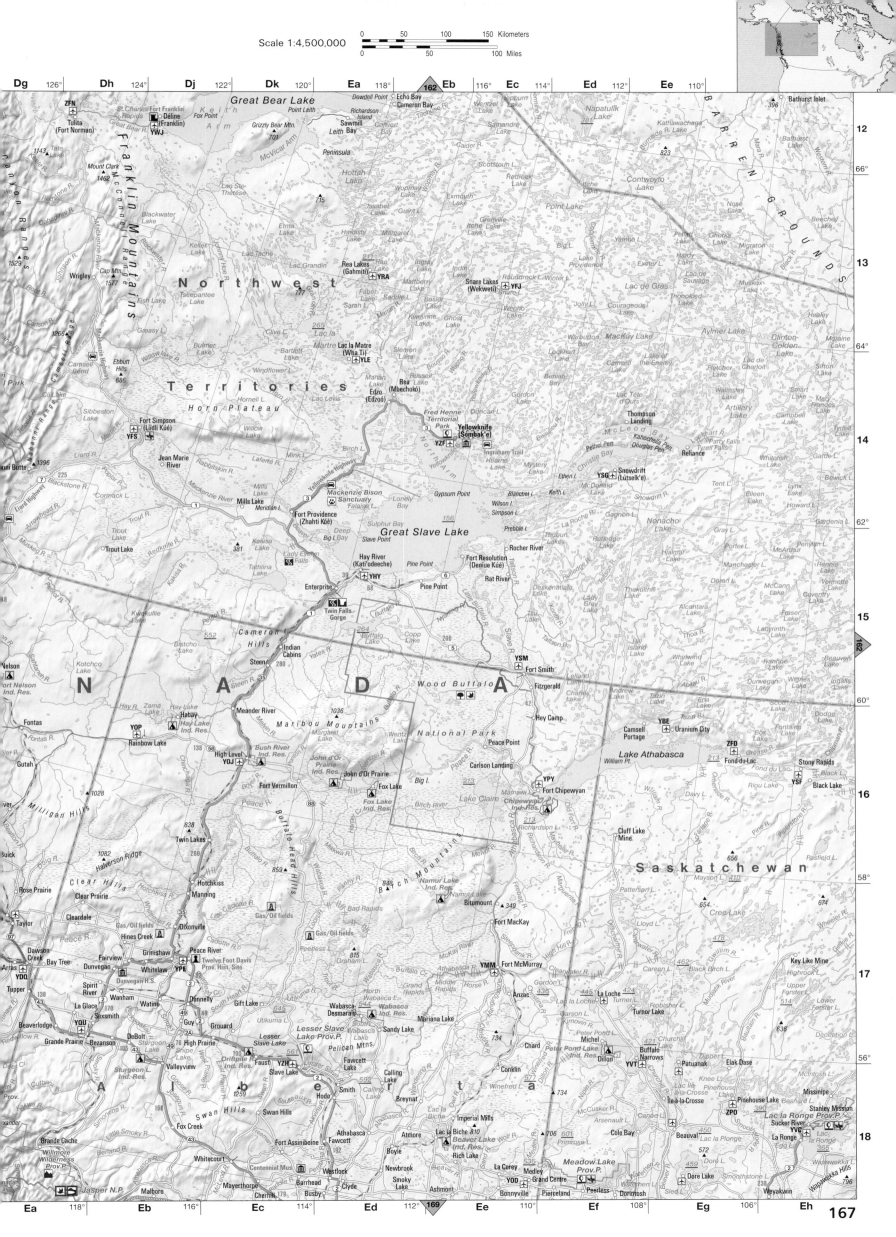

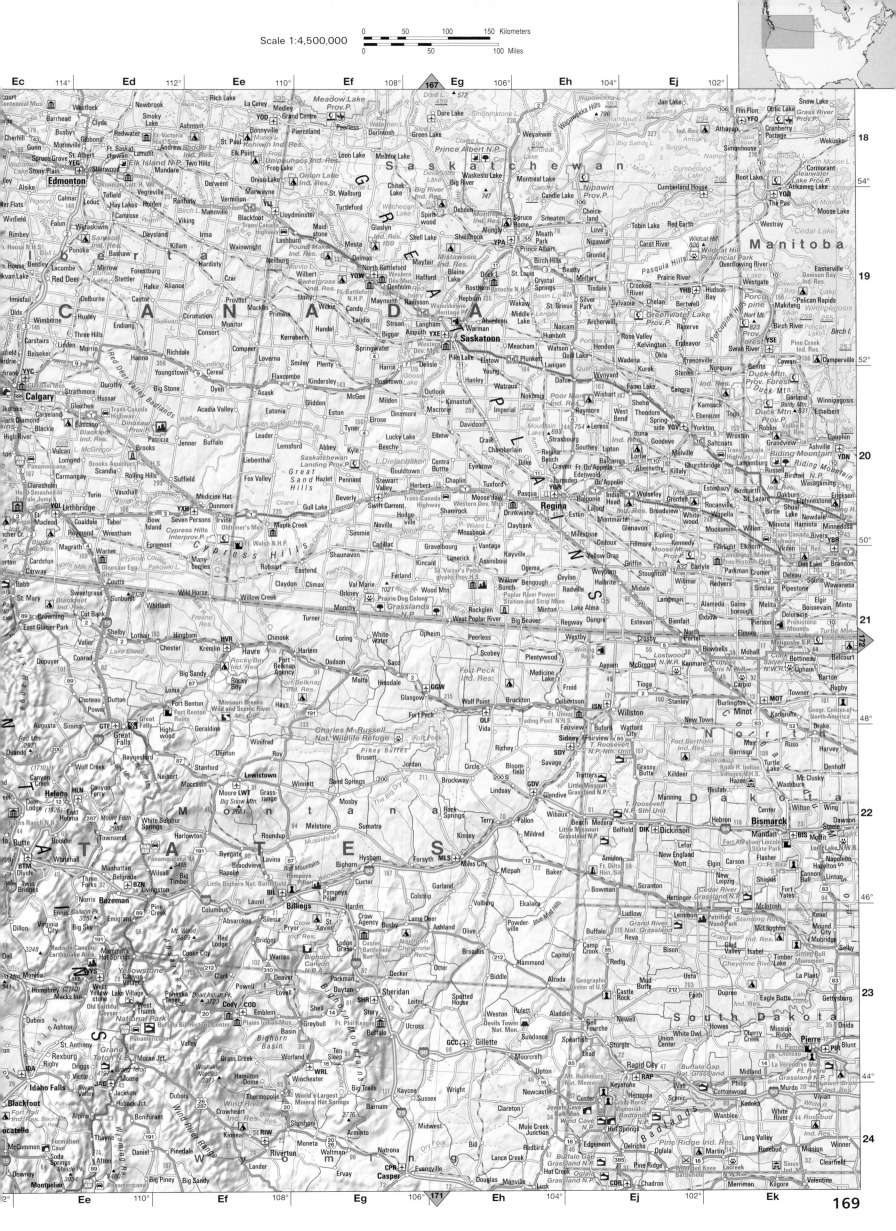

Southwestern USA, Hawaiian Islands

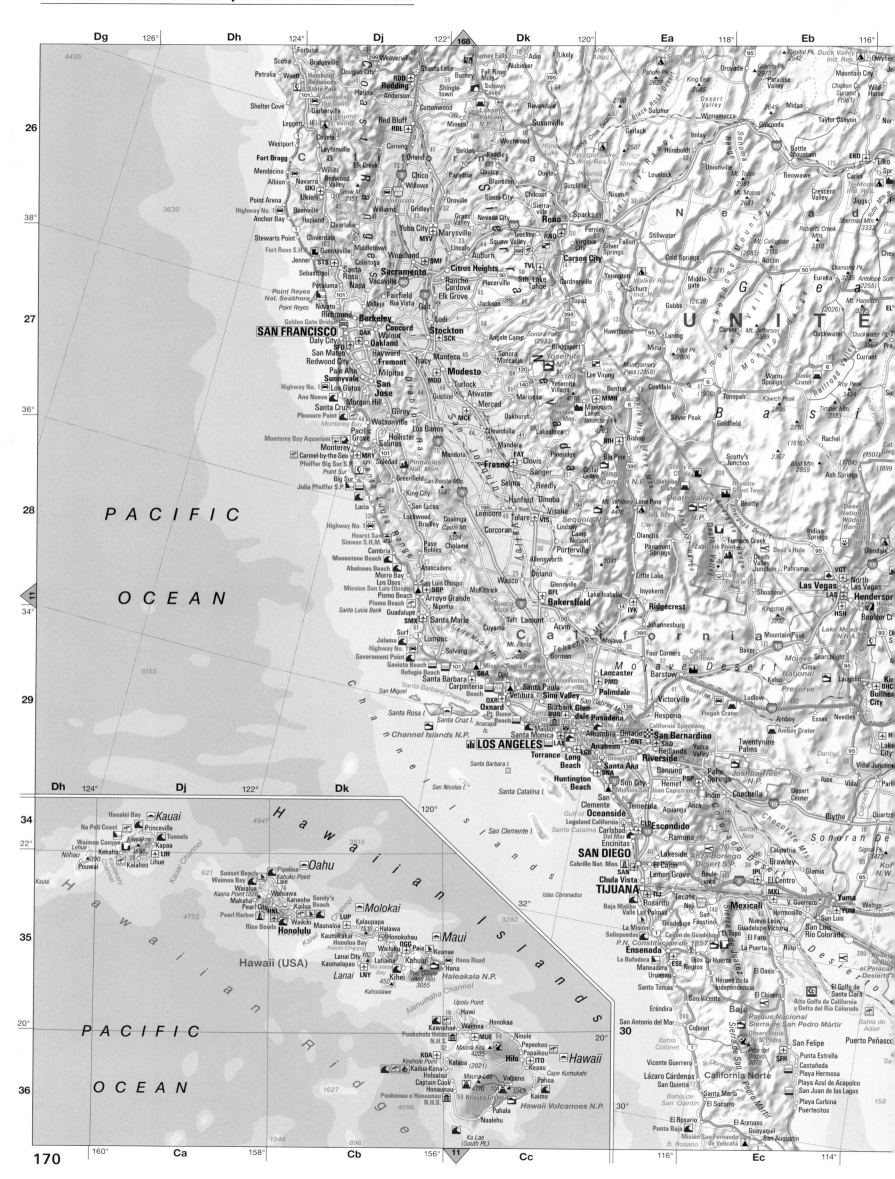

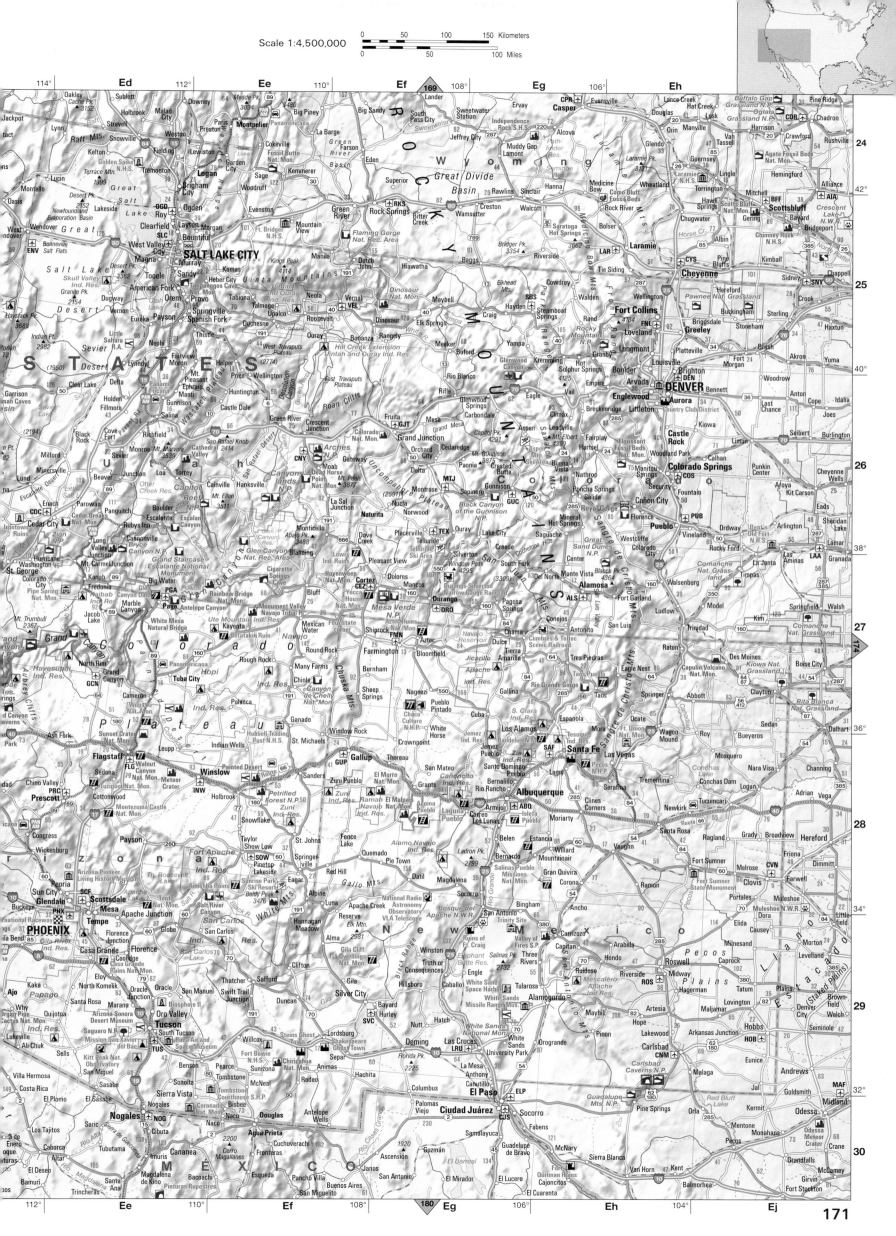

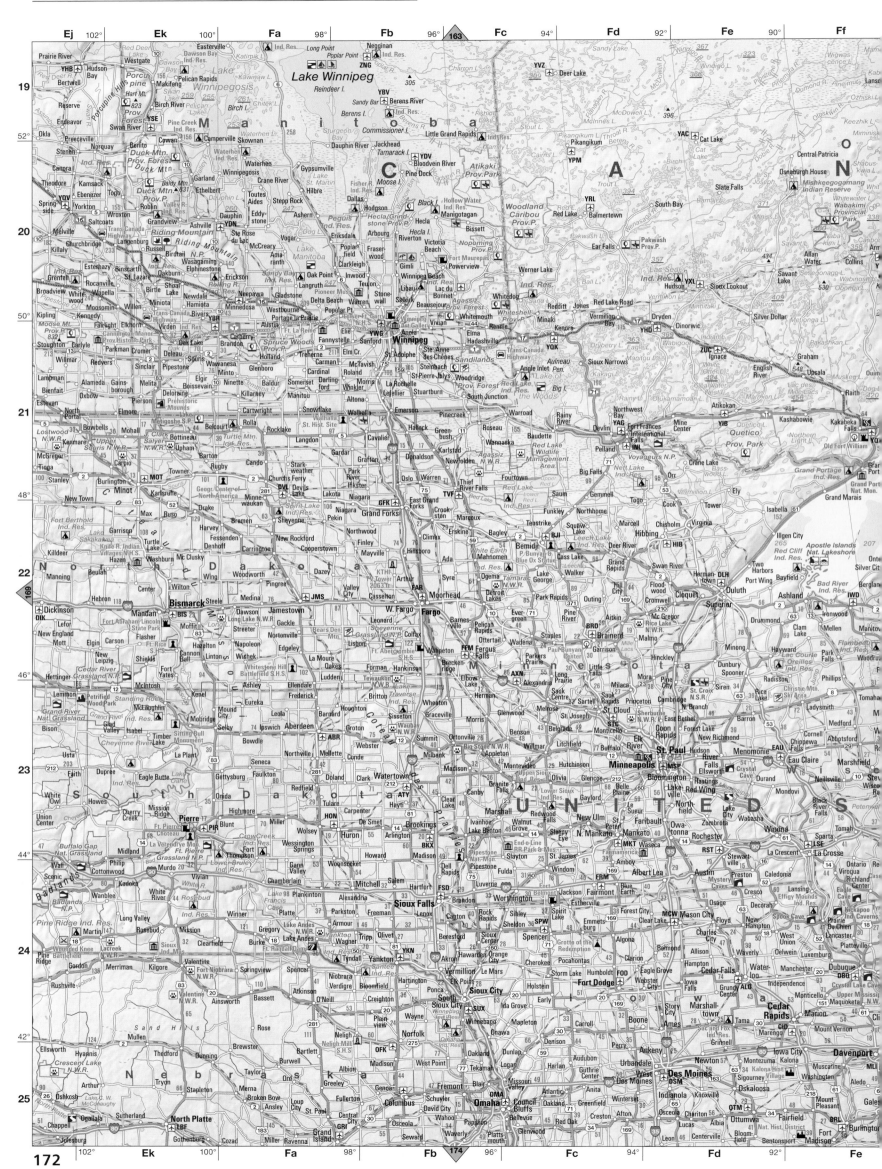

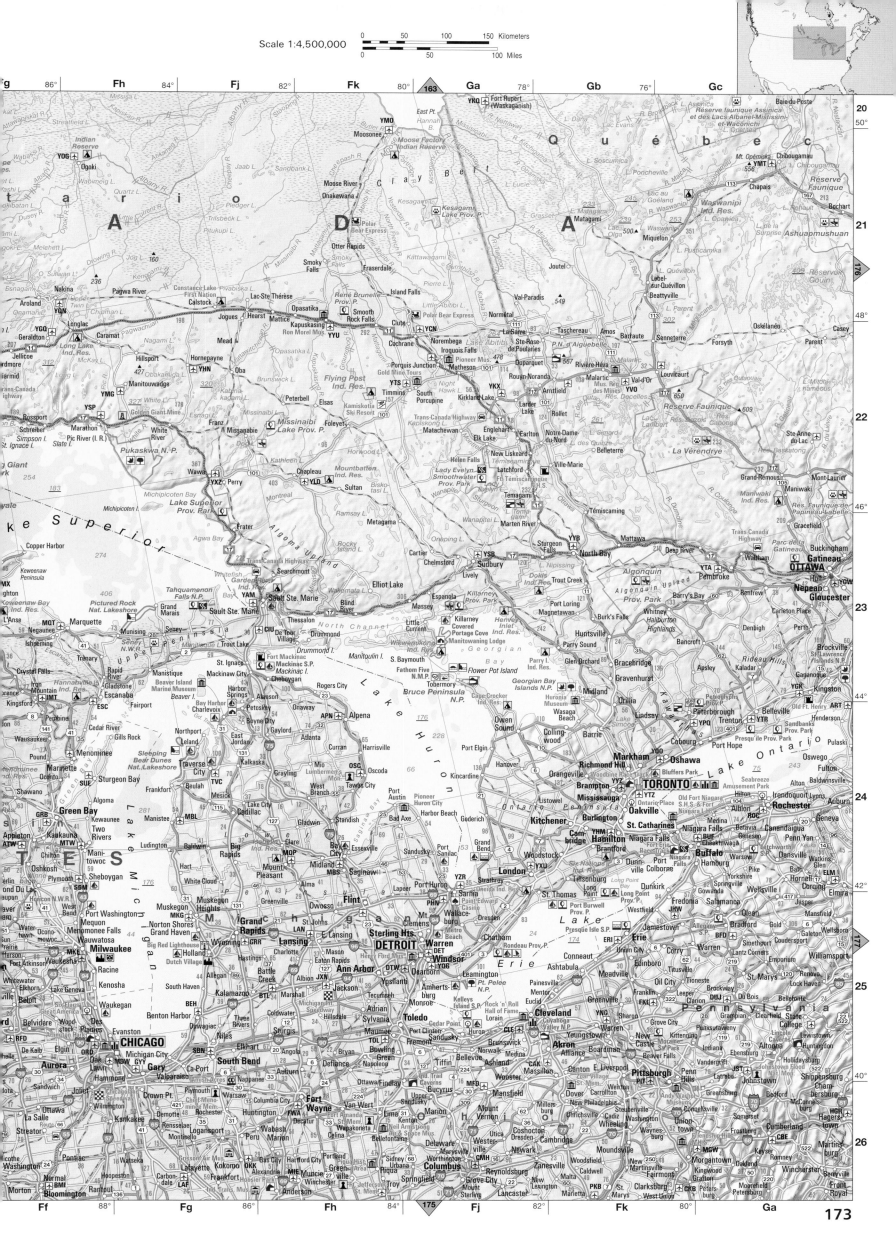

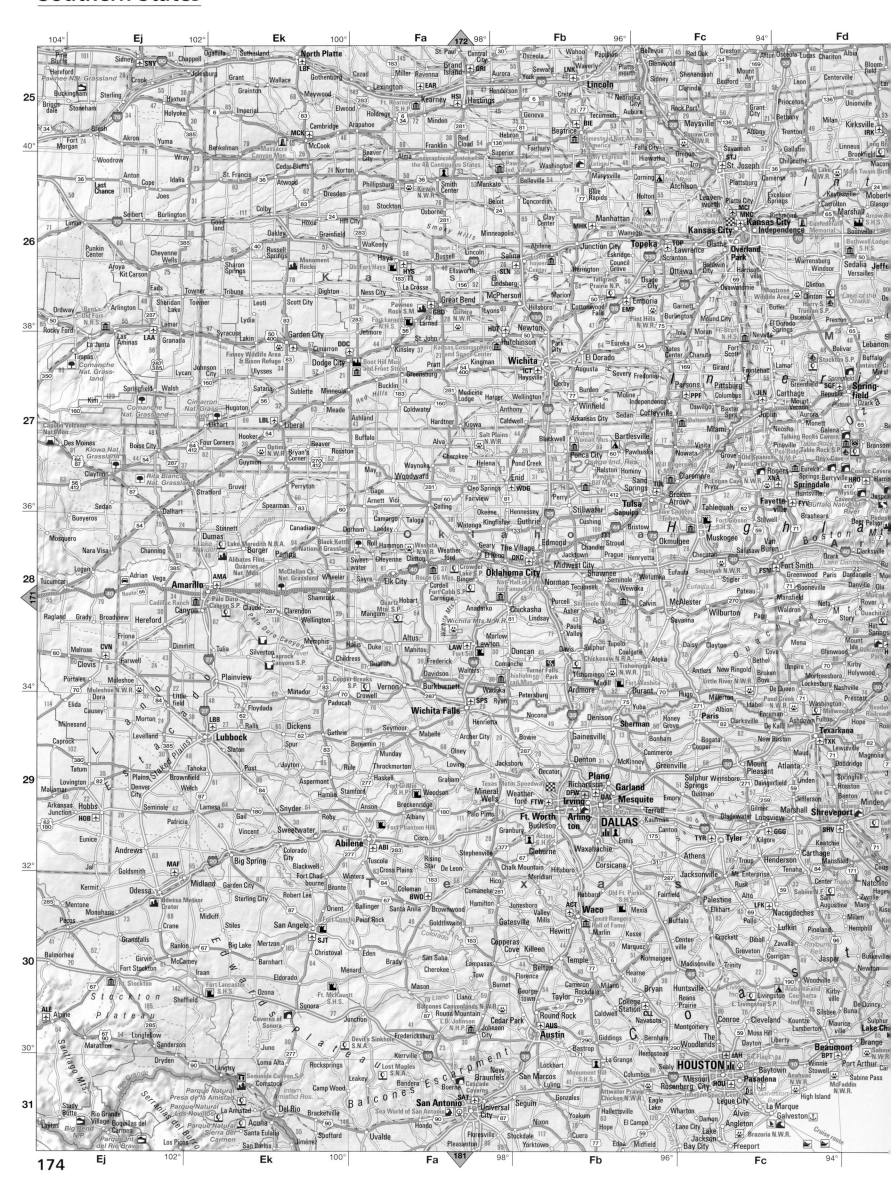

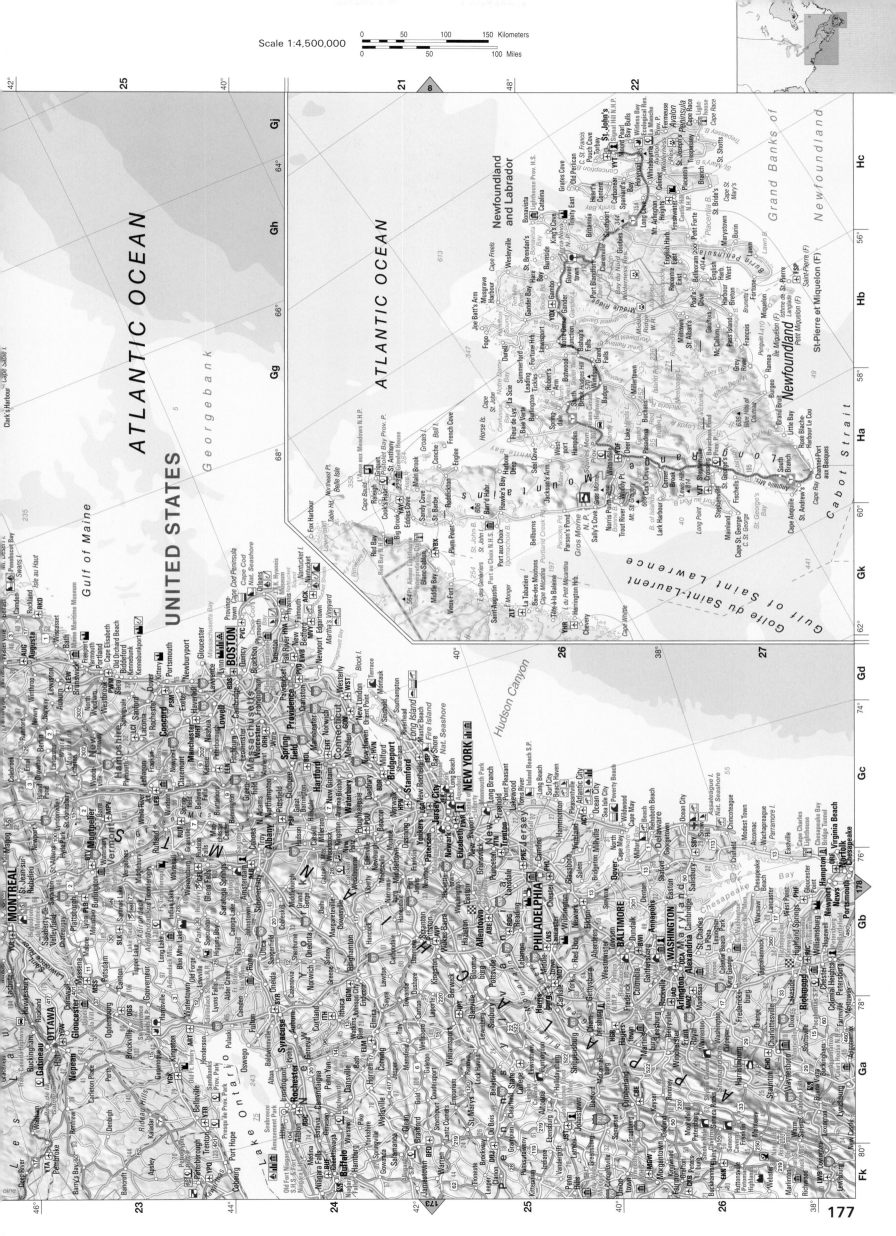

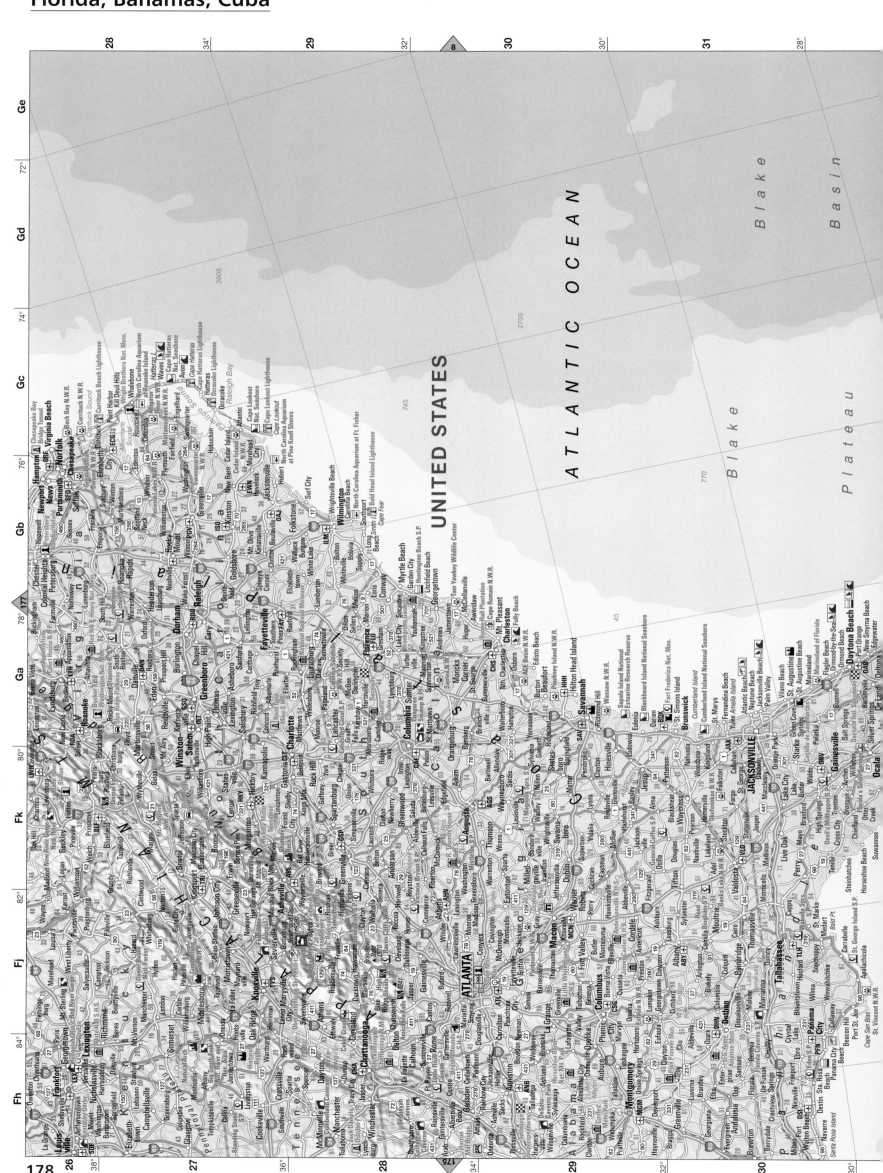

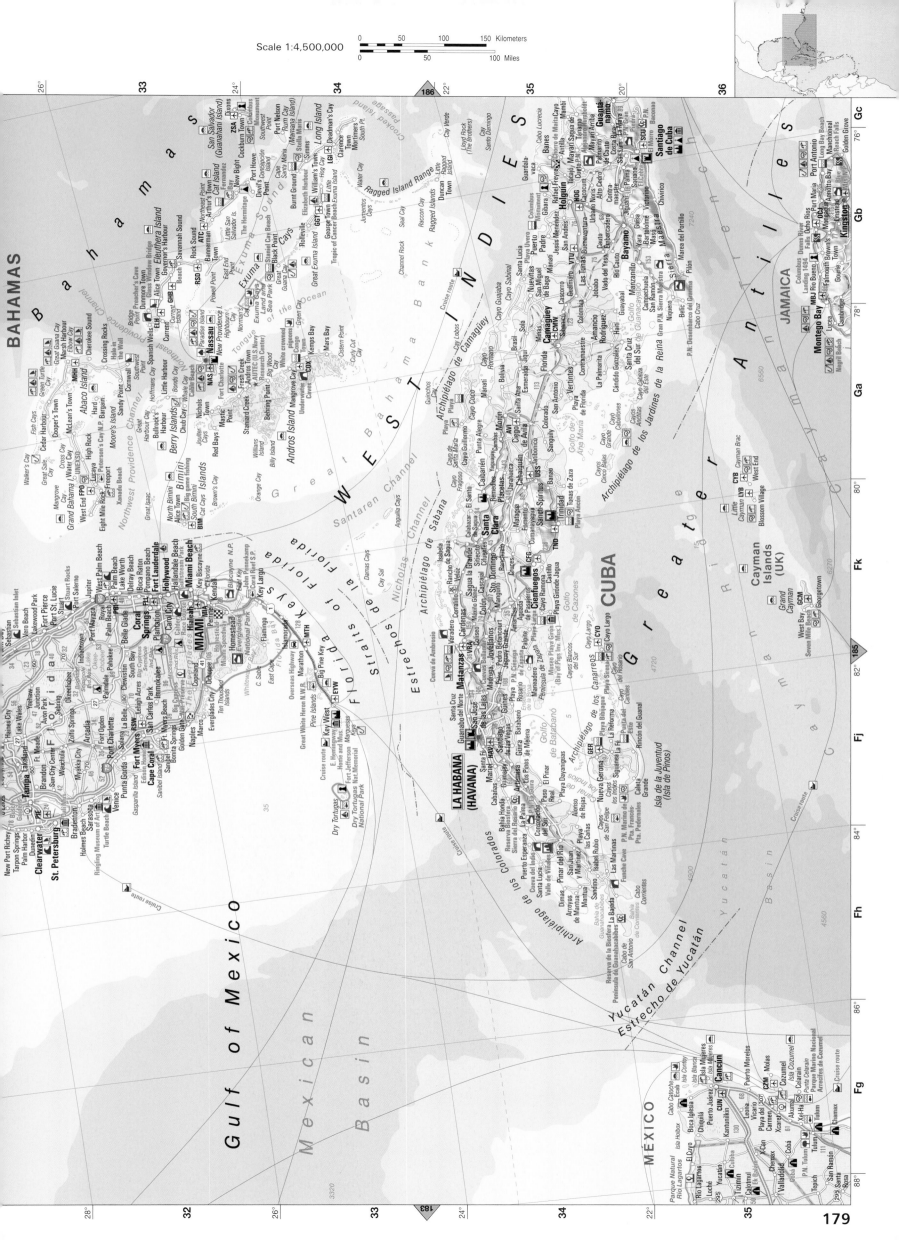

Northern Mexico

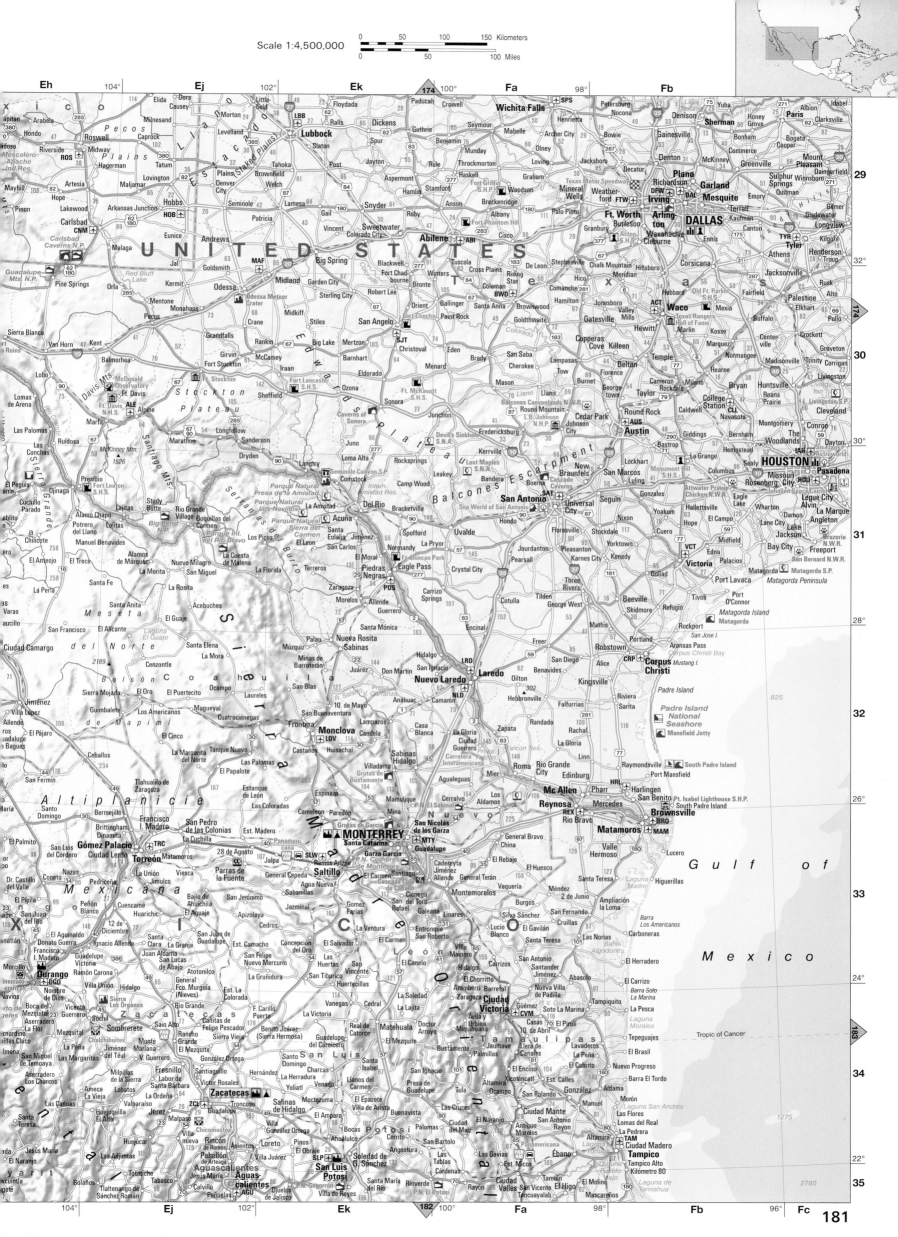

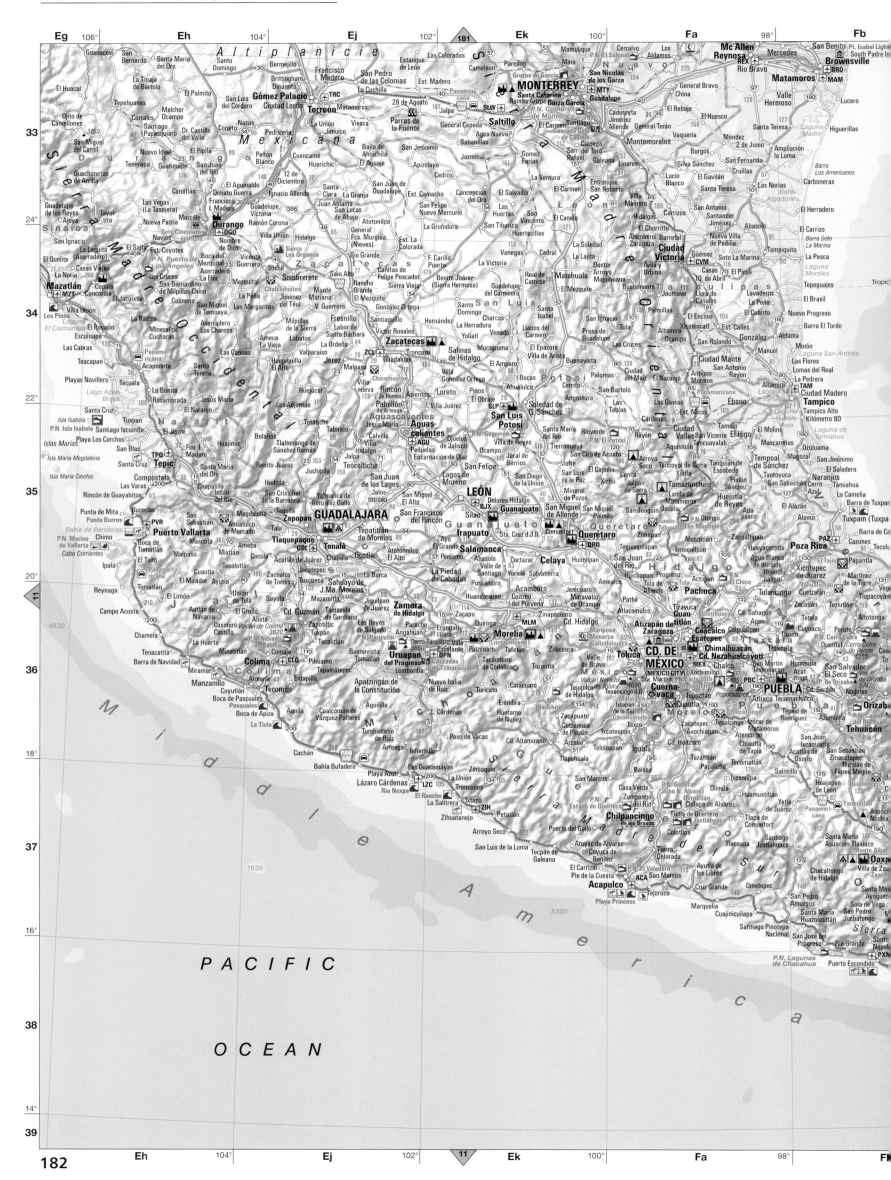

Central America

MÉXICO

Isla Arena
La Costa
Chunchucmil
Oxkintoc
Maxcanú
Halachó
Calkiní
Hecelchakán
Jaina

Sotuta
Mayapan
Chichén Itzá
Cobá
Akumal
Isla Cozumel
Celarain
Punta Celarain
Parque Marino Nacional
Arrecifes de Cozumel

Muna
Ticul
Grutas de Loltún
Labna
Tekax
Tihosuco
Tepich
Tulum
P.N. Tulum
Tulum
Xel-Ha

Yaxcabá
Chikindzonot

Yucatán

Chamax
Vigía
Chico
Punta Allen

Bolonchén de Rejón
Tenabó
Hecelchakán

Tzucacab
Peto
Chumil
Presumida
Sabana
Rosa
San Ramón
San Francisco
Polyuc
Felipe Carrillo
Puerto
Bahia de la Ascensión
Reserva de
Punta Pájaros
la Biosfera
Sian Ka'an
Punta Herrero

Campeche
Lerma
Baluarte de Santiago
CPE
Tiquimul
Hopel
Edzná chén
Pich
Xochob
Río Verde
Champotón
Villa Madero
Villa de Guadelupe
Hool
Pustunich
Santa Maria
Sabancuy
Pixoyal
Carrillo Puerto
Santa
Maria
79
Yohaltún

Quintana
Roo

Gulf of
Campeche

Península

Campeche

Reserva de
la Biosfera
Pantanos de Centa
Laguna
de Términos
Isla de
Aguada
Puerto Real
CME
Chicbul
Francisco
Escárcega
Kilometro 59
Candelaria
Constitución
Balamkú
Calakmul
Xpujil
Morocoy
Corozal
Chicanná
Xpujil
Río Bec
Tomás
Garrido
Kohunlich

BELIZE

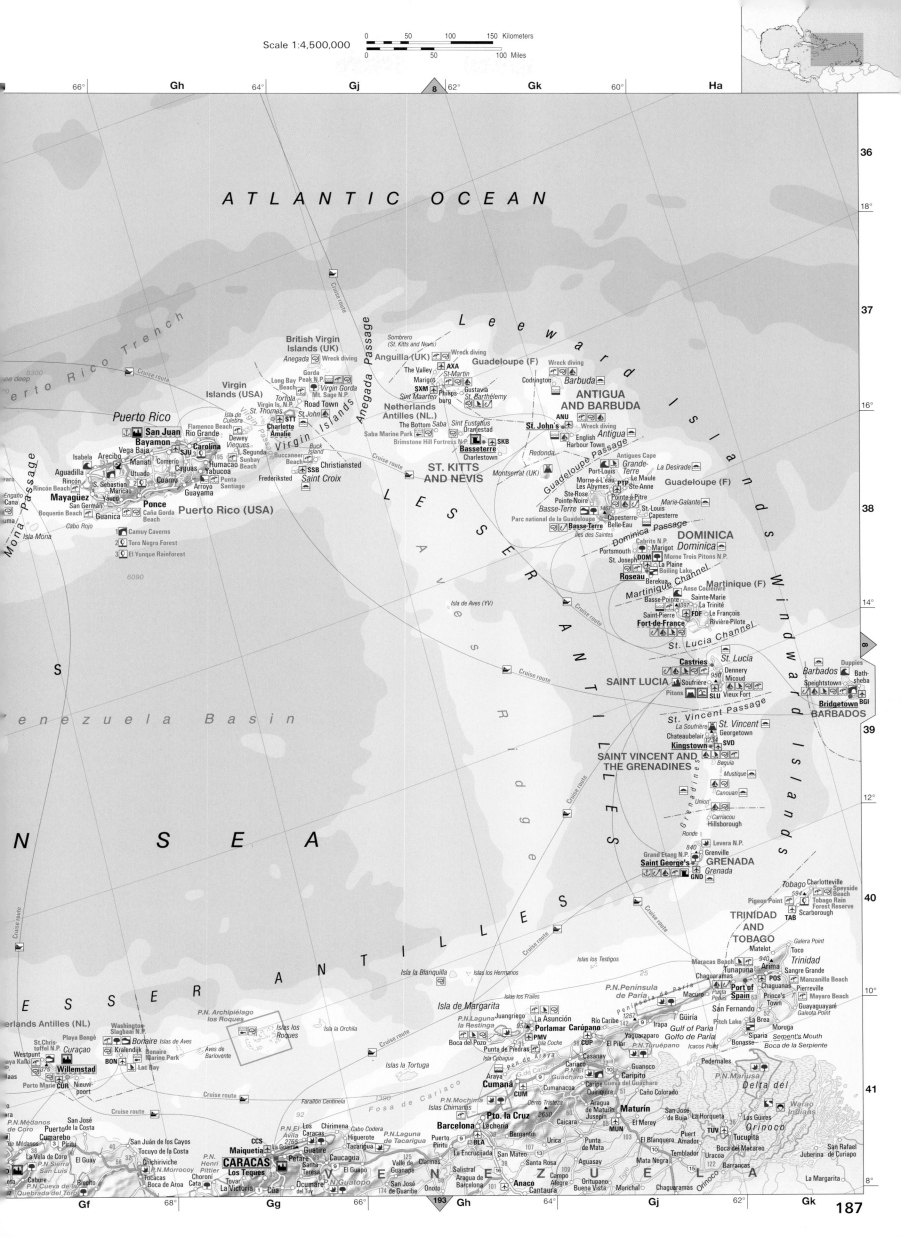

A rainbow spans the cascading Iguaçu falls amid the primeval forest.

Brazil's metropolis Rio de Janeiro: Co-
pacabana and Sugarloaf Mountain.

SOUTH AMERICA

MAGNIFICENT PASSIONS, STUNNING LANDSCAPES

Compared to the other continents South America is a relatively compact landmass. It has smooth coastlines and a consistently flat relief – outside of the Andes. The southern continent of the western hemisphere is 7,500 kilometers long from north to south and the greatest distance from east to west measures 4,800 kilometers. The continent borders Central (and North) America at the Isthmus of Panama.

The Andes, the world's second highest mountain range after the Himalayas, rise to the east of the continent's Pacific coast. Aconcagua in Argentina is the highest mountain in the Western Hemisphere. Other significant mountain ranges in South America include the Pakaraima Mountains in the north and the Serra do Mar in Brazil. Between these two mountainous regions lies the vast basin of the Amazon River. With a length of 6,400 kilometers, the Amazon is the second longest river in the world after the Nile. The marshy land of the Gran Chaco is located north of the fertile Pampas and the sparsely populated region of Patagonia. The flat basin of the Orinoco River (2,140 km) occupies a large area in northern South America.

There are twelve independent nations in South America as well as French Guiana, a territory of France. South America is home to 304 million people, more than half of whom live in Brazil. Centuries of contact between Europeans, Amerindians and Africans has made the population of South America the most ethnically and racially mixed in the world. No other continent is as religiously homogeneous as South America. Almost 90 % of the continent's people are Roman Catholics. Migration from rural areas to cities continues to expand the population of cities in the region. In recent decades, the continent's cities have grown explosively. Most of South America's large cities are surrounded by large distirct of slums, home to the poorest members of society.

The Quechua live in the South American Andes.

South America

Fa 90° Fb 80° Ga 70° Gb 60° 160 Ha 50° Hb 40° Ja 30° Jb 20°

Coastal Plain
NEW ORLEANS
HOUSTON
Mississippi Delta
Cape Canaveral
5223
S a r g a s s o S e a
N o r t h
A m e r i c a n B a s i n
Mi d

07
Gulf of
Mexico
MIAMI
Bahamas
Nassau
Nares Abyssal Plain
7107

HAVANA
Cuba
Tropic of Cancer
A T L A N T I C

3265
MÉRIDA
Yucatán Peninsula
Greater Antilles
West Indies
Puerto Rico Trench
Cayman Isands

20
Isthmus of Tehuantepec
Cayman Trench
SANTO DOMINGO
Jamaica
Hispaniola
PUERTO RICO
Leeward Islands
Venezuela Basin
Barbados
G u i a n a B a s i n
Cape Verde Basin
6246
Cape Verde Islands

08
CIUDAD DE GUATEMALA
6663
TEGUCIGALPA
Caribbean Sea
Colombia Basin
Lesser Antilles
Windward
Trinidad
2177
O C E A N

MANAGUA
Lago de Nicaragua
4032
P.Cólon
5775
MARACAIBO
CARACAS
Ciudad Guayana

Middle America Trench
Guatemala Basin
Panamá
MEDELLÍN
Llanos del Orinoco
C.Yavi 2441
Georgetown
Mt.Roraima 2810
Paramaribo
Cayenne
Demeraraplateau

09
Cocos Ridge
Nev.del Ruiz 5325
BOGOTÁ
5120
Nev.del Huila 5750
Guiana Highlands
Boa Vista
Orinoco
Rio Negro
Macapá
I.de Marajó
Ceara Abyssal Plain

Cocos Island
QUITO
Vol.Cotopaxi 5897
Pico da Neblina 3014
Amazon Lowlands
MANAUS
BELÉM
São Luís
4527
FORTALEZA
Equator

0
Archipiélago de Colón/Galápagos-Islands
Chimborazo 6310
GUAYAQUIL
Maynas
Iquitos
Amazon
Madeira
Tapajós
Amazon
Xingu
Teresina
Atol das Rocas
Ilha Fernando de Noronha

I.Isabela
Pta.Negra
S E L V A
Cabo de São Roque
Natal
RECIFE
Pernambuco Abyssal Plain

10
3711
TRUJILLO 6768
Señal Huascarán
Porto Velho
Rio Branco
La Montaña
Araguaia
Tocantins
Caatinga
São Francisco
Aracaju
5294

Peru Basin
LIMA
Cuzco
Llanos de Mojos
Campos Cerrados
Sertão
SALVADOR
B r a z i l

10
3444
Peru-Chile Trench
Lake Titicaca
Yungas
Arequipa
Planalto do Mato Grosso
PLANALTO
Ilhéus
Campos
B a s i n

11
Nev.Sajama 6520
LA PAZ
Altiplano
Cuiabá
GOIÂNIA
BRASÍLIA
Brazilian
2033

11
Nazca Ridge
Chile Basin
7523
Sucre
SANTA CRUZ DE LA SIERRA
Pantanal
CENTRAL
Highlands
BELO HORIZONTE 2890
Vitória
Pico da Bandeira 2797
Ilhas Martim Vaz (BR)

PACIFIC
A T A C A M A
A N D E S
Gran Chaco
Campo Grande
Paraguay
20
Vitória Seamount

20
483
Antofagasta
San Miguel de Tucumán 6887
Nev.Ojos del Salado
Asunción
Paraná
Londrina
Serra do Mar
SÃO PAULO
RIO DE JANEIRO
Tropic of Capricorn

Sala-y-Gomez Fracture Zone
497
Corrientes
Entre Ríos
Uruguay
CURITIBA
1808

12
Islas de los Desventurados
La Serena
Aconcagua 6963
Serras de Córdoba
CÓRDOBA
ROSARIO
Pampa
PORTO ALEGRE

Roggeveen Basin
Islas Juan-Fernández
SANTIAGO
Mendoza
MONTEVIDEO
660
Rio Grande Plateau

30
Concepción
Vol.Domuyo 4709
Río de la Plata
BUENOS AIRES
4413
A T L A N T I C

OCEAN
Vol.Lanín 3747
Rio Negro
Mar del Plata
Bahía Blanca

13
Puerto Montt
Chiloé
Chonos Archipelago
Patagonia
Península Valdés
4400
A r g e n t i n e B a s i n
5585
Tristan da Cunha

Chile Rise
San Valentín 4058
Comodoro Rivadavia

40
Mornington Abyssal Plain
4295
Punta Arenas
Strait of Magellan
Tierra del Fuego
Falkland Islands
120
Falkland Plateau
6245
OCEAN

East Pacific Rise
Chile Trench
Cape Horn
Drake Passage
S c o t i a S e a
Scotia Ridge
5100
South Georgia

50
5160
South Shetland Islands
Scotia Sea
South Sandwich Islands
South Orkney Islands

15
South East Pacific Basin
2920
Antarctic Peninsula
Larsen Ice Shelf
Mt.Jackson 4190
Bellingshausen Sea
W e d d e l l S e a
Antarctic Circle

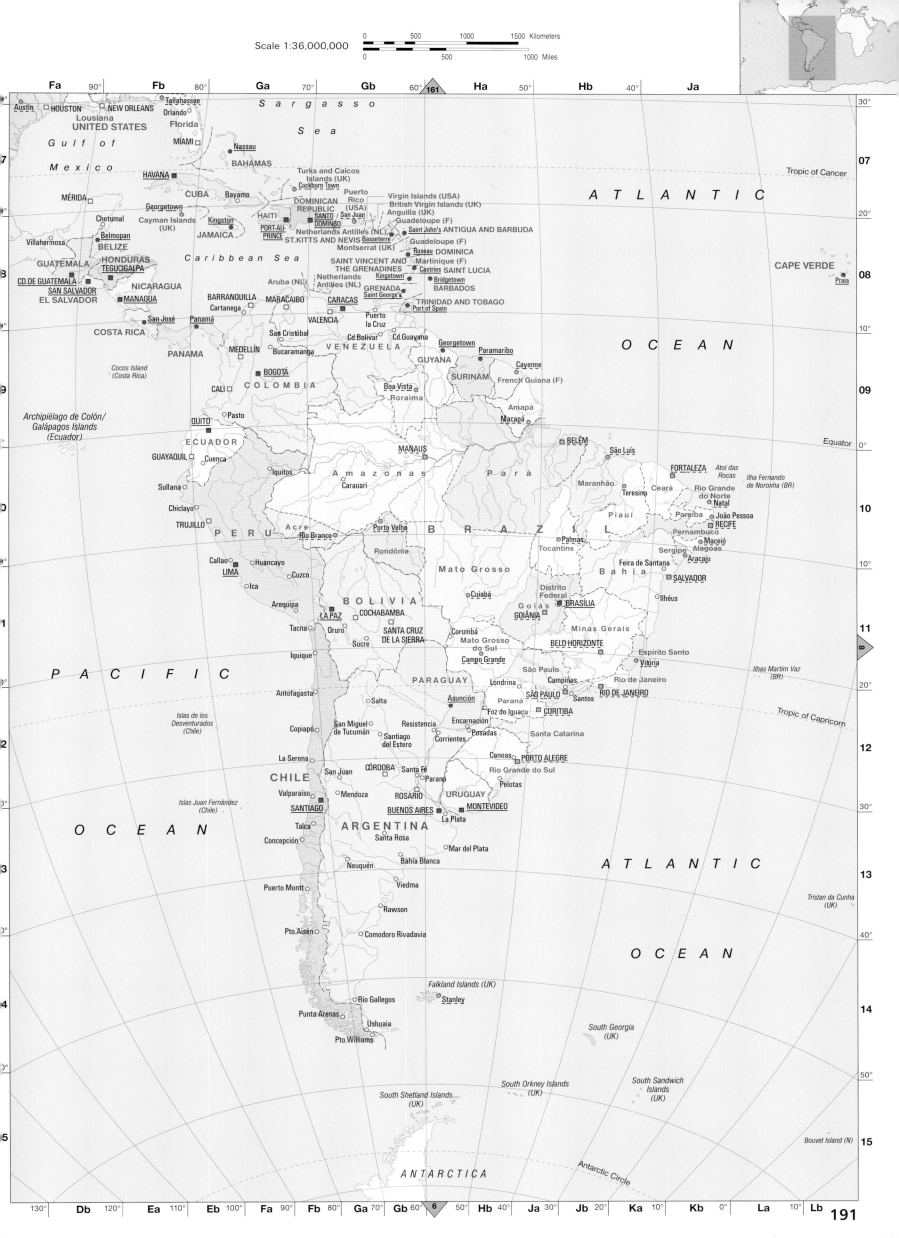

Colombia, Venezuela

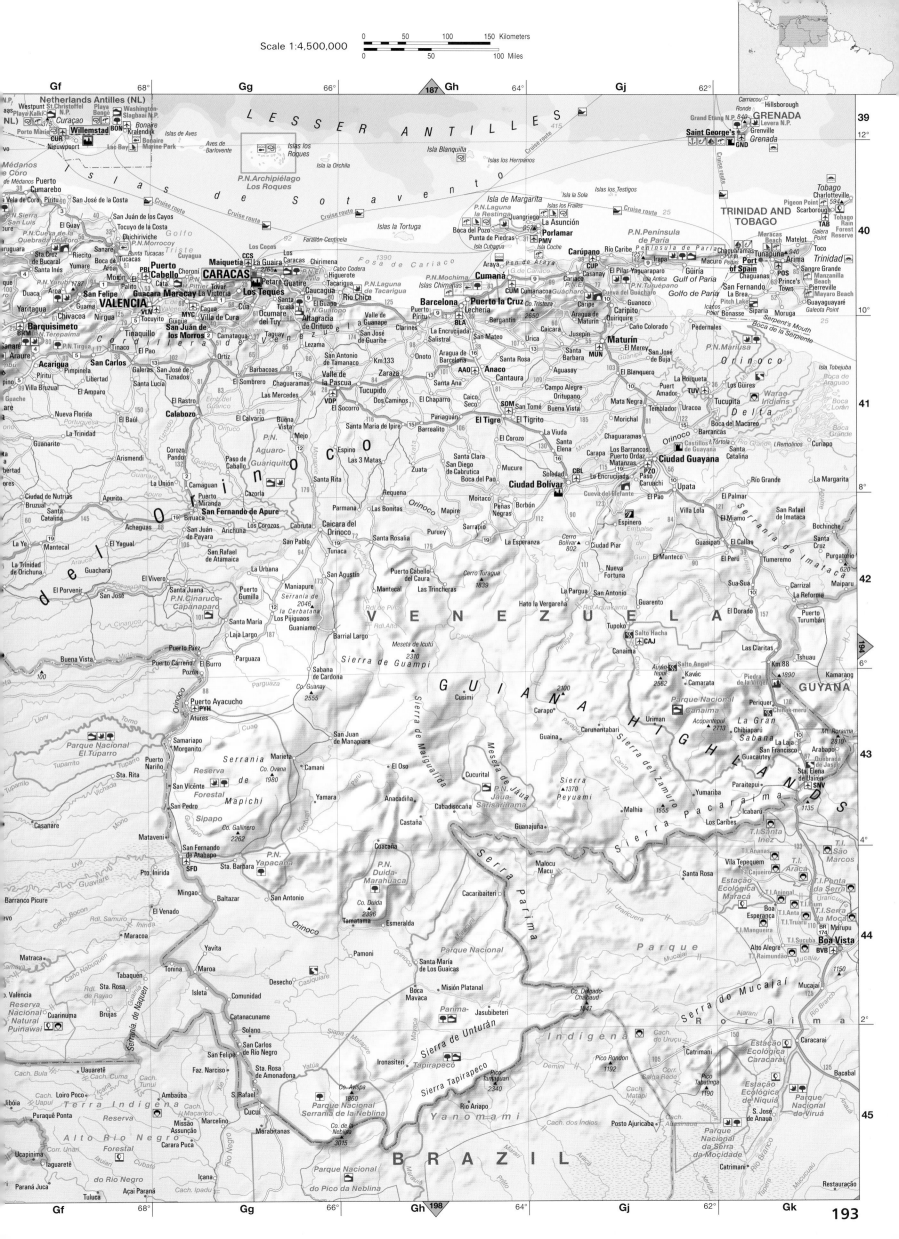

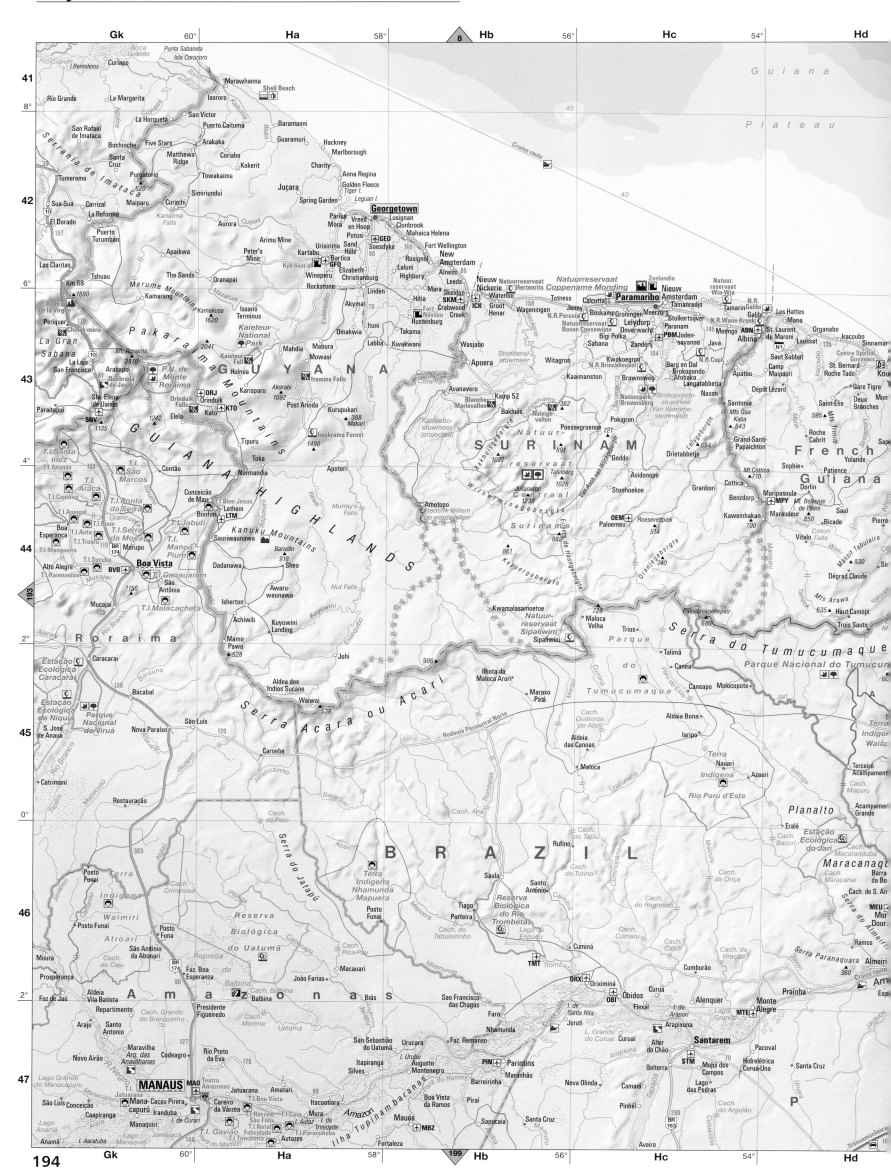

Guyana, Surinam, Mouths of the Amazon

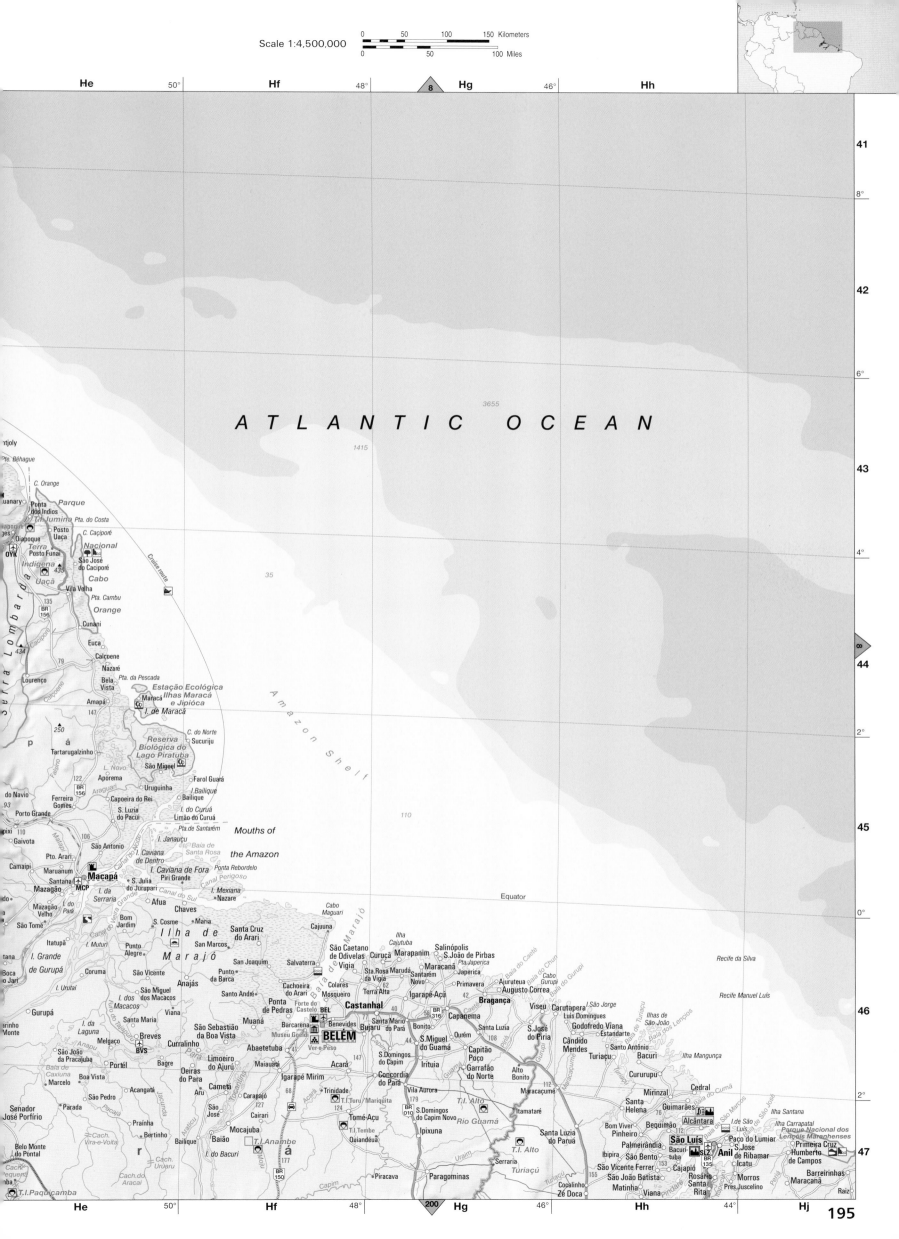

Amazon Lowlands

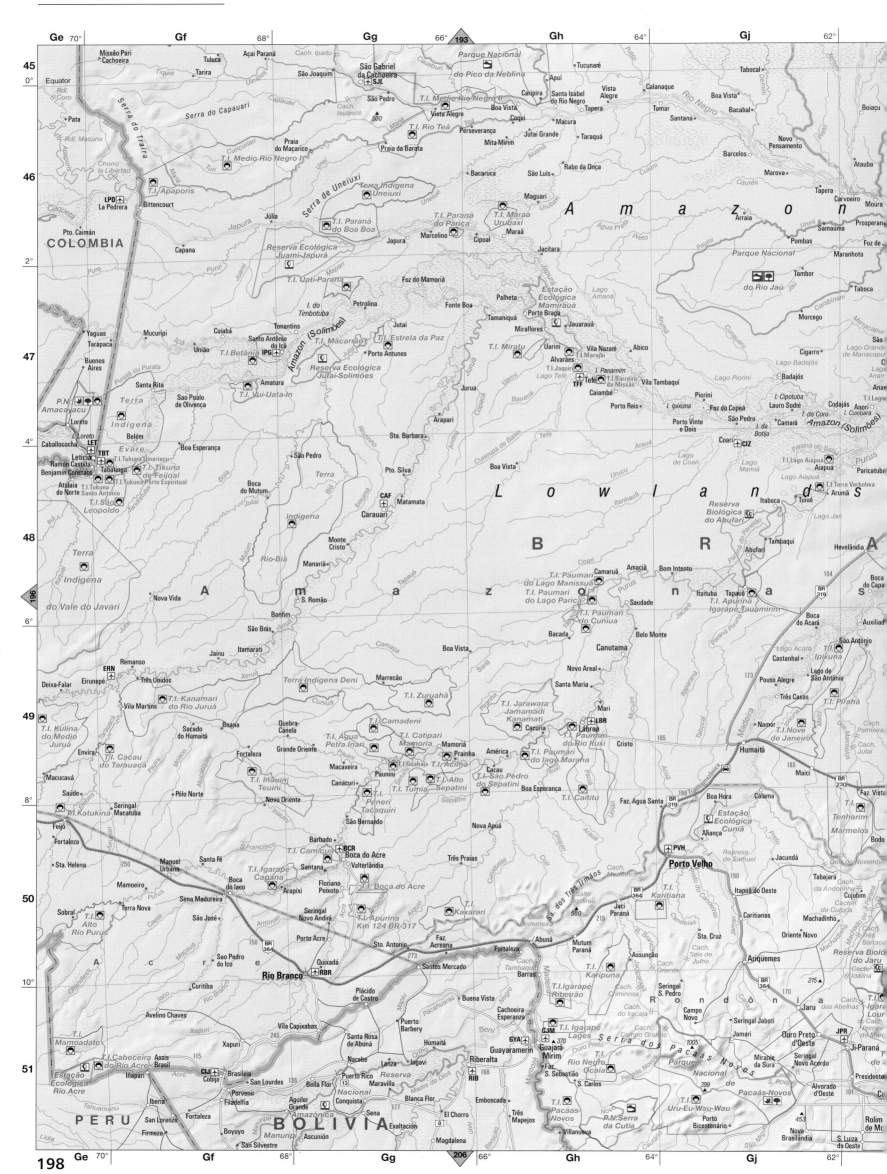

Scale 1:4,500,000

0 50 100 150 Kilometers
0 50 100 Miles

60° **Ha** 58° **Hb** ▼194 56° **Hc** 54° **Hd**

Planalto
45
Acampamento Grande
0°
Eralé
Taperaba
Estação Ecológica do Jari
Maracanaquará
Pançudo
Rufino
Santa Clara
Cach. do Tapiú
Maçaranduba
Cach. Bacuri
Santo Antônio
Cach. do Torino
366
Saula
Barraca da Boca
de S. Antônio
MEU Monte Dourado
Beiradão
46
Terra Indígena Nhamundá Mapuera
Tiago
Porteira
Cach. do Regresso
Cach. da Onça
Pagas Divisas
Santana
Reserva Biológica do Rio Trombetas
Cumaru
Cach. Cajuti
Ramos
Boca do Jari

Cach. do Pato
Baracuxi
Cach. Ana
Cach. do Tapiú
Cach. Cumaru
Serra do Almeirim
Posto Funai
Acari
Pitinga
Cuminá
Cach. da Viração
Serra Paranaquara
Reserva Biológica do Uatumã
Macauari
Cach. Pica-Pau
TMT Trombetas
Cumburão
Almeirim
Cruise route
I. Urucuri
Gurupá
Cach. Grande do Branquinho
João Farias
Brás
São Francisco das Chagas
ORX Oriximiná
Curuá
Prainha
PTQ Vilarinho do Monte
Amazon
Esperança
Porto do Moz
BR 174
Faz. Boa Esperança
Cach. Balbina
Cach. Morena
Balbina
Faro
Flexal
OBI Óbidos
Alenquer
Monte Alegre
MTE
2°
Presidente Figueiredo
Nhamundá
Juruti
I. do Arapari
Lago Grande
São Sebastião do Uatumã
Urucará
Faz. Remanso
L. Grande do Curuai
Curuaí
Arapixuna
Pacoval
Codegro
Rio Preto da Eva
I. Urubu
Belterra
STM Santarém
Hidrelétrica Curuá-Una
Senador José Porfírio
MANAUS MAO
Teatro Amazonas
PIN Parintins
Nova Olinda
Camará
Lago das Pedras
Aricaria
47
Cacau Pirera
Careiro da Várzea
T.I. Boa Vista
Itacoatiara
Boa Vista da Ramos
Piraí
Pinhél
Cach. do Argolão
Vitoria
Belo Monte do Pontal
Irunduba
T.I. Recreio
Mura
Barreirinha
Maranhão
ATM Altamira
Paquiçamba
Autazes
Maués
Sapucaia
Santa Cruz
Aveiro
BR 230 Transamazônica
T.I. Paquiçamba
Nova Olinda do Norte
Fortaleza
T.I. Juara
Repartimento
Rurópolis Pres. Médici
Caima
T.I. Arara
Careiro
Axinim
Osório da Fonseca
Andirá
Marau
Pedreiras
Cach. Grande do Iriri
T.I. Kararaô
4°
BR 319
Vila Sagrado Coração de Jesus
ITB Itaituba
BR 230
Cach. Inferno
T.I. Koatinemo
RBB Borba
Inaja
Parque Nacional de Amazônia
São Luís do Tapajós
Cach. Sem-Tripa
Cach. Soledade
T.I.
Sta. Maria
Campina
Buiucu
Pouso Grande
Praia
Jatobá
Aiaweté
48
Novo Aripuanã
Usina São Francisco
Porto Alegre
Cach. do Caí
Cach. Tacupare
Entre Rios
Igarapé Ipixuna
São João
Ariranha
Vila Meriti
Agapo Açu
Cach. Mutum
Cach. da Boca São Francisco
Bonfim
Z I
Miramar
Cach. Moura
Mamãe Ana
L I P a r á
200
Tucuriba
Corr. Onça
Terra Preta
150
JCR Jacareacanga
Morais de Almeida
Araras
6°
Tucumã
Paraíso
T.I. Sai-Cinza
Mundico Coelho
Cach. das Capivaras
Bomsucesso
São Felix do Xingu
SXX
Mutum
BR 230
Primero Salto
R.F. Mundurucânia
Barraca de A. Lopes
Barra de S. Manuel
Cach. Araras
Posto Cocraimore
Apuí
Vila Porto Franco
Bom Lugar
428
São Antonio
Terra Indígena Kayapó
49
Prainha Nova
Cach. Matamatá
Maloca do Gonçalo
Florestal
Sumaúma
Terra Preta
Visita
Serra do Cachimbo
Mundurucânia
Terra Indígena
50
Jacaretinga
Pereirinha
I. Marengo om Pavilhão
São João do Paraná
Baú-Mekragroti
Barracão do Barreto
433
640
T.I. Escondido
Apiacás
Paranaita
Alta Floresta
Guarantã do Norte
Faz. Primavera
10°
AIR Aripuanã
T.I. **M**
Loreto
Juruena
Usina Apiacás
AFL
Peixoto de Azevedo
MBK Matupá
Terra Indígena Capoto Jarina
Faz. Muraquitã
a t o G r o s s o
Nova Canaã do Norte
Terra Nova do Norte
S. José do Xingu
PBX
517
T.I. Japuíra
T.I. Apiaka Kayabi
Colíder
Porto Alegre do Norte
205
Castanheira
Itauba
Marcelândia
Parque Indígena do Xingu
JUA Juara
Itapiúna
Novo Paraná
430
JIA Juína
T.I. Rikbaktsa
Cláudia
T.I. Wawi
Porto dos Gaúchos
Sinop **OPS**
335
Parque do
Cach. Nove de Abril
Brasnorte
T.I. Marãiwatsede

60° **Ha** 58° **Hb** ▼202 56° **Hc** 54° **Hd** 52° **He**

199

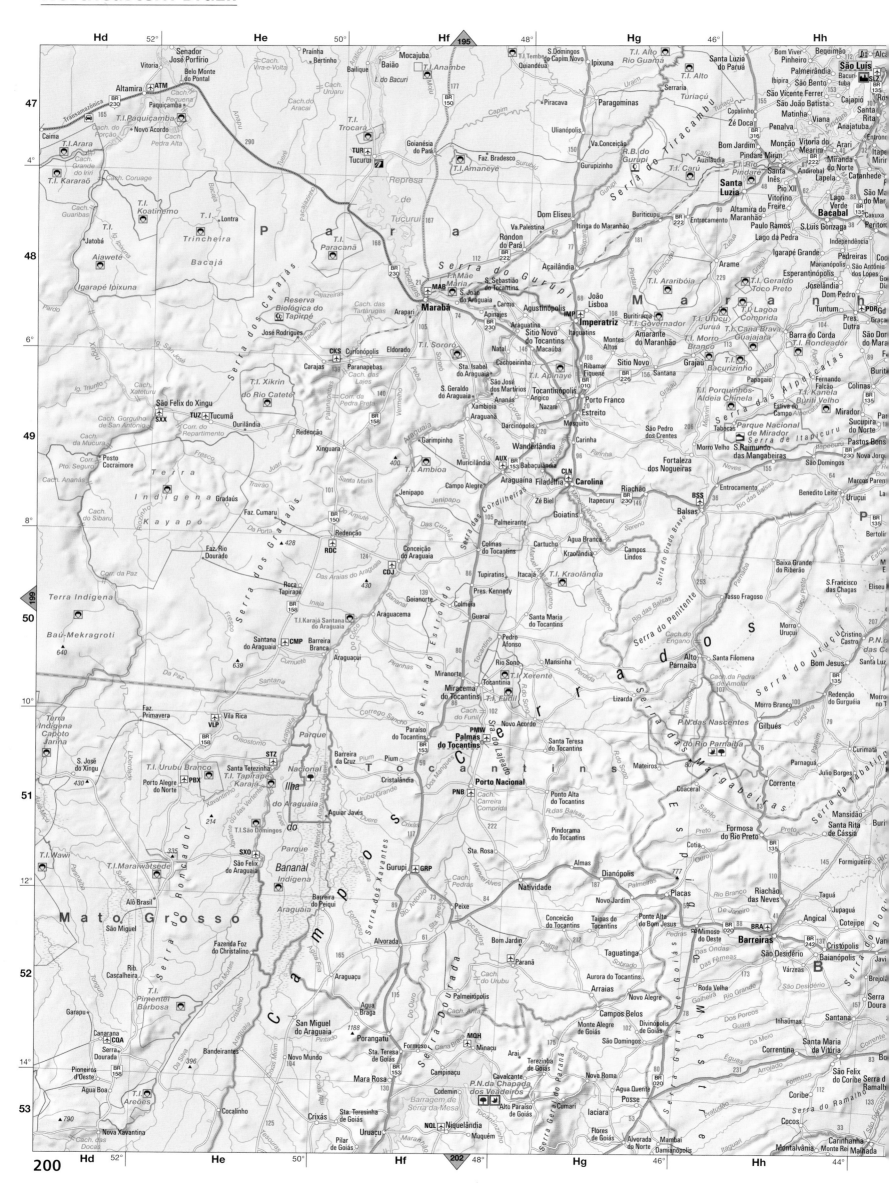

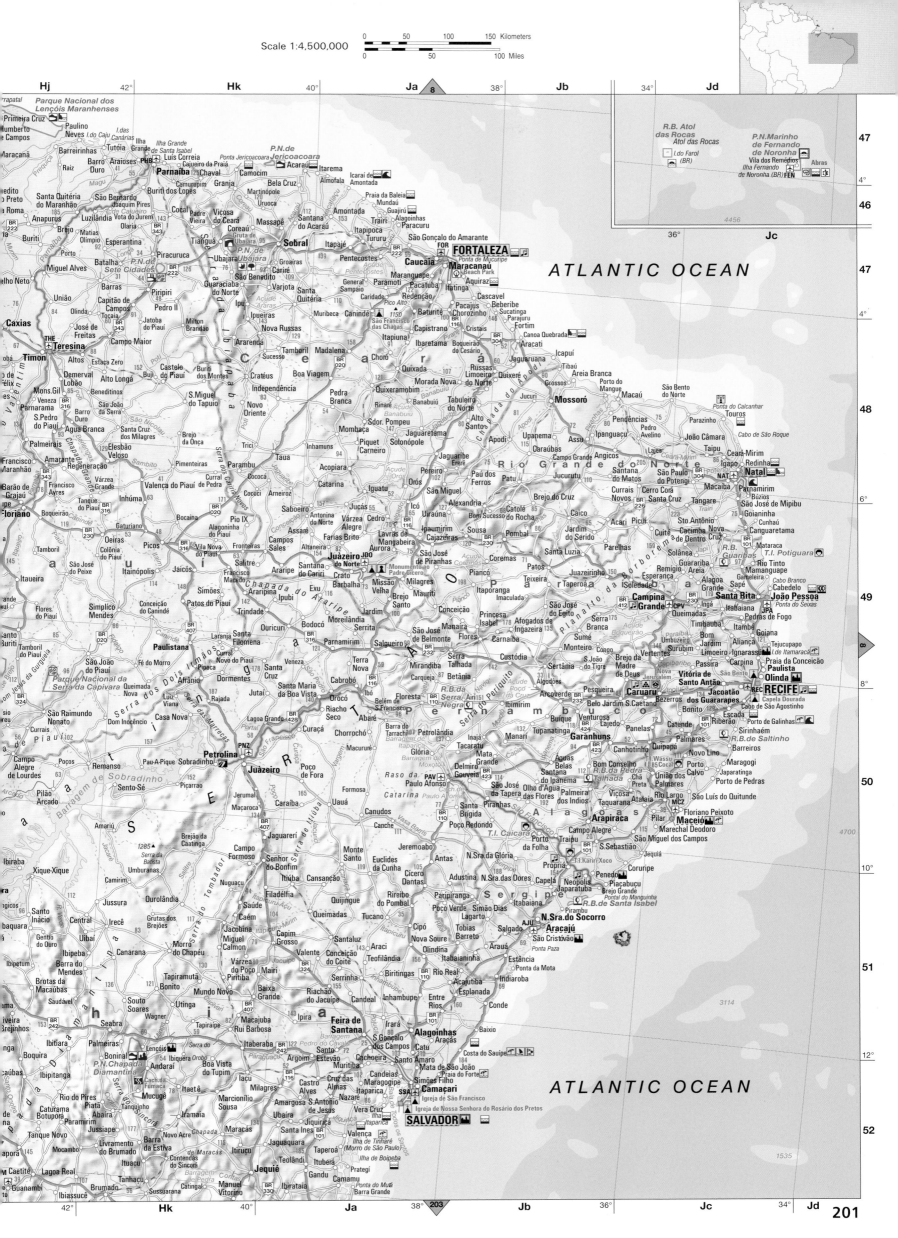

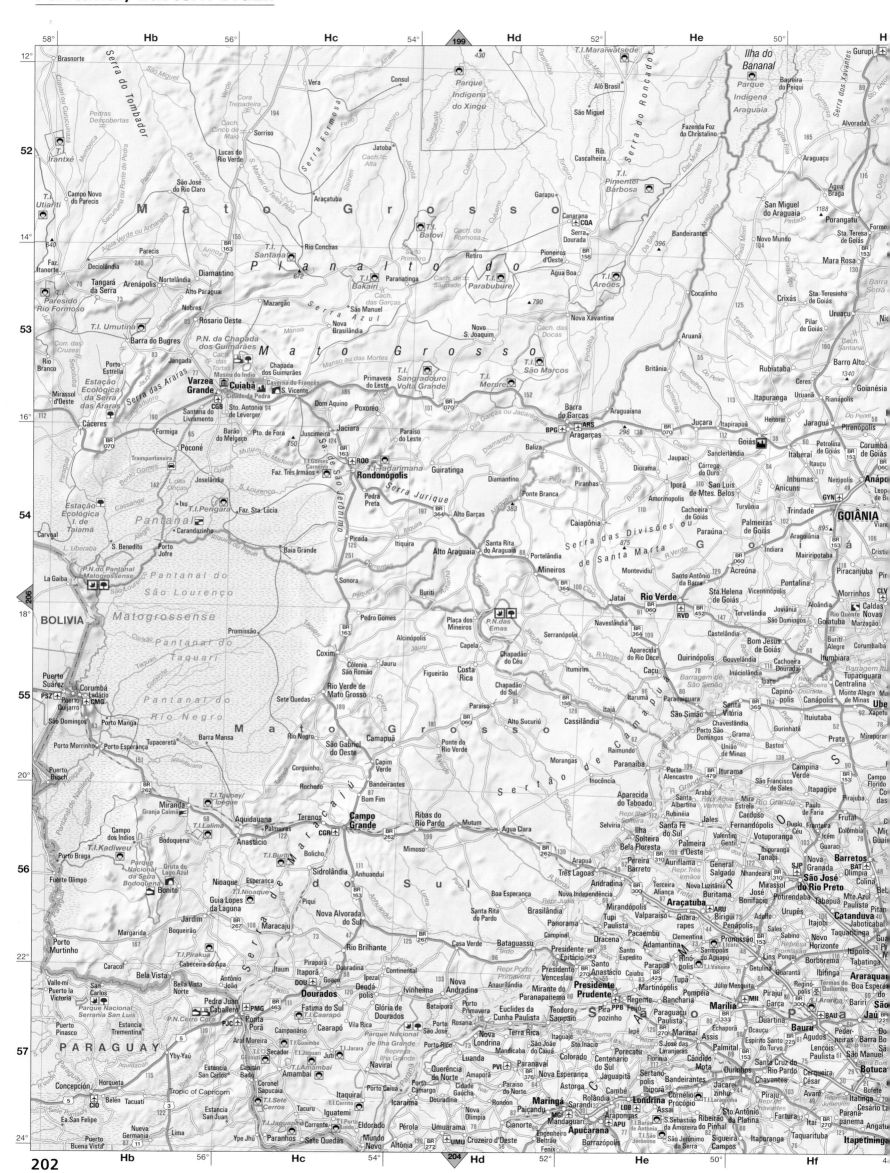

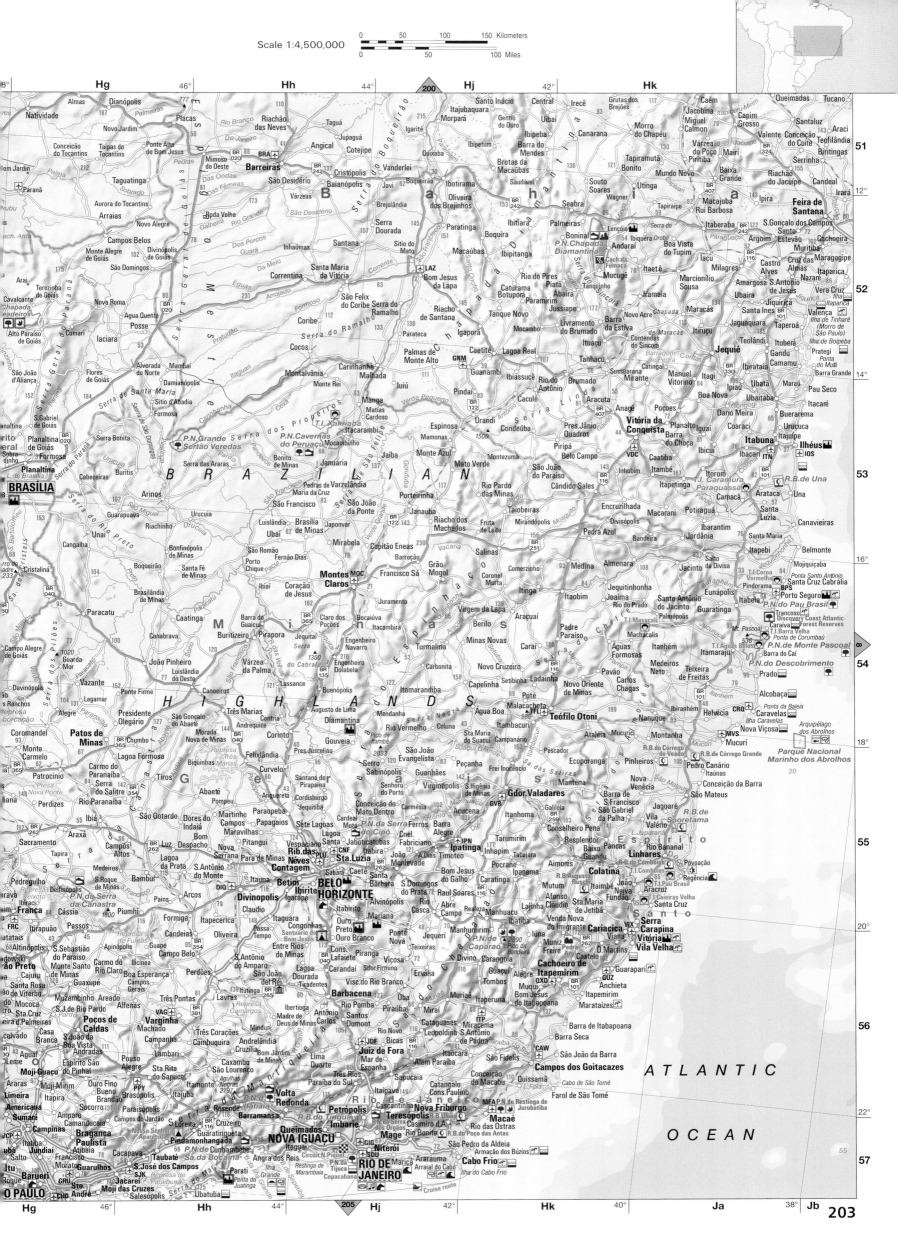

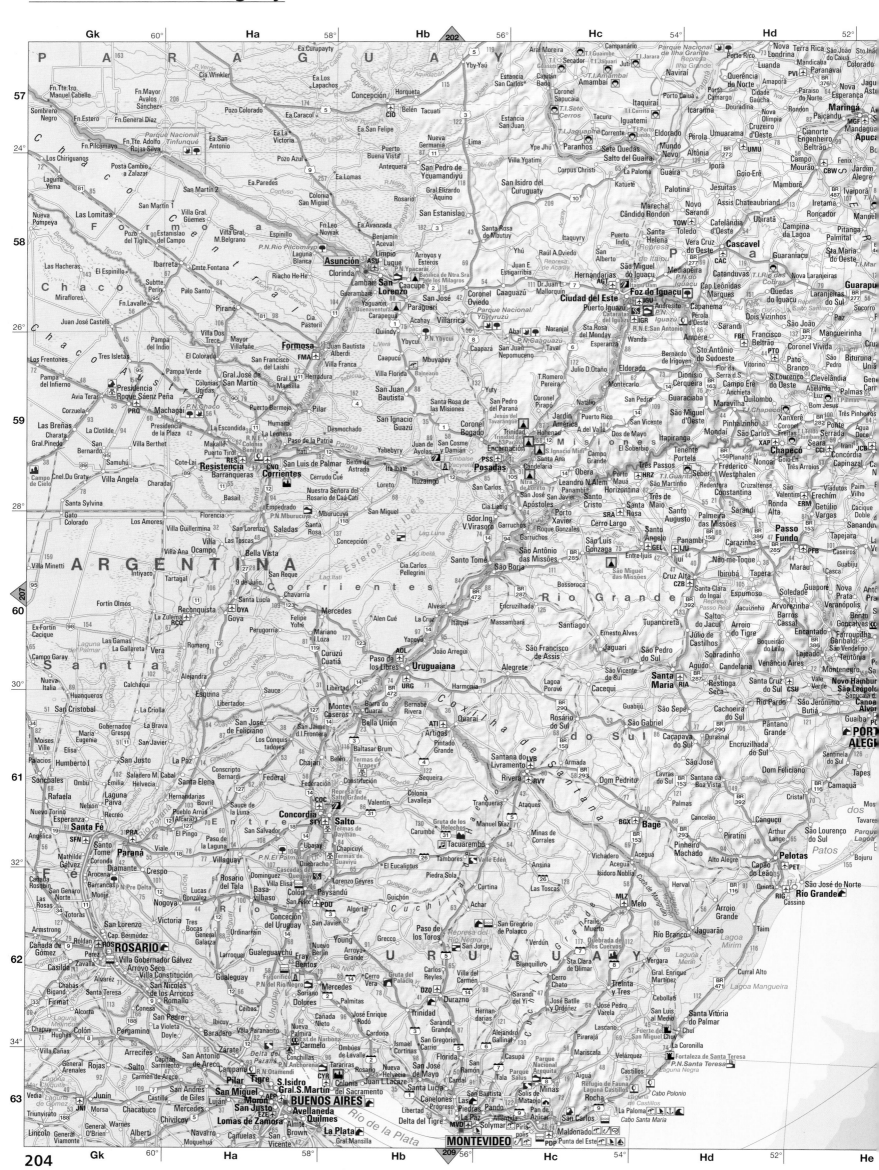

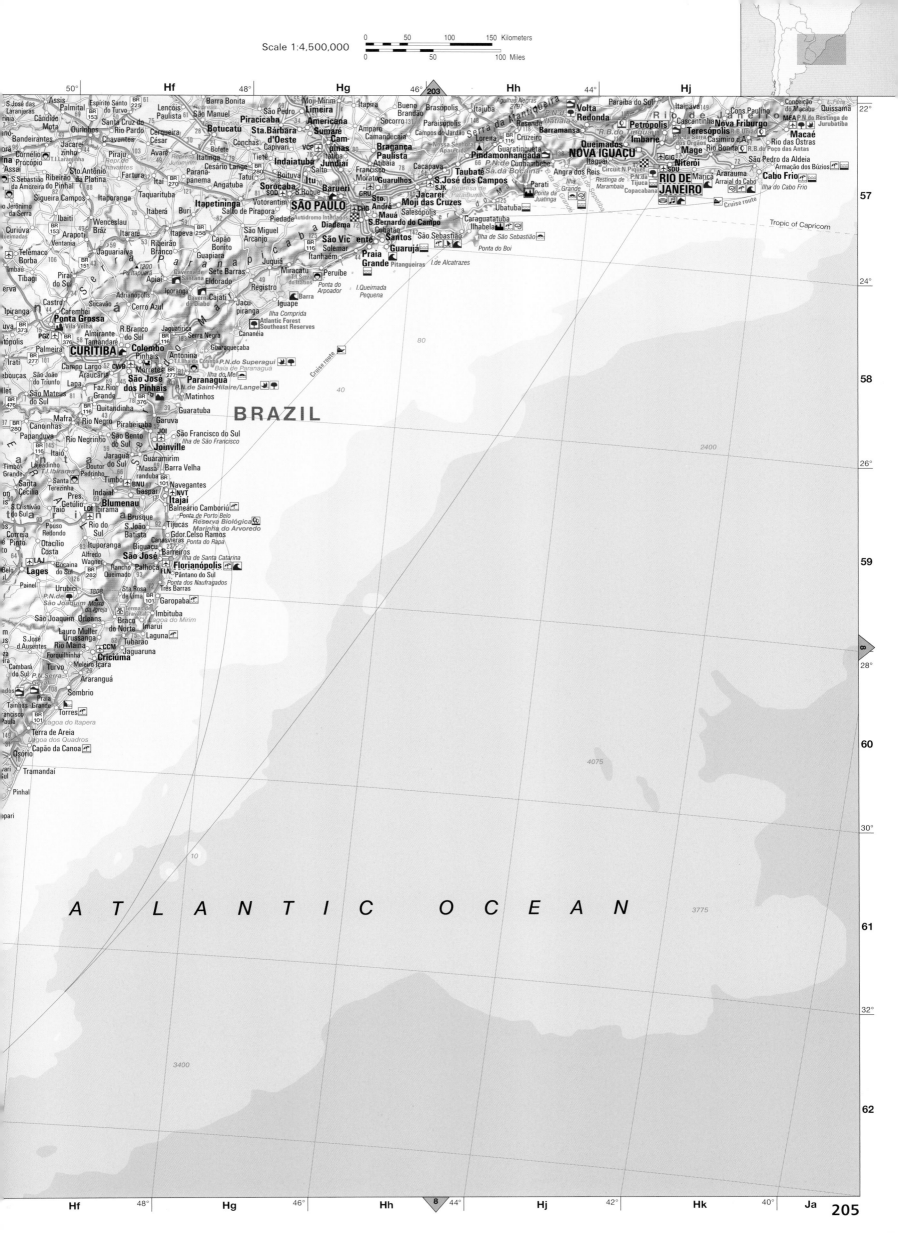

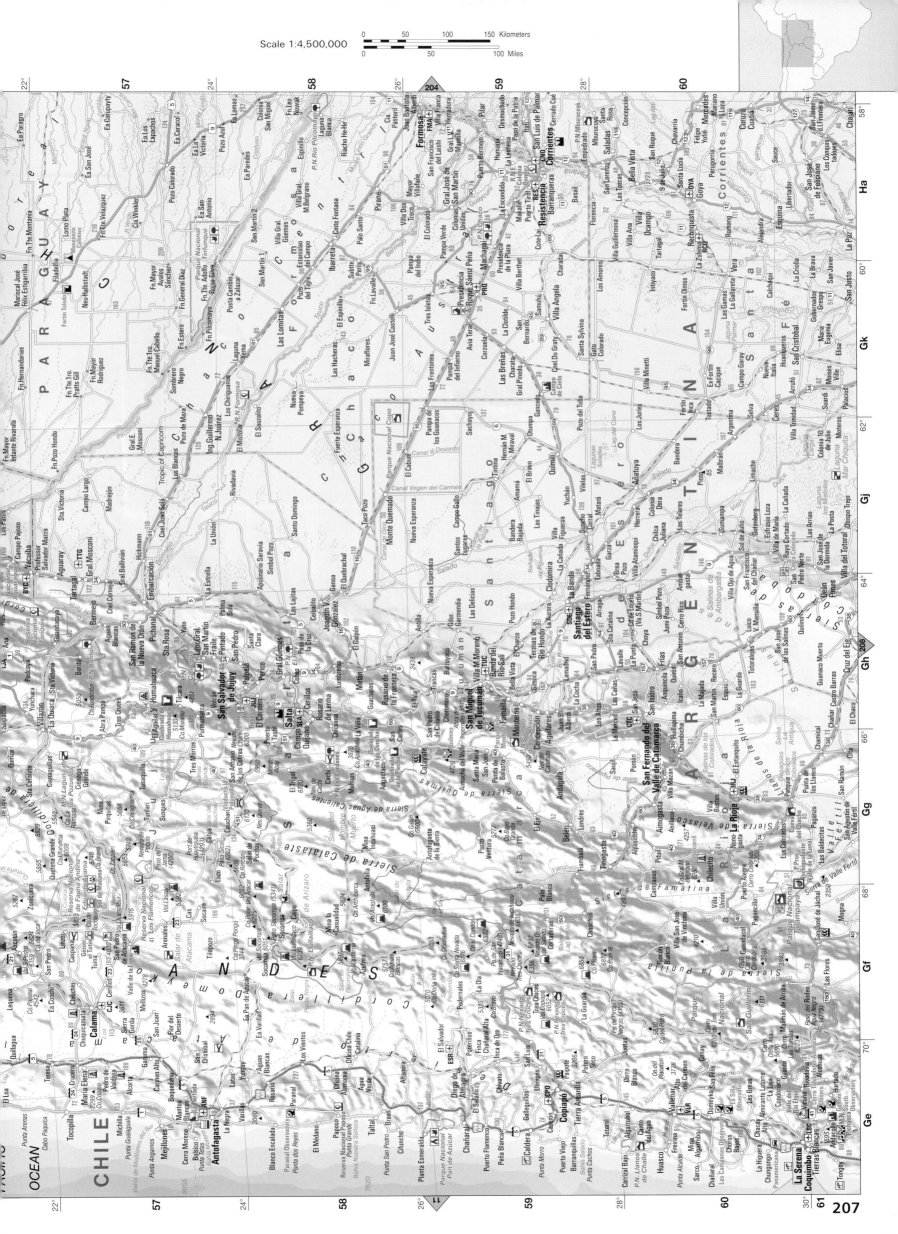

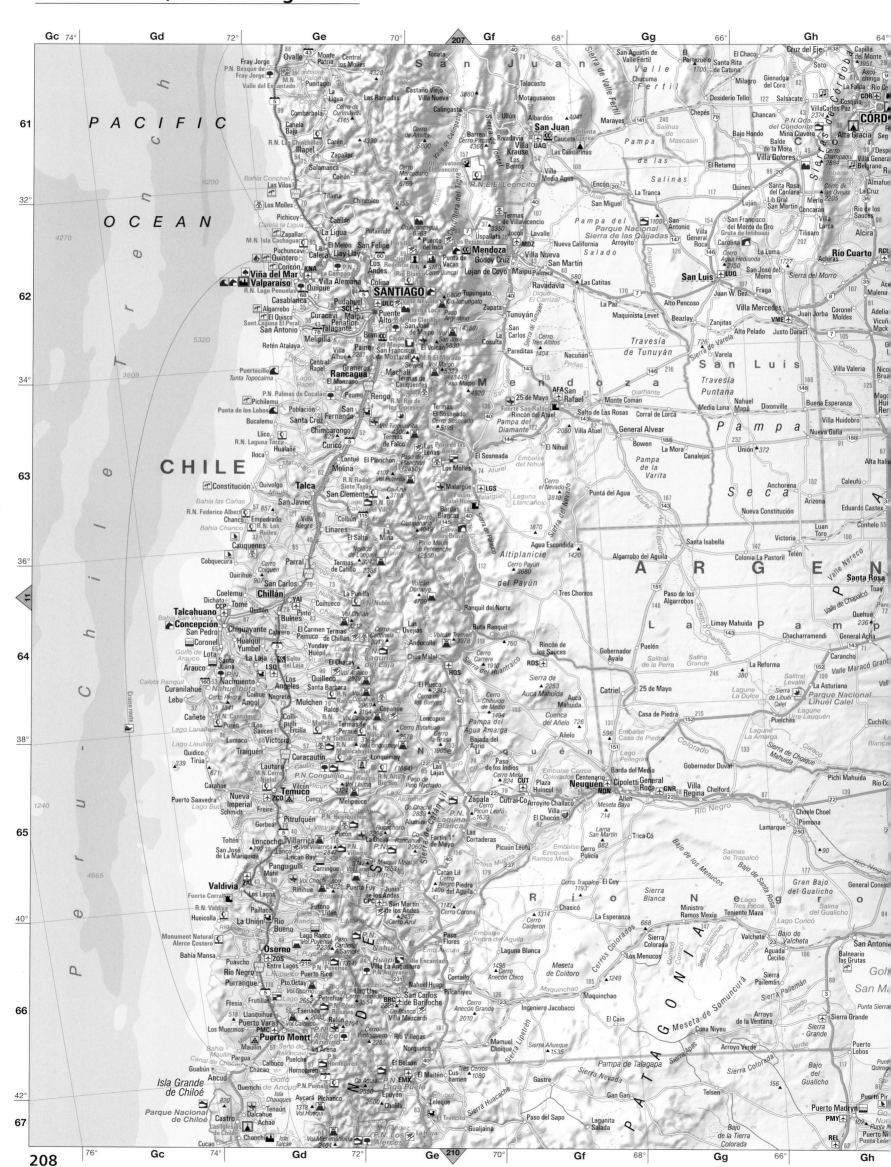

Southern Chile, Southern Argentina, Falkland Islands

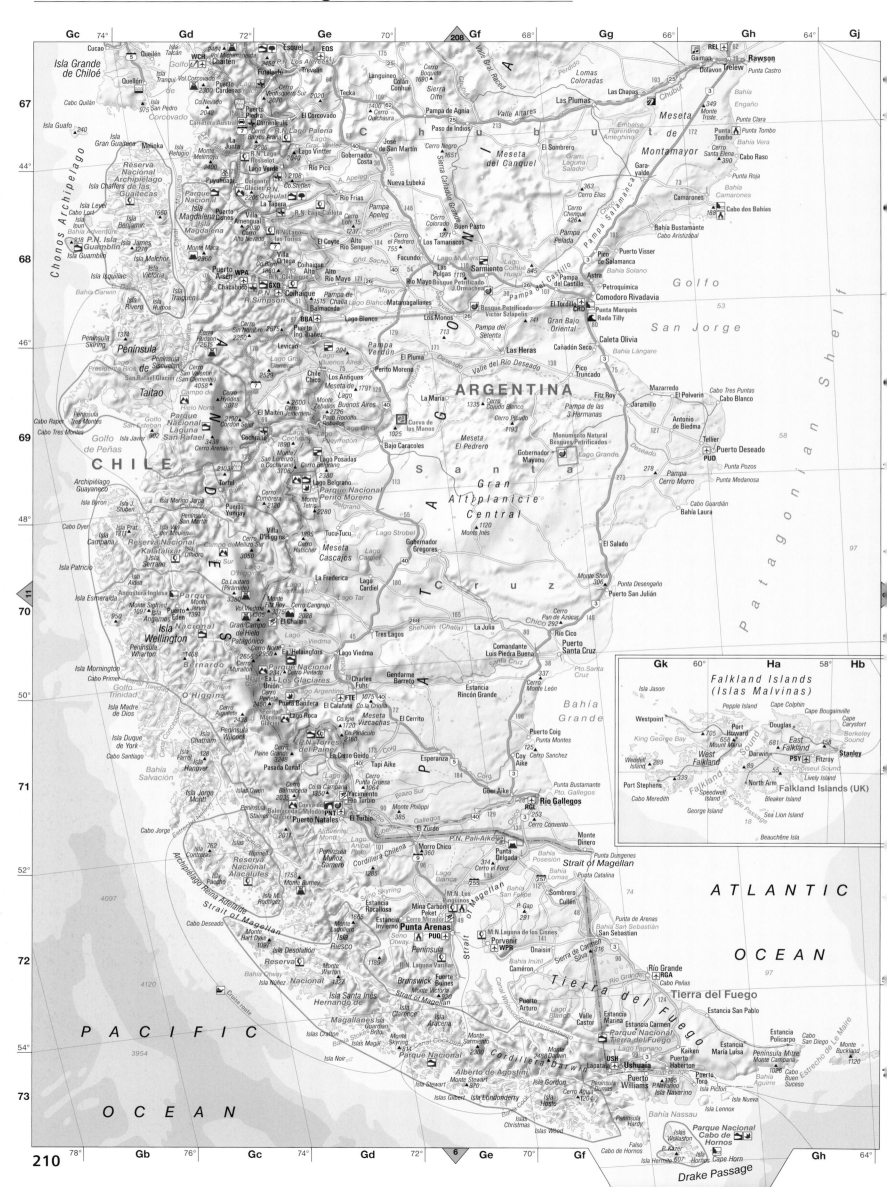

NATIONS OF THE WORLD

Facts and figures

There were 195 sovereign nations on six continents at the start of the 21st century. During the 20th century, the political makeup of our planet changed frequently and the borders of many nations were redrawn. Two world wars, the end of European colonialism, and the decline of communism led to the creation and collapse of numerous nations and political entities.

Although most of Africa was under the control of European powers at the start of the 20th century, it is now the continent with the most states: 54. Asia is only slightly behind Africa with 47 states, and is followed by Europe (45), North America (23), Australia/Oceania (14), and South America (12). Inhospitable Antarctica is the only "stateless" continent.

Index of local country names

English	Local	Continent	Page	English	Local	Continent	Page
Afghanistan	Afghānistān	Asia	216	Cyprus	Kypros/Kibris	Europe	241
Albania	Shqipëria	Europe	260	Czech Republic	Česká Republika	Europe	226
Algeria	Al-Ġazā'ir/Algérie	Africa	216	Denmark	Danmark	Europe	229
Andorra	Andorra	Europe	218	Djibouti	Djibouti	Africa	230
Angola	Angola	Africa	218	Dominica	Dominica	Central America	230
Antigua and Barbuda	Antigua and Barbuda	Central America	218	Dominican Republic	República Dominicana	Central America	256
Argentina	Argentina	South America	219	East Timor	Timor-Leste	Asia	266
Armenia	Armenija (Hayastan)	Asia	219	Ecuador	Ecuador	South America	230
Australia	Australia	Australia	220	Equatorial Guinea	Guinea Ecuatorial	Africa	236
Austria	Österreich	Europe	253	Egypt	Al-Miṣr/Egypt	Africa	217
Azerbaijan	Azerbajdzan	Asia	220	El Salvador	El Salvador	Central America	232
Bahamas	Bahamas	Central America	220	Eritrea	Eritrea	Africa	232
Bahrain	Al-Bahrain	Asia	216	Estonia	Eesti	Europe	231
Bangladesh	Bangladesh	Asia	220	Ethiopia	Îtyopya	Africa	239
Barbados	Barbados	Central America	221	Fiji	Fiji	Australia/Oceania	233
Belarus	Belarus	Europe	221	Finland	Suomi/Finland	Europe	263
Belgium	België/Belgique	Europe	222	France	France	Europe	234
Belize	Belize	Central America	222	Gabon	Gabon	Africa	234
Benin	Benin	Africa	222	The Gambia	Gambia	Africa	234
Bhutan	Bhutan	Asia	222	Georgia	Gruzija (Sakartvelo)	Asia	235
Bolivia	Bolivia	South America	223	Germany	Deutschland	Europe	230
Bosnia-Herzegovina	Bosna i Hercegovina	Europe	223	Ghana	Ghana	Africa	234
Botswana	Botswana	Africa	223	Greece	Elláda (Hellás)	Europe	232
Brazil	Brasil	South America	224	Grenada	Grenada	Central America	234
Brunei	Brunei	Asia	224	Guatemala	Guatemala	Central America	235
Bulgaria	Bŭlgarija	Europe	224	Guinea	Guinée	Africa	236
Burkina Faso	Burkina Faso	Africa	224	Guinea-Bissau	Guinea-Bissau	Africa	236
Burundi	Burundi	Africa	225	Guyana	Guyana	South America	236
Cambodia	Kâmpŭchéa	Asia	240	Haiti	Haïti	Central America	236
Cameroon	Cameroun/Cameroon	Africa	225	Honduras	Honduras	Central America	237
Canada	Canada	North America	226	Hungary	Magyarország	Europe	244
Cape Verde	Cabo Verde	Africa	225	Iceland	Ísland	Europe	238
Central African Republic	République Centrafricaine	Africa	256	India	India (Bhărat)	Asia	237
Chad	Tchad	Africa	266	Indonesia	Indonesia	Asia	238
Chile	Chile	South America	226	Iraq	'Irāq	Asia	238
China	Zhongguo	Asia	272	Iran	Îrân	Asia	238
Colombia	Colombia	South America	227	Ireland	Éire/Ireland	Europe	231
Comoros	Comores	Africa	228	Israel	Yi'sra'el	Asia	271
Congo	Congo	Africa	228	Italy	Italia	Europe	239
Congo, Dem. Rep.	Congo, Rép. Démocratique	Africa	228	Ivory Coast	Côte d'Ivoire	Africa	228
Costa Rica	Costa Rica	Central America	228	Jamaica	Jamaica	Central America	240
Croatia	Hrvatska	Europe	237	Japan	Nippon/Nihon	Asia	252
Cuba	Cuba	Central America	229	Jordan	Urdunn	Asia	270

English	Local	Continent	Page	English	Local	Continent	Page
Kazakhstan	Kazahstan	Asia	240	Rwanda	Rwanda	Africa	257
Kenya	Kenya	Africa	240	Saint Kitts and Nevis	Saint Kitts and Nevis	Central America	257
Kiribati	Kiribati	Australia/Oceania	241	Saint Lucia	Saint Lucia	Central America	258
Korea, North	Choson	Asia	226	St. Vincent and the Grenadines	St. Vincent and the Grenadines	Central America	258
Korea, South	Taehan-Min'guk	Asia	264	Samoa	Samoa	Australia/Oceania	258
Kuwait	Al-Kuwait	Asia	216	San Marino	San Marino	Europe	258
Kyrgyzstan	Kyrgyzstan	Asia	241	São Tomé and Principe	São Tomé e Príncipe	Africa	259
Laos	Lao	Asia	242	Saudi Arabia	Al-Mamlaka	Asia	217
Latvia	Latvija	Europe	242		al-'Arabiya as-Sa'ūdiya		
Lebanon	Al-Lubnān	Asia	216	Senegal	Sénégal	Africa	259
Lesotho	Lesotho	Africa	242	Serbia	Srbija	Europe	262
Liberia	Liberia	Africa	242	Seychelles	Seychelles	Africa	260
Libya	Lîbîyâ	Africa	242	Sierra Leone	Sierra Leone	Africa	260
Liechtenstein	Liechtenstein	Europe	243	Singapore	Singapore	Asia	260
Lithuania	Lietuva	Europe	243	Slovakia	Slovenská Republika	Europe	261
Luxembourg	Luxembourg	Europe	243	Slovenia	Slovenija	Europe	260
Macedonia	Makedonija	Europe	244	Solomon Islands	Solomon Islands	Australia/Oceania	261
Madagascar	Madagasíkara	Africa	244	Somalia	Soomaaliya	Africa	262
Malawi	Malawi	Africa	244	South Africa	South Africa/Suid-Afrika	Africa	262
Malaysia	Malaysia	Asia	245	Spain	España	Europe	232
Maldives	Maldives (Divehi Rajje)	Asia	245	Sri Lanka	Šrī Laṅkā	Asia	262
Mali	Mali	Africa	245	Sudan	As-Sūdān	Africa	219
Malta	Malta	Europe	246	Suriname	Suriname	South America	263
Marshall Islands	Marshall Islands	Australia/Oceania	246	Swaziland	Swaziland (kaNgwane)	Africa	264
Mauritania	Mawrītāniyah	Africa	246	Sweden	Sverige	Europe	264
Mauritius	Mauritius	Africa	246	Switzerland	Suisse/Schweiz/Svizzera	Europe	262
Mexico	México	Central America	247	Syria	Sūriya	Asia	264
Micronesia	Micronesia	Australia/Oceania	247	Taiwan	Taiwan	Asia	265
Moldova	Moldova	Europe	248	Tajikistan	Tadžikistan	Asia	264
Monaco	Monaco	Europe	248	Tanzania	Tanzania	Africa	265
Mongolia	Mongol Ard Uls	Asia	248	Thailand	Muang Thai	Asia	249
Montenegro	Crna Gora	Europe	228	Togo	Togo	Africa	266
Morocco	Al-Maġrib/Maroc	Africa	217	Tonga	Tonga	Australia/Oceania	266
Mozambique	Moçambique	Africa	248	Trinidad and Tobago	Trinidad and Tobago	Central America	266
Myanmar (Burma)	Myanmar	Asia	249	Tunisia	Tūnisiyah/Tunisie	Africa	267
Namibia	Namibia	Africa	250	Turkey	Türkiye	Europe	267
Nauru	Nauru (Naoero)	Australia/Oceania	250	Turkmenistan	Turkmenistan	Asia	268
Nepal	Nepal	Asia	250	Tuvalu	Tuvalu	Australia/Oceania	268
Netherlands	Nederland	Europe	250	Uganda	Uganda	Africa	268
New Zealand	New Zealand	Australia/Oceania	251	Ukraine	Ukrajina	Europe	268
Nicaragua	Nicaragua	Central America	251	Uruguay	Uruguay	South America	270
Niger	Niger	Africa	252	Uzbekistan	Uzbekistan	Asia	270
Nigeria	Nigeria	Africa	252	Vanuatu	Vanuatu	Australia/Oceania	270
Norway	Norge	Europe	252	Vatican City	Città del Vaticano	Europe	227
Oman	Salṭanat 'Umān	Asia	258	Venezuela	Venezuela	South America	270
Pakistan	Pākistān	Asia	253	Vietnam	Viêt-Nam	Asia	271
Palau	Palau	Australia/Oceania	254	United Arab Emirates	Daulat al-Imārāt	Asia	229
Panama	Panamá	Central America	254		al-'Arabiya Al-Muttahida		
Papua New Guinea	Papua New Guinea	Australia/Oceania	254	United Kingdom	United Kingdom	Europe	268
Paraguay	Paraguay	South America	254	United States of America	United States of America	North America	269
Peru	Perú	South America	254	Western Sahara	Al-Saharaw	Africa	218
Philippines	Pilipinas	Asia	254	Yemen	Al-Yaman	Asia	218
Poland	Polska	Europe	255	Zambia	Zambia	Africa	272
Portugal	Portugal	Europe	255	Zimbabwe	Zimbabwe	Africa	272
Qatar	Qaṭar	Asia	256				
Romania	România	Europe	256				
Russia	Rossija	Europe	256				

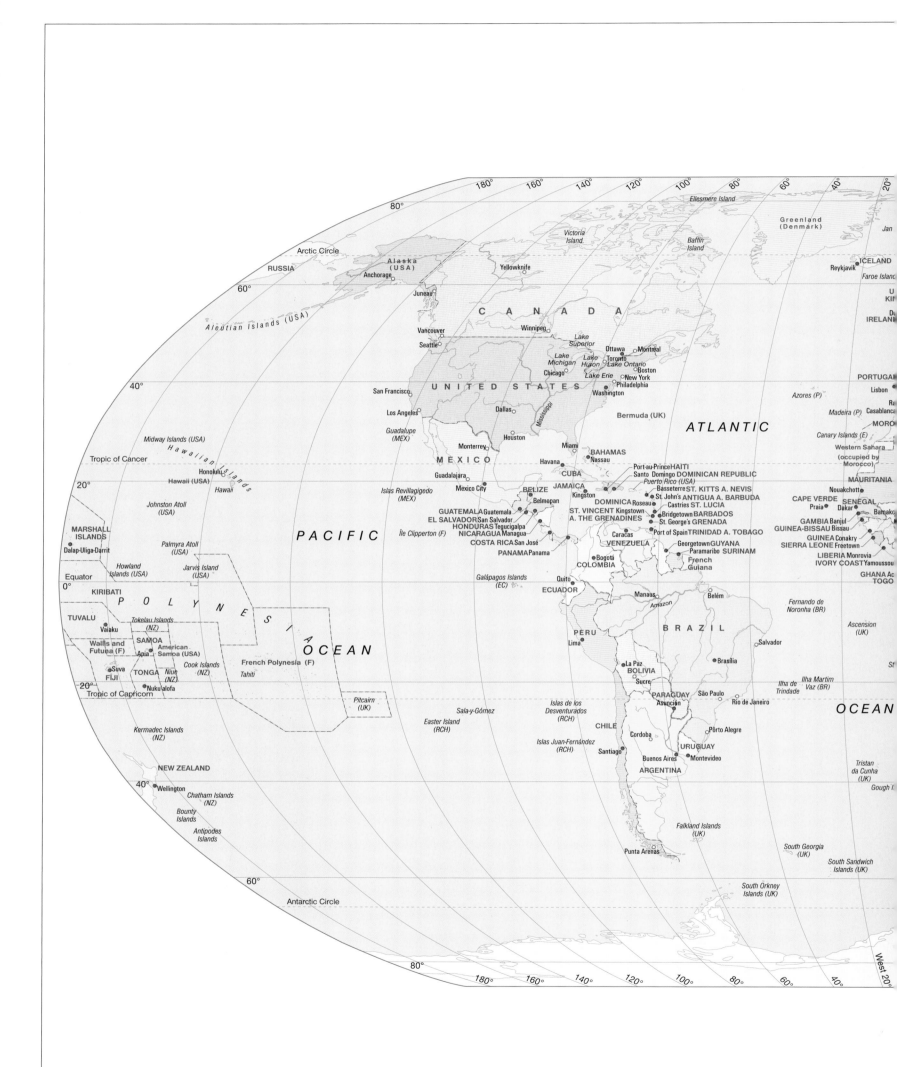

Scale 1:80,000,000

0 1000 2000 3000 Kilometers

0 1000 2000 Miles

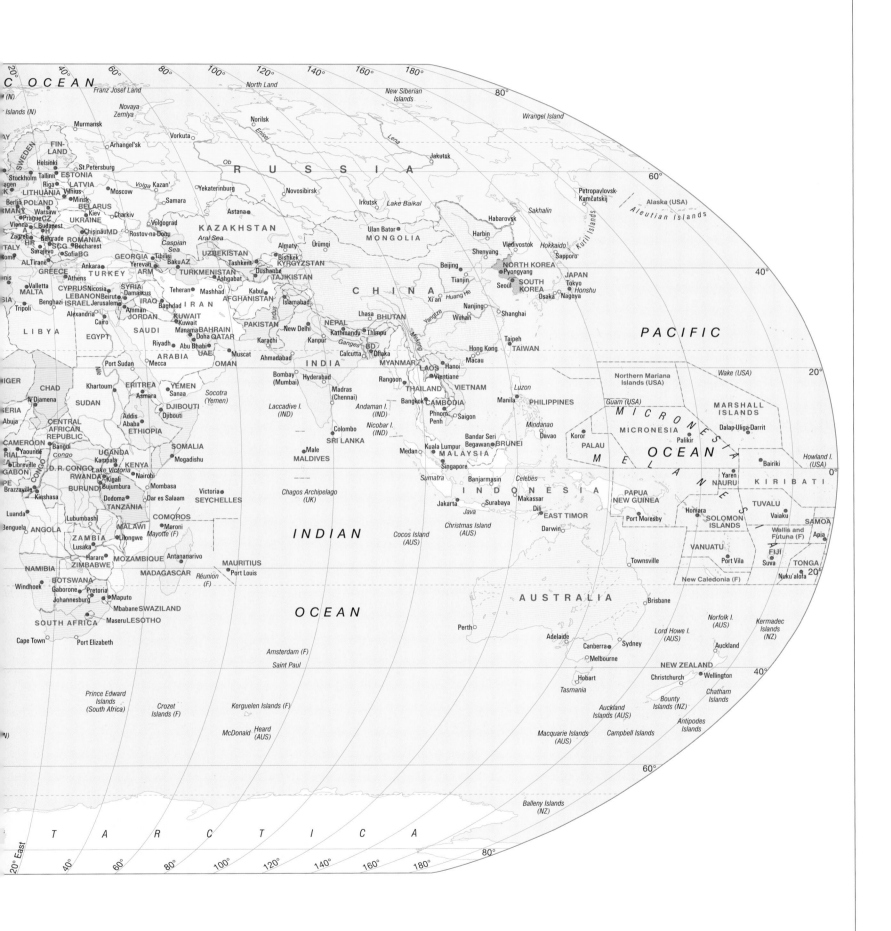

C OCEAN

Franz Josef Land

North Land

New Siberian Islands

80°

Islands (N)

Novaya Zemlya

Norilsk

Wrangel Island

Murmansk

Vorkuta

Enisej

Lena

SWEDEN FIN-LAND

Arhangel'sk

Jakutsk

60°

Helsinki

Ob

R U S S I A

St. Petersburg

Yekaterinburg

Petropavlovsk-Kamčatskij

Stockholm Tallinn ESTONIA

Novosibirsk

Alaska (USA)

K Riga LATVIA

Volga Kazan'

Aleutian Islands

LITHUANIA Vilnius Moscow

Samara

Irkutsk Lake Baikal

Habarovsk

Sakhalin

Berlin POLAND Minsk BELARUS

KAZAKHSTAN

MONGOLIA

Sapporo

60°

MANY Warsaw Kiev Charkiv UKRAINE

Volgograd

Astana

Ulan Bator

Vladivostok Hokkaido Kuril Islands

Vienna Prague CZ Budapest

Rostov-na-Donu

Harbin

Shenyang

NORTH KOREA

Zagreb H Chişinău MD

Caspian Sea

Aral Sea

Almaty Ürümqi

Pyongyang JAPAN Tokyo

40°

ITALY Belgrade SCG Bucharest ROMANIA

GEORGIA Tbilisi

Bishkek KYRGYZSTAN

Beijing

Seoul SOUTH KOREA Osaka Honshu Nagoya

Rome Sarajevo SofiaBG

UZBEKISTAN

Tianjin

AL Tirane GREECE

Ankara Yerevan ARM Baku AZ

Tashkent

Xi'an Huang He

Nanjing

Shanghai

Athens TURKEY TURKMENISTAN

Dushanbe TAJIKISTAN

CHINA

Wuhan

Valletta CYPRUS Nicosia SYRIA Teheran Mashhad

Ashgabat

Lhasa BHUTAN

Yangtze

Taipeh

MALTA LEBANON Beirut Damascus

Kabul AFGHANISTAN

PACIFIC

Benghazi ISRAEL Jerusalem IRAQ Baghdad I R A N

Islamabad

NEPAL

Hong Kong Macau TAIWAN

SIA Alexandria Amman JORDAN KUWAIT

PAKISTAN New Delhi

Kathmandu Thimpu

Cairo Kuwait

Ganges BD

LIBYA EGYPT SAUDI Manama BAHRAIN Doha QATAR

Karachi Kanpur

Calcutta Dhaka

20°

Riyadh Abu Dhabi

Ahmadabad

MYANMAR Hanoi

NIGER CHAD

ARABIA UAE Muscat

Mecca OMAN

INDIA

LAOS

Vientiane

Northern Mariana Islands (USA)

Wake (USA)

20°

N'Djamena SUDAN

Port Sudan

ERITREA YEMEN

Bombay (Mumbai) Hyderabad

Rangoon

THAILAND VIETNAM

Luzon

MARSHALL ISLANDS

ERIA

Khartoum

Asmara Sanaa

Madras (Chennai)

Bangkok CAMBODIA

Manila PHILIPPINES

Guam (USA)

Abuja CENTRAL AFRICAN REPUBLIC

Addis Ababa DJIBOUTI Djibouti

Socotra (Yemen)

Laccadive I. (IND)

Andaman I. (IND)

Phnom Penh Saigon

Mindanao

MICRONESIA

Dalap-Uliga-Darrit

CAMEROON Yaounde ETHIOPIA

Colombo

Nicobar I. (IND)

Bandar Seri Begawan BRUNEI

Davao

Koror PALAU

OCEAN

RIAL Bangui

SOMALIA

SRI LANKA

Medan MALAYSIA

Bairiki

Libreville UGANDA

Kampala

Male

Kuala Lumpur

Howland I. (USA)

GABON CONGO D.R. CONGO

Lake Victoria

Nairobi KENYA

MALDIVES

Singapore

Yaren NAURU KIRIBATI

0°

PE Brazzaville

Kigali RWANDA

Mombasa

Sumatra

Banjarmasin Celebes

PAPUA NEW GUINEA

Kinshasa BURUNDI Bujumbura Dodoma Dar es Salaam

Victoria SEYCHELLES

Makassar

INDONESIA

TUVALU

Luanda

Lubumbashi TANZANIA

Chagos Archipelago (UK)

Jakarta Surabaya Java

Dili EAST TIMOR

Honiara SOLOMON ISLANDS

Vaiaku

Benguela ANGOLA COMOROS Moroni

Port Moresby

Wallis and Futuna (F) Apia SAMOA

ZAMBIA MALAWI Mayotte (F)

Lilongwe

I N D I A N

Darwin

VANUATU

Port Vila FIJI Suva

Lusaka Harare ZIMBABWE MOZAMBIQUE

Antananarivo

Christmas Island (AUS)

TONGA

NAMIBIA

MAURITIUS Port Louis

Townsville

New Caledonia (F) Nuku'alofa 20°

Windhoek BOTSWANA

MADAGASCAR Réunion (F)

OCEAN

A U S T R A L I A

Brisbane

Gaborone Pretoria

Johannesburg Maputo

Norfolk I. (AUS)

Kermadec Islands (NZ)

Mbabane SWAZILAND

Amsterdam (F)

Perth

Adelaide

Sydney

Lord Howe I. (AUS)

SOUTH AFRICA Maseru LESOTHO

Saint Paul

Canberra

Auckland

Cape Town

Port Elizabeth

Melbourne

NEW ZEALAND

40°

Hobart

Christchurch Wellington

Prince Edward Islands (South Africa)

Crozet Islands (F)

Kerguelen Islands (F)

Tasmania

Auckland Islands (AUS)

Bounty Islands (NZ)

Chatham Islands

N)

McDonald Heard (AUS)

Antipodes Islands

Macquarie Islands (AUS)

Campbell Islands

60°

Balleny Islands (NZ)

T A R C T I C A

80°

20° East

40° 60° 80° 100° 120° 140° 160° 180°

Afghānistān Afghanistan

Teacher and disciple: *Although Saudi Arabia, as a modern industrialized country, is provided with a fully developed and structured educational system (at one of the six universities in the country English is actually the language of instruction), getting instruction in the rules of the Koran is a very important matter for young Arabs. The Koran, together with the Sunna (traditions of the prophet Mohammed) serve as the country's constitution.*

Afghānistān
Afghanistan

Area: 647,500 sq km
Population: 28.5 million
GDP per capita: 700 US$
Capital: Kabul
Government: Republic
Languages: Pushtu, Dari
Currency: 1 afghani = 100 puls

Geography: The mountainous interior includes the mighty Hindu Kush range, whose summits rise to over 7,000 meters culminating in Mount Tirich Mir on the Pakistan border. Great climatic differences exist in a relatively limited space, ranging from arid to subtropical and alpine climates depending on altitude. Tourist destinations include the Islamic buildings in Ghazni, the Caliph Mausoleums in Kabul and the pilgrimage sites of Kandahar and Mazar-e Sharif.

Politics: Settled by Iranian tribes since the 2nd millennium BC, Afghanistan has been under a succession of foreign dominations. The Afghan Emirate, established in 1747, later came under English influence. In 1919 it became a kingdom independent of Great Britain, and in 1973 a republic. The civil war from 1979 to 1992 and the struggle against the Russian army on its own soil to 1989 have brought lasting changes; the radical Islamist Taliban gained increasing influence from 1994. Their terror regime was overthrown at the end of 2001 in an offensive by the US and the Afghan Northern Alliance.

Economy: Afghanistan is one of the poorest countries in the world. Agriculture and fruit cultivation is practiced in the irrigated valleys, and livestock breeding in the mountain areas. Natural resources include coal, lapis lazuli, petroleum and natural gas. The continuous fighting has wreaked enormous damage on the economy – more than three quarters of the industrial plants lie in ruins today.

Al-Bahrain
Bahrain

Area: 665 sq km
Population: 677,800
GDP per capita: 17,100 US$
Capital: Al-Manama
Government: Emirate
Language: Arabic
Currency: 1 Bahrain dinar = 1,000 fils

Geography: The Emirate in the Persian Gulf is composed of 33 islands, 13 of which are inhabited. Bahrain, the main island, has a desert-like landscape with expansive salt marshes and sand dunes, whilst the archipelago enjoys a mild desert climate. Artesian wells permit oasis agriculture in the northern coastal area. Tourism is concentrated in the capital Al-Manama.

Politics: The city of Dilmun was a trading hub as early as the 3rd century BC. Occupied by the Portuguese in the 16th century and later by the Persians, the emirate was a British protectorate from 1816 to 1971 and joined the Arab League after declaring independence in 1971. The Emir in power since 1999 has ushered in political reforms including a constitution (in force since 2002), making the country a constitutional monarchy. Around 40% of Bahrain's population comprises non-nationals.

Economy: The rich petroleum reserves discovered in 1932 have provided a solid base for the country's economy, with the oil and gas sector generating 80% of exports but only 2% of employment. Because of the climatic conditions, the agricultural sector accounts for only 1% of GDP, while industry contributes 41%. The services sector (banking) plays an important role as part of diversification, anticipating the end of the oil reserves.

Albania see Shqipëria

Al-Ǧazā'ir/Algérie
Algeria

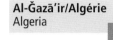

Area: 2,381,741 sq km
Population: 32.1 million
GDP per capita: 5,900 US$
Capital: Algiers
Government: Presidential republic
Language: Arabic
Currency: 1 Algerian dinar = 100 centimes

Geography: Settlements are concentrated in the Mediterranean climate of the fertile coastal areas to the north, extending along 1,300 kilometers of bays and inlets. 85% of the south is occupied by the

Saudi Arabia: The Ka'bah in Mecca, the religious center of the Islam.

Sahara. In addition to the Sahara's unique landscape and beautiful oases, other places of interest are the many cultural sites from the Roman and Phoenician eras.

Politics: First settled by the Phoenicians and later by Carthaginians and Romans, the coastal areas fell under Arab rule from the 7th to 15th centuries, were conquered by the French in 1830 and became French territory from 1881 to 1962. Although uprisings and resistance activities reached their peak in 1945 and 1958, political unrest continued after 1962 and terrorism by Islamic fundamentalists has increased since 1990, despite the election of a National Assembly in 1997.

Economy: Although constraints of climate and soil quality restrict agriculture to a narrow coastal area, it is the country's second largest industry. Algeria is among the world's largest cork exporters; the sparse forests are state-run. Natural gas and petroleum exports from the Sahara's extensive reserves form Algeria's main source of foreign currency. The country is now the world's second largest exporter of natural gas. Recent reforms may eventually help to diversify the economy, but Algeria's unemployment and poverty rates remain critically high.

Al-Kuwait
Kuwait

Area: 17,820 sq km
Population: 2.3 million
GDP per capita: 18,100 US$
Capital: Kuwait City
Government: Emirate
Language: Arabic
Currency: 1 Kuwait dinar = 100 dirhams = 1,000 fils

Geography: This emirate on the Persian Gulf consists of dry steppes and sandy deserts. Summers inland are extremely hot and dry, while the more humid coastal areas have some of the lowest precipitation on the planet. Destinations include the old town of Kuwait City as well as the Island of Faylakah (holiday facilities with beaches). The 1991 Gulf War left ecological devastation in its wake.

Politics: A British protectorate from 1899, Kuwait gained independence in 1961. Executive power lies with the Emir, a member of the Al Sabbah dynasty that has reigned since 1756, and has been elected by it; a house of representatives, elected in 1996, enjoys limited powers. Invaded and occupied by Iraq in 1990, Kuwait was freed by allied forces in the (first) Gulf War in early 1991.

Economy: 62% of the people living and working in Kuwait come from neighboring countries. Because of the terrain, agricultural use is limited to only 0.2% of the overall area where there is coastal irrigation. Most food is imported. Oil, drilled in Kuwait since 1946, accounts for the country's wealth. Kuwait has many large-scale oil harbors. Shrimps also form an important export. Kuwait does not levy taxes or social security contributions.

Al-Lubnān
Lebanon

Area: 10,452 sq km
Population: 3.8 million
GDP per capita: 4,800 US$
Capital: Beirut
Government: Republic
Languages: Arabic (official), French
Currency: 1 Lebanese pound = 100 piasters

Geography: Dominated by mountain ranges on the eastern edge of the Mediterranean, the country has only a narrow, fertile coastal strip, with a Mediterranean climate in this region and a continental climate in the hinterland, with high snowfalls in the winter. Tourist destinations include Baalbek (excavations of Roman sites), the old harbor city of Beirut, and Tripoli.

Politics: After the end of the Ottoman Empire, Lebanon came under a French mandate in 1920 until it gained independence in 1944. Since 1958 it has been continuously shaken by external political crises and internal conflicts, attributable to the overall Middle East conflict. After a peace treaty with neighboring Syria, Lebanon is also negotiating a comprehensive peace settlement with Israel.

Economy: The country's economic fabric and infrastructure was almost completely destroyed by the civil war. Agriculture covers only part of the country's needs. Fruit and vegetables are grown on the irrigated land on the coast. Industry is limited to products for domestic consumption. Services are the largest contributor to GDP.

Unveiled beauty: Although most of the Berber are Muslims, the women do not wear veils; their clothes are more colorful and decorated than those of the men. They enjoy more freedom than is usual for women in Arab countries. Berber society is based on the tribe and the clan, with blood relationships and the extended family of paramount importance.

Al-Maġrib/Maroc
Morocco

Area: 446,550 sq km
Population: 32.2 million
GDP per capita: 4,000 US$
Capital: Rabat
Government: Constitutional monarchy
Languages: Arabic, French (both official), Berber dialects
Currency: 1 dirham = 100 centimes

Geography: Fertile countryside with a Mediterranean climate extends to the Rif Mountains in the north. To the south of the coastal strip, three chains of the Atlas Mountains mark the transition to the steppes and deserts in the extreme southwest. The most popular tourist destinations are Agadir, Fès, Marrakesh, Meknès and Rabat.

Politics: Conquered by the Arabs in the 7th century, Morocco fell under the rule of Islamic dynasties until the end of the 19th century, became a French protectorate from 1912, and gained independence in 1956. The country's monarch is its political and spiritual leader. In 1996, the monarch Hassan II. then ushered in a phase of liberalization. Morocco's claim to the former Spanish colony of Western Sahara, source of a long-standing conflict, is still unresolved.

Economy: Agriculture accounts for less than 20% of GDP, with the chief exports being citrus fruit, wine, fruit and vegetables. Industry, though underdeveloped, contributes 32% of GDP. Morocco has the largest phosphate reserves in the world. Services, principally tourism, form the chief economic sector at 53%. Trade with Europe is an important economic factor for the country.

Al-Mamlaka al-'Arabiya as-Sa'ūdiya
Saudi Arabia

Area: 1,960,582 sq km
Population: 25.8 million
GDP per capita: 11,800 US$
Capital: Riyadh
Government: Islamic absolute monarchy (Koran and Sunna serve as constitution)
Language: Arabic

Currency: 1 Saudi riyal = 20 qirshes = 100 hallalas

Geography: The country's territory, covering a large part of the Arabian Peninsula, features stony and sandy deserts traversed by wadis (watercourses that flow only after rains), in a hot and dry climate. The only natural vegetation is found in the oases. Tourist destinations almost entirely concentrate to pilgrimages to the holy sites in Mecca and Medina.

Politics: The history of Saudi Arabia begins with the Prophet Mohammed, who in the 7th century not only founded the new religion of Islam, but also united various Arab tribes. The Ottomans conquered the north and west of the peninsula, as well as the holy sites, in the 16th century. The ruling Saud dynasty, still in power today, founded the Islamic State of the Wahhabites in the 18th century. The Kingdom of Saudi Arabia was proclaimed in 1932. Its ruler is also the head of government and Keeper of the Holy Places.

Economy: More than three-quarters of the almost exclusively Muslim population live in the cities. A small proportion engage in nomadic livestock breeding (sheep, camels, goats), and 13% generate nearly one-tenth of GDP through agriculture in the widely scattered oases. The gigantic petroleum and natural gas reserves in the Persian Gulf make Saudi Arabia the world's largest oil exporter. Water shortages and population growth represent areas of concern.

Al-Miṣr/Egypt
Egypt

Area: 1,001,450 sq km
Population: 76.1 million
GDP per capita: 3,900 US$
Capital: Cairo
Government: Presidential republic
Language: Arabic
Currency: 1 Egyptian pound =100 piasters

1 The Blue Mosque in Mazar-e Sharif, Afghanistan.

2 Egypt: The Sphinx near the Pyramid of Cheops in Gizeh, 2500 BC.

3 Carpet manufacturing is still highly estimated in Morocco. The most valuable pieces decorate the floors and walls of the mosques.

4 The emirate of Kuwait has become one of the richest Persian Gulf states by exporting petroleum and natural gas.

Heirs to a legend: The times when gauchos rode over the pampas are long gone. These skilled horsemen and cattle drovers led a nomadic life, but over time were replaced with poorly paid farm laborers by the Argentinian ranchers, who frequently mistrusted the gauchos' fiercely independent spirit and cavalier attitude to property.

Geography: The fertile Nile valley, between three and 20 kilometers wide and extending over 1,000 kilometers from the river delta in the north deep into the south, has been settled since earliest times. The Arabian Desert lies to the northwest, while the Libyan Desert in the west occupies one quarter of the country's area. Egypt is in a subtropical zone of high pressure, with only the Mediterranean coastal areas receiving rain in winter. The Aswan Dam enables the country's agricultural areas to be irrigated.

Politics: The cradle of one of the earliest major cultures from the 3rd millennium BC, Egypt fell under Libyan, Persian and Assyrian rule. At the turn of the millennium, the fertile Nile region was the granary of Ancient Rome. Islam took effect after the conquest by the Arabs in the 7th century. In 1517 the country came under Ottoman rule. British influence increased after the opening of the Suez Canal in 1869. Egypt became an independent kingdom in 1922. After conflicts with Israel over the latter's occupation of the Sinai peninsula in 1967, a peace treaty was concluded in 1979, and Sinai was returned in 1982.

Economy: The high level of education in the cities contrasts with the lifestyle of the nomads. Only the fertile Nile valley yields grain, sugar-cane and cotton – the latter being Egypt's principal export after oil. Agriculture accounts for 18% of GDP. The Suez Canal is a major source of revenue. Tourism is suffering from Islamic extremist acts of terrorism. Economic reforms in the 1990s led to an increase in foreign investment levels and growth rates.

Al-Saharaw
Western Sahara

Area: 266,000 sq km
Population: 267,000
GDP per capita: 9,300 US$
Capital: El Aaiún
Government: Republic/ annexed by Morocco in 1979
Languages: Arabic, Spanish, Hassani
Currency: Saharaui peseta; unofficial currency: 1 Moroccan dirham = 100 centimes

Geography: This almost uninhabited country largely consists of semi-desert. Rocky outcrops feature in the north, sand deserts in the south.

Politics: The territory belonged to the Islamic empires that ruled over what is now Morocco from the 11th century. It was declared Spanish in 1885 and became the overseas province of Spanish Sahara in 1958. The Polisario Liberation Front was founded in 1973. Spain withdrew in 1975 and designated Morocco and Mauretania as administrative powers. In 1979 Mauretania waived its share in favor of Polisario, only to have its share annexed by Morocco. After a UNO peace plan Polisario and Morocco agreed a cease-fire in 1991, to be followed by a referendum on independence planned for 2008 after a period of extensive autonomy. The country is recognized by 29 OAU states and 77 states worldwide.

Economy: The country has rich phosphate reserves and fishing grounds in coastal waters. Oasis cultivation and nomadic animal husbandry are practised as subsistence farming.

Al-Yaman
Yemen

Area: 527,970 sq km
Population: 20 million
GDP per capita: 800 US$
Capital: Sanaa
Government: Republic
Languages: Arabic (official), English
Currency: 1 Yemen rial = 100 fils

Geography: Yemen lies at the southwestern edge of the Arab peninsula. North Yemen occupies a coastal strip on the Red Sea, behind which rise highlands and the Rub al-Khali desert. The South extends behind a narrow, coastal area with high rainfall to meet a mountain plateau, giving way to the sandy desert in the north. The country enjoys a tropical desert climate. Tourists can visit numerous Islamic and ancient sites of the Kingdom of Sheba.

Politics: In pre-Christian times, Yemen belonged to the Kingdom of the Minoans and Shebans. In the 7th century it was conquered by the Abbasids, and in the 16th century became part of the Ottoman Empire. Under British control, the Kingdom of Yemen was created in 1918 in Northern Yemen, and became a republic in 1962. A socialist republic was created in South Yemen in 1967. The process of unification to the Republic of Yemen lasted from 1990 to 1994. The first direct presidential elections were held in 1999.

Economy: Yemen is one of the most underdeveloped countries in the world. Agriculture is still the most important sector. Nomads roam the hinterland and industrialization is still in its infancy, with the export of oil playing the most important role.

Andorra
Andorra

Area: 467.7 sq km
Population: 69,900
GDP per capita: 19,000 US$
Capital: Andorra la Vella
Government: Parliamentary principality
Language: Catalan (official), Spanish, French

Argentina: The Patagonian Andes in the southern part of the country.

Currency: 1 euro = 100 cents

Geography: The small principality of Andorra consists of three valleys surrounded by high mountains in the eastern Pyrenees (highest peak: Coma Pendrosa, 2,946 m). More than half of the country is above the tree line.

Politics: Several states vied for control of Andorra before the 13th century. An agreement in 1278 left the area under the joint control of the French monarchy and the bishops of d'Urgell in Catalonia. In 1993 Andorra was established as an independent parliamentary democracy.

Economy: Andorra's topography limited the growth of industrial activity and large-scale agriculture. Sheep herding and tourism are the country's largest industries.

Angola
Angola

Area: 1,246,700 sq km
Population: 11 million
GDP per capita: 1,900 US$
Capital: Luanda
Government: Republic
Languages: Portuguese (official), Bantu languages
Currency: 1 kwanza = 100 lwei

Geography: The high plateau is traversed by rivers and slopes steeply down to the rain forests along the narrow coastal region. The tropical climate of Angola's interior is moderated by the altitude. Savanna to the far southwest gives way to desert. Nine national parks and animal reserves provide protection for indigenous wildlife.

Politics: Discovered in 1483 by Diego Cao, Angola remained a Portuguese province. Its independence in 1975 triggered a civil war lasting more than 15 years. The country is currently ruled by UN mandate, but the peace process is making only slow progress. In 2002 a peace treaty was signed by the two warring factions, stabilizing the political situation. Angola now faces a long process of reconstruction.

Economy: The long civil war has ravaged the economy, and the population depends on foreign aid. Agricultural products are sisal, sugar and tobacco. Key exports are coffee, diamonds, petroleum, and iron ores. The small industral sector primarily processes agricultural goods. Development of the country's poor infrastructure is desperately needed for greater economic progress.

Antigua and Barbuda
Antigua and Barbuda

Area: 442 sq km
Population: 68,300
GDP per capita: 11,000 US$
Capital: St. John's
Government: Constitutional monarchy within the Commonwealth
Languages: English (official), Creole
Currency: 1 Eastern Caribbean dollar = 100 cents

Geography: This tiny country in the Caribbean Ocean includes the islands of Antigua, Barbuda and Redonda in the Lesser Antilles. Uninhabited Redonda is part of the region's volcanic arc. In the south there are craggy mountains with lush vegetation. The climate is tropical, moderated by the sea winds but with frequent hurricanes. Beaches and ocean are ideal for bathing and diving, and the coastline is fringed by coral banks.

Politics: Discovered by Columbus in 1493, the islands were settled 150 years later by the English, who established plantations there. Antigua and Barbuda was a British colony from 1667 and did not gain independence until 1981. The country is governed by a bicameral parliament, elected every five years; the British monarch is the head of state.

Economy: The majority of the population is of African descent. Various plants are cultivated. The largest contribution to the economy comes from tourism. Exports include petroleum products.

Mysterious glances: Traditional dress is becoming rare in modern Yemen, but the veil is still an important part of women's clothing.

Many islamic women do not regard it as a symbol of suppression, but as an expression of their Muslim identity and growing autonomy in public life.

Argentina
Argentina

Area: 2,766,889 sq km
Population: 39.1 million
GDP per capita: 11,200 US$
Capital: Buenos Aires
Government: Federal republic
Language: Spanish
Currency: 1 Argentinian peso = 100 centavos

Geography: The country is around 3,700 kilometers long from north to south; the Andean mountains form its western border with Chile. To the southeast, the main settlement area is the treeless plains of the pampas, with their fertile steppes, giving way in the south to Patagonia's tableland. In the north, the pampas meets the densely wooded, rainy area between the Paraná and Uruguay rivers and the swamp forests along their banks, terminating in the Brazilian mountains. Favorite destinations are the beaches along the Atlantic Ocean, the ski resorts and nature reserves in the Andes and the game reserves on Tierra del Fuego.

Politics: The arrival of the Spanish in 1516 heralded two centuries of foreign rule that ended in 1816 with the Proclamation of Independence by the United Provinces. After conquering Patagonia in 1880, Argentina became a major destination for immigrants. Until 1982 the country was ruled by a succession of military juntas and conservative large-scale landowners. Argentina's defeat by Britain in the Falklands War led to the end of military rule and to free presidential elections in 1983. Since 1999 Argentina has faced a deep economic recession, resulting in the country's inability to pay back foreign debts and an exploding crime rate.

Economy: 90% of Argentina's population are descended from European immigrants. The country has extensive agricultural and industrial capacities. Agriculture (principally livestock) accounts for 8% of GDP, and services 63%. The country's industry concentrates on processing agricultural products and on mechanical engineering. Exports are primarily from the agricultural sector.

Armenija (Hayastan)
Armenia

Area: 29,800 sq km
Population: 3 million
GDP per capita: 3,900 US$
Capital: Yerevan
Government: Republic
Languages: Armenian (official), Russian, Kurdish
Currency: 1 dram = 100 luma

Geography: The Ararat highlands extend to the west, with the peaks of the Lesser Caucasus in the north. The central depression in the southeast is dominated by Lake Sevan.

The south has fertile farmlands and a favorable climate. Owing to the continental climate, steppe and semi-desert vegetation dominate. Armenia frequently suffers earthquakes and drought.

Politics: In the 7th century Turks and Persians contested the country; in the 19th century, Russia's attempt at conquest was repulsed. In 1922 Armenia was divided, with one part becoming a Soviet Republic, and the other remaining with Turkey. Armenia declared its independence in 1991, but retained the socialist-tinted constitution. The predominantly Christian enclave of Nagorno Karabakh has in recent times been the object of conflict with Armenia's Islamic neighbor Azerbaijan.

Economy: The economy is characterized by the difficult transition from the Soviet planned economy to a market economy. Half of GDP is generated by industry, only a fifth by services. Important exports are light industry products and diamonds. The country imports oil, gas, and foodstuffs.

As-Sūdān
Sudan

Area: 2,505,813 sq km
Population: 39.1 million
GDP per capita: 1,900 US$
Capital: Khartoum
Government: Republic
Languages: Arabic (official),

1 Agriculture is the most important economic sector in Sudan. The south, however, is suffering from aridity and is therefore dependent on aid from the north.

2 The mini state of Antigua and Barbuda belongs to the "islands above the wind" (Lesser Antilles). The economy is mostly dependent on cruise tourism.

3 Argentina: Perito Moreno Glacier in Los Glaciares National Park.

4 The adobe houses of Wadi Hadramaut (UNESCO World Heritage Site) in the south of Yemen reach up to 30 meters high and are nearly 300 years old.

Land of the plains: In Bangladesh heavy rainfalls during monsoon periods flood the rivers. Like islands, dry spots are only accessible by boat. Paddies cover the fertile alluvial soil, the largest river delta of the world formed by the rivers of Ganges and Bramaputra. Sylhet in the north, surrounded by rolling hills on the border to the Indian province of Assam, houses the largest tea plantations of the country.

English, Hamitic, and Nilotic languages
Currency: 1 Sudanese pound = 100 piastres

Geography: The Sudan is the largest African country in terms of area. It is divided into north and south by the great swamps of the Sudd, a flood plain of the White Nile. Almost one-third of the country consists of barren sand desert, although rain forests grow in the mountainous southern regions. The climate is largely continental tropical. The game reserves in the south are the chief tourist destinations. Desertification is a major environmental issue throughout the country.

Politics: Sudan's early history was shaped by Egypt; an independent kingdom was not formed until 1000 BC. Christian empires ruled from the 6th century onwards until the country was Islamicized by Arab settlers at the end of the 13th century. Sudan was ruled by the British in the 19th and 20th centuries. Since Sudan acheived independence in 1956, religious and ethnic differences have led to frequent political unrest and armed conflicts; human rights violations and famine are commonplace in the country.

Economy: Subsistence agriculture and nomadic animal husbandry are practised. Agricultural products are the chief exports, comprising cotton, peanuts, sesame, and oilseed as well as 80% of the world's gum resin production. The small industrial sector, which did not begin its slow development until after independence, is rudimentary and employs 5% of the workforce. Services are the most significant sector, accounting for 50% of GDP, and the new oil industry boosts exports.

Australia
Australia

Area: 7,686,850 sq km
Population: 19.9 million
GDP per capita: 28,900 US$
Capital: Canberra
Government: Parliamentary democracy
Languages: English, Asian and Aboriginal languages

Currency: 1 Australian dollar = 100 cents

Geography: Deserts and semi-arid land cover around 70% of the world's smallest continent, including most of western and central Australia. The 3,000-kilometer-long Great Dividing Range stretches along the continent's east coast, while the Great Barrier Reef extends 2,000 kilometers from north to south, directly off the coast. Northern Australia features extensive grassy and forested savannas as well as humid rain forests along the coast. The Murray and Darling rivers in the south are Australia's most important rivers. The island state of Tasmania is located south of mainland Australia's southeastern coast. In addition to numerous national parks and wilderness areas, Australia also features countless beaches and diving sites open to tourists.

Barbuda: Sandy beaches make the Island a holiday paradise.

Politics: The Aborigines, Australia's indigenous inhabitants, arrived on the continent during the last ice age. In 1770, British captain James Cook claimed the colony of New South Wales for Great Britain. The colony served as a British penal colony until 1865. The first free settlers arrived – in the Sydney area – in 1793. The six Australian colonies united in 1901 to form the Commonwealth of Australia. In the following decades, Australia achieved increased political independence but the British monarch remains the country's official head of state. The Aborigines have been granted increased political rights in recent decades, including citizenship and voting rights after generations of political and social neglect.

Economy: Immigrants from more than 120 nations have settled in Australia during the past two centuries. The country's standard of living is one of the world highest. The country's leading export products include agricultural goods, and mineral resources such as iron, uranium, nickel, bauxite, raw diamonds, and opals. Australia, the world's leading wool and beef exporter, is also an important producer of grain, wine meat and dairy products. Around 25% of the country's labor force works in the manufacturing sector, while at least 70% of Australians now work in the service sector, including tourism.

Azerbajdzan
Azerbaijan

Area: 86,600 sq km
Population: 7.9 million
GDP per capita: 3,400 US$
Capital: Baku
Government: Republic
Languages: Azeri (official), Turkish, Russian
Currency: 1 manat = 100 gepik

Geography: Over half the country's area is covered by the Greater Caucasus (4,466 m) in the north, the Lesser Caucasus with Karabakh in the west, and the southern mountains extending to Iran. The plains of the Kura and Arax rivers in the east are bordered by the Caspian Sea in the south. The climate ranges from subtropical and humid to arid-dry. Large-scale irrigation is necessary for agriculture.

Politics: A settlement in early times, the area was briefly a Roman province. Islamization commenced in the 7th century. After 300 years of Mongol rule, Azerbaijan was besieged first by the Ottomans and then by the Russians, who in 1813 divided the country with the Persians. The Soviet Republic of Azerbaijan was founded in 1920. Ethnic conflicts over the Nagorno Karabakh enclave and its annexation by Armenia in 1988 led to the declaration of independence in 1991 and to a more pronounced turn towards Islam.

Economy: The economy concentrates on winemaking, cotton, tobacco, vegetables, olives, and tea. Canned fish products (caviar) from the Caspian Sea are exported. The country's real wealth, however, lies in its mineral resources such as oil, iron ore, copper, and manganese, for which development is planned. These resources form the basis of the remaining industry (chemical, mechanical engineering). The main oil fields lie in the Apseron peninsula and to the west of Baku. Environmental issues are an increasing concern.

Bahamas
Bahamas

Area: 13,939 sq km
Population: 300,000
GDP per capita: 16,800 US$
Capital: Nassau
Government: Parliamentary monarchy within the Commonwealth
Language: English
Currency: 1 Bahamian dollar = 100 cents

Geography: The island state comprises 30 large and 700 small to tiny islands, most with sandy beaches and thousands of reefs extending over 1,200 kilometers from Florida's east coast down to Haiti. Tourist centers with bathing or sailing facilities can be found on the Exumas and around Nassau. Angling is popular around the Bimini Islands, and the Inagua Islands have a rich variety of tropical fauna.

Politics: It was here that Columbus first stepped onto American soil in 1492. The islands were depopulated by Spanish slave traders; the British established a crown colony in the 17th century. The Bahamas have been independent since 1973. The parliament is bicameral, modeled on its British counterpart, with elections held every five years.

Economy: Agriculture is restricted by the barrenness of the steppes. In addition to tourism, which accounts for around half of GDP, the economy is principally driven by the resale of imported petroleum and petroleum products, chiefly to the USA.

Bahrain see Al-Bahrain

Bangladesh
Bangladesh

Area: 144,000 sq km
Population: 141.3 million
GDP per capita: 1,900 US$
Capital: Dhaka
Government: Republic
Languages: Bengali (official), Urdu and Hindi
Currency: 1 taka = 100 poisha

Geography: The entire country consists of fertile lowlands in a monsoon region with high rainfall (June to October); the unprotected coast, with few harbors, is threatened by flooding, often with catastrophic consequences. The southwest at the Indian border comprises part of the flood plains of the Ganges and Brahmaputra. Tourist destinations include Dhaka with its interesting old town, and the coastal city of Chittagong for swimming. Part of the Sundarban National Park, with unique fauna, is on Bangladeshi territory.

Politics: The former Bengal belonged to the British colony of India (1757–1947). In the division that followed Indian independence, West Bengal

Dreamtime: The Aborigines of Australia inhabited the continent for 30,000 years. The myths of the semi-nomadic clans are evidence of their lifestyle in harmony with the forces of nature. Today many of the sacred landscapes of the Aborigines again carry their mythical names.

remained part of India, whereas East Bengal went to Pakistan. After bloody riots following the great flood of 1970, East Bengal separated from Pakistan, and the Republic of Bangladesh was declared in 1971. After 15 years of authoritarian presidential rule, characterized by frequent coups d'état, the first democratically elected government took office in 1991. Relations with neighboring India have visibly improved in recent years.

Economy: The education system has been seriously neglected, and only a quarter of the population is literate. One of the poorest national economies and highest population densities in the world, Bangladesh relies essentially on agriculture, which employs 66% of the working population in small companies and generates one third of GDP. The most important exports are rice, jute and seafood. 12% of the workforce are employed in industry, comprising small handicraft concerns (jute products, cotton yarn and fabrics, textiles, sugar, and tea), and generating about one third of GDP. Heavy industry processes the available raw materials (natural gas, oil, coal, and ores) but is of minor importance.

Barbados
Barbados

Area: 430 sq km
Population: 276,000
GDP per capita: 16,200 US$
Capital: Bridgetown
Government: Parliamentary monarchy within the Commonwealth
Languages: English (official), Bajan
Currency: 1 Barbados dollar = 100 cents

Geography: The easternmost island of the Lesser Antilles, 36 kilometers long and 24 kilometers wide, is volcanic in origin and largely (80%) composed of fossilized coral and fringed by coral reefs. The impermeable bedrock prevents the formation of watercourses. Only the north of the island has rolling hills, some up to 340 meters high. The island's climate and natural features make it a holiday paradise.

Politics: Discovered in the 16th century by Spain, Barbados became a British crown colony in 1652. In the 17th century the first settlers established sugar-cane plantations worked by imported African slaves; the slave economy ended in 1838. Barbados gained independence in 1966.

Economy: The traditional sugar-cane cultivation employs only 6% of the workforce and is dwindling in significance. The island is heavily dependent on imports, including foodstuffs, timber, consumer goods, paper, machinery, and crude oil. Its exports include sugar, cotton, and peanuts, but

also electronic components and petroleum from deposits in the interior and the north and east coasts. Services, principally tourism, contribute two-thirds of GDP. The island has an international airport and seaport.

Belarus
Belarus

Area: 207,600 sq km
Population: 10.3 million
GDP per capita: 6,000 US$
Capital: Minsk
Government: Republic
Language: Belarusian (official), Russian, minority languages
Currency: 1 Belarusian rouble = 100 kopecks

Geography: Belarus is located on the vast East European Plain and consists largely of flat lowlands. The country features numerous rivers, canals and lakes in all of its regions. The Palesse marsh in southern

Belarus is the largest marshland in Europe. The capital city of Minsk and the country's lakes are Belarus' principal tourist attractions.

Politics: The Slavic ancestors of the modern Belarusians were able to preserve their language and culture despite

 The Great Barrier Reef near the northeastern coast of Australia.

2 **Uluru-kata Tjuta National Park** in Central Australia features the famous monolith Ayers Rock (Uluru) and other interesting natural attractions.

3 **The Sydney Opera House** is dominated by skyscrapers of the Australian metropolis. Port Jackson (also known as Sydney Harbour) saw the first penal colonists at the end of the 18th century.

België/Belgique Belgium

Caribbean joie de vivre: The small country of Belize is noted for its easygoing lifestyle, its snow-white beaches picturesquely fringed by coconut palms, and untouched tropical landscapes in the interior.

The multi-ethnic population, augmented by Europeans and Americans, lives an unhurried, carefree life in tune with the tropical climate.

centuries of foreign domination by the Polish and Lithuanian Commonwealth. The country came under the control of the Russian Empire at the end of the 18th century. In 1922, Belarus became a Soviet republic in the USSR. Belarus was declared an independent republic in 1991, following the collapse of the Soviet Union. The repressive policies of Belarus' government have been repeatedly criticized by the European Union and numerous human rights organizations and have isolated the country.

Economy: Belarus faced a severe economic crisis, including high inflation rates and rising foreign debts, during most of the 1990s. The country has experienced stable growth in recent years, but the economy remains heavily regulated and is largely closed to foreign investment. The agricultural sector accounts for approximately one third of the country's GDP. Manufacturing produces just over half (56%) of the national GDP. The government has failed to implement the reforms neccesary for stable economic development.

België/Belgique
Belgium

Area: 30,528 sq km
Population: 10.3 million
GDP per capita: 29,000 US$
Capital: Brussels
Government: Parliamentary monarchy
Languages: French, Flemish, German
Currency: 1 euro = 100 cents

Geography: Belgium's smooth North Sea coast is lined by sand dunes and sandy beaches. The west and north are dominated by fertile marshy plains, polders, and moorlands. Farther south lies the central plateau, a region of fertile valley crossed by numerous rivers and canals. The third major region of Belgium, the Ardennes, is a heavily forested area of low mountains. Belgium's major tourist attractions include the historic towns of Flanders, the Ardennes countryside, and the capital city of Brussels.

Politics: The cities of Flanders were among Europe's leading

commercial and cultural centers during the late Middle Ages. From then, until the 19th century, Belgium was under the control of several foreign nations – Spain between the 16th and 17th centuries, followed by Austria, France, and finally the Netherlands. Belgium became an independent kingdom in 1833. Modern Belgium is a federal state divided into three distinct regions – Flanders, Brussels, and Wallonia, each of which has extensive political autonomy and its own government. The capital city of Brussels houses the European Union and NATO headquarters.

Economy: Belgium's highly productive agricultural sector produces less than 2% of the country's GDP. The industrial areas along the Sambre and Meuse (Maas) Rivers are important centers of the chemical, glass, and machinery industries. The expanding service sectors currently account for around 68% of the country's

Brussels: The city is the cultural and political center of Belgium.

annual GDP. Belgium has one of the world's most modern transportation networks.

Belize
Belize

Area: 22,965 sq km
Population: 273,000
GDP per capita: 4,900 US$
Capital: Belmopan
Government: Const. monarchy

Languages: English (official), Creole, Spanish, minorities
Currency: 1 Belize dollar = 100 cents

Geography: Belize, to the southeast of the Yucatán Peninsula, is composed of swampy coastland with large rivers and countless lagoons enclosing hilly landscapes (altitudes around 1,000 m) in the interior. Rain forests and dense mangrove forests flourish in the humid, tropical climate. A major natural phenomenon is an island chain of coral reefs extending 300 kilometers down the coastline. Hurricanes are frequent.

Politics: Before its discovery by Columbus in the 16th century and colonization by the Spanish conqueror Cortèz (1524/25) the region was the heartland of the Mayan civilization. Settled from the 17th century by British colonists, it became a crown colony in 1862 as British Honduras. Renamed Belize in 1973, it

gained independence in 1981. The Governor-General of Belize represents the British monarch.

Economy: While 38% of the area is suitable for cultivation, only around 12% is actually utilized. Citrus fruits, seafood, bananas, sugarcane, cocoa, and tropical hardwoods are key exports. The underdeveloped industrial sector employs 10% of

the workforce and is primarily oriented toward products for export, comprising sawmills, sugar factories, rum distilleries, and textiles. Services, including tourism, account for 57% of GDP.

Benin
Benin

Area: 112,622 sq km
Population: 7.2 million
GDP per capita: 1,100 US$
Capital: Porto Novo
Government: Presidential republic
Languages: French (official), Fon, Yoruba, and other tribal languages
Currency: 1 CFA franc = 100 centimes

Geography: Benin's coast along the Gulf of Guinea consists of humid, swampy lowlands fringed by lagoons. To the north fertile clay highlands rise to form a plateau. In the west the land slopes gently down to the Niger basin. Tourist destinations are the nature parks in the north, and the cities of Ouidah and Porto Novo in the south.

Politics: In the 17th century the kingdom of the Fon, based in the city of Aborney, increased in power. The Fon delivered slaves to European trading centers. In 1899 the region became part of the colony of French West Africa under the name Dahomey, and was decolonized and awarded independence in 1960. The Republic of Benin was established in 1975 after a coup d'ètat. Torn by tribal wars, the country held its first free parliamentary elections in 1991.

Economy: Benin is inhabited by more than 60 ethnic populations. Attempts to nationalize the economy in the 1970s failed. The country primarily lives from the agricultural sector, which produces for the domestic market, as well as coffee, oils, and cotton for export. The industrial and service sectors are both relatively undeveloped. Tourism is receiving increasing promotion. The country has experienced impressive growth rates in recent years but the high popu-

lation growth has prevented a significant rise in living standards.

Bhutan
Bhutan

Area: 47,000 sq km
Population: 2.2 million
GDP per capita: 1,300 US$
Capital: Thimphu
Government: Constitutional monarchy
Languages: Dzongkha (official), Tibetan dialects
Currency: 1 ngultrum = 100 chetrum

Geography: This small kingdom on the southern incline of the Himalayas is accessible only with extreme difficulty. The mighty mountain chains (Jomo Lhari, 7,314 m) flank the high plateau, which slopes down only gradually to the southern foothills on the Indian border. Interesting destinations include the monasteries and temples in the vicinity of the capital.

Politics: In a country initially ruled by Indian princes, Tibetan conquerors founded a lamaist state in the 9th century. In the wake of 19th century civil wars, a hereditary monarchy emerged under British influence, which today governs the land together with the National Assembly (parliament of estates). There is close cooperation with India over foreign affairs and defense. The country did not receive television until 1999 – a gift from the reigning monarch to his people.

Economy: Nearly half of GDP is generated by agriculture, which also accounts for 90% of all jobs and covers domestic needs. A few products (maize, wheat, cardamom) are also exported. Wood from the extensive forest is exported to India. The poorly developed industrial sector consists of small handicraft concerns (weaving, metalwork, mask carving). Bhutan has been open to tourism to a limited extent since 1974, and the 5,000 annual tourists are the most important source of foreign currency. Technical and mechanical work traditionally occupies a lowly status.

Mysterious: The people of Bhutan call their kingdom Druk Yul, "land of the thunder-dragon". White prayer banners and countless sacred buildings bear witness to the deeply religious nature of the mostly Buddhist population. The people of the almost inaccessible valleys of the southern Himalayas have been able to preserve their traditional way of life. Nomadic yak-herds live in the upper regions.

Bolivia
Bolivia

Area: 1,098,581 sq km
Population: 8.7 million
GDP per capita: 2,400 US$
Capital: Sucre
Government: Presidential republic
Languages: Spanish, Quechua and Aymará (all official)
Currency: 1 boliviano = 100 centavos

Geography: The west of the country is taken up by the Bolivian Andes, divided by the Altiplano plateau with an average altitude of 3,000–4,000 meters. The lowlands to the east of the Andes give way to the plain of La Plata in the south and the Amazon basin in the north. The climate ranges from cold to tropical. Tourist attractions are Lake Titicaca, Inca sites in Tiahuanaco, and the ancient silver-mining center of Potosí.

Politics: Bolivia's history has always been closely linked to that of neighboring Peru. The end of the 18th century saw the first Indian uprisings against Spanish colonial rule, brought to an end in 1825 with the foundation of the republic. The present-day political situation is marked by ideological conflicts, guerilla warfare and military coups. Bolivia has had around 200 governments since it was founded. The unicameral parliament, like the president, is elected every five years.

Economy: Almost 40% of the workforce supply 17% of GDP in agriculture on the plateau and in the valleys. The most important crop is probably illegal coca cultivation. Mining includes zinc, tin, lead, and precious metals. Petroleum and natural gas exports are an important economic factor. The processing industry primarily comprises small and medium-size enterprises (foodstuffs, textiles).

Bosna i Hercegovina
Bosnia-Herzegovina

Area: 51,129 sq km
Population: 4 million
GDP per capita: 6,100 US$ (estimated)

Capital: Sarajevo
Government: Republic
Languages: Bosnian, Croatian, Serbian (all official)
Currency: 1 mark

Geography: Bosnia-Herzegovina is a largely mountainous country with large stretches of dense forests and a continental climate. Because of poor soils and the mountainous terrain, only a few sections of the country, such as the Sava Valley, are suitable for large-scale agriculture.

Politics: Bosnia was dominated by foreign powers during most of its history. A large percentage of Bosnia's population converted to Islam during the more than 400 years that the region was under the control of the Turkish Ottoman Empire from 1463. The region was ruled by the Austro-Hungarian Empire in the 19th century. Bosnia was part of the republic of Yugoslavia during most of the 20th century. Following the collapse of Yugoslavia, Bosnia experienced a period of ethnic conflict that escalated into a bloody war and widespread "ethnic cleansing." The country has been divided into an ethnic Serb republic and a Croat-Muslim federation since 1995. Many refugees are now returning to the country despite continuing hostility between the ethnic groups.

Economy: Most of the country's infrastructure and industrial facilities were damaged in the civil war of the 1990s. Foreign aid remains important to the country, but post-war recovery is rapidly progressing.

Botswana
Botswana

Area: 600,370 sq km
Population: 1.6 million
GDP per capita: 8,800 US$
Capital: Gaborone
Government: Republic
Languages: Setswana, English (both official)
Currency: 1 pula = 100 thebe

Geography: The Kalahari semi-desert covers almost 80% of Botswana, which extends over the chiefly flat continental plateau (800–1,300 m). Agriculture is restricted to small areas in the southeast. Around one-fifth of the country is a registered national park. The Okavango forms a freshwater delta on the northern rim of the Kalahari. The climate is subtropical and extremely dry, with maximum temperatures of 40° C in summer and 6° C in winter. Temperatures in the capital range from 13° C (July) to 26° C (January).

1 Marginal rainfall generated vast salt-pans in the Makarikari Basin of Botswana.

2 The impressive ruins of the Maya city Xunantunich, one of Belize's main attractions, perch on a mountain in the jungle.

3 The traditional ponchos and blankets of the Bolivian Indios are produced from naturally dyed llama or sheep's wool.

4 In the Kingdom of Bhutan, temples are not only places of worship but also administrative centers for the small country. The picture shows the 17th-century Paro Dzong.

At Carnival time in Brazil: Samba sets the pace. Processions may last for days and are crammed with gorgeous costumes that are lovingly fashioned throughout the year.

Politics: English missionary territory since 1820, Botswana became a British protectorate in 1885 because of its key strategic location to the north of the Boer state. The country was administered by the British Ambassador to South Africa from 1964, and gained independence in 1966 as the Republic of Botswana. The government comprises the National Assembly and the House of Chiefs.

Economy: 95% of the population are Bantu, with over 80% living outside the urban centers. Agriculture largely consists of extensive cattle farming, frequently beset by drought. However, the backbone of the economy are the rich diamond mines of the Kalahari, which have made Botswana the second largest exporter of these gems in the world. Iron ore and anthracite are also important export commodities. Botswana is a member of the Southern African Customs Union.

Brasil
Brazil

Area: 8,511,996 sq km
Population: 184 million
GDP per capita: 7,600 US$
Capital: Brasília
Government: Federative rep.
Languages: Portuguese (official), regional Indian languages
Currency: 1 real = 100 centavos

Geography: The Atlantic forms the eastern border of the world's fifth largest country; the narrow coastal strip is densely populated. To the north, in the mountains of Guyana, tropical rain forest dominates the landscape. Farther south is the rain forest area of the Amazon basin, home to a unique ecosystem with countless animal species. Tourist centers are Rio de Janeiro, the coastal regions, the Amazon and the southwestern Iguazú Falls.

Politics: Brazil was settled as early as the 8th century BC. The Spanish reached the coast in 1500, the first Europeans to do so; however, the region became a Portuguese colony in the 17th century. In 1825 Brazil declared independence, and

economic prosperity began as coffee exports grew. The military seized power in 1961; the first general elections were held in 1982, and the country had a civil president in 1985. The new constitution of 1988 confirmed the presidential system, although the military still retains extensive influence. Voting is compulsory between the ages of 18 and 69.

Economy: The country is inhabited by many ethnic groups, the smallest of which are the indigenous Indians. Agriculture is highly profitable; coffee, cocoa, soybeans, sugar, tobacco, maize, and cotton are cultivated in addition to livestock farming. Rich natural resources (iron, manganese) are as yet not fully exploited. Economic reforms introduced from the mid-1990s are showing initial success. The industrial sector of this highly industrialized country (textiles, leather goods) is dominated by the automotive industry and its suppliers. Other key exports are metals and metal products.

Brunei
Brunei

Area: 5,765 sq km
Population: 365,000
GDP per capita: 18,600 US$

Brunei comprises two non-adjoining territories on the northern coast of Borneo, surrounded by the Malaysian Sarawak mountains. The hill country, covered by tropical rain forests, is the habitat of a rich fauna. The densely settled coast consists of alluvial land with mangrove forests, broken by coral sand beaches. The country has an equatorial rainy climate. The capital with its old town, Sultan's palace and mosque, is worth visiting.

Politics: Muslim Malays founded the Sultanate of Brunei in the 15th century and it became a British protectorate in 1888. After Japanese occupation in 1941–1945, it became a British colony until the constitution of 1959, which initially guaranteed autonomy. Brunei finally gained independence in 1984. Enthroned in 1967, the Sultan took over the affairs of state in 1973, and has reigned as an absolute monarch since 1984, supported by a council. He is one of the world's richest men. The country has no political parties and no suffrage.

Economy: Islam plays an important role in the life of the predominantly Malay population, which, owing to the country's enormous riches, enjoys full social protection. Agricul-

Bŭlgarija
Bulgaria

Area: 110,910 sq km
Population: 7.5 million
GDP per capita: 7,600 US$
Capital: Sofia
Government: Republic
Language: Bulgarian
Currency: 1 lev = 100 stotinki

Geography: The marshy Danube basin forms the northern border of Bulgaria. South of this region lie vast fertile plains. Southern Bulgaria is largely mountainous: the Balkans, Rhodope Mountains, and other highlands cover over a third of the country. Bulgaria has a continental climate, with warm summers and cold winters. The country's major tourist attractions include the beaches along the Black Sea and the cities of Varna and Sofia, as well as the landscapes of Pirin National Park.

Politics: The first Bulgarian state was formed in the 7th century by Slavs and Bulgars from the Volga basin. Bulgaria was dominated by the Turkish Ottoman Empire for more than five centuries before it achieved independence in 1878. After decades as a kingdom, Bulgaria was declared a people's republic in 1947. The country was closely aligned to

transition to democracy in the early 1990s. The fall of the socialist government in 1996 was followed by fiscal discipline and economic reforms. Despite recent impressive growth and successful reforms, most Bulgarians still live in poverty. Manufacturing and services account for more than 75% of GDP. Major agricultural products include wine, fruits, and tobacco. Lignite, iron ore, lead, and zinc are mined. Key exports include chemicals and textiles.

Burkina Faso
Burkina Faso

Area: 274.200 sq km
Population: 13.6 million
GDP per capita: 1,100 US$
Capital: Ouagadougou
Government: Republic
Languages: French (official), Fulbe, More and other tribal languages
Currency: 1 CFA franc = 100 centimes

Geography: Wet savannas in the southwest give way to dry savannas in the country's center and main settlements. The Black Volta is the only river that carries water all year. Part of the Sahel desert region lies in the northeast, where a semi-desert climate reigns. Tourist centers are the cities of Ouagadougou and Bobo-Dioulasso and the national parks with their rich wildlife.

Politics: The heart of today's Burkina Faso was the state of Ouagadougou, founded in the 11th century by the Mossi and conquered by the French in the 19th century. The former colony of Upper Volta (1919–1960) was renamed Burkina Faso in 1984. After independence, Burkina Faso was weakened by frequent attempted coups followed by years of military dictatorship; the political situation seems to have stabilized.

Economy: Among the most densely populated countries in West Africa, Burkina Faso is inhabited by around 160 tribes, around half of whom practice natural religions. Illiteracy is high at around 80%. Despite regular periods of drought, the country's economy is based on

Rio de Janeiro: The Sugarloaf's peak towers 395 meters over Guanabara Bay.

Capital: Bandar Seri Begawan
Government: Sultanate
Languages: Malay (official), English
Currency: 1 Brunei dollar = 100 cents
Geography: The Sultanate of

ture is of subordinate importance. A large proportion of the foodstuffs are imported. Brunei has extensive petroleum and natural gas reserves and 56% of GDP is generated in this sector. Tourism is as yet limited.

the Soviet Union before 1991. Bulgaria is now a multi-party parliamentary republic and a candidate for EU membership.

Economy: Bulgaria has faced several economic crises since its

Tax-heaven: The vast wealth of the small Sultanate of Brunei is solely founded upon the exploitation of the country's petroleum resources.

Its inhabitants pay no taxes, enjoy free housing and receive a basic salary from the state.

agriculture, with 90% of the population practising subsistence farming to account for 35% of GDP. Small amounts of cotton are exported. Apart from gold, the rich natural resources are largely untapped. The country's poor infrastructure and widespread corruption have impaired development. 48% of GDP is generated by the services sector and 17% by industry.

Burundi
Burundi

Area: 27,834 sq km
Population: 6.2 million
GDP per capita: 600 US$
Capital: Bujumbura
Government: Presidential republic
Languages: Kirundi, French (official), Kiswaheli
Currency: 1 Burundi franc = 100 centimes

Geography: Lying to the northeast of Lake Tanganyika, the country comprises uplands with wet and dry savannas in the interior and humid tropical rain forests to the northeast. The humid, tropical climate is moderated by the country's relatively high average elevation above sea level.

Politics: Tutsi tribes invaded the territory of Burundi in the 15th century and established feudal rule over the indigenous Hutus. In 1890, the country became part of the German colony of East Africa, and subsequently fell under Belgian administration. Since Burundi's independence in 1962, the political situation has been determined by repeated conflicts between the Hutu (85% of the population) and Tutsi (15%). Despite a new constitution (1992) and international efforts, the civil war cannot be regarded as over.

Economy: Agriculture is the chief economic sector. The mild climate favors tropical fruit farming and extensive animal husbandry. The industrial center around the city of Bujumbura produces textiles and small amounts of agricultural products for export, with coffee the most important of these. The government of Burundi is heavily dependent on foreign aid.

Cabo Verde
Cape Verde

Area: 4,033 sq km
Population: 415,000
GDP per capita: 1,400 US$
Capital: Praia
Government: Republic
Languages: Portuguese (official), Creole
Currency: 1 Cape Verde escudo = 100 centavos

Geography: Cape Verde, an archipelago off the west coast of Africa, comprises nine large islands and five uninhabited islets, all of volcanic origin. The landscape is dominated by bush, plains and semi-desert vegetation. Cape Verde has one of the lowest rainfalls in the world, and drought periods often last for years. The sandy beaches on Sal, Boa Vista, and Maio and the island of Fogo attract tourists.

Politics: After the islands' discovery by the Portuguese in 1460, it remained under Portuguese rule for more than 500 years. The slave trade with America brought long prosperity. Cape Verde did not become independent until 1975. The parliament, elected for a five-year term, elects the executive body and the President.

Economy: More than 70% of the population are descended from Portuguese immigrants and African slaves. More than 60% live and work abroad owing to the sparse natural resources. The rich fishing grounds off the coast account for 50% of export revenues, but almost all foodstuffs must be imported. There is a small textile industry. Most of the country's GDP is generated by the service sector. The country's local tourism industry is expanding.

Cameroun/Cameroon
Cameroon

Area: 475,442 sq km
Population: 16.1 million
GDP per capita: 1,800 US$
Capital: Yaoundé
Government: Presidential republic
Languages: French, English (both official), Bantu languages
Currency: 1 CFA franc = 100 centimes

Geography: The narrow coastal plain is covered by tropical rain forests that give way to wet savanna in the largely mountainous interior. To the north are dry grassland savannas that meet Lake Chad in the northeast and the Sahel to the far north. The highest point is the volcano Mount Cameroon (4,070 m). Cameroon's natural

1 The ritual dances and other traditions of eastern Africa arose as a way of making tribal territorial claims.

2 The Mosque of Bandar Seri Begawan, with its 44-meter-high minaret, lies amidst an artificial lagoon.

3 Burkina Faso is one of the poorest countries of the world.

4 The large monastery complex of Rila, most of which was reconstructed in the 19th century, is an important Bulgarian national monument.

Colombia: The year in this South American country is punctuated by numerous ethnic feasts: Five days before Ash Wednesday, Barranquilla turns into "the foolish city" and thousands of visitors come for the parades and dance competitions. Medellín is home to the second largest bullfighting arena in Latin America, where the popular corridas take place.

beauty and diversity of cultures offer a wide range of tourist attractions.

Politics: In the 15th century the coast of Cameroon was a center of the slave and ivory trade for European colonial powers. It became a German protectorate in 1884. From 1918 Britain and France shared the former colony under the mandate of the League of Nations, awarding the country independence in 1960. After a period as a federal republic, Cameroon became a presidential republic in 1972.

Economy: The population is composed of roughly 200 tribes. Agriculture plays a significant role, with coffee and cocoa, the principal exports. The country's petroleum resources brought only temporary economic growth. The industrial and services sectors are underdeveloped. Cameroon has experienced steady and strong growth in recent years and the country has made progress in reducing its foreign debt burden.

Central African Republic see République Centrafricaine

Chad see Tchad

Canada
Canada

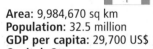

Area: 9,984,670 sq km
Population: 32.5 million
GDP per capita: 29,700 US$
Capital: Ottawa
Government: Parliamentary monarchy in the Commonwealth
Languages: English, French (both official)
Currency: 1 Canadian dollar = 100 cents

Geography: Canada is the second largest country in the world, fringed to east and west by two great mountain chains. The foothills of the Appalachian Mountains extend to the Atlantic coast in the east, giving way in the west to the broad plains and lakes of the Great Plains and bounded by Hudson Bay to the north. The plains rise further to the west, meeting the Rocky Mountains (highest peak: Mt. Logan (6,050 m) at an altitude of 1,500 meters. To the far

north, the Arctic islands border the North Polar Sea. 80% of the country consists of forests and tundra; the remainder is arable land and the polar islands. The continental climate fluctuates considerably, with average winter temperatures often falling below zero. Canada offers many tourist attractions: countless national parks of unspoiled scenery, Niagara Falls and cosmopolitan cities such as Toronto, Québec, Montreal, and Vancouver.

Politics: Up to the arrival of the first settlers in the 17th century, the country was inhabited by First Nations tribes and Inuit. Conflicts over British and French territorial claims were decided in 1763 by the British. Canada did not gain full political independence until 1931. The country is governed by a bicameral parliament, the lower house of which is elected every five years, with the British monarch as the formal Head of State. Given increasing calls for autonomy in the province of Québec (although the 1995 referendum narrowly rejected independence), a key goal of domestic politics is to achieve equilibrium between the French Canadian and English-speaking populations.

Prague: View of the Charles Bridge to the old town.

Economy: Canada is one of the world's most prosperous nations, with rich natural resources, forests and vast tracts of arable land. Agriculture employs 3% of the work-force; in addition to extensive livestock farming, grain (wheat, maize), and potatoes are cultivated. Ontario,

Québec and British Columbia are the main industrial areas, where 22% of the workforce produces around 30% of GDP. Petroleum and natural gas drilling are important. The commercial and services sector accounts for 60% of GDP.

Cap Verde see Cabo Verde

Česká Republika
Czech Republic

Area: 78,866 sq km
Population: 10.2 million
GDP per capita: 15,700 US$
Capital: Prague
Government: Republic
Language: Czech (official), Slovakian
Currency: 1 Czech koruna = 100 haleru

Geography: The central plateau and the populous Bohemian basin are surrounded by the Sudetes, Bohemian forest, and the Ore Mountains. Moravia, in the east, is a fertile and largely hilly region. The Elbe and Vltava (Moldau) rivers are the most important waterways. The Czech Republic's leading tourist attractions include the historic towns of Bohemia, the natural landscapes of the country's mountainous regions, and the capital city Prague, one of Europe's most visited cities.

Politics: Great Moravia, a powerful Slavic state, emerged in the 9th century and was closely aligned to the German-

dominated Holy Roman Empire for most of its history. Following the domination of the Hussites in the 15th century, the Czech lands were ruled by the Austrian Habsburg Empire. They united with Slovakia to form the first Czechoslovak republic in 1918 following the collapse of the Austro-Hungarian Empire. Czechoslovakia was occupied by Germany during the Second World War and assigned to the Soviet bloc in 1945. In 1948, Czechoslovakia was declared a socialist republic under the Communist party. An attempt at political liberalization during the Prague Spring of 1968 was brutally repressed by Soviet troops. Czechoslovakia was dissolved in 1993 and the Czech Republic joined the NATO in 1999 and the EU in 2004.

Economy: The Czech Republic is one of the most successful transition countries in Europe, with steady growth and an increase in living standards since the 1990s. Manufacturing accounts for a third of GDP, and services for more than 60%. Agriculture generates 5% of GDP. Leading industries include the production of textiles, glass, and metal. Coal, lignite, and metal ores are mined.

Chile
Chile

Area: 756,950 sq km
Population: 15.8 million
GDP per capita: 9,900 US$
Capital: Santiago de Chile
Government: Presidential republic
Language: Spanish
Currency: 1 Chilean peso = 100 centavos

Geography: Chile extends 4,230 kilometers along the west coast of South America, with an average width of only 176 kilometers. The country encompasses five highly diverse climatic zones. The northern desert zone is among the most arid places on earth; the semi-desert can only be cultivated with the help of irrigation. The main cities are in Central Chile between Illapel and Concepción; to their south is a panorama of lakes. The great forests of the south have high rainfall and a cold cli-

mate. The south also has many active volcanoes. The Easter Islands are a travel destination worth adding to Chile's many areas of natural beauty.

Politics: Conquered in 1544 by the Spanish, Chile gained independence in 1818 after a long struggle. The following decades were dominated by conflicts between the great landowners and farm workers. The socialist President Allende was overthrown in 1973 and power was seized by a military regime; after the brutal dictatorship of Pinochet, the country has faced the painful duty of addressing its political heritage since the process of democratization began in 1990. Chile has been a presidential republic since 1925, with a bicameral parliament. Voting is compulsory from age 18.

Economy: Only 23% of the area is fertile; in Central and South Chile fruit is grown for export and grain (wheat, maize) for subsistence. Yields from the rich fishing grounds are chiefly for export. Industry primarily consits of food processing (fishmeal, fish canning). Natural resources form the main economic sector (minerals, natural gas). Chile is the world's largest copper exporter (40% of foreign trade). Commerce and services account for more than half of GDP.

Choson
Korea, Democratic People's Republic

Area: 120,538 sq km
Population: 22.7 million
GDP per capita: 1,000 US$
Capital: Pyongyang
Government: People's democracy
Language: Korean
Currency: 1 won = 100 chon

Geography: The country covers the north of the Korean peninsula and a part of the Asian mainland. It is largely mountainous, with peaks of up to 2,541 meters (Gwammo), but becomes considerably flatter to the southwest. It has a cool, moderate monsoon climate. The country's flora and fauna have been seriously affected by industrialization.

Life in the polar region: The Inuit people of the eastern Canadian Arctic were highly skilled at surviving in the hostile environment. Isolated from other indiginous peoples, they developed a unique culture and language. Today, they chiefly live in mixed settlements, and their traditional clothing, language, and customs are gradually being forgotten. They are in a minority in the population.

Primary destinations for the scarcely developed tourist trade are Pyongyang and the old capital of Kaesong.

Politics: Owing to the country's geographic location, the history of Korea has always been influenced by the tensions between China and Japan. After the Japanese occupation (1910–1945), the north of the country was occupied by Soviet troops, and the Democratic People's Republic was established in 1948. The conflict with South Korea reached a climax during the Korean War (1950–1953). Initially close to China and the Soviet Union, the country has become increasingly isolated; relations with the USA are strained by Korea's nuclear arms programs.

Economy: The country has a Socialist planned economy. 65% of the population live in cities. Agriculture, which employs 34% of the workforce population and generates 20% of GDP, produces staples (rice, corn, potatoes) for domestic consumption. 7% of the industrial production is state run. The industrial sector generates two thirds of GDP; main branches include heavy industry (non-ferrous metals, coal), food, textiles, and increasingly the electrical goods industry. Reasons for the food shortages which led to a serious famine in 1997 include poor planning and enormous arms spending.

Città del Vaticano
Vatican City

Area: 0.44 sq km
Population: 920
GDP per capita: not available
Capital: Vatican City
Government: Sovereign diocese since 1929
Language: Latin, Italian
Currency: 1 euro = 100 cents, and own currency

Geography: The world's smallest sovereign state is located in the center of the Italian capital city, Rome. Vatican City's major tourist attractions include St. Peter's Basilica, St. Peter's Square, and the Sistine Chapel.

Politics: The history of the Vatican begins with the founding of the Roman Catholic Church. For centuries, popes ruled the Papal States on the Italian peninsula. The territory of the Vatican and the popes was mostly lost in the creation of the modern Italian state. An agreement with Italy in 1928 guaranteed Vatican sovereignty. Vatican City, the center of the Roman Catholic church, is ruled by the Pope.

Economy: Vatican City's existence as a sovereign state is funded mostly by church investments and holdings as well as contributions from around the world. Tourism is also an important sources of income.

Croatia see Hrvatska

Cyprus see Kypros

Czech Republic
see Česká Republica

Colombia
Colombia

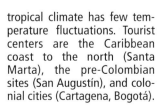

Area: 1,138,910 sq km
Population: 42.3 million
GDP per capita: 6,300 US$
Capital: Bogotá
Government: Republic
Language: Spanish
Currency: 1 Colombian peso = 100 centavos

Geography: The northern foothills of the Andes divide the country into a western coastal plain and eastern lowlands, extending in the far southeast into the Amazon basin through the pastures of Llanos del Orinoco. Tropical rain forests flourish here and on the Pacific coast. The main settlements are in the Andes basins. The tropical climate has few temperature fluctuations. Tourist centers are the Caribbean coast to the north (Santa Marta), the pre-Colombian sites (San Augustín), and colonial cities (Cartagena, Bogotá).

Politics: Colombia was the site of early Indian civilizations. Discovered by the Europeans in

1 The llamas and alpacas of Chile's uplands were bred by the area's native Indians as hardy beasts of burden, but chiefly for their meat and wool.

2 Rio Magdalena and its tributaries in the coastal plains of Colombia were traditionally important trade routes.

3 Banff National Park in the Canadian Rockies: Founded in 1885, Canada's oldest nature reserve contains the glacial Lake Louise and Lake Moraine.

4 Lake Ontario and the Toronto skyline are dominated by the elegant CN Tower, the highest tower in the world.

Everyday life in Cuba: *An essential for everyone is the "libreta," the supply booklet for cheap, state-subsidized food and clothing. Everyday life is fraught with organizational difficulties for Cuban families.*

Equanimity is essential in Cuba. With public transportation almost always crammed, an old car is a precious asset; getting spare parts is an art in itself.

1499, it became a Spanish colony in the mid-16th century. After successfully fighting for independence under Simon Bolivar in 1819, the country gained its first republican constitution in 1886. Reforms in the 1930s were succeeded by years of bloody civil war. The military junta which took over power resigned in 1957; however, the uprisings and civil war which characterized the 1960s still recur today.

Economy: Agriculture accounts for 20% of GDP and employs 30% of the workforce. Colombia is the world's second largest coffee exporter, with bananas and flowers also cultivated for export. 30% of agricultural production is devoted to livestock farming. The industrial sector (automotive, foodstuffs, petroleum processing) accounts for 20% of GDP. Imports include machinery and chemicals. The rich natural resources (gold, iron ore, oil) are almost untouched. Services produce 40% of GDP.

Comores
Comoro Islands

Area: 2,170 sq km
Population: 652,000
GDP per capita: 700 US$
Capital: Moroni
Government: Islamic Presidential republic
Languages: Comorian, French (both official), minority languages
Currency: 1 Comorian franc = 100 centimes

Geography: The territory comprises the three large islands of Ngazidja, Ndzuani and Mwali and other islets off the East African coast. They are largely of volcanic origin, with the highest volcano the still-active Karthala (2,361 m). Rain forests cover the craggy mountain massifs. The narrow coastlines are fringed by coral reefs.

Politics: The islands fell under Persian and Arab rule from the 16th century. The colony founded by France in 1843 on the neighboring island of Mayotte was extended in 1912 to encompass the Comoro Islands. Most of the Islands declared their independence in 1975, while Mayotte remained French.

Economy: The educational, health and social security systems are inadequate (50% of the population are illiterate). 78% of the population work in agriculture which accounts for 41% of GDP. Large areas of the agricultural land are under state control. Major agricultural export commodities include vanilla, coconuts, and spices.

Congo
Congo

Area: 342,000 sq km
Population: 3 million
GDP per capita: 700 US$
Capital: Brazzaville
Government: Republic
Languages: French (official), Bantu languages
Currency: 1 CFA franc = 100 centimes

Geography: A narrow coastal plain where mangroves and tropical rain forests flourish gives way in the country's interior to rolling hills of an average height of 800 meters, with savanna vegetation. The swampy lowlands of the Congo Basin are covered mostly by vast tropical rain forests.

Politics: After the Congo was discovered by Europeans in the 15th century, European explorers established trading posts there. The region did not become a French colony until 1880. After independence in 1960, the republic first modeled itself on France, but declared itself a Socialist People's Republic in 1970. 1991 saw the introduction of democracy and a multiple-party system.

Economy: The agricultural sector accounts for 12% of GDP, with crops being yams, plantains, and grain. Petroleum forms the basis of the economy, with drilling, processing and export bringing in around 80% of foreign currency. The country's industrial sector produces chemicals and foodstuffs. Services account for 51% of GDP. Political instability has been a major hindrance to economic development in Congo.

Congo, République Démocratique
Congo, Democratic Republic

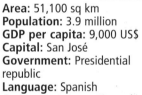

Area: 2,345,410 sq km
Population: 58.3 million
GDP per capita: 600 US$
Capital: Kinshasa
Government: Republic
Language: French
Currency: 1 Congo franc

Geography: The third largest country in Africa is shaped by

Cuba: The Old City's colonial architecture.

its location in the Zaire Basin, a plain at an altitude of 200–400 meters, which extends to the Central African rift valley in the east and is bounded to the west by the Congo and Kwango rivers. The highest peaks are the Virunga volcano (4,507 m) and the Ruwenzori (5,109 m). Tourism is restricted to the capital and the national parks. Tropical rain forests cover much of the country.

Politics: In 1885 the Congo was owned by the King of Belgium, but received independence in 1960 as Congo-

Kinshasa. A military coup in 1965 was followed in 1971 by the foundation of the Republic of Zaire. The dictator Mobutu was finally overthrown in 1997 by rebels, whose leader Kabila proclaimed the Democratic Republic of Congo; after his murder in 2001, responsibility for solving the Congo conflict now lies with his son Joseph Kabila.

Economy: In agriculture, subsistence farming produces the bare minimum necessary, with coffee and rubber produced for export. The country is rich in natural resources, including copper, zinc, precious metals, diamonds, and petroleum.

Costa Rica
Costa Rica

Area: 51,100 sq km
Population: 3.9 million
GDP per capita: 9,000 US$
Capital: San José
Government: Presidential republic
Language: Spanish
Currency: 1 Costa Rica colón = 100 centavos

Geography: Humid savannas up to 700 meters in altitude and dry forest lie on the Pacific side of Costa Rica, while the main settlements are found in the Valle Central, with fertile land and a mild climate. Rain forests dominate the Caribbean coast.

Politics: Costa Rica was discovered by Columbus in 1502 and became a Spanish colony in the mid-16th century. It became a republic ten years after gaining independence (1838). The constitution of 1949 stipulates political neutrality. The country is governed by the parliament and a directly elected president. It has no army.

Economy: Costa Rica is one of Latin America's richest countries. The predominantly white population is relatively well-educated. Agriculture accounts for 16% of GDP and 64% of export revenues. The industrial sector contributes 26% of GDP from processing agricultural products, and textile and chemical production. Tourism is undergoing a dramatic increase.

Côte d'Ivoire
Ivory Coast

Area: 322,462 sq km
Population: 17.3 million
GDP per capita: 1,400 US$
Capital: Yamoussoukro
Government: Presidential republic
Languages: French (official), Dioula and further languages
Currency: 1 CFA franc = 100 centimes

Geography: From its 550 kilometers of coastline, fringed by lagoons to the east, the country rises to an altitude of 300–400 meters. Around half the country's area consists of tableland covered by wet savannas. Intensive farming is practiced along the coast. Tourist destinations include the animal reserves (Comoé, Nimba) and beaches.

Politics: Before its colonization by the French from 1893, the north belonged to the old kingdom of Mali and the south was ruled by the Ashanti. European influences were introduced by missionaries who traveled through the country from the 17th century. The Republic of the Ivory Coast gained independence in 1960.

Economy: 33% of national GDP is produced by the agriculture and fishery sectors, in which more than half of the workforce is employed. Ivory Coast is the world's fourth largest producer of coffee and has the highest level of industrialization in West Africa.

Crna Gora
Montenegro

Area: 13,812 sq km
Population: 620,000
GDP per capita: 3100 US$
Capital: Podgorica
Government: Republic
Language: Serbian, Albanian
Currency: 1 Euro = 100 cents

Geography: The highlands of central Montenegro are situated up to 2500 metres above sea level and extend to the country's coast along the Adriatic. Lake Skadar, the largest lake in the Balkans extends along the border with Albania.

United Arab Emirates **Daulat Al-Imārāt al-'Arabiya Al-Muttahida**

Ethnic Variety: Côte d'Ivoire is populated by 60 clans that have developed and preserved their own traditions and contribute to the cultural variety of the nation. The Dan, who are settled in the West, are well known *for their traditional masks. The Lobi, who live in the northeast, developed a certain kind of adobe architecture that is also common in West African countries.*

Politics: Before 2006, Montenegro was united politically with neighbouring Serbia for more than 80 years. The country declared its independence after a referendum in May 2006.

Economy: The country's economy was greatly weakened by the break-up of Yugoslavia and the wars that followed during the 1990s. Tourism, the metals industry, agriculture, and sheep herding are the most important segments of the economy.

Cuba
Cuba

Area: 110,860 sq km
Population: 11.3 million
GDP per capita: 2,800 US$
Capital: La Habana
Government: Socialist republic
Language: Spanish
Currency: 1 Cuban peso = 100 centavos

Geography: The largest island of the Western Antilles, Cuba has an interior of craggy mountain chains (over 1,900 m) met by a swampy, fertile plain that gives way to the rain forests of the mountainous east. High, rolling hills dominate the west. Arable land and savannas have replaced much of the rain forests. The climate is tropical and humid. Tourist centers are La Habana (Havana), Trinidad, and Santiago de Cuba.

Politics: Discovered in 1492 by Columbus, the island was settled by the Spanish from 1511. In 1902 the republic of Cuba fell under the influence of the United States, but became a Socialist republic after Castro's revolution (1959). The disintegration of the USSR has caused Cuba many economic problems, particularly since the trade embargo by the USA, although the country has emerged from isolation since the end of the Cold War.

Economy: The healthcare and educational system are exemplary. 80% of agricultural operations are owned by the state. The main crop is sugarcane. The processing industry (textiles, leather, tobacco goods) accounts for 46% of GDP. Tourism is now the second largest source of foreign currency.

Danmark
Denmark

Area: 43,094 sq km; Greenland 2.176 million sq km; Faroe Islands 1,398 sq km
Population: 5.4 million; Greenland 55,400; Faeroes 43,700
GDP per capita: 31,200 US$
Capital: Copenhagen
Government: Parliamentary monarchy
Language: Danish
Currency: 1 Danish krone = 100 Øre

Geography: The Kingdom of Denmark consists of the Jutland peninsula and at least 400 islands located between the North and Baltic seas. Only a quarter of Denmark's islands are inhabited and 40% of the country's population live on the most populous island, Seeland. Denmark is a flat country and consists mostly of meadows, moorlands, sandy coastlines, and forests. The capital city, Copenhagen, and the beaches of Jutland are the country's major tourist attractions.

Politics: The history of the Danish kingdom begins around AD 800. In the 14th century, the Danish monarchy was able to expand its territory through a series of conquests and unions. The country was occupied by Germany during the Second World War. Both Greenland and the Faeroe Islands are currently administered by Denmark.

Economy: The generous welfare state of modern Denmark guarantees all Danish citizens access to excellent social services. Only around 5% of the country's population works in the agricultural sector. Textile, machinery, and metal production are among the country's leading industries. The service sector, including tourism, currently generates more than 70% of the country's annual GDP.

Daulat al-Imārāt al-'Arabiya Al-Muttahida
United Arab Emir.

Area: 82,880 sq km
Population: 2.5 million
GDP per capita: 23,200 US$

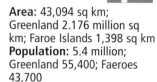

Capital: Abu Dhabi
Government: Federation of independent sheikdoms
Language: Arabic (official)
Currency: 1 dirham = 100 fils

Geography: The flat, coastal strip on the Persian Gulf is backed by salty clay plains inland, which meet the extensive dunes of Rub' al-Khali. On

1 In the rural districts of the United Arab Emirates camels are the most effective traditional means of transportation.

2 Copenhagen, Denmark's capital: The Nyhavn and Frederiksstaden district contain the city's old harbor, with its picturesque views and well-preserved historic buildings.

3 In Dubai the modern mosques are modeled on those of ancient Persia.

4 Costa Rica: The Central American Cordilleres are largely covered by tropical evergreen mountain and rain forests, with a wide variety of flora and fauna.

Deutschland Germany

Ecuador: Most of the agricultural products of the smallest country in the Andes are sold at local markets, whereas the crops from the extensive plantations of bananas and cocoa are exported. The core of the economy, however, is provided by the export of petroleum which is driving ahead the development of the country.

the eastern border, the Al-Hajar mountains rise to 1,100 meters. Vegetation in this hot, dry climate is possible only in the irrigated coastal area. The chief tourist destination is the Emirate of Dubai.

Politics: The seven sheikdoms of Abu Dhabi, Dubai, Sharjah, Ajman, Umm-el-Qaiwain, Fudjaira, und Ras' al-Khaimah became a British protectorate in the 19th century. When the British withdrew, the emirates formed a federation in 1971. The seven emirates have constituted the Upper Council since the adoption of the constitution (1975), electing one of their number as president.

Economy: Three quarters of the inhabitants are migrant workers from the Indian subcontinent. Agriculture plays only a subordinate role, and contributes 2.5% to GDP. Oil has been drilled in the Persian Gulf since 1962. This industry employs 2% of the working population, and generates 40% of GDP. The modest processing industries produce textiles, leather goods and clothing.

East Timor see Timor-Leste

Deutschland
Germany

Area: 357,021 sq km
Population: 83.2 million
GDP per capita: 27,600 US$
Capital: Berlin
Government: Parliamentary federal republic
Language: German
Currency: 1 euro = 100 cents

Geography: The northernmost region of Germany includes coastal areas along the North and Baltic seas and numerous islands. Germany's south is dominated by the Alps and Alpine foothills. Most of northern Germany consists of flat and fertile plains, bordering a series of mountains that stretch through much of central and eastern Germany. Farther south low rolling hills give way to the higher Alpine foothills and the Alps. The country's major waterways include the Rhine, Elbe, and Weser rivers. Germany's tourist

attractions include the capital city, Berlin, and the capital of Bavaria, Munich, as well as important cultural centers such as Dresden, Weimar, and Cologne. The Bavarian Alps, the Black Forest, and the coastal areas along the North and Baltic seas are also popular attractions.

Politics: Germany was originally settled by a variety of Germanic, Celtic, and later Slavic peoples. Large areas were controlled for centuries by the Romans, who founded many of Germany's oldest cities. Charlemagne was able to unite much of Germany into one empire during the 9th century. Between the 10th and 12th century, German nobles and the popes vied for control. During most of the Middle Ages, Germany was a collection of kingdoms known as the Holy Roman Empire, ruled by an elected Kaiser. The Thirty Years War, which devastated

The Brandenburg Gate: Symbol of Germany's new unified status.

Germany and left a third of its population dead, weakened the Holy Roman Empire and left Germany divided for many centuries. The formation of the German Empire in 1871 was followed by a period of rapid economic and social progress. Following Germany's defeat in the First World War, the Kaiser was forced to abdicate and the country became a republic. One of the darkest chapters in German history began in 1933 when the National Socialist party and Adolf Hitler came to power, leading the country to a devastating defeat in the Se-

cond World War and to the Holocaust. Following the Second World War, the country was divided into two states — East and West Germany. While West Germany, an ally of the USA, prospered under capitalism and democracy, the East was transformed into a repressive communist state. After the fall of communism, the two German states were reunited in 1990 and the country currently consists of sixteen federal states.

Economy: Germany is one of the world's wealthiest industrialized nations and has the largest economy in Europe. Agriculture plays only a marginal role in the national economy, while services (principal sectors include finance and insurance, commerce and transportion) and manufacturing account for most of Germany's GDP. Tourism is an important sector of the economy in several German regions.

Djibouti
Djibouti

Area: 23,200 sq km
Population: 467,000
GDP per capita: 1,300 US$
Capital: Djibouti
Government: Republic
Languages: French, Arabic (both official), Cushitic languages
Currency: 1 Djibouti franc = 100 centimes

Geography: The Tadjoura Basin, among the world's hottest areas, is covered by sand and

stony deserts in the interior. 95% of the country consits of steppe. Continuous vegetation (acacia and shrubs) is found only above 1,200 meters. Hot springs and active volcanos can be found throughout the country, and earthquakes are frequent.

Politics: In 1896, French protectorates on the Gulf of Aden were merged to form the state of Djibouti. Although the country became independent in 1977, the French army maintains a number of military bases there and is still responsible for national defense.

Economy: More than half the population are nomads. Djibouti has to cope with waves of Ethiopian refugees who make up almost one-fifth of the population. Frequent drought means that agriculture accounts for only around 2% of GDP, while industry contributes around 18%. The country aims to concentrate on services, which already account for 80% of GDP thanks to the French military presence. Djibouti has a large national debt and remains dependent on foreign aid. Its economy is based on its strategic location and status as free trade zone.

Egypt see Al-Misr

Equatorial Guinea see Guinea Ecuatorial

Dominica
Dominica

Area: 750 sq km
Population: 70,000
GDP per capita: 5,400 US$
Capital: Roseau
Government: Republic within the Commonwealth
Languages: English (official), Patois, Cocoy
Currency: 1 East Caribbean dollar = 100 cents

Geography: This volcanic island is part of the Lesser Antilles. It is predominantly mountainous (Morne Diablotins, 1,447 m), almost untouched at the center and covered with evergreen rain forests. The main settlements are on the coast. The climate is tropical and humid; cyclo-

nes may occur in the rainy season from June to November. The country's principal attraction is the Morne-Trois-Pitons National Park in the interior, with over 100 species of birds. The island has many hot springs and a crater lake giving evidence of its volcanic origins.

Politics: Discovered by Columbus on a Sunday ("Domingo") in 1493 (hence the name), Dominica successfully resisted all attempts at colonization into the 18th century. Faught over by the British and French, it became a British colony in 1805 and gained independence in 1978.

Economy: The economy is founded on agriculture, with 50% of export revenues produced by small farmers from banana cultivation. Other crops such as ginger, coconuts, copra, fruit juices, cocoa, and citrus fruits are industrially processed and contribute to exports. Plans to expand the underdeveloped industrial sector through incentives for foreign investors are under way. Trade and tourism generate 63% of GDP.

Ecuador
Ecuador

Area: 283,560 sq km
Population: 13.2 million
GDP per capita: 3,300 US$
Capital: Quito
Government: Presidential republic
Languages: Spanish (official), Indian dialects
Currency: 1 sucre = 100 centavos

Geography: The country is divided into three main geographical zones: the densely settled coastal region on the Pacific, the mountainous Andean region (Chimborazo 6,310 meters, an extinct volcano) and the Oriente lowlands, in which tropical rain forests flourish up to the Peruvian border. The climate has no significant temperature fluctuations. Ecuador's territory includes the Galapagos Islands, around 1,000 kilometers away in the Pacific, with their unique animal life (tortoises, giant lizards, birds). The country's chief tour-

Ireland: In the 1970s the folk music group "The Dubliners" made traditional Irish folk music internationally known. Some of the traditional dance music is centuries old. Typical instruments are Irish bagpipes, fiddle, flute and harp – the emblem of Ireland. The lively music can often be heard in Ireland's pubs.

ist attractions are these islands, rain forest areas of natural beauty and the old colonial cities of Cuenca and Quito, today a world heritage site).

Politics: Ecuador was conquered in the 15th century, first by the Incas and 100 years later by the Spanish, who founded today's capital of Quito. The country received independence in 1822 but found only brief interludes of peace; not until the second half of the 20th century did Ecuador have long periods of political stability. The 1979 constitution appoints the parliament as the legislative power, elected every four years; the President is the head of government.

Economy: Agriculture accounts for 18% of GDP and employs one-third of the workforce. In addition to grain, potatoes, vegetables, and fruit as subsistence crops, coffee, cocoa, sugar-cane, and bananas are cultivated for export. Shrimp are also exported. A major source of foreign currency is the natural resources in the Amazon basin, where gold, silver, zinc, and copper are mined. Around 60% of the population live below the poverty line.

Eesti
Estonia

Area: 45,226 sq km
Population: 1.3 million
GDP per capita: 12,300 US$
Capital: Tallinn
Government: Parliamentary republic
Language: Estonian (official), Russian
Currency: 1 Estonian krone = 100 senti

Geography: Estonia consists primarily of low-lying plains, moorlands, and marshes. More than 1,500 islands are located off the country's coast. The cool temperate climate gives way to a continental climate in the country's interior. The country's principal tourist attractions are the capital city, Tallinn, and the cities of Narva and Tartu.

Politics: The small country on the Baltic Sea was conquered by the Danes in the 13th century. During the 15th century it was ruled by Sweden and after 1721 by Russia. Estonia declared its independence from Russia in 1918 but was occupied by the Soviet Union in 1940. Estonia was declared an independent republic in 1991. The country is now a multi-party democracy with a unicameral parliament.

Economy: Estonia has been largely successful with its transition from a planned economy to free market capitalism. The country experienced strong growth and foreign investment rates in the 1990s. The service sector now accounts for most of Estonia's GDP with agriculture and wood processing industries (paper, furniture) also key. Estonia is the world's second largest oil shale producer.

Éire/Ireland
Ireland

Area: 70,280 sq km
Population: 4 million
GDP per capita: 29,800 US$
Capital: Dublin
Government: Parliamentary republic
Language: Irish (Gaelic), English (both official)
Currency: 1 euro = 100 cents

Geography: Ireland is a medium-sized island in the North Atlantic with a temperate maritime climate. The country's terrain consists mostly of rolling hills, meadows, and moorlands. The northern half of the island features numerous lakes. Ireland's historic monuments and attractive countryside are the island's leading tourist attractions.

Politics: Archeological finds show the island was settled by

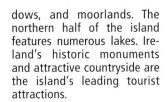

1 Lough Corrib, the largest lake in Eire, offers great prospects for angling. It lies in the wild counties of Galway and Mayo amid spectacular scenery.

2 Today Tallinn's medieval city is a protected monument. The church of St. Nicholas was built in the 13th/14th century.

3 Quechua-speaking Indians in Peru and Ecuador live from potato farming and alpaca breeding. Woollen garments are their chief trade at city markets.

4 High above the Moselle in one of the largest winegrowing districts in Germany towers the restored Burg Cochem.

Corrida de toros: *Today the classic corrida in its traditional form is solely held in Spain. It is separated into several parts; only in the last part, when the toreros have tantalized the bull to the limit, is it killed by the deadly stroke of the matador. In southern France and Portugal bloodless corridas are held. The bullfight is a complex ritual which many claim is central to Spain's culture.*

Celts no later than the 3rd century BC. The island's people were converted to Christianity during the 5th century. The English conquest of Ireland in 1171 was followed by a series of revolts and centuries of British domination. Devastating famines in the mid-19th century decimated the population and caused thousands of people to emigrate, mostly to the United States. In 1921, the Republic of Ireland was declared an independent state, while several northern Irish countries in the province of Ulster remained within the United Kingdom. In 1937 Ireland became a sovereign state with its own constitution.

Economy: Traditionally one of the poorest regions of Western Europe, Ireland experienced a remarkable economic transition in the 1990s. The country is now one of Europe's richest due to foreign investment, competitive tax rates, and EU regional aid. While agriculture once dominated the Irish economy, services and manufacturing (primarily the computer, chemical and pharmaceuticals industries) now account for more than 90% of Ireland's GDP. Tourism is a key economic factor on the "Emerald Isle."

El Salvador
El Salvador

Area: 21,041 sq km
Population: 6.6 million
GDP per capita: 4,800 US$
Capital: San Salvador
Government: Presidential republic
Languages: Spanish (official), Indian languages
Currency: 1 El-Salvador colón = 100 centavos

Geography: El Salvador largely consists of fertile hills and grassland, apart from a narrow coastal strip of mangrove forest with a hot, humid climate. In the interior, a high plateau, with grassland enclosed by mountains, forms the main settlement area. Much of the natural vegetation has given way to arable land. The humid, hot climate extending to an altitude of 1,800 meters is ideal for agriculture. The country has one of the most frequent incidences of earthquakes in the world. Tourist destinations are the volcanoes and the Indian cult sites.

Politics: From the country's conquest in 1524 to its independence in 1821, El Salvador was part of the Spanish colony of Guatemala. Its history is marked by recurring periods of unrest, in which the economic and social situation deteriorated considerably. A military dictatorship ruled from 1931 to 1967. The military coup in 1979 resulted in 14 years of civil war, with a high toll of victims. The 1983 constitution states that the president is directly elected by the people for a term of five years.

Economy: 95% of the population of Central America's most densely populated country are mestizos. Agriculture employs 50% of the workforce and generates 14% of GDP. Rice, maize, beans, and millet are grown for domestic markets, and coffee, sugar, cotton, and more recently flowers and ornamental plants for export. The industrial sector chiefly comprises small and medium-size processing companies which account for 3% of GDP. Considerably more than half the population is employed in the services sector. The tourism industry is still in its infancy. High unemployment and government corruption are critical problems.

Elláda (Hellás)
Greece

Area: 131,940 sq km
Population: 10.6 million
GDP per capita: 19,900 US$
Capital: Athens
Government: Parliamentary republic
Language: Modern Greek
Currency: 1 euro = 100 cents

Geography: Greece consist of the large peninsula Peloponnese on the southern edge of the Balkans and numerous islands. Heavily forested mountains and hills cover more than three-quarters of the land. The Pindus Mountains occupy much of central and western mainland Greece. Most of the country has a warm Mediterranean climate, while the northernmost regions have a continental climate. Ancient monuments and the Greek islands are the country's main attractions.

Politics: The powerful Greek city-states of the classical era profoundly influenced European culture. Alexander the Great (356–323 BC) conquered vast territories and spread Greek (Hellenic) culture through the Near East and Mediterranean. Greece was a Roman province from 148 BC to 396 BC, then a province of the Byzantine Empire. Conquered by the Ottoman Turks in 1356, Greece remained an Ottoman province for almost five centuries. A sovereign Greek kingdom was created in 1832. After a military coup in 1967, the monarchy reintroduced in 1946 was abolished. Greece became a democratic republic in 1974 after several years of repressive dictatorship. Tension remains between Greece and Turkey over Cyprus.

Economy: Despite a move towards greater privatization a large segment of Greece's economy is under government control. Traditional crops including olives, wine, citrus fruits and tobacco account for more than a quarter of Greece's exports. Greece's manufacturing sector is dominated by small businesses. The rapidly growing service sector accounts for more than 60% of the country's GDP. Greece currently has the world's largest fleet of commercial sailing vessels. Its main trading partners are the European Union and the USA. Tourism remains an important sector of the economy. Greece joined the European currency union in 2000.

Eritrea
Eritrea

Area: 121,320 sq km
Population: 4.5 million
GDP per capita: 700 US$
Capital: Asmara
Government: Republic
Languages: Arabic, Tigrinja (official)
Currency: 1 birr = 100 cents

Geography: The Red Sea forms the country's northeastern border. The narrow coastal plain extends in the north to the Abyssinian Highlands, with mountains more than 2,600 meters in height. The main settlements are here because of the relatively high rainfall. Desert lowlands are found to the south in the foothills of the Denakil Mountains. The Dahlak Islands in the Red Sea also belong to Eritrea. Tourist destinations are Asmara, the nearby ancient city of Cohaito, the historic colonial architecture in Massawa and the coral reefs of the Dahlak archipelago.

Politics: What is today Eritrea was part of the Italian colony from 1890 to 1941, and subsequently under British administration until 1952. After ten years as an autonomous region within Ethiopia, it was annexed as the 14th province, finally gaining independence as a republic in 1993 after a long battle for freedom. The Provisional National Council, in power since 1991, is working on a democratic constitution and the establishment of a multiple-party system.

Economy: Illiteracy is around 80%. The war caused particularly extensive damage to agriculture; while 80% of the population are traditionally small farmers, millet, wheat, and pulse production is currently sufficient for only about 20% of the population. A current development program subsidizes coffee and tobacco farming for export. Industrial processing and consumer goods production account for 18% of GDP. Quarrying (marble) is planned for expansion. There are hopes of attracting foreign investors to support the reconstruction of the infrastructure, which was completely destroyed in the war. Tourism is in its infancy.

Ethiopia see Ityopya

España
Spain

Area: 504,782 sq km
Population: 40.3 million
GDP per capita: 22,000 US$
Capital: Madrid
Government: Parliamentary monarchy
Language: Spanish (Castilian), Catalan, Basque (Euskara), Galician
Currency: 1 euro = 100 cents

Geography: The Pyrenees mountains form a natural boundary between the mountainous Iberian Peninsula and the rest of Europe. Northern Spain is dominated by the plateaus of Castille, while the Sierra Nevada mountains stretch over much of the country's south. The south consists largely of semi-arid areas with steppe vegetation. The northernmost coastal areas have a distinct temperate climate with heavy rainfall. Spain is one of the world's most popular tourist destinations, with its leading attractions including islands such as Majorca in the Mediterranean or the Canary Islands, and large cities such as Barcelona.

Mykonos: The best-known Cycladic island in the Aegean Sea.

South Seas: In spite of the modern infrastructure due to tourism, the inhabitants of Fiji have preserved their traditional way of life to this day. On mostly small farms grain and fruit are cultivated for subsistence.

In addition, the people on the Islands breed pigs and small livestock.

Politics: Spain was settled by a variety of European groups including Basques, Celts, and Iberians before the 3rd century BC. Most of Iberia became a Roman province in the 1st century BC. Large sections of the country fell under the control of Muslim Arabs during the 8th century. The Reconquista, a long military campaign led by Christian nobles, eventually succeeded in expelling the Arabs by 1492. Spain was Europe's most powerful nation by the 16th century and the ruler of vast territories in the Americas. By the 18th century, however, Spain was in a period of decline that culminated in the loss of its empire in the 19th century. A civil war between nationalists and Spanish republicans ended with a victory for the reactionary nationalists. The country returned to democracy following the dictator Franco's death in 1978.

Economy: After a period of high unemployment and rising foreign debts, the Spanish economy has become increasingly strong in recent years. Agriculture and fishing account for around one-tenth of the country's GDP, although this is falling. Manufacturing produces around a third of the GDP, and the service sector more than half. Tourism remains a major industry and provides employment for a large number of Spaniards.

Estonia see Eesti

Finland see Suomi

Fiji
Fiji

Area: 18,270 sq km
Population: 880,874
GDP per capita: 5,800 US$
Capital: Suva
Government: Republic
Languages: English, Fijian, Hindi
Currency: 1 Fijian dollar = 100 cents

Geography: Fiji consists of more than 320 islands, including volcanic and coral islands. Around 110 of the islands are inhabited. The mountains on the largest islands, Viti Levu and Vanua Levu, rise above 1,300 meters. Fiji is a major tourist attraction with a tropical climate and countless sandy beaches.

Politics: In 1643, Abel Tasman was the first European to visit the islands. More than a century later, James Cook claimed the islands for Great Britain. From 1874 to 1970 the islands were a British colony. Following independence, the country experienced periods of political instability including several military coups. A new constitution was created in 1997 in an attempt to ease tensions

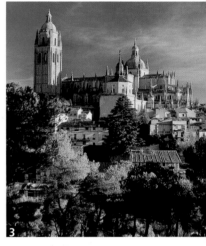

between the country's indigenous Melanesian population and the large Indo-Fijian community. Political power is now divided between the Senate, House of Representatives, and President. Fiji's President, the official head of state, is chosen by the national council of chiefs, a non-elected body of mostly hereditary members. This council also appoints one-third of the country's senators. The role of the council is controversial because it excludes the country's Indo-Fijian majority. Elections to the House of Representatives are based on a mixture of universal direct elections and electoral rolls divided between the country's ethnic groups.

Economy: Around half of the Fijian labor force works in the country's large agricultural sector. Sugar and fish are among the country's main exports. The industrial sector consists primarily of sugar refining, rice milling, and textile production. Mining

– mostly gold and copper – also plays a limited but important role in Fiji's economy. The service sector generates at least 62% of Fiji's GDP. Tourism remains an important industry and a major source of employment for many Fijians. the islands are home to a host of holiday centers and resorts.

1 The Parthenon on the Acropolis was founded in 3000 BC. The City, host of the 2004 Olympic Games, is home to more than four million residents.

2 The Straits of Gibraltar link the Atlantic Ocean and the Mediterranean Sea. The view extends to the North of Africa.

3 The construction of the late Gothic cathedral of Segovia started in 1525. The tower is 110 meters high.

4 Many of Fiji's Islands are covered by lush tropical rain forests.

French savoir-vivre: Since Roman times wine making has been common in France. Today the largest wine producing areas are to be found in Bordeaux, the Bourgogne, Champagne and Alsace, as well as the Loire and Rhône valleys. The harvest and pressing lasts from September to December. Whether it is to accompany haute or rustic cuisine, wine is regarded as a staple in France.

France
France

Area: 547,030 sq km
Population: 60.4 million
GDP per capita: 27,500 US$
Capital: Paris
Government: Parl. republic
Language: French
Currency: 1 euro = 100 cents

Geography: France is a mostly hilly country situated between the Atlantic Ocean, English Channel, and the Mediterranean Sea. Two high mountain ranges form natural borders along the country's edges – the Pyrenees in the south and the Alps in the east. Large basins cover a large segment of France's territory, including the densely populated Paris Basin. The Rhône, Seine, and Loire rivers are the country's principal rivers. France is an extremely popular tourist destination and its main attractions include the city of Paris, the Loire river valley, the French Riviera, and the country's Atlantic coast.

Politics: The history of modern France can be directly connected to the division of the Frankish Empire in the year AD 843. France emerged victorious from the Hundred Years' War (1338–1453) with England. In the centuries that followed, France greatly expanded its territory and was ruled by absolutist monarchs. The French Revolution of 1798 brought an end to the monarchy and established the first French republic. The French general Napoleon was declared emperor in 1804 and launched a series of military campaigns that changed the political structure of Europe. The country switched between monarchy and republicanism several times during the 19th century. The country was occupied by Germany during the Second World War. France is currently governed by the so-called Fifth Republic, a presidential democracy established in 1958.

Economy: France rapidly made the transition from a largely agricultural economy to an industrialized nation following the Second World War. Modern France is now one of the world's most affluent nations, with a diverse economy. Despite the country's wealth, unemploy-

ment remains high and the French are heavily taxed. Tourism continues to play an important role in the national economy. The French government retains significant influence over the economy. The service sector now accounts for most of France's GDP.

Germany see Deutschland

Greece see Elláda (Hellás)

Hungary see Magyaroszag

Gabon
Gabon

Area: 267,667 sq km
Population: 1.4 million
GDP per capita: 5,500 US$
Capital: Libreville
Government: Pres. republic
Languages: French (official), Bantu languages
Currency: 1 CFA franc = 100 cent.

The Eiffel Tower: Peak of civil engineering in the 19th century.

Geography: The landscape is marked by River Ogooué and its tributaries. The mangrove swamps and lagoons of the coastal lowlands give way to coastal savanna. The interior tableland with an altitude of up to 1,000 meters is largely covered with tropical rain forests (Birougou Mountains 1,190 m). There are dry savannas in the southeast. The climate is tropical. Tourist destinations are the capital city, the Albert Schweitzer Hospital in Lambaréné and the three national parks.

Politics: After the coast was discovered by the Portuguese in 1470, several European powers established trading points for raw materials principally ivory and exotic woods, and slave trading. The country became a French colony in 1885, and gained independence in 1960. Under the new constitution (1991), the National Assembly is elected for five years and the President is appointed by direct election.

Economy: Around half of the predominantly Bantu population lives in the cities. Agriculture accounts for only 8% of GDP; 20% of the country's area is taken up by subsistence crops of manioc, yams, plantains and maize, and coffee, cocoa, sugar-cane, and palms for export. Rain forest lumber is a major source of export revenue. The backbone of the economy, however, is the export of petroleum and refinery products, which accounts for 80% of GDP and makes

Gabon one of Africa's richest countries. The mining industry produces uranium, manganese, iron ore, and gold. Tourism is relatively underdeveloped.

Gambia
The Gambia

Area: 11,295 sq km
Population: 1.5 million
GDP per capita: 1,700 US$
Capital: Banjul
Government: Pres. republic

Languages: English (official), Mandingo, Wolof, other local languages
Currency: 1 dalasi = 100 butut

Geography: Africa's smallest country, along the banks of the Gambia River, is completely enclosed by Senegal, and no more than 50 kilometers wide at its widest point. Mangrove swamps extend far inland from the Gambia delta. The Atlantic beaches, said to be the most beautiful in Africa, attract tourists. The national parks, with their rich fauna, are also popular.

Politics: In the 8th century a number of kingdoms arose in what is today The Gambia, and were annexed to the kingdom of Mali in the 12th century. The Gambia was discovered by the Portuguese in the 15th century and became a British colony in 1765, received independence in 1965 as a Commonwealth state and became a republic in 1970. The British-style constitution (1970) was repealed in 1994 after the military coup. Parliamentary elections were resumed in 1997.

Economy: The majority of the population are small farmers growing subsistence crops of millet, sorghum, rice, and maize; peanuts are the main export product, and like fishery products are processed by the underdeveloped industry. Tourism accounts for 15% of GDP and the industry has largely recovered from a major decline that followed a military coup in the 1990s.

Ghana
Ghana

Area: 239,460 sq km
Population: 20.8 million
GDP per capita: 2,2000 US$
Capital: Accra
Government: Presidential republic
Languages: English (official), over 70 further languages and dialects
Currency: 1 cedi = 100 pesewas

Geography: The 535-kilometer-long coastline along the Gulf of Guinea, rendered near-impassable by lagoons, forms

a natural border to the south. From here, grassland gives way to the tropical rain forests that cover the Ashanti Highlands rising to the west. Lake Volta lies in the wet savanna to the east. The climate is tropical. Tourism concentrates on the partly preserved forts at the colonial trading outposts of Cape Coast, Elmina, and Accra.

Politics: The Ashanti people founded a powerful kingdom in what is now Ghana, engulfing neighboring tribes to extend their territory to the coast, from where they conducted slave trading with Europe from the 15th century. In 1850 the British conquered the country and founded the colony of Gold Coast. After early independence in 1957, the republic initially profited from its rich natural resources until economic decline set in from 1966. The new constitution (1993) is intended to promote the process of democratization by introducing a multiple-party system. Ghana has enjoyed a period of political stability since 1993 and is now one of the most open democracies in Africa.

Economy: Half of the population are small farmers, cultivating basic subsistence crops of rice, millet, yams, and plantains. 50% of the agricultural land is taken up by cocoa. Animal husbandry is primarily conducted in the north. Tropical rain forest lumber is exported. The mining industry supplies mineral raw materials (bauxite, manganese) and rich yields of gold. The small industrial processing sector produces foodstuffs, textiles, and shoes for the country's own needs. The service sector accounts for almost half of GDP.

Grenada
Grenada

Area: 344 sq km
Population: 89,300
GDP per capita: 5,000 US$
Capital: St. George's
Government: Constitutional monarchy
Languages: English (official), Patois
Currency: 1 East Caribbean dollar = 100 cents

Ancestor worship: While in the cities of western Africa the traditional beliefs are widely replaced by Islam and Christianity, in the countryside they are largely still alive. The numerous rites and dances are evidence of a powerful community and closeness to the natural rhythms of life. They are to a large extent characterized by ancestor worship, which serves to foster cohesion within families.

Geography: This volcanic island with countless crater-lakes, sulphur springs and earthquakes, is part of the Lesser Antilles. The highest peak in its mountainous interior (Mount St. Catherine) is 840 meters high. Mountain and rain forests grow in the mountainous interior. The climate is tropical, with an extended rainy season. The island's many beaches are visited primarily by cruise tourists.

Politics: Discovered in 1498 by Columbus, Grenada was first settled by the French. The island was occupied by the British in 1762 and remained a British crown colony until its independence in 1974. It was invaded by US American troops in 1983 following a Socialist revolution. According to the reinstated constitution of 1974, the parliament is composed of the Senate and the House of Representatives. The British monarch is the head of state.

Economy: The majority of Grenada's inhabitants are descended from African slaves. The country's flag depicts its main export: nutmeg (25% of the world's production), cultivated by small farmers in addition to bananas and cocoa. The underdeveloped industrial sector chiefly manufactures semi-luxury goods, but also electronic components and pharmaceuticals. Tourism is gaining a foothold.

Gruzija (Sakartvelo)
Georgia

Area: 69,700 sq km
Population: 4.7 million
GDP per capita: 2,500 US$
Capital: Tbilisi (Tiflis)
Government: Republic
Languages: Georgian (official), Russian, Ar
Currency: Lari

Geography: The western border is formed by the Black Sea coast, which runs into the Kura lowlands. The climate here is sub-tropical and humid. The north is dominated by the southern slope of the Greater Caucasus (Kasbe 5,033 m). The country extends into part of the Lesser Caucasus in the south. To the east of Tbilisi, the country is characterized by dry forests in an increasingly continental climate, becoming grassy steppe. In addition to 15 nature reserves, winter sports, and hiking regions, towns such as Suchumi and Batumi on the Black Sea coast are very popular. Important historic sites are at Kutaisi and Mzcheta.

Politics: After the Roman era (from 65 BC), the country became part of the Byzantine Empire in the 4th century. In the 14th century it came under Mongol rule. Following the division of the country between the Ottomans, Persians, and Russians (1555), an Eastern Georgian Kingdom was founded in the 18th century and annexed by the Russian Empire (1801–1810). Georgia declared its independence in 1918, and the Soviet Socialist Republic of Georgia was founded in 1921. Since independence (1991), efforts towards autonomy by the Islamoriented Republics of Abkhazia and South Ossetia have led to warring confrontations, largely settled with the aid of international intervention.

Economy: Most of the agricultural land consists of grain, beet and potato fields. In addition, tropical fruits, tea, tobacco, and grapes are cultivated, with eucalyptus, bamboo and bay trees on the coast. Mining yields coal, copper, manganese, barite, diatomite and semi-precious stones. The processing industry produces foodstuffs, wines and textiles. Chief exports are raw materials and foodstuffs. A third of the population lives from the traditionally important sector of tourism.

Guatemala
Guatemala

Area: 108,889 sq km
Population: 14.3 million
GDP per capita: 4,100 US$

1 Mont Saint Michel monastery is on a small island off the coast of Normandy.

2 The steep, towering temples of Tikal in Guatemala are a relic of the mighty and powerful civilization of the Mayas.

3 Carriacou island, off the Caribbean island of Grenada; ideal for diving and swimming.

4 The 13th-century Metechi Church in Georgia's capital Tblisi.

Ancient wisdom: In India there are many ascetics who have abjured the world for religious reasons and live off the alms of their fellow men. Hinduism, which esteems respect for all life and nonviolence as the highest values, teaches this way of life as a way to escape the eternal cycle of rebirth and gain salvation.

Capital: Guatemala City
Government: Presidential republic
Languages: Spanish (official), Maya languages
Currency: 1 quetzal = 100 centavos

Geography: The plains to the north are covered with tropical rain forests. The Central American Andes traverse the country's south from east to west. To the far south, the high plains of the Sierra Madre extend to the vertile Pacific coastal plains. Tourist attractions are the intact Indian cultures (Chichicastenango), sites of the Mayan civilizations (Tikal), and the colonial architecture in the cities of Antigua and Quezaltenango.

Politics: The center of the ancient Mayan culture was conquered by the Spanish in 1524 and remained a Spanish colony until its independence in 1821. Since then Guatemala has been ruled by a succession of military dictatorships. The government has been democratically elected since 1986, but the war led by the left-wing guerrilla movement URNG did not end until a peace treaty was signed in 1997.

Economy: More than half of the inhabitants work in agriculture; peas, broccoli, tobacco, and flowers are cultivated in addition to traditional export crops of coffee, sugar, bananas, and cardamom. Natural resources are largely untapped. The industrial sector processes foodstuffs, rubber, and textiles for export. Tourism is the main source of foreign revenue.

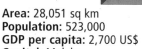

Guinea Ecuatorial
Equatorial Guinea

Area: 28,051 sq km
Population: 523,000
GDP per capita: 2,700 US$
Capital: Malabo
Government: Presidential republic
Languages: Spanish (official), pidgin English, Bantu languages
Currency: 1 CFA franc = 100 centimes

Geography: The country's territory comprises the mountainous region of Mbini and the volcanic islands of Bioko and Pagalu. The higher elevated areas of Mbini are covered with savanna and the rest with tropical rain forests, giving way to mangrove swamps on the coast. In the rainy season violent storms are frequent.

Politics: Discovered in 1470, Bioko and Pagalu became Spanish in 1778, and the mainland in 1885. After independence (1968) the country was ruled by a dictatorship until a military coup in 1979. The 1991 constitution's plans for a democratic multi-party system were limited prior to the country's first free elections in 1993.

Economy: The majority of the population are Bantu speakers and 85% are Catholic. The economy is founded on cocoa and coffee plantations and valuable lumber reserves. Livestock farming on the mainland is gaining in significance. 5% of the population is employed in industry, primarily processing agricultural products. Modest gold reserves are mined. The service sector accounts for 42% of employment but the export of oil now accounts for most economic growth.

India's Taj Mahal: Impressive mausoleum for a queen.

Guinea-Bissau
Guinea-Bissau

Area: 36,125 sq km
Population: 1.4 million
GDP per capita: 900 US$
Capital: Bissau

Government: Presidential republic
Languages: Portuguese (official), Creole, dialects
Currency: 1 Guinea peso = 100 centavos

Geography: The broad coastal plain traversed by rivers is bounded to the east by wet savanna and to the southeast by hills. Freshwater swamps in the interior give way to mangrove swamps at the coast. The country is rich in wildlife. Tourist attractions are the old colonial city of Bissau and the islands of the Bijagos Archipelago off the coast.

Politics: Portuguese outposts for the slave trade were founded in the 16th century. Guinea-Bissau was a Portuguese colony from 1879–1974 and later became a parliamentary democracy after gaining independence, which ended abruptly in a military coup. Following the approval of new parties in 1991, the first free elections of a National Assembly were held in 1994.

Economy: 80% of the population cultivate subsistence crops of rice, maize, and other grain. Animal husbandry accounts for nearly a third of GDP, and peanuts and cashews are significant exports. There are plans to attract foreign investors to tap the bauxite, phosphate, and petroleum reserves. The country's economy was thrown into a major crisis by a civil war in the late 1990s.

Guinée
Guinea

Area: 245,857 sq km
Population: 9.2 million
GDP per capita: 2,170 US$
Capital: Conakry
Government: Republic
Languages: French (official), tribal languages
Currency: 1 Guinea franc = 100 cauris

Geography: The coastal plain to the west gives way to the plateau of Fouta Djalon, up to 1,500 meters high and the source of the Senegal, Niger, and Gambia rivers, which slopes away to the east. The coast is swampy; the country's northeast is covered by savanna and the southeast by tropical rain forests.

Politics: For centuries, the Fulbe people defended their territory against the mighty kingdoms of Ghana and Mali. In the 19th century Guinea became a French colony. After independence in 1958 a single-party system was established which was overturned by a military coup in 1984. The republican constitution of 1991 led to the first democratic elections in 1995. Conflicts in neighboring states could threaten Guinea's current stability.

Economy: Three-quarters of the population live from agriculture, which barely covers domestic needs despite the extenive fertile areas. The country has rich natural resources and is the second largest bauxite producer in the world. Other mining products are iron ore, uranium, cobalt, gold. The small industrial sector produces foodstuffs and textiles.

Guyana
Guyana

Area: 214,969 sq km
Population: 706,000
GDP per capita: 4,000 US$
Capital: Georgetown
Government: Presidential republic within the Commonwealth
Languages: English (official), Hindi, Urdu, dialects
Currency: 1 Guyana dollar = 100 cents

Geography: The fertile coastal region gives way to mountain chains in the west and far south. Savannas dominate the southwest. 80% of the country is covered by largely untouched rain forest. Land reclamation for arable use has been practiced since the 17th century.

Politics: Guyana's history of colonization began in the early 17th century, when British colonizers were followed by French and Dutch. Following Dutch rule, the country returned to Great Britain, gaining independence in 1966 and adopting South America's only socialist constitution in 1980.

Economy: More than half the population is descended from Indian immigrants, who were imported in the 19th century to work in the plantations. A quarter of the workforce is employed in agriculture, cultivating the chief exports of cane sugar and rice. Hardwoods from the extensive forests, gold, sugar, bauxite, and manganese are the primary sources of export revenue. Trade, services, and transportation are underdeveloped. Regional airlines operate between the largest cities.

Haïti
Haiti

Area: 27,750 sq km
Population: 7.6 million
GDP per capita: 1,600 US$
Capital: Port-au-Prince
Government: Presidential republic
Languages: French (official), Creole
Currency: 1 gourde = 100 centimes

Geography: Haiti occupies the western third of the island of Hispaniola and includes the two neighboring islands of Gonâve and Tortue. The country is divided from east to west by four mountain chains, accounting for around 80% of the country's area. Vegetation is dominated by savannas, with the remaining tropical rain forests limited to a few mountain areas. Cruise ship tourism concentrates on the capital of Port-au-Prince.

Bidjogo: The Bidjogo people on the Bissago Islands off the coast of Guinea-Bissau are said to be expert fishers, boat builders and craftspeople. Apart from cult objects and elaborate figures of ancestors, they also manufacture naturalistic animal masks, which they wear at initiation ceremonies.

Politics: After its discovery by Columbus, Hispaniola was a Spanish colony; the western part became a French colony in 1697, rose to prosperity and declared its independence in 1804 as the Empire of Haiti. After an era of revolutions, dictatorships and civil war the country now appears to be gaining political stability. Democratic parliamentary elections were introduced in 1996.

Economy: Agriculture, although employing more than half the population, is barely at subsistence level. Sugar cane, coffee, coca, and sisal are exported. Industry principally comprises small trade companies operating for the national market. Raw materials and semifinished products (textiles, electrical goods) are processed for re-export. Services are also gaining in significance, although tourism figures have dropped in recent years.

Honduras
Honduras

Area: 112,088 sq km
Population: 6.8 million
GDP per capita: 2,600 US$
Capital: Tegucigalpa
Government: Pres. republic
Languages: Spanish (official), English, Indian languages
Currency: 1 lempira = 100 centavos

Geography: Honduras is bounded to the north by the Caribbean and to the southwest by the Pacific. Its territory includes the Bahía and Swan islands. The country is primarily mountainous, with only a narrow coastal strip along the Pacific, and rivers, lagoons and swamps on the Caribbean side. The main settlement area is concentrated in the valleys of the Central American Andes.

Politics: In 1524 the country was conquered by Spain; in 1821 Honduras proclaimed its independence and became an independent republic in 1838 after leaving the Central American Federation. Over 100 governments and military dictatorships have seized power as a result of coups to the present day. The 1982 constitution specifies a term of four years for elected members of the National Assembly.

Economy: Agriculture primarily produces bananas and coffee for export, with seafood the second most important export. Extensive livestock farming also exports its surplus. The rich natural resources (lead, zinc, silver) are almost untapped. Industry is insignificant, directed chiefly at the domestic market.

Hrvatska
Croatia

Area: 56,542 sq km
Population: 4.5 million
GDP per capita: 10,700 US$
Capital: Zagreb
Government: Republic
Language: Croatian
Currency: 1 kuna = 100 lipa

Geography: Croatia borders the Adriatic Sea to the west. The country's narrow coastal stip stretches south from Dalmatia to the Bay of Kotor. Croatia's territory also includes at least 600 islands in the Adriatic. Northeastern Croatia is a largely mountainous region that borders the fertile plains between the Sava and Danube rivers. The Croatian coast is an increasingly popular tourist destination.

Politics: Croatia was first settled by Slavic groups in the 7th century. The first Croatian kingdom was established in the 9th century. The country came under the control of the Habsburg Empire in 1527. Between 1918 and 1991, Croatia was a republic in the kingdom and later socialist republic of Yugoslavia. The country's declaration of independence was followed by a brutal civil war that lasted until 1995.

Economy: Croatia's economy was severely affected by the war of the early 1990s but has since made a gradual recovery. Agriculture remains an important economic sector, although the service sector is the fastest growing segment of the economy. Key exports are engineering and shipping. Tourism declined dramatically during the violent breakup of Yugoslavia but the industry is now growing rapidly.

India (Bhărat)
India

Area: 3,287,263 sq km
Population: 1.065 billion
GDP per capita: 2,900 US$
Capital: New Delhi
Government: Republic
Languages: Hindi, English
Currency: 1 Indian rupee = 100 paisa

1 Varanasi (Benares) is one of the most important sites of pilgrimage in India: devout Hindus purify themselves every year in the holy water of the Ganges with ritualistic ablutions.

2 Off the Honduran coast lie the mostly unspoiled Isles of Bahía, which stretch across one of the largest coral reefs in the world.

3 The Plitvic lakes and their surroundings in Croatia were declared a National Park in 1949. Since 1979 they have belonged to the UNESCO World Nature Heritage.

4 Rovinj, seaport and seaside resort in western Istria, is one of the most beautiful cities on the Croatian part of the Adriatic coast.

In the gods' honor: The temple dances of Bali employ fantastic masks and make-up and magnificent costumes to tell the traditional legends of the Hindu gods. The dances are performed at the islands' religious sites and shrines to entertain these gods. The Balinese value their ancient theater traditions, including Indonesian shadow plays.

Geography: The Indian subcontinent is divided into three regions: the mountain area of the Himalayas; the plain of the Indus and the Ganges; and the southern plateau, crossed by rivers, whose coasts are hemmed by wide plains. The climate is sub-tropical to tropical. In addition to nature reserves with a rich variety of fauna, India has countless cultural and historical monuments.

Politics: Aryan nomads displaced the Indus civilization from the 15th century BC. The Islamization of India began in the 12th century AD. The advance of the Europeans in the beginning of the 16th century led to the weakening of the Mogul rulers. In 1858 India was brought directly under the British crown. The struggle for independence started at the end of the 19th century, and inspired Mahatma Gandhi's movement after World War I. After Islamic Pakistan broke away, India finally gained independence in 1950. Although the country has enjoyed relative political stability since then, the conflict with Pakistan over Kashmir still continues until today.

Economy: The caste system dominates the life of the population. Three quarters of the inhabitants live from agriculture, generating some 32% of GDP. India is the world's number one tea exporter, and second largest exporter of dairy produce as well as a major fishing nation. The rich natural resources, which are little exploited, constitute the basis for the largely state-owned heavy industry. India has highly developed weapons, nuclear and space exploration industries. Tourism is an important branch of the services sector (40% of GDP).

Indonesia
Indonesia

Area: 1,919,440 sq km
Population: 238.4 million
GDP per capita: 3,200 US$
Capital: Jakarta
Government: Pres. republic
Languages: Indonesian (official), Javanese, other
Currency: 1 rupiah = 100 sen

Geography: More than 13,600 islands, about half of which are inhabited, span the Equator in a 5,000 kilometer arc. More than half the overall area is covered by forests, and the lowland plains of Sumatra and Borneo also feature extensive marsh and freshwater swamp forests. Chains of volcanoes (around 70 of which are active) extend through Western Sumatra. The climate is tropical and always humid. Indonesia is a popular tourist destination, especially Bali, the main island of Java, with Borobudur Temple, and the Lesser Sunda islands.

Politics: In early times, the country was under Hindu and Buddhist influence, becoming Islamic in the 13th century, with the exception of Hindu Bali. The Dutch took over the entire archipelago in the 16th–19th centuries to control the spice trade. In World War II,

The fertile fields of Bali yield two crops of rice every year.

Japan occupied the Dutch East Indies, which became independent in 1949 as the Republic of Indonesia. The country's history since then has been characterized by unrest and military coups. The military hold extensive power, and occupy several seats in the unicameral government.

Economy: The multiethnic state is predominantly inhabited by Malays, with Polynesian-Melanesian peoples in the eastern islands. More than half of the population work in agriculture, producing rice, corn, cassava, and sweet potatoes for domestic consumption, and coffee, cocoa, tea, and rubber from the plantations for export. Other important exports include wood, rattan and copal from the rain forest regions. Rich ore, mineral, oil and natural gas reserves form the basis of the highly developed heavy industry, which produces solely for export. Inland waterways are an important mode of transport.

Îrân
Iran

Area: 1,648,000 sq km
Population: 69 million
GDP per capita: 7,000 US$
Capital: Teheran

Government: Islamic republic
Languages: Farsi (official), Luri, Balochi, Kurdish
Currency: 1 rial = 100 dinar

Geography: Iran, between the Caspian Sea and the Persian Gulf, is bordered to the north by the Elburz Mountains (up to 5,064 m high), and the Zagros Mountains to the south. The arid highlands in the interior meet the Lût Desert in the east. In addition to the pilgrim cities of Qom and Masshad, popular destinations include the ancient ruins of Persepolis and Parsagadae, and the royal mosque in Isfahan.

Politics: The country's chequered history began with its settlement in the 2nd millennium BC by Iranians, who established the first Persian empire in the 6th century. Islamization began with the Arab conquest in the 7th century AD. In 1907 Russia and Great Britain divided the country into areas of influence. Extensive western-style reforms were introduced by Shah Pahlewi from 1925. The Islamic Revolution (1978) led to the flight of the Shah and the establishment of the Islamic Republic.

Economy: Only 10% of the area is used for agriculture through irrigation. In addition to wheat, barley, vegetables and sugar beet, tobacco, tea, pistachios, and dates are grown for export; the Caspian Sea yields caviar, whitefish, and ray. The country's heavy industry is based on rich petroleum and natural gas reserves, together with coal, copper, nickel, and chromium mining, and accounts for 85% of exports. Traditional crafts (e.g. carpetmaking) are declining.

'Īrāq
Iraq

Area: 437,072 sq km
Population: 25.3 million
GDP per capita: 1,600 US$
Capital: Baghdad
Government: Pres. republic
Language: Arabic
Currency: 1 Iraqi dinar = 1,000 fils

Geography: The heartland of the country in the northeast of the Arabian Peninsula is formed by the floodplain of the Tigris and Euphrates rivers, which turns into semi-desert and then desert to the west. There is a narrow access route to the Persian Gulf in the southeast. The sites of ancient Mesopotamia are of immense cultural and historical importance.

Politics: Mesopotamia was founded in the 3rd millennium BC by the Sumerians; in the 2nd and 1st millennium BC, the area was ruled by the Babylonians and Assyrians, and then conquered by the Persians in the 6th century BC. In the 7th century AD, the country fell under the Arabo-Islamic sphere of influence; the Ottomans ruled from the 16th to the 19th century. The monarchy established by the British in 1921 was overthrown by a bloody coup in 1958. Under the dictatorial president Saddam Hussein (in power from 1979), Iraq waged war with Iran over the oil regions from 1980–88. In 1990 Iraq annexed Kuwait. This led to the First Gulf War (1991), which ended with the defeat of Iraq by the US-led coalition. The conflict with the US escalated in 2002 when the latter suspected Iraq of harboring weapons of mass destruction. In 2003, the US, Great Britain and other countries launched a war which soon brought down the regime and investigated the democratic process.

Economy: Iraq has the third largest oil reserves in the world. The country is only slowly recovering from the consequences of the wars and from decades of a war economy, so economic reconstruction can only succeed with international help. Important industrial branches, other than the oil industry, are processing and construction.

Ísland
Iceland

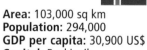

Area: 103,000 sq km
Population: 294,000
GDP per capita: 30,900 US$
Capital: Reykjavik
Government: Republic
Language: Icelandic
Currency: 1 Icelandic krone = 100 aurar

Geography: Iceland is a volcanic island in the Atlantic Ocean. The northernmost sections of the country are located above the Arctic Circle. Most of the population is concentrated on the coast, while the rugged interior is largely uninhabited. Approximately 27 of the country's 140 volcanoes are active. Geysers, hot springs, lava, and ash fields are common throughout the country. About half of the island is covered by glaciers.

Multi-ethnic nation: Ethiopia is populated by more than 80 different ethnic groups which often differ widely. More than 90% of the inhabitants live from nomadic livestock breeding such as the small ethnic group of the Karo.

Among the most important peoples are the politically influential Oromo, the Amhara and the Tigrines.

Politics: Norwegians, the first permanent settlers of Iceland, arrived on the island during the 9th and 10th centuries. The Althing, an assembly of chiefs, was founded in 930 BC and exists to this day. The population of Iceland was converted to Christianity around AD 1000. The island was ruled by Denmark between the 13th century and 1944, when independence was declared.

Economy: Fishing and the manufacture of fish products is the largest industry in Iceland. Around a quarter of the workforce are directly or indirectly employed in the fishing industry. Livestock (sheep and horses) is also an important industry. The few mining operations are carefully regulated and limited. The economy has become increasingly diverse in recent years.

Israel see Yi'sra'el

Italia
Italy

Area: 301,230 sq km
Population: 58 million
GDP per capita: 26,800 US$
Capital: Rome
Government: Republic
Language: Italian
Currency: 1 euro = 100 cents

Geography: The Alps stretch along the northern border of Italy. Farther south, the Alpine foothills extend to the fertile Po River Valley. The Apennine Mountains stretch from north to south through the center of the Italian peninsula. In addition to mainland Italy, the country also consist of several large islands such as Sicily and Sardinia, and many smaller islands in the Mediterranean and Adriatic seas. The western coastline bears evidence of volcanic activity (Etna, Vesuvius). Italy is a popular tourist destination – major attractions include the country's ancient cities and coastal areas.

Politics: Italy was dominated by the Catholic Church for centuries following the collapse of the Roman Empire. Several Italian city-states – including Venice and Florence – emerged

as important centers of cultural and commercial progress during the late Middle Ages. The popes and several foreign powers vied for control of Italy between the 16th and 19th centuries. A united Italian kingdom was created in 1861 and Rome was declared the capital in 1870. A series of domestic crises led to the rise of Mussolini's fascist government in the 1920s. The country was occupied by German troops before the end of World War II. In 1946, Italy was declared a republic. Despite frequent changes in government during recent decades, Italy remains an open multi-party democracy.

Economy: The dramatic wealth gap between the industrialized north and the poorer, agricultural south of the country remains a major problem for Italy. Italy's highly productive agriculture sector now contributes less than 3% of the country's GDP, while the diverse service sector accounts for at least 70% of national GDP. Major exports include automobiles, electric goods, chemical products, textiles, and machinery. Tourism is a major industry in numerous Italian regions.

Îtyopya
Ethiopia

Area: 1,127,127 sq km
Population: 67.8 million
GDP per capita: 700 US$
Capital: Addis Ababa
Government: Federal republic
Languages: Amharic (official), 70 further languages

and dialects
Currency: 1 birr = 100 cents

Geography: The territory of Ethiopia extends over a mountain range divided by the East African Rift Valley. The north is dominated by desert and savanna, the south by rain forests. The chief tourist destinations are the landscapes and fauna of the national parks

1 The Roman Colloseum, which provided space for 50,000 spectators in the ancient world, was badly destroyed by an earthquake in 1348 and stripped of its decorations in subsequent centuries.

2 Italy: Vernazza on the Ligurian coast, one of five towns in the Cinque Terre region.

3 The north of Ethiopia encompasses vast dry savannas; water is a scarce commodity.

4 Jökulsá á Fjöllum, Iceland's second largest river, flows into the Greenland Sea.

Jamaica Jamaica

Cyprus: The vast majority of the island's Greek inhabitants belong to the Greek Orthodox Church, which can trace its origins back to the 5th century. Starvo Abbey near Larnaca is one of Cyprus' numerous religious buildings, with mosques during established Osmanic times.

(Omo, Awash, Bale), the ruins at Axum and the Christian sites at Lalibela.

Politics: The legendary Kingdom of Sheba was succeeded in the 1st century by the mighty Axum, which lasted for more than 1,000 years, was Christianized as early as the 4th century and subsequently defied Islamization. Not until the 19th century did a mighty state again rise to resist colonialization. A Socialist people's republic was founded after the 1974 abdication of the last emperor; its leader was overthrown in 1991.

Economy: Agriculture accounts for more than half of GDP and employs 80% of the labor force, yet barely produces the basic foodstuffs. Coffee is the main export. The country's underdeveloped service industry primarily produces goods for the domestic market; a further obstacle is that the majority of large-scale companies are still state-owned.

Jamaica
Jamaica

Area: 10,990 sq km
Population: 2.7 million
GDP per capita: 3,800 US$
Capital: Kingston
Government: Parl. monarchy within the Commonwealth
Languages: English (official), Patois
Currency: 1 Jamaica dollar = 100 cents

Geography: The 235-kilometer-long island extends from east to west. The east is dominated by the volcanic Blue Mountains (up to 2,257 m); impenetrable gorges cleave the densely wooded western foothills. Rolling karst highlands in the west slope down to craggy sea cliffs. It's a Caribbean holiday paradise, with its tropical climate and idyllic sandy beaches.

Politics: Jamaica was discovered in 1494 by the Spanish, who eradicated the indigenous population and introduced slaves. The island was conquered by the British in 1655 and became a crown colony in 1866, one of the richest thanks to its sugar-

cane and cocoa plantations. Jamaica has been independent since 1962 and has a bicameral parliament, with elections held every five years.

Economy: The educational and social systems are well-developed. Export crops are bananas, citrus fruits, coffee, cocoa, coconuts, and allspice, as well as large-scale sugar-cane plantations. Jamaica is the world's third largest bauxite supplier. The industrial sector comprises foodstuffs, electronics, and data processing products. Tourism is significant, accounting for just under 50% of GDP.

Japan see Nippon

Jordan see Urdunn

Kâmpǔchéa
Cambodia

Area: 181,035 sq km
Population: 13.4 million
GDP per capita: 1,700 US$
Capital: Phnom Penh
Government: Const. monarchy

Languages: Khmer (official), Vietnamese
Currency: 1 riel = 10 kak = 100 sen

Geography: The lowlands of the Tônlé-Sap basin and the Mekong Delta are bounded

to the north by the Dangrek mountain range, and to the southwest by the Cardamom mountains, sloping down to the Gulf of Thailand. In the tropical, humid climate, vegetation ranges from mangrove forest swamps on the coast to monsoon forests in the central region and rain forests in the mountains. The most important travel destination is Angkor, the former capital of the old Khmer Empire.

Politics: The Khmer Empire was established in the 7th century and was overrun in the 17th century after repeated attacks by neighboring countries. In 1867 it was occupied by the French and incorporated into the Union of Indochina. The country gained independence in 1964. The civil war triggered in 1970 by the Indochina conflict was won by the communist forces of the Khmer Rouge. In 1975, they set up a terror regime, which was ended only when Vietnamese troops marched in. Despite free elections in 1993, the democratization process launched with the Vietnamese withdrawal and the introduction of a new constitution in 1989 has still not stabilized to the present day. The country is a constitutional monarchy.

Economy: The Agriculture accounts for 50% of GDP and

employs 85% of the workforce, who, in addition to growing rice, cultivate soybeans, corn, and pepper for export. Tobacco, seafood, and valuable tropical hardwoods are also exported. The industrial sector comprises small companies and factories supplying the domestic market. Lack of infrastructure has hampered its growth. Tourism is an increasingly important sector.

Kazahstan
Kazakhstan

Area: 2,717,300 sq km
Population: 15.1 million
GDP per capita: 7,000 US$
Capital: Astana
Government: Republic
Languages: Kazakh, Russian
Currency: 1 tenge = 100 tiin

Geography: Much of the country, which comprises extensive steppes and deserts and includes part of the Tianshan Mountains in the southeast, has a continental, dry climate. The southwest border is formed by the Caspian Sea.

Politics: In the mid-18th century, the country, settled since the 6th century, came under Russian sovereignty, and was incorporated into the Czarist empire in 1873. The autonomous Socialist Republic was proclaimed in 1920 and joined

the USSR in 1936. It again gained independence in 1991.

Economy: Grain, sugar beet, tobacco, and fruit are cultivated by means of irrigation, with vineyards in the northern mountain areas. Large copper and iron deposits, oil, and natural gas form the basis of the country's heavy industry. There are extensive road and rail networks and inland waterways. Pollution and ecological problems caused by industry and irrigation needs are a serious threat.

Kenya
Kenya

Area: 582,646 sq km
Population: 32 million
GDP per capita: 1,000 US$
Capital: Nairobi
Government: Pres. republic
Languages: Kiswaheli (official), English, tribal languages
Currency: 1 Kenya shilling = 100 Cents

Geography: Kenya on Africa's eastern coast, is divided into four distinct geographic zones: dry plains in the northeast; mountainous foothills around Lake Turkana to the northwest; southeastern savannas with forests and thorny scrub vegetation, and high plateaus in the west that rise to altitudes above 3,000 meters and then slope down to Lake Victoria.

Politics: The former British colony gained full independence in 1963, and proclaimed itself a republic. From 1982 the single-party system was gradually broadened in favor of democracy, at the urging of international aid contributors. The 2002 elections were a major transition in Kenyan politics and ended the decades of government by the KANU political party.

Economy: Kenya's agriculture produces tea, coffee, sisal, and sugar-cane for export. Cattle farming is practised at a high level. Processing industries (petroleum, agricultural products) account for 11% of GDP. The service sector, including tourism, is the largest segment of the national economy.

The west coast of Cyprus still offers unspoiled beaches.

Life in the savanna: In the arid lands in the north of Kenya, agriculture is all but impossible. The 80,000 or so Samburu who live here subsist from livestock, farming goats and cattle and more recently camels as well.

The Samburu National Park is home to numerous big game species and is said to be one of the most beautiful in Africa.

Kiribati
Kiribati

Area: 810.5 sq km
Population: 100,800
GDP per capita: 800 US$
Capital: Tarawa
Government: Presidential republic
Languages: I-Kiribati, English
Currency: 1 Australian dollar = 100 cents

Geography: Kiribati consists of 33 atolls scattered over an area of five million km² in the Pacific Ocean. Kiribati is generally divided into the Gilbert, Phoenix, and Line island groups. Most of the islands are unsuited for large scale agriculture because of their poor soils. The capital is located on the island of Tarawa.

Politics: The islands of Kiribati were first settled during the prehistoric era. During the 19th century, the first European traders arrived on the islands. They were declared a British protectorate in 1892, together with the Ellice Islands. After several decades as a British colony, the islands were granted independence in 1979.

Economy: The majority of Kiribati's population works in agriculture. Coconuts and fish are the leading exports. Manufacturing currently generates less than 10% of the country's gross domestic product. The country's geographic isolation is an obstacle to trade and increased foreign investments as is the shortage of skilled workers and weak infrastructure. Tourism accounts for around one-fifth of GDP. Aid from the industrialized countries, principally the UK and Japan, is an important source of income.

Kuwait see Al-Kuwait

Kypros/Kibris
Cyprus

Area: 9,250 sq km
Population: 776,000
GDP per capita: 16,000 US$
Capital: Nicosia
Government: Pres. republic

Language: Greek, Turkish (both official), English
Currency: 1 Cypriot pound = 100 cents

Geography: The island of Cyprus is in the Mediterranean Sea to the south of Turkey. Mesaoria, a large plain, stretches through central Cyprus and borders the Kyrenia mountains to the north. The Troodos Mountains, with Mount Olympus (1,953 m), stretch through most of southern and western Cyprus. Cyprus has a Mediterranean climate. The island is a popular tourist destination with many historic sites.

Politics: Cyprus has been dominated by numerous foreign powers throughout most of its history including Persians, Romans, Arabs, and Christian crusaders. It was a British colony (1925–1960). In 1974, Turkey occupied the northern sections of the island. Since then, the island has been divided between a Greek-speaking republic in the south and an ethnic Turkish state.

Economy: Greek Cyprus has experienced rapid growth in recent decades, while the Turkish north has stagnated due to its political isolation and corruption. The service sector dominates the economy of both areas and tourism is important.

Kyrgyzstan
Kyrgyzstan

Area: 198,500 sq km
Population: 5 million

GDP per capita: 1,600 US$
Capital: Biskek
Government: Presidential republic
Languages: Kyrghyz (official), Russian, and other minority languages
Currency: 1 Kyrghyzstan som = 100 tyin

1 Angkor has the largest complex of buildings in Southeast Asia, the Angkor Wat temple, began in the 12th century. From the 9th to the 15th centuries it was the religious and political center of the Khmer Empire.

2 Coconut palms are the predominant vegetation on Kiribati.

3 The majority of Jamaica's population are descended from slaves imported up to the mid-18th century to work in the country's many plantations.

4 The grassy savannas of the Serengeti cover a total of 14,500 square kilometers.

Laos: The majority of the inhabitants of Laos are Thai. In this communist country, Buddhism is joined by traditional tribal religions, particularly prevalent among the peasants. Nomadic cultivation is practised, with slash and burn methods causing damage to the tropical rainforest.

Geography: This Central Asian republic lies mostly in the Tianshan mountains. 50% of the landmass is at an altitude of above 3,000 meters, with only the western and northern promontories falling under 1,200 meters. At 3,000 meters, the landscape turns from desert and semi-desert into mountain steppes, meadows, and forests. The mountainous tundra lying beyond gives way to a glaciated region.

Politics: The country, settled early by nomadic peasants and hunters, achieved modern statehood only after the October Revolution of 1917. The Soviet Socialist Republic (from 1936) proclaimed its independence from the USSR in 1991. The amendment of the 1993 constitution granted far-reaching powers to the head of state.

Economy: Agriculture, which is possible in only 7% of the area, is the most important sector of the economy, accounting for 47% of GDP. In addition to grain and fodder for the extensive livestock breeding, fruit, vegetables, cotton, hemp, poppies, oil-giving plants, and tobacco are grown for export and for domestic consumption. Light industry is of great importance in this country with few natural resources.

Lao
Laos

Area: 236,800 sq km
Population: 6 million
GDP per capita: 1,700 US$
Capital: Vientiane
Government: People's republic
Languages: Lao (official), minority languages
Currency: 1 kip

Geography: The country is bordered in the north by the Tramin Plateau, which rises up to 2,820 meters, and in the south by the Boloven Plateau, about 2,000 meters high with a tropical monsoon climate. The rainy season (with temperatures of around 27° C) lasts from May to September. 40% of the area is covered by forests; dense deciduous growth gives way to rain forests at higher altitudes. The most important travel destination is Luang Prabang.

Politics: Buddhism was introduced in the 14th century with the establishment of the first Laotian Kingdom. After occupation by the Thais, Laos became a French protectorate in the 19th century and gained independence in 1954. During the Vietnam War, Communist revolutionary troops overran large parts of the country. The last king abdicated when the People's Republic was established in 1975.

Economy: Laos has experienced strong economic growth since 1986. Around 78% of the population work in agriculture, which accounts for 57% of GDP. A large part of the arable land comprises rice fields. Wood such as rattan and bamboo is felled for export.

Latvija
Latvia

Area: 64,589 sq km
Population: 2.3 million

Kyrghyzstan: Stock farming is run on the most remote high-pastures.

GDP per capita: 10,100 US$
Capital: Riga
Government: Republic
Language: Latvian (official), Russian
Currency: 1 lats = 100 santims

Geography: Latvia is bordered to the west by the Baltic Sea. The country's coast is mostly smooth and lined by wide sandy beaches. Latvia's interior is dominated by large fertile plains. Around 40% of the land area is covered by forests of birch, fir, and pine trees. Riga, the historic capital city, and Latvia's national parks are the country's leading tourist attractions.

Politics: The German speaking Teutonic Knights and the Hanseatic League dominated Latvia during the Middle Ages. Latvia was annexed by Russia in the 18th century and became independent in 1920. The country was reoccupied by Russia in 1940 and declared a republic of the USSR. Latvia declared its independence from the Soviet Union in 1991.

Economy: Agriculture and fishing remain important sectors of the Latvian economy and together account for around 10% of national GDP. The services sector now accounts for 66% of the country's GDP and is expanding. Major exports include agricultural produce, electronics, and machinery. Cargo handling in the Baltic ports is an important economic factor. The vast majority of former state enterprises have been privatized since 1991.

Lebanon see Al-Lubnān

Lesotho
Lesotho

Area: 30,355 sq km
Population: 1.9 million
GDP per capita: 3,000 US$
Capital: Maseru
Government: Constitutional monarchy within the Commonwealth
Languages: Sesotho, English
Currency: 1 loti = 100 lisente

Geography: Lesotho is completely enclosed by South Africa and is in the extreme south of the continent. There is little forest and scrub; the predominant forms of vegetation are grass savanna and mountain pastures. The country's territory consists largely of highlands and elevated plateaus.

Politics: The kingdom of the Basotho was formed in the 19th century and gained independence from British rule in 1966. It has been a constitutional monarchy since 1993. The close relationship to South Africa colors its political landscape.

Economy: Owing to the limited land area and repeated droughts, agriculture (maize, wheat, millet, and livestock) is poorly developed; supplies are imported. The majority of the country's GDP is derived from the wages of Lesotho citizens working in South Africa. Textile and leather processing is undergoing expansion.

Liberia
Liberia

Area: 111,369 sq km
Population: 3.4 million
GDP per capita: 1,000 US$
Capital: Monrovia
Government: Pres. republic
Languages: English (official), tribal languages
Currency: 1 Liberian dollar = 100 cents

Geography: The coastal areas are characterized by savanna, while much of the interior is covered by tropical rain forest. The climate is humid and tropical. The nature reserves in the Nimba Mountains were once tourist attractions, but the tourist industry is now virtually non-existent due to political instability.

Politics: Africa's oldest republic, Liberia was established in 1822 by freed American slaves. The country gained independence in 1847 but retained close ties to the USA for many years. After nine years of civil war following the 1990 fall of President Doe, the dictator who had ruled since 1986, a peacekeeping force was provided by ECOWAS.

Economy: Agriculture (rice, manioc) barely covers two-thirds of the country's needs. Large-scale plantations principally supply rubber for export. Other exports are coffee, cocoa, and palm kernels. Timber and iron ore are also exported. The services sector profits from the world's largest trading fleet in terms of tonnage.

Lîbîyâ
Libya

Area: 1,759,540 sq km
Population: 5.6 million
GDP per capita: 6,400 US$
Capital: Tripoli
Government: Islamic people's republic
Languages: Arabic (official), Berber dialects
Currency: 1 Libyan dinar = 1,000 dirham

Geography: The Mediterranean climate favors relatively lush vegetation along the narrow coastal region, which gives way in the south to plains and ultimately to the desert that cover 90% of the country's area. In the extreme south, foothills of the Tibesti Massif on the northern fringes of the Sahara reach altitudes of up to 2,285 meters. The ancient historical sites along the coast (Leptis Magna, Cyrene) and the capital of Tripoli are the main tourist destinations.

Politics: Settlements were established in the coastal regions by the 9th century BC, and fell to Roman rule in the 1st century AD. Libya was conquered by the Ottomans (1517) and ruled by an Islamic order in the 19th century. The country was an Italian protectorate for 40 years before receiving independence as a monarchy. The king was overthrown in 1969 by a military coup led by Colonel al-Gaddafi.

Economy: 90% of the population lives in the coastal area. Only 2% of the land is cultivatable, and the majority of farmland is irrigated. Privati-

Desert areas: While the densely populated coastal regions of Libya are sufficiently developed for traffic, travelling into the south of the country requires suitable cross-country vehicles to cope with the enormous distances between the oasis settlements. Despite the exertions involved, the beauty of the landscape makes the journey well worth while.

zation of most state-owned operations is planned to secure subsistence quantities of fruit, vegetables, grain, and fruit. The Libyan economy is centered on the country's enormous petroleum reserves, which produce 25% of the annual GDP.

Liechtenstein
Liechtenstein

Area: 160 sq km
Population: 33,400
GDP per capita: 25,000 US$
Capital: Vaduz
Government: Parliamentary monarchy
Language: German
Currency: 1 Swiss franc = 100 rappen

Geography: Liechtenstein is a small principality in the highlands of the Alps, located between Austria and Switzerland. The Rhine River forms the country's northwestern border. Liechtenstein is a year-round destination for skiers.

Politics: Liechtenstein's existence as a sovereign principality began in 1719. The country remained neutral during both world wars and joined a customs and monetary union with Switzerland in 1923. Liechtenstein's ruling monarch has broad sweeping powers in contrast to most other European constitutional monarchies.

Economy: Workers from neighbouring Switzerland, Germany and Austria form a third of the country's population. The majority of the country's people work in the service and manufacturing sectors. Modern Liechtenstein has a diverse and highly developed economy and its people enjoy a high standard of living.

Lietuva
Lithuania

Area: 65,200 sq km
Population: 3.6 million
GDP per capita: 11,200 US$
Capital: Vilnius
Government: Parliamentary republic
Language: Lithuanian (official), Russian

Currency: 1 litas = 100 centas

Geography: Lithuania has a 100-kilometer coastline along the Baltic Sea and the Curonian Lagoon. The country is largely flat. Most of the country's terrain is covered by forests, moorlands, and meadows. The coastal areas have a mild maritime climate, while the interior has a drier continental climate.

Politics: The Polish-Lithuanian Commonwealth ruled a vast territory stretching from the Baltic to the Black Sea during the 17th and 18th centuries. Lithuania came under the control of the Russian Empire in 1772. The country declared its independence from Russia in 1918 and was annexed by the Soviet Union in 1940. Lithuania became the first Soviet republic to declare its independence (1991).

Economy: Lithuania experienced a difficult transition to free market capitalism in the 1990s but the country has recently experienced strong growth levels. Although not plentiful in natural resources, Lithuania is developing an oil reserve discovered in the Baltic Sea. Agriculture accounts for 10% of Lithuania's GDP, while the service sector contributes approximately 66% of GDP.

Luxembourg
Luxembourg

Area: 2,586 sq km
Population: 462,700
GDP per capita: 55,100 US$
Capital: Luxembourg
Government: Constitutional monarchy
Language: Letzebuergesch, French, German (all official)
Currency: 1 euro = 100 cents

Geography: Luxembourg, one of the smallest states in Europe, shares borders with France, Germany, and Belgium. Northern Luxembourg is a heavily forested area with rolling hills while the south is dominated by river valleys. The country's main attractions include its river valleys and capital city.

Politics: Once a region of the German-dominated Holy Roman Empire, Luxembourg came under the control of France in the 18th century. The country achieved its formal independence in 1867. It was occupied by the German army in both world wars and abandoned its neutrality when it joined the NATO defence alliance in 1949. The Grand Duke

1 Vast seas of dunes and sandy plains known as ergs cover large parts of the Libyan Sahara.

2 Riga, the capital city of Latvia, is near the country's Baltic Sea coast and boasts an attractive medieval city center.

3 The inhabitants of Lesotho paint their houses with colorful traditional patterns.

4 Monks are highly regarded in Laos, although it's a communist state; two-thirds of the population are Buddhists.

"Small Tiger": A booming economy led to the Islamic country of Malaysia being classified as one of the "four small tigers," Southeast Asia's most successful newly industrialized countries. The country is home to a range of Asiatic cultures which coexist largely peacefully; the population comprises two-thirds Malays and almost one-third Chinese, in addition to Indians and Pakistanis.

of Luxembourg is the country's official head of state.

Economy: Foreign workers – most from other EU countries – form more than a quarter of Luxembourg's population. The country's economy is heavily dependent on foreign trade. The steel industry was once the largest in the country, but the economy is now dominated by the service industries, including the large banking and financial services sector, in which around 70% of the workforce are employed. Luxembourg is the seat of the European Court of Auditors as well as other European organizations.

Madagasíkara
Madagascar

Area: 587,041 sq km
Population: 17.5 million
GDP per capita: 800 US$
Capital: Antananarivo
Government: Republic
Languages: Malagasy, French (both official official), Howa
Currency: 1 Madagascar franc = 100 centimes

Geography: The world's fourth largest island is largely composed of sloping mountains, with coastal plains to the west. The climate is tropical; the island's east has high rainfall and is covered with lush rain forest. The unique, partly endemic flora and fauna of the island is threatened by slash and burn agricultural techniques, cyclones, flooding, and earthquakes. Areas of tourist interest are the many nature reserves and the capital city.

Politics: Originally settled by South Asian peoples, the island was discovered in 1500 by the Portuguese, who established settlements with the French on the coast. The indigenous population successfully resisted colonization until 1896; then a colony of France, the country gained independence in 1960. Its 1992 constitution specifies a bicameral parliament, with elections held every five years.

Economy: Social and healthcare services are as inadequate as the provision of basic foodstuffs. Agriculture forms the basis of existence for 75%

of the largely Malayan/ Indonesian population, who cultivate rice, cassava, maize, sweet potatoes, mangos, bananas, and sugar cane in smallholdings. Key exports are coffee, vanilla, cotton, and tobacco. Shrimp, tuna and lobster are processed by the poorly developed industrial sector. The not inconsiderable natural resources are largely untapped. Recent political instability in the country has slowed economic growth. The government is now liberalizing the economy and challenging corruption.

Magyarország
Hungary

Area: 93,030 sq km
Population: 10 million
GDP per capita: 13,900 US$
Capital: Budapest

Kuala Lumpur: The economic and cultural center of Malaysia.

Government: Parliamentary republic
Language: Hungarian
Currency: 1 forint

Geography: The vast Pannonian plain/Carpathian Basin stretches over most of Hungary's national territory. Low mountains rising up to 1,000 meters stretch along the Slovakian border and through

northern Hungary. The Danube and Theiss river are the country's principal waterways. Budapest, Lake Balaton (the largest lake in Central Europe) and the pristine landscapes of Hortobagy National Park are the country's leading tourist attractions.

Politics: The Magyar ancestors of the Hungarians arrived in the Carpathian Basin during the 9th century. Hungary was one of Europe's most powerful states by the 13th century. The country was divided and controlled by the Habsburg Empire and Ottoman Turks during the 16th century. After a failed Hungarian revolution in 1867, the Habsburg Empire was reorganized into the Austro-Hungarian Empire. Hungary became an independent kingdom in 1918 at the end of the First World War and was governed by a reactionary nationalist government in the 1930s. Hungary was allied to the Axis powers in World War II and was placed in the Soviet sphere of influence after the war. Hungary was the first communist state in Eastern Europe to begin the transition to democracy and capitalism, and joined NATO in 1999 and the European Union in 2004.

Economy: Hungary is one of the wealthier transition countries in Europe. The country has privatized most former state industries and receives impressive levels of foreign investment. The service sector accounts for more than 62% of Hungary's GDP, while the manufacturing sector accounts for 34%.

Makedonija
Macedonia

Area: 25,333 sq km
Population: 2 million
GDP per capita: 6,700 US$
Capital: Skopje
Government: Republic
Language: Macedonian (official), Albanian, Turkish, Serbian
Currency: 1 Macedonian denar = 100 deni

Geography: The former Yugoslav republic of Macedonia is a largely mountainous republic with several peaks rising 2,000 meters or more. The southern sections of the country and the Vadar Valley have a Mediterranean climate, while the rest of the country has a cooler continental climate. More than a third of the country is covered by forests. The monasteries around Lake Ohrid, the country's national parks, and the almost Oriental-style capital city, Skopje, are Macedonia's leading attractions.

Politics: Macedonia was a region in the Ottoman Empire between the 14th and 19th centuries. The country was widely known as Vadarska before 1929 when it was renamed Macedonia. The country has been in dispute with Greece over the name Macedonia since its independence in 1991.

Economy: Macedonia was one of the poorer republics in Yugoslavia. The country's economy stagnated throughout the 1990s because of its poor infrastructure, conflicts in the Balkans, and a Greek embargo. Ethnic conflict and instability continue to undermine sustained economic development. Textiles, steel, and agricultural produce (the latter chiefly from small farms in the Pelargonija basin) are the country's leading export commodities. Services are gaining in importance in this transit country.

Malawi
Malawi

Area: 118,484 sq km
Population: 11.9 million
GDP per capita: 600 US$
Capital: Lilongwe
Government: Presidential republic within Commonwealth
Languages: Chichewa, English (both official), Chitumbuka, other Bantu languages
Currency: 1 Malawi kwacha = 100 tambala

Geography: The majority of the country's area is occupied by Lake Nyasa. The regions to the west and south of the lake are mountainous, with peaks of up to 2,670 meters (Nylka Plateau). Grasslands and dry forests are the principal forms of vegetation; dense forests can be found in the mountains. The rich animal life is protected in four national parks; tourist centers are Lake Nyasa and Blantyre, with its beautiful surroundings.

Politics: In 1891 the region surrounding Lake Nyasa became a British protectorate, and was incorporated into Rhodesia as Nyasaland in 1907. Malawi was declared independent in 1964. The president's extensive powers awarded by the Constitution in 1966 were repealed in 1993, partly at the urging of creditor countries. The first free elections were held in 1994.

Economy: 70% of Malawi's population lives from smallholder farming, producing 35% of GDP. Subsistence is threatened by periods of drought. 90% of export revenues are derived from coffee; other exports are tea, sugar, and tobacco. Subsistence fishing is practiced on the country's three lakes. The industrial sector processes domestic agricultural products (tea, beer, tobacco, textiles, shoes). Tourism is well-developed, contributing 25% to GDP. The service sector is underdeveloped but now contributes almost half of GDP. Malawi is heavily indebted and remains dependent on foreign aid.

The art of horsemanship: Although horse-breeding has diminished somewhat in importance, the herds of horses roaming the puszta are a typical image of traditional Hungarian life. Even today, the equestrian skills of *the Magyars are a popular attraction at Hungary's numerous festivals and at circus performances all over the world.*

Malaysia
Malaysia

Area: 329,758 sq km
Population: 23.5 million
GDP per capita: 9,000 US$
Capital: Kuala Lumpur
Government: Constitutional elected monarchy in the Commonwealth
Languages: Malay (official), Chinese, Tamil, Iban, English
Currency: 1 Malay ringgit = 100 sen

Geography: Malaysia extends over the southern part of the Malacca Peninsula and the northwestern part of the island of Borneo 600 kilometers away, separated by the China Sea. The predominantly mountainous country is largely covered by evergreen tropical rain forests, which flourish in lush abundance in the hot and humid climate with average temperatures of 27° C. Flora and fauna are highly varied. With many beaches, nature reserves and cities such as Kuala Lumpur or Malacca, Malaysia has a host of tourist destinations.

Politics: Malaysia was created in 1963 from the union of newly independent principalities on the Malacca peninsula, the British territories of Sabah and Sarawak, Borneo and Singapore, which, however, left the union two years later. The country is governed by a king elected from the Nine Sultans for a five-year term. The king then appoints the head of government, nominated by the lower house, and also appoints some members of the upper house. The more influential lower house is elected directly for a five-year term.

Economy: Exported forestry and agricultural products such as tropical hardwoods, rubber, palm oil, and coconut products, plus petroleum and natural gas, have helped Malaysia gain an economic upswing. The country is also the world's leading producer of tin. The backbone of Malaysia's economy is formed by the high-tech and automotive industries. The services sector, which has hitherto generated 20% of GDP, will gain in importance in future as the infrastructure of this emerging country expands.

Maldives (Divehi Rajje)
Maldives

Area: 298 sq km
Population: 339,300
GDP per capita: 3,900 US$
Capital: Malé
Government: Presidential republic in the Commonwealth
Languages: Divehi (official), English
Currency: 1 rufiyaa = 100 laari

Geography: The country's territory is divided into 19 atoll groups with about 2,000 islands, only about one tenth of which are inhabited. The tropical climate ensures an average annual temperature of 30° C. In contrast to the limited land fauna, there are many species of sea life in the coral reefs. The Maldives have a very well developed tourism industry, and a site of cultural and historical interest is the 17th-century mosque in the capital, Malé, as well as idyllic beaches.

Politics: The expansion of Islam, which has been the state religion since 1153, dates back to traveling Arab merchants of the 12th century. The British protectorate, on the other hand, which ruled from 1887 until independence in 1965, had little influence on the state system. The 1975 constitution vests the directly elected president with extensive powers. There are no political parties or parliamentary supervisory authorities.

Economy: A quarter of the population live in the capital. Owing to soil conditions, agriculture can only cover domestic needs (coconuts and betel nuts, cassava, onions, and chili peppers). Part of the fishing catches are processed for export, the second highest foreign currency earner after tourism. The Maldives have no railroad, and cars only on Malé and Gan. The most important economic sector on the Maldives is tourism, with 20% of GDP.

Mali
Mali

Area: 1,240,192 sq km
Population: 12 million

GDP per capita: 900 US$
Capital: Bamako
Government: Presidential republic
Languages: French (official), Bamakan, farther Mandé languages
Currency: 1 CFA franc = 100 centimes

Geography: Between Ségou and Timbuktu, the Niger forms

1 The capital city of Hungary is divided by the Danube River into two distinct sections, Buda in the west and Pest in the east.

2 Hardy plants like the coconut palm chiefly thrive in the sandy soil of the Maldives' 2,000-plus islands.

3 Malawi is chiefly populated by Bantu tribes and is among the most densely populated countries in Africa.

4 Sunset off the shore of Madagascar; the island, with its unique flora and fauna, is an increasingly popular destination.

Pre-Colombian heritage: Indigenous communities, such as the Maya, make up only around ten percent of Mexi-co's 105 million inhabitants. As their numbers dwindle, their ancient cultural heritage and its legacy of countless archeological treasures has become an inspiration for contemporary artists and architects.

a large freshwater delta with fertile alluvial deposits. Mali's north is dominated by dry Saharan zones, while the south has tree savannas and gallery forests. These areas are home to a richly diverse range of wildlife. Tourist attractions are the areas of natural beauty and the ancient royal cities of Timbuktu, Mopti, and Bamako. Desertification is a major environmental issue in the country.

Politics: The legendary kingdom of the Mali arose in the 11th century. Its trading center – Timbuktu – became famous far beyond the borders of Africa in the 14th century. At the end of the 19th century the French conquered the country and incorporated it into the colony of French West Africa. The Republic of Mali gained independence in 1960 and was ruled by a dictatorship until 1991. After the first free elections in 1992, conflicts with the Tuareg were reconciled by the assurance of partial autonomy.

Economy: The north is inhabited only by the Tuareg, while 90% of the largely Islamic population live in the south. Because of Mali's poverty migration into neighboring countries is very high. Over 80% of the population subsists from agriculture. Desertification is reducing the amount of cultivatable land, and grain cultivation in the savannas is frequently affected by drought. Nomadic animal husbandry in the Sahel and fishing in the Niger delta and lakes are major contributions to subsistence. The industrial sector processes domestic agricultural products. Mali is heavily dependent on foreign aid, remittances from overseas workers, and global prices for agricultural goods. Government reforms have led to steady growth rates in recent years.

Malta
Malta

Area: 316 sq km
Population: 397,000
GDP per capita: 17,700 US$
Capital: Valletta
Government: Republic
Language: Maltese, English
Currency: 1 Maltese lira = 100 cents

Geography: The island republic of Malta in the southern Mediterranean, consists of three islands – Malta, Gozo, and Comino. The ancient islands are the remnants of a large land bridge that once stretched between North Africa and Europe. Malta has few freshwater sources and most of the islands consist of arid plains with poor soils. Most of Malta's indigenous vegetation was cleared during the Middle Ages. All of the Maltese islands have a distinctly Mediterranean climate with hot, dry summers and mild winters.

Politics: The ancient megaliths of Malta are remnants of an ancient stone age culture that once inhabited the islands. Malta was ruled by numerous foreign powers throughout its history, including the Romans, Egyptians, Phoenicians, Arabs, Spaniards, and the British. In the possession of the Knights of Malta, the country was an important center of the Christian wars against the Ottoman Turks between 1530 and 1798 and a bulwark of the West. It was a British colony from 1800 to 1964 and declared independence in 1974. Malta joined the EU in 2004.

Economy: Malta's agricultural sector consists mostly of small farms and produces less than 5% of the country's GDP. The services sector accounts for more than 74% of GDP. Tourism remains the single most important industry in the country and provides jobs for more than a quarter of the population. The country's leading export commodities include citrus fruits and machinery.

Marshall Islands
Marshall Islands

Area: 181 sq km
Population: 57,700
GDP per capita: 1,600 US$
Capital: Majuro
Government: Republic
Languages: Marshallese dialects, English
Currency: 1 US dollar = 100 cents

Geography: The Marshall Islands consist of two atolls that stretch over a distance of 1,200 kilometers. The Ratak island group comprises 16 atolls, while the large Ralik group consists of 18 atolls and more than 100 coral reefs. The Marshall Islands all have humid tropical climate with heavy rainfall.

Politics: The islands were first visited by Europeans in 1529 and became a German protectorate in 1884. After the First World War the islands were transferred to Japanese control. Between 1945 and 1980 they were administered by the United States. In 1980 the Marshall Islands were declared an independent state but the United States provides the country's defense and much development aid.

Economy: More than half of the Marshall Islands' population is concentrated on the islands of Ebeye and Majuro. Much of the population works in agriculture. Bananas, papayas, and coconuts are the most widely produced crops. The islands have few mineral resources, but phosphate is mined on the Ailinglaplap atoll. Coconuts and fish are the leading exports. Tourism is a small but important industry for the islands and the industrial sector consists mostly of fish processing. Development aid from the United States is the country's main source of government funding.

Mauritius
Mauritius

Area: 2,040 sq km
Population: 1.2 million
GDP per capita: 11,400 US$
Capital: Port Louis
Government: Republic
Languages: English (official), Creole, Hindi, Urdu
Currency: 1 Mauritius rupee = 100 cents

Geography: The tropical island, a volcanic formation in the Indian Ocean, has a humid tropical climate. Its highest mountain is the Cocotte (771 m) in the south. The white beaches of the coastline's many bays are fringed by lagoons. Parts of the original rain forest have survived only in the nature reserves. The island's capital is the center of its thriving tourism industry, and the nature reserves at Rivière Noire and Ile Aigrettes are easily accessible. The other islands in the group also attract holiday-makers and diving fans.

Politics: The island was conquered in the 16th century by the Dutch, who introduced plantation cultivation. The French took over the colony in the 18th century, while Mauritius came under British rule from 1810 until its independence in 1968. The Republic of Mauritius was founded in 1992, although the country remained a member of the Commonwealth.

Economy: Sugar-cane cultivation has primary importance, employing 14% of the labor force. Three-quarters of foodstuffs are imported; cultivation of potatoes, vegetables, bananas, and pineapple is subsidized. The country's industrial sector focuses on textile production and sugar-cane processing. 10% of the workforce are employed in the tourism sector. The island's infrastructure is well-developed, with road networks and shipping and air links to the other islands.

Mawrītāniyah
Mauritania

Area: 1,030,700 sq km
Population: 3 million
GDP per capita: 1,800 US$
Capital: Nouakchott
Government: Islamic presidential republic
Languages: Arabic (official), Niger-Congo languages
Currency: 1 ouguiya = 5 khoums

Geography: The eastern Atlantic coast gives way to flat coastal plains and extensive tableland with steppe vegetation. The majority of the country is occupied by the Sahara with sand and scree deserts. Its highest elevations are the plateaus of Adrar and Tagant, at around 500 meters. Owing to the extremely dry climate, palms and baobab flourish only in the far south in the savannas on the Senegal. Of interest for tourists are the cities of Chinguetti, Oualâta, Tîchît and Oudâne. The bird sanctuary of Djoudj and Banc d'Arguin national park are on the coast. Desertification is a major environmental problem in Mauritania.

Mexico City: The fourth largest city in the world.

Beautiful island: Beaches and lagoons make Mauritius a popular holiday destination. Today tourism is the most important source of income for the population. Two-thirds of them are descendants of the Indian plantation workers who were recruited in the 19th century for the dominant sugarcane cultivation; the remainder are Creoles, Europeans, and Chinese.

Politics: The country, part of the wealthy Ghana Empire, was Islamicized by Arab settlers in the 11th century. It was ruled by Moorish sultans until the end of the 19th century. In 1902 the French acquired the territory and incorporated it into the colony of French West Africa in 1920. Mauritania gained independence in 1960. The new constitution of 1991 smoothed the path from dictatorship to democracy; the first elections were held in 1992.

Economy: Persistent droughts have reduced the proportion of traditional nomadic populations; urbanization is increasing. Only 0.2% of the country's area is cultivatable. The fertile land in the catchment area of the Senegal and the oases of the south is cultivated for subsistence agriculture supplying basic needs. Animal husbandry is practised in the southern steppe belt. Fishery accounts for the majority of export revenues, and forms the basis of a small processing industry. Iron ore exports are the major source of foreign currency.

México
Mexico

Area: 1,972,550 sq km
Population: 105 million
GDP per capita: 9,000 US$
Capital: Mexico CIty
Government: Presidential federal republic
Languages: Spanish (official), minority languages
Currency: 1 Mexican new peso = 100 centavos

Geography: Mexico lies between the Gulf of Mexico and the Pacific. A ridge of high mountains, with the Sierra Madre to the west, south and east, surround the tableland that comprises most of the country's interior, with the highest peak – Popocatépetl (5,452 m) – at its center. The peninsula of Yucatán, bordering the Caribbean in the southeast, is composed of a chalk layer. The southern foothills of the coastal American Cordilleras form the peninsula of Baja California, divided from the remaining territory by the Gulf of California. Northern Mexico has desert vegetation; tropical rain forests grow along the coast of the Gulf of Mexico. Tourist attractions are principally the capital, the many sites of ancient civilizations (Uxmal, Teotihuacán, Palenque) and the lively beaches (Acapulco, Tampico).

Politics: At the start of the 16th century the Spanish conquered the seat of the Maya and Aztec civilizations and plundered its rich silver reserves, overthrowing the native ruler to establish an extensive colony under Hernán Cortez. Mexico declared independence in 1821. The civil war in the following era culminated in 1911 in a bloody revolution, which ended in 1920 after the proclamation of a presidential federal republic. The country's states have their own constitutions, with a relatively high degree of autonomy. The president is elected by a bicameral parliament for a term of six years.

Economy: Agriculture forms the livelihood of half the population, with maize, wheat, pulses, vegetables and fruit grown for subsistence in smallholdings and private plantations cultivating coffee, tobacco and cotton for export. Extensive and largely untapped reserves of minerals and ores have already made Mexico a major supplier of silver, feldspar, and graphite. The rich petroleum and natural gas reserves make a significant contribution to the economy, accounting for around 30% of export revenues and forming the basis of the chemical industry. Tourism is well-developed and accounts for a large share of the services sector.

Micronesia
Micronesia

Area: 702 sq km
Population: 108,200
GDP per capita: 2,000 US$
Capital: Palikir
Government: Constitutional government

1 The Maya temple of Tulúm is picturesquely located on the Caribbean coast of Mexico in the northern part of the Yucatan peninsula.

2 Vast parts of Mauritania are occupied by dunes and rocky deserts; the country borders the Sahara to the northwest.

3 The storehouses and sanctuaries in the cliffs of Bandiagara, constructed some centuries ago of clay bricks, belong to the cultural heritage of the people of Dogon in Mali.

4 Ferries play an important role in the traffic system of Malta.

Moçambique Mozambique

Mongolian traditions: Although the majority of the Mongolian people have now settled, hunting and horse-riding are still living traditions among these former nomads and equestrians who once ruled the whole of Asia.

Today the various ethnic groups and tribes of the Mongols, who have a single language in common, live scattered over the national territories of Mongolia, China, and Russia.

Languages: English, local Polynesian and Micronesian languages
Currency: 1 US dollar = 100 cents

Geography: The territory of the Federated States of Micronesia are scattered over an area of 2.6 million km² in the Pacific Ocean. The country comprises four states – Chuuk (294 islands), Yap (145 islands), Kosrae (five islands), and Pohnpei (163 islands). The country consists of both volcanic and coral island groups. All of the islands have a humid tropical climate with heavy rainfall, and tropical storms are common in the regions. Ancient ruins and the diverse marine life in Micronesia's coral reefs are the country's main tourist attractions.

Politics: The islands of Micronesia were under Spanish control for centuries before they were sold to Germany in the 19th century. The islands were administered by Japan after the end of the First World War, and were transferred to the United States after the Second World War. Micronesia became an independent federal republic in 1990, although the United States continues to maintain responsibility for the country's defense. The constitution of 1979 applies. There are no formal political parties.

Economy: Small-scale farming of coconuts, cassava, and other crops provides most of Micronesia's food demands and employs a significant segment of the local population. The selling of fishing licenses to foreign companies, chiefly Japan, is an important source of income for the country. Tourism and the export of crops are both major industries in Micronesia.

Moçambique
Mozambique

Area: 801,590 sq km
Population: 18.8 Million
GDP per capita: 1,200 US$
Capital: Maputo
Government: Republic
Languages: Portuguese (official), Bantu languages
Currency: 1 metical = 100 centavos

Geography: The many bays of the coast along the Indian Ocean give way to savanna and dry forests inland. To the north are mountains of up to 2,000 meters. Mangrove forests grow in the swampy regions of the river deltas. In the summer, monsoons dominate the tropical climate. The once rich animal life (antelopes, gazelles, elephants, leopards) has been decimated by big game hunting. Tourism concentrates on nature reserves such as Gorongosa and the broad beaches, but also the old colonial cities of Moçambique and Maputo. The country's climate ranges from subtropical to tropical with significant differences between the coastal and interior regions. Severe flooding and periods of drought are common in many regions.

Politics: Occupied in the 16th century by the Portuguese, the country did not gain independence until 1975 after a long guerilla war. In the same year the liberation movement proclaimed a people's republic, which was replaced in 1990 by a parliamentary democracy with a new constitution. After a long civil war, a peace treaty was signed with the right-wing rebels in 1992.

Economy: Although the largest sector of the economy, agriculture is barely at subsistence level. Over half the export revenues are derived from shrimps, which are processed by the industrial sector. The rich natural resources (precious and semiprecious stones, iron ores, minerals, metals) are largely untouched. Improvements to the infrastructure since the 1990s have benefited the services sector as tourism and the cargo handling trade have increased.

Morocco see Al-Magrib/Maroc

Moldova
Republic of Moldova

Area: 33,700 sq km
Population: 4.4 million
GDP per capita: 1,800 US$
Capital: Chisinau
Government: Republic

Language: Moldovan (official), Russian
Currency: 1 Moldoan leu = 100 bani

Geography: The small country in Eastern Europe consists primarily of plains and marshes. Moldova is crossed by several rivers including the Danube, the Dniester, and the Prut. Most of the country is covered by grasslands, marshes, and deciduous forests. Tourism focuses on the capital, and on the historic castles.

Politics: The area of modern Moldova was part of the Principality of Moldova during the Middle Ages. Moldova was conquered by the Ottomans in the 16th century. The eastern part of the country was annexed by Russia in 1812 and became a Soviet republic in 1918. The country declared its independence from the Soviet Union in 1991.

Economy: Moldova is one of the poorest states in Europe despite strong growth in recent years. The country has few mineral resources and agriculture contributes more than a quarter of national GDP and occupies over 70% of Moldova's area. The country's agricultural sector stagnated during the 1990s due to a loss of its traditional markets in the former Soviet republics. Privatization is progressing slowly. Moldova's service sector remains undeveloped and manufacturing is relatively unproductive. Major exports include fruits, grain, wine, tobacco, and machinery.

Monaco
Monaco

Area: 1.95 sq km
Population: 32,300
GDP per capita: 27,000 US$
Capital: Monaco City
Government: Constitutional hereditary monarchy
Language: French (official), Monegasque, Italian
Currency: 1 euro = 100 cents

Geography: Monaco is a small principality on the Mediterranean coast of Southern France. Most of the country's land area was created by reclaiming land from the sea. The densely populated country consists mostly of urban landscapes, although wines and olives are grown in a few areas. Monaco is a popular tourist destination.

Politics: The ruling Grimaldi dynasty gained control of Monaco in 1454. Monaco achieved complete independence in 1861 after periods of Spanish and French domination. Monaco lost most of its territory to France during the 19th century. The constitutions of 1911 and 1962 limited the power of Monaco's princes

Monaco: Tax haven on the Côte d'Azur.

and transformed the country into a modern constitutional monarchy.

Economy: Only around 17% of Monaco's residents are citizens of the country. Monaco has a high standard of living and low taxes that attract many residents and investors. Tourism is an important industry for the country and the principality's famous casino in the Monte Carlo area is the country's largest single business. Other economic pillars are the real estate and financial sectors.

Mongol Ard Uls
Mongolia

Area: 1,565,000 sq km
Population: 2.8 million
GDP per capita: 1,800 US$
Capital: Ulan Bator
Government: Republic
Languages: Mongolian, Kazakh, Russian, other languages
Currency: 1 tugrik = 100 mongo

Geography: The country also known as Outer Mongolia is dominated in the west by the Altai Mountains, up to 4,300 meters in height, and the Changai Mountains (over 3,500 m). Highlands with peaks of 1,000–1,500 meters cover the east, and taiga vegetation grows in the northeast. The mountain desert and steppe vegetation that dominates the remaining area gives way to the Gobi Desert in the south.

Politics: Inhabited early by nomadic horsemen, Mongolia was united in 1206 by Genghis Khan and formed the core of a large empire with Beijing at its center. After the fall of the Mongolian imperial dynasty in 1368, the country fell under Chinese rule. In 1911, Outer Mongolia separated from China. The People's Republic of Mongolia was created in 1924. After the collapse of the USSR, a multi-party system was introduced and the Republic of Mongolia founded in 1992. The country has a unicameral parliament.

Economy: The population consists predominantly of Mongols, followed by Kazakhs, Chinese, and Russians. The transition from a socialist planned

"Golden triangle": The Shan people, Thai in origin, have populated northeastern Myanmar on the borders of Laos, Thailand, and China since the 13th century. Extensive smuggling of opium by troops of rebels from the world's largest production area has repeatedly led to armed conflict with the central government. Limited autonomy was granted to the Shan State in 1993, within a cease-fire agreement.

economy to a market economy has proved difficult. Traditional animal husbandry (goats, sheep, camels, and horses) predominates, as only 1% of the area can be used for agriculture (grains, vegetables, feedstuffs). The rich coal, copper, molybdenum, gold, and tin deposits are mined and form the basis of the industry. Tourism is almost non-existent; services account for 34% of GDP.

Montenegro see Crna Gora

Muang Thai
Thailand

Area: 513,115 sq km
Population: 64.8 million
GDP per capita: 7,400 US$
Capital: Bangkok
Government: Constitutional monarchy
Languages: Thai (official), English, Chinese dialects
Currency: 1 baht = 100 stangs

Geography: The west of the country consists of foothills of the Southeast Asian central mountain range, which reaches as far as the Malacca peninsula. The fertile lowland plain, running from north to south and watered by the Menam, is the most densely populated area of the country. The Korat plateau lies to the east, sloping gently into the Mekong. Rain and monsoon forests flourish in the tropical climate, with high temperatures all year round. In addition to tourist sites like Pattaya and Phuket, Thailand boasts numerous cultural sights such as Ayutthaya and Sukhotai. Rare animals can be seen in the Khao-Yai National Park.

Politics: The Kingdom of Siam was founded in the 13th century. Bangkok became its capital in 1782. In the 19th century, Siam ceded areas to France and Great Britain, without being colonized itself. In 1932, a coup d'état led to a constitutional monarchy. The emergence of a modern state since the Second World War has been delayed time and again by unrest. A new constitution has been in force since 1998, vesting power in a bicameral parliament. The monarch is the head of state and is much revered and respected. All but 5% of Thais are Buddhists.

Economy: 80% of the population live outside the cities. Some 60% of the workforce are employed in agriculture, cultivating rice, corn, manioc, sugar cane, and rubber. The country's main exports are rubber and tin. Illegal poppy growing is a not insignificant economic factor. In addition to foodstuffs, the industry produces paper, computer parts, building materials, and motor vehicles, and accounts for 40% of GDP. Tourism is the main branch of the services sector which contributes 50% of GDP.

Myanmar
Myanmar (Burma)

Area: 678,500 sq km
Population: 42.7 million
GDP per capita: 1,900 US$
Capital: Yangon
Government: Republic
Languages: Burmese (official), local languages
Currency: 1 kyat = 100 pyas

Geography: The land is surrounded by high mountains at the borders and opens up on the coast. The Arakan Mountains in the southwest (Hkakabo Razi, 5,881 m), covered with virgin forest, are foothills of the Himalayas. The Irawadi river valley flows through a densely populated lowland plain to the east, irrigating the world's largest rice-growing region. Myanmar belongs to the tropical monsoon zone. Popular tourist destinations include the Buddhist monuments in Yangon and Pagan and the beautiful landscapes on the Shan Plateau.

Politics: Settled by Burmese invaders from China in the 8th century, the country was conquered by the Mongols in the 13th century. Power struggles between the Arakan and Ava empires ended in 1752 with the union of the entire country under a Burmese dynasty. Burma was under British rule from 1866 to 1948. In the civil war that followed after independence, the military emerged victorious and has hampered all attempts at democratization since 1962 under a succession of leaders.

Economy: The leading economic sector of Myanmar is agriculture, the main products of which (rice, pulses, beans) are processed by the small-scale industrial sector for export. Forests yield hardwoods such as teak for export. Diamonds and natural gas reserves generate the highest export earnings. Illegal opium is grown in the area known

1 The Caroline Islands are the largest island group in Micronesia, with more than 963 islands, including some of volcanic origin and coral atolls. Archeological discoveries have indicated a long history of human settlement.

2 The buildings of the royal palace are in the center of Bangkok.

3 Predominantly Buddhist Myanmar is home to numerous important art treasures.

4 In agricultural Mongolia, the people primarily live from livestock breeding.

Guided by the stars: *Polynesians call their legendary country of origin "Hawaiki." Exceptionally skilled shipbuilders and navigators, they extended their territory as far as New Zealand, using the position of the sun and* *stars, the currents and winds to guide them through the vastness of Oceania. Their descendants still employ the same techniques.*

as the Golden Triangle. The country has well-developed rail and air networks.

Namibia
Namibia

Area: 825,418 sq km
Population: 1.9 million
GDP per capita: 7,100 US$
Capital: Windhoek
Government: Republic within Commonwealth
Languages: English (official), Afrikaans, German
Currency: 1 Namibian dollar = 100 cents

Geography: The sandy, rocky expanse of the Namib Desert extends parallel to the coast. A steep escarpment (Brandberg, 2,574 m) rises in the interior in rolling highlands that slope down in the east to the Kalahari basin at 1,000 meters. To the north is the Etoscha Pan, one of Africa's largest salt pans. The climate is subtropical. Around 7% of the country's area comprises animal reserves principally inhabited by antelopes, lions, and elephants. The country's major attractions include the seaside towns of Swakopmund and Walvis Bay as well the extensive desert wildernesses in the interior.

Politics: European traders and missionaries first entered the country in the mid-19th century; Namibia became a German colony in 1884. It was occupied by South Africa during the First World War and was subsequently annexed as the Boer state's 5th province. The guerilla war that raged from the 1960s ended in a cease-fire in 1989; Namibia gained independence in 1990, and a democratic constitution followed. SWAPO, which led the resistance movement from the outset (1959), is today the most influential political force.

Economy: The economy is still suffering from the separation from South Africa, although it has retained close links with that country. Agriculture is the most important area, accounting for 73% of employment, and beef is the main agrarian export. Mining forms the backbone of the economy, with natural resources of diamonds, uranium, copper, zinc, and gold

contributing 20% to GDP and plentiful foreign exchange revenues. The profitable fishing industry is expanding further after the inclusion of the port of Walvis Bay in the country's territory (1994). Government reforms are now liberalizing the economy and privatizing many state industries.

Nauru (Naoero)
Nauru

Area: 21.3 sq km
Population: 12,800
GDP per capita: 5,000 US$
Capital: Yaren
Government: Parliamentary democracy
Languages: Nauruan, English
Currency: 1 Australian dollar = 100 cents

Geography: This small coral island is surrounded by a large reef. Nauru's coast consists of sandy beaches that border a broad strip of fertile land stretching between 150 and 300 meters inland. Most of the island is a plateau that rises 70 meters above sea level. Large sections of Nauru's interior are uninhabitable, covered with barren patches of land that are

Amsterdam's many canals are the most famous landmarks of the city.

the result of phosphate mining. The island has neither rivers nor natural harbors.

Politics: In 1798, after centuries of isolation, European whale hunters arrived on the island. Nauru was incorpora-

ted into the German protectorate of the Marshall Islands in 1888. The island's first phosphate mining operation began in 1905. Nauru achieved independence in 1968 after decades of Japanese and later Australian administration. The country's parliament is directly elected every three years. The traditional Polynesian clan system is still in operation on the island.

Economy: The economy of Nauru is dominated almost entirely by phosphate mining. The local mining industry is controlled by the Nauru Phosphate Corporation, the country's largest company and employer and a major investor in fishing and tourism. With most of its phosphate deposits depleted, Nauru is now facing serious economic challenges that could threaten its survival as a viable independent nation.

Nederland
Netherlands

Area: 41,526 sq km
Population: 16.3 million
GDP per capita: 28,600 US$

Capital: Amsterdam
Government: Parliamentary monarchy
Language: Dutch
Currency: 1 euro = 100 cents

Geography: The Netherlands is situated on a vast plain that

extends through large sections of western and central Europe. Reclaimed land that is below sea level comprises more than a quarter of the country's territory. The highest point in the country, the Vaalserberg hill, rises just 320 meters above sea level. Several major rivers flow through the country including the Rhine and the Meuse. Inland waters account for one sixth of its area. The Netherlands has a temperate-maritime climate with frequent precipitation throughout the year. The capital city, Amsterdam, is by far the most visited destination in the country.

Politics: The Netherlands gained its independence from the rulers of the German-dominated Holy Roman Empire in 1648. During much of the 16th and 17th centuries, the Dutch controlled Europe's most powerful trading and naval fleet. The country lost control of Belgium in 1831 but retained control of its largest overseas territories until the 1950s. The strictly neutral country was occupied by Germany during the Second World War. The Netherlands was one of the founding members of NATO and the EU. The Hague is the seat of government and the International Court of Justice.

Economy: The Netherlands has one of the most diverse and highly developed economies in the world. The people of the Netherlands enjoy one of the highest standards of living in Europe. Most of the country's population is concentrated in the heavily-populated Randstad, an urban conglomerate in the western section of the country. The country's service sector contributes more than 70% of national GDP. The Rhine Delta is one of the world's busiest centers of shipping and Rotterdam is the site of Europe's busiest harbor. Agriculture employs less than 4% of the workforce but is highly developed; the Netherlands is the world's third largest agricultural exporter, with major exports including flowers and hothouse vegetables. Fishing also remains an important industry. Machinery, electronics, and chemical products are important industrial exports.

Nepal
Nepal

Area: 140,800 sq km
Population: 27 million
GDP per capita: 1,400 US$
Capital: Kathmandu
Government: Constitutional monarchy
Languages: Nepali (official), Maithili, Bhojpuri
Currency: 1 Nepalese rupee = 100 paisa

Geography: Nepal consists of a narrow strip of land 853 kilometers long and 160 kilometers wide, on the southern slopes of the Central Himalayas. The flood plain of the Terai to the far south follows the Siwalik chain and the broad, medium-altitude Lower Himalayas. The national territory ends in the north at the crest of the Himalayas with some of the world's highest peaks (Mt. Everest, 8,846 m). The core economic and social region is the Kathmandu Valley, extending through the Fore-Himalayas for 30 kilometers in length and 25 kilometers breadth. Increasing numbers of Himalayan trekking tours are beginning to take their toll on the environment.

Politics: The principalities and tribal societies in the Valley of Kathmandu were united for the first time in 1756 under the rule of the Gurkhas. From the beginning of the 19th century, Great Britain exercised its influence on the Nepalese government. A constitutional monarchy followed a change of dynasty in 1951. The democratic constitution of 1959 was replaced in 1962 by a markedly monarchist constitution. Civil war has raged for years between the government and Maoist rebels. Political parties have been permitted since 1990, with representatives running for election to the National Assembly every five years.

Economy: The Nepalese economy is based on the poorly developed agricultural production (livestock breeding). Gold, copper, and iron ore deposits are mined and slate and limestone quarried for export. The modest industrial sector consists of textile companies, carpet weaving concerns, and brick-works, plus jute, tobacco,

Ovamboland: The largest population in Namibia is the Ovambo, a Bantu people from the fertile north of the country. They were leaders in the formation of the popular opposition movement SWAPO at the end of the 1950s. The organization fought a long and bitter guerilla war against the South African administration and military.

and grain processing. Tourism is emerging as the leading economic sector.

New Zealand
New Zealand

Area: 268,680 sq km
Population: 4 million
GDP per capita: 21,600 US$
Capital: Wellington
Government: Parliamentary democracy
Languages: English, Maori
Currency: 1 New Zealand dollar = 100 cents

Geography: New Zealand consists of two large islands (North and South Islands) separated by the Cook Strait, and several smaller islands. The terrain on both of the large islands is dominated by a series of mountain ranges. The North Island has several active volcanoes as well as numerous hot springs and geysers. The South Island features the 300-kilometer chain of the Southern Alps, New Zealand's largest mountain system. The country's largest mountain, Mount Cook, rises 3,764 meters. Most of New Zealand's virgin forests were cleared by settlers to create farmland. New Zealand is home to an array of unique flora and fauna, with a host of fascinating bird species including the Kiwi. The North Island has a mild subtropical climate, while the South Island features a cooler, more temperate climate.

Politics: The Polynesian ancestors of today's Maori first arrived in New Zealand during the 9th century. During the late 18th century, Captain James Cook explored the islands, and the first European settlers, mostly British, arrived on the islands shortly thereafter. The Treaty of Waitangi (1840) granted Great Britain control over most of New Zealand. A series of violent conflicts between the Maori and British forces was brought to an end in 1874. New Zealand achieved independence in 1931 but the British monarch remains the country's official head of state. New Zealand has one of the few unicameral parliaments in the world and elections are

held every three years. It was the first country in the world to introduce female suffrage.

Economy: New Zealanders of European descent comprise around 78% of the country's population. The country's advanced agricultural sector is one of the world's most productive. New Zealand is now the only developed nation which does not subsidize its domestic agricultural industry. Important crops include grains, fruits, and dairy products. The South Island has extensive sheep farming and wool production. The manufacturing and service sectors have both grown substantially

in recent decades. Important industrial exports include chemical, electronic, and wood products. The country's extensive hydroelectric resources are being increasingly exploited and could eventually have a major impact on New Zealand's economy.

Nicaragua
Nicaragua

Area: 129,494 sq km
Population: 5.3 million
GDP per capita: 2,200 US$
Capital: Managua
Government: Presidential republic
Languages: Spanish (official), Chibcha
Currency: 1 córdoba = 100 centavos

Geography: Central America's largest country is bounded to the west by the Pacific, to the

east by the Caribbean. Two-thirds of the population live on the plains of the Pacific coast. A 240-kilometer-long arc of volcanic mountains, 11 of which are active, lie to the east. Earthquakes are relatively frequent. The Caribbean coast is rich in lagoons and swamps, with savannas on the

1 The Netherlands is traditionally the country of windmills. Their sails stand out amid the vast plains.

2 The Nepalis call the highest mountain in the world, first climbed in 1953, Sagarmatha or "King of Heaven."

3 The Namib desert extends along the Atlantic coast of Namibia.

4 The glaciers in the west of the Alps on New Zealand's South Island stretch almost to the coast of the Tasmanian Sea.

Priests of the mountains: Devotees of the popular Japanese faith of shugendo, a combination of Buddhist and Shinto elements, regularly go to the mountains to perform ascetic practices. They chant incantations, meditate and fast as a means of accumulating spiritual power.

Pacific coast. 40% of the country is covered by rain forests. Tourist destinations are the Pacific and Caribbean beaches, the capital Managua and the nearby Lake Nicaragua.

Politics: Nicaragua was discovered by Columbus in 1502 and conquered 20 years later by the Spanish. In the early 19th century the country joined the Central American Federation. Nicaragua was torn by civil war from the early 20th century; the overthrow of the dictator Somoza in 1979 after 40 years' rule triggered military conflict between the left-wing Sandinistas and the Contra rebel forces, which did not end until 1990. The first free democratic elections, won by the opposition party UNO, were held the same year.

Economy: Nicaragua suffers under a large foreign trade deficit. Agriculture supplies 28% of GDP and comprises basic food crops, but also coffee, sugarcane, cotton, and bananas for export. The industrial sector is poorly developed and chiefly processes foodstuffs. Tourism, although as yet in its infancy, is undergoing gradual expansion. 80% of the population live in poverty.

Niger
Niger

Area: 1,267,000 sq km
Population: 11.4 million
GDP per capita: 800 US$
Capital: Niamey
Government: Pres. republic
Languages: French (official), Haussa and further tribal languages
Currency: 1 CFA franc = 100 centimes

Geography: The country extends from the middle reaches of the Niger through the Sahel and deep into the Sahara. Oases are fed by rivers rising in the Aïr Mountains (1,944 m) to dry up in the desert. The north is dominated by sand and stony deserts, the south by dry savanna inhabited by elephants, lions and other wildlife. The chief settlement areas are the Niger and Komadougo basins. Popular tourist sights are the ancient city of Agadez, former hub of caravan routes, prehistoric rock drawings in the Aïr Massif and the "W" nature reserve.

Politics: In the 16th century, the political structure that had stood in the Niger area since the 12th century came under Islamic influence before the country was conquered by the Fulbe in the 19th century. The French colony of Niger was founded in 1922. The constitution brought in after independence in 1960 was suspended until 1991. The National Assembly was dissolved in 1996 following a coup. A new constitution restored civilian rule to the country in 1999.

Economy: The country's economy is dominated by traditional nomadic animal husbandry and small-scale farming, principally in the Niger Valley and largely for subsistence. Fisheries and the fishing licence business are profitable. The mining industry supplies the country's main exports in the form of diamonds, copper, and uranium.

Geography: The country on the Gulf of Guinea has a humid tropical climate. The coast is fringed by a strip of mangroves 15–90 kilometers wide, which gives way to primeval forest farther inland. The plateau in the country's interior is marked by savannas, steppes and desert-like regions. Lake Chad lies to the northeast. The Niger flows through the country for 1,168 kilometers and ends in 24,000 km² of delta. Tourist destinations are the northern Haussa cities of Kano and Katsina.

Politics: The kingdoms of Nigeria, in existence since the early Middle Ages, were gradually conquered by the Fulbe. In 1885 the country was declared a British protectorate. Since its independence in 1960 Nigeria has been ravaged by military coups, unrest and religious conflict. The elections of 1992 were annulled by the country's leaders but the military dictatorship ended in 1999 with new elections.

A japanese landmark: The Torii in front of the Itsukushima-shrine.

Nigeria
Nigeria

Area: 923,768 sq km
Population: 137.3 million
GDP per capita: 800 US$
Capital: Abuja
Government: Presidential federal republic
Languages: English (official), Arabic, tribal languages
Currency: 1 naira = 100 kobo

Economy: Nigeria is inhabited by three major peoples: the Christian Yoruba and Igbo in the south, and the Muslim Haussa in the north. Agriculture consists of subsistence smallholdings and plantations that supply export goods such as cocoa and rubber. The main basis of the economy, at 90% of export revenue, is the petroleum and natural gas reserves that have been exploited since the 1970s.

Corruption and the poor infrastructure are major obstacles to the country's economic development. Tourism has been hampered by the unrest in the country, it is still a key source of foreign revenue.

Nippon/Nihon
Japan

Area: 377,801 sq km
Population: 127.3 million
GDP per capita: 28,000 US$
Capital: Tokyo
Government: Constitutional monarchy
Language: Japanese
Currency: 1 yen = 100 sen

Geography: Japan's territory comprises some 4,100 mainly mountainous islands, the peaks of an underwater mountain range. The highest mountain is the volcano Fuji (3,776 m); in addition to countless hot springs, there are also some 40 active volcanoes in this earthquake-prone country. Industrialization has almost completely destroyed the original natural landscapes. The extensive geographical area includes a variety of climates; the south is subtropical and hot, the north temperate and cool. Monsoon winds bring rain in summer, which falls as snow in winter. The numerous tourist destinations range from hot springs in the Beppu spa, to the ancient imperial cities of Nara and Kyoto and the metropolis Tokyo.

Politics: An early target for settlement, the country came under Chinese influence in the 6th–7th centuries, and was ruled by powerful warring clans from the 12th century. From the 16th to the 19th century, under the rule of the Tokugawa Shogunate, Japan moved into international isolation. After the restoration of imperial power (1868), the country underwent industrialization. At the end of World War II, two American atomic bombs were dropped on Japan (Hiroshima, Nagasaki). A new constitution was introduced in 1947, and the emperor is now only a figurehead.

Economy: Japan is one of the richest industrialized nations in the world. Agriculture (grains, rice, tea, fruit, and vegetables) is practiced primarily for domestic consumption. The northern island of Hokkaido is the center of an extensive cattle breeding industry. Part of the fleet of this major fishing nation is stationed abroad. The highly developed industry of this country with little materials produces the most important export products: ships, cars, steel, computers, and artificial fibers and materials.

Norge
Norway

Area: 324,220 sq km
Population: 4.6 million
GDP per capita: 37,700 US$
Capital: Oslo
Government: Parliamentary monarchy
Language: Norwegian
Currency: 1 Norwegian krone = 100 Øre

Geography: Norway occupies the western section of the Scandinavian peninsula and has more than 2,650 kilometers of coastline. The northernmost sections are above the Arctic Circle. Most of Norway's landscapes were formed by glaciers during the last ice age. Large fjords cut deep into the country, and it is surrounded by numerous islands. Most of Norway's interior is dominated by mountains and hills. Northern Norway has a severe sub-arctic climate, and the far north consists of treeless tundras. Most of the country, however, has a mild maritime-temperate climate. The country's main tourist attractions include its impressive landscapes as well the cities of Bergen and Oslo.

Politics: Norway came under the control of the Danish monarchy in the late 14th century. The country was joined with Sweden in a political union between 1814 and 1915. Norway was neutral during the First World War but was occupied by Germany in the Second World War. The country was a founding member of NATO in the 1950s. Norway is a constitutional monarchy and a multi-party democracy.

Economy: Less than 3% of Norway's terrain consists of arable land. The agricultural sector is protected from for-

Fulbe: The largest ethnic group in Western Africa is composed of several peoples differing in economic, cultural, and religious aspects. The Bororo or Fulani people of Niger are traditionally nomadic cattle farmers, less Islamicized than the sedentary Fulbe people. They often form economic communities with farmers. The Bororo men are noted for their complex face painting.

eign competition by tariffs and subsidies. Oil from Norway's North Sea reserves is the country's most important export commodity, and the country is the third largest oil and natural gas exporter in the world. The service sector accounts for most of the country's GDP.

Oman see Saltanat 'Uman

Österreich
Austria

Area: 83,870 sq km
Population: 8.2 million
GDP per capita: 30,000 US$
Capital: Vienna
Government: Federal republic
Language: German
Currency: 1 euro = 100 cents

Geography: Austria is a small mountainous republic located in Central Europe. The Alps and Alpine foothills cover more than half of the country's terrain. A small section of the flat Carpathian Basin stretches through eastern Austria. The Danube and Inn rivers are the most important waterways. Austria's major tourist attractions include the capital city Vienna and the country's many excellent winter sports facilities.

Politics: Austria emerged as the center of the Habsburg Empire in the 13th century. The Habsburgs were able to rapidly expand their empire through numerous alliances and marriages. The vast multi-cultural empire was reorganized into the Austro-Hungarian Empire during the 19th century. The German-speaking provinces of the empire became the Republic of Austra in 1918. A second Austrian republic gained its sovereignty in 1955. Austria joined the European Union in 1995.

Economy: Austria has a highly developed and diverse economy. The country has attracted significant levels of foreign investment in recent years because of its proximity to the transition countries of Central Europe. The service sector contributes more than 65% of the national GDP. Tourism alone contributes 8% of Austria's GDP.

Pākistān
Pakistan

Area: 803,940 sq km
Population: 159.2 million
GDP per capita: 2,100 US$
Capital: Islamabad
Government: Islamic republic
Languages: Urdu (official), English, Punjabi, Sindhi, other minority languages
Currency: 1 Pakistani rupee = 100 paisa

Geography: Pakistan is bounded to the north by part of the Himalayas, the Hindu Kush and Karakorum, and to the West by the mountains bordering Iran

and Afghanistan. The eastern part of the country is taken up by the Indus basin. The country has a high-altitude climate in the mountains, and a dry hot to arid climate in the Indus basin. Only 4% of the area is wooded. In addition to Lahore, possible tourist destinations include the ancient sites of Mohenjodaro and the northern mountains.

Politics: Pakistan was created in 1947 by the partition of former British India. After a civil war, the eastern part split off in 1971 as Bangladesh. Not even free elections since 1988 have succeeded in bringing peace to the country, which has been torn by politically motivated acts of violence since its independence. Atomic bomb tests and the Kashmir conflict affect relations with neighboring India.

Economy: Agriculture, which employs half the population, generates 25% of GDP. A fifth

of the land is used for agriculture. The Indus basin has one of the largest irrigation systems in the world. In addition to wheat, cotton, and sugar cane, the main product is rice. The industrial sector, which is gaining in importance, processes agricultural products for export. The key exports are textiles, carpets, and clothing.

1 Architectural treasures from the baroque and classical eras are typical of the historic city of Salzburg.

2 Breathtaking Mount Fuji is Japan's highest mountain, at 3,776 meters. Every year the country's most sacred mountain attracts 4 million visitors.

3 Just recognizable under the decoration: a bus in Pakistan.

4 The seaport Ålesund, which is spread over a range of skerries off the west coast of Norway, is the fishing center of the country.

Highlands of the Andes: The majority of Peru's indigenous population are Quechuans. These breeders of llamas and alpacas inhabit the entire Andean highlands. Their religion and myths indicate the importance of their animals; for example, they believe that a decline in the size of their herds will indicate the end of the world, as the llamas return to their original homes under the earth.

Palau
Palau

Area: 458 sq km
Population: 20,000
GDP per capita: 9,000 US$
Capital: Koror
Government: Democratic state associated with the United States
Languages: Palauan, English, Japanese
Currency: 1 US dollar = 100 cents

Geography: Palau consists of 343 islands stretching over a distance of 200 kilometers. Most of the islands are volcanic in origin. Many of the country's coral islands feature extensive sand beaches and interesting diving sites, including numerous coral reefs.

Politics: The islands were settled as early as 1000 BC and were first visited by European explorers in the 18th century. Palau was administered by the German Empire at the beginning of the 20th century and came under Japanese control after 1914. The islands were under American administration between 1947 and 1982, when they became an independent republic with close ties to the United States.

Economy: Fishing and agriculture (fruit, manioc, coconuts) generate around half of Palau's GDP. Most of the country's national budget, however, is generated from annual payments from the United States government.

Panamá
Panama

Area: 78,200 sq km
Population: 3 million
GDP per capita: 6,300 US$
Capital: Panama City
Government: Presidential republic
Languages: Spanish (official), English
Currency: 1 balboa = 100 centésimos

Geography: The west of Panama is taken up by the foothills of the Central Cordilleras, with peaks of up to 3,475 meters, falling to the tropical lowlands of the Darien Jungle. In the northern rain forests, rainfall is high owing to the climatic divide formed by the Cordilleras. Only 46 kilometers wide, the Panama isthmus is the narrowest point between the Atlantic and Pacific Oceans.

Politics: 1501 saw the first Spanish colonies on Panama coast. The country joined Greater Colombia in 1821. After the Panama Canal was completed, Panama became nominally independent in 1903 on intervention from USA, and has been a sovereign state since 1982. The US military maintained a strong presence in the canal region (part of US territory until 1977) until 2000.

Economy: The commercial and services sector is the economy's largest at 70% of GDP, thanks to the Canal, opened in 1914, and the free trade area around Colón. Bananas, cane sugar, coffee, cocoa, shrimp, and tuna are the main exports. Industries process foodstuffs and petroleum.

Papua New Guinea
Papua New Guinea

The historic market square in Warsaw's scenic old town.

Area: 462,840 sq km
Population: 5.4 million
GDP per capita: 2,200 US$
Capital: Port Moresby
Government: Democracy
Languages: Pidgin, English, Motu
Currency: 1 kina = 100 toea

Geography: Papua New Guinea comprises the eastern half of New Guinea, the Bismarck Archipelago, and numerous small Melanesian islands. The mainland is dominated by volcanic mountain ranges and large swampy plains. The majority of the population is concentrated in the central highlands. Vast tropical rainforests and savannas cover most of the islands.

Politics: The island of New Guinea has been continuously inhabited for at least 40,000 years. In 1884 the eastern section of the island was divided and occupied by Germany and Great Britain. In 1975, Papua New Guinea became an independent nation after decades of Australian administration.

Economy: A significant percentage of Papua New Guinea's population continues to live in isolated rural communities with little or no access to modern technology or education. At least 66% of the population works in the agricultural sector, which generates 33% of the country's GDP. Major export crops include coconuts, coffee, and tea. Around 80% of the country's income from exports is generated by mineral resources including gold, copper, and oil. Other major exports include timber and palm oil. Economic growth has slowed in recent years, but the government is now working to reform the economy.

Paraguay
Paraguay

Area: 406,752 sq km
Population: 6.2 million
GDP per capita: 4,600 US$
Capital: Asunción
Government: Presidential republic
Languages: Spanish, Guaraní (all official)
Currency: 1 guaraní = 100 céntimos

Geography: The Río Paraguay divides Paraguay into an eastern region, with mountains and plateaus, and the western plains of Gran Chaco. The northwest has tropical rain forests giving way to savanna and grassland in the south. Tourist destinations are the areas of natural beauty and many sites dating from the colonial era.

Politics: Conquered by the Spanish in 1536, Paraguay housed a Jesuit state in the early 17th century until 1759. Paraguay became independent in 1811. 1989 saw the end of more than 30 years of dictatorship.

Economy: Agriculture is the principal economic sector, dominated by monocultures (livestock farming, coffee, rice, soybean, and cotton cultivation). The profitable export of tropical hardwoods has led to widespread clearing of rain forest areas. Industrial development has advanced little owing to lack of exploitation of the rich natural resources. River shipping is a popular transportation method in trading with neighboring countries.

Perú
Peru

Area: 1,285,216 sq km
Population: 27.5 million
GDP per capita: 5,200 US$
Capital: Lima
Government: Presidential republic
Languages: Spanish, Quechua (official), Aymará
Currency: 1 nuevo sol = 100 céntimos

Geography: The Andes Mountains (Nevado Huascarán, 6,768 m) in Peru's interior follow the coastline and slope down to the broad expanse of the Amazon basin in the northwest. Grasslands are found at higher altitudes. Tourist destinations are cultural monuments such as Machu Picchu and Chan-Chan, and colonial cities such as Lima and Trujillo. The coast comprises desert and steppes.

Politics: The Inca's kingdom was destroyed by Spanish conquerors in 1572. In 1821 Peru declared its independence from Spanish colonial rule, and since then the country has been ruled by a succession of military and civil governments. Moves towards neoliberalism have been met by social unrest.

Economy: The main agricultural crops are sugar-cane, maize, cotton, and coffee. Illegal coca cultivation is increasing dramatically. Fisheries account for 24% of export revenues; other key exports are copper, zinc, silver, and petroleum. The industrial sector processes textiles, foodstuffs, chemicals, and metals.

Pilipinas
Philippines

Area: 300,000 sq km
Population: 86.2 million
GDP per capita: 4,600 US$
Capital: Manila
Government: Presidential republic
Languages: Filipino (official), Spanish, English
Currency: 1 Philippine peso = 100 centavos

Geography: The Philippines extend along the northern part of the Malaysian Archipelago. The predominantly mountainous islands are often hit by earthquakes and volcanic eruptions. The humid climate favors tropical forests, which have largely been replaced by grass savanna as a result of land clearing. Primary tourist destinations are the scenic areas and the capital Manila.

Politics: The Philippines were under Spanish rule from the 16th to the 19th century. The colony was transferred to the United States in the late 19th century and granted independence in 1946. A 30-year dictatorship that ruined the country's economy was overturned in 1986.

Economy: 45% of the population live from agriculture, cultivating grains, vegetables, and coconut trees – the country is

Stone age: In the mountainous parts of the rainforests of Papua New Guinea there are still tribes living in complete isolation in neolithic-style settlements. These peoples largely practice ancestor worship and have systems of taboos. Many choose their leaders for their generosity and success in war.

the world's biggest producer of coconut products. The rich natural resources (copper, nickel, and petroleum) form the basis of a major industrial sector; high-tech electronic products generate the highest export revenues. The country's domestic air network is well developed.

Polska
Poland

Area: 312,685 sq km
Population: 38.6 million
GDP per capita: 11,000 US$
Capital: Warsaw
Government: Republic
Language: Polish
Currency: 1 zloty = 100 groszy

Geography: Poland consists mostly of vast plains and is bordered to the north by the Baltic Sea. A series of medium-height mountains stretches along the country's southern border. Several major rivers, including the Oder and the Vistula, flow through Poland. Poland's leading tourist attractions include the country's Baltic coast, the mountainous regions in the south, and historic cities such as Gdansk, Warsaw, and Krakow.

Politics: Poland emerged as a distinct nation around the 10th century. The country, together with Lithuania, ruled a vast empire that stretched from the Baltic to the Black Sea. Poland was divided between Prussia, Austria, and Russia in 1795 and did not exist as an independent state during most of the 19th century. The country regained its independence in 1918. Poland was occupied by Germany in the Second World War and 5 million Poles died during the war. The post-war period of communist rule was ended in 1989. Poland joined the EU in 2004.

Economy: Around 40% of the country's terrain is used for agricultural purposes. More than a quarter of the Polish labor force works in the agricultural sector, although agriculture contributes less than 5% of GDP. Major industries in the country include the chemical, steel, and shipbuilding industries. The rapidly growing service sector now contributes

more than half of the country's GDP. Reforms in the 1990s have opened the economy to increased foreign investment.

Portugal
Portugal

Area: 92,391 sq km
Population: 10.5 million
GDP per capita: 18,000 US$
Capital: Lisbon
Government: Republic
Language: Portuguese
Currency: 1 euro = 100 cents

Geography: Portugal occupies the westernmost section of the Iberian Peninsula. The

Sierra de Estrela mountain range stretches through the center of the country. The Tejo, Portugal's principal river, flows from Spain to its delta at the Atlantic Ocean near Lisbon. The country has a Mediterranean climate with hot, dry summers. In addition to the mainland, Portugal also consists of two island groups in the Atlantic Ocean: the Azores and Madeira Islands. Lisbon, the Algarve region, and the coastal areas are the country's most important tourist destinations.

Politics: Portugal was dominated by Arabs between the 8th and 13th centuries. The country gained its independence from the Spanish kingdom of Castille in the 12th century. Portugal was one of Europe's most powerful nations during the 15th and 16th centuries. Portugal was

declared a republic in 1910 but a military coup in 1926 left the country under military rule for decades. Portugal is now a multi-party democracy.

Economy: The areas between the Tejo and Duoro rivers are an important agricultural area

1 Machu Picchu, Peru's "Forgotten City" at an altitude of 2,900 meters. The countless artifacts give an insight into the ancient civilization.

2 Porto is one of the most beautiful cities of the Iberian peninsula.

3 Traditional island village off the coast of the island of Cebu at the heart of the Philippines.

4 The Iguaçu Falls cascade 70 meters down over two giant "steps."

where wine, olives, and citrus fruits are produced. Maize, potatoes and livestock are the products of the rainy northern regions. The country's economy, which was once dominated by agriculture, has become increasingly diverse since the 1980s. Today, the service sector accounts for more than 65% of national GDP. Major exports include textiles, cork (for which Portugal supplies half the world's requirements), machinery and agricultural products. Tourism is taking on increasing significance.

Qaṭar
Qatar

Area: 11,437 sq km
Population: 840,00
GDP per capita: 21,500 US$
Capital: Doha
Government: Emirate (absolute monarchy)
Language: Arabic
Currency: 1 Qatar riyal = 100 dirham

Geography: The small peninsular country extends into the Persian Gulf from Arabia's east coast. Rolling hills about 100 meters high are found only in the east of this otherwise flat country, which has a hot, dry desert climate. Of the small islands off Qatar's coast, only Halul is inhabited.

Politics: The peninsula has been ruled by the al-Thani family since the 18th century. After interruptions by Ottoman (1872–1916) and British occupations (until 1971), members of the family have returned to reign over the stable country as a hereditary monarchy. Islam is the state religion, of which around 90% of Qatar's inhabitants are adherents.

Economy: More than 50% of the population are migrant workers from neighboring Arab states. Social security, health, and education systems are very good. Agriculture is insignificant; the majority of foodstuffs are imported. The economy as a whole is based on oil; Qatar's natural gas reserves are thought to be the largest in the world. The country is visited only by business travelers and has almost no tourism.

República Dominicana
Dominican Republic

Area: 48,730 sq km
Population: 8.8 million
GDP per capita: 6,000 US$
Capital: Santo Domingo
Government: Presidential republic
Language: Spanish
Currency: 1 Dominican peso = 100 centavos

Geography: The Dominican Republic covers two-thirds of the island of Hispaniola, and is bounded by Haiti to the west. The highest peaks of the four parallel mountains that cross the island are on Dominican territory. The dense forests have largely been replaced by sugar-cane plantations. Although frequently hit by earthquakes, the Dominican Republic is a popular tourist destination thanks to its beautiful beaches.

Politics: The island's history from the 17th century was dominated by colonial conflicts, revolutions and US military intervention, the latter continuing after independence (1844). The murder of the dictator Trujillo in 1961 led to a period of deceptive stability, but social tensions continually disrupt the peace.

Economy: 32% of the workforce is employed in the agricultural sector, with the main exports being sugar, honey, coffee, and cocoa. Despite rich natural resources (gold and silver ores, ferronickel) mining is poorly developed. The services sector (tourism) is the only growth industry and a major source of revenue; it accounts for 24% of jobs.

République Centrafricaine
Central African Republic

Area: 622,984 sq km
Population: 3.7 million
GDP per capita: 1,200 US$
Capital: Bangui
Government: Presid. republic
Languages: French, Sangho (both official), Bantu, and Sudan languages
Currency: 1 CFA franc = 100 centimes

The Caribbean: The Dominican Republic is one of the poorest countries in the Antilles. Its inhabitants have had to relearn subsistence agriculture since the prices of once-flourishing export crops such as sugar cane, tobacco, and coffee have dropped on the world market. Nevertheless, many economic refugees from Haiti immigrate to the country.

Geography: The interior consists of low, rolling hills 500–1,100 meters in height, broken by isolated outcrops. Great rain forests flourish in the humid tropical climate of the south. The remaining country is covered by wet savannas, giving way to dry savanna in the northeast. Manovo-Gounda St. Floris National Park and the capital are the chief areas of interest for tourism, a sector that remains largely undeveloped. Floods are common throughout the country.

Politics: The French conquered the country and incorporated the region into what is now Chad; liberation movements gained the country's independence in 1960. The single-party system, in place since 1962, was

Dominican Republic: Idyllic sandy beaches.

replaced after a military coup in 1965 by a dictatorship under General Bokassa, who was overthrown in 1979. The country's first multi-party democratic elections were held in 1993.

Economy: Agriculture is primarily subsistence, with coffee and cotton cultivated for export. Small quantities of uranium, iron, copper, and nickel are mined, as are diamonds. The poorly developed industrial sector produces foodstuffs, leather, and wood products. The service sector also remains largely undeveloped.

România
Romania

Area: 237,500 sq km
Population: 22.4 million
GDP per capita: 6,900 US$
Capital: Bucharest
Government: Republic
Language: Romanian (official), Hungarian, German
Currency: 1 leu = 100 bani

Geography: Romania is in southeastern Europe and borders the Black Sea in the east. The Transylvanian basin is surrounded by the Carpathian Mountains and other highland areas. Several large plains dominate the rest of the country including the hilly Moldavian plain in the north and fertile Wallachian plain in the south. The Danube flows along most of the country's southern border. Most of the country has a continental climate. The historic towns of Transylvania and the monasteries of Moldova are important tourist attractions.

Politics: The principalities of Moldavia, Wallachia, and Transylvania were conquered by the Ottoman Empire in the 14th century. In 1878, Wallachia and Moldavia united to form the Kingdom of Romania. The country was dominated by the Soviet Union after the Second World War and was declared a socialist republic in 1947. Romania was ruled by the dictator Nicolae Ceausescu for more than 24 years before he was overthrown in 1989. The country is now a candidate for membership in the EU.

Economy: Romania's economy is now gradually developing, after year of difficult transition to free market capitalism. The country's industry is largely antiquated and inefficient but the service sector now contributes more than half of Romania's GDP. Major exports include natural resources, machinery, and agricultural products.

Rossija
Russia

Area: 17,075,200 sq km
Population: 143.7 million
GDP per capita: 8,900 US$
Capital: Moscow
Government: Federated presidential republic
Language: Russian (official), other national languages
Currency: 1 rouble = 100 kopecks

Geography: Russia, the largest nation on Earth, stretches west from the Baltic Sea to the Pacific Ocean in the east and north from the Black Seato the Arctic Ocean in the north. The country's territory includes vast areas on two continents and a variety of climate and vegetation zones. The Caucasus Mountains stretch along the country's southeastern border while the Urals separate the European and Asian sections of Russia. Most of northern Russia consists of forested taiga areas and arctic tundras. Steppes and desert cover the southeast. Moscow and St. Petersburg, are the country's most popular tourist destinations.

Politics: The Kiev Rus, an alliance of Slavic groups, emer-

Siberia: The Yakuts who live in the north of Siberia subsist by breeding cattle, horses, and reindeer, hunting and fishing. Their language belongs to the Altaic-Turkic family of languages. The Yakuts have been members of the Russian Orthodox faith for nearly two centuries and adopted the Cyrillic script, yet still retain a number of shamanistic practices and believe in spirits.

ged in the 9th century and gained power and influence through its trade with the Byzantine Empire. Christianity arrived in Russia during the 10th century and encouraged the formation of a formal state. The duchy of Moscow gained increased political power in the 14th century. Russia developed into a vast empire in the following centuries. The imperial era, however, came to an end in 1918 during the Bolshevik Revolution. The Russian-dominated Soviet Union was one of the world's two superpowers before it collapsed in 1991. Russia is now a multi-party democracy consisting of 21 republics.

Economy: Russia has an incredible wealth of natural resources and a large manufacturing sector. Services are increasing in importance. The country faced a series of economic crises throughout the 1990s. The effects of a severe financial crisis in 1997 have mostly been overcome. High global oil prices and foreign investment have led to stable growth in recent years but the country's economy is still in need of major reforms. A particular problem is the underground economy.

Rwanda
Rwanda

Area: 26,338 sq km
Population: 7.9 million
GDP per capita: 1,300 US$
Capital: Kigali
Government: Presidential republic
Languages: Kinyarwanda, French (both official), Kiswaheli, English
Currency: 1 Rwanda franc = 100 centimes

Geography: The highest peaks in this mountainous country are the Virunga volcanoes (4,507 m) in the west. Much of central and eastern Rwanda consists of low, hilly tableland. Rain forests and wet savannas flourish in the humid tropical climate up to a height of 2,500 meters, giving way to bamboo forests at higher altitudes. Virunga National Park is the home of the mountain gorilla, a rare species that is now threatened with extinction due to widespread poaching.

Politics: In the 15th century the Tutsi people established feudal rule in the territory settled by the Hutu, which survived colonization by the Germans and Belgians. When the Tutsi (19% of the population) lost their position of power in the 1950s, sustained and bloody conflicts erupted that have continued to the present day and that reached a terrible climax in the 1994 massacres. Despite UNO's peace efforts, unrest continues.

Economy: A civil war that began in the spring of 1994 completely destroyed the economy in Africa's most densely populated country; rebuilding

of the economy with foreign aid began in 1996. Coffee is the main export, followed by tea, pyrethrum, beans, maize, and bananas. The developing industrial sector mostly processes agricultural products in small and medium-sized enterprises.

Saint Kitts and Nevis
St. Kitts and Nevis

Area: 261.6 sq km
Population: 39,000
GDP per capita: 8,800 US$
Capital: Basseterre
Government: Federation/constitutional monarchy within the Commonwealth
Language: English
Currency: 1 East Caribbean dollar = 100 cents

Geography: The islands, five kilometers apart in the Eastern Caribbean, are volcanic in ori-

gin (Mount Liamuiga, 1,156 m; an extinct volcano with crater lake) and have many sulphurous springs. Rain forests grow at higher altitudes; the coastal plains are used for agriculture. The white, sandy beaches represent the main tourist attractions. The islands have a tropical climate, with high rainfall in the mountains.

1 The winter sports regions in the Caucasus Mountains are still largely unknown to vacationers.

2 The Kremlin, originally a fortress, is the seat of Russia's government.

3 The Winter Palace on the Neva River in St. Petersburg was built for Czar Peter the Great by the Italian architect Rastelli.

Saint Lucia Saint Lucia

Windward Islands: The island states of Saint Lucia, Saint Kitts and Nevis lie in the crescent of the Lesser Antilles. Tourism is an increasingly important factor for all three countries, which present the perfect Caribbean idyll with their white sandy beaches and blue sea. While Saint Kitts has a well-developed tourist infrastructure, many of the Grenadine islands are largely undiscovered.

Politics: Discovered by Columbus in 1493, the islands were ruled for centuries by the Spanish, who enslaved the indigenous population. The islands became Britain's first West Indian colony in 1623. Long years of striving for independence were finally successful in 1983. A Governor-General still represents the British monarch. Nevis also has its own parliament and prime minister.

Economy: Illiteracy has been reduced to 10%, a key condition for advanced economic development. The islands' economy is principally based on agriculture (sugarcane) and tourism. Cruise passengers are the main source of foreign currency, so that the services sector employs 43.1% of the workforce. Exports are sugarcane and textiles.

Saint Lucia
Saint Lucia

Area: 616.3 sq km
Population: 164,000
GDP per capita: 4,500 US$
Capital: Castries
Government: Constitutional monarchy within the Commonwealth
Languages: English (official), Patois
Currency: 1 East Caribbean dollar = 100 cents

Geography: Located in the East Caribbean, St. Lucia is volcanic in origin. Agriculture is practiced in the coastal regions and in the broad mountain valleys in the north and south. Rain forests are confined to higher altitudes and are home to many species of birds. The climate, influenced by the northwest Trade winds, has average temperatures of 25–30° C. The main tourist destination is the cruise terminal of Pointe Seraphine in Castries.

Politics: The indigenous Caribbean inhabitants were wiped out by colonial rulers in the 17th century; the island was subsequently British and French in succession before finally becoming a British colony in 1814. A member of the West Indian Federation in 1958, St Lucia gained independence in 1979.

Economy: The economy chiefly consists of banana exports and tourism, with other exports being sugar and citrus fruits. While tourism has delivered around half of St. Lucia's foreign currency revenues since the early 1990s, banana cultivation and export is primarily practiced on smallholdings and is highly vulnerable to crises.

Saint Vincent and the Grenadines
St. Vincent and the Grenadines

Area: 389 sq km
Population: 117,000
GDP per capita: 2,900 US$
Capital: Kingstown
Government: Constitutional monarchy in the Commonwealth
Language: English

Saint Lucia: Picturesque view of Soufrière Bay.

Currency: 1 East Caribbean dollar = 100 cents

Geography: Part of the arc of the Lesser Antilles, the islands consist of the main island of St. Vincent, 345 km² in area, and the smaller Grenadine Islands, seven of which are inhabited. The active volcano Soufrière (1,234 m) lies in the north of St. Vincent. The mountains there are covered with tropical rain forests with a moist tropical climate: home to a rich variety of bird species, while the Grenadines are considerably drier. The land slopes down to the sea in the east.

Politics: St. Vincent was discovered by Christopher Columbus in 1498. Fought over by the French and English in the 17th century, in 1748 the island was initially awarded to the Carib Indians as neutral territory, before becoming a British colony in 1783. From 1958 to 1962 the islands joined the West Indian Federation, and became an Associated State of the British Commonwealth in 1969 it gained independence in 1979.

Economy: The islands' principal sources of revenue are agriculture and tourism, 28% of the area is given over to agriculture. The banana crop is frequently endangered by hurricanes. Other important exports are flour, cotton, and arrowroot. Tourism, primarily comprising cruise visitors and sailing enthusiasts, is increasing in importance as a source of foreign currency.

Salṭanat 'Umān
Oman

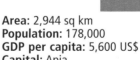

Area: 212,457 sq km
Population: 2.9 million
GDP per capita: 13,400 US$
Capital: Muscat
Government: Sultanate (absolute monarchy)
Languages: Arabic (official), Farsi, Urdu
Currency: 1 Omani rial = 1,000 baizas

Geography: Oman's natural borders are the Gulf of Oman in the east, the Arabian Sea in the south, and the Rub' al-Khali Desert in the west. 15 kilometers of fertile coast extend to the 3,000-meter-high Oman Mountains. The territory includes the Mussandam exclave, enabling Oman to control the Straits of Hormuz, the exit from the Persian Golf. Oman has an extreme desert climate, with temperatures of up to 50° C in summer, and a subtropical climate in the highlands. Monsoon rains fall in the south and west.

Politics: Settled around 2500 BC, the region fell under Islamic influence in the 7th century and became independent in 751. Ahmed bin Said founded the current reigning dynasty after the end of Portuguese rule, from the 16th century. Oman was a British protectorate from 1891 to 1951. Progress has been registered in all areas since Sultan Qabus became the ruling monarch in 1970.

Economy: Oman's economy is a liberal free market economy with some state influence. Only 5% of the national territory is inhabited. The oil sector has dominated the economy since oil was discovered in the 1950s, and registers a 38% share of GDP. As the oil reserves will be exhausted in 30 years at most, efforts are already under way to diversify the economy.

Samoa
Samoa

Area: 2,944 sq km
Population: 178,000
GDP per capita: 5,600 US$
Capital: Apia
Government: Constitutional monarchy
Languages: Somoan, English
Currency: 1 tala = 100 sene

Geography: Samoa consists of two large islands – Upoli and Savai'i – and seven small islands in the southern Pacific Ocean. All of Samoa's islands are of volcanic origin, and the country's tallest mountain, Silisili, rises to 1,857 meters. The island group has a tropical climate with high humidity and warm temperatures throughout the year. Tourist centers are the islands of Lifuka and Ha'apai.

Politics: Samoa was frequently visited by European traders and explorers throughout the 18th century. During the 19th century, the island was disputed between Germany, the United States, and Great Britain. Samoa became an independent nation in 1961, after decades under the administration of New Zealand. Samoa is now a constitutional monarchy, where local traditions play an important role in the nation's government, as befits what is probably Polynesia's oldest culture.

Economy: More than 70% of Samoa's people live on Upolu. Fishing and agriculture are the primary sources of income for most of the population. Coffee and bananas have traditionally been the leading export crops of Samoa but cocoa production is becoming increasingly important for the economy. Tourism is now a major source of income, but Samoa still maintains a large trade deficit.

San Marino
San Marino

Area: 61.2 sq km
Population: 28,500
GDP per capita: 34,600 US$
Capital: San Marino Città
Government: Republic
Language: Italian (official), Romagnol
Currency: 1 euro = 100 cents

Geography: The smallest republic in Europe is dominated by Mount Titano (756 m). The country comprises ten separate towns, including the small capital city San Marino Città. The principal rivers are the Marano and the Ausa. The country's small and historic capital city is a popular destination.

Politics: San Marino was first settled around AD 600. The country achieved its independence in 1400 and become a republic in 1600. San Marino's independence was affirmed at the Congress of Vienna in 1815. The neutral country was occupied by the German army and later the Allies during the

Samoa: The islands of the Samoan archipelago are home to probably the oldest Polynesian culture. Before the advent of colonialism, the social system comprised a complex network of family and social bonds. The head of the family was also a member of the village council, which in turn appointed a representative to the regional council. Many of the ancient customs and traditional structures have been preserved in present-day Samoa.

Second World War. San Marino's status as an Italian protectorate was ended in 1968. The country became a member of the Council of Europe in 1998 and of UNO in 1992.

Economy: Tourism and the sale of postage stamps are the two largest industries in San Marino, with tourist visits accounting for more than half of the country's GDP. Agriculture is entirely small scale and contributes little to the economy. San Marino has a relatively high standard of living and per capita GDP.

São Tomé e Príncipe
São Tomé and Príncipe

★ ★

Area: 1,001 sq km
Population: 182,000
GDP per capita: 1,200 US$
Capital: São Tomé
Government: Republic
Languages: Portuguese (official), Creole
Currency: 1 dobra = 100 centimos

Geography: The archipelago off the coast of Gabun near the Equator consists of the two main islands of São Tomé and Príncipe and some smaller islands, all volcanic in origin and part of the Cameroon line. The landscape is dominated by rain forests, favored by the climate and the numerous rivers. A leisure and sports fishing center was built in the north of Príncipe in 1992. Soil erosion due to farming is a major environmental issue in the country.

Politics: The islands were settled by the Portuguese from 1485, and from the 16th to the 18th centuries were the world's largest sugar suppliers and a center of the slave trade with Brazil. A Portuguese overseas province from 1951, the islands became independent in 1975. Recent years have seen major political reforms. In 1990 a multiple-party system was established and Príncipe received a statute of autonomy in 1995.

Economy: Cocoa, the principal crop from its introduction in the 19th century, is still almost the only significant economic factor, accounting for 78% of export revenues. Agricultural land passed into state control in 1975 and was partly awarded to small farmers; foreign investors receive administration licences. Since 1987 the slump in world cocoa prices has generated structural reorganization initiatives supported by the World Bank. However, 80% of foodstuffs consumed in the country are imported. Portugal remains a key trading partner. Tourism and offshore oil reserves could both become important economic factors.

Saudi Arabia see Al-Mamlaka al-'Arabiya as-Sa'udiya

Serbia see Srbija

Sénégal
Senegal

★

Area: 196,722 sq km
Population: 10.8 million
GDP per capita: 1,600 US$
Capital: Dakar
Government: Presidential republic
Languages: French, Wolof
Currency: 1 CFA franc = 100 centimes

Geography: Senegal, bounded by the Senegal River and its tributary, the Falémé, is at the western extremity of the continent of Africa. Largely flat, it rises in the northeast to the Guinean Fouta Djalon. Senegal is in the Sahel zone; rainfall increases to the south, while Casamance has a humid tropical climate. Tourism is chiefly concentrated in Casamance, Dakar, and Petite Côte.

Politics: Home to European settlements, Senegal came under French colonial rule from the 17th to the 19th centuries. In 1958 it was awarded autonomy within the French Communauté and became independent in 1960. Senegal became a single-party state in real terms in 1966; opposition parties were not permitted until 1975. The country joined with Gambia to form the confederation of Senegambia.

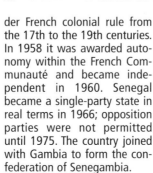

1 San Marino: The small capital city is 750 meters above sea level atop Mount Titato. The city has preserved most of its medieval character, including fascinating narrow lanes and historic buildings.

2 The island of Gorée off the coast of Senegal was one of the most important bases of the West African slavetraders.

3 Muscat: The seaport on the Gulf of Oman is the cultural and economic center of the sultanate.

4 The islands of Western Samoa are among the most unspoiled in the southern Pacific. The country also boasts a well-preserved and vibrant local culture.

Fruits of paradise: The main product in the Seychelles is coconuts, from which copra is extracted. In the valley of Mai, on the island of Praslin, gigantic palms known as "coco de mer" grow. Their fruits can reach weights of 25 kg and take up to ten years to ripen; they are governed by a special export licence.

Economy: Agriculture and fishery account for the majority of export revenues, with raw materials (gold, iron ore) increasing in significance. The service sector (tourism) is the country's primary economic focus, at 61% of GDP. Senegal realized full Internet connectivity in 1996, triggering a minor boom in information technology based services. Key economic tasks for the future are the reduction of subsidies and industrial privatization. Government reforms have led to strong growth rates in recent years and the country's government has successfully held inflation in check since the 1990s.

Seychelles
Seychelles

Area: 454 sq km
Population: 81,000
GDP per capita: 7,800 US$
Capital: Victoria
Government: Republic within the Commonwealth
Languages: English, French, Creole
Currency: 1 Seychelles rupee = 100 cents

Geography: The archipelago consists of more than 90 islands, fewer than half of which are inhabited. Only the larger islands are mountainous and covered with sparse vegetation. The climate is tropical marine. The territory covered by the archipelago includes more than a million km² in the Indian Ocean. The sandy beaches of Mahé, the nature reserve on Praslin, and the island of Silhouette are the primary tourist destinations.

Politics: Discovered by Vasco da Gama in 1501, the islands were colonized by the French from 1756 and by the British from 1794–1811, and became a British Crown colony in 1903. Independence in 1976 was followed by years of political unrest in which the constitution was overturned by a coup. Although other parties have been allowed since 1991, the Unity Party SPPF has held power since 1977.

Economy: The main exports continue to be fish, cinnamon, and copra. The greatest econ-omic potential lies in tourism services. The economy has stagnated since 1991, leading to an extensive program of privatization intended to replace the previous government controls. The government is now attempting to diversify the economy by establishing the islands as a center for financial services and cargo handling.

Shqipëria
Albania

Area: 28,748 sq km
Population: 3.5 million
GDP per capita: 4,500 US$
Capital: Tirana
Government: Republic
Language: Albanian
Currency: 1 lek = 100 quindarka

Geography: Albania is in southeastern Europe along the Ionian and Adriatic Seas. The country is largely mountainous and features more than 40 peaks rising to more than 2,000 meters. Numerous rivers flow through the country, most of which are not navigable. The country's coast is bordered by expansive marshlands and swampy plains. Albania boasts several large man-made and natural

The Slovenian spa of Bled is in the Julian Alps.

lakes and reservoirs including Lake Ohrid.

Politics: The area of modern Albania was once a region of the Roman and later Byzantine Empire. Albania was dominated by the Ottoman Empire for several centuries after 1502.

The country declared its independence from the empire in 1913. Albania was occupied by German and Italian forces during the Second World War and was declared a communist republic in 1946. The country returned to democracy in 1991 after decades of dictatorship and repression.

Economy: Albania remains one of the poorest countries in Europe and has one of the continent's least developed infrastructures. Agriculture (grain, beans, cotton, and tobacco) is an important industry and contributes more than a third of GDP. The majority of the labor force works in agriculture.

Sierra Leone
Sierra Leone

Area: 71,740 sq km
Population: 5.9 million
GDP per capita: 500 US$
Capital: Freetown
Government: Republic within the Commonwealth
Languages: English (official), Creole
Currency: 1 leone = 100 cents

Geography: Sierra Leone is on Africa's west coast, and includes small islands off the flat, wooded coastal region with strips of alluvial deposits. The higher savannas in the country's interior are traversed by rivers that rise in the Talla and Falaba plateaus in the north and east. The tropical climate on the coast provides relatively constant temperatures.

Politics: England acquired land in the region from 1787–1788 and established settlements of freed slaves. The country was a British crown colony from 1808, and gained independence in 1961. A one-party state after 1973, Sierra Leone received a democratic constitution in 1991, shortly followed by a military coup and another in 1997. A system of parliamentary democracy was reintroduced in 1998.

Economy: Sierra Leone is one of the poorest countries in the world, with an economy originating from colonial times, based on raw materials and oriented to global markets. Mining products are titanium ore, diamonds, bauxite, and gold. Initial signs of economic stabilization were destroyed by the Liberian war. The industrial sector remains undeveloped, despite the country's mineral wealth. Destruction of the rain forests has caused severe environmental damage. Sierra Leone's service sector contributes one-fifth of national GDP and its development is blocked by political instability.

Singapore
Singapore

Area: 692.7 sq km
Population: 4.4 million
GDP per capita: 23,700 US$
Capital: Singapore
Government: Republic in the Commonwealth
Languages: Malay, English, Chinese, Tamil (all official)
Currency: 1 Singapore dollar = 100 cents

Geography: The main island of Singapore, with 54 smaller islands, only two dozen of which are inhabited, lies at the southern outlet of the Malacca Straits. The country is low-lying. A railroad and road causeway connects the main island with the Malaysian peninsula. The tropical flora and fauna have been seriously affected by settlement.

Politics: The first British trading settlement was founded in 1819, and in 1824 the East India Company took over Singapore. In 1955 the British crown colony was given a constitution with election rights for the entire population, as well as extensive self-government. After gaining autonomy in 1959 and independence in 1963, Singapore became a republic in 1965. Its president has been elected in general elections since 1991. The parliament is elected every five years.

Economy: Inhabited largely by Chinese, the city-state of Singapore is a leading industrial and service center, as well as an important air traffic hub in Asia. The agricultural sector today accounts for less than 1% of GDP, owing to rapid industrialization in the 1960s and 1970s. Export revenues are predominantly generated by electronic products in addition to tools, machinery, and shipbuilding. The services sector (banks) accounts for 62% of GDP.

Slovenija
Slovenia

Area: 20,273 sq km
Population: 2 million
GDP per capita: 18,300 US$
Capital: Ljubljana
Government: Republic
Language: Slovenian
Currency: 1 tolar = 100 stotin

Geography: The Julian Alps dominate much of northern Slovenia. More than half of the country is covered by forests, one of the highest ratios of woodland coverage in Europe. The flat Pannonian Plain covers sections of eastern Slovenia. Slovenia's narrow Adriatic coast has a Mediterranean climate, while the rest of the country has a cooler continental climate. The Slovenian Alps, Ljubljana, and the coast are all major tourist destinations.

Politics: The territory of modern Slovenia was under Austrian domination between the 13th century and 1918. Slovenia was joined in a united kingdom with Serbia, Croatia, and Macedonia after the First World War. The Yugoslav regions were reunited after the Second World War as a communist federation. Slovenia was the first Yugoslav republic to declare its independence, in 1991, with a constitution

Male and female social and community groups are formed according to traditions; here to organize religious ceremonies.

modeled on Western European democracy. The country is now a member of NATO and the EU.

Economy: Slovenia has a highly developed and diversified economy and a high standard of living. The country also boasts the highest GDP per capita of any former communist state in Europe. Agriculture and forestry contribute around 5% of national GDP, while the services sector accounts for 65%. Slovenia's major exports include machinery, electronic goods, and chemical products. Tourism is an important industry in several regions.

Slovenská Republika
Slovakia

Area: 48,845 sq km
Population: 5.4 million
GDP per capita: 13,300 US$
Capital: Bratislava
Government: Republic
Language: Slovakian (official), Hungarian, Ruthenian
Currency: 1 Slovakian krone = 100 heller

Geography: Slovakia is a largely mountainous country, its terrain dominated by the western Carpathian Mountains. Large basins separated by mountains also cover sections of the country. The Vah is the longest river, while the Danube flows along the country's southwestern border. Slovakia has a continental climate. The mountains and the towns of eastern Slovakia are the main tourist destinations.

Politics: Slovakia was settled by Slavs in the 6th century AD and came under the control of Hungary in 908. With Hungary, became a region of the Habsburg Empire in 1526. The country was merged with the Czech lands in 1918 to form Czechoslovakia. After the Second World War, Czechoslovakia became a communist state. Democracy was restored to Czechoslovakia in 1989 and Slovakia became an independent state in 1993.

Economy: Like many other former communist states in Europe, Slovakia experienced

a difficult transition to capitalism in the 1990s. Major reforms in recent years have opened the economy to foreign investment and led to stable growth. Most of the country's former state enterprises have been privatized and the service sector now contributes 60% of the country's GDP. High levels of unemployment are a major challenge for the country.

Solomon Islands
Solomon Islands

Area: 28,450 sq km
Population: 523,600
GDP per capita: 1,700 US$
Capital: Honiara
Government: Parliamentary democracy
Languages: Pidgin, English
Currency: 1 Solomon Islands dollar = 100 cents

Geography: The Solomon Islands comprise two long island chains stretching over 1,450 kilometers in the western Pacific. The largest islands – including Guadalcanal, San Cristobal, Santa Isabel, Malaita, New Georgia and Choiseul – are all of volcanic origin. The country also comprises numerous small coral islands and islets. Because of their tropical climate, heavy rainfall and high humidity are common throughout the year on the islands.

Politics: Originally settled more than 30,000 years ago, the Solomons are home to a blend of Polynesian and Melanesian cultures. The isolated island group was largely avoided by Europeans until the 19th century. Towards the end of that century, the islands were declared a British protectorate. Since independence in 1978, the Solomon Islands have experienced sporadic periods of political instability, including a coup in 2000. In response to civil unrest in 2003, international peacekeeping forces restored stability.

Economy: The economy of the Solomon Islands is dominated by agriculture, which generates 70% of the country's GDP. The most important crops include cocoa, coconuts, rice, and spices. Fishing accounts

for at least 25% of the country's gross domestic product and is a major source of foreign income. Forestry is a rapidly growing industry on the island, while the government strictly regulates the exploitation and export of mineral resources which include lead, zinc, nickel, and gold.

1 Mahé is the only island of the Seychelles with steep granite crags as well as palm-fringed beaches. The largest island is an ideal resort for divers.

2 The city-state of Singapore is characterized by contrasts. At the feet of the air-conditioned skyscrapers, rickshaws are a

common means of transportation in the narrow Chinese markets.

3 The High Tatra in the Slovakia was formed by glacial movement. Unique mountain flora and rare wildlife are protected in the Tatra National Park.

Soomaaliya Somalia

Land of tea: Tea connoisseurs all over the world are familiar with Sri Lanka under its old name of Ceylon. Tea is still a key factor in the island's economy; it is the world's second largest tea producer and third largest tea exporter. The vast plantations are mostly located in the south of the island.

Soomaaliya
Somalia

Area: 637,657 sq km
Population: 8.3 million
GDP per capita: 500 US$
Capital: Mogadishu
Government: Republic
Languages: Somali (official), Arabic, English, Italian
Currency: 1 Somalia shilling = 100 centesimi

Geography: The largely steep, craggy coast of Somalia runs along the Gulf of Aden and Indian Ocean for more than 3,000 kilometers. The country's highest peak is Surud Add (2,408 m). The two largest rivers, Yuba and Shebeli, form great swamps along the flat southern coast. The climate is desert-like in the northwest, with monsoon conditions in other regions. Before the civil war, the beaches, natural landscapes and cultural heritage sites were important tourist destinations.

Politics: Following Portuguese and Turkish influences in the 16th century, the country came under the rule of the Sultan of Oman from the 17th to the 19th centuries. At the end of the 19th century the colonial territories of French and British Somaliland were founded on the Gulf of Aden, and Italian Somaliland on the Indian Ocean. The Republic of Somalia was founded in 1960. The military dictatorship in power from 1969 was overthrown in 1991. The civil war which has raged since then has resisted even UN intervention.

Economy: One of the world's poorest countries, Somalia has seen its animal husbandry and agriculture destroyed by drought and the long civil war. UN aid provided only temporary relief in the famines of 1992–1993. Political instability impedes substantial development.

South Africa/Suid-Afrika
South Africa

Area: 1,219,912 sq km
Population: 43.6 million
GDP per capita: 10,700 US$
Capital: Pretoria
Government: Republic

Languages: English, Afrikaans, Zulu, Bantu languages (all official)
Currency: 1 rand = 100 cents

Geography: South Africa is divided into three main regions: the plateau of the interior, the Rand ridge, and the coastal area. The extensive interior plateau of the Karoo (veld), 1,000–1,800 meters in height, is broken by isolated peaks and bordered by the Drakensberg mountains to the east. The coastal region, generally narrow and straight, joins this region farther east. The country has a warm, temperate subtropical climate. Krüger National Park and Cape Town are only two of South Africa's many tourist attractions.

Politics: The Dutch colony was founded in the 17th century. Conquered by the British in 1795, the region was divided into the crown colony of Natal and the Boer republics of Transvaal and Oranje, which were defeated in the Second

Sri Lanka: Flower sacrifice in front of the statue of the Aukana Buddha.

Boer War. The racist apartheid policy introduced in 1911 was fiercely opposed by the ANC. The policy of reconciliation launched in 1989 led in 1993 to a new constitution and the end of government-enforced racial discrimination.

Economy: Agriculture (citrus fruits, wine, fruit, wool, and cotton) accounts for only 4.6% of GDP and covers subsistence needs, but is increasing in importance for export. More than a third of exports come from mining; South Africa is the world's primary supplier of gold and platinum. The industrial sector (metal processing, automobiles, textiles) contributes 44% of GDP. The service sector now contributes most of country's GDP and provides employment for most of the labor force.

Spain see España

Srbija
Serbia

Area: 88,361 sq km
Population: 10.2 million
GDP per capita: 5,200 US$
Capital: Belgrade
Government: Federal republic
Language: Serbian (official)
Currency: Serbia: 1 novi dinar,

Geography: Landlocked Serbia is the largest of the former Yugoslav republics. The country encompasses both mountainous regions and flat lowlands on the Pannonian Plain. Kosovo is now under UN administration. The Danube is the country's most important waterway. Most of Serbia's regions have a continental climate, while the southernmost region has a warmer climate.

Politics: The first Serbian kingdom emerged in the 12th century and was later conquered by the Ottoman Empire. Serbia first regained its independence in the 19th century and formed a united kingdom with Croatia and Slovenia after the First World War. The communist Yugoslav federation existed from 1946 until its collapse in the 1990s. Slovenia and Croatia's separation from Yugoslavia unleashed a long period of violent conflict in the Balkans. The repression of Serbia's Albanian minority in Kosovo led to the Kosovo conflict, after which NATO forced Serbia to turn the region over to the control of the United Nations. A new constitution in 2003 abolished the name Yugoslavia and replaced it with the new title Serbia and Montenegro. Both republics enjoyed a high degree of autonomy but the union was finally dissolved after Montenegro declared its independence in June of 2006.

Economy: Agriculture (25% of GDP) and industry (45%) are the key economic sectors. The country has extensive natural resources. Serbia's economy stagnated throughout the 1990s due to international embargoes, corruption, and the country's political isolation. Increases in foreign investment and political stability are needed to help the country's economy recover.

Ṣrī Lankā
Sri Lanka

Area: 65,610 sq km
Population: 19.9 million
GDP per capita: 3,700 US$
Capital: Colombo
Government: Socialist presidential republic in the Commonwealth
Languages: Singhalese, Tamil
Currency: 1 Sri Lankan rupee = 100 cents

Geography: Sri Lanka is separated from the Indian subcontinent by the Palk Straits and the Gulf of Mannar. Its territory includes 22 smaller islands off its coasts. Extensive lowlands, broken by isolated peaks, join the coastal areas to the north and the east. The central mountain region rises over several terraces to the Pidurutalagala peak (2,524 m). The country has a monsoon-influenced tropical climate. The Buddhist sites of Kandy, Polonnaruva, and Dambulla are fascinating.

Politics: Settled by Tamils since the 2nd century, the island was discovered by the Portuguese in 1505. At the end of the 18th century, it became a British crown colony. The country gained its independence in 1948. Discrimination of Tamils by the Singhalese is destabilizing, resulting in terrorist acts and military conflict. Before the introduction of the republican constitution in 1972, Sri Lanka was named Ceylon.

Economy: Compared with the percentage of GDP generated by agriculture (tea and rubber plantations; 24%), industry (15%) is still insignificant, although steadily growing. The most important industrial exports are textiles. The services sector accounts for nearly half of GDP. However, the economic growth is threatened by its population explosion, crippling poverty and civil unrest.

Sudan see As-Sūdān

Suisse/Schweiz/Svizzera
Switzerland

Area: 41,290 sq km
Population: 7.3 million
GDP per capita: 32,800 US$
Capital: Bern
Government: Parliamentary federation
Languages: German, French, Italian, Rhaeto-Romance (all official)
Currency: 1 Swiss franc = 100 rappen/centimes

Geography: Switzerland is a mostly mountainous country and contains some of the highest peaks in Europe. The country consists of three distinct geographic regions: the Jura mountains, the central plateau, and the Alps. Several of Switzerlands's higher mountains rise to 4,000 meters or more, including the famous Matterhorn (4,478 m). The densely populated central plateau between the Jura mountains and the Alps is home to several large lakes including Lake Geneva and Lake Constance. Switzerland is a popular tourist destination with an excellent tourism infrastructure. Its climate is continental to alpine.

Somalia: Since 1991 civil war has raged in the country between the warlords of the developed north and the tumultuous south. A humanitarian effort by the UN from 1993–95 alleviated some famine conditions, but could not restore order. Famine is a constant threat, and lining up for food is a way of life.

Politics: In 1291, three German-speaking areas – Uri, Schwyz, Unterwalden – formed a confederation that would later evolve into Switzerland. The country later acquired French and Italian speaking regions in the 18th century. Switzerland became a federal republic in 1848 and maintained its neutrality through both world wars. The individual cantons maintain a large degree of sovereignty and referendums play an important role in Swiss democracy.

Economy: Switzerland is one of the world's wealthiest nations and its people enjoy a high standard of living. The small but productive agricultural sector accounts for less than 3% of the country's GDP. Despite its landlocked location, Switzerland is a major trading nation and an important center of the global banking and financial services industries. Major exports include timepieces, machinery, chemical products, and electronic goods. Tourism is an important industry in many Swiss regions.

Suomi/Finland
Finland

Area: 337,031 sq km
Population: 5.2 million
GDP per capita: 27,300 US$
Capital: Helsinki
Government: Republic
Language: Finnish, Swedish (both official)
Currency: 1 euro = 100 cents

Geography: Finland is in northern Europe and borders the Gulf of Bothnia in the east as well as the Gulf of Finland and Baltic Sea in the south. The country's terrain is dominated by forests and thousands of lakes and swamps. Its craggy coastline is lined with islets, with the Åland Islands to the southwest. The northernmost section of the country consist of treeless tundra with an arctic climate. While most of the country is flat, central and some eastern sections feature rolling hills. Finland's pristine landscapes attract numerous tourists to the country. Helsinki and the country's rural areas are its most popular tourist attractions.

Politics: Finland was under the control of the Swedish monarchy between the 12th and 18th centuries. Sweden relinquished control of the country to Russia after a series of wars. Finland achieved independence from Russia in 1918. Finland, a capitalist country, was closely aligned to its powerful neighbour, the USSR, after the Second World War. The country joined the EU in 1995.

Economy: Finland has a diverse and advanced free market economy. The country suffered a major economic crisis in the early 1990s but quickly rebounded and has experienced steady growth since then. Trade is vital for the Finish economy with exports accounting for around 15% of the national GDP. Major exports include paper, electronics, and machinery. Together with Russia, Finland is developing the petroleum and natural gas reserves to its northeast.

Suriname
Suriname

Area: 163,265 sq km
Population: 437,000
GDP per capita: 3,500 US$
Capital: Paramaribo
Government: Presidential republic
Languages: Dutch (official), Hindustani, Javanese, English
Currency: 1 Suriname guilder = 100 cents

Geography: Suriname, on the Caribbean, is named after the Suriname River that forms a great lake at Brokopondo before flowing into the Atlantic at Paramaribo. Behind the coastal plain, where around 80% of the population live, the interior rises to meet the Tumuc-Humac Mountains, covered with dense rain forest and largely unexplored. The climate is tropical and humid, moderated only by the northeastern trade winds.

Politics: After a turbulent colonial history from the 16th century, Suriname fell to the Dutch in 1814. In 1974 around 50,000 Surinamese utilized their Dutch citizenship to emigrate to Europe, after which, in 1975, Suriname became independent. Bitter ethnically motivated power struggles developed, as a result of which a third of the population continued to emigrate in the following years in search of a better life. The 1992 overthrow of Desi Bouterse, who had gained power in 1980 in a military coup, failed to restore

1 The majestic Matterhorn in the Valais Alps was first conquered in 1865.

2 South Africa's breathtaking Drakensberg Mountains reach heights of 3,376 meters. To the east, they slope dramatically down to the coastline.

3 The port, with its impressive neo-classical architecture, is the center of Finland's capital, Helsinki. The city's historic architecture was strongly influenced by the country's neighbours Sweden and Russia.

Chinese heritage: Traditional Korean education includes Confucianism, the Chinese philosophy that is widespread throughout Korea, and every other culture influenced by China. Confucian schools were introduced in the 4th century, serving as a reserve of resources for the civil service. Today, education is still held to be the key to a great career.

stability. Parliamentary elections are held every five years.

Economy: The agricultural sector produces key exports of rice, sugar, bananas, and coffee. Bauxite reserves, exploited almost exclusively by US companies, generate the majority of export revenues. The country also has some oil and gold reserves. Waterways are an important method of transportions. Tourism is almost nonexistent. The consumer goods industry is directed solely at the home market. Since 85% of the country is wooded, forestry could be a potential factor, given appropriate development.

Sūriya
Syria

Area: 185,180 sq km
Population: 18 million
GDP per capita: 3,300 US$
Capital: Damascus
Government: Presidential republic
Languages: Arabic (official), Kurdish, Armenian
Currency: 1 Syrian pound = 100 piasters

Geography: 90% of Syria is uncultivated; while steppes dominate in the north and northwest, the Syrian Desert extends through the southeast. The remaining territory to the west is essentially mountainous (Mount Hermon, 2,814 m). Rising in Turkey, the Euphrates and its tributaries flow for 675 kilometers through the northeast. Syria lies at the transition zone between the Mediterranean climate, with its moist winters, and the continental dry climate. Chief travel destinations include important historical and cultural cities such as Damascus, Aleppo and Palmyra.

Politics: A Persian satrapy since the 6th century BC, the country became the centre of the Seleucid Empire in 323, and later came under Roman, Byzantine, Arab, and Ottoman rule. Declared part of the French mandate in 1922, Syria gained independence in 1946. The politically unstable years up to 1970 were marked by coups, a temporary union with Egypt and the Six Days' War in June 1967. The possibility of reconciliation with Israel did not emerge until the 1990s.

Economy: The socialist-planned economy provides for an amalgam of state, collective, and private ownership. Economic reforms and attempts at industrialization and diversification are progressing only slowly. Agriculture, which is still the mainstay of the economy at 28% of GDP, is dependent on highly fluctuating rainfall, and irrigation is employed to produce cotton and fruit for export in addition to grain. Oil extraction and processing account for the highest export revenues.

Sverige
Sweden

Area: 449,964 sq km
Population: 9 million
GDP per capita: 26,800 US$
Capital: Stockholm
Government: Constitutional monarchy

Seoul: More than 11 million people live in the metropolis.

Language: Swedish
Currency: 1 Swedish krone = 100 Ore

Geography: Sweden is in northern Europe between the Gulf of Bothnia and Norway. More than two-thirds of the country's land area is covered by forests. In addition to the mainland, Sweden also consists of numerous islands including Gotland and Öland. The country's interior has a continental climate with often severe winters, while the southern coasts have a milder maritime climate. The capital city of Stockholm as well as the country's many lakes and pristine forests are the most popular tourist destinations in Sweden.

Politics: Sweden was united with Norway and Denmark in the Kalmar Union between 1389 and 1520. The country emerged as a major European power during the 17th century. Sweden eventually lost its role as the leading power of northern Europe to Russia. The country remained neutral through both world wars, despite the occupation of its neighbors Finland and Denmark during the Second World War. Sweden joined the EU in 1995.

Economy: Sweden faced a major economic crisis in the 1990s but remains one of world's most prosperous nations. Citizens have access to a generous social network and an excellent public education system. Sweden has a modern infrastructure and a wealth of hydroelectric power sources and natural resources. The country's diverse service sector accounts for more than 70% of the Swedish national GDP.

Swaziland (kaNgwane)
Swaziland

Area: 17,363 sq km
Population: 1.2 million
GDP per capita: 4,900 US$
Capital: Mbabane
Government: Constitutional monarchy within the Commonwealth
Languages: English, Siswati (both official)
Currency: 1 lilangeni = 100 cents

Geography: Swaziland, enclosed by South Africa and Mozambique, is on the eastern side of the Drakensberg Mountains and has a warm, moderately subtropical climate. The country is divided into four zones of varying altitudes; the western highlands have large forestry plantations, while the main settlement area is the savanna of the adjacent Middle Veld, giving way to the Low Veld to the east on the border with Mozambique. The dry savanna of the Lebombo Plateaus is used for grazing. The mountains and game reserves (Mlilwane and Ehlane) are popular tourist destinations.

Politics: The area was settled by the Bantu people of Swazi from the mid-18th century before the first Boers entered the country in 1868, followed by the British in 1877. Swaziland was named a British protectorate in 1907 and gained independence in 1968. The constitution of 1978 gives the King extensive executive and legislative powers.

Economy: Swaziland's economy is dependent on global markets and its neighbor South Africa. It is traditionally dominated by the cultivation of agricultural and forestry products, which are processed by the industrial sector, contributing 38% to GDP. Services (tourism) account for 47% of GDP and are set to expand as a result of the changing economic structure. More than 75% of the population works in agriculture and animal husbandry.

Tadžikistan
Tajikistan

Area: 143,100 sq km
Population: 7 million
GDP per capita: 1,000 US$
Capital: Dushanbe
Government: Pres. republic
Language: Tajik
Currency: 1 Tajik rouble = 100 kopeks

Geography: An extremely mountainous land to the south of the CIS, 90% of which has an altitude of over 1,000 meters; almost the entire population lives in the narrow mountain valleys. In the southeast, the Pamir mountains cover an area of 64,000 km^2. The western mountain ranges boast the highest peaks of the CIS: Communism Peak (7,495 m), and Lenin Peak (7,134 m). The climate is continental, giving way to an arctic climate in the mountainous regions. Tourism is largely limited to trekking expeditions from the capital.

Politics: Settled as early as the 1st millennium BC, the region was ruled by the Persians, Greeks, Macedonians, and Arabs until the 9th century. After centuries of Mongol and Uzbek rule, the north of Tajikistan came under Russian control in 1870, and in 1918 became part of the Soviet Republic of Turkestan. In 1929, the Tajik Soviet Socialist Republic became part of the USSR, from which it broke away in 1991 to become an independent state and a member of CIS. It underwent changes of government and a civil war, before achieving relative stability.

Economy: Owing to poor infrastructure and the cotton monoculture of the USSR era, Tajikistan is today the poorest republic of the CIS. Agriculture still accounts for some 40% of GDP. The important industries are wool processing, foodstuffs and textiles. Raw materials include uranium and gold, and to a small extent petroleum, natural gas, lead, zinc, tungsten, and tin.

Taehan-Min'guk
Republic of Korea (South)

Area: 98,480 sq km
Population: 48.6 million
GDP per capita: 17,700 US$
Capital: Seoul
Government: Pres. republic
Language: Korean
Currency: 1 won = 100 chon

Geography: The landscape in the southern part of the Korean peninsula is predominantly mountainous. Unlike the east

Nordic nomads: *For the past 2,000 years, nomadic peoples from Lapland have inhabited the vast, sparsely populated marshy highlands of the tundra covering the north of Norway, Sweden, and Finland. They call them-* *selves Sami ("marsh people"), have their own language and subsist from breeding reindeer and fishing.*

coast, the south and west coasts are highly fragmented. A hilly, fertile basin in the south is traversed by the Naktong, with 50–100 kilometers of coastal plain to the west. Extensive coniferous forests dominate the landscape. The major rivers flow into the Yellow Sea and are only partly navigable. With the exception of the subtropical south, the climate is continental and cool to moderate. Cultural cities of interest other than Seoul include Taegu or Kyongju.

Politics: Tradition dates the founding of the Korean Empire to 2333 BC, although the date 57 BC is historically documented. Under the influence of China and Japan, Korea has nonetheless developed its own independent culture. In 1910 Korea was annexed by Japan. In 1945, occupation by the USSR and the USA led to the division of the country, then in 1948 to the establishment of the Republic of Korea in the US-controlled south. After the Korean War (1950–53), the military held sway in South Korea. Democratization, launched in the mid 1980s, led to a new constitution in 1988.

Economy: Rice cultivation in smallholdings cannot meet domestic needs. Industrialization has taken off in the last 30 years; initially in cheap, labor-intensive products, now export production is shifting from manufactured products in the food, textile, and clothing industry to individualized technologies and brand articles for the automotive and electronics industry. In addition, the share of the financial, service, and real-estate sector in GDP is rising (48%).

Taiwan
Taiwan

Area: 35,980 sq km
Population: 22.7 million
GDP per capita: 23,400 US$
Capital: Taipei
Government: Republic
Language: Chinese
Currency: 1 New Taiwanese dollar = 100 cents

Geography: Taiwan lies off the southeast coast of China. The center has thickly wooded mountain ranges with more than 60 peaks above 3,000

meters in height (Jade Mountain or Yushan, 3,997 m). The climate is subtropical with high rainfall in the north, but tropical with winter monsoons in the south. In addition to the capital, chief tourist destinations are the magnificent inland and coastal landscapes.

Politics: Settled by the Chinese in the 9th century and the focus of colonization attempts by Portugal, Spain, and Holland, Taiwan became part of the Chinese Empire in 1661. China ceded the island to Japan in 1895, but it became Chinese territory again in 1945. Defeated in the civil war, the Kumointang moved its seat of government to Tai-

wan in 1949. Relations between the People's Republic and Taiwan remain tense. Despite the constitution of 1946, the president retains significant political power.

Economy: Privatization is gradually replacing state economic control. On this densely populated island with few natural resources, agriculture mainly produces rice to cover domestic needs. The core of this highly capitalist economy is its enormously productive industry, primarily for export. While industry accounts for 37% of GDP, services generate 60%, and 50% of employment.

Tanzania
Tanzania

Area: 945,087 sq km
Population: 36.6 million

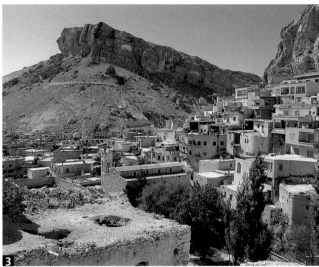

GDP per capita: 600 US$
Capital: Dodoma
Government: Federal Presidential republic
Language: Kiswaheli
Currency: 1 Tanzanian shilling = 100 cents

Geography: Situated on the Indian Ocean, the country rises

1 The historic province of Bohuslän on the Kattegat is one of Sweden's most popular holiday regions.

2 The Chiang-Kai Shek Monument, built 1980, commemorates Taiwan's first president.

3 Probably the oldest Christian monastery in the world, near the Syrian village of Ma'aloula.

4 Isolated umbrella thorn trees are typical of the Tanzanian Serengeti.

Tchad Chad

Caravans: The Tuareg call themselves Imushagh or "free men." They are noted for their head and face coverings. The Sahara and Sahel area is inhabited by a number of nomadic peoples. The resilient dromedaries are essential beasts of burden and means of transportations in the harsh climate. Although Islamicized at an early stage, the Tuareg have retained their belief in nature-spirits.

from the coast toward the west and is divided by highland plateaus and mountains. Its highest peak is Kilimanjaro (5,895 m). It is bordered by the three great lakes of Lake Victoria, Lake Nyasa and Lake Tanganyika. The territory also includes the islands of Zanzibar, Pemba, and Mafia. The climate is tropical, and temperate in the uplands. Tanzania is a popular safari destination.

Politics: In 1884 Tanganyika became the main constituent of the colony of German East Africa. The country was taken over by Britain in 1920 under a League of Nations mandate and became a UN trustee territory in 1946, and acheived independence in 1962. The presidential republic of Tanzania was formed in 1964 by merging Tanganyika and the British protectorate of Zanzibar, independent since 1963. The one-party system of the 1977 constitution was replaced by a multiple party system in 1992.

Economy: Agriculture, forestry and fishery account for around 53% of GDP and 60–70% of export revenue. Tanzania's food production is self-sufficient. Industry, at 4.3% of GDP, is insignificant, while services account for 23%. The government has endeavoured since 1986 to accelerate development in line with IMF requirements by restructuring the economy as a market economy. Major export commodities include gold and coffee. Government reforms have led to higher growth rates in recent years.

Tchad
Chad

Area: 1,284,000 sq km
Population: 9.5 million
GDP per capita: 1,200 US$
Capital: N'Djamena
Government: Presidential republic
Languages: French, Arabic (both official)
Currency: 1 CFA franc = 100 centimes

Geography: The Republic of Chad lies in the Sahara, Sahel, and Sudan regions along the east of the Chad Basin. The basin is broken by a few isolated peaks. Lake Chad to the west is

an important source of water. Tourist centers include the national parks of Zakouma and Manda, the game reserves of Abou-Teflan, Siniaka-Minia, and Bahr-Salamat and the northern desert regions.

Politics: Chad was settled by Arabs, Berber, and Bantu from the 15th century and became a French protectorate in 1900. After gaining independence in 1960 the country was torn by military struggles. After international pressure the introduction of a multiple party system became possible.

Economy: The country today is one of the poorest and least-developed in the world. Agriculture is still at subsistence level, and is dominated by arable farming and animal husbandry. The economy is dependent on foreign aid, although the establishment of oil drilling and export offers a perspective for the future. The service industry is the main source of growth.

Istanbul: The Hagia Sophia was built in 532.

Thailand see Muang Thai

Timor-Leste
East Timor

Area: 15,007 sq km
Population: 1 million
GDP per capita: Estimated at 500 US$
Capital: Dili
Government: Republic
Languages: Indonesian, Portuguese
Currency: 1 US dollar = 100 cents

Geography: The island republic occupies the eastern part of the Lesser Sunda Island of Timor. The central mountains attain an altitude of 2,960 meters in Ramelan.

Politics: East Timor was a Portuguese colony from 1695; the west of the island was occupied by the Dutch. After World War II, this part was given to Indonesia. When the Portuguese withdrew in 1975, civil war broke out, with the Fretilin Party fighting for independence. Indonesia annexed East Timor in 1975/76, resulting in a bloody conflict with many lives lost. In 1999 the majority of the population voted for independence, and East Timor became a sovereign state in 2002.

Economy: There are great hopes for the petroleum and natural gas reserves in the Timor Sea. Hitherto the economy has relied on the cultivation of coffee, rice, manioc, and coconut palms.

Togo
Togo

Area: 56,785 sq km
Population: 5.5 million
GDP per capita: 1,500 US$
Capital: Lomé
Government: Presidential republic
Languages: French (official), Kabyé, Ewe
Currency: 1 CFA franc = 100 centimes

Geography: Togo lies in West Africa. Its narrow, 53-kilome-

ter-long coastal region gives way to a 50-kilometer-wide strip of hills and a sandstone plateau traversed by the Togo-Atakora Mountains. The wet savanna in the south merges into dry savanna in the north. Forests are found only in the mountains and along the rivers. The major tourist destinations are the sandy beaches and former colonial cities such as Lomé.

Politics: Discovered by the Portuguese in 1481 and first settled by Europeans from the 16th century, Togo became a German protectorate in 1884. In 1922 the region was divided between the French and British under a League of Nations mandate, and became a UN territory of the French Union in 1946. Since its independence (1960) oppositional forces have battled for democracy. The 1992 constitution was planned as a transition from the dictatorship to a democratic republic.

Economy: The 40 or so tribes and peoples that make up Togo's population live in one of the poorest countries in the world. The less developed north is chiefly given over to subsistence farming. Agriculture accounts for 70% of employment, yet generates only 36% of GDP. Togo is highly dependent on the export of a few raw materials. Trade and services account for 42.7% of GDP.

Tonga
Tonga

Area: 748 sq km
Population: 110,200
GDP per capita: 2,200 US$
Capital: Nuku'alofa
Government: Constitutional monarchy
Languages: English, Tonga dialect
Currency: 1 pa'anga = 100 seniti

Geography: Tonga consist of two long island chains encompassing 172 islands in the southern Pacific. While the western islands are mostly of volcanic origin, the eastern chain mostly consits of flat coral islands. Tonga's capital city, Nuku'alofa, is located on Tongatapu, the country's largest and most populous island. Tonga has a tropical climate and

the country's beaches and coral reefs attract many tourists.

Politics: Polynesian Tongans constitute 98% of the ethnically homogenous population. The Tongans once ruled vast sections of the southern Pacific. In 1793, the British Captain James Cook visited and explored the islands. During the 19th century European missionaries exerted major control on the islands and converted the majority of the population to Christianity. The islands became a British protectorate in 1900 and an independent kingdom in 1970.

Economy: Agriculture dominates the local economy. Key export crops are bananas and coconuts. Much of the country's food must be imported. Foreign aid and wages from Tongans working abroad are the country's two most important sources of income. Tourism remains minor and undeveloped.

Trinidad and Tobago
Trinidad and Tobago

Area: 5,128 sq km
Population: 1.1 million
GDP per capita: 9,600 US$
Capital: Port of Spain
Government: Presidential republic within the Commonwealth
Language: English
Currency: 1 Trinidad-and-Tobago dollar = 100 cents

Geography: The islands of Trinidad and Tobago, off the coast of Venezuela, form the southern end of the East Caribbean island arc. Trinidad's mountainous north has rain forests, while the flat east coast at the Gulf of Paria is mainly occupied by industrial plants and harbors. Tobago too has hilly rain forest country. The climate is tropical, with minor seasonal temperature fluctuations. Tourism focuses on Tobago as a diving paradise.

Politics: Discovered by Columbus in 1498, the islands were initially ruled by the Spanish before becoming a notorious center of piracy in the 17th century and a British crown colony in 1803. From 1958-

Joie de vivre: Trinidad's annual carnival is the island's major cultural event, with fascinating parades rivaling Rio de Janeiro in their riotously colorful, elaborate costumes. The origins lie in the Christian religion of the Spanish Colonialists but the exuberance is rooted in the African tradition: The descendants of African slaves represent the majority of the population.

1962 Trinidad and Tobago were members of the West Indian Federation, gaining independence in 1962 as a British Commonwealth state. The country received a republican constitution in 1976. Tobago has held autonomy since 1987. The islands have a bicameral parliament elected for a five-year term.

Economy: The population is heterogeneous, with 41% black and 41% Indian. Although export-oriented, agriculture (cocoa, sugar, citrus fruits) and fisheries contribute a mere 2.7% to GDP. Trinidad's economy remains dependent on petroleum and natural gas exports from the relatively small deposits in the country's ocean shelf, generating at least 23% of GDP. The country also has the world's largest natural asphalt deposits at Pitch Lake, a 38.5-hectare tar lake. Other exports include chemical products and rum. Tourism is also an important economic factor. The economy has grown at around 5% p. a. in recent years.

Tūnisiyah/Tunisie
Tunisia

Area: 163,610 sq km
Population: 9.9 million
GDP per capita: 6,900 US$
Capital: Tunis
Government: Pres. republic
Language: Arabic (official)
Currency: 1 Tunesian Dinar = 1000 Millimes

Geography: The Tell-Atlas Mountains, up to 1,200 m in height, join the north coast and give way to the Medjerda plain in the south, an agricultural area. Farther south is a central ridge of mountains up to 1,500 meters in height, which also marks the boundary of the humid Mediterranean climate. Beyond this border the south is characterized by dry steppes and deserts. Tourist centers are Tunis, Sousse, Kairouan, and Djerba.

Politics: A country with a great Carthaginian and Roman past, Tunisia experienced Arab and Turkish rule from the 7th century before becoming a French protectorate in 1881. Independent since 1956, Tunisia finally began to abandon

the single-party system in 1981. The constitutional reform of 1987 was aimed at increasing democracy. Tunisia's largest political party, the Constitutional Democratic Assembly, has dominated politics since independence.

Economy: Agriculture accounts for around 15% of GDP and is export-oriented, cultivating grain, fruit, wine, and olives. Products from the textiles, food, and electrical engineering industries deliver around half of export revenues and have increased in importance over petroleum and natural gas exports. Phosphate mining has resulted in a network of narrow-gauge railroads for its transportation. The service sector, including the tourism industry, has a share of 50% of GDP.

Türkiye
Turkey

Area: 780,580 sq km
Population: 68.9 million
GDP per capita: 6,700 US$
Capital: Ankara
Government: Republic
Language: Turkish
Currency: 1 Turkish lira = 100 kurus

Geography: Turkey occupies the Anatolian peninsula, a small section of Europe, and numerous islands in the Mediterranean Sea. A large central plateau covers most of mainland Turkey and is surrounded by the Taurus and Pontus mountains. The country has a Mediterranean climate with mild winters, although some areas on the Black Sea coast have a distinctly humid subtropical climate. Turkey is a popular tourist destination and its major attractions include countless ancient historic sites and popular beach resorts.

Politics: The first Turkish state emerged around 552. The Ottoman Empire became one of the world's most powerful states in the centuries that followed. After centuries of conquest, however, the Ottoman Empire faced a series of military defeats and territorial losses in the 19th century. Mustafa Atatürk, a young soldier, founded the Turkish republic in 1923 after the

country's defeat in the First World War. The republic has experienced several military coups in its history; the last took place in 1980.

Economy: Turkey is in the midst of a rapid transition from an agrarian economy to one centered on industry and services. Around 40% of the Turkish

1 Tourism on Tobago benefits from its unique diving and swimming locations.

2 Camels and dromedaries are still essential productive livestock in the vast desert regions of Chad.

3 The people of the Fulbe populate the whole western part of the Sudan. In the multiethnic state of Chad they are only a minority.

4 Antalya, center of tourism on the Turkish Mediterranean, has one of the most beautiful old towns in the country.

labor force currently works in the agricultural sector, which accounts for a fifth of the country's GDP. The rapidly growing service sector now accounts for just over half of GDP. The country's leading exports include both agricultural products and mineral resources. Other export areas are textiles and clothing, contributing one-third of GDP and primarily privately owned. Tourism is a rapidly growing industry in many parts of the country.

Turkmenistan
Turkmenistan

Area: 488,100 sq km
Population: 4.9 million
GDP per capita: 5,700 US$
Capital: Ashgabat
Government: Presidential republic
Language: Turkmen
Currency: 1 manat = 100 tenge

Geography: Turkmenistan is located between the Caspian Sea in the west and the Amu-Darja River on the Uzbek border in the east. 80% of the country is lowlands covered by the Karakum sand desert. The coastal area on the Caspian Sea is flat and sandy. The country has a continental desert climate with extreme temperature fluctuations.

Politics: Settled by Turkic peoples since the 5th century and Islamic since the 7th century, Turkmenistan became part of Czarist Russia during that country's expansion in 1877–1881. In 1918 it became a part of the Autonomous Soviet Republic of Turkestan and in 1991, after the dissolution of the USSR, an independent member of the CIS. However, the old Communist regime is still in power, even after the new constitution of 1992.

Economy: Turkmenistan's health and social services are well-developed. The economy shows little diversification; agriculture is concentrated around cotton production in irrigated areas. Formerly supplying raw materials to the USSR, industry is still underdeveloped. Key economic factors are the natural gas, petroleum, sulphur, and mineral reserves. The petrochemicals and textile sectors are also major industries in the country.

Tuvalu
Tuvalu

Area: 26 sq km
Population: 11,500
GDP per capita: 1,100 US$
Capital: Vaiaku (Funafuti)
Government: Constitutional monarchy
Languages: Tuvaluan, English
Currency: 1 Australian dollar = 100 cents

Geography: The island group in the southwestern Pacific consists of nine beautiful atolls and numerous coral islets. Most of the islands are surrounded by coral reefs and are just a few meters above sea level. Tuvalu has a hot and humid tropical climate.

London: Britain's Houses of Parliament with "Big Ben."

Politics: The population of Tuvalu was devastated by slave traders and diseases following the arrival of European traders and explorers in the 16th century. Great Britain declared the islands a protectorate in 1892 and officially annexed Tuvalu in 1916. Tuvalu was formally granted its independence from Great Britain in 1978.

Economy: The population of Tuvalu consists primarily of Polynesians and a Melanesian minority. Most of the country's people work as small-scale farmers. Fishing and the sale of postage stamps are major sources of income for Tuvalu but the country remains highly dependent on foreign aid. Export of mineral resources could help develop the country's economy, but the country's isolated location prevents the development of large-scale tourism and industry. A significant number of Tuvalan citizens now work in other countries and contribute to the economy through remittances. The licensing of the internet domain tv. has become another important source of income.

Uganda
Uganda

Area: 236,040 sq km
Population: 26.4 million
GDP per capita: 1,400 US$
Capital: Kampala
Government: Presidential republic within the Commonwealth
Languages: Kiswaheli, English (both official), Luganda
Currency: 1 Uganda shilling = 100 cents

Geography: Most of the country is made up of a high plateau from 1,000–3,000 meters, broken by isolated peaks. The highest elevations in this savanna landscape are Mount Elgon (4,321 m) to the east and the Ruwenzori Massif in the west, up to 5,119 meters high. Half of Lake Victoria lies within the southeast of Uganda's territory. The climate is temperate owing to the altitude. The rich wildlife of Ruwenzori National Park is a magnet for tourists.

Politics: A number of centralized African kingdoms had already existed for centuries in Uganda when the British conquered the country and declared it a protectorate in 1894. After independence (1962) the situation in the 1970s and 1980s under the terror regimes of Amin and Obote was characterized by civil war before the political situation stabilized in the 1990s.

Economy: Agricultural production dominates the economy, although half of agriculture's 50% share of GDP is accounted for by subsistence farming. Only 5% of agricultural products are exported, chiefly coffee (90% of export revenues), but also cotton, tea and tobacco. The industrial sector contributes only 11–12% to GDP. Since 1987 the government has applied a policy of economic liberalization in coordination with the IMF, and an economic community with Kenya and Tanzania has been in existence since 2001.

Ukrajina
Ukraine

Area: 603,700 sq km
Population: 47.7 million
GDP per capita: 5,300 US$
Capital: Kiev
Government: Republic
Language: Ukrainian (official), Russian
Currency: 1 hryvnia = 100 kopijken

Geography: Ukraine is in Eastern Europe and has a long coastline along the Black Sea. Most of the country consists of plains and scattered plateaus. The country is crossed by many significant rivers including the Dniepr, Donets, and Dnister. Odessa in southern Ukraine has one of the largest harbors on the Black Sea. The Crimean Peninsula is a popular destination for tourists from Ukraine and neighboring countries.

Politics: Much of Ukraine was once controlled by the Kievan Rus. Later the country came under the control of the Mongols, the Polish-Lithuanian Commonwealth, and eventually the Russian Empire. Ukraine was declared a Soviet Republic in 1922 and remained one of the most influential republics in the USSR up until the union's collapse in the 1990s. Ukraine declared independence in 1991.

Economy: Ukraine's economy has mostly stagnated since the country achieved independence in 1991. The economy remains largely closed to foreign investment and previous governments have been ineffective at implementing desperately needed reforms. Ukraine is rich in mineral resources and arable land; agriculture accounts for a large percentage of its national GDP. Russia is the country's leading trading partner and supplies most of its energy imports. Natural resources and agricultural products are the country's leading exports.

United Arab Emirates see Daulat al-Imārāt al-'Arabiya Al-Muttahida

United Kingdom
United Kingdom

Area: 244,820 sq km
Population: 60.3 million
GDP per capita: 27,700 US$
Capital: London
Government: Constitutional monarchy within Commonwealth
Language: English (official), Welsh, Scots Gaelic
Currency: 1 pound sterling = 100 pence

Geography: Great Britain is separated from mainland Europe by the English Channel and the North Sea. The United Kingdom consists of four main divisions: England, Wales, Scotland, and Northern Ireland. England, which comprises around two-thirds of Great Britain's land area, consists mostly of rolling hills. Scotland and Wales both feature

"People of the fireplaces": A member of the Potawatomie tribe is painted for a ritual. This nation lived south of the Great Lakes before it was forced to move to Oklahoma and Kansas in the 19th century.

Words like "wigwam," "moccasin," and "totem" derive from the language of the Algonquin people.

medium-height mountain systems and numerous valleys. The capital city of London and scenic rural areas such as the Scottish Highlands are the country's leading tourist destinations.

Politics: England was successfully invaded by a Norman army in 1066 AD. The end of the English Civil War left England without a monarchy before its restoration less than two decades later. England emerged as an important world power by the early 1700s and the 1800 Act of Union united Britain and Ireland. Great Britain was the world's premier power throughout the 19th century and ruled a vast empire with large territories on several continents. The country emerged exhausted but victorious from both world wars. Britain's vast colonial empire was gradually relinquished in the decades after the Second World War and Queen Elizabeth II was crowned in 1952. The country is now a member of NATO and the EU.

Economy: Britain was the world's first industrialized nation and the leading trading nation throughout much of the 19th century. The country experienced a painful transition during the 1970s and 1980s as it shifted from a manufacturing to a services-based economy. London is one of the world's most important financial services and banking centers. The country has a small but productive agricultural sector. The diverse service sector produces more than 70% of the country's GDP and provides employment for most of the population.

United States of America
United States
of America

Area: 9,631,418 sq km
Population: 293 million
GDP per capita: 37,800 US$
Capital: Washington
Government: Presidential federal republic
Languages: English (official), Spanish, tribal languages
Currency: 1 US dollar = 100 cents

Geography: The United States extend from the Canadian border in the north to the Carib-

bean Sea in the south, a distance of 2,500 kilometers; the country is 4,500 kilometers wide from the eastern Atlantic to the western Pacific coast. The USA can be divided into six major landforms: the coastal plains on the Atlantic and Gulf of Mexico, the craggy, low Appalachian Mountains, the inland plains, the high Rocky Mountains, the basins and plateaus of the west, and the Coastal Cordilleras. The country's territory includes the mountainous Arctic and sub-Arctic region of Alaska, and Hawaii, a group of tropical volcanic islands. Almost every climatic type, with the exception

of tropical, is represented. The USA offers an enormous variety of tourist destinations, from major cities such as New York, Chicago or Los Angeles to Florida's bathing beaches and the breathtaking scenery of the Colorado plateau.

Politics: Since the first European settlers arrived in the early 17th century, the country's history has been dominated by the rivaling interests of European colonists. The Declaration of Independence in 1776 heralded the USA's new status as an independent power. In the 19th century the country extended its territory significantly by waging war, acquiring lands and displacing the Native American population, and expanded toward the west coast. The civil war of 1861–1865 (War of Secession) led to the abolition of slavery. The USA became a military and economic superpower by entering the global political stage in both world wars. The Constitution of 1788 and Bill

of Rights of 1791 still determine the political system today. The country has a bicameral parliament, with direct elections to the House of Representatives held every two years. At the start of the new millennium, the USA regards itself as the world's economic and military leader and strives to implement western ideals of democracy

1 The peaks of the Rocky Mountains form a chain that stretches more than 4,300 kilometers from north to south.

2 For decades the Statue of Liberty, unveiled in 1886, saluted incoming ships bringing immigrants from Europe. The picture shows the skyline of New York as it was until

September 11, 2001, when the twin towers of the World Trade Center were destroyed in a terrorist attack.

3 The giant rocks (300–600 m) in Monument Valley in Arizona in the USA were shaped by erosion over millions of years.

Urdunn Jordan

The Promised Land: *Since 1948 the Jewish people, persecuted for centuries, have lived in their own country. The "Wailing Wall," the western wall of the ancient temple in Jerusalem, is a central sanctuary, not only for* orthodox Jews. It has been open to the public again since 1967, a reminder of where King Solomon ordered the first temple to be built to house the Ark of the Covenant.

and human rights throughout the world. The country was confronted by a new situation on September 11, 2001, when terrorists attacked the World Trade Center in New York and the Pentagon in Washington.

Economy: The country has the richest economy in the world. The geographical structure of the USA enables a variety of agriculture to be practiced in all areas, with large-scale livestock farming and highly mechanized grain cultivation (wheat, rice) playing key roles. Agriculture takes up around 47% of the country's total area. Vast natural resources (petroleum, coal, ores) have hastened the development of high-performance industries, particularly in the north (chemicals, mechanical engineering, automotive, electronics). In the USA's post-industrial economic structure, services account for almost 80% of GDP, employing an equivalent percentage of the workforce. The United States has around 13,400 airports, 180 of which are international.

Urdunn
Jordan

Area: 92,300 sq km
Population: 5.6 million
GDP per capita: 4,300 US$
Capital: Amman
Government: Constitutional monarchy
Language: Arabic
Currency: 1 Jordanian dinar = 1,000 fils

Geography: The Jordan valley separates the country at the northwest of the Arabian peninsula into a hilly landscape in the west, and a mountain range in the east, gradually sloping down to the Arabian desert. The twisting, non-navigable River Jordan flows into the Dead Sea. Jordan has an outlet to the Red Sea through a small coastal strip on the Gulf of Aqaba. Most areas have a desert climate, although the Mediterranean climate in the west enables agriculture. Tourist destinations, other than the capital Aqaba and Amman, include the ruins of Petra in the south.

Politics: Jordan's monarchy has existed since the country

gained independence in 1946. According to the constitution (since 1952), only the king exercises executive power, and in theory shares legislative power with the national assembly. In 1994 King Hussein concluded a peace treaty with Israel.

Economy: Jordan consists mostly of non-arable deserts and mountainous landscapes. Because it has no oil reserves, it is one of the poorest states in the Arab world. Economic activities concentrate in the services sector. Tourism is one of the most important sources of foreign revenue.

Uruguay
Uruguay

Area: 176,215 sq km
Population: 3.4 million
GDP per capita: 12,600 US$
Capital: Montevideo
Government: Presidential republic

Jerusalem is the holy City of three world religions.

Language: Spanish
Currency: 1 Peso Uruguayo = 100 centésimos

Geography: Uruguay lies to the north of the Río de la Plata. The foothills of the Brazilian highlands extend into the country from the north, creating rolling hills. Wet grasslands or pampas dominate the landscape at the coast and along the Uruguay River. Uruguay is the least forested country in South America. The climate is temperate, in-

fluenced by the ocean. March, April, October, and November are particularly good months to visit coastal resorts or the capital of Montevideo.

Politics: Discovered in 1515 by the Spanish, Uruguay was part of the viceroy of Rio de la Plata after 1777, passed to Brazil in 1817, and gained independence in 1830. In 1967, Uruguay regained the status of a presidential republic with a bicameral parliament, under its fifth constitution since its independence. A civil head of state was not elected until 11 years after the 1973 coup d'état. In the intervening period, two presidents were appointed by a "Council of Ministers."

Economy: Around 80% of Uruguay's land area is used for agriculture, mainly grazing. Despite this, only 8.5% of the population work in agriculture. Chief exports are agricultural products (beef, rice) and pro-

Uzbekistan
Uzbekistan

Area: 447,400 sq km
Population: 26.4 million
GDP per capita: 1,700 US$
Capital: Tashkent
Government: Pres. republic
Language: Uzbek

ducts from the processing industries (leather goods, wool, and textiles). The services sector accounts for 69% of GDP.

Currency: 1 Uzbek sum = 100 tijin

Geography: This Central Asian republic comprises the center of the Turan basin with the southwestern part of the Kysyl-Kum Desert. The Amu-Darja River flows through the desert on the southwest border and into the Aral Sea. In the east, the country is bounded by the foothills of the Tianshan and Altai mountains. The climate is continental.

Politics: When Uzbekistan was made a republic of the USSR (1924), the term "Uzbeks" was introduced for the Turkic speaking populations round Bukhara and Kokand. When the Soviet Union collapsed in 1991, Uzbekistan declared its independence.

Economy: Uzbekistan is an agricultural country with little industry. The cultivation of cotton plays a major role in the economy – Uzbekistan is the world's third largest exporter of cotton. Agriculture accounts for 32% of GDP and employs at least 44% of the workforce. Aside from the manufacture of cotton harvesting machinery, the industrial sector also produces fertilizers. Gold and oil production are becoming more important sectors.

Vanuatu
Vanuatu

Area: 12,190 sq km
Population: 203,000
GDP per capita: 2,900 US$
Capital: Port Villa
Government: Republic
Languages: English, French, Bislama
Currency: 1 vatu = 100 centimes

Geography: Vanuatu comprises 12 main islands and at least 70 smaller ones located 2,000 kilometers east of Australia. The country includes both coral islands and islands of volcanic origin, some still active. Except for the more arid islands of Eromanga and Aneityum in the south, most of Vanuatu has a humid tropical climate. The country's major tourist attractions include volcanic landscapes and beaches plus resorts such as the Mamanuca and Yasawa Islands.

Politics: The islands were visited by Portuguese explorers in 1606 and Captain James Cook in 1774, who named them the New Hebrides. In 1906, France and Great Britain agreed to jointly administer the islands. An independent state since 1980, Vanuatu is governed by an elected parliament and a council of local chiefs.

Economy: Agriculture and fishing are the most important segments of Vanuatu's economy and the sources of employment for most of the country's people. Cocoa and coconuts are the most important export crops produced on the islands, with sawmills for processing timber. The local service industry is rapidly expanding because of increased tourism. Vanuatu has become a minor financial services center because of its lax financial disclosure and tax laws, but the country has faced pressure to regulate the industry.

Venezuela
Venezuela

Area: 912,050 sq km
Population: 25 million
GDP per capita: 4,800 US$
Capital: Caracas
Government: Presidential federal republic
Language: Spanish
Currency: 1 bolívar = 100 céntimos

Geography: To the northwest is the oil-rich Maracaibo Basin with shallow Maracaibo Lake, 13,600 km^2 in area. These lowlands are bordered by the Cordillera de Mérida (Pico Bolívar, 5,002 m). To the southeast are the Orinoco lowlands and the Llanos, giving way in the south to the Guayana mountains, which occupy almost half the country's area. Canaima National Park is the main tourist attraction.

Politics: Discovered in 1498 by Columbus, Venezuela has been independent since 1830 following a succession of colonial and territorial claims. The 1961 constitution places legislative power with the National Congress, comprising the Senate and House of Representatives. The country

Endangered people: The Yanomami live in the Amazon forests of Venezuela and Brazil. Landgrabbing and slash-and-burn clearance is threatening their homeland and lifestyle. Gold deposits have attracted countless treasure-hunters. Many Yanomami die of illnesses carried by outsiders, which their immune systems are not able to cope with.

is still dogged by attempted coups, high crime and inflation and social unrest. General strikes in 2003 triggered an economic crisis and almost brought oil production to a standstill.

Economy: Long neglected, agriculture is now receiving new attention. Venezuela depends highly on its agricultural sector. The country has the potential to become a major exporter of coffee and cocoa. Petroleum and its derivates account for 71% of GDP. The government's efforts to promote industry have met with little success despite the country's rich natural resources.

Viêt-Nam
Vietnam

Area: 329,560 sq km
Population: 82.6 million
GDP per capita: 2,500 US$
Capital: Hanoi
Government: Socialist republic
Language: Vietnamese
Currency: 1 dong = 10 hào = 100 xu

Geography: The Red and Black River delta lies on the Gulf of Tongking. To the south extends the central region of Annam, formed by a deeply indented costal strip that is 40 kilometers wide at its narrowest point. In the south lies the Mekong Delta, 70,000 km² in area. In the long rainy season, tropical rain forests and mangrove forests flourish in the coastal areas. Vietnam has a host of cultural monuments in Ho Chi Minh City (Saigon) and Hue, plus areas of natural beauty.

Politics: In the 10th century, Vietnamese rebels drove out their Chinese overlords. Rivalries between two families caused a split in the country in the 15th century, which was reunited only in 1802 with French help. After World War II, the country was partitioned into communist-ruled North Vietnam, and dictator-led South Vietnam. The Vietnam War (1957/58–1975), in which the USA and the SEATO states played an important role, ended with the Vietcong taking power in South Viet-

nam and the unification of the country under communist leadership. The invasion of Cambodia in 1979 led to acts of war with China.

Economy: The transition from the socialist-planned economy has meant a surplus in rice production in recent years. Vietnam is today the world's third largest rice exporter. Wood and rubber reserves are industrially processed. Private companies are increasing, but the economy remains underdeveloped.

Yemen see Al-Yaman

Yi'sra'el
Israel

Area: 21,946 sq km
Population: 6.2 million
GDP per capita: 19,700 US$
Capital: Jerusalem
Government: Republic
Languages: Hebrew, Arabic (official), English
Currency: 1 new shekel = 100 agorot

Geography: The highlands of Galilee extend to the Mediterranean in the north, with a narrow, fertile coastal strip to the south that meets the Negev Desert, occupying the country's largest area. Israel is bounded to the east by the Red Sea and the Jordan plains. The coast has a Mediterranean climate, while a desert climate reigns to the south. Important tourist destinations, other than the Dead Sea scenery, are sites from Jewish, Roman, and Byzantine eras and the Crusades.

Politics: The Republic of Israel was proclaimed in 1948 at the end of the British Mandate in Palestine. A large number of the Arabs living in the national territory, who had fought for the creation of their own state thereupon left the country. Irreconcilable differences with their neighbors have led to a total of four Israeli-Arab wars. The peace process, initiated in 1993 by Arafat and Rabin with a mutual agreement to recognize Israel and the PLO, slowed down in 1996 when a conservative coalition came to power. Clashes escalated in 2001, and Palestinian suicide bombers aggrava-

ted the situation. The establishment of a Palestinian State has become the focus of international efforts, with a crucial aspect being how to draw the borders of a country when large areas are still under Israeli control. Time will tell whether the 2005 Israeli withdrawal from Gaza will help find a peaceful conclusion. The influence of PLO can scarcely be over-estimated.

1 Parts of the tropical rain forests in the mountainous parts of Vietnam have given way to terraced cultivated rice fields.

2 Impressive rock graves in Petra, Jordan, bear witness to the Nabatean culture of the 2nd century BC.

3 Vanuatu: The islands – formerly known as the New Hebri-

des – have been settled by more than 100 Melanesian peoples.

4 The 3 million hectures of tropical forests in Venezuela's Canaima National Park are home to many endangered species. Countless waterfalls are typical of the landscape.

Picture perfect: The river Li in southern China, with its craggy mountains and cormorant fishers, is one of China's most popular holiday destinations. The more liberal economic policy that has developed in recent years allows culturally and scenically attractive, but commercially underdeveloped regions to benefit from tourist revenues.

Economy: Once solely agricultural, Israel is developing into a modern industrialized country; cooperative agriculture accounts for just 3% of GNP; industry for more than 30%. Important areas of industry include the food, metal, and aircraft industries. Tourism is the most reliable source of foreign exchange, at 2 billion US$.

Zambia
Zambia

Area: 752,614 sq km
Population: 10.4 million
GDP per capita: 800 US$
Capital: Lusaka
Government: Presidential republic within Commonwealth
Languages: English (official), Bantu languages
Currency: 1 kwacha = 100 ngwee

Geography: The high plateau (1,000–1,500 m) gradually rising from south to north is broken up by isolated outcrops and mountains of up to 2,300 meters. The basins of the Zambezi and Kafue rivers have shallow lakes and swamps. The altitude causes a moderately tropical climate; the highland savannas experience prolonged dry periods. Tourist attractions include Victoria Falls, Lake Tanganika and the national parks.

Politics: The country was formed from the original territories of Barotseland, Northwest Rhodesia and Northeast Rhodesia to the north of the Zambesi River, which were declared a British protectorate in 1911. In 1923 the region came under direct British colonial rule. From 1953 to 1963 North Rhodesia was part of the Central African Federation before gaining independence in 1964. Its president, K.D. Kaunda, established a single-party system in 1972–1973. National and international pressure for democracy led in 1990 to the approval of opposition parties. A new constitution guarantees the multi-party system and specifies the simultaneous holding of presidential and parliamentary elections. Forceful investigation into corruption has been championed by the current president, Levy Mwanawasa.

Economy: The majority of the African population, composed of 73 different ethnic groups, practices subsistence farming. Only the minority of European farmers use modern methods of cultivation. Zambia's economy is based on copper mining and export, which accounts for 65% of the total export volume. The government has privatized the country's largest mining company. Service industries, including tourism, are the country's fastest growing industries.

Zhongguo
China

Area: 9,596,960 sq km
Population: 1.3 billion.
GDP per capita: 5,000 US$
Capital: Beijing
Government: Socialist people's republic
Language: Mandarin Chinese (official), Cantonese and other dialects
Currency: 1 yuan renminbi = 10 jiao = 100 fen

Geography: From the fertile lowlands in the east, the landscape rises to meet the Himalayas in the west. High plateaus and mountains of more than 1,000 meters occupy one third of the area. The coastline on the Yellow Sea is flat at the mouths of China's two major rivers, the Huanghe and the Yangze. The southern coast is mountainous, with many offshore islands. The testimonials to 5,000 years of civilization and a richly varied landscape offer a vast number of fascinating travel destinations. Rapid industrialization,

erosion and pollution have decimated the rich flora and fauna.

Politics: As early as 2000 BC, small states existed in what is now China. Since the formation of a united empire in 221 BC, accompanied by standardized systems for weights, measures and writing, China has twice fallen to foreign rule; the Mongols governed from 1280 to 1368, and the Manchurians from 1644 to 1911. The fall of the empire was followed by a republic in 1911. After the end of World War I, the country was the scene of repeated civil wars. In 1937 war broke out with Japan, and in 1941 China declared war on Germany. The Chinese civil war between Kuomintang and the communists ended in 1949 with the withdrawal of the Kuomintang to Taiwan, later the National Republic of China. In October 1949, the People's Republic of China was established under

Mao Tse Tung. In the 1960s internal struggles resulted in the Cultural Revolution. Since 1978, the communist leadership has been pursuing economic liberalization, although without relinquishing any of its political power. In 1997, China took over the former British crown colony of Hong Kong, undertaking to retain the existing economic system for another 50 years.

Economy: Most of the population lives and works in rural regions. Rice and grain cultivation covers basic needs, and surpluses are exported. The country is opening up to world markets and undergoing major structural upheavals as its economy develops. In a low-wage country such as China, the lion's share of exports is accounted for by processed goods, chiefly machinery and electronic appliances, but also textile products. Thanks to foreign trade and tourism, the services sector is gaining in importance.

Zimbabwe
Zimbabwe

Area: 390,757 sq km
Population: 12.6 million
GDP per capita: 1,900 US$
Capital: Harare
Government: Presidential republic
Languages: English (official), Bantu languages
Currency: 1 Zimbabwe dollar = 100 cents

Geography: Zimbabwe, bounded to the north by the Zambesi and to the south by the Limpopo lowlands, mainly consists of a high plateau belonging to the rim of the Kalahari Basin. The highlands of the interior consist of rolling tableland with rocky outcrops and savanna vegetation. The climate is tropical, but moderate thanks to the altitude. Tourist destinations include the nature reserves, Victoria Falls and the ruins of Great Zimbabwe.

Politics: A British protectorate from 1891, the country became the colony of Rhodesia in 1923, named after the British South African colonial politician Cecil Rhodes. In 1930 Rhodesia was divided into European and African territories, favoring the Europeans. After long negotiations and battles against minority rule, the country gained independence in 1980 under the name of Zimbabwe.

Economy: Zimbabwe's economy, with an export-oriented agriculture, well-developed processing industries and a variety of mineral resources, is more highly diversified than many other African countries. The main crops include sugar, maize, cotton, tobacco, tea, peanuts, and citrus fruits; livestock farming is also profitable. Important natural resources in the country, comparatively highly industrialized by African standards, include iron, nickel, chromium, gold, asbestos and anthracite. Government corruption and repression is now undermining the country's economy. The agricultural sector has deteriorated due to land seizures and emigration.

1 Tiananmen Square is of central significance for China; here Mao Tse Tung proclaimed the People's Republic in 1949.

2 Hong Kong: The breathtaking view from the 554-meter-high Victoria Peak to the peninsula of Kowloon.

Secretary-Generals until 1981: The first Secretary-General of the UN was Tygve Lie from Norway (1946–1952, no picture) followed by the Swede Dag Hammersköld (1953–1961), Sihtu U Thant from Myanmar (1962–1971, pictured with John F. Kennedy), Kurt Waldheim from Austria (1972–1981).

UNO
United Nations Organization
Founded: 1945
Members: 192 countries
Headquarters: New York
In 1942, the effects of the Second World War moved 26 countries to form a joint organization. On October 24, 1945, 45 countries signed the United Nations Charter transforming the former war alliance into a global forum to replace the 1919 League of Nations.

The goals of the Organization are the establishment of world peace and international security, the promotion of human rights and basic freedoms "without distinction of race, sex, language or religion." In 1948 it formulated the Universal Declaration of Human Rights, under the heading of "all human rights for all." Peaceful resolution of conflicts is a key goal. The UN may not intervene in the right to self-determination of peoples.

The UN General Assembly (UNGA), in which each member is represented by one vote, meets annually. China, France, Great Britain, Russia, and the USA are permanent members of the Security Council, with ten further members elected for a two-year term. The Security Council acts on behalf of all members and awards and extends mandates of the UN forces. In 1988 the UN peace-keeping forces were awarded the Nobel Peace Prize.

IAEA
International Atomic Energy Agency
Founded: 1957
Members: 137 countries
Headquarters: Vienna
Monitoring of nuclear power plants and their waste disposal policies, plus compliance with the non-proliferation treaty of 1970.

IMF
International Monetary Fund
Founded: 1944
Members: 184 countries
Headquarters: Washington DC
Organization responsible for fostering monetary cooperation, facilitating international trade, monitoring the international currency system and promotion of development aid. The IMF also produces bi-annual reports on the international economic situation.

UNCTAD
United Nations Conference on Trade and Development
Founded: 1964
Members: 192 countries
Headquarters: Geneva
Promotion of international trade, particularly with developing countries, and interrelated issues of finance, technology, investment, and sustainable development.

UNDP
United Nations Development Programme
Founded: 1965
Headquarters: New York
Executive Council for the coordination and financing of technological and other forms of aid for developing countries. Its global network seeks to ensure the most effective use of UN and international aid resources. Voluntarily funded; largest multilateral source of grant technical assistance in the world.

UNEP
United Nations Environment Programme
Founded: 1972
Headquarters: Nairobi
Administrative council for international environmental issues, including those outside the UN system.

UNESCO
United Nations Educational, Scientific and Cultural Organization
Founded: 1946

Members: 190 countries
Headquarters: Paris
Special UN organization fostering cooperation with member states on cultural affairs and managing the continuously expanding "World Heritage List" of cultural and natural sites. Also contributes special support to educational and learning programs in developing countries and works on forging universal agreements on ethical issues.

UNHCR
United Nations High Commissioner for Refugees
Founded: 1949
Headquarters: Geneva
Assists those persecuted for reasons of race, religions or political views. Regular monitoring of refugee movements throughout the world and organization of aid campaigns. Leads and coordinates international action to protect refugees and internally

Many UN organizations are headquartered in the Palace of Nations in Geneva.

displaced persons (IDPs) and resolve refugee problems worldwide.

UNICEF
United Nations International Children's Fund
Founded: 1946
Headquarters: New York
Secures food and medical supplies for children and mothers in need in around 160 countries and is largely financed by private donations. Demands ban on recruitment of "child sol-

diers." Educational, child development and training programs, promotion of children's rights, emergency assistance in crises.

World Bank Group
Headquarters: Washington
Comprises five institutions:

• IBRD
International Bank for Reconstruction and Development
Founded: 1944
Members: 184 countries

• IDA
International Development Association
Founded: 1959
Members: 163 countries

• IFC
International Finance Corporation
Founded: 1956
Members: 176 countries

• MIGA
Multilateral Investment Guarantee Agency
Founded: 1985
Members: 163 countries

• ICSID
International Centre for Settlement of Investment Disputes
Founded: 1966
Members: 154 countries
The World Bank Group supports economic development in less developed member countries by

granting loans and supplying consulting and technical assistance, with the goals of combating poverty and improving the standard of living. The World Bank Group institutions are governed by a single president.

WHO
World Health Organization
Founded: 1948
Members: 193 countries
Headquarters: Geneva
WHO's objective, as set out in its constitution, is the attainment by all peoples of the highest possible level of health. Its constitution defines health as a state of complete physical, mental, and social well-being, and not merely the absence of disease or infirmity. The WHO maintains a global atlas of infectious diseases and is active in expanding medical research and care, for example in the struggle against Aids (UNAIDS Program). It also supplies emergency aid in disease outbreaks and crises.

Arab League
Founded: 1945
Members: 22 Arab countries in Africa and Asia
Headquarters: Cairo
Voluntary association of independent Arab countries fostering cooperation on cultural, economic, political, and scientific issues and representing common interests.

ASEAN
Association of South East Asian Nations
Founded: 1967
Members: Brunei, Cambodia, Indonesia, Malaysia, Philippines, Myanmar, Singapore, Thailand, Vietnam, Laos
Headquarters: Jakarta
Promotion of economic growth, social progress and political stability by means of political and security dialogue and cooperation. A free trade area is planned by 2010.

Commonwealth of Nations
Founded: 1931
Members: 53 countries
Headquarters: London
Fostering of political, economic, and cultural cooperation as well as the securing of democracy in the former territories of the British Empire. The foundation of the Commonwealth in 1931 coincided with the beginning of decolonization. Most colonies

Secretary-Generals since 1982: Javier Pérez de Cuéllar (1982–1991) from Peru and Boutros Boutros-Ghali from Egypt (1992–96). Seventh Secretary-General is Kofi Annan from Ghana. He took office in 1997 and was re-elected in June 2001.

had gained independence by 1984 but retained their close ties to Great Britain and the Commonwealth.

ECO
Economic Cooperation Organization
Founded: 1985
Members: Afghanistan, Azerbaijan, Iran, Kazakhstan, Kyrgyz Republic, Pakistan, Tajikistan, Turkey, Turkmenistan, Uzbekistan
Headquarters: Teheran
Cooperation of Islamic nations on economic, agricultural, industrial, transport, technological, scientific, and educational issues.

EFTA
European Free Trade Association
Founded: 1960
Members: Iceland, Liechtenstein, Norway, Switzerland
Headquarters: Geneva
Promotion of an extensive network of free trade agreements between member states and associated EU and non-EU countries.

EP
European Parliament
Founded: 1952
Members: total of 732 elected members from all EU countries
Headquarters: Strasbourg, Luxembourg, Brussels
The EP has far-reaching legislative powers and supervises the executive. Together with the European Council, it forms the EU budgetary authority and supervises budget spending. The EP also presides over EU issues of foreign and security policy and plays a key role in the enlargement discussion.

COE
Council of Europe
Founded: 1949
Members: 46 nations
Headquaters: Strasbourg
Organization with almost all European countries as members. Based on the law of nations and founded in London as a private initiative. Its goal is to foster cooperation, preserve items of common cultural heritage, defend human and minority rights as well as support the spread of democracy throughout Europe.

EU
European Union
Founded: 1993
Members: Germany, France, Great Britain, Finland, Italy, Spain, Netherlands, Belgium, Austria, Sweden, Denmark, Portugal, Greece, Ireland, Luxembourg, Latvia, Estonia, Lithuania, Hungary, Poland, Czech Republic, Slovakia, Slovenia, Malta, and Cyprus
Headquarters: Strasbourg, Brussels, Luxembourg
The EU is a development of the original European Coal and Steel Community, which joined with the European Economic Community (EEC) in 1957. In 1967, these bodies merged with the European Atomic Energy Commission (EURATOM) to form the European Community – renamed the EU in 1993. The organization strives toward a common foreign and security policy and fosters cooperation in issues of national policy and law.

European Court of Justice
Headquarters: Luxembourg
The highest legal institution in the EU deals with disputes involving EU law, ensuring that it is uniformly interpreted and applied throughout the Union. The Court hears actions against member countries, the EP, the Council or Commission. Its verdicts cannot be overturned by national courts. All member states are represented by one judge, presided over by a president.

FTAA
Free Trade Area of the Americas
Members: USA, Canada, all Latin and South American countries
Headquarters: none
The agreement signed in Miami in 1994 is aimed at interconnecting the planned North and South American free trade areas (NAFTA and Mercosur), with the goal of incorporating most countries in the Americas to create the world's largest international free trade zone by 2005.

CEFTA
Central European Free Trade Association
Founded: 1993
Members: Poland, Slovakian Republic, Slovenia, Czech Republic, Hungary, Bulgaria, Romania
Headquarters: none
The Free Trade Agreement came into force in 1993. The long-term goal of all members is EU and NATO membership, whereupon CEFTA would be dissolved.

IOC
International Olympic Committee
Founded: 1894
Members: 201 National Olympic Committees (NOCs)
Headquarters: Lausanne
International, non-governmental, non-profit organization and umbrella organization of the Olympic Movement. Decides the locations, rules and programs of the Summer and Winter Olympic Games and supervises their organization.

NATO
North Atlantic Treaty Organization
Founded: 1955
Members: 19
Headquarters: Brussels
The military pact was initiated by the USA and several Western European states in response to the formation of the Warsaw Pact during the Cold War. NATO has cooperated with the former Eastern Bloc countries since the early 1990s within the NATO Partnership for Peace. The organization has also extended membership to several former Warsaw Pact members. NATO's fundamental role is the safeguarding of its members' freedom and security by political and military means as well as upholding democracy, political stability and the rule of law.

OECD
Organization for Economic Cooperation and Development
Founded: 1961
Members: 30 countries
Headquarters: Paris
Successor to the Organization for European Economic Cooperation (OEEC) founded in 1948. Its goal is the economic development and improvement of living standards in member countries, fostering good governance and multilateral agreement. It produces individual country reviews and surveys, monitors trends and analyzes economic developments. It spearheads efforts to help countries respond to new economic challenges.

OPEC
Organization of Petroleum Exporting Countries
Founded: 1960
Members: 11 countries
Headquarters: Vienna
Oil cartel organization serving the interests of its member states with economies heavily reliant on oil. Aims to bring stability and harmony to the oil market by adjusting oil output to help ensure a balance between supply and demand.

OSCE
Organization for Security and Cooperation in Europe
Founded: 1975 (CSCE), since 1995 OSCE
Members: 56 countries
Headquarters: Vienna
The world's largest regional security organization, the Conference for Security and Cooperation in Europe, began its work with the signing of the Helsinki Final Act. It deals with many security and stability-related issues, early warning and crisis prevention and management. The OCSE has played an important role in assisting the former communist states of Europe in their transition to democracy.

WTO
World Trade Organization
Founded: 1995
Members: 149 countries and the EU Commission
Headquarters: Geneva
Replaced the GATT world trade agreement of 1947 and since then has supervised multilateral agreements concerning exchange of goods and services and agreements on patents and other property rights. The WTO also provides arbitration services in trade conflicts. Its promotion of global trade prompts many countries to apply for membership.

The banner of the European Union.

European Union: Parade of the banners of the members in front of the EU building in Brussels and in front of the European Parliament in Strasbourg.
25 countries are members of the European Union (EU) with a total of 450 million inhabitants.

All of the places named on the maps in the atlas are listed in the atlas index. The place names are listed alphabetically. Special symbols and letters including accents and umlauts are ignored in the order of the index. For example, the letters Á, Ä, Â are all categorized under A, and è, ˚, Î are all treated as the standard Latin letter Z. Written characters consisting of two letters joined together (ligatures) are treated as two separate characters in the index: for example, words beginning with the character Æ would be indexed under AE.
The most commonly used abbreviations in the atlas – including N.P. for national park or N.W.R. for national wildlife refuge – are also used in the index. These abbreviations are listed and explained on this page (below). Generic geographic terms (sea, bay, etc.) and word articles (the, le, el, etc.)

were used in the order of the index: for example, the Gulf of Mexico is listed under G and Le Havre, France is listed under L.
A special aspect of the atlas is the detailed and specially developed system of pictograms it features. These pictograms highlight famous travel routes, scenic landscapes, natural attractions, man-made attractions, cultural sites, as well as sporting, vacation, and recreation facilities. These pictograms also appear in the index (up to three per place name). The pictograms provide a basic overview of the attractions featured in a particular area. The meanings of all of the pictograms featured in the atlas are explained on the following page. In addition to these pictograms, the index also features special symbols to provide information about the political status of certain

places including states, provinces, and capital cities. Virtually all of the places listed in the atlas have a country reference; these nations are identified by their international license (registration) plate codes. The various international license codes are identified on page 276. In the case of communities and areas that are located on or between the borders of two nations, the license

plate codes of both nations are listed and separated by a backslash.
The names of areas and geographic features that cannot be assigned to specific states, such as the Atlantic Ocean, are followed by the page number of a map featuring the area and the number of the map grid box in which the area is depicted on the map.

Antigua	⌂ ⛴ ⚓	**AG**	187	Gk37
Place name	Pictograms	Nation	Page	Map grid

Abbreviations

Abb.	Abbey, abbaye (French), abbadia (Span.), abbazia (Ital.)	Ind.	Indian/ Native Americans, First Nation	N.R.	Nature Reserve, Natuurreservaat (Dutch)	Sr.	Sredn -e, -ij, -jaja (Russian) = central, middle
Abor.	Aboriginal (indigenous inhabitants of Australia)	Ind.Res.	Indian Reservation = Native American land reserves in North America	N.R.A.	National Recreation Area	Sra.	Sierra (Span.), serra (Port./Ital.) = mountain range
Aborig.	Aboriginal (indigenous inhabitants of Australia)	Is.	Islands	N.S.	National Seashore	St./St	Saint (English and French), sankt (German, Dutch)
Ad.	Adas (Turkish) = Island	Îs.	Îles (French) = islands	N.Sra.	Nossa Senhora (Port.) = our lady (Mary, the mother of Jesus)	Sta.	Santa (Span./Port./Ital.) = saint
Ág.	Ági -os, -a, -i (Greek) = Saint	Jaz.	Jazovir (Bulg.) = reservoir	Nva.	Nueva (Span.) = new-	Star.	Star -o, -yj, -aja, -oe (Russian) = old-
A.L.	Aboriginal Land = Aboriginal land reserve in Australia	Jct.	Junction	Nvo.	Nuevo (Span.) = new-	Ste	Sainte (French) = saint
Ban.	Banjaran (Malaysian) = mountain range	Jez.	Jezioro (Pol.), jezero (Czech/Slovak./Serb./Croat./Slov.) = lake	N.W.R.	National Wildlife Refuge	Sth.	South, southern
Bol'.	Bol'-šoj, -šaja, -šoe (Russian) = large-	Kan.	Kanal (Turk./Rus.), kanaal (Dutch), kana (Pol.) = canal	o.	Ostrov (Rus.) = island	St.Mem.	State Memorial
C.	Cape, cap (French), cabo (Span./Port., capo (Ital.)	Kep.	Kepulauan (Malaysian) = archipelago	P.	Port (English and French), puerto (Span./Port.), porto (Ital.) = harbor	Sto.	Santo (Span./Port.) = Saint
Can.	Canal	Kg.	Kampong (Malaysian), kampung (Khmer) = village	Peg.	Pegunungan (Indonesian) = mountain	Str.	Street, Strait, stretto (Italian), stræde (Danish), stret (Norwegian)
Cast.	Castle, castel (French.), castillo (Span.), castelo (Port.), castello (Ital.)	Kör.	Körfezi (Turk.) = gulf, bay	Pen.	Peninsula, péninsule (franz.), península (Span.), penisola (Ital.)	t.	tau (Kaz.) = mountain
Cd.	Ciudad (Span.), cidade (Port.) = city	L.	Lake, lac (French), lago (Ital./Span./Port.), loch, lough (Gaelic)	Pk.	Peak	T.	Take (Jap.) = peak, summit
Co.	Cerro (Span.) = mountain, hill	M.	Mys (Rus./Ukr.) = cape	P.N.	Parc National (French), parque nacional (Span./Port.), parco nazionale (Ital.) = national park	T.	Temple
Conv.	Convento (Span.) = monastery	Mal.	Malo, -yj, -aja, -oe (Rus.) = small	p-ov.	Poluostrov (Rus.) = peninsula	Tel.	Teluk (Indonesian) = bay
Cord.	Cordillera (Span.) = mountain range	Mem.	Memorial	Pres.	Presidente (Span./Port.) = president	Tg.	Tanjung (Indonesian) = cape
Corr.	Corrente (Port.), corriente (Ital./Span.) = river	Mon.	Monastery, monastère (French.), monasterio (Span.), monastero (Ital.)	Prov.	Provincial, Province	T.I.	Terra Indígena (Port.), territorio indigena (Span.) = indigenous land reservation in Latin America
Cr.	Creek	M.P.	Milli Parki (Turk.) = national park	Pse.	Passe (French) = Pass	
D.	Dake (Jap.) = mountain	Mt.	Mount, mont (French)	Pso.	Paso (Span.), passo (Ital.) = Pass	Vdhr.	Vodohranilišče (Russian) = reservoir
D.	Danau (Indonesian) = lake	Mta.	Montagna (Ital.), montaña (Span.) = mountain range	Pt.	Point	Vel.	Velik -o, -ij, -yki, -oe (Rus.) = large-
Dağ.	Dağlar, dağlari (Turkish) = mountain range	Mte.	Monte (Ital./Span./Port.), montagne (French) = mountain	Pta.	Punta (Span./Port.) = point	Verh.	Verhn -ee, -ie, -ij, -jaja (Rus.) = mountain
Ea.	Estancia (Span.) = estate	Mtes.	Montes (Span./Port.), montagnes (French) = mountains	Pte.	Pointe (French) = point	Vill.	Village
Emb.	Embalse (Span.), embassament (catalonian) = reservoir	Mţi.	Munţii (Romanian) = mountain range	Pto.	Punto (Ital.) = point	vlk.	Vulkan (Rus.) = volcano
Ens.	Ensenada (Span./Port.) = small bay	Mti.	Monti (Ital.) = mountain range	Q.N.P.	Quasi National Park (Jap.) = national park	Vol.	Volcano, volcan (French), volcán (Span.)
Erm.	Ermita (Span.) = hermitage	Mtn.	Mountain	R.	River, rivière (French), río (Span.), ribeiro, rio (Port.), rîu (Romanian), reka (Bulgarian)	Vul.	Vulkan (German), Vulcano (Ital./Romanian) = volcano
Est.	Estación (Span.) = train station	Mtns.	Mountains	Ra.	Range	W.A.	Wilderness Area
Faz.	Fazenda (Port.) = estate	Mts.	Mountains, Monts (French)	Rep.	Republic, république (French), república (Span./Port.), republicca (Ital.)	Wildl.	Wildlife
Fl.	Fleuve (French) = river	Mus.	Musée (French), museo (Span.), museu (Port.) = museum	Repr.	Represa (Port.) = dam	W.S.	Wildlife Sanctuary
Fs.	waterfalls			Res.	Reserva (Span.), réserve (French) = nature reserve	Y.	Yama (Jap.) = mountain, mountain range
g.	gawa (Jap.) = river	N.	North, Northern, Norte (Ital./Span./Port.), Norra (Swedish), Nørdre (Norwegian), Nørre (Danish), Nord (German)	Res.	Reservoir, réservoir (French)	Zal.	Zaliv (Russian), zalew (Polish) = bay
G.	Gora (Russian), góra (Polish), gunung (Indonesian) = mountain	Nac.	Nacional (Span.), Nacional'-nyj, -aja, -oe (Russian) = national	Resp.	Respublika (Russian) = Republik	Zap.	Zapovednik (Russian) = nature reserve
Gde.	Grande (Span./French) = large	Naz.	Nazionale (Ital.) = national	s.	San (Jap.) = mountain	Z.B.	Nature reserve in the People's Republic of China
Geb.	Gebirge (German), gebergte (Dutch) = mountain range	N.B.C.A.	National Biodiversity and Conservation Area = protected natural area	S.	San (Span./Ital.), são (Port.) = saint	Zp.	Zapadn -e, -ji, -aja, -noe (Russian) = west, western
Grd.	Grand (French) = large	Nev.	Nevado (Span.) = snow-covered mountain peaks	Sanc./Sanct.	Sanctuary		
Gt.	Great-	N.H.P.	National Historic Park	Sd.	Sound, sund (German, Danish, Norwegian, Swedish)		
Hist.	Historic, historical	N.H.S.	National Historic Site	Sel.	Selat (Indonesian) = strait		
Hr.	Hrebet (Russian) = high	Niž.	Niž-e, -nij, -naja, -neje (Russian) = lower-	Sg.	Song (Vietnamese) = river		
Ht.	Haut (French) = high-	Nižm.	Nižmennosť (Rus.) = plain	S.H.P.	State Historic Park		
Hte.	Haute (French) = high-	N.M.P.	National Military Park	S.H.S.	State Historic Site		
Hts.	Haut -s, -es (French) = high-	N.P.	National Park, Nationalpark (Swedish), nasjonal park (Norwegian), Nemzeti Park (Hungarian)	Sk.	Shuiku (Chinese) = reservoir		
Hwy.	Highway			S.M.	State Monument		
I.	Isla (Span.), ilha (Port.) = island			S.P.	State Park		
Î.	Île (French) = island						

The index explained

International license (registration) plate code

A	Austria	CR	Costa Rica	GR	Greece	MD	Moldova	RCH	Chile	THA	Thailand
AFG	Afghanistan	CV	Cape Verde	GUY	Guyana	MEX	Mexico	RDC	Dem. Republic of the Congo	TJ	Tajikistan
AG	Antigua and Barbuda	CY	Cyprus	H	Hungary	MH	Marshall Islands	RG	Guinea	TLS*	East Timor
AL	Albania	CZ	Czech Republic	HN	Honduras	MK	Macedonia	RH	Haiti	TM	Turkmenistan
AND	Andorra	D	Germany	HR	Croatia	MNG	Mongolia	RI	Indonesia	TN	Tunisia
ANG	Angola	DARS	Western Sahara	I	Italy	MOC	Mozambique	RIM	Mauritania	TO	Tonga
ARM	Armenia	DJI	Djibouti	IL	Israel	MS	Mauritius	RL	Lebanon	TR	Turkey
AUS	Australia	DK	Denmark	IND	India	MV	Maldives	RM	Madagascar	TT	Trinidad and Tobago
AZ	Azerbaijan	DOM	Dominican Republic	IR	Iran	MW	Malawi	RMM	Mali	TUV	Tuvalu
B	Belgium	DY	Benin	IRL	Ireland	MYA	Myanmar (Burma)	RN	Niger	UA	Ukraine
BD	Bangladesh	DZ	Algeria	IRQ	Iraq	N	Norway	RO	Romania	UAE	United Arab Emirates
BDS	Barbados	E	Spain	IS	Iceland	NAM	Namibia	ROK	Korea, South	USA	United States of
BF	Burkina Faso	EAK	Kenya	J	Japan	NAU	Nauru	ROU	Uruguay		America
BG	Bulgaria	EAT	Tanzania	JA	Jamaica	NEP	Nepal	RP	Philippines	UZ	Uzbekistan
BH	Belize	EAU	Uganda	JOR	Jordan	NIC	Nicaragua	RSM	San Marino	V	Vatican City
BHT	Bhutan	EC	Ecuador	K	Cambodia	NL	Netherlands	RUS	Russia	VN	Vietnam
BIH	Bosnia and Herzegovina	ER	Eritrea	KIR	Kiribati	NZ	New Zealand	RWA	Rwanda	VU	Vanuatu
BOL	Bolivia	ES	El Salvador	KNA*	Saint Kitts and Nevis	OM	Oman	S	Sweden	WAG	Gambia
BR	Brazil	EST	Estonia	KS	Kyrgyzstan	P	Portugal	SD	Swaziland	WAL	Sierra Leone
BRN	Bahrain	ET	Egypt	KSA	Saudi Arabia	PA	Panama	SGP	Singapore	WAN	Nigeria
BRU	Brunei	ETH	Ethiopia	KWT	Kuwait	PAL	Palau	SCG**	Serbia and Montenegro	WD	Dominica
BS	Bahamas	F	France	KZ	Kazakhstan	PE	Peru	SK	Slovakia	WG	Grenada
BU	Burundi	FIN	Finland	L	Luxembourg	PK	Pakistan	SLO	Slovenia	WL	Saint Lucia
BY	Belarus	FJI	Fiji	LAO	Laos	PL	Poland	SME	Suriname	WS	Samoa
C	Cuba	FL	Liechtenstein	LAR	Libya	PNG	Papua New Guinea	SN	Senegal	WV	Saint Vincent and
CAM	Cameroon	FSM	Micronesia	LB	Liberia	PRK*	Korea, North	SOL	Solomon Islands		the Grenadines
CDN	Canada	G	Gabon	LS	Lesotho	PY	Paraguay	SP	Somalia	YE	Yemen
CH	Switzerland	GB	Great Britain	LT	Lithuania	Q	Qatar	STP	São Tomé and Príncipe	YV	Venezuela
CHN*	China	GCA	Guatemala	LV	Latvia	RA	Argentina	SUD	Sudan	Z	Zambia
CI	Cote d'Ivoire	GE	Georgia	M	Malta	RB	Botswana	SY	Seychelles	ZA	South Africa
CL	Sri Lanka	GH	Ghana	MA	Morocco	RC	Taiwan	SYR	Syria	ZW	Zimbabwe
CO	Colombia	GNB	Guinea-Bissau	MAL	Malaysia	RCA	Central Africa Republic	TCH	Chad		
COM	Comoros	GQ	Equatorial Guinea	MC	Monaco	RCB	Republic of the Congo	TG	Togo		

* Some countries do not have official vehicle registration codes. In these cases, the international three-letter code (ISO 3166) is shown.

** Montenegro and Serbia were without individual license plate codes at the time of publication. As a result, locations in these two countries are listed here under the code SCG.

Symbols used in the index

○ City
■ State
● Capital
□ Province
◉ Provincial Capital

Principal travel routes

Auto route
Rail road
Highspeed train
Shipping route

Remarkable landscapes and natural monuments

UNESCO World Natural Heritage
Mountain landscape
Rock landscape
Ravine/canyon
Extinct volcano
Active volcano
Geyser
Cave
Glacier
River landscape
Waterfall/rapids
Lake country
Desert
Oasis
Fossil site
Depression
Nature park
National park (landscape)
National park (flora)
National park (fauna)
National park (culture)
Biosphere reserve
Wildlife reserve
Whale watching

Turtle conservation area
Protected area for sea-lions/seals
Protected area for penguins
Zoo/safari park
Crocodile farm
Coastal landscape
Beach
Coral reef
Island
Underwater reserve

Remarkable Cities and cultural monuments

UNESCO World Cultural Heritage
Pre- and early history
Prehistoric rockscape
The Ancient Orient
Ancient Egypt
Ancient Egyptian pyramids
Minoan culture
Phoenecian culture
Early African culture
Etruscan culture
Greek antiquity
Roman antiquity
Nabatean culture
Vikings
Ancient India
Ancient China
Ancient Japan
Mayan culture
Inca culture
Aztec culture
Other ancient American cultures
Places of Jewish cultural interest
Places of Christian cultural interest
Places of Islamic cultural interest
Places of Buddhist cultural interest
Places of Hindu cultural interest

Places of Jainist cultural interest
Places of Sikh cultural interest
Places of Shinto cultural interest
Places of cultural interest to other religions
Places of cultural interest to indigenous peoples (native peoples)
Aborigine reservation
Places of Aboriginal cultural interest
Indian reservation
Indian Pueblo culture
Places of Indian cultural interest
Amazonian Indians/protected area
Cultural landscape
Historical city scape
Impressive skyline
Castle/fortress/fort
Caravanserai
Palace
Technical/industrial monument
Dam
Remarkable lighthouse
Remarkable bridge
Tomb/grave
Theater of war/battlefield
Monument
Memorial
Space mission launch site
Space telescope
Market
Festivals
Museum
Theater
World exhibition
Olympics

Sport and leisure destinations

Arena/stadium
Race track

Golf
Horse racing
Skiing
Sailing
Diving
Windsurfing
Surfing
Canoeing/rafting
Seaport
Deep-sea fishing
Waterskiing
Beach resort
Mineral/thermal spa
Amusement/theme park
Casino
Hill resort
Lodge

Special index pictograms

Bodies of Water
Canal
Other physical names
Pass
Underwater topography

Belet Weyne – Bisauli

Belet Weyne SP 143 Nc43
Belev RUS 48 Mj19
Bèleya RG 136 Ke40
Belezma, P.N. de DZ 126 Lc28
Belfast GB 19 Kp36
Belfast USA (MA) 177 Gf23
Belfast ZA 155 Mf58
Belfield USA (ND) 169 Ej22
Belfir RO 43 Mb44
Belfodiyo ETH 142 Mh40
Belford GB 20 Kt35
Belfort F 25 Lg43
Belgachhi IND (BIH) 83 Pd33
Belgaum IND (KTK) 82 Oh38
Belgaum Fort IND (KTK) 82 Oh38
Belgern D 32 Lo39
Belgium B 23 Le40
Belgo SUD 135 Mg40
Belgodère F 34 Lk48
Belgorod RUS 48 Mj20
Belgrade SCG 44 Ma46
Belgrade USA (MN) 172 Fc23
Belgrade USA (MT) 169 Ee23
Belgrano, Cerro RA 210 Ge69
Belgrano II ANT (RA) 6 Jb34
Belhar IND (BIH) 83 Pd33
Belhatti IND (KTK) 82 Oh38
Belhirane DZ 126 Ld30
Béli GNB 136 Kd40
Beli WAN 139 Lf42
Belic C 179 Gb36
Belica MK 44 Ma49
Belidzi RUS (DAG) 57 Ne25
Belifang CAM 138 Lf42
Beli Izvor BG 44 Md47
Beli Manastir HR 35 Lt45
Belimbing RI 93 Qc48
Belin-Béliet F 24 Ku46
Belinga G 139 Lg45
Belinyu RI 93 Qc46
Beliş RO 43 Md44
Belišće HR 35 Lt45
Belitsaka RM 157 Nc54
Belitung RI 95 Qd47
Belize ANG 148 Lg48
Belize 184 Ff37
Belize Barrier Reef System BH 184 Fg37
Belize City BH 184 Ff37
Beljanovo BG 45 Mf47
Belkar IND (MHT) 82 Og37
Belkhera IND (MPH) 83 Ok34
Bel'ki BY 39 Mh35
Bel'kovo RUS 48 Mg19
Bell AUS (QLD) 109 Sf59
Bell ZA 155 Md62
Bella CAM 138 Lf44
Bella Bella CDN (BC) 166 Df19
Bellac F 24 Lb44
Bella Coola CDN (BC) 166 Dg19
Belladère DOM 186 Ge36
Bella Flor BOL 198 Gg51
Bellágio I 34 Lk45
Bellalie AUS (QLD) 108 Sb59
Bellária-Igea Marina I 34 Ln46
Bellary IND (KTK) 84 Oj38
Bellata AUS (NSW) 109 Se60
Bella Unión ROU 204 Hb61
Bellavista CO 192 Gb42
Bellavista PE 196 Ga48
Bellavista PE 196 Gb49
Bella Vista RA (CR) 204 Ha60
Bella Vista RA (TU) 207 Gh59
Bella Vista Norte PY 202 Hb57
Bell Brook AUS (NSW) 109 Sg61
Bellburns CDN (NF) 177 Hb20
Belle Anse RH 186 Gd36
Belleden Ker AUS (QLD) 107 Sc54
Bellefontaine USA (OH) 173 Fj25
Bellefonte USA (PA) 177 Gb25
Bellegarde F 25 Lc43
Bellegarde-sur-Valserine F 25 Lf44
Belle Glade USA (FL) 179 Fk32
Belle-Île F 22 Kr43
Belle Isle CDN 177 Hc20
Bellême F 22 La42
Bellenden Ker N.P. AUS (QLD) 107 Sd54
Belleoram CDN (NF) 177 Hc22
Belle Plaine USA (MN) 172 Fd23
Belleterre CDN (QC) 173 Ga22
Belleville CDN (ON) 177 Gb23
Belleville F 25 Le44
Belleville USA (IL) 175 Fe26
Belleville USA (KS) 174 Fb26
Belleville ZA 154 Lk62
Belleville-sur-Vie F 24 Kt44
Bellevue AUS (QLD) 107 Sc54
Bellevue USA (ID) 168 Ec24
Bellevue USA (NE) 172 Fc25
Bellevue USA (OH) 173 Fj25
Bellevue USA (WA) 168 Dj22
Belley F 25 Lf45
Belle Yella LB 136 Kf42
Bellfield AUS (QLD) 107 Sb55
Bell Fourche USA (SD) 169 Ej23
Bellingham USA (WA) 168 Dj21
Bellingrath Gardens USA 175 Ff30
Bellingshausen ANT (RUS) 6 Ha30
Bellingshausen Sea ANT 6 Fd32
Bellinzona CH 34 Lk44
Bell Island CDN 177 Hc20
Bell Island Hot Springs USA (AK) 166 De18
Bello CO 192 Gc42
Bellocq RA (BA) 209 Gk63
Bellows Falls USA (VT) 177 Gd24
Bellpat PK 65 Od31
Bell Peninsula CDN 163 Fd06
Bellpuig E 29 Lb49
Bell River CDN (YT) 165 Db12
Bell Rock 20 Ks34
Bellrose AUS (QLD) 109 Sd59
Bells Beach AUS (VIC) 111 Sc65
Belluno I 34 Ln44
Bell Ville RA (CD) 209 Gj62
Bélmez E 27 Kp52
Belmond USA (IA) 172 Fd24
Belmont GB 20 Ku30
Belmont USA (NC) 178 Fk28
Belmont ZA 155 Mc60
Belmonte BR (BA) 203 Ja53
Belmonte E 29 Ks51
Belmonte P 26 Kn50
Belmonte de Miranda E 26 Ko47
Belmont Park USA (NY) 177 Gd25
Belmont Park Racecourse AUS (WA) 104 Qh61
Belmopan BH 184 Ff37
Belmopan BH 184 Ff37
Belmore AUS (NSW) 110 Sa62
Belmullet IRL 19 Kl36
Belo RM 157 Nc56
Belobaka RM 157 Nc55
Belo Campo BR (BA) 203 Hk53
Belœil B 23 Ld40
Belogorsk RUS 71 Re20
Belogradčik BG 44 Mc47
Belogradčiški Skali BG 44 Mc47
Beloha RM 157 Nc58
Belo Horizonte BR (MG) 203 Hj55
Beloit USA (KS) 174 Fa26
Beloit USA (WI) 173 Ff24
Belo Jardim BR (PE) 201 Jb50
Belojarovo RUS 71 Re20
Belojarskij RUS 54 Ob06
Béloko RCA 140 Lh43
Belo Monte BR (AM) 198 Gh49
Belo Monte do Pontal BR (PA) 195 He47
Belonge RDC 149 Ma47
Belorado E 28 Kr48
Beloreček RUS 49 Mk23
Beloslav BG 45 Mh47
Belotinci BG 44 Mc47
Belo Tsiribihina RM 157 Nc55
Belovodskoe KS 66 Oh24
Belpasso I 37 Lp53
Belper GB 21 Kt37
Belpre USA (OH) 175 Fk26
Belsay GB 20 Kt35
Bel'skaja vozvyšennost' RUS 48 Mg18
Beltana AUS (SA) 108 Rk61
Belterra BR (PA) 199 Hc47
Beltinci SLO 42 Lr44
Beltiug RO 43 Mc43
Belton USA (SC) 178 Fj28
Belton USA (TX) 174 Fb30
Beltov Qirlari UZ 62 Oa24
Belturbet IRL 19 Kn36
Beluguppa IND (APH) 84 Oj38
Belur IND (KTK) 84 Oh39
Beluran MAL 94 Qj43
Beluru MAL 94 Qh44
Belvedere Maríttimo I 37 Lq51
Belvès F 24 La46
Belvidere USA (IL) 173 Ff24
Belvidere Kerk ZA 154 Mb63
Belyj RUS 48 Mg18
Belz UA 41 Me40
Belzig D 32 Ln38
Belzoni USA (MS) 175 Fe29
Bełżyce PL 41 Mc39
Béma RMM 130 Kf38
Bémal RCA 140 Lj42
Bemanevika RM 156 Ne52
Bemanevika RM 156 Nf53
Bemaraha RM 157 Nc55
Bemarivo RM 157 Nc56
Bembe ANG 148 Lh49
Bembeche TCH 133 Lk36
Bembesi ZW 152 Me56
Bemboka AUS (NSW) 111 Se64
Bemetara IND (CGH) 83 Pa35
Bemidji USA (MN) 172 Fc22
Bemonto RM 157 Nc55
Ben BF 137 Kh39
Bena WAN 138 Lc40
Benabarre E 28 La48
Bena-Dibele RDC 149 Mb48
Benagerie AUS (SA) 108 Sa61
Ben-Ahmed MA 125 Kg29
Bena-Kamba RDC 149 Mc47
Ben Alberts Nature Reserve ZA 155 Md58
Benalla AUS (VIC) 111 Sc64
Benalup de Sidonia E 27 Kp54
Benamaurel E 27 Ks53
Ben Amera RIM 130 Kd35
Benato-Toby RM 157 Nc57
Bena-Tshadi RDC 149 Mb48
Benavente E 26 Kp49
Benavides E 26 Kp48
Benavides USA (TX) 181 Fa32
Ben Badis DZ 125 Kk28
Ben Boyd N.P. AUS (NSW) 111 Se64
Bencés főapátság H 42 Ls43
Bencha CHN (JGS) 78 Ra29
Bencheng CHN (HBI) 73 Qk26
Bencubbin AUS (WA) 104 Qj61
Bend USA (OR) 168 Dk23
Béndana TCH 140 Lk41
Benda Range AUS 110 Sa62
Bendela RDC 149 Lj47
Bendeleben Mts. USA 165 Bj13
Bendemeer AUS (NSW) 109 Sf61
Bender Beyla SP 143 Nf41
Bendigo AUS (VIC) 111 Sc64
Bend of the Boyne IRL 19 Ko37
Bendorf D 32 Lh40
Bendugu WAL 136 Ke41
Bene MOC 152 Mg53
Beneditinos BR (PI) 201 Hj48
Benedito Leite BR (MA) 200 Hh49
Benejama E 29 Ku52
Benemérito de las Américas MEX (CHP) 183 Fe37
Bénéna RMM 137 Kh39
Bénéníkényi RMM 137 Kh39
Benenitra RM 157 Nc57
Benešov CZ 42 Lp41
Benevento I 37 Lp49
Benevides BR (PA) 195 Hf46
Benga MOC 152 Mg54
Benga MW 146 Mh52
Bengabad IND (JKD) 83 Pd33
Bengala CO 192 Gd43
Bengala IND (AAN) 88 Pg41
Bengamisa RDC 141 Mc45
Bengbis CAM 139 Lg44
Bengbu CHN (AHU) 78 Qj29
Benge USA (WA) 168 Ea22
Benghazi LAR 127 Ma29
Bengkalis RI 93 Qb45
Bengkalis RI 93 Qb45
Bengkulu RI 93 Qb47
Bengoi RI 97 Rf47
Bengough CDN (SK) 169 Eh21
Beng Per W.S. K 89 Qc39
Bengtsfors S 30 Ln31
Benguela ANG 150 Lg52
Ben Guerdane TN 126 Lf29
Ben Guerir MA 125 Kg29
Beni BOL 198 Gh51
Beni NEP 81 Pb31
Beni RDC 141 Me45
Beni-Abbès DZ 125 Kj30
Beni Barka TN 126 Lf29
Benicarló E 29 La50
Benicasim = Benicàssim E 29 La50
Benicàssim E 29 La50
Benidorm E 29 Ku52
Benifaió E 29 Ku51
Beni Hammad DZ 126 Lc28
Beni Haoua DZ 126 La27
Beni Hassan ET 129 Mf32
Beni Hassan el Shuruq ET 129 Mf32
Beni Kheddache TN 126 Lf29
Beni Mazâr ET 129 Mf31
Beni-Mellal MA 125 Kg29
Benin WAN 138 Lc43
Benin 123 La08
Benin City WAN 138 Lc42
Benin Iya WAN 138 Lc42
Beni-Ounif DZ 125 Kk29
Beni Saf DZ 125 Kk28
Benisheikh WAN 139 Lg40
Beni Slimane DZ 126 Lb27
Beni-Smir DZ/MA 125 Kk29
Beni Suêf ET 129 Mf31
Beni-Tajjite MA 125 Kj29
Benito CDN (MB) 172 Ek20
Benito Juárez MEX (CHH) 180 Eg30
Benito Juárez MEX (CHH) 180 Eg31
Benito Juárez MEX (TB) 183 Fd37
Benito Juárez MEX (ZCT) 182 Ej35
Benito Juárez RA (BA) 209 Ha64
Benito Juárez, P.N. MEX 182 Fb37
Benito Juárez (Sierra Hermosa) MEX (ZCT) 182 Ek34
Beni-Yal MA 125 Kj29
Benjamin USA (TX) 174 Fa29
Benjamín Aceval PY 204 Hb58
Benjamin Constant BR (AM) 196 Ge48
Benjamin Hill MEX (SO) 180 Ee30
Benjina RI 114 Rh49
Benkayang RI 95 Qe45
Benkelman USA (NE) 174 Ek25
Benkovac HR 35 Lq46
Ben Lavin Nature Reserve ZA 152 Me57
Ben Lawers GB 20 Kq34
Ben Lomond N.P. AUS (TAS) 111 Sd66
Ben Luc VN 89 Qd40
Ben Macdui GB 20 Kr33
Benmara AUS (NT) 106 Rj54
Ben Mehidi DZ 126 Ld27
Ben More GB 20 Ko34
Ben More GB 20 Kq34
Ben More Assynt GB 20 Kq32
Ben Moussa MA 125 Kg29
Benndale USA (MS) 175 Ff30
Bennetsville USA (SC) 178 Ga28
Bennett CDN (BC) 166 Dc16
Bennett USA (CO) 171 Eh26
Bennett Dam, W.A.C. CDN 166 Dj17
Ben Nevis GB 20 Kq34
Bennichchâb RIM 130 Kc36
Bennington USA (VT) 177 Gd24
Bénodet F 22 Kq43
Benoni ZA 155 Me59
Benoud DZ 125 La29
Bénoué = Benue WAN 138 Le42
Bénoué, P.N. de la CAM 139 Lg41
Bénoye TCH 140 Lj41
Ben Quang VN 87 Qd37
Ben S'Bour DZ 126 Lc28
Bensékou DY 138 Lb40
Bensheim D 33 Lj41
Ben-Slimane MA 125 Kg29
Benson USA (AZ) 171 Ee30
Benson USA (MN) 172 Fc23
Ben Starav GB 20 Kp34
Bent IR 64 Nk32
Benteng RI 96 Ra49
Benteng Belgica RI 97 Rf48
Bentia RMM 131 La38
Bentick Island MYA 88 Pj40
Bentinck Island AUS (QLD) 107 Rk54
Bentinck Sound MYA 88 Pj38
Bentiu SUD 141 Me41
Bentley CDN (AB) 169 Ec19
Bento Gonçalves BR (RS) 204 He60
Benton USA (AR) 174 Fd28
Benton USA (CA) 170 Ea27
Benton USA (IL) 175 Ff27
Benton USA (LA) 174 Fd29
Bentong MAL 92 Qa44
Benton Harbor USA (MI) 173 Fg24
Bentonsport USA (MO) 172 Fe25
Bentonsport Nat. Hist. District USA (MO) 172 Fe25
Bentota Beach CL 85 Ok42
Bentuang Karimun Nature Reserve RI 94 Qg45
Benty RG 136 Kd41
Benua RI 95 Qd45
Benue WAN 138 Ld41
Benwee Head IRL 19 Kl36
Benxi CHN (LNG) 76 Rb25
Benza ANG 148 Lg49
Benzdorp SME 194 Hc44
Ben-Ziareg DZ 125 Kk30
Beo RI 91 Rd43
Beoga RI 114 Rj47
Beograd SCG 44 Ma46
Beograd-Surcin SCG 44 Ma46
Beohari IND (MPH) 83 Pa33
Béoumi CI 137 Kh42
Beowawe USA (NV) 170 Eb25
Beppu J 79 Rf29
Beqa FJI 119 Tk55
Bequia WV 187 Gk39
Bequimão BR (MA) 195 Hh47
Ber RMM 131 Kj37
Berabevu RA (SF) 209 Gk62
Berahle ETH 142 Mk39
Beraketa RM 157 Nc58
Berakit Beach RI 93 Qc45
Beramanja RM 156 Ne52
Bérandjokou RCB 140 Lj44
Berangang RI 93 Qb46
Berasia IND (MPH) 82 Oj34
Beraspapan RI 95 Qh46
Berastagi RI 92 Pk44
Berat AL 46 Lu50
Berat Fortesë AL 46 Lu50
Beravina RM 157 Nc55
Beravy RM 157 Nc56
Berazino BY 48 Me19
Berazino BY 39 Mj36
Berbak National Park RI 93 Qb46
Berber SUD 135 Mg36
Berbera SP 143 Nc40
Berbérati RCA 140 Lh43
Berbinzana E 28 Kt48
Berceto I 34 Lk46
Berchtesgaden D 33 Ln43
Berchtesgaden, N.P. D 33 Ln43
Berck-Plage F 23 Lb40
Berdaale SP 145 Nb44
Berdale SP 143 Nd42
Berdía E 26 Km48
Berdjans'k UA 49 Mj22
Berdjans'ka kosa UA 49 Mj22
Berdsk RUS 54 Pa08
Berdyčiv UA 49 Me21
Bére TCH 140 Lj41
Berea USA (KY) 175 Fh27
Béréba BF 137 Kj40
Berebere RI 91 Re44
Bereeda SP 143 Nf40
Berega EAT 147 Mj49
Berehomet UA 43 Mf42
Berehove UA 43 Mc42
Bereina PNG 115 Sd50
Bereketa RM 157 Nc57
Bereku EAT 147 Mh48
Berekua WD 187 Gk38
Berekum GH 137 Kj42
Berendi TR 56 Mh27
Berenice ET 129 Mh34
Berens Island CDN 172 Fb19
Berens River CDN (MB) 172 Fb19
Berenty RM 157 Nc57
Bere Regis GB 21 Ks40
Beresford USA (SD) 172 Fb24
Berestečko UA 41 Mf40
Berestjane UA 41 Mf40
Berettyóújfalu H 43 Mb43
Berevo RM 157 Nc55
Berezanka UA 49 Mf22
Berezanskaja RUS 49 Mk23
Berežany UA 43 Me41
Berezinsky Biosphere Nature Reserve BY 39 Mj36
Berezna UA 48 Mf20
Berezne UA 48 Md20
Bereznehuvate UA 49 Mg22
Berezniki RUS 54 Nd07
Berežnycja UA 41 Mg39
Berga E 28 Lb48
Bergama TR 47 Mh51
Bergamo I 34 Lk45
Bergantin YV 193 Gh41
Bergantiños E 26 Km47
Bergara E 28 Ks47
Bergen D 32 Lk38
Bergen D 31 Lo36
Bergen N 30 Lf30
Berg en Dal SME 194 Hc43
Bergen op Zoom NL 23 Le39
Bergensbanen N 17 Ld15
Berger N 30 Ll31
Bergerac F 24 La46
Bergheim D 32 Lg40
Bergland CDN (ON) 172 Fc21
Bergland NAM 154 Lj57
Bergland USA (MI) 172 Ff22
Bergo FIN 38 Mb28
Bergo FIN 38 Mb28
Bergshamra S 31 Lt31
Bergsig NAM 150 Lh56
Bergsjö S 17 Lj15
Bergues F 23 Lc40
Bergville ZA 155 Me60
Berhait IND (JKD) 83 Pd33
Berhamapur IND (ORS) 83 Pc36
Berilo BR (MG) 203 Hj54
Beringarra AUS (WA) 104 Qj59
Beringen B 23 Lf39
Bering Glacier USA 166 Cj15
Bering Land Bridge National Preserve USA 165 Bh13
Bering Sea USA/RUS 162 Ba06
Bering Strait USA/RUS 160 Ba03
Berisu IR 57 Nc27
Berja E 27 Ks54
Berkåk N 16 Lf14
Berkane MA 125 Kj28
Berkeley USA (CA) 170 Dj27
Berkh MNG 70 Qf22
Berkner Island 6 Hc34
Berkovica BG 44 Md47
Berkovici BIH 44 Lt47
Berlanga E 27 Kp52
Berlanga de Duero E 28 Ks49
Berlenga P 27 Kl51
Berlevåg N 16 Me10
Berlin CO 192 Gd42
Berlin D 32 Lo38
Berlin USA (NH) 177 Ge23
Berlin USA (WI) 173 Ff24
Berlin, Mount 6 Da34
Bermagui AUS (NSW) 111 Sf64
Bermejillo MEX (DGO) 181 Ej33
Bermejo BOL 207 Gh57
Bermejo BOL/RA 207 Gh57
Bermejo PE 197 Gb51
Bermejo PE 197 Gb51
Bermejo RA 207 Gf61
Bermeo E 28 Ks47
Bermillo de Sayago E 26 Ko49
Bermo RN 132 Ld38
Bermuda GB 161 Gb06
Bermuda Islands GB 160 Gb06
Bern CH 34 Lh44
Bernabé Rivera ROU 204 Hb61
Bernalda I 37 Lr50
Bernalillo USA (NM) 171 Eg28
Bernardo C 186 Gc35
Bernardo USA (NM) 171 Eg28
Bernardo de Irigoyen RA (MI) 204 Hd59
Bernardo O'Higgins, P.N. RCH 210 Gc70
Bernartice CZ 42 Lp41
Bernāti LV 39 Ma34
Bernau D 32 Lo38
Bernaville F 23 Lc40
Bernay F 22 La41
Bernburg D 32 Lm39
Berndorf A 35 Lr43
Berne CH 34 Lh44
Berner Alpen CH 34 Lh44
Berneray GB 20 Kn33
Berner Oberland CH 34 Lg44
Bernham USA (TX) 174 Fb30
Bernice USA (LA) 175 Fd29
Bernier Island AUS 104 Qg58
Bernkastel-Kues D 33 Lh41
Bernsdorf D 32 Lp39
Berón de Astrada RA (CR) 204 Hb59
Beronovo BG 45 Mg48
Beroroha RM 157 Nc56
Beroun CZ 42 Lp41
Berounka CZ 42 Lo41
Berovo MK 44 Mc49
Berraha DZ 126 Ld27
Berraondo RA (BA) 209 Gj65
Berrechid MA 125 Kg29
Berre-l'Étang F 25 Lf47
Berri AUS (SA) 110 Sa63
Berriane DZ 126 Lb29
Berridale AUS (NSW) 111 Se64
Berrigan AUS (NSW) 111 Sc63
Berrima AUS (NSW) 111 Sf63
Berrouaghia DZ 126 Lb27
Berrydale USA (FL) 175 Fg30
Berry Islands BS 179 Gb33
Berryville USA (AR) 174 Fd27
Berryville USA (VA) 177 Gb26
Beršad' UA 49 Me21
Berseba NAM 154 Lj59
Bersenbrück D 32 Lh38
Berteştii de Jos RO 45 Mh46
Bertincourt F 23 Ld40
Bertinho BR (PA) 195 He47
Bertolínia BR (PI) 201 Hj49
Bertoua CAM 139 Lg43
Bertrand CDN (NB) 176 Gh22
Bertrix B 23 Lf41
Bertwell CDN (SK) 169 Ej19
Beruniy UZ 62 Oa25
Beruri BR (AM) 198 Gk47
Beruwala CL 85 Ok42
Berwick AUS (VIC) 111 Sc64
Berwick CDN (NB) 176 Gh23
Berwick USA (PA) 177 Gb25
Berwick-upon-Tweed GB 20 Ks35
Beryslav UA 49 Mg22
Berzence H 42 Ls44
Bērzpils LV 39 Mh34
Besakih RI 95 Qh50
Besalampy RM 157 Nc54
Besalú E 28 Lc48
Besançon F 25 Lg43
Besani IND (MPH) 83 Pa33
Bešankovičy BY 48 Me18
Besar MAL 92 Qb44
Besar MAL 92 Qc44
Besar RI 96 Rb50
Besar, Gunung RI 95 Qg48
Besassi DY 138 Lb40
Beschoky tau KZ 62 Ng23
Besedino RUS 48 Mj20
Besenyszög H 43 Ma43
Beshahr IR 62 Ng27
Besham PK 63 Og28
Beshariq UZ 63 Of25
Beshkent UZ 63 Oc26
Beshneh IR 64 Nh31
Beshtom UZ 62 Oa24
Besikama RI 97 Rc50
Besir RI 97 Rf46
Beskid Mountains PL/SK 43 Mb41
Beskid Wysoki PL 41 Lu41
Beslan RUS (SOA) 57 Nc24
Besni TR 56 Mj27
Bessa Monteiro ANG 148 Lg49
Béssao TCH 140 Lh42
Bessarabia MD 48 Me22
Bessaz tau KZ 63 Oe24
Bessèges F 25 Le46
Bessemer USA (AL) 175 Fg29
Bessoung Kang CAM 138 Le43
Best NL 23 Lf39
Bestavarapeta IND (APH) 85 Ok38
Bestwig D 32 Lj39
Besuki RI 95 Qg49
Beswick AUS (NT) 106 Rg53
Beswick A.L. AUS 106 Rg53
Beta IND (BIH) 83 Pb33
Betafo RM 157 Nd55
Betalevana RM 157 Ne54
Betanantanana RM 157 Nc55
Betancuria E 124 Kc31
Betânia BR (MT) 206 Gk53
Betânia BR (PE) 201 Ja50
Betania CO 192 Gd43
Betânia, T.I. BR 198 Gf47
Betanty RM 157 Nc58
Betanzos BOL 206 Gh55
Betanzos E 26 Km47
Betarara VU 118 Te53
Bétaré Oya CAM 139 Lh43
Betatakin Ruin USA 171 Ee27
Bete Hor ETH 142 Mk40
Betein WAN 138 Le43
Bétera E 29 Ku51
Beteta E 29 Ks50
Bethal ZA 155 Me59
Bethanie NAM 154 Lj59
Bethany USA (MO) 174 Fc25
Bethel USA (AK) 164 Bk15
Bethel USA (OK) 174 Fc28
Bethlehem IL 58 Mh30
Bethlehem ZA 155 Me60
Bethulie ZA 155 Mc61
Béthune F 23 Lc40
Betim BR (MG) 203 Hh55
Betioky RM 157 Nc57
Betita DZ 126 Ld28
Betong MAL 94 Qf45
Betong THA 89 Qa43
Betoota AUS (QLD) 108 Sa58
Bétou RCB 140 Lk44
Betpak Dala KZ 54 Ob09
Betrandraka RM 157 Nd54
Betroka RM 157 Nd57
Betsaa RB 151 Mb55
Bet Shean IL 56 Mh29
Betsiaka RM 156 Ne52
Betsy Bay BS 186 Gd34
Bettiah IND (BIH) 83 Pc32
Bettié CI 137 Kj42
Bettiesdam ZA 155 Me59
Bettles USA (AK) 165 Ce12
Bettloua DZ 125 Kk28
Bettna S 31 Lr32
Béttola I 34 Lk46
Betton F 22 Kt42
Bettyhill GB 20 Kq32
Betul IND (MPH) 82 Oj35
Betulia CO 192 Gb42
Betung RI 93 Qc47
Betws-y-Coed GB 21 Kr37
Betzdorf D 32 Lh40
Béu ANG 148 Lh49
Beulah AUS (VIC) 110 Sb63
Beulah USA (MI) 173 Fg23
Beulah USA (ND) 172 Ek22
Beulaville USA (NC) 178 Gb28
Beurfou TCH 133 Lh38
Beurkia TCH 133 Lj38
Beurkié TCH 133 Lj36
Bevato RM 157 Nd55
Beveren B 23 Le39
Beverley AUS (WA) 104 Qj62
Beverley GB 21 Ku37
Beverly CDN (SK) 169 Ef20
Beverly Hills USA (FL) 178 Fj31
Beverly Springs AUS (WA) 103 Rc54
Beverstedt D 32 Lj37
Beverungen D 32 Lk39
Bevoalavo Andrefana RM 157 Nc58
Bevoay RM 157 Nb56
Bewani PNG 115 Sa47
Bewar IND (UPH) 81 Ok32
Bewar IND (UPH) 83 Ok33
Beyağaç TR 47 Mj53
Beyazçeşme Şelâlesi TR 57 Nb26
Beyçayırı TR 45 Mg50
Beydağ TR 47 Mj52
Bey Dağları TR 56 Mf27
Beykoz TR 45 Mk49
Beyla RG 136 Kf41
Beylaqan AZ 57 Nd26
Beylul ER 142 Nb39
Beypazarı TR 56 Mf25
Beypore IND (KER) 84 Oh40
Beyra SP 143 Nd42
Beyşehir TR 56 Mf27
Beyşehir Gölü TR 56 Mf27
Beytüşşebap TR 57 Nb27
Bezaha RM 157 Nc57
Bežanickaja vozvyšennost' RUS 48 Me17
Bežanicy RUS 48 Me17
Bezanson CDN (AB) 167 Ea18
Bezas E 29 Kt50
Bezdan SCG 44 Lt45
Bežeck RUS 48 Mj17
Bežeckij verhnij RUS 48 Mj17
Bezeklik Qianfo Dong CHN 67 Pe24
Bezerros BR (PE) 201 Jc50
Béziers F 25 Ld47
Bez'va RUS 38 Mj32
Bhabbar IND (GUJ) 82 Of33
Bhabua IND (BIH) 83 Pb33
Bhadasar IND (RJT) 80 Oh31
Bhadora IND (MPH) 83 Pa34
Bhadra IND (RJT) 80 Oh31
Bhadrachalam IND (APH) 83 Pa37
Bhadrakh IND (ORS) 83 Pd35
Bhadrapur NEP 86 Pe32
Bhadravati IND (KTK) 84 Oh39
Bhadra W.S. IND 84 Oh39
Bhadreswar IND (WBG) 86 Pe34
Bhag PK 65 Od31
Bhagalpur IND (BIH) 83 Pd33
Bhagamandala IND (KTK) 84 Oh39
Bhaguapura IND (MPH) 83 Ok32
Bhainsrorgarh IND 82 Oh33
Bhai Pheru PK 65 Og30
Bhairab Bazar BD 86 Pf33
Bhairamgarh IND (CGH) 83 Pa36
Bhairi Hol PK 65 Oc33
Bhaisa IND (APH) 82 Oj36
Bhakarapeta IND (APH) 85 Ok39
Bhakkar PK 65 Of30
Bhaktapur NEP 81 Pc32
Bhalki IND (KTK) 82 Oj37
Bhaluka BD 86 Pf33
Bhalwal PK 65 Og29
Bhamo MYA 86 Pj33
Bhanbore PK 65 Od33
Bhandara IND (MHT) 83 Ok35
Bhandari IND (NGL) 86 Ph32
Bhandarwah 80 Oh29
Bhander IND (MPH) 83 Ok33
Bhanga BD 86 Pf34
Bhanjanagar IND (ORS) 83 Pc36
Bhanpura IND (MPH) 82 Oj33
Bhanupratappur IND (CGH) 83 Pa35
Bhaptiahi IND (BIH) 83 Pd32
Bharatpur IND (RJT) 81 Oj32
Bharatpur NEP 81 Pc32
Bharatpur National Park = Keoladeo National Park IND 80 Oj32
Bharda NEP 83 Pd32
Bharthana IND (UPH) 83 Ok32
Bharuch IND (GUJ) 82 Og35
Bhata NEP 83 Pc32
Bhatagli IND (MHT) 82 Oj36
Bhatapara IND (CGH) 83 Pa35
Bhatgaon IND (CGH) 83 Pb35
Bhatiapara BD 86 Pe34
Bhatkal IND (KTK) 84 Oh39
Bhattiprolu IND (APH) 83 Pa37
Bhaun PK 65 Og29
Bhavani IND (TNU) 84 Oj40
Bhavnagar IND (GUJ) 82 Og35
Bhawal N.P. BD 86 Pf33
Bhawana PK 65 Og30
Bhawanipatna IND (ORS) 83 Pb36
Bhawra IND (MPH) 82 Oj34
Bheemunipatnam IND (APH) 83 Pb37
Bheemunipatnam Beach IND 83 Pb37
Bhelsi IND (MPH) 83 Ok33
Bhera PK 65 Og29
Bherdaghat Marble Rocks IND 83 Ok34
Bheri River Rafting NEP 81 Pb31
Bhigvan IND (MHT) 82 Oh36
Bhikamkor IND (RJT) 80 Og32
Bhilai IND (CGH) 83 Pa35
Bhilwara IND (RJT) 82 Oh33
Bhim IND (RJT) 82 Oh33
Bhimavaram IND (APH) 83 Pa37
Bhimbar PK 65 Oh29
Bhimbetka IND 82 Oj34
Bhimpur IND (MPH) 82 Oj35
Bhind IND (MPH) 83 Ok32
Bhinmal IND (RJT) 82 Og33
Bhisi IND (MHT) 83 Ok35
Bhita IND 83 Pa33
Bhitarkanika Sanctuary IND 83 Pd35
Bhitarwar IND (MPH) 83 Ok33
Bhiwandi IND (MHT) 82 Og36
Bhiwani IND (HYA) 80 Oj31
Bhognipur IND (UPH) 83 Ok32
Bhojpur IND (ORS) 83 Pc35
Bhojpur IND 82 Oj34
Bhokar IND (MHT) 82 Oj36
Bhola BD 86 Pf34
Bholari PK 65 Oe33
Bhongaon IND (UPH) 81 Ok32
Bhongir IND (APH) 83 Ok37
Bhopal IND (MPH) 82 Oj34
Bhopalpatnam IND (CGH) 83 Pa36
Bhoramdeo IND (CGH) 83 Pa34
Bhore IND (BIH) 83 Pc32
Bhorvadi IND (MHT) 82 Oh36
Bhuban IND (ORS) 83 Pc35
Bhubaneswar IND (ORS) 83 Pc35
Bhuj IND (GUJ) 82 Oe34
Bhusawal IND (MHT) 82 Oh35
Bhutan BHT 86 Pe32
Biadola IND (WBG) 86 Pe33
Biafra WAN 138 Le43
Biak RI 96 Rb46
Biak RI 114 Rj46
Biak RI 114 Rj46
Biak Utara Nature Reserve RI 114 Rh46
Biała Piska PL 41 Mc37
Biała Podlaska PL 41 Md38
Białka PL 41 Ma41
Białobrzegi PL 41 Ma39
Białobrzegi PL 41 Mc40
Białogard PL 40 Lq36
Białopole PL 41 Md40
Białowieski P.N. PL 41 Md37
Białowieża PL 41 Md38
Biały Bór PL 40 Lr37
Białystok PL 41 Md37
Bianco I 37 Lr52
Bianga RCA 140 Ma43
Biankouma CI 137 Kg42
Bia N.P. GH 137 Kj42
Biaora IND (MPH) 82 Oj34
Biaranga RDC 149 Lk46
Biaro RDC 141 Mc45
Biaro RI 91 Rc44
Biarritz F 24 Kt47
Biasca CH 34 Lj44
Biawak MAL 94 Qe45
Bibâ ET 129 Mf31
Biba RI 93 Qc48
Bibai J 77 Sa24
Bibala ANG 150 Lg53
Bibas G 139 Lf45
Bibbiena I 34 Lm47
Bibé CAM 139 Lg43
Bibémi CAM 139 Lg41
Biberach D 33 Lk42
Bibiani GH 137 Kj42
Bibi-Jawindi Mausoleum PK 65 Of31
Bibikovo RUS 71 Rd20
Bibile CL 85 Pa42
Bibi Nani PK 65 Od31
Biboohra AUS (QLD) 107 Sc54
Bibora G 148 Lf47
Bibrka UA 43 Me41
Bicade F 194 Hd44
Bicaj AL 44 Ma49
Bicanak asr. ARM/AZ 57 Nc26
Bicas BR (MG) 203 Hj56
Bicaz RO 49 Md22
Bicester GB 21 Kt39
Bičevaja RUS 77 Rh22
Bichena ETH 142 Mk40
Bicheng CHN (CGQ) 74 Qd31
Bicheno AUS (TAS) 111 Se66
Bichhia IND (MPH) 83 Pa34
Bichhua IND (MPH) 83 Ok35
Bichi WAN 138 Le39
Bickerton Island AUS 106 Rj52
Bicol N.P. RP 90 Rb39
Bicske H 43 Lt43
Bicuar, P.N. do ANG 150 Lh53
Bičura RUS (BUR) 70 Qd20
Bid IND (MHT) 82 Oh36
Bida WAN 138 Ld41
Bida WAN 139 Lg39
Bidar IND (KTK) 82 Oj37
Bidar Fort IND 82 Oj37
Bidbid OM 61 Nk34
Bidde SP 145 Nb45
Biddeford USA (ME) 177 Ge24
Biddle USA (MT) 169 Eh23
Bideford GB 21 Kq39
Bidgemia AUS (WA) 104 Qh58
Bidokht IR 64 Nk28
Bidon V DZ 132 La34
Bidor MAL 92 Qa43
Bidukbiduk RI 91 Qk45
Bidžan RUS (YAO) 76 Rf22
Bie S 31 Lr31
Biebrzański Park Narodowy PL 41 Mc37
Biecz PL 41 Mb41
Biedenkopf D 32 Lj40
Biéha BF 137 Kk40
Biei J 77 Sb24
Biel = Bienne CH 34 Lh43
Biel E 28 Ku48
Bielawa PL 40 Lr40
Bielefeld D 32 Lj38
Bieler See CH 34 Lh43
Bielice PL 41 Lu37
Biella I 34 Lj45
Biélou CI 137 Kg41
Bielsa E 28 La48
Bielsk PL 41 Lu38
Bielsko-Biała PL 41 Lu41
Bielsk Podlaski PL 41 Md38
Bienenbüttel D 32 Ll37
Bienfait CDN (SK) 169 Ej21
Bienge RDC 149 Lk48
Bien Hoa VN 89 Qd40
Bieniów PL 40 Lq39
Bienne = Biel CH 34 Lh43
Bierbank AUS (QLD) 109 Sc59
Bierdzany PL 40 Lt40
Biertan RO 43 Me44
Bierutów PL 40 Ls39
Biescas E 28 Ku48
Biesiekierz PL 40 Lr36
Biesiesvlei ZA 155 Mc59
Bieszczady PL 43 Mc41
Bieszczadzki P.N. PL 43 Mc41
Bièvre B 23 Lf41
Bieżuń PL 41 Lu38
Bifoulé CAM 139 Lg43
Bifoun G 148 Lf46
Bifuka J 77 Sb23
Biga TR 45 Mh50
Bigadiç TR 47 Mj51
Big Ambergris Cay GB 186 Ge35
Bigand RA (SF) 209 Gk62
Biga Yarımadası TR 45 Mg50
Big Baldy USA 168 Ec23
Big Bear Creek CDN (BC) 168 Dj20
Big Beaver CDN (SK) 169 Eh21
Big Belt Mts. USA 169 Ee22
Big Bend SD 155 Mf59
Big Bend N.P. USA 181 Ej31
Big Branch Marsh N.W.R. USA 175 Fe30
Big Brook CDN 177 Hb20
Big Creek CDN (BC) 168 Dj20
Big Creek USA (ID) 168 Ec23
Big Cypress Seminole Ind. Res. USA 179 Fk32
Big Desert AUS 110 Sa63
Big Desert Wilderness Park AUS 110 Sa63
Bigene GNB 136 Kc39
Big Falls USA (MN) 172 Fd21
Bigfork USA (MT) 168 Ec21
Biggar CDN (SK) 169 Eg19
Biggar GB 20 Kr35
Bigge Island AUS 103 Rc53
Biggenden AUS (QLD) 109 Sg58
Biggleswade GB 21 Ku38
Big Hole ZA 155 Mc60
Big Hole Nat. Battlefield USA 168 Ed23
Bighorn USA (MT) 169 Eg22
Bighorn Basin USA 169 Ef23
Bighorn Canyon N.R.A. USA 169 Ef23
Bighorn Mountains USA 169 Eg23
Bight of Bangkok T 88 Qa39
Bight of Benin 138 Lb43
Bight of Biafra 138 Ld43
Bigi Polka SME 194 Hc43
Big Island CDN (AB) 167 Ed16
Big Island CDN 167 Eb15
Big Island CDN 172 Fc21
Big Koniuji Island USA 164 Ca18
Big Lagoon Z 146 Mg52
Big Lake USA (TX) 174 Ek30
Big Lake Ranch CDN (BC) 168 Dk19
Bignona SN 136 Kb39
Bigo Bya Mugenyei EAU 144 Mf45
Big Pine USA (CA) 170 Ea27
Big Pine USA (FL) 179 Fk33
Big Piney USA (WY) 171 Ee24
Big Pond CDN (NS) 176 Gk23
Big Rapids USA (MI) 173 Fh24
Big Red Lighthouse USA 173 Fg24
Big River CDN (SK) 169 Eg19
Big River Ind. Res. CDN 169 Eg19
Big River Roadhouse USA (AK) 165 Cc14
Big Rock USA (CA) 170 Eb29
Big Salmon Range CDN 166 Dd15
Big Salmon River CDN 166 Dc15
Big Sandy USA (MT) 169 Ee21
Big Sandy USA (WY) 171 Ef24
Big Sky USA (MT) 169 Ee23
Big Smokey Valley USA 170 Eb26
Big Snow Mtn. USA 169 Ef22
Big South Fork Nat. River and Rec. Area USA 175 Fh27
Big Spring USA (TX) 174 Ek29
Big Stone CDN (AB) 169 Ee20
Big Stone N.W.R. USA 172 Fb23
Big Sur USA (CA) 170 Dk27
Big Timber USA (MT) 169 Ef23
Big Trails USA (WY) 169 Eg24
Biguaçu BR (SC) 205 Hf59
Big Water USA (UT) 171 Ee27
Big Wood Cay BS 179 Gb33
Bihać BIH 35 Lq46
Bihar IND 83 Pc33
Biharamulo EAT 144 Mf47
Biharamulo Game Reserve EAT 144 Mf47
Biharia RO 43 Mb43
Bihariganj IND (BIH) 83 Pd33
Biharkeresztes H 43 Mb43
Biharnagybajom H 43 Mb43
Bihar Sharif IND (BIH) 83 Pc33
Bihé Plateau ANG 150 Lj52
Bihoro J 77 Sc24
Bihoua RCB 148 Lg47
Bihpur IND (BIH) 83 Pd33
Bijainagar IND (RJT) 82 Oh33
Bijaipur IND (MPH) 82 Oj32
Bijapur IND (CGH) 83 Pa36
Bijapur IND (KTK) 82 Oh37
Bijapur IND (ORS) 83 Pb36
Bijar IR 57 Nd28
Bijawar IND (MPH) 83 Ok33
Bijbehara 80 Oh29
Bijeljina BIH 44 Lu46
Bijelo Polje SCG 44 Lu47
Bijie CHN (GZH) 87 Qc32
Bijnapalli IND (APH) 82 Ok37
Bijnor IND (UPH) 81 Ok31
Bijoutier SY 145 Ng49
Bijsk RUS 54 Pb08
Bikaner IND (RJT) 80 Og31
Bikapur IND (UPH) 83 Pb32
Bikin RUS 77 Rh22
Bikini Atoll MH 10 Ta08
Bikita ZW 152 Mf56
Bikok CAM 139 Lf44
Bikori SUD 135 Mh40
Bikoro RDC 149 Lk46
Bikou CHN (GSU) 72 Qc29
Bikramganj IND (BIH) 83 Pc33
Bikubiti LAR/TCH 133 Lk34
Bikumpur IND (RJT) 80 Og32
Bila Cerkva UA 49 Mf21
Bilad Bani Bu Ali OM 61 Nk34
Bilad Bani Bu Hasan OM 61 Nk34
Bilala RCB 148 Lg48
Bilanga BF 137 Kk39
Bilanga G 148 Lf47
Bilara IND (RJT) 80 Og32
Bilaspur IND (CGH) 83 Pb34
Bilaspur IND (HPH) 81 Oj30
Bilaspur IND (UPH) 81 Pa32
Bilassana RG 136 Kf41
Bilauktaung Range MYA/THA 88 Pk39
Bilbao = Bilbo E 28 Ks47
Bilbeis ET 129 Mf30
Bilbo = Bilbao E 28 Ks47
Bilbor RO 43 Mf43
Bílčice CZ 42 Ls41
Bíldudalur IS 18 Jr25
Bileća BIH 44 Lt48
Bilecik TR 56 Me25
Biled RO 44 Ma45
Bilehra IND (UPH) 81 Pa32
Bilesha Plain EAK 145 Na45
Bilesuvar AZ 57 Ne26
Biłgoraj PL 41 Mc40
Bilgorod-Dnistrovs'kij UA 49 Mf22
Bilgram IND (UPH) 81 Pa32
Bilhaur IND (UPH) 83 Pa32
Bili RDC 140 Lk43
Bili RDC 141 Mc43
Biliali Koyra RMM 131 Kk37
Bilibino RUS 55 Tb05
Bilin MYA 88 Pj37
Bílina CZ 42 Lo40
Biling La CHN/NEP 68 Pa30
Biliran Island RP 90 Rc40
Biliri WAN 139 Lf41
Bilisht AL 46 Ma50
Bilis Qoogaaoi SP 145 Na45
Bilje HR 35 Lt45
Bilka BG 45 Mh48
Bill USA (WY) 169 Eh24
Billabong Roadhouse AUS (WA) 104 Qh59
Billa Kalina AUS (SA) 108 Rj60
Billdal S 30 Lm33
Billengarrah AUS (NT) 106 Rh53
Billiluna AUS (WA) 103 Rd55
Billiluna A.L. AUS 103 Rd55
Billingen S 31 Lo32
Billingnooka AUS (WA) 102 Ra57
Billings USA (MT) 169 Ef23
Billingsfors S 30 Ln32
Bill of Portland GB 21 Ks40
Billom F 25 Ld45
Billun IND (RJT) 80 Oh31
Billy Island BS 179 Ga33
Bilma RN 133 Lg36
Biloela AUS (QLD) 109 Sf58
Bilohors'k UA 49 Mh23
Bilokurakyne UA 48 Mk21
Biloo SP 145 Nb45
Bilopillja UA 48 Mh20
Bílovec CZ 42 Ls41
Bilovods'k UA 48 Mk21
Biloxi USA (MS) 175 Ff30
Bilqâs Qism Auwal ET 129 Mf30
Biltine TCH 134 Ma38
Bilto N 16 Ma11
Bilugyun MYA 88 Pj37
Bilungala RI 91 Rb45
Bilverdi IR 57 Nd26
Bilwi = Puerto Cabezas NIC 185 Fj38
Bima RI 96 Qk50
Bimba CAM 139 Lh43
Bimbe ANG 150 Lh51
Bimbéréke DY 138 Lb40
Bimbijy AUS (WA) 104 Qk60
Bimbila GH 137 La41
Bimbo RCA 140 Lk43
Bimini Islands BS 179 Ga33
Bina Etawa IND (MPH) 83 Ok33
Binalbagan RP 90 Rb40
Binanga RI 93 Pk45
Binarowa PL 41 Mb41
Binauhan Falls RP 90 Rc39
Binbee AUS (QLD) 107 Sd56
Binche B 23 Le40
Binchuan CHN (YUN) 87 Qa33
Bindé BF 137 Kk40
Binder TCH 140 Lh41
Bindi Bindi AUS (WA) 104 Qj61
Bindki IND (UPH) 83 Pa32
Bindloe = Isla Marchena EC 197 Fe45
Bindoy RP 90 Rb41
Bindu RDC 149 Lk49
Bindura ZW 152 Mf54
Binéfar E 28 La49
Bin-el-Ouidane MA 125 Kg29
Binga EAT 147 Mk49
Binga ZW 152 Md54
Bingara AUS (NSW) 109 Sf60
Bing Bong AUS (NT) 106 Rj53
Bingen D 33 Lh41
Binger USA (OK) 174 Fa28
Bingham GB 21 Ku38
Bingham USA (MA) 176 Gf23
Bingham USA (NM) 171 Eg29
Binghamton USA (NY) 177 Gc24
Bin Ghashir LAR 127 Lg29
Bin Ghaylan YE 60 Nc38
Bingintelok RI 93 Qb47
Binglingsi Shiku CHN 72 Qb28
Bingmei CHN (GZH) 74 Qe33
Bingöl TR 57 Na26
Bingöl Dağları TR 57 Na26
Bingsjö S 17 Lh15
Binhai CHN (JGS) 78 Qk28
Binh Chanh VN 89 Qd40
Binh Chau Hot Springs VN 89 Qd40
Binh Dinh VN 89 Qe39
Binh Gia VN 87 Qd35
Binh Lu VN 87 Qb34
Binh Son VN 89 Qe38
Binibihali PNG 116 Sf51
Bini Erde TCH 133 Lk35
Binjai RI 92 Pk44
Bin Jawwad LAR 127 Lk30
Binkolo WAL 136 Ke41
Bin Lam VN 89 Qe38
Binnaway AUS (NSW) 109 Se61
Binneringie AUS (WA) 105 Rb61
Binongko RI 97 Rc48
Binpur IND (WBG) 83 Pd34
Binscarth CDN (MB) 172 Ek20
Bintagoungou RMM 131 Kj37
Bintan RI 93 Qc45
Binthalya AUS (WA) 104 Qh58
Bintuhan RI 93 Qb48
Bintulu MAL 94 Qg44
Bintumani, Mount WAL 136 Ke41
Bintuni RI 114 Rg47
Binur IND (CGH) 83 Pa36
Bin Xian CHN (HLG) 76 Rd23
Bin Xian CHN (SAA) 72 Qe28
Binyang CHN (GZG) 74 Qe34
Binz D 32 Lo36
Binzhou CHN (SDG) 73 Qk27
Bio Addo SP 145 Nc44
Bioča SCG 44 Lu48
Biograd na moru HR 35 Lq47
Biogradska Gora, N.P. SCG 44 Lu48
Biokovo HR 35 Ls47
Biosphärenreservat Pfälzerwald Nordvogesen D/F 33 Lh41
Biosphere II USA 171 Ee29
Biosphere Reserve (Issyk-Kul) KS 66 Oj24
Biotopo del Quetzal GCA 184 Fe38
Biotopo Monterrico-Hawaii GCA 184 Fe39
Biougra MA 124 Kf30
Bipindi CAM 138 Lf44
Bipok CAM 138 Lf43
Biquinhas BR (MG) 203 Hh55
Bira RUS (YAO) 76 Rg21
Bira Beach Resort RI 96 Ra48
Bi'r Abu Zaïma SUD 134 Me38
Birak LAR 127 Lh32
Bi'r al 'Akkariyah LAR 127 Lk30
Bi'r al 'Alaqah LAR 127 Lh31
Bi'r al 'Atrun SUD 134 Md36
Bi'r al Awyan LAR 128 Mc30
Bi'r al Banakish LAR 127 Ma30
Bi'r al Fatiyah LAR 127 Lh31
Bi'r al Ghanam LAR 127 Lg29
Bi'r al Ghararah LAR 127 Ma30
Bir al Guzayyil LAR 126 Lf31
Bir 'Ali YE 60 Ne38
Bir Ali Ben Khélifa TN 126 Lf28
Bi'r al Jadid LAR 127 Lg32
Bi'r al Kammuniyan LAR 127 Lj31
Bi'r al Khawr LAR 127 Lg30
Bi'r Allaq LAR 126 Lf30
Bi'r al Mastutah LAR 127 Lh33
Bi'r al Muwaylih LAR 127 Lk31
Bi'r al Qaf LAR 127 Lh31
Bi'r al Qataf LAR 128 Mb30
Bi'r al 'Utaylah LAR 127 Lj30
Bi'r al Washkah LAR 127 Lh31
Birampur IND (WBG) 83 Pd35
Bîr 'Amrâne RIM 131 Kf34
Biramsar IND (RJT) 80 Of32
Bir Anzarane DARS 130 Kc34
Birao RCA 134 Mb40
Bi'r ar Rijl LAR 127 Lh31
Bi'r ash Shahwi LAR 127 Lh30
Biratnagar NEP 83 Pd32
Biratori J 77 Sb24
Bi'r A'yad LAR 127 Lg29
Bîr Bel Guerdâne RIM 124 Ke33
Bi'r Ben Ghimah LAR 127 Ma30
Bir Beria TN 126 Le29
Bi'r Bin 'Isa LAR 127 Lh30
Bi'r Bu al Ghurab LAR 127 Lg30
Birch Creek USA (AK) 165 Ch12
Birchenough Bridge ZW 152 Mg55
Birches USA (AK) 165 Cd13
Birch Hills CDN (SK) 169 Eh19
Birchi WAN 138 Ld39
Birchip AUS (VIC) 111 Sb63
Birchiş RO 44 Mc45
Birch Island CDN 172 Fa19
Birch Mountains CDN (AB) 167 Ed17
Birch River CDN (MB) 169 Ek19
Bircot ETH 143 Nb42
Bircza PL 41 Mc41
Bi'r Dhu'fan LAR 127 Lh30
Bir Di SUD 141 Me42
Bird Island = Île aux Vaches SY 145 Nh47
Bird Island ZA 154 Lk62
Bir Djedid DZ 126 Ld29
Bir Dolmane DZ 126 Le30
Bird Rock Lighthouse BS 186 Gc34
Birdsville AUS (QLD) 108 Rk58
Birdsville Race AUS 108 Rk58
Birdtail CDN (MB) 172 Ek20
Birecik TR 56 Mk27
Bire Kpatuos Game Reserve SUD 141 Me43
Bir el Amdar DZ 126 Ld29
Bir El-Ater DZ 126 Le28
Bir el Fakama SUD 135 Mg37
Bir el Gâreb RIM 130 Kb35
Bir el Ghorifa TN 126 Lf29
Bir el Hasa SUD 129 Mh34
Birendranagar NEP 81 Pa31
Bir en Nugeim SUD 135 Mh36
Biretwa EAK 144 Mh45
Bireuen RI 92 Pj43
Bir Fadil KSA 61 Ne34
Bir Fanoidig SUD 135 Mh36
Bir Faysan KSA 60 Ne35
Bir Fegoussi TN 126 Le29
Birfel'd RUS (YAO) 76 Rg21
Bi'r Furawiya SUD 134 Mb38
Bir Gandouz DARS 130 Kb35
Birganj NEP 83 Pc32
Birgi TR 47 Mj52
Birgudi IND (CGH) 83 Pa35
Bir Hadi KSA 61 Nf36
Birhan ETH 142 Mj40
Bi'r Hasanah ET 129 Mg30
Bir Hatab SUD 129 Mg35
Bir Hismet ,Umar SUD 129 Mh35
Biri N 17 Lf15
Biri SUD 141 Md42
Biria EAT 146 Mg50
Birigüi BR (SP) 202 He56
Biri Island RP 90 Rc39
Birini RCA 140 Mb42
Biritingas BR (BA) 201 Ja51
Birjand IR 64 Nk29
Bir Jaydah KSA 58 Mj32
Bir-Jdid MA 125 Kg29
Bi'r Jimi LAR 127 Lh29
Bi'r Jubni LAR 128 Mc30
Birka S 31 Ls31
Birkat al 'Aqabah IRQ 59 Nb30
Birkat al Jumaymah KSA 59 Nb31
Birkat Saira SUD 134 Mb39
Birkeland N 30 Lh32
Birkeland N 30 Lj32
Birkelane SN 130 Kc38
Birkenau PL 41 Lu41
Birkenfeld D 33 Lh41
Birkenhead AUS (QLD) 109 Sd58
Birkenhead GB 21 Kr37
Birkerød DK 30 Ln35
Bi'r Khalaf Allah LAR 127 Lg32
Bir Kiau SUD 135 Mh35
Bir Labasoi SUD 129 Mh35
Birlik KZ 66 Og23
Birlik KZ 66 Og24
Bir Mahmoud TN 126 Le29
Birmingham GB 21 Ks38
Birmingham USA (AL) 175 Fg29
Birmitrapur IND (ORS) 83 Pc34
Bîr Mogreïn RIM 124 Ke33
Bi'r Mudakim LAR 127 Lg29
Bir Nawari SUD 135 Mh35
Bir Nazsirah LAR 126 Lf30
Birni Gwari WAN 138 Ld40
Birni-Keebi WAN 138 Lc39
Birnim RN 132 Le38
Birnin Gaouré RN 132 Lb39
Birnin Konni RN 132 Lc39
Birnin Kudu WAN 138 Le40
Birnin Lallé RN 132 Ld38
Birnin-Yauri WAN 138 Lc40
Birniwa WAN 138 Lf39
Birnni DY 138 La41
Birnon IND (UPH) 83 Pb33
Biro DY 138 Lb41
Birobidžan RUS (YAO) 76 Rg21
Birou RMM 130 Kf38
Bir Ounâne RMM 131 Kj35
Birpara IND (WBG) 86 Pe32
Bir Qar'at ad Dibah LAR 126 Le31
Bi'r Qaryas LAR 127 Lj31
Birr IRL 19 Kn37
Birricannia AUS (QLD) 109 Sc57
Birrimba Out Station AUS (NT) 106 Rg53
Birrindudu AUS (NT) 103 Re55
Bir Salala SUD 129 Mh35
Birsay GB 20 Kr31
Bir Senia DZ 125 Kk29
Bir Shalatayn ET 129 Mh34
Bir Shari KSA 59 Nb32
Birsilpur IND (RJT) 80 Og31
Bir Slougui TN 126 Lf29
Bir Soltane TN 126 Le29
Birštonas LT 39 Me36
Bi'r Tabankurt LAR 127 Lg32
Bir Taleb RIM 130 Kf37
Bir-Tam-Tam MA 125 Kh29
Bi'r Tanjdar LAR 128 Mb30
Bi'r Taziet LAR 127 Lg33
Bir Tegheri LAR 126 Lf32
Birthplace of Mahatma Gandhi IND 82 Oe35
Birthplace of Sun Yat-sen CHN 75 Qg34
Birti SUD 135 Mg36
Bi'r Tin Abunda LAR 127 Lg32
Bi'r Tlakshin LAR 127 Lg30
Birtle CDN (MB) 172 Ek20
Bi'r Tuhab LAR 127 Ma29
Biruaca YV 193 Gg42
Birufu RI 114 Rk48
Bi'r Umar LAR 127 Ma30
Biržai LT 39 Me34
Bi'r Zaltan LAR 127 Lk31
Bir Zar TN 126 Lf30
Birži LV 39 Mf34
Biržų pilis LT 39 Me34
Bisa RI 97 Rd46
Bisáccia I 37 Lq49
Bisagana WAN 133 Lg39
Bisai IND (ORS) 83 Pd34
Bisalpur IND (UPH) 81 Ok31
Bisambharpur IND (CGH) 83 Pb34
Bisanadi National Reserve EAK 145 Mk45
Bisane RMM 131 Kk37
Bišapur IR 59 Nf31
Bisauli IND (UPH) 81 Ok31

Boulogne-sur-Gesse F 24 La47
Boulogne-sur-Mer F 23 Lh40
Bouloire F 22 La43
Boulonnais F 23 Lb40
Boulouba RCA 140 Ma43
Boulouparis F 118 Td56
Boulsa F 137 Kh39
Boultoum RN 132 Lf38
Boumaïne Dadès MA 125 Kh30
Boumango G 148 Lg47
Bouma N.P. FJI 119 Ua54
Boumbou RMM 131 Kk38
Boumbé II RCA 140 Mb42
Boumedine RIM 130 Kf37
Boumerdès DZ 126 Lc27
Bou Mertala RIM 130 Kf35
Boumia MA 125 Kh29
Bou Kabir TCH 139 Lk40
Bou Mréga RMM 130 Ke37
Bou Nâga RIM 131 Kj36
Bounafla CI 137 Kh42
Boû Nâga RIM 131 Kj36
Boundary CDN (BC) 166 De17
Boundary Bend AUS (VIC) 111 Sb63
Boundary Mts. USA 177 Ge23
Boundary Peak USA 170 Ea27
Boundary Range CDN 166 Df18
Boundiali CI 137 Kg41
Boundioba RMM 137 Kg40
Boundji RCB 148 Lh46
Boundjiaire RMM 131 Kg38
Boundoukui BF 137 Kj40
Bongou RCA 140 Mb42
Bounkiling SN 136 Ke39
Bountiful USA 171 Ee25
Bountiful Islands AUS (QLD) 107 Rk54
Bounty Islands 100 Tb14
Bounty Trough 100 Tb14
Bouquet F 25 Lf43
Boura RMM 137 Kh39
Boura RMM 137 Kh39
Bourail F 118 Td56
Bourbon-Lancy F 25 Ld44
Bourbon-l'Archambault F 25 Ld44
Bourbonnais F 25 Lf43
Bourbriac F 22 Kr42
Bourdeaux F 25 Lf46
Bouré RMM 132 La39
Bourem RMM 131 Kh38
Bourem-Inali RMM 131 Kj37
Bourganeuf F 24 La45
Bourg-en-Bresse F 25 Lf44
Bourg-st-Comin F 23 Ld41
Bourg-Madame F 24 Lb48
Bourgneuf-en-Retz F 24 Kk43
Bourgoin-Jallieu F 25 Lf45
Bourg-Saint-Andéol F 25 Le46
Bourg-Saint-Maurice F 25 Lg45
Boû Rjéimât RIM 130 Kc36
Bourke AUS (NSW) 109 Se61
Bournda N.P. AUS (NSW) 111 Se64
Bournemouth GB 21 Kt40
Bourou TCH 140 Lj41
Bouroum BF 137 Kh39
Bouroum-Bouroum BF 137 Kj40
Bourrah CAM 139 Lg40
Bourscheid L 23 Lg41
Bourzanga BF 137 Kh39
Bou Saada DZ 126 Lc28
Bou Salem TN 126 Le27
Bouse USA (AZ) 170 Ed29
Bou Sfer DZ 125 Kk28
Boussac F 25 Lc44
Boussé BF 137 Kh39
Boussens F 24 La47
Boussou TCH 139 Lj40
Boussou F 137 Kj39
Boussoum BF 137 Kh39
Boutilimit RIM 130 Kc37
Boutilier F 23 Ld42
Boutougou Fara SN 136 Kd39
Bouvet Island 190 La15
Bouvellier F 23 Lh42
Bouza RN 132 Le37
Bouzghaïa DZ 126 Lc27
Bovalino Mare I 37 Lr52
Bovbjerg Fyr DK 30 Lj34
Bovec SLO 42 Lo45
Boves F 23 Lc41
Bovino F 37 Lq49
Bovra N.P. (ER) 204 Ha61
Bowa Falls AUS 107 Sd62
Bowbells USA (ND) 169 Ej21
Bowdle USA (SD) 172 Fa23
Bowdon USA (ND) 169 Ej21
Bowen RA (MD) 208 Gg63
Bowerville USA (VIC) 111 Sf59
Bowes GB 21 Kt36
Bow Island CDN (AB) 169 Ee21
Bowling Green USA (KY) 175 Fg27
Bowling Green USA (MO) 173 Fj25
Bowling Green USA (OH) 173 Fj25
Bowling Green Bay AUS (QLD) 107 Sd55
Bowling Green Bay N.P. AUS (QLD) 107 Sd55
Bowman USA (ND) 169 Ej22
Bowman GB 20 Ko35
Bowning AUS (NSW) 111 Se63
Bowraville AUS (NSW) 109 Sg61
Bowron Lake Prov. Park CDN 168 Dk19
Bowser CDN (BC) 168 Dh21
Bowthorn AUS (QLD) 106 Rk55
Boxberg D 32 Lj29
Boxholm S 31 Lq32
Boxmeer NL 23 Lg39
Boxtel NL 23 Lf39
Boxwood Hill AUS (WA) 104 Qk63
Boyabat TR 56 Mh25
Boyabo RDC 140 Lk44
Boyaca CO 192 Gd43
Bo Yai Hot Spring LAO 87 Qb36
Boyalıca CI 137 Kh42
Boyalıca TR 45 Mk50
Boyang CHN (JGX) 75 Qj31
Boyellé CDN (AB) 167 Ed18
Boyle IRL 19 Km37
Boylston CDN (NS) 176 Ha23
Boyne City USA (MI) 173 Fh23
Boyo RI 95 Qg44
Boyolali RI 95 Qf49
Boysun UZ 63 Oc26
Boyu Brook USA 107 Sa55
Boyuibe BOL 206 Gj56
Boyup Brook USA 104 Qj62
Boyuyo BOL 198 Gf51
Boza EAT 147 Mk49
Bozanbai RO 43 Mc44
Bozashchy Köbegi A KZ 62 Nd23
Božava HR 35 Lp46
Bozburun Yarımadası TR
Bozburun TR 47 Mh53
Bozcaada I TR 47 Mg51
Bozdağ TR 47 Mj53
Bozdoğan TR 47 Mj53
Bozeman USA (MT) 169 Ee23

Bozen = Bolzano I 34 Lm46
Bozene RDC 140 Lk44
Bozhou CHN (AHU) 73 Qh29
Bozi CHN (SCH) 69 Qa30
Bozk TR 56 Mg27
Bozköl KZ 62 Oa23
Bozkurt F 25 Lc46
Bozoum RCA 140 Lj42
Bozova TR 56 Mg28
Bozüyük TR 56 Mf26
Bozzolo I 34 Ll45
Bra I 34 Lh46
Braås S 31 Lq33
Brabova RO 44 Md46
Brač HR 35 Lr47
Bracciano I 36 Ln48
Bracebridge CDN (ON) 173 Ga28
Brachlewo PL 40 Lt37
Bräcke S 17 Lh14
Bracketville USA (TX) 181 Ek31
Brackley GB 21 Ku39
Bracknell GB 21 Ks38
Braco do Norte BR (SC) 205 Hf60
Bräden RO 43 Mc44
Bradenton USA (FL) 179 Fj32
Bredaryd S 31 Lo33
Bredasdorp ZA 154 Ma63
Bradford GB 21 Kt37
Bradford USA (AR) 174 Fe28
Bradley USA (CA) 170 Dk28
Bradley Reef SOL 117 Ta49
Bradleyville USA (MO) 174 Fd27
Brady USA (TX) 174 Fa30
Brae GB 20 Kt30
Braedstrup DK 30 Lk35
Braemar AUS (SA) 110 Rk62
Braemar GB 20 Kr35
Braga P 26 Km49
Bragadiru RO 45 Mf46
Bragado BR (BA) 209 Gk63
Bragança BR (PA) 195 Hg46
Bragança P 26 Ko49
Bragança Paulista BR (SP) 208 Hg57
Braggs USA (AL) 175 Fg29
Brahestad FIN 16 Mc13
Brahim RI 94 Pj44
Brahmanbaria BD 86 Pf34
Brahmapuri IND (MHT) 83 Ok35
Brahmaputra IND 86 Pg32
Brahmour F 25 Lf45
Braidwood AUS (NSW) 111 Se63
Bräila RO 45 Mh45
Braine F 23 Ld41
Brainerd USA (MN) 172 Fc22
Braintree GB 21 La39
Brakas CI 137 Kj39
Brak S 32 Lj37
Brakmakund PL 40 Lt37
Brakpan ZA 155 Md59
Brakwater NAM 150 Lj57
Brålanda S 30 Ln32
Brålos GB 46 Mc52
Bramming I 26 Ko33
Brampton CDN (ON) 173 Ga24
Brampton GB 20 Ks36
Bramsche D 32 Lj38
Bramwell AUS (QLD) 107 Sb52
Bran RO 45 Mf45
Branca USA (SC) 178 Fk29
Brancaleone Marina I 37 Lr53
Branch CDN (NF) 177 Hd22
Branchville USA (SC) 178 Fk29
Brandberg NAM 150 Lh56
Brandbu N 30 Ll30
Brande DK 30 Lk35
Brandenburg D 32 Lo38
Brand-Erbisdorf D 32 Lo40
Brandfort ZA 155 Md60
Brandon USA (MS) 175 Ff29
Brandon USA (FL) 179 Fj32
Brandon USA (MS) 175 Ff29
Brandon Bay IRL 19 Kk38
Brandon Head IRL 19 Kk38
Brandvlei ZA 154 Mb61
Brandýs nad Labem-Stará Boleslav CZ 42 Lp40
Branford USA (FL) 178 Fj31
Bransk PL 41 Ma38
Branitzer Park D 32 Lp39
Bransan S 30 Ln32
Branson USA (MO) 174 Fd27
Brantford CDN (AB) 167 Ed18
Brantôme F 24 La45
Brantholme USA (VIC) 110 Sa64
Brás BR (AM) 194 Ha46
Brashears USA 198 Gf51
Brasil C 179 Gb35
Brasilândia BR (MS) 202 Hd56
Brasília de Minas BR (MG) 203 Hh54
Brasiléia BR (AC) 198 Gf51
Brasília BR (DF) 203 Hg53
Brasília de Minas BR (MG) 203 Hh54
Brasília, P.N. de BR 203 Hg53
Braslandia D.H. BR (PI) 202 Hf53
Braslaw BY 39 Mh35
Braslav Lakes N.P. BY 39 Mh35
Brasnorte D BR 199 Hd51
Brasópolis BR (MG) 205 Hh57
Braşov RO 45 Mf45
Brasschaat B 23 Le39
Brassey, Mount MAL 93 Qj44
Brasstown Bald USA 178 Fh28
Brastad S 30 Lm32
Brąszewice PL 40 Lt39
Bratca RO 43 Md44
Bratislava SK 42 La42
Bratislavský hrad SK 42 La42
Bratovoešti RO 44 Md46
Bratsk RUS 54 Qd07
Bratskoje-vodohranilišče RUS
Bratteborg S 31 Lp33
Brattleboro USA (VT) 177 Gd24
Brattvåg N 16 Ld14
Bratul Chilia RO 45 Mk45
Braţul Sfântu Gheorghe RO 45 Mk45
Braunau A 42 Lo42
Braunfels D 32 Lj40
Braunschweig D 32 Ll38
Braunton GB 21 Kq39
Braunlage D 32 Ll39
Braunton GB 21 Kq39
Braúlio Carrillo, P.N. CR 185 Fj40

Brazil 191 Ha10
Brazil Basin 190 Ja11
Brazilian Highlands BR
Brazilian City USA (UT) 171 Eb25
Brazoria N.W.R. USA 174 Fc31
Brazos USA 174 Fb30
Brazzaville RCB 148 Lh48
Brbinj RI 35 Lp46
Brčko BIH 44 Lt46
Breadalbane AUS (QLD) 108 Sa57
Breaksea Sound NZ 113 Td68
Brea Pozo RA (SE) 207 Gj60
Breas PE 207 Ge25
Breaux Bridge USA (LA) 175 Fe31
Breaza RO 43 Me44
Breaza RO 45 Mf45
Brebes RI 95 Qe49
Brechen D 32 Lj39
Brechin GB 20 Ks34
Breckenridge USA (TX) 174 Fa29
Breckenridge USA (CO) 171 Eh25
Breclav CZ 42 La42
Brecon GB 21 Kr39
Brecon Beacons N.P. GB 21 Kr39
Breda NL 23 Le39
Bredaryd S 31 Lo33
Bredasdorp ZA 154 Ma63
Bredbo AUS (NSW) 111 Se63
Bredstedt D 32 Lj36
Bree B 23 Lf39
Breil-sur-Roya F 25 Lh47
Breisach D 33 Lh42
Breitenbrunn A 42 La42
Breja RUS 38 Nb08
Brejão de Caatinga BR (BA) 201 Hk51
Brejinho BR (MA) 201 Hj47
Brejo da Madre de Deus BR (PE) 201 Hk48
Brejo da Onça BR (PI) 201 Hk48
Brejo de São Félix BR (MA) 201 Hja43
Brejo do Cruz BR (PB) 201 Hk48
Brejo Grande BR (SE) 201 Jb51
Brejolândia BR (BA) 200 Hj52
Brejo Santo BR (CE) 201 Ja49
Brejões BR (BA) 200 Hja48
Brekka BR (SE) 201 Hk48
Brekken N 17 Lf14
Brekstad N 16 Le14
Bremen D USA (IN) 173 Fg25
Bremen USA (ND) 172 Fa22
Bremer Bay AUS (WA) 104 Ra61
Bremerhaven D 32 Lj37
Bremerton USA (WA) 168 Dj22
Bremervörde D 32 Lk37
Brénes USA (PE) 196 Gb48
Brenner A/I 34 Lm43
Breno I 34 Ll44
Brentey USA (AL) 175 Fg30
Brentwood USA (TN) 175 Fg27
Brep PK 63 Og27
Bréscia I 34 Ll44
Bressanone = Brixen I 34 Lm44
Bressuire F 24 Kk44
Brest BY 41 Md38
Brest F 22 Kq42
Brestova BG 45 Me47
Brestovac PE 196 Gd48
Bretenoux F 24 Lb46
Breteuil F 23 Lc41
Breteuil-sur-Iton F 22 La43
Breton N.W.R. USA 175 Ff31
Bretten D 33 Lj41
Breueh RI 92 Ph43
Breuil-Cervinia I 34 Lh45
Breuna D 32 Lk39
Brevard USA (NC) 178 Fj28
Brewarrina AUS (NSW)
Brewer USA (ME) 176 Gf23
Brewton USA (AL) 175 Fg31
Breynat CDN (AB) 167 Ed18
Breza BIH 44 Lt46
Breznica SLO 42 Lq45
Brezina DZ 125 La29
Brezno SK 43 Lu42
Březová BG 45 Me47
Brezová nad Hronom SK 43 Lt42
Brezovo BG 45 Mf48
Briançon F 25 Lg46
Briare F 25 Lc43
Bribbaree AUS (NSW) 111 Sf62
Bribie Island AUS 109 Sg59
Bribir HR 35 Lq47
Bribri CR 185 Fj40
Bricquebec F 22 Kk41
Bridge End IRL 19 Kn35
Bridgecity USA (TX) 175 Fd31
Bridgend GB 21 Kr39
Bridgenorth CDN (ON) 173 Ga24
Bridgeport USA (CT) 170 Ec28
Bridgeport USA (NE) 171 Eh24
Bridger USA (MT) 169 Ef23
Bridgetown AUS (WA) 104 Qj63
Bridgewater AUS (VIC) 111 Sb64
Bridgewater AUS (TAS) 111 Sd66
Bridgwater GB 21 Kr39
Bridlington GB 21 Ku36
Bridport GB 21 Kr40
Bridport AUS (TAS) 111 Sd66
Brie-Comte-Robert F 23 Lc42
Brienne-le-Château F 23 Le42
Brieska DZ 128 Le30
Brienz CH 34 Lh44
Brier RO 43 Lf41
Brie F 23 Lf42

Brig CH 34 Lh44
Briggsdale USA (CO) 171 Eh25
Brigham City USA (UT) 171 Ee25
Bright AUS (VIC) 111 Sd64
Brighton GB 21 Ks40
Brighton USA (CO) 171 Eh26
Brighton Downs AUS (QLD) 108 Sa57
Brighton Seminole Ind. Res. USA 179 Fk32
Brignogan-Plages F 22 Kq42
Brignoles F 25 Lg47
Brihadisvara Temple IND 85 Ok40
Brihuega E 29 Kr50
Brijuni, N.P. HR 35 Lo46
Brikama WAG 136 Kd39
Brilon D 32 Lj39
Brimnes IS 18 Kd02
Brindabella-in-Furness GB 21 Kr36
Brindisi I 37 Ls50
Brinje HR 35 Lq46
Brinkley USA (AR) 174 Fe28
Brinkmann RA (CD) 209 Gj61
Brinkworth AUS (SA) 110 Rk62
Brinlack IRL 19 Km35
Brinnon USA (WA) 168 Dj22
Brioude F 25 Ld45
Briouze F 22 La41
Brisbane AUS (QLD) 109 Sg59
Brisighella I 34 Lm46
Bristol CDN (NB) 176 Gg22
Bristol GB 21 Ks39
Bristol USA (CT) 177 Gd25
Bristol USA (VA) 178 Fj27
Bristol Bay USA 164 Ca17
Bristol Channel GB 21 Kr39
Bristow USA (OK) 174 Fb28
Britania BR (GO) 202 Hd53
Britannia CDN (NF) 177 Hd21
British Columbia CDN 162 Dc07
British Mountains CDN (YT) 165 Ck11
British Virgin Islands 181 Gg36
Brito Godins ANG 148 Lj50
Brits ZA 155 Md58
Britstown ZA 154 Mb61
Brittany I F 22 Kr42
Brittany F 22 Kr43
Brittingham MEX (DGO)
Britton USA (SD) 172 Fa23
Brive-la-Gaillarde F 24 La45
Briviesca E 28 Kr48
Brixen = Bressanone I 34 Lm44
Brixen RO 21 Kr40
Brjanceninovo RUS 39 Mj33
Brjanka UA 49 Mk21
Brjanskoe USA 181 Gg41
Brjansk RUS 48 Mh19
Brjanslækur IS 18 Jr25
Brkan I 35 Lq48
Brmaze IS 18 Jr25
Brno CZ 42 Lr41
Bro S 31 Lt33
Broach = Bharuch IND (GUJ)
82 Og35
Broad Arrow AUS (WA) 104 Ra61
Broadbent's Mission ZA 155 Mc59
Broadbent's Sending ZA 155 Mc59
Broadford GB 20 Kp33
Broad Peak PK 63 Oj28
Broad Sound AUS 109 Se57
Broad Sound Channel AUS 109 Sf57
Broadstairs GB 21 Lb39
Broadview USA (SK) 169 Ej20
Broadview USA (MT) 169 Ef23
Broadwater USA (NE) 171 Eh24
Brobo CI 137 Kh42
Broby S 31 Lp34
Brocēni LV 39 Mc34
Brochow PL 40 Lu38
Brocken D 32 Ll39
Brockman, Mount AUS 102 Qj57
Brockton USA (MA) 177 Ge24
Brockton USA (MT) 169 Eh21
Brockville CDN (ON) 177 Gc24
Brockway USA (PA) 173 Ga25
Brockway USA (MT) 169 Eh22
Brod BIH 44 Lt47
Brod MK 44 Mb49
Brodadeevo RA (SC) 174 Fd30
Brodarevo SCG 44 Lu47
Brodce CZ 42 Lp40
Brodec'ke UA 49 Me21
Brodeur Peninsula CDN 163 Fd04
Brodick GB 20 Kp35
Brodina de Jos RO 43 Mf43
Brodnica PL 41 Lu37
Brody UA 41 Mf40
Broken Arrow USA (OK) 174 Fc27
Broken Bay AUS (NSW)
111 Sf62
Broken Bow USA (NE) 174 Fa25
Broken Bow USA (OK) 174 Fc29
Broken Head AUS 109 Sg60
Broken Hill AUS (NSW)
108 Sa61
Broken Ridge 9 Pb13
Broki USA (AR) 179 Ga33
Brokind S 31 Lq33
Brokopondo SME 194 Hc43
Brokoyo CI 137 Kg43
Bromary FIN 38 Mc31
Bromby Islands AUS 106 Rj51
Brome CDN (QUE) 177 Gd23
Bromölla S 31 Lp34
Bromontville TCH 130 Lg42
Brommö S 31 Lp32
Bromo, Gunung RI 95 Qg49
Bromo-Tengger-Semeru N.P. RI 95 Qg50
Brömsebro S 31 Lr34
Bromsgrove GB 21 Ks38
Bromyard GB 21 Ks38
Brønderslev DK 30 Lk33
Brønnøysprut ZA 155 Mc58
Brønnøysund N 16 Lf12
Brønnøy I 16 Lf12
Broni I 34 Lk45
Bronkhorstspruit ZA 155 Md58
Bronte I 37 Lp53
Bronte AUS (TAS) 111 Sd66
Brookeville USA (MS)
Brookfield USA (MO) 174 Fd26
Brookgreen Gardens USA
178 Ga29
Brookings USA (OR) 168 Dh24
Brookings USA (SD) 172 Fb23
Brooklyn USA (MS)
Brookneal USA (VA) 178 Fk27
Brooks CDN (AB) 169 Ee20
Brooks Aqueduct Prov. H.S. CDN 169 Ee20
Brooks Range USA 165 Cc11
Brooksville USA (FL) 179 Fj31

Brooksville USA (MS) 175 Ff29
Brookton AUS (WA) 104 Qj63
Broome AUS (WA) 102 Rb54
Broome Crocodile Park AUS 90 Rd41
Broomehill AUS (WA) 104 Qj63
Broons S 22 Ks42
Brora GB 20 Kr32
Brørup DK 30 Lk35
Brosarp S 31 Lp35
Brosna I RO 44 Mc46
Brosten RO 43 Mf43
Brotas BR (SP) 202 Hf57
Brotas BR (BA) 201 Hj52
Brotas da Macaúbas BR (BA) 201 Hj52
Brothers USA (OR) 168 Dk24
Brotterode D 33 Ll40
Brottby S 31 Lt31
Brou F 23 Lb42
Broughton USA (IL)
Broughton-in-Furness GB 21 Kr36
Broulee AUS (NSW) 111 Sf63
Broulkou TCH 133 Lk37
Broumov CZ 42 Lr40
Broutzékia E 46 Mc53
Brouwershaven NL 23 Ld39
Brovary UA 48 Mf20
Brovina E 46 Mf21
Brovst DK 30 Lk33
Brown Bank ZA 90 Qj40
Brown's Cay ZA 90 Qj40
Brownell USA (KS) 174 Fa27
Browning USA (MT) 169 Ee22
Brownlow Point USA (AK)
165 Ch10
Browns USA (AL) 175 Fg29
Brown's Town JA 186 Gb36
Brownsville USA (KY) 175 Fg27
Brownsville USA (TX) 181 Fb33
Brownsweg SME 194 Hc43
Browse Island AUS 102 Rb53
Brozas E 27 Ko51
Brú IS 18 Jt25
Bruay-la-Buissière F 23 Lc40
Bruce USA (MS) 175 Ff29
Bruce Crossing USA (MI)
173 Ff22
Bruce Highway AUS (QLD)
107 Sd55
Bruce, Mount AUS 102 Qk57
Bruce Peninsula N.P. CDN
173 Fk23
Bruce Rock AUS (WA) 104 Qk61
Bruchsal D 33 Lj41
Bruck A 35 Lr43
Bruck D 33 Ln41
Bruck an der Leitha A 42 Lr42
Bruck an der Mur A 35 Lq44
Brüel D 32 Lm37
Brugg CH 34 Lj43
Brugge B 23 Ld39
Bruges = Brugge B 23 Ld39
Brühl D 32 Lh40
Brui'in RI 91 Rd43
Bruit, Pulau MAL 94 Qh45
Bruja Beach MEX 180 Eg34
Brujas CO 193 Gf44
Brukkaros NAM 154 Lj58
Brukkaros NAM 154 Lj58
Bruksljö S 31 Lp33
Brûlon F 22 Ku43
Brumado BR (BA) 203 Hk53
Brumath F 25 Lh42
Brumovice-Bylnice CZ 42 Ls41
Brunchilly AUS (NT) 106 Rh55
Bruneau USA (ID) 168 Ea24
Brunei BRU 94 Qh43
Brunette Downs AUS (NT)
106 Rh55
Brunflo S 16 Lh14
Brunico = Bruneck I 34 Lm44
Brunkild CDN (MB) 169 Fb21
Brunna S 31 Lr31
Brunnen CH 35 Lr47
Brunner, Lake NZ 113 Te67
Brunnsvik S 31 Lq30
Brunsbüttel D 32 Lk37
Brunssum NL 23 Lf40
Brunswick D USA (ME) 177 Ge24
Brunswick USA (GA) 178 Fk30
Brunswick USA (MO) 174 Fd26
Brunswick, Peninsula de RCH
208 Gd72
Brunswick, Lake USA 173 Fh25
Brunswick Junction AUS
Bruntál CZ 42 Ls41
Brus SCG 44 Mb47
Brusarci BG 44 Md47
Brusa ANG 148 Lh48
Brusaque BR (SC) 205 Hf59
Brus Laguna HN 185 Fh38
Brusque BR (SC) 205 Hf59
Brussel = Brussels B 23 Le40
Brussels B 23 Le40
Brussel = Brussels B 23 Le40
Brusselton AUS (WA) 104 Qh62
Bruthen AUS (VIC) 111 Sd64
Bruxelles = Brussels B 23 Le40
Bruyères F 25 Lg42
Bruz F 22 Kt42
Bruzaholm S 31 Lq33
Bry USA 193 Gh41
Brwinów PL 40 Lu38
Bryan USA (OH) 173 Fh25
Bryan USA (TX) 174 Fb30
Bryan Coast 6 Fd33
Bryan, Mount AUS 110 Rk62
Bryan's Corner USA (TX)
174 EK27
Bryansk USA (AR) 175 Fd28
Bryce Canyon N.P. USA
171 Ee27
Brynderwyn NZ 112 Th64
Bryne NO 16 Lf31
Brysetra TR 23 Mc57
Brzeg PL 40 Ls39
Brzeg Dolny PL 40 Lr39
Brzesko PL 41 Ma41
Brzeszcze PL 41 Lu41
Brzeziny PL 40 Lu39
Brzostek PL 41 Mb41
Brzóza PL 41 Ma39
Brzozów PL 41 Mc41

Bucalemu RCH 208 Gd63
Bucaramanga CO 192 Gd42
Bucas Grande Island RP 90 Rd41
Bucasia USA (QLD) 109 Se56
Buccaneer Archipelago AUS
102 Rb53
Buccaneer Beach USA 187 Gk37
Bucecea RO 43 Mf43
Bucegi, P.N. RO 45 Mf45
Bucerias MEX (NYT) 182 Eh35
Buccas da Madre BR (BA)
201 Hj52
Buchan AUS (VIC) 111 Sd64
Buchanan CDN (SK) 169 Eb20
Buchanan USA (MI) 173 Fg25
Buchanan Gulf CDN 163 Gb04
Buchanan Highway AUS
106 Rh54
Buchans CDN (NF) 177 Hb21
Buchen D 33 Lk41
Buchholz D 33 Lk41
Bucholz D 33 Lk41
Buchs CH 34 Lk43
Buchy F 23 Lb41
Buçinyris LT 39 Me35
Bucium RO 43 Md43
Buckeye USA (AZ) 171 Ee29
Buckeye USA (WV) 175 Fk26
Buckhaven GB 20 Kr34
Buckhorn USA (GA)
Buckingham GB 21 Ku39
Buckingham USA (VA) 177 Ga27
Buckingham Downs AUS
108 Sa56
Buckland USA (AK) 165 Cg10
Buckland Tableland AUS
109 Sd58
Buckle Island 6 Sd33
Bucklin USA (KS) 174 Fa27
Bucklin USA (MO) 174 Fd26
Bucksport USA (ME) 177 Gf23
Buckwaroon AUS (NSW)
Buco Zau ANG 148 Lg48
Bucșani RO 45 Mf46
Bucharest RO 45 Mg46
Buckye USA (AR) 174 Fd28
Bucureşti RO 45 Mg46
Bucurica CHN (QHI)
Bud USA (ID) 168 Ec24
Budaka EAU 144 Mg45
Budalin MYA 86 Ph34
Budapest H 43 Lu43
Buda VN 89 Qd40
Budaörs H 43 Lt43
Budaun IND (UPH) 81 Ok31
Buddha Park THA 87 Qb37
Buddhist Temple PK 81 Oj29
Buddon Ness AUS 20 Ks34
Budduso I 36 Lk50
Budel NL 23 Lf39
Budennovsk RUS 57 Nc23
Budelsdorf D 32 Lk36
Büdingen D 32 Lk40
Budir IS 18 Jt26
Budjala RDC 140 Lk44
Budogošč RUS 48 Mg16
Buducan CHN (QHI)
69 Qg28
Búðrdir IS 18 Jt26
Bu Dúc VN 89 Qd40
Bududu EAU 144 Mg45
Budva SCG 44 Lt48
Budweis CZ IR 57 Nd27
Budyne PL 40 Lt38
Budyoni AL R 36 Mb56
Budzyn PL 40 Lr38
Buen USA (TX) 174 Fd30
Bueche USA (LA) 175 Fd30
Buenaventura CO 179 Gb35
Buena Vista BOL 206 Gj54
Buenavista MEX (CHH)
180 Ej32
Buena Vista BOL 206 Gf54
Buena Vista Island SOL
117 Sk50
Buenavista Tomatlán MEX
(MHC) 182 Eh37
Buendía E 29 Kr50
Bueno Brandão BR (MG)
203 Hg57
Buenópolis BR (MG) 203 Hh54
Buenos Aires CO 192 Gd44
Buenos Aires CO 192 Gd44
Buenos Aires RA 209 Ha64
Buenos Aires YV 193 Gf42
Buenos Aires YV 193 Gf41
Buenos Aires MEX (CHH)
180 Ef30
Buenos Aires PE 196 Gb49
Buenos Aires RA 209 Gd64
Buenos Aires RA (CB) 210 Gf68
Buerarema BR (BA) 203 Ja53
Buesaco CO 192 Gb44
Bueu E 26 Km48
Bueyeros USA (NM) 174 Ej28
Bueno, Cerro de los RA
208 Ge64
Bufarek RI 114 Rk47
Bufels-s Point USA 94 Qj41
Buffalo USA (TX) 174 Fb30
Buffalo CDN (AB) 169 Ee20
Buffalo USA (MN) 172 Fc23
Buffalo USA (MO) 174 Fd27
Buffalo USA (NY) 173 Ga24
Buffalo USA (SD) 169 Ej23
Buffalo USA (WY) 169 Eg24
Buffalo Gap Grassland N.P.
USA 169 Ej24
Buffalo Head Hills CDN
167 Eb17

Buffalo Narrows CDN (SK)
167 Ef18
Buffalo National River USA
174 Fd28
Buffalo River CDN (AB)
167 Ed17
Buffalo Springs National Reserve
EAK USA 145 Mj45
Buflé Noir CAM 139 Lg41
Buford USA (GA)
Buford USA (CO) 171 Eg26
Buford USA (GA) 175 Fh28
Buford USA (ND) 169 Ej22
Buftea RO 45 Mf46
Buga CO 192 Gb44
Buga WAN 138 Ld41
Bugaba PA 185 Fj41
Bugala Island EAU 144 Mg46
Bugana RWA 146 Me47
Bugasong RP 90 Rb40
Buganda WAN 138 Ld42
Bugant MNG 70 Qd21
Bugdaly TM 62 Nh26
Bugdaylı TR 56 Mg29
Bugeat F 24 Lb45
Bugel, Tanjung RI 95 Qf49
Bugg RO 45 Mh45
Buggerru I 36 Lj51
Bugojno BIH 35 Ls46
Bugønes N 17 Me11
Bu In RI 57 Sh28
Bugrino RUS 38 Nc06
Bugsuk Island RP 90 Qk41
Bugt CHN (NMZ) 71 Ra21
Bugt Shan CHN 71 Ra21
Buguda IND (ORS) 83 Pc36
Bugué RP 90 Ra36
Bugul'ma RUS (BUR) 71 Qh19
Bugungan Game Reserve EAU
144 Mf44
Buhaka EAU Mf45
Buharkent TR 47 Mk53
Bu Hasa UAE 61 Ng34
Buhera ZW 152 Mf56
Buhi RP 90 Rb39
Buhl USA (ID) 168 Ea24
Bui GH 137 Kj41
Buhore EAT 146 Mf48
Buhovci BG 45 Mg47
Bui N.P. GH 137 Kj41
Buindependa sukojmasy KZ 67 Pa21
Buick CDN (BC) De17
Buigiri EAT 147 Mh49
Buin GH 137 Sh49
Bu'in ZIR 57 Nd28
Bukadaban Feng CHN 69 Pf27
Bukakata EAU 144 Mg47
Bukama RDC 149 Me48
Bu Kammash LAR 126 Lf29
Bukavu RDC 141 Md46
Bukawa PNG 115 Sd49
Bukima EAU 144 Mf46
Bukit Barisan Selatan National
Park RI 93 Qb47
Bukit Batu MAL 94 Qh45
Bukit Larut MAL 93 Qa43
Bukittinggi RI 93 Qa46
Bukit Ujungan CI 93 Qa46
Bükk MNG 67 Pa23
Bukkapatna IND (KTK)
84 Oj39
Bukku RI 91 Rd44
Bukoba EAU 144 Mf46
Bukova RUS (DAG) 57 Nd24
Bukuru WAN 138 Le41
Bukwa EAU 144 Mg45
Bulan RP 90 Rb39
Bulalacao RP 90 Ra40
Bulalakao RP 90 Ra40
Bulan USA (NM) 174 Fd28
Bulak RP 90 Rb40
Bulan CHN (XUZ) 66 Oh26
Bulancak TR 56 Mg25
Bulaq ET 129 Mf33
Bulari MNG 67 Pb23
Bu'ale SP 145 Nd45
Buali GH 137 Kj42
Bulan SOL 117 Sk50
Buram SUD 141 Mc39
Buao RP 90 Rb40
Bulanık TR 57 Nb26
Bulawayo ZW 152 Me56
Bulusan RP 90 Rb39
Bulyan TR 56 Mc27

Bullabulling AUS (WA) 104 Ra61
Bulla Regia TN 126 Le27
Bullaring AUS (WA) 104 Qj62
Bullas E 29 Kr52
Bullaxaar SP 143 Nc40
Bulle CH 34 Lh44
Bullen USA (AK) 165 Cg10
Buller USA (AK) 165 Cg10
Bullfinch AUS (WA) 104 Qk61
Bullhead City USA (AZ)
170 Ec28
Bulli AUS (NSW) 111 Sf63
Bullis Out Station USA (NT)
106 Rh54
Bull Mountains USA 169 Ef22
Bullo River USA (NT) 103 Re53
Bulloo Downs AUS (QLD)
108 Sb60
Bulloo Downs AUS (WA)
104 Qk58
Bullock's Harbour BS 179 Gb33
Bulnes RCH 208 Gd64
Bulolo PNG 115 Sd49
Bulolo RDC 149 Ma48
Bultfontein ZA 155 Md60
Buluama RI 95 Qf49
Buludawa Mountains RI 91 Rd45
Bulukumba EAT 146 Mf48
Bulukumi RI 95 Qh49
Bulunkol CHN (XUZ) 66 Oh26
Bulun RUS 55 Rb09
Bulungu RDC 149 Lk48
Bulungur UZ 63 Od26
Buluri RP 90 Rb39
Buma RI 114 Rk47
Bumba RDC 140 Ma44
Bumbah, Khalij al LAR 127 Ma29
Bümberg-yön RO 44 Md46
Bumbire Island EAT 144 Mf46
Bumba MAL 94 Qh45
Bumiayu RI 95 Qe49
Bun Hills PNG 115 Sd49
Bun N.P. AUS 109 Se60
Bunatari RP 90 Rb40
Bunbury AUS (WA) 104 Qh62
Bunclody IRL 19 Kn38
Buncrana IRL 19 Kn35
Bunda EAT 144 Mg47
Bundaberg AUS (QLD) 109 Sf58
Bundadara RP 109 Sg60
Bunde D 32 Lj38
Bunde D 32 Lj38
Bundena D (AUS) (QLD) 108
Bundi IND (RJT) 82 Oh33
Bundibugyo EAU 144 Mf45
Bundjalung N.P. AUS (NSW)
109 Sg60
Bundu IRL 19 Km36
Bungay GB 21 Lb38
Bünge D 32 Lj38
Bunge Bay RUS 52 Ra04
Bungku RI 96 Rb46
Bungo EAU 144 Mg47
Bungoma EAK 144 Mg46
Bungo-suidō J 79 Rh29
Bungowannah THA 88 Qa38
Bunguran & Blue Ox Statue USA 172 Ez23
Bünyan TR 56 Mg26
Bunia RDC 144 Me45
Bunji RI 91 Rd44
Bunker Hill USA (AK) 164 Bh13
Bunker Hill USA (OR) 168 Ea24
Bunkeroon USA (LA) 175 Fd30
Bunkie USA (LA) 175 Fd30
Bunnell USA (FL) 178 Fk31
Bunnerinege USA (NSW)
110 Sa62
Bun Neua LAO 87 Qa35
Bunó IS 18 Jt26
Buñol E 29 Ks51
Buntaru SP 145 Nc43
Bunta RI 96 Rb46
Bunun TA 89 Qc46
Buntingfordtgh GB 21 Ks39
Bunun EAK 144 Mh46
Bunya Mountains N.P. AUS
(QLD) 109 Sf59
Bunyan AUS (NSW) 111 Se63
Bünyan TR 56 Mg26
Bünz S 17 Lb14
Buoch Don VN 89 Qd39
Buôn Đôn VN 89 Qd39
Buôn Ma Thuột VN 89 Qd39
Buon Don Elephants VN
Bura ET 142 Na41
Bura KBT 44 Md46
Buran BSS 57 Nd27
Burang CHN 81 Pa31
Burang CHN 81 Pa31
Burao SP 143 Nc41
Buras USA (LA) 175 Fd31
Buraydah KSA 59 Na31
Burayevo RUS 50 Nf17
Burbage GB 21 Kt39
Burco SP 143 Nc41
Burd USA (KS) 174 Fa27
Burdalyk TM 63 Oc26
Burdaökköiba CHN (XUZ) 66 Oh26
Burden USA (KS) 174 Fb27
Burdur TR 56 Mf27
Burdur Gölü TR 56 Mf27
Bure ETH 142 Mk40
Bure GB 21 Lb38

Bürenkhayrkhan MNG 67 Pb22
Büren Togtokh Uul MNG
70 Pk21
Bürentsogt MNG 70 Qf22
Bürenrog YV 192 Gd49
Bürewestnik RUS 77 Sd23
BürfelheiÖ IS 18 Ke25
Burg D 32 Ll38
Burg D 32 Lm38
Bur Gabo SP 145 Na46
Burgas BG 45 Mh48
Burgawa VI USA (NC) 178 Sb28
Burg Burghausen D 33 Ln42
Burgdorf CH 34 Lh43
Burgdorf D 32 Ll38
Burgdorf USA (ID) 168 Ec23
Burgebrach D 33 Lm41
Burg Eltz D 33 Lh40
Burgersfort ZA 155 Mf58
Burgersdorp ZA 155 Md61
Burghausen D 33 Ln42
Burghill GB 21 Ks38
Burgio I 36 Lo53
Burglengenfeld D 33 Ln41
Burgo E 27 Km50
Burgohondo E 27 Kp50
Burgos E 28 Kr48
Burgos MEX (TM) 181 Fa33
Burgos RP 90 Qk37
Burgstädt D 32 Ln40
Burg Querfurt D 32 Lm39
Burgstädt D 32 Ln40
Burgsvik S 31 Lt34
Burgstall S 28 Kt48
Burgundy F 25 Le43
Burgundy A 7 La40
Burg zu Nürnberg D 33 Lm41
Burhana D TR 47 Mk51
Burhana D (UPH) 81 Oj31
Burhan Budai Shan CHN
69 Pk29
Burhan buubay Uul MNG
67 Pj23
Burhaniye TR 47 Mg51
Burhanpur IND (MPH) 82 Oj35
Burias Island RP 90 Rb39
Buri RI (SP) 205 Hf57
Burgi Game Reserve EAT
144 Mf47
Buriša Mare RO 44 Mc46
Burin CDN (NF) 177 Hc22
Burin Peninsula CDN 177 Hc22
Buritama THA 80 Qb38
Buritama BR (SP) 202 Hd56
Buritá BR (MT) 202 Hd54
Buri BR (MT) 202 Hd54
Buri Alegre BR (GO) 202 Hf55
Buritá BR (BA) 200 Hj48
Buri dos Lopes BR (PI)
201 Hk47
Buritirama BR (BA) 200 Hj51
Buritizeiro BR (MG) 203 Hh54
Buriti, T.I. BR 202 Hc56
Buritizeiro BR (MG) 203 Hh54
Burj al Arab UAE 61 Nh33
Burjassot E 29 Ks51
Burk WAN 138 Le41
Burketown AUS (QLD) 107 Sa55
Burketown AUS (QLD) 107 Sa54
Burkina Faso 123 Kb08
Burk's Falls CDN (ON) 173 Ga23
Burleigh AUS (QLD) 107 Sb56
Burlington USA (CO) 174 Ej26
Burlington USA (CO) 174 Ej26
Burlington USA (IA) 173 Fe24
Burlington USA (KS) 174 Fc27
Burlington USA (NC) 175 Fk26
Burlington CDN (NF) 177 Hb22
Burlington USA (VT) 177 Gd23
Burma = Myanmar MYA
Burney Caves KSA 59 Nd33
Burnet USA (TX) 174 Fa30
Burnett Heads AUS (QLD)
Burnett Range AUS 109 Sf58
Burnham USA (PA) 173 Ga25
Burnham-on-Crouch GB
21 La39
Burnham-on-Sea GB 21 Ks39
Burnie AUS (TAS) 111 Sc66
Burnley GB 21 Ks37
Burnpur IND (WBG) 83 Pd34
Burns USA (OR) 168 Ea24
Burns Junction USA (OR)
168 Eb24
Burns Lake CDN (BC) 166
Dh18
Burns Paiute Ind. Res. USA
168 Ea24
Burnside CDN (NC) 178 Ga29
Burnt Mountain NAM 150 Lh56
Burnt Ground BS 186 Gc34
Burnt Ranch USA (CA)
168 Dj25
Burns USA (SA) 103 Rf55
Burns USA (SD) 172 Fa23
Burra AUS (SA) 110 Rk62
Burrel AL 44 Ma49
Burren Junction USA (NSW)
109 Se61
Burren N.P. IRL 19 Kl37
Burngham Hill AUS 109 Sg58
Burg Eck F 23 Lg41
Burried Village BR N.Z 112 Th65
Bürrsvik S 31 Lt34
Burruyacú RA (TU) 207 Gh59
Bürs A 34 Lk43
Burstall CDN (SK) 169 Ef20
Burton S 17 Mk40
Bûr Safajah ET 129 Mg32
Bûr Safâga ET 129 Mg32
Buru RI 96 Re46
Burugwo SP 145 Nd46
Burund av CI 137 Kj42
Burundi 123 Md10
Burwash Landing CDN (YT)
165 Ck14
Burwell GB 21 La38
Burwick GB 20 Ks32
Bury GB 21 Ks37

Cay Lobos ⌂ 179 Gb34
Caylus ◻ F 24 Lb46
Cayman Brac ⌂◻⊟ GB 179 Ga36
Cayman Islands ◻ GB 179 Fk36
Cayman Ridge ⌂ 179 Fj36
Cay Marino ◻ RA 207 Ge47
Caynabo ◻ SP 143 Nd41
Cayo Arenas ⌂ MEX 183 Fa34
Cayo Becerro ⌂ HN 185 Fj38
Cayo Becerro ⌂ HN 184 Ff38
Cayo Caballones ⌂ C 179 Ga35
Cayo Cabeza del Este ⌂ C 179 Ga35
Cayo Cantiles ⌂ C 179 Fj35
Cayo Caratasca ⌂ HN 185 Fj37
Cayo Caratasca ⌂ HN 185 Fj37
Cayo Centro ⌂ MEX 185 Ff35
Cayo Coco ⌂ C 179 Ga34
Cayo del Rosario ⌂ C 179 Fj35
Cayo de Santa María ⌂ C 179 Ga34
Cayo Fragoso ⌂ C 179 Ga34
Cayo Gorda ⌂ HN 185 Fj38
Cayo Gorda ⌂ HN 185 Fj38
Cayo Grande ⌂ C 179 Ga35
Cayo Guajaba ⌂ C 179 Gb35
Cayo Guillermo ⌂ C 179 Ga34
Cayo Largo ⌂ C 179 Fj35
Cayo Largo ⌂ C 179 Fj35
Cayo Lobos ⌂ MEX 185 Ff35
Cayo Mambi ⌂ C 186 Gc35
Cayo Nuevo ⌂ MEX 183 Fb35
Cayo Ramona ⌂ C 179 Fk34
Cayo Romano ⌂ C 179 Ga35
Cayo Sabinal ⌂ C 179 Gb35
Cayos Blancos del Sur ⌂ C 179 Fk34
Cayos Cajones ⌂ HN 185 Fj37
Cayos Cinco Balas ⌂ C 179 Ga35
Cayos Cocorocuma ⌂ HN 185 Fj38
Cayos Cocorocuma ⌂ HN 185 Fj38
Cayos de Albuquerque ⌂ CO 185 Fk35
Cayos de E.S.E. ⌂ CO 185 Fk35
Cayos de Perlas ⌂ NIC 185 Fj39
Cayos de Roncador ⌂ C 185 Fk35
Cayos de San Felipe ⌂ C 179 Fj35
Cayos Guerrero ⌂ NIC 185 Fj39
Cayos King ⌂ NIC 185 Fj39
Cayos los Indios ⌂ C 179 Fj35
Cayos Mayores del Cabo Falso ⌂ HN 185 Fj38
Cayos Mayores del Cabo Falso ⌂ HN 185 Fj38
Cayos Miskitos ⌂ NIC 185 Fj38
Cayos Morrison Dennis ⌂ NIC 185 Fj38
Cayos NASA ⌂ NIC 185 Fj38
Cayo Tyara ⌂ NIC 185 Fj39
Cayo Vivorillo ⌂ HN 185 Fj38
Cayo Vivorillo ⌂ HN 185 Fj38
Cay Sal ⌂ BS 179 Fk34
Cay Santo Domingo ⌂ BS 186 Gc35
Cay Verde ⌂ BS 186 Gc35
Cazage ◻ ANG 151 Ma51
Cazalla de la Sierra ◻ E 27 Kp53
Cazalá ◻ GE 57 Nb24
Cazaubon ◻ F 24 Ku47
Cazenovia ◻ USA (NY) 177 Gc24
Cazin ◻ BIH 35 Lq46
Čazma ◻ HR 35 Lr45
Cazombo ◻ ANG 151 Mb51
Cazones ◻ MEX (VC) 182 Fb35
Cazorla ◻ E 27 Ks53
Cazula ◻ YV 193 Gg41
Cazula ◻ MOC 152 Mg54
Cazuza Ferreira ◻ BR (RS) 205 Hd60
Ccatca ◻ PE 197 Ge52
Cea ◻ E 26 Kq48
Ceahláu, P.N. ⌂ RO 49 Mc22
Ceanu Mare ◻ RO 43 Md44
Ceará ◻ BR 191 Hb10
Ceará Abyssal Plain ⌂ 190 Hb09
Ceará-Mirim ◻ BR (RN) 201 Jc48
Ceará-Mirim ◻ BR 201 Jc48
Ceatalchioi ◻ RO 45 Mj45
Ceballos ◻ MEX (DGO) 181 Eh32
Čeboksary ◻ RUS (CHU) 48 Nd17
Cebolatí ◻ ROU 204 Hd62
Cebreros ◻ E 27 Kp50
Cebu ◻ RP 90 Rb40
Čečava ◻ BIH 35 Ls46
Ceccano ◻ I 36 Lo49
Ceceľ'nyk ◻ UA 49 Me21
Čechtice ◻ CZ 42 Lq41
Cecil Plains ◻ AUS (QLD) 109 Sf59
Cécina ◻ I 34 Ll47
Cedar Bay N.P. ⌂ AUS 107 Sc53
Cedar Bluffs ◻ USA (KS) 174 Fa26
Cedar Breaks Nat. Mon. ⌂ USA 171 Ed27
Cedar City ◻ USA (UT) 171 Ed27
Cedaredge ◻ USA (CO) 171 Eg26
Cedar Falls ◻ USA (IA) 172 Fd24
Cedar Grove ◻ USA (CA) 170 Ea27
Cedar Harbour ◻ BS 179 Gb32
Cedar Island ◻ USA (NC) 178 Gb28
Cedar Island N.W.R. ⌂ USA 178 Gb28
Cedar Key ◻ USA (FL) 178 Fj31
Cedar Lake ⌂ CDN 169 Fa19
Cedar Park ◻ USA (TX) 174 Fb30
Cedar Point ◻ USA 173 Fj25
Cedar Rapids ◻ USA (IA) 172 Fe24
Cedar River ◻ USA (ND) 172 Fg23
Cedar River Grassland N.P. ⌂ USA 172 Ek22
Cedartown ◻ USA (GA) 175 Fh29
Cedarvale ◻ CDN 166 Df18
Cedarville ◻ USA (CA) 168 Dk24
Cedarville ◻ ZA 155 Me61
Cedeira ◻ E 26 Km47
Cedeño ◻ HN 184 Ff39
Cederberg ◻ ZA 154 Lk62
Cederberg Wilderness Area ⌂ ZA 154 Lk62
Cedillo ◻ E 27 Ko51
Cedoux ◻ CDN (SK) 169 Ej21
Cedral ◻ BR (MA) 195 Hh46
Cedral ◻ MEX (SLP) 182 Ek34
Cedrillas ◻ E 29 Ku50
Cedros ◻ BR (BA) 201 Hj52
Cedros ◻ HN 184 Ff38
Cedros ◻ MEX (ZCT) 181 Eh33
Cedros Trench ⌂ 180 Ea31
Ceduna ◻ AUS (SA) 110 Rg62
Cée ◻ E 26 Km47
Ceek ◻ SP 143 Nc41
Ceel Afweyn ◻ SP 143 Nd41
Ceelaanyo ◻ SP 143 Ne41
Ceel Baxay ◻ ETH 143 Nb40
Ceelbuur = El Bur ◻ SP 145 Nd43
Ceel Dhaab ◻ SP 143 Nd41
Ceeldheer ◻ SP 145 Nd44
Ceeldheere ◻ SP 145 Nd44
Ceel Dudbo ◻ SP 145 Nd44
Ceel Gaal ◻ SP 143 Nf40
Ceel Gaan ◻ SP 143 Nd45
Ceel Garas ◻ SP 145 Nd43
Ceel Huur ◻ SP 145 Nd43
Cefalù ◻ I 37 Lp52
Ceglédbercel ◻ H 43 Lu43
Céglie Messápico ◻ I 37 Lt50
Cehegín ◻ E 29 Kt53
Ceheng ◻ CHN (GZH) 87 Qd33
Čehov ◻ RUS 48 Mj18

Cehu Silvaniei ◻ RO 43 Md43
Ceibalito ◻ RA (SA) 207 Gh58
Ceibal, P.N. ⌂ GCA 183 Ff37
Ceibas ◻ RA (ER) 204 Ha62
Céide Fields ⌂ IRL 19 Kl36
Čejč ◻ CZ 42 Lr42
Čekerek ◻ TR 56 Mh25
Cekidake ⌂ J 87 Rd28
Čekurdah ◻ RUS 55 Sb04
Celanova ◻ E 26 Kn48
Čelebi ◻ TR 56 Mf26
Celaya ◻ MEX (GJT) 182 Ek35
Celbridge ◻ IRL 19 Ko37
Čelebes Basin ⌂ RP 91 Ra44
Celebes Sea ⌂ RI 52 Ra09
Čelinac Donji ◻ BIH 35 Ls46
Čeljabinsk ◻ RUS 54 Oa07
Čeljachany ◻ BY 41 Mf40
Čella ◻ E 29 Kt50
Celldömölk ◻ H 42 Ls43
Celle ◻ D 32 Ll38
Celle Ligure ◻ I 34 Lj46
Celorico da Beira ◻ P 26 Kn50
Čerkoce ◻ SCG 44 Mb50
Čelten Sea ⌂ 19 Kn40
Cemaru, Gunung ⌂ RI 94 Qh45
Cemerno ◻ BIH 44 Lt47
Çemişgezek ◻ TR 57 Mk26
Cemolgan ◻ KZ 64 Oh23
Cemorowanki Marine Reserve ⌂ RI 114 Rh47
Čenei ◻ RO 43 Mb45
Centani ◻ ZA 155 Me62
Centelles ◻ E 29 Lc49
Centani ◻ RA (NE) 208 Gf65
Centenario do Sul ◻ BR (PR) 202 Hd57
Centenary ◻ ZW 152 Mf54
Centennial Museum, Barrhead ⌂ CDN 167 Ec18
Center ◻ USA (CO) 171 Eg27
Center ◻ USA (ND) 172 Ek22
Center ◻ USA (TX) 174 Fe30
Centerville ◻ USA (IA) 174 Fd25
Centerville ◻ USA (MO) 175 Fe27
Centerville ◻ USA (TN) 175 Fg28
Centerville ◻ USA (TX) 174 Fc30
Centinela ◻ PE 197 Gb51
Centinela, Cerro ⌂ RA 208 Ge64
Centra Buttte ◻ CDN (SK) 169 Eg20
Centrale ◻ BR (BA) 201 Hj51
Central African Republic ◻ RCA 123 Lb09
Central Australia A.L. ⌂ AUS 103 Re57
Central Balkan, N.P. ⌂ BG 45 Me48
Central Brahui Range ⌂ PK 65 Od31
Central City ◻ USA (KY) 175 Fg27
Central City ◻ USA (NE) 172 Fa25
Central Desert A.L. ⌂ AUS 103 Rf55
Central Eastern Rainforest Reserves ⌂ AUS 109 Sg60
Centralia ◻ USA (IL) 175 Ff26
Centralia ◻ USA (WA) 168 Dj22
Central Kalahari Game Reserve ⌂ RB 151 Mb10
Central Karakorum N.P. ⌂ PK 81 Oj28
Central los Molles ◻ RCH 208 Ge61
Central Makran Range ⌂ PK 65 Oc32
Central Mosque (Pattani) ⌂ THA 89 Qa42
Central Mount Wedge ⌂ AUS 103 Rf57
Central'nojakutskaja ravnina ⌂ RUS 55 Qd06
Central'notunguskoe plato ⌂ RUS 54 Pd06
Central Pacific Basin ⌂ 10 Ba08
Central Patricia ◻ CDN 172 Fe20
Central Range ⌂ LS 155 Me60
Central Range ⌂ PNG 115 Sb48
Central Reserve A.L. ⌂ EAK 144 Mj44
Central Siberian Plateau ⌂ RUS 54 Pc05
Centre ◻ F 22 Lb43
Centre ◻ USA (AL) 175 Fh29
Centre Island ◻ AUS 106 Rj53
Centre minier de Lewarde ⌂ F 23 Ld40
Centre Spatial Guyanais ⌂ F 194 Hd43
Centreville ◻ USA (AL) 175 Fg30
Centreville ◻ USA (MS) 175 Fe30
Cenxi ◻ CHN (GZG) 74 Qf34
Cenzontle ◻ MEX (COH) 181 Eh32
Cepigovo ◻ MK 44 Mb49
Čepin ◻ HR 35 Lt45
Cepu ◻ RI 95 Qg44
Cerachovka ◻ BY 48 Mf19
Cercal ◻ P 27 Km53
Cercle mégalithique ⌂ SN 136 Kc39
Cerdon ◻ F 26 Kn50
Cereal ◻ CDN (AB) 169 Ee20
Cerejeiras ◻ BR (RO) 206 Gk52
Čeremhovo ◻ RUS 70 Qd19
Ceremonija Pečina ⌂ SCG 44 Md45
Čerencovo ◻ RUS 48 Mg16
Čerepanovo ◻ RUS 54 Pa08
Čerepovec ◻ RUS 48 Mj16
Čereso ◻ BG 45 Mg47
Ceresole Reale ◻ I 34 Lh45
Cereté ◻ CO 192 Gc41
Cerezo de Abajo ◻ E 26 Kr49
Cerfontaine ◻ B 23 Le40
Cerignola ◻ I 37 Lq49
Çerikli ◻ TR 56 Mg26
Cerillos ◻ RA 207 Gh57
Cerillos ◻ RCH 207 Gf51
Cerito ◻ CO 192 Gd42
Cerisay ◻ F 24 Ku44
Čerkasskoe ◻ RUS 38 Mj30
Čerkasy ◻ UA 49 Mg21
Čerkessk ◻ RUS (KCH) 57 Nb23
Čerkes Marijinega oznanjanja ⌂ SLO 42 Lp44
Čerknica ◻ SLO 42 Lp45
Čermik ◻ TR 57 Mk26
Cern' ◻ RUS 48 Mj19

Cerna ◻ HR 35 Lt45
Cerna ◻ RO 45 Mj45
Cerna-Sat ◻ RO 44 Mc45
Černava ◻ RUS 48 Mk19
Cernavodă ◻ RO 45 Mj46
Černay ◻ F 25 Lh43
Cernégula ◻ E 26 Kr48
Černica ◻ RUS 38 Mj32
Černica ◻ UA 49 Mk41
Černivci ◻ UA 49 Mc21
Černjachiv ◻ UA 49 Me20
Černjachovsk ◻ RUS 71 Rd19
Černjanka ◻ RUS 48 Mj20
Černobaj ◻ UA 49 Mg21
Černoholovka ◻ RUS 71 Qi19
Černyškovskij ◻ RUS 48 Nb21
Cerovačke Špilje ⌂ HR 35 Lq46
Cerovica ◻ SCG 44 Mc47
Čerquqira César ◻ BR (SP) 202 Hf57
Cerralvo ☒ (NL) 181 Fa32
Cerrigydrudion ◻ GB 21 Kr37
Cerrito ◻ CO 192 Gd42
Cerrito ◻ MEX (SLP) 182 Ek34
Cerrito, T.I. ⌂ BR 202 Hc57
Cerro Aconcagua ⌂ RA 208 Ge62
Cerro Agua Hedionda ⌂ RA 208 Gg62
Cerro Aguas Blancas ⌂ RA/RCH 207 Gf58
Cerro Aguja ⌂ RA/RCH 208 Ge67
Cerro Aguja ⌂ RCH 210 Gd73
Cerro Aguilete ⌂ RCH 210 Gd71
Cerro Atalaya ⌂ PE 197 Ge52
Cerro Alto Nevado ⌂ RCH 210 Gd68
Cerro Anecón Chico ⌂ RA 208 Gf66
Cerro Anecón Grande ⌂ RA 208 Gf65
Cerro Apacheta ⌂ RA 207 Gg58
Cerro Archibarca ⌂ RA 207 Gg58
Cerro Arenales ⌂ RCH 210 Gd69
Cerro Atajama ⌂ RCH 206 Ge55
Cerro Aucanquilcha ⌂ RCH 206 Gg55
Cerro Avispa ⌂ BR/YV 193 Gh45
Cerro Ayapungo ⌂ PE 196 Gc47
Cerro Azanaques ⌂ BOL 206 Gg55
Cerro Azul ◻ BR (PR) 205 Hf58
Cerro Azul ◻ EC 197 Fk46
Cerro Azul ◻ MEX (VC) 182 Fb35
Cerro Azul ◻ PE 197 Gb52
Cerro Azul ⌂ RA 208 Ge63
Cerro Balmaceda ⌂ RCH 210 Gd71
Cerro Barros Arana ⌂ RCH 210 Gd67
Cerro Bayo ⌂ RA 208 Gg59
Cerro Belgrano ⌂ RA 208 Ge69
Cerro Blanco ⌂ RA 208 Ge66
Cerro Blanco ⌂ RA 208 Gf61
Cerro Bolívar 802 ⌂ YV 193 Gj42
Cerro Bonete ⌂ RA 207 Gf58
Cerro Boquete ⌂ RA 208 Ge67
Cerro Bravo ⌂ BOL 206 Gf54
Cerro Bravo ⌂ BOL 206 Gh54
Cerro Butahuao ⌂ RA 208 Ge67
Cerro Calpún ⌂ PE 196 Ga49
Cerro Caltama ⌂ BOL 206 Gf56
Cerro Campanario ⌂ RA/RCH 208 Ge63
Cerro Cangrejo ⌂ RA 210 Gd70
Cerro Carrera ⌂ RA 208 Gf64
Cerro Centinela ⌂ RA 208 Ge64
Cerro Cerrón ⌂ YV 192 Ge40
Cerro Chachil ⌂ RA 208 Gf63
Cerro Chacras ⌂ RA 208 Gd64
Cerro Champaquí ⌂ RA 208 Gh61
Cerro Chato ⌂ ROU 204 Hc62
Cerro Chenque ⌂ RA 210 Ge71
Cerro Chihuido de Medio ⌂ RA 208 Gf62
Cerro Chocca ⌂ PE 197 Gc52
Cerro Chulluncani ⌂ BOL 206 Gf56
Cerro Cibaray ⌂ BOL 206 Gf54
Cerro Cinque ⌂ BOL 206 Gf54
Cerro Cofre de Perote ⌂ MEX 182 Fb36
Cerro Cofre, P.N. ⌂ MEX 182 Fb36
Cerro Cojudo Blanco ⌂ RA 210 Gd69
Cerro Colorado ☒ MEX (SO) 180 Ef32
Cerro Colorado ⌂ RA 210 Gd68
Cerro Colorado ⌂ RA 207 Gd68
Cerro Colorados ⌂ RA/RCH 208 Gf63
Cerro Colquen ⌂ RCH 208 Gd64
Cerro Colupo ⌂ RCH 206 Gf55
Cerro Convento ⌂ RA 210 Gf71
Cerro Copa ⌂ BOL/RCH 206 Gf56
Cerro Coposa ⌂ RCH 206 Gf56
Cerro Corá ⌂ BR (RN) 201 Jb49
Cerro Corá (MA) 204 Ho57
Cerro Corá, P.N. ⌂ PY 202 Hb57
Cerro Cordobés ⌂ RA 207 Gf60
Cerro Corona ⌂ RA 208 Gf64
Cerro Cotacachi ⌂ CO 192 Gd45
Cerro Cowan ⌂ EC 197 Fe46
Cerro Coyaquiama ⌂ RA 207 Gf57
Cerro Criterion ⌂ PE 197 Gd53
Cerro Cumbrera ⌂ RCH 210 Gd69
Cerro Cupisnique ⌂ PE 196 Ga49
Cerro de Ansantúa ⌂ RA 208 Gf61
Cerro de Anáitna ⌂ BOL 207 Gf58
Cerro de la Neblina ⌂ EC 196 Fk46
Cerro de las Ovejas ⌂ RA 208 Gd62
Cerro Delgado-Chalbaud ⌂ BR/YV 193 Gj44
Cerro del Inca ⌂ BOL/RCH 207 Gd55
Cerro de los Bueyes ⌂ RCH 207 Gd56
Cerro del Potro ⌂ RA/RCH 207 Gd60
Cerro del Toro ⌂ RA/RCH 207 Gf60
Cerro de Pasco ◻ PE 197 Gb51
Cerro de Pomasí ⌂ PE 197 Gd54
Cerro de Tocopuri ⌂ BOL 206 Gf55
Cerro Doña Ana ⌂ RCH 207 Gd60
Cerro Doña Inés ⌂ RA 207 Gd58
Cerro Duida ⌂ YV 193 Gh44
Cerro el Cóndor ⌂ RA 207 Gd59
Cerro el Fraile ⌂ RCH 210 Gd72
Cerro Elías ⌂ RA 210 Gd68
Cerro el Nevado ⌂ RA 208 Gf63
Cerro el Fundición ⌂ RA 207 Gf57
Cerro Galán ⌂ RA 207 Gf58
Cerro Galliero ⌂ YV 193 Gh42
Cerro General M. Belgrano ⌂ RA 207 Gg60

Cerro Guanay ⌂ YV 193 Gg43
Cerro Hatscher ⌂ RA 210 Gd70
Cerro Hoya, P.N. ⌂ PA Pa44
Cerro Hudson ⌂ RA 210 Gd69
Cerro Hyades ⌂ RCH 210 Gd70
Cerro Igle ⌂ RA 210 Gd71
Cerro Illesca ⌂ PE 196 Fk49
Cerro Jeinememi ⌂ RCH 210 Gd69
Cerro Juncal ⌂ RA/RCH 208 Ge62
Cerro la Campana ⌂ RCH 210 Gd71
Cerro la Criolla ⌂ RA 210 Ge71
Cerro la Grasa ⌂ RA 208 Ge65
Cerro La Ramada ⌂ BOL/RA 207 Gg57
Cerro Largo ◻ BR (RS) 204 Hc60
Cerro Las Torolas ⌂ RA/RCH 207 Gd60
Cerro Lautaro ⌂ RCH 210 Gd70
Cerro León ◻ CO 193 Gf44
Cerro León ⌂ PY 206 Gk56
Cerro Lique ⌂ BOL 206 Gh56
Cerro Lliscaya ⌂ BOL 206 Gf55
Cerro Lote 15 ⌂ RA 210 Ge68
Cerro Magallanes ⌂ MEX 180 Ef50
Cerro Mellizo Sur ⌂ RCH 210 Gd70
Cerro Mercedario ⌂ RA 208 Ge61
Cerro Mesa ⌂ RA 208 Gf65
Cerro Mina ⌂ CO 192 Gd41
Cerro Mirador ⌂ RCH 210 Ge72
Cerro Monte León ⌂ RA 210 Gf71
Cerro Morado ⌂ RA 207 Gf57
Cerro Moreno ⌂ RCH 207 Ge57
Cerro Murallón ⌂ RA/RCH 210 Gd70
Cerro Nanchital ⌂ MEX (VC) 183 Fc37
Cerro Negro ⌂ RA 210 Gd70
Cerro Negro ⌂ RA 210 Gf68
Cerro Nevado ⌂ RCH 210 Gd71
Cerro Norte ⌂ RA 210 Gd70
Cerro Ovana ⌂ YV 193 Gg43
Cerro Paine Grande ⌂ RCH 210 Gd71
Cerro Pan de Azúcar ⌂ RA 210 Gd70
Cerro Payún ⌂ RA 208 Gf64
Cerro Peineta ⌂ RA 210 Gd71
Cerro Picudo ⌂ RA 210 Gf69
Cerro Picún Leufú ⌂ RA 208 Gf65
Cerro Piedra ⌂ RCH 208 Gd64
Cerro Pináculo ⌂ RA 210 Gd71
Cerro Pingi Pongo ⌂ RA 207 Gf58
Cerro Pintado ⌂ RA 210 Gd70
Cerro Pircas ⌂ RA 208 Gf61
Cerro Pissis ⌂ RA 207 Gf58
Cerro Policia ⌂ RA (RN) 208
Cerro Prieto ⌂ PE 196 Fk48
Cerro Pular ⌂ RCH 207 Gf58
Cerro Punta ⌂ PA 185 Fj41
Cerro Punta Gruesa ⌂ RA 210 Gf71
Cerro Quichaura ⌂ RA 210 Ge68
Cerro Rancahué ⌂ RA 208 Ge65
Cerro Rico ⌂ BOL 206 Gh55
Cerro Rico ⌂ RA (SE) 207 Gh60
Cerro Rincón ⌂ RA/RCH 208 Gf55
Cerro Rucachoroil ⌂ RA 208 Gf66
Cerro Sanchez ⌂ RA 210 Gf71
Cerro San Cirilo ⌂ PE 196 Ga49
Cerro San Joaquín ⌂ EC 197 Ff46
Cerro San Lorenzo ⌂ PE 196 Ga49
Cerro Santa Elena ⌂ RA 210 Gh68
Cerro San Valentín ⌂ RCH 210 Gd69
Cerro Saroche, P.N. ⌂ YV 193 Gf40
Cerros Colorados ⌂ RA 208 Gf66
Cerros de Amotape ⌂ PE 196 Fk48
Cerros de Amotape, P.N. ⌂ PE 196 Fk48
Cerros de Bala ⌂ BOL 206 Gg53
Cerros de Campanquiz ⌂ PE 196 Gb48
Cerros de Canthuyaya ⌂ PE 196 Ga49
Cerros Sierra Nevada ⌂ RCH/RA 208 Gf66
Cerro Sin Nombre ⌂ RCH 208 Gf66
Cerro Sosneado ⌂ RA 208 Gf63
Cerro Steffen ⌂ RA/RCH 210 Gd70
Cerro Tamaná ⌂ CO 192 Gb43
Cerro Tatajachura ⌂ RCH 206 Gf55
Cerro Tazna ⌂ BOL 206 Gg56
Cerro Tetari ⌂ CO/YV 192 Ge40
Cerro Toldo Inter-American Observatory ⌂ RCH 207 Gd60
Cerro Trapalco ⌂ RA 208 Gf65
Cerro Tres Altitos ⌂ RA 208 Gf62
Cerro Tres Cruces ⌂ MEX 183 Fd38
Cerro Tres Picos ⌂ RA 209 Gj65
Cerro Tristeza ⌂ YV 193 Gj40
Cerro Tronador ⌂ RA/RCH 208 Ge66
Cerro Tunapa ⌂ BOL 206 Gg55
Cerro Tupungato ⌂ RA/RCH 208 Ge62
Cerro Turagua ⌂ YV 193 Gh42
Cerro Uhuruncu ⌂ BOL 207 Gg57
Cerro Ventisquero ⌂ RA 208 Gd67
Cerro Ventisquero Sur ⌂ RCH 210 Gd67
Cerro Vera ⌂ ROU 204 Hb62
Cerro Vizcaroya ⌂ RCH 206 Gf56
Cerro Yarupaja ⌂ PE 197 Gb51
Cerro Zapaleri ⌂ BOL/RA/RCH 207 Gg57
Cerrudo Cué ⌂ RA (CR) 204 Ha60
Čerský ◻ RUS 55 Ta05
Certaldo ◻ I 34 Ll47
Certižné ◻ SK 43 Mb41
Čertkovo ◻ RUS 48 Na21
Certosa di Padula ⌂ I 37 Lq50
Certosa di Pavía ⌂ I 34 Lk45
Cervales ⌂ E 27 Kp51
Cervantes ◻ AUS 104 Qh61
Cervantes ◻ RP 90 Ra37
Červen' ◻ BY 48 Mf19
Červená Skala ◻ SK 43 Ma42
Červená Voda ◻ CZ 42 Lr41
Cervera ◻ E 29 Lb49
Cervera del Río Alhama ◻ E 28 Kt48
Cervera de Pisuerga ◻ E 26 Kq47
Cervia ◻ I 36 Ln46
Cervignano del Friuli ◻ I 35 Lo45

Cérykav ◻ BY 48 Mf19
Cesário Lange ◻ BR (SP) 205 Hg57
Česavljia ◻ BY 41 Mf37
Cesena ◻ I 36 Ln46
Cēsis ◻ LV 39 Mf33
Česká Kamenice ◻ CZ 42 Lp40
Česká Kubice ◻ CZ 42 Ln41
Česká Lípa ◻ CZ 42 Lp40
České Budějovice ◻ CZ 42 Lp42
Cēsvaine ◻ LV 39 Mf33
České Švýcarsko, N.P. ⌂ CZ 42 Lp42
České Velenice ◻ CZ 42 Lp42
Český Brod ◻ CZ 42 Lp40
Český Dub ◻ CZ 42 Lp40
Český Krumlov ◻ CZ 42 Lp42
Český ráj ⌂ CZ 42 Lq41
Çeşme ◻ TR 56 Mg28
Cessnock ◻ AUS (NSW) 111 Sf62
Cestos Point ⌂ LB 136 Kf43
Cētār ◻ CHN (NEI) 72 Qa27
Cetatea de Baltă ◻ RO 43 Me44
Cetatea Heracleea ⌂ RO 45 Mj46
Cetingrad ◻ HR 35 Lq45
Cetinje ◻ SCG 44 Lt48
Cetraro ◻ I 37 Lq51
Ceuta ◻ E 125 Kn28
Ceuta ◻ E 125 Kh28
Ceuta ⌂ YV 192 Ge41
Cevdale = Zufallspitze ⌂ I 34 Ll44
Cévennes ⌂ F 25 Ld46
Cévennes, P.N. des ⌂ F 25 Ld46
Cevizli ◻ TR 56 Mf27
Cewice ◻ PL 40 Ls36
Ceyhan ◻ TR 56 Mh27
Ceyhan Nehri ⌂ TR 56 Mj27
Ceylanpınar ◻ TR 57 Na27
Ceylon ◻ CDN (SK) 169 Eh21
Ceylon ◻ CL 52 Pa09
Chaacha ◻ TM 62 Oa27
Cha-am ◻ THA 88 Qa38
Chababar ⌂ IR 64 Oa33
Chabanais ◻ F 24 Lb45
Chabás ◻ RA (SF) 209 Gk62
Chabe ⌂ J 146 Mg31
Chabi ◻ THA (NBI) 171 Eg27
Chaboksar ◻ IR 57 Nf27
Chabovicy ◻ BY 41 Me38
Chabris ◻ F 25 Lb43
Chacabuco ◻ RA (BA) 209 Gk62
Chacabuco ◻ RCH 210 Gd68
Chacaltaya ⌂ BOL 206 Gf54
Chacao ◻ RCH 208 Gd66
Chacarilla ◻ RCH 206 Gf56
Chacas ◻ PE 197 Gb50
Chaca Sur ◻ RCH 206 Gf55
Chacay Alto ◻ RA 208 Gf64
Chачани, Volcán ⌂ PE 197 Ge54
Chachapoyas ◻ PE 196 Ga49
Chacharan ◻ PK 65 Of31
Chacharramendi ◻ RA (LP) 208 Gf64
Chachi, Cerro ⌂ RA 208 Gd64
Chachoengsao ◻ THA 88 Qa39
Chachro ◻ PK 65 Of33
Chaco ◻ RA 207 Gj58
Chaco Austral ⌂ RA 207 Gk59
Chaco Boreal ⌂ PY 206 Gj56
Chacomer ◻ MOC 153 Mj53
Chacon ◻ CDN 166 Dd18
Chaco Central ⌂ PY 206 Gj56
Chaco Culture N.H.P. ⌂ USA 171 Ef28
Chacra del Atakora ⌂ RA 207 Gj57
Chaco, P.N. ⌂ RA 207 Gj59
Chacras, Cerro ⌂ EC 197 Fe46
Chacuey ◻ DOM 186 Ge36
Chad ◻ 123 Lb08
Chadakan ◻ RN 132 La38
Chadaounka ◻ RN 132 La38
Chad Basin N.P. ⌂ WAN 139 Lg39
Chadegan ◻ IR 59 Nf29
Chadiza ◻ Z 152 Mg53
Chadron ◻ USA (NE) 171 Ej24
Chae Hom ◻ THA 88 Pk36
Chaek ◻ KS 66 Oh25
Chaeryong ◻ PRK 78 Rd26
Chae Son N.P. ⌂ THA 87 Pk36
Chafe ◻ WAN 138 Lc40
Chafo ◻ WAN 138 Lc40
Chagai ◻ PK 65 Oc31
Chagai Hills ⌂ PK 65 Ob31
Chagalamarri ◻ IND (APH)
Chaghanbadi ⌂ IR 57 Ne29
Chagla ◻ PE 197 Gc52
Chagny ◻ F 25 Le44
Chagoda ◻ RUS 48 Mh16
Chagos Archipelago ◻ GB 52 Oi10
Chagos-Laccadive Ridge ⌂ 52 Oi11
Chagres, P.N. ⌂ PA 185 Ga41
Chaguanas ◻ TT 187 Gk40
Chaguaramas ⌂ TT 187 Gk40
Chaguaramas ◻ YV 193 Gg42
Chaguaramas ◻ YV 193 Gg41
Chaguaramba ⌂ EC 196 Ga47
Chahabad ⌂ IR 64 Oa30
Chahar Borjak ⌂ AFG 64 Ob30
Chahar Burjak ⌂ AFG 64 Ob30
Chahbounia ◻ DZ 126 Lb28
Chahe ◻ CHN (YUN) 87 Qb32
Chah-e Ab ⌂ AFG 63 Oe27
Chah-e-Mosafar ◻ IR 64 Nj28
Chahjam ◻ IR 62 Nh28
Chah Pahn ◻ IR 59 Nf32
Chah Sagak ◻ IR 64 Nj29
Chah Zardar ◻ IR 64 Nk32
Chah Zebar ◻ IR 64 Nh31
Chai ◻ MOC 147 Na51
Chai Badan ◻ THA 88 Qa38
Chaibasa ◻ IND (JKD) 83 Pc34
Chaill ◻ IND (UPH) 83 Pa33
Chaillé-les-Marais ◻ F 24 Ku44
Chainat ◻ THA 88 Qa38
Chaine des Biban ⌂ DZ 126 Lc27
Chai Pra Kan ◻ THA 87 Pk36
Chaiqiao ◻ CHN (ZJG) 75 Ra31
Chaitén ◻ RCH 210 Gd67
Chaiwopu ◻ CHN (XUZ) 67 Pd24
Chaiya ◻ THA 88 Pk41
Chaiyaphum ◻ THA 89 Qb38
Chajari ◻ RA (ER) 204 Ha60
Chajian ◻ CHN (AHU) 78 Qk29
Chajlakol ◻ KZ 63 Oe23
Chakai ◻ IND (JKD) 83 Pc33
Chak Chake ◻ EAT 147 Na47
Chakdaha ◻ IND (WBG) 86 Pe34
Chak Jhumra ◻ PK 65 Og30
Chakkarrat ◻ THA 89 Qb38

Chakradharpur ◻ IND (JKD) 83 Pc34
Chakrata ◻ IND (UTT) 81 Oj30
Chaksu ◻ IND (RJT) 80 Oh32
Chak Swari ◻ 65 Og29
Chakur ◻ IND (MHT) 82 Oj36
Chakwal ◻ PK 65 Og29
Chakwale ◻ EAT 146 Mf49
Chakwenga ◻ Z 152 Me53
Chala ◻ EAT 146 Mf49
Chala ◻ MOC 153 Mh52
Chala ◻ PE 197 Gc53
Chalais ◻ F 24 Lb45
Chalakudi ◻ IND (KER) 84 Oj40
Chalalou ◻ PNG 116 Sd47
Chalamera ◻ E 29 La49
Chalamont ◻ F 21 Lf45
Chalatenango ◻ ES 184 Ff38
Chalaua ◻ MOC 153 Mk54
Chalbi Desert ⌂ EAK 144 Mj44
Chalcatzingo ⌂ MEX 182 Fa36
Chalchihuites ◻ MEX (ZCT) 181 Eh34
Chalco ◻ MEX (MEX) 182 Fa36
Chalinze ◻ EAT 147 Mk49
Chalisgaon ◻ IND (MHT) 82 Oh36
Chalk Mountain ⌂ USA (TX) 174 Fb29
Chalky Inlet ⌂ NZ 113 Td69
Chalkyitsik ◻ USA (AK) 165 Cj12
Challa ◻ AUS (WA) 104 Qj60
Challakere ◻ IND (KTK) 84 Oj38
Challakudi ◻ IND (KER) 84 Oj40
Challalle ◻ IND (APH) 83 Pa37
Challapalca ◻ BOL 206 Gf54
Challapata ◻ BOL 206 Gg55
Challenger Deep ⌂ 10 Sa08
Challis ◻ USA (ID) 168 Ec23
Chalma ◻ MEX 182 Fa36
Châlons-en-Champagne ◻ F 23 Le42
Chalon-sur-Saône ◻ F 25 Le44
Chalt ◻ 80 Oj27
Cha Lugala ◻ MOC 153 Mj54
Châlus ◻ F 24 Lb45
Chalus ◻ IR 57 Nf27
Cham ◻ CH 34 Lj43
Chama ◻ USA (NM) 171 Eg27
Chama ◻ Z 146 Mg51
Chamah, Gunung ⌂ MAL 92 Qa43
Chaman ◻ PK 65 Oe30
Chamanga ◻ EC 196 Fj46
Chaman Soltan ⌂ IR 59 Ne29
Chamarel ⌂ MEX 183 Fg36
Chamba ◻ EAT 147 Mj51
Chamba ◻ IND (HPH) 80 Oj29
Chamba ◻ MOC 153 Mj53
Chambamba ◻ RIM 132 Kj37
Chamba ◻ RIM 130 Kh38
Chamical ◻ RA (LR) 207 Gg61
Chamberlain ◻ CDN (SK) 169 Eh20
Chamberlain ◻ USA (SD) 172 Fa24
Chamberlain Lake ⌂ USA 177 Gf22
Chambersburg ◻ USA (PA) 177 Gb26
Chambers Pillar ⌂ AUS 108 Rg58
Chambéry ◻ F 25 Lf45
Chambi ⌂ TN 126 Le28
Chambley ◻ F 23 Lf41
Chambly ◻ CDN (QC) 176 Gd23
Chambord ◻ CDN (QC) 176 Gd21
Chamboré ⌂ F 24 La43
Chamdo ◻ CHN (TIB) 87 Qb30
Chamela ◻ MEX (JLC) 182 Eh36
Chameteng ◻ MOC 153 Mk54
Chamesson ◻ F 23 Le43
Chamgordy ⌂ IR 57 Nd27
Chami ◻ RIM 130 Kh35
Chamical ◻ RA (LR) 207 Gg61
Cham Ka ◻ THA 87 Pk36
Cham Kabud ⌂ IR 59 Nd29
Chamkani ◻ AFG 65 Oe29
Chamoli ⌂ IND (UTT) 81 Ok30
Chamonix-Mont-Blanc ◻ F 25 Lg45
Champagne ◻ CDN (BC) 166 Dc16
Champagne ◻ F 23 Le42
Champagne-Ardenne ◻ F 23 Ld42
Champagne-Mouton ◻ F 24 La45
Champagne Pools ⌂ NZ 113 Tj65
Champagnole ◻ F 25 Lf44
Champaign ◻ USA (IL) 175 Ff25
Champal (MZR) 86 Pd34
Champaign ◻ CDN (IL) 175 Ff25
Champ-du-Boult ◻ F 22 Ku42
Champerico ◻ GCA 184 Fe38
Champhai ◻ IND (MIZ) 86 Ph34
Champhon ◻ LAO 89 Qc38
Champlitte-et-le-Prélot ◻ F 25 Lc43
Champotón ◻ MEX (CAM) 183 Fe36
Champua ◻ IND (ORS) 83 Pc34
Chamrajnagar ◻ IND (KTK) 84 Oj40
Chamuris ⌂ IND (MHT) 83 Ok36
Chamusca ◻ P 27 Km51
Chanac ◻ F 25 Ld46
Chanakvilla ⌂ IND (APH) 83 Pa37
Chan-Chan ⌂ PE 197 Ga50
Chancay ◻ PE 197 Gb51
Chanchayllo ◻ PE 197 Gb52
Chanch ◻ MNG 70 Qf21
Chanchra ◻ BD 86 Pf34
Chanco ◻ RCH 208 Gd63
Chandalar ◻ USA (AK) 165 Cf12
Chandavila ⌂ IND (MHT) 82 Oj37
Chandbali ◻ IND (ORS) 83 Pd35
Chandel ◻ IND (MNP) 86 Ph33
Chandeleur Islands ⌂ USA 175 Ff31
Chandeleur Sound ⌂ USA 175 Ff31
Chandemagore ◻ IND (WBG) 86 Pe34
Chanderi ⌂ IND (MPH) 83 Ok33
Chandigarh ◻ IND (PJB) 81 Oj30
Chandil ◻ IND (JKD) 83 Pc34
Chandler ◻ CDN (QC) 176 Gg22
Chandler ◻ USA (AZ) 171 Ee29
Chandler ◻ USA (OK) 174 Fb28
Chandlers Falls ⌂ EAK 144 Mj45
Chandni Chowk ⌂ IND (DEL) 80 Oj31
Chandod ◻ IND (GUJ) 82 Og34
Chandpur ◻ BD 86 Pf34
Chandpur ◻ IND (UPH) 81 Ok31
Chandrabhaga ◻ IND (MHT)
Chandragiri ◻ IND (APH) 84 Ok39
Chandragutti ◻ IND (KTK) 84 Oh39
Chandraghona ◻ BD 86 Pg34
Chandrakona ◻ IND (WBG) 86 Pe34
Chandranath Temple ⌂ BD 86 Pf34
Chandrapur ◻ IND (MHT) 83 Ok35

Chandraprabha Wildlife Sanctuary ⌂ IND 83 Pc33
Chapfuche ◻ ZW 152 Mf56
Chapicuy ◻ ROU 204 Hb61
Chaplin ◻ CDN (SK) 169 Eg20
Chaplin ◻ USA (NE) 174 Ej25
Chapleau ◻ CDN (MPH) 82 Oj34
Chapuy ◻ RA (ST) 209 Gk62
Chār ◻ RIM 130 Kd35
Charadai ◻ RA (CH) 204 Ha59
Charagua ◻ BOL 206 Gj55
Charala ◻ CO 192 Gd42
Charama ◻ IND (CGH) 83 Pa35
Charara Safari Area ⌂ ZW 152 Me54
Charata ◻ RA (CH) 207 Gk59
Charcas ◻ MEX (SLP) 182 Ek34
Chard ◻ CDN (AB) 167 Ee18
Chardon ◻ USA (GA) 175 Fh26
Charikar ◻ AFG 65 Oe28
Chariton ◻ USA (IA) 172 Fd25
Charity ◻ GUY 194 Ha42
Charkhari ◻ IND (UPH) 83 Ok33
Charkhari ◻ IND (UPH) 83 Ok33
Charkhi Dadri ◻ IND (HYA) 80 Oj31
Charleroi ◻ B 23 Le40
Charlesbourg ◻ CDN (QC) 176 Ge22
Charles City ◻ USA (IA) 172 Fd24
Charles Fort ⌂ IRL 19 Km39
Charles Fuhr ◻ RA (SC) 210 Ge71
Charles Lake ⌂ CDN (AB) 167 Ee16
Charleston ◻ NZ 113 Td66
Charleston ◻ USA (MO) 175 Ff27
Charleston ◻ USA (SC) 178 Ga29
Charleston ◻ USA (WV) 175 Fk26
Charleston ◻ KNA 187 Gi37
Charlestown ◻ USA (IN) 175 Fh26
Charleville ◻ AUS (QLD) 109 Sd59
Charleville ◻ IRL 19 Km38
Charleville-Mézières ◻ F 23 Le41
Charlevoix ◻ USA (MI) 173 Fh23
Charlieu ◻ F 25 Le44
Charlotte ◻ USA (MI) 173 Fh24
Charlotte ◻ USA (NC) 178 Fk28
Charlotte Bank ⌂ 89 Qd42
Charlotte Bank ◻ 100 Tb11
Charlottenberg ◻ S 30 Lm31
Charlotte Plains ◻ AUS (QLD) 109 Sd60
Charlottesville ◻ USA (VA) 177 Ga26
Charlottetown ◻ CDN (PE) 176 Gg22
Charlotteville ◻ TT 187 Gk40
Charlton ◻ USA (IL) 175 Ff26
Charmco ◻ USA (WV) 175 Fk26
Charmes ◻ F 23 Lg42
Charminar ⌂ IND 82 Ok37
Charny ◻ F 25 Ld43
Charolles ◻ F 25 Le44
Charost ◻ F 25 Lc44
Charouïne ◻ DZ 125 Kj31
Char Rah ◻ AFG 64 Ob29
Charrud ◻ IR 64 Nj29
Chasrada ◻ PK 65 Of28
Charsadda ◻ IND (AK) 164 Bh15
Chegaraski ◻ UZ 63 Od27
Chegga ◻ DZ 126 Lc29
Chegga ◻ RIM 125 Kh30
Chegge ◻ RIM 130 Kc36
Cheghe ◻ ZW 152 Mf55
Chehalis ◻ USA (WA) 168 Dj22
Cheheo ◻ CHN (SAA) 72 Qd33
Cheia ◻ RO 45 Mh44
Cheile Bicazului-Hășmaș, P.N. ⌂ RO 49 Mg22
Cheile Nerei-Beușnița, P.N. ⌂ RO 44 Mb46
Cheju ◻ ROK 78 Rd28
Cheju do ◻ ROK 78 Rd28
Chelabó ◻ DZ 126 Lc29
Chelan ◻ USA (WA) 168 Dk21
Chela, Serra da ⌂ ANG 150 Lg53
Cheleken ◻ TM 62 Ng26
Cheles ◻ E 27 Kn52
Chelford ◻ RA (SC) 208 Gg65
Chelghoum-El Aïd ◻ DZ 126 Ld27
Cheliff ⌂ DZ 126 Lb27
Chelm ◻ PL 41 Md39
Chelmno ◻ PL 40 Lt37
Chelmsford ◻ GB 21 La39
Chelmsford Public Resort Nature Reserve ⌂ ZA 155 Me59
Chełmża ◻ PL 40 Lt37
Cheltenham ◻ GB 21 Ks39
Chelva ◻ E 29 Ku51
Chemaia ◻ MA 125 Kg29
Chemax ◻ MEX (YT) 183 Fg35
Chembe ◻ Z 146 Md51
Chemillé ◻ F 24 Ku43
Chemin de Saint-Jacques-de-Compostelle ⌂ F 24 Kt47
Chemnitz ◻ D 32 Ln40
Chemtou ⌂ TN 126 Le27
Chenachane ◻ DZ 125 Kh32
Chena Hot Springs ◻ USA (AK) 165 Cg13
Chena River State Recreation Area ⌂ USA 165 Cg13
Chenar Shahijan ◻ IR 59 Nf31
Chen Barag Qi ◻ CHN (NMZ) 71 Qk21
Chencha ◻ ETH 142 Mj42
Chéneralles ◻ F 25 Lc44
Chenereilles ◻ F 25 Le44
Chengam ◻ IND (TNU) 85 Ok39
Chengbu ◻ CHN (HUN) 74 Qf32
Chengcheng ◻ CHN (SAA) 72 Qe28
Chengde ◻ CHN (HBI)
Chengdu ◻ CHN (SCH) 74 Qc30
Chenggong ◻ CHN (YUN) 87 Qa33
Chenghai ◻ CHN (SAA) 72 Qf29
Chenghai ◻ CHN (GDG) 75 Qj34
Chengjiang ◻ CHN (YUN) 87 Qa33
Chengmai ◻ CHN (HAI) 75 Qf36
Chengshan Jiao ◻ CHN 73 Rb27
Cheng Xian ◻ CHN (GSU) 72 Qd29
Chengyang Bridge ⌂ CHN 74 Qe33
Chenik ◻ USA (AK) 164 Cc16
Chenini ◻ TN 126 Lf29
Chenjiagang ◻ CHN (JGS)

Chennakeshava Temple ⌂ IND 84 Oh39

Column 1

Chenonceaux ⊙ F 24 Lb43
Chenôve F 25 Le43
Chenpur NEP 81 Pa31
Chenque, Cerro RA 210 Gg68
Chenxi CHN (CGG) 74 Qd30
Chenzhou CHN (HUN) 75 Qg33
Cheo Reo VN 89 Qe39
Chepen PE 196 Ga49
Chepes RA (LR) 208 Gg61
Chepo PA 185 Ga41
Chepsikunya EAU 144 Mh45
Cheptow GB 21 Ks39
Cher F 24 Lb43
Cheranchi WAN 132 Ld39
Cherangani Hills EAK 144 Mh45
Cherating Beach MAL 92 Qb43
Cheraw USA (SC) 178 Ga28
Cherbourg-Octeville F 22 Kt41
Cherchell DZ 126 Lb27
Cherhill GB 169 Ec19
Chéri RN 133 Lf39
Cheria DZ 126 Ld28
Cheripon GH 137 La40
Chernobyl KZ 62 Nk23
Cherkee USA (IA) 172 Fc24
Cherokee USA (OK) 174 Fa27
Cherokee USA (TX) 174 Fa30
Cherokee Sound BS 179 Gb32
Chéroy F 23 Ld42
Cherry Creek USA (NV) 170 Ec26
Cherry Creek USA (SD) 172 Ek23
Cherryfield USA (ME) 176 Gg23
Cherryville CDN (BC) 168 Ea20
Cherskiy Range RUS 55 Rd05
Cherson UA 49 Mg23
Chersonesus UA 49 Mg23
Cheru Konda IND 83 Pb37
Chesapeake USA (VA) 178 Gb27
Chesapeake Bay USA 177 Gb26
Chesapeake Bay Bridge Tunnel USA 178 Gc27
Chesapeake Beach USA (VA) 177 Gb27
Cheshmeh Malek IR 64 Nk30
Chesht-e Sharif AFG 65 Ob28
Chesmeh Kabud IR 57 Nd29
Cheste E 29 Ku51
Chester CDN (NS) 176 Gh23
Chester GB 21 Ks37
Chester USA (MT) 169 Ee21
Chester USA (PA) 177 Gc26
Chester USA (CA) 170 Dk26
Chester USA (VA) 178 Gb27
Chesterfield GB 21 Kt37
Chesterfield Inlet CDN 163 Fb06
Chesterton Range AUS (QLD) 109 Sd58
Chesterton N.P. AUS 109 Sd59
Chetaïbi DZ 126 Ld27
Chete ZW 152 Md54
Chetlat Island IND 84 Og40
Chetput IND (TNU) 85 Ok39
Chetumal MEX (QTR) 183 Ff36
Chetwynd CDN (BC) 166 Dk18
Chevak USA (AK) 164 Bh05
Chevanceaux F 24 Lb43
Cheverny F 24 Lb43
Cheviot CDN (QC) 176 Ha20
Cheviot NZ 113 Tg67
Chew Bahir ETH 144 Mj43
Chewelah USA (WA) 168 Eb21
Chewore Safari Area ZW 152 Me53
Cheyenne USA (OK) 174 Fa28
Cheyenne USA (WY) 171 Eh25
Cheyenne USA 169 Ef22
Cheyenne River Ind. Res. USA 172 Ek23
Cheyenne Wells USA (CO) 174 Ej26

Column 2

Chichagof Island USA 166 Dc17
Chichaouanni MA 124 Kf30
Chichawatni PK 65 Og30
Chicheng CHN (HBI) 73 Qh25
Chichén Itzá MEX 183 Ff35
Chichester GB 21 Ku40
Chichibu J 77 Rk27
Chichibu-Tama J 79 Rk28
Chichicastenango GCA 184 Fe38
Chichirivichi YV 193 Gf40
Chichola EC 196 Gb47
Chicholi IND (MPH) 83 Pa35
Chickaloon USA (AK) 165 Cf15
Chickamauga & Chattanooga N.M.P. USA 175 Fh28
Chickasaw N.R.A. USA 174 Fb28
Chickasaw USA (OK) 174 Fb29
Chickasha CDN (OK) 165 Ck13
Chicken Cr. Summit USA 170 Eg25
Chiclana de la Frontera E 27 Ko54
Chiclayo PE 196 Ga49
Chico USA (MOC) 152 Mg56
Chico RA 210 Gf70
Chico USA (CA) 170 Dk26
Chicoana RA (SA) 207 Gh58
Chicoasén MEX (CHP) 183 Fd37
Chicocca ANG 150 Lh54
Chicomba ANG 150 Lh53
Chicomo MOC 152 Mg56
Chicomostoc MEX 182 Ej34
Chicomuselo MEX (CHP) 183 Fd38
Chiconono MOC 147 Mh52
Chicopee USA (MA) 177 Gd24
Chicoral CO 192 Gc43
Chicotte CDN (QC) 176 Gj21
Chicoutimi CDN (QC) 176 Ge21
Chicualacuale MOC 152 Mf57
Chicuma ANG 150 Lh52
Chicundo Z 146 Mf51
Chicupa ANG 150 Lj52
Chicuti MOC 153 Mh52
Chidambaram IND 85 Ok40
Chidenguele MOC 152 Mh58
Chidu ROK 78 Rd28
Chidu SUD 142 Mf41
Chidya EAT 147 Mk51
Chiede ANG 150 Lh54
Chiefland USA (FL) 178 Fj31
Chief Menominee Mem. USA 173 Fg25
Chief's Island RB 151 Mb55
Chiemsee D 33 Ln43
Chieng Cang VN 87 Qb35
Chiengi Z 146 Me50
Chiengo Z 152 Mf53
Chiesa di San Pio J 37 Lq49
Chieti I 37 Lp48
Chifango ANG 150 Lj53
Chifeng CHN (NMZ) 71 Qk24
Chiftak USA (AK) 164 Bj15
Chifu WAN 138 Lc40
Chifukunya Hills Z 152 Me53
Chifunda Z 146 Mg51
Chihama ANG 150 Lj52
Chig RIM 130 Kd35
Chigamane MOC 152 Mg53
Chigingak, Mount USA 164 Cb17
Chigmit Mountains USA 164 Cd15
Chignik USA (AK) 164 Ca17
Chigongwe EAT 146 Mh49
Chigorodó CO 192 Gb42
Chiguana, Volcán BOL 206 Gg56
Chiguayante RCH 208 Gd64
Chigubo MOC 152 Mg57
Chigugu EAT 147 Mf51
Chigwe Z 146 Mf51
Chigwell GB 21 La39
Chihili Zina J AFG 65 Oc30
Chihsing Yen RC 75 Ra35
Chihuahua MEX (CHH) 180 Eg31
Chihuahua MEX 180 Eg31
Chihuído de Medio, Cerro RA 208 Gf64
Chihulo MOC 153 Mj53
Chijmuni BOL 206 Gg54
Chikali Kalan IND (MPH) 83 Ok34
Chikamamudi IND (APH) 83 Ok37
Chikaballapur IND (KTK) 84 Oj39
Chikhli IND (GUJ) 82 Og35
Chikhli IND (MHT) 82 Oj35
Chikitzonoot MEX (YT) 183 Ff35
Chikmagalur IND (KTK) 84 Oj39
Chikodi IND (KTK) 82 Oh37
Chikombedzi ZW 152 Mf56
Chikupalle IND (APH) 83 Pa36
Chikwa Z 146 Mg51
Chikwanda Z 146 Mf51
Chikwawa MW 153 Mh54
Chila ANG 150 Lh52
Chilanko Forks CDN (BC) 166 Dh19
Chilapa de Alvarez MEX (GUR) 182 Fa37
Chilapa de Corzo MEX (CHP) 183 Fd37
Chilas PK 65 Og28
Chilaw CL 85 Ok42
Chilca PE 197 Gb52
Chilca Juliana RA (SE) 207 Gj60
Chilcoot USA (CA) 170 Dk26
Chilcotin CDN (BC) 166 Dh20
Chilches E 29 Ku51
Childers AUS (QLD) 109 Sg58
Childress USA (TX) 174 Fa29
Chile S 191 Ga13
Chile Basin 190 Ga12
Chile Chico RCH 210 Ge69
Chilecito RA (LR) 207 Gg60
Chilhowie USA (VA) 178 Fk27
Chilia RN 133 Lh39
Chilete PE 196 Ga49
Chilhiore PA 185 Ga41
Chilika Lake IND (WI) 172 Fe23
Chililicote MEX (CHH) 181 Eh31
Chilin J 89 Qc40
Chiling RA (CA) 170 Dk28
Chiliwack CDN (BC) 168 Dk21

Column 3

Chilpancingo de los Bravos MEX (GUR) 182 Fa37
Chilpi IND (MPH) 80 Pa37
Chiltern AUS (VIC) 111 Sd64
Chiltern Hills GB 21 Ku39
Chiluage ANG 149 Ma50
Chilumbulwa Z 151 Md52
Chilupar IND (UPH) 83 Pb32
Chil-Ustun KS 63 Og25
Chimaila EAT 146 Mg50
Chimaltenango GCA 184 Fe38
Chimán PA 185 Ga41
Chimanimani N.P. ZW 152 Mg55
Chimamba Z 152 Me53
Chimay B 23 Le40
Chimba Z 146 Mg51
Chimbana CO 163 Ga08
Chimbas RA (SJ) 207 Gf61
Chimborazo, Volcán EC 196 Ga46
Chimbote PE 197 Ga50
Chimboy UZ 62 Nk24
Chimel MEX (JLC) 182 Eh35
Chimoio MOC 152 Mg54
Chimpamba MW 146 Mf51
Chimur IND (MHT) 83 Ok35
Chimusimbe ZW 152 Mf55
China CHN 53 Pa06
Chinácota CO 192 Gd42
Chinak-meru YV 193 Gk43
Chinandega NIC 184 Fg39
Chincha Alta PE 197 Gb52
Chinchero PE 197 Gd52
Chinchilla AUS (QLD) 109 Sf59
Chinchilla de Monte Aragón E 29 Ks52
Chinchina CO 192 Gc43
Chinchon E 27 Kr50
Chinchorro, Reserva de la Biósfera Banco MEX 183 Fg36
Chincoteague USA 177 Gc27
Chinde MOC 153 Mj55
Chin Do ROK 78 Rd28
Chindo ROK 78 Rd28
Chindrikir IND 81 Oj27
Chindwin MYA 86 Ph33
Chingaza, P.N. CO 192 Gd43
Chingnal IND (NGL) 86 Ph32
Chingo ANG 150 Lj53
Chinguar ANG 150 Lj52
Chinguetti RIM 130 Kd35
Chingune ANG 150 Lj52
Chinhae ROK 78 Rd28
Chini CO 192 Gd41
Chinibulak KS 63 Oh25
Chinin CO 192 Gd40
Chinju ROK 79 Re28
Chinko RCA 141 Md43
Chinle USA (AZ) 171 Ef27
Chinmen CHN (FJN) 75 Qk33
Chinmen Tao RC 75 Ra35
Chinnur IND (APH) 83 Ok36
Chinobampo MEX (SL) 180 Ef32
Chin Hills MYA 86 Pg35
Chinhoyi ZW 152 Mf54
Chinhoyi Caves ZW 152 Mf54
Chinida Z 152 Mg53
Chinsali Z 146 Mg51
China PL USA 164 Cd16
Chinju R ROK 79 Re28
Chino USA (CA) 170 Eb28
Chino RCA 141 Md43
Chino Valley USA (AZ) 171 Ee28
Chinobo Z 152 Mf54
Chinook CDN (AB) 169 Ef20
Chinsali Z 146 Mg51
Chinturi NEP 83 Pb32
Chinquite USA 49 Md21
Chinsali Z 146 Lg52
Chintalapudi IND (APH) 83 Pa37
Chintalnar IND (CGH) 83 Pa36
Chintamani IND (KTK) 84 Oj39
Chintapalle IND (APH) 83 Pb37
Chintheche MW 146 Mh51
Chinú CO 192 Gc41
Chinunje EAT 147 Mj51
Chinyama Litapi Z 151 Mb52
Chioco MOC 152 Mg54
Chióggia I 34 Ln45
Chipaia PE 197 Gb51
Chione RO 45 Mg45
Chiona IND (MHT) 84 Oj37
Chipata Z 146 Mg52
Chipepo Z 152 Me53
Chipewyan Ind. Res. CDN 167 Ee16
Chiphen Hot Springs RC 75 Ra34
Chipinda Z 146 Me51
Chipindo ANG 150 Lj52
Chipinga ZW 152 Mg55
Chipinga Safari Area ZW 152 Mg56
Chipiona E 27 Ko54
Chipley USA (FL) 175 Fh30
Chiplun IND (MHT) 82 Og37
Chipman CDN (NB) 176 Gh22
Chipogolo Z 146 Mh50
Chipoia ANG 150 Lj52
Chipoka MW 153 Mh53
Chipola USA (FL) 175 Fh30
Chippenham Falls GB 21 Kt39
Chippewa Falls USA (WI) 172 Fe23
Chiprana E 29 Ku49
Chiprovtsi BG 44 Mc47
Chiquila MEX 183 Ff35
Chiquián PE 197 Gb51
Chiquila N.P. BR 194 Ff37
Chira ETH 142 Mj44
Chiramba MOC 153 Mh54
Chirapatla IND (MPH) 82 Oj34
Chiraz IRN 57 Ng30
Chirdzi MW 153 Mh53
Chire CO 192 Gd42
Chirfa RN 133 Lg35
Chirgaon IND (UPH) 83 Ok33
Chiribiquete, P.N. CO 192 Gd45
Chirikof Island USA 164 Cb17

Column 4

Chiricahua Nat. Mon. USA 171 Ef29
Chiriguana CO 192 Gd41
Chirinos PE 196 Ga48
Chiri YV 193 Gg40
Chiripó, P.N. CR 185 Fj41
Chiri San ROK 78 Rd28
Chirisa Safari Area ZW 152 Me54
Chirivel E 27 Ks53
Chiroqchi UZ 63 Oc26
Chiriró, P.N. CR 185 Fj41
Chirumanzu ZW 152 Mf55
Chirundu Z 152 Me53
Chirundu Fossil Forest Z 152 Me54
Chisamba Z 152 Me53
Chisamba Z 146 Mg51
Chisana USA (AK) 165 Ck14
Chisasibi CDN (QC) 163 Ga08
Chisec GCA 184 Fe38
Chisekesi Z 152 Md54
Chisenga MW 146 Mg51
Chisenga MW 146 Mh51
Chisholm USA (MN) 172 Fd22
Chisholm Trail Mus. USA 174 Fb28
Chishui CHN (SCH) 87 Qc32
Chishiba Falls Z 146 Mf51
Chisinau MD 49 Me22
Chislaz RO 43 Mc43
Chisoso Z 146 Mf51
Chisov MOC 155 Mg58
Chissibuce Z 146 Mf51
Chissinguane MOC 152 Mh56
Chistian Mandy PK 65 Og31
Chisvingo ZW 152 Mf55
Chitanli PE 196 Ga48
Chitalpa MEX (TB) 183 Fd37
Chitanda Z 152 Md53
Chi Tanh VN 89 Qe39
Chitedze MW 146 Mg52
Chitek Lake CDN (SK) 169 Eg19
Chitina USA (AK) 165 Ck15
Chitengo MOC 153 Mh55
Chitina Z 151 Mc52
Chitipa MW 146 Mg51
Chitobe MOC 152 Mg54
Chitonga Z 152 Md54
Chitose J 77 Sa24
Chitradurga IND (KTK) 84 Oj38
Chitrakut IND (MPH) 83 Pa33
Chitral PK 63 Of28
Chitral PA 185 Fk42
Chittagong BD 86 Pf34
Chittaranjan IND (JKD) 83 Pd34
Chittaurgarh IND (RJT) 82 Oh33
Chittaurgarh Fort IND (RJT) 82 Oh33
Chittoor IND (APH) 85 Ok39
Chittoor = Chittaurgarh IND (RJT) 82 Oh33
Chitungwiza ZW 152 Mf55
Chiúcha MOC 152 Mg56
Chityal IND (APH) 83 Ok36
Chiuchiu RCH 207 Gf57
Chiuchiu RCH 207 Gf57
Chiúmbo ANG 150 Lj52
Chiúmbo Z 152 Md54
Chiúre Novo MOC 147 Mk52
Chiúre Velho MOC 147 Mk52
Chiusa = Klausen I 34 Lm44
Chiusi I 34 Lm47
Chiuta Z 146 Mg51
Chiva E 29 Ku51
Chivacoa YV 193 Gf40
Chivasso I 34 Lh45
Chivato RCH 207 Gf59
Chivay PE 197 Gd53
Chivhu ZW 152 Mf55
Chivicloy PA (BA) 209 Ha63
Chivirico C 179 Ga36
Chizarira ZW 152 Md54
Chizarira N.P. ZW 152 Md54
Chizu J 79 Rh28
Chizwina RB 152 Md56
Chlef DZ 126 La27
Chlebiów USA 164 Dd42
Chłmo Bung CAM 139 Lh43
Chlumec nad Cidlinou CZ 42 Lq41
Chmel'nyc'kyj UA 49 Md21
Chmielnik PL 41 Ma40
Chmil'nyk UA 49 Md21
Cham Khsant K 89 Qc38
Choam Sla K 89 Qb40
Chobe RB 151 Mc55
Chobe = RB/NAM 151 Mc55
Chobe N.P. RB 151 Mc55
Chocca, Cerro PE 197 Gc52
Chocianów PL 40 Lq39
Chocó CO 192 Gb41
Chocolate Hills RP 90 Rc41
Chocolate Mts. USA 170 Ec29
Chocontá CO 192 Gd43
Chocope PE 196 Ga49
Chocua N.W.R. USA 175 Ff30
Chodavaram IND (APH) 83 Pb37
Chodová Planá CZ 42 Ln41
Chodzież PL 40 Lr38
Choele Choel RA (RN) 208 Gg65
Choharwa MOC 153 Mh54
Choir MNG 71 Qg24
Choiceland CDN (SK) 169 Eh19
Choiroikoitía CY 56 Mg28
Choiseul SOL 117 Sj49
Choix MEX (SL) 180 Ef32
Chojbalsan MNG 71 Qn21
Chojna PL 40 Lp38
Chojnice PL 40 Ls37
Chojnów PL 40 Lq39
Chok Chai THA 88 Qb38
Chokai J 77 Sa26
Chokai-san J 77 Sa26
Chok Chai THA 88 Qb38
Chókue MOC 152 Mg56
Chokwe = Chókué MOC 155 Mg58
Chola Shan CHN 69 Pk30
Chola Shankou CHN 69 Pk30
Cholila RA (CB) 208 Gd67
Cholila RA 208 Ge67
Cholollan Desert PK 65 Of31
Cholopyçi UA 41 Mc40
Chom Bung THA 88 Pk39
Chomen IND 82 Oj33
Chomo Lhari CHN 85 Pe32
Chom Thong THA 87 Pk36

Column 5

Chongjin PRK 76 Re25
Chongju PRK 76 Rc26
Ch'ongju ROK 78 Rd27
Chongju ROK 78 Rd28
Chongjong S CHN (SCH)
Chongqong CHN (JGS) 78 Ra30
Chongoene MOC 152 Mg58
Chongoni Rock Art MW 153 Mh53
Chongorói ANG 150 Lh52
Chongoyape PE 196 Ga49
Ch'ŏngp'yŏng PRK 76 Rd26
Chongqing CHN (CGQ) 74 Qd31
Chongqing CHN 74 Qd31
Chong Qing-Temple CHN 72 Qb28
Chongren CHN (JGX) 75 Qj32
Chong Samui THA 88 Pk41
Chongsan Do ROK 78 Rd28
Chongwe Z 146 Mf52
Chongwe Z 152 Me53
Chonhum CHN 74 Qb30
Chongyi CHN (JGX) 75 Qh33
Chongzhou CHN (SCH) 74 Qb30
Chonju ROK 78 Rd28
Chonkham IND (ARP) 86 Pj32
Chonogol MNG 71 Qn23
Chonos Archipélago RCH 210 Gd68
Chontali PE 196 Ga48
Chontalpa MEX (TB) 183 Fd37
Chon Thanh VN 89 Qd40
Cho Oyo NEP/CHN 81 Pd31
Chopda IND (MHT) 82 Oh35
Chopda IND (MHT) 82 Oh35
Choqa Zanbil IR 57 Ne30
Chorea MA 125 Kh30
Chorlú IND (MHT) 83 Pa34
Chorzele PL 41 Ma37
Chorzów PL 41 Lt40
Ch'osan PRK 76 Rc25
Choshi J 79 Sa28
Choshuenco, Volcán RCH 208 Ge66
Chos Malal RA (NE) 208 Gf64
Chosica PE 197 Gb51
Chosroes Bajos CRCH 207 Ge60
Chosroes Bajos RCH 207 Ge60
Chos Malal RA 208 Gf64
Chosroes Bajos RCH 207 Ge60
Choszczno PL 40 Lq37
Chota PE 196 Ga49
Chota Nagpur Plateau IND 83 Pa34
Chota Udaipur IND (GUJ) 82 Oh34
Choteau USA (MT) 169 Ed22
Chotilsko CZ 42 Lp41
Chott Ech Chergui DZ 126 La29
Chott el Fedjadj TN 126 Le28
Chott el Gharbi DZ 125 Kk29
Chott el Gharsa TN 126 Ld29
Chott el Hodna DZ 126 Lc28
Chott el Jerid TN 126 Le29
Chott Melrhir DZ 126 Ld28
Chott Merouane DZ 126 Ld28
Chou RL 56 Mh29
Chouf RL 56 Mh29
Chowan CO 192 Gd40
Chowchilla USA (CA) 170 Dk27
Choya RA (SE) 207 Gh60
Choyr MNG 71 Qg24
Chralú CZ 42 Lq40
Chréa DZ 126 Lb27
Chréa, P.N. de DZ 126 Lb27
Chreirik IR 64 Nk30
Chris Ammoudia CY 56 Mf28
Chrisman USA (IL) 175 Ff26
Chrissiesmeer ZA 155 Mf59
Chrismat Khsant ZA 89 Qc38
Christchurch GB 21 Kt40
Christchurch NZ 113 Tg67
Christiana ZA 155 Mc59
Christian GUY 194 Ha42
Christiana USA 178 Fk27
Christiansburg USA 178 Fk27
Christiansholm DK 30 Lk35
Christiansø DK 31 Lq35
Christiansted USA (VI) 187 Gh37
Christie Mt. AUS 108 Rg58
Christie Mtn. Ski Area USA 172 Fe23
Christmas Creek AUS (WA) 103 Rc55
Christmas Island USA 10 Bb08
Christmas Valley USA (OR) 168 Dk24
Christoval USA (TX) 174 Ek30
Christovos USA (TX) 174 Ek30
Chrudim CZ 42 Lq41
Chrystynivka UA 49 Me21
Chrzanów PL 41 Lu40
Chu = Shu KZ 63 Oe23
Chuadanga BD 86 Pe34
Chuave PNG 115 Sc49
Chuba Uray BS 179 Gb33
Chubu-Sangaku N.P. J 79 Rj27
Chubut RA 210 Gg67
Chuchilnga GH 137 Kk40
Chucurpo CH 208 Gf63
Chucuito PE (SL) 208 Gg61
Chucunaque PA 185 Gb41
Chuchilnga GH 137 Kk40
Chudskoe, Oz. EST/RUS 38 Mf32
Chugach Is. USA 164 Ce16
Chugach Mountains USA 165 Cf15
Chugay PE 196 Ga49
Chugoku-sanchi J 79 Rg28
Chugwater USA (WY) 171 Eh24
Chühli CHN 69 Pk30
Chui BR (RS) 204 Hd62
Chuitna IND (MHT) 83 Pa34
Chuiquitan MEX
Chuita J 77 Sa26
Chui Z 146 Mg50
Chuitayo PE 196 Ga48
Chuka EAK 144 Mj46
Chukai MAL 92 Qb43
Chukchi Autonomous District RUS 55 Tb05
Chukchi Peninsula RUS 55 Uc04
Chukchi Sea RUS 55 Uc04
Chukhá BD 86 Pe34
Chukhá BD 86 Pe34
Chukhrapalli IND (MHT) 83 Pa36
Chuknagar BD 86 Pe34
Chukotsky Poluostrov RUS 55 Tc04
Chukwani EAT 147 Mk49
Chula Vista USA (CA) 170 Eb29
Chulak-Orda KZ 63 Og23
Chula Vista USA 170 Eb29
Chulucanas PE 196 Ga48
Chulumani BOL 206 Gg54
Chulym RUS 54 Pa07
Chumba ETH 144 Mk43
Chumbicha RA (CA) 207 Gg60
Chum Phae THA 88 Qb37
Chumphon Buri THA 89 Qc38
Chum Phuang THA 88 Qb38
Chumuch PE 196 Ga49
Chur THA 87 Qb35
Chuchi CHN (QHI) 69 Pj29
Chumikel K 89 Qb39
Chuor Phnom Kravanh K 89 Qb39
Chuor Phnom Dangrek K 89 Qc38
Chupaca PE 197 Gc52
Chupán IR 64 Nh29
Chu Prong VN 89 Qd39
Chuquibamba PE 197 Gd53
Chuquicamata RCH 207 Gf57
Chuquis PE 197 Gb50
Chur CH 34 Lk44
Churachandpur IND (MNP) 86 Pg34
Churchbridge CDN (SK) 172 Fa19
Churchill CDN 163 Fa07
Churchill CDN 163 Fb07
Churchill Falls CDN (NF) 176 Gg19
Churchill Lake CDN 167 Ef17
Churchill Mountains 7 Tc34
Churchill River CDN 167 Eg18
Churchs Ferry USA (ND) 172 Fa21
Church Stretton GB 21 Ks38
Churia Range NEP 81 Pb32
Churín PE 197 Gb51
Churu IND (RJT) 80 Oh31
Churubamba PE 197 Gb50
Chute-des-Passes CDN (QC) 176 Ge21
Chutes d'Abourou RCA 140 Ma43
Chutes d'Antafofo RM 157 Nd55
Chutes de Béla RCB/RDC 148 Ld48
Chutes de Betsiboka RM 157 Nd54
Chutes de Boali RCA 140 Ma43
Chutes de Bouenza RCB 148 Lg47
Chutes de Dibouangui G 148 Lf46
Chutes de Félou RMM 130 Kd38
Chutes de Gouina RMM 130 Kd38
Chutes de Gozobangui RDC 140 Mb43
Chutes de Kembé RCA 140 Mb43
Chutes de Kinkon RG 136 Kd40
Chutes d'Ekom CAM 138 Ld43
Chutes de Kongou G 148 Lg45
Chutes de Kotto RCA 140 Mb43
Chutes de la Kagera BU 146 Me47
Chutes de la Kiubo RDC 146 Md50
Chutes de la Lobé CAM 138 Lc44
Chutes de la Lofoi RDC 146 Md50
Chutes de la Lufira RDC 146 Md50
Chutes de la Madelaine F 148 Td57
Chutes de Lancrenon CAM 139 Lh42
Chutes de l'Ankofia RM 156 Ne53
Chutes de l'Ivindo de Tsengué Leledi G 148 Lg46
Chutes de Livingstone RDC 148 Lg48
Chutes de Lokoho RM 156 Ne53
Chutes Ko RCA 140 Ma43
Chutes de Loufoulakari RCB/RDC 148 Lh48
Chutes de Makateli RCA 140 Ma41
Chutes de Mbi RCA 140 Lj43
Chutes de Mingouli RCB 148 Lg45
Chutes de Nachtigal CAM 139 Lf43
Chutes de Ngolo RCA 140 Mb43
Chutes de Papara RMM 130 Ke38
Chutes de Poubara G 148 Lg46
Chutes de Sakaleona RM 157 Nd55
Chutes de Tanougou DY 137 La40
Chutes de Tinkisso RG 136 Ke40
Chutes de Touboutou RG 136 Kd40
Chutes de Zongo RCB/RDC 148 Lh48
Chutes d'Iga USA 165 Ck15
Chutes d'Iga USA 165 Ck15
Chutes du Tello CAM 139 Lg42
Chutine Landing CDN (BC) 166 De17
Chuvashia RUS 48 Nd18
Chuwangsan N.P. ROK 79 Re27
Chuxiong CHN (YUN) 87 Qb33
Chuy ROU 204 Hd62
Chuzhou CHN (AHU) 78 Qj29
Chwała Dolna PL 41 Lt38
Chwaka EAT 147 Mk49
Chwarzno PL 41 Mb40
Chwałowice PL 41 Mb40

Column 6

Chwaszczyno PL 40 Lt36
Chynów PL 41 Mb39
Chynhiana CHN (KY) 175 Fh26
Chyriv UA 43 Mc41
Chyulu Hills N.P. EAK 144 Mj47
Ciamis CI 95 Qd49
Cianjur RI 95 Qd49
Cianorte BR (PR) 202 Hd57
Ciawi RI 95 Qd49
Cibadak RI 95 Qd49
Cibadak USA (AK) 206 Gf55
Cibinong RI 95 Qd49
Cibit RUS (ALT) 67 Pd20
Cibuta MEX (SO) 180 Ee30
Cicero Dantas BR (BA) 201 Ja51
Čičevac SCG 44 Mb47
Čičevo CHN (ZJG) 79 Ra31
Cicia FJI 119 Ua54
Cide TR 56 Mg25
Cidade Medieval de Évora P 27 Kn52
Cidade Velha CV 136 Jf38
Cide TR 56 Mg25
Ciechanów PL 41 Ma38
Ciechanowiec PL 41 Mc38
Ciechocinek PL 40 Lt38
Ciego de Ávila C 179 Ga34
Ciego de Ávila C 179 Ga34
Ciemnik PL 40 Lq37
Ciempozuelos PL 41 Ma40
Ciénaga CO 192 Gc40
Ciénaga de Oro CO 192 Gc41
Ciénaga de Zapata, P.N. C 179 Fk34
Ciénaga Grande D YV 192 Gd40
Ciénagas de Catatumbo, P.N. YV 192 Ge41
Cienega RA (PJ) 207 Gh57
Cienaguillas RA (PJ) 207 Gh57
Cienega RA 207 Gg57
Ciénega de Flores MEX (NL) 181 Ek33
Ciénega de Toro MEX (NL) 181 Ek33
Ciénega Prieta MEX (CHH) 180 Eg32
Cienfuegos C 179 Fk34
Cieply Balog SK 43 Lu42
Cieplice Śl. PL 41 Mb40
Cieszyn PL 41 Lt41
Cieza E 29 Kt52
Cigŭk CHN (ZJG) 79 Ra31
Ciężkowice PL 41 Ma41
Cifrapalota H 43 Ld44
Çiftkale TR 56 Na26
Çifteler TR 56 Md26
Cigliano I 34 Lh45
Çifteler TR 56 Md26
Ciguetes C 179 Fk34
Çıfunçho PE 207 Ge58
Cigarette Springs Cave USA 171 Ee27
Cigarro BR (AM) 198 Gj47
Cigŭk KS 43 Kb43 Mf41
Cigliano I 34 Lh45
Çihanbeyli TR 56 Mf27
Cihuatlán MEX (JLC) 182 Eh36
Çıldır TR 57 Nb26
Cijara, Emb. de E 27 Kq51
Čili CHN (HUN) 74 Qf31
Cill Chiaráin IRL 19 Kl37
Cillas E 29 Kt50
Cimaltepec MEX (HDG) 182 Fa35
Cimaltepec MEX (HDG) 182 Fa35
Çimenlik TR 57 Nb26
Çımışlıya MD 49 Me22
Cimarron USA (KS) 174 Ek27
Cimarron Nat. Grassland USA 174 Ej27
Cimbur TR 57 Nd26
Çımenlik TR 57 Nb26
Cimislia MD 49 Me22
Cimone, Monte I 34 Ll46
Cimpia Turzii RO 43 Md44
Cimpulung Moldovenesc RO 43 Me43
Çımošķi PL 41 Md37
Çınar TR 57 Na27
Cıncır CHN (ZJG) 78 Ra30
Cinco Saltos RA (RN) 208 Gf65
Cinconosa RO 44 Md46
Cinco Saltos RA 208 Gf65
Cine TR 56 Mh27
Ciney B 23 Lf40
Cinfães P 26 Km49
Cingus Island AUS (QLD) 109 Se57
Cíntalapa MEX (CHP) 183 Fd37
Cinto, Mont F 25 Lj48
Cintra, Serra de BR (AM) 198 Gh46
Cipó BR (BA) 201 Ja51
Cipoletti RA (RN) 208 Gf65
Cipolletti RA 208 Gf65
Circeo, P.N. del I 36 Ln49
Circle USA (MT) 169 Eh22
Circleville USA (OH) 175 Fj26
Circleville USA (UT) 171 Ee26
Circuit de Catalunya E 29 Lc49
Circuit Nelson Piquet BR 203 Hj57
Circuito de Jerez E 27 Ko54
Circuit Ricardo Tormo E 29 Ku51
Cirebon RI 95 Qd49
Cirencester GB 21 Kt39
Cirey-sur-Vezouze F 23 Lg42
Ciriè I 34 Lh45
Cir Kuad SP 145 Nb44
Ciro Marina I 37 Lr51
Cırpan BG 45 Mf48
Cirque, Cerro RCH 208 Ge64
Cırpan BG 45 Mf48
Cirque de Jaffar MA 125 Kh29
Cirque Rouge RM 156 Nd53
Cirque de Navacelles F 25 Ld47
Çişane PL 41 Mb40
Ciskei RCA 155 Me61
Cisneros CO 192 Gc42
Cistergine IT 37 Lr50
Cislău RO 44 Mf45
Cisnes RCH 208 Gd68
Cisneros USA (TX) 174 Ek31
Cistern Point BS 179 Ga33
Citá RUS 70 Qg18
Citadelle de Calvi F 34 Lj48
Citadelle/Sans Souci RH 186 Gd36

Column 7

Citluk BIH 35 Ls47
Citronelle USA (AL) 175 Fh30
Citrusdal ZA 154 Lk62
Citrus Heights USA (CA) 170 Dk26
Città Alta di Bergamo I 34 Lk45
Cittadella I 34 Lm45
Città dei Palladio I 34 Lm45
Città di Castello I 37 Ln47
Città Sant'Angelo I 37 Lp48
City Palace (Jaipur) IND 80 Oh32
City Palace (Udaipur) IND 82 Og33
Ciucea RO 43 Mc44
Ciucurova RO 45 Mh46
Ciudad Altamirano MEX (GUR) 182 Ek36
Ciudad Bolívar YV 193 Gj41
Ciudad Bolivia YV 192 Ge41
Ciudad Camargo MEX (CHH) 181 Eg32
Ciudad Constitución MEX (BCS) 180 Ee33
Ciudad Cortes CR 185 Fj41
Ciudad de Guatemala GCA 184 Fe38
Ciudad del Carmen MEX 183 Fe36
Ciudad del Este PY 204 Hc58
Ciudad del Maíz MEX (SLP) 182 Fa34
Ciudad de Loreto RA (SE) 207 Gh60
Ciudad de México MEX 182 Fa36
Ciudad de México MEX 182 Fa36
Ciudad de Nutrias YV 193 Gf41
Ciudad Encantada E 29 Ks50
Ciudad Guayana YV 193 Gj41
Ciudad Guerrero MEX (TM) 181 Fa32
Ciudad Guzmán MEX (JLC) 182 Eh36
Ciudad Hidalgo MEX 183 Fd38
Ciudad Hidalgo MEX (MHC) 182 Ek36
Ciudad Huitzuco MEX (GUR) 182 Fa36
Ciudad Insurgentes MEX (BCS) 180 Ee33
Ciudad Ixtepec MEX (OAX) 183 Fc37
Ciudad Juárez MEX (CHH) 180 Eg30
Ciudad Lerdo MEX (DGO) 181 Eh32
Ciudad Lerdo de Tejada MEX (VC) 183 Fc36
Ciudad Madero MEX (TM) 182 Fb34
Ciudad Mante MEX (TM) 182 Fb34
Ciudad Melchor de Mencos GCA 183 Ff37
Ciudad monumental de Cáceres E 27 Ko51
Ciudad Mutis = Bahía Solano CO 192 Gb42
Ciudad Nezahualcóyotl MEX 182 Fa36
Ciudad Obregón MEX (SO) 180 Ef32
Ciudad Ojeda YV 192 Ge40
Ciudad Perdida CO 192 Gd40
Ciudad Piar YV 193 Gj42
Ciudad Real E 27 Kr52
Ciudad Rodrigo E 26 Ko50
Ciudad Sahagún MEX (HDG) 182 Fa35
Ciudad Serdán MEX (PUE) 182 Fb36
Ciudad Valles MEX (SLP) 182 Fa35
Ciudad Victoria MEX (TM) 182 Fa34
Ciuperceni RO 44 Md46
Ciutadella E 29 Lc50
Ciudad de Friuli I 34 Ln44
Civil'sk RUS (CHU) 48 Nd18
Civita Castellana I 36 Ln48
Civitanova Marche I 37 Lo47
Civitavecchia I 36 Lm48
Civitella del Tronto I 35 Lo49
Civray F 24 La44
Civril TR 56 Mi26
Cıxi CHN (ZJG) 78 Ra30
Cizre TR 57 Na27
Çjurupynsk UA 49 Mg22
Ckalov RUS 78 Rb19
Çki-Naryn KS 66 Oj25
Clacton-on-Sea GB 21 Lb39
Clairière RA (QLD) 109 Se57
Clamecy F 25 Ld43
Clanton AUS (QLD) 109 Se57
Clanton USA (AL) 175 Fh29
Clanwilliam ZA 154 Lk61
Claonaig GB 20 Ko35
Clara IRL 19 Kn37
Clara Island MYA 88 Pj40
Clara, Mount NZ 113 Tg67
Clara RO 45 Mg45
Claraville AUS (QLD) 107 Sb56
Clare AUS (SA) 110 Rk62
Clare IRL 19 Kl36
Claremont USA (CA) 170 Eb28
Claremont USA (NH) 177 Gd24
Claremont Point AUS 107 Sb52
Claremore USA (OK) 174 Fc27
Claremorris IRL 19 Kl37
Clarence CDN (AB) 169 Ed20
Clarence Island GB 6 Hb31
Clarence Cannon N.W.R. USA 175 Fe26
Clarence Strait AUS 106 Rf52
Clarence Strait USA 166 Dd18
Clarence Town BS 179 Gb34
Clarendon USA (TX) 174 Ek29
Clarens ZA 155 Me60
Clareté BR (MG) 203 Hj56
Cláudia BR (MT) 199 Hc51
Claudio BR (MG) 203 Hh56
Claverley RO 45 Mf46
Claveria RP 90 Rb38
Claxton USA (GA) 178 Fk29
Clay USA (WV) 175 Fk26
Clay Belt CDN (ON) 173 Fh20
Clay Center USA (KS) 174 Fb26
Claydon CDN (SK) 169 Ef20
Clayhole USA 178 Fk30
Clayton USA (AL) 175 Fh30
Clayton USA (GA) 178 Fj28
Clayton USA (NM) 174 Ej27
Clayton USA (NM) 174 Ej27
Clearco USA (AB) 167 Ea17
Clear Lake USA (PA) 173 Ga25
Clearfield USA (PA) 173 Ga25
Clearfield USA (UT) 171 Ed25
Clear Hills CDN (AB) 167 Ea17
Clear Lake USA (IA) 163 Fd66
Clear Lake USA (SD) 172 Fb23
Clear Lake USA (UT) 171 Ed26
Clear Prairie CDN (AB)
Clearwater CDN (BC) 168 Dk20
Clearwater USA (FL)
Clearwater Lake Prov. Park CDN 169 Ek18
Clearwater Mountains USA 168 Ec22
Cleburne USA (TX) 174 Fb29
Cle Elum USA (WA) 168 Dk22
Cleethorpes GB 21 Ku37
Clejani RO 45 Mf46
Clelles F 25 Le46
Clementina BR (SP) 202 He56
Cleopatra Needle RP 90 Qk40
Cleo Springs USA (OK) 174 Fa27
Clerke Reef AUS (QLD) 109 Se57
Clermont F 23 Ld41
Clermont USA (FL) 179 Fk31
Clermont-en-Argonne F 23 Lf41
Clermont-Ferrand F 25 Ld45
Clermont-l'Hérault F 25 Ld47
Cléry-St-André E 23 Lc42
Clervaux L 23 Lg40
Cles I 34 Lm44
Cleugh Passage IND 88 Pg39
Cleve AUS (SA) 110 Rj62
Clevedon GB 21 Ks39
Cleveland USA (MS) 175 Fe29
Cleveland USA (OH) 173 Fk25
Cleveland USA (TN) 175 Fh28
Cleveland USA (TX) 174 Fc30
Clevedon BR (PR) 204 Hd60
Clevelan Pen. USA 166 Dd18
Cleveleys GB 21 Ks37
Clew Bay IRL 19 Kl37
Cleveland AUS (QLD) 109 Sg59
Clifden IRL 19 Kk36
Clifden Castle IRL 19 Kk36
Cliffs of Moher IRL 19 Kl38
Cliffs of the Nullarbor AUS 105 He61
Clifton USA (AZ) 171 Ef29
Clifton USA (TX) 174 Fb30
Clifton Bridge GB 21 Ks39
Clifton Hills AUS (SA) 108 Rk59
Climax CDN (SK) 169 Ef21
Climax USA (CO) 171 Eg26
Climax USA (MN) 172 Fb22
Clinch Mts. USA 178 Fj27
Clines Corners USA (NM) 171 Eh28
Clinton CDN (BC) 168 Dk20
Clinton USA (AR) 175 Fd28
Clinton USA (IA) 172 Fe25
Clinton USA (MO) 174 Fd26
Clinton USA (NC) 178 Ga28
Clinton USA (OK) 174 Fa28
Clinton-Colden Lake CDN 167 Eg13
Clinton Creek CDN 165 Da14

Column 8

Claro dos Poções BR (MG) 203 Hh54
Claromecó RA (BA) 209 Gk65
Classical Gardens CHN 78 Ra30
Clear USA (TX) 174 Ek28
Clear Lake USA (UT) 171 Ed26
Clear Prairie CDN (AB)
Clearwater CDN (BC) 168 Dk20
Clearwater USA (FL)
Clearwater Lake Prov. Park CDN 169 Ek18
Clearwater Mountains USA 168 Ec22
Cleburne USA (TX) 174 Fb29
Clarksburg USA (WV) 173 Fk26
Clark's Harbour CDN (NS) 176 Gh24
Clark River Lake USA 175 Ff27
Clark River CDN 176 Gh22
Clarke River AUS (QLD)
107 Sc55
Clarksdale USA (MS) 175 Fe28
Clarke City CDN (QC) 176 Gg21
Clarke Island AUS 111 Se66
Clarke River AUS (QLD) 107 Sc55
Clarkesdale USA (MS) 175 Fe28
Clarks Summit USA (PA) 177 Gc25
Clarksville USA (AR) 175 Fd28
Clarksville USA (TN) 175 Fg27
Clatskanie USA (OR)
Claude USA (TX) 174 Ek29
Cloudy Mount LK 85 Ok39
Clovelly GB 21 Kq40
Cloverdale USA (CA) 170 Dj26
Clovis USA (CA) 170 Ea27
Clovis USA (NM) 174 Ej28
Cluj-Napoca RO 43 Md44
Cluny GB 21 Kt39
Clunes AUS (VIC) 111 Sb64
Clusone I 34 Lk45
Clutha NZ 113 Td69
Clwyd GB 21 Ks37
Clyde CDN (AB) 167 Ed18
Clyde GB 20 Kq35
Clyde USA (NY) 177 Gb24
Clydebank GB 20 Kq35
Coachella USA (CA) 170 Eb29
Coahuila MEX (MEX) 182 Fa34
Coal Creek USA (NM) 165 Cj13
Coaldale CDN (AB) 169 Ed21
Coal River CDN (BC) 166 Dg16
Coamo USA (PR) 187 Gg36
Coari BR (AM) 198 Gj48

Column 9 (right edge)

Coast Mountains CDN/USA 160 Db04

Coast of Labrador ⊠ CDN 163 Gd07
Coast Ranges ▲ USA 168 Dj25
Coata ⊠ PE 206 Gf53
Coatepeque ⊠ MEX (VC) 182 Fb36
Coatepeque ■ GCA 184 Fe38
Coaticook ⊠ CDN (QC) 177 Ge23
Coats Island ▲ CDN 163 Fd06
Coats Land ▲ ANT 6 Jb34
Coatzacoalcos ⊠ MEX (VC) 183 Fc36
Cobá ▲ MEX (QTR) 183 Fj35
Cobá ⊞ MEX 183 Fj35
Cobadin ⊠ RO 45 Mj46
Cobalt ⊠ USA (ID) 168 Ec23
Cóbano ⊠ CR 185 Fh41
Cobar ⊠ AUS (NSW) 109 Sc61
Cobblestones ▲ AUS 104 Qh62
Cobden ⊠ AUS (VIC) 111 Sb65
Cobh ⊠ IRL 19 Km39
Cobham ⊠ AUS (NSW) 108 Rg51
Cobija ⊠ BOL 198 Gf51
Coblenz ⊠ NAM 150 Lk56
Cobleskill ⊠ USA (NY) 177 Gc24
Cobos ⊠ RA (SA) 207 Gh58
Cobourg ⊠ CDN (ON) 173 Ga24
Cobourg Peninsula ▲ AUS 106 Rg51
Cobquecura ⊠ RCH 208 Gd64
Cóbué ⊠ MOC 146 Mh52
Coburg ⊠ D 33 Ll40
Coburn ⊠ AUS (WA) 104 Qh59
Coca ⊞ E 26 Kq49
Coca ⊠ EC 196 Gb46
Cocachacra ⊠ PE 197 Gb51
Cocalinho ⊠ BR (PI) 201 Hk47
Cocalinho ⊠ BR (MA) 195 Hh47
Cocalinho ⊠ BR (MT) 202 He53
Cocameira ⊠ BR (AC) 196 Ge50
Cochabamba ⊠ BOL 206 Gh54
Cochabamba ⊠ PE 196 Ga49
Cochem ⊠ D 33 Lh40
Cochetopa Hills ▲ USA 171 Eg27
Cochin = Kochi ⊠ IND (KER) 84 Oj41
Cochran ⊠ USA (GA) 178 Fj29
Cochrane ⊠ CDN (AB) 169 Ec20
Cochrane ⊠ CDN (ON) 173 Fe21
Cochrane ⊠ RCH 210 Gd69
Cockatoo ⊠ AUS (QLD) 109 Sf58
Cockatoo Island ▲ AUS 102 Rb54
Cockburn Harbor ⊠ GB 186 Ge35
Cockburn Town ■ BS 186 Gc33
Cockburn Town ⊠ GB 186 Ge35
Cockermouth ⊠ GB 20 Kr36
Cocklebiddy ⊠ AUS (WA) 105 Rd62
Coco ⊠ CDN 184 Fh40
Cocobeach ⊠ G 148 Le45
Cococá ⊠ BR (CE) 201 Hk49
Cocodrie ⊠ USA (LA) 175 Fe31
Cocoland ⊠ NIC 185 Fj36
Cocona ■ MEX 183 Fd37
Cocoparra N.P. ✦ AUS (NSW) 111 Sd63
Cocorna ⊠ CO 192 Gc42
Cocos ⊠ BR (BA) 203 Hh53
Cocos Island ▲ CR 190 Fb09
Cocos Islands ▲ AUS 52 Pb11
Cocos Ridge ▲ 190 Fb09
Coculle ⊠ MEX (VC) 183 Fb36
Cocula ⊠ MEX (JLC) 182 Ej35
Codajás ⊠ BR (AM) 198 Gd47
Codemin ⊠ BR (AM) 199 Gk47
Codfish Island ▲ NZ 113 Td69
Codigoro ⊠ I 34 Lm46
Codlea ⊠ RO 45 Mf45
Codó ⊠ BR (MA) 200 Hj48
Codo del Pozuzo ✦ PE 197 Gc50
Codogno ⊠ I 34 Lk45
Codozinho ⊠ BR (MA) 200 Hh48
Codpa ⊠ RCH 206 Gf55
Codrington ⊠ AG 187 Gk37
Codrópio ⊠ I 34 Lk45
Cody ⊠ USA (WY) 169 Ef23
Coelemu ⊠ RCH 208 Gd64
Coelho Neto ⊠ BR (MA) 201 Hj48
Coenbult ⊠ NAM 154 La59
Coeur d'Alene Ind. Res. ▲ USA 168 Eb22
Coeur d'Alene ⊠ USA 168 Eb22
Coesfeld ⊠ D 32 Lh39
Coetivy ▲ SY 145 Nj49
Coeur d'Alene ⊠ USA (ID) 168 Eb22
Coevorden ⊠ NL 23 Lg38
Coffee Bay ⊠ ZA 155 Me62
Coffee Bay Beach Point ▲ ZA 155 Me62
Coimara ⊞ F 25 Lg45
Coffee Creek ⊠ CDN (YT) 165 Da14
Coffeyville ⊠ USA (KS) 174 Fc27
Coffin Bay ⊠ AUS (SA) 110 Rh63
Coffin Bay ▲ AUS 110 Rh63
Coffin Bay N.P. ✦ AUS 110 Rh63
Coffs Harbour ⊠ AUS (NSW) 109 Sg61
Cofimvaba ⊠ ZA 155 Md61
Cofre de Perote, Cerro ▲ MEX 182 Fb36
Cogdala ⊞ IR 59 Nf31
Coghlan ⊠ RA (BA) 209 Ha61
Cogla Downs ⊠ AUS (WA) 104 Qj59
Cognac ⊞ F 24 Ku45
Cogne ⊠ I 34 Lh45
Cogolin ⊠ F 25 Lg47
Cogunu ⊠ MOC 152 Mh58
Cohoes ⊠ USA (NY) 177 Gd24
Cohuna ⊠ AUS (VIC) 111 Sc63
Coihaique ⊠ RCH 210 Gd68
Coihaique Alto ⊠ RCH 210 Ge68
Coihueco ⊠ RCH 208 Ge64
Coimbatore ⊠ IND (TNU) 84 Oj40
Coimbra ⊞ P 26 Km50
Coin ⊞ E 27 Kq54
Coipasa, Cerro ▲ BOL 206 Gf55
Coirón ⊠ RCH 208 Ge61
Cojata ⊠ PE 206 Gf53
Cojimies ⊠ EC 196 Fk45
Cojúa ⊞ YV 192 Ge40
Cojudo Blanco, Cerro ▲ RA 210 Gf69
Çokak ⊠ TR 56 Mj27
Coker Creek ⊠ USA 175 Fh28
Cokeville ⊠ USA (WY) 169 Ee24
Colac ⊠ AUS (VIC) 111 Sb65
Colán Conhué ⊠ RA 210 Gf67

Col des Chandeliers ⊠ RN 133 Lg35
Col de Tafori ⊠ DZ 126 Ld28
Col de Telmet ⊠ DZ 126 Ld28
Col de Yel Lulu ⊞ RN 133 Lh35
Coldfiz ⊠ D 32 Lm39
Coldspring Mtn. ▲ CDN 165 Db14
Cold Springs ⊠ USA (NV) 170 Eb24
Coldstream ⊞ GB 20 Ks35
Col du Galibier ⊠ F 25 Lg45
Col du Grand Saint-Bernard ⊠ I/CH 34 Lh45
Col du Lautaret ⊞ F 25 Lg45
Col du Petit St-Bernard ⊞ F/I 25 Lg45
Col du Pourtalet ⊞ F 24 Ku48
Col du Tourmalet ⊞ F 24 La48
Col du Zad ⊞ MA 125 Kh29
Coldwater ⊠ USA (KS) 174 Fa27
Coldwater ⊠ USA (MI) 173 Fh25
Coleambally ⊠ AUS (NSW) 111 Sd63
Cole Bay ⊠ CDN (SK) 167 Ef18
Colebrook ⊠ USA (NH) 177 Gd23
Colegiata de Santa María de Calatayud ⊞ E 26 Kt49
Colekeplaas ⊠ ZA 155 Mc62
Colenso ⊠ ZA 155 Me60
Cole La Pagoda ▲ MYA 87 Qd35
Colera ⊞ E 28 Ld48
Coleraine ⊞ GB 19 Ko35
Coleraine ⊠ AUS (TAS) 111 Se67
Colesberg ⊠ ZA 155 Mc61
Colfax ⊠ USA (NY) 172 Fd22
Colfax ⊠ USA (WA) 168 Eb22
Colfontaine ⊞ B 23 Ld40
Colgante Glacier ✦ RCH 210 Gd68
Colgong ⊞ IND (BIH) 83 Pd33
Coliguala ⊞ SP 143 Nh49
Colha ⊞ BH 184 Ff37
Colider ⊠ BR (MT) 199 Hc51
Colidor ⊠ BR (MT) 199 Hc51
Coligny ⊠ ZA 155 Md59
Colima ⊞ MEX (COL) 182 Ej36
Colima, Volcán de ▲ MEX 182 Ej36
Colima ⊠ MEX (SP) 202 Hf56
Colina ⊠ BR (SP) 202 Hf56
Colina ⊠ RCH 208 Ge62
Colinas ⊠ BR (MA) 200 Hh49
Colinas do Tocantins ⊠ BR (TO) 200 Hf50
Colinet ⊞ CDN (NF) 177 Hd22
Colintraive ⊠ GB 20 Kp34
Coll ▲ GB 20 Ko34
Collado Bajo ▲ E 29 Kt50
Collado-Villalba ⊞ E 27 Kr50
Collao ⊞ RCH 208 Ge62
Collarenebri ⊠ AUS (NSW) 109 Se60
Collary ⊠ AUS (QLD) 109 Se57
Colle de Rates ▲ E 29 Ku50
Colléchio ⊠ I 34 Ll46
Colle della Maddalena ⊞ F/I 25 Lg46
Colle di Val d'Elsa ⊠ I 34 Lm47
Colleferro ⊠ I 36 Lo49
College Place ⊠ USA (WA) 168 Ea22
College Ridge ⊠ USA 179 Ga35
College Station ⊠ USA (TX) 174 Fb30
Collembar ⊠ D 32 Lm38
Collgata di San Cándido ⊞ I 34 Ln44
Colli Albani ▲ I 36 Ln49
Collie ⊠ AUS (WA) 104 Qj62
Collier Range N.P. ✦ AUS 104 Qk58
Collier Range ▲ AUS 104 Qk58
Collierville ⊠ USA (TN) 175 Ff28
Collines Baoule ▲ CI 137 Kh42
Collines de Bongouanou ▲ CI 137 Kh42
Collingwood ⊠ AUS (NSW) 111 Sd63
Collingwood ⊠ CDN (ON) 173 Fk23
Collingwood ⊠ NZ 113 Tg66
Collingwood Bay ⊠ PNG 116 Se50
Collins ⊠ CDN (ON) 172 Ff21
Collins ⊠ USA (MS) 175 Ff30
Collins ⊠ AUS (QLD) 107 Sd56
Colliguilli ⊠ RCH 208 Gd63
Collo ⊠ DZ 126 Ld37
Colloma ⊠ BOL 206 Gg55
Collooney ⊠ IRL 19 Km37
Colmar ⊞ F 25 Lh43
Colmbia ⊠ BR (TO) 200 Hf50
Colmena ⊠ RA (SC) 210 Gf70
Colmenar ⊞ E 27 Kq54
Colmenar Viejo ⊞ E 27 Kr50
Colnett ⊞ F 32 Lg40
Colo-Suva Forest Reserve ✦ FJI 119 Tk54
Colomb-Béchar ⊠ DZ 125 Kh29
Colombey-les-Belles ⊞ F 23 Lf42
Colombey-les-Deux-Églises ⊞ F 23 Le42
Colombia ⊞ BR (SP) 202 Hf56
Colombia ⊞ CO 192 Gc44
Colombo ■ CL 85 Ok42
Colombia ⊠ BR (TO) 200 Hf50
Colombo ⊠ BR (TO) 205 Hf58
Colomboula ⊠ BR (PR) 205 Hf58
Colón ⊞ PA 185 Ga41
Colón ⊠ RA (BA) 209 Gk62
Colón ⊠ RA (ER) 204 Ha62
Colón ⊠ RA (ER) 204 Ha62
Colonganj ⊞ IND (UPH) 83 Pa32
Colonel Hill ⊠ BS 186 Ge34
Colonel ⊞ MEX (BC) 180 Eb30
Colônia ⊞ FSM 101 Rb09
Colonelganj ⊞ IND (UPH) 83 Pa32
Colonia Angamos ⊠ PE 196 Gd48
Colonia Carlos Pellegrini ⊠ RA (CR) 204 Ha58
Colonia Caroya ⊠ RA (CD) 208 Gj61
Colonia del Sacramento ⊞ ROU 209 Hb63
Colonia de Sant Jordi ⊞ E 29 Lc51
Colonia do Piauí ⊠ BR (PI) 201 Hj49
Colonia Dora ⊠ RA (SE) 207 Gj60
Colonia La Esperanza ⊠ RA 208 Gg64
Colonia Lavalleja ⊠ ROU 204 Hb61
Colonial Beach ⊠ USA (VA) 177 Gb26
Colonial Heights ⊠ USA (VA) 178 Gb27
Colonia Liebig ⊠ RA (CR) 204 Ha59
Colonial Williamsburg ⊞ USA (VA) 177 Gb26
Colonia Marina ⊠ RA (CD) 208 Gj61
Colonia Pastoril ⊠ RA 204 Ha58
Colonia San Miguel ⊞ PY 204 Ha58
Colônia São Romão ⊞ BR (MS) 202 Hc55
Colonia Unidas ⊠ RA (CH) 204 Ha59

Colonia Winkler ⊠ PY 207 Ha57
Colonsay ⊞ GB 20 Ko34
Colorado ⊠ BR (PR) 202 He57
Colorado ⊠ BR 206 Gj52
Colorado ⊠ USA 179 Ga35
Colorado ⊠ RA 210 Gf68
Colorado ⊠ USA 171 Ee27
Colorado ⊠ USA 174 Fa30
Colorado City ⊠ USA (AZ) 171 Ed27
Colorado City ⊠ USA (CO) 171 En27
Colorado City ⊠ USA (TX) 174 Ek29
Colorado Desert ▲ USA 170 Ec29
Colorado Nat. Mon. ✦ USA 171 Ee27
Colorado, Cerro ▲ RA/RCH 207 Gf59
Colorado Springs ⊠ USA (CO) 171 Eg27
Color Sand Forest ✦ CHN 87 Qh33
Colossal ⊠ AUS (WA) 105 Rb61
Colotenango ⊠ GCA 184 Fe38
Colotlipa ⊠ MEX (GUR) 182 Fa37
Coloured Canyon ✦ ET 129 Mh57
Coloqueuchaca ⊠ BOL 206 Gh55
Coluqen, Cerro ▲ RCH 208 Gd64
Col Quijoux ⊠ F 25 Lg45
Colquiri ⊠ BOL 206 Gg54
Colquitt ⊠ USA (GA) 175 Fh30
Colston Park ✦ AUS (QLD) 206 Gj54
Colstrip ⊠ USA (MT) 169 Eg22
Columbia ⊠ USA (KY) 175 Fh27
Columbia ⊠ USA (LA) 175 Fd29
Columbia ⊞ USA (MD) 177 Gb26
Columbia ⊠ USA (MO) 174 Fd26
Columbia ⊠ USA (MS) 175 Ff30
Columbia ⊞ USA (PA) 177 Gb25
Columbia ⊞ USA (SC) 178 Fk28
Columbia ⊞ USA (TN) 175 Fg28
Columbia Falls ⊠ USA (MT) 168 Ec21
Columbia Glacier ⊞ USA 165 Cg15
Columbia Icefield ✦ CDN 169 Eb20
Columbia, Mount ▲ CDN 168 Eb19
Columbia Mountains ▲ CDN 168 Eb24
Columbiana ⊞ USA (AL) 175 Fg29
Columbia Plateau ▲ USA 168 Eb24
Columbia River ⊞ CDN 168 Ea20
Columbia River ⊠ USA 168 Ea21
Columbus ⊠ USA (GA) 175 Fh29
Columbus ⊞ USA (IN) 175 Fh26
Columbus ⊠ USA (KS) 174 Fc27
Columbus ⊞ USA (MS) 175 Ff29
Columbus ⊠ USA (NE) 172 Fb25
Columbus ⊞ USA (NM) 171 Eg30
Columbus ⊞ USA (OH) 173 Fk25
Columbus ⊞ USA (TX) 174 Fb31
Columbus Landing 1494 ⊞ JA 186 Gb36
Columbus Monument ⊞ BS 186 Gc33
Columbus Monument ⊞ C 179 Gb35
Columbus ⊞ MEX 172 Fb25
Columbus ⊞ USA (TX) 181 Eh35
Columbus ⊠ USA (WI) 172 Fe24
Coluna ⊞ BR (MG) 203 Hj55
Colunga ⊞ E 26 Kq47
Colupo, Cerro ▲ RCH 207 Gf58
Colville ⊠ USA (WA) 168 Eb21
Colville Ind. Res. ▲ USA 168 Ea21
Colwyn Bay ⊞ GB 21 Kr37
Comácchio ⊠ I 34 Lm46
Comácha ⊞ MOC 152 Mg54
Comala ⊞ MEX (COL) 182 Ej36
Comalcalco ⊠ MEX (TB) 183 Fd37
Comalcalco ▲ MEX 183 Fd36
Comallo ⊠ RA (RN) 208 Ge66
Comanche ⊠ USA (OK) 174 Fb28
Comanche Nat. Grassland ✦ USA 174 Fa27
Comandante Fontana ⊠ RA (FO) 204 Ha58
Comandante Luis Piedra Buena ⊠ RA (SC) 210 Gf70
Comandatuba ▲ BR 45 Mm49
Comanesti ⊠ RO 45 Mf44
Comarnic ⊠ RO 45 Mf45
Comas ⊠ PE 197 Gc51
Comayagua ⊠ HN 184 Fg38
Comayaguela ⊞ HN 184 Fg38
Combapata ⊠ PE 197 Ge53
Combarbalá ⊠ RCH 208 Ge61
Combeaufontaine ⊞ F 25 Lf43
Combe de Lavaux ⊞ F 25 Le43
Combles ⊞ F 23 Lc41
Combol ⊞ RI 93 Qb45
Combo, T.I. ⊠ BR 203 Hk55
Combolmhe ⊞ MOC 152 Mg57
Combourg ⊞ F 22 Kt42
Come by Chance ⊠ AUS (NSW) 109 Se61
Comedero ⊠ MEX (SL) 180 Eg33
Comercio ⊞ BR (AM) 197 Gf36
Comerzinho ⊞ BR (MG) 203 Hk54
Comet ⊞ AUS (QLD) 109 Se57
Cometa ⊞ MOC 152 Mh60
Cometela ⊞ MOC 152 Mh56
Comfort ⊞ USA (TX) 174 Fa31
Comilla ⊞ BGD 86 Pf34
Comines ⊞ F 37 Lg54
Comitán de Domínguez ⊠ MEX (CHP) 183 Fd37
Commentry ⊞ F 25 Lc44
Commerce ⊞ USA (GA) 178 Fj28
Commerce ⊞ USA (TX) 174 Fc29
Commissioner Island ▲ CDN 172 Fb19
Committee Bay ⊞ CDN 163 Fc05
Commonwealth Bay ⊠ ANT (AUS) 7 Sa32
Commonwealth Hill ⊠ AUS (SA) 108 Rh60
Como ⊞ I 34 Lk45
Como Bluff Fossil Beds ✦ USA 169 Eg24
Comodoro ⊞ BR (MT) 206 Ha52
Comodoro Py ⊞ RA (BA) 209 Gk63
Comodoro Rivadavia ⊠ RA (CB) 210 Gg68
Comoé ⊞ CI 137 Kh43
Comoé, P.N. de la ✦ CI 137 Kj41
Comondú ⊠ MEX (BC) 180 Ec34
Comorin, Cape ▲ IND 84 Oj42
Comoros ⊞ COM 156 Nb51
Comox ⊞ CDN (BC) 168 Dh21
Compeer ⊞ CDN (AB) 169 Ee20
Complex of Monuments (Hue) ✦ VN 89 Qd37
Comporta ⊞ P 27 Km52

Composela ⊞ MEX (NYT) 182 Eh35
Compostela ⊞ RP 91 Rd42
Comps-sur-Artuby ⊞ F 25 Lg47
Comrat ⊞ MD 49 Me22
Comstock ⊞ USA (TX) 181 Ek31
Comunidad ⊞ YV 193 Gg44
Cona ⊞ CHN (TIB) 86 Pf32
Conakry ■ RG (NV) 171 Ec25
Conambo ⊞ EC 196 Gb46
Conanicut ⊞ EC 196 Ga46
Cona Niyeu ⊞ RA (RN) 208 Pj35
Conara ⊞ AUS (TAS) 111 Sd66
Conargo ⊞ AUS (NSW) 111 Sc63
Conca ⊞ MEX (HDG) 182 Fa35
Concarneau ⊞ F 22 Kr43
Concepción ⊞ BR (ES) 203 Ja55
Conceição da Barra ⊞ BR (ES) 203 Ja55
Conceição das Alagoas ⊞ BR (MG) 202 Hf55
Conceição de Mau ⊞ BR (RR) 194 Ha44
Conceição do Araguaia ⊞ BR (PA) 200 Hf50
Conceição do Canindé ⊞ BR (PI) 201 Hk49
Conceição do Coité ⊞ BR (BA) 201 Ja51
Conceição do Macabu ⊞ BR (RJ) 203 Hk57
Conceição do Mato Dentro ⊞ BR (MG) 203 Hj55
Conceição do Tocantins ⊞ BR (TO) 200 Hg52
Concepción ⊞ BOL 206 Gj54
Concepción ⊞ CO 196 Gd46
Concepción ⊞ PE 197 Gc51
Concepción ⊞ PY 202 Hd57
Concepción ⊞ RA (CR) 204 Hb60
Concepción ⊞ RA (TU) 207 Gh59
Concepción ⊞ RCH 208 Gd64
Concepción de la Vega ⊞ DOM (ZCT) 181 Ga33
Concepción Island ▲ BS 186 Gc34
Concepción, Volcán ▲ NIC 185 Fh39
Conches-en-Ouche ⊞ F 23 La42
Conchillas ⊞ ROU 209 Ha63
Concho ⊞ CDN 177 Hc20
Concord ⊞ USA (CA) 170 Dj27
Concord ⊞ USA (NC) 178 Fk28
Concordia ⊞ USA (KS) 174 Fb26
Concórdia ⊞ BR (SC) 204 Hd59
Concordia ⊞ MEX (SL) 180 Eg34
Concórdia ⊞ PE 196 Ge48
Concórdia ⊞ BR 204 Ha61
Concordia ⊞ ZA 154 Lj60
Concordia do Pará ⊞ BR (PA) 200 Hf47
Con Cuong ⊞ VN 87 Qc36
Conda ⊞ ANG 150 La51
Condamine ⊞ AUS (QLD) 109 Sf59
Con Dao ⊞ VN 89 Qd41
Con Dao ⊞ VN 89 Qd41
Condat ⊞ F 25 Lc45
Conde ⊞ BR (BA) 201 Jb51
Conde ⊞ BR (PB) 201 Jb49
Condé-en-Brie ⊞ F 23 Ld42
Condega ⊞ NIC 185 Fh38
Condeúba ⊞ BR (BA) 203 Hk53
Condingup ⊞ AUS (WA) 105 Rb62
Condobolin ⊞ AUS (NSW) 111 Sd62
Condom ⊞ F 24 La47
Condon ⊞ USA (OR) 168 Dk23
Condór, Cerro el ▲ RA 207 Gf59
Condoriaco ⊞ RCH 207 Ge60
Conegliano ⊞ I 34 Lm45
Conejos ⊞ USA (CO) 171 Eg27
Conesa ⊞ RA (BA) 209 Gk63
Conesa ⊞ MEX (DGO) 181 Ek33
Confederate Memorial Park ✦ USA 175 Fg29
Confederate Memorial S.H.S. ✦ USA 174 Fc27
Conflict Group ▲ PNG 116 Sf51
Confucius Temple & Tomb ✦ CHN 78 Qj28
Congaree Swamp N.P. ✦ USA 178 Fk29
Congerenge ⊞ MOC 153 Mh53
Conghua ⊞ CHN (GDG) 75 Qj34
Congleton ⊞ GB 21 Ks37
Congo ⊞ BR (PB) 201 Jb49
Congo ■ RDC 140 Ma45
Congonhas ⊞ BR (MG) 203 Hj56
Congostrina ⊞ E 29 Ks49
Congo Town ⊞ BS 179 Gb33
Congress ⊞ USA (AZ) 171 Ed28
Conguillio, P.N. ✦ RCH 208 Gd64
Conhelo ⊞ RA (LP) 208 Gh64
Coni el la Frontera ⊞ E 27 Ko54
Conimbriga ⊞ P 26 Km50
Coniston ⊞ AUS (QLD) 107 Sc55
Conjuboy ⊞ AUS (QLD) 107 Sd54
Conklin ⊞ CDN (AB) 167 Ee18
Conkouati-Douli, P.N. de la ✦ RCB 148 Lf47
Connah's Quay ⊞ GB 21 Kr37
Conneaut ⊞ USA (OH) 173 Fk25
Connecticut ⊞ USA 177 Gd25
Connell ⊞ USA (WA) 168 Ea22
Connellsville ⊞ USA (PA) 173 Ga26
Connemara ⊞ AUS (QLD) 108 Sb58
Connemara ▲ IRL 19 Kl37
Connemara N.P. ✦ IRL 19 Kl37
Conner ⊞ RP 90 Ra37
Connerré ⊞ F 22 La42
Conner, Mount ▲ AUS 103 Rd53
Conques ⊞ F 25 Lc46
Conquista ⊞ BOL 198 Gg51
Conrad ⊞ USA (MT) 169 Ee21
Conroe ⊞ USA (TX) 181 Fc30
Conscripto Bernardi ⊞ RA (ER) 204 Ha61
Conselheiro Lafaiete ⊞ BR (MG) 203 Hj56
Conselheiro Paulino ⊞ BR (RJ) 203 Hj57
Consolación del Sur ⊞ C 179 Fj34
Consort ⊞ CDN (AB) 169 Ee20
Constanc City ⊞ USA (CO) 169 Ef24
Constance Lake First Nation ⊞ CDN 173 Fj21
Constanta ⊞ RO 45 Mj46
Constance ⊞ RS (MA) 203 Hh55
Constantina ⊞ E 27 Kp53
Constantine ⊞ DZ 126 Ld27
Constitución ⊞ RCH (BIO) 208 Gd63
Constitución ⊞ ROU 204 Hb60
Constitución ⊞ MEX (PBL) 182 Fa36
Coração de Jesus ⊞ BR (MG) 203 Hj54
Coração de Maria ⊞ BR (BA) 201 Ja51
Coracora ⊞ PE 197 Gc52
Coracora ⊞ RCH 208 Gd63
Coral Basin ▲ 100 Sa11

Constitución ⊞ MEX (CAM) 183 Fe36
Constitución ⊞ ROU 204 Hb61
Corales del Rosario y San Bernardo, P.N. ✦ CO 192 Gc40
Coral Harbour ⊞ CDN 163 Fd06
Coral Heights ⊞ BS 186 Gd34
Coral Sea ⊞ 100 Sb11
Coral Sea Islands Territory ⊞ AUS 101 Sb11
Coral Springs ⊞ USA (FL) 179 Fk32
Corato ⊞ I 37 Lr49
Corbeil-Essonnes ⊞ F 23 Lc42
Corbelled House ▲ ZA 154 Ma61
Corbett N.P. ✦ IND 81 Ok31
Corbières ▲ F 25 Lc48
Corbigny ⊞ F 25 Ld43
Corbin ⊞ USA (KY) 175 Fh27
Corbridge ⊞ GB 20 Ks36
Corby ⊞ GB 21 Ku38
Corcaigh = Cork ⊞ IRL 19 Km39
Corcoran ⊞ USA (CA) 170 Ea27
Corcovado, P.N. ✦ CR 185 Fj41
Corcovado, Volcán ▲ RCH 208 Gd66
Cordele ⊞ USA (GA) 178 Fj30
Cordell ⊞ USA (OK) 174 Fa28
Cordes ⊞ F 24 Lb47
Cordillera Bética ▲ E 27 Kq54
Cordillera Blanca ▲ PE 197 Gb50
Cordillera Central ▲ CO 192 Gc43
Cordillera Central ▲ CR 185 Fh40
Cordillera Central ▲ DOM 186 Ge36
Cordillera Central ▲ PE/BOL 196 Ga48
Cordillera Central ▲ RP 90 Ra37
Cordillera Chilena ▲ RCH 210 Gd72
Cordillera Chontaleña ▲ NIC 185 Fh40
Cordillera Darwin ▲ RCH 210 Gf73
Cordillera de Aguaragüe ▲ BOL 207 Gj56
Cordillera de Ampato ▲ PE 197 Ge52
Cordillera de Carabaya ▲ PE 197 Ge52
Cordillera de Chicas ▲ BOL 206 Gg56
Cordillera de Chilca ▲ PE 197 Ge53
Cordillera de Guamaní ▲ PE 196 Gb48
Cordillera de Guanacaste ▲ CR 185 Fh40
Cordillera del Cóndor ▲ PE 196 Ga48
Cordillera de Lipez ▲ BOL 206 Gg56
Cordillera de los Picachos, P.N. ✦ CO 192 Gc44
Cordillera del Tigre ▲ RA 208 Gf62
Cordillera de Mérida ▲ YV 192 Ge41
Cordillera de San Pablo de Balzar ▲ EC 196 Ga46
Cordillera de Talamanca ▲ CR 185 Fj41
Cordillera de Venezuela ▲ YV 193 Gg41
Cordillera Domeyko ▲ RCH 207 Gf58
Cordillera Entre Ríos ▲ HN 184 Fh38
Cordillera Isabella ▲ NIC 184 Fh39
Cordillera Negra ▲ PE 197 Gb50
Cordillera Nombre de Dios ▲ HN 184 Fg38
Cordillera Occidental ▲ CO 192 Gb43
Cordillera Occidental ▲ PE 196 Ga49
Cordillera Oriental ▲ BOL 206 Gg54
Cordillera Oriental ▲ CO 192 Gc43
Cordillera Oriental ▲ PE 196 Gb49
Cordillera Real ▲ EC 196 Ga47
Cordillera Vilcabamba ▲ PE 197 Ge52
Cordillera Central ▲ PA 185 Fk41
Cordillera de San Blas ▲ PA 185 Ga41
Cordilla Downs ⊞ AUS (QLD) 108 Sa57
Cordisburgo ⊞ BR (MG) 203 Hj55
Córdoba ⊞ E 27 Kq53
Córdoba ⊞ MEX (VC) 182 Fb36
Córdoba ⊞ CO 192 Gc44
Córdoba ⊞ RA 208 Gh61
Cordobés, Cerro el ▲ RA 207 Gf60
Córdoba ⊞ CO 171 Ef27
Cordón Seler ⊞ RCH 210 Gd69
Córdova ⊞ USA (AK) 165 Ch15
Cordova Peak ▲ USA 165 Ch15
Coreaú ⊞ BR (CE) 201 Hk47
Corella ⊞ E 28 Kt48
Coremas ⊞ BR (PB) 201 Jb49
Corfield ⊞ AUS (QLD) 108 Sb56
Corfu = Kérkira ⊞ GR 46 Lu51
Corguinho ⊞ BR (MS) 202 Hc55
Coria ⊞ E 27 Ko51
Coribe ⊞ BR (BA) 200 Hh52
Corinth ⊞ USA (MS) 175 Ff28
Corinth = Kórinthos ⊞ GR (MS) 175 Ff28
Corinto ⊞ CO 192 Gb44
Corinto ⊞ NIC 184 Fg39
Coripata ⊞ BOL 206 Gg54
Cork = Corcaigh ⊞ IRL 19 Km39
Corlay ⊞ F 22 Kr42
Corleone ⊞ I 36 Lo53
Corleto Perticara ⊞ I 37 Lr50
Çorlu ⊞ TR 45 Mg49
Corlu, P.N. ✦ RO 207 Gf58
Cornaredo ⊞ I 34 Lk45
Corn Island ⊞ NIC 185 Fj39
Corneliç Procópio ⊞ BR (PR) 202 He57
Cornélio ⊞ USA (WI) 172 Fe23
Corner Brook ⊞ CDN 177 Hc21
Corners Cove ▲ USA (TX) 174 Fb30
Cornești ⊞ RO 45 Mf46
Corniche Kabyle ▲ DZ 126 Lc27
Cornimont ⊞ F 25 Lg43
Corning ⊞ USA (AR) 175 Fe27
Corning ⊞ USA (CA) 170 Dj26
Corning ⊞ USA (NY) 177 Gb24
Cornish, Mount ▲ AUS 103 Rd52
Corno Grande ▲ I 34 Ln48
Cornomors'ke ⊞ UA 49 Mg23
Cornwall ⊞ CDN 177 Gd23
Cornwall ▲ GB 21 Kp40
Cornwall Island ▲ CDN 163 Fb03

Coral Bay ⊞ AUS (WA) 102 Qg57
Coral City ⊞ USA (FL) 179 Fk32
Coral Fiji 119 Tj55
Coral, P.N. ✦ CDN 206 Gf54
Coral, Cerro ▲ RCH 206 Gf54
Coral Verde ▲ P 26 Kl49
Costeşti ⊞ RO 43 Mb44
Coral Sea ⊞ 100 Sb11
Costeşti ⊞ RO 40 Md45
Costeşti ⊞ RO 45 Mj45
Costiera Amalfitana ▲ I 37 Lp50
Costineşti ⊞ RO 45 Mj47
Coswig ⊞ D 32 Ln39
Cotabambas ⊞ PE 197 Gd52
Cotagaita ⊞ BOL 206 Gg56
Cotabato, Cerro ▲ CO 192 Ga45
Cotagaita ▲ RI 93 Qc48
Coteana ⊞ RO 45 Me46
Coteau des Prairies ▲ USA 172 Fb23
Coteau du Missouri ▲ USA 172 Fa23
Côte d'Argent ▲ F 24 Kt47
Côte d'Azur ▲ F 25 Lh47
Côte de Granit Rose ▲ F 22 Kr42
Côte d'Emeraude ▲ F 22 Ks42
Côte d'Opale ▲ F 23 Lb40
Côte Fleurie ▲ F 22 Ku41
Côte-la-Di ▲ RA (CH) 204 Ha59
Côte d'Or ▲ F 25 Le43
Cotigao ▲ IND 84 Oh38
Cotila ▲ RA (LP) 208 Gh64
Cotoca ⊞ BOL 206 Gj54
Coto de Doñana ✦ E 27 Ko54
Cotonou ⊞ DY (AT) 138 La43
Cotopaxi, P.N. ✦ EC 196 Ga46
Cotopaxi, Volcán ▲ EC 196 Ga46
Cotswold Hills ▲ GB 21 Ks39
Cottage Grove ⊞ USA (OR) 168 Dj24
Cottbus ⊞ D 32 Lp39
Cottesloe Beach ⊞ AUS (WA) 104 Qh61
Cottian Alps ▲ F/I 34 Lh46
Cottiella ▲ E 28 La48
Cottonwood ⊞ USA (AZ) 171 Ed28
Cottonwood ⊞ USA (ID) 168 Eb22
Cottonwood ⊞ USA (SD) 172 Ek24
Cottonwood Falls ⊞ USA (KS) 174 Fb26
Cotuí ⊞ DOM 186 Ge36
Couchman Range ▲ AUS 103 Rd53
Coudekerque-Branche ⊞ F 23 Lc40
Coudersport ⊞ USA (PA) 177 Ga25
Couffles ▲ F 24 Lb48
Couhé ⊞ F 24 Lq44
Couiza ⊞ F 24 Lc48
Coulman Island ▲ 7 Tc33
Couloir 1 ▲ DZ 126 Lc44
Coulommiers ⊞ F 23 Ld42
Coulonges-sur-l'Autize ⊞ F 24 Ku44
Coulta ⊞ AUS (SA) 108 Rh63
Council ⊞ USA (AK) 164 Bj13
Council ⊞ USA (ID) 168 Eb23
Council Bluffs ⊞ USA (IA) 174 Fb25
Council Grove ⊞ USA (KS) 174 Fb26
Country Club District ⊞ USA (CO) 171 Eh26
Coupar Anguse ⊞ GB 20 Kr34
Courchevel ⊞ F 25 Lg45
Courland Lagoon = RUS/LT 39 Ma35
Courmayeur ⊞ I 34 Lg45
Cournon-d'Auvergne ⊞ F 25 Ld45
Coursan ⊞ F 25 Lc47
Courseulles-sur-Mer ⊞ F 22 Ku41
Cours-la-Ville ⊞ F 25 Le44
Cours Mirabeau ▲ F 25 Lf47
Courtenay ⊞ CDN (BC) 168 Dh21
Courtenay ⊞ F 23 Ld42
Courtomer ⊞ F 23 La42
Coushatta ⊞ USA (LA) 174 Fd30
Coutada Pública do Longa – Mavinga ✦ ANG 151 Mb54
Coutada Pública do Luengué ✦ ANG 151 Ma54
Coutada Pública do Mucusso ✦ ANG 151 Ma54
Coutances ⊞ F 22 Kt41
Coutras ⊞ F 24 Ku45
Coutts ⊞ CDN (AB) 169 Ee21
Couvin ⊞ B 23 Le40
Covadonga y Picos de Europa, P.N. de ✦ E 26 Kp47
Covasna ⊞ RO 45 Mf45
Covelo ⊞ USA (CA) 170 Dh26
Coventry ⊞ GB 21 Kt38
Covered Portage Cove ✦ CDN 173 Fk23
Coves del Drac ✦ E 29 Ld51
Coves de Sant Josep ✦ E 29 Ku51
Covilhã ⊞ P 26 Kn50
Covington ⊞ USA (GA) 178 Fj29
Covington ⊞ USA (KY) 175 Fh26
Covington ⊞ USA (LA) 175 Fe30
Covington ⊞ USA (TN) 175 Ff28
Covington ⊞ USA (VA) 178 Ga27
Cowal Creek ⊞ AUS (QLD) 107 Sc52
Cowan ⊞ CDN (MB) 169 Ek19
Cowan, Cerro ▲ EC 197 Fe46
Cowan Downs ⊞ AUS (QLD) 107 Sa55
Cowarie ⊞ AUS (SA) 108 Rk59
Cowdrey ⊞ USA (CO) 169 Eg24
Cowell ⊞ AUS (SA) 110 Rj62
Cowes ⊞ GB 21 Kt40
Cowpens National Battlefield ✦ USA 178 Fk28
Cowper Point ▲ AUS 106 Rg51
Cowra ⊞ AUS (NSW) 111 Se62
Coxen Hole ⊞ HN 184 Fg37
Coxilha de Santana ▲ BR 204 Hc61
Cox's Bazar ⊞ BGD 86 Pf35
Cox's Cove ⊞ CDN (NF) 177 Hc21
Coyaguaima, Cerro ▲ RA 207 Gg57
Coyah ⊞ RG (NV) 136 Kd39
Coy Aike ⊞ RA (SC) 210 Gf71
Coyame ⊞ CO 192 Gb44
Coyame ⊞ MEX (CHH) 181 Eh31
Coyhaique ⊞ RCH 210 Gd68
Coyle ⊞ USA (OK) 174 Fb28
Coyote ⊞ USA (NM) 171 Eg28
Coyoteipec ⊞ MEX (OAX) 182 Fb37
Coyuca de Benítez ⊞ MEX (GUR) 182 Fa37

Coroa Vermelha, T.I. ⊞ BR 203 Ja54
Corocito ⊞ HN 184 Fh38
Corocoro ⊞ BOL 206 Gg54
Corocoro ⊞ NZ 112 Th64
Coromandel ⊞ BR (MG) 203 Hg55
Coromandel ⊞ NZ 112 Th64
Coromandel Coast ▲ IND 85 Pa40
Coromandel Peninsula ▲ NZ 112 Th64
Coron ⊞ RP 90 Ra40
Corona, Cerro la ▲ RA 208 Gf64
Corona ⊞ USA (NM) 171 Eh28
Coronado Nat. Mem. ✦ USA 171 Ee30
Coronation ⊞ CDN (AB) 169 Ee19
Coronation Gulf ⊞ CDN 162 Eb05
Coronation Island ▲ USA 166 Dc18
Coronation Island ▲ 7 Ha34
Coronda ⊞ RA (SF) 209 Gk61
Coronel ⊞ RCH 208 Gd64
Coronel Bogado ⊞ PY 204 Hb59
Coronel Brandsen ⊞ RA (BA) 209 Ha63
Coronel Cornejo ⊞ RA (SA) 207 Gj57
Coronel Dorrego ⊞ RA (BA) 209 Gk65
Coronel du Graty ⊞ RA (CH) 207 Gk59
Coronel Fabriciano ⊞ BR (MG) 203 Hj55
Coronel Freitas ⊞ BR (SC) 204 Hd59
Coronel Juan Solá ⊞ RA (SA) 207 Gk58
Coronel Moldes ⊞ RA (CD) 208 Gh62
Coronel Murta ⊞ BR (MG) 203 Hj54
Coronel Oviedo ⊞ PY 204 Hb58
Coronel Pirapó ⊞ PY 204 Hb59
Coronel Pringles ⊞ RA (BA) 209 Gk64
Coronel Sapucaia ⊞ BR (MS) 204 Hc57
Coronel Suárez ⊞ RA (BA) 209 Gk64
Coronel Vidal ⊞ RA (BA) 209 Ha64
Coronel Vivida ⊞ BR (PR) 204 Hd58
Corongo ⊞ PE 197 Gb50
Coron Island ▲ RP 90 Ra40
Coropuna, Nevado ▲ PE 197 Gd52
Corovodë ▲ AL 46 Ma50
Corowa ⊞ AUS (NSW) 111 Sd63
Corozal ⊞ BH 183 Ff36
Corozal ⊞ CO 192 Gc41
Corozo Pando ⊞ YV 193 Gg41
Corporales ▲ E 26 La44
Corpus ⊞ RA (MS) 204 Hc58
Corpus Christi ⊞ USA (TX) 181 Fb32
Corpus Christi Bay ⊞ USA 181 Fb32
Corque ⊞ BOL 206 Gg55
Córrego do Ouro ⊞ BR (GO) 202 He54
Correia Pinto ⊞ BR (SC) 205 He59
Corrente ⊞ BR (MS) 202 Hc57
Corrente ⊞ BR (BA) 200 Hh52
Corrente ⊞ BR (GO) 202 Hf54
Correntina ⊞ BR (BA) 200 Hh52
Correze ⊞ F 25 Lb45
Corrib, Lough ⊞ IRL 19 Kl37
Corrie Downs ⊞ AUS (QLD) 108 Sa57
Corrientes ⊞ RA 204 Ha60
Corrigan ⊞ USA (TX) 174 Fc30
Corrigin ⊞ AUS (WA) 104 Qj62
Corriverton ⊞ GUY 194 Ha43
Corry ⊞ USA (PA) 173 Ga25
Corryong ⊞ AUS (VIC) 111 Se63
Corse = Corsica ▲ F 34 Lj48
Corsica ▲ F 34 Lj48
Corsicana ⊞ USA (TX) 174 Fb29
Cortaderas ▲ RA (CD) 207 Gf59
Cortazar ⊞ MEX (GJT) 182 Ej35
Corte ⊞ F 34 Lk48
Cortemilia ⊞ I 34 Lj46
Cortes ⊞ RP 90 Rd41
Cortes ⊞ CO 171 Ef27
Cortes Nuevos ▲ E 27 Ks52
Cortina d'Ampezzo ⊞ I 34 Ln44
Çörtkiv ⊞ UA 43 Mf41
Cortland ⊞ USA (NY) 177 Gc24
Cortona ⊞ I 34 Lm47
Corubal ⊞ GNB (MG) 203 Hh55
Corum ⊞ BR (MG) 202 Hd55
Çorum ⊞ TR 56 Mh25
Corumbá ⊞ BR (MS) 202 Hb55
Corumbá de Goiás ⊞ BR (GO) 202 Hf53
Corumbaíba ⊞ BR (GO) 202 Hf54
Corumbau ▲ BR 203 Ja55
Coruña, A ⊞ E 26 Km47
Coruripe ⊞ BR (AL) 201 Jb51
Corvallis ⊞ USA (OR) 168 Dj23
Corve ⊞ USA (MO) 175 Fe27
Corzuela ⊞ RA (CH) 207 Gk59
Cosalá ⊞ MEX (SL) 180 Eg33
Cosamaloapan ⊞ MEX (VC) 183 Fc36
Cosenza ⊞ I 37 Lr51
Coshocton ⊞ USA (OH) 173 Fk25
Cosmo Newberry ⊞ AUS (WA) 105 Rb59
Cosne-Cours-sur-Loire ⊞ F 25 Lc43
Cosolea caque ⊞ MEX (VC) 183 Fc36

Cozia, P.N. ✦ RO 43 Me44
183 Fg35
Costa Rica ⊞ MEX (SL) 180 Eg33
Costa Rica ⊞ MEX (SO) 180 Ed30
Cozumel ⊞ MEX (QTR) 183 Fg35
Cozumel, Parque Marino Nacional Arrecifes de ✦ MEX 183 Fg35
Crab Orchard N.W.R. ✦ USA 175 Ff27
Crabtree Falls ✦ USA 177 Ga27
Crabwood Creek ⊞ GUY 194 Ha43
Crac des Chevaliers ✦ SYR 56 Mj28
Cracow ⊞ AUS (QLD) 109 Sf58
Cracow ⊞ PL 41 Lu40
Cradle Mountain National Park ✦ AUS (TAS) 111 Sd66
Cradle Mount Lake Saint Clair N.P. ✦ AUS (TAS) 111 Sd66
Cradock ⊞ AUS (SA) 110 Rk62
Cradock ⊞ ZA 155 Mc62
Crăiesti ⊞ RO 43 Me44
Craig ⊞ USA (AK) 166 Dc18
Craig ⊞ USA (CO) 171 Ef25
Craigie ⊞ USA (UT) 171 Ef25
Craigieburn ⊞ AUS (VIC) 111 Sc64
Craigmont ⊞ USA (ID) 168 Eb22
Craigsville ⊞ USA 173 Fk26
Crail ⊞ GB 20 Ks34
Crailsheim ⊞ D 33 Ll41
Craiova ⊞ RO 44 Md46
Craiva ⊞ RO 43 Mb44
Cramer Island ▲ AUS 106 Rg51
Cramond ▲ ZA 154 Ma59
Cranberry Junction ⊞ CDN (BC) 166 Df18
Cranberry Portage ⊞ CDN (MB) 169 Ek18
Cranbrook ⊞ AUS (WA) 104 Qh62
Cranbrook ⊞ CDN (BC) 168 Ec21
Cranbrook ⊞ GB 21 Lb39
Cranburne ⊞ AUS (VIC) 111 Sc65
Crandon ⊞ USA (WI) 173 Ff23
Crane ⊞ USA (OR) 168 Ea24
Crane ⊞ USA (TX) 181 Ej30
Crane Lake ⊞ USA (MN) 172 Fd21
Crane River ⊞ CDN (MB) 172 Fa20
Cranganore = Kodungallur ⊞ IND (KER) 84 Oj41
Crans-sur-Sierre ⊞ CH 34 Lh44
Cran ⊞ USA (CA) 170 Dj25
Craon ⊞ F 22 Kt43
Craponne-sur-Arzon ⊞ F 25 Ld45
Crary Mountains ▲ 6 Ec34
Crasna ⊞ RO 43 Mc43
Crater Hot Springs Resort ✦ RI 95 Qb49
Crater Lake ⊞ USA 168 Dj24
Crater Lake ▲ WAN 139 Lg40
Crater Lake N.P. ✦ USA 168 Dj24
Crater Mount ▲ USA 164 Cd14
Craters of the Moon Nat. Mon. ✦ USA 168 Ed24
Crateús ⊞ BR (CE) 201 Hk48
Crathie ⊞ GB 20 Kr33
Crato ⊞ BR (CE) 201 Ja49
Crato ⊞ P 27 Kn51
Craven ⊞ CDN (SK) 169 Eh20
Craven Arms ⊞ GB 21 Ks38
Crawford ⊞ USA (NE) 172 Ek24
Crawfordsville ⊞ USA 175 Fg25
Crawley ⊞ GB 21 Ku39
Creagorry ⊞ GB 20 Kn33
Crediton ⊞ GB 21 Kr40
Cree Lake ⊞ CDN (SK) 167 Eg27
Creek Town ⊞ WAN 138 La43
Creel ⊞ MEX (CHH) 180 Eg32
Cree Lake ⊞ CDN 167 Eg17
Creighton ⊞ USA (NE) 172 Fb24
Creil ⊞ F 23 Lc41
Crema ⊞ I 34 Lk45
Crémieu ⊞ F 25 Lf45
Cremona ⊞ CDN (AB) 169 Ec20
Cremona ⊞ I 34 Ll45
Creole ⊞ USA (LA) 174 Fd31
Créon ⊞ F 24 Ku46
Crepaja ⊞ SCG 44 Ma45
Crépy-en-Valois ⊞ F 23 Lc41
Cres ▲ HR 35 Lp46
Crescent ⊞ USA (OR) 168 Dj24
Crescent City ⊞ USA (CA) 168 Dh25
Crescent Junction ⊞ USA (UT) 171 Ef26
Crescent Lake ⊞ USA 168 Be24
Crescent Spur ⊞ CDN (BC) 168 Dk19
Crescent Valley ⊞ USA (NV) 170 Eb25
Cresco ⊞ USA (IA) 172 Fd24
Crespi d'Adda ✦ I 34 Lk45
Crespo ⊞ RA (ER) 209 Gk62
Cresti ⊞ BR (RS) 205 Hb65
Crest ⊞ F 25 Lf46
Crested Butte ⊞ USA (CO) 171 Eg26
Creston ⊞ CDN (BC) 168 Eb21
Creston ⊞ USA (IA) 172 Fc25
Crestview ⊞ USA (FL) 175 Fg30
Creswell Downs ⊞ AUS (NT) 106 Rh54
Creswick ⊞ AUS (VIC) 111 Sb64
Crete ⊞ USA (NE) 174 Fb25
Crete = Kríti ▲ GR 47 Me55
Créteil ⊞ F 23 Lc42
Creußen ⊞ D 33 Ln41
Creutzwald ⊞ F 23 Lg41
Crèvecœur-le-Grand ⊞ F 23 Lc41
Crevillente ⊞ E 29 Ku52
Crewe ⊞ GB 21 Ks37
Crewkerne ⊞ GB 21 Ks39
Crianlarich ⊞ GB 20 Kq34
Criciúma ⊞ BR (SC) 205 Hf60
Crickhowell ⊞ GB 21 Kr39
Crieff ⊞ GB 20 Kr34
Crikvenica ⊞ HR 35 Lp45
Crimea ⊞ UA 48 Mg23
Crimmitschau ⊞ D 32 Ln39
Criolla, Cerro la ▲ RA 210 Gf71
Cripple ⊞ USA 164 Cb14
Crişcior ⊞ RO 43 Mc44
Crişeni ⊞ RO 43 Md43
Crisfield ⊞ USA (MD) 177 Gc27
Cristais ⊞ BR (RS) 204 Hd61
Cristal, Monts de ▲ RCB 148 Lf45
Cristalândia ⊞ BR (TO) 200 Hf51
Cristalândia ⊞ BR (BA) 203 Hg54
Cristalândia do Piauí ⊞ BR (PI) 201 Hj50
Cristalia ⊞ BR (MG) 203 Hj54
Cristalina ⊞ BR (GO) 202 Hf54
Cristian ⊞ RO 45 Me44
Cristina ⊞ BR (MG) 203 Hh56
Cristino Castro ⊞ BR (PI) 200 Hj50
Cristo ⊞ BR (AM) 198 Gd49
Cristobal ⊞ PA 185 Ga41
Cristobal ⊞ BR (BA) 200 Hh52
Cristóbal Colón, Pico ▲ CO 192 Gd40
Cristo Redentor ✦ BR 203 Hj57
Cristuru Secuiesc ⊞ RO 43 Mf44
Criterion, Cerro ▲ RA 210 Gf68
Crivitz ⊞ D 32 Lm37
Crixás ⊞ BR (GO) 202 He53
Crixás Açu ⊞ BR 202 He53
Crna Bara ⊞ SCG 44 Ma45
Crni vrh ▲ BIH 35 Lr46
Črni vrh ▲ SLO 42 Lp44
Črnomelj ⊞ SLO 42 Lp44
Croajingolong N.P. ✦ AUS 111 Se64
Crocker Range N.P. ✦ MAL 94 Qj43
Crockett ⊞ USA (TX) 174 Fc30

Crocodile Camp ⊡ RB 151 Mb56
Crocodile Farm ⊡ AUS 106 Rf52
Crocodile Farm (Abaya Hayk') ⚑ ETH Mj42
Crocodile Pond ⊡ GH 137 Kk40
Crocq ⊡ F 25 Lc45
Croissilles ⊡ GB 20 Kq33
Cromer-Co ⊡ RA (LP) 208 Gh65
Cromer ⊡ CDN (MB) 172 Ek21
Cromwell ⊡ NZ 113 Te68
Cromwell ⊡ GB 21 Lb38
Cronulla Point ⊡ AUS (MN) 172 Fd22
Crooked Creek ⊡ USA (AK) 164 Ca15
Crooked Island ⊡ BS 186 Gc34
Crooked Island ⊡ AUS 164 Bk16
Crooked Island Passage ⊟ BS 186 Gc34
Crookhaven ⊡ IRL 19 Kj39
Crookston ⊡ USA (MN) 172 Fg22
Crookwell ⊡ AUS (NSW) 111 Se63
Crosby ⊡ USA (MS) 175 Fh28
Crosby ⊡ USA (ND) 169 Ej21
Cross City ⊡ USA (FL) 178 Fj31
Cross Creeks N.W.R. ⚑ USA 175 Fg27
Crossett ⊡ USA (AR) 175 Fe29
Cross Fell ⊿ GB 21 Ks36
Crossfield ⊡ CDN (AB) 169 Ec20
Cross Hands ⊡ GB 21 Kq39
Crossing Rocks ⊡ BS 179 Gb32
Crossmore ⊡ AUS (QLD) 109 Sc57
Crosson Ice Shelf ⊟ 6 Ec33
Cross Plains ⊡ USA (TX) 174 Fa29
Cross River N.P. ⚑ WAN 138 Le42
Crossville ⊡ USA (TN) 175 Fh28
Crotone ⊡ I 37 Ls51
Crow Agency ⊡ USA (MT) 169 Eg23
Crow Creek Ind. Res. ⚑ USA 172 Fa23
Crowder Lake S.P. ⚑ USA 174 Fa28
Crowdy Bay N.P. ⚑ AUS 109 Sg61
Crowheart ⊡ USA (WY) 169 Ef24
Crow Ind. Res. ⚑ USA 169 Ef23
Crowley ⊡ USA (LA) 175 Fd30
Crown Island ⊡ PNG 115 Sd48
Crown Point ⊡ USA (IN) 173 Fg25
Crownpoint ⊡ USA (NM) 171 Ef28
Crown Prince Range ⊿ PNG 117 Sh44
Crowpara ⊡ BD 86 Pg34
Crows Nest ⊡ AUS (QLD) 109 Sg59
Crowsnest Pass ⊟ CDN 168 Ec21
Croydon ⊡ SD 155 Mf59
Crozet Islands ⊡ 9 Nb14
Crozet Plateau ⊟ 9 Na14
Crozon ⊡ F 22 Kq42
Cruces ⊡ RO 45 Mj46
Crucero ⊡ PE 206 Gf53
Crucero ⊡ C 179 Fk34
Crucita ⊡ EC 196 Fk46
Cruden Bay ⊡ GB 20 Kt33
Cruillas ⊡ MEX (TM) 181 Fa33
Cruise Route ⊡ 184 Fh37
Cruise route ⊡ USA 179 Fj33
Cruise route ⊡ 184 Hd62
Cruise route (Irrawaddy) ⊡ MYA 86 Ph35
Cruz Alta ⊡ BR (RS) 204 Hd60
Cruz Alta ⊡ RA (CD) 209 Gk62
Cruzaltense ⊡ BR (RS) 204 Hd62
Cruzamento de Pegões ⊡ P 27 Km52
Cruz das Almas ⊡ BR (BA) 201 Ja52
Cruz del Eje ⊡ RA (CD) 207 Gh61
Cruzeiro ⊡ BR (SP) 205 Hh57
Cruzeiro ⊡ MOC 153 Mh56
Cruzeiro d'Oeste ⊡ BR (PR) 202 Hd57
Cruzeiro do Sul ⊡ BR (AC) 196 GG49
Cruz Grande ⊡ MEX (GUR) 182 Fa37
Cruzília ⊡ BR (MG) 203 Hh56
Cruz Machado ⊡ BR (PR) 204 He59
Creni cot ⊿ SCG 44 La45
Cryon ⊡ AUS (NSW) 109 Se60
Crysdale, Mount ⊿ CDN 166 Dj17
Crystal Brook ⊡ AUS (SA) 110 Rk62
Crystal Cave ⊡ USA 172 Fd23
Crystal City ⊡ USA (TX) 181 Fa31
Crystal Falls ⊡ USA (MI) 173 Ff22
Crystal Lake ⊡ USA (FL) 175 Fh30
Crystal Lake Cave ⊡ USA 172 Fe24
Crystal River ⊡ USA (FL) 178 Fj31
Crystal River N.W.R. ⚑ USA 178 Fj31
Crystal Springs ⊡ CDN (SK) 169 Eh19
Crystal Springs ⊡ USA (MS) 175 Fe30
Csakvár ⊡ H 42 Lt43
Csánytelek ⊡ H 43 Ma44
Csaroda ⊡ H 43 Mc42
Csátalja ⊡ H 43 Lu44
Csenger ⊡ H 43 Mc42
Csesznek ⊡ H 42 Ls43
Csigar-heg ⊿ H 43 Ma44
Csongrad ⊡ H 43 Ma44
Csorna ⊡ H 42 Ls43
Csorvás ⊡ H 43 Mb44
Csót ⊿ H 42 Ls43
Ctesiphon ⊡ IRQ 59 Nc29
Cúa ⊡ YV 193 Gg42
Cuacama ⊡ YV 193 Gf40
Cuale ⊡ ANG 150 Lj50
Cuamato ⊡ ANG 150 Lh54
Cuamba ⊡ MOC 153 Mj53
Cuando ⊡ RB 151 Mb54
Cuango ⊡ ANG 150 Lk49
Cuango ⊡ ANG 150 Lj48
Cuango ⊡ ANG 149 Lj50
Cuango ⊡ ANG 148 Lk49
Cuanza ⊡ ANG 148 Lh49
Cuanza ⊡ ANG 150 Lk51
Cuanza ⊡ ANG 150 Lh49
Cuanza Sul ⚑ MEX 180 Ef31
Cuarinuma ⊡ C 193 Gd44
Cuarteron Reef ⊡ 94 Qg41
Cua Song Cuu Long ⊟ MEX 181 Ej32
Cuatrociénegas ⊡ MEX (COH) 181 Ej32
Cuauhtémoc ⊡ MEX (CHH) 180 Eg31
Cuautla ⊡ MEX (MOR) 182 Fa36
Cuautla ⊡ MEX (JLC) 182 Eh35
Cuba ⊡ USA (AL) 175 Ff29
Cuba ⊡ C 179 Ek35
Cuba ⊡ USA (NM) 171 Ef27
Cubango ⊡ ANG 150 Lj53
Cubango ⊡ ANG 150 Lh54
Cubatão ⊡ BR (SP) 205 Hg57
Cubati ⊡ C 179 Ek49
Cubculo ⊡ GA 184 Ga54
Cucao ⊡ RCH 210 Gc67

Cuchagua ⊡ BOL 206 Gg55
Cuchi ⊡ ANG 150 Lj53
Cuchilla de Haedo ⊿ ROU 204 Hb61
Cuchilla de Mangrullo ⊿ ROU 204 Hd62
Cuchilla Grande ⊿ ROU 204 Hb61
Cúdnite mostove ⊡ BG 45 Me49
Cudnav ⊡ UA 49 Me20
Cúdovo ⊡ RUS 48 Mf16
Cue ⊡ AUS (WA) 104 Qj59
Cuéllar ⊡ E 26 Kq49
Cuenca ⊡ ANG 150 Lk52
Cuenca ⊡ E 29 Ks50
Cuenca ⊡ EC 196 Ga47
Cuenca del Añelo ⚑ RA 208 Gf65
Cuencamé ⊡ MEX (DGO) 182 Fa36
Cuerne ⊡ MEX (MOR) 182 Fa36
Cuero ⊡ USA (TX) 181 Fb31
Cuers ⊡ F 25 Lg47
Cuerva ⊡ E 27 Kq51
Cuestecitas ⊡ CO 192 Gd40
Cueto ⊡ C 186 Gc35
Cuetzalán ⊡ MEX (PUE) 182 Fb35
Cueva de Altamira ⊡ E 26 Kq47
Cueva de Ambrosio ⊡ C 179 Fk34
Cueva de la Quebrada del Toro ⊡ YV 193 Gf40
Cueva de las Brujas ⊡ RA 208 Gf63
Cueva de las Manos ⊡ RA 210 Ge69
Cueva del Chacho ⊡ RA 207 Gg61
Cueva del Elefante ⊡ YV 193 Gj42
Cueva del Guácharo ⊡ YV 193 Gj40
Cueva del Indio ⊡ C 179 Fj34
Cueva del Milodón ⊡ RCH 210 Gd71
Cueva de los Guácharos, P.N. ⚑ CO 192 Gb45
Cueva de Nerja ⊡ E 27 Kr53
Cuevas Bellamar ⊡ C 179 Fk34
Cuevas Candelaria ⊡ GCA 184 Fe38
Cuevas del Almanzora ⊡ E 29 Kt53
Cuevas de los Tayos ⊡ EC 196 Ga47
Cugir ⊡ RO 44 Md45
Cugnaux ⊡ F 24 Lb47
Cuhujiv ⊡ UA 48 Mg21
Cuiabá ⊡ BR (AM) 198 Gf47
Cuiabá ⊡ BR (MT) 202 Hb53
Cuiabá ⊡ BR 202 Hb54
Cuia, T.I. ⚑ BR 199 Ha47
Cuicatlán ⊡ MEX (OAX) 182 Fb37
Cuieiras ⊟ BR 198 Ha47
Cuijabo ⊡ CDN 35 Li39
Cuilo ⊡ ANG 149 Lk50
Cuilo Pombo ⊡ ANG 148 Lh49
Cuima ⊡ ANG 150 Lh52
Cuima-Cavungo ⊡ ANG 150 Lh52
Cuio ⊡ ANG 150 Lh52
Cuipo ⊡ PA 185 Fk41
Cuira o Monos ⊡ CO 196 Gd46
Cuiseaux ⊡ F 25 Lf44
Cuito ⊡ ANG 150 Lj53
Cuito Cuanavale ⊡ ANG 150 Lk53
Cuitzeo del Porvenir ⊡ MEX (MIC) 182 Eh36
Çukurca ⊡ TR 57 Nd27
Çukurköprü ⊡ TR 56 Mh27
Çukurova ⊡ TR 56 Mh27
Culanegia ⊡ ANG 148 Lh49
Culan ⊡ F 25 Lc44
Cu Lao Cham ⊡ VN 89 Qe38
Cu Lao Thu = Phu Quy ⊡ VN 89 Qf39
Culasi ⊡ RP 90 Rb40
Culasian ⊡ RP 94 Qk41
Culburra ⊡ AUS (NSW) 111 Sf63
Culcairn ⊡ AUS (NSW) 111 Sd63
Culebra ⊡ PE 197 Ga56
Culemborg ⊡ NL 23 Lf39
Culfa ⊿ AZ 57 Nd26
Culgoa N.P. ⚑ AUS 109 Sd60
Culiacán ⊡ MEX (SL) 180 Eg33
Cúllar-Baza ⊡ E 27 Ks53
Cullen ⊡ GB 20 Ks33
Cullera ⊡ RCH 210 Gf72
Cullera ⊡ E 29 Ku51
Cullinan ⊡ ZA 155 Me58
Cullman ⊡ USA (AL) 175 Fg28
Culuene ⊡ BR 200 Hd52
Culuene ⊿ BR 202 Hd52
Çuluwuru Island ⊡ AUS 106 Rj51
Culverden ⊡ NZ 113 Tg67
Culzean Castle ⊡ GB 20 Kq35
Culzean ⊿ F 25 Lf45
Cuman ⊡ UA 41 Mf40
Cumanacoa ⊡ YV 193 Gj40
Cumanayagua ⊡ C 179 Fk34
Cumar ⊡ SP 145 Nd44
Cumari ⊡ BR (GO) 203 Hg53
Cumaru ⊡ BR (GO) 203 Hg53
Cumba ⊡ PE 196 Ga48
Cumbal, Volcán de ⊿ CO 192 Gb45
Cumbe ⊡ EC 196 Ga47
Cumberland ⊡ USA (MD) 177 Ga26
Cumberland Caverns ⊡ USA 175 Fh28
Cumberland Downs ⊡ AUS (QLD) 109 Sd57
Cumberland Gap N.H.P. ⚑ USA 178 Fj27
Cumberland House ⊡ CDN (SK) 169 Ej19

Cumberland Island ⚑ USA 178 Fk30
Cumberland Island National Seashore ⚑ USA 178 Fk30
Cumberland Islands ⊡ AUS 107 Se56
Cumberland Peninsula ⊿ CDN 163 Gc05
Cumbernauld ⊡ GB 20 Kr35
Cumbi ⊡ ANG 148 Lg49
Cuborah ⊡ AUS (NSW) 109 Sd60
Cumbrera, Cerro ⊿ RCH 210 Gd69
Čučkovo ⊡ RUS 48 Na18
Cuc Phuong N.P. ⚑ VN 87 Qc35
Cucui ⊡ BR 193 Gg45
Cucurbeta ⊿ YV 193 Gh43
Cucurta ⊡ YV 193 Gf41
Čučuta ⊡ CO 192 Gd42
Cuddalore ⊡ IND (TNU) 85 Ok40
Cuddapah ⊡ IND (APH) 83 Ok38
Cudillero ⊡ E 26 Ko47
Cúdnite mostove ⚑ BG 45 Me49
Čudnav ⊡ UA 49 Me20
Cue ⊡ AUS (WA) 104 Qj59
Cuéllar ⊡ E 26 Kq49
Cuemba ⊡ ANG 150 Lj52
Čuenca ⊡ E 29 Ks50
Cuenca ⊡ EC 196 Ga47
Čuhloma ⊡ RUS 48 Na16
Čuhuiv ⊡ BR (RN) 201 Jc49
Čumica ⊡ ANG 150 Ma53
Čumphon ⊡ THA 88 Pj41
Čuna ⊡ RUS 54 Pd07
Cunani ⊡ BR (AP) 195 He44
Cuñare ⊡ CO 192 Gd44
Cunco ⊡ RCH 208 Gd65
Cunday ⊡ CO 192 Gc43
Cundeelee A.L. ⚑ AUS 105 Rb61
Cunderdin ⊡ AUS (WA) 104 Qj61
Cunducán ⊡ MEX (TB) 183 Fd36
Cunene ⊡ ANG 150 Lg54
Cunene ⊿ ANG 150 Lg53
Cunene ⊡ ANG 150 Lh53
Cúneo ⊡ I 34 Lh46
Cunhambebe ⊡ BR (RJ) 205 Sa47
Čunhaú ⊡ BR (RN) 201 Jc49
Cunnamulla ⊡ ANG 150 Ma53
Cunnamulla ⊿ AUS (QLD) 109 Sd59
Cunningham Islands ⊡ AUS 106 Rj51
Cupar ⊡ GNB 136 Kc39
Cupar ⊡ GB 20 Kr34
Cupica ⊡ CO 192 Gb42
Cupica ⊿ CO 192 Gb42
Cupisnique, Cerro ⊿ PE 196 Ga49
Cupixi ⊡ BR (AP) 195 He45
Čuprija ⊡ SCG 44 Mb47
Curaçá ⊡ BR (BA) 201 Ja50
Curaçao ⊡ NL 193 Gf39
Curacautin ⊡ RCH 208 Gd65
Curacavi ⊡ RCH 208 Ge62
Curahuara de Carangas ⊡ BOL 206 Gf54
Curale ⊡ ETH 143 Nd42
Cural Velho ⊡ CV 136 Jj37
Curanilahué ⊡ RCH 208 Gd64
Curanilla ⊡ F 24 Lh47
Čuhujiv ⊡ UA 48 Mg21
Curaray ⊡ EC 196 Ga46
Curaray ⊿ PE 196 Gc47
Curaru ⊡ RA (AM) 198 Gf47
Curburba ⊡ AUS (WA) 104 Qh59
Curdimurka ⊡ AUS 107 Se54
Curepipe ⊡ MS 157 Nj56
Curiapo ⊡ YV 193 Gk41
Curibaya ⊡ PE 197 Ge54
Curicó ⊡ RCH 208 Ge63
Curimatá ⊡ BR (PI) 200 Hh51
Curionópolis ⊡ BR (PA) 200 Hf48
Curitiba ⊡ BR (AC) 196 GG49
Curitiba ⊡ BR (PR) 205 He59
Curitibanos ⊡ BR (SC) 205 He59
Curiúva ⊡ BR (PR) 205 He58
Curk Cut Cay ⊡ BS 179 Gb34
Curnamona ⊡ AUS (SA) 108 Rk61
Curragh Racetrack ⊡ IRL 19 Ko37
Currais ⊡ BR (PI) 201 Hj50
Currais Novos ⊡ BR (RN) 201 Jb49
Curral Alto ⊡ BR (RS) 204 Hd62
Curral de Pedra ⊡ BR (PI) 201 Hk49
Curralinho ⊡ BR (PA) 195 Hf46
Currant Novo do Piauí ⊡ BR (PI) 201 Hh50
Curran ⊡ MTJ 173 Fj23
Currant ⊡ USA (NV) 170 Ec26
Curranyalpa ⊡ AUS (NSW) 109 Sc61
Currawinya ⊡ AUS (QLD) 109 Sc60
Currawinya N.P. ⚑ AUS 109 Sc60
Current ⊡ BS 179 Gb33
Current Island ⊡ AUS (TAS) 111 Sb65
Currie ⊡ AUS (VIC) 111 Sb65
Currie ⊡ USA (NV) 171 Ec25
Curtici ⊡ RO 43 Mc44
Curtea de Argeş ⊡ RO 43 Me45
Curtici ⊡ ROU 44 Mb44
Curtis Island ⊡ AUS (VIC) 111 Sd65
Curtis Island ⊡ NZ 112 Ua61
Curtin Springs ⊡ AUS (NT) 105 Rf58
Curuá ⊡ BR (PA) 199 Hc47
Curuaí ⊡ BR (PA) 199 Hc47
Curug Sewu ⊡ RI 95 Qf49
Curup ⊡ RI 93 Qb47
Curuzú Cuatiá ⊡ RA (CR) 204 Hb60
Cusco ⊡ RCH 210 Gc67

Cuttack ⊡ IND (ORS) 83 Pc35
Cutta Cutta Caves ⊡ AUS 106 Rg53
Cutzamala de Pinzón ⊡ MEX (GUR) 182 Eh36
Cuvelar ⊡ ANG 150 Lh53
Cuveta de Doany ⊿ RM 156 Nj53
Cuvier Island ⊡ NZ 112 Th64
Cuxhaven ⊡ D 32 Lj37
Cuya ⊡ RCH 206 Gd55
Cuyaguta ⊡ YV 193 Gj40
Cuyahoga Valley N.P. ⚑ USA 173 Fk25
Cuyamel ⊡ HN 184 Ff38
Cuyo ⊡ RP 90 Ra40
Cuyo East Passage ⊟ RP 90 Ra40
Cuyo ⊡ MEX (PUE) 182 Fb36
Cuyo 'English Game' Subterranean N.P. ⚑ RP 90 Ra40
Cuyo Islands ⊡ RP 90 Ra40
Cuyo West Passage ⊟ RP 90 Ra40
Cuyotenango ⊡ GCA 184 Fe38
Cuyutlán ⊡ MEX (COL) 182 Eh36
Cuzco ⊡ PE 197 Ge52
Cwmcarn ⊡ GB 21 Kr39
Cyangugu ⊡ RWA 146 Me47
Cybinka ⊡ PL 40 Lp38
Cyclades ⊡ GR 47 Md53
Cyclops Mountains ⊿ RI 115
Čyhryn ⊡ UA 49 Mg21
Cylinder ⊡ USA 109 Sg59
Cypress Gardens ⊡ USA (QLD) 109 Sf58
Cypress Hills ⊿ CDN 169 Ef21
Cypress Hills Interprov. Park ⚑ CDN 169 Ef21
Cyprus ⊡ CY 56 Mg28
Cyran ⊡ BY 41 Mg37
Cyrenaica ⊿ LAR 127 Ma31
Cyrene = Shahhāt ⊡ LAR 127 Ma29
Czarny ⊡ UA 49 Mg21
Czarna ⊡ PL 41 Mc41
Czarna Białostocka ⊡ PL 41 Md37
Czarna Dąbrówka ⊡ PL 40 Ls36
Czarnków ⊡ PL 40 Lr38
Czarny Dunajec ⊡ PL 41 Lu41
Czchów ⊡ PL 41 Ma41
Czech Republic ⊡ CZ 42 Lp41
Czekanowice ⊡ PL 41 Mb39
Czermno ⊡ PL 41 Ma39
Czersk ⊡ PL 40 Ls37
Czerwieniék ⊡ PL 41 Lu38
Czerwińsk ⊡ PL 40 Lt38
Czerwonka-Leszczyny ⊡ PL 40 Lt40
Czerwony Dwór ⊡ PL 41 Mc36
Częstochowa ⊡ PL 41 Lu40
Człopa ⊡ PL 40 Lr37
Człuchów ⊡ PL 40 Ls37
Czyżew-Osada ⊡ PL 41 Mc38

D

Da'an ⊡ CHN (JLN) 76 Rc23
Daan Viljoen Game Park ⚑ NAM 150 Lj57
Dabaga ⊡ EAT 147 Mh50
Dabaga ⊿ RN 132 Le47
Dabagram ⊡ IND (WBG) 86 Pe34
Dabai ⊡ WAN 138 Lc40
Dabakala ⊡ CI 137 Kh41
Dabaklala ⊡ IND (ASM) 86 Pg32
Dabancheng ⊡ CHN (XUZ) 67 Pe24
Dabane-ye-Qoloman ⊿ IR 64 Oa30
Daban Shan ⊿ CHN 72 Qe29
Dabas ⊡ H 43 Lu43
Dabatou ⊡ RG 136 Ke40
Dabdab ⊡ LAR 127 Lh32
Dabeiba ⊡ CO 192 Gb42
Dabeiyuan Monastery ⊡ CHN 73 Qg26
Dabenoris ⊡ ZA 154 Lk60
Dabie ⊡ PL 40 Lu39
Dabie Shan ⊿ CHN 73 Qh30
Dabija ⊡ MK 44 Mc49
Dabiss ⊡ RG 136 Kc40
Dabo ⊡ SN 136 Kc38
Dabola ⊡ RG 136 Kd40
Dabolatounka ⚑ RG 136 Kd40
Daborow ⊡ CI 137 Kh43
Dabra ⊡ IND (MPH) 83 Ok33
Dabrava ⊡ SOL 117 Ta50
Dabravolja ⊡ RI 91 Me38
Dąbrowa ⊡ RI 91 Me38
Dąbrowa Górnicza ⊡ PL 41 Lu40
Dąbrowa Tarnowska ⊡ PL 41 Ma40
Dabryn' ⊡ BY 48 Me20
Dabugam ⊡ IND (ORS) 83 Pb36
Dabuk ⊡ RI 93 Qb47
Dacata ⊿ ETH 143 Nb40
Dachau ⊡ D 33 Ll42
Dachepalle ⊡ IND (APH) 83 Ok37
Dachigam N.P. ⚑ IND (JKT) 80 Oh30
Dachiken ⊡ IND (JKT) 80 Oh30
Dachstein ⊿ A 42 Lo43
Dachsteinhöhlen ⊡ A 81 Ok29
Dachung Yogma ⊡ 81 Ok29
Dacia Seamount ⊿ 124 Kd30
Daçi ⊡ CZ 42 Lq41
Dac Song ⊡ VN 89 Qd39
Dac To ⊡ VN 89 Qd38
Dadaab ⊡ EAK 145 Na45
Dadaku ⊡ CI 137 Kg42
Dadeldhura ⊡ NEP 81 Pa32
Dadra and Nagar Haveli ⚑ IND 82 Og35
Dadu ⊡ PK 65 Oc31
Dadu ⊿ CHN 73 Qa30
Daduku ⊡ CHN (AHU) 78 Qk30

Dafni ⊡ GR 45 Md53
Dafo ⊡ CHN (SK) 169 Eh20
Dafo Si ⊡ CHN (SAA) 72 Qe28
Dafra ⊡ TCH 139 Lk40
Daga ⊡ IND (MPH) 83 Pd33
Daga Istephanos Monastery ⊡ ETH 142 Mj40
Dagana ⊡ SN 130 Kc37
Daga Post ⊡ SUD 142 Mg41
Dagasuli ⊡ RI 91 Re44
Dagash ⊡ SUD 135 Mg39
Dagba ⊡ YV 39 Mh34
Dagda ⊡ LV 39 Mj52
Daget ⊡ ETH 129 Mf32
Dagbreek ⊡ ZA 155 Me58
Dagestan ⊿ RUS 57 Nd24
Dageb ⊡ IND (WBG) 83 Pd33
Dagestanskij zapovednik ⚑ RUS 57 Nd23
Daghar ⊡ OM 61 Nk34
Daghmar ⊡ OM 61 Nk34
Dagkhenga ⊡ IND (MHT) 82 Og36
Daging Chi ⊡ CHN 66 Pb24
Dalmacija ⊿ HR 35 Lq46
Dalmalin ⊡ BH 138 Lf39
Dalmatia ⊿ 14 Lo05
Dalmeny ⊡ AUS (NSW) 111 Sf64
Dalmose ⊡ DK 30 Ll35
Dan Gulbi ⊡ WAN 138 Lc40
Dangur ⊡ ETH 142 Mj40
Dalton ⊡ USA (GA) 175 Fh28
Dalton Highway ⊡ USA (AK) 164 Cd12
Dalton Mus. ⊡ USA 178 Fc27
Dalu ⊡ CHN (GSU) 72 Qc27
Dalu ⊡ IND (MGA) 86 Pf33
Daludalu ⊡ RI 92 Qa44
Dalupiri Island ⊡ RP 90 Ra36
Dalupiri Island ⊡ RP 90 Rc39
Dal'verzin Tepe ⊡ UZ 63 Od27
Dalwa ⊡ ETH 142 Na38
Daly ⊿ AUS (NT) 106 Rf53
Daly City ⊡ USA (CA) 170 Dj27
Daly River ⊿ AUS (NT) 106 Rf53
Daly River ⊡ AUS (NT) 106 Rf53
Daly River A.L. ⚑ AUS 106 Rf53
Daly Waters ⊡ AUS (NT) 106 Rg54
Damaik ⊿ IND (ASM) 86 Pg32
Dalyup ⊡ AUS (WA) 105 Ra62
Damagarambe ⊿ WAN 138 Lf40
Damamulai ⊿ IR 57 Ne26
Damachim ⊡ IR 59 Nf29
Daman ⊡ AFG 65 Oc30
Daman ⊡ IND 82 Og35
Daman ⊿ CHN (HUB) 74 Qf30
Damanhūr ⊡ ET 129 Mf30
Damao ⊡ CHN 72 Qf26
Damar ⊡ RI 97 Rb48
Damaraland ⊿ NAM 150 Lg56
Damas ⊿ RN 138 Le41
Damascus = Dimashq ⊡ SYR 56 Mj29
Damaturu ⊡ WAN 139 Lg40
Damau ⊡ RI 91 Rd44
Damba ⊡ ANG 148 Lh50
Damba Island ⊡ EAU 144 Mg46
Dambam ⊡ WAN 138 Lf40
Dambaslar ⊡ TR 45 Mh49
Damboa ⊡ WAN 139 Lg40
Dambi Wuqala ⊡ ETH 142 Mk41
Dambulla ⊡ CL 85 Pa42
Dame Marie ⊡ RH 186 Gc36
Damergou ⊿ RN 132 Le40
Damerow ⊡ D 32 Lo36
Damietta = Dumyāt ⊡ ET 129 Mf30
Damietta ⊡ ET 129 Mf30
Damion ⊡ TCH 139 Lh40
Damjong ⊡ CHN (QHI) 72 Qb28
Damman ⊡ KSA 59 Ne32
Damme ⊡ D 32 Lj38
Dämning ⊿ N 30 Lm30
Damodar ⊿ IND 83 Pc34
Damoh ⊡ IND (MPH) 83 Ok34
Damongo ⊡ GH 137 Kk41
Damoure ⊡ ET 129 Mf30
Damqawt ⊡ YE 61 Ng37
Damroh ⊡ IND (ARP) 86 Ph31

Dalhousie ⊡ CDN (NB) 176 Gg21
Dalhousie Springs ⚑ AUS (SA) 108 Rh59
Dali = Xiaguan ⊡ CHN (YUN) 76 Rc25
Dali ⊡ RMM 131 Kg38
Dalian ⊡ CHN (LNG) 76 Rc26
Dalianhe ⊡ CHN (HLG) 76 Re22
Dali ⊡ E 27 Ks54
Dali ⊡ CHN (SAA) 72 Qf29
Dali Museum (Saint Petersburg) ⊡ USA 179 Fj32
Dali Sharafat ⊡ SUD 135 Mg39
Dalja ⊡ ET 129 Mf32
Dalkeith ⊡ GB 20 Kr35
Dalkhaki ⊡ AFG 63 Oc30
Dalkola ⊡ IND (WBG) 83 Pd33
Dallas ⊡ USA (OR) 168 Dj23
Dall Island ⊡ USA 166 Dd18
Dalli ⊡ UAE 61 Ng33
Dalli ⊡ WAN 138 Lf41
Dalma Reef ⊟ 94 Qg42
Dalmacija ⊿ HR 35 Lq46
Dalupiri ⊿ RP 90 Ra36
Daling River ⊿ AUS 111 Sc62
Dalmally ⊡ GB 20 Kq34
Dalmellington ⊡ GB 20 Kq35
Dalnerecensk ⊡ RUS 76 Rg22
Daloa ⊡ CI 137 Kg42
Dalol Crater ⊿ ER 142 Na39
Dalol Saltlake and Hot Springs ⚑ ETH 142 Na38
Dalong ⊡ CHN (HUN) 74 Qe32
Dalong Chi ⊿ CHN 66 Pb24
Dalrymple, Mount ⊿ AUS 109 Se56
Dahana Beach ⊡ IND (MHT) 82 Og36
Daheba ⊡ CHN (QHI) 69 Pk28
Dahebian ⊡ CHN (SCH) 74 Qd31
Dahei ⊿ CHN (SCH) 87 Qa27
Dahei ⊿ CHN (GSU) 72 Qd27
Dahei ⊿ CHN (YUN) 87 Qa27
Dahlak Archipelago ⊡ ER 142 Na38
Dahlak Marine N.P. ⚑ ER 142 Na38
Dahme ⊡ D 32 Ln38
Dahme ⊿ D 32 Lo38
Dahnshür ⊡ ET 129 Mf31
Dahod ⊡ IND (GUJ) 82 Oh34
Dahod ⊡ IND (GUJ) 82 Oh34
Dai Loc ⊡ VN 89 Qd38
Dai al'Rīh ⊿ SUD 135 Mf40
Dahra ⊡ DZ 126 Lc28
Dai Chang ⊡ THA 88 Qa37
Dahūk ⊡ IRQ 57 Nc28
Dai Dao ⊡ CHN 78 Rb30
Dahua ⊡ CHN (GZG) 74 Qe34
Dahuaishu ⊿ IND (ARP) 86 Pf33
Dai Hai ⊿ CHN 72 Qf25
Dai Huoai ⊡ VN 89 Qd40
Dai Island ⊡ SOL 117 Ta49
Dai Lanh Beach ⊡ VN 89 Qe39
Daileki ⊡ NEP 81 Pa31
Daimiel ⊡ E 27 Kr51
Daingerfield ⊡ USA (TX) 174 Fc29
Daintree N.P. ⚑ AUS 107 Sc54
Dai Island ⊿ CHN (HAN) 75 Qf34
Dai Xian ⊡ CHN (SAA) 73 Qf26
Daiyun Shan ⊿ CHN 75 Qj33
Daja ⊡ CHN (QHI) 69 Pg27
Dajarra ⊡ AUS (QLD) 108 Rk56
Dajabon ⊡ DOM 186 Gf36
Daju ⊡ CHN (GSU) 72 Qd27
Da Juh ⊡ CHN 69 Pg27
Dak Glei ⊡ VN 89 Qd38
Dakar ⊿ SN 130 Kb38
Dak Doa ⊡ VN 89 Qd39
Dakawa ⊡ EAT 147 Mj49
Dak Kherja Sherif Ziarat Mosque ⊡ AFG 65 Oc30
Dakhla ⊿ DARS 130 Kc34
Dakhla Oasis ⊿ ET 129 Me33
Dakhlet Nouâdhibou ⚑ RIM 130 Kb35
Dakingari ⊡ WAN 138 Lc40
Dakor ⊡ IND (GUJ) 82 Og34
Dak Mil ⊡ VN 89 Qd39
Dakota ⊿ WAN 138 Ld41
Dak Pek ⊡ VN 89 Qd38
Dakpam ⊡ GH 137 Kk41
Dakshin Gangotri ⚑ ANT (IND) 7 Lc32
Daku, Gunung ⊿ RI 91 Rd45
Dala ⊡ ANG 150 Ma51
Dala ⊡ RMM 131 Kj38
Dala ⊡ SOL 117 Ta50
Dalaba ⊡ RG 136 Kd40
Daladag Maligawa (Kandy) ⊡ CL 85 Pa42
Dalai ⊿ CHN (NMZ) 72 Qf25
Dalai ⊿ CHN 76 Rb22
Dalai Nur ⊿ CHN 73 Qj24
Dalai Shan ⊿ CHN 69 Pj26
Dalaki ⊡ IR 59 Nf31
Dalam ⊡ SP 143 Nf40
Dalama ⊡ RM 156 Na54
Dalamxung ⊿ CHN (TIB) 68 Pe30
Dalandzadgad ⊡ MNG 71 Qg29
Dalangyun ⊡ MYA 86 Ph36
Dana ⊡ RI 96 Ra51
Dana Nature Reserve ⚑ JOR 58 Mh30
Dane ⊿ CI 136 Kf42
Da Nang ⊡ VN 89 Qe38
Dana Point ⊡ USA (CA) 170 Ec29

Dandarah ⊡ ET 129 Mg32
Dandale ⊡ CI 137 Kh41
Dande ⊿ ANG 150 Lj51
Dande ⊡ ETH 144 Mj43
Dandeli ⊡ IND (KTK) 82 Oh38
Dandenong ⊡ AUS (VIC) 111 Sc64
Dandeli Nat. Res. ⚑ CHN (NMZ) 72 Qf25
Dando ⊡ CHN (LNG) 76 Rc25
Dando ⊡ CHN (LNG)
Danfa ⊡ RMM 131 Kg38
Danfeng ⊡ CHN (SAA) 72 Qf29
Danforth ⊡ USA (ME) 176 Gg23
Danga ⊡ IND (WBG) 86 Pe33
Dangan ⊡ ETH 142 Mj40
Dangan ⊿ CHN 75 Qh34
Dangara ⊡ TJ 63 Oe26
Dangchang ⊡ CHN (GSU) 72 Qc28
Danggali Conservation Park ⚑ AUS 108 Sa60
Danghara ⊡ RO 43 Mf44
Dangla ⊡ CHN (LNG) 78 Re26
Darke Peak ⊡ AUS (SA) 108 Rj62
Darkhadyn Khotgor ⊿ MNG 70 Pk20
Darkhan ⊡ MNG 70 Qd21
Darkhovin ⊡ IR 59 Ne30
Darkot ⊡ IND (HPH) 81 Oj30
Darkovici ⊡ IND (MHT) 82 Og36
Danguy ⊿ ETH 142 Mj40
Dangyang ⊡ CHN (HUB) 74 Qf30
Dani ⊡ CI 137 Kg42
Daniel Boone Natl. Forest ⚑ USA 178 Fj27
Daniel Johnson Dam ⊡ CDN 176 Gf20
Danielskuil ⊡ ZA 154 Mb60
Danilov ⊡ RUS 48 Na16
Danilovgrad ⊡ SCG 44 Lu48
Daning ⊡ CHN 72 Qf27
Danish Fort ⊡ IND 85 Ok40
Dankama ⊡ EAK 145 Na44
Dan Issa ⊡ RN 132 Le40
Dankov ⊡ RUS 48 Mk19
Danling ⊡ CHN (SCH) 74 Qc30
Danli ⊡ HN 184 Fg38
Dannenberg ⊡ D 32 Ln37
Dannevirke ⊡ NZ 113 Tj66
Danshui ⊡ CHN 73 Qh28
Dan Sadau ⊡ WAN 138 Ld40
Dantan ⊡ IND (WBG) 83 Pd35
Dante = Xaafuun ⊡ SP 143 Nf40
Dantewara ⊡ IND (CGH) 83 Pa36
Danube ⊿ 14 Ma05
Danubyu ⊡ MYA 88 Ph37
Danum Valley Conservation Area ⚑ MAL 94 Qj43
Danville ⊡ USA (IN) 174 Fd26
Danville ⊡ USA (KY) 175 Fh27
Danville ⊡ USA (IL) 175 Fg25
Danville ⊡ USA (VA) 177 Gb27
Danwan ⊡ CHN 72 Qd28
Danxiashan ⊡ CHN 75 Qg33
Danyang ⊡ CHN (JGS) 78 Qk29
Danyi-Apéyémé ⊡ TG 137 La42
Danzé ⊡ EAK 145 Na47
Danzhou ⊡ CHN 75 Qf34
Dao ⊡ RP 90 Ra40
Danzhou ⊡ CHN (HAN) 75 Qf34
Dao Bari ⊿ RP 90 Ra40
Dao Hon Lon La ⊡ VN 89 Qe39
Dao Phu Quoc ⊡ VN 89 Qc40
Daotanghe ⊡ CHN (QHI) 72 Qb27
Daoukro ⊡ CI 137 Kh42
Daoulas ⊡ F 22 Kq42
Dapango ⊡ TG 137 La41
Daparola ⊿ 143 Nf41
Dapchi ⊡ WAN 139 Lf39
Dapélogo ⊡ BF 137 Kk39
Dapdap ⊡ RP 90 Rb41
Daping ⊿ CHN (HLG) 76 Rf22
Dapoli ⊡ IND (MHT) 82 Og37
Dapuchaihe ⊡ CHN (JLN) 76 Re24
Da Qaidam ⊡ CHN (QHI) 69 Pj28
Daqing ⊡ CHN (HLG) 76 Rc22
Daqing Shan ⊿ CHN 72 Qf25
Daqu ⊡ CHN 78 Ra30
Daqu Dao ⊡ CHN 78 Rb30
Dara ⊿ IRQ 57 Nc28
Dar'a ⊡ SYR 56 Mj29
Darab ⊡ IR 64 Ng31
Daraban ⊡ PK 65 Of30
Darabani ⊡ RO 43 Mg42
Darabani ⊡ DZ 126 Lc28
Darangal ⊿ RCA 141 Mc43
Daradou ⊡ RCA 141 Mc43
Daraina ⊡ RM 156 Ne52
Darajani ⊿ EAK 145 Na47
Dara-Lac = Dalat ⊿ VN 89 Qe39
Daramanil ⊿ RI 114 Rg46
Daran ⊡ IR 59 Nf29
Dar-el-Barka ⊡ RIM 130 Kd37
Dar es Salaam ⚑ EAT 147 Mk49
Darfur ⊿ SUD 134 Mc39
Dargai ⊡ PK 65 Of29

Daurskij hrebet ⊿ RUS 71 Qg20
Dausa ⊡ IND (RJT) 80 Oj32
Dau Thieng ⊡ VN 89 Qd40
Dautlbos ⊡ MEX (SL) 180 Eg33
Davangere ⊡ IND (KTK) 84 Oh38
Davao ⊡ RP 91 Rc42
Davarzan ⊡ IR 62 Nj27
Davenas ⊡ RUS 71 Oh19
Davenport ⊡ USA (IA) 175 Fe25
Davenport ⊡ USA (WA) 168 Ea22
Davenport Downs ⊡ AUS (QLD) 108 Sa58
Davenport Range ⊿ AUS
Davenport Range N.P. ⚑ AUS 106 Rh56
Daventry ⊡ GB 21 Kt38
Davhinava ⊡ BY 39 Mh36
David ⊡ PA 185 Fj41
Davidson ⊡ CDN (SK) 169 Eh19
David City ⊡ USA (NE) 172 Fb25
David Garedza ⊡ GE 57 Nc25
Davidson Mountains ⊿ USA (AK) 165 Cj11
Davis City ⊡ USA (IA) 174 Fd25
Davis ⊡ ANT (AUS) 7 Od32
Davis, Mount ⊿ USA 105 Re59
Davis Mts. ⊿ USA 181 Eh30
Davis Strait ⊟ 163 Ha05
Davyd-Haradok ⊡ BY 48 Md19
Davlekanovo ⊿ TJ 76 Rg25
Dawa ⊡ GH 137 La43
Dawai ⊿ ETH 142 Na41
Dawei ⊡ SUD 141 Mj41
Dawa ⊿ KSA 59 Ne33
Dawei ⊿ EAK 145 Na47
Dawes Range ⊿ AUS 109 Sf58
Dawera Range ⊿ AUS 109 Sf58
Dawera ⊡ RI 97 Rf49
Dawhenya ⊡ GH 137 La43
Dawu ⊡ CHN (HUB) 75 Qg30
Dawu ⊡ SUD 141 Mj41
Dawu ⊡ CHN (NMZ) 88 Pj37
Dawu ⊡ CHN (SCH) 72 Qb30
Dawu ⊿ E 29 Kl49
Dawson Bay Ind. Res. ⚑ CDN 169 Ej19
Dawson City ⊡ CDN (YT) 165 Da13
Dawson Creek ⊡ CDN (BC) 167 Dk18
Dawson Landing ⊡ CDN (BC) 166 Dj17
Dawson River ⊿ AUS 109 Sf58
Dawson Springs ⊡ USA (KY) 175 Fg27
Dawu ⊡ CHN (HUB) 73 Qh30
Dawu ⊡ CHN (SCH) 69 Qa30
Dawwa ⊡ CHN (SCH) 69 Qa30
Daxian ⊡ CHN (SCH) 74 Qd30
Daxin ⊡ CHN (GZG) 74 Qd34
Daxing ⊿ CHN (BJG) 73 Qj26
Daxue Shan ⊿ CHN (YUN) 87 Qa32
Dayang Bunting ⊡ MAL 92 Pk42
Dayangshu ⊡ CHN (NMZ) 71 Qk21
Dayao ⊡ CHN (YUN) 87 Qa32
Dayaxa ⊡ SP 143 Nd40
Daye ⊡ CHN (HUB) 75 Qg30
Dayi ⊡ CHN (SCH) 74 Qc30
Dayingjiang ⊿ CHN (YUN) 87 Pk32
Daylesford ⊡ AUS (VIC) 111 Sc64
Dayr az Zawr ⊡ SYR 56 Mk28
Dayton ⊡ USA (OH) 175 Fh26
Dayton ⊡ USA (TX) 175 Fc30
Dayton ⊡ USA (WA) 168 Ea22
Daytona Beach ⊡ USA (FL) 178 Fk31
Dayu ⊡ CHN (JGX) 75 Qh33
Dayville ⊡ USA (OR) 168 Ea23
Dayyer ⊡ IR 59 Nf31
Dayinnah ⊡ UAE 61 Ng33
Dazhu ⊡ CHN (SCH) 74 Qd30
Dazu Rock Carvings ⊡ CHN 74 Qd31
Dchira ⊡ DARS 124 Kd32
De Aar ⊡ ZA 155 Mc61
Deadhorse ⊡ USA (AK) 165 Cf10
Dead Horse Point Mon. ⊡ USA 171 Ef27
Deadman Hill ⊿ AUS 102 Rh49
Deadman's Cr. Ind. Res. ⚑ CDN 168 Dk20
Dead Sea ⊟ IL 58 Mh30
Deakin ⊡ AUS (WA) 105 Re61
Deal ⊡ GB 21 Lb39
Dealurile Silvaniei ⊿ RO 43 Mc43
Dean ⊿ CHN (JGX) 75 Qh31
Deán Funes ⊡ RA (CD) 207 Gh61
Dearborn ⊡ USA (MI) 173 Fj24
Dease ⊿ CDN (BC) 166 Dg16
Dease Strait ⊟ CDN 162 Ec05
Deasy ⊿ IND (JKT) 81 Pa29
Death Railway ⊡ THA 88 Pk38
Death Valley ⊿ USA (CA) 170 Eb27
Death Valley Junction ⊡ USA (CA) 170 Eb27
Death Valley N.P. ⚑ USA 170 Ea27
Deauville ⊡ F 22 Lb41
Debali ⊡ RG 136 Kd41
Debar ⊡ MK 44 Ma49
Debark ⊡ ETH 142 Mk39
Debark Mts. ⊿ ETH 142 Mk39
Debawa ⊡ RI 115
Debden ⊡ CDN (SK) 169 Eg18
Deben ⊿ GB 21 Lb39
Debica ⊡ PL 41 Mb40
Debiar ⊡ BD 86 Pf35
Debidwar ⊡ BD 86 Pg34
Debin ⊡ RUS 55 Sc06
Dębica ⊡ PL 41 Mb40
Dębno ⊡ PL 40 Lp38
Dębno ⊡ PL 41 Ma41
Debolt ⊡ CDN (AB) 167 Ea18
Debre Birhan ⊡ ETH 142 Na40
Debre Bizen ⊡ ER 142 Na38
Debre Libanos ⊡ ETH 142 Mk40
Debre Markos ⊡ ETH 142 Mj40
Debre Sina ⊡ ETH 142 Mj40

Eemshaven ☒ NL 23 Lg37
Eendekuil ☒ ZA 154 Lk62
Eenhana ☒ NAM 150 Lj54
Éfaté ☒ VU 118 Te54
Effigy Mounds Ind. Res. ◫ USA 172 Fe24
Effingham ☒ USA (IL) 175 Ff26
Efkarpía ☒ GR 45 Me55
Eflâni ☒ TR 56 Mg25
Efon Alaye ☒ WAN 138 Lc42
Efrémov ☒ RUS 48 Mk19
Efteling ☒ NL 23 Lf39
Eg ☒ MNG 70 Qf21
Egayit ☒ MYA 88 Ph36
Egbe ☒ WAN 138 Lc41
Egbunda ☒ RDC 141 Md44
Egbunda ☒ RDC 141 Me44
Egby ☒ S 31 Lr34
Egeln ☒ D 32 Lm39
Eger ⊞ H 43 Ma43
Egersund ☒ N 30 Lg32
Egeskov ⊞ DK 30 Ll35
Eggedal ☒ N 30 Lk30
Eggenburg ☒ A 42 Lq42
Eggenfelden ☒ D 33 Ln42
Eggesin ☒ D 32 Lp37
Egg Lagoon ☒ AUS (TAS) 111 Sb65
Egholo ☒ SOL 117 Sj50
Eghra ☒ IND (JKD) 83 Pc33
Egilsstaðir ☒ IS 18 Kf25
Egína ☒ GR 45 Md53
Egína ☒ GR 45 Md53
Eginbah ☒ AUS (WA) 102 Qk56
Egínio ☒ GR 46 Mc50
Egío ☒ GR 46 Mc51
Egirdir ☒ TR 56 Mf27
Egirdir Gölü ⊟ TR 56 Mf27
Egito Praia ☒ ANG 150 Lg51
Egizkara tau ▲ KZ 62 Oc22
Egletons ☒ F 24 Lc45
Egmond aan Zee ☒ NL 23 Le38
Egor'e ☒ RUS 48 Mj18
Egor'evsk ☒ RUS 48 Mk18
Egorlykskaja ☒ RUS 49 Na22
Egré ☒ IND (WBG) 83 Pd35
Egtved ☒ DK 30 Lk35
Egum Atoll ⊞ PNG 116 Sf50
Egvekinot ☒ RUS 55 Ua05
Egyed ☒ H 42 Ls43
Egypt ■ ET 123 Ma07
Eha-Amufu ☒ WAN 138 Lc42
Ehi ☒ GH 137 Ld42
Ehingen ☒ D 33 Lk42
Ehinos ☒ GR 45 Me49
Ehrenbreitstein ⊞ D 33 Lh40
Ehrwald ☒ A 34 Ll43
Eibar ☒ E 28 Ks47
Eibergen ☒ NL 23 Lg38
Eibiswald ☒ A 35 Lq44
Eichenried ☒ D 33 Lm42
Eichstätt ☒ D 33 Lm42
Eiðar ☒ IS 18 Kf25
Eide ☒ N 16 Ld14
Eidfjord ☒ N 30 Lh30
Eid-Gah-Masjid ⊞ PK 65 Of30
Eiði ☒ DK 18 Kp28
Eidsvåg ☒ N 16 Le14
Eidsvold ☒ AUS (QLD) 109 Sf58
Eidsvoll ☒ N 30 Lf32
Eifel ☒ D 33 Lg40
Eiffel Flats ☒ ZW 152 Me55
Eigerøya ☒ N 30 Lf32
Eigg ☒ GB 20 Ko34
Eight Degree Channel ⊟ IND 84 Og42
Eight Mile Rock ☒ BS 179 Ga32
Eights Coast ⊟ 6 Fa33
Eighty Mile Beach ⊞ AUS 102 Ra55
Eijsden ☒ B 23 Lf40
Eikon ☒ N 30 Lf32
Eikonaskanskij hrebet ▲ MNG 70 Qe21
Eilai ☒ SUD 135 Mf37
Eilean Donan Castle ⊞ GB 20 Kp33
Eilenburg ☒ D 32 Ln39
Eilerts de Haangebergte ▲ SME
Eil Malk ☒ PAL 90 Rh42
Eilsleben ☒ D 32 Lm38
Eina ☒ N 30 Ll30
Einasleigh ☒ AUS (QLD) 107 Sc55
Einbeck ☒ D 32 Lk39
Eindyaza ☒ MYA 88 Pk38
Eindhoven ☒ NL 23 Lf39
Eindpaal ☒ NAM 150 La56
Ein Mansur ☒ SUD 134 Md38
Eina ☒ MYA 88 Ph37
Éire ☒ 15 Ko34
Eiriksjökull ☒ IS 18 Ju26
Eirikstaðir ⊞ IS 18 Jt25
Eirunepé ☒ BR (AM) 198 Gf49
Eiseb ☒ NAM 150 La56
Eisenberg ☒ D 32 Ln40
Eisenerz ☒ A 35 Lq43
Eisenerzer Alpen ▲ A 35 Lp43
Eisenhower Center ⊞ USA 174 Fb26
Eisenhüttenstadt ☒ D 32 Lp38
Eisenstadt ☒ A 35 Lr43
Eisenwurzen ▲ A 35 Lp43
Eisfeld ☒ D 33 Ll40
Eišiškés ☒ LT 39 Mf36
Eisriesenwelt ⊞ A 35 Lo43
Eivissa = Ibiza ☒ E 29 Lb51
Eivissa ☒ E 29 Lb52
Ejaji ☒ ETH 142 Mj41
Ejea de los Caballeros ☒ E 28 Kt48
Ejeda ☒ RM 157 Nc58
Ejer Bavnehøj ▲ DK 30 Lk35
Ejido ☒ YV 192 Ga41
Ejidogari ☒ WAN 138 Lc41
Ejido La Concha ☒ MEX (CHH) 180 Eg31
Ejin Horo Qi ☒ CHN (NMZ) 72 Qe26
Ejin Qi ☒ CHN (NMZ) 72 Qa25
Ejirin ☒ WAN 138 Lb42
Ejisu ☒ GH 137 Kk42
Ejsk ☒ RUS 49 Mk22
Ejule ☒ WAN 138 Lc42
Ejutla ☒ MEX (JAL) 182 Eh36
Ekalaka ☒ USA (MT) 169 Eh23
Ekamour ☒ RIM 131 Kg36
Ekang ☒ WAN 138 Ld43
Ekata ☒ G 140 Ld44
Ekaterinoslavka ☒ RUS 71 Re20
Ekaterinovka ☒ RUS 48 Mk19
Ekaterinovka ☒ RUS 48 Na19
Ekaterininskij dvorec ⊞ RUS 48 Mf16
Ek Balám ⊞ MEX 183 Ff35
Ekeby ☒ S 30 Ln35
Ekélfi ☒ RN 132 Ld37
Ekenäs = Tammisaari ☒ FIN 38 Md31
Ekenäs ☒ S 31 Lo32
Ekenäs skärgårds n.p. = Tammisaaren saariston kansallipuisto ⊞ FIN 38 Md31
Ekeröl ☒ S 31 Ln31
Eket ☒ WAN 138 Lc43
Ekibastuz ☒ KZ 54 Oc08
Ekimoviči ☒ RUS 113 Pb66
Ekinanec ☒ RN 132 Ld38
Ekluma Village Hist. Park ⊞ USA 165 Cf15
Ekma ☒ IND (BIH) 83 Pc33
Eknö ☒ S 31 Lp33
Ekoka ☒ RDC 149 Mc46

Ekombe ☒ RDC 140 Ma45
Ekondo Titi ☒ CAM 138 Le43
Ekouata ☒ G 148 Lc46
Ekrafanen ☒ RN 132 Lb38
Eksi dzamija ⊞ BG 45 Mf49
Eksjö ☒ S 31 Lp33
Eku ☒ WAN 138 Lc43
Ekukola ☒ RDC 140 Mb47
Ekumakoko ☒ GH 137 Kj43
Ekuropon ☒ GH 137 Kj43
Ekwa ☒ CAM 139 Lg44
Ekwendeni ☒ MW 146 Mg51
Ekylamenfurom ☒ GH 137 Kk42
Ekzarh Antimovo ☒ BG 45 Mg48
El Abiodh-Sidi-Cheikh ☒ DZ 125 La29
El Abred ☒ ETH 145 Nc43
El Adeb Larache ☒ DZ 126 Ld32
Elafónissos ☒ GR 46 Mc54
El Agrud ☒ ET 129 Mg30
El Aguila ☒ BOL 206 Gj53
El Aguilar ☒ RA (JU) 207 Gh57
El Aguinaldo ☒ MEX (DGO) 181 Eh33
Elahera ☒ CL 85 Pa42
El Aïadia ☒ SUD 135 Mg36
El-Aïoun ☒ MA 125 Kj28
Elak Oase ☒ CDN 167 Eg18
El-Alamein ☒ ET 129 Me30
El-Alamein War Cemetery ⊞ ET 129 Me30
El Alazán ☒ MEX (VC) 182 Fb35
El Alicante ☒ MEX (COH) 181 Ej32
El Almendral ⊞ PE 196 Ga48
El Alto ☒ MEX (JLC) 182 Ej35
Elamanchili ☒ IND (APH) 83 Pb37
El Amirah ☒ ET 129 Mf31
El Amparo ☒ MEX (SLP) 182 Ek34
El Amparo ☒ YV 193 Gf41
El Amparo de Apure ☒ YV 192 Ge42
El Cubo de Tierra del Vino ☒ E 26 Kp49
El Cuco ☒ ES 184 Ff39
El Cuy ☒ RA (RN) 208 Gf65
El Cuyo ☒ MEX (YT) 183 Fg35
Elda ☒ E 29 Ku52
El Dab'ah ☒ ET 129 Me30
El Darien ☒ CO 192 Gc42
Elde ☒ D 32 Lm37
El Deir ☒ ET 129 Mg33
Eldersile ☒ AUS (QLD) 108 Sb57
El Descanso ☒ PE 197 Ge53
El Desemboque ☒ MEX 180 Ed30
El Deseo ☒ MEX (SO) 180 Ed30
Eldgjá ▲ IS 18 Kb27
El Divisadero ☒ MEX (CHH) 180 Eg32
El Djem ☒ TN 126 Lf28
El Doncello ☒ CO 192 Gc45
Eldon Hazlet S.P. ⊞ USA 175 Ff26
Eldorado ☒ BR (MS) 200 Hd58
Eldorado ☒ BR (PA) 200 Hd48
Eldorado ☒ BR (SP) 205 Hf58
El Dorado ☒ HN 184 Fh38
El Dorado ☒ MEX (SL) 180 Ee32
El Dorado ☒ RA (MI) 204 Hc59
El Dorado ☒ RA (SA) 475 Fd29
El Dorado ☒ USA (AR) 175 Fe29
El Dorado ☒ USA (KS) 174 Fb27
El Dorado ☒ USA (TX) 174 Ek30
El Dorado ☒ YV 193 Gk42
El Dorado River ☒ USA 164 Bh13
El Dorado Springs ☒ USA (MO) 174 Fc27
Eldoret ☒ EAK 144 Mh45
Eldorrã ☒ TM 62 Nb26
Elec ☒ RUS 48 Mk19
Elefsína ☒ GR 46 Mc52
Eleftheroúpoli ☒ GR 45 Me50
El Eje ☒ RA (LP) 204 Gg64
Elékta ☒ RUS (MB) 48 Mk18
Elektrénai ☒ LT 39 Me36
Elele ☒ WAN 138 Lc43
El Empalme ☒ EC 196 Ga48
El Empedrado ☒ YV 192 Gd41
Elemi ☒ SUD 135 Mg38
El Encanto ☒ CO 192 Gd46
El Encino ☒ MEX (PJ) 182 Fa34
El Epazote ☒ MEX (SLP) 182 Ek34
Elephanta Island ⊞ ☒ IND 82 Og36
Elephant Butte Res. ☒ USA 171 Eg26
Elephant Island ☒ 6 Hb31
Elephant Island ☒ USA (AK) 165 Bk12
Elephant Training Centre ⊞ RI 93 Qc48
Elesbão Veloso ☒ BR (PI) 201 Hj49
El Blanquero ☒ YV 193 Gj41
El Blanquito ☒ NIC 185 Fj39
El Bolsón ☒ RA (RN) 208 Ge66
El Bonillo ☒ E 27 Ks52
El Bordj ☒ DZ 125 La28
El Bordo ☒ MEX 192 Gb44
El Borma ☒ TN 126 Le30
El Borouj ☒ MA 125 Kh29
El Bosque ☒ MEX 184 Fg39
El Brasil ☒ MEX (TM) 182 Fb34
El'brus ☒ RUS (KBA) 57 Nb24
El Burgo de Osma ☒ E 28 Kr49
Elburgon ☒ EAK 144 Mh46
El Burro ☒ YV 193 Gg42
El Burumbul ☒ ET 129 Mf31
El Cabrito ☒ MEX (TM) 182 Fb34
El Cabure ☒ RA (SE) 207 Gj59
El Cain ☒ RA (RN) 208 Gf66
El Cajas, P.N. ⊞ EC 196 Ga48
El Cajon ☒ USA (CA) 170 Eb29
El Calafate ☒ RA (SC) 210 Gd71
El Callao ☒ YV 193 Gk42
El Calvario ☒ YV 193 Gg41
El Campin ☒ CO 192 Gd43
El Campo ☒ USA (TX) 181 Fb31
El Canelo ☒ MEX (SL) 181 Eg33
El Caño ☒ PA 185 Fk41
El Canton ☒ YV 192 Ge42
El Capulín ☒ MEX (GJT) 182 Ek35
El Carbón ☒ HN 184 Fh38
El Carmen ☒ BOL 206 Gj52
El Carmen ☒ BOL 206 Ha55
El Carmen ☒ CO 192 Gc44
El Carmen ☒ CO 192 Gd44
El Carmen ☒ EC 196 Ga46
El Carmen ☒ MEX (COH) 181 Ek33
El Carmen ☒ MEX (NL) 181 Ek33
El Carmen ☒ NIC 184 Fj39
El Carmen ☒ MEX (PJ) 207 Gd58
El Carmen ☒ RCH (CHH) 180 Eg30
El Carrizal ☒ MEX (GUR) 182 Ek37
El Carrizo ☒ MEX (TM) 181 Fa33
El Castillo ☒ MEX (SL) 180 Eg33
El Cayo ▲ MEX 183 Fe37

El Cayuco ☒ MEX (BCS) 180 Ee33
El Ceibal ▲ GCA 183 Ff37
El Centro ☒ USA (CA) 170 Ec29
El Cerrito ☒ CO 192 Gb44
El Cerrito ☒ RA (SJ) 206 Ge71
El Cerro de Concepción ☒ BOL 206 Gk54
Elchacay ☒ RCH 208 Ge64
El Chaco ☒ EC 196 Gb46
El Chaco ☒ RA (CD) 208 Gh61
El Chaltén ☒ RA (SC) 210 Gd70
El Chaparro ☒ YV 193 Gh41
El Charco ☒ MEX (SLP) 182 Ek35
Elche = Elx ☒ E 29 Ku52
Elche de la Sierra ☒ E 27 Ks52
El Chico, P.N. ⊞ MEX (HDG) 182 Fa35
El Chilar ☒ NIC 185 Fh39
El Chinero ☒ MEX (BC) 180 Ec30
Elcho Island ☒ AUS (NT) 106 Rg51
El Chorrito ☒ MEX (TM) 181 Fa33
El Chorro ☒ BOL 198 Gg51
El Ciento Veinticinco ☒ MEX (BCS) 180 Ee33
El Cinco ☒ MEX (COH) 181 Ej32
El Cisne ☒ EC 196 Ga48
El Cisne ☒ MEX 196 Ga47
El Cobre ☒ CO 192 Gd42
El Cocuy, P.N. ⊞ CO 192 Gd42
El Colorado ☒ RA (FO) 204 Ha59
El Comitán ☒ MEX 180 Ee33
El Cope ☒ PA 185 Fk41
El Corazón ☒ EC 196 Ga46
El Corcovado ☒ RA (CB) 210 Ge67
El Corozo ☒ YV 193 Gh41
El Coyote ☒ MEX (BCS) 180 Ed32
El Coyote ☒ MEX (SO) 180 Ed31
El Coyte ☒ RA (CB) 210 Ge68
El Crispín ☒ RA (CD) 209 Gj61
El Cruce ☒ GCA 183 Ff37
El Crucero ☒ MEX (BC) 180 Ec31
El Cuarenta ☒ MEX (SLP) 182 Ek34

El Guapo ☒ YV 193 Gh40
El Guay ☒ YV 193 Gf40
El Guayabo ☒ YV 192 Gd41
El Guerara ☒ DZ 125 Lb31
El Guettar ☒ TN 126 Le28
El Guettar ☒ TN 126 Le28
El Hadjar ☒ DZ 126 Ld27
El Hagounia ☒ DARS 124 Kd32
El-Hajeb ☒ MA 125 Kh29
El Hamma ☒ DZ 126 Lc30
El Hamma ☒ TN 126 Le30
El Hammám ☒ ET 129 Me30
El Hammám ☒ RIM 130 Ke34
El Hamraâwein ☒ ET 129 Mf31
El Hank ☒ RIM/RMM 131 Kg33
El Haouaria ☒ TN 126 Le27
El-Harcha ☒ DZ 126 Lc29
El Haouita ☒ SUD 135 Mh39
El Hawata ☒ SUD 135 Mh39
El Herradero ☒ MEX (TM)
El Higo ☒ MEX (VC) 182 Fa35
El Homr ☒ DZ 125 La31
El Hovo ☒ BG 45 Mg48
El Huacal ☒ MEX (DGO) 180 Eg33
El Hierro ☒ RA (NE) 208 Ge64
El Huesco ☒ MEX (TM) 181 Fa33
El Humume ☒ SP 143 Ne42
Eliá ☒ GR 46 Mb53
Elías, Cerro ▲ RA 210 Gg68
Eliase ☒ RI 97 Rf50
Elías Gracia ☒ ANG 149 Ma50
Elida ☒ CDN (MB) 172 Fa21
El Idrisiia ☒ DZ 126 Lc28
El Idrisiia ☒ DZ 126 Lc28
Eliki Gounda ☒ RN 132 Le38
El Ingenio ☒ PE 197 Gc53
Elin Pelin ☒ BG 44 Md48
Elionka ☒ RUS 48 Mg19
Elipa ☒ RDC 149 Mc46
Elípa ☒ RDC 149 Mc46
El Isiro ☒ BR (PI) 200 Hj50
El Iskandarïya = ☒ ET 129 Me30
Eliye Springs ☒ EAK 144 Mj44
Elizabeth ☒ GUY 194 Ha47
Elizabeth ☒ USA (NJ) 177 Gc25
Elizabeth City ☒ USA (NC) 178 Gb27
Elizabeth Downs ☒ AUS (NT) 106 Rf52
Elizabeth Harbour ☒ BS 186 Gc34
Elizabethton ☒ USA (TN) 178 Fj27
Elizabethtown ☒ USA (KY) 175 Fh27
Elizabethtown ☒ USA (NC)
Eljadida ☒ MEX (DGO) 181 Eh34
El-Jadida ☒ MA 125 Kf29
El Jadidah ☒ ET 129 Mf31
El-Jemaa ☒ MA 124 Kf30
El Jicaral ☒ NIC 184 Fh39
El Jobean ☒ USA (NYT) 182 Eh35
El Jordán ☒ CO 192 Gd46
Etk ☒ PL 41 Mc37
El Kab ☒ SUD 135 Mg36
El Kab (Nekheb) ⊞ ET 129 Mg33
El Kala, P.N. d' ⊞ DZ 126 Ld27
El Kantara ☒ DZ 126 Lc28
El Karabi ☒ SUD 135 Mg36
Elk City ☒ USA (ID) 168 Ec23
Elk City ☒ USA (OK) 174 Fa28
Elk Creek ☒ USA (CA) 170 Dj26
El Kebab ☒ MA 125 Kh29
Elkedra ☒ AUS (NT) 106 Rh56
El Kef ☒ TN 126 Le28
El-Kelaâ-des-Sraghna ☒ MA 125 Kg29
El Kere ☒ ETH 145 Nb43
Elkford ☒ CDN (BC) 168 Ec20
Elk Grove ☒ USA (CA) 170 Dk26
Elkhart ☒ USA (IN) 173 Fh25
Elkhart ☒ USA (KS) 174 Ek27
Elkhart ☒ USA (TX) 174 Fc30
El Khatouat ☒ MA 125 Kj29
El Khatt ☒ RIM 130 Ke34
Elkhorn ☒ CDN (MB) 172 Ek21
Elkhorn ☒ USA (WI) 173 Fg24
Elkhorn N.P. ☒ CDN 169 Ed19
El Khroub ☒ DZ 126 Ld27
El Khufrah ☒ LAR 128 Mb33
Elkin ☒ USA (NC) 178 Fk27
El Kinta ☒ MEX (YT) 183 Fg36
Elk Island N.P. ☒ CDN 169 Ed19
El Kir ☒ CAM ...
Elko ☒ CDN (BC) 168 Ec21
Elko ☒ USA (NV) 170 Ec25
Elkol ☒ USA (WY) 169 Ef24
Elkton ☒ USA (MD) 177 Gb26
Elkton ☒ USA (OR) 168 Dj24
El Kurah Oasis ☒ LAR 128 Mb33
Ellababa ☒ USA (GA) 175 Fh29
Ellaville ☒ USA (GA) 175 Fh29
Ellendale ☒ AUS (WA) 103 Rc54
Ellendale ☒ USA (ND) 172 Fa23
Ellen, Mount ▲ USA 171 Ee26
Ellenburg ☒ USA 180 Ek34
Ellenville ☒ USA (NY) 177 Gc25
Ellerbe ☒ USA (NC) 178 Ga28
Ellerslie Racecourse ⊞ NZ 112 The4
Ellesmere Island ☒ CDN 163 Fd02
Elphinstone ☒ CDN (MB) 172 Ek20
El Limón ☒ MEX (JLC) 182 Fb36
El Limón ☒ MEX (MO) 175 Fe27
El Pilar de la Mola ☒ E 29 Lb52
El Pinar ☒ C 179 Fj34
El Pingo ☒ RA (EA) 209 Ha61
El Pipila ☒ MEX (DGO) 181 Eh33
El Platanal ☒ MEX (SO) 180 Ef31
El Plomo ☒ RA (SA) 207 Gd58
El Pocito ☒ MEX (DGO)
El Portón ☒ BOL 206 Gk53
El Porvenir ☒ PA 185 Ga41
El Porvenir ☒ RA (SC) 210 Ge71
El Porvenir ☒ YV 193 Gf42

Ellsworth ☒ USA (MA) 177 Gf23
Ellsworth ☒ USA (NE) 172 Ej25
Ellsworth ☒ USA (WI) 172 Fd23
Ellsworth Mountains ▲ 6 Fa33
El Lucero ☒ MEX (CHH) 180 Eg30
Ellwangen ☒ D 33 Ll42
Elma ☒ USA (WA) 168 Dh22
El Maand ☒ DZ 126 Lc29
El Macao ☒ DOM 186 Gf36
El-Mahalla el-Kubra ☒ ET 129 Mf30
El Maitén ☒ YV 192 Mg33
El Maitén ☒ RA (CB) 208 Ge66
El Malah ☒ DZ 125 Kk28
El Malah ☒ DZ 125 Kk28
Elmalı ☒ TR 56 Mf27
El Mallale ☒ ETH 145 Nd43
El Mansour ☒ DZ 125 La31
El Mansûra ☒ ET 129 Mf30
Elmar ☒ RI 97 Rf50
El Manzano ☒ RCH 208 Ge63
El Maragha ☒ ET 129 Mf31
El Maria ☒ PA 185 Fk41
El Marsa ☒ DZ 125 La27
El Matariyah ☒ ET 129 Mf30
El May ☒ TN 126 Lf29
El Medo ☒ ETH 145 Na43
El Meghaier ☒ DZ 126 Lc29
El Meki ☒ SUD 135 Mg38
El Mékí ☒ RN 132 Le37
El Melhes ☒ RIM 130 Kd36
El Melón ☒ RCH 208 Ge61
El Mellah ☒ DZ 125 Lb30
El Mereïe ☒ YV 193 Gj41
El Mesellemiya ☒ SUD 135 Mg38
El Mezquite ☒ MEX (SLP) 182 Ek34
El Mezquite ☒ MEX (ZCT) 182 Ej34
El Milagro ☒ RA (SL) 207 Gg61
Elmina ☒ GH 137 Kk43
El-Minia ☒ ET 129 Mf31
El Minshäh ☒ ET 129 Mf32
Elmira ☒ CDN (ON) 173 Fk24
Elmira ☒ USA (NY) 177 Gb24
El Mirador ▲ GCA 183 Ff37
El Mistolar ☒ RA (FO) 207 Gk58
El Moinane ☒ RIM 130 Ke34
Elmo ☒ USA (UT) 171 Ee26
El Molino ☒ MEX (CHH) 180 Eg31
El Molino ☒ E 27 Kr51
El Molino ☒ MEX (PJ) 182 Fa34
Elmore ☒ AUS (VIC) 111 Sc64
Elmore City ☒ USA (OK) 174 Fb28
El Morrión ☒ MEX (CHH) 181 Eh31
El Morro ☒ EC 196 Fk47
El Morro Nat. Mon. ⊞ USA 171 Ef28
El Morro = San Pedro de la Roca Castle ⊞ C 186 Gc35
El Mraïti ☒ RMM 131 Kj36
El Mreiti ☒ RIM 131 Kg34
El Munia ☒ ET 129 Mf31
El Muti'a ☒ ET 129 Mf33
El Mzereb ☒ RMM 131 Kg33
El Nakhl ☒ ET 129 Mg31
El Naranjo ▲ GCA 183 Fe38
El Naranjo ☒ MEX (SLP) 182 Fa34
El Nevado, P.N. ☒ YV 192 Ge42
El Nihuil ☒ RA 208 Gf63
El-Obeid ☒ SUD 135 Mf39
El Obraje ☒ MEX (ZCT) 182 Ek34
El Ocotito ☒ MEX 182 Fa37
El Ogla Gasses ☒ DZ 126 Lc28
El Ologo ☒ RCH 140 Lh45
El Olvido ☒ CO 192 Gc44
El Oro ☒ MEX (SLP) 182 Ek33
Elorza ☒ YV 193 Gf42
El Oso ☒ YV 193 Gh43
El Ostional ☒ NIC 184 Fh40
El Ouata ☒ DZ 125 Kk31
El Ouata ☒ DZ 124 Ke31
El Oued ☒ DZ 126 Lc29
El Palmar ☒ YV 193 Gk42
El Palmar ☒ YV 193 Gf43
El Palmar, P.N. ☒ RA 204 Ha61
El Palmito ☒ MEX (DGO) 181 Eh33
El Pangui ☒ EC 196 Ga47
El Papalote ☒ MEX (COH)
El Paraíso ☒ BOL 206 Gk53
El Paso ☒ USA (TX) 171 Eg29
El Paso de la Laguna ☒ MEX 182 Fb34
El Pato ☒ CO 192 Gc44
El Pedregal ☒ MEX (TB) 183 Fe37
El Pedregal ☒ E 28 Ks49
El Pensamiento ☒ BOL 206 Gk53
El Perú ▲ GCA 183 Fe37
El Pilar ☒ YV 193 Ga42
El Pilar ☒ YV 193 Gj40
El Porvenir ☒ BOL 206 Gk53

El Potosí, P.N. ☒ MEX 182 Fa35
El Progreso ▲ GCA 184 Fe38
El Progreso ☒ GCA 184 Fe38
El Progreso ☒ HN 184 Fg38
El Progreso ☒ MEX (BC) 180 Eg30
El Puente ☒ BOL 206 Gh56
El Puente ☒ MEX (MB) 172 Fc21
Puerto del Arzobispo ☒ E 27 Kp51
El Puertecito ☒ MEX (BC) 181 Ej32
Puerto de Santa María ☒ E 27 Ko54
El-Qahira ☒ ☒ ET 129 Mf30
El Qanatir el Khayriya ☒ ET 129 Mf30
El Qaser ☒ ET 129 Me33
Quebrachal ☒ RA (SA) 207 Gh58
El Quelite ☒ MEX (SL) 180 Eg33
Embalse de Alange ⊟ E 27 Ko52
El Questro ☒ AUS (WA) 103 Rd53
El Quisco ☒ RCH 208 Ge62
El Rancho ☒ MEX 182 Ek37
El Rastro ☒ YV 193 Gg42
El Real de la Jara ☒ E 27 Ko53
El Real de San Vicente ☒ E 27 Kp50
El Rebaje ☒ MEX (NL) 181 Fa33
El Re'ia ☒ ET 129 Mf30
El Reno ☒ USA (OK) 174 Fb28
El Retamo ☒ RA (SL) 208 Gg62
El Rey, P.N. ⊞ RA 207 Gh58
El Ridisiya Bahari ☒ ET 129 Mg33
El Rio ☒ MEX (DGO) 181 Eh33
El Roble ☒ E 27 Kp53
El Rodeo ☒ E 27 Kp50
El Rosario ☒ MEX (BC) 180 Ec30
El Rosario ☒ MEX (SL) 180 Eh34
Embalse de Gabriel y Galán ⊟ E 27 Ko51
El Rubio ☒ E 27 Kp53
El Sabinal, P.N. ☒ MEX 181 Fa32
El Safi ☒ ET 129 Mf31
El Salado ☒ RA 207 Gh58
El Salado ☒ RCH 207 Ge59
El Salado ☒ RA (SA) 210 Gg70
El Salto ☒ MEX (DGO) 181 Eh33
El Salto ☒ RCH 208 Ge60
El Salvador ■ ES 184 Fe39
El Salvador ☒ RCH 207 Gf59
El Salvador ☒ RCH 207 Gf59
El Sargento ☒ MEX (BCS) 180 Ee33
El Sauce ☒ NIC 184 Fh39
El Saucejo ☒ E 27 Ko53
El Sauz ☒ MEX (CHH) 180 Eg31
El Sauzalito ☒ RA (CD) 207 Gj58
El Seibo ☒ DOM 186 Gf36
El Semillero ☒ GCA 184 Fe38
Elsenborn ☒ B 23 Lg40
Elsey N.P. ☒ AUS 106 Rg52
El Soberbio ☒ RA (MI) 204 Hc59
El Socorro ☒ MEX 180 Ee32
El Socorro ☒ YV 193 Gh41
El Sombrero ☒ RA (CB) 210 Gd68
El Sombrero ☒ YV 193 Gg41
El Sosneada ☒ RA (MD) 208 Gf63
Elsterwerda ☒ D 32 Lo39
Elstow ☒ CDN (SK) 169 Eg20
El Subin ☒ GCA 184 Fe38
El Sueco ☒ MEX (CHH) 180 Eg31
El-Suwais = Suez ☒ ET 129 Mg31
El-Suwais ☒ ET 129 Mg31
El Tabo ☒ RCH 208 Ge62
El Taji ☒ MEX (SL) 181 Eg33
El Tama, P.N. ⊞ YV 192 Ge42
El Tambo ☒ CO 192 Gb44
El Tanque ☒ NIC 184 Fj39
El Tejar ☒ GCA 184 Fe38
El Tejel ☒ RA (SA) 207 Gj59
El Tenam Puente ⊞ MEX 183 Fd37
El Tepuche ☒ MEX (SL) 180 Eg33
El Thamad ☒ ET 129 Mg31
El Tichilili ☒ RIM 130 Kd37
El Tigre ☒ BOL 206 Gd51
El Tigre ☒ MEX (SO) 180 Ef31
El Tigre ☒ YV 193 Gh41
El Tigrito ☒ YV 193 Gh41
El Tintal ⊞ GCA 183 Fe37
El Tío ☒ RA (CD) 209 Gj61
El Tlacuache ☒ MEX
Eltmann ☒ D 33 Ll41
El Tocuyo ☒ YV 193 Gf41
El Tor ☒ ET 129 Mg31
El Toro ☒ MEX (CB) 210 Gg68
El Toro ☒ E 27 Kt51
El Transcantábrico ⊞ E 28 Kr47
El Trece ☒ RA (SA) 208 Gg67
El Trifinio ☒ ES/GCA/HN 184 Ff38
El Triunfo ☒ EC 196 Ga48
El Triunfo ☒ MEX (TB) 183 Fe37
El Troncal ☒ CO 192 Gd42
El Trune ☒ RA (NSW) 109 Sd61
El Tuparro, P.N. ☒ CO 193 Gf43
El Turbio ☒ RA (SC) 210 Gc71
Eltville ☒ D 33 Lj40
El 'Uteishan ☒ SUD 135 Mf37
El Vado ☒ E 28 Kr49
El Vapor ☒ CO 192 Gd42
El Vapor ☒ CO 192 Gd42
El Vado ☒ E 27 Kp52
El Valle ☒ CO 192 Gb43
El Valle ☒ PA 185 Fk41
El Valle ☒ YV 193 Gh41
El Vergel ☒ MEX (CHH) 180 Eg32
El Vigía ☒ YV 192 Gd41
El Villar de Arnedo ☒ E 28 Ks48
El Viejo ☒ NIC 184 Fh39
Elvira ☒ BR (AM) 196 Ge49
El Volcán ☒ RCH 208 Ge62
El Wak ☒ EAK 145 Nb44
El Wara ☒ SUD 135 Mg38
El Wâsitah ☒ ET 129 Mf31
Elwood ☒ USA (NE) 174 Fa25
Ely ☒ GB 21 La38
Ely ☒ USA (MN) 172 Fd22
Ely ☒ USA (NV) 170 Ec26
El Yaqui ☒ MEX (SO) 180 Ee32
El Yunque ☒ C 186 Gc35
Emam Abbas ☒ IR 57 Nc28
Emam Hasan ☒ IR 59 Nf31
Emam Saheb ☒ AFG 63 Oe27
Emam Taqi ☒ IR 62 Nc27
Emamzui ☒ RA 155 Kg59
El Progreso ☒ GCA 184 Fe38

Emam Abbas ☒ IR 57 Nc28
Emam Hasan ☒ IR 59 Nf31
Emam Saheb ☒ AFG 63 Oe27
Emam Taqi ☒ IR 62 Nc27
Emamzui ☒ RA 155 Kg59
Emamrud ☒ IR 62 Ng27
Emas, P.N. das ☒ BR 202 Hd53
Embarse Alicura ☒ RA 208 Ge66
Emmiganuru ☒ IND (APH) 82 Oj38
Embalse Amaluza ☒ EC 196 Ga47
Embalse Boconó Tucupido ⊟ YV 193 Gf41
Embalse Cabra Corral ⊟ RA 207 Gh58
Embalse Camatagua ⊟ YV 193 Gg41
Embalse Casa de Piedra ⊟ RA 208 Gf64
Embalse Cerros Colorados ⊟ RA 208 Gf63
Embalse Cogoti ⊟ RCH 208 Ge61
Embalse de Aguilar de Campóo ⊟ E 26 Kq48
Embalse de Alarcón ⊟ E 29 Ks51
Embalse de Alcántara ⊟ E 27 Ko51
Embalse de Almendra ⊟ E 26 Ko49
Embalse de Arbón ⊟ E 26 Ko47
Embalse de Belesar ⊟ E 26 Kn48
Embalse de Bembézar ⊟ E 27 Kp53
Embalse de Buendía ⊟ E 28 Kr50
Embalse de Cíjara ⊟ E 27 Kp51
Embalse de Contreras ⊟ E 29 Kt51
Embalse de El Cajon ⊟ HN 184 Fg38
Embalse de El Grado ⊟ E 28 Lá48
Embalse de Entrepeñas ⊟ E 28 Kr50
Embalse de Gabriel y Galán ⊟ E 27 Ko51
Embalse de García de Sola ⊟ E 27 Kp51
Embalse de Giribaile ⊟ E 27 Kr52
Embalse de Guadalcacín ⊟ E 27 Ko54
Embalse de Guadalhorce ⊟ E 27 Kp54
Embalse de Gurí ☒ YV 193 Gk42
Embalse de Jándula ⊟ E 27 Kr52
Embalse de la Serena ⊟ E 27 Kp52
Embalse de la Sotonera ⊟ E 28 Ku48
Embalse de las Portas ⊟ E 26 Kn48
Embalse del Cenajo ⊟ E 29 Kt52
Embalse del Chanza ⊟ E 27 Kn53
Embalse de Ricobayo ⊟ E 26 Kp49
Embalse de Riaño ⊟ E 26 Kp48
Embalse de Santa Teresa ⊟ E 27 Kp50
Embalse de Sierra Boyera ⊟ E 27 Kp52
Embalse de Sierra Brava ⊟ E 27 Kp51
Embalse de Urrunaga ⊟ E 28 Ks48
Embalse de Valdecañas ⊟ E 27 Kp51
Embalse de Valdemojón ⊟ E 27 Kp52
Embalse Ezequiel Ramos Mexia ⊟ RA 208 Gf63
Embalse Florentino Ameghino ⊟ RA 209 Ha65
Embalse Paso de las Piedras ⊟ RA 209 Gj64
Embalse Peñol ⊟ CO 192 Gd42
Embalse Piedra del Águila ⊟ RA 208 Ge66
Embalse Poechos ⊟ PE 196 Fk48
Embalse Río Hondo ⊟ RA 207 Gj59
Embalse Yacyretá Apipé ☒ PY/RA 204 Hb59
Embarcación ☒ RA (SA) 207 Gj57
Embarcadero ☒ MEX (CHP) 183 Fd38
Embarcadero ☒ MEX (OAX) 183 Fd38
Embi ☒ KZ 54 Nd09
Embira ☒ BR (AC) 198 Gf50
Embley ☒ AUS (QLD) 107 Sb52
Emborio ☒ GR 45 Mf54
Embrun ☒ F 25 La46
Embu ☒ EAK 144 Mj46
Embu ☒ BR (SP) 205 Hg57
Emden ☒ D 32 Lh37
Emerald ☒ AUS (QLD) 109 Se57
Emereau ☒ C 186 Gc35
Emerald Mound ⊞ USA 175 Fe29
Emerau Point ☒ PNG 116 Sf47
Emeralue Mound ☒ PNG 116 Sf47
Emerson ☒ CDN (MB) 172 Fa21
Emesa = Homs ☒ SYR 56 Mj28
Emet ☒ TR 56 Mf26
Emi Fezzane ☒ RN 132 Ld35
Emilia-Romagna ☒ I 34 Ll46
Emi Koussi ▲ TCH 134 Lk36
Emirau Island ☒ PNG 116 Sf47
Emirau Rainforest ☒ PNG 116 Sf47
Emir Dağları ▲ TR 56 Mf26
Emirdağ ☒ TR 56 Mf26
Emita ☒ AUS (TAS) 111 Sc65
Emken ☒ TR 57 Nb28
Emlichheim ☒ D 23 Lg38
Emmaboda ☒ S 31 Lq34
Emmaste ☒ EST 38 Mc32
Emmaste ☒ EST 38 Mc32
Emmeloord ☒ NL 23 Lf38
Emmelshausen ☒ D 33 Lh40
Emmen ☒ NL 23 Lg38
Emmendingen ☒ D 33 Lh42
Emmerich ☒ D 32 Lg39
Emmetsburg ☒ USA (IA) 172 Fc24
Emmet ☒ USA (ID) 168 Eb24
Emmonak ☒ USA (AK) 164 Bh14
Emory ☒ RN 132 Ld38
Empada ☒ GNB 136 Kc40
Empalme ☒ MEX (SO) 180 Ee32
Empangeni ☒ ZA 155 Mf60
Empedrado ☒ RA (CR) 204 Hb59
Empedrado ☒ RCH 208 Gd63
Emperor Range ▲ PNG 117 Sk48
Empesós ☒ GR 46 Mb52
Empire ☒ USA (OR) 168 Dh24
Empire ☒ USA (VA) 178 Fk26
Emporium ☒ USA (PA) 173 Ga25
Empress Augusta Bay ⊟ PNG 117 Sh49
Empress Mine ☒ ZW 152 Me55
Ems ☒ D 32 Lh38
Ems-Jade-Kanal ☒ D 32 Lh37
Emu Hill ☒ AUS (WA) 104 Qk62
Emu Junction ☒ AUS (SA) 105 Rf59
Emuranga ☒ RN 132 Ld38
Ena ☒ J 79 Rj28
Ena de Ros ☒ RUS 16 Mg11
Enänger ☒ S 17 Lj15
Enarca ☒ ET 143 Mj41
Enarotali ☒ RI 114 Rj47
Ena-san Tunnel ☒ J 79 Rj28
Enawene-Nawe, T.I. ☒ BR 206 Ha52
Enchi ☒ GH 137 Kk43
Encinal ☒ USA (TX) 181 Fa31
Encinitas ☒ USA (CA) 170 Eb29
Enciso ☒ E 28 Ks48
Encontrados ☒ YV 192 Gd41
Encrucijada ☒ BR (SC) 204 He59
Encruzilhada ☒ BR (BA) 203 Hk53
Encruzilhada do Sul ☒ BR (RS) 204 Hd61
Encs ☒ H 43 Mb42
Endako ☒ CDN (BC) 166 Dh18
Endalaghneti ☒ EAT 146 Mh48
Endau ☒ EAK 145 Mk46
Endau Rompin N.P. ☒ ☒ MAL 92 Qb44
Ende ☒ RI 96 Ra50
Endeavor ☒ CDN (SK) 169 Ej19
Endeavour Strait ☒ AUS 107 Sb51
Endelave ☒ DK 30 Ll35
Enderby ☒ CDN (BC) 168 Ea20
Enderby Land ☒ ANT 7 Na32
Endiang ☒ CDN (AB) 169 Ed20
Endibir ☒ ETH 142 Mk41
Endicott ☒ USA (NY) 177 Gb24
Endicott Mountains ▲ USA 165 Cd12
Endöki ☒ RCB 148 Lh46
End-o-Line RR Park & Mus. ☒ USA 172 Fc23
Endom ☒ CAM 139 Lg44
Eneabba ☒ AUS (WA) 104 Qh60
Enebakk ☒ N 30 Ll31
Enerhodar ☒ UA 49 Mh22
Eneryda ☒ S 31 Lp34
Enez ☒ TR 45 Mg50
Enfida ☒ TN 126 Lf28
Enfield ☒ CDN (NS) 176 Gj23
Engadin ☒ CH 34 Lk44
Engan ☒ N 16 Le14
Engaño, Cabo ☒ DOM 186 Gf36
Engaru ☒ J 77 Sc24
Engcobo ☒ ZA 155 Md61
Engel's ☒ RUS 48 Nd20
Engelberg ☒ CH 34 Lj44
Engelhartszell ☒ A 35 Lo42
Engen ☒ CDN (BC) 166 Dh18
Enger ☒ D 32 Lj38
Enggano ☒ RI 93 Qa47
Enghien ☒ B 23 Le40
Engineer Group ☒ PNG 116 Sf51
England ☒ USA (AR) 175 Fe28
England ☒ GB 21 Ks38
Englee ☒ CDN (NF) 177 Hb20
Englefield ☒ CDN (ON) 173 Ga22
Engle ☒ USA (NM) 171 Eg29
English Bay ☒ USA (AK) 164 Ce16
English Channel ☒ 22 Kr41
English Coast ☒ 6 Gb33
English Harbour East ☒ CDN (NF) 177 Hc22
English Harbour Town ☒ AG (NF) 177 Hc22
English River ☒ CDN (ON) 172 Fd20
Engonga ☒ ZA 155 Md61
Engozero ☒ RUS 16 Mg12
Engravings ⊞ RB 155 Md58
Engre Ríos = Malema ☒ MOC 153 Mj53
Engstingen ☒ D 33 Lk42
Enguera ☒ E 29 Kt51
Enguídanos ☒ E 29 Kt51
Enguri ☒ GE 57 Na24
Enid ☒ USA (OK) 174 Fb27
Enid ☒ USA (MS) 175 Fe28
Enilda ☒ CDN (AB) 167 Ec18
Enis ☒ TR 57 Nc28
Enitsa ☒ BG 45 Me48
Enjiang ☒ CHN (JGX) 74 Qh32
Enkeldoorn = Chivhu ☒ ZW 152 Mf55
Enkhuizen ☒ NL 23 Lf38
Enköping ☒ S 31 Lr31
Enna ☒ I 37 Lp53
Ennadai ☒ CDN (NT) 167 Fa15
Ennadai Lake ☒ CDN 167 Fa15
Ennedi ☒ TCH 134 Mb37
Enngonia ☒ AUS (NSW) 109 Sc60
Ennigerloh ☒ D 32 Lj39
Enniraana ☒ RMM 131 Kh35
Ennis ☒ IRL 19 Kn38
Ennis ☒ USA (TX) 174 Fb29
Ennis ☒ USA (MT) 169 Ee23
Enniscorthy ☒ IRL 19 Ko38
Enniskillen ☒ GB 19 Kn36
Ennistymon ☒ IRL 19 Kn38
Enns ☒ A 42 Lp42
Enns ☒ A 35 Lp43
Enontekiö ☒ FIN 16 Mc11
Enping ☒ CHN (GDG) 74 Qg34
Enrekang ☒ RI 96 Qk47
Enrile ☒ RP 90 Ra37
Enriquillo ☒ DOM 186 Ge37
Ensched ☒ NL 23 Lg38
Ensenada ☒ MEX (BC) 180 Eb30
Ensenada de Garachiné ☒ PA 185 Ga41
Ensenada de la Broa ☒ C 179 Fj34
Ensenada de Mompiche ☒ EC 196 Fk45
Ensenada de Tumaco ☒ CO 192 Ga45
Ensenada Los Muertos ☒ MEX (BCS) 180 Ee34
Ensenada Pabellones ☒ MEX 181 Eg33
Enshi ☒ CHN (HUB) 74 Qd30
Ensisheim ☒ F 33 Lh43
Entebbe ☒ EAU 144 Mg45
Entenbühl ▲ D 33 Ln41
Enterprise ☒ CDN 167 Ed15
Enterprise ☒ USA (AL) 175 Fh30
Enterprise ☒ USA (OR) 168 Ea22
Enterprise ☒ USA (UT) 171 Ed27
En Tmadé ☒ RIM 130 Ke36
Entrance ☒ CDN (AB) 168 Eb19
Entraygues-sur-Truyère ☒ F 25 Lc46
Entre-Ijjas ☒ RIM 204 Hc60
Entre Lagos ☒ RCH 208 Gd66
Entre-os-Rios ☒ P 26 Km49
Entre Ríos ☒ BOL 207 Gh56
Entre Ríos ☒ BR (BA) 201 Ja51
Entre Ríos ☒ BR (PA) 199 Ho48
Entre Ríos ☒ RA 204 Ha61
Entre Ríos de Minas ☒ BR (MG) 203 Hh56
Entrevaux ☒ F 25 La47
Entroncamento ☒ BR (MA) 200 Hg48
Entroncamento ☒ BR (MA) 200 Hh47
Entronque San Roberto ☒ MEX (NL) 181 Ek33
Entumeni ☒ ZA 155 Mf60
Entwistle ☒ CDN (AB) 169 Ec19
Enugu ☒ WAN 138 Ld42
Enugu Ezike ☒ WAN 138 Ld42
Enumclaw ☒ USA (WA) 168 Dj22
Envermeu ☒ F 23 Lä44
Envira ☒ BR (AC) 198 Gf50
Enviken ☒ S 17 Lh15
Enxudé ☒ GNB 136 Kc40
Enyamba ☒ RDC 149 Mc47
Enyellé ☒ RCB 140 Lk44
Enz ☒ D 33 Lj42
Eo ☒ E 26 Ko47
Epako ☒ NAM 150 Lj56
Epe ☒ NL 23 Lf38
Epe ☒ WAN 138 Lb42
Epéna ☒ RCB 140 Lj45
Epenarra ☒ AUS (NT) 106 Rh56
Épernay ☒ F 23 Ld41
Ephraim ☒ USA (UT) 171 Ee26
Ephrata ☒ USA (WA) 168 Ea22
Epi ☒ RDC 141 Md44
Epila ☒ VU 118 Te54
Epidavros ⊞ GR 47 Mj26
Épinal ☒ F 25 Lg42
Épineuil ☒ F 23 Ld43
Epi ☒ RDC 141 Md45
Epiphania ☒ SYR 56 Mj28
Episkopí ☒ GR 47 Me55
Epoleokoso ☒ RDC 148 Lj47
Epoma ☒ RCB 140 Lh45
Eppingen ☒ D 33 Lj41
Epping Forest ☒ AUS (QLD) 109 Sd57
Epsom ☒ GB 21 Ku39
Epu-pel ☒ RA (LP) 208 Gg64
Epukiro ☒ NAM 150 Lj56
Epupa Falls ☒ NAM 150 Lg54
Epuyén ☒ RA (CB) 208 Ge66
Equatorial Guinea ■ 123 La09
Equator Monument ⊞ RI 95 Qe45
Équeurdreville-Hainneville ☒ F 22 Kt41
Eraballi ☒ IND (KTK) 84 Oj38
Eraclea Minoa ⊞ I 37 Lo53
Erahtur ☒ RUS 48 Na18
Eralé ☒ BR (PA) 194 Hd45
Erandol ☒ IND (MHT) 82 Og35
Erandique ☒ HN 184 Fg38
Erantis ☒ PNG 116 Sd49
Eravikulam N.P. ☒ IND 84 Oj40
Eravur ☒ CL 85 Pa42
Erawan Cave ⊞ THA 88 Pk38
Erawan N.P. ☒ THA 88 Qa39
Erba ☒ I 34 Lk45
Erba ☒ TR 56 Mj25
Erbach ☒ D 33 Lk41
Erbach ☒ D 33 Lj42
Erba Lugang ☒ CHN (AHU) 73 Qj29
Erbil ☒ IRQ 57 Nb28
Erbrach ☒ D 33 Lm41
Erbeskopf ▲ D 33 Lh41
Erçek ☒ TR 57 Nb26
Ercikeş ☒ D 33 Lh41
Ercek Gölü ☒ TR 57 Nb26
Ercilla ☒ RCH 208 Gd65
Ercis ☒ TR 57 Nb26
Ercolano ⊞ I 37 Lp50
Erd ☒ H 43 Lt43
Erdaobaihe ☒ CHN (JLN) 76 Re24
Erdao Jiang ☒ CHN (JLN) 76 Rd24
Erdek ☒ TR 45 Mg50
Erdemli ☒ TR 56 Mh27
Erdenet ☒ MNG 70 Qg22
Erdenet ☒ MNG 66 Mh07
Erdenet ☒ TR 56 Mh27
Erdenetsogt ☒ MNG 70 Qd22
Erdene Zuu Monastery ⊞ MNG 70 Qf22
Erding ☒ D 33 Lm42
Erdre ☒ F 24 Kt43
Erdut ☒ HR 35 Lu45
Ereğli ☒ TCH 134 Lj41
Erebus, Mount ▲ 7 Tc34
Erebus ☒ IR 60 Nf29
Erechim ☒ BR (RS) 204 Hd59
Ered ☒ IR 59 Nf31
Ereğli ☒ TR 56 Mg25
Ereğli ☒ TR 56 Mh27
Eregli Ovası ☒ TR 56 Mg27
Eremitu ☒ RO 43 Me44
Eréndira ☒ MEX (BC) 180 Eb30
Erenhot ☒ CHN (NMZ) 73 Qg24
Ereñozar ▲ E 28 Ks47
Erepecuru ☒ BR (PA) 199 Hc47
Erere ☒ BR (CE) 201 Ja48
Erer Gota ☒ ETH 142 Nb41
Eressós ▲ GR 47 Mf52
Erfoud ☒ MA 125 Kh30
Erg Atouila ☒ RMM 131 Kg35
Ergani ☒ TR 57 Na26
Azennezar ☒ DZ 132 Lb33
Ergene ☒ TR 56 Me25
Erg Chech ▲ DZ 125 Kj32
Erg d'Amguid ☒ DZ 132 Lc33
Erg du Djourab ☒ TCH 133 Lk37
Erg el Ahmar ☒ DZ 126 Lc30
Erg er Raoui ☒ DZ 125 Kj31

Erg labes ◻ DZ 125 Kj32
Erg Iguidi ◻ DZ 125 Kg32
Erg i-n-Sâkâne ◻ RMM 131 Kk35
Erg in Techerène ◻ RMM 131 Kk35
Ergli ◻ LV 39 Mf34
Erg Issaouane ◻ DZ 132 Le32
Erg Kilian ◻ DZ 132 Le34
Erg Mehedjibat ◻ DZ 126 Lb33
Erg n'Ataram ◻ DZ 132 La34
Ergolsbach ◻ D 33 Ln42
Ergoldsbach ◻ D 33 Ln42
Erg Tassedjefit ◻ DZ 132 Lb33
Erg Thihodaine ◻ DZ 126 Ld33
Erg Tidjidit ◻ DZ 132 La34
Erg Tifernine ◻ DZ 126 Ld32
Ergun Youqi ◻ CHN/RUS 71 Ra20
Ergun Zuoqi ◻ CHN (NMZ) 71 Ra20
Er Hai ◻ CHN 87 Qa33
Erheib ◻ SUD 135 Mj36
Eric ◻ CDN (QC) 176 Gb20
Erice ◻ I 36 Lq32
Ericeira ◻ P 27 Kl52
Erickson ◻ CDN (MB) 172 Fa20
Eridu ◻ IRQ 59 Nd30
Erigat ◻ RMM 131 Kh36
Erikli ◻ TR 45 Mg50
Erikoussa ◻ GR 46 Lu51
Eriksdale ◻ CDN (MB) 172 Fa20
Erimitage Père de Foucauld ◻ DZ 132 Lc34
Erimo ◻ J 77 Sb24
Erimo-misaki ◻ J 77 Sb25
Erimo Seamount ◻ J 77 Sc25
Eringsboda ◻ S 31 Lq34
Erithree ◻ GR 45 Md52
Eritrea ◻ ER 123 Mb08
Erkelenz ◻ D 32 Lg40
Erkhet ◻ MNG 70 Qb31
Erkhet Uul ◻ MNG 70 Qa22
Erkilet ◻ TR 56 Mh26
Erkner ◻ D 32 Lo38
Erkowcy ◻ RUS 77 Re20
Erkovit ◻ SUD 135 Mj36
Erla ◻ E 28 Ku48
Erlangen ◻ D 33 Lm41
Erldunda ◻ AUS (NT) 108 Rg58
Erlistoun ◻ AUS (WA) 104 Rb60
Ermelo ◻ ZA 155 Mf59
Ermenek ◻ TR 56 Mf27
Ermesinde ◻ 26 Km49
Ermil Post ◻ SUD 134 Md39
Ermióni ◻ GR 45 Md53
Ermoúpoli ◻ GR 47 Me53
Ernakulam ◻ IND (KER) 84 Oj41
Erne ◻ IRL 22 Ka42
Ernesto Alves ◻ BR (RS) 204 Hc60
Ernest Sound ◻ USA 166 Dz18
Erode ◻ IND (TNU) 84 Oj40
Eromanga ◻ AUS (QLD) 108 Sb59
Eromanga Island ◻ VU 118 Te55
Erongari-cuaro ◻ MEX (MHC) 182 Ek36
Erongo ◻ NAM 150 Lh56
Erongo ◻ NAM 150 Lh57
Erongoberge ◻ NAM 150 Lh56
Eroro ◻ PNG 116 Se50
Erpengdianzi ◻ CHN (LNG) 76 Rc25
Erquy ◻ F 22 Ks42
Errabiddy ◻ AUS (WA) 104 Qj58
Erragondapalem ◻ IND (APH) 83 Ok37
Erraguntla ◻ IND (APH) 85 Ok38
Errego ◻ MOC 153 Mj54
Errigal ◻ IRL 19 Km35
Erris Head ◻ IRL 19 Kk36
Er Roged ◻ SUD 135 Mh38
Errol ◻ USA (NH) 177 Ge23
Er Roseires ◻ SUD 135 Mh40
Ersaf ◻ MA 125 Kj28
Ersekë ◻ AL 46 Ma50
Erskine ◻ USA (MN) 172 Fb22
Erstein ◻ F 23 Lh42
Ertix Ale ◻ ETH 142 Na39
Ertil' ◻ RUS 48 Na19
Ertis ◻ 54 Pa08
Ertuğrul ◻ TR 47 Mh51
Eruda ◻ WAN 138 Lc41
Eruwa ◻ WAN 138 Lb42
Ervália ◻ BR (MG) 203 Hj56
Ervay ◻ USA (WY) 169 Eg24
Ervenik ◻ HR 35 Lq46
Ervy-le-Chatel ◻ F 23 Ld42
Erwang ◻ RI 97 Re46
Erwin ◻ USA (TN) 178 Fj27
Erwitte ◻ D 32 Lj39
Erythrai ◻ GR 47 Md53
Erzgebirge ◻ D/CZ 33 Ln40
Erzin ◻ RUS (TUV) 67 Ph20
Erzincan ◻ TR 57 Na26
Erzurum ◻ TR 57 Na26
Esa'ala ◻ PNG 116 Sf50
Esan ◻ J 77 Sa25
Esashi ◻ J 77 Sa25
Esashi ◻ J 77 Sb23
Esbjerg ◻ DK 30 Lj35
Escada ◻ BR (PI) 201 Jc50
Escalada ◻ E 28 Kr48
Escalante ◻ RP 90 Rb40
Escalante ◻ USA (UT) 171 Ee27
Escalante Canyons ◻ USA 171 Ee27
Escalante Desert ◻ USA 171 Ed27
Escalaplano ◻ I 36 Lk51
Escalona ◻ E (CH) 206 Gf56
Escalona ◻ E 27 Kq50
Escalos de Cima ◻ P 27 Km50
Escanaba ◻ USA (MI) 173 Fg23
Escároz ◻ E 28 Ks47
Eschede ◻ D 32 Ll38
Esche-Alzette ◻ L 23 Lf41
Eschscholtz Bay ◻ USA 165 Bk12
Esch-s-Sûre ◻ L 23 Lf41
Eschwege ◻ D 32 Ll39
Eschweiler ◻ D 32 Lg40
Escocesa ◻ BOL 206 Gg54
Escondido ◻ MEX 183 Ff36
Escondido ◻ NIC 185 Fh39
Escondido ◻ USA (CA) 170 Eb29
Escondido, T.I. ◻ BR 199 Ha50
Escort ◻ ZA 155 Mf60
Escoumins ◻ CDN (QC) 176 Gf21
Escravos ◻ WAN 138 Lc43
Escudero ◻ ANT (RCH) 6 Ha30
Escuinapa ◻ MEX (SI) 180 Eh34
Escuintla ◻ GCA 184 Fe38
Escuintla ◻ MEX (CHP) 183 Fd38
Escuminac ◻ CDN (NB) 176 Gh22
Escus Th Bd 45 Mm47
Esdraelon ◻ 58 Mh29
Eséka ◻ CAM 138 Lf44
Eseli ◻ PNG 116 Se49
Esenada ◻ RCH 208 Gd66
Esens ◻ D 32 Lh37
Esentepe ◻ RI 51 Nf29
Esfand Abad ◻ IR 64 Ng30
Esfand Abad ◻ IR 62 Nj27
Esfarayen ◻ IR 64 Ng26
Esha ◻ CHN (YUN) 87 Qb33
Esha No 6 ◻ RB 151 Mb55

Eshiba ◻ RDC 149 Mc48
Eshkamesh ◻ AFG 63 Oe29
Eshkashem ◻ AFG 63 Of27
Eshowe ◻ ZA 155 Mf60
Eshq Abad ◻ IR 62 Nd27
Eshtahard ◻ IR 57 Nf28
Esiama ◻ GH 137 Kj43
Esigodin ◻ ZW 152 Me56
Esik ◻ KZ 66 Oj24
Esikuma ◻ GH 137 Kk43
Esino ◻ I 35 Lo47
Esira ◻ RM 157 Nd58
Esk ◻ AUS 18 J26
Esk ◻ AUS 109 Sg59
Eskdale ◻ AUS (VIC) 111 Sd64
Esker ◻ CDN (NF) 176 Gg19
Eskifjörður ◻ IS 18 Kg25
Eskifjörður ◻ IS 18 Kg25
Eskil ◻ TR 56 Mg28
Eskilstuna ◻ S 31 Lr31
Eskipazar ◻ TR (KS) 174 Fb26
Eskişehir ◻ TR 56 Mf26
Eslam Abad ◻ IR 57 Nd28
Eslam Qal'eh ◻ AFG 64 Oa28
Eslamshahr ◻ IR 57 Nf28
Eslohe ◻ D 32 Lj39
Eslöv ◻ S 30 Lo35
Eşme ◻ TR 47 Mj52
Esmeralda ◻ AUS (QLD) 107 Sb55
Esmeralda ◻ BR (RS) 204 He60
Esmeralda ◻ C 179 Ga55
Esmeralda ◻ YV 193 Gh44
Esmeraldas ◻ EC 196 Ga46
Es Mercadal ◻ E 29 La50
Espadon ◻ IR 64 Oa32
Espalion ◻ F 25 Lc46
Espalmador ◻ AUS 150 Lg54
Espanha ◻ E 28 Kr48
Espanola ◻ CDN (ON) 173 Fk22
Espanola ◻ USA (NM) 171 Eg28
Espargos ◻ CV 136 Jg37
Espartillar ◻ RA (BA) 209 Gj64
Espejo ◻ E (AN) 25 Lq56
Espelkamp ◻ D 32 Lj38
Espenberg ◻ USA (AK) 165 Bj12
Esperança ◻ BR (MS) 202 Hc56
Esperança ◻ BR (PA) 199 Hd46
Esperança ◻ BR (PB) 201 Jc49
Esperance ◻ AUS (WA) 105 Ra62
Esperance Bay ◻ AUS 105 Ra62
Esperance Highway ◻ AUS 104 Ra62
Esperantina ◻ BR (PI) 201 Hj47
Esperantinópolis ◻ BR (MA) 200 Hh48
Esperanza ◻ MEX (SO) 180 Ef32
Esperanza ◻ PE 197 Ge50
Esperanza ◻ RA (MI) 204 Hc59
Esperanza ◻ RA (SF) 209 Gk61
Esperanza ◻ RP 90 Rc40
Esperanza ◻ RP 91 Rc41
Esperanza ◻ ANT (RA) 6 Ha31
Espiel ◻ E 27 Kp52
Espigão do Oeste ◻ BR (RO) 199 Gk51
Espigão Mestre ◻ BR 200 Hh52
Espinal ◻ CO (VAC) 192 Gd44
Espinal ◻ E 28 Kr48
Espinama ◻ E 26 Kp47
Espinazo ◻ MEX (NL) 181 Ek32
Espinhaço ◻ BR 200 Hj52
Espinho ◻ P 26 Km50
Espinillo ◻ RA (FO) 204 Ha58
Espinosa ◻ BR (MG) 203 Hj53
Espinosa ◻ YV 193 Gh41
Espinosa de los Monteros ◻ E 26 Kr47
Espírito Santo ◻ BR 191 Hb51
Espírito Santo do Turvo ◻ BR (SP) 202 Hf57
Espiritu Santo ◻ VU 118 Td53
Estevan Group ◻ CDN 166 Df19
Espita ◻ MEX (YT) 183 Ff35
Es Pla ◻ E 29 Ld51
Esplanada ◻ BR (BA) 201 Jb51
Espoo = Esbo ◻ FIN 38 Me30
Esposende ◻ P 26 Km49
Espunaberg ◻ MOC 152 Mg56
Espungabera ◻ MOC 152 Mg56
Esquel ◻ RA (CB) 210 Ge67
Esquina ◻ RA (CR) 204 Ha60
Esquipulas ◻ GCA 184 Ff38
Esquina ◻ RA (CR) 204 Ha60
Essaouira ◻ MA 124 Kf29
Es Salihiya ◻ ET 129 Mg30
Essé ◻ CAM 139 Lf43
Essen ◻ B 23 Le39
Essen ◻ D 32 Lh39
Essendon, Mount ◻ AUS 104 Ra58
Essentuki ◻ RUS 57 Nb23
Essex ◻ GB? GUY 194 Ha43
Essex ◻ CDN (ON) 173 Fj24
Essexville ◻ USA (MI) 173 Fj24
Esslingen ◻ D 33 Lk42
Essouk ◻ RMM 132 La36
Essoyes ◻ F 23 Le42
Es Suki ◻ SUD 135 Mg39
Estação de Narbona ◻ ROU 204 Ha62
Estação Ecológica Caracaraí ◻ BR 193 Gh46
Estação Ecológica Cuniã ◻ BR 198 Gj50
Estação Ecológica da Serra das Araras ◻ BR 202 Hb53
Estação Ecológica de Niquiá ◻ BR 193 Gh45
Estação Ecológica do Jari ◻ BR 199 Hd46
Estação Ecológica Ilha de Taiamã ◻ BR 202 Hb53
Estação Ecológica Ilhas Maracá e Jipioca ◻ BR 199 He45
Estação Ecológica Iquè-Juruena ◻ BR 206 Ha52
Estação Ecológica Mamirauá ◻ BR 198 Gf47
Estação Ecológica Maracá ◻ BR 194 Ha44
Estação Ecológica Rio Acre ◻ BR 197 Ge51
Estaca Zero ◻ BR (PI) 201 Hj48
Estación Baquéira-Beret ◻ E 28 La48
Estación biológica Charles Darwin ◻ EC 197 Fe45
Estación Calles ◻ MEX (TH) 182 Fa34
Estación Camacho ◻ MEX (ZCT) 181 Ek34
Estación Cerler ◻ E 28 La48
Estación Coyotes ◻ MEX (DGO) 181 Eh34
Estación Dimas ◻ MEX (SL) 180 Eg34
Estación La Colorada ◻ MEX (ZCT) 182 Ej34
Estación la Molina ◻ E 28 La48
Estación Masella ◻ E 28 Lb48
Estación Micos ◻ MEX (SLP) 182 Fa34
Estación Ordino-Arcalis ◻ AND 28 Lb48
Estación Pintados ◻ RCH 206 Gf56

Estación Sierra Nevada ◻ E 27 Kr53
Estado de Guerrero, P.N. ◻ MEX 182 Fa37
Esteban ◻ IR 64 Nh31
Estaing ◻ F 25 Lc46
Estambul ◻ TR 56 Mf25
Estância ◻ BR (SE) 201 Jb51
Estancia Avanzada ◻ PY 204 Hb58
Estancia Caracol ◻ PY 207 Ha51
Estancia Carmen ◻ RA (TF) 210 Gf73
Estancia Cerrito Jara ◻ PY 206 Ha55
EstanciaCerro Guido ◻ RA 210 Gd71
Estancia Conchi ◻ RCH 207 Gf57
Estancia Curupayty ◻ PY 207 Ha57
Estancia Invierno ◻ RCH 210 Ge72
Estancia La Patria ◻ PY 207 Ha56
Estancia La Victoria ◻ PY 207 Ha56
Estancia Lomas ◻ PY 204 Ha58
Estancia los Lapachos ◻ PY 207 Ha57
Estancia L.Unión ◻ RA (SC) 210 Gf73
Estancia María Luisa ◻ RA (TF) 210 Gf73
Estancia Marina ◻ RA (TF) 210 Gf73
Estancia Noric ◻ PY 207 Ha56
Estancia Pan de Azucár ◻ PE 207 Gf58
Estancia Paragro ◻ PY 207 Ha56
Estancia Paredes ◻ PY 204 Ha58
Estancia Policarpo ◻ RA (TF) 210 Gh73
Estancia Rincón Grande ◻ RA (SC) 210 Ge71
Estancia Rocallosa ◻ RCH 210 Ge72
Estancia San Antonio ◻ PY 207 Ha57
Estancia San Carlos ◻ PY 202 Hc57
Estancia San Felipe ◻ PY 202 Hb57
Estancia San José ◻ PY 207 Hc57
Estancia San Juan ◻ PY 202 Hc57
Estancia San Pablo ◻ PY 210 Gg73
Estancia Santa Teresa ◻ PY 210 Gf73
Estancia Trementina ◻ PY 202 Hb57
Estancia Varillas ◻ PE 207 Gf58
Estanción ◻ BR (MA) 195 Hh46
Estanislao del Campo ◻ RA (FO) 207 Gk58
Estanque de León ◻ MEX (COH) 181 Ej32
Estapilla ◻ MEX (COL) 182 Ej36
Estaquinha ◻ MOC 153 Mh55
Estarreja ◻ P 26 Km50
Estcourt ◻ ZA 155 Me60
Este ◻ I 35 Lm46
Estela ◻ ANG 150 Lg54
Estepa ◻ E 27 Kq53
Este, P.N. del ◻ DOM 187 Gf36
Estevadinho, T.I. ◻ BR 206 Ha53
Estêvão do Campo ◻ BR (MA) 200 Hh49
Estlin ◻ CDN (SK) 169 Ef20
Eston ◻ CDN (SK) 169 Ef20
Estonia ◻ EST 38 Me32
Estoril ◻ P 27 Kl51
Estrecho de la Maire ◻ RA 210 Gh73
Estrecho de Yucatán ◻ 179 Fh35
Estrecho Nelson ◻ RCH 210 Gc71
Estrechos de la Florida ◻ 179 Fk34
Estreito ◻ BR (MA) 200 Hg49
Estrela da Paz, T.I. ◻ BR 198 Gf47
Estremadura ◻ P 27 Kl52
Estremoz ◻ P 27 Km52
Estuario de Virrita ◻ PE 196 Fk48
Esztergom ◻ H 43 Lt43
Etadunna ◻ AUS (SA) 108 Rk60
Étain ◻ F 23 Lf41
Etais ◻ F 23 Lc42
Etawah ◻ IND (PUT) 82 Oj32
Etawah ◻ IND (UPH) 83 Ok32
Etchojoa ◻ MEX (SO) 180 Ef32
Etemba Cave ◻ NAM 150 Lh56
Etembue ◻ GQ 138 Le45
Ethelbert ◻ CDN (MB) 172 Fa20
Ethel Creek ◻ AUS (WA) 104 Qk57
Etheldale ◻ AUS (QLD) 107 Sb55
Ethels wreck ◻ AUS 110 Rd63
Ethen Island ◻ CDN 167 Ee14
Ethiopia ◻ ETH 123 Mb09
Ethiopian Highlands ◻ ETH 142 Mj40
Etili ◻ TR 47 Mg51
Etjo ◻ NAM 150 Lj56
Etna ◻ I 30 Lf31
Etne ◻ N 30 Lf31
Etoile ◻ AUS (SA) 106 Bk16
Etolin Island ◻ USA 166 Dd17
Etolin Pt. ◻ USA 164 Ca15
Etorofu = Iturup ◻ RUS 77 Sc23
Etosha N.P. ◻ NAM 150 Lh55
Etoumbi ◻ RCB 140 Lh45
Etowah ◻ USA (TN) 175 Fh28
Étrépagny ◻ F 23 Lb41
Etretat ◻ F 22 La41
Etrœungt ◻ F 23 Ld40
Étroubles ◻ I 34 Lh46
Etsch = Adige ◻ I 34 Ll44
Ettelbruck ◻ L 23 Lf41
Etten-Leur ◻ NL 23 Le39
Et-Tieta-de-Oued-Laou ◻ MA 124 Kh27
Ettlingen ◻ D 33 Lj42
Et-Tnine ◻ MA 124 Kf30

Ettumanur ◻ IND (KER) 84 Oj41
Etumba ◻ RDC 149 Ma47
Etumba ◻ RDC 149 Mc48
Eturnagaram ◻ IND (APH) 83 Ok36
Eu ◻ F 23 Lb40
Euca ◻ BR (AP) 195 He44
Eucalyptus ◻ BOL 206 Ga54
Eucla ◻ AUS (WA) 105 Re61
Eucla Basin ◻ AUS 105 Rc62
Euclid ◻ USA (OH) 173 Fk25
Euclides da Cunha ◻ BR (BA) 201 Jb50
Euclides da Cunha Paulista ◻ BR (SP) 202 Hd57
Eudora ◻ USA (AR) 175 Fe29
Eudunda ◻ AUS (SA) 110 Rk63
Eufaula ◻ USA (AL) 175 Fh30
Eufaula ◻ USA (OK) 174 Fc28
Eufaula ◻ USA (TX) 175 Fh29
Eufrasio Loza ◻ RA (CD) 207 Gj60
Eufrasijeva bazilika ◻ HR 35 Lo45
Eugene ◻ USA (OR) 168 Dj23
Eugowra ◻ AUS (NSW) 111 Se62
Eulo ◻ AUS (QLD) 109 Sc60
Eulonia ◻ USA (GA) 178 Fk30
Eumara Springs ◻ AUS (QLD) 107 Sd55
Eumungerie ◻ AUS (NSW) 109 Se61
Eunápolis ◻ BR (BA) 203 Ja54
Eungella ◻ AUS (QLD) 109 Se56
Eungella N.P. ◻ AUS 109 Se56
Eunice ◻ USA (NM) 174 Ej29
Eunice ◻ USA (LA) 175 Fd30
Euphrates ◻ SYR 129 Md29
Eupora ◻ USA (MS) 175 Ff29
Eura ◻ FIN 38 Mc29
Eurady ◻ AUS (WA) 104 Qh59
Eurajoki ◻ FIN 38 Mb29
Eureka ◻ USA (CA) 168 Dh25
Eureka ◻ USA (KS) 174 Fa27
Eureka ◻ USA (MT) 168 Ec21
Eureka ◻ USA (NV) 170 Ec26
Eureka ◻ USA (SD) 172 Fa23
Eureka ◻ USA (UT) 171 Ed26
Eureka Springs ◻ USA (AR) 174 Fd27
Eurimbula N.P. ◻ AUS 109 Sf58
Euromba ◻ AUS (QLD) 109 Se58
Europa Park ◻ D 33 Lh42
Europe ◻ 14 La05
Europoort ◻ NL 23 Ld39
Europos parkas ◻ LT 39 Mf36
Eurora ◻ AUS (VIC) 111 Sc64
Euro Speedway ◻ D 32 Lo39
Euskirchen ◻ D 32 Lg40
Euston ◻ AUS (NSW) 111 Sb63
Eutaw ◻ USA (AL) 175 Fg29
Eutin ◻ D 32 Ll37
Eva Downs ◻ AUS (NT) 106 Rh55
Evakkokeskus ◻ FIN 40 Mh28
Evandale ◻ CDN (NB) 176 Gg23
Evangelistria ◻ GR 47 Md53
Evans Strait ◻ CDN 163 Fc06
Evanston ◻ USA (IL) 173 Fg24
Evanston ◻ USA (WY) 171 Ee24
Evansville ◻ USA (IN) 175 Fg27
Evare, T.I. ◻ BR 198 Gf47
Evart ◻ USA (MI) 173 Fh24
Evenkis-Bains ◻ F 25 Ld44
Evaz ◻ IR 64 Ng32
Evciler ◻ TR 47 Mg51
Évdilos ◻ GR 47 Mf53
Evenki Autonomous District ◻ RUS 54 Pc05
Everard ◻ USA (WY) 169 Eg24
Everard Junction ◻ AUS (WA) 105 Rc58
Everard Park ◻ AUS (SA) 105 Rg59
Everard Ranges ◻ AUS 105 Rg59
Everest, Mount ◻ NEP/CHN 81 Pd31
Everett ◻ USA (WA) 168 Dj22
Evergem ◻ B 23 Ld39
Everglades City ◻ USA (FL) 179 Fk33
Everglades National Park ◻ USA 179 Fk33
Evergreen ◻ USA (AL) 175 Fg30
Evergreen ◻ USA (MT) 168 Ec21
Eversberg ◻ S 17 Lg15
Evesham ◻ GB 21 Ks39
Évia ◻ GR 45 Md52
Évia ◻ GR 47 Me53
Évinayong ◻ GQ 138 Lf44
Evitäki ◻ FIN 38 Md27
Evje ◻ N 30 Lh32
Evksinograd ◻ BG 45 Mh47
Evo ◻ Oghli ◻ IR 57 Nc26
Evoikós Kólpos ◻ GR 45 Md52
Evolène ◻ CH 34 Lh44
Évora ◻ P 27 Km52
Évora Romana ◻ BR 200 Hj49
Évreux ◻ F 23 Lb41
Évron ◻ F 22 La42
Evros ◻ GR 45 Mg49
Ewan ◻ AUS (WA) 168 Eb22
Ewaso Ngiro ◻ EAK 144 Mh46
Ewaso Ngiro ◻ EAK 145 Mk45
Ewasse ◻ PNG 116 Sf48
Ewo ◻ RCB 148 Lh46
Ewuru Bugt ◻ DK 30 Lo35
Exaltación ◻ BOL 198 Gg51
Exaltación ◻ BOL 206 Gg51
Exe ◻ GB 21 Kr39
Exeter ◻ GB 21 Kr40
Exeter ◻ USA (NH) 177 Ge24
Ex-Fortín Cacique ◻ RA (SF) 204 Gk58
Exit-Home of the Dalai Lama ◻ IND 81 Og29
Exmoor N.P. ◻ GB 21 Kr39
Exmouth ◻ AUS (WA) 102 Qg56
Exmouth Gulf ◻ AUS 102 Qh57
Exmouth Plateau ◻ AUS 100 Qb11
Exsmouth ◻ GB 21 Kr39
Extremadura ◻ E 27 Kn52
Extxemadura ◻ E 27 Kn52
Extremo ◻ P 26 Km49
Exu ◻ BR (PE) 201 Ja49
Exuma Cays ◻ BS 179 Gb33
Exuma Cays Land and Sea Park ◻ BS 179 Gb33
Eyasi ◻ EAT 146 Mg47
Eyebrow ◻ CDN (SK) 169 Ef21
Eydhafushi ◻ MV 84 Og43
Eyemouth ◻ GB 19 Ks35
Eye of Kuruman ◻ ZA 154 Mb59
Eye Peninsula ◻ GB 18 Ko33
Eygurande ◻ F 25 Lc45
Eyl ◻ SP 143 Ne42
Eymet ◻ F 24 Lc46
Eymoutiers ◻ F 24 Lb45
Eysturoy ◻ DK 18 Kk28
Eyrarbakki ◻ IS 18 Jj27
Eyre Highway ◻ AUS 105 Rc62
Eyre Mountains ◻ NZ 113 Te68

Eyre Peninsula ◻ AUS 110 Rh62
Eysturoy ◻ DK 18 Kk28
Eyu-mojok ◻ CAM 138 Le43
Eyvan ◻ IR 57 Nd29
Eyvanakey ◻ IR 64 Ng28
Ezba Hasaballa ◻ ET 129 Mf33
Ezbet Ain ◻ ET 129 Mf33
Ezbet Dûsh ◻ ET 129 Mf33
Ezbet el Jâjah ◻ ET 129 Mf33
Ezcaray ◻ E 28 Ks48
Ezere ◻ LV 39 Mc34
Ezereki ◻ LV 39 Mk36
Ezhou ◻ CHN (HUB) 75 Qh30
Ezibeleni ◻ ZA 155 Md61
Ezine ◻ TR 47 Mg51
Ezo ◻ SUD 141 Md43
Ezt, la ◻ SYR 56 Mj29
Ezulwini Valley ◻ SD 155 Mf59
Ezzangbo ◻ WAN 138 Ld42
Ez-Ziliga ◻ MA 125 Kg29

F

Faaborg ◻ DK 30 Ll35
Faadippolhu Atoll = Lhaviyani Atoll ◻ MV 84 Og43
Fabens ◻ USA (TX) 171 Eg30
Fåberg ◻ N 17 Lf15
Fåbersebovstyen ◻ H 43 Ma44
Fåboda ◻ FIN 16 Mb14
Fa Bouré ◻ DY 138 Lb40
Fåbrica ◻ BR (AP) 195 He44
Fábricas de Riópar ◻ E 27 Ks52
Fabrichnyj ◻ KZ 66 Oj24
Facatativa ◻ CO 192 Gc43
Facho ◻ RM 133 Lf36
Facundo ◻ RA (CB) 210 Gf68
Fada ◻ TCH 134 Ma37
Fada-Ngourma ◻ BF 137 La41
Fada at Mislah ◻ KSA 60 Na34
Fadan Gora ◻ WAN 138 Ld41
Fada-Noun ◻ CDN 176 Gg18
Fadghami ◻ SYR 56 Mj29
Fadhi ◻ OM 61 Nh37
Fadiadougou ◻ CI 137 Kg41
Fadugu ◻ WAL 136 Ke41
Fa ◻ CDN 74 Qe35
Fafa ◻ I 34 Lm46
Fafadun ◻ SP 145 Na44
Fafakourou ◻ SN 136 Sn39
Fafe ◻ P 26 Km49
Fágáras ◻ RO 43 Me45
Fagerhult ◻ S 31 Lq34
Fagernes ◻ N 17 Le15
Fagersta ◻ S 31 Lq30
Fagge ◻ WAN 138 Lc41
Fagne ◻ B 23 Le40
Fagnkotti ◻ SUD 135 Mf37
Fagudu ◻ RI 97 Rd46
Fagwir ◻ SUD 141 Mf41
Fahahel ◻ KWT 59 Ne31
Faiaka Island ◻ KWT 59 Ne31
Faille de Nyakazu ◻ BU 146 Mf47
Fairbairn Reservoir ◻ AUS 109 Sd57
Fairbury ◻ USA (AK) 165 Cg13
Fairbury ◻ USA (NE) 174 Fb25
Fairfax ◻ USA (CA) 170 Dj26
Fairfield ◻ USA (AL) 175 Fg29
Fairfield ◻ USA (IA) 172 Fd25
Fairfield ◻ USA (ID) 168 Ec23
Fairfield ◻ USA (MT) 168 Ed22
Fairfield ◻ USA (NC) 178 Gb28
Fairfield ◻ USA (TX) 174 Fb30
Fairfield Sapphire Valley ◻ USA 178 Fj28
Fair Harbour ◻ CDN (BC) 168 Dg20
Fair Head ◻ GB 19 Ko35
Fairlie ◻ AUS (QLD) 109 Se57
Fairlie ◻ NZ 113 Tf68
Fairlight ◻ AUS (QLD) 107 Sc53
Fairlight ◻ CDN (SK) 172 Ec21
Fairmont ◻ USA (MN) 172 Fc24
Fairmont ◻ USA (WV) 173 Fk26
Fairmont Hot Springs ◻ CDN (BC) 168 Ec20
Fairo ◻ WAL 136 Ke42
Fair Oaks ◻ USA (AR) 175 Fe28
Fairplay ◻ USA (CO) 171 Eh26
Fairview ◻ USA (MI) 173 Fk24
Fairview ◻ CDN (AB) 167 Ea17
Fairview ◻ USA (MT) 169 Eh22
Fairview ◻ USA (OK) 174 Fa27
Fairview ◻ USA (UT) 171 Ee26
Fairweather, Mount ◻ CDN 166 Dc16
Fairy Harbour ◻ AUS 108 Rk60
Fairyhouse Racetrack ◻ IRL 19 Ko37
Faith ◻ USA (SD) 169 Ek23
Fasahabe ◻ PK 65 Og30
Faisalabad ◻ AFG 63 Of27
Faiyiba ◻ SUD 135 Mf38
Faizabad ◻ AFG 63 Of27
Faje ◻ WAN 138 Lc41
Fakakina Atoll ◻ F 11 Cb11
Fakenham ◻ GB 21 La38
Fakfak = Onin Peninsula ◻ RI 97 Rf47
Fakh Abad ◻ IR 64 Ng31
Fakhrabad ◻ IR 64 Ng31
Fakija ◻ BG 45 Mh48
Fakkeh ◻ IR 59 Nd29
Fakola ◻ RMM 137 Kg40
Faku ◻ CHN (LNG) 76 Rb24
Fakse Bugt ◻ DK 30 Lm35
Fala ◻ THA 87 Qa37
Falaba ◻ WAL 136 Ke41
Faladié ◻ RMM 136 Kf39
Falagountou ◻ BF 131 La38
Falaise ◻ F 22 Ku42
Falaise d'Amont ◻ F 22 La41
Falaise d'Angamma ◻ TCH 133 Lj37
Falaise d'Aval ◻ F 22 La41
Falaise de Banadiagara ◻ RMM 131 Kk38
Falaise de Banfora ◻ BF 137 Kh40
Falaise de l'Aguer-Tay ◻ TCH 133 Lj35
Falaise de Tambaoura ◻ RMM 136 Ke39
Falaise de Tiguidit ◻ RN 132 Ld37
Falaise du Gobnangou ◻ BF 138 La40
Falaise et grottes de l'Isandra ◻ RM 157 Nc58
Fäläné Deep ◻ GB? 131 Lr30
Fälénesthe n.p. ◻ S 31 Lr30
Fälene Islands ◻ GB 21 Kn39
Fälénham ◻ GB 21 Kt39
Falémé ◻ RMM 136 Ke39
Faléa ◻ RMM 131 Kj38
Faleá ◻ SN 130 Kd38
Faldwirthshaus ◻ A 34 Lo43
Falcarragh ◻ IRL 19 Km35
Falkenberg ◻ S 30 Ln34
Falkenberg ◻ D 32 Lo39
Falkenhain ◻ D 32 Lo39
Falkensee ◻ D 32 Ln38
Falkenstein ◻ D 33 Ln40
Falkland ◻ CDN (BC) 168 Ea20
Falkland Islands ◻ GB 191 Ha15
Falkland Plateau ◻ 190 Ha15
Falkland Sound ◻ GB 210 Ha71

Farquharson, Mount ◻ AUS 106 Rf54
Farranfore ◻ IRL 19 Kl38
Fällingbostel ◻ D 32 Lk38
Fallon ◻ USA (MT) 169 Eh22
Fallon ◻ USA (NV) 170 Ea26
Fall River ◻ USA (MA) 177 Ge25
Falls City ◻ USA (NE) 174 Fc25
Falo de Measach ◻ IRL ◻ GB 20 Kp33
Falmey ◻ RN 138 Lb39
Falmouth ◻ JA 186 Gb36
Falmouth ◻ USA (KY) 175 Fh26
Falmouth ◻ USA (MA) 177 Ge25
Falo ◻ RMM 137 Kg39
False Bay ◻ BC 168 Dh21
False Oxford Ness ◻ AUS 107 Sb51
False Pass ◻ USA (AK) 164 Bj18
Falset ◻ E 29 La49
Falso Cabo de Hornos ◻ RCH 210 Gf73
Falster ◻ DK 30 Ln36
Falsterbo ◻ S 30 Ln35
Falticeni ◻ RO 49 Md22
Falu gruva ◻ S 31 Lq30
Falun ◻ S 31 Lq30
Fasha ◻ IR 62 Nj27
Fashola ◻ WAN 138 Lc42
Fasht ◻ YE 60 Nb37
Fasil Ghebbi ◻ ETH 142 Mj39
Fask ◻ MA 124 Kd30
Fasku ◻ MA 124 Kd30
Fasskrúðsfjörður ◻ IS 18 Kf26
Fassala Néré ◻ RIM 131 Kh38
Fassanu ◻ LAR 127 Lg30
Fastiv ◻ UA 49 Me20
Fataki ◻ RDC 144 Mf44
Fatahabad ◻ IND (HYA) 80 Oh31
Fatehgarh ◻ IND (UPH) 81 Ok32
Fatehjang ◻ PK 65 Og29
Fatehpur ◻ IND (RJT) 80 Oh32
Fatehpur ◻ IND (UPH) 83 Pa33
Fatehpur Sikri ◻ IND (UPH) 81 Oj32
Fath Abad ◻ IR 64 Nh31
Fathom Five N.M.P. ◻ CDN 173 Fk23
Fatick ◻ SN 130 Kb38
Fatima ◻ RC 75 Ra34
Fátima ◻ P 27 Km51
Fatima Masume ◻ IR 57 Nf28
Fatmé ◻ RMM 137 Kh39
Fatoto ◻ WAG 136 Kd39
Fatsa ◻ TR 56 Mj25
Fattasha ◻ SUD 134 Md39
Fatumafuti ◻ IND (PUB) 80 Oh30
Fatumu ◻ RDC 146 Mf44
Fatunda ◻ RDC 148 Lj48
Fatural ◻ RI 130 Kc30
Fatutaka ◻ SOL 118 Tf51
Fatwa ◻ IND (BIH) 83 Pd33
Faulkton ◻ USA (SD) 172 Fa23
Faulquemont ◻ F 23 Lg41
Faurderfe ◻ S 31 Lq30
Fáureti ◻ RO 45 Mf45
Fauresmith ◻ ZA 155 Mc60
Fauske ◻ N 16 Lj12
Fauville-en-Caux ◻ F 22 La41
Faux Cap = Betanty ◻ RM 157 Nd58
Faraba ◻ RMM 131 Kj37
Faradady ◻ ANT (UK) 6 Gd32
Farafangana ◻ RM 157 Nd58
Farafenni ◻ WAG 136 Kc39
Farafra Oasis ◻ ET 129 Me32
Farägi Samariás ◻ GR 45 Md55
Farágoi Vouriakoú ◻ GR 46 Mc52
Farah ◻ AFG 64 Ob29
Farahalana ◻ RM 156 Nf53
Faraka ◻ IND (WBG) 83 Pd33
Faranah ◻ RG 136 Ke40
Farasan Centinela ◻ YV 193 Gg40
Faraba ◻ RMM 131 Kj37
Farahan ◻ RG 136 Ke40
Farasan ◻ KSA 60 Na37
Faratsiho ◻ RM 157 Nd55
Fárau ◻ RO 43 Me44
Faraulep ◻ FSM 116 Sa43
Fárbel F ◻ BR (CE) 201 Ja49
Fárceara ◻ RO 43 Md43
Faraga ◻ RO 44 Md43
Fareham ◻ GB 21 Kt40
Faresund ◻ N 30 Lg32
Farestad ◻ N 30 Lh33
Farewell Spit ◻ NZ 113 Tg66
Färgelanda ◻ S 30 Lm32
Fargo ◻ USA (GA) 178 Fk30
Fargo ◻ USA (ND) 172 Fb22
Farg'ona ◻ UZ 63 Of25
Farias Brito ◻ BR (CE) 201 Ja49
Faribault ◻ USA (MN) 172 Fd23
Faridabad ◻ IND (HYA) 80 Oj31
Faridkot ◻ IND (PJB) 80 Oh30
Faridpur ◻ BD 86 Pe34
Farié ◻ RI 114 Rg47
Farihy Alaotra ◻ RM 157 Ne54
Farihy Antanavo ◻ RM 156 Nf53
Farihy Ihotry ◻ RM 157 Nb57
Farihy Itasy ◻ RM 157 Nd55
Farihy Kinkony ◻ RM 157 Nc55
Farihy Tritriva ◻ RM 157 Nd56
Farilhões ◻ P 27 Kl51
Farim ◻ GNB 136 Kc39
Farinanga Iharoub ◻ IR 64 Ng31
Farindon ◻ GB 21 Kt39
Faringdon ◻ GB 21 Kt39
Farini ◻ I 34 Lk46
Fárjestaden ◻ S 31 Lr34
Farka ◻ RN 132 Lb38
Fárliug ◻ RO 44 Mb45
Farma ◻ ET 129 Mg30
Farmakas ◻ GR 46 Mc54
Farmamérica ◻ USA 172 Fd24
Farmerville ◻ USA (LA) 175 Fd29
Farmington ◻ USA (NM) 177 Ee27
Farmington ◻ USA (MO) 175 Fe27
Farmington ◻ USA (NM) 171 Ef27
Farmville ◻ USA (VA) 178 Ga27
Fárnes ◻ S 31 Lr30
Fárne Islands ◻ GB 19 Kt36
Farnham ◻ GB 21 Kt39
Faro ◻ BR (PA) 199 Hb47
Faro ◻ CDN (YT) 166 Dd14
Faro ◻ P 27 Km53
Feda ◻ N 30 Lg32
Federación ◻ RA (ER) 204 Hb60
Federal ◻ RA (ER) 204 Hb60
Fé do Morro ◻ BR (PI) 201 Hj50
Fertőszentmiklós ◻ H 42 Lr43
Fès ◻ MA 125 Kh28
Fé-Solidária ◻ BR (RR) 193 Gh45
Fessenden ◻ USA (ND) 172 Fa22
Fessessma ◻ CI 137 Kg42

Fehring ◻ A 35 Lr44
Feidh el botma ◻ DZ 126 Lb28
Feidong ◻ CHN (AHU) 78 Qj30
Feijó ◻ BR (AC) 196 Ge50
Feilding ◻ NZ 113 Th66
Feira de Santana ◻ BR (BA) 201 Ja52
Feiran Oasis ◻ ET 129 Mf32
Feitok ◻ CAM 138 Le43
Feixi ◻ CHN (AHU) 78 Qj30
Fei Xian ◻ CHN (SDG) 78 Qj28
Felanitx ◻ E 29 Ld51
Féase ◻ DZ 132 Le36
Feldbach ◻ A 35 Lr44
Feldberg ◻ D 33 Lj43
Feldberg ◻ D 32 Ln37
Feldkirch ◻ A 34 Lk43
Feldkirchen ◻ A 35 Lp44
Felegenway ◻ ETH 142 Mj42
Félicité ◻ SY 145 Nh48
Felidhoo Atoll ◻ MV 84 Og44
Felidhoo Channel ◻ MV 84 Og44
Felipe Carrillo Puerto ◻ MEX (QTR) 183 Ff36
Felipe Yofré ◻ RA (CR) 204 Ha60
Felixburg ◻ ZW 152 Mf55
Felixlândia ◻ BR (MG) 203 Hh55
Felixstowe ◻ GB 21 La39
Fellabær ◻ IS 18 Kf25
Fellbach ◻ D 33 Lk42
Fellheim ◻ F 23 Lg43
Fellingsbro ◻ S 31 Lq31
Felnac ◻ RO 43 Mb44
Felsberg ◻ D 32 Lk39
Felsőcsatár ◻ H 43 Lr43
Femer Bælt ◻ DK 30 Lm36
Femer Burnu ◻ TR 56 Mh27
Femund ◻ N 17 Lf14
Feng'an ◻ CHN (GDG) 75 Qg34
Fengcheng ◻ CHN (JGX) 75 Qh31
Fengcheng ◻ CHN (LNG) ...
Fengdu ◻ CHN 74 Qd31
Fengelo ◻ CI 137 Kg41
Fengguo Monastery ◻ CHN 76 Ra25
Fenghua ◻ CHN (ZJG) 75 Ra31
Fenghuang ◻ CHN (GDG) 75 Qd34
Fenghuang ◻ CHN (HUN) 74 Qd32
Fengkou ◻ CHN (HUB) 75 Qh30
Fengjieng ◻ CHN (GDG) 75 Qg34
Fengjian ◻ CHN (HBI) 73 Qg25
Fenglin ◻ RC 75 Ra34
Fengkou ◻ CHN (HUB) 75 Qh30
Fengxin ◻ CHN (JGX) 75 Qh31
Fengning ◻ CHN (SHG) 78 Ra30
Fenggang ◻ CHN 74 Qd31
Fengqiu ◻ CHN (YUN) 87 Pk33
Fengqing ◻ CHN (HEN) 73 Qg28
Fengrun ◻ CHN (HBI) 73 Qh25
Fengshan ◻ CHN (GZG) 74 Qd32
Fengsheng ◻ CHN 74 Qd31
Fengnan ◻ CHN 77 Rb19
Fengtai ◻ CHN (AHU) 78 Qh29
Fenging ◻ CHN (HUN) 74 Qe32
Fengxi ◻ CHN (JGX) 75 Qh31
Feng'xian ◻ CHN (JGS) 78 Qj28
Feng Xian ◻ CHN (SAA) 72 Qd29
Fengxiang ◻ CHN (SHG) 78 Ra30
Fengyang ◻ CHN (AHU) 78 Qj29
Fengxin ◻ CHN (JGX) 75 Qh31
Fengyi ◻ CHN (GZH) 74 Qd31
Feng-yüan ◻ RC 75 Ra33
Fenggun ◻ CHN (SAA) 72 Qg25
Fenoarivo ◻ RM 157 Nd56
Fenoarivo Atsinanana ◻ RM 157 Ne54
Fenoarivobe ◻ RM 157 Nd55
Fenwick ◻ CDN (ON) 173 Fk24
Feodosija ◻ UA 49 Mh23
Feres ◻ GR 45 Mg50
Fergana ◻ UZ 63 Of25
Ferganskaja dolina ◻ UZ 63 Og25
Fergus ◻ CDN (ON) 173 Fk24
Fergusson Island ◻ PNG 116 Sf50
Ferizaj ◻ SRB 44 Mb48
Ferkane ◻ DZ 126 Lc28
Ferkéssédougou ◻ CI 137 Kh41
Ferland ◻ CDN (SK) 169 Ej21
Ferland ◻ CDN (ON) 172 Ff20
Fermoselle ◻ E 26 Ko49
Fermoy ◻ IRL 19 Km38
Fernandina Beach ◻ USA (FL) 178 Fk30
Fernandópolis ◻ BR (SP) 202 He56
Fernão Dias ◻ BR (MG) 203 Hh55
Fernao Veloso ◻ MOC 153 Mk53
Ferndale ◻ USA (WA) 168 Dj21
Fernie ◻ CDN (BC) 168 Ec21
Fernhill ◻ INR (KER) 84 Oh40
Ferokh ◻ IND (KER) 84 Oh40
Ferozepore ◻ IND 80 Oh30
Ferrara ◻ I 34 Lm46
Ferreira do Alentejo ◻ P 27 Km52
Ferreira Gomes ◻ BR (AP) 195 He44
Ferrenafe ◻ PE 196 Ga49
Ferrette ◻ F 23 Lh43
Ferreira ◻ I 34 Le46
Ferro ◻ I 35 Lp47
Ferrol ◻ E 26 Km47
Ferros ◻ BR (MG) 203 Hj55
Ferryhill ◻ GB 20 Kt36
Fertile ◻ USA (MN) 172 Fb22
Fertility ◻ ES 186 Gc33
Fés ◻ MA 125 Kh28
Festenburg ◻ D 32 Ll40
Festesics ◻ H 42 Ls44
Festival Folclórico (Parintins) ◻ BR (AM) 199 Hb47
Fété Bowé ◻ SN 130 Kd38
Fetesti ◻ RO 45 Mh46
Fethard ◻ IRL 19 Kn38
Fethiye ◻ TR 56 Me27
Fetisovo ◻ KZ 62 Ng24
Fetlar ◻ GB 20 Ku30
Fetsund ◻ N 30 Lm31
Feuchtwangen ◻ D 33 Ll41
Feyzabad = Faizabad ◻ AFG 63 Of27
Feyz Abad ◻ IR 64 Nk28
Fezna ◻ MA 125 Kh30
Fezzan ◻ LAR 127 Lg33
Fiadanana ◻ RM 157 Nd56
Fiadanana II ◻ RM 157 Nd56
Fiambalá ◻ RA (CA) 207 Gg59
Fianarantsoa ◻ RM 157 Nd56
Fiananarantsoa ◻ RM 157 Nd56
Fianga ◻ TCH 140 Lh41
Fiaia ◻ RO 44 Mb45
Fiche ◻ ETH 142 Mk41
Fichtelgebirge ◻ D 33 Lm40
Ficksburg ◻ ZA 155 Md60
Ficuár ◻ P 196 Fk48
Fidenza ◻ I 34 Ll46
Fielding ◻ USA (UT) 171 Ed25
Fields ◻ USA (OR) 168 Ea24
Fier ◻ AL 46 Lu50
Fierenana ◻ RM 157 Nc55
Fiery Cross Reef ◻ 94 Qg41
Fierzë ◻ AL 44 Ma48
Fiesole ◻ I 34 Lm47
Fifa ◻ RG 136 Kf40
Fife Ness ◻ GB 20 Ks34
Fifield ◻ AUS (NSW) 111 Sd62
Fifinda ◻ CAM 138 Lf44
Figari ◻ F 36 Lk49
Figeac ◻ F 24 Lc46
Figeholm ◻ S 31 Lr33
Figalás ◻ GR 47 Me52
Figtree ◻ ZW 152 Me56
Figueira da Foz ◻ P 26 Km50
Figueira de Castelo Rodrigo ◻ P 26 Ko50
Figueiró ◻ BR (MS) 202 Hd56
Figueiras, T.I. ◻ BR 206 Ha53
Figueiró dos Vinhos ◻ P 27 Km51
Fiji ◻ 101 Tb11
Fiji Islands ◻ 100 Tb11
Fik ◻ ETH 142 Nb41
Fika ◻ WAN 139 Lg40
Filabres ◻ E 27 Ks53
Filadélfia ◻ BOL 198 Gf51
Filadélfia ◻ BR (BA) 201 Hk51
Filadélfia ◻ BR (TO) 200 Hg49
Filadelfia ◻ PY 207 Gk57
Fil'akovo ◻ SK 43 Lu42
Filchner ◻ ANT 6 Hb34
Filchner Ice Shelf ◻ 6 Hd35
Filer ◻ USA (ID) 168 Ec24
Filey ◻ GB 20 Ku36
Filiátes ◻ GR 46 Ma51
Filiatrá ◻ GR 46 Mb53
Filingué ◻ RN 132 Lb38
Filiouse ◻ RUS 48 Nb18
Filipiada ◻ GR 46 Mb52
Filipstad ◻ S 31 Lp31
Filiya ◻ WAN 139 Lg41
Fillmore ◻ CDN (SK) 169 Ej21
Fillmore ◻ USA (UT) 171 Ed26
Fillnekho ◻ LB 136 Kf43
Fillmore ◻ USA (NT) 108 Rh58
Filós ◻ GR 47 Mf53
Filtu ◻ ETH 145 Na43
Fimbulheimen ◻ 7 Lb33
Finale Emília ◻ I 34 Lm46
Finale Ligure ◻ I 34 Lj46
Finaly Ranges ◻ CDN 166 Dh17
Finca Chañaral Alta ◻ RCH 207 Gf59
Finchaa ◻ ETH 142 Mk41
Fincham ◻ AUS (QLD) 109 Se56
Finch Hatton ◻ AUS (QLD) 109 Se56
Findikli ◻ TR 45 Mg50
Findlay ◻ USA (OH) 173 Fj25
Findlay, Mt. ◻ CDN 166 De15
Fingoe ◻ MOC 152 Mf53
Fingas ◻ OM 61 Nk34
Finike ◻ TR 56 Mf27
Finisterre Range ◻ PNG 115 Sd49
Fink Creek ◻ USA (AK) 165 Bj13
Finke ◻ AUS (NT) 108 Rh58
Finke Gorge N.P. ◻ AUS 103 Rg58
Finke Pmer Ulperre Ingwemirne Arletherre A.L. ◻ AUS 108 Rh58
Finkolo ◻ RMM 137 Kg40
Finland ◻ 15 Ma03
Finlay Forks ◻ CDN (BC) 166 Dj17
Finnmarksvidda ◻ N 16 Mb11
Finnøy ◻ N 30 Lf31
Finnsnes ◻ N 16 Lk11
Finnveden ◻ S 31 Lo34
Fins ◻ OM 61 Nk34
Finsch Island ◻ PNG 115 Sd49
Finskiy zaliv ◻ RUS 38 Mg31
Finspang ◻ S 31 Lq32
Finsterwalde ◻ D 32 Lo39
Fintona ◻ GB 19 Kn36
Fintown ◻ IRL 19 Km36
Finyolé ◻ CAM 139 Lg41
Fiordland ◻ NZ 113 Td68
Fiordland N.P. ◻ NZ 113 Td68
Firat Nehri ◻ TR 57 Mk26
Fire Island Nat. Seashore ◻ USA 165 Ca15
Fire Island N.S. ◻ USA 165 Ce15
Firenze ◻ I 34 Lm47
Firat ◻ RN 131 Lg38
Firovo ◻ RUS 48 Mj17
Firminy ◻ F 25 Le45
Firovo ◻ RUS 48 Mj17
Firozabad ◻ IND (UPH) 81 Ok32
Firozpur ◻ IND (PJB) 80 Oh30
Firuzabad ◻ IR 64 Nh31
Firuzabad ◻ IR (HYA) ...
First Coffee Plantations ◻ B ...
First of Forth ◻ GB 20 Ks34
Fisht of Thames ◻ GB? ...
Firuz Abad ◻ IR 57 Nd29
Firuz Bey Camii ◻ TR 47 Mh53

297

Glória ☐ BR (BA) 201 Ja50
Glória ☐ RP 90 Ra39
Glória de Dourados ☐ BR (MS) 202 Hc57
Gloucester ☐ GB 45 Md51
Gloucester ☐ AUS (NSW) 111 Sf62
Gloucester ☐ CDN (ON) 177 Gc23
Gloucester ☐ GB 21 Ks39
Gloucester ☐ USA (MA) 177 Ge24
Gloucester Island ☐ AUS 107 Se56
Gloucester Point ☐ USA (VA) 177 Gb27
Glovers Reef ☐ BH 184 Fg37
Glovertown ☐ CDN (NF) 177 Hc21
Głowczyce ☐ PL 40 Ls36
Głowno ☐ PL 41 Lu39
Gloženski manastir ☐ BG 45 Me48
Głubczyce ☐ PL 40 Ls40
Głubokij ☐ RUS 48 Na31
Głuchołazy ☐ PL 40 Ls40
Głuchowo ☐ PL 40 Lf38
Glücksburg ☐ D 32 Lk37
Glückstadt ☐ D 32 Lk37
Gluhove ☐ RUS 48 Nb18
Glymur ☐ IS 18 Jt26
Gmünd ☐ A 35 Lo44
Gmünd ☐ A 42 Lp42
Gmunden ☐ A 34 Ln37
Gnadenkapelle Altötting ☐ D 33 Ln42
Gnaraloo ☐ AUS (WA) 104 Qg57
Gnarp ☐ S 17 Lj14
Gnarrenburg ☐ D 32 Lk38
Gniazdowo ☐ PL 41 Mb38
Gniben ☐ DK 30 Lm34
Gnibi ☐ DY 138 Lb41
Gniechowice ☐ PL 40 Lr40
Gniew ☐ PL 40 Lt37
Gniezno ☐ PL 40 Ls38
Gnjilane ☐ SCG 44 Mb48
Gnoien ☐ D 32 Ln37
Gnonsamoridou ☐ RG 136 Kf41
Gnosjö ☐ S 31 Lo33
Gnowangerup ☐ AUS (WA) 104 Qk62
Goa ☐ IND 82 Og38
Goageb ☐ NAM 154 Lj59
Goal Mtn. ☐ USA 169 Ed22
Goalpara ☐ IND (ASM) 86 Pf32
Goaltor ☐ IND (WBG) 83 Pd34
Goaso ☐ RMM 137 Kh39
Goari ☐ PNG 115 Sc49
Goaso ☐ GH 137 Kj42
Goat Fell ☐ GB 20 Kp35
Goat Horn Mosque (Chahar Borjak) ☐ AFG 64 Ob30
Goba ☐ ETH 142 Mk42
Goba ☐ MOC 155 Mg59
Gobabeb ☐ NAM 154 Lh57
Gobabis ☐ NAM 150 Lk57
Gobe ☐ PNG 116 Se50
Gobernador Ayala ☐ RA (LP) 208 Gg64
Gobernador Costa ☐ RA (CB) 210 Gd68
Gobernador Duval ☐ RA (LP) 208 Gg65
Gobernador Gregores ☐ RA (SC) 210 Ge70
Gobernador Grespo ☐ RA (SF) 207 Gk61
Gobernador Mayano ☐ RA (SC) 210 Gf69
Gobesh ☐ AL 46 Ma50
Gobi Desert ☐ 68 Ph24
Gobindgur ☐ IND (JKD) 83 Pd34
Gobindpur ☐ IND (ORS) 83 Pc34
Gobo ☐ J 79 Rh29
Gobo ☐ ZW 152 Mf55
Gobonoboseberge ☐ NAM 150 Lh56
Gobra Nawapara ☐ IND (CGH) 83 Pa35
Gobur ☐ SUD 144 Mf43
Göçbeyli ☐ TR 47 Mh51
Goce Delčev ☐ BG 45 Md49
Goce Delčev ☐ BG 45 Md49
Goch ☐ D 32 Lg39
Gochang Dolmen Site ☐ ROK 78 Rd28
Gochas ☐ NAM 154 Lk58
Go Cong Dong ☐ VN 89 Qd40
Göd ☐ H 43 Lu43
Godafoss kil IS 18 Kc25
Godar-e Alizak ☐ IR 62 Nj27
Godatatir ☐ SUD 141 Md41
Godavari ☐ IND 83 Pa34
Godawari ☐ NEP 81 Pa31
Godbout ☐ CDN (QC) 176 Gg21
Godby ☐ FIN 38 Lu30
Godda ☐ IND (JKD) 83 Pd33
Goddalir ☐ IS 18 Ka25
Goddo ☐ SME 194 Hc41
Göde ☐ BF 137 Kj39
Gode ☐ ETH 143 Nb42
Godeanu ☐ RO 44 Mc46
Godeč ☐ BG 44 Mc47
Godegode ☐ EAT 147 Mj49
Godeli ☐ ETH 143 Nb42
Goderich ☐ CDN (ON) 173 Fk24
Goderville ☐ F 22 La41
Godhavn = Qeqertarsuaq ☐ DK 163 Hb05
Godhra ☐ IND (GUJ) 82 Og34
Godinlabe ☐ SP 145 Nd43
Godofredo Viana ☐ BR (MA) 195 Hh46
Godong ☐ RI 95 Qf49
Godoy Cruz ☐ RA (MD) 208 Gf62
Gods Lake Narrows ☐ CDN (MB) 163 Fb08
Godthåb = Nuuk ☐ DK 163 Hb06
Godwin Austen, Mount ☐ PK 81 Oj28
Goe ☐ PNG 115 Sa50
Goegap Nature Reserve ☐ ☐ ZA 154 Lk60
Goëlettes ☐ SY 156 Nf51
Goes ☐ NL 23 Ld39
Goes ☐ ETH 142 Mk42
Gogango ☐ AUS (QLD) 109 Se57
Gogo ☐ AUS (WA) 103 Rc55
Gogo ☐ BF 137 Kk40
Gogol ☐ WAN 138 La41
Gogol ☐ RP 157 Nc58
Gogoi ☐ BR (GO) 202 Hg55
Gogolin ☐ PL 40 Ls40
Gogore ☐ DY 138 Lb41
Gogorūn, P.N. de ☐ MEX 182 Ek35
Gogrial ☐ SUD 141 Me41
Gogui ☐ RMM 130 Ke38
Goh ☐ IND (BIH) 83 Pc33
Gohad ☐ IND (MPH) 83 Oj32
Gohana ☐ IND (HYA) 80 Oj31
Gohitafla ☐ CI 137 Kg41
Göhren ☐ D 32 Lo36
Goiabeiras ☐ BR (PE) 201 Jc49
Goiandira ☐ BR (GO) 203 Hf55
Goianésia ☐ BR (GO) 202 Hf53
Goianésia do Pará ☐ BR (PA) 200 Hf47
Goiânia ☐ BR (GO) 202 He54
Goianira ☐ BR (GO) 202 He54
Goianorte ☐ BR (TO) 200 Hf50
Goiás ☐ BR (GO) 202 Hd53
Goiás ☐ BR 191 Ha51
Goiatins ☐ BR (TO) 200 Hg49
Goiatuba ☐ BR (GO) 202 Hf54

Goidhoo Atoll ☐ MV 84 Og43
Goilkera ☐ IND (JKD) 83 Pc34
Golo de Dourados ☐ BR (MS) 202 Hc57
Goio-En ☐ BR (RS) 204 Hd59
Goi-Pula ☐ RDC 146 Md49
Góis ☐ P 26 Kn50
Goito ☐ I 34 Ll45
Gojra ☐ PK 65 Og30
Gojeb ☐ PL 41 Lu38
Gojyo ☐ J 79 Rh28
Gokak ☐ IND (KTK) 82 Oh37
Gokavaram ☐ IND (APH) 83 Pa37
Gökçeada ☐ TR 45 Mf50
Gökçedağ ☐ TR 47 Mj51
Gökcek ☐ TR 57 Me26
Gökçekaya Baraji ☐ TR 56 Mf25
Gökçen ☐ TR 47 Mf53
Gök Medrese ☐ TR 56 Mj26
Gökova ☐ TR 47 Mi53
Gökova Körfezi ☐ TR 47 Mh54
Göksu ☐ TR 57 Nb26
Göksu Millî Park ☐ TR 56 Mg27
Göksun ☐ TR 56 Mj26
Göktepe ☐ TR 47 Mf53
Gokwe ☐ ZW 152 Me55
Gol ☐ N 17 Le15
Gola ☐ IND (JKD) 83 Pc34
Golaghat ☐ IND (ASM) 86 Ph32
Gola Hills ☐ WAL 136 Kd42
Golan al ☐ SYR 56 Mh29
Golapalle ☐ IND (CGH) 83 Pa37
Golashkerd ☐ IR 64 Nj31
Golbaf ☐ IR 64 Nj31
Golbahar ☐ AFG 63 Oe28
Golborne ☐ GB 21 Ks37
Golconda ☐ USA (NV) 170 Eb25
Golconda Fort ☐ IND 82 Ok37
Gölcük ☐ TR 56 Me25
Gölcük ☐ TR 56 Mh26
Gölcük ☐ TR 57 Mh51
Gölcük ☐ TR 57 Mk26
Gölcüv Jenikov ☐ CZ 42 Lq41
Gölcük ☐ USA (IN) 177 Gb25
Golela ☐ RCA 140 Lk41
Golotí ☐ RUS (Dag) 57 Nd27
Golovin ☐ USA (AK) 164 Bj13
Golovina ☐ RUS (YAO) 76 Rg21
Golovnino ☐ RUS 77 Sc24
Golpayegan ☐ IR 59 Nf29
Golra ☐ PL 41 Mb38
Golßen ☐ D 32 Lo39
Gol Tappeh ☐ IR 57 Nc27
Gol Tappeh ☐ IR 57 Nc28
Göltzschtalbrücke ☐ D 33 Ln40
Golubac ☐ SCG 44 Mb46
Golub-Dobrzyń ☐ PL 41 Lu37
Golumet' ☐ RUS 70 Qe17
Golungo Alto ☐ ANG 148 Lh50
Golymin-Ośrodek ☐ PL 41 Ma38
Goma ☐ RDC 146 Me47
Gomamuwang Caves ☐ MAL 94 Qj43
Gómara ☐ E 28 Ks49
Gombe ☐ G 148 Le45
Gombe ☐ WAN 139 Lf40
Gombela ☐ EAT 147 Mj49
Gombe-Matadi ☐ RDC 148 Lh48
Gombe Streams N.P. ☐ EAT 146 Me48
Gombo ☐ RG 136 Ke39
Gombe ☐ BF 137 Kj39
Gomboussougou ☐ BF 137 Kk40
Gomes Carneivo, T.I. ☐ BR 202 Hc54
Gómez Farías ☐ MEX (CHH) 180 Eg31
Gómez Farías ☐ MEX (COH) 181 Ek33
Gómez Palacio ☐ MEX (DGO) 181 Ej33
Gómez Rendón = Progreso ☐ EC 196 Ff47
Gommen ☐ D 32 Ln38
Gomon ☐ D 32 Lm38
Gomph ☐ PK 81 Oj28
Gomumu ☐ RI 97 Rd46
Gona ☐ CI 137 Kg41
Gonabad ☐ IR 64 Nk28
Gonaïves ☐ RH 186 Gd36
Gonarezhou N.P. ☐ ZW 152 Mf56
Gonâte ☐ CI 137 Kg42
Gonbad-e Ghaffarieh ☐ IR 57 Nd27
Gonbad-e-Qabus ☐ IR 62 Nh27
Gonçalves Dias ☐ BR (MA) 200 Hh48
Goncelin ☐ F 25 Lf45
Gonda ☐ IND (UPH) 83 Pc35
Gonda ☐ IND (UPH) 83 Pa32
Gonda-e-Gonâve ☐ RH 186 Gd36
Gonde ☐ ETH 142 Mk41
Gonden ☐ ETH 142 Mj39
Gondia ☐ IND (MHT) 83 Pa35
Gondola ☐ MOC 152 Mg55
Gondolahun ☐ LB 136 Ke41
Gondomar ☐ P 26 Km49
Gondomar ☐ P 26 Km49
Gondrecourt-le-Château ☐ F 23 Lf42
Gondwana ☐ ANT (D) 7 Tc33
Gönen ☐ TR 45 Mh50
Gönen ☐ TR 57 Mk27
Góngbyam ☐ CAM 139 La43
Gong'an ☐ CHN (HUB) 74 Qg30
Gongbogyamda ☐ CHN (TIB) 69 Pg31
Gongcheng ☐ CHN (GZG) 74 Qf32
Gonghe ☐ CHN (QHI) 72 Qa27
Gongar Monastery ☐ CHN 69 Pf31
Gongliu ☐ CHN (HBI) 73 Qh25
Gongliu ☐ CHN (XUZ) 66 Pb24
Gongo ☐ EAT 147 Mh49
Gongo ☐ CHN 140 Lk41
Gongola ☐ WAN 138 Lf40
Gongolgon ☐ AUS (NSW) 109 Sd61
Gongopquan ☐ CHN (GSU) 67 Pj25
Gongshan ☐ CHN (YUN) 87 Pk32
Gongwe ☐ RI 95 Qd49
Gong Xian ☐ CHN (HNN) 73 Qg28
Gong Xian ☐ CHN (SCH) 72 Qc30
Gongzhuling ☐ CHN (JLN) 76 Rc24
Goniądz ☐ PL 41 Mc37
Gonnesa ☐ I 36 Lj51
Gonohe ☐ J 79 Sa25
Gonzaga ☐ USA (NSW) 111 Sd62
Goobies ☐ CDN (NF) 177 Hc21
Goodenough Bay ☐ PNG 116 Sf50

Goodenough Island ☐ PNG 116 Sf50
Goodeve ☐ CDN (SK) 169 Ej20
Good Hope ☐ CDN (BC) 168 Dg20
Good Hope ☐ RB 155 Mc58
Goodhouse ☐ ZA 154 Lk60
Gooding ☐ USA (ID) 168 Ec24
Goodland ☐ USA (KS) 174 Ek26
Goodlands ☐ MS 157 Nj56
Goodnews Mining Camp ☐ USA (AK) 164 Bk16
Goodooga ☐ AUS (NSW) 109 Sd60
Goodwood ☐ AUS (NSW) 108 Sb61
Goodwood ☐ GB 21 Ku40
Goold Island ☐ AUS (QLD) 107 Se56
Goole ☐ GB 21 Ku37
Goolgowi ☐ AUS (NSW) 111 Sc63
Goolma ☐ AUS (NSW) 111 Nc41
Goomalling ☐ AUS (WA) 104 Qj61
Goomeri ☐ AUS (QLD) 109 Sg59
Goondiwindi ☐ AUS (NSW) 109 Sf60
Goondooblue ☐ AUS (NSW) 109 Se60
Goongarrie N.P. ☐ ☐ AUS 104 Ra61
Goongarrie ☐ AUS (WA) 104 Ra61
Goonyella Mine ☐ AUS (QLD) 107 Sd56
Goose ☐ NL 23 Lg38
Goose Bay ☐ CDN 163 Gd08
Goose Creek ☐ USA (SC) 178 Ga29
Gooty ☐ IND (APH) 84 Oj38
Gooty Fort ☐ IND 84 Oj38
Gop ☐ IND (ORS) 83 Pd36
Gopalganj ☐ IND (BIH) 83 Pc32
Gopalpur ☐ IND 86 Pe33
Gopalpur-on-Sea ☐ IND (ORS) 83 Pc36
Gopichettipalaiyam ☐ IND (TNU) 84 Oj40
Göppingen ☐ D 33 La42
Góra ☐ PL 40 Lr39
Góra ☐ PL 41 Mb38
Gora Ackasar ☐ ARM 57 Nb25
Gora Ak-Ojuk ☐ RUS 67 Pe20
Gora Aragac ☐ ARM 57 Nc25
Gora Arlang ☐ TM 64 Nh26
Gora Bazazbjuzi ☐ AZ/RUS 57 Nd25
Gora Bekmurat ☐ TM 64 Ng26
Gora Blednaja ☐ RUS/KZ 67 Pd21
Gora Čenova ☐ RUS 70 Qb19
Gora Čeravja ☐ RUS 77 Rh24
Gora Chokhrak ☐ TM 62 Nk26
Gora Čehova ☐ RUS 77 Sb22
Gora Dyhtau ☐ RUS 57 Nb24
Gora El'brus ☐ RUS 57 Nb24
Gora G'amys ☐ AZ 57 Nd25
Goragorskij ☐ RUS (CHE)
gora Han-Ula ☐ RUS 70 Qb18
gora Huhak ☐ RUS 70 Qe19
gora Kamuj ☐ RUS 77 Sa25
gora Karabil ☐ TM 63 Oc27
gora Karakus ☐ RUS/GE 57 Nc24
gora Kedrovaja ☐ RUS 76 Rf23
Gorakhpur ☐ IND (UPH) 83 Pb32
gora Ko ☐ RUS 77 Rj22
gora Konžakovskij Kamen' ☐ RUS 54 Nd07
gora Ledjanaja ☐ RUS 55 Tc06
gora Manas ☐ KS 63 Of24
Gora Munku-Sardyk ☐ MNG/ RUS 70 Pk19
gora Munku-Sasan ☐ RUS 70 Pk19
gora Narodnaja ☐ RUS 54 Oa05
Goráni ☐ GR 46 Mc54
gora Oblačnaja ☐ RUS 77 Rh24
gora Pajer ☐ RUS 54 Oa05
Gora Reza ☐ IR/TM 62 Nh27
gora Sabantuj ☐ RUS 70 Qc19
Gora Skalistyj ☐ RUS (CHE)
55 Qd07
gora Snežnaja ☐ KS 63 Oh25
gora Sohor ☐ RUS 70 Qc20
gora Stokan ☐ RUS 77 Sd23
Gora Tagarev ☐ TM/IR 62 Nj27
gora Taskyl-Sajlyg ☐ RUS 67 Pf22
Gora Tastau ☐ KZ 66 Pb22
gora Tel'posiz ☐ RUS 54 Nd06
Gorau ☐ IND (RJT) 80 Oh32
Goražde ☐ BIH 44 Lt47
Gorbea ☐ RCH 208 Gd65
Gorbica ☐ RUS 71 Qk19
Gorczański Park Narodowy ☐ PL 41 Ma41
Gorda Peak N.P. ☐ GB 187 Gh36
Gördes ☐ TR 47 Mj51
Gordion ☐ TR 56 Mg26
Gordo ☐ USA (AL) 165 Ck11
Gordon ☐ USA (NE) 172 Ej24
Gordon ☐ AUS (WA) 103 Rc55
Gordon, Mount ☐ AUS 104 Ra62
Gordon's Bay ☐ ZA 154 Lk63
Gordonvale ☐ AUS (QLD) 107 Sc54
Gore ☐ ETH 142 Mh41
Gore ☐ NZ 113 Te69
Gore ☐ TCH 140 Lq42
Gore Highway ☐ AUS 109 Sf59
Gorelki ☐ RUS 48 Mj18
Gorey ☐ GBJ 22 Kr43
Gorey ☐ IRL 19 Ko38
Gorgadji ☐ BF 131 Kk38
Gorgan ☐ IR 62 Nh27
Gorge d'Arak ☐ DZ 126 Lb33
Gorge Island ☐ AUS 123 Kb13
Gorgé ☐ RN 132 La38
Gorgnowa ☐ PL 40 Ls39
Gorgona ☐ I 34 Lk45
Gorgona, Isla de ☐ CO 192 Gb44
Gorgora ☐ ETH 142 Mj39
Gorham ☐ USA (ME) 177 Ge23
Gori ☐ PK 65 Of27
Gori ☐ GE 57 Nc25
Gorica ☐ AL 46 Ma51
Goricy ☐ RUS 48 Mj17
Gori Hills ☐ WAL 136 Kd41
Gorin ☐ ARM 57 Nd26
Gorisa ☐ SY 46 Mc53
Goritsa ☐ BG 45 Mh48
Gorizia ☐ I 35 Lo45
Gorizdowskij ☐ BG 45 Md48
Gorj ☐ RO 44 Md46
Gorja ☐ RUS 48 Na21
Gorji Hills ☐ WAL 136 Kd41
Gorki ☐ ARM 57 Nd26
Gorki ☐ BY 48 Mf18
Gorkij Reservoir ☐ RUS 48 Nb17
Gorlevo ☐ RUS 48 Mj17
Gorlice ☐ PL 41 Mb41
Görlitz ☐ D 32 Lp39

Goozuela ☐ DZ 126 La27
Gouraya ☐ DZ 126 La27
Gouraya, P.N. de ☐ DZ 126 Lc27
Gourdon ☐ F 24 Lb46
Gourdon ☐ F 24 Lb46
Gouré ☐ RN 132 Lf38
Gouri ☐ PK 65 Of27
Gourma ☐ RMM 131 Kk38
Gourma-Rharous ☐ RMM 131 Kk37
Gourmeur ☐ TCH 134 Ma37
Gournay-en-Bray ☐ F 23 Lb41
Gournia ☐ GR 47 Mf55
Gourrama ☐ MA 125 Kh29
Goush ☐ LAR 126 Lf29
Gouveia ☐ BR (MG) 203 Hj55
Gouveia ☐ P 26 Kn50
Gouvêlandia ☐ BR (GO) 202 He55
Gouverneur ☐ USA (NY) 177 Gc23
Gouzé ☐ RCA 140 Lj42
Gouzon ☐ F 25 Lc44
Gov'-Altay ☐ MNG 67 Ph22
Gov' Altayn Nuruu ☐ MNG 52 Pb05
Govedari ☐ HR 35 La48
Gove Peninsula ☐ AUS 106 Rj52
Gov' Altayn Nuruu ☐ MNG 52 Pb05
Govena ☐ RUS 48 Nb21
Gore ☐ ETH 142 Mh41
Gore ☐ NZ 113 Te69
Governor ☐ USA (CA)
Governor's Harbour ☐ BS 179 Fk33
Governor Generoso ☐ RP 91 Rd42
Governor's Harbour ☐ BS 179 Fk33
Govindapalle ☐ IND (ORS) 83 Pb36
Govorovo ☐ RUS 75 Pd47
Govorogoro ☐ RUS 57 Nd46
Gowa ☐ PNG 115 Sc49
Gorom-Gorom ☐ BF 131 Kk38
Gorondoma ☐ ZW 152 Me54
Gorongosa ☐ MOC 152 Mh55
Gorongoza, P.N. de ☐ MOC 153 Mh55
Gorontalo ☐ RI 93 Rb46
Goronyo ☐ WAN 132 Lc39
Górowo Iławeckie ☐ PL 41 Ma36
Gorowa ☐ NT 106 Rg53
Gorron ☐ F 22 Ku42
Goršečnoe ☐ RUS 48 Mj20
Gor Stokovych, P.N. ☐ RUS 54 Nb22
Gort ☐ IRL 19 Km37
Görtis ☐ GR 47 Mf55
Görükle ☐ TR 45 Mj50
Gorumna Island ☐ IRL 19 Kl37
Gorwmal Kalay ☐ AFG 65 Oe29
Gorum Park ☐ IRL 19 Kn38
Gowrie Park ☐ AUS (TAS) 111 Sd66
Goryčkin ☐ RUS 77 Rh24
Gorzów Wielkopolski ☐ PL 40 Lq38
Gorzyń ☐ PL 40 Lq38
Gosau ☐ A 34 Ln43
Goschen Strait ☐ PNG 116 Sf51
Góścikowo Jordanowo ☐ PL 40 Lq38
gora Aranha ☐ BR (MA) 200 Hh48
Gosforth ☐ GB 21 Kr36
Goshogawara ☐ J 77 Sa25
Goshute Ind. Res. ☐ USA 171 Ec26
Gospić ☐ HR 35 Lq46
Gospel ☐ HR 35 Lq46
Gossas ☐ SN 130 Kb38
Gossau ☐ CH 34 Lk43
Gossel ☐ RMM 131 Kf38
Gostivar ☐ MK 44 Ma49
Gostomia ☐ PL 40 Lr37
Gostotmia ☐ PL 40 Lr37
Gostynin ☐ PL 40 Lt38
Gósta kanal ☐ S 31 Lq33
Gotel Mountains ☐ WAN 139 Lf42
Gotha ☐ D 32 Ll40
Gothuburg = Göteborg ☐ S 30 Ln33
Gotland ☐ S 31 Lk32
Gotô-rettô ☐ J 79 Rd29
Gotse-Dełčev ☐ BG 45 Md49
Gotska Sandön ☐ S 31 Lr32
Gotska Sandön n.p. ☐ S 31 Lk32
Gott ☐ J 79 Sa28
Göttingen ☐ D 32 Lk39
Gottolengo ☐ I 34 Ll45
Gottwaldov = Zlín ☐ CZ 42 Ls41
Gotvand ☐ IR 62 Ne29
Gou ☐ PL 41 Mc40
Gouagoussou ☐ BF 137 Kj39
Goubangui ☐ CYN (LNG)
76 Ra25
Goubi ☐ TG 137 La41
Goubouna ☐ DY 138 La41
Gouchang ☐ CHN (GZH) 87 Qc33
Gouchi ☐ ETH 142 Mh41
Gouda ☐ NL 23 Le39
Gouda ☐ ZA 154 Lk62
Goudomp ☐ SN 136 Kb39
Goudoumaria ☐ RN 133 Lf39
Gouée ☐ ☐ ZA 155 Md62
Graiguenamanagh ☐ IRL 19 Ko38
Grain Coast ☐ LB 136 Ke43
Grainton ☐ USA (KS) 174 Ek26
Gralla ☐ CI 137 Kg42
Gramalote ☐ CO 192 Gd42
Gramada ☐ BG 44 Mc47
Gramados ☐ BR (MG) 202 He55
Gouldtown ☐ CDN (SK) 169 Gouli ☐ RCB 148 Lf47
Goumère ☐ CI 137 Kh41
Goumori ☐ GR 46 Ma51
Goumra ☐ TCH 140 Lk41
Goundam ☐ RMM 131 Kh37
Goundi ☐ TCH 140 Lj41
Goundiodou ☐ RN 133 Lf39
Gouékon ☐ RIM 130 Kf41
Gouéké ☐ RG 136 Kf41
Goúmenissa ☐ GR 46 Mc50
Goumbou ☐ RMM 131 Kh38
Goudou ☐ DY 138 La41
Goumori ☐ GR 46 Ma51

Granard ☐ IRL 19 Kn37
Gran Bajo del Gualicho ☐ RA 208 Gg66
Gran Bajo Oriental ☐ RA 210 Gd69
Granbury ☐ SME 194 Hc44
Granbury ☐ USA (TX) 174 Fb29
Granby ☐ USA (CO) 171 Eh25
Granby ☐ USA (CO) 171 Eh25
Gran Caldera Aguada ☐ ☐ GQ 138 La44
Gran Campo de Hielo Patagónico ☐ RA/RCH 210 Gd70
Gran Canaria ☐ E 124 Kc32
Gran Chaco ☐ RA/PY 207 Gj58
Grandas de Salime ☐ E 26 Ko47
Gran Desierto ☐ MEX 180 Ee30
Grand Bahama Island ☐ BS 179 Ga32
Grand Ballon ☐ F 25 La43
Grand Banks of Newfoundland ☐ CDN 177 Hc22
Grand-Bassam ☐ CI 137 Kj43
Grand Bend ☐ CDN (ON) 173 Fk24
Grand Bérard ☐ F 25 Lg46
Grand-Béréby ☐ CI 137 Kg43
Grand Bruit ☐ CDN (NF) 177 Hc21
Grandcamp-Maisy ☐ F 22 Kt41
Grand Canal ☐ IRL 19 Kn37
Grand Canyon ☐ USA (AZ) 171 Ed27
Grand Canyon ☐ ☐ USA 171 Ed28
Grand Canyon Caverns ☐ USA 171 Ed28
Grand Canyon du Verdon ☐ F 25 Lg47
Grand Cayman N.P. ☐ ☐ GB 179 Fk36
Grand Cayman ☐ GB 179 Fk36
Grand Centre ☐ CDN (AB) 169 Ee18
Grand Cess ☐ LB 136 Kf43
Grand Colombier ☐ F 25 Lg45
Grand Combin ☐ CH 34 Lh45
Grand Coulee ☐ USA (WA) 168 Ea22
Grand Erg de Bilma ☐ RN 133 Lg36
Grande ☐ RA (CR) 204 Ha60
Grande ☐ USA (TX) 181 Ed30
Grande ☐ USA (TX) 181 Ed30
Grandes Bergeonnes ☐ CDN (QC) 176 Gf21
Grande Sertão Veredas, P.N. ☐ BR 203 Hh53
Grande Terre ☐ F 187 Gk37
Grande Terre ☐ SY 156 Nd58
Grande-Vallée ☐ CDN (QC) 176 Gg21
Grand Etang N.P. ☐ WG 187 Gk39
Grand Falls ☐ CDN (NB) 176 Gg22
Grand Falls ☐ CDN (NF) 177 Hc21
Grandfalls ☐ USA (TX) 181 Ed30
Grand Forks ☐ CDN (BC) 169 Ea21
Grand Forks ☐ USA (ND) 172 Fb22
Grand Gorge ☐ USA (NY) 177 Gd24
Grand Haven ☐ USA (MI) 173 Fg24
Grand Island ☐ USA (NE) 174 Fa25
Grand Isle ☐ USA (LA) 175 Ff31
Grand Junction ☐ USA (CO) 171 Ef26
Grand-Lahou ☐ CI 137 Kh43
Grand Lake ☐ CDN (NB) 176 Gh22
Grand Lake ☐ CDN (NF) 177 Hb21
Grand Lake ☐ USA (CO) 171 Eh25
Grand Lake ☐ USA (MI) 173 Fh23
Grand Marais ☐ USA (MN) 172 Fe22
Grand Marais ☐ USA (MI) 173 Fh22
Grand-Mère ☐ CDN (QC) 176 Gd22
Grand Mesa ☐ USA 171 Eg26
Grândola ☐ P 27 Km52
Grand-Popo ☐ DY 138 La42
Grand Portage ☐ USA (MN) 172 Ff22
Grand Portage Ind. Res. ☐ USA 172 Ff22
Grand Portage Nat. Mon. ☐ USA 172 Ff22
Grand Rapids ☐ CDN 167 Ed17
Grand Rapids ☐ USA (MI) 173 Fg24
Grand Rapids ☐ USA (MN) 172 Fd22
Grand Récif de Cook ☐ F 118 Td55
Grand Récif de Koumac ☐ F 118 Tc56
Grand Récif Mathieu ☐ F 118 Tc56
Grand Récif Mengalia ☐ F 118 Td56
Grand Récif Sud ☐ F 118 Td57
Grand-Remous ☐ CDN (QC) 176 Gc22
Grand River Nat. Grassland ☐ USA 169 Ek23
Grand Rivière Noire ☐ MS 157 Nj56
Grand Ronde ☐ USA (OR) 168 Dj23
Grand-Santi-Papaïchton ☐ F 194 Hc43
Grand Staircase Escalante National Monument ☐ USA 171 Ee27
Grand Teton ☐ USA 169 Ee24
Grand Teton N.P. ☐ USA 169 Ee24
Grand Traverse Bay ☐ USA 173 Fh23
Grand Turk ☐ GB 186 Ge35
Grand Turk Island ☐ GB 186 Ge35
Grandview ☐ CDN (MB) 172 Fa20
Grand View ☐ USA (ID) 168 Eb24
Graneros ☐ RCH 208 Ge62
Grangeville ☐ USA (ID) 168 Eb23
Granite Peak ☐ USA 171 Ed25
Granite Mine, The ☐ AUS (NT) 103 Rf56
Granite ☐ CR (CE) 201 Hk47
Grânja ☐ BR (CE) 201 Hk47
Granja Caimá ☐ BR 202 Hb56
Gränna ☐ S 31 Lp32
Granö ☐ S 16 Lk13
Granollers ☐ E 29 Lc49
Gran Pajatén ☐ PE 196 Gb49
Gran Pajonal ☐ PE 197 Gc51
Gran Pampa Salada ☐ BOL 206 Gg56
Gran Paradiso ☐ I 34 Lh45
Gran Paradiso, P.N. del ☐ ☐ I 34 Lh45
Gran Pilastro = Hochfeiler ☐ A/I 34 Lm44
Gran Quivira ☐ USA (NM) 171 Eg28
Gran Sasso d'Italia ☐ I 36 Lo48
Gran Sasso e Monti della Laga, P.N. del ☐ ☐ I 35 Lo48
Gransee ☐ D 32 Lo37
Gransherad ☐ N 30 Lk31
Grant ☐ USA (NE) 174 Ek25
Grant City ☐ USA (MO) 174 Fc25
Grantham ☐ GB 21 Ku38
Grant Mercury Island ☐ NZ 112 Th64
Grant Mosque ☐ CHN 72 Qf25
Great Nicobar Island ☐ IND
Grantown-on-Spey ☐ GB 20 Kr33
Grant's Birthplace St. Mem. ☐ USA 175 Fh26
Grants Pass ☐ USA (OR) 168 Dj24
Granville ☐ AUS (QLD) 109 Sc59
Granville ☐ F 22 Ks42
Granville ☐ USA (NY) 177 Gd24
Grão Mogol ☐ BR (MG) 203 Hj54
Grão Pará ☐ BR (SC) 205 Hf59
Grasa, Cerro la ☐ RA 208 Ge65
Gräsgård ☐ S 31 Lr34
Graskop ☐ ZA 155 Mf58
Grasmere ☐ USA (ID) 168 Eb24
Grass Creek ☐ USA (WY) 169 Ef24
Grasse ☐ F 25 Lg47
Grass Patch ☐ AUS (WA) 105 Ra62
Grassrange ☐ USA (MT) 169 Ef22
Grass River Prov. Park ☐ CDN 169 Ek18
Grass Valley ☐ USA (CA) 170 Dk26
Grässy Butte ☐ USA (ND) 169 Ej22
Grass Sand Hills ☐ CDN 169 Ef20
Grassy Island N.H.S. ☐ CDN 176 Gk23
Grassy Island N.H.S. ☐ CDN 176 Gk23
Grästorp ☐ S 30 Ln33
Grates Cove ☐ CDN (NF) 177 Hc21
Gratwein ☐ A 35 Lq43
Grauhet ☐ F 24 Lb47
Graus ☐ E 28 La48
Gravatai ☐ BR (RS) 204 He60
Gráveumersello ☐ I 34 Lk44
Gravedona ☐ I 34 Lk44
Gravelbourg ☐ CDN (SK) 169 Eg21
Gravelines ☐ F 23 Lc40
Gravelotte ☐ ZA 152 Mf57
Gravenhurst ☐ CDN (ON) 173 Ga23
Gravesend ☐ GB 21 La39
Gravià ☐ GR 46 Mc52
Gravina ☐ F 194 Hd43
Gravina in Púglia ☐ I 37 Lr50
Gravina di ☐ USA (TX)
Grà̀vsko ☐ CDN 176 Gd18
Gravures rupestres (Aozou) ☐ TCH 133 Lj35
Gravures rupestres (Bambari) ☐ RCA 140 Mb43
Gravures rupestres de Dabous ☐ RN 132 Le37
Gravures rupestres de Gonoa ☐ TCH 133 Lj35
Gravures rupestres de Kongo Moumba ☐ G 148 Lf46
Gravures rupestres de Laghouat ☐ DZ 126 Lb29
Gravures rupestres (Lengo) ☐ RCA 140 Mb43
Gravures rupestres (Mapé) ☐ F 118 Td57
Gravures rupestres (Nzako) ☐ RCA 140 Mb43
Gravures rupestres (Oued Ouret) ☐ DZ 126 Lc33
Gravures rupestres (Pobe Mengao) ☐ BF 137 Kk38
Gravures rupestres (Taghit) ☐ DZ 125 Kj30
Gravures rupestres (Zouar) ☐ TCH 133 Lj35
Gray ☐ F 25 Lf43
Grayling ☐ USA (AK) 164 Bk14
Grayling ☐ USA (MI) 173 Fh23
Grayling Fork ☐ USA/CDN (AK/YT) 165 Ck12
Graz ☐ A 35 Lq43
Grdelica ☐ SCG 44 Mb48
Great Artesian Basin ☐ AUS
Great Astrolabe Reef ☐ FIJI 119 Tk55
Great Australian Bight ☐ AUS 100 Ra13
Great Ayton ☐ GB 21 Kt36
Great Bahama Bank ☐ BS 179 Ga33
Great Barrier Island ☐ NZ 112 Th64
Great Barrier Reef ☐ AUS 100 Sa11
Great Barrier Reef Marine Park ☐ ☐ AUS 107 Se52
Great Basalt Wall N.P. ☐ AUS (QLD) 107 Sc55
Great Bear Lake ☐ CDN 162 Ea05
Great Bend ☐ DK 30 Ll35
Great Bend ☐ USA (KS) 174 Fa26
Great Bitter Lake ☐ ET 129 Mg30
Great Britain ☐ GB 14 La04
Great Channel ☐ 88 Ph42
Great Coco Island ☐ MYA 88 Pg38
Great Dismal Swamp N.W.R. ☐ USA (VA) 178 Gb27
Great Dividing Range ☐ AUS 100 Sa11
Great Eastern Erg ☐ 122 La07
Great Eastern Highway ☐ AUS 104 Qj61
Great Exuma Island ☐ BS 179 Gb34
Great Falls ☐ USA (MT) 169 Ee22
Great Falls ☐ USA (SC) 178 Fk28
Great Fish River Reserves ☐ ZA 155 Md62
Great Guana Cay ☐ BS 179 Gb32
Great Harbour Cay ☐ BS 179 Ga33
Great Himalaya N.P. ☐ IND 81 Oj29
Great Inagua Island ☐ BS 186 Gd35
Great Isaac ☐ BS 179 Ga32
Great Karoo ☐ ZA 154 Ma62
Great Keppel Island ☐ AUS 109 Sf57
Great Limpopo Transfrontier Park ☐ ☐ ZW/ZA/MOC 152 Mf57
Great Malvern ☐ GB 21 Ks38
Great Mercury Island ☐ NZ 112 Th64
Great Mosque ☐ CHN 72 Qf25
Great Nicobar Island ☐ IND
Great North East Channel ☐ AUS 107 Sb51
Great Northern Highway ☐ AUS 102 Qk57
Great Northern Highway ☐ AUS 104 Qk57
Great Ocean Road ☐ AUS 111 Sb65
Great Ormes Head ☐ GB 21 Kr37
Great Oyster Bay ☐ AUS (TAS) 111 Sd67
Great Palm Island ☐ AUS 107 Sd55
Great Papuan Plateau ☐ PNG 115 Sb49
Great Pedro Bluff ☐ JA 186 Gb37
Great Plain of the Koukdjuak ☐ CDN 163 Gb05
Great Plains ☐ CDN/USA 160 Ea04
Great Rift Valley ☐ 122 Ma08
Great Rift Valley ☐ 122 Mb10
Great Ruaha ☐ EAT 147 Mh49
Great Sale Cay ☐ BS 179 Ga32
Great Salt Lake ☐ USA 171 Ed25
Great Salt Lake Desert ☐ USA 171 Ed25
Great Sand Dunes N.P. ☐ USA 171 Eh27
Great Sandy Desert ☐ AUS 100 Ra12
Great Sandy Desert ☐ USA 168 Ea24
Great Sandy N.P. ☐ AUS 109 Sg58
Great Sea Reef ☐ FIJI 119 Tk54
Great Slave Lake ☐ CDN 162 Ea06
Great Smoky Mts. ☐ USA 178 Fh27
Great Smoky Mts. Railroad ☐ USA 178 Fi28
Great Tiras ☐ NAM 154 Lj59
Great Valley ☐ USA 177 Gb25
Great Victoria Desert ☐ AUS 100 Ra13
Great Victoria Desert Nature Reserve ☐ AUS 105 Re60
Great Wall ☐ ANT 6 Ha30
Great Western Erg ☐ DZ 125 Kk30
Great Western Tiers ☐ AUS (TAS) 111 Sd66
Great Western Torres Island ☐ MYA 88 Pf42
Great White Heron N.W.R. ☐ USA 179 Fk33
Great Yarmouth ☐ GB 21 Lb38
Great Zimbabwe National Monument ☐ ☐ ZW 152 Mf56
Grebbestad ☐ S 30 Lm32
Grebenhain ☐ D 32 Lk40
Grebocin ☐ PL 40 Lt37
Grébou ☐ RN 132 Le35
Greece ☐ RO 204 Hb02
Greeley ☐ USA (CO) 171 Eh25
Greeley ☐ USA (NE) 174 Fa25
Green Bay ☐ USA (WI) 173 Fg23
Green Bay ☐ USA 173 Fg23
Green Bay ☐ USA 173 Fg23
Greenbush ☐ USA (MN) 172 Fb21
Green Cape ☐ AUS 111 Sf64
Green Cape Lighthouse ☐ AUS 111 Sf64
Green Cove Springs ☐ USA (FL) 178 Fk31
Greeneville ☐ USA (NY) 177 Gc24
Greeneville ☐ USA (TN) 178 Fj27
Greenfield ☐ USA (CA) 170 Dk27
Greenfield ☐ USA (IA) 174 Fc25
Greenfield ☐ USA (IN) 177 Gb26
Greenfield ☐ USA (MA) 177 Gd24
Greenfield ☐ USA (OH) 177 Fj26
Greenfield ☐ USA (TN) 175 Ff27
Greenhill Island ☐ AUS 106 Rg51
Green Island ☐ USA 107 Sd54
Green Island = Lutao ☐ RC 90 Ra34
Green Island Bay ☐ RP 90 Qk40
Green Lake ☐ USA (SK) 169 Sh48
Green Lake ☐ USA (SK) 169 Eg18
Greenland ☐ DK 163 Hd03
Greenland Sea ☐ 14 Kb02
Greenly Island ☐ AUS 110 Rh63
Green Mts. ☐ USA 177 Gd24
Greenock ☐ GB 21 Kr35
Greenodd ☐ GB 21 Kr36
Greenough ☐ AUS 104 Qh60
Green Point ☐ ZA 155 Mf61
Green River ☐ PNG 115 Sb47
Green River ☐ USA (UT) 171 Ee26
Green River ☐ USA (WY) 171 Ef25
Green River ☐ USA (WY) 171 Ef25
Green River Basin ☐ USA 169 Ef24
Greensboro ☐ USA (AL) 175 Fg29
Greensboro ☐ USA (NC) 178 Ga27
Greensburg ☐ USA (IN) 175 Fh26
Greensburg ☐ USA (KS) 174 Fa27
Greensburg ☐ USA (KY) 175 Fh27
Greensburg ☐ USA (PA) 173 Ga25
Great Turtle Cay ☐ BS 179 Gb32
Greenvale ☐ AUS (QLD) 107 Sc55

Greenview ◻ USA (CA) 168 Dj25
Greenville ◻ CDN (BC) 166 Df18
Greenville ◻ LB 136 Kf43
Greenville ◻ USA (AL) 175 Fg30
Greenville ◻ USA (GA) 175 Fh29
Greenville ◻ USA (KY) 175 Fg27
Greenville ◻ USA (MI) 173 Fh24
Greenville ◻ USA (MO) 175 Fe27
Greenville ◻ USA (MS) 175 Fe29
Greenville ◻ USA (NC) 178 Gb28
Greenville ◻ USA (PA) 173 Fk25
Greenville ◻ USA (TX) 174 Fb29
Greenwater ◻ USA (WA) 168 Dk22
Greenwater Lake Prov. Park ◻ CDN 169 Ej19
Greenwich ◻ GB 21 La39
Greenwood ◻ AUS (WA) 104 Qj59
Greenwood ◻ CDN (BC) 168 Ea21
Greenwood ◻ USA (AR) 174 Fc28
Greenwood ◻ USA (IN) 175 Fg26
Greenwood ◻ USA (MS) 175 Fe29
Greenwood ◻ USA (SC) 178 Fj28
Greer ◻ USA (ID) 168 Eb22
Greer ◻ USA (SC) 178 Fj28
Greetsiel ◻ D 32 Lh37
Gregbeu ◻ CI 137 Kg42
Gregory ◻ USA (SD) 172 Fa24
Gregory Downs ◻ AUS (QLD) 106 Rh53
Gregory N.P. ◻ AUS 106 Rf53
Gregory N.P. ◻ AUS 106 Rf54
Gregory Range ◻ AUS (QLD) 107 Sb55
Gregory Range ◻ AUS 102 Ra56
Gregory Springs ◻ AUS (QLD) 107 Sc55
Greifenburg ◻ A 35 Lo44
Greifswald ◻ D 32 Lo36
Greifswalder Bodden ◻ D 32 Lo36
Grein ◻ A 42 Lp42
Grein ◻ D 33 Ln40
Gremjačinsk ◻ RUS 54 Md05
Gremjač'e ◻ RUS 48 Mk20
Grenaa ◻ DK 30 Ll34
Grenada ◻ CO 192 Ge42
Grenada ◻ USA (MS) 175 Fe29
Grenada ◻ WG 187 Gk40
Grenada ■ 187 Gk39
Grenade ◻ F 24 Lb47
Grenade-sur-l'Adour ◻ F 24 Ku47
Grenadines ◻ WV 187 Gk39
Grenchen ◻ CH 34 Lh43
Grenen ◻ DK 30 Ll33
Grenfell ◻ AUS (NSW) 111 Se62
Grenfell ◻ CDN (SK) 169 Ej20
Grenfell House ◻ CDN 177 Hc20
Grenivík ◻ IS 18 Kb25
Grenoble ◻ F 25 Lf45
Grenville ◻ WG 187 Gk39
Gresford ◻ AUS (NSW) 111 Sf62
Gresham ◻ USA (OR) 168 Dj23
Gresham ◻ USA (SC) 178 Ga29
Gresham ◻ ZW 152 Me56
Gresik ◻ RI 95 Qg49
Gressamoen n.p. ◻ N 16 Lg13
Gressoney-la-Trinité ◻ I 34 Lh45
Gretna Green ◻ GB 20 Kr36
Greve in Chianti ◻ I 34 Lm47
Greven ◻ D 32 Lh38
Grevená ◻ GR 46 Mb50
Grevenbroich ◻ D 32 Lg40
Grevenmacher ◻ L 23 Lg41
Grevesmühlen ◻ D 32 Ll37
Greve Strand ◻ DK 30 Ll35
Grevie ◻ S 30 Ln34
Greybull ◻ USA (WY) 169 Ef23
Grey Cairns ◻ GB 20 Kr32
Grey Hunter Peak ◻ CDN 165 Dc14
Greylingstad ◻ ZA 155 Me60
Grey Mare's Tail ◻ GB 20 Kr35
Greymouth ◻ NZ 113 Tf67
Grey Range ◻ AUS 108 Sb60
Grey River ◻ CDN (NF) 177 Hb22
Greystone ◻ ZW 152 Me56
Greystones ◻ IRL 19 Ko37
Greyton ◻ ZA 154 Lk63
Greytown ◻ ZA 155 Mf60
Grgurnica ◻ MK 44 Mb49
Grianan of Aileach ◻ IRL 19 Kn35
Gribanovskij ◻ RUS 48 Na20
Gribbell Island ◻ CDN 166 Df19
Gridley ◻ USA (CA) 170 Dk26
Griekwastad ◻ ZA 154 Mb60
Grieskirchen ◻ A 42 Lo42
Griffin ◻ USA (GA) 175 Fh29
Griffin ◻ USA (GA) 175 Ej21
Griffin Point ◻ USA (AK) 165 Cj10
Griffith ◻ AUS (NSW) 111 Sd63
Grigor'evskoe ◻ RUS 48 Nb17
Grigoriopol ◻ MD 49 Me22
Grik ◻ MAL 92 Qa43
Grillby ◻ S 31 Ls31
Grillon, Mount ◻ USA 166 Db16
Grimari ◻ RCA 140 Ma43
Grimmen ◻ D 32 Lo36
Grimsby ◻ GB 21 Ku37
Grimsey ◻ IS 18 Kb24
Grimsey ◻ IS 18 Kb24
Grimshaw ◻ CDN ( ) 167 Eb17
Grimstad ◻ N 30 Lj32
Grimsvötn ◻ IS 18 Kc26
Grindavík ◻ IS 18 Jz27
Grindsted ◻ DK 30 Lk35
Grinkiškis ◻ LT 39 Md35
Grinnel Peninsula ◻ CDN 163 Fb03
Grintavec ◻ SLO 42 Lp44
Gripsholm ◻ S 31 Ls31
Griquatown ◻ ZA 154 Mb60
Griquet ◻ CDN 177 Hc20
Grise Fiord ◻ CDN 163 Fc03
Griškabūdis ◻ LT 39 Md36
Grisolles ◻ F 24 Lb47
Grisslehamn ◻ S 31 Lt30
Grissom Air Mus. ◻ USA
Grivenskaja ◻ RUS 49 Mk23
Grivita ◻ RO 45 Mh49
Grizzly Bear Mountain ◻ CDN 167 Ea15
Grjada ◻ RUS 48 Mf16
Grjazi ◻ RUS 48 Mk19
Grmeč ◻ BIH 35 Lr46
Grmeč ◻ BIH (CE) 201 Hk47
Groais Island ◻ CDN 177 Hc20
Grobina ◻ LV 39 Mb34
Groblersdal ◻ ZA 155 Me58
Groblershoop ◻ ZA 154 Mb60
Grobnica ◻ BG 45 Mf48
Grocka ◻ SCG 44 Ma47
Gródek ◻ PL 41 Md37
Grodzisk ◻ PL 41 Ma39
Grodzisk Mazowiecki ◻ PL 41 Mb38
Grodzisk Wielkopolski ◻ PL 40 Lr38
Groening-Museum ◻ B 23 Le39
Groenrivier ◻ ZA 154 Lj61
Grošea ◻ ZA 152 Me50
Groix ◻ F 24 Kr43
Groix ◻ F 22 Kr43

Grójec ◻ PL 41 Ma39
Grombalia ◻ TN 126 Lf27
Grömitz ◻ D 32 Ll36
Gromnik ◻ PL 41 Ma41
Gröna Lund ◻ S 31 Ls31
Gronau ◻ D 32 Lh38
Grong ◻ N 16 Lg13
Grong Grong ◻ AUS (NSW) 111 Sd63
Groningen ◻ D 32 Lm39
Groningen ◻ NL 23 Lg37
Groningen ◻ SME 194 Hc43
Gronlid ◻ CDN (SK) 169 Eh19
Grønligrotta ◻ N 16 Lh12
Grönskära ◻ S 31 Lq33
Grootberg ◻ NAM 150 Lh55
Grootfontein ◻ ZA 154 Ma60
Groote Eylandt ◻ AUS 106 Rj53
Groote Eylandt A.L. ◻ AUS 106 Rj53
Grootfontein ◻ NAM 150 Lk55
Groot Hemar ◻ SME 194 Hb43
Groot Jongensfontein ◻ ZA 154 Ma63
Groot Karasberge ◻ NAM 154 Lk59
Grootkraal ◻ ZA 154 Mb62
Groot Marico ◻ ZA 155 Md58
Grootrivierhoogte ◻ ZA 154 Lk62
Groot Waterberg ◻ NAM 150 Lj55
Groot Winterhoek Wilderness Area ◻ ZA 154 Lk62
Gropeni ◻ RO 45 Mh49
Gros Morne ◻ CDN 177 Hb21
Gros Morne ◻ RH 186 Gd36
Gros Morne N. P. ◻ CDN 177 Hb21
Gross Barmen Hot Springs ◻ NAM 150 Lh55
Großenhain ◻ D 32 Lo39
Großenkneten ◻ D 32 Lj38
Großer Arber ◻ D 33 Lo41
Großer Beerberg ◻ D 32 Ll40
Großer Feldberg ◻ D 33 Lj40
Großer Inselsberg ◻ D 32 Ll40
Großer Peilstein ◻ A 42 Lq42
Großer Plöner See ◻ D 32 Ll36
Großer Pyhrgas ◻ A 35 Lp43
Großer Rachel ◻ D 33 Lo41
Grosses ◻ AUS (SA) 108 Rh61
Große Sandspitze ◻ A 35 Ln44
Grosseto ◻ I 34 Lm47
Grosseto Prugna ◻ F 36 Lj49
Groß-Gerau ◻ D 33 Lj41
Groß Gerungs ◻ A 42 Lp42
Groß Gerungs ◻ A 42 Lp42
Großglockner ◻ A 35 Ln43
Großglockner Straße ◻ A 35 Ln43
Grossos ◻ BR (RN) 201 Jb48
Großpetersdorf ◻ A 35 Lr43
Großräschen ◻ D 32 Lo39
Gross Ums ◻ NAM 154 Lk57
Großvenediger ◻ A 34 Ln43
Grosuplje ◻ SLO 42 Lp45
Groton ◻ USA (SD) 172 Fa23
Grotta Azzurra ◻ I 37 Lp50
Grotta di Nettuno ◻ I 36 Lj50
Grotta di San Michele ◻ I 36 Lk50
Grottaglie ◻ I 37 Ls50
Grottammare ◻ I 35 Lo47
Grotte di Clamouse ◻ F 25 Ld47
Grotte de Clamouse ◻ F 24 La46
Grotte de Lascaux ◻ F 24 La46
Grotte de Niaux ◻ F 24 Lb48
Grotte de Pech Merle ◻ F 24 Lb46
Grottes des Demoiselles ◻ F 25 Ld47
Grotte de Villars ◻ F 24 La45
Grotte di Castellana ◻ I 37 Ls50
Grotte di Catullo ◻ I 34 Ll45
Grotte di Frasassi ◻ I 35 Ln47
Grotte du Mas-d'Azil ◻ F 24 Lb47
Grottes (Bangbali) ◻ RCA 140 Ma41
Grottes d'Azé ◻ F 25 Le44
Grottes de Béni-Add ◻ DZ 126 Kr28
Grottes de Bétharram ◻ F 24 Ku47
Grottes de Bongolo ◻ G 148 Lf47
Grottes de Dimba et Ngovo ◻ RDC 148 Lh48
Grottes de Matupi ◻ RDC 141 Me45
Grottes de Missirikoro ◻ RMM 137 Kh43
Grottes de Remouchamps ◻ B 23 Lf40
Grottes de Yambala ◻ RCA 140 Ma41
Grottes du Galo Boukoy ◻ RCA 140 Lk43
Grouard ◻ CDN (AB) 167 Eb18
Groumania ◻ CI 137 Kg42
Groundbirch ◻ CDN (BC) 167 Dk18
Groupe d'Abdabra ◻ SY 156 Nf50
Grove ◻ USA (OK) 174 Fc27
Grove City ◻ USA (OH) 173 Fj26
Grove City ◻ USA (PA) 173 Fk25
Grove Hill ◻ USA (AL) 175 Fg30
Grove Mountains ◻ 7 Oc32
Groveton ◻ USA (TX) 174 Fc30
Grožnjan ◻ HR 35 Lo45
Grozny ◻ RUS (CHE) 57 Nc24
Grube ◻ GM 137 Kf40
Grube Messel ◻ D 33 Lj41
Grubišno Polje ◻ HR 35 Ls45
Grudusk ◻ PL 41 Mb37
Grudziądz ◻ PL 40 Lt37
Grumento Nova ◻ I 37 Lq50
Grums ◻ S 30 Lo31
Grünau ◻ NAM 154 Lk59
Grünberg ◻ D 32 Lj40
Grundarfjörður ◻ IS 18 Jz26
Grundforsen ◻ S 30 Lo29
Grünheide ◻ D 32 Lo38
Grundkallen ◻ S 31 Lt30
Grundy ◻ USA (VA) 178 Fj27
Grundy Center ◻ USA (IA) 172 Fc24
Grünstadt ◻ D 33 Lj41
Grünwald ◻ PL 41 Ma37
Grupe ◻ CH 137 Kj41
Grupo di Sella ◻ I 34 Lm44
Gruta de Intihuasi ◻ RA 208 Gh62
Gruta de la Paz ◻ EC 196 Gb45
Gruta las Maravillas ◻ E 27 Ko53
Gruta de los Helechos ◻ ROU 204 Hb61
Gruta del Palacio ◻ ROU 204 Hb61
Gruta La Goja Azul ◻ BR 202 Hb56
Grutas de Bustamante ◻ MEX 181 Ek32
Grutas de García ◻ MEX 181 Ek33
Grutas de Lanquín ◻ GCA 184 Ff38

Grutas de Loltún ◻ MEX 183 Ff35
Grutas de Xtacumbilxunán ◻ MEX 183 Fe36
Grutas dos Brejões ◻ BR (BA) 201 Hk51
Grutas Lázaro Cárdenas ◻ MEX 183 Fc37
Gruver ◻ USA (TX) 174 Ek27
Gruža ◻ SCG 44 Ma47
Gruždžiai ◻ LT 39 Md34
Grybów ◻ PL 41 Ma41
Gryckebro ◻ S 31 Lo32
Gryfice ◻ PL 40 Lq37
Gryfino ◻ PL 40 Lq38
Gryfów Śląski ◻ PL 40 Lq39
Grykë ◻ AL 46 Lu50
Grythyttan ◻ S 31 Lp31
Grytøya ◻ N 16 Lj11
Gryllefjord ◻ N 16 Lj11
Gstaad ◻ CH 34 Lh44
Gua ◻ EAT 146 Mf49
Guabalá ◻ PA 185 Fk41
Guabijú ◻ BR 204 Hc61
Guabiju ◻ BR 204 He60
Guabún ◻ RCH 208 Gd66
Guacamayas ◻ CO 192 Ge44
Guacamayas ◻ CO 192 Ge43
Guacara ◻ YV 193 Gg40
Guacautey ◻ YV 193 Gk43
Guachara ◻ YV 193 Gj43
Gua Charah ◻ MAL 92 Qb43
Guachichas de Arriba ◻ MEX (DGO) 180 Eg33
Guachochi ◻ MEX (CHH) 180 Eg32
Guachucal ◻ CO 192 Gb45
Guacochi ◻ MEX (CHH) 180 Eg32
Guadal ◻ RA 205 Gh59
Guadalajara ◻ MEX 182 Ej35
Guadalajara ◻ E 27 Kr50
Guadalajara ◻ E (JLC) 182 Ej35
Guadalcanal ◻ E 27 Kp52
Guadalcanal ◻ SOL 117 Sk50
Guadalcanal ◻ E 27 Kp52
Guadalupe ◻ PI (PI) 201 Hj49
Guadalupe ◻ MEX (NL) 181 Ek33
Guadalupe ◻ MEX (ZCT)
Guadalupe ◻ PE 196 Ga49
Guadalupe de Bagues ◻ MEX (CHH) 181 Eh32
Guadalupe Mts. N.P. ◻ USA 171 Eh30
Guadalupe y Calvo ◻ MEX (CHH) 180 Eg32
Guadalupe de Bravo ◻ MEX (CHH) 180 Eg32
Guadalupe del Carnicero ◻ MEX (SLP) 182 Ek34
Guadalupe Victoria ◻ MEX (BC) 180 Ec29
Guadalupe Victoria ◻ MEX (DGO) 181 Eh33
Guadas ◻ CO 192 Gc43
Guadix ◻ E 27 Kr53
Guadua de Miaux ◻ F 24 Lb48
Guadua ◻ CO 192 Gc43
Guafo, I. ◻ RCH 208 Gc66
Guaguapan ◻ BR (CE) 201 Ja47
Guaguapan ◻ GCA 184 Ff38
Guale ◻ EC 196 Fk46
Gualdira ◻ BR (ER) 204 Ha62
Gualea ◻ RA (CB) 208 Ge67
Gualjaina ◻ RCH 208 Ge66
Gualletti, Volcán ◻ RCH 206 Gf55
Gualmatán ◻ CO 192 Gb45
Gualoque ◻ USA 101 Sa08
Gualy ◻ YV 193 Gh40
Guamal ◻ CO 192 Gc41
Guamal San Martin ◻ CO 192 Gd44
Guamanga ◻ CO 192 Gc44
Guamini ◻ RA (BA) 209 Gj64
Guamo ◻ CO 192 Gc43
Guamote ◻ EC 196 Ga46
Guanabacoa ◻ MEX (SL) 180 Ed33
Gua Musang ◻ MAL 92 Qb43
Gu'an ◻ CHN (HBI) 73 Qj26
Guanabacoa ◻ C 179 Ga34
Guanacaste, N.P. ◻ BR 184 Ff37
Guanacevi ◻ MEX (DGO) 180 Eg33
Guanaco Muerto ◻ RA (CD) 207 Gh61
Guanajibo Island = San Salvador ◻ BS 186 Gc33
Guanaja ◻ HN 184 Fh37
Guanajay ◻ C 179 Fj34
Guanajuato ◻ MEX 182 Ek35
Guanajuato ◻ MEX (GJT) 182 Ek35
Guanambi ◻ BR (BA) 203 Hj53
Guanare ◻ YV 193 Gf41
Guanarito ◻ YV 193 Gf42
Guanay, Cerro ◻ YV 193 Gg43
Guandacay ◻ RA (LR) 207 Gf60
Guandu ◻ IND (MPH) 82 Oj35
Guandacaya ◻ RA (LR) 207 Gf60
Guanding ◻ CHN (HUN)
Guanghua ◻ CHN 75 Qg34
Guangde ◻ CHN (AHU) 76 Qk31
Guangfeng ◻ CHN (JGX)
Guanghan ◻ CHN (SCH) 74 Qd30
Guangling ◻ CHN (SHA) 72 Qh27
Guangmao Shan ◻ CHN 75 Qa33
Guangnan ◻ CHN (YUN) 87 Qd33
Guangrao ◻ CHN (SDG) 73 Qk27
Guangshan ◻ CHN (HNN) 73 Qh30
Guangshui ◻ CHN (HUB) 73 Qg30
Guangshun ◻ CHN (HUB) 74 Qf32
Guangyuan ◻ CHN (SCH) 74 Qd29
Guangze ◻ CHN 75 Qj32
Guangzhou ◻ CHN 75 Qh34

Guanze ◻ CHN (FJN) 75 Qj32
Guangzhou ◻ CHN 75 Qh34
Guanhães ◻ BR (MG) 203 Hj55
Guaní ◻ CO 192 Ge44
Guaniano ◻ YV 193 Gg42
Guanica ◻ USA (PR) 187 Gg37
Guanizuela ◻ CHN (GZH) 87 Qc33
Guano ◻ YV 193 Gj40
Guanqiao ◻ CHN (NHZ) 72 Qc27
Guanta ◻ RCH 206 Ge60
Guantánamo ◻ C 186 Gc36
Guantánamo Bay US Naval Base ◻ USA 186 Gc36
Guantao ◻ CHN (HBI) 73 Qh27
Guanxi ◻ CHN (GDG) 75 Qh33
Guapé ◻ BR (MG) 203 Hh56
Guapí ◻ CO 192 Gb44
Guapiaçu ◻ BR (SP) 205 Hf58
Guapiles ◻ CR 185 Fj40
Guapó ◻ BOL 206 Gk52
Guaporé ◻ BR (RS) 204 Hd60
Guaporé ◻ BR 204 Hd60
Guaqui ◻ BOL 206 Ha53
Guara ◻ E 28 Ku48
Guarabira ◻ BR (SP) 203 Hg56
Guaraciaba ◻ BR (SC) 204 Hd59
Guaraciaba do Norte ◻ BR (CE) 201 Hk48
Guaraí ◻ BR (TO) 200 Hf50
Guaramacal, P.N. ◻ YV 192 Ge41
Guarambaré ◻ PY 204 Hb59
Guaramirim ◻ BR (SC) 205 Hf59
Guaranda ◻ EC 196 Ga46
Guaranda ◻ BOL 206 Gj55
Guaraniaçu ◻ BR (PR) 204 Hd58
Guaranta ◻ BR (ES) 203 Hk54
Guarantã do Norte ◻ BR (MT) 199 Hc50
Guarapari ◻ BR (ES) 203 Hk56
Guarapuava ◻ BR (MG) 203 Hg54
Guarapuava ◻ BR (PR) 204 He58
Guaraqueçaba ◻ BR (PR) 205 Hf58
Guararapes ◻ BR (SP) 202 He56
Guaratiba ◻ BR (PB) 201 Jc49
Guaratinga ◻ BR (BA) 203 Ja54
Guaratinguetá ◻ BR (SP) 205 Hh57
Guaratuba ◻ BR (PR) 205 Hf58
Guarayos ◻ BOL 206 Gf52
Guarda ◻ P 26 Ko50
Guardamar del Segura ◻ E 27 Ks52
Guarda-Mor ◻ BR (MG) 203 Hg54
Guardiagrele ◻ I 37 Lp48
Guardia Mitre ◻ RA (RN) 209 Gj66
Guardian Seamounts ◻ 184 Fg41
Guardo ◻ E 26 Kq48
Guareña ◻ E 27 Kp51
Guariba ◻ PNG 115 Sd50
Guariba ◻ BR (SP) 202 Hf56
Guarico ◻ YV 193 Gh41
Guaricana, T.I. ◻ BR 204 Hd59
Guarujá ◻ BR (SP) 205 Hg58
Guarulhos ◻ BR (SP) 205 Hg57
Guarumales ◻ BR (MA) 195 Hh47
Guasave ◻ MEX (SL) 180 Ef33
Guasca ◻ CO 192 Gd43
Guasdualito ◻ YV 192 Ge42
Guasipati ◻ YV 193 Gk42
Guasizaco ◻ MEX (CHH) 180 Ef32
Guastalla ◻ I 34 Ll46
Guasti, T.I. ◻ BR 202 Hf56
Guatacondo ◻ RCH 206 Gf56
Guataquí ◻ CO 192 Gc43
Guatemala ■ 184 Fe38
Guatimapé ◻ MEX (DGO) 181 Eh33
Guataré ◻ YV 193 Gg40
Guato, P.N. ◻ YV 193 Gj40
Guatrache ◻ RA (LP) 209 Gj64
Guávare ◻ CO 193 Gd44
Guáyape ◻ BR (MG) 203 Hg56
Guayabal ◻ CO 192 Gc43
Guayabones ◻ YV 192 Ge41
Guayaguayaré ◻ TT 187 Gk40
Guayana ◻ USA (PR) 187 Gg37
Guayaquil ◻ EC 196 Ga47
Guayaramerín ◻ BOL 198 Gh50
Guayllabamba ◻ EC 196 Ga46
Guaymas ◻ MEX (SO) 180 Ee32
Guayubin ◻ DOM 186 Ge36
Guayumil ◻ MEX (SL) 180 Ed33
Guba ◻ ETH 142 Mh40
Guba ◻ RDC 146 Md51
Guban ◻ SP 143 Nb40
Gubao ◻ RP 90 Rc39
Gubatas Hills ◻ RP 90 Rc39
Gubbio ◻ I 34 Ln47
Gubdor ◻ RUS 48 Nc06
Gubei ◻ WAN 138 Ld40
Gubio ◻ WAN 139 Lg39
Gubin ◻ PL 40 Lp39
Gubkin ◻ RUS 48 Mj20
Gubkinskij ◻ RUS 54 Od05
Gučevo ◻ SCG 44 Lu46
Guchab ◻ NAM 150 Lj55
Gücük ◻ TR 56 Na26
Gudalur ◻ IND (APH) 84 Oj40
Gudbrandsdalen ◻ N 30 Lj29
Guder ◻ ETH 142 Mj41
Guder Falls ◻ ETH 142 Mj41
Gudermes ◻ RUS (CHE) 57 Nd24
Gudhem ◻ S 30 Lo32
Gudja ◻ IND (MPH) 82 Oj32
Gudivada ◻ IND (APH) 83 Pa37
Gudiyattam ◻ IND (TNU) 85 Ok39
Gudō ◻ BOL 206 Gh52
Gudur ◻ IND (APH) 85 Pa38
Guebwiller ◻ F 25 Lh43
Guéckédou ◻ RG 136 Kf41
Guelb El Rhein ◻ RIM 130 Ke35
Guelb er Richât ◻ RIM 130 Ke35
Guélb Ragoum ◻ RIM 131 Kf36
Guélb Zednes ◻ RIM 130 Ke35
Guélé ◻ TCH 140 Lk41
Gueledignang ◻ TCH 139 Lj40
Guélengdeng ◻ TCH 139 Lj40
Guélta d'Archei ◻ TCH 134 Ma37
Guelmim ◻ MA 124 Kd30
Guelph ◻ CDN (ON) 173 Fk24
Guéméné-Penfao ◻ F 22 Kt43
Guéméné-sur-Scorff ◻ F 22 Kr42
Guémené-Penfao ◻ F 22 Kt43
Guémé ◻ DZ 126 Lc32
Guénange ◻ F 23 Lg41
Guépaoué ◻ CI 137 Kh42
Guéra ◻ TCH 139 Lk40
Guérande ◻ F 22 Ks43

Guera ◻ DZ 126 Lc29
Guercif ◻ MA 125 Kj28
Guérédaa ◻ TCH 134 Mb38
Guerende ◻ LAR 128 Ma34
Guéret ◻ F 24 Lb44
Guérguarat ◻ DARS 130 Kb35
Guérin-Kouka ◻ TG 137 La41
Guermessa ◻ TN 126 Lf29
Guernsey ◻ GB 22 Ks41
Guernsey ◻ USA (WY) 171 Eh24
Guerrero ◻ MEX (COH) 181 Ek31
Guerrero ◻ MEX (COH) 181 Ek31
Guerrero Del ◻ CHN (HNN) 73 Qh27
Guerrero ◻ MEX 182 Ek36
Guerrero Negro ◻ MEX (BCS) 180 Ec32
Guettara ◻ DZ 125 Kk31
Gueskerou ◻ RN 133 Lg39
Guéssébo ◻ CI 137 Kg42
Guessou South ◻ DY 138 La40
Guéxigna ◻ F 25 Le44
Guezaoua ◻ RN 132 Le38
Guffertspitze ◻ A 34 Lm43
Gufudalur ◻ IS 18 Jz25
Guge, Mount ◻ ETH 142 Mj42
Gugesti ◻ RO 45 Mh45
Gugionesi ◻ I 37 Lp48
Guguan ◻ USA (Guam) 91 Qi44
Gugu, Mount ◻ ETH 142 Mk41
Gugurtli ◻ UZ 62 Ob25
Guhagar ◻ IND (MHT) 82 Og37
Guia Lopes da Laguna ◻ BR (MS) 202 Hb56
Guiana Basin ◻ 190 Ha08
Guiana Highlands ◻ 190 Gb09
Guiana Plateau ◻ 194 Hc41
Guiarote ◻ BOL 206 Gj55
Guiba ◻ BF 137 Kk39
Guibéroua ◻ CI 137 Kg42
Guichi ◻ CHN (AHU) 78 Qj30
Guichón ◻ ROU 204 Hb62
Guidan-Roumji ◻ RN 132 Ld39
Guider ◻ CAM 139 Lh41
Guidiguir ◻ RN 132 Le39
Guidimaka ◻ RIM/RMM 130 Ke38
Guidimouni ◻ RN 132 Le39
Guiding ◻ CHN (GZH) 74 Qd33
Guidjiba ◻ CAM 139 Lg41
Guidong ◻ CHN (HUN) 75 Qg32
Guienga ◻ MEX 183 Fc37
Guiffa ◻ RCA 140 Lk42
Guiging ◻ CHN (GZG) 74 Qe34
Guiglo ◻ CI 137 Kg42
Guigou ◻ YV 193 Gg40
Guihua Temple ◻ CHN 69 Pk31
Guihuayuan ◻ CHN (SCH) 74 Qh30
Guijuelo ◻ E 27 Kp50
Guilderton ◻ AUS (WA) 104 Qh61
Guildford ◻ GB 21 Ku39
Guilin ◻ CHN (GZG) 74 Qf33
Guillaumes ◻ F 25 Lg46
Guillestre ◻ F 25 Lg45
Guimarães ◻ BR (MA) 195 Hh47
Guimarães ◻ P 26 Km49
Guimba ◻ RP 90 Ra38
Guimiliau ◻ F 22 Kr42
Guimacouru ◻ DY 138 La41
Guinchos Cay ◻ BS 179 Ga34
Guindulman ◻ RP 90 Rc41
Guines ◻ C 179 Fj34
Guinea ■ 123 Ka08
Guinea-Bissau ■ 123 Ka08
Guinea Basin ◻ 160 Fa08
Guingamp ◻ F 22 Kr42
Guinea ◻ SN 130 Kc38
Guipavas ◻ F 22 Kr42
Guiping ◻ CHN (GZG) 74 Qf34
Guira de Melena ◻ C 179 Fj34
Guiratinga ◻ BR (MT) 202 Hd54
Gûira ◻ YV 193 Gh40
Guirol ◻ RIM 130 Kd37
Guisborough ◻ GB 21 Kt36
Guiscard ◻ F 23 Ld41
Guise ◻ F 23 Ld41
Guishan ◻ CHN 75 Qg31
Guishui ◻ CHN 75 Qh34
Gui Yuan Si ◻ CHN 75 Qh30
Guixi ◻ CHN (JGX) 78 Qj31
Guiyang ◻ CHN (HUN) 75 Qg33
Guiyang ◻ CHN (GZH) 74 Qe33
Guizhou ◻ CHN (HUB) 74 Qf31
Guizhou ◻ CHN 74 Qc33
Gujan-Mestras ◻ F 24 Kt46
Gujar Khan ◻ PK 65 Og29
Gujiao ◻ CHN (SAX) 72 Qg27
Gujranwala ◻ PK 65 Oh29
Gujrat ◻ PK 65 Oh29
Gujrat ◻ IND (MPH) 80 Oh34
Gujra ◻ PK 65 Og29
Gukasjan ◻ RUS 49 Mk22
Gulang ◻ CHN (GSU) 72 Qb27
Gulaothi ◻ IND (UPH) 81 Ok31
Gulbarga ◻ IND (KTK) 82 Oj37
Gulbene ◻ LV 39 Mf33
Gul'ca ◻ KS 63 Og25
Guledagudd ◻ IND (KTK) 82 Oh38
Gulfe ◻ RI 95 Qh46
Gülek ◻ TR 56 Na27
Gulf Islands National Seashore ◻ USA 175 Ff30
Gulf of Aden ◻ 135 Nd08
Gulf of Aqaba ◻ ET/KSA 58 Mh31
Gulf of Arab ◻ ET 128 Mc30
Gulf of Bahrain ◻ KSA 59 Nf33
Gulf of Bone ◻ RI 96 Ra47
Gulf of Boothia ◻ S/FIN 17 Lk15
Gulf of Bothnia ◻ S 31 Lt30
Gulf of California ◻ MEX 180 Ec33
Gulf of Carpentaria ◻ AUS 106 Rk53
Gulf of Darién ◻ PA/CO 185 Gd41
Gulf of Finland ◻ S 31 Mf31
Gulf of Gdansk ◻ PL 41 Ltu6
Gulf of Genoa ◻ I 34 Lj46
Gulf of Guinea ◻ 122 La09
Gulf of Hikma ◻ ET 126 Mc30
Gulf of Kachchh ◻ IND 82 Od34
Gulf of Khambhat ◻ IND 82 Og35
Gulf of Liaotong ◻ CHN 76 Ra25
Gulf of Maine ◻ USA 177 Ge24
Gulf of Manaar ◻ IND/CY 85 Ok41
Gulf of Martaban ◻ MYA 88 Pj38
Gulf of Masirah ◻ OM 61 Nh35
Gulf of Mexico ◻ 160 Fa07
Gulf of Oman ◻ 50 Ob08
Gulf of Papua ◻ PNG 115 Sc49
Gulf of Paria ◻ YV 193 Gj40

Gulf of Riga ◻ EST/LV 39 Md33
Gulf of Saint Lawrence ◻ CDN 176 Gj21
Gulf of Sallum ◻ ET 128 Mc30
Gulf of Salonica ◻ GR 46 Mc50
Gulf of Suez ◻ ET 129 Mg31
Gulf of Taranto ◻ I 37 La50
Gulf of Tehuantepec ◻ MEX 183 Fc38
Gulf of Thailand ◻ T 88 Qa40
Gulf of Tolo ◻ RI 96 Ra47
Gulf of Tomini ◻ RI 96 Ra46
Gulf of Tonkin ◻ VN/CHN 87 Qd30
Gulf of Valencia ◻ E 29 La51
Gulf of Venezuela ◻ YV 192 Ge40
Gulian ◻ CHN (HLG) 76 Ra22
Gulgong ◻ AUS (NSW) 111 Se62
Gulian ◻ CHN (MPH) 83 Ok33
Gulistan ◻ UZ 63 Oe25
Guljanci ◻ BG 45 Me47
Gulkevíči ◻ RUS 49 Na23
Gull Lake ◻ CDN (SK) 169 Ef20
Gullspång ◻ S 31 Lp32
Güllük Dağları ◻ TR 57 Na25
Güllük ◻ TR 47 Mh53
Gulmarg ◻ IND 80 Oh28
Gulnare ◻ RI 93 Qk47
Gülpinar ◻ TR 47 Mg51
Gulshat ◻ KZ 66 Oi22
Gulsvík ◻ N 30 Lk30
Gulu ◻ EAU 144 Mg44
Gulumba Gana ◻ WAN 139 Lh40
Gulwe ◻ EAT 147 Mj49
Guma = Pishan ◻ CHN (XUZ) 66 Ok27
Gumare ◻ RP 90 Ra39
Gumare ◻ RB 151 Mb55
Gumba ◻ ANG 151 Li44
Gumbiro ◻ EAT 146 Mh51
Gumdag ◻ TM 62 Nh26
Gumel ◻ WAN 138 Lf39
Gumgarhi ◻ NEP 81 Pb31
Gumi ◻ RI 91 Rd45
Gumia ◻ IND (JGT) 83 Pc34
Gummer ◻ PNG 115 Sc49
Gummi ◻ WAN 138 Lc39
Gumuia ◻ IND (MPH) 83 Pb36
Gümüşçay ◻ TR 45 Mh50
Gümüşhane ◻ TR 57 Na25
Gumu Uen ◻ SP 145 Nb46
Gumzai ◻ RI 91 Rd46
Guna ◻ IND (MPH) 82 Oj33
Guna ◻ ETH 142 Mk40
Gunbad-e-Harunieyeh ◻ IR
Gundabooka N.P. ◻ AUS (NSW) 109 Sc61
Gundardehi ◻ IND (GGC) 83 Pa35
Gundelfingen ◻ D 33 Ll42
Gundupet ◻ IND 84 Oj40
Güney ◻ TR 47 Mj53
Güney ◻ TR 47 Mk52
Güney Doğu Toroslar ◻ TR 56 Mj26
Gunga ◻ ANG 150 Lk53
Gungu ◻ RDC 149 Lk49
Gungung Trus Madi ◻ MAL 94 Qj43
Gunib ◻ RUS (DAG) 57 Nd24
Gunnarn ◻ S 16 Lk12
Gunnedah ◻ AUS (NSW) 111 Sf61
Gunnison ◻ USA (CO) 171 Eg26
Gunnison ◻ USA (UT) 171 Ee26
Gunnison ◻ USA (UT) 171 Ee26
Gunpowder ◻ AUS (QLD) 106 Rk55
Guntakal ◻ IND (APH) 84 Oj38
Guntersville ◻ USA (AL) 175 Fg28
Guntur ◻ IND (APH) 83 Pa37
Guntín de Pallares ◻ E 26 Ko48
Gunungsitoli ◻ RI 93 Pj45
Gunupur ◻ IND (ORS) 83 Pc36
Gunza ◻ ANG 150 Lh52
Gunzenhausen ◻ D 33 Ll41
Guocheng ◻ CHN (GSU) 72 Qb27
Guodao ◻ CHN (SAX) 73 Qg27
Guoquanyan ◻ CHN 72 Qb30
Guoyang ◻ CHN (AHU) 78 Qj29
Guozhen ◻ CHN (SAX) 68 Qe28
Gupeng ◻ CHN (GZG) 74 Qe34
Gupis ◻ 80 Og27
Guptapur ◻ IND (ORS) 83 Pc36
Guraghe, Mount ◻ ETH 142 Mk41
Gura Haiții ◻ RO 43 Mf43
Gurahonț ◻ RO 43 Mc44
Gura Humorului ◻ RO 43 Mg43
Gurais ◻ 80 Oh28
Guramputci ◻ IND (APH) 84 Ok37
Guran ◻ IR 64 Nh32
Guranda ◻ RO 44 Mc45
Gurban-Obo ◻ CHN (NMZ) 72 Qh25
Gurban ◻ IR 64 Nh32
Gurbantäggät Shamo ◻ CHN 67 Pg23
Gurdaspur ◻ IND (PJB) 80 Oh29
Gurdon ◻ USA (AR) 174 Fd29
Gurdžaani ◻ GE 57 Nc25
Gur'evsk ◻ RUS (KGD) 41 Mb36
Gurgan ◻ IND (HYA) 80 Oj31
Gürgentepe ◻ TR 57 Na25
Guri ◻ WAN 139 Lg41
Gurig N.P. & Cobourg Marine Park ◻ AUS 106 Rg51
Gurimático ◻ CHN (MB)
Guriri ◻ BR (ES)
Gurla Mandata ◻ CHN (TIB) 68 Pb31
Gurlan ◻ UZ 62 Nk25
Gurmatkal ◻ IND (KTK) 82 Oj37
Gurskoe ◻ RUS (KHA) 77 Rd20
Gürün ◻ TR 56 Mj26
Gurupa ◻ BR (PA) 195 Hd47
Gurupá, Ilha Grande de ◻ BR 195 Hd47
Gurué ◻ MOC 153 Mj53
Guruguru ◻ IND (APH) 84 Ok37
Guruguru ◻ IR 64 Nh33
Gurué ◻ MOC 153 Mj53
Gurun ◻ MAL 92 Qa43
Gurupi ◻ BR (TO) 200 Hf50
Gurupi ◻ BR 195 Hg48
Guru Shikhar ◻ IND 82 Og33
Gurupuri ◻ BR (PA) 200 Hg47
Gurupa ◻ BR 195 Hd47
Gurvan Sai Bada ◻ MNG 70 Qa24
Gurvan Saykhan N.P. ◻ MNG 70 Qa24
Gurwa ◻ ZW 152 Mf54
Gurzuf ◻ UA 49 Mh24
Gusau ◻ WAN 138 Ld39
Gusev ◻ RUS (KGD) 41 Mc36
Gushan ◻ CHN 75 Qj33
Gushgy ◻ TM 63 Oa28
Gushan ◻ CHN (LNG) 73 Ra26
Gushi ◻ CHN (HNN) 73 Qh29
Gushikawa ◻ J 79 Re32
Gus'-Khrustal'nyj ◻ RUS 48 Na18
Gusinoozërsk ◻ RUS (BUR)
Güssing ◻ A 35 Lr43
Gustavia ◻ F 187 Gk36
Gustavus ◻ USA (AK) 166 Dc16
Gustrow ◻ D 32 Ll37
Güterfelde ◻ D 32 Lo38
Gutenberg ◻ RA (CD) 207 Gj60
Gutenberg ◻ USA (IA) 172 Fe25
Güterbock ◻ D 32 Ln38
Gutian ◻ CHN (FJN) 75 Qk32
Gutierrez ◻ BOL 206 Gj55
Gutland al L. ◻ L 23 Lg41
Gutsuo ◻ CHN (TIB) 68 Pd31
Gützkow ◻ D 32 Lo37
Guuijá ◻ MOC 155 Mg58
Guwahati (IND) (ASM) 86 Pf32
Guwer ◻ SUD 135 Mg37
Guwer ◻ IRQ 57 Nb27
Guya ◻ ZW 152 Me56
Guyana ■ 191 Ha09
Guyang ◻ CHN (NMZ) 72 Qf25
Güyang ◻ ETH 142 Nb41
Guyra ◻ AUS (NSW) 109 Sf61
Guyuan ◻ CHN (NHZ) 72 Qd28
Güzelçamli ◻ TR 47 Mh53
Güzelpinar ◻ TR 57 Nb26
Güzelyurt = Morfou ◻ CY 56 Mg28
Guzev ◻ CHN (GZG) 87 Qc33
Guzhang ◻ CHN (AHU) 78 Qj29
Guzhen ◻ CHN (XUZ) 68 Pd27
Guzmán ◻ MEX (CHH) 180 Eg30
Gvardejsk ◻ RUS (KGD) 39 Mb36
Gvarv ◻ N 30 Lj31
Gvasjugi ◻ RUS 77 Rd20
Gwa ◻ MYA 88 Ph37
Gwadar ◻ PK 64 Ob33
Gwadar East Bay ◻ PK 64 Ob33
Gwaii Haanas South Moresby National Park Reserve & Marine Conservation Area Reserve ◻ CDN 166 De19
Gwalior Fort ◻ IND 83 Ok32
Gwalior ◻ IND (MPH) 81 Ok32
Gwambaria ◻ WAN 138 Le40
Gwambara ◻ WAN 138 Ld40
Gwanda ◻ ZW 152 Me56
Gwane ◻ RDC (MPH) 83 Pa34
Gwaram ◻ WAN 138 Le40
Gwararo ◻ WAN 138 Ld40
Gwasero ◻ WAN 138 Ld40
Gwatar Bay ◻ PK 64 Ob33
Gwayi River ◻ ZW 152 Md55
Gwembe ◻ Z 152 Md54
Gweru ◻ ZW 152 Me55
Gweta ◻ RB 151 Mc56
Gwi, WAN 138 Le40
Gwoza ◻ WAN 139 Lg40
Gyaca ◻ CHN (TIB) 69 Pg31
Gyali ◻ GR 47 Mh54
Gyali ◻ H 43 Lu43
Gyandzha ◻ CHN (TIB) 69 Pg31
Gyangze ◻ CHN (TIB) 68 Pe31
Gyaring Hu ◻ CHN 69 Pg28
Gyaros ◻ GR 47 Me53
Gydanskij Poluostrov ◻ RUS 54 Od04
Gydanskij Poluostrov ◻ RUS 54 Od04
Gyigang ◻ CHN (TIB) 68 Pe31
Gyldanskaj guba ◻ RUS 54 Od04
Gyékényes ◻ H 42 Ls44
Gylling ◻ DK 30 Ll35
Gympie ◻ AUS (QLD) 109 Sg59
Gyōbutsuji ◻ J 79 Rd32
Gyömöre ◻ H 43 Ls43
Gyömrő ◻ H 43 Lu43
Gyöngyös ◻ H 43 Ma43
Gyopárosfürdő ◻ H 44 Mb44
Győr ◻ H 43 Ls43
Győrtelek ◻ H 43 Mc43
Gyula ◻ H 44 Mb44
Gyzyldepe ◻ TM 62 Ng26
Gyzylsu ◻ TM 62 Ng26
Gżatsk ◻ RUS 48 Mh18

Haa-Alifu Atoll ◻ MV 84 Og42
Häädemeeste ◻ EST 39 Me32
Haa-Dhaalu Atoll ◻ MV 84 Og42
Haag ◻ A 42 Lp42
Haag, Niederösterreich ◻ A 42 Lp42
Haag Nunataks ◻ 6 Ga34
Haakon VII Land ◻ N 16 Lp06
Haaksbergen ◻ NL 23 Lg38
Haanja kõrgustik ◻ EST 39 Mf33
Haapajärvi ◻ FIN 16 Me14
Haapamäki ◻ FIN 16 Mc14
Haapavesi ◻ FIN 16 Me13
Haapsalu ◻ EST 38 Md32
Haarlem ◻ ZA 154 Mb62
Haarlem ◻ NL 23 Le38
Haast ◻ NZ 113 Td67
Haast Bluff ◻ AUS 103 Rf57
Haast Bluff A.L. ◻ AUS 103 Rf57
Haasts Bluff ◻ AUS 103 Rf57
Hab ◻ PK 65 Oe33
Habana ■ 179 Fj34
Habaswein ◻ EAK 145 Mk45
Habay-la-Neuve ◻ B 23 Lf41
Habban ◻ YE 60 Nd39
Habarane ◻ CL 85 Pa42
Habarovsk ◻ RUS (KHA) 77 Rd20
Habaswein ◻ EAK 145 Mk45
Hab Chauki ◻ PK 65 Oe33
Habiganj ◻ BD 86 Pf33
Habirag ◻ CHN (NMZ) 73 Qj24
Habo ◻ S 30 Lo33
Haboro ◻ J 77 Sb23
Habshan ◻ UAE 61 Ng34
Habur ◻ TR 57 Nb27
Hachenburg ◻ D 32 Lh40
Hachijō-jima ◻ J 79 Rk29
Hachinohe ◻ J 77 Sb25
Haci Zeynalabdin ◻ AZ 57 Ne25
Hacıbektaş ◻ TR 56 Mk26
Hack, Mount ◻ AUS 108 Rk61
Hacking Downs ◻ AUS 108 Rk58
Hadabat al Jilf al Kabir ◻ ET 129 Md33
Hadabat al Jilf al Kabir ◻ ET 129 Md33
Haco ◻ ANG 148 Li51
Haco ◻ ANG 150 Lh51
Hadagalli ◻ IND (KTK) 84 Oh38

Hadakata ◻ RUS 70 Qg20
Hadaluma ◻ ETH 143 Nb42
Hadamar ◻ D 33 Lj40
Hadar (site of Lucy) ◻ ETH 142 Na39
Hadban ◻ CDN (MB)
Hadboram ◻ OM (NMZ) 71 Qk21
Hadbin ◻ OM 61 Nh37
Hadd ◻ KSA 58 Mk35
Hadda' ◻ KSA 58 Md35
Haddad Bani Malik ◻ KSA 60 Na35
Had-des-Oulad-Frej ◻ MA 125 Kf29
Haddington ◻ GB 20 Ks35
Hadejia ◻ WAN 138 Lf39
Hadejia ◻ WAN 138 Lf39
Haderslev ◻ DK 30 Lk35
Hadgaon ◻ IND (MHT) 82 Oj36
Hadhah ◻ KSA 60 Na34
Hadh Bani Zaynan ◻ KSA 60 Ne35
Hadhdhunmathee Atoll = Laamu Atoll ◻ MV 84 Og45
Hadiboh ◻ YE 61 Ng39
Hadithah ◻ CHN (SAX) 72 Qf27
Hadilik ◻ CHN (XUZ) 68 Pd27
Hadim ◻ TR 56 Mg27
Hadmkõy ◻ TR 45 Mj49
Hadjer Bandala ◻ TCH 134 Ma40
Hadjer el Hamis ◻ TCH 139 Lh39
Hado Dan ◻ PRK 76 Rd26
Hadraniyah ◻ IRQ 57 Nb28
Hadrian's Wall ◻ GB 20 Ks36
Hadseleya ◻ N 16 Lj11
Hadrian's Wall ◻ GB 20 Ks36
Hadsund ◻ DK 30 Ll34
Hadxhi ◻ BIH 44 Lt47
Haegeland ◻ N 30 Lh32
Haeinsa Temple ◻ ROK 78 Re28
Haeju ◻ PRK 78 Rc26
Haena ◻ USA (HI) 170 Ca34
Haenertsburg ◻ ZA 152 Me57
Haenam ◻ ROK 78 Rd28
Haerbin ◻ CHN 132 Le37
Hafar al Batin ◻ KSA 59 Nc31
Hafford ◻ CDN (SK) 169 Eg19
Haffouz ◻ TN 126 Le28
Hafik ◻ TR 56 Mj26
Hafit al Ayda ◻ KSA 58 Mk32
Hafit al Hamis ◻ TCH 139 Lh39
Hafizabad ◻ PK 65 Og29
Hafiz Sa'adi ◻ IR 64 Nj31
Hafjell alpincenter ◻ N 17 Lf15
Hafnaberg ◻ IS 18 Jz25
Hafnarfjörður ◻ IS 18 Jz26
Haftgel ◻ IR 59 Ne30
Haft Tappeh ◻ IR 59 Ne30
Hag Abdallah ◻ SUD 135 Mg38
Hagar Banga ◻ SUD 134 Mb40
Hagar Nish Plateau ◻ ER 135 Mj37
Hagelberg ◻ D 32 Ln38
Hagemeister Island ◻ USA 164 Bk16
Hagen ◻ D 32 Lh39
Hagenow ◻ D 32 Ll37
Hage Qaltan Pir Gandom Beryan ◻ IR 64 Oa30
Hagere Hiywot ◻ ETH 142 Mj41
Hagerman ◻ USA (ID) 168 Ec24
Hagerstown ◻ USA (MD) 177 Gb26
Hagetmau ◻ F 24 Ku47
Hagewood ◻ USA (LA) 174 Fd30
Hagfors ◻ S 31 Lo30
Häggenås ◻ S 16 Lh14
Haggin ◻ 7 Qd33
Hagiyama ◻ J 79 Rd32
Hagonange ◻ F 23 Lg41
Hagonoy ◻ RP 90 Ra38
Haguenau ◻ F 23 Lh42
Hahndorf ◻ AUS (SA) 110 Rk63
Hai ◻ PNG 115 Sc49
Hai'an ◻ CHN (JGS) 78 Ra29
Haibao Ta ◻ CHN 72 Qd26
Haibei ◻ CHN (HLG) 76 Rb24
Haicheng ◻ CHN (LNG) 76 Rb25
Haidargarh ◻ IND (UPH) 83 Pa32
Hai Dong ◻ CHN 75 Qg33
Haidra ◻ TN 126 Le28
Hai Duong ◻ VN 87 Qd35
Haifa ◻ IL 56 Mh29
Haiger ◻ D 32 Lj40
Haikang ◻ CHN (GDG) 74 Qf35
Haikou ◻ CHN (HAN) 87 Qf35
Hai'l ◻ KSA 58 Na32
Hailakandi ◻ IND (ASM) 86 Pg33
Hailar ◻ CHN (NMZ) 71 Qk22
Hailin ◻ CHN (HLG) 76 Rd24
Hailun ◻ CHN (HLG) 76 Rb23
Hainan Strait ◻ CHN 74 Qf35
Hainburg ◻ A 42 Lr42
Haines ◻ USA (AK) 166 Dc16
Haines ◻ USA (OR) 168 Eb23
Haines City ◻ USA (FL) 179 Fk31
Haines Junction ◻ CDN (YT) 166 Db15
Hainfeld ◻ A 42 Lq42
Hainichen ◻ D 32 Lo40
Hainich, N.P. ◻ D 32 Ll39
Haiphong ◻ VN 87 Qd35
Haisnes ◻ F 23 Ld40
Haiti ■ 186 Gd36
Haiya ◻ SUD 135 Mj37
Haiyan ◻ CHN (QHI) 72 Qa27
Haiyang ◻ CHN (SDG) 73 Ra27
Haiyuan ◻ CHN (NHZ) 72 Qc27
Hajdúböszörmény ◻ H 43 Mb43
Hajar ◻ KSA 58 Mk34
Hajdúdorog ◻ H 43 Mc43
Hajdúhadház ◻ H 43 Mb43
Hajdúnánás ◻ H 43 Mb43
Hajdúsámson ◻ H 43 Mb43
Hajdúszoboszló ◻ H 43 Mb43
Hajeb el Aioun ◻ TN 126 Le28
Hajek ◻ CZ 42 Ln40
Haji Abad ◻ IR 64 Nh31
Haji Abad ◻ IR 64 Nh29
Haji Jafar Shahid ◻ PK 65 Oe32
Hajiki-saki ◻ J 77 Rk26
Hajjah ◻ YE 60 Nb38

Hajnówka ◻ PL 41 Md38
Hajo ◻ IND (ASM) 86 Pf32
Hajo Do ▲ ROK 78 Rd28
Hajós ◻ H 43 Lu44
Hajrah ◻ KSA 60 Na35
Hajr ▲ USA 49 Me21
Hajyr ◻ RUS 55 Rc04
Hakai Recreation Area ◻ ▦ CDN 168 Df20
Hakha ◻ MYA 86 Pg34
Hakkâri ◻ TR 57 Nb27
Hakkári Daǧları ▲ TR 57 Nb27
Hakken-san ▲ J 79 Rh28
Hakodate ◻ J 77 Sa25
Hakui ◻ J 77 Rj27
Hakusan ◻ J 79 Rj27
Hala ◻ PK 65 Oe33
Halab ◻ SYR 56 Mj27
Halab ◻ SYR 56 Mj28
Halaban ◻ KSA 60 Nc34
Halabiyeh ▲ SYR 56 Mk27
Halabja ◻ IRQ 57 Nc28
Halacho ◻ MEX (YT) 183 Fe35
Halacun ◻ CHN (NMZ) 71 Qk24
Halaib ◻ SUD 129 Mj34
Halali ◻ NAM 150 Lj55
Halástra ◻ GR 46 Mc50
Halat 'Ammar ◻ KSA 58 Mj31
Halawa ◻ USA (HI) 170 Cb35
Haberstadt ◻ D 32 Lm36
Halbrite ◻ CDN (SK) 169 Ej21
Halden ◻ N 30 Lm31
Haldia ◻ IND (WBG) 86 Pe34
Haldikhora ◻ IND (BIH) 83 Pd32
Haldwani ◻ IND (UTT) 81 Ok31
Hale ◻ EAT 147 Mk48
Haleakala N.P. ◻ USA 170 Cb35
Halebid ◻ IND 84 Oj39
Halejí Bird Reserve ◻ PK 65 Od33
Halembe ◻ EAT 146 Me48
Hale, Mount ▲ AUS 104 Qj58
Halesworth ◻ GB 21 Lb38
Half Assini ◻ GH 137 Kj43
Half Moon Bay ◻ NZ 113 Te67
Halfmoon Bay ◻ CDN (BC) 168 Dj21
Halfmoon Bay ◻ NZ 113 Te69
Halfweg ◻ ZA 154 Md61
Halgeri ◻ IND (KTK) 84 Oh38
Haliburton Highlands ▲ CDN 173 Ga23
Halic ◻ UA 43 Me41
Halidon ◻ AUS (SA) 110 Sa63
Halifax ◻ CDN 177 SdT55
Halifax ◻ GB 21 Kt37
Halifax Bay ◻ AUS (QLD) 107 Sd55
Halikarnassos ◻ TR 47 Mh53
Halikko ◻ FIN 38 Md30
Halimun, Gunung ▲ RI 95 Qd49
Haliyal ◻ IND (KTK) 82 Oh38
Hajala ◻ EAT 38 Mg31
Halke Shan ▲ CHN 66 Pa24
Hálki ◻ GR 47 Mh54
Halkida ◻ GR 45 Md52
Halkirk ◻ CDN (AB) 169 Ed19
Halkirk ◻ GB 20 Kr32
Halland ◻ S 30 Ln33
Hallandale ◻ USA (FL) 179 Fk33
Hallasan ◻ ROK 78 Rd29
Hallasan A.P. ▲ ROK 78 Rd29
Hall Beach ◻ CDN 163 Fd05
Halle ◻ B 23 Le40
Halleck ◻ USA (NV) 170 Ec25
Hällefors ◻ S 31 Lp31
Hälleforsnäs ◻ S 31 Lr31
Hallein ◻ A 35 Lo43
Hallekis ◻ S 31 Lo32
Hallen ◻ S 16 Ln14
Hallersville ◻ USA (AR) 164 Cb16
Halle (Saale) ◻ D 32 Lm39
Hallett ◻ USA 110 Rk62
Hallettsville ◻ USA (TX) 181 Fb31
Halley ◻ ANT 6 Jc34
Halligen ◻ D 32 Lj36
Hallingdal ▲ N 30 Lk30
Hällingsåfallet ◻ ▦ S 16 Lh13
Hall in Tirol ◻ A 34 Lm43
Hall Island ◻ USA 164 Bd15
Hall Islands ◻ FSM 10 Sb06
Hällnäs ◻ S 16 Lk13
Hallock ◻ USA (MN) 172 Fb21
Hallormsstaður ◻ IS 18 Kf25
Hall Peninsula ▲ CDN 163 Gc06
Point ◻ AUS 103 Rc53
Hall Point ▲ AUS 106 Rg51
Halls ◻ USA (TN) 175 Fe28
Hallsberg ◻ S 31 Lp31
Halls Creek ◻ AUS (WA) 103 Rc53
Halls Gap ◻ AUS (VIC) 110 Sb64
Hallsta ◻ S 31 Lr31
Hallstahammar ◻ S 31 Lr31
Hallstatt ◻ A 35 Lo43
Hallstatt-Dachstein Salzkammergut ◻ ▦ A 35 Lo43
Hältättter See ◻ A 35 Lo43
Hallstavik ◻ S 31 Ls30
Hallyo Haesang N.P. ◻ ROK 79 Re28
Halmahera ◻ RI 91 Re45
Halmahera Sea ◻ RI 97 Re46
Halmstad ◻ S 30 Ln34
Halol ◻ IND (GUJ) 82 Og34
Halong Bay ◻ ▦ VN 87 Qd35
Halong City ◻ VN 87 Qd35
Hals ◻ DK 30 Ll34
Hal Saflieni Hypogeum ◻ ▦ M 37 Lp55
Hälsingland ◻ S 17 Lh15
Halsön ◻ FIN 38 Mb28
Halstead ◻ GB 21 La39
Halsteren ◻ NL 23 Le39
Halton Bank ◻ 16 Lh13
Hälttern ◻ D 32 Lh39
Halthwhistle ◻ GB 20 Ks36
Haluagghat ◻ BD 86 Pf33
Halul ◻ Q 61 Ng33
Halvad ◻ IND (GUJ) 82 Of34
Halverson Ridge ◻ CDN (AB) 167 Ea17
Halvmåneøya ◻ N 16 Mb07
Ham ◻ F 23 Ld41
Ham ◻ TCH 139 Lh40
Hama ◻ SYR 56 Mj28
Hamab ◻ NAM 154 Lk60
Hamada ◻ J 79 Rg28
Hamada al Hamrah ◻ LAR 126 Lf31
Ham ada de la Dao ura ◻ DZ 125 Kj31
Hamada de Tindouf ◻ DZ 124 Kf32
Hamada deTinrhert ◻ DZ 126 Ld31
Hamada du Draâ ◻ DZ 125 Kg33
Hamada du Guir ◻ DZ 125 Kj33
Hamada el Douakel ◻ DZ 124 Kg32
Hamada el Harich ◻ RMM 131 Kh34
Hamada Mangeni ◻ RN 133 Lg34
Hamada Marzuq ◻ LAR 127 Lf34
Hamadan ◻ IR 57 Ne28
Hamada Tounassine ◻ DZ 125 Kg34

Hamadat Tingarat ◻ LAR 126 Lf31
Hamada Zegher ◻ LAR 126 Lf32
Hamadet Bet Touadjine ◻ DZ 126 Lc30
Hamaguir ◻ DZ 125 Kj30
Hamamah ◻ LAR 127 Ma29
Hamamatsu ◻ J 77 Sa24
Hamamatsu ◻ J 79 Rj28
Hamar ◻ N 17 Lf15
Hamardomen ◻ N 17 Lf15
Hamarro Hadad ◻ ETH 143 Nb42
Hamasaka ◻ J 79 Rh28
Hama-Tombetsu ◻ J 77 Sb24
Hambidge Conservation Park ◻ AUS 110 Rh62
Hamburg ◻ D 32 Ll37
Hamburg ◻ USA (AR) 175 Fe29
Hamburg ◻ USA (IA) 168 Dj25
Hamburg ◻ USA (NY) 173 Ga24
Hamdah ◻ KSA 60 Na36
Hamdallaye ◻ RMM 131 Kt33
Hamdallay ◻ RN 132 Lc39
Hamdanah ◻ KSA 60 Na36
Hamdibey ◻ TR 47 Mh51
Hämeenkyrö ◻ FIN 38 Md29
Hämeenlinna ◻ FIN 38 Me30
Hämeensselkä ◻ FIN 38 Me30
Hamelin ◻ AUS (WA) 104 Qh59
Hameln ◻ D 32 Lk38
Hamersley Gorge ▲ AUS 102 Qk57
HamersleyRange ▲ AUS 102 Qj57
Hamhung ◻ PRK 76 Rd28
Hami ◻ CHN (XUZ) 67 Pg24
Hamid ◻ IR 59 Ne30
Hamid ◻ SUD 135 Mf35
Hamidiye ◻ TR 45 Mg49
Hamidiyeh ◻ IR 59 Ne30
Hamilton ◻ AUS (TAS) 111 Sd67
Hamilton ◻ AUS (VIC) 111 Sb64
Hamilton ◻ CDN (ON) 173 Ga24
Hamilton ◻ GB 20 Kq35
Hamilton ◻ NZ 112 Th64
Hamilton ◻ USA (AK) 164 Bj14
Hamilton ◻ USA (IL) 175 Fe25
Hamilton ◻ USA (MT) 168 Ed22
Hamilton ◻ USA (OH) 175 Fh26
Hamilton ◻ USA (TX) 174 Fa30
Hamilton ◻ USA (WA) 168 Dj21
Hamilton Dome ◻ USA (WY) 169 Ef24
Hamilton Downs ◻ AUS (QLD) 108 Sb56
Hamilton Hotel ◻ AUS (QLD) 108 Sa57
Hamilton Island ◻ AUS 107 Se56
Hamilton, Mount ▲ USA 170 Ec26
Hamilton River ◻ AUS (QLD) 107 Rj56
Hamina ◻ FIN 38 Mg30
Hamin ◻ UAE 61 Nh34
Hamiota ◻ CDN (MB) 172 Ek20
Hamirpur ◻ IND (HP) 81 Oj30
Hamirpur ◻ IND (UPH) 81 Qj30
Hamju ◻ PRK 76 Rd25
Hamlin ◻ USA (WV) 175 Fh26
Hamlin Bay ◻ AUS 104 Qh62
Hamm ◻ D 32 Lh39
Hammam al Alif ◻ TN 126 Lf37
Hammam al Alif ◻ IRQ 57 Nb27
Haotan ◻ CHN (SAA) 72 Qe27
Hammam ad Damt ◻ YE 60 Nd38
Hammamet ◻ TN 126 Lf37
Hammam Meskoutine ◻ DZ 131 La37
Hammam-Righa ◻ DZ 126 Ld27
Hammam Salahine ◻ DZ
Hammar ◻ S 31 Lp32
Hammarn ◻ S 31 Lo31
Hammarsland ◻ S 31 Lo35
Hammel ◻ DK 30 Lk34
Hammelburg ◻ D 33 Lk40
Hammerdal ◻ S 16 Lh14
Hammeren ◻ DK 31 Lp35
Hammerfest ◻ N 16 Mb10
Hamminkeln ◻ D 32 Lg39
Hammon ◻ USA (OK) 174 Fa28
Hammond ◻ USA (IL) 173 Fg25
Hammond Island ◻ AUS 107
Hammonton ◻ USA (NJ) 177 Gc25
Hamnvik ◻ N 16 Lj11
Hamoud ◻ RIM 130 Ke38
Hampden ◻ CDN (NF) 177 Hb23
Hampenanperak ◻ RI 92 Pk44
Hampi ◻ ▦ IND 82 Oj37
Hampton ◻ CDN (NB) 176 Gh23
Hampton ◻ USA (FL) 175 Fj29
Hampton ◻ USA (IA) 172 Fd24
Hampton ◻ USA (SC) 178 Fk28
Hampton ◻ USA (VA) 178 Gb27
Hamra ◻ SUD 134 Me40
Hamra ◻ S 17 Lh13
Hamrat al-Wuzz ◻ SUD 135 Mf38
Hamrat as Shaykh ◻ SUD 134 Md38
Hamriya ◻ UAE 61 Nh33
Ham Tan ◻ VN 89 Qe40
Ham Thuam Nam ◻ VN 89 Qe40
Hamtic ◻ RP 90 Ra40
Hamün-e-Jazmuriyan ◻ IR 64 Nk32
Hamun N.P. ◻ IR 64 Oa30
Han Yen ◻ VN 87 Qd35
Hamyski ◻ RUS (ADY) 49 Na23
Hana ◻ USA (HI) 170 Cb35
Hanagal ◻ IND (KTK) 84 Oj38
Hanahan ◻ PNG 117 Sh48
Hanak ◻ KSA 58 Mj33
Hanak ◻ TR 57 Nb26
Hanalei Bay ◻ USA (HI) 170 Ca34
Hanamaki ◻ J 77 Sa26
Hanam Plateau ▲ NAM 154 Lj58
Hanang, Mount ▲ EAT 146 Mh48
Hana Road ◻ USA 170 Cc35
Hanau ◻ D 33 Lj40
Hancavičy ◻ BY 41 Mg38
Hance ◻ USA (MI) 173 Fh22
Hancheng ◻ CHN (SAA) 72 Qf28
Hancheng ◻ CHN (HUB) 75 Qg30
Handa ◻ USA (MI) 173 Ff22
Handa ◻ J 79 Rj28
Handa ◻ SYR 56 Mj28
Handagajty ◻ RUS (TUV) 67 Pg20
Handan ◻ EAT 147 Nh49
Handali ◻ CHN (HBI) 73 Qh27
Handapa ◻ IND (ORS) 83 Pc35
Handeni ◻ EAT 147 Mk48
Handewitt ◻ D 32 Lk36
Handha ◻ SP 143 Nf40
Handlova ◻ SK 43 Lt42
Handsworth ◻ CDN (SK) 169 Ej20
Handyga ◻ RUS 55 Rd06
Hanford ◻ USA (CA) 170 Ea27
Hangal ◻ IND (KTK) 84 Oh38
Han Gangui ◻ CHN (NMZ) 72 Qd25

Hanggin Qi ◻ CHN (NMZ) 72 Qe26
Hanging Rock ▲ AUS 102 Ra57
Hanging Trail ◻ LB 136 Kf43
Hangö = Hanko ◻ FIN 38 Mc31
Hangu ◻ CHN (TJN) 73 Qj26
Hangzhou ◻ CHN (ZJG) 78 Ra30
Hani ◻ TR 57 Na26
Haniótis ◻ GR 47 Md55
Haniótis ◻ GR 45 Md50
Hankasalmi ◻ FIN 38 Mg28
Hankinson ◻ USA (ND) 172 Fb22
Hankensbüttel ◻ D 32 Ll38
Hanker ◻ IND (GUJ) 82 Pa35
Hankey ◻ ZA 155 Mc62
Hankinson ◻ USA (ND) 172 Fb22
Hanko = Hangö ◻ FIN 38 Mc31
Hanksville ◻ USA (UT) 171 Ee26
Hanley ◻ CDN (SK) 169 Eg20
Hammer Springs ◻ NZ 113 Tg67
Hanna ◻ CDN (AB) 169 Ed20
Hanna ◻ USA (WY) 171 Eg25
Hannagan Meadow ◻ USA (AZ) 171 Ef29
Hannahville Ind. Res. ◻ USA 173 Fg23
Hannibal ◻ USA (MO) 175 Fe26
Hannik ◻ SUD 135 Mg36
Hann, Mount ▲ AUS 103 Rc53
Hannover ◻ D 32 Lk38
Hannoversch Münden ◻ D 32 Lk39
Hannur ◻ IND (MHT) 82 Oj37
Hannut ◻ B 23 Lf40
Hanö ◻ S 31 Lp35
Hanöbukten ◻ S 31 Lp35
Hanoi ◻ CHN (YN) 173 Fk23
Hanover ◻ CDN (ON) 173 Fk23
Hanover ◻ ZA 155 Mc61
Hanover Road ◻ ZA 155 Mc61
Han Pijesak ◻ BIH 44 Lt46
Hanshou ◻ CHN (HN) 74 Qf31
Hansi ◻ IND (HYA) 80 Oh31
Hansnäs ◻ N 80 Oh31
Hans Merensky Nature Reserve ◻ ZA 152 Mf57
Hanson Bay ◻ AUS 110 Rj64
Hansthoim ◻ DK 30 Lj33
Han-sur-Nied ◻ F 23 Lg42
Hanten ◻ CHN (HUN) 74 Qf31
Hantamsberg ▲ ZA 154 Lk61
Hantau ◻ KZ 66 Og23
Hanti ◻ IND (BIH) 83 Pd33
Han Tombs ◻ CHN 74 Qf33
Hantoukoura ◻ BF 137 La39
Hanty-Mansijsk ◻ RUS 54 Ob06
Han UI ◻ CHN (NMZ) 71 Qk23
80 Oh31
Hanumana ◻ IND (MPH)
Hanumanesa nad Topl'ou ◻ SK 43 Mb41
Hanuovice ◻ CZ 42 Lr40
Hanwang ◻ CHN (SAA) 74 Qd30
Hanyin ◻ CHN (SAA) 72 Qe29
Hanyuan ◻ CHN (SAA) 74 Qb31
Hanzhong ◻ CHN (SAA) 72 Qe29
Hao Atoll ◻ F 11 Cb11
Haora ◻ IND (WBG) 86 Pe34
Haotan ◻ CHN (SAA) 72 Qe27
Haouch ◻ TCH 134 Ma39
Haousa-Foulane ◻ RMM 131 La37
Haoxue ◻ CHN (HUB) 74 Qg30
Háø̆ya ▲ N 16 Ma07
Hapai ◻ SOL 117 Sj50
Hapanda skärgårds n.p. ◻ ▦ S 16 Mb13
Hapçeranga ◻ RUS 70 Qg21
Hapo ◻ RI 91 Re44
Happy Camp ◻ USA (CA) 168 Dj25
Happy Corner ◻ USA (NH) 177 Ge23
Happy's Inn ◻ USA (MT) 168 Ec21
Happy Valley ◻ CHN (GDG) 75 Qh34
Happy Valley ◻ IND (UPH) 81 Oj31
Haputale ◻ CL 85 Pa42
Haql ◻ KSA 58 Mh31
Harabarjan ◻ IR 64 Nh30
Harad ◻ KSA 59 Ne33
Harad ◻ YE 60 Nb37
Harada ◻ KSA 60 Nd34
Haradok ◻ BY 48 Me18
Häradsbäck ◻ S 31 Lp34
Haradzdča ◻ BY 41 Mg37
Härakas ◻ GR 47 Mf55
Haramachi ◻ J 77 Sa27
Harappa ◻ ▦ PK 65 Og30
Harar (Babille) Elephant Sanctuary ◻ ETH 143 Nb41
Harar = Harrar ◻ ETH 143 Nb41
Haraukali ◻ PL 41 Mc40
Harat ◻ ER 135 Mk37
Harau Canyon ◻ RI 93 Qa46
Haraz-Djombo ◻ TCH 133 Lk39
Harbang ◻ BD 86 Pg35
Harbel ◻ LB 136 Kf43
Harberton ◻ RA (TDF) 210 Gf73
Harbin ◻ CHN (HLG) 76 Rb23
Harbo ◻ S 31 Ls30
Harbour Beach ◻ USA (MI) 173 Fl24
Harbour Breton ◻ CDN (NF) 177 Hc22
Harbour Deep ◻ CDN (NF) 177 Hb21
Harcourt ◻ AUS (VIC) 111 Sc64
Harda ◻ IND (MPH) 82 Oj34
Hardangerfjorden ◻ N 30 Lf31
Hardangervidda ▲ N 30 Lh30
Hardangervidda N.P. ◻ ▦ N 30 Lh30
Hardap ◻ NAM 154 Lj58
Hardap Recreational Resort ◻ NAM 154 Lj58
Hardapdam ▧ NAM 154 Lj58
Hard Bargain ◻ BS 179 Gb32
Hardelot-Plage ◻ F 23 Ld40
Hardenberg ◻ NL 23 Lg38
Harden, Gunung ▲ RI 94 Rh45
Hardin ◻ USA (KY) 175 Fg27
Hardin ◻ USA (IL) 175 Fe26
Hardin ◻ USA (MT) 169 Ef23
Harding ◻ ZA 155 Me61
Hardman ◻ USA (OR) 168 Ea23
Hardner ◻ USA (KS) 174 Fa27
Hardoi ◻ IND (UPH) 81 Pa32
Hardtner ◻ USA (KS) 174 Fa27
Hardwar ◻ IND 81 Ok31
Hardy ◻ CDN (AB) 169 Eg19
Harwood ◻ AUS (NSW) 109 Sg60
Hare Bay ◻ CDN (NF) 177 Hd21
Haren(Ems) ◻ D 32 Lh38
Harer ◻ ETH 142 Na41
Harewood ◻ CDN 169 Ea19
Harganı ◻ IND (KTK) 84 Oh38
Hargas nuur ◻ MNG 67 Pg21
Hasa Abdal ◻ PK 65 Og30

Hargele ◻ ETH 145 Nb43
Hargeysa ◻ SP 143 Nc41
Hargigo ◻ ER 142 Mk38
Harghasmam ◻ S 31 Lt30
Hangō = Hanko ◻ FIN 38 Mc31
Haridwar ◻ IND 81 Ok31
Haridspur ◻ IND (ORS) 83 Pd35
Haridwar ◻ IND (UTT) 81 Ok31
Harikanassou ◻ RN 132 Lb39
Harippad ◻ IND (KER) 84 Oj41
Harisah ◻ KSA 60 Nb34
Harisal ◻ IND (MHT) 82 Oj34
Harjavalta ◻ FIN 38 Mc29
Härjedalen ◻ S 16 Lg14
Harkány ◻ H 42 Lt45
Har-ki-Pauri ◻ IND 81 Ok31
Harlan ◻ USA (IA) 172 Fb25
Harlan ◻ USA (KY) 178 Fj27
Hârlau ◻ RO 44 Md22
Harlech Castle ◻ ▦ GB 21 Kq38
Harleigh Farm ◻ ZW 152 Mg55
Harlem ◻ USA (MT) 169 Ef21
Harlingen ◻ NL 23 Lf37
Harlingen ◻ USA (TX) 181 Fb32
Harlow ◻ GB 21 La39
Harlowton ◻ USA (MT) 169 Ef22
Harmancık ◻ TR 47 Mj51
Harmankiya ◻ FIN 16 Me13
Harmanli ◻ BG 45 Mf49
Harmelo ◻ S 17 Lj14
Harmonia ◻ BR 205 Hb60
Harmu ◻ PK 65 Oe30
Harnai ◻ PK 65 Oe30
Harnes ◻ F 23 Lc40
Harney Basin ◻ USA 168 Ea24
Haro ◻ E 28 Ks48
Haro Shiikh ◻ SP 143 Nc41
Harpanahalli ◻ IND (KTK) 84 Oh38
Harper ◻ LB 136 Kg43
Harper ◻ USA (KS) 174 Fa27
Harper ◻ USA (OR) 168 Eb24
Harpers Ferry N.H.P. ◻ USA 177 Ga26
Harpersville ◻ USA (AL) 175 Fg29
Harpeth Narrows Historic Area ◻ USA 175 Fg27
Harput Kalesi ◻ TR 57 Na26
Harqin ◻ CHN (NMZ) 73 Qk25
Harqin Qi ◻ CHN (NMZ) 73 Qk25
Harrat al Buqum ◻ KSA 60 Na35
Harrat al Kishb ◻ KSA 60 Na34
Harrat al ,Uwayrid ◻ KSA 58 Mj32
Harrat Hadan ◻ KSA 60 Na35
Harrat Khaybar ◻ KSA 58 Mk33
Harrat Kurama ◻ KSA 58 Mk33
Harrat Lunayyir ◻ KSA 58 Mj33
Harrat Nawasif ◻ KSA 60 Na35
Harratola ◻ IND (MPH) 83 Pa34
Harrat Rahat ◻ KSA 60 Na34
Harrel ◻ IND (MPH) 83 Ok34
Harriburg ◻ LB 136 Ke42
Harriman ◻ USA (TN) 175 Fh28
Harrington ◻ AUS (NSW)
Harrington Harbour ◻ CDN (QC) 176 Ha20
Harripur ◻ PK 65 Og29
Harris ◻ GB 20 Ko33
Harris, Mount ◻ CDN (AB) 175 Fe28
Harrisburg ◻ USA (AR) 175 Fe28
Harrisburg ◻ USA (IL) 175 Ff27
Harrisburg ◻ USA (PA) 177 Gb25
Hasslö ◻ S 31 Lq34
Harris, Mount ▲ AUS 103 Re58
Harrisonburg ◻ USA (VA) 177 Ga26
Harrisonville ◻ USA (MO) 174 Fc26
Harrodsburg ◻ USA (KY) 175 Fh27
Harrogate ◻ CDN (BC) 168 Eb20
Harrogate ◻ GB 21 Kt37
Harrow ◻ AUS (VIC) 110 Sa64
Harrström ◻ FIN 38 Mb28
Harry S. Truman S.P. ◻ USA 174 Fd26
Harsani ◻ IND (RJT) 80 Of32
Harsefeld ◻ D 32 Lk37
Harsin ◻ IR 57 Nd28
Harsor ◻ IND (RJT) 80 Oh32
Hårsovo ◻ BG 45 Mg47
Harstad ◻ N 16 Lj11
Harsum ◻ D 32 Lk38
Harsvik ◻ N 16 Lf13
Hart ◻ USA (MI) 173 Fg24
Harta ◻ H 43 Lu44
Hartbeesfontein ◻ ZA 155 Md59
Hartford ◻ A 35 Lq43
Hartford ◻ LB 136 Ke42
Hartford ◻ USA (CT) 177 Gd25
Hartford City ◻ USA (IN) 173 Fh25
Hartheigh ◻ GB 21 Kq40
Hartbei ◻ USA (UPH) 81 Oh32
Ha Tinh ◻ VN 87 Qd36
Hatkhamba ◻ IND (MHT) 82 Og37
Hartland Covered Bridge ◻ ▦ CDN 176 Gg22
Hartland ◻ IND (UPH) 81 Oj30
Hartlepool ◻ GB 21 Kt36
Hartley Bay ◻ CDN (BC)
Hartmannberge ◻ ▦ NAM 150 Lf55
Hart, Mount ◻ AUS 103 Rc53
Hart, Mount ▲ CDN 169 Ek19
Hart Mtn. Nat. Antelope Refuge ◻ USA 168 Ea24
Hartola ◻ FIN 38 Mg29
Hart Ranges ◻ CDN 166 Dj18
Hartseer ◻ NAM 150 Lj56
Hartselle ◻ USA (AL) 175 Fg28
Harts Range ◻ AUS (NT) 108 Rh57
Harts Range ◻ AUS 108 Rh57
Hartsville ◻ USA (MO) 174 Fd27
Hartsville ◻ USA (SC) 178 Fk28
Hartwell ◻ USA (GA) 178 Fk28
Haruku ◻ RI 97 Re47
Harun = Gunung Harden ▲ RI 94 Qh43
Harun ◻ KSA 60 Nb37
Harunabad ◻ PK 65 Og31
Har nuur = Har nuur ◻ MNG 67 Pg21
Harvale ◻ IND (GOA) 82 Oh38
Harvey ◻ AUS (WA) 104 Qh62
Harvey ◻ CDN (NB) 176 Gg23
Harvey ◻ USA (ND) 172 Fa22
Harvest Home ◻ AUS (QLD) 107 Sd56
Harwich ◻ GB 21 Lb39
Har Yai ◻ THA 88 Qa42
Harz N.P. ◻ ▦ D 32 Ll39
Harzgerode ◻ D 32 Ll39
Hargas nuur ◻ MNG 67 Pg21

Hasaat ◻ MNG 70 Qc23
Hasama ◻ J 77 Sa26
Hasanabad ◻ IR 57 Nf28
Hasan Abad ◻ IR (APH) 80 Ok36
Hasan Abad ◻ IR 64 Ng29
Hasan Abad ◻ IR 64 Ng28
Hasançelebi ◻ TR 56 Mj26
Hasankale ◻ TR 57 Nb27
Hasankale ◻ TR 57 Na27
Hasankeyf ◻ TR 57 Na27
Hasanpur ◻ IND (UPH) 81 Ok31
Hasarah ◻ KSA 60 Nb34
Hasdang Reserve ◻ TR 62 Kj29
Hasavjurt ◻ RUS (DAG) 57 Nd24
Haselünne ◻ D 32 Lh38
Hashab ◻ SUD 134 Mc39
Hashimoto ◻ J 79 Rh29
Hasik ◻ OM 61 Nh37
Haskell ◻ USA (TX) 174 Fa29
Haskovo ◻ BG 45 Mf49
Hasle ◻ DK 31 Lp35
Haslev ◻ DK 30 Lm35
Haslo ◻ USA (MT) 169 Ef21
Harlingen ◻ NL 23 Lf37
Harlowton ◻ USA (MT) 169 Ef22
Härlev ◻ DK 30 Ln35
Harley ◻ IR 64 Nk30
Haslemere ◻ GB 21 Kt40
Härnä ◻ S 17 Lj14
Haro ◻ E 28 Ks48
Haslamah ◻ SUD 134 Md40
Hassasparren ◻ F 24 Kt47
Hassa ◻ TR 56 Mj27
Hassan ◻ IND (KTK) 84 Oj39
Hassanli ◻ IRQ 61 Ng30
Hasselo ◻ S 31 Lr34
Hasselt ◻ B 23 Lf40
Hasselt ◻ NL 23 Lg38
Havlíčkův Brod ◻ CZ 42 Lq41
Hassfurt ◻ D 33 Ll40
Hassi Bahbah ◻ DZ 126 Lb28
Hassi Barroukah ◻ DZ 126 Lc29
Hassi Bel Guebbour ◻ DZ 126 Ld31
Hassi Berrekhem ◻ DZ 126 Lc29
Hassi-Bou-Allala ◻ DZ 125 Kj29
Hassi Daoula ◻ DZ 126 Lc29
Hassi Delia ◻ DZ 126 Lc29
Hassi-el-Belerm ◻ DZ 125 Kj29
Hassi el Ghella ◻ DZ 125 Kk28
Hassi-el-Hadjar ◻ DZ 126 Lc28
Hassi el Khannfous ◻ DZ
Hassi el-Khenig ◻ DZ 126 Lc30
Hassi el Klebi ◻ DZ 125 Kj29
Hassi el Mounir ◻ DZ 125 Kg31
Hassi-Fahl ◻ DZ 126 Lc30
Hassi Fougani ◻ MA 125 Kh30
Hassi Fouini ◻ RIM 131 Kj37
Hassi Habadra ◻ DZ 126 Lc30
Hassi Hadhour ◻ DZ 126 Lb30
Hassi Ifertas ◻ DZ 126 Lb30
Hassi Inifel ◻ DZ 126 Lb30
Hassi Ismoulaye ◻ DZ 126 Lc29
Hassi Issendjel ◻ DZ 126 Lb29
Hassi Karkabane ◻ RMM 131 Kk37
Hassi Kord Myriem ◻ DZ 125 Kj31
Hassi-Mahzez ◻ DZ 125 Kh31
Hassi Marraket ◻ DZ 126 Lb30
Hassi Messaoud ◻ DZ 126 Lc29
Hassi Moussa ◻ DZ 125 La31
Hassi Ntsel ◻ DZ 126 Ld32
Hassi Ramad ◻ DZ 126 Lc28
Hassi el Erg ◻ DZ 126 Lb29
Hassi-R'Mel ◻ DZ 126 Lb29
Hassi Safiei Iniguel ◻ DZ 126 Lc30
Hassi Settafa ◻ DZ 126 Lc29
Hassi Tabankort ◻ DZ 126 Lb30
Hassi Tabelbalet ◻ DZ 126 Ld30
Hassi Tartrat ◻ DZ 124 Kg32
Hassi Touil ◻ RIM 131 Kh37
Hasslo ◻ S 31 Lq34
Hasslö ◻ S 31 Lq34
Hastings ◻ GB 21 La40
Hastings ◻ NZ 113 Tj65
Hastings ◻ USA (MI) 173 Fh24
Hastings ◻ USA (MN) 172 Fd23
Hastings ◻ USA (NE) 174 Fa25
Hastings Island ◻ MYA 88 Pk40
Hastings Island ◻ PNG 116 Sf51
Hastpar ◻ IR 57 Ne27
Hästvadā ◻ S 31 Lo34
Hasvayn ◻ YE 61 Ng38
Hasy Hague ◻ LAR 128 Lf32
Hasy in Aguel ◻ LAR 128 Lf32
Hasy Tissan ◻ LAR 127 Lg31
Hata ◻ IND (UPH) 83 Pb32
Hatanga ◻ RUS 54 Qa04
Hatangskij zaliv ◻ RUS 55 Qb04
Hatay ◻ TR 56 Mj27
Hatches Creek ◻ AUS (NT) 106 Rh56
Hatch Creek ◻ USA (WY) 171 Eh24
Hat Creek Hist. Ranch ◻ CDN 167 Ea17
Hateg ◻ RO 44 Mc45
Hatfield al ◻ AUS 111 Sb62
Hat Gamaria ◻ IND (JKD) 83 Pc34
Hathazari ◻ BD 86 Pf34
Hat Head N.P. ◻ AUS 109 Sg61
Hathersleigh ◻ GB 21 Kq40
Hathras ◻ IND (UPH) 81 Ok32
Hatia ◻ IND 83 Pd34
Hatiman ◻ J 79 Rj29
Hatinh ◻ VN 87 Qd36
Hatkulkyne N.P. ◻ AUS 111 Sb63
Hato Corozal ◻ CO 199 Gd43
Hato la Vergareña ◻ YV 193 Gj42
Hato Mayor ◻ DOM 186 Gf36
Hatpasa ◻ RI 97 Re49
Hatra ◻ ▦ IRQ 57 Nb28
Hatreal ◻ DZ 126 Lc29
Hatsheur, Cerro ▲ RA 210 Gd70
Hatta ◻ IND (MPH) 82 Ok33
Hatta ◻ UAE 61 Nh34
Hattah ◻ AUS (VIC) 110 Sb63
Hattah-Kulkyne N.P. ◻ AUS 111 Sb63
Hatten ◻ USA (CO) 171 Eh26
Hattfjelldal ◻ N 16 Lh13
Hat Thai Muang N.P. ◻ THA 88 Pk41
Hattiesburg ◻ USA (MS) 175 Ff30
Hattingen ◻ D 32 Lh39
Hatton-Dikoya ◻ CL 85 Pa42
Hattula ◻ FIN 38 Me29
Hattusas ◻ ▦ TR 56 Mh26
Hatvan ◻ H 43 Lu43
Hat Wanakon N.P. ◻ THA 88 Qa41
Hatzfeldt-Wildenburg ◻ D 32 Lj40
Hatzic ◻ CDN (BC) 168 Dj21
Hatyai ◻ THA 88 Qa42
Hatzfeldhaven ◻ PNG 115 Sc48
Hatztat Island ◻ USA 178 Gc28
Hau Bon ◻ VN 89 Qe39
Haugastøl ◻ N 30 Lh30
Haugesund ◻ N 30 Lf31
Hauho ◻ FIN 38 Me30
Haukelseter ◻ N 30 Lh31
Haukipudas ◻ FIN 16 Me12
Haukivuori ◻ FIN 38 Mg28

Hauraha ◻ SOL 117 Ta51
Hauraki Gulf ◻ NZ 112 Th64
Hausach ◻ D 33 Lj42
Hausdiha ◻ IND (JKD) 83 Pd33
Hausen ◻ D 33 Lk42
Haut Atlas ◻ MA 124 Kf30
Haut Campi ◻ F 24 Kt41
Hautefort ◻ F 24 Lb39
Hautes Fagnes ◻ B 23 Lf40
Haut-Kœnigsbourg ◻ ▦ F 25 Lh42
Hauts Plateaux ◻ DZ 126 Lb28
Hauts Plateaux de l'Ouest ◻ WAN 138 Le42
Hauzenberg ◻ D 33 Lo42
Havalli ◻ KSA 60 Na36
Havana ◻ USA (IL) 175 Fe25
Havana ◻ USA (FL) 175 Fj30
Havant ◻ GB 21 Kt40
Havasupai Ind. Res. ◻ USA 171 Ed27
Havdhem ◻ S 31 Lt33
Havel ◻ D 32 Lm38
Havelberg ◻ D 32 Lm38
Havelian ◻ PK 65 Og29
Haveli Lakkha ◻ PK 65 Og30
Havelock ◻ USA (NC) 178 Gb28
Havelock ◻ CDN (ON) 173 Gb23
Havelock Island ◻ IND 88 Pg40
Haven ◻ IND (KTK) 84 Oh38
Haverfordwest ◻ GB 21 Kp39
Haverhill ◻ GB 21 La38
Haverhill ◻ USA (MA) 177 Ge24
Haversin ◻ B 23 Lf41
Haveselö ◻ S 31 Lr34
Hasselt ◻ B 23 Lf40
Havířov ◻ CZ 42 Lt41
Havíkvuori ◻ FIN 38 Mg28
Havneby ◻ DK 30 Lk35
Havøysund ◻ N 16 Mc10
Havran ◻ TR 47 Mh51
Havre ◻ USA (MT) 169 Ef21
Havre-Aubert ◻ CDN 176 Gj21
Havre-Saint-Pierre ◻ CDN (QC) 176 Gj20
Havrylivka ◻ UA 49 Mj21
Hawaii ◻ TR 56 Mj26
Hawza ◻ TR 56 Mj25
Hawaii ◻ USA (HI) 170 Ca35
Hawaiian Islands ◻ USA 170
Hawaiian Ridge ◻ USA 170 Bk34
Hawaii Volcanoes N.P. ◻ USA 170 Cc36
Hawalli ◻ KWT 59 Nd31
Hawa Mahal ◻ ▦ IND 80 Oh32
Hawarden ◻ CDN (SK) 169 Eg20
Hawer Islands ◻ BRN 59 Nf33
Hawera ◻ NZ 113 Th65
Hawesville ◻ USA (KY) 175 Ff30
Hawi ◻ USA (HI) 170 Cb35
Hawick ◻ GB 20 Ks35
Hawke Bay ◻ NZ 113 Tj65
Hawker ◻ AUS (SA) 108 Rk61
Hawke's Bay ◻ CDN (NF) 177 Hb20
Hawkes Bay Green Turtle Beach ◻ PK 65 Od33
Hawkesbury ◻ CDN (ON) 177 Gc23
Hawkeye ◻ USA 166 Df19
Hawkes Nest ◻ AUS (NSW) 111 Sg62
Hawk Inlet ◻ USA (AK) 166 Dc16
Hawkins Bay ◻ USA 165 Cg15
Hawkinsville ◻ USA (GA)
Hawks Head Lookout ◻ AUS 104 Qh59
Hawk Springs ◻ USA (WY) 171 Eh25
Hawrah ◻ YE 60 Ne38
Hawrat Sudayr ◻ KSA 59 Nc33
Hawthorne ◻ USA (NV) 170 Ea26
Hawza ◻ DARS 124 Kg32
Hawzen ◻ ETH 142 Mk39
Haxtun ◻ USA (CO) 174 Ej25
Haya ◻ SUD 135 Mk38
Haya ◻ TR 56 Mg26
Hayange ◻ F 23 Lg41
Hayang ◻ SUD 135 Mf40
Haydar ◻ KSA 58 Mj32
Hayden ◻ USA (CO) 171 Eg25
Haydere ◻ TR 56 Me27
Haycock Park ◻ AUS 21 Ks37
Hayes Creek ◻ AUS (NT) 106 Rf52
Hayes Halvø ◻ DK 163 Gc09
Hayes, Mount ◻ USA 165 Cg14
Hayfield ◻ PNG 115 Sb49
Hayle ◻ GB 21 Ko40
Hay, Mount ◻ AUS 103 Rc53
Hayman ◻ YE 60 Ne38
Haynesville ◻ USA (LA) 175 Fd29
Hayrabolu ◻ TR 47 Mh49
Hay River ◻ CDN 167 Ec15
Hays ◻ USA (KS) 174 Fa26
Hay Springs ◻ USA (NE) 169 Ek24
Hays Mountains ◻ 6 Cc36
Haystack Mount ◻ USA 165 Cd13
Haystack Peak ◻ USA 174 Fc27
Haysville ◻ USA (KS) 174 Fa27
Hayti ◻ USA (MO) 175 Fe27
Hayuliang ◻ IND (ARP) 86 Ph31
Hayward ◻ USA (CA) 170 Dj27
Hayward ◻ USA (WI) 172 Fe23
Haywards Heath ◻ GB 21 Kt40
Hazard ◻ USA (KY) 178 Fj27
Hazarduari Palace ◻ IND 86 Pe33
Hazaribagh ◻ IND (JKD) 83 Pc34
Hazaribagh ◻ IND (HPH) 81 Oj30
Hazaroanjı Chiltan N.P. ◻ PK 65 Od30
Hazarganji N.P. Markhor Leopard ◻ PK 65 Od30
Hazarganji N.P. Markhor ◻ PK 65 Od30
Hazbek ◻ RL 56 Mj28
Hazazou ◻ TR 56 Mj29
Hazrat Khairuddin Mausoleum ◻ ▦ PK 65 Og32
Hazebrouck ◻ F 23 Lc40
Hazelton ◻ CDN (BC) 166 Dg18
Hazelton ◻ USA (ND) 172 Ek22
Hazelton Mtns. ◻ CDN 166 Dg18
Hazen Bay ◻ USA 164 Bh15
Hazen Strait ◻ CDN 162 Ec03
Hazin ◻ KSA 59 Ne33
Hazira ◻ IND (GUJ) 82 Og35
Hazleton ◻ USA (PA) 177 Gc25
Hazlet ◻ CDN (SK) 169 Ef20
Hazmiya ◻ RL 56 Mh29
Hazmbaba Duhaym ◻ KSA 58 Mk31
Hazu ◻ TR 56 Mj29
Hazlehurst ◻ USA (MS) 175 Fe30

Hebbe Falls ◻ ▦ IND 84 Oh39
Hebbronville ◻ USA (TX) 181 Fa32
Helvécia ◻ BR (BA) 203 Ja54
Hebbronville ◻ USA (TX) 181 Fa32
Hebei ◻ CHN 73 Qj26
Hebel ◻ AUS (QLD) 109 Sd60
Hebenshausen ◻ D 32 Lk39
Hebenshausen ◻ D 33 Lk39
Heber City ◻ USA (UT) 171 Ee25
Heber Springs ◻ USA (AR) 175 Fe28
Heber ◻ S 30 Lm34
Hebrides ◻ GB 14 Ko34
Hebron ◻ CDN 163 Gd07
Hebron ◻ IL 58 Mh30
Hebron ◻ USA (ND) 169 Ej22
Hebron ◻ USA (NE) 174 Fb25
Heby ◻ S 31 Lr31
Hecate Strait ◻ CDN 166 De19
Hecelchakán ◻ MEX (CAM) 183 Fe35
Hechi ◻ CHN 73 Qd33
Hechingen ◻ D 33 Lj42
Hechuan ◻ CHN (CGQ) 74 Qd30
Hecla ◻ CDN (MB) 172 Fb20
Hecla/Grindstone Prov. Park ◻ CDN 172 Fb20
Hecla Island ◻ CDN 172 Fb20
Hector ◻ NZ 113 Tf66
Hectorspruit ◻ ZA 155 Mf58
Hector Tejada ◻ PE 197 Ge53
Heddal ◻ N 31 Lk31
Heddal stavkirke ◻ ▦ N 30 Lk31
Hédé ◻ F 24 Kt42
Hede ◻ S 17 Lg14
Hedemora ◻ S 31 Lq30
Hedensted ◻ DK 30 Lk35
Hedesunda ◻ S 31 Lr30
Heek ◻ D 32 Lh38
Heerde ◻ NL 23 Lg38
Heerenveen ◻ NL 23 Lf38
Heerhugowaard ◻ NL 23 Le38
Heerlen ◻ NL 23 Lg40
Heeze ◻ NL 23 Lf39
Heezen Fracture Zone ◻ ANT 6 Ea30
Hefa ◻ IL 56 Mh29
Hefei ◻ CHN (AHU) 78 Qk29
Hefeng ◻ CHN (HUB) 74 Qf31
Heffley Creek ◻ CDN (BC) 168 Dk20
Heflin ◻ USA (AL) 175 Fh29
Hegang ◻ CHN (HLG) 76 Rf22
Hegura-jima ◻ J 77 Rj27
Hegytelő ◻ H 42 Lt43
Hehelek ◻ CHN (XUZ) 68 Pb27
Heho ◻ MYA 86 Ph35
Hehua ◻ CHN (HUB) 74 Qf31
Heide ◻ D 32 Lk36
Heidelberg ◻ D 33 Lj41
Heidelberg ◻ ZA 154 Lk62
Heidelberg ◻ ZA 155 Md59
Heidenau ◻ D 32 Lo40
Heidenheim ◻ D 33 Ll42
Heiðmörk ◻ IS 18 Jz27
Heihe ◻ CHN (HLG) 71 Rd20
Heijing ◻ CHN (YUN) 74 Qb32
Heijiang ◻ CHN (SCH) 74 Qc31
Heikendorf ◻ D 32 Lc38
Heilbron ◻ ZA 155 Md59
Heilbronn ◻ D 33 Lk41
Heiligenblut ◻ A 35 Ln43
Heiligenhafen ◻ D 32 Ll36
Heiligenstadt ◻ D 32 Ll39
Heilongjiang ◻ CHN 53 Ra05
Heilong Jiang ◻ CHN 76 Rf22
Heiloo ◻ NL 23 Le38
Heimaey ◻ IS 18 Jt27
Heimahe ◻ CHN (QHI) 69 Pk27
Heimefrontfjella ◻ 6 Ka33
Heinola ◻ FIN 38 Mg29
Heinsberg ◻ D 32 Lg40
Heira Chaung ◻ MYA 88 Pj38
Heishan ◻ CHN (LNG) 76 Rb24
Heishantou ◻ CHN (NMZ) 71 Qk20
Heishui ◻ CHN (SCH) 72 Qb28
Heitoral ◻ BR (GO) 202 Hf53
Heitske ◻ D 114 Rh49
Heituinaitu ◻ FIN 38 Md30
Hejanneh ◻ SYR 56 Mj29
Hejaz ◻ KSA 58 Mj32
Hejian ◻ CHN (HBI) 73 Qj26
Hejiang ◻ CHN (SCH) 74 Qc31
Hejing ◻ CHN (XUZ) 67 Pd24
Hekimhan ◻ TR 56 Mj26
Hekla ◻ IS 18 Jz27
Hekou ◻ CHN (GSU) 72 Qc27
Hekou ◻ CHN (HUB) 75 Qg30
Hekou ◻ CHN (SAX) 73 Qg28
Hekou ◻ CHN (YUN) 74 Qc34
Hel Abad ◻ IR 57 Ne27
Helan ◻ CHN (NHZ) 72 Qd26
Helan Shan ◻ CHN 72 Qc26
Helan Z.B. ◻ CHN 72 Qc26
Helbra ◻ D 32 Ll39
Helen ◻ USA (GA) 178 Fj28
Helena ◻ USA (AR) 175 Fe28
Helena ◻ USA (MT) 169 Ed22
Helen Springs Roadhouse ◻ AUS (NT) 106 Rg54
Helen Springs ◻ AUS 106 Rg54
Helensburgh ◻ GB 20 Kq34
Helensville ◻ NZ 112 Th64
Helgoland ◻ D 32 Lj36
Helgolander Bucht ◻ D 32 Lj36
Heli ◻ CHN (HLG) 76 Rf22
Heliopolis ◻ ET 129 Mf31
Helixi ◻ CHN (AHU) 78 Qk30
Hella ◻ IS 18 Jz27
Hella ◻ USA (AHU) 78 Qk30
Hellin ◻ E 29 Kt52
Hell Ville = Andoany ◻ ▦ RM
Hellissandur ◻ IS 18 Jt26
Hells Canyon ◻ USA 168 Eb23
Hells Canyon Nat. Rec. Area ◻ USA 168 Eb23
Hells Gate Airtram ◻ ▦ CDN
Hellsvik ◻ N 17 Ld14
Hellvoetsluis ◻ NL 23 Le39
Hellín ◻ E 29 Kt52
Helmand ◻ AFG 64 Ob29
Helmbrechts ◻ D 32 Lm40
Helmond ◻ NL 23 Lf39
Helmsdale ◻ GB 20 Kr32
Helmsdal ◻ S 31 Lp31
Helmstedt ◻ D 32 Ll38
Helodrano Antongila ◻ RM 157 Nb56
Helodrano Antsiranana ◻ RM 157 Nd53
Helodrano Fanemotra ◻ RM 157 Nd54
Helong ◻ CHN (JLN) 76 Rd24
Helper ◻ USA (UT) 171 Ee26
Helsingborg ◻ S 30 Ln34
Helsingfors = Helsinki ◻ FIN 38 Me30
Helsingør ◻ DK 30 Ln34
Helsinki = Helsingfors ◻ FIN 38 Me30
Helston ◻ GB 21 Kp40

Heltermaa ◻ EST 38 Md32
Helvécia ◻ BR (BA) 203 Ja54
Helvellyn ◻ GB 21 Kr36
Helvenjärven kansallispuisto ◻ ▦ FIN 38 Md28
Hemau ◻ D 33 Lm41
Hemavan ◻ S 16 Lh13
Hemel Hempstead ◻ GB 21 Kt39
Hemet ◻ USA (CA) 170 Eb29
Hemingford ◻ USA (NE) 171 Ej24
Hemis Monastery ◻ ▦ IND 81 Oj29
Hemling ◻ S 16 Lk14
Hemmoor ◻ D 32 Lk37
Hemnes ◻ N 16 Lg12
Hemnesberget ◻ N 16 Lg12
Hemphill ◻ USA (TX) 174 Fc30
Hempstead ◻ USA (TX) 174 Fb30
Herónia ◻ GR 46 Mc52
Heron Island ◻ 109 Sf57
Herradura ◻ RA (FO) 204 Ha59
Herrenchiemsee ◻ D 33 Ln43
Herrera de la Ros ◻ E 27 Kt49
Herrera del Duque ◻ E 27 Kp51
Herrera de los Navarros ◻ E 29 Kt49
Herrera de Pisuerga ◻ E 26 Kq48
Hendaye ◻ F 24 Kt47
Hendek ◻ TR 56 Mf25
Herrljunga ◻ S 30 Lo32
Henderson ◻ RA 209 Gk64
Henderson ◻ USA (KY) 175 Fg27
Herschel ◻ ZA 155 Md61
Henderson ◻ USA (NC) 178 Ga27
Herschel Akrotiri ◻ GR 47 Mc55
Henderson ◻ USA (NE) 174 Fb25
Herschel ◻ ZA 155 Md61
Hendiján ◻ IR 59 Ne30
Hersónisos Rodópou ◻ GR 46 Mc55
Hendon ◻ USA (MB) 169 Ej19
Hersónisos Tiganis ◻ GR 45 Md55
Hendijan ◻ IR 64 Ng29
Herstal ◻ B 23 Lf40
Hendorabi ◻ IR 64 Ng32
Hendrina ◻ ZA 155 Me59
Hervás ◻ E 27 Kp50
Hendersonville ◻ USA (TN) 175 Fg27
Hervey Bay ◻ AUS (QLD) 109 Sg58
Hendijan ◻ IR 64 Ng29
Hervey Junction ◻ CDN (QC) 176 Gd22
Henganofi ◻ PNG 115 Sc49
Herzberg ◻ D 32 Lm39
Hengduan Shan ◻ CHN 87 Px32
Herzberg ◻ D 32 Lm39
Hengelo ◻ NL 23 Lg38
Herzliya ◻ IL 56 Mh29
Heng Shan ◻ CHN 73 Qg28
Herzogenaurach ◻ D 33 Ll41
Heng Shan ◻ CHN 74 Qg32
Herzogswalde ◻ CHN 75 Qf32
Henderson ◻ USA (TX) 174 Fc29
Hesdin ◻ F 23 Lc40
Hendersonville ◻ USA (NC)
Heshan ◻ CHN 73 Qd33
Hendijan ◻ IR 64 Ng29
Heshengqiao ◻ CHN (GZG) 74 Qe34
Hengyang ◻ CHN (HUN) 74 Qg32
Hengyang ◻ CHN (HUN) 74 Qg32
Henices'k ◻ UA 49 Mh22
Héni-Beaumont ◻ F 23 Lc40
Hénin-Beaumont ◻ F 23 Lc40
Heiðdé-Park ◻ D 32 Lf39
Heiðin há ◻ IS 18 Jz27
Hennan ◻ S 17 Lh14
Hennef ◻ D 32 Lh40
Hennessey ◻ USA (OK) 174 Fb27
Henoles ◻ F 25 Lh44
Henrichemont ◻ F 25 Lc43
Henneborn ◻ D 33 Lt44
Henrietta ◻ USA (TX) 174 Fa29
Henrique ◻ BR (AM) 198 Gk48
Herschel ◻ ZA 155 Md61
Henry Lawrence Island ◻ ▦ IND
Henryetta ◻ USA (OK) 174 Fc28
Henry Ford Museum (Dearborn, MI) ◻ USA 173 Fj24
Hevelándia ◻ BR (AM) 198 Gk48
Henties Bay ◻ NAM 150 Lf57
Heves ◻ H 43 Ma43
Hesdin ◻ F 23 Lc40
Henty ◻ AUS (NSW) 111 Sd63
Hevron ◻ IL 58 Mh30
Henvey Inlet Ind. Res. ◻ CDN 173 Fj23
Hewart Downs ◻ AUS (NSW) 108 Sa60
Hen Xian ◻ CHN (HNN) 73 Qg28
Hexham ◻ GB 20 Ks36
Henzada ◻ MYA 88 Ph37
Hexi ◻ CHN (SCH) 87 Qb32
Hepburn ◻ CDN (SK) 169 Eg20
He Xian ◻ CHN (AHU) 78 Qk30
Heping ◻ CHN (GDG) 75 Qh33
Hexigten Qi ◻ CHN (NMZ) 73 Qj24
Hepner ◻ USA (OR) 168 Ea23
Heqing ◻ CHN (GZG) 74 Qe35
Hervieierberge ◻ ZA 154 Ld62
Heping ◻ CHN (GZG) 74 Qe34
Hey Camp ◻ USA (AD) 167 Ea16
Hepu ◻ CHN (GZG) 73 Qf34
Heydaliar ◻ IR 57 Ne28
Heqing ◻ CHN (GZG) 74 Qe35
Heydār ◻ IR 57 Ne28
Heraclea ◻ MK 46 Mb50
Heydar ◻ ZA 155 Mc61
Heradalir ◻ IS 18 Jz27
Heyrieux ◻ F 25 Le45
Herald Cays ◻ AUS 107 Se54
Heys Xian ◻ CHN (HNN) 73 Qg28
Heraneny ◻ BY 41 Mf38
Heywood ◻ CHN (GDG) 75 Qh34
Herbagat ◻ CHN (GDG) 75 Qh34
Heywood ◻ AUS (VIC) 110 Sa65
Herbert ◻ CDN (SK) 169 Ef20
Heywood Islands ◻ AUS 103 Rc53
Herbert ◻ NZ 113 Tf68
Herbertabad ◻ IND (UTT) 81 Ok30
Hialeah ◻ USA (FL) 179 Fk33
Herbertdale ◻ ZA 154 Lk62
Hiawassee ◻ USA (GA) 178 Fj28
Herbertville ◻ USA (TX) 174 Fc29
Hiawatha ◻ USA (KS) 174 Fc26
Herceg-Novi ◻ ▦ SCG 44 Lt48
Hiawatha ◻ IRQ 57 Nb28
Herbert Vale ◻ AUS (QLD) 106 Rk55
Hibbing ◻ USA (MN) 172 Fd22
Herceg-Novi ◻ ▦ SCG 44 Lt48
Hibberdene ◻ ZA 155 Mf61
Hercilópolis ◻ BR (SC) 204 He59
Hibbing ◻ USA (MN) 172 Fd22
Hercules Bay ◻ PNG 115 Sd49
Hibbs, Point ◻ AUS 111 Sc67
Hercílio ◻ BR 204 Hg57
Hibernia Reef ◻ AUS 102 Rb50
Hickman, Mount ◻ CDN 166 De17
Herdubreid ◻ IS 18 Ka26
Hickory Motor Speedway ◻ USA 178 Fk28
Hereford ◻ GB 21 Ks38
Hereford ◻ USA (CO) 171 Eh25
Hicks Bay ◻ NZ 112 Tk64
Hereford ◻ USA (TX) 174 Ej28
Hick's Cays ◻ BH 184 Fg37
Herefoss ◻ N 30 Lk31
Hico ◻ USA (TX) 174 Fa30
Hereke ◻ TR 45 Mk50
Hidaka ◻ J 77 Sb24
Herentals ◻ B 23 Le39
Hidalgo ◻ MEX (COH) 180 Eg30
Hérford ◻ D 32 Lk39
Hidalgo ◻ MEX (COH) 181 Fa32
Hergla ◻ TN 126 Lg27
Hidalgo ◻ MEX (NL) 181 Fa33
Héricourt ◻ F 25 Lg43
Hidalgo ◻ MEX (ZCT) 182 Ej34
Hermagor ◻ A 35 Lo44
Hidalgo ◻ MEX (SO)
Herman ◻ USA (MN) 172 Fb23
Hidalgo del Parral ◻ MEX (CHH) 180 Eg32
Hermanburg ◻ AUS (NT)
Hidalgo ◻ MEX (SO)
Hidalgo ◻ RA (FO) 208 Gj62
Hidas-sanmyaku ◻ J 79 Rj27
Hermannsdenkmal ◻ ▦ D 32 Lj39
Hidden Bay ◻ USA (AK) 165 Ca17
Hermansó ◻ S 17 Lj14
Hidden Valley ◻ AUS (QLD) 107 Sd55
Hermel ◻ RL 56 Mj28
Hidden Valley ◻ AUS (NT)
Hermidale ◻ AUS (NSW) 107 Sd55
Hidden Valley ◻ AUS (QLD) 107 Sd55
Hermiston ◻ USA (OR) 168 Ea22
Hidden Valley N.P. = Mirima National Park ◻ AUS 103 Rd53
Hermon, Mount ▲ RL 56 Mh29
Hermosa ◻ MEX (SO) 180 Ee31
Hidrelétrica Curuá-Una ◻ BR (PA) 199 Hc47
Hieflau ◻ A 35 Lp43
Hienghène ◻ F 118 Tc56
Hermannsfjorden ◻ N 87 Qg37
Hermannsfjorden ◻ ZA 155 Md58
Hierapolis ◻ ▦ TR 47 Mk53
Higgins Bay ◻ CDN (MB) 172 Fa19
Higashine ◻ J 77 Sa26
Hermitage Bay ◻ CDN (NF)
Highborn Cay ◻ BS 179 Gb33
Highbury ◻ AUS (QLD) 107 Sc53
Highbury ◻ GUY 194 Ha42
Highflats ◻ ZA 155 Mf61
High Island ◻ USA (TX) 174 Fc31
High Island ◻ USA 164 Bd16
Highland Plains ◻ AUS 106 Rj55

Hvanneyri – Isla de los Riachos

Hvanneyri IS 18 Jt26
Hvanngiljafoss IS 18 Ka26
Hvar HR 35 Lr47
Hvar HR 35 Lr47
Hvastoviči RUS 48 Mh19
Hveragerði IS 18 Jt27
Hveravellir IS 18 Ka26
Hvide Sande DK 30 Lj35
Hvittingfoss N 30 Lk31
Hvolsvöllur IS 18 Ju27
Hvostovo RUS 77 Sb22
Hwali ZW 152 Me56
Hwange ZW 152 Md55
Hwange N.P. ZW 152 Md55
Hwaseong Fortress ROK 78 Rd27
Hwasun Dolmen Site ROK 78 Rd28
Hwedza ZW 152 Mf55
Hweiziyeh SYR 57 Na27
Hyades, Cerro RCH 210 Gd69
Hyannis USA (MA) 177 Ge25
Hyannis USA (NE) 172 Ek25
Hydaburg USA (AK) 166 Dd18
Hyden AUS (WA) 104 Qk62
Hyden USA (KY) 178 Fj27
Hyde Park USA (VT) 177 Gd23
Hyder USA (AK) 166 De18
Hyderabad IND (APH) 82 Ok37
Hyderabad PK 65 Oe33
Hyères F 25 Lg47
Hyesan PRK 76 Re25
Hyland Plateau CDN 166 Df15
Hyltebruk S 30 Lo34
Hyperittfossen N 16 Lj06
Hyrax Hill EAK 144 Mj46
Hysham USA (MT) 169 Eg22
Hyuga J 79 Rf29
Hyvinkää FIN 38 Me30

I

Ía GR 47 Mf54
Iaciara BR (GO) 203 Hg53
Iaçu BR (BA) 201 Hk52
Iagain Island PNG 117 Sh48
Iaguaretê BR (AM) 193 Gf45
Iakora RM 157 Nd57
Iamara PNG 115 Sb50
Ianabinda RM 157 Nc57
Ianakafy RM 157 Nc57
Ianapera RM 157 Nc57
Ianca RO 45 Mh45
Iapim BR (AC) 196 Gd49
Iaripo BR (PA) 194 Hc45
Iași RO 49 Md22
Íasmos GR 45 Mf49
Iba RP 90 Qk38
Ibacarí BR (BA) 203 Ja53
Ibadan WAN 138 Lb42
Ibague CO 192 Gc43
Ibaiti BR (PR) 205 He57
Iballë AL 44 Lu48
Ibanda EAU 144 Mf46
Ibanda Game Reserve EAT 144 Mf46
Ibanga RDC 146 Md47
Ibarantim BR (BA) 203 Ja53
Ibaretama BR (CE) 201 Ja48
Ibarra EC 196 Ga45
Ibarreta RA (FO) 204 Ha58
Ibatiba BR (ES) 203 Hk56
Ibb YE 60 Nc39
Ibba SUD 141 Me43
Ibbenbüren D 32 Lh38
Ibeas de Juarros E 28 Kr48
Ibembo RDC 141 Mb44
Iberia PE 196 Gc48
Iberia PE 198 Gf51
Iberian Basin 8 Ka05
Ibertioga BR (MG) 203 Hj56
Ibeto WAN 138 Lc40
Ibi E 29 Ku52
Ibi WAN 138 Le41
Ibiá BR (MG) 203 Hg55
Ibiaí BR (MG) 203 Hh54
Ibiassucê BR (BA) 203 Hj53
Ibibobo BOL 207 Gj56
Ibicuí BR (BA) 203 Ja53
Ibicuy RA (ER) 204 Ha62
Ibimirim BR (PE) 201 Jb50
Ibindy RM 157 Nd56
Ibipeba BR (BA) 201 Hj51
Ibipetum BR (BA) 201 Hj51
Ibipira BR (MA) 195 Hh47
Ibipitanga BR (BA) 201 Hj52
Ibiporã BR (PR) 202 He57
Ibiporanga BR (SP) 202 Hf56
Ibiquera BR (BA) 201 Hk52
Ibiraba BR (BA) 201 Hj51
Ibiraci BR (MG) 203 Hg56
Ibirama BR (SC) 205 Hf59
Ibirama, T.I. BR 205 Hf59
Ibiranhém BR (BA) 203 Hk54
Ibirataia BR (BA) 203 Ja53
Ibirite BR (MG) 203 Hh56
Ibirubá BR (RS) 204 Hd60
Ibitiara BR (BA) 201 Hj52
Ibitinga BR (SP) 202 Hf56
Ibiza = Eivissa E 29 Lb51
Ibiza = Eivissa E 29 Lb52
Ibó BR (PE) 201 Ja50
Ibo MOC 147 Na52
Ibohamane RN 132 Lc38
Iboih Beach RI 92 Ph43
Iboko RDC 149 Lk46
Ibologelo EAT 146 Mg48
Ibonma RI 114 Rg47
Iboro WAN 138 Lb42
Ibotirama BR (BA) 201 Hj52
Ibra OM 61 Nk34
Ibra RI 114 Rg48
Ibrahimpatan IND (APH) 82 Ok37
Ibrahim Rauza IND 82 Oh37
Ibri OM 61 Nj34
Ibrice TR 45 Mg50
Ibu RI 91 Rd45
Ibusuki J 79 Rf30
Ica PE 197 Gc53
Icabarú YV 193 Gk43
Icacos Point YV 193 Gj40
Içana BR (AM) 193 Gg45
Icaño RA (CA) 207 Gh60
Icapuí BR (CE) 201 Jb48
Içara BR (SC) 205 Hf60
Icaraí de Amontada BR (CE) 201 Ja47
Icaraíma BR (PR) 202 Hd57
Icatu BR (MA) 195 Hh47
Icatú, T.I. BR 202 He56
Ice Caves USA 168 Dk23
Icefield Ctr. CDN 168 Eb19
Içel TR 56 Mh27
Iceland IS 18 Ju24
Iceland IS 18 Ka26
Iceland Basin 14 Jb04
Iceland Faeroe Rise 163 Kb06
Icelandic Plateau 160 Ka03
Icém BR (SP) 202 Hf56
İçeriçumra TR 56 Mg27
Ice Stream A 6 Cd35
Ice Stream B 6 Cc35
Ice Stream C 6 Cd35
Ice Stream D 6 Cd35
Ice Stream E 6 Cd35
Ichabo-eiland NAM 154 Lh59
Ichabo Island NAM 154 Lh59
Ichalkaranji IND (MHT) 82 Oh37
Ichchapuram IND (APH) 83 Pc36
Iche MA 125 Kk29
Ichenhausen D 33 Ll42
Icheu WAN 138 Ld42
Ichhawar IND (MPH) 82 Oj34
Ichinomiya J 79 Rj28
Ichinos J 77 Sa26
Ichkeul, P.N. de l' TN 126 Le27
Ich'on PRK 78 Rd26
Ich'on ROK 78 Rd27
Ichuña PE 197 Ge54
Iclod RO 43 Md44
İçmeler TR 47 Mj54
Ičnja UA 48 Mg20
Icó BR (CE) 201 Ja49
Icoca ANG 148 Lj49
Icy Cape USA (AK) 165 Bk10
Icy Cape USA 166 Ck16
Icy Reef USA (AK) 165 Ck11
Ida SP 145 Nb45
Idabato CAM 138 Le43
Idabel USA (OK) 174 Fc29
Idabo ETH 142 Na42
Idaga Hamus ETH 142 Mk38
Ida Grove USA (IA) 172 Fc24
Idah WAN 138 Ld42
Idaho USA 168 Ec24
Idaho Falls USA (ID) 169 Ee24
Idalia USA (CO) 174 Ej26
Idalia N.P. AUS (QLD) 109 Sc58
Idanre WAN 138 Lc42
Ida-Oumarkt MA 124 Kf31
Idar IND (GUJ) 82 Og34
Idar-Oberstein D 33 Lh41
Ida Valley AUS (WA) 104 Ra60
Idd al-Ghanam SUD 134 Mc40
Idelès DZ 132 Lc34
Idenao CAM 138 Le43
Idgaon BD 86 Pg35
Idgarh BD 86 Pg35
Idi RI 92 Pj43
Ididole ETH 145 Nb43
İdil TR 57 Na27
Idîni RIM 130 Kc37
Idiofa RDC 149 Lk48
Id-Kah-Mosque CHN 66 Oj26
Idlib SYR 56 Mj28
Idoani WAN 138 Lc42
Idodi EAT 146 Mh49
Idodoma EAT 147 Mj49
Idogo WAN 138 Lb42
Idongo RCA 140 Ma42
Ídra GR 45 Md53
Ídra GR 45 Md53
Idracowra AUS (NT) 108 Rg58
Idre S 17 Lg15
Idrefjäll S 17 Lg15
Idrija SLO 42 Lp45
Idstein D 33 Lj40
Idumba RDC 149 Ma47
Idutywa ZA 155 Me62
Idvor SCG 44 Ma45
Iecava LV 39 Me34
Ie-jima J 79 Rd32
Iepê BR (SP) 202 He57
Ieper B 23 Lc40
Ierápetra GR 47 Mf55
Ierissós GR 45 Md50
Iernut RO 43 Me44
Ieud RO 43 Me43
Ifakara EAT 147 Mj50
Ifaki WAN 138 Lc42
Ifanadiana RM 157 Nd56
Ifanirea RM 157 Nd57
Ifaty RM 157 Nb57
Ife WAN 138 Lc42
Ifenat TCH 133 Lk39
Iferouâne RN 132 Le36
Ifetedo WAN 138 Lc42
Ifetesene DZ 126 Lc33
Iffezheim D 33 Lj42
Iffley AUS (QLD) 107 Sa55
Ifjord N 16 Md10
Ifon WAN 138 Lc42
Ifrane MA 125 Kh29
Ifumbe EAT 146 Mg49
Igabi WAN 138 Ld40
Igalukila EAT 146 Mf49
Igalulu EAT 146 Mg48
Iganga EAU 144 Mg45
Igangan WAN 138 Lb42
Igapo BR (RN) 201 Jc48
Igaporã BR (BA) 201 Hj52
Igarapava BR (SP) 203 Hg56
Igarapé BR (MG) 203 Hh56
Igarapé-Açú BR (PA) 195 Hg46
Igarapé Capana, T.I. BR 198 Gf50
Igarapé do Caucho, T.I. BR 196 Ge50
Igarapé Grande BR (MA) 200 Hh48
Igarapé Lages, T.I. BR 198 Gh51
Igarapé Lourdes, T.I. BR 198 Gk51
Igarapé Mirim BR (PA) 195 Hf46
Igarapé Ribeirão, T.I. BR 198 Gh51
Igarité BR (BA) 200 Hj51
Igarka RUS 54 Pb05
Igarra WAN 138 Ld42
Igatpuri IND (MHT) 82 Og36
Igawa EAT 146 Mh50
Igbeti WAN 138 Lc41
Igbogor WAN 138 Lc42
Igboho WAN 138 Lb41
Igbo-Oro WAN 138 Lb42
Igbor WAN 138 Le42
Iğdır TR 57 Nc26
Igherm MA 124 Kf30
Ighiu RO 43 Md44
Igichuk Hills USA 165 Bj12
Igina RDC 141 Md44
Igina RDC 141 Me44
Igiugig USA (AK) 164 Cc16
Igle, Cerro RA 210 Gd71
Iglésias I 36 Lj51
Igli DZ 125 Kj30
Ignace CDN (ON) 172 Fe21
Ignacio Allende MEX (DGO) 181 Ej33
Ignalina LT 39 Mg35
Ignarassú BR (PE) 201 Jc49
Ignašino RUS 71 Rb19
İğneada TR 45 Mh49
Igoma EAT 146 Mg50
Igoumenitsa GR 46 Ma51
Igporin WAN 138 Lc41
Igreja de Boroma MOC 152 Mg53
Igreja de Nossa Senhora do Rosário dos Pretos BR 201 Ja52
Igreja de São Francisco BR 201 Ja52
Igrita WAN 138 Ld43
Iguaçu, P.N. do BR 204 Hd58
Iguaí BR (BA) 203 Hk53
Iguala MEX (GUR) 182 Fa36
Igualada E 29 Lb49
Iguape BR (SP) 205 Hg58
Iguatemi BR (MS) 202 Hc57
Iguatu BR (CE) 201 Ja49
Iguazú, P.N. BR/RA 204 Hc58
Iguéla G 148 Le46
Igüeña E 26 Ko48
Iguetti RIM 124 Kf33
Iguguna EAT 146 Mh48
Iguidi Ouan Kasa LAR 133 Lf33
Igunga EAT 146 Mg48
Igusule EAT 144 Mg47
Iharana RM 156 Ne52
Iharosberény H 42 Ls44
Iheret EAK 144 Mj43
Iherir DZ 126 Le33
Iheya J 79 Rd32
Iheya-jima J 79 Rd32
Ihiala WAN 138 Ld43
Ihitsa LAR 127 Lg33
Ihlara TR 56 Mh26
Ihode FIN 38 Mb30
Ihosy RM 157 Nd57
Ihu PNG 115 Sc49
Ihugh WAN 138 Le42
Ihumbu EAT 147 Mh49
Ihuo WAN 138 Ld43
Iida J 79 Rj28
Iidaan SP 143 Ne42
Iide-san J 77 Rk27
Iisalmi FIN 16 Md14
Iittala FIN 38 Me29
Ij IND (APH) 82 Oj37
Ijâfene RIM 131 Kf35
Ijara EAK 145 Na46
Ijebu-Igbu WAN 138 Lb42
Ijebu-Ode WAN 138 Lb42
Ijen-Merapi Maelang Reserves RI 95 Qh50
Ijevan ARM 57 Nc25
IJmuiden NL 23 Le38
Ijoubban RIM 131 Kg34
Ijoukak MA 125 Kf30
IJssel NL 23 Lg38
IJsselmeer NL 23 Lf38
IJsselstein NL 23 Lf38
Ijuí BR (RS) 204 Hd60
Ikaalinen FIN 38 Md29
Ikalamavony RM 157 Nd56
Ikali RDC 149 Ma47
Ikalto Monastery GE 57 Nc25
Ikanbujimal CHN (XUZ) 67 Pe26
Ikanda RDC 149 Ma47
Ikang WAN 138 Le43
Ikanga EAK 144 Mk46
Ikare WAN 138 Lc42
Ikaría GR 47 Mg53
Ikast DK 30 Lk34
Ikauna IND (UPH) 83 Pa32
Ikebe WAN 138 Ld42
Ikeda J 77 Sb24
Ikeja WAN 138 Lb42
Ikela RDC 149 Mb46
Ikelenge Z 151 Mc51
Ikem WAN 138 Ld42
Ikengué G 148 Le46
Ikere WAN 138 Lc42
Ikh Bogd Uul MNG 70 Pk21
Ikh Bogd Uul MNG 70 Qa23
Ikh Bulag MNG 70 Qd24
Ikh Gazaryn Chuluu MNG 70 Qd23
Ikh Khayrkhan MNG 70 Qc22
Ikh Khenteyn Nuruu MNG 70 Qe21
Ikh Nuuruudyn Khotgor MNG 67 Ph21
Ikhsüüj MNG 70 Qd21
Iki J 79 Re29
Ikiak USA (AK) 165 Cc10
Ikire WAN 138 Lc42
Ikirun WAN 138 Lc42
Iki-Tsushima Q.N.P. J 79 Re28
Ikiztepe TR 56 Mj25
Ikola EAT 146 Mf49
Ikole WAN 138 Lc42
Ikom WAN 138 Le43
Ikoma EAT 144 Mh47
Ikomu WAN 138 Lb41
Ikongo RM 157 Nd56
Ikonogo EAT 146 Mh49
Ikonongo RDC 140 Lk45
Ikoo EAK 144 Mk46
Ikorodu WAN 138 Lb42
Ikot Ekpene WAN 138 Ld43
Ikoto SUD 144 Mg43
Ikšķile LV 39 Me34
Ikuba EAT 146 Mf49
Ikungi EAT 146 Mh48
Ikutha EAK 144 Mk47
Ilaga RI 114 Rj47
Ilagan RP 90 Ra37
Ilaiyankudi IND (TNU) 84 Ok41
Ilaji WAN 138 Lb42
Ilaka Afovoany RM 157 Nd56
Ilaka Atsinanana RM 157 Ne55
Ilakaka RM 157 Nc57
Ilam IR 57 Nd29
Ilam NEP 83 Pd32
Ilan RC 75 Ra33
Ilangali EAT 146 Mh49
Ilanz CH 34 Lk44
Ila-Orangun WAN 138 Lc41
Ilara WAN 138 Lc42
Ilaro WAN 138 Lb42
Ilaura PNG 115 Sd49
Ilaut EAK 144 Mj45
Ilava SK 42 Lt41
Ilave PE 206 Gf54
Iława PL 41 Lu37
Ilawe WAN 138 Lc42
Ilbilbie AUS (QLD) 109 Se56
Ilbisil EAK 144 Mj47
Ilchester GB 21 Ks40
Il'ci UA 43 Me42
Ildır TR 47 Mg52
Ile KZ 66 Oj23
Ile KZ 66 Ok24
Île-à-la-Crosse CDN (SK) 167 Eg18
Ile-Ala-Toosu KS 63 Og26
Île Aoba VU 118 Td53
Île Aride SY 145 Nh48
Île Art F 118 Tb55
Île aux Serpents MS 157 Nj55
Île aux Vaches SY 145 Nh47
Île-à-Vache RH 186 Gd36
Île Baaba F 118 Tb56
Île Balabio F 118 Tc56
Île Beautemps-Beaupré F 118 Td56
Ilebo RDC 149 Ma48
Île Brion CDN 176 Gk22
Île Chesterfield RM 156 Nb54
Île d'Ambre MS 157 Nj56
Île d'Anticosti CDN 176 Gj21
Île de France F 23 Lc41
Île de France F 23 Lc42
Île de Gorée SN 130 Kb38
Île de Jerba TN 126 Lf29
Île de la Gonâve RH 186 Gd36
Île de la Tortue RH 186 Gd35
Île Denis SY 145 Nh47
Île-d'Entrée CDN (QC) 176 Gk22
Île de Ré F 24 Kt44
Île des Genévriers CDN 176 Ha20
Île des Pins F 118 Td57
Île Desroches SY 145 Ng48
Île de Tiagba CI 137 Kh43
Île de Tumba RG 136 Kd41
Île d'Orléans CDN 176 Ge22
Île du Diable F 194 Hd43
Île du Nord SY 156 Nf51
Île du Nord SY 145 Nh48
Île du Petit Mécantina CDN 176 Ha20
Île du Sud SY 156 Nf51
Île d'Yeu F 24 Ks44
Île Esumba RDC 140 Ma45
Île Europa F 153 Na57
Île Joinville 6 Hb31
Île Kiji RIM 130 Kb36
Île Kôtomo F 118 Td57
Île Lamèque Island CDN 176 Gh22
Île Matthew F 10 Tb12
Île Miquelon F 177 Hb22
Île Miscou Island CDN 176 Gh22
Île Monger CDN 176 Ha20
Île Moucha DJI 143 Nb40
Île Plate MS 157 Nj55
Île Plate SY 145 Nh48
Île Pott F 118 Tb55
Île Raiatea F 11 Ca11
Ilesa WAN 138 Lb41
Ilesa WAN 138 Lc42
Îles Belep F 118 Tb55
Îles Chausey F 22 Kt42
Îles Daos F 118 Tb55
Îles de Glénan F 22 Kr43
Îles de Kerkenah TN 126 Lf28
Îles de la Madeleine CDN 176 Gj22
Îles de la Madeleine, P.N. SN 130 Kb38
Îles de Los RG 136 Kd41
Îles des Saintes F 187 Gk38
Îles d'Hyères F 25 Lg48
Îles du Désappointement F 11 Cb11
Îles du Salut F 194 Hd43
Îles Ehotilés, P.N. des CI 137 Kj43
Îles flottantes du Lac Tchad TCH 133 Lh39
Îles Glorieuses F 156 Nd51
Îles Glorieuses F 156 Nd51
Îles Juân de Nova F 157 Nb54
Îles Loyauté F 118 Td56
Îles Tristao RG 136 Kc40
Île Sumba RDC 140 Lk45
Île Surprise F 118 Tb55
Île Tîdra RIM 130 Kb36
IletsJérémie CDN (QC) 176 Gf21
Île Yandé F 118 Tb56
Ilfeld D 32 Ll39
Ilford AUS (NSW) 111 Se62
Ilfracombe AUS (QLD) 109 Sc57
Ilfracombe GB 21 Kq39
Ilgaz TR 56 Mg25
Ilgaz Dağları TR 56 Mg25
Ilgaz Dağı Milli Parkı TR 56 Mg25
Ilgın TR 56 Mf26
Ilha Aaratuba BR 199 Gk47
Ilha Autaz BR 199 Ha47
Ilha Bailique BR 195 Hf45
Ilhabela BR (SP) 205 Hh57
Ilha Cajutuba BR 195 Hg46
Ilha Caravela GNB 136 Kb40
Ilha Caravelas BR 203 Ja54
Ilha Carrapatal BR 195 Hj47
Ilha Caviana de Dentro BR 195 He45
Ilha Caviana de Fora BR 195 He45
Ilha Cipotuba BR 198 Gj47
Ilha Comprida BR 205 Hg58
Ilha Cuxiuara BR 198 Gk47
Ilha da Boa Vista CV 136 Jj37
Ilha da Botija BR 198 Gj47
Ilha da Cotinga, T.I. BR 205 Hf58
Ilha da Inhaca MOC 155 Mg59
Ilha da Laguna BR 195 He46
Ilha das Canárias BR 201 Hj47
Ilha da Serraria BR 195 He46
Ilha da Trinidade BR 199 Ha47
Ilha de Alcatrazes BR 205 Hh58
Ilha de Benguerra MOC 153 Mh56
Ilha de Boipeba BR 201 Ja52
Ilha de Bolama GNB 136 Kc40
Ilha de Brava CV 136 Jh38
Ilha de Curari BR 199 Gk47
Ilha de Fogo CV 136 Jh38
Ilha de Itamaracá BR 201 Jc49
Ilha de Jeta GNB 136 Kb40
Ilha de Maio CV 136 Jj38
Ilha de Maracá BR 195 He44
Ilha de Marajó BR 195 He46
Ilha de Moçambique MOC 153 Na53
Ilha de Orango GNB 136 Kb40
Ilha de Orangozinho GNB 136 Kc40
Ilha de Pecixe GNB 136 Kb40
Ilha de Santa Catarina BR 205 Hf59
Ilha de Santa Luzia CV 136 Jh37
Ilha de Santa Rita BR 199 Hc47
Ilha de Santiago CV 136 Jj38
Ilha de Santo Antão CV 136 Jh37
Ilha de São Francisco BR 205 Hf59
Ilha de São Luís BR 195 Hh47
Ilha de São Nicolau CV 136 Jh37
Ilha de São Sebastião BR 205 Hh57
Ilha de São Vicente CV 136 Jh37
Ilha de Tinharé BR 201 Ja52
Ilha de Uno GNB 136 Kb40
Ilha do Arapori BR 199 Hc47
Ilha do Bacuri BR 195 Hf47
Ilha do Bananal BR 200 He51
Ilha do Bazaruto MOC 153 Mh56
Ilha do Cabo Frio BR 203 Hk57
Ilha do Caju BR 201 Hj47
Ilha do Coro BR 198 Gj47
Ilha do Curuá BR 195 Hf45
Ilha do Farol BR 201 Jd47
Ilha do Farol BR 201 Jd47
Ilha do Ibo MOC 147 Na52
Ilha do Mel BR 205 Hf58
Ilha do Pará BR 195 He46
Ilha do Porto Santo P 124 Kb29
Ilha do Sal CV 136 Jj37
Ilha dos Macacos BR 195 He46
Ilha Fernando de Noronha BR 201 Jd47
Ilha Fernando de Noronha BR 201 Jd47
Ilha Formosa GNB 136 Kb40
Ilha Grande BR (PI) 201 Hk47
Ilha Grande BR 205 Hh57
Ilha Grande de Gurupá BR 195 He46
Ilha Grande de Santa Isabel BR 201 Hk47
Ilha Grande, P.N. de BR 202 Hd57
Ilha Ipixuna BR 198 Gj47
Ilha Itaparica BR 201 Ja52
Ilha Janauçu BR 195 He45
Ilha Loreto BR 196 Ge47
Ilha Magaruque MOC 153 Mh56
Ilha Mangunça BR 195 Hh46
Ilha Marengo om Pavilhão BR 199 Hb50
Ilha Metemo MOC 147 Na52
Ilha Mexiana BR 195 Hf46
Ilha Muturi BR 195 He46
İlhanköy TR 45 Mh50
Ilha Panamim BR 198 Gh47
Ilha Queimada Pequena BR 205 Hg58
Ilha Queramimbi MOC 147 Na51
Ilha Quirimba MOC 147 Na52
Ilha Roxa GNB 136 Kc40
Ilha Santa Carolina MOC 153 Mh56
Ilha Santana BR 195 Hj47
Ilha São Jorge BR 195 Hh46
Ilhas de Barlavento CV 136 Jh37
Ilhas de São João BR 195 Hh46
Ilhas Desertas P 124 Kb29
Ilhas de Sotavento CV 136 Jh38
Ilhas Martim Vaz BR 190 Jb12
Ilha Solteira BR (SP) 202 He56
Ilhas Selvagens P 124 Kc30
Ilha Tupinam baranas BR 199 Ha47
Ilha Urubu BR 199 Hb47
Ilha Urucuri BR 199 Hd46
Ilha Urutaí BR 195 He46
Ilha Vamizi MOC 147 Na51
Ílhavo P 26 Km50
Ilhéu Branco CV 136 Jh37
Ilhéu Razo CV 136 Jh37
Ilhéus BR (BA) 203 Ja53
Ilheu Secos e Rombo CV 136 Jh38
Ilhota da Maloca Arori BR (PA) 194 Hb45
Iliamna Vol. USA 164 Cd16
Iliç TR 57 Mk26
Ilıca TR 47 Mh51
Ilicínea BR (MG) 203 Hh56
Iligan RP 91 Rc41
Iligan Bay RP 91 Rb41
Ilijaš BIH 44 Lt47
Ilimo PNG 115 Sd50
Ilin Island RP 90 Ra39
Il'ino RUS 48 Mf18
Il'inovka RUS 71 Re21
Il'insko- Zaborskoe RUS 48 Nc17
Iliokómi GR 45 Me50
Ilirska Bistrica SLO 42 Lp45
Il'ja BY 39 Mh36
Ilkal IND (KTK) 82 Oj38
Illapel RCH 208 Ge61
Illawong AUS (WA) 104 Qh60
Illbillee, Mount AUS 105 Rg59
Illea WAN 132 Lc39
Illéla RN 132 Lc38
Iller D 33 Ll43
Illertissen D 33 Ll42
Illesca, Cerro PE 196 Fk49
Illescas E 27 Kr50
Ille-sur-Têt F 24 Lc48
Illgen City USA (MN) 172 Fe22
Illičivs'k UA 49 Mf22
Illiers-Combray F 22 Lb42
Illimani, Nevado del BOL 206 Gg54
Illimo Túcume PE 196 Ga49
Illiniza, Volcán EC 196 Ga46
Illinois USA 175 Fe25
Illizi DZ 126 Le32
Illkirch-Graffenstaden F 23 Lh42
Illueca E 28 Kt49
Illzach F 25 Lh43
Ilm D 32 Lm39
Ilmajoki FIN 38 Mc28
Ilmenau D 33 Ll40
Ilminster GB 21 Ks40
Ilnik USA (AK) 164 Ca17
Ilo PE 197 Ge54
Ilobasco ES 184 Ff39
Ilobu WAN 138 Lc42
Iloca RCH 208 Gd63
Ilofa WAN 138 Lc41
Ilog RP 90 Rb40
Iloilo RP 90 Rb40
Ilok HR 44 Lu45
Ilomantsi FIN 38 Ml28
Ilonga EAT 147 Mj50
Ilongero EAT 146 Mh48
Ilorin WAN 138 Lc41
Îlots Nosy Faho et Nosy Longo RM 156 Nd53
Ilphofen D 33 Ll41
Ilsbo S 17 Lj15
Iluka AUS 109 Sg60
Ilūkste LV 39 Mg35
Ilulissat = Jakobshavn DK 163 Hc05
Ilulissat Icefjord DK 163 Hc05
Ilupu IND (ARP) 86 Ph31
Ilur RI 97 Rf48
Ilushi WAN 138 Ld42
Ilva Mare RO 43 Me43
Ilwaco USA (WA) 168 Dh22
Ilwaki RI 97 Rd49
Ilwendo Z 151 Mc54
Iłża PL 41 Mb39
Imabari J 79 Rg28
Imaculada BR (PB) 201 Jb49
Imaichi J 77 Rk27
Imajo J 79 Rj28
Imakane J 77 Rk24
Imala MEX (SL) 180 Eg33
Imala MOC 153 Mk53
Imam al Hamzah IRQ 59 Nc30
Imamganj IND (BIH) 83 Pc33
İmamoğlu TR 56 Mh27
Imam Zadeh Ali IR 64 Ng28
Imamzadeh Qolam Rasuli IR 64 Oa33
Imamzaeh Jafar IR 57 Nf28
Imanombo RM 157 Nc58
Imari J 79 Re29
Imarui BR (SC) 205 Hf60
Imasa SUD 135 Mj36
Imasgo BF 137 Kj39
Imata PE 197 Ge53
Imatong Mountains SUD 144 Mg43
Imatra FIN 38 Mj29
Imatrankoski FIN 38 Mj29
Imavere EST 38 Mf32
Imbarie BR (RJ) 205 Hj57
Imbaú BR (PR) 205 He58
Imbert DOM 186 Ge36
Imbituba BR (SC) 205 Hf60
Imbituva BR (PR) 205 He58
Imboden USA (AR) 175 Fe27
Imbwae Z 151 Mc54
Iménas RMM 131 La37
Imerimandroso RM 157 Ne54
Imese RDC 140 Lk44
Imi ETH 142 Nb42
Imilchil MA 125 Kh29
Imi-n-Ifri MA 125 Kg30
Imi-n'Ouasif MA 125 Kg30
Imi-n-Tanoute MA 124 Kf30
Imishli AZ 57 Nd26
Imja Do ROK 78 Rd28
Imlay USA (NV) 170 Ea25
Imlili DARS 130 Kc34
Immenstadt D 33 Ll43
Immingham GB 21 Ku37
Immokalee USA (FL) 179 Fk32
Imnaha USA (OR) 168 Eb23
Ímola I 34 Lm46
Imonda PNG 115 Sa47
Imotski HR 35 Ls47
Imouzzèr-des-Ida-Outanane MA 124 Kf30
Imouzzèr-Kandar MA 125 Kh29
Impasugong RP 91 Rc41
Imperatriz BR (MA) 200 Hg48
Impéria I 34 Lj47
Imperial CDN (SK) 169 Eh20
Imperial USA (NE) 174 Ek25
Imperial Mills CDN (AB) 167 Ee18
Imperial Palace CHN 73 Qj25
Imperial Palace CHN 76 Rc24
Imperieuse Reef AUS 102 Qk54
Impfondo RCB 140 Lk45
Imphal IND (MNP) 86 Ph33
Imphy F 25 Ld44
Impulo ANG 150 Lg52
İmrali Adası TR 45 Mj50
Imran YE 60 Nc39
İmroz TR 45 Mf50
Imst A 34 Ll43
Imuris MEX (SO) 180 Ee30
Imusho Z 151 Mb54
Imvouba RCB 148 Lh47
Ina J 79 Rj28
Inaafrmadow SP 143 Nc41
I-n-Abaléha RMM 131 Kj37
I-n-Abangharit RN 132 Ld37
Ináciolândia BR (GO) 202 Hf55
Inácio Martins BR (PR) 205 He58
I-n-Adiattafene RMM 131 Kj38
In Afellahlah DZ 132 Le34
Inagua N.P. BS 186 Gd35
Inaja BR (AM) 199 Ha48
Inajá BR (PE) 201 Jb50
In Akamil DZ 126 Le31
In Akeouet DZ 126 Le32
I-n-Akhmed RMM 131 Kk36
I-n-Akli RMM 131 Kk35
Inâl RIM 130 Kc35
I-n-Aleï RMM 131 Kj37
Inalik USA (AK) 164 Bf13
I-n-Amazzagh RMM 131 Kh37
Inambari PE 206 Gf52
In Amenas DZ 126 Le31
In A'mguel DZ 132 Lc34
Inangahua NZ 113 Tf66
Inanwatan RI 114 Rg47
Iñapari PE 198 Gf51
Inari FIN 16 Md11
Inarijärvi FIN 16 Md11
Inarungtong MAL 94 Qj42
In Atteï DZ 132 Ld35
Inauini Teuini, T.I. BR 198 Gf49
I-n-Azaoua RN 132 Ld35
In-Belbel DZ 125 La32
Inca, Cerro del BOL/RCH 207 Gf56
Inca E 29 Lc51
Inca de Oro RCH 207 Gf59
Incahuasi BOL 206 Gh56
Incahuasi PE 196 Ga49
Incahuasi PE 197 Gc52
Incahuasi, Nevado RA/RCH 207 Gf59
Incallajta BOL 206 Gh54
Incaracay BOL 206 Gg54
İncebel Dağları TR 56 Mj26
İnce Burnu TR 45 Mh50
İnce Burun TR 56 Mh24
İncekum Burnu TR 56 Mg27
Incense Route KSA 58 Mk34
Incense Route KSA 58 Mk34
Incense Route YE 60 Nd38
Inchadèn MA 124 Kf30
Inchbonnie NZ 113 Tf67
Inchnadamph GB 20 Kq32
Inch'on ROK 78 Rd27
Inchope MOC 152 Mg55
Inciems LV 39 Me33
Incisioni rupestri I 34 Ll44
Indagaon IND (CGH) 83 Pb35
Indaial BR (SC) 205 Hf59
Indaiatuba BR (SP) 203 Hg57
Indalsälven S 16 Lh14
Indapur IND (MHT) 82 Oh36
Inda Silase ETH 142 Mk38
Indaw MYA 86 Ph34
Indaw MYA 86 Pj33
Indaw MYA 86 Pj35
Indawgyi Lake Wildlife Sanctuary MYA 86 Ph35
Indefatigabla Bank 21 Lc37
Indefatigable o Chávez = Isla Santa Cruz EC 197 Ff46
I-n-Délimane RMM 132 La38
I-n-Délimane RMM 132 La38
Independence USA (IA) 172 Fe24
Independence USA (KS) 174 Fc27
Independence USA (KY) 175 Fh26
Independence USA (MO) 174 Fc26
Independence USA (OR) 168 Dj23
Independence Hall USA 177 Gc26
Independence Mine USA 165 Cf15
Independence Rock S.H.S. USA 171 Eg24
Independencia BOL 206 Gg54
Independência BR (CE) 201 Hk48
Independência BR (MA) 200 Hh48
Inderaba SUD 135 Mg39
Inderborskij KZ 54 Nc09
Indi IND (KTK) 82 Oh37
India IND 53 Ob07
Indiana AUS (NT) 108 Rh57
Indiana USA (PA) 173 Ga25
Indiana USA 175 Fg26
Indianapolis USA (IN) 175 Fg26
Indianapolis Speedway USA 175 Fg26
Indiana Territory S.H.S. USA 175 Fg26
Indiana Transportation Mus. USA 173 Fg25
Indian Cabins CDN (AB) 167 Eb16
Indian Grave Mountain USA (AK) 165 Ck13
Indian Head CDN (SK) 169 Ej20
Indian Lake CDN 172 Fe21
Indian Lake USA (NY) 177 Gc24
Indian Mosque IR 64 Nj32
Indian Mounds S.H.S. (Etowah) USA 175 Fh28
Indian Ocean 9 Nb13
Indianola USA (IA) 172 Fd25
Indianola USA (MS) 175 Fe29
Indianópolis BR (MG) 203 Hg55
Indian-Pacific (Western Australia) AUS 105 Rb61
Indian-Pacific (South Australia) AUS 105 Rg61
Indian Pt. USA 171 Ed26
Indian Pt. USA 171 Ed26
Indian Res. 159 CDN 169 Ef19
Indian Springs USA (NV) 170 Ec27
Indiantown USA (FL) 179 Fk32
Indian Township Ind. Res. USA 176 Gg23
Indian Trail Caverns USA 173 Fj25
Indian Wells USA (AZ) 171 Ee28
Indiara BR (GO) 202 He54
Indiaroba BR (SE) 201 Jb51
Indigirka RUS 55 Sb05
Inđija SCG 44 Ma45
Indio USA (CA) 170 Eb29
Indio-Maíz, Reserva de Biosfera CR 185 Fj40
Indio Rico RA (BA) 209 Gk65
Indipur IND (ORS) 83 Pd35
Indira Gandhi Canal IND 80 Og31
Indira Sagar Reservoir IND 82 Oj34
Indispensable Strait SOL 117 Ta50
Indochina Peninsula 10 Qa08
Indombo G 148 Lg45
Indonesia RI 53 Qa10
Indooroopilly AUS (SA) 108 Rg60
Indore IND (MPH) 82 Oh34
Indramayu RI 95 Qe49
Indre Arna N 17 Lc15
Induanjat RI 95 Qj46
Indura BY 41 Md37
Indus PK 65 Of31
Indwe ZA 155 Md61
In Ebeggi DZ 132 Ld35
İnebolu TR 56 Mg25
İnece TR 45 Mh49
I-n-Échaï RMM 131 Kj35
In Ecker DZ 132 Lc33
İnegöl TR 45 Mk50
Inékar RMM 132 Lb38
Ineu RO 43 Mb44
Inewari ETH 142 Mk41
Inezgane MA 124 Kf30
In Ezzane DZ 133 Lf34
Infanta RP 90 Ra38
Infantado P 27 Km52
I-n-Farba RIM 130 Ke38
Infiernillo MEX (MHC) 182 Ek36
Ingá BR (PB) 201 Jc49
Ingå = Inkoo FIN 38 Me30
Ingal RN 132 Ld37
Inganda RDC 149 Ma46
Ingapirca EC 196 Ga47
Ingavi BOL 198 Gg51
Ingawa WAN 138 Le39
Ingelheim D 33 Lj41
Ingelstad S 31 Lp34
Ingende RDC 149 Lk46
Ingeniero Guillermo N.Juárez RA (FO) 207 Gk57
Ingeniero Jacobacci RA (RN) 208 Gf66
Ingeniero Mora BOL 206 Gj55
Ingenieur Woudagemaal NL 23 Lf38
Ingham AUS (QLD) 107 Sd55
In Ghar DZ 125 La32
Inginiyagala CL 85 Pa42
Inglewood AUS (QLD) 109 Sf60
Ingoka Bum MYA 86 Pj33
Ingólfshöfði IS 18 Kd27
Ingolstadt D 33 Lm42
Ingomar AUS (SA) 108 Rh60
Ingonish Beach CDN (NS) 176 Gk22
Ingoré GNB 136 Kc39
Ingraham Trail CDN 167 Ed14
Ingraj Bazar IND (WBG) 86 Pe33
Ingushetia RUS 57 Nc24
Ingwe Z 151 Md52
Inhafenga MOC 152 Mg56
Inhambane MOC 153 Mh57
Inhambupe BR (BA) 201 Ja51
Inhaminga MOC 153 Mh55
Inhamitanga MOC 153 Mh55
Inhamuns BR (CE) 201 Hk48
Inhapim BR (MG) 203 Hj55
Inharrime MOC 153 Mh58
Inhassoro MOC 153 Mh56
Inhaúmas BR (BA) 200 Hh52
Inhauna IND (UPH) 83 Pa32
Inhaunho MOC 152 Mh55
In Herene LAR 126 Lf32
Inhobim BR (BA) 203 Hk53
Inhúma BR (PI) 201 Hk49
Inhumas BR (GO) 202 Hf54
Iniö FIN 38 Mb30
Inishbofin IRL 19 Kk37
Inisheer IRL 19 Kl37
Inishmaan IRL 19 Kl37
Inishmore IRL 19 Kl37
Inishowen IRL 19 Kn35
Inishtrahull IRL 19 Kn35
Inishturk IRL 19 Kk37
Inja RUS (ALT) 67 Pd20
Injanah IRQ 57 Nc28
Inje ROK 78 Re26
Injibara ETH 142 Mj40
I-n-Jitane RN 132 Ld37
Injune AUS (QLD) 109 Se58
Inkauk MYA 88 Pj37
Inkerman AUS (QLD) 107 Sa54
Inkerman AUS (QLD) 107 Sd55
Inkoo = Ingå FIN 38 Me30
Inkouélé RCB 148 Lh46
Inkster USA (ND) 172 Fb21
Inland Kaikoura Range NZ 113 Tg67
Inlandsbanan S 16 Lh13
Inlandsbanan S 17 Lh15
Inle Lake MYA 86 Pj35
I-n-Milach RMM 131 Kk37
Innamincka AUS (SA) 104 Ra59
Innamincka Regional Reserve AUS 108 Sa59
Innbygda N 17 Lg15
Inndyr N 16 Lh12
Inner Hebrides GB 20 Ko34
Innerleithen GB 20 Kr35
Inner Mongolia CHN 53 Qb05
Inner Silver Pit 21 La37
Inner Sister Island AUS (VIC) 111 Sd65
Inner Sound GB 20 Kp33
Innes N.P. AUS 110 Rj63
Innesowen AUS (NSW) 109 Sc61
Inneston AUS (SA) 110 Rj63
Innfield IRL 19 Ko37
Innisfail AUS (QLD) 107 Sd54
Innisfail CDN (AB) 169 Ed19
Innisvale AUS (NSW) 109 Sd61
Innokent'evka RUS 76 Re21
Innoko N.W.R. USA 164 Ca14
Innouendy AUS (WA) 104 Qj58
Innsbruck A 34 Lm43
Innset N 16 Lk11
Innviertel A 33 Ln42
Innviertel A 42 Lo42
Inobonto RI 91 Rc45
Inocência BR (MS) 202 He55
Inói GR 46 Mb53
Inongo RDC 149 Lk46
Inoni RCB 148 Lh47
Inoro ZW 152 Mf55
I-n-Ouagar RN 132 Ld37
I-n-Ouchef RMM 131 Kk37
Inoús GR 47 Mg52
Inowłódz PL 41 Ma39
Inowrocław PL 40 Lt38
I-n-Quezzam DZ 132 Lc36
Inquisivi BOL 206 Gg54
Inriville RA (CD) 209 Gj62
Insaca = Mecanhelas MOC 153 Mh53
In Salah DZ 126 Lb32
Insar RUS (MOR) 48 Nc19
Insculas PE 196 Ga48
Insein MYA 88 Pj37
Inside Passage USA 166 Dd17
Insjön S 31 Lq30
Inskip Point AUS 109 Sg58
Insula Mică a Brăilei, P.N. RO 45 Mh46
Însurăţei RO 45 Mh46
Inta RUS 54 Nd05
I-n-Tadéra RN 132 Le35
I-n-Talak RMM 132 Lb37
I-n-Tebezas RMM 132 La37
I-n-Techerène RMM 131 Kk35
I-n-Tédéïni RN 132 Le37
I-n-Tékélit RMM 132 La38
I-n-Telli RMM 132 Lb37
I-n-Témegui RMM 132 Lb37
Intendante Alvelar RA (LP) 209 Gj63
İntepe TR 45 Mg50
Interior Highlands USA 174 Fc27
Interior Plateau CDN 166 Dh19
Interlaken CH 34 Lh44
International Amistad Resational USA 181 Ek31
International Falls USA (MN) 172 Fd21
Intervew Island IND 88 Pg39
Intich'o ETH 142 Mk38
I-n-Tillit RMM 131 Kk38
Intiyaco RA (SF) 207 Gk60
Întorsura Bauzăului RO 45 Mg45
Intutu PE 196 Gc47
Inubo-saki J 79 Sa28
Inukjuak CDN 163 Ga07
Inuo PNG 115 Sb49
Inuvik CDN 162 Db05
Inveraray GB 20 Kp34
Inveraray Castle GB 20 Kp34
Invercargill NZ 113 Te69
Inverell AUS (NSW) 109 Sf60
Inverewe Gardens GB 20 Kp33
Invergarry GB 20 Kq33
Invergordon GB 20 Kq33
Inverleigh AUS (QLD) 107 Sa54
Inverleigh AUS (VIC) 111 Sc65
Inverloch AUS (VIC) 111 Sc65
Invermoriston GB 20 Kq33
Inverness AUS (QLD) 109 Sc57
Inverness CDN (NS) 176 Gk22
Inverness CDN (PE) 176 Gh22
Inverness GB 20 Kq33
Inverness USA (FL) 178 Fj31
Inverurie GB 20 Ks33
Inverway AUS (NT) 103 Re54
Investigator Channel MYA 88 Pj40
Investigator Passage MYA 88 Pj39
Investigator Shoal 94 Qh41
Investigator Strait AUS 110 Rj63
Inwood CDN (MB) 172 Fb20
Inyala EAT 146 Mg50
Inyangani ZW 152 Mg55
Inyathi ZW 152 Me55
Inylchek Glacier KS 66 Pa24
Inyokern USA (CA) 170 Eb28
Inyo Mts. USA 170 Ea27
Inyonga EAT 146 Mg49
Inza RUS 48 Nd19
Inžavino RUS 48 Nb19
In Ziza DZ 132 Lb34
Ioánina GR 46 Ma51
Io-jima J 79 Rf30
Iola USA (KS) 174 Fc27
Iona ANG 150 Lg54
Iona GB 20 Ko34
Iona, P.N. do ANG 150 Lg54
Iongo ANG 149 Lj50
Ionian Basin 46 Lu53
Ionian Islands GR 46 Lu51
Ionian Sea 14 Lb06
Ion Roată RO 45 Mg46
Iori PNG 115 Sc49
Íos GR 47 Mf54
Íos GR 47 Mf54
Iouîk RIM 130 Kb36
Iowa USA 172 Fc24
Iowa City USA (MO) 172 Fe25
Iowa Falls USA (IA) 172 Fd24
Ipaçu BR (MG) 202 Hf55
Ipala MEX (JLC) 182 Eh35
Ipala, Volcán HN 184 Ff38
Ipameri BR (GO) 203 Hf54
Ipanema BR (MG) 203 Hk55
Ipanema BR 201 Jb50
Ipanguaçu BR (RN) 201 Jb48
Ipao VU 118 Tf55
Iparia PE 197 Gc50
Ipatinga BR (MG) 203 Hj55
Ipatjevskij monastyr RUS 48 Na17
Ipaumirim BR (CE) 201 Ja49
Iperu WAN 138 Lb42
Ipetu-Ijesha WAN 138 Lc42
Ipezal BR (MS) 202 Hc57
Ipiales CO 196 Gb45
Ipiaú BR (BA) 203 Ja53
Ipil RP 91 Rb42
Ipira BR (BA) 201 Ja52
Ipiranga BR (PR) 205 He58
Ipixuna BR (AM) 196 Ge49
Ipixuna BR (PA) 195 Hg47
Ipixuna , T.I. BR 198 Gj49
Ipogoro EAT 146 Mh50
Ipoh MAL 92 Qa43
Iporã BR (GO) 202 He54
Iporã BR (PR) 204 Hd58
Iporanga BR (SP) 205 Hf58
Ipota VU 118 Te55
Ippy RCA 140 Ma42
İpsala TR 45 Mg50
Ipswich AUS (QLD) 109 Sg59
Ipswich GB 21 Lb38
Ipswich USA (SD) 172 Fa23
Ipu BR (CE) 201 Hk48
Ipuã BR (SP) 202 Hf56
Ipubi BR (PE) 201 Hk49
Ipueiras BR (CE) 201 Hk48
Ipuh RI 93 Qa47
Iqaluit CDN 163 Gc06
Iqe CHN (QHI) 69 Ph26
Iquipi PE 197 Gd53
Iquique RCH 206 Ge56
Iquitos PE 196 Gd47
Iraan USA (TX) 174 Ek30
Ira Banda RCA 140 Mb43
Iracema PE 196 Gd48
Iracoubo F 194 Hd43
Iraifia DARS 124 Kc33
Iraka WAN 138 Le40
Iráklia GR 44 Md49
Iráklia GR 47 Mf54
Iráklia GR 47 Mf54
Iráklio GR 47 Mf55
Iráklio GR 47 Mf55
Iramaia BR (BA) 201 Hk52
Iran IR 53 Nb06
Iranduba BR (AM) 199 Gk47
Irani BR (SC) 204 He59
Iran Shahr IR 64 Oa32
Irantxé, T.I. BR 206 Ha52
Irapa YV 193 Gj40
Irapuato MEX (GJT) 182 Ek35
Iraq IRQ 53 Na06
Irará BR (BA) 201 Ja52
Irarraren DZ 126 Lc32
Irati BR (PR) 205 He58
Irau, Gunung RI 114 Rg46
Irbene LV 39 Mb33
Irbid JOR 56 Mh29
Irbit RUS 54 Oa07
Irebu RDC 149 Lj46
Irecê BR (BA) 201 Hk51
Irečekovo BG 45 Mg48
Ireland 15 Kb04
Ireland 14 La04
Irene RA (BA) 209 Gk65
Iretama BR (PR) 204 Hd58
Ireupuow VU 118 Te55
Irgakly RUS 57 Nc23
Irhil M'Goun MA 125 Kg30
Irian Jaya RI 114 Rk48
Iriba TCH 134 Mb38
Iriga RP 90 Rb39
Irigui RMM 131 Kh37
Iriji RIM 130 Kd36
Irimote Jima J 79 Rb33
Iringa EAT 147 Mh49
Irinjalakuda IND (KER) 84 Oj40
Iriona HN 184 Fh38
Iriri BR 199 Hd48
Iriri EAU 144 Mh44
Irish Sea 21 Kp37
Iritty IND (KER) 84 Oh40
Irituia BR (PA) 195 Hg46
Irkeštam CHN (XUZ) 66 Og26
Irklijiv UA 49 Mg21
Irklinskoe vodohranilišče RUS 54 Nd08
Irkutsk RUS 70 Qc19
Irma CDN (AB) 169 Ee19
Irmath AL 44 Lu49
Irminger Basin 163 Jb06
Irmo USA (SC) 178 Fk28
Irobo CI 137 Kh43
Iroko WAN 138 Lb42
Ironasiteri YV 193 Gh45
Ironbridge GB 21 Ks38
Iron Creek USA (AK) 164 Bh13
Irondequoit USA (NY) 177 Gb24
Irondro RM 157 Nd56
Iron Mountain USA (MI) 173 Ff23
Ironona RM 156 Ne52
Iron Range N.P. AUS 107 Sb52
Iron River USA (MI) 173 Ff22
Ironton USA (MO) 175 Fe27
Ironton USA (OH) 175 Fj26
Ironwood USA (WI) 172 Fe22
Iroquois Falls CDN (ON) 173 Fk21
Iro-saki J 79 Rk28
Irosin RP 90 Rc39
Ir Ovot IL 58 Mh30
Irrawaddy MYA 86 Ph36
Irrua WAN 138 Ld42
Iršava UA 43 Md42
Irsina I 37 Lr50
Irsta S 31 Lr31
Irtyš 54 Oc07
Irtysh RUS 54 Oc07
Irtysh = Ertis 54 Pa08
Irugwa Island EAT 144 Mg46
Irumu RDC 141 Me45
Irun E 28 Kt47
Iruñea E 28 Kt48
Irupana BOL 206 Gg54
Irurita E 28 Kt47
Irurzun E 28 Kt48
Irvine CDN (AB) 169 Ee21
Irvine GB 20 Kq35
Irvinestown GB 19 Kn36
Irving USA (TX) 174 Fb29
Irwinton USA (GA) 178 Fj29
Isa WAN 132 Ld39
Isaba E 28 Ku48
Isabel USA (SD) 172 Ek23
Isabela RP 91 Ra42
Isabela RP 90 Rb40
Isabela USA (PR) 187 Gg36
Isabela de Sagua C 179 Fk34
Isabella USA (MN) 172 Fe22
Isabella Ind. Res. USA 173 Fh24
Isabel Pass USA 165 Ch14
Isabel Rubio C 179 Fh34
Isaccea RO 45 Mj45
Ísafjörður IS 18 Jr25
Isagarh IND (MPH) 83 Oj33
Isahaya J 79 Rf29
Isaka EAT 144 Mg47
Isa Khel PK 65 Of29
Isaku EST 38 Mh31
Isalo RM 157 Nc57
Isalo, P.N. de l' RM 157 Nc57
Isambe RDC 141 Md46
Isandhlwana ZA 155 Mf60
Isandja RDC 149 Ma46
Isandja RDC 149 Ma47
Isang RDC 141 Mc45
Isanga RDC 149 Mb46
Isangano N.P. Z 146 Mf51
Isangate EAT 146 Mg50
Isango RDC 141 Me46
Isanlu WAN 138 Lc41
Isanlu-Esa WAN 138 Lc41
Isar D 33 Ln42
I Sassi di Matera I 37 Lr50
Iscar E 26 Kq49
Iscayachi BOL 207 Gh56
İscehisar TR 56 Mf26
Ischgl A 34 Ll43
Íschia I 36 Lo50
Ise J 79 Rj28
Isebania EAK 144 Mh46
Iselin Bank ANT 6 Ba33
Iseo I 34 Ll45
Iseramagazi EAT 146 Mg48
Iserlohn D 32 Lh39
Isérnia I 37 Lp49
Ise-shima N.P. J 79 Rj28
Isesy RM 156 Ne52
Iseyin WAN 138 Lb42
Isfahan IR 59 Nf29
Isfjord Radio N 16 Lg06
Isha PK 65 Of29
Ishaka EAU 144 Mf46
Ishak Paşa Sarayı TR 57 Nc26
Ishasha EAU 141 Me46
Ishenga RDC 149 Mb47
Isherton GUY 194 Ha44
Ishiara EAK 144 Mj46
Ishigaki Jima J 79 Rc33
Ishikari J 77 Sa24
Ishikawa J 79 Rd32
Ishinomaki J 77 Sa26
Ishioka J 77 Sa27
Ishizuchi-san J 79 Rg29
Ishotellet S 16 Ma12
Ishpeming USA (MI) 173 Fg22
Ishtgah-e Na'in IR 64 Ng29
Ishtixon UZ 63 Od26
Ishurdi BD 86 Pe33
Isibaki Z 146 Mg52
Isiboro Sécure, P.N. BOL 206 Gh54
Isidoro Noblía ROU 204 Hc61
Isigny-sur-Mer F 22 Kt41
Isikari-santi J 77 Sb24
Isikisia EAT 146 Mg48
Işıklar Dağı TR 45 Mh50
Ísili I 36 Lk51
Isil'kul' KZ 54 Oc08
Išim RUS 54 Ob07
Isimila EAT 147 Mh49
Isimu RI 91 Rb45
Isinga RUS (BUR) 70 Qg19
Isiolo EAK 144 Mj45
Isipingo ZA 155 Mf60
Isiro RDC 141 Md44
Isiro RDC 141 Me44
Isisford AUS (QLD) 109 Sc58
Isisi EAT 147 Mh49
Isispynten N 16 Md06
Iskagundam IND (APH) 82 Ok38
Iskanwaya BOL 206 Gf53
İskenderun TR 56 Mj27
İskenderun Körfezi TR 56 Mh27
İskilip TR 56 Mh25
Iskushuban SP 143 Nf40
Isla MEX (VC) 183 Fc36
Isla Aji CO 192 Gb44
Isla Aldea RCH 210 Gc70
Isla Alejandro Selkirk RCH 197 Fk62
Isla Amantani PE 206 Gf53
Isla Angamos RCH 210 Gc70
Isla Ángel de la Guarda MEX 180 Ed31
Isla Antica YV 193 Gj40
Isla Aracena RCH 210 Ge73
Isla Arena MEX (CAM) 183 Fe35
Isla Baltra EC 197 Fe46
Isla Barro Colorado, Monumento Nacional PA 185 Fk41
Isla Barú CO 192 Gc40
Isla Bastimentos PA 185 Fj41
Isla Beata DOM 186 Ge37
Isla Benjamin RCH 210 Gc68
Isla Blanca MEX 183 Fg35
Isla Blanquilla YV 193 Gh40
Isla Byron RCH 210 Gc69
Isla Cabritos, P.N. DOM 186 Ge36
Isla Campana RCH 210 Gc70
Isla Carmen MEX 180 Ee32
Isla Cayambre CO 192 Gb44
Isla Cedros MEX 180 Ec31
Isla Cerralvo MEX 180 Ef33
Isla Chaffers RCH 210 Gc68
Isla Chao PE 197 Ga50
Isla Chatham RCH 210 Gc71
Isla Chauques RCH 208 Gd67
Isla Chiquitina PE 197 Gb51
Isla Clarence RCH 210 Ge73
Isla Coche YV 193 Gj40
Isla Coiba, P.N. PA Fk42
Isla Colón PA 185 Fj41
Isla Contoy MEX 183 Fg35
Isla Contreras RCH 210 Gc71
Isla Corocoro YV 194 Gk41
Isla Coronados MEX 180 Ee32
Isla Cozumel MEX 183 Fg35
Isla Cubagua YV 193 Gh40
Isla de Aguada MEX (CAM) 183 Fe36
Isla de Altamura MEX 180 Ef33
Isla de Aves YV 187 Gj38
Isla de Bioko GQ 138 Le44
Isla de Cabrera E 29 Lc51
Isla de Cébaco PA 185 Fk42
Isla de Coiba PA 185 Ga42
Isla de Cojimíes EC 196 Fk45
Isla de Corisco o Mandyi GQ 138 Le45
Isla de Culebra USA 187 Gh36
Isla de Guanaja HN 184 Fh37
Isla de la Independencia PE 197 Gb53
Isla de la Juventud C 179 Fj35
Isla del Alborán E 125 Kj28
Isla de la Plata EC 196 Fk46
Isla del Caño CR 185 Fh41
Isla de los Césares RA 209 Gj66
Isla de los Riachos RA 209 Gj66

Isla del Sol ▲ BOL 206 Gf54
Isla de Macabí ⬜ PE 196 Ga49
Isla de Maiz Grande ⬛ NIC 185 Fj39
Isla de Maiz Pequeña ⬜ NIC 185 Fj39
Isla de Margarita ⬜ YV 193 Gh40
Isla de Ometepe ⬜ NIC 185 Fh39
Isla de Pagalu ⬜ GQ 138 Lc46
Isla de Pinos = Isla de la Juventud ⬜ C 179 Fj35
Isla de Providencia ⬜ CO 185 Fk39
Isla de Rey ⬜ PA 185 Ga41
Isla de Roatán ⬜ HN 184 Fg37
Isla de Salamanca, P.N. 🏞 CO 192 Gc40
Isla de San Andrés ⬜ CO 185 Fk39
Isla de San Ignacio ⬜ MEX 180 Ef33
Isla de Santa Cruz ⬜ MEX 180 Ed33
Isla de Tachichilte ⬜ MEX 180 Ef33
Isla de Todos Santos ⬜ MEX 180 Eb30
Isla de Utila ⬜ HN 184 Fg37
Isla de Tintómboba ⬜ PE 198 Gg47
Isla Duque de York ⬜ RCH 210 Gc71
Isla Escudo de Veraguas ⬜ PA 185 Fk41
Isla Esmeralda ⬜ RCH 210 Gc70
Isla Española ⬜ EC 197 Ff46
Isla Espíritu Santo ⬜ MEX 180 Ee33
Isla Farrel ⬜ RCH 210 Gc71
Isla Fernandina ⬜ EC 197 Fe46
Isla Flamenco ⬜ RA 209 Gj66
Isla Foca ⬜ PE 196 Fk48
Isla Fuerte ⬜ CO 192 Gb40
Isla Gama ⬜ RA 209 Gj66
Isla Genovesa ⬜ EC 197 Ff45
Isla Gordon ⬜ RCH 210 Gf73
Isla Gorge N.P. ⬜ RCH 210 Gd73
Isla Gorgona ⬜ CO 192 Ga44
Isla Gorgona, P.N. 🏞 CO 192 Ga44
Isla Grande de Chiloé ⬜ RCH 210 Gc67
Isla Gran Guaiteca ⬜ RCH 210 Gc67
Isla Guafo ⬜ RCH 210 Gc67
Isla Guamblin ⬜ RCH 210 Gc67
Isla Guamblin, P.N. 🏞 RCH 210 Gc67
Isla Guardian Brito ⬜ RCH 210 Gd73
Isla Hanover ⬜ RCH 210 Gc71
Isla Hermite ⬜ RCH 210 Gg73
İslahiye ⬜ TR 56 Mj27
Isla Holbox ⬜ MEX 183 Fg35
Isla Hornos ⬜ RCH 210 Gg73
Isla Hoste ⬜ RCH 210 Gg73
Isla Huivulai ⬜ MEX 180 Ee32
Isla Humos ⬜ RCH 210 Gc68
Isla Ipun ⬜ RCH 210 Gc68
Isla Isabela ⬜ RCH 197 Fe46
Isla Isabela ⬜ MEX 182 Eg35
Isla Isabela, P.N. 🏞 RCH 182 Eh35
Isla Isquiliac ⬜ RCH 210 Gc68
Isla Jabali ⬜ RA 209 Gj66
Isla James ⬜ RCH 210 Gc68
Isla Jason ⬜ GB 210 Gk71
Isla Javier ⬜ RCH 210 Gc68
Isla Jicarón ⬜ RA 185 Fk42
Isla Jorge Montt ⬜ RCH 210 Gc71
Isla J. Stuben ⬜ RCH 210 Gc69
Isla la Orchila ⬜ YV 193 Gg40
Isla la Sola ⬜ YV 193 Gg40
Isla Lennox ⬜ RCH 210 Gg73
Isla Level ⬜ RCH 210 Gc68
Isla Lobos de Afuera ⬜ PE 196 Fk49
Isla Lobos de Tierra ⬜ PE 196 Fk49
Isla Londonderry ⬜ RCH 210 Ge73
Islamabad ⬛ PK 65 Og29
Isla Macapule ⬜ MEX 180 Ef33
Isla Madre de Dios ⬜ RCH 210 Gc71
Isla Magdalena ⬜ MEX 180 Ed33
Isla Magdalena ⬜ RCH 210 Gc68
Isla Magdalena, P.N. 🏞 RCH 210 Gd68
Isla Marchena ⬜ EC 197 Fe45
Isla Margarita ⬜ CO 192 Ga41
Isla Maria Cleofas ⬜ MEX 182 Eg35
Isla Maria Madre ⬜ MEX 180 Eg35
Isla Maria Magdalena ⬜ MEX 182 Eg35
Isla Más a Tierra ⬜ RCH 197 Ga62
Isla Mazorca ⬜ PE 197 Gb51
Isla Melchor ⬜ RCH 210 Gc68
Isla Merino Jarpa ⬜ RCH 210 Gc69
Islamorth FL ⬜ USA 177 Gc26
Isla Mona ⬜ USA 187 Gf36
Isla Monserrate ⬜ MEX 180 Ee33
Isla Montecristo ⬜ ES 184 Ff39
Isla Montuosa ⬜ PA 185 Fj42
Islamorada ⬜ USA (FL) 179 Fk33
Isla Mornington ⬜ RCH 210 Gc70
Islampur ⬜ IND (BIH) 83 Pc33
Islampur ⬜ IND (WBG) 86 Pe32
Isla M. Rodriguez ⬜ RCH 210 Gd72
Isla Mujeres ⬜ MEX (QTR)
Isla Mujeres ⬜ MEX 183 Fg35
Isla Natividad ⬜ MEX 180 Ec31
Isla Navarino ⬜ RCH 210 Gg73
Island Beach S.P. ⬜ USA 177 Gc26
Island Falls ⬜ CDN (ON) 173 Fk21
Island Lake ⬜ CDN 163 Fa08
Island Pond ⬜ USA (VT) 177 Ge23
Island Safari Lodge ⬜ RB 151 Mb55
Isla Nueva ⬜ RCH 210 Gd73
Isla Nueva ⬜ RCH 210 Gg73
Isla Núñez ⬜ RCH 210 Gc71
Isla Ofhidro ⬜ RCH 210 Gc70
Isla Paecho ⬜ RCH 210 Gc72
Isla Parida ⬜ PA 185 Fj41
Isla Patricio Lynch ⬜ RCH 210 Gc70
Isla Pedro González ⬜ PA 185 Ga41
Isla Picton ⬜ RCH 210 Gg73
Isla Pinta ⬜ EC 197 Fe45
Isla Pizon ⬜ EC 197 Fe46
Isla Popa ⬜ PA 185 Fk41
Isla Prat ⬜ RCH 210 Gc70
Isla Puna ⬜ EC 196 Fk47
Isla Refugio ⬜ RCH 210 Gd67
Isla Remolinos ⬜ YV 193 Gk41
Isla Riesco ⬜ RCH 210 Gd72
Isla Rivera ⬜ RCH 210 Gc68
Isla S. de Dragonera ⬜ E 29 Lc51
Isla San Ambrosio ⬜ RCH 197 Ga59
Isla San Cristóbal ⬜ EC 197 Ff46
Isla San Esteban ⬜ MEX 180 Ed31
Isla San Francisco ⬜ MEX
Isla San Juan ⬜ PE 197 Gb52
Isla San José ⬜ MEX 180 Ee33
Isla San José ⬜ PA 185 Ga41

Isla San Juanito ⬜ MEX 180 Eg35
Isla San Lorenzo ⬜ MEX 180 Ed31
Isla San Lorenzo ⬜ PE 197 Gb52
Isla San Marcos ⬜ MEX Ee32
Isla San Pedro ⬜ RCH 210 Gd67
Isla San Pedro Nolasco ⬜ MEX 180 Ee32
Isla San Salvador ⬜ EC 197 Fe46
Issati ⬜ TG 137 La41
Issia ⬜ CI 137 Kg42
Isla Santa Catalina ⬜ MEX 180 Ee33
Isla Santa Clara ⬜ RCH 197 Ga62
Isla Santa Cruz ⬜ EC 197 Ff46
Isla Santa Fé ⬜ EC 197 Fe46
Isla Santa Inés ⬜ RCH 210 Gd72
Isla Saona ⬜ DOM 186 Gf36
Isla Santa María ⬜ EC 197 Fe46
Isla Santa Rosa ⬜ EC 196 Ga45
Islas Ballestas ⬜ PE 197 Gb52
Islas Chafarinas ⬜ E 125 Kj28
Islas Chimanas ⬜ YV 193 Gh40
Islas Christmas ⬜ RCH 210 Ge73
Islas Cumbretes ⬜ E 29 La51
Isolane Erarenine ⬜ DZ 132 Lb34
Islas Coronados ⬜ MEX 180 Eb29
Islas Crafton ⬜ RCH 210 Gd73
Islas de Aves ⬜ YV 193 Gg40
Islas de la Bahia ⬜ HN 184 Fg37
Islas de los Desventurados ⬜ RCH 190 Fb12
Islas de San Bernardo ⬜ CO 192 Gb41
Islas Serrano ⬜ RCH 210 Gc70
Islas S'Espalmador ⬜ E 29 Lb52
Islas S'Esperdell ⬜ E 29 Lb52
Islas Gilbert ⬜ RCH 210 Gd67
Islas Guañape ⬜ PE 197 Ga50
Islas Juan-Fernández ⬜ RCH 190 Fb13
Islas Juan Fernández ⬜ RCH 197 Fk62
Islas Lavanderas ⬜ HN 185 Fj37
Islas Santanilla ⬜ HN 185 Fj37
Islas Secas ⬜ PA 185 Ga42
Islas Stewart ⬜ RCH 210 Ge73
Islas Wollaston ⬜ RCH 210 Gg73
Islas Wood ⬜ RCH 210 Gf73
Islas Tiburón ⬜ MEX 180 Ed31
Isla Tigre ⬜ PE 196 Ge47
Isla Tobejuba ⬜ YV 193 Gk41
Isla Tórtola ⬜ YV 193 Gk41
Isla Tortuga ⬜ EC 197 Fe46
Isla Tortuga ⬜ MEX 180 Ee32
Isla Tranqui ⬜ RCH 210 Gd67
Isla Trinidad ⬜ RA 209 Gk65
Isla Uvas ⬜ PA 185 Fk42
Isla Van der Meulen ⬜ RCH 210 Gc70
Isla Victoria ⬜ RCH 210 Gd68
Isla Wellington ⬜ RCH 210 Gc70
İslahyę ⬜ PE 197 Gd54
Islaz ⬜ RO 45 Me47
Isla Zapatera ⬜ NIC 184 Fh40
Isle au Haut ⬜ USA 177 Gf23
Isle of Lewis ⬜ GB 20 Ko32
Isle of Man ⬜ GB 20 Kq36
Isle of Noss ⬜ GB 21 Kq38
Isle of Sheppey ⬜ GB 21 La39
Isle of Wight ⬜ GB 21 Kt40
Isle Royale N.P. 🏞 USA 173 Ff21
Isles of Scilly ⬜ GB 21 Ko41
Isleta ⬜ CO 193 Gg44
Isleta Pueblo ⬜ USA 171 Eg28
Isletes-Caribou ⬜ CDN (NF)
Isle Woodah ⬜ AUS 106 Rj52
Islilitas ⬜ USA 187 Gh36
Isluga, Volcán ⬜ RCH 206 Gf55
Ismael Cortinas ⬜ ROU 204
Ismâ'iliya ⬜ ET 129 Mg30
Ismavill ⬜ AZ 57 Nc26
Isny ⬜ D 33 Ll43
Isoanala ⬜ RM 157 Nc57
Isojoen kansallispuisto 🏞 FIN 38 Mf29
Isoka ⬜ Z 146 Mg51
Isokyrö ⬜ FIN 38 Mb28
Isokyrö ⬜ FIN 38 Md28
Isola ⬜ F 25 Lh46
Isola 2000 ⬜ F 25 Lh46
Isola Alicudi ⬜ I 37 Lo52
Isola Asinara ⬜ I 36 Lj50
Isola Caprera ⬜ I 36 Lk49
Isola d'Elba ⬜ I 34 Ll48
Isola del Giglio ⬜ I 34 Ll48
Isola delle Stagnone ⬜ I 36 Ln53
Isola di Capo Rizzuto ⬜ I 37 Ls52
Isola di Capràia ⬜ I 34 Lk47
Isola di Giannutri ⬜ I 36 Ll48
Isola di Gorgona ⬜ I 34 Lk47
Isola di Lampedusa ⬜ I 36 Lm54
Isola di Lévanzo ⬜ I 36 Ln53
Isola di Linosa ⬜ I 36 Ll54
Isola di Montecristo ⬜ I 34 Ll48
Isola di Pantelleria ⬜ I 36 Ln54
Isola di Ponza ⬜ I 36 Lo49
Isola di Procida ⬜ I 36 Lp50
Isola di Sant'Antioco ⬜ I 36 Lj52
Isola Favignana ⬜ I 36 Ln53
Isola Filicudi ⬜ I 37 Lo52
Isola Lipari ⬜ I 37 Lo52
Isola Molara ⬜ I 36 Lk49
Isola Mortório ⬜ I 36 Lk49
Isola Palmarola ⬜ I 36 Lo49
Isola Panarea ⬜ I 37 Lp52
Isola Salina ⬜ I 37 Lo52
Isola San Dómino ⬜ I 37 Lq48
Isola Tavolara ⬜ I 36 Lk49
Isola Ventoténe ⬜ I 36 Lp50
Isola Zannone ⬜ I 36 Lo50
Iole Éolie o Lìpari ⬜ I 37 Lo52
Isole Ponziane ⬜ I 36 Lo49
Isole Trémiti ⬜ I 37 Lq48
Isola ⬜ UZ 62 Oa25
Isole ⬜ PE 197 Gc54
Isortog ⬜ DK 163 Hc06
Isorto ⬜ GUY 194 Ha43
Isparta ⬜ TR 56 Mf27
İsperih ⬜ BG 45 Mg47
İspir ⬜ TR 57 Na25
İsperih ⬜ BG 45 Mh39
Isrealite Bay ⬜ WA 105 Rb62
Isriyeh ⬜ SYR 56 Mj28
Issano Terminus ⬜ GUY 194 Hd43
Isla Zapatera ⬜ NIC 184

Itete ⬜ EAT 146 Mg50
Itezhi-Tezhi Dam ⬜ Z 152 Md53
Ithaca ⬜ USA (NY) 177 Gb24
Ithäki ⬜ GR 44 Ma52
Itigi ⬜ EAT 146 Mh47
Itiki ⬜ (KTK) 84 Oj38
Itoigawa ⬜ J 77 Rk28
Itoko ⬜ RDC 149 Lk46
Itondy ⬜ RM 157 Nc55
Itororó ⬜ BR (BA) 203 Hk53
Itquiy ⬜ DARS 124 Kd32
Itsukushima ⬜ J 79 Rg28
Ittiri ⬜ I DS 32 Lk37
Ittoqqortoormiit = Scoresbysund ⬜ DK 163 Jd04
Itu ⬜ BR (SP) 205 Hg57
Ituaçu ⬜ BR (BA) 201 Hk52
Ituango ⬜ CO 192 Gc42
Ituberá ⬜ BR (BA) 201 Ja52
Itui/taba ⬜ BR (MG) 202 Hf55
Itula ⬜ CI 146 Md47
Itumbiara ⬜ BR (GO) 202 He56
Itumirim ⬜ BR (GO) 202 Hd55
Itungi Port ⬜ EAT 146 Mg50
Ituni ⬜ GUY 194 Ha43
Ituporanga ⬜ BR (SC) 205 Hf59
Iturbide ⬜ MEX (CAM) 183 Ff36
Ituri ⬜ RDC
Itutinga ⬜ BR (MG) 203 Hh56
Ituverava ⬜ BR (SP) 203 Hg56
Itzehoe ⬜ D 32 Lk37
Iuiú ⬜ BR (BA) 203 Hj53
Itu ⬜ WAN 138 Ld43
Ivaí ⬜ BR (PR) 204 He58
Ivanava ⬜ BY 41 Mf38
Ivancice ⬜ CZ 42 Lr41
Ivangorod ⬜ RUS 38 Mj31
Ivanhoe ⬜ AUS (NSW) 111 Sc62
Ivanhoe Lake ⬜ CDN (SK)
Ivanic Grad ⬜ HR 35 Lr45
Ivankiv ⬜ UA 49 Me40
Ivano-Frankivsk ⬜ UA 43 Me42
Ivanovka ⬜ RUS 71 Qk20
Ivanovo ⬜ RUS 71 Re20
Ivanovo ⬜ RUS (MS) 175 Fe29
Ivanovo ⬜ RUS (OH) 61 Nj34
Ivanovo ⬜ BIH 35 Ls46
Ivanské ⬜ BIH 35 Ls45
Ivanjica ⬜ SCG 44 Lu47
Ivanpah Lake ⬜ USA
Ivatsevičy ⬜ BY 41 Mf38
Ivdel' ⬜ RUS 54 Na17
Ivinhema ⬜ BR (MS) 202 Hc57
Ivittuut ⬜ DK 163 Ha06
Ivohibe ⬜ RM 157 Nd56
Ivory Coast = Côte d'Ivoire ⬜ CI 137 Kf42
Ivory Coast ⬜ CI 123 Kb09
Ivrea ⬜ I 34 Lh45
İvrindi ⬜ TR 47 Mh51
Ivujivik ⬜ CDN 163 Ga06
Ivvavik National Park 🏞 CDN
Iwaizumi ⬜ J 77 Sa26
Iwaki ⬜ USA (SA) 108 Rg59
Iwakuni ⬜ J 79 Rg28
Iwamizawa ⬜ J 77 Sa24
Iwanai ⬜ J 79 Rg28
Iwase ⬜ RDC 149 Mc47
Iwo ⬜ WAN 138 Lc42
Iwungu ⬜ RDC 149 Lk48
Ixcamilpa ⬜ MEX (GUR) 182 Fa32
Ixcateopan ⬜ MEX (GUR) 182 Fa36
Ixcún ⬜ GCA 183 Ff37
Ixiamas ⬜ BOL 206 Gf52
Ixmiquilpan ⬜ MEX (HDG) 182 Fa35
Ixopo ⬜ ZA 155 Mf61
Ixtapa ⬜ MEX (GUR) 182 Ek37
Ixtapan de la Sal ⬜ MEX (MEX) 182 Fa36
Ixtlán de Juárez ⬜ MEX (OAX) 183 Fb37
Ixtlán del Río ⬜ MEX (NYT) 182 Eh35
Izabal, L. de ⬜ GCA 184 Ff38
Izamal ⬜ MEX (YUC) 183 Ff35
Izara ⬜ MEX (HDG)

Izsák ⬜ H 43 Lu44
Iztočni Rodopi ⬜ BG 45 Mf39
Izúcar de Matamoros ⬜ MEX (PUE) 182 Fa36
Izu-hantō ⬜ J 79 Rk28
Izu-Shotō ⬜ J 79 Rg28
Izumi ⬜ J 77 Sa26
Izumi ⬜ J 79 Rg28
Izumo ⬜ J 79 Rg28
Izvestkovyj ⬜ RUS (YAO) 76 Rf21
Izvor ⬜ BG 44 Md48
Izvor ⬜ MK 44 Ma48
Izvor ⬜ BG 45 Mf45
Izvoru Dulce ⬜ RO 45 Mg45

J

Jaala ⬜ FIN 38 Mg29
Ja'ar ⬜ YE 60 Nc39
Jabal os Sara ⬜ AFG 63 Oe28
Jabalpur ⬜ IND (MPH) 83 Ok34
Jabarona ⬜ SUD 134 Md37
Jabbrah Fara ⬜ WAN
Jabbaren ⬜ DZ 132 Lc33
Jaberos ⬜ PE 196 Gb48
Jabiru ⬜ AUS (NT) 106 Rg52
Jablah ⬜ SYR 56 Mh28
Jablanica ⬜ BG 45 Me47
Jablanica ⬜ SCG 44 Ma48
Jablanica ⬜ BIH 35 Ls47
Jabłoniec ⬜ PL 41 Lu41
Jabłonowo Pomorskie ⬜ PL 41 Lu37
Jabluniv ⬜ UA 43 Me42
Jablunkov ⬜ CZ 43 Lt41
Jabłun ⬜ CAM 138 Lf42
Jaboatão ⬜ BR (PE) 201 Jc50
Jaboticabal ⬜ BR (SP) 202 Hf56
Jabotiçatubas ⬜ BR (MG) 203 Hj55
Jabra ⬜ IND (JKD) 83 Pc33
Jabrin ⬜ SYR 56 Mh34
Jabugo ⬜ E 27 Ko53
Jaburu ⬜ BR (AM) 198 Gh48
Jabukovac ⬜ SCG 44 Mc46
Jabukovik ⬜ SCG 44 Md46
Jaburi, T.I. ⬜ BR 194 Gk44
Jaca ⬜ E 28 Ku44
Jacala ⬜ MEX (HDG) 182 Fa35
Jacareacanga ⬜ BR (PA) 199 Hb49
Jacaré ⬜ BR (SP) 205 Hh57
Jacareí ⬜ BR (AM) 199 Ha50
Jacarezinho ⬜ BR (PR) 202 Hf57
Jacaretinga ⬜ BR (AM) 198 Gj48
Jáchal ⬜ RA 208 Gf61
Jaciara ⬜ BR (MT) 202 Hc54
Jacinto ⬜ BR (MG) 203 Hk54
Jaci Paraná ⬜ BR (RO) 198 Gh50
Jacitara ⬜ BR (AM) 198 Gh47
Jack Daniels Distillery ⬜ USA 175 Fg28
Jackhead ⬜ CDN (MB) 172 Fb20
Jackman Station ⬜ USA (ME) 176 Ge23
Jacks ⬜ USA (NV) 171 Ec25
Jacksboro ⬜ USA (TX) 174 Fa29
Jackson ⬜ USA (CA) 170 Dk26
Jackson ⬜ USA (KY) 178 Fj27
Jackson ⬜ USA (MN) 172 Fc24
Jackson ⬜ USA (MS) 175 Fe26
Jackson ⬜ USA (OH) 173 Fj26
Jackson ⬜ USA (WY) 169 Ee24
Jackson ⬜ USA (TN) 175 Ff28
Jackson's Arm ⬜ CDN (NF) 177 Hb21
Jacksonville ⬜ USA (AL) 175 Fh29
Jacksonville ⬜ USA (FL) 178 Fk28
Jacksonville ⬜ USA (FL) 178 Fk30
Jacksonville ⬜ USA (GA)
Jacksonville ⬜ USA (IL) 175 Fe26
Jacksonville ⬜ USA (NC) 178 Gb28
Jacksonville ⬜ USA (TX) 174 Fc30
Jacksonville Beach ⬜ USA (FL) 178 Fk30
Jacmel ⬜ USA (OK) 174 Fa28
Jack Wade ⬜ USA (AK) 165 Ck13
Jacmel ⬜ RH 186 Gd36
Jaco ⬜ CR 185 Fh41
Jacó ⬜ CR 185 Fh41
Jacobabad ⬜ PAK (BA) 201 Hk51
Jacobina ⬜ BR (BA) 201 Hk51
Jacob Lake ⬜ USA (AZ) 171 Ed27
Jacobsdal ⬜ ZA 155 Mc60
Jacques Cartier, Mount ⬜ CDN 176 Gh21
Jacuizinho ⬜ BR (RS) 204 Hd60
Jacundá ⬜ BR (RO) 198 Gj50
Jacup ⬜ AUS (WA) 104 Qk62
Jacupiranga ⬜ BR (SP) 205 Hf58
Jada ⬜ WAN 139 Lg41
Jadcherla ⬜ IND (APH) 83 Ok37
Jadebusen ⬜ D 32 Lj37
Jadowniki ⬜ PL 41 Ma41
Jadraque ⬜ E 28 Kr50
Jaén ⬜ E 27 Kr53
Jaén ⬜ PE 196 Gb48
Jaffna ⬜ CL 85 Pa42
Jafr, Al- ⬜ JOR 58 Mj30
Jafura ⬜ KSA 61 Nf33

Jahangira ⬜ PK 65 Og29
Jahangirabad ⬜ IND (UPH) 81 Ok31
Jahangirganj ⬜ IND (UPH) 83 Pb32
Jahazpur ⬜ IND (RJT) 82 Oj33
Jahotyn ⬜ UA 49 Mf20
Jahrah ⬜ KWT 59 Nd31
Jahrom ⬜ IR 64 Ng31
Jaicós ⬜ BR (PI) 201 Hk49
Jaigarh Fort ⬜ IND 80 Oh32
Jailolo ⬜ RI 91 Rd45
Jailolo = Halmahera ⬜ RI 91 Re45
Jaina ⬜ MEX (CAM) 183 Fe35
Jainca ⬜ CHN (QHI) 72 Qc28
Jainti ⬜ IND (WBG) 86 Pe33
Jaintiapur ⬜ BD 86 Pf33
Jainu ⬜ BR (AM) 198 Gf49
Jaipur ⬜ IND (RJT) 82 Oj32
Jaipur ⬜ IND (ASM) 86 Ph32
Jaipurhat ⬜ BD 86 Pe33
Jais Aben Resort ⬜ PNG 115 Sc48
Jaisalmer ⬜ IND (RJT) 80 Of32
Jaisalmer Fort ⬜ IND 80 Of32
Jaisamand Sanctuary 🏞 IND 82 Oh33
Jaisinghnagar ⬜ IND (MPH) 83 Pa34
Jaiyuhun ⬜ IND (MPH)
Jajarkot ⬜ NEP 81 Pb31
Jajarm ⬜ IR 62 Nj27
Jajce ⬜ BIH 35 Ls46
Jakabszállás ⬜ H 43 Lu44
Jakalį ⬜ SCG 44 Lu46
Jakar ⬜ BHT 86 Pf32
Jakarta ⬛ RI 95 Qd49
Jakes Point ⬜ LAR 127 Ma31
Jakharrah ⬜ LAR 128 Ma31
Jakiri ⬜ CAM 138 Lf42
Jakkvik ⬜ S 16 Lj12
Jan Mayen ⬜ N 14 Kb02
Jan Mayen ⬜ N 14 Kb02
Jan Mayen ⬜ N 14 Kb02
Jana-indijirskaja nizmennost' ⬜ RUS 55 Sa04
Janakpur ⬜ IND (UPH) 81 Ok32
Janaúba ⬜ BR (MG) 203 Hj54
Janaucú, Ilha ⬜ BR (AP) 200 He45
Janda, La ⬜ E 27 Kp54
Jandanku ⬜ IND (ORS) 83 Pd35
Jandaia do Sul ⬜ BR (PR) 202 Hd57
Jandiala ⬜ IND (PJB) 80 Oh30
Jandola ⬜ PK 65 Of29
Jandowae ⬜ AUS (QLD) 109 Sd57
Janducu ⬜ BR (AM) 198 Gj48
Janesville ⬜ USA (WI) 173 Ff24
Janga ⬜ GH 137 Kk40
Jangada ⬜ BR (MT) 202 Hb54
Jangamo ⬜ MOC 153 Mh58
Jangany ⬜ RM 157 Nc56
Jangaon ⬜ IND (APH) 83 Ok36
Jangany ⬜ IND (WBG) 86 Pe33
Jangi ⬜ IND 81 Oj30
Jangir ⬜ RI 95 Qh49
Jangkar ⬜ RI 95 Qh49
Jangngai ⬜ RI 95 Qh49
Jani Khel ⬜ AFG 63 Oe29
Janīn ⬜ IND (ORS) 83 Pd35
Janja ⬜ BIH 44 Lu46
Jankovci ⬜ HR 35 Lt45
Janneh ⬜ IRQ 59 Nc30
Jansath ⬜ IND (UPH) 81 Oj31
Janakpur ⬜ NEP 81 Pc32
Jannah ⬜ UAE 61 Ng33
Janjanbureh ⬜ GAM
Jannatabad ⬜ IR 62 Nj28
Janos ⬜ MEX 180 Eg30
Jánoshalma ⬜ H 43 Lu44
Jánosháza ⬜ H 42 Ls43
Jánossomorja ⬜ H 42 Ls43
Jánów Lubelski ⬜ PL 41 Mc40
Janowo ⬜ PL 41 Ma37
Janów Podlaski ⬜ PL 41 Mc39
Jans ⬜ E 29 Kt51
Jansenville ⬜ ZA 155 Mc62
Janski zaliv ⬜ RUS 55 Rd04
Jantan ⬜ RI 114 Rh47
Jantarnyj ⬜ RUS 39 Ma36
Jantia Hills ⬜ IND 86 Pf33
Jantinguie ⬜ MOC 155 Mg58
Januária ⬜ BR (MG) 203 Hj54
Janville ⬜ F 25 Lb43
Janze ⬜ F 23 Kt42
Japan ⬜ J 73 Sa08
Japan Basin ⬜ 77 Rh24
Japanese World War II Bunker ⬜ RI 91 Rd45
Japan Trench ⬜ 51 Sa06
Japan World War II Headquarter ⬜ RI 91 Rd45
Japaratuba ⬜ BR (AL) 201 Jc50
Japarica ⬜ BR (TI) 195 Hg46
Jápiba ⬜ FIN 38 Mh28
Jápuria, T.I. ⬜ BR 199 Ha51
Japurá ⬜ BR (AM) 198 Ga46
Japurá ⬜ BR 198 Gd46
Jaqué ⬜ PA 185 Ga42
Jaquirí, T.I. ⬜ BR 194 Gh45
Jara, La ⬜ E 27 Kq51
Jarabacoa ⬜ DOM 186 Gd36
Jarablos ⬜ SYR 56 Mj27
Jaraguá ⬜ BR (GO) 202 Hd53
Jaraguá do Sul ⬜ BR (SC) 205 Hf59
Jaragua, P.N. 🏞 DOM 186 Gd36
Jarahueca ⬜ C 179 Ga34
Jaraicejo ⬜ E 27 Kp51
Jaral de la Vera ⬜ E 27 Kp50
Jaral de Berrios ⬜ MEX (GJT) 182 Ek35
Jaramataia ⬜ BR (AL) 201 Jc50
Jaramillo ⬜ RA (SC) 210 Gf69
Ja'ranah ⬜ KSA 59 Na29
Jarandilla de la Vera ⬜ E 27 Kp50
Jarānwāla ⬜ PAK (PJB) 65 Og30
Jarabub ⬜ LAR 128 Mc32

Jamnagar ⬜ IND (GUJ) 82 Of34
Jamnagar Fort ⬜ IND (GUJ) 82 Of34
Jamnice ⬜ CZ 42 Lq41
Jamno ⬜ PL 40 Ls38
Jampur ⬜ PK 65 Og31
Jamsah ⬜ ET 129 Mg31
Jämsä ⬜ FIN 38 Mf29
Jämsänkoski ⬜ FIN 38 Mf29
Jamshedpur ⬜ IND (JKD) 83 Pd34
Jamtara ⬜ IND (JKD) 83 Pd34
Jämtland ⬜ S 16 Lh14
Jamu ⬜ ETH 142 Mh42
Jamui ⬜ IND (BIH) 83 Pd33
Jamund ⬜ CO 192 Gb44
Jamunkira ⬜ IND (ORS) 83 Pc35
Jamur ⬜ KSA 59 Na28
Jana ⬜ RUS 55 Rb06
Janab ⬜ SYR 56 Mi27
Janakpur Road ⬜ NEP 81 Pc32
Janapur ⬜ RUS 39 Mb35
Jan Mayen ⬜ N 14 Kb02
Jan Mayen ⬜ N 14 Kb02
Jan Mayen ⬜ N 14 Kb02

Jasaan ⬜ RP 91 Rc41
Jasa ⬜ AL 44 Lu48
Jasa Tornić ⬜ SCG 44 Ma45
Jasenica ⬜ HR 35 Mk22
Jasenskaja ⬜ RUS 49 Mk25
Jashpurnagar ⬜ IND (CGH) 83 Pc34
Jasień ⬜ PL 40 Lq39
Jasin ⬜ MAL 92 Qa43
Jasinja ⬜ UA 43 Me42
Jašiūnai ⬜ LT 39 Mf36
Jask ⬜ IR 61 Nj33
Jasło ⬜ PL 41 Mb41
Jasmund, N.P. 🏞 D 32 Lo36
Jasnaja Poljana ⬜ RUS 39 Mb35
Jasnogorsk ⬜ RUS 48 Mj18
Jasnoe ⬜ RUS 39 Mb35
Jasonovo ⬜ RUS 77 Sa22
Jasper ⬜ CDN (AB) 168 Ea19
Jasper ⬜ USA (AL) 175 Fg29
Jasper ⬜ USA (AR) 174 Fd27
Jasper ⬜ USA (FL) 178 Fj30
Jasper ⬜ USA (IN) 175 Fg26
Jasper ⬜ USA (TX) 174 Fd30
Jasper ⬜ USA (NY) 177 Gb24
Jasper Lake ⬜ CDN 168 Ea19
Jasper N.P. 🏞 CDN 168 Ea19
Jasper Tramway ⬜ CDN 168 Eb19
Jasra ⬜ IND (UPH) 81 Ok32
Jassan ⬜ IRQ 59 Nc30
Jassira ⬜ SP 145 Nc45
Jastarnia ⬜ PL 40 Lt36
Jasterbarsko ⬜ HR 35 Lg45
Jastrebarsko ⬜ HR 35 Lq45
Jastrzębia ⬜ PL 41 Mb37
Jastrzębie Gora ⬜ PL 40 Lt36
Jastrzębie-Zdrój ⬜ PL 40 Lt41
Jászapáti ⬜ H 43 Ma43
Jászárokszállás ⬜ H 43 Lu43
Jászberény ⬜ H 43 Lu43
Jászladány ⬜ H 43 Ma43
Jaszczów ⬜ PL 41 Mc40
Jata ⬜ BR (GO) 202 Hd56
Jati ⬜ PK 65 Oe33
Jatibonico ⬜ C 179 Ga35
Jatijajar Cave ⬜ RI 95 Qd49
Jatiragá ⬜ RI 95 Qd49
Jatwangi ⬜ RI 95 Qe49
Jatni ⬜ IND (ORS) 83 Pd35
Jatobá ⬜ BR (AM) 199 Hj48
Jatobá ⬜ BR (BA) 201 Hj50
Jatobá ⬜ BR (MT) 202 Hc52
Jatobá ⬜ BR (PA) 199 Hd48
Jatobá do Piauí ⬜ BR (PI) 201 Hk48
Jatobal ⬜ BR
Jatupatina ⬜ IND (WBG) 86 Pe33
Jatuarana, T.I. ⬜ BR 199 Ha47
Jaú ⬜ BR (SP) 202 Hf57
Jauaperi ⬜ BR (AM) 199 Ha46
Jaua-Sariraninama, P.N. 🏞 YV 193 Gh43
Jauca ⬜ BR (BA) 201 Hk52
Jauja ⬜ PE 197 Gc51
Jaumave ⬜ MEX (TAM) 182 Fa34
Jaungulbene ⬜ LV 39 Mg33
Jaunjelgava ⬜ LV 39 Mf33
Jaunpiebalga ⬜ LV 39 Mg33
Jaunpils ⬜ LV 39 Me33
Jaunpur ⬜ IND (UPH) 83 Pb33
Jaupaci ⬜ BR (GO) 202 Hc54
Jauru ⬜ BR (MS) 202 Hc55
Jauru ⬜ BR (MT) 206 Ha53
Java ⬜ RI 95 Qd49
Javari ⬜ BR (AM) 196 Gd48
Java Sea ⬜ RI 95 Qf48
Javarthushuu ⬜ MNG 70 Qg21
Java Trench ⬜ 52 Pb10
Jávea = Xàbia ⬜ E 29 Ku52
Javhlant ⬜ MNG 70 Qf21
Javhlant ⬜ MNG 70 Qf21
Jávkhlant ⬜ MNG 70 Qe21
Javorie ⬜ SK 43 Lu42
Javoriv ⬜ UA 43 Md41
Javornik ⬜ CZ 42 Ls40
Javron ⬜ F 25 La42
Jawand ⬜ AFG 63 Ob28
Jawhar ⬜ IND (MHT) 82 Og36
Jawhar ⬜ SP 145 Nd45
Jawor ⬜ PL 40 Lr39
Jaworki ⬜ PL 41 Ma41
Jaworzno ⬜ PL 41 Lu40
Jayanca ⬜ PE 196 Ga49
Jayapatna ⬜ IND (ORS) 83 Pb36
Jayapura ⬜ RI 115 Sa47
Jayawijaya, Pegunungan ⬜ RI 114 Rj47
Jayb, Al- ⬜ JOR
Jaynagar ⬜ IND (BIH) 83 Pd32
Jayrud ⬜ SYR 56 Mj29
Jayton ⬜ USA (TX) 174 Ek29
Jaza'ir al Farasan ⬜ KSA 60 Na37
Jazirah ⬜ KSA 60 Nb36
Jazirat al Batinah ⬜ KSA 59 Ne32
Jazireh-ye Abu Musa ⬜ IR
Jazireh-ye Hendorabi ⬜ IR 64 Ng32
Jazireh-ye Hengam ⬜ IR 64 Nh32
Jazireh-ye Hormoz ⬜ IR 64 Nh32
Jazireh-ye Kish ⬜ IR 64 Ng32
Jazireh-ye Lavan ⬜ IR 64 Ng32
Jazireh-ye Qeshm ⬜ IR 64 Nh32
Jazireh-ye Sirri ⬜ IR 64 Ng32
Jazminal ⬜ MEX (COH) 181 Ek33
Jbel ⬜ RO 44 Md45
Jbel ⬜ PK 65 Qc46
Jean ⬜ USA (NV) 170 Ec28
Jeannin ⬜ BR (SC)

Jemaa Ida Oussemial ⬜ MA 224 Kf31
Jemaja ⬜ RI 92 Qd44
Jemaluang ⬜ MAL 92 Qb44
Jember ⬜ RI 95 Qf50
Jembongan ⬜ GMB 136 Kc40
Jemez Ind. Res. ⬜ USA 171 Eg28
Jemez Pueblo ⬜ USA (NM) 171 Eg28
Jemielno ⬜ PL 40 Lr39
Jeminay ⬜ CHN (XUZ) 67 Pc22
Jemna ⬜ WAN 138 Ld42
Jempara ⬜ RI 95 Qh47
Jen ⬜ WAN 139 Lf41
Jena ⬜ USA (LA) 175 Fd30
Jenakijeve ⬜ UA 49 Mk21
Jenbach ⬜ A 34 Lm43
Jenda ⬜ MW 146 Rg2
Jendouba ⬜ TN 126 Le27
Jengish Chokusu ⬜ KS 66 Pa24
Jenin ⬜ IL 56 Mh29
Jenipapo ⬜ BR (BA) 201 Hj48
Jenipapo ⬜ BR (TO) 200 Hf49
Jenlulse Bank ⬜ 7 Qb31
Jenner ⬜ CDN (AB) 169 Ee20
Jennersdorf ⬜ A 35 Lr44
Jennings ⬜ USA (LA) 175 Fd30
Jenny Lind I. ⬜ CDN 163 Ed05
Jepara ⬜ RI 95 Qf49
Jeppener ⬜ RA (BA) 209 Ha63
Jepua ⬜ FIN 38 Me27
Jequeri ⬜ BR (MG) 203 Hj56
Jequié ⬜ BR (BA) 201 Hk52
Jequitibá ⬜ BR (MG) 203 Hj55
Jequitinhonha ⬜ BR (MG)
Jerangle ⬜ AUS (NSW) 111 Se63
Jerantut ⬜ MAL 92 Qa44
Jerba ⬜ SUD 144 Mf43
Jercevo ⬜ RUS 54 Na06
Jeréctico ⬜ MEX (GJT) 182
Jereh ⬜ IR 59 Nf31
Jérémie ⬜ RH 186 Gc36
Jeremoabo ⬜ BR (BA) 201 Jb50
Jeres ⬜ BR (AM) 196 Ge48
Jerez de la Frontera ⬜ E 27 Ko54
Jerez de los Caballeros ⬜ E 27 Ko52
Jericho ⬜ AUS 108 Rh54 — uncertain
Jericho ⬜ IL 58 Mh30
Jericó ⬜ CO 192 Gc43
Jericoacoara, P.N. de 🏞 BR 201 Hk47
Jeriquara ⬜ GH 137 Kk41
Jerilderie ⬜ AUS (NSW) 111 Sc63
Jerkoh ⬜ MAL 92 Qa43
Jerle La ⬜ CHN 68 Pa30
Jerome ⬜ USA (ID) 168 Ec24
Jerome ⬜ USA (AZ) 171 Ee28
Jersey ⬜ GB 21 Ks41
Jersey City ⬜ USA (NJ) 177 Gc25
Jerseyville ⬜ USA (IL) 175 Fe26
Jersey Zoo ⬜ GB 22 Ks41
Jerudong Park ⬜ BRU 94 Qd43
Jerusalem ⬜ IL 58 Mh30
Jerusalem ⬛ IL 58 Mh30
Jervis Bay ⬜ AUS (NSW) 111 Sf63

Jefferson, Mount ⬜ USA 170 Eb26
Jeffersontown ⬜ USA (KY) 175 Fh26
Jeffersonville ⬜ USA (GA) 178 Fj29
Jeffersonville ⬜ USA (IN) 175 Fh26
Jeffrey City ⬜ USA (WY) 171 Ef25
Jeffrey's Bay ⬜ ZA 155 Mc63
Jef-Jef el Kébir ⬜ TCH 134 Ma35
Jega ⬜ WAN 138 Lc40
Jege ⬜ WAN 138 Lc41
Jehanabad ⬜ IND (BIH) 83 Pc33
Jeinemeni, Cerro ⬜ RCH 210 Gd69
Jejevo ⬜ SOL 117 Sk50
Jekabpils ⬜ LV 39 Mf34
Jelanec' ⬜ UA 49 Mf22
Jelcz-Laskowice ⬜ PL 40 Ls39
Jelenakowska Góra ⬜ PL 40 Lq40
Jelena Góra ⬜ PL 40 Lq40
Jelgava ⬜ LV 39 Me34
Jeli ⬜ MAL 92 Qa43
Jellicoe ⬜ CDN (ON) 173 Fg21
Jelšava ⬜ SK 43 Ma42
Jelø ⬜ N 30 Lk31
Jelsa ⬜ N 30 Lg31
Jelutong ⬜ RI 95 Qd47
Jemaa ⬜ GH 137 Kk42

Jew Town ◻ IND 84 Oj41
Jeypur ◻ IND (ORS) 83 Pb36
Jeziorany ◻ PL 41 Ma37
Jezioro Bukowo ◻ PL 40 Lr36
Jezioro Jamno ◻ PL 41 Lu37
Jeziorko Jeziorak ◻ PL 41 Lu37
Jeziorko Kopan ◻ PL 40 Lt39
Jeziorko Lebsko ◻ PL 40 Ls36
Jeziorko Śniardwy ☑ ◻ PL 41 Mb37
Jeziorko Wicko ◻ PL 40 Lr36
Jeziorko Zegrzyńskie ◻ PL 41 Mb38
Jeżów ◻ PL 41 Lu39
Jezzine ◻ L 56 Mn29
Jhabua ◻ IND (MPH) 82 Oh34
Jhajha ◻ IND (BIH) 83 Pd33
Jhajjar ◻ IND (HYA) 80 Oj31
Jhal ◻ PK 65 Od31
Jhalakati ◻ BD 86 Pf34
Jhalawar ◻ IND (RJT) 82 Oj33
Jhalida ◻ IND (WBG) 83 Pd34
Jhalod ◻ IND (GUJ) 82 Oh34
Jhang ◻ PK 65 Og30
Jhanjharpur ◻ IND (BIH) 83 Pd32
Jhansi ◻ IND (UPH) 83 Ok33
Jhanzi Fort ◻ IND 83 Ok33
Jhanzi ◻ IND (ASM) 86 Ph32
Jhargram ◻ IND (WBG) 83 Pd34
Jharkhand ◻ IND 83 Pc34
Jharol ◻ IND (RJT) 82 Oh33
Jharsuguda ◻ IND (ORS) 83 Pc35
Jhatpat ◻ PK 65 Oe31
Jhelum ◻ PK 65 Og29
Jhenaidah ◻ BD 86 Pe34
Jhimpir ◻ PK 65 Oe33
Jhudo ◻ PK 65 Oe33
Jhunjhunun ◻ IND (RJT) 80 Oh31
Jiachuan ◻ CHN (GZH) 74 Qd33
Jiading ◻ CHN (SHG) 78 Ra30
Jiahe ◻ CHN (HUN) 74 Qg33
Jiamusi ◻ CHN (HLG) 76 Rf22
Jiajiang ◻ CHN (SCH) 75 Qh32
Ji'an ◻ CHN (JLN) 76 Rd23
Jian ◻ IR 64 Ng30
Jianchang ◻ CHN (LNG) 73 Qk25
Jianchaxi ◻ CHN (GZH) 74 Qe31
Jianchi ◻ CHN (HUB) 74 Qe30
Jianchuan ◻ CHN (YUN) 87 Pk32
Jiande ◻ CHN (ZJG) 75 Qj33
Jiang'an ◻ CHN (SCH) 74 Qc31
Jiangcheng ◻ CHN (YUN) 87 Qa33
Jiangchuan ◻ CHN 87 Qb33
Jiangdi ◻ CHN (YUN) 87 Qa32
Jiangdu ◻ CHN (JGS) 78 Qk29
Jiange ◻ CHN (SCH) 74 Qc30
Jiangjin ◻ CHN (CQG) 74 Qd31
Jiangkou ◻ CHN (GZG) 74 Qe35
Jianghua ◻ CHN (HUN) 74 Qg33
Jiangjunmiao ◻ CHN (XUZ) 67 Pf23
Jiangkou ◻ CHN (CQG) 74 Qe30
Jiangkou ◻ CHN (GZH) 74 Qe32
Jiang'ou ◻ CHN (FJN) 75 Qk31
Jianping ◻ CHN (LNG) 73 Qk25
Jianshui ◻ CHN (YUN) 87 Qb34
Jianwuluo ◻ CHN (GSU) 72 Qc29
Jianmen ◻ CHN (GDG) 75 Qg34
Jiangsu ◻ CHN 78 Qk29
Jiangxi ◻ CHN 75 Qh32
Jiangyou ◻ CHN (SCH) 74 Qc30
Jianhe ◻ CHN (GZH) 74 Qe33
Jianhu ◻ CHN (JGS) 78 Ra30
Jianle ◻ CHN (HUB) 75 Qj32
Jianli ◻ CHN (HUB) 74 Qg31
Jianmen Path ◻ CHN 74 Qc29
Jianmen ◻ CHN (GZH) 74 Qe32
Jian'ou ◻ CHN (FJN) 75 Qk31
Jianping ◻ CHN (LNG) 73 Qk25
Jianshui ◻ CHN (YUN) 87 Qb34
Jianyang ◻ CHN (SCH) 74 Qc30
Jianyang ◻ CHN (FJN) 75 Qk32
Jiaohe ◻ CHN (JLN) 76 Rd24
Jiaohe Gucheng ◻ CHN 67 Pe24
Jiaojiang ◻ CHN (ZJG) 75 Ra31
Jiaokou ◻ CHN (SAX) 72 Qf27
Jiaoling ◻ CHN (GDG) 75 Qj33
Jiaozhou ◻ CHN (SDG) 78 Qk28
Jiaotebo ◻ CHN (TIB) 68 Pd31
Jiaozhou ◻ CHN (SDG) 73 Qg27
Jiaozuo ◻ CHN (HNN) 73 Qg28
Jiasa ◻ CHN (YUN) 87 Qa32
Jiashan ◻ CHN (AHU) 78 Qj29
Jiashan ◻ CHN (ZJG) 78 Ra30
Jiashi ◻ CHN (XUZ) 66 Oj26
Jia Xian ◻ CHN (HNN) 73 Qg28
Jia Xian ◻ CHN (SAX) 72 Qf27
Jiaxing ◻ CHN (ZJG) 78 Ra30
Jiayin ◻ CHN (HLG) 76 Rf21
Jiayu ◻ CHN (HUB) 75 Qg32
Jiayuguan ◻ CHN (GSU) 69 Pk26
Jibert ◻ RO 43 Mf45
Jiberu ◻ WAN 139 Lg41
Jiblya ◻ UZ 132 Lo39
Jibou ◻ RO 43 Md43
Jibóia ◻ BR (AM) 193 Gf45
Jibou ◻ BR 43 Md43
Jicarilla Apache Ind. Res. ☑ USA 171 Eg27
Jícaro Galán ◻ HN 184 Fg39
Jichang ◻ CHN (GZH) 74 Qd33
Jichang ◻ CHN (GZH) 74 Qd33
Jičín ◻ CZ 42 Lo40
Jiddah ◻ KSA 58 Mk35
Jiddat al-Harasis ◻ OM 61 Nh36
Jiele Golden Pagoda ☑ CHN 86 Pj33
Jielong ◻ CHN (CQG) 74 Qd31
Jieshi ◻ CHN (GDG) 75 Qh34
Jieshou ◻ CHN (AHU) 73 Qh29
Jiexi ◻ CHN (GDG) 75 Qh34
Jiexiu ◻ CHN (SAX) 72 Qf28
Jieznas ◻ LT 39 Me36
Jiggalong ◻ AUS (WA) 102 Ra57
Jiggalong Aboriginal Reserve ☑ AUS 102 Ra57
Jiggs ◻ USA (NV) 170 Ec25
Jigme Dorji N.P. ☑ BHT 86 Pe32
Jigongshan ◻ CHN 73 Qh30
Jiguaní ◻ C 179 Ga35
Jihanah ◻ YE 60 Nc38
Jihlava ◻ CZ 42 Lq41
Jihua Dao ◻ CHN 76 Rd24
Jiigley ◻ SP 145 Nc43
Jijel ◻ DZ 126 Lc27
Jijiga ◻ ETH 143 Nb41
Jijona = Xixona ◻ E 29 Ku52
Jiju ◻ CHN (YUN) 87 Qa33
Jilamo ◻ HN 184 Fg40
Jilan ◻ IR 62 Ng27
Jilava ◻ RO 45 Mf46
Jilbadji Nature Reserve ☑ AUS (WA) 104 Qk61
Jilib ◻ SP 145 Na45
Jilin ◻ CHN (JLN) 76 Rd24
Jilin ◻ CHN 76 Rd24
Jiliu He ◻ CHN 76 Rc21
Jima ◻ ETH 142 Mj42
Jim Abad ◻ DOM 186 Ge36
Jimani ◻ DOM 186 Gd36
Jimata ◻ ETH 142 Mj41

Jimbe ◻ ANG 151 Mb51
Jimbolia ◻ RO 44 Ma45
Jimda ◻ CHN (FJN) 75 Qd33
Jimei ◻ CHN (FJN) 75 Qk33
Jiménez de la Frontera ◻ E 27 Kp54
Jiménez ◻ MEX (CHH) 181 Eh32
Jiménez ◻ MEX (COH) 181 Ek31
Jiménez ◻ RP 91 Rb41
Jiménez del Téul ◻ MEX (ZCT) 182 Ej34
Jimena Waterfall ☑ DOM 186 Ge36
Jimeta ◻ WAN 139 Lg41
Jim Jim Falls ☑ AUS 106 Rg52
Jimsar ◻ CHN (XUZ) 67 Pe24
Jimulco ◻ MEX (COH) 181 Ej33
Jinan ◻ CHN (SDG) 73 Qj27
Jinchai ◻ CHN (GZG) 74 Qd33
Jinchang ◻ CHN (GSU) 72 Qb26
Jincheng ◻ CHN (SAA) 72 Qe27
Jincheng ◻ CHN (YUN) 87 Qb33
Jinchuan ◻ CHN (SCH) 72 Qb30
Jinci Si ☑ CHN 72 Qg27
Jind ◻ IND (HYA) 80 Oj31
Jindabyne ◻ AUS (NSW) 111 Sd63
Jindayris ◻ SYR 56 Mj28
Jindera ◻ AUS (NSW) 111 Sd63
Jindiana ◻ IND (GUJ) 82 Of34
Jindo ◻ ROK 78 Rc27
Jindřichov ◻ CZ 42 Ls40
Jindřichův Hradec ◻ CZ 42 Lq41
Jinfo Shan ◻ CHN 74 Qd31
Jing'an ◻ CHN (JGX) 75 Qh31
Jingbian ◻ CHN (SAA) 72 Qe27
Jingde ◻ CHN (AHU) 78 Qk30
Jingdezhen ◻ CHN (JGX) 75 Qj31
Jingdong ◻ CHN (YUN) 87 Qa33
Jinghai ◻ CHN (AUS) (NSW) 111 Sd63
Jinggangshan ◻ CHN (JGX) 75 Qh32
Jinggangdaizu ◻ CHN (YUN) 87 Qa34
Jinghe ◻ CHN (XUZ) 66 Pb23
Jinghong ◻ CHN (YUN) 87 Qa34
Jingjiang ◻ CHN (JGS) 78 Ra29
Jingle ◻ CHN (SAX) 72 Qg27
Jingmen ◻ CHN (HUB) 74 Qg30
Jingpo ◻ CHN (HLG) 76 Re24
Jingshan ◻ CHN (HUB) 74 Qg30
Jingtai ◻ CHN (GSU) 72 Qc27
Jingtieshan ◻ CHN (GSU) 69 Pj26
Jingxi ◻ CHN (GZG) 74 Qc34
Jingxi ◻ CHN (GZG) 74 Qd33
Jingxian ◻ CHN (AHU) 78 Qk30
Jingxing ◻ CHN (HBI) 73 Qg27
Jingxing ◻ CHN (HLG) 71 Pd32
Jingyu ◻ CHN (JLN) 76 Rd24
Jingyuan ◻ CHN (GSU) 72 Qc27
Jingzhou Nao ◻ CHN 74 Qf31
Jinhe ◻ CHN (NMZ) 71 Qa24
Jinhu ◻ CHN (JGS) 75 Qk30
Jinhua ◻ CHN (ZJG) 75 Qj32
Jining ◻ CHN (NMZ) 73 Qg25
Jining ◻ CHN (SDG) 73 Qj27
Jinja ◻ EC 196 Fk46
Jinja ◻ EAU 144 Mg45
Jinja War Cemetery ☑ EAU 144 Mg45
Jinjiang = Panzhihua ◻ CHN (SCH) 87 Qa32
Jinjiang ◻ CHN 75 Qk31
Jinka ◻ ETH 144 Mj43
Jinkouhe ◻ CHN (SCH) 87 Qb33
Jinmu ◻ CHN (HUB) 75 Qh33
Jinnah Barrage ☑ PK 65 Og29
Jinotega ◻ NIC 184 Fg40
Jinotepe ◻ NIC 184 Fg40
Jinping ◻ CHN (YUN) 74 Qe32
Jinping ◻ CHN (YUN) 87 Qb34
Jinping ◻ CHN (GZH) 74 Qe33
Jin'ou ◻ CHN (JGX) 75 Qh31
Jinsha ◻ CHN (GZH) 74 Qd32
Jinsha Jiang ◻ CHN 87 Qa32
Jinshi ◻ CHN (HUN) 74 Qf31
Jinshanlin ◻ CHN 73 Qj25
Jinshatan ◻ CHN (SAX) 73 Qg26
Jinta ◻ CHN (GSU) 69 Pj26
Jintan ◻ CHN (HUN) 74 Qf32
Jintan ◻ CHN (JGS) 78 Qk30
Jintotolo Channel ◻ RP 90 Rb40
Jintur ◻ IND (MHT) 82 Oj36
Jinxi ◻ CHN (JGX) 75 Qj32
Jinxi ◻ CHN (LNG) 76 Ra25
Jinxiang ◻ CHN (ZJG) 75 Ra31
Jinyun ◻ CHN (ZJG) 75 Ra31
Jinzhou ◻ CHN (LNG) 76 Ra25
Jinzhou ◻ CHN (HBI) 73 Qh27
Ji-Paraná ◻ BR (RO) 198 Gk51
Jipijapa ◻ EC 196 Fk46
Jiqui ◻ C 179 Ga35
Jiquilillo ◻ NIC 184 Fg39
Jiquilpan de Juárez ◻ MEX (MHC) 182 Ej35
Jiquipilco ◻ BR (BA) 201 Ja52
Jiquirica ◻ BR (BA) 201 Ja52
Jira Alem ◻ ETH 142 Mk42
Jirga Adel ◻ ETH 142 Mj43
Jiroft ◻ IR 64 Nj31
Jirriban ◻ SP 143 Ne42
Jishan ◻ CHN (SAX) 72 Qf28
Jishou ◻ CHN (HUN) 74 Qe31
Jisitang ◻ CHN 74 Qd32
Jitarning ◻ AUS (WA) 104 Qj62
Jitia ◻ RO 45 Mg44
Jitra ◻ MAL 92 Qa42
Jitzamuri ◻ MEX (SL) 180 Ef32
Jiucai Ling ◻ CHN 74 Qf33
Jiuchang ◻ CHN (GZH) 74 Qd32
Jiudong ◻ CHN (GSU) 72 Qb27
Jiufu ◻ CHN (AHU) 78 Qk30
Jiuhuashan ◻ CHN 78 Qj30
Jiujiang ◻ CHN (JGX) 75 Qj31
Jiuling Shan ◻ CHN 75 Qh31
Jiulong = Kowloon ◻ CHN (HKG) 75 Qh34
Jiulong Shan ◻ CHN 75 Qk33
Jiupu ◻ CHN (SDG)
Jiurongcheng ◻ CHN (SDG) 73 Ra27
Jiutai ◻ CHN (JLN) 76 Rd23
Jiutepec ◻ MEX (GZG) 74 Qd33
Jiuyishan ◻ CHN 74 Qg33
Jiuzhaigou ◻ CHN (SCH) 72 Qb29
Jiuzhou ◻ CHN (HLG) 71 Pk20
Jiwani ◻ PK 65 Oa33
Jiwen ◻ CHN (NMZ) 71 Rb20
Jixian ◻ CHN (HLG) 76 Rf23
Jixian ◻ CHN (HBI) 73 Qj26
Ji Xian ◻ CHN (JLN) 76 Rd23
Jiyang ◻ CHN (SDG) 73 Qj27
Jizan ◻ KSA 60 Nb37
Jizzakh ◻ UZ 63 Od25
Jizzax ◻ UZ 63 Od25

Joal-Fadiout ◻ SN 130 Kb38
Joanna Beach ◻ AUS 111 Sc65
Joanópolis ◻ BR (SP) 205 Hf57
João Arregui ◻ BR (RS) 204 Hb60
João Câmara ◻ BR (RN)
João Chagas ◻ ANG 151 Mb51
João Lisboa ◻ BR (AM) 194 Ha46
João Monlevade ◻ BR (MG) 203 Hj55
João Neiva ◻ BR (ES) 203 Hk55
João Pataço ◻ MOC 153 Mh55
João Pessoa ◻ BR (PB) 201 Jc49
João Pinheiro ◻ BR (MG) 203 Hg54
Joaquim Pires ◻ BR (PI)
Joaquim V.González ◻ RA (SA) 207 Gj58
Joara ◻ IND (MPH) 82 Oh34
Jobabo ◻ C 179 Ga35
Jobal ◻ IND (MPH) 82 Oh34
Jobelt ◻ WAN 138 Le41
Jocoli ◻ RA (MD) 208 Gf62
Jocotepec ◻ MEX (JLC) 182 Ej35
Jocotán ◻ GCA 184 Ff38
Jodhpur ◻ IND (RJT) 80 Og32
Jodlo ◻ RJ 97 Rf46
Jodoigne ◻ B 23 Le40
Joe Batt's Arm ◻ CDN (NF) 177 Hc21
Joensuu ◻ FIN 38 Mk28
Joetsu ◻ J 77 Rk27
Jofane ◻ MOC 152 Mh56
Jõf di Montásio ◻ I 35 Lo44
Joffre, Mount ◻ CDN 168 Ed20
Jogana ◻ WAN 138 Le39
Joghah ◻ IND (BIH) 83 Pd32
Jõgeva ◻ EST 38 Mg32
Jog Falls ☑ IND 84 Oh38
Joghdan ◻ IR 64 Nj32
Joghdan Nagar ☑ IND (HPH) 81 Oj29
Jogjakarta ◻ RI 92 Qg50
Jogogo ◻ GH 137 La41
Jogues ◻ CDN (ON) 173 Fj21
Johan ◻ PK 65 Od31
Johanna Beach ◻ AUS 111 Sc65
Johannesburg ◻ USA (CA) 170 Eb28
Johannesburg ☑ ZA 155 Md59
Johanngeorgenstadt ◻ D 33 Ln40
John ◻ GUY 194 Ha45
John ◻ PK 65 Od32
Johnnie Shan ◻ CHN 69 Pj26
Johngxi ◻ CHN (GZG) 74 Qd33
Johngxing ◻ CHN (AHU) 78 Qk30
Johngxing ◻ CHN (HLG) 71 Pd32
Jingyu Nao ◻ CHN (GZG) 72 Qc27
John Day ◻ USA 168 Dk23
John Day Fossil Beds Nat. Mon. Clarno Unit ☑ USA 168 Dk23
John Day Fossil Beds Nat. Mon. Painted Hills Unit ☑ USA 168 Dk23
John Day Fossil Beds Nat. Mon. Sheep Rock Unit ☑ USA 168 Ea23
John Deere H.S. ☑ USA 173 Ff21
John Deere Pavilion ☑ USA (IL) 172 Fe25
John d'Or Prairie ◻ CDN (AB) 167 Ec16
John d'Or Prairie Ind. Res. ☑ CDN (AB) 167 Ec16
John Fitzgerald Kennedy Hyannis Museum ☑ USA 177 Gd25
John Flynn Memorial ☑ ☑ AUS 106 Rh55
John Henry Statue ☑ USA 178 Fk27
John Hopkins Glacier ☑ USA (AK) 166 Db16
John o'Groats ◻ GB 20 Kr32
John Pennekamp Coral Reef S.P. ☑ USA 179 Fa33
Johnson City ◻ USA (KS) 174 Ek27
Johnson City ◻ USA (NY) 177 Gd24
Johnson City ◻ USA (TX) 178 Fj27
Johnson City ◻ USA (TX) 174 Fa30
Johnsonburg ◻ USA (PA) 173 Ga24
Johnson N.H.P. ☑ USA 174 Fa30
Johnson River ◻ CDN 167 Di14
Johnsons ◻ CAS (QLD) 108 Dj25
Johnsons Crossing ◻ CDN (YT) 166 Dd15
Johnson Space Center ☑ USA 174 Fc31
Johnstone ◻ GB 20 Kq35
Johnstone ◻ AUS (NSW) 111 Sa63
Johnstown ◻ USA (NY) 177 Gc24
Johnstown ◻ USA (PA) 173 Ga25
Johnstown Flood Nat. Mon. ☑ USA 173 Ga25
Johor Bahru ◻ MAL 93 Qb45
Jõhvi ◻ EST 38 Mg31
Joiasy ◻ F 25 Ld43
Joinville ◻ F 23 Lf42
Joita ◻ RO 45 Mf46
Jokau ◻ SUD 142 Mg41
Jokhang ☑ CHN 69 Pf31
Jokoa Cupriją ◻ SCG 44 La47
Jokkmokk ◻ S 16 Lj13
Jôksûršârlõn ◻ IS 18 Kf26
Jolfa ◻ IR 57 Nc29
Joliet ◻ USA (IL) 173 Ff25
Joliette ◻ CDN (QC) 176 Gd22
Jolo Group ◻ RP 91 Ra43
Jolo Island ◻ RP 91 Ra43
Jomala ◻ FIN 38 Ld30
Jombang ◻ RI 95 Qg49
Jombory ◻ AFG 65 Oc28
Jomda ◻ CHN (TIB) 87 Pk30
Jomal Bazar ◻ IND (ASM) 86 Ph32
Jonava ◻ LT 39 Me36
Jondal ◻ N 30 Lg31
Jondó ◻ CHN (GSU) 70 Qa26
Jonesboro ◻ USA (AR) 175 Fe28
Jonesboro ◻ USA (LA) 175 Fd30
Jones Islands ◻ USA (AK) 165 Ch10
Jones Mountains ◻ ANT 6 Ha31
Jonesport ◻ USA (ME) 176 Gg23
Jones Sound ◻ CDN 163 Fd3
Jonglei Canal ◻ SUD 142 Mf41
Jonglong Shrine ☑ ROK 78 Rd27
Joniškis ◻ LT 39 Me34
Jõnkõping ◻ S 30 Ln34
Jonquière ◻ CDN (QC) 176 Ge21
Jonzac ◻ F 24 Ku45

Joplin ◻ USA (MO) 174 Fc27
Jora ◻ IND (MPH) 83 Oj32
Jordan ◻ IL 56 Mh29
Jordan ◻ JOR 58 Mj30
Jordan ◻ RP 90 Rb40
Jordània ◻ BR (MG) 203 Hk53
Jordan Valley ◻ USA (ID)
Jordbro ◻ S 31 Lt31
Jorf ◻ MA 125 Kh30
Joriapandi ◻ NEP 81 Pa31
Jorigam ◻ IND (ORS) 83 Pb36
Joriorepal ◻ IND (GUJ) 82 Of34
Jorm ◻ AFG 63 Oe27
Jörn ◻ S 16 Ma13
Joroinen ◻ FIN 38 Mh28
Jærpeland ◻ N 30 Lg31
Joru ◻ WAL 136 Ke42
Jos ◻ WAN 138 Le41
Josânica Banja ◻ SCG 44 Mb44
José Abad Santos ◻ RP 91 Rc43
José Battle y Ordóñez ◻ ROU 204 Hc62
José Bonifacio ◻ BR (SP) 202 Hf56
José Cardel ◻ MEX (VC) 183 Fb36
José de Freitas ◻ BR (PI) 201 Hj48
José del Carmen Ramírez, P.N. ☑ DOM 186 Ge36
José de San Martín ◻ RA (CB) 210 Ge68
José Enrique Rodó ◻ ROU 204 Hb62
Joselândia ◻ BR (MA) 200 Hh48
Joselândia ◻ BR (MT) 202 Hb54
Josení Bârgăului ◻ RO 43 Me43
Jose Panganiban ◻ RP 90 Rb38
José Paso ◻ RA (BA) 209 Gj63
José Pedro Varela ◻ ROU 204 Hc62
Joseph Bonaparte Gulf ◻ AUS 103 Re53
Josephstaal ◻ PNG 115 Sc48
José Rodrigues ◻ BR (PA) 200 Hd48
José Soriano ◻ IND (UTT) 81 Ok30
Joshin Etsu Kogen N.P. ☑ J 77 Rk27
Joshipur ◻ IND (ORS) 83 Pd35
Joshua Tree N.P. ☑ USA 170 Eb29
Joskar-Ola ◻ RUS (MEL)
Jos Plateau ◻ WAN 138 Le41
Josselin ◻ F 22 Ks43
Jostedalsbreen ◻ N 17 Ld15
Jostedalsbreen n.p. ◻ N 17 Le15
Joubertberge ◻ NAM 150 Lj55
Joubertina ◻ ZA 154 Mb62
Joulter Cays ◻ BS 179 Ga33
Joungs Cove ◻ CDN (NF) 176 Gh23
Jourdanton ◻ USA (TX) 181 Fa31
Joure ◻ NL 23 Lf38
Joutsa ◻ FIN 38 Mg29
Joutseno ◻ FIN 38 Mj29
Jovellanos ◻ C 179 Fk34
Jovânia ◻ BR (GO) 202 Hf54
Jowai ◻ IND (MHT) 82 Oh36
Jowzjân ◻ AFG 63 Oc27
Joya de Cerén ☑ ES 184 Ff39
Joyag ◻ BD 86 Pf34
Jozani-Chwaka Bay Conservation Area ☑ EAT 147 Mk49
Jozefów ◻ PL 41 Mb38
Jozefów ◻ PL 41 Md39
Jozefów ◻ PL 41 Ma39
Jozini ◻ ZA 155 Mg59
Jreida ◻ RIM 130 Kb36
Jreif ◻ RIM 130 Kb36
Juancheng ◻ CHN (SDG) 73 Qh28
Juangriego ◻ YV 193 Gj40
Juan Guerra ◻ PE 196 Gb49
Juani Island ◻ EAT 147 Mk49
Juan Island ◻ USA 168 Dj21
Juan Jorba ◻ RA (SL) 208 Gh62
Juan José Castelli ◻ RA (CH) 207 Gk58
Juan Fernández ◻ RCH 206 Ge53
Juanjuí ◻ PE 196 Gb49
Juan L.Lacaze ◻ ROU 209 Hb63
Juan N.Fernández ◻ RA (BA) 209 Ha65
Juan W.Gez ◻ RA (SL) 208 Gg62
Juapon ◻ GH 137 La42
Juárez ◻ MEX (MHT) 199 Hb51
Juárez ◻ BR (AM) 198 Gf47
Juárez ◻ MEX (COH) 181 Ek32
Juarina ◻ BR 200 Hd49
Juazeirinho ◻ BR (PB) 201 Jb49
Juàzeiro ◻ BR (BA) 201 Hk50
Juàzeiro do Norte ◻ BR (CE) 201 Ja49
Juba ◻ SUD 142 Mf43
Jubaíl al Sinaíyah ◻ KSA 59 Na32
Jubany ◻ ANT (RA) 6 Ha31
Jubba ◻ EAT 144 Mg47
Jübek ◻ D 32 Lk36
Jubilee Lake ◻ AUS 105 Rd60
Juçara ◻ BR (GO) 202 He53
Juçara ◻ GUY 194 Ha44
Júcar ◻ E 29 Ku51
Juchavičy ◻ BY 39 Mj34
Juchen ◻ D 32 Lh39
Juchitán de Zaragoza ◻ MEX (OAX) 183 Fc37
Juckwyaker Doley ☑ PL 41 Md38
Jucurucú ◻ BR (BA) 201 Jb49
Judah ◻ KSA 59 Ne33
Judaidat al Hamir ◻ IRQ 57 Nb30
Judayyidat 'Ar'ar ◻ KSA 58 Na30
Judenburg ◻ A 35 Lp43
Juderina ◻ SCG 44 Lu47
Jüdin ◻ RUS 48 Nf16
Juelsminde ◻ DK 30 Ll35
Juglorski Poluostrov ◻ RUS 77 Sa22
Jugorskij Šar ◻ RUS 49 Nd19
Juhnov ◻ RUS 48 Mh18
Juichiana ◻ CA 49 Nd22
Juigalpa ◻ NIC 184 Fh39
Juillac ◻ F 24 La45
Juína ◻ BR (MT) 199 Ha51

Juininha, T.I. ◻ BR 206 Ha53
Juist ◻ D 32 Lg37
Juiz de Fora ◻ BR (MG) 203 Hj56
Juina ◻ IRI 93 Qa47
Jujuy ◻ RA (JY) 207 Gh57
Jukagirskoe ploskogor'e ◻ RUS 55 Sc05
Jukkasjärvi ◻ S 16 Ma12
Jukonglukong ◻ RI 95 Qf44
Jülich ◻ D 32 Lg40
Julca ◻ MAL 94 Qf44
Julcán ◻ PE 196 Ga50
Juldessa ◻ ETH 145 Mk44
Julesburg ◻ USA (CO) 174 Ej25
Juli ◻ PE 206 Gf54
Julia Creek ◻ AUS (QLD) 107 Sa56
Luis Tamayo ◻ EC 196 Fk47
Julia Pfeiffer S.P. ☑ USA 170 Dk27
Juliasdale ◻ ZW 152 Mg55
Júlich ◻ D 32 Lg40
Juliães Alpe ◻ SLO 42 Lo45
Julimes ◻ MEX (CHH) 181 Eh31
Júlio Borges ◻ BR (PI) 200 Hh51
Júlio de Castilhos ◻ BR (RS) 204 Hd60
Júlio D.Otaño ◻ PY 204 Hc59
Julm Mesquita ◻ BR (PI)
Julong Shan ◻ CHN 72 Qf30
Julwania ◻ IND (MPH) 82 Oh35
Juma ◻ UZ 63 Od26
Jumali ◻ RP 90 Rb38
Jumla in Mtwana ◻ EAK 145 Mk47
Jumbe Foume ◻ EAT 147 Mj51
Jumbe Salims ◻ EAT 147 Mj51
Jumbilla ◻ PE 196 Ga48
Jumboo ◻ SP 145 Nb46
Jumeaux ◻ F 25 Ld45
Jumentos Cays ◻ BS 186 Gc34
Jumilla ◻ E 29 Ks52
Jumjum ◻ BR (BA) 195 Ha43
Jumla ◻ NEP 81 Pb31
Jumma Masjid (Gulbarga) ☑ IND 82 Oj37
Jumunde ◻ IR 64 Nh34
Jun Abad ◻ IR 64 Oa31
Juna Downs ◻ AUS (WA) 102 Qk57
Junagadh ◻ IND (GUJ) 82 Of35
Junagarh ◻ IND (ORS) 83 Pb36
Junan ◻ CHN (SDG) 78 Qk28
Juncal, Cerro ◻ RA/RCH 208 Gf62
Junction ◻ USA (TX) 174 Fa30
Junction ◻ USA (UT) 171 Ed26
Junction Bay ◻ AUS 106 Rg51
Junction ◻ USA (KS)
Junction City ◻ USA (LA)
Junction City ◻ USA (OR)
Jundah ◻ AUS (QLD) 108 Sb58
Jundee ◻ AUS (WA) 104 Qk59
Jundiaí ◻ BR (SP) 203 Hg57
Juneau ◻ USA (AK) 166 Dc17
Jungar Qi ◻ CHN (NMZ) 72 Qf26
Jungfrau ◻ CH 34 Lh44
Junglebrähn ◻ CH 34 Lh44
Jungolev Canal ◻ SUD 141 Mf41
Jungshahi ◻ PK 65 Oe33
Junigau ◻ ANG 150 Lh51
Junín ◻ CO 192 Gd45
Junín ◻ PE 196 Gb51
Junín ◻ RA (BA) 209 Gj63
Junín de los Andes ◻ RA (NE) 208 Ge66
Juniper Dunes Wilderness ☑ USA 168 Ea22
Juniper Forests ☑ PK 65 Od30
Juniyah ◻ RL 56 Mn29
Junlian ◻ CHN (SCH) 74 Qc31
Junnar ◻ IND (MHT) 82 Og36
Junovo ◻ RUS 48 Nb17
Junqueiro ◻ BR (AL) 201 Jc50
Junquillo ◻ CR 185 Fh40
Juntas ◻ RCH 207 Gf60
Juntas ◻ RA (CA) 207 Gg59
Jupagua ◻ BR (BA) 200 Hh51
Jupiter ◻ USA (FL) 179 Fk32
Juquiá ◻ BR (SP) 205 Hg58
Jur ◻ SUD 141 Me41
Jura ◻ F 25 Lg43
Juracidki ◻ BY 39 Mj37
Jurado ◻ CO 192 Gb44
Juramento ◻ BR (MG) 203 Hj54
Jur'ev-Pol'skij ◻ RUS 48 Mk17
Jurbarkas ◻ LT 39 Mc35
Jurbise ◻ B 23 Le40
Jurdabel ◻ EST 38 Mf31
Jureia ◻ NEP 83 Pc32
Jurema ◻ BR (MT) 199 Ha51
Jurema ◻ BR (PI) 200 Hj49
Jurerê ◻ BR (SC) 205 He59
Jürgin ◻ S 31 Lt31
Jussara ◻ BR (BA) 201 Hk52
Jussiape ◻ BR (BA) 201 Hk52
Justiniano Posse ◻ RA (CD) 209 Gj62
Jutaí ◻ BR (AM) 192 Gh47
Juter ◻ MAR (MS) 202 Hc57
Jüterbog ◻ D 32 Ln39
Jûtî ◻ BR (MS) 202 Hc57
Juticalpa ◻ HN 184 Fg38
Jutuba ◻ BR (PA)
Juúara ◻ FIN 38 Mg29
Juva ◻ FIN 38 Mh28
Jüxian ◻ CHN (SDG) 73 Qk28
Juxtlahuaca ◻ MEX 182 Fa37
Júžna-Alićurskij hrebet ◻ TJ 63 Og27
Južno Azorskaja ◻ RUS 53 Mg43
Južno-Sahalinsk ◻ RUS 77 Sb22
Juzno Mountains ◻ USA 165 Cd14
Južno-Kuril'sk ◻ RUS 77 Sc23
Južno-Kamyšovyj hrebet ◻ RUS 77 Sb22
Južnyj ◻ RUS 49 Mg18
Južnyj ◻ RUS (DAG) 57 Nc23
Južnyj ◻ RUS 49 Nd22

Juzzak ◻ PK 64 Oa31
Jwalamukhi Temple ☑ IND 81 Oj29
Jwaneng ◻ RB 155 Mc58
Jyderup ◻ DK 30 Ll35
Jyllland Bank ◻ 30 Lk33
Jyväskylä ◻ FIN 38 Mf28

K

K2 ◻ PK 81 Oj28
Kaaba ◻ KSA 58 Mk35
Kaabong ◻ EAU 144 Mg44
Kaech'on ◻ PRK 78 Rc26
Kaedi ◻ RIM 130 Kd37
Kaélé ◻ CAM 139 Lg40
Kaena Point ◻ USA 170 Ca35
Kafa Kingi ◻ SUD 141 Mc41
Kaena Point ◻ USA 170 Ca35
Kaeo ◻ NZ 112 Tg63
Kao Kaji ◻ SUD 144 Mf44
Kaesong ☑ PRK 78 Rd27
Kaevanga ◻ SOL 117 Sk50
Kaew Kho Rum Cave ☑ THA
Kafa Kingi ◻ SUD 141 Mc41
Kafakumba ◻ RDC 149 Mb50
Kafanchan ◻ WAN 138 Le41
Kafar-Jar-Ghar Range ◻ AFG
Kaffin-Saru ◻ WAN 138 Le41
Kaffrine ◻ SN 130 Kc38
Kafin-Chana ◻ WAN 132 Lc39
Kafindibei ◻ WAN 138 Le41
Kafiné ◻ CI 137 Kh41
Kafin Hausa ◻ WAN 138 Lf39
Kafireas, Akra ◻ GR 47 Mf53
Kafountine ◻ SN 136 Kb39
Kafr el-Dawuár ◻ ET 129 Mf30
Kafr el-Sheikh ◻ ET 129 Mf30
Kafue ◻ Z 146 Me52
Kafue ◻ Z 152 Me53
Kafukata ◻ LB 136 Ke42
Kafuchinga ◻ MW 146 Mg53
Kafuka ◻ J 79 Rk28
Kafue N.P. ☑ Z 146 Md53
Kaga ◻ J 79 Rk27
Kaga Bandoro ◻ RCA 140 Lk42
Kagadi ◻ EAU 144 Mf45
Kagan ◻ PK 65 Og28
Kagaru ◻ BF 137 Kk40
Kågeroma-jima ◻ J 79 Re31
Kagitna ◻ EAK 144 Mh44
Kago Kaji ◻ SUD 144 Mf44
Kagoshima ◻ J 79 Rf30
Kagoshima wan ◻ J 79 Rf30
Kaguvi ◻ ZW 152 Me56
Kagugu ◻ EAT 146 Mj49
Kagugu ◻ EAT 146 Mj48
Kaha ◻ ETH 143 Nb41
Kahak Cave ☑ IR 57 Nf28
Kal Tabelbala ◻ DZ 125 Kj31
Kahaman ◻ EAT 146 Mh48
Kahani ◻ IND (MPH) 83 Ok34
Kaharlyk ◻ UA 49 Mf21
Kaharoa ◻ NZ 113 Tg64
Kahatola ◻ RI 94 Rd46
Ka-Hem = Malyj Enisej ◻ RUS 67 Pd20
Kahemba ◻ RDC 149 Lk49
Kahir ◻ IR 64 Oa33
Kahkaman ◻ D 32 Lj39
Kahler Asten ◻ D 32 Lj39
Kahnoo ◻ IND (JLD) 109 Sc60
Kahnui ◻ IR 64 Nj32
Kai Besar ◻ RI 114 Rg49
Kaiapoi ◻ NZ 113 Tf67
Kaibola ◻ PNG 116 Sf50
Kaichui, Mount ◻ SOL 117 Ta50
Kaidu He ◻ CHN 67 Pd25
Kaieteur Fall ☑ GUY 194 Ha43
Kaieteur National Park ☑ GUY 194 Ha43
Kaifeng ◻ CHN (HNN) 73 Qh28
Kaihua ◻ USA (AK) 166 Dd18
Kaiken ◻ RA (TF) 210 Gg72
Kaikohe ◻ NZ 112 Tg63
Kaikoura ◻ NZ 113 Tg67
Kaikoura Peninsula ◻ NZ 113 Tg67
Kailahun ◻ WAL 136 Ke41
Kailas = Kangrinboqê Feng ◻ CHN 68 Pa30
Kailash, Mount ◻ CHN 68 Pa30
Kaili ◻ CHN (GZH) 74 Qd32
Kailu ◻ CHN (NMZ) 76 Ra24
Kailua-Kona ◻ USA (HI) 170 Cc36
Kaimana ◻ RI 114 Rd48
Kaimanawa Forest National Park ☑ NZ 113 Tg65
Kaimur Range ◻ IND 83 Pb33
Kainan ◻ J 79 Rh28
Kainantu ◻ PNG 115 Sc49
Kainde ◻ PNG 116 Sf50
Kaingaroa ◻ NZ 113 Th64
Kaini Reservoir ◻ WAN 138 Ld40
Kaiparowits Plateau ◻ USA 171 Ee27
Kaipara Harbour ◻ NZ 112 Tg64
Kaiping ◻ CHN (GDG) 75 Qg34
Kairana ◻ IND (UPH) 80 Oj31
Kairi ◻ AUS (QLD) 107 Sc55
Kairoan ◻ TN 126 Lf28
Kairuku ◻ PNG 115 Sd50
Kaisepakte ◻ S 16 Lk12
Kaiserslautern ◻ D 33 Lh41
Kaiserstuhl ☑ D 33 Lh42
Kaitaia ◻ NZ 112 Tg63
Kaitangata ◻ NZ 113 Te69
Kaitawa ◻ NZ 113 Th65
Kaithal ◻ IND (HYA) 80 Oj31
Kaitum ◻ S 16 Lk12
Kaiwi Channel ◻ USA (HI) 170 Cb35
Kaiyang ◻ CHN (GZH) 74 Qd32
Kaiyuan ◻ CHN (LNG) 76 Rb24
Kaiyuan ◻ CHN (YUN) 87 Qb33
Kaiyuan Temple ☑ CHN 75 Qk33

Kadyj ◻ RUS 48 Nb17
Kadzidło ◻ PL 41 Mb37
Kaédi ◻ RIM 130 Kd37
Kaena Point ◻ USA 170 Ca35
Kaena Tana N.P. ☑ THA 89 Qc38
Kaeo ◻ NZ 112 Tg63
Kaesong ☑ PRK 78 Rd27
Kaëvanga ◻ SOL 117 Sk50
Kabalega Falls N.P. = Murchison Falls N.P. ☑ EAU 144 Mf44
Kabala ◻ TR 56 Mj25
Kabale ◻ EAU 144 Me46
Kabalo ◻ RDC 146 Md49
Kabambare ◻ RDC 146 Me49
Kabamba ◻ Z 152 Md54
Kabanga ◻ RDC 149 Lk49
Kabanga ◻ Z 152 Md54
Kabanjahe ◻ RI 93 Pk44
Kabangu ◻ RDC 149 Mb51
Kabankalan ◻ RP 90 Rb41
Kabanpe ◻ GH 137 La41
Kabaovaj ◻ LT 39 Mc35
Kabaro ◻ Z 151 Mb52
Kabaro ◻ LAR 126 Lg30
Kabale ◻ EAU 144 Me46
Kabardino-Balkaria ◻ RUS 57 Nb24
Kabardino-Balkarskij zapovednik ☑ RUS 57 Nb24
Kabare ◻ RDC 146 Me47
Kabarei ◻ RI 97 Rf46
Kabasalan ◻ RP 91 Rc47
Kabatepe ☑ TR 47 Mg51
Kabbäli ◻ S 16 Ma12
Kabe ◻ WAN 138 Lc40
Kabelvåg ◻ N 16 Lh11
Kaberamaido ◻ EAU 144 Mg45
Kabetan ◻ RI 94 Ra48
Kabeya ◻ RDC 149 Mb50
Kabib ◻ LV 39 Mc34
Kabinda ◻ RDC 149 Mc49
Kabir ◻ RI 97 Rf46
Kabirwala ◻ PK 65 Og30
Kabkabiya ◻ SUD 141 Mb39
Kabnebryce ◻ S 16 Lk12
Kabo ◻ RCA 140 Lk41
Kabobi ◻ RN 132 Lc39
Kabol ◻ AFG 65 Oe29
Kabompo ◻ Z 151 Mb52
Kabompo ◻ Z 151 Mb52
Kabondo-Dianda ◻ RDC 149 Mc50
Kabong ◻ MAL 94 Qf45
Kabongo ◻ RDC 149 Mc49
Kaboré Tambi (Pó), P.N.de ☑ BF 137 Kk40
Kabou ◻ TG 137 La41
Kabou ◻ RCA 140 Lk42
Kaboudia ◻ TN 126 Lf28
Kabowe ◻ PNG 115 Sb49
Kabran ◻ IR 64 Oa33
Kabul ◻ AFG 65 Oe29
Kabumbu ◻ RDC 146 Mc48
Kabunda ◻ RDC 146 Me49
Kabunduk ◻ RDC 149 Mc50
Kabûngu ◻ EAT 146 Mh48
Kaburuang ◻ RI 91 Rd44
Kabushiya ◻ SUD 135 Mg37
Kabwe ◻ Z 146 Me53
Kabwum ◻ PNG 115 Sd49
Kabwoya ◻ EAU 144 Mf45
Kacanik ◻ SCG 45 Mb48
Kaçarli ◻ TR 47 Mh52
Kacelovo ◻ BG 45 Mg47
Kačer ◻ SCG 44 Ma47
Kači ◻ PK 65 Od30
Kachisi ◻ ETH 142 Mj41
Kacholola ◻ Z 146 Mf53
Kachovka ◻ UA 49 Mg22
Kachovs'kyj kanal ◻ UA 49 Mg22
Kachung ◻ EAU 144 Mg45
Kacketar Dag ◻ TR 57 Nb25
Kaczory ◻ PL 40 Lt38
Kadaň ◻ CZ 42 Ln40
Kadapongan ◻ RI 95 Qh48
Kadayanallur ◻ IND (TNU) 84 Oj41
Kadarkút ◻ H 42 Ls44
Kadavu ◻ FJI 119 Tk55
Kadé ◻ GH 137 Kk42
Kadegaon ◻ IND (MHT) 82 Oh37
Kadei ◻ RCA 140 Lj43
Kadina ◻ AUS (SA) 110 Rj62
Kadinamkulam ◻ IND 84 Oj42
Kadiolo ◻ RMM 137 Kh40
Kadirana ◻ IND (UPH) 80 Oj31
Kadiri ◻ IND (APH) 85 Ok38
Kadirli ◻ TR 56 Mj27
Kadiwéu, T.I. ◻ BR 202 Hb56
Kadoka ◻ USA (SD) 172 Ek24
Kado ◻ WAN 138 Le41
Kadok ◻ MAL 92 Qb44
Kadoma ◻ J 79 Rh28
Kadoma ◻ ZW 152 Me55
Kadrus ◻ BG 45 Mf48
Kaduguli ◻ SUD 141 Me40
Kaduna ◻ WAN 138 Le40
Kaduna ◻ WAN 138 Le40
Kadur ◻ IND (KTK) 84 Oj39

Kajang ◻ MAL 92 Qa44
Kajaani ◻ FIN 38 Mh26
Kajaki ◻ AFG 65 Oc29
Kajang ◻ RI 96 Ra48
Kajebo ◻ RCA 140 Lk42
Kajiado ◻ EAK 144 Mj46
Kajikawa ◻ IND (RJT) 80 Og32
Kajnar ◻ KZ 66 Pg23
Kajo Kaji ◻ SUD 144 Mf44
Kajok ◻ SUD 141 Me42
Kajokya ◻ WAN 138 Le42
Kajola ◻ WAN 138 Lc42
Kaju Saba ◻ SUD 135 Mg37
Kajuru ◻ WAN 138 Le40
Kaka ◻ TM 62 Nk27
Kaka ◻ AZ 171 Ed27
Kakaban ◻ RI 94 Qk44
Kakamas ◻ ZA 154 Mb60
Kakamega ◻ EAK 144 Mh45
Kakamega Forest National Reserve ☑ EAK 144 Mh45
Kakanda ◻ RDC 146 Md50
Kakani ◻ BIH 44 Ls46
Kakanj ◻ BIH 44 Lt46
Kakata ◻ LB 136 Ke42
Kakegawa ◻ J 79 Rk28
Kakenge ◻ RDC 149 Mb49
Kakamega ◻ EAK 144 Mh45
Kakdwip ◻ IND (WBG) 86 Pe35
Kakelé ◻ RI 94 Qk46
Kaki ◻ IR 59 Ng31
Kakia ◻ GH 137 La42
Kakielo ◻ RDC 146 Me50
Kakinada ◻ IND (APH) 83 Pb37
Kakisa ◻ CDN 167 Ea14
Kakisa Lake ◻ CDN 167 Ea14
Kakkiriigumma ◻ IND (ORS) 83 Pb36
Kakobola ◻ RDC 149 Lk48
Kakogawa ◻ J 79 Rh28
Kakosi ◻ EAT 146 Mj47
Kakovatos ◻ GR 47 Mc53
Kakpin ◻ CI 137 Kj41
Kakrala ◻ IND (UPH) 81 Ok32
Kaktovik ◻ USA (AK) 165 Cj10
Kakuma ◻ EAK 144 Mh44
Kakunodate ◻ J 77 Sa26
Kakwa Prov. Rec. Area ☑ CDN 167 Dk18
Kala ◻ EAK 145 Mk46
Kala ◻ RDC 149 Mc50
Kalaa-i-Darab ◻ IR 64 Nj31
Kalaallit ◻ USA (HI) 170 Cb35
Kalabagh ◻ PK 65 Of29
Kalabahi ◻ RI 97 Rc50
Kalabakan ◻ MAL 94 Qj44
Kalabo ◻ Z 151 Mb53
Kalabsha Temple ☑ ET 129 Mf36
Kalač ◻ RUS 48 Na20
Kalach ◻ RUS (ON) 177 Gb23
Ka Lae ◻ USA 170 Cc37
Kalafafiata ◻ SOL 117 Ta50
Kalabo ◻ Z 151 Mb53
Kalafat ◻ GH 137 Kk43
Kalagi ◻ SN 136 Kc39
Kalai ◻ IND 82 Of35
Kalajoki ◻ FIN 38 Md25
Kalak ◻ IR 64 Oa33
Kala-Mor ◻ TM 62 Nk28
Kálamos ◻ GR 47 Mc52
Kalanguy ◻ RUS 71 Qh20
Kalam ◻ PK 65 Og28
Kalamos ◻ GR 46 Mb52
Kalamáki ◻ GR 46 Mc51
Kalamalos ◻ GR 46 Mb52
Kalamaria ◻ GR 46 Md50
Kalamata ◻ GR 46 Mc53
Kalamazoo ◻ USA (MI) 173 Fh24
Kalamba ◻ RDC 149 Lk49
Kalambáka ◻ GR 46 Mb51
Kalambi ◻ RDC 146 Me48
Kalamnuri ◻ IND (MHT) 82 Oj36
Kalana ◻ RMM 136 Kg40
Kálanda ◻ GR 47 Mf54
Kalanguy ◻ RUS 71 Qh20
Kalándra ◻ GR 46 Md51
Kalannie ◻ AUS (WA) 104 Qj61
Kalao ◻ RI 96 Ra49
Kaláthos ◻ GR 47 Mh54
Kalavárda ◻ GR 47 Mh54
Kalávryta ◻ GR 46 Mc52
Kalawao ◻ USA (HI) 170 Cb35
Kalba ◻ UAE 61 Nj33
Kalbarri ◻ AUS 104 Qg60
Kalbarri N.P. ☑ AUS 104 Qg59

Kalbay ◻ RP 91 Rc43
Kalbe ◻ D 32 Lm38
Kalabinskij togleri ◻ KZ 66 Pg21
Kalc ◻ IND (APH) 82 Of37
Kale ◻ TR 56 Me27
Kale ◻ TR 47 Mj53
Kaledibu ◻ TR 57 Na25
Kalehe ◻ DY 138 Ld40
Kalema ◻ RDC 146 Me48
Kalemegdan ◻ SCG 44 Ma46
Kalemie ◻ RDC 146 Me48
Kalena ◻ UA 41 Mf39
Kalengwa ◻ Z 151 Mc52
Kaleo ◻ GH 137 Kk41
Kalewa ◻ MYA 86 Ph34
Kalfou ◻ CAM 139 Lg40
Kalga ◻ RUS 71 Qk20
Kalgaur Island ◻ AUS (WA) 104 Qj61
Kalgoorlie ◻ AUS (WA) 104 Ra61
Kalgudishy ◻ USA (AK) 165 Cd14
Kali Gandaki River Rafting ☑ NEP 81 Pb31
Kali Gandaki (World's deepest gorge) ☑ NEP 81 Pb31
Kaligiri ◻ IND (APH) 85 Ok38
Kalikata = Calcutta ◻ IND 86 Pe34
Kalimala ◻ IND (ORS) 83 Pa36
Kalimantan ◻ RI 92 Qg48
Kálimnos ◻ GR 47 Mg54
Kálimnos ◻ GR 47 Mg54
Kalimpong ◻ IND (WBG)
Kalinda ◻ Z 146 Mg53
Kalindi ◻ IND (QLD) 107 Sb53
Kalingia ◻ IND (ORS) 83 Pc35
Kaliningrad ◻ RUS 39 Ma36
Kalininskoe ◻ RUS 76 Rc21
Kalinjara ◻ IND (RJT) 82 Oh34
Kalinkovičy ◻ BY 48 Me19
Kalinko ◻ RG 136 Kf40
Kalinovik ◻ BIH 44 Lt47
Kaligi ◻ PNG 116 Sf48
Kalipefang ◻ RI 96 Qj49
Kaliptan ◻ PK 80 Oh31
Kalir ◻ EAU 144 Mg45
Kalisch ◻ SYR 56 Mj27
Kalisangko ◻ RP 91 Rd45
Kalisko ◻ PL 41 Lu39
Kalispell ◻ USA (MT) 168 Ec21
Kalisty ◻ PL 40 La37
Kalisz Pomorski ◻ PL 40 Lq37
Kalisz ◻ PL 41 Lt39
Kalitna ◻ EAT 146 Mh48
Kalitva ◻ RUS 48 Na21
Kalix ◻ S 16 Mb13
Kalixälven ◻ S 16 Mb12
Kaljazin ◻ RUS 48 Mj17
Kalkalpen, N.P. ☑ A 35 Lp43
Kalkan ◻ IND (HYA) 81 Ok30
Kalkaring ◻ AUS (NT) 106 Rf54
Kalkaroo ◻ AUS (SA) 108 Sa61
Kalken ◻ B 23 Ld39
Kalkfeld ◻ NAM 150 Lj56
Kalkfontein = Tshootsha ◻ RB 151 Ma57
Kalkfontein Dam Nature Reserve ☑ ZA 155 Mc60
Kalkudah Beach ◻ CL 85 Pa42
Kalkveld ◻ NAM 150 Lj56
Kallakkurichchi ◻ IND (TNU) 85 Ok40
Kallang ◻ IND (MHT) 82 Of36
Kallambella ◻ IND (KTK) 84 Oj38
Kallands halvö ◻ S 30 Ln32
Kallar Kahar ◻ PK 65 Og29
Kallbådagrund ◻ FIN
Kalle Kado ◻ PNG 116 Sf50
Kalletal ◻ LB 136 Kg43
Kallinge ◻ S 31 Lp34
Kallioa ◻ IND (MPH) 82 Of33
Kallithéa ◻ GR 47 Mf53
Kallmet ◻ AL 44 Lu49
Kallo ◻ RP 90 Rc41
Kallsjön ◻ S 16 Lk14
Kalmar ◻ S 31 Lp34
Kalmar ◻ S 31 Lp34
Kalmalo ◻ WAN 138 Le39
Kalmthout ◻ B 23 Le39
Kalmunai ◻ CL 85 Pa42
Kalmykia ◻ RUS 53 Na05
Kalmykovo ◻ KZ 53 Nd21
Kalná nad Hronom ◻ SK 42 Lt42
Kalná Roztoka ◻ SK 43 Mc42
Kalnciems ◻ LV 39 Md33
Kalocsa ◻ H 43 Lu44
Kalofer ◻ BG 45 Mf48
Kalohi Channel ◻ USA (HI) 170 Cb35
Kalol ◻ IND (GUJ) 82 Og34
Kalolimnos ◻ GR 47 Mg53
Kalomo ◻ Z 152 Md55
Kalona ◻ USA (MO) 172 Fe25
Kalona Hist. Village ☑ USA 172 Fe25
Kaloleni ◻ EAK 144 Mj47
Kaloma ◻ RDC 146 Me48
Kalomo ◻ Z 152 Md55
Kalona Island ◻ PNG 116 Sf50
Kalong ◻ RI 94 Qk46
Kalpa ◻ IND (HPH) 81 Oj30
Kalpetta ◻ IND (KER) 84 Oj40
Kalpi ◻ IND (UPH) 83 Ok32
Kalpin ◻ CHN 66 Oj26
Kalsdorf ◻ A 35 Lq43
Kaltag ◻ USA (AK) 165 Cb13
Kaltennach ◻ D 32 Lm37
Kaltenkirchen ◻ D 32 Lk37
Kaltern = Caldaro ◻ I 34 Lm44
Kaltungo ◻ WAN 139 Lg41
Kalu ◻ RUS 48 Mj18
Kalugerovo ◻ BG 45 Me48
Kaluku ◻ RI 96 Ra47
Kalulushi ◻ Z 146 Me52

Kalumburu ☐ AUS (WA) 103 Rd53
Kalumburu A.L. ☐ AUS 103 Rd53
Kalundborg ☐ DK 30 Lm35
Kalundu ☐ RDC 149 Mc49
Kalundwe ☐ RDC 146 Me47
Kalur Kot ☐ PK 65 Of29
Kalus ☐ UA 43 Me41
Kaluvaye ☐ IND (APH) 85 Qk38
Kalvåg ☐ N 17 Lc15
Kalvarija ☐ LT 39 Md36
Kalvitsa ☐ FIN 38 Me29
Kalvola ☐ FIN 38 Me29
Kalwakurti ☐ IND (APH) 82 Ok37
Kalwaria Zebrzydowska ☐ 🏛 PL 41 Lu41
Kalya ☐ EAT 146 Mme45
Kalyan ☐ IND (MHT) 82 Og36
Kalyandrug ☐ IND (APH) 84 Oj38
Kalynivka ☐ UA 49 Me43
Kalzhat ☐ KZ 66 Pa24
Kamat ☐ RMM 138 Ld36
Kamablon ☐ RMM 136 Kf40
Kamada ☐ TCH 133 Lf37
Kamaday ☐ TCH 134 Ma40
Kamaishi ☐ J 77 Sa26
Kamakura ☐ J 79 Rk28
Kamakusa ☐ GUY 194 Ha43
Kamakwie ☐ WAL 136 Kd41
Kamal ☐ RI 95 Qe43
Kamal ☐ PK 65 Of30
Kamalia ☐ PK 65 Og30
Kamalpur ☐ IND (TRP) 86 Pf33
Kaman ☐ IND (RJT) 80 Oj32
Kaman ☐ TR 56 Mg26
Kamanga ☐ EAT 144 Mf45
Kamanjab ☐ NAM 150 Lh55
Kamanola ☐ RDC 146 Me47
Kamapanda ☐ Z 151 Mc51
Kamaran ☐ RI 95 Qe43
Kamarang ☐ GUY 194 Ga43
Kamaredelli ☐ IND (APH) 82 Ok36
Kamáres ☐ GR 46 Mb52
Kamáres ☐ GR 45 Me50
Kamáres ☐ GR 47 Mt54
Kamári ☐ GR 47 Mt54
Kamaron ☐ WAL 136 Ke41
Kamaru ☐ RI 97 Rb48
Kamas ☐ USA (UT) 171 Ee25
Kamasin ☐ IND (UPH) 83 Pa33
Kamatvi ☐ ZW 152 Md55
Kamba ☐ ETH 142 Mj42
Kamba Kota ☐ RCA 140 Lj42
Kamba ☐ IND 138 Lj40
Kambalda ☐ AUS (WA) 104 Ra61
Kambam ☐ IND (TNU) 84 Oj41
Kambambe ☐ ANG 148 Lh50
Kambánis ☐ GR 46 Mc50
Kambeng ☐ IND (APH) 86 Ph31
Kamberatoro ☐ PNG 115 Sa47
Kambia ☐ WAL 136 Kd41
Kambikatoto ☐ EAT 146 Mg49
Kambode ☐ RI 97 Rb48
Kamboló ☐ TG 137 La41
Kambove ☐ RDC 146 Md51
Kambuku ☐ PNG 116 Sg48
Kambuno, Gunung ☐ RI 96 Ra47
Kamburu ☐ EAK 144 Mj46
Kambut ☐ LAR 128 Mc30
Kambwata ☐ Z 151 Mb54
Kamcha-t ☐ THA 89 Qc37
Kamchatka Peninsula ☐ RUS 55 Sc07
Kamčija ☐ BG 45 Mh47
Kamčija ☐ BG 45 Mh47
Kamdara ☐ IND (JKD) 83 Pc34
Kamdesh ☐ AFG 63 Of28
Kameel ☐ ZA 155 Mc60
Kamélé ☐ CI 137 Kj41
Kameme ☐ MW 146 Mg50
Kamen ☐ D 32 Lh39
Kamena ☐ EAT 144 Mg47
Kamena ☐ RDC 146 Mc49
Kamenec ☐ RUS 39 Mj32
Kameng ☐ AFG 65 Oc29
Kamenica ☐ BG 44 Md49
Kamenica ☐ SCG 44 Lu46
Kamenica nad Lipou ☐ CZ 42 Lq41
Kamenka ☐ RUS 45 Mh47
Kamenka ☐ RUS 38 Mk30
Kamenka ☐ RUS 48 Nb19
Kamen'-na-Ob' ☐ RUS 54 Pa08
Kamennïe gäbi ☐ RUS 49 Mt49
Kamennogorsk ☐ RUS 38 Mk30
Kamenný Přívoz ☐ CZ 42 Lq40
Kamenoo ☐ CI 137 Kj44
Kamen'Rybolov ☐ RUS 76 Rg23
Kamenskoe ☐ RUS 55 Tb06
Kamensk-Sahtinskij ☐ RUS 49 Na21
Kamensk-Ural'skij ☐ RUS 48 Oa18
Kamenz ☐ D 32 Lp39
Kameshia ☐ RDC 146 Md50
Kameškovo ☐ RUS 48 Na17
Kamet ☐ IND 81 Ok35
Kamianka-lnieckaja vieza ☐ BY 41 Md38
Kamień ☐ PL 41 Ma39
Kamiendo ☐ WAL 136 Ke41
Kamień Pomorski ☐ PL 40 Lp37
Kamieskroon ☐ ZA 154 Lj61
Kamiha ☐ TG 137 La41
Kamiiso ☐ J 77 Sa26
Kamiji ☐ RDC 149 Mb49
Kamikawa ☐ J 77 Sa25
Kami-koshiki-jima ☐ J 79 Re30
Kamileroi ☐ AUS (QLD) 107 Rk55
Kamina ☐ PNG 115 Sb46
Kamina ☐ RDC 146 Mb49
Kamina Base ☐ RDC 149 Mc50
Kamin'-Kašyrs'kyj ☐ UA 41 Me39
Kaminokuni ☐ J 77 Sa25
Kámiros ☐ J 79 Rj27
Kámiros ☐ GR 47 Mt54
Kami-Shihoro ☐ J 77 Sa24
Kamiskotia Ski Resort ☐ CDN 173 Fk21
Kamitsushima ☐ J 79 Re28
Kamituga ☐ RDC 146 Me47
Kami-Yaku ☐ J 79 Rf30
Kam'janec-Podil's'kyj ☐ UA 49 Md21
Kamjaniec ☐ BY 41 Md38
Kamjanjuki ☐ SCG 41 Md38
Kamjanka ☐ UA 49 Mg43
Kamjanka-Buz'ka ☐ UA 41 Me40
Kamjanske ☐ BY 41 Md38
Kamloops ☐ CDN (BC) 168 Dk20
Kamloops Ind. Res. ☐ CDN 168 Dk20
Kamloops Plateau ☐ CDN 168 Dk20
Kammanassieberge ☐ ZA 154 Mb62
Kamnarok National Reserve ☐ EAK 144 Mh46
Kamnik ☐ SLO 42 Lp44
Kamob Sanha ☐ SUD 135 Mj36
Kamoke ☐ PK 65 Oh30
Kamola ☐ RDC 146 Mc49
Kamoto ☐ Z 146 Mg52
Kamp 52 ☐ SME 194 Hb44
Kampa do Rio Amônea, T.I. ☐ BR 197 Ge50
Kampa e Isolados do Rio Envira, T.I. ☐ BR 197 Ge50
Kampala ☐ EAU 144 Mg45
Kampala ☐ SUD 134 Mf41
Kampampi ☐ Z 146 Mf50
Kampar ☐ MAL 92 Qa43
Kampar ☐ RI 96 Qa45
Kampen ☐ NL 23 Lf38
Kampene ☐ RDC 146 Me47
Kamphaeng Phet ☐ THA 88 Pk37

Kamphaeng Phet Historical Park ☐ THA 88 Pk37
Kamphambale ☐ MW 146 Mg52
Kampinoski P.N. ☐ PL 41 Ma38
Kampli ☐ IND (KTK) 82 Oj38
Kampong Padawan ☐ MAL 94 Qf45
Kampong Sirik ☐ MAL 94 Qf44
Kampong Sralao ☐ K 89 Qc38
Kampong Taben ☐ MAL 94 Qc39
Kampong Thom ☐ K 89 Qc40
Kampti ☐ BF 137 Kj40
Kampumbu ☐ Z 146 Mg51
Kampung Ayer Puteh ☐ MAL 92 Qb43
Kampung Batu Enam ☐ MAL 92 Qb44
Kampung Batu Satu ☐ MAL 94 Qg43
Kampung Buloh ☐ MAL 92 Qb43
Kampung Chenereh ☐ MAL 92 Qb43
Kampung Damak ☐ MAL 92 Qb44
Kampung Gading ☐ MAL 92 Qa43
Kampung Gajah ☐ MAL 92 Qa43
Kampung Gajah ☐ MAL 92 Qa43
Kampung Jerangau ☐ MAL 92 Qb43
Kampung Kemara ☐ MAL 92 Qa43
Kampung Koh ☐ MAL 92 Qa43
Kampung Landak ☐ MAL 92 Qa44
Kampung Laut ☐ RI 93 Qb46
Kampung Merang ☐ MAL 92 Qb43
Kampung Merting ☐ MAL 92 Qb43
Kampung Nibong ☐ MAL 92 Qb43
Kampung Palas ☐ MAL 92 Qb43
Kampung Penarik ☐ MAL 92 Qb43
Kampung Permas Kecil ☐ MAL 92 Qb43
Kampung Punggai ☐ MAL 92 Qb45
Kampung Relok ☐ MAL 92 Qb43
Kampung Sawagan ☐ MAL 94 Qh43
Kampung Seri Gading ☐ MAL 92 Qb43
Kampung Sook ☐ MAL 94 Qj43
Kampung Sungai Ayer Deras ☐ MAL 92 Qb44
Kampung Tanjung Batu ☐ MAL 92 Qb44
Kampung Tekek ☐ MAL 92 Qb44
Kampung Telupid ☐ MAL 94 Qj43
Kamsack ☐ CDN (SK) 172 Ek20
Kamsamba ☐ EAT 146 Mg50
Kamsandra ☐ IND (KTK) 84 Ok35
Kamsar ☐ RG 136 Kc40
Kamsuko vodohranilišče ☐ RUS 54 Nd07
Kamsuma ☐ SP 145 Nb45
Kamthi ☐ IND (MHT) 83 Ok35
Kamudi ☐ IND (TNU) 84 Oj41
Kamuli ☐ EAT 144 Mg44
Kamuli ☐ EAU 144 Mg45
Kamuwongo ☐ EAK 144 Mk46
Kamyaran ☐ IR 57 Nd28
Kamysanovka ☐ KS 66 Oh24
Kan ☐ IR 57 Nf28
Kanacea ☐ RI 119 Ua54
Ka Nae ☐ THA 89 Qc37
Kanal ☐ PK 65 Od30
Kanaima Falls ☐ GUY 194 Ga42
Kanaka ☐ RI 114 Rg47
Kanakanak Mount ☐ USA 165 Bk12
Kanannui ☐ IND (UPH) 81 Oh32
Kanayakumari ☐ IND (TNU) 84 Oh41
Kannod ☐ IND (MPH) 82 Oj34
Kanno ☐ IND (KER) 84 Oh40
Kano ☐ NAM 150 Lh55
Kano ☐ RI 96 Ra50
Kanombe ☐ RWA 144 Mf46
Kanoni ☐ RDC 146 Md51
Kanoroba ☐ CI 137 Kg41
Kanowit ☐ MAL 94 Qg44
Kanowit ☐ MAL 94 Qg44
Kanoya ☐ J 79 Rf30
Kanpur ☐ IND (UPH) 83 Pa32
Kansanshi ☐ Z 151 Mc51
Kansar ☐ IND (RJT) 80 Oh33
Kanshanoo ☐ RDC 146 Md51
Kansas ☐ USA 174 Ek26
Kansas City ☐ USA (KS) 174 Fc26
Kansas Cosmosphere and Space Center ☐ USA 174 Fa27
Kansas Speedway ☐ USA (KS) 174 Fc26
Kansenia ☐ RDC 146 Md51
Kanseth ☐ BD 86 Pe33
Kanshengel ☐ KZ 66 Oh23
Kansk ☐ RUS 54 Pd07
Kant ☐ KS 66 Oh24
Kantal Temple ☐ BD 86 Pe33
Kantala ☐ IND 83 Od32
Kantanagar Temple ☐ BD 86 Pe33
Kantbalu ☐ MYA 86 Ph34
Kanchari ☐ BF 137 La39
Kantemirovka ☐ RUS 48 Mk21
Kantishna ☐ USA (AK) 165 Ce14
Kantunil ☐ MEX (YT) 183 Ff35
Kantunilkin ☐ MEX (QTR) 183 Fg35
Kanturk ☐ IRL 19 Km38
Kanuku Mountains ☐ GUY 194 Ha44
Kanum Monastery ☐ IND 81 Ok30
Kanungu ☐ EAU 144 Mf46
Kanus ☐ NAM 154 Lh59
Kanwat ☐ IND (RJT) 80 Oh32
Kanyakubja ☐ IND (UPH) 83 Pa32
Kanyameza ☐ Z 146 Mf51
Kanyemba ☐ ZW 152 Mf53
Kanyilámbi ☐ Z 146 Md51
Kanyš-Kija ☐ UZ 63 Of25
Kanil Bagh ☐ AFG 65 Kd39
Kanzu-Bel ☐ KS 66 Mc25
Kao Chaison ☐ THA 88 Pk39
Kaohsiung ☐ RC 75 Ra34
Kaolovei ☐ CI 137 Kg42
Kaole Ruins ☐ EAT 147 Mk48
Kaolinovo ☐ BG 45 Mh47
Kaoma ☐ Z 151 Mc52
Kaoma ☐ SCG 44 Mf47
Kapadvanj ☐ IND (GUJ) 82 Og34

Kanfarandé ☐ RG 136 Kc40
Kang ☐ AFG 64 Oa30
Kang ☐ RB 154 Mb57
Kanga ☐ EAT 146 Mg52
Kanga ☐ IND (KTK) 82 Oj38
Kangal ☐ TR 56 Mj26
Kangan ☐ IR 57 Nf32
Kanganpur ☐ PK 65 Oh30
Kangar ☐ MAL 92 Qa42
Kangaré ☐ RMM 136 Kf40
Kangaroo Island ☐ AUS 110 Rj63
Kangasniemi ☐ FIN 38 Mg28
Kangasniemi ☐ FIN 38 Mg29
Kangayam ☐ IND (TNU) 84 Oj40
Kangding ☐ CHN (SCH) 69 Qa30
Kangen ☐ PRK 78 Rd26
Kanger ☐ SUD 141 Md41
Kangirsuk ☐ CDN 163 Gc07
Kangri Karpo Pass ☐ CHN/IND 86 Pg32
Kangar ☐ Z 151 Mc54
Kangxian ☐ CHN (GSU) 72 Qc29
Kan Gyi ☐ MYA 86 Pg34
Kangz'gyai ☐ CHN 69 Pj26
Kanha N.P. ☐ IND 83 Pa34
Kani ☐ CI 137 Kg41
Kaniama ☐ RDC 149 Mc49
Kani-Gogouna ☐ RMM 131 Kj38
Kanika ☐ IND (ORS) 83 Pb35
Kanioume ☐ RMM 131 Kj38
Kanisa ☐ UA 49 Mf21
Kaniv ☐ UA 49 Mf21
Kaniva ☐ AUS (VIC) 110 Sa64
Kaniya ☐ PNG 115 Sb49
Kanjan Cham ☐ IR 59 Nd29
Kanjiža ☐ SCG 44 Ma44
Kankaanpää ☐ FIN 38 Mc29
Kankakee ☐ USA (IL) 173 Fg25
Kankalabé ☐ RG 136 Kd40
Kankan ☐ RG 136 Ke40
Kankan ☐ RI 95 Qh49
Kankesanturai ☐ CL 85 Pa41
Kankossa ☐ RIM 130 Ke38
Kankyldaung ☐ MYA 88 Ph37
Kanmaw Island ☐ MYA 88 Pj36
Kan Nack ☐ VN 89 Qe38
Kannad ☐ IND (MHT) 82 Oh35
Kannapolis ☐ USA (NC) 178 Fk28
Kapelni ☐ RI 117 Re45

Karamian ☐ RI 95 Qh48
Karanpura ☐ AUS 104 Qk62
Karchewan ☐ CDN (ON) 163 Fd08
Karlino ☐ PL 40 Lq36
Karlova ☐ TR 57 Na26
Karlivka ☐ UA 49 Mg22
Karlovac ☐ HR 35 Lq46
Karlovássi ☐ GR 46 Mf53
Karlovice ☐ CZ 42 Ls40
Karlovo ☐ BG 45 Me48
Karlovy Vary ☐ 🏛 CZ 42 Ln40
Karlsberg ☐ S 31 Lp32
Karlsborg ☐ S 31 Lp32
Karlshamn ☐ S 31 Ln32
Karlskoga ☐ S 31 Lp31
Karlskrona ☐ S 31 Ln32
Karlsóarna ☐ S 31 Ls33
Karlstad ☐ S 31 Ln31
Karlstad ☐ USA (MN) 172 Fa21
Karluk ☐ USA (AK) 164 Cc17
Karma ☐ RN 132 Lc38
Karma ☐ SUD 135 Mf36
Karmala ☐ IND (MHT) 82 Oh36
Karmana ☐ UZ 63 Oc25
Karmé ☐ TCH 129 Lh38
Karnaj ☐ IR 59 Nf31
Karnafuli ☐ IND (APH) 81 Oj30
Karaikudi ☐ IND (TNU) 85 Ok40
Karaimata ☐ RI 95 Qe46
Karamata Strait ☐ RI 95 Qf46
Karimganj ☐ IND (ASM) 86 Pg33
Karimnagar ☐ IND (APH) 83 Ok36
Karimu ☐ IR 62 Nd27
Karimun ☐ RI 93 Qb45
Karimunjawa ☐ RI 95 Qf48
Karimun, Mount ☐ PNG 115 Sc49
Karin ☐ SP 143 Nc40
Karina ☐ WAL 136 Ke41
Karinagar ☐ RI 91 Rc44
Karimata ☐ RI 95 Qf46
Karis = Karjaa ☐ FIN 38 Mc30
Karisia Hills ☐ EAK 144 Mj45
Kariya ☐ J 79 Rj28
Karjat ☐ IR 64 Nj32
Kašiwazaki ☐ J 77 Rk27
Kashmar ☐ IR 64 Nk28
Kashmor ☐ PK 65 Oe31
Kashwal ☐ SUD 141 Me42
Kasi ☐ LAO 87 Qb36
Kasia ☐ IND (UPH) 83 Pb32
Kasigluk ☐ USA (AK) 164 Bj15
Kašin ☐ RUS 48 Mj17
Kašira ☐ RUS 48 Mk18
Kasiul ☐ RI 97 Rf48
Kaskas ☐ SN 130 Ke38
Kaskasia River St. Fish and Wildlife Area ☐ USA 175 Ff26
Kaskelen ☐ KZ 66 Oj24
Kaskii ☐ FIN 38 Mj29
Kasköö = Kaskö ☐ FIN 38 Mb28
Kasoma ☐ RDC 151 Mc50
Kasomalale ☐ RDC 146 Md47
Kasomo ☐ RDC 146 Me47
Kasongo ☐ RDC 146 Md48
Kasongo-Lunda ☐ RDC 149 Lj49
Kasonkomona ☐ Z 146 Md53
Kaspi ☐ GE 57 Nc25
Kaspijsk ☐ RUS (DAG) 57 Nd24
Kassala ☐ SUD 135 Mj36
Kassama ☐ RMM 136 Ke39
Kassari ☐ EST 38 Mc32
Kassarola ☐ RMM 137 Kh39
Kassel ☐ D 32 Lk39
Kassou ☐ BF 137 Kk40
Kasson ☐ USA (MN) 172 Fc24
Kastaniá ☐ GR 46 Mb51
Kastaniá ☐ GR 46 Mc50
Kastaniá ☐ GR 46 Mb51
Kastélli ☐ GR 47 Md53
Kastellaun ☐ D 33 Lh40
Kaštel-Stari ☐ HR 35 Lr47
Kastel ☐ D 33 Lm41
Kastéli ☐ GR 46 Mb53
Kástro ☐ GR 46 Mc53
Kástro ☐ GR 44 Md52
Kastron Mefa'a = Umm al-Rasas ☐ JOR 58 Mh30
Kasuga ☐ J 79 Rk28
Kasugai ☐ J 79 Rj28
Kašuku ☐ RDC 146 Me48
Kasulu ☐ EAT 146 Mf47
Kasumbalesa ☐ RDC 151 Md51
Kasumi ☐ J 79 Rh28
Kasumpti ☐ IND (HPH) 81 Oj30
Kasungu ☐ MW 146 Mg52
Kasungu N.P. ☐ MW 146 Mg52
Kasur ☐ PK 65 Oh30
Kata ☐ THA 88 Pj42

Kasganj ☐ IND (UPH) 81 Ok32
Kashambie ☐ ZW 152 Me54
Kato Nevrokópi ☐ GR 45 Md49
Kata ☐ THA 88 Pj42
Kataba ☐ Z 151 Mc53
Katábasi, Umm al- ☐ JOR 58 Mh30
Katako-Kombe ☐ RDC 146 Mc47
Katákolo ☐ GR 46 Mb53
Katakwi ☐ EAU 144 Mg45
Katalla ☐ USA (AK) 166 Ch15
Katangli ☐ RUS 71 Sa08
Katanning ☐ AUS (WA) 104 Qj62
Katastári ☐ GR 46 Ma53
Katátapola ☐ GR 47 Mf54
Katavi N.P. ☐ EAT 146 Mf48
Katawaz ☐ AFG 65 Oc29
Katchall Island ☐ IND 88 Pg43
Kateel ☐ IND 82 Oh39
Katende ☐ RDC 146 Md49
Katen ☐ RDC 149 Lj49
Katerero ☐ EAT 144 Mf46
Katerini ☐ GR 46 Mc50
Kates Needle ☐ CDN 166 Dc16
Katete ☐ Z 152 Mg53
Kathama Lake ☐ CDN 167 Ec12
Katha ☐ MYA 87 Pj34
Katherine Gorge ☐ AUS (NT) 106 Rg53
Kathiawar Peninsula ☐ IND 82 Of34
Kathmandu ☐ NEP 83 Pc32
Kathu ☐ ZA 154 Mb59
Kati ☐ RMM 136 Kf39
Katima Mulilo ☐ NAM 151 Mc54
Katiola ☐ CI 137 Kh41
Kato Achaïa ☐ GR 46 Mb52
Káto Figalía ☐ GR 46 Mb53
Katonda = Hay River ☐ CDN 167 Ec15
Katoomba ☐ AUS (NSW) 111 Sf62
Katoposo, Gunung ☐ RI 96 Ra46
Katorku hhoi Darvoz ☐ TJ 63 Of26
Katorkuhhoi Hisar ☐ TJ 63 Oe26
Katorkuhhoi Quarama ☐ TJ 63 Oc25
Katorkuhhoi Turkistan ☐ TJ 63 Od26
Katorkuhhoi Zarafšon ☐ TJ 63 Of26
Katowice ☐ PL 41 Lt40
Katrançğ Daği ☐ TR 56 Md27
Katrineholm ☐ S 31 Lr32
Katse ☐ EAK 144 Mk46
Katse Dam ☐ LS 155 Md60
Katsepy ☐ RM 156 Nd53
Katsiveli ☐ UA 49 Mf23
Katsina ☐ WAN 132 Ld39
Katsina-Ala ☐ WAN 138 Le42
Katsumoto ☐ J 79 Re29
Katsuta ☐ J 77 Sa27
Katsuura ☐ J 79 Sa28
Kattagoʻrgʻon ☐ UZ 63 Oc26
Kattavía ☐ GR 47 Mh55
Kattegat ☐ S/DK 30 Lm33
Kattehammarsvik ☐ S 31 Lt33
Kattimavadi ☐ IND (TNU) 85 Ok40
Katumbi ☐ MW 146 Mg51
Katun Abad ☐ IR 64 Nh30
Katunayaka ☐ CL 85 Ok42
Katungu ☐ EAU 144 Mf46
Katunskij hrebet ☐ RUS/KZ 67 Pd21
Katupa ☐ RI 96 Qk50
Katuria ☐ IND (BIH) 83 Pd33
Katwa ☐ IND (WBG) 86 Pe34
Katwe ☐ EAU 144 Mf46
Katwijk aan Zee ☐ NL 23 Le38
Katy Wrocławskie ☐ PL 40 Lr39
Katzenbuckel ☐ D 33 Lk41
Kauai ☐ USA (HI) 170 Ca35
Kauai Channel ☐ USA 170 Ca35
Kaufbeuren ☐ D 33 Ll43
Kauhajoki ☐ FIN 38 Mc28
Kauhanevan-Pohjankankaan kansallispuisto ☐ FIN 38 Mc28
Kauhava ☐ FIN 38 Md27
Kaukaveld ☐ NAM/RB 151 Ma55
Kaukel ☐ KZ 63 Oa27
Kaula ☐ USA 170 Bk35
Kaulakahi Channel ☐ USA 170 Ca35
Kaulishishi ☐ Z 152 Me53
Kaulsdorf ☐ D 33 Lm40
Kaumalapau ☐ USA (HI) 170 Cb35
Kauna Point ☐ USA (HI) 170 Cc36
Kaunakakai ☐ USA (HI) 170 Cb35
Kaunas ☐ LT 39 Md36
Kaunos ☐ TR 47 Mj54
Kaup ☐ PNG 115 Sc49
Kaupena ☐ PNG 115 Sb49
Kaurai ☐ PNG 116 Sg50
Kaura-Namoda ☐ WAN 138 Ld39
Kauri Museum ☐ NZ 112 Th64
Kauriralamp ☐ IND (MHT) 83 Pb32
Kaurissalo ☐ FIN 38 Mb30
Kausala ☐ FIN 38 Mg30
Kautokeino ☐ N 16 Mc11
Kau-Ye Island ☐ MYA 88 Pj38
Kavača ☐ YV 193 Hj13
Kavacık ☐ TR 47 Mj51
Kavadarci ☐ MK 44 Mc49
Kavak ☐ TR 47 Mj52
Kavaklidere ☐ TR 47 Mj53
Kavála ☐ GR 45 Me50
Kavalerovo ☐ RUS 77 Rh23
Kavali ☐ IND (APH) 85 Ok39
Kavaratti ☐ IND 84 Og41
Kavaratti Island ☐ IND 84 Og41
Kavarna ☐ BG 45 Mj47
Kavdanbeli ☐ RI 95 Qh48
Kavendou, Mont ☐ RG 136 Kd40
Kaveri ☐ IND 84 Oj40
Kaveripattinam ☐ IND 85 Ok40
Kavieng ☐ PNG 116 Sf47
Kavir = Abarkuh ☐ IR 64 Nh29
Kavir-e Daranjir ☐ IR 64 Nj29
Kavir-e Siyah Kuh ☐ IR 59 Nf29
Kavir-i Namak ☐ IR 64 Nk28
Kavkaz ☐ RUS/GE ...
Kaviti ☐ IND (ORS) 83 Pc35
Kavuluvadu Kariem ☐ IND 84 Oh40
Kavumu ☐ F 156 Nd43
Kaw ☐ F 194 Hd43
Kawa ☐ SUD 135 Mf37
Kawagama Lake ☐ CDN 173 Ga23
Kawagoe ☐ J 79 Rk28
Kawahabo ☐ RI 96 Qk50
Kawaihae ☐ USA (HI) 170 Cc36
Kawaikini ☐ USA (HI) 170 Ca35
Kawambwa ☐ Z 146 Me50
Kawanoe ☐ J 79 Rh28
Kawardha ☐ IND (CGH) 83 Pa34
Kawasa ☐ RDC 146 Me49
Kawasaki ☐ J 79 Rk28
Kawasso ☐ CDN 173 Ga23
Kawauchi ☐ J 77 Sa25
Kawawachikamach ☐ CDN 163 Gd08
Kawazu ☐ J 79 Rk29
Kawela Bay ☐ USA (HI) 170 Ca35
Kawene ☐ CDN (ON) 172 Fe22
Kawhia ☐ NZ 113 Tj65
Kawich Peak ☐ USA 170 Eb26
Kawio ☐ RI 97 Rd45
Kawir ☐ IR 57 Ne28
Kawm Umbū ☐ ET ...

Kaxinawá Nova Olinda, T.I. ☐ BR 197 Ge50
Kaya ☐ BF 137 Kk39
Kayah ☐ MYA 88 Pj36
Kayaki ☐ RI 93 Qd48
Kayak Island ☐ USA 166 Ch16
Kayama ☐ Z 146 Mf50
Kayan ☐ MYA 86 Ph33
Kayan Bung ☐ MAL 94 Qj43
Kayan ☐ EAT 144 Mf46
Kayankulam ☐ IND (KER) 84 Oj41
Kayan-Sungai Mentarang Reserve ☐ RI 94 Qj44
Kayapa ☐ TR 47 Mh51
Kayapó, T.I. ☐ BR 200 Hc49
Kayar ☐ IND (MHT) 82 Oh36
Kayasan N.P. ☐ ROK 79 Re28
Kayattar ☐ IND 84 Oj41
Kaycee ☐ USA (WY) 169 Eg24
Kayeli ☐ RI 97 Rd47
Kayembe Mukulu ☐ RDC 149 Mc50
Kaye, Mount ☐ AUS 111 Se64
Kayenta ☐ USA (AZ) 171 Ee27
Kayes ☐ EAT 144 Mg47
Kayes ☐ RCB 148 Lg48
Kayes ☐ RMM 130 Kd38
Kayima ☐ WAL 136 Ke41
Kaymakçı ☐ TR 47 Mj52
Kaymor ☐ SN 136 Kc39
Kayna-Bayonga ☐ RDC 141 Me46
Kayo ☐ RI 91 Rd45
Kayogoro ☐ BU 146 Me48
Kayombo ☐ Z 151 Mb52
Kayonza ☐ RWA 144 Mf46
Kay Point ☐ CDN (YT) 165 Ck11
Kayrunnera ☐ AUS (NSW) 108 Sb61
Kayserbergerbge ☐ SME 194 Hb44
Kayseri ☐ TR 56 Mh26
Kaysersberg ☐ F 25 Lh42
Kayuadi ☐ RI 96 Ra49
Kayuagung ☐ RI 93 Qc47
Kayuwawa ☐ EAU 144 Mg45
Kayville ☐ CDN (SK) 169 Eh21
Kazachka ☐ RUS 48 Nb20
Kazakhstan ☐ KZ 53 Oa05
Kazak shyghanaghy ☐ KZ 62 Nf24
Kazanka ☐ UA 49 Mg23
Kazanlák ☐ BG 45 Mf48
Kazanskaja ☐ RUS 48 Na21
Kazas ☐ KS 66 Oh25
Kazbegi ☐ GE 57 Nc24
Kaz Daği ☐ TR 47 Mj52
Kaz Daği Milli Parkı ☐ TR 47 Mj51
Kazerun ☐ IR 59 Nf31
Kazı Kazı ☐ EAT 146 Mg48
Kazıklı ☐ TR 47 Mh53
Kazimierza Wielka ☐ PL 41 Ma40
Kazimierz Dolny ☐ PL 41 Mb39
Kazımkarabekir ☐ TR 56 Mg27
Kazincbarcika ☐ H 43 Ma42
Kaziranga ☐ IND 86 Pg32
Kaziza ☐ RDC 151 Mb51
Kazlu Rūda ☐ LT 39 Md36
Kaznakovka ☐ KZ 67 Pd21
Kaznéjov ☐ CZ 42 Lo41
Kazuma Pan N.P. ☐ ZW 152 Mc55
Kazuno ☐ J 77 Sa25
Kazygurt ☐ KZ 63 Oe25
Keavy ☐ USA (HI) 170 Ca35
Kbor Roumia ☐ 🏛 DZ 126 La28
Kcynia ☐ PL 40 Ls38
Kdyně ☐ CZ 42 Lo41
Kéa ☐ GR 46 Me53
Kea ☐ GR 46 Me53
Keaau ☐ USA (HI) 170 Cc36
Keahole Point ☐ USA (HI) 170 Cc36
Kearney ☐ USA (NE) 174 Fa25
Keatchie ☐ USA (LA) 174 Fd29
Keating Point ☐ AUS ...
Keauhou = Hay River ☐ CDN 167 Ec15
Kebara ☐ 🏛 IL 58 Mh29
Kebemer ☐ SN 130 Kc38
Kébi ☐ CI 137 Kg42
Kébili ☐ TN 126 Le29
Kebilgiollewa ☐ CL 85 Pa41
Kebir, Nahr al- ☐ SYR 58 Mh28
Kebnekaise ☐ S 16 Lq12
Kebola ☐ RCB 148 Lf46
Kébou ☐ RI 96 Qk50
Kébra Dehar ☐ ETH 143 Nc42
Kebumen ☐ RI 95 Qe49
Keele Peak ☐ CDN 166 Da13
Keel ☐ IRL 19 Kj37
Keeley Lake ☐ CDN (SK) ...
Keeley ☐ USA (NH) 177 Gd24
Keene ☐ USA (NH) 177 Gd24
Keeneland Race Course ☐ USA (KY) 175 Fh26
Keer-Weer, Cape ☐ AUS ...
Keerabah ☐ AUS (QLD) ...
Keeroongooloo ☐ AUS (QLD) ...
Keet Seel ☐ 🏛 USA ...
Keetmanshoop ☐ NAM 154 Lh59
Keewatin ☐ CDN (ON) ...
Kefalonia ☐ GR 46 Ma52
Kefalos ☐ GR 47 Mg54
Keffi ☐ WAN 138 Ld41
Kef Mimouna ☐ DZ 126 Lc30
Keftya ☐ ETH 142 Mj39
Kegalla ☐ CL 85 Ok42
Kegaška ☐ CDN (QC) ...
Kegdzierzyn-Kozle ☐ PL 40 Ls40
Kegeti ☐ KS 66 Oh24
Kegums ☐ LV 39 Me34
Kegworth ☐ GB 21 Kt38

Kitami-Yamato-tai J 77 Sc23
Kita-Nagato Q.N.P. J 79 Rf28
Kitanda RDC 146 Md49
Kitangari EAT 147 Mk51
Kitani EAK 144 Mj47
Kitaotao RP 91 Rc42
Kit Carson USA (CO) 174 Ej26
Kitchener AUS (WA) 105 Rc61
Kitchener CDN (ON) 173 Fk24
Kiteba RDC 149 Mc49
Kitee FIN 38 Mf28
Kitembé RCB 148 Lh47
Kitendwe RDC 146 Me49
Kitenga RDC 148 Lj48
Kitengo RDC 149 Mc49
Kiteto EAT 147 Mj48
Kitgum EAU 144 Mg44
Kithairónas Óros GR 45 Md52
Kithira GR 46 Mc54
Kithnos GR 47 Me53
Kithnos GR 47 Me53
Kitia RCA 140 Mb43
Kitimat CDN (BC) 166 Df18
Kitimat Ranges CDN 166 Df19
Kitimat-Stikine CDN (BC) 166 Df18
Kitiu GH 137 Kk40
Kitmore Range AUS 103 Re57
Kitob UZ 63 Od26
Kitomanga EAT 147 Mk50
Kitou J 79 Rh29
Kitros GR 46 Mc52
Kitsuki J 79 Rf29
Kitteljäll S 16 Lh13
Kittenning USA (PA) 173 Ga25
Kittilä FIN 16 Mc12
Kitt Peak Nat. Observatory USA 171 Ee30
Kitui EAK 144 Mk50
Kitumba EAT 147 Mk50
Kitumba EAT 146 Mg49
Kitunga RDC 149 Me49
Kitutu RDC 146 Me47
Kitwancool Totem Poles CDN 166 Dg18
Kitwanga CDN (BC) 166 Dg18
Kitwanga EAU 144 Mg45
Kitwe Z 146 Me44
Kitzbühel A 34 Ln43
Kitzbüheler Alpen A 34 Ln43
Kitzingen D 33 Ll41
Kiumbila RDC 146 Md48
Kiumba EAT 147 Mk50
Kiunga PNG 115 Sa49
Kiunga Marine National Reserve EAK 145 Na46
Kiuruvesi FIN 16 Md14
Kivalina USA (AK) 165 Bh12
Kiverci UA 41 Mf40
Kivijärvi FIN 38 Mf27
Kivik S 31 Lj35
Kiviks marknad S 31 Lj35
Kivióli EST 38 Mg31
Kiwale EAT 146 Mg50
Kiwalik USA (AK) 165 Bk12
Kiwaru Island EAK 145 Na47
Kiwirrkurra A.L. AUS 103 Rd57
Kiworo RI 114 Rk49
Kiyamaki Dagh IR 57 Nd26
Kiyasar IR 62 Ng27
Kiyev WAN 138 La40
Kiyembwe RDC 146 Md47
Kiyköy TR 45 Mj49
Kizbeyl TR 57 Mk27
Kizildağ Milli Parkı TR 56 Mg25
Kizilçahamam TR 56 Mg25
Kizilirmak TR 56 Mg25
Kizilyurt RUS (DAG) 57 Nd24
Kizil Kala TM 62 Nz25
Kizil Gianfo Dong CHN 66 Pb25
Kiziltepe TR 57 Na27
Kizimkazi EAT 147 Mk50
Kizimkazi EAT 147 Mk49
Kizinga RUS (BUR) 70 Qe20
Kız Kalesi TR 56 Mh27
Kizljar RUS (DAG) 57 Nd24
Kjahta RUS (BUR) 70 Qd20
Kjellerup DK 30 Lk34
Kjøllefjord N 30 Ln30
Kjøllefjord N 16 Md10
Kjølur IS 18 Ka26
Kjustendil BG 44 Mc48
Klaarbeck RI 97 Re46
Klaarstroom ZA 154 Mb62
Kladanj BIH 44 Lu46
Kladar RI 114 Rj50
Kladnica SCG 44 Ma47
Kladno CZ 42 Lp40
Kladovo SCG 44 Mc46
Klaeng THA 89 Qa39
Klagenfurt A 35 Lp44
Klagetoh USA (AZ) 171 Ee28
Klakah RI 95 Qg49
Klaksvik DK 16 Ko28
Klamath USA (CA) 168 Dj25
Klamath Falls USA (OR) 168 Dk24
Klamath Mountains USA 168 Dj25
Klamono RI 97 Rf46
Klampa RI 94 Qj45
Klanac HR 35 Lq46
Klappa RI 94 Qd45
Klaserie Nature Reserve ZA 155 Mf58
Klasies River Caves ZA 155 Mc63
Kläšterec nad Ohří CZ 42 Lo40
Klasztor Paulinów PL 41 Lu40
Klasztor Świętej Anny PL 40 Lt40

Kliprondawel NAM 154 Lk59
Klipskool CI 154 SM58
Klissoura GR 46 Ma51
Klisura BG 45 Me48
Klitmøller DK 30 Lj33
Kljuè BIH 35 Lr46
Ključevskaja Sopka, vulkan RUS 55 Ta07
Klobuck PL 41 Lt40
Klodawa PL 40 Lt38
Klodzko PL 40 Lr41
Klofças TR 45 Ma49
Klofele ETH 142 Mk42
Koffi-Amankro CI 137 Kj42
Koffielontein ZA 155 Mc60
Kofiau RI 97 Re46
Köflach A 35 Lq43
Koforidua GH 137 Kk42
Kofu J 79 Rg28
Kofu J 79 Rk27
Koga J 77 Rk27
Kogan AUS (QLD) 109 Sf59
Koge DK 30 Ln35
Køge Bugt = Pikiutdleq DK 163 Ja06
Kogheily Nature Reserve ZA 154 Lk63
Koghaly KZ 66 Ok23
Kogon UZ 63 Oc26
Kogula EST 39 Mc32
Koguryo, Capital Cities and Tombs of the Ancient Kingdom PRK 70 Ed29
Koguryo Tombs, Complex of PRK 76 Rd25/Rd26
Koguva EST 39 Md32
Kogyae Strict Nature Reserve GH 137 Kk42
Kohatpur NEP 81 Pa31
Kohan PK 65 Od32
Koh Ang Tong THA 88 Pk41
Kohat PK 65 Oe32
Kohila EST 38 Me31
Kohima IND (NGL) 86 Ph33
Koh-i-Patandar PK 65 Oc32
Koh Kong K 89 Qb40
Kohler Range F 6 Eb33
Kohlu PK 65 Oe31
Kohma RUS 48 Na17
Kohol RI 97 Rd47
Kolombangara SOL 117 Sj49
Koh Phalual THA 88 Pk41
Koh Phangan THA 88 Qa41
Kohrud IR 62 Ng27
Koh Rung K 89 Qa40
Koh Rung Samloem K 89 Qb40
Koh Samui THA 88 Qa41
Koh Tang THA 88 Pk40
Koh Tao THA 88 Pk40
Koh Thmei K 89 Qb40
Kohtla-järve EST 38 Mg31
Kohung EAT 146 Mg49
Kohunlich MEX 183 Ff36
Koidu CDN (YT) 166 Ck15
Koidu-Sefadu WAL 136 Ke41
Koi Island PNG 115 Sc47
Koilkundla IND (APH) 85 Ok38
Koilovci BG 45 Me47
Koimbani COM 156 Nb51
Koindu WAL 136 Ke41
Koi Sanjaq IRQ 57 Nc27
Kojadik USA 164 Bk12
Koje Do ROK 79 Re28
Kojetin CZ 42 Ls41
Kojgorod RUS 48 Nd18
Kojonup AUS (WA) 104 Qj62
Kojori GE 57 Nb25
Kok K 89 Qd39
Koka ETH 142 Mj41
Koka ETH 142 Mk41

Koduru IND (APH) 85 Ok39
Kodyma UA 49 Me21
Koébomou CI 137 Kj41
Koegelbeen Caves ZA 154 Mb60
Koegelbeengrotte ZA 154 Mb60
Koehula ZA 154 Lk61
Koelwar IND (BIH) 83 Pc33
Koés NAM 154 Lk58
Kofa N.W.R. USA 170 Ed29
Kofarnihon TJ 63 Oe26
Kofças TR 45 Ma49
Kohala ZA 35 Lq43
Kohan TR 45 Ma49
Ko Kha Khao THA 88 Pj41
Kokinomblèa GR 45 Md52
Kokish CDN (BC) 168 Dg20
Kok-Jangak KS 63 Og25
Kökken FIN 16 Mb14
Koklot LV 39 Mh35
Kokrach RI 95 Qg48
Kokrajhar IND (ASM) 86 Pf32
Kokrines Hills USA 165 Cc13
Kokruagarok USA (AK) 165 Cd10
Köksajok RUS (MEL) 48 Nd17
Köksaras IND (ORS) 83 Pb36
Köksarai TJ 63 Oe26
Köksengir tau KZ 62 Nj23
Kokstad ZA 155 Me61
Kokomedua GH 137 Kk43
Komendá GH 137 Kk42
Komárno SK 42 Lt43
Komárom H 42 Ls43
Komarówka Podlaska PL 41 Mc39
Komarno PL 41 Mc40
Komatipoort ZA 155 Mf58
Komatipeta IND (ORS) 83 Pb37
Komatsu J 79 Rj27
Komba RI 97 Rb49
Kombat NAM 150 Lj55
Kombissiri BF 137 Kk39
Kombo-Itindi CAM 138 Le43
Kombone CAM 138 Lc43
Kombongou CI 137 Kh41
Komebyo CI 137 Kj41
Kome Island EAT 144 Mg47
Kome Island EAT 144 Mg46
Komejan IR 57 Ne28
Kom el Ahmar (Nekhen) ET 129 Mg33
Komenda GH 137 Kk43
Komga ZA 155 Md62
Komi 53 Nb03
Komin-Yanga BF 137 La40
Ko Miang THA 88 Pj41
Ko Pha Ngan THA 88 Qa41
Kominternivs'ke UA 49 Mf22
Kolafa Fora NEP 81 Ob34
Kolafa CI 137 Kg40
Kolaczyce PL 41 Md39
Kolahun LB 136 Ke41
Kolana RI 97 Rc50
Ko Lanta THA 88 Pk42
Ko Lanta Marine N.P. THA
Kolaras RI 95 Qf47
Kolarovo SK 42 Ls43
Kolásin SCG 44 Lu48

Koldinghus DK 30 Lk35
Kole RDC 149 Md47
Kolebira IND (JKD) 83 Pc34
Kolen IR 59 Ne30
Kolèntèn IR 59 Ne30
Kolha IR 43 Ll44
Kolga-Jaani EST 38 Mf32
Kolgaon IND (MHT) 82 Oh36
Kolhapur IND (APH) 82 Ok37
Kolhapur IND (MHT) 82 Oh37
Kolhar IND (KTK) 82 Oh37
Kolia CI 137 Kg41
Koliganek USA (AK) 164 Cb16
Kolin CZ 42 Lp40
Kolka LV 39 Mc33
Kolkasrags LV 39 Mc33
Kolkata IND 86 Pe34
Kolkhetis Nakrdzali GE 57 Na24
Kolky UA 41 Mf39
Kollafjarðarnes IS 18 Jd25
Kollam IND (KER) 84 Oj41
Kollegal IND (KTK) 84 Oj39
Kollo RN 132 Lb39
Kollur IND (KTK) 84 Oj39
Kolmanskop ZA NAM 154 Lh59
Kolmården S 31 Lj32
Kolnáqur CI 137 Kg40
Kolno PL 41 Mb37
Kolo EAT 147 Mh48
Koto PL 40 Lt38
Kolobane SN 130 Kc38
Kolobeke RDC 149 Lk46
Kolobrzeg PL 40 Lq36
Kolocava UA 43 Md43
Kolokani RMM 137 Kg40
Kolokolovo BG 45 Mh48
Kolokondé DY 138 La41
Kolomyia UA 43 Me42
Kolomna RUS 48 Mh18
Kolomyji RDC 149 Mb48
Kolomyji RDC 149 Mf42
Kolon CI 137 Kh41
Kolondièba CI 137 Kg40
Kolon CI 137 Kg42
Kolondzi RMM 137 Kh39
Kolonidale RI 96 Ra46
Kolondale RI 96 Ra46
Koloro, V. = Pamporovo BG 45 Me49
Koloa CI 137 Kh41
Kolka THA 88 Pk42
Kolski Poluostrov RUS 54 Md05
Kolsva S 31 Lj31
Koltur DK 18 Kn29
Kolufoss IS 18 Ju25
Kolulu EST 142 Na38
Kolur IND (CGH) 83 Pb36
Koluszki PL 41 Lu39
Kolwezi RDC 151 Mc51
Kolychiva UA 48 Nd19
Kolyma RUS 55 So06
Kolyma Range RUS 55 So05
Kolyšlej RUS 48 Nc19
Koma RI 97 Rf47
Komadougou Yobe RN/WAN 133 Lg39

Koopan Sud ZA 154 Ma59
Koopmansfontein ZA 155 Mc60
Komsomol'sk TM 62 Ob26
Komsomol'skaja ANT (RUS) 7 Pd33
Komsomol'sk RUS 39 Ma36
Komsomol'skij RUS (DAG) 57 Nd24
Komsomol'skij RUS (KAL) 57 Nd23
Komsomol'skij RUS (MOR) 48 Nc18
Komsomol'sk-na-Amure RUS 55 Rd08
Komsomolskoye ZA 63 Oe25
Komsomol'skiy Zapovednik RUS 39 Ma36
Kön Burnu TR 45 Mf50
Körümlani TR 45 Mf50
Kon CAM 139 Lf43
Kona BF 137 Kj39
Kona RN 132 Le39
Konada IND (APH) 83 Pb36
Konakovo RUS 48 Mj17
Konakpinar TR 47 Mh51
Konandikro CI 137 Kh42
Konankro CI 137 Kh42
Konareta IND (APH) 85 Ok38
Konarak IND 84 Pa36
Konare BG 45 Mj47
Konarzyny PL 40 Lr37
Konch IND (UPH) 83 Ok33
Kondagaon IND (CGH) 83 Pa36
Kondakamberu IND (ORS) 83 Pb36
Kondamkro IND (CGH) 83 Pa36
Kondamp IND 83 Pg37
Kondembia WAL 136 Ke41
Kondhali IND (MHT) 83 Ok35
Kondinin AUS (WA) 104 Qk62
Kondoa EAT 147 Mh48
Kondobé M 48 Nc19
Kondolole RDC 149 Md48
Kondrovo RUS 48 Mh18
Kondue RDC 149 Mb48
Konduga WAN 139 Lg40
Köneürgench TM 62 Nk24
Koneng RI 92 Pk53
Koné F 118 Tc56
Konévka RUS 48 Nd18
Kongaso CI 137 Kg42
Kongolo RDC 146 Me47
Kong Christian IX Land DK 163 Ja05
Kong Christian X Land DK 163 Jb04
Konga EAT 144 Mh45
Kong Frederik IX Land DK 163 Hc05
Kong Frederik VIII Land DK 163 Jc03
Kong Frederik VI Kyst DK 163 Hd03
Kong Karls Land N 16 Md06
Kong Krallat THA 88 Qa37
Konglong CHN (HUB) 75 Qh31
Kongo LB 136 Ke42
Kongolo RDC 146 Md48
Kongor SUD 141 Mf42
Kongoussi BF 137 Kk39
Kongsberg N 30 Lk31
Kongsvege Kongbreen N 16 Lg06
Kongugal IND (MNP) 86 Pg34
Kongu Shan CHN 66 Oh26
Kongwa EAT 147 Mj49
Koni RDC 146 Md51
Koniborom TJ 63 Of25
Koniecpol PL 41 Lu40
Königsbrück D 32 Lo40
Königsbrunn D 33 Ll42
Königstein D 32 Lo40
Königswiesen D 42 Lp42
Königswinter D 32 Lh40
Königs Wusterhausen D 32 Lo38
Konimex UZ 63 Oc25
Konin PL 40 Lt38
Konina RMM 137 Kh39
Konina RMM 137 Kh39
Könitsa GR 45 Mb51
Konj BIH 35 Lr47
Konjed dan IR 59 Nf29
Konjic BIH 35 Ls47
Konkoure CI 137 Kh41

Korovniki RUS 48 Mk17
Korovou FJI 119 Tk54
Korošci SOL 117 Sh49
Koryaninu N.P. FJI 119 Tj54
Korpilahti FIN 38 Mf28
Korppoo = Korppoo FIN 38 Mb30
Korppoo FIN 38 Mb30
Korppoo II FIN 38 Mb30
Korsakow RUS 77 Sb22
Korsberga S 31 Lg33
Korsnäs FIN 38 Ma29
Korsör DK 30 Lm35
Korsun'-Ševčenkivs'kyj UA 49 Mf21
Korsze PL 41 Mb36
Kortala SUD 135 Mf48
Korte BG 45 Mf48
Kórthio GR 47 Me53
Kortrijk B 23 Ld40
Korucu TR 47 Mh51
Korup, P.N. de CAM 138 Le43
Koruyeh IR 59 Nf30
Koryak Autonomous District RUS 55 Tb06
Koryak Range RUS 55 Tb06
Korycany CZ 42 Ls41
Korycin PL 41 Mc37
Korzybie PL 40 Lr36
Kós GR 47 Mh54
Kós GR 47 Mh54
Kosa ETH 142 Mj42
Koš-Agač RUS (ALT) 67 Pe21
Kosbad RG 136 Kf41
Kościan PL 40 Lr38
Kościelec PL 40 Lt38
Kościerzyna PL 40 Ls36
Kościół Sytersów PL 40 Lt36
Kosciusko USA (MS) 175 Ff29
Kosciuszko, Mount AUS 111 Se64
Kösciuszko N.P. AUS (NSW) 111 Se63
Köse EST 38 Mf32
Köse Dağları TR 57 Mk25
Kösen SUD 135 Md48
Kosi Bay Nature Reserve ZA 155 Mg59
Košice SK 43 Mb42
Košiicka Belá SK 43 Mb42
Koslohovce SK 43 Lu42
Kosji RUS 38 Ng18
Köşk Maracki IQ 76 Ea20
Köşkerli SCG 44 Lu48
Kosol HR 35 Lr45
Kosor FIN 38 Mb28
Kosovska Mitrovica SCG 44 Ma48
Kosow Lacki PL 41 Mc38
Koserao al FSM 10 Td36
Kosrayl IR 57 Nc28
Kosse USA (TX) 174 Fb30
Kossen RDC 146 Md51
Kossou, Lac de CI 137 Kh42
Kostajnica SLO 42 Lo45
Kostanjevica na Krki SLO 42 Lq45
Kostelec nad Černými Lesy CZ 42 Lp41
Kostenec BG 45 Md48
Kostopilʹ UA 41 Mf40
Kostrzyn PL 40 Lp38
Kostrzyn PL 40 Lt38
Kostyantynivka UA 48 Mj21
Kostyukovichi BY 48 Mf19

Ko Yao Yai THA 88 Pk42
Koyasan sacred site (Koya) J 79 Rh28
Köycegiz TR 47 Mf54
Koygolo RN 132 Lb39
Koyuk USA (AK) 165 Bk13
Koyukuk National Wildlife Refuge USA 165 Cb13
Koyukuk USA (AK) 165 Cb13
Koyyuuru IND (APH) 83 Pb37
Koza CAM 139 Lg40
Kozak TR 47 Mh51
Kozaki TR 56 Mh26
Kozan TR 56 Mh27
Kozarci GR 46 Md50
Kozara, N.P. BIH 35 Lr45
Kozara, N.P. BIH 35 Lr46
Kozel'sk RUS 48 Mh19
Kozelets UA 48 Me20
Koziki BY 41 Mf40
Kozjak German MK 44 Mc48
Kozjatyn UA 48 Me21
Kozloduj BG 44 Mc47
Kozlov PL 41 Lu40
Kozlupinar TR 57 Mk26
Kozmin PL 40 Ls39
Kozy modem'jansk RUS (MEL) 48 Nc17
Kožuchów PL 40 Lp39
Kozu-jima J 79 Rk28
Kozyn UA 41 Mf40
Kpagato GH 137 Kk41
Kpalbusi GH 137 Kk41
Kpalimé TG 137 La42
Kpando GH 137 La41
Kpariigu GH 137 La41
Kpaso GH 137 La41
Kpassagon GH 137 Lb42
Kpatawee Falls LB 136 Kf42
Kpatinga GH 137 Kk41
Kpèssi TG 137 La41
Kpetoe GH 137 La42
Kpetuo LB 136 Kf42
Kpeve GH 137 La42
Kraankuil ZA 155 Mc60
Krabi THA 88 Pk41
Kra Buri THA 88 Pk40
Krafla IS 18 Ka25
Kraftstation S 16 Lk12
Kragemäs DK 30 Lm36
Kragero N 30 Lk32
Kragujevac SCG 44 Mb48
Krajište SCG 44 Mc48
Krajnovka RUS (DAG) 57 Nd24
Krakatau Island = Rakata RI 93 Qc49
Krakau Volcano RI 93 Qc49
Kraké DY 138 Lb42
Kräklingbo S 31 Lj33
Krakór RMM (AK) 165 Bk13
Krakovec CZ 42 Lo40
Kraków PL 41 Lu40
Kraków am dem S 32 Ln37
Kralendijk NL 193 Gf34
Kralický Sněžník CZ 42 Lr41
Kraljevica HR 35 Lp45
Kraljevo SCG 44 Mb48
Kralovice CZ 42 Lo41
Král'ovský Chlmec SK 43 Mb42
Kralupy nad Vltavou CZ 42 Lp40
Kramators'k UA 49 Mj21
Kramfors S 16 Lj14
Kramjanica BY 41 Me37
Krani SLO 42 Lp44
Kranj SLO 42 Lp44
Kranjska Gora SLO 42 Lo44
Kranovodskoye plato TM 62 Ng25
Kransfontein ZA 155 Me60
Kranskop ZA 155 Mf60
Kranuan THA 89 Qb37
Kranza RI 94 Qj45
Krapina HR 35 Lq44
Krapinske Toplice HR 35 Lq44
Krapkowice PL 40 Ls40
Kraskino RUS 76 Rf24
Kras'lava LV 39 Mh35
Krasnaja Horka SK 43 Ma42
Krašna Hôrka SK 43 Ma42
Krasna jaruga Gornadóm SK 43 Ma42
Kránja N.P. RUS 48 Nb18
Krása nad Hornádom SK
Krásna baki RUS 48 Nc17
Krasný Holm RUS 48 Mj17
Krasnaj Mançt RUS 48 Mk18
Krasavin Beach RUS (KER) 84 Oj41
Krasnoarmejsk RUS 48 Mk17
Krasnoarmijs'k UA 49 Mj21
Krasnobród PL 41 Md40
Krasnodar RUS 49 Mk22
Krasnodarskoe Vodohranilišče RUS 49 Mk22
Krasnodon UA 49 Mk21
Krasnogorodskoe RUS 39 Mj34
Krasnogvardejskoe RUS 49 Na22
Krasnogorsk RUS 71 Re20
Krasnohrad UA 49 Mh21
Krasnohvardijs'ke UA 49 Mh23
Krasnojarsk RUS 54 Pc07
Krasnoj ulus RUS (TU) 48 Nd17
Krasnoodokuysk UA 41 Mf40
Krasnokamensk RUS 71 Qk20
Krasnokamsk RUS 48 Nf17
Krasnomajskij RUS 48 Mh17
Krasnoozernoe RUS 38 Mj30
Krasnoperekops'k UA 49 Mg23
Krasnopillya UA 48 Mh20
Krasnoselʹsk UA 49 Me22
Krasnoselʹkup RUS 54 Ob05
Krasnoslobodsk RUS (MOR) 48 Nb18
Krasnoslobodsk RUS 39 Lu36
Krasnoznamensk RUS 39 Mc36
Krasnyi Baki RUS 48 Nc17
Krasovce UA 49 Mh23
Kratie K (TBO) 200 Hg50
Krating Falls THA 88 Pj40
Kravica PNG 115 Sc49
Krau RI 115 Sd49
Kraženʹ J 79 Rh28
Krebs Bekati al Bässä RMM 132 Lc35
Krefeld D 32 Lg39
Kreganuare NAM 150 La55
Krek K 89 Qc40
Krekenava LT 39 Me35
Kremaste vodosvetys CHN 48 Mf40
Kremenchuk UA 49 Mg21
Kremenec UA 41 Mf40
Kremenivci RUS BG 44 Md48
Kremenki RUS 48 Mk18
Kremnica SK 43 Lu42
Kremnesegni UA 49 Me21
Kremsmünster A 42 Lp42

Kreml Novgorod – La Flor y Río Escalante

Kreml Novgorod ⬚ RUS 48 Mf16
Kremmen ⬚ D 32 Lo38
Kremmling ⬚ USA (CO) 171 Eg25
Kremna ⬚ SCG 46 Lu47
Kremnický hrad ⬚ SK 43 Lu42
Krems ⬚ A 35 Lo44
Krems ⬚ A 42 Lq42
Krepoljin ⬚ SCG 44 Mb46
Krepsko ⬚ PL 40 Lr37
Kréševo ⬚ BIH 44 Lt47
Kresk-Królowa ⬚ PL 41 Md38
Kresna ⬚ BG 44 Md49
Krestcy ⬚ RUS 48 Mg16
Kréstena ⬚ GR 46 Mb53
Kretinga ⬚ LT 39 Mb35
Kreuzeck ⬚ A 35 Lo44
Kreuzenstein ⬚ A 42 Lr42
Kreuzlingen ⬚ D 32 Lj40
Kriátsi ⬚ GR 46 Mc52
Kribi ⬚ CAM 138 Le44
Kriel ⬚ ZA 155 Me59
Kriens ⬚ CH 34 La43
Krikelos ⬚ GR 46 Ma52
Krim-Krim ⬚ TCH 140 Lh41
Krimmler Fälle ⬚ A 34 La43
Krini ⬚ GR 46 Mc51
Krishna ⬚ IND (AP) 83 Ok36
Krishnagiri ⬚ IND (TNU) 84 Ok39
Krishnai ⬚ IND (ASM) 86 Pf33
Krishnanagar ⬚ IND (WBG) 86 Pe34
Krishnarajanagara ⬚ IND (KTK) 84 Oj39
Kristdala ⬚ S 31 Lr33
Kristiansand ⬚ N 30 Lh32
Kristiansund ⬚ S 31 Lp34
Kristiansund ⬚ N 16 Ld14
Kristiinankaupunki = Kristinestad ⬚ FIN 38 Mb28
Kristineham ⬚ S 31 Lp31
Kristinestad = Kristiinankaupunki ⬚ FIN 38 Mb28
Kriva Feja ⬚ SCG 44 Mc48
Kriva Palanka ⬚ MK 44 Mc48
Krivodol ⬚ BG 44 Md47
Krivolak ⬚ MK 44 Mc48
Krivoroz'e ⬚ RUS 48 Na21
Kriz ⬚ TN 126 Le28
Křižanov ⬚ CZ 42 Lr41
Kříževci ⬚ HR 35 Lr44
Krízpolje ⬚ HR 35 Lq45
krjaž Cekanovskogo ⬚ RUS 55 Ra04
Krk ⬚ HR 35 Lp46
Krka, N.P. ⬚ HR 35 Lq47
Krkonošský N.P. ⬚ CZ 42 Lq40
Krn ⬚ SLO 42 Lo44
Krnja ⬚ SCG 44 Lu48
Krnov ⬚ CZ 42 Ls40
Krobia ⬚ PL 40 Lr39
Kraderen ⬚ N 30 Lk30
Krokek ⬚ S 31 Lr32
Krokilio ⬚ GR 46 Mc52
Kokom ⬚ S 16 Ln14
Króksfjarðarnes ⬚ IS 18 Jt25
Krolevec' ⬚ UA 48 Mg20
Kromdraai ⬚ ZA 155 Md59
Kroměříž ⬚ CZ 42 Ls41
Kronach ⬚ D 33 Lm40
Kronauce ⬚ LV 39 Md34
Kronberg ⬚ DK 30 Lu14
Krong Buk ⬚ VN 89 Qe39
Krong Pach ⬚ VN 89 Qe40
Kronprins Christian Land ⬚ DK 163 Jd02
Kronprins Olav kyst ⬚ 7 Na32
Kronshagen ⬚ D 32 Ll36
Kronstadt ⬚ RUS 38 Mk31
Kroonstad ⬚ ZA 155 Md59
Kröpelin ⬚ D 32 Lm36
Kropotkin ⬚ RUS 49 Na23
Krośnice ⬚ PL 40 Ls39
Krośniewicz ⬚ PL 41 Lu39
Krosno ⬚ PL 41 Mb41
Krosnojarskoe vodohraniliŝče ⬚ RUS 54 Pc08
Krosno Odrzańskie ⬚ PL 40 Lq38
Kross ⬚ IS 18 Jz27
Krotoszyn ⬚ PL 40 Ls39
Krotz Springs ⬚ USA (LA) 175 Fe30
Kráko ⬚ SLO 42 Lp45
Krstac ⬚ SCG 44 Lt47
Krueng Raya ⬚ RI 92 Ph43
Kruger N.P. = Nasionale Krugerwildtuin ⬚ ZA 152 Mf57
Krugersdorp ⬚ ZA 155 Md59
Kruhla ploska ⬚ UA 49 Mh21
Krui ⬚ RI 93 Qb48
Kruidfontein ⬚ ZA 154 Ma62
Kruje ⬚ AL 44 Lu49
Krukenyči ⬚ UA 43 Md41
Krukowo ⬚ PL 41 Mb37
Krumbach ⬚ D 33 Ll42
Krung Ching Waterfall ⬚ THA 88 Pk41
Krung Thep = Bangkok ⬚ THA 88 Qa39
Krupa na Vrbasu ⬚ BIH 35 Ls46
Krupanj ⬚ SCG 44 Lu46
Krupinská planina ⬚ SK 43 Lu42
Krušari ⬚ BG 45 Mh47
Krušari ⬚ BG 45 Mh47
Krusedol Selo ⬚ SCG 44 Lu45
Krŭševac ⬚ MK 44 Md49
Krušné hory ⬚ D/CZ 33 Ln40
Kruševo ⬚ BG 45 Me47
Kruševica ⬚ SCG 44 Md47
Krustpils ⬚ LV 39 Mf34
Kruszwica ⬚ PL 40 Lt38
Kruszyna ⬚ PL 41 Lu40
Kruszyniany ⬚ PL 41 Md37
Kruzof Island ⬚ USA 166 Dc17
Krygav ⬚ BY 48 Mf19
Krylov ⬚ RUS 39 Mb36
Krymsk ⬚ RUS 49 Mj23
Kryms'ky hory ⬚ UA 49 Mh23
Krynica ⬚ PL 41 Ma41
Krynica Morska ⬚ PL 41 Lu36
Krynki ⬚ PL 41 Md37
Krynyčne ⬚ UA 45 Mj40
Kryry Ozero ⬚ UA 49 Mf22
Kryvčyy ⬚ BY 39 Mh36
Kryvsk ⬚ BY 48 Mf19
Kryvyj Rih ⬚ UA 49 Mg22
Kryžiu kalnas ⬚ LT 39 Md34
Kryžopol' ⬚ UA 49 Me21
Krzepice ⬚ PL 40 Lt40
Krzeszów ⬚ PL 41 Mb41
Krzepice ⬚ PL 40 Lt40
Krzywa ⬚ PL 40 Lq40
Krzyz ⬚ PL 40 Lq38
Krzyż ⬚ CZS Kk31
'Ksan Ind. Village ⬚ CDN 166 Dg18
Ksar Chellala ⬚ DZ 126 Lb28
Ksar El Barka ⬚ RIM 130 Kd36
Ksar el Boukhari ⬚ DZ 126 Lb28
Ksar El Hirane ⬚ DZ 126 Lb28
Ksar-el-Kebir ⬚ MA 125 Kh28
Ksar-es-Seghir ⬚ MA 27 Kp45
Ksar Ghilane ⬚ TN 126 Lf29
Ksar Lamsa ⬚ TN 126 Le27
Ksar Ouled Soltane ⬚ TN 126 Lf29
Ksenski ⬚ RUS 48 Mj20
Ksiepol ⬚ PL 41 Md40
Ksour Djedidat ⬚ TN 126 Lf29
Ksour Essaf ⬚ TN 126 Lf28
Kstovo ⬚ RUS 48 Nc17
KTHI-TV Tower ⬚ USA 172 Fb22

La Follet – Lan Sang

La Follet USA (TN) 175 Fh27
la Font de la Figuera E 29 Ku52
La Francia RA (CD) 209 Gj61
La Frederica RA (SC) 210 Gd70
La Fría YV 192 Gd41
Laft-e Nou IR 64 Nh32
La Fuente de San Esteban E 26 Ko50
La Gacilly F 22 Ks43
La Gaiba BOL 202 Hb54
Lagako-Topeko CI 137 Kh43
Lagalaga FJI 119 Tk54
La Galite TN 126 Le27
La Gallareta RA (SF) 207 Gk60
La Gallega E 26 Kr49
Lagamar BR (MG) 203 Hg55
Lagan S 31 Lp34
Lagangilang RP 90 Ra37
Lagarto BR (SE) 201 Jb51
Lagash IRQ 59 Nd30
La Gateada NIC 185 Fh39
Lagawe RP 90 Ra37
Lagbar SN 130 Kc38
Lagçayb DARS/MA 124 Ke32
Lagdo CAM 139 Lg41
Lage D 32 Lj39
Lages BR (SC) 205 He59
Lages USA (NV) 171 Ec25
Lageuen RI 92 Ph43
Laggan AUS (NSW) 111 Se63
Lagh Bogal EAK 145 Na45
Laghouat DZ 126 Lb29
La Gineta E 29 Ks51
La Glace CDN (AB) 167 Ea18
Laglan AUS (QLD) 109 Sd57
La Glória CO 192 Gd41
La Gloria MEX (NL) 181 Fa32
La Gloria USA (TX) 181 Fa32
Lågneset N 16 Lg07
Lagnieu F 25 Lf45
Lagny-sur-Marne F 23 Lc42
Lago WAL 136 Ke41
Lagoa P 27 Km53
Lago Acará BR 198 Gj49
Lagoa Comprida, T.I. BR 200 Hh48
Lagoa da Prata BR (MG) 203 Hh55
Lagoa do Itapera BR 205 Hf60
Lagoa do Mirim BR 205 Hf60
Lagoa Dongane MOC 153 Mh58
Lagoa do Peixe BR 204 He61
Lagoa do Peixe, P.N. BR 204 He61
Lagoa dos Brincos, T.I. BR 206 Gk52
Lagoa dos Patos BR 204 He61
Lagoa dos Quadros BR 205 Hf60
Lagoa Dourada BR (MG) 203 Hh56
Lagoa Formosa BR (MG) 203 Hg55
Lagoa Grande BR (PE) 201 Hk50
Lagoa Grande BR (PI) 200 Hj50
Lago Agrio EC 196 Gb45
Lago Agua Brava MEX 180 Eh34
Lago Aiapuá BR 198 Gj48
Lago Aiapuá, T.I. BR 198 Gj48
Lago Aluminé RA 208 Ge65
Lago Amanã BR 198 Gh47
Lagoa Mangueira BR 204 Hd62
Lago Amaramba MOC 153 Mj53
Lagoa Mirim BR 204 Hd62
Lago Anamã BR 198 Gk47
Lago Ananta PE 197 Ge53
Lago Anibal Pinto RCH 210 Gd72
Lagoa Poelela MOC 153 Mh58
Lagoa Porové BR (RS) 204 Hc60
Lago Arapa PE 197 Ge53
Lagoa Real BR (BA) 203 Hj53
Lago Arenal CR 185 Fh40
Lago Argentino RCH 210 Gd71
Lagoa Santa BR (MG) 203 Hj55
Lagoa Uembje MOC 155 Mg58
Lagoa Vermelha BR (RS) 204 He60
Lago Badajós BR 198 Gj47
Lago Baia Grande BOL/BR 206 Gk53
Lago Banamana MOC 152 Mg57
Lago Bayano PA 185 Ga41
Lago Belgrano RA (SC) 210 Gd69
Lago Bianca RCH 210 Ge72
Lago Blanco RA (CB) 210 Ge68
Lago Blanco RA 210 Ge68
Lago Blanco RCH 210 Gf73
Lago Budi RCH 208 Gd65
Lago Buenos Aires RA 210 Ge69
Lago Caburgua RCH 208 Ge65
Lago Calafquén RCH 208 Ge65
Lago Calbún RCH 208 Ge63
Lago Cardiel RA (SC) 210 Ge70
Lago Cardiel RA 210 Ge70
Lago Chasicó RA 209 Gj65
Lago Chioa PE 197 Gc50
Lago Cochrane RCH 210 Gd69
Lago Colhué Huapi RA 210 Gf68
Lago Colorada BOL 207 Gg57
Lago Concepción BOL 206 Gk54
Lago Conceptión BOL 206 Gj53
Lago Coricó RA 208 Gh66
Lago Coríco RCH 208 Gd65
Lago da Pedra BR (MA) 200 Hh48
Lago das Onças BR 202 Hb54
Lago das Pedras BR (PA) 199 Hc47
Lago de Atitlan GCA 184 Fe38
Lago de Brasília BR 203 Hg53
Lago de Cabora Bassa MOC 152 Mf53
Lago de Cajueiro BR 201 Hj47
Lago de Coari BR 198 Gj48
Lago de Eripucu BR 194 Hb46
Lago de Izabal GCA 184 Ff38
Lagodekhis Nakrdzali GE 57 Nc24
Lago del Abra RA 209 Gj66
Lago del Coghinas I 36 Lk50
Lago del Maule RCH 208 Ge64
Lago del Toro RCH 210 Gd71
Lago de Managua NIC 184 Fg39
Lago de Maracaibo YV 192 Ge41
Lago de Nicaragua NIC 185 Fh40
Lago de Poopó BOL 206 Gg55
Lago de San Luis BOL 206 Gj52
Lago de São Antônio BR (AM) 198 Gj49
Lago de Valencia YV 193 Gg40
Lago di Bolsena I 34 Lm48
Lago di Bracciano I 36 Ln48
Lago di Como I 34 Lk44
Lago di Garda I 34 Ll45
Lago di Lessina I 37 Lq49
Lago Dilolo ANG 151 Mb51
Lago di Lugano CH/I 34 Lj45
Lago di Mulárgia I 36 Lk51
Lago di Occhito I 37 Lp49
Lago di Sabáudia I 36 Lo49
Lago d'Iseo I 34 Ll45
Lago di Varano I 37 Lq49
Lago do Beruri, T.I. BR 198 Gk47
Lago d'Orta I 34 Lj45
Lago Enriquillo DOM 186 Ge36
Lago Epequén RA 209 Gj64
Lago Fagnano RCH 210 Gf73
Lago Feia BR 203 Hk57
Lago Gatún PA 185 Ga41
Lago General Carrera RCH 210 Gd69
Lago General Vintter RA 210 Ge67
Lago Ghio RA 210 Ge69
Lago Grande BR 199 Hc47
Lago Grande RA 210 Gg69
Lago Grande de Manacapuru BR 198 Gk47
Lago Grande do Curuai BR 199 Hc47
Lago Huachi BOL 206 Gj53
Lago Huatunas BOL 206 Gg52
Lago Huechulafquén RA 208 Ge65
Lago Huiñaymarcá BOL/PE 206 Gf54
Lago Inuria PE 197 Gc50
Lago Janauacá BR 199 Gk47
Lago Jari BR 198 Gj48
Lago Junín PE 197 Gc51
Lago Juparanã BR 203 Hk55
Lago La Argentina RA 209 Hb64
Lago Lagunillas PE 197 Ge53
Lago Lanalhue RCH 208 Gd64
Lago Languí Layo PE 197 Ge53
Lago Llanquihue RCH 208 Gd66
Lago Lleulleu RCH 208 Gd65
Lago Loriscota PE 206 Gf54
Lagolovo RUS 38 Mk31
Lago Macucocha PE 197 Gd53
Lago Maggiore CH/I 34 Lj45
Lago Maihue RCH 208 Ge66
Lago Mamiá BR 198 Gj48
Lago Mamori BR 199 Gk47
Lago Manaquiri BR 199 Gk47
Lago Menéndez RA 208 Ge67
Lago Musters RA 210 Gf68
Lago Nahuel Huapi RA 208 Ge66
Lagonegro I 37 Lq50
Lagong RI 94 Qe44
Lago Novo BR 195 He45
Lago O'Higgins RCH 210 Gd70
Lago Omodeo I 36 Lj50
Lagoon Point USA 164 Bk17
Lago Orcococha PE 197 Gc52
Lago Panguipulli RCH 208 Gd65
Lago Parinacochas PE 197 Gd53
Lago Pellegrini RA 208 Gg65
Lago Petén Itzá GCA 183 Ff37
Lago Piorini BR 198 Gj47
Lago Pirehueico RCH 208 Gd65
Lago Ponte Ribeiro BR 206 Ha53
Lago Posadas RA (SC) 210 Ge69
Lago Presidente Ríos RCH 210 Gc69
Lago Puelo, P.N. RA 208 Ge67
Lago Pueyrredón RA 210 Ge69
Lago Punrun PE 197 Gb51
Lago Puyehue RCH 208 Gd66
Lago Ranco RCH 208 Gd66
Lago Ranco RCH 208 Gd66
Lago Rapel RCH 208 Ge63
Lago Roca RA (SC) 210 Gd71
Lago Rogana BOL 206 Gg52
Lago Rogoaguado BOL 206 Gh52
Lago Rupanco RCH 208 Gd66
Lágos GR 45 Mf49
Lagos P 27 Km53
Lagos WAN 138 Lb42
Lagosa EAT 146 Me48
Lago Salinas PE 197 Ge54
Lago San Martín RA 210 Gd70
Lagos de Moreno MEX (JLC) 182 Ek35
Lagos Entry MOC 153 Mh53
Lagos Lagoon WAN 138 Lb42
Lago Strobel RA 210 Ge70
Lago Taciuã BR 199 Gk48
Lago Tar RA 210 Ge70
Lago Tefé BR 198 Gh47
Lago Todos los Santos RCH 208 Gd66
Lago Traful RA 208 Ge66
Lago Trasimeno I 34 Ln47
Lago Tres Picos RA 208 Gg66
Lago Uberaba BOL/BR 202 Hb54
La Gouira DARS 130 Kb35
Lago Uru Uru BOL 206 Gg55
Lago Verá PY 204 Hb59
Lago Verde BOL 207 Gg57
Lago Verde BR (MA) 195 Hh47
Lago Verde RCH 210 Ge68
Lago Verde RCH 207 Gf59
Lago Viedma RA (SC) 210 Gd70
Lago Viedma RA 210 Gd70
Lago Villarrica RCH 208 Gd65
Lago Vintter RA (CB) 210 Ge67
Łagów PL 40 Lq38
Łagów PL 41 Mb40
Lågøya N 16 Lk05
Lago Yelcho RCH 210 Gd67
Lago Yusala BOL 206 Gg53
la Granadella E 29 La49
La Grand-Combe F 25 Le46
La Grande USA (OR) 168 Ea23
La Grande-Motte F 25 Le47
La Grande Rivière CDN 176 Gd19
Lagrange AUS (WA) 102 Ra55
La Grange USA (GA) 175 Fh29
La Grange USA (KY) 175 Fh26
La Grange USA (TX) 181 Fb31
La Granja MEX (DGO) 181 Ej33
La Gran Sabana YV 193 Gk43
La Griba TN 126 Lf29
La Grita YV 192 Gd41
La Gruñidora MEX (ZCT) 181 Ek33
Lågskär 31 Lu31
La Guadelupe CDN (QC) 176 Ge23
La Guaira YV 193 Gg40
La Guarda RA (CA) 207 Gh60
La Guardia BOL 206 Gj54
La Guardia E 27 Kr51
Laguardia E 28 Ks48
La Guardia RCH 207 Gf59
Laguarta E 28 Ku48
La Guerche-de-Bretagne F 22 Kt43
La Guerche-sur-l'Aubois F 25 Lc44
Laguié CI 137 Kh42
Laguiole F 25 Lc46
La Güira, P.N. C 179 Fj34
L'Agulhas ZA 154 Ma63
Laguna BR (SC) 205 Hf60
Laguna Bismuna NIC 185 Fj38
Laguna Blanca RA (FO) 204 Ha58
Laguna Blanca RA (RN) 208 Gf66
Laguna Blanca, P.N. RA 208 Ge65
Laguna Campos PY 206 Gk56
Laguna Canachi MEX (SL) 180 Eg33
Laguna Catemaco MEX 183 Fc36
Laguna de Bay RP 90 Ra38
Laguna de Brus HN 185 Fh38
Laguna de Caratasca HN 185 Fj38
Laguna de Castillos ROU 209 Hd63
Laguna de Chapala MEX 182 Ej35
Laguna de Chiriquí PA 185 Fj41
Laguna de Coipasa BOL 206 Gf55
Laguna de Duero E 26 Kq49
Laguna de Gómez RA 209 Gk63
Laguna de Guayatayoc RA 207 Gh57
Laguna de Huaunta NIC 185 Fj39
Laguna de La Laja RCH 208 Ge64
Laguna de las Perlas NIC 185 Fj39
Laguna del Cisne RA 207 Gj60
Laguna del Laja, P.N. RCH 208 Ge64
Laguna del Monte RA 209 Gj64
Laguna de los Pozuelos RA 207 Gh57
Laguna del Palmar RA 207 Gk60
Laguna de Negrillos E 26 Kp48
Laguna de Perlas NIC 185 Fj39
Laguna de Tacarigua, P.N. YV 193 Gh40
Laguna de Tamiahua MEX 182 Fb35
Laguna de Términos MEX 183 Fe36
Laguna di Orbetello I 34 Lm48
Laguna di Venézia I 35 Ln45
Laguna El Caimanero MEX 180 Eg34
Laguna El Cuervo MEX 180 Eg31
Laguna El Guaje MEX 181 Ej32
Laguna Grande PE 197 Gb53
Laguna Gri Gri DOM 186 Ge36
Laguna Guatavita CO 192 Gd43
Laguna Iberá RA 204 Hb60
Laguna Itati RA 204 Ha60
Laguna Karatá NIC 185 Fj39
Laguna la Blanca Grande RA 208 Gj65
Laguna la Brava RA 209 Gj62
Laguna La Cocha CO 192 Gb45
Laguna la Restinga, P.N. YV 193 Gh40
Laguna Larga RA 207 Gj61
Laguna La Tortuga MEX 182 Fa34
Laguna Llancañelo RA 208 Gf63
Laguna los Mistoles RA 207 Gj61
Laguna Luna RA 204 Hb60
Laguna Madre MEX 181 Fb33
Laguna Mar Chiquita RA 207 Gj61
Laguna Mar Chiquita RA 209 Gk63
Laguna Mar Chiquitq RA 209 Hb64
Laguna Melincue RA 209 Gk62
Laguna Merín BR/ROU 204 Hd62
Laguna Morales MEX 182 Fb34
Laguna Negra ROU 209 Hd63
Laguna Paiva RA (SF) 209 Gk61
Laguna Pueblo USA 171 Eg28
Laguna Pueblo Viejo MEX 182 Fb34
Laguna Quistococha PE 198 Gf47
Laguna Ramón PE 196 Fk48
Lagunas PE 196 Ga49
Lagunas PE 196 Gc48
Laguna San Andrés MEX 182 Fb34
Laguna San Ignacio MEX (BCS) 180 Ed32
Laguna San Ignacio MEX 180 Ed32
Laguna San Rafael, P.N. RCH 210 Gd69
Lagunas de Chacahua, P.N. MEX 182 Fb38
Lagunas de Montebello, P.N. MEX 183 Fe37
Lagunas las Tunas Grandes RA 209 Gj63
Lagunas Saladas RA 207 Gj60
Laguna Taberis NIC 185 Fj38
Laguna Tarapaya BOL 206 Gh55
Laguna Trinidad PY 206 Gk56
Laguna Yema RA (FO) 207 Gk58
Lagundri RI 93 Pj45
Lagune Abi CI 137 Kj43
Lagune Banio G 148 Lf47
Lagune Ebrié CI 137 Kh43
Lagune Iguéla G 148 Le46
Lagune La Amarga RA 208 Gg65
Lagune La Dulce RA 208 Gg64
Lagune Ndogo G 148 Lf47
Lagune Nkomi G 148 Le46
Lagune Tadio CI 137 Kh43
Lagune Urre Lauquén RA 208 Gh65
Lagunillas BOL 206 Gj55
Lagunillas YV 192 Ge40
Lagunillas YV 192 Ge41
Lagunita Salada RA (CB) 208 Gf67
Laha CHN (HLG) 71 Rc21
La Habana C 179 Fj34
Lahad Datu MAL 91 Qk43
La Hai VN 89 Qe39
Lahaina USA (HI) 170 Cb35
Lahar IND (MPH) 83 Ok32
Laharpur IND (UPH) 81 Pa32
Lahat RI 93 Qb47
La Haye-du-Puits F 22 Kt41
Lahdenpoh'ja RUS (KAR) 38 Ml29
Lahe MYA 86 Ph32
Lahema rahvuspark EST 38 Mf31
La Hermosa CO 192 Ge43
La Herradura MEX (SLP) 182 Ek34
Lahewa RI 93 Pj45
La Higuera BOL 206 Gh55
La Higuera RCH 207 Ge60
Lahij YE 60 Nc39
Lahijan IR 57 Ne27
Lahinch IRL 19 Kl38
Lahišyn BY 41 Mf38
Lahlangubo ZA 155 Me61
Lahmar DZ 125 Kj30
Lahn D 32 Lj40
Lahnstein D 33 Lh40
Lahojsk BY 39 Mh36
Laholm S 30 Lo34
Laholmsbukten S 30 Ln34
Lahore PK 65 Oh30
Lahore Fort PK 65 Oh30
La Horqueta YV 193 Gj41
La Horqueta YV 193 Gk42
La Horquilla BOL 206 Gh52
La Hoya RA 208 Ge67
Lahr D 33 Lh42
Lahri PK 65 Oe31
Lahtheh SYR 56 Mj29
Lahti FIN 38 Mf30
La Huerta MEX (BC) 180 Eb30
La Huerta MEX (JLC) 182 Eh36
Lahugala N.P. CL 85 Pa42
Laï TCH 140 Lj41
Laiagam PNG 115 Sb48
Lai'an CHN (AHU) 78 Qk29
Laibanghe CHN (AHU) 78 Qj30
Laibin CHN (GZG) 74 Qe34
Lai Chau VN 87 Qb34
Laide GB 20 Kp33
Laie USA (HI) 170 Cb35
Laifeng CHN (HUB) 74 Qe31
L'Aigle F 22 La42
Laignes F 25 Le43
Laiguéglia I 34 Lj47
L'Aiguillon-sur-Mer F 24 Kt44
Laihia FIN 38 Mc28
Laihia FIN 38 Md28
Lai-hka MYA 86 Pj35
Laikipia Nature Reserve EAK 144 Mj45
Laiküla EST 38 Me32
Lailaba WAN 138 Lc39
La Independencia EC 196 Ga45
Laingsburg ZA 154 Ma62
Laininir RI 114 Rh49
Laird River CDN 166 De15
Lairg GB 20 Kq32
Lais RI 93 Qb47
La Isabela DOM 186 Ge36
Laisamis EAK 144 Mj45
Laissac F 25 Lc46
Laitila FIN 38 Mb30
Laitse EST 38 Me31
Laiverero EAT 147 Mj48
Laiwu CHN (SDG) 73 Qj27
Laiwui RI 97 Rd46
Laiyang CHN (SDG) 73 Ra27
Laiyuan CHN (HBI) 73 Qh26
Laizhou CHN (SDG) 73 Qk27
Laizhou Wan CHN 73 Qk27
Laja BOL 206 Gf54
La Jagua CO 192 Gd41
Laja Largo YV 193 Gg42
Lajamanu AUS (NT) 103 Rf55
La Jaram DARS 124 Ke32
Lajas PE 196 Ga49
Lajeadinho BR (SC) 205 He59
Lajeado BR (RS) 204 He60
Lajeado Grande BR (RS) 205 He60
Lajedo BR (PE) 201 Jb50
Lajes BR (RN) 201 Jb48
Lajinha BR (MG) 203 Hk56
Lajitas MEX (CHH) 181 Ej31
Lajitas USA (TX) 181 Ej31
Lajkovac SCG 44 Ma46
la Jonquera E 28 Lc48
Lajord CDN (SK) 169 Eh20
La Joya de los Sachas EC 196 Gb46
La Julia RA (SC) 210 Gf70
La Junta BOL 206 Gk53
La Junta RCH 210 Gd67
La Junta USA (CO) 174 Ej27
La Juridiction F 24 Ku46
Lakala RDC 148 Lh48
Lakamané RMM 130 Kf38
Lăkatnik BG 44 Md47
Lake USA (ID) 169 Ee23
Lake Abaya ETH 142 Mj42
Lake Abijatta ETH 142 Mk42
Lake Abitibi CDN 173 Ga21
Lake Acraman AUS 110 Rh62
Lake Aerodrome AUS 104 Ra58
Lake al Asad SYR 56 Mk27
Lake Albert EAU 144 Mf45
Lake Albert USA 168 Dk24
Lake Alexandrina AUS 110 Rk63
Lake Alma CDN (SK) 169 Eh21
Lake Amadeus AUS 103 Rf58
Lake Amadeus A.L. AUS 103 Rf58
Lake Amboseli EAK 144 Mj47
Lake Andes USA (SD) 172 Fa24
Lake Andes N.W.R. USA 172 Fa24
Lake Annean AUS 104 Qk59
Lake Anthony AUS 108 Rg60
Lake Argyle AUS (WA) 103 Re54
Lake Argyle AUS 103 Re54
Lake Arthur USA (LA) 175 Fd30
Lake Athabasca CDN 162 Ec07
Lake Auld AUS 103 Rb57
Lake Austin AUS 104 Qj59
Lake Awasa ETH 142 Mk42
Lakeba FJI 119 Ua55
Lake Baikal RUS 55 Qb08
Lake Baker AUS 105 Rd59
Lake Balkhash KZ 54 Oc09
Lake Ballard AUS 104 Ra60
Lake Bangweulu Z 146 Me51
Lakeba Passage FJI 119 Ua54
Lake Baringo EAK 144 Mj45
Lake Barlee AUS (WA) 104 Qk60
Lake Barlee AUS 104 Qk60
Lake Belajau RI 95 Qg47
Lake Benmore NZ 113 Tf68
Lake Bennett AUS 103 Rf57
Lake Benton USA (MN) 172 Fb23
Lake Biddy AUS (WA) 104 Qk62
Lake Bindegolly N.P. AUS 109 Sc59
Lake Bisina EAU 144 Mg45
Lake Bistineau S.P. USA 174 Fd29
Lake Blanche AUS 102 Rb57
Lake Blanche AUS 108 Rk60
Lake Boga AUS (VIC) 111 Sb63
Lake Bogoria EAK 144 Mj45
Lake Bogoria National Reserve EAK 144 Mj45
Lake Bolac AUS (VIC) 111 Sb64
Lake Borgne USA 175 Ff30
Lake Bosumtwi GH 137 Kk42
Lake Breaden AUS 105 Rc58
Lake Buchanan AUS 105 Rb58
Lake Buck AUS 103 Rf55
Lake Bunyonyi EAU 141 Me46
Lake Burigi EAT 144 Mf46
Lake Burnside AUS 105 Rb58
Lake Burullus ET 129 Mf30
Lake Butler USA (FL) 178 Fj31
Lake Cadibarrawirracanna AUS 108 Rh60
Lake Callabonna AUS 108 Sa60
Lake Carey AUS 105 Rb60
Lake Cargelligo AUS (NSW) 111 Sd62
Lake Carnegie AUS 105 Rb59
Lake Cave AUS 104 Qh63
Lake Chad 139 Lh39
Lake Chamo ETH 144 Mj43
Lake Champlain USA 177 Gd23
Lake Changane MOC 155 Mg58
Lake Charles USA (LA) 174 Fd30
Lake Chelan USA 168 Dk21
Lake Chilengwa and Lake Kashiba Z 146 Me52
Lake Chilwa MW 153 Mh53
Lake Chivero ZW 152 Mf54
Lake Chivero Wildlife Park ZW 152 Mf54
Lake Christopher AUS 103 Rd58
Lake City USA (CO) 171 Eg27
Lake City USA (FL) 178 Fj30
Lake City USA (MI) 173 Fh23
Lake City USA (MN) 172 Fd23
Lake City USA (SC) 178 Ga29
Lake Claiborne S.P. USA 174 Fd29
Lake Claire CDN (AB) 167 Ed16
Lake Clark USA 164 Cc15
Lake Clark National Park and Preserve USA 164 Cd15
Lake Clifton AUS 104 Qh62
Lake Cobb AUS 103 Rd58
Lake Coleridge AUS 113 Tf67
Lake Cowan AUS 105 Rb61
Lake Cowichan CDN (BC) 168 Dh21
Lake Cumberland USA 175 Fh27
Lake C. W. McConaughy USA 172 Ek25
Lake Dakataua PNG 116 Sf48
Lake Dalrymple AUS (QLD) 107 Sd56
Lake D'Arbonne S.P. USA 175 Fd29
Lake Dardanelle USA 174 Fd28
Lake Dartmouth AUS 109 Sc59
Lake Deborah East AUS 104 Qk61
Lake Deborah West AUS 104 Qk61
Lake De Burgh AUS 106 Rh55
Lake Dennis AUS 103 Re56
Lake de Temazcal, P.N. MEX 182 Fb36
Lake Dey Dey AUS 105 Rf60
Lake Diefenbaker CDN 169 Eg20
Lake Dissapointment AUS 102 Rb57
Lake District N.P. GB 21 Kr36
Lake Dora AUS 102 Rb57
Lake Dundas AUS 105 Ra62
Lake Edward RDC/EAU 141 Me46
Lake Eildon N.P. AUS 111 Sc64
Lake Elwell USA 169 Ee21
Lake Erie USA/CDN 173 Fk24
Lake Etamunbanie AUS 108 Rk59
Lake Everard AUS (SA) 108 Rh61
Lake Everard AUS 108 Rh61
Lake Eyasi EAT 144 Mh47
Lake Eyre Basin AUS 108 Rj59
Lake Eyre North AUS 108 Rj60
Lake Eyre N.P. AUS 108 Rj60
Lake Eyre South AUS 108 Rj60
Lakefield AUS (QLD) 107 Sc53
Lakefield N.P. AUS 107 Sc53
Lake Francis Case USA 172 Fa24
Lake Frome AUS 108 Rk61
Lake Frome Regional Reserve AUS 108 Rk61
Lake Gairdner AUS 108 Rh61
Lake Gairdner N.P. AUS 108 Rh61
Lake Gardens MAL 92 Qa43
Lake Geneva CH/F 34 Lg44
Lake Geneva USA (WI) 173 Ff24
Lake George USA (MN) 172 Fc22
Lake George USA 177 Gd24
Lake Giles AUS 104 Qk60
Lake Gilles AUS 110 Rj62
Lake Gilles Conservation Park AUS 110 Rj62
Lake Gordon AUS 111 Sd67
Lake Grace AUS (WA) 104 Qk62
Lake Grace AUS 104 Qk62
Lake Gregory AUS 104 Qk58
Lake Gregory AUS 103 Rd56
Lake Gregory AUS 108 Rk60
Lake Gregory A.L. AUS 103 Rd56
Lake Guinas NAM 150 Lj55
Lake Halbert AUS 105 Rb62
Lake Hanson AUS 108 Rj61
Lake Harris AUS 108 Rh61
Lake Hart AUS 108 Rj61
Lake Havasu City USA (AZ) 170 Ec28
Lake Hawea NZ 113 Te68
Lake Hawea NZ 113 Te68
Lake Hope AUS 104 Ra62
Lake Hopkins AUS 103 Re58
Lake Howitt AUS 108 Rk59
Lake Huron USA/CDN 173 Fj23
Lake Ikimba EAT 144 Mf46
Lake Indawgyi MYA 86 Pj33
Lake Isabella USA (CA) 170 Ea28
Lake Isom N.W.R. USA 175 Ff27
Lake Issyk-Kul KS 66 Oj24
Lake Jackson USA (TX) 174 Fc31
Lake Jempang RI 95 Qj46
Lake Johnston AUS 104 Ra62
Lake Julius AUS (QLD) 107 Rk56
Lake Kampo- longo Z 146 Me51
Lake Kariba Z/ZW 152 Md54
Lake Kariba Recreational Park ZW 152 Md54
Lake Kerinci RI 93 Qa47
Lake Khanka RUS/CHN 76 Rg23
Lake Kijanebalola EAU 144 Mf46
Lake King AUS (WA) 104 Qk62
Lake Kitangiri EAT 146 Mh48
Lake Kittakittaooloo AUS 108 Rk60
Lake Kivu RDC/RWA 141 Me46
Lake Koka ETH 142 Mk41
Lake Koocanusa USA 168 Ec21
Lake Koolkootinnie AUS 108 Rj59
Lake Kutubu PNG 115 Sb49
Lake Kutubu N.P. PNG 115 Sb49
Lake Kwania EAU 144 Mg45
Lake Kyoga EAU 144 Mg45
Lake Laberge CDN 166 Dc15
Lake Labyrinth AUS 108 Rh61
Lake Ladoga RUS 54 Mc06
Lake Lanao RP 91 Rc42
Lakeland USA (FL) 179 Fk32
Lakeland USA (GA) 178 Fj30
Lakeland Downs AUS (QLD) 107 Sc53
Lake Langano ETH 142 Mk42
Lake Leaghur AUS 111 Sc62
Lake Lefroy AUS 104 Ra61
Lake Liambezi NAM 151 Mc54
Lake Lincoln S.P. USA 175 Fe30
Lake Livingston USA 174 Fc30
Lake Livingston S.P. USA 174 Fc30
Lake Louise CDN (AB) 168 Eb20
Lake Louise USA 165 Cg14
Lakelse Lake CDN (BC) 166 Df18
Lake Luar RI 94 Qg45
Lake Mabesi WAL 136 Ke42
Lake Macdonald AUS 103 Re57
Lake Macfarlane AUS 110 Rj62
Lake Mackay AUS 103 Re57
Lake Mackay A.L. AUS 103 Re57
Lake Macleod AUS 104 Qg58
Lake Magadi EAK 144 Mj46
Lake Magenta AUS 104 Qk62
Lake Mainit RP 90 Rc41
Lake Malawi MW/EAT 146 Mh52
Lake Malawi N.P. MW 153 Mh52
Lake Malombe MW 153 Mh53
Lake Manapouri NZ 113 Td68
Lake Maninjau RI 93 Qa46
Lake Manitoba CDN 172 Fa20
Lake Manyara EAT 144 Mh47
Lake Manyara N.P. EAT 144 Mh47
Lake Manzala ET 129 Mf30
Lake Mape WAL 136 Kd42
Lake Marmion AUS 104 Ra60
Lake Martin USA 175 Fh29
Lake Mason AUS 104 Qk59
Lake Matano RI 96 Ra47
Lake Maurice AUS 105 Rf60
Lake Mburo N.P. EAU 144 Mf46
Lake McChattie AUS 108 Rk58
Lake McDougal ZW 152 Mf56
Lake McGregor CDN 169 Ed20
Lake Mead N.R.A. USA 170 Ec27
Lake Melintang RI 95 Qj46
Lake Melville CDN 163 Ha08
Lake Meranda AUS 104 Ra59
Lake Meredith N.R.A. USA 174 Ek28
Lake Meridith USA 174 Ek28
Lake Michigan USA 173 Fg23
Lake Minchumina USA (AK) 165 Cd14
Lake Minchumina USA 165 Cd13
Lake Minigwal AUS 105 Rb60
Lake Mipia AUS 108 Rk58
Lake Moeraki NZ 113 Te67
Lake Mondurran AUS (QLD) 109 Sf58
Lake Moore AUS 104 Qj60
Lake Mujunju EAT 144 Mf46
Lake Mulapula AUS 108 Rk60
Lake Murray PNG 115 Sa49
Lake Murray PNG 115 Sa49
Lake Mutirikwi ZW 152 Mf56
Lake Mweru RDC/Z 146 Me50
Lake Mweru Wantipa Z 146 Me50
Lake Naivasha EAK 144 Mj46
Lake Nakivali EAU 144 Mf46
Lake Nakuru N.P. EAK 144 Mj46
Lake Nash AUS (NT) 106 Rj56
Lake Nasser ET 129 Mg34
Lake Natron EAT 144 Mj47
Lake Navar AFG 65 Od29
Lake Neale AUS 103 Rf58
Lake Newell AUS 103 Rd58
Lake Ngami RB 151 Mb56
Lake Nipigon CDN 172 Ff21
Lake Nipissing CDN 173 Ga22
Lake Noondie AUS 104 Qk60
Lake Nunavaugaluk USA 164 Cb16
Lake Nyassa MOC 146 Mh52
Lake Oahe USA 172 Ek23
Lake of 1000 Isles CHN 75 Qk31
Lake of the Enemy CDN 167 Ee14
Lake of the Ozarks USA 174 Fd26
Lake of the Woods CDN 172 Fc21
Lake Ohau NZ 113 Te68
Lake Ohrid AL/MK 44 Ma49
Lake Okeechobee USA 179 Fk32
Lake Onega RUS 54 Md06
Lake Ontario USA/CDN 173 Ga24
Lake Opeta EAU 144 Mh45
Lake Ophelia N.W.R. USA 175 Fe30
Lake Otjikoto NAM 150 Lj55
Lake Ouachita S.P. USA 174 Fd28
Lake Owyhee USA 168 Eb24
Lake Palace (Udaipur) IND 82 Og33
Lake Paoay N.P. RP 90 Ra36
Lake Pedder AUS 111 Sd67
Lake Peipus EST/RUS 38 Mh32
Lake Philippi AUS 108 Rk58
Lake Placid USA 177 Gc23
Lake Pontchartrain USA 175 Fe30
Lake Poso RI 96 Ra46
Lake Powell USA 171 Ee27
Lake Prespa AL/MK 46 Ma50
Lake Providence CDN 167 Ed13
Lake Providence USA (LA) 175 Fe29
Lake Pskov RUS 39 Mh32
Lake Pukaki AUS 113 Tf67
Lake Pure AUS (QLD) 108 Sa59
Lake Pyramid AUS 104 Ra62
Lake Raeside AUS 104 Ra60
Lake Ranau RI 93 Qb48
Lake Rebecca AUS 105 Rb61
Lake Riamkanan RI 95 Qh47
Lake Rotorua NZ 112 Tj65
Lake Rudolf = Lake Turkana EAK 144 Mh44
Lake Rukwa EAT 146 Mg49
Lake Sagara EAT 146 Mf48
Lake Saint Lucia ZA 155 Mg60
Lake Saint Martin CDN 172 Fa20
Lake Sakakawea USA 169 Ej21
Lake Sakakawea USA 172 Ek22
Lake Scutari SCG/AL 44 Lu48
Lake Seabrook AUS 104 Qk61
Lake Sebu RP 91 Rc42
Lake Semayang RI 94 Qj46
Lake Seminole USA 175 Fh30
Lake Sentarum RI 94 Qg45
Lakes Entrance AUS (VIC) 111 Sd64
Lake Seul CDN 172 Fe20
Lake Sevan ARM 57 Nc25
Lake Shalla ETH 142 Mk42
Lake Sharpe AUS 104 Ra62
Lakeshore USA (CA) 170 Ea27
Lake Sibaya ZA 155 Mg59
Lakeside AUS (WA) 104 Qj59
Lakeside USA (CA) 170 Eb29
Lakeside USA (OR) 168 Dh24
Lakeside USA (UT) 171 Ed25
Lakeside USA (VA) 177 Gb27
Lake Simcoe CDN 173 Ga23
Lake Singkarak RI 93 Qa46
Lake Smoky River CDN 167 Eb18
Lake St. Clair National Park AUS (TAS) 111 Sc66
Lake Stephanie ETH 144 Mj43
Lake Superior USA/CDN 173 Ff22
Lake Sylvester AUS 106 Rh55
Lake Taal RP 90 Ra38
Lake Tahoe USA 170 Dk26
Lake Tana ETH 142 Mj39
Lake Tanganyika EAT/RDC 146 Me49
Lake Tarrabool AUS 106 Rh55
Lake Taupo NZ 112 Th65
Lake Teague AUS 104 Ra58
Lake Te Anau NZ 113 Td68
Lake Tekapo AUS 113 Tf67
Lake Tekapo NZ 113 Tf68
Lake Tempe RI 96 Qk48
Lake Texoma USA 174 Fb29
Lake Thac Ba VN 87 Qc35
Lake Throssel AUS 105 Rc59
Lake Titicaca PE 206 Gf53
Lake Toba RI 93 Pk44
Lake Torquinie AUS 108 Rk58
Lake Torrens AUS 108 Rj61
Lake Torrens N.P. AUS 108 Rj61
Lake Towuti RI 96 Ra47
Lake Traverse Ind. Res. USA 172 Fb23
Lake Turkana EAK 144 Mh44
Lake Uloowaranie AUS 108 Rk59
Lake Urmia IR 57 Nc27
Lake Victoria EAU/EAT 144 Mg46
Lakeview USA (OR) 168 Dk24
Lake Village USA (AR) 175 Fe29
Lake Village USA (WY) 169 Ee23
Lakeville USA (MN) 172 Fd23
Lake Violet AUS (WA) 104 Ra59
Lake Volta GH 137 Kk42
Lake Wakatipu NZ 113 Te68
Lake Wales USA (FL) 179 Fk32
Lake Wanaka NZ 113 Te68
Lake Warrandirrinna AUS 108 Rj59
Lake Waukarlycarly AUS 102 Ra56
Lake Way AUS 104 Ra59
Lake Wells AUS (WA) 105 Rb59
Lake Wells AUS 105 Rb59
Lake White AUS 103 Re56
Lake Wills AUS 103 Re56
Lake Winnebago USA 173 Ff23
Lake Winnipeg CDN 172 Fa19
Lake Winnipegosis CDN 169 Ek19
Lake Wisdom PNG 115 Sd48
Lake Wonchi ETH 142 Mj41
Lakewood USA (CO) 171 Eh26
Lakewood USA (NJ) 177 Gc25
Lakewood USA (NM) 171 Eh29
Lakewood Park USA (FL) 179 Fk32
Lake Woods AUS 106 Rg54
Lake Worth USA (FL) 179 Fk32
Lake Xau RB 151 Mc56
Lake YammaYamma AUS 108 Sa59
Lake Yindarlgodda AUS 104 Rb61
Lake Ziway ETH 142 Mk41
Lakhadaria DZ 126 Lb27
Lakhamara IND (ORS) 83 Pb35
Lakhbahat IND (ORS) 83 Pb36
Lakheri IND (RJT) 82 Oj33
Lakhimpur IND (UPH) 81 Pa32
Lakhipur IND (ASM) 86 Pf32
Lakhisarai IND (BIH) 83 Pd33
Lakhnador IND (MPH) 83 Ok34
Lakhni IND (MHT) 83 Ok35
Lakhpat IND (GUJ) 82 Oe34
Lakhra PK 65 Od33
Laki AZ 57 Nd25
Lăki BG 45 Me49
Laki IS 18 Kb26
Lakin USA (KS) 174 Ek27
Lakinsk RUS 48 Mk17
Lakkí GR 47 Mg53
Lakki PK 65 Of29
Lákkoma GR 45 Mf50
Lakohembi RI 96 Ra50
Lakor RI 97 Re50
Lakota CI 137 Kh43
Lakota USA (ND) 172 Fa21
Lakselv N 16 Mc10
Lakshadweep IND 84 Og41
Lakshadweep Sea IND 84 Oh41
Laksham BD 86 Pf34
Lakshmeshwar IND (KTK) 82 Oh38
Lakshmipur BD 86 Pf34
Lakshmipur IND (AAN) 88 Pg39
Laktaši BIH 35 Ls46
Lakuramau PNG 116 Sf47
Lak Xao LAO 87 Qc36
Lalafuta Z 151 Mc53
Lalago EAT 144 Mg47
La Laguita (Aserradero) MEX (DGO) 180 Eh34
La Laguna E 124 Kb31
La Laguna MEX (VC) 183 Fb36
La Laguna RA (CD) 209 Gj62
La Laja RCH 208 Gd64
La Laja RCH 207 Ge60
La Laja YV 193 Gk43
La Lajita MEX (NL) 182 Ek34
Lala Musa PK 65 Og29
Lalandai RI 96 Rb46
Lalapansi ZW 152 Mf55
Lalapaşa TR 45 Mg49
Lálas GR 46 Mb53
Lalaua MOC 153 Mk53
Lalauli IND (UPH) 83 Pa33
Lalbagh Fort BD 86 Pf34
Lalbert AUS (VIC) 111 Sb63
Lalbiti NEP 83 Pc32
l'Alcora E 29 Ku50
l'Alcúdia E 29 Ku51
Laleham AUS (QLD) 109 Se57
Lalem EAU 144 Mf44
La Leonesa RA (CH) 204 Ha59
Lalganj IND (BIH) 83 Pc33
Lalganj IND (UPH) 83 Pa32
Lalganj IND (UPH) 83 Pb33
Lalgarh Palace IND 80 Og31
Lalgay BF 137 Kk40
Lali IR 59 Ne29
Lalibela ETH 142 Mk39
Lalibela Cave churches ETH 142 Mk39
La Libertad ES 184 Ff39
La Libertad HN 184 Fg38
La Libertad MEX (CHH) 180 Eg32
La Libertad NIC 185 Fh39
Lalibu PNG 115 Sc49
La Ligua RCH 208 Ge61
La Ligua RCH 208 Ge62
Laliki RI 97 Rd49
La Lima HN 184 Fg38
Lalima, T.I. BR 202 Hb56
Lalin CHN (HLG) 76 Rd23
Lalín E 26 Km48
Lalinde F 24 La46
La Línea de la Concepción E 27 Kp54
Lalitagiri IND 83 Pd35
Lalitpur IND (UPH) 83 Ok33
Lalla Outka MA 125 Kh28
Lalla Rookh AUS (WA) 102 Qk56
Lal-Lo RP 90 Ra36
Lalmanir Hat BD 86 Pe33
Lalo DY 138 La42
La Lobería RA (RN) 209 Gj66
La Loche CDN (SK) 167 Ef17
La Loma RA (SL) 208 Gh62
La Lonja de València E 29 Ku51
Aloşu RO 44 Me46
La Loupe F 22 Lb42
La Louvière B 23 Le40
L'Alpe-d'Huez F 25 Lg45
Lalsot IND (RJT) 82 Oj32
Lal-Suharna N.P. PK 65 Og31
Laluin RI 97 Rd46
Laluni GUY 194 Hb42
La'l va Sar Jangal AFG 65 Od28
Lalyo SUD 144 Mf43
Lam CAM 139 Lf42
La Machine F 25 Ld44
Lamadai EAT 144 Mg47
la Maddalena I 36 Lk49
Lamadi CHN (YUN) 87 Pk32
Lamadrid RA (TU) 207 Gh59
La Majada RA (CA) 207 Gh60
Lamakan RP 94 Qj41
Lamalaga DARS 130 Kb34
La Malbaie CDN (QC) 176 Ge22
La Malène F 25 Ld46
Lama Monastery CHN 69 Pk30
Lamanai BH 184 Ff37
La Mancha E 29 Ks51
La Manche Prov. Park CDN 177 Hd22
Lamandongahao CHN (NMZ) 72 Qf26
La Manta CO 192 Gc41
Lamanuna RI 97 Rb50
Lamap VU 118 Td54
La Máquina MEX (CHH) 181 Eh30
Lamar USA (CO) 174 Ej26
Lamar USA (MO) 174 Fc27
Lamarche F 25 Lf42
Lamard IR 64 Ng32
La Margarita YV 193 Gk41
La Margarita del Norte MEX (COH) 181 Ej32
La María RA (SC) 210 Gf69
Lamarque RA (RN) 208 Gh65
La Marque USA (TX) 174 Fc31
La Marsa TN 126 Lf27
La Martorana I 36 Lo52
Lamas PE 196 Gb49
Lamas PE 196 Gc47
Lama San Martín RA 208 Gf65
La Masica HN 184 Fg38
Lamassa PNG 116 Sg48
Lamastre F 25 Le46
La Mata CO 192 Gd41
Lamau MAL 94 Qj43
La Maya C 186 Gc35
Lamayuru Monastery PK 81 Oj28
Lambach A 35 Lo43
Lambafell IS 18 Kf26
Lambak RI 93 Pk45
Lamballe F 22 Ks42
Lambaré PY 204 Hb58
Lambaréné G 148 Lf46
Lambari BR (MG) 203 Hh56
Lambayeque PE 196 Ga49
Lambay Island IRL 19 Ko37
Lambell, Mount AUS 106 Rg53
Lambertsbaai ZA 154 Lk62
Lamberts Bay ZA 154 Lk62
Lambesc F 25 Lf47
Lambi SOL 117 Sk50
Lámbia GR 46 Mb53
Lambidou RMM 130 Kf38
Lambina AUS (SA) 108 Rj59
Lambrama PE 197 Gd52
Lambu PNG 116 Sf47
Lambubalano RI 96 Rb48
Lambunao RP 90 Rb40
Lambuya RI 96 Rb47
Lamdesar RI 97 Rf49
Lamé TCH 140 Lh41
Lame WAN 138 Le40
Lame Burra Game Reserve WAN 138 Le40
Lame Deer USA (MT) 169 Eg23
Lamego P 26 Kn49
Lamen Bay VU 118 Te54
Lamèque CDN (NB) 176 Gh22
La Merced PE 197 Gc51
La Merced RA (CA) 207 Gh60
La Mesa CO 192 Gc43
La Mesa USA (NM) 171 Eg29
Lamesa USA (TX) 174 Ek29
l'Ametlla de Mar E 29 La50
Lamézia Terme-Nicastro I 37 Lr52
Lami FJI 119 Tk55
Lamía GR 46 Mc52
Lamie RI 92 Pj44
La Mina RCH 208 Ge63
Lamindo SUD 144 Mf43
Lamington N.P. AUS 109 Sg60
La Misa MEX (SO) 180 Ee31
La Misión MEX (BC) 180 Eb29
La Mitad del Mundo EC 196 Ga45
Lamitan RP 91 Rb42
Lamlam RI 97 Rf46
Lammerkop ZA 155 Me58
Lammermuir Hills GB 20 Ks35
Lammeulo RI 92 Ph43
Lammhult S 31 Lp33
Lammi FIN 38 Mf29
Lamno RI 92 Ph43
Lamongan RI 95 Qg49
La Mongie F 24 La48
Lamont CDN (AB) 169 Ed19
Lamont USA (CA) 170 Ea28
Lamont USA (WY) 171 Eg24
La Montaña PE 190 Ga10
La Mora MEX (COH) 181 Ej32
La Mora RA (MD) 208 Gg63
La Morita MEX (COH) 181 Ej31
La Mothe-Achard F 24 Kt44
La Motte F 25 Lg46
Lamotte-Beuvron F 25 Lc43
La Moure USA (ND) 172 Fa22
Lampa PE 197 Ge53
Lampanaih RI 92 Ph43
Lampang THA 87 Pk36
Lampasas USA (TX) 174 Fa30
Lampazos MEX (NL) 181 Ek32
Ísola di Lampedusa I 37 Ln55
Lampedusa I 37 Ln55
Lampeland N 30 Lk31
Lampeter GB 21 Kq38
Lam Phai THA 89 Qa42
Lamphun THA 87 Pk36
Lampia RI 96 Ra47
Lam Plaimat THA 89 Qb38
Lampman CDN (SK) 169 Ej21
Lamta IND (MPH) 83 Pa34
Lamti BHT 86 Pf32
Lam tok MYA 86 Pg34
Lamu EAK 145 Na47
Lamud PE 196 Gb49
Lamu Island EAK 145 Na47
La Muralla de Ávila E 27 Kq50
La Muralla, P.N. HN 184 Fg38
La Mure F 25 Lf46
Lamuru RI 96 Ra48
Lamy USA (NM) 171 Eh28
Lana I 34 Lm44
Lanai USA 170 Cb35
Lanai City USA (HI) 170 Cb35
Lanaja E 28 Ku49
Lanark GB 20 Kr35
Lanas MAL 94 Qj43
La Nava de Ricomalillo E 27 Kq51
La Nava de Santiago E 27 Ko51
Lanbi Island MYA 88 Pk40
Lancang CHN (YUN) 87 Qa34
Lancang Jiang CHN 87 Qa34
Lancaster GB 21 Ks36
Lancaster USA (CA) 170 Ea28
Lancaster USA (MO) 174 Fd25
Lancaster USA (NH) 177 Ge23
Lancaster USA (OH) 173 Fj26
Lancaster USA (SC) 178 Fk28
Lancaster USA (VA) 177 Gb27
Lancaster USA (WI) 172 Fe24
Lancaster Sound CDN 163 Fd04
Lance Creek USA (WY) 169 Eh24
Lancefield AUS (VIC) 111 Sc64
Lancelin AUS (WA) 104 Qh61
Lancester USA (PA) 177 Gb25
Lánchíd H 43 Lu43
Lanciano I 37 Lp48
Lanco RCH 208 Gd65
Łańcut PL 41 Mc40
Landa de Matamoros MEX 182 Fa35
Landana ANG 148 Lg48
Landau D 33 Lj41
Landau D 33 Ln42
Landay AFG 65 Ob30
Land Between The Lakes USA 175 Ff27
Landeck A 34 Ll43
Landeh IR 59 Nf30
Lander USA (WY) 169 Ef24
Landerneau F 22 Kq42
Lander River AUS 103 Rg56
Landeryd S 31 Lo33
Landes F 24 Kt47
Landete E 29 Kt51
Landfall Island IND 88 Pg39
Land Glacier 6 Cc33
Landi RG 136 Ke40
Landi Kotal PK 65 Of28
Landis CDN (SK) 169 Ef19
Landivisiau F 22 Kq42
Landless Corner Z 152 Me53
Landmannalaugar IS 18 Ka27
Land O'Lakes USA (FL) 179 Fj31
Landor AUS (WA) 104 Qj58
Landrecies F 23 Ld40
Landri Sales BR (PI) 200 Hj49
Landsberg D 33 Ll42
Landsberg D 32 Ln39
Landsbro S 31 Lp33
Landscheid D 33 Lg41
Land's End GB 21 Kp40
Landsford Canal S.P. USA 178 Fk28
Landshut D 33 Ln42
Landskrona S 30 Ln35
Landsortsdjupet 31 Lt32
Landvetter S 30 Ln33
Lane City USA (TX) 181 Fb31
La Negra RA (BA) 209 Ha64
La Negra RCH 207 Ge57
Lane Poole Conservation Res. AUS (WA) 104 Qj62
Lanfiéra BF 137 Kj39
Langå DK 30 Lk34
Langa PE 197 Gb52
Langabou TG 137 La41
Langadás GR 44 Md50
Langa de Duero E 26 Kr49
Langa-Langa RDC 148 Lj47
Langanes IS 18 Kf24
Langar UZ 63 Oc25
Langar UZ 63 Od26
Langara RI 97 Rb48
Langara Island USA 166 Dd18
Langarud IR 57 Nf27
Langarud IR 57 Nf28
Långås S 30 Ln34
Langatabbetja SME 194 Hc43
Langberg ZA 154 Ma62
Langberg ZA 154 Mb60
Langbinsi GH 137 Kk40
Lang Cay VN 87 Qc34
Lang Cung VN 87 Qc35
Langdon USA (ND) 172 Fa21
Langeac F 25 Ld45
Langeais F 24 La43
Lange Anna D 32 Lh36
Langebaan ZA 154 Lj62
Langeberg ZA 154 Ma62
Langedijk NL 23 Le38
Langeland DK 30 Ll35
Längelmäki FIN 38 Me29
Langen D 32 Lj37
Langen D 33 Lj41
Langenau D 33 Ll42
Langenberg D 32 Lj39
Langenburg CDN (SK) 172 Ek20
Langenhagen D 32 Lk38
Langenlois A 42 Lq42
Langenthal CH 34 Lh43
Langenzenn D 33 Ll41
Langeoog D 32 Lh37
Langesund N 30 Lk32
Langevåg N 30 Lf31
Langfang CHN (HBI) 73 Qj26
Långfjället S 17 Lg14
Langford CDN (BC) 168 Dj21
Langga RI 96 Qk47
Langgam RI 93 Qa45
Langgapayung RI 93 Pk45
Langgur RI 114 Rg48
Langham CDN (SK) 169 Eg19
Langholm GB 20 Ks35
Langjökull IS 18 Ju26
Langka RI 92 Pj43
Langkahan RI 92 Pj43
Langkawi MAL 92 Pk42
Langklip ZA 154 Ma60
Langkofel = Sasso Lungo I 34 Lm44
Langlo Crossing AUS (QLD) 109 Sc59
Langmusi CHN (GSU) 72 Qb28
Langnau CH 34 Lh44
Lango RCB 140 Lh45
Langogne F 25 Ld46
Langon F 24 Ku46
Langøya N 16 Lh11
Langqên Zangbo CHN 68 Pa30
Langres F 25 Lf43
Langruth CDN (MB) 172 Fa20
Langsa RI 92 Pj43
Lang Shan CHN 72 Qd25
Långshyttan S 31 Lr30
Långsjöby S 16 Lj13
Lang Son VN 87 Qd35
Lang Suan THA 88 Pk41
Langtang NEP 81 Pc31
Langtang WAN 138 Le41
Langtang N.P. NEP 81 Pc31
Långträsk S 16 Ma13
Langtry USA (TX) 181 Ek31
Langu THA 88 Pk42
Langue de Barbarie, P.N. de la SN 130 Kb38
Languedoc F 25 Lc47
Languedoc-Roussillon F 25 Ld46
Languineo RA (CB) 210 Ge67
Langxi CHN (AHU) 78 Qk30
Langxiang CHN (HLG) 76 Re22
Langzhong CHN (SCH) 72 Qc30
Lanigan CDN (SK) 169 Eh20
Lanín, P.N. RA 208 Ge65
Lanín, Volcán RCH 208 Ge65
Lanja GH 137 La41
Lanji IND (MPH) 83 Pa35
Lanka IND (ASM) 86 Pg33
Lankadonkhang CHN (TIB) 68 Pa30
Lankao CHN (HNN) 73 Qh28
Lankoé BF 137 Kj39
Lankong MAL 94 Qj42
Lan Krabu THA 88 Pk37
Lanna S 31 Lp31
Länna S 31 Ls31
Lannemezan F 24 La47
Lannion F 22 Kr42
La Noria MEX (SL) 180 Eg34
Lan Sak THA 88 Pk38
Lan Sang N.P. THA 88 Pk37

Lansdale ☒ USA (PA) 177 Gc25
Lansdowne ☒ AUS (WA) 103
Lansdowne ☒ IND (UTT) 81 Ok31
Lansdowne House ☒ CDN (ON) 172 Fg19
L'Anse ☒ USA (MI) 173 Ff22
L'Anse aux Meadows N.H.P. ☐ CDN 177 Hc20
Länsi-Aure ☒ FIN 38 Md29
Lansing ☒ USA (MI) 173 Fh24
Lanškroun ☒ CZ 42 Lf41
Lanslebourg-Mont-Cenis ☒ F 25 Lg45
Lantau ☒ CHN (HKG) 75 Qf34
Lantewa ☒ WAN 139 Lf39
Lantian ☒ CHN (SAA) 72 Qe28
Lantz Corners ☒ USA (PA) 173 Ga25
Lanu ☒ RI 91 Ra45
Lanusei ☒ I 36 Lk51
Lanxi ☒ CHN (HLG) 76 Rd22
Lanxi ☒ CHN (ZJG) 75 Qh31
Lan Xian ☒ CHN (SAX) 72 Qf26
Lány ☒ CZ 42 Lo40
Lanyu ☒ RC 75 Ra34
Lanyu ☒ RC 75 Ra34
Lanza BOL 198 Gg51
Lanzat ☒ WAN 139 Le41
Lanzhou ☒ CHN (GSU) 72 Qc27
Lanzo Torinese ☒ I 34 Lh45
Lanzual ☒ MA 125 Kg28
Laoag ☒ RP 90 Ra36
Laoang ☒ RP 90 Rc39
Laobie Shan ☒ CHN 87 Pk34
Laohekou ☒ CHN (HUB) 72 Qf29
Laokas ☒ TCH 140 Lh41
La Ola ☒ RCH 207 Gf59
Laon ☒ F 23 Ld41
Lao Ngam ☒ LAO 89 Qd38
Laoora ☒ RI 96 Rd48
La Ordeña ☒ MEX (ZCT) 182 Ef32
La Oroya ☒ PE 197 Gc51
Laos ■ LAO 53 Qa08
Laoshan ☒ CHN 73 Ra27
Laoshuhui ☒ CHN (YUN) 87 Pk33
Laotieshan Shedao Z.B. ☒ CHN 73 Ra26
L'Ardouikouba ☒ DJI 142 Nb40
Laredo ☒ E 27 Ks47
Laredo ☒ USA (TX) 181 Fa32
La Reforma ☒ C 179 Fj35
La Reforma ☒ MEX (SL) 180 Ef33
La Reforma ☒ MEX (ZCT) 180 Ed31
La Reforma ☒ RA (LP) 208 Gg64
La Reforma ☒ YV 193 Gk42
La Réole ☒ F 24 Ku44
La Ribera ☒ MEX (BCS) 180 Ef34
La Rica ☒ C 192 Gc42
Larino ☒ I 37 Lp49
La Rioja ☒ E 28 Ks48
La Rioja ☒ RA 207 Gf60
Lárissa ☒ GR 46 Mc51
Larkana ☒ PK 65 Oe30
La Lisas ☒ GCA 184 Fe39
Las Lomas ☒ RA (NY) 207 Gk58
Las Margaritas ☒ MEX (DGO) 181 Eh34
Las Marismas ☒ E 27 Ko53
Las Martinas ☒ C 179 Fh35
Las Médulas ☐ E 26 Ko48
Las Mercedes ☒ YV 193 Gg41
Las Minas ☒ PA 185 Fk42
Las Navas ☒ RP 90 Rc39
Las Navas de la Concepción ☒ E 27 Kp53
Las Negras ☒ E 29 Ks53

[índice continúa en múltiples columnas]

Los Santos – Mahbubabad

Mahbubnagar – Maranguape

Mahbubnagar IND (APH) 82 Oj37
Mahdah OM 61 Nh33
Mahdalynivka UA 49 Mh21
Mahdia GUY 194 Ha43
Mahdia TN 126 Lf28
Mahdija-Plage MA 125 Kg28
Mahdi's Tomb SUD 135 Mg38
Mahé IND (PND) 84 Oh40
Mahé SY 145 Nh48
Mahébourg MS 157 Nj56
Mahendragarh IND (CGH) 83 Pb34
Mahendragarh IND (HYA) 80 Oj31
Mahenge EAT 147 Mj50
Mahé Pondicherry IND 84 Oh40
Maheshwar IND (MPH) 82 Oh34
Maheskhali Island BD 86 Pf35
Mahfuzbhendaru IND (APH) 83 Pb36
Mahgawan IND (MPH) 83 Ok32
Mahia Peninsula NZ 113 Tj65
Mahibadhoo MV 84 Og44
Mahidasht IR 57 Nd28
Mahien SYR 56 Mj28
Mahila RDC 146 Me48
Mahilëv BY 48 Mf19
Mahin WAN 138 Lc42
Mahina RMM 136 Ke39
Mahirija MA 125 Kj29
Mahisama IND (APH) 82 Ok37
Mahitsy RM 157 Nd55
Mahjub LAR 127 Lh29
Mahlaing MYA 86 Ph35
Mahmiya SUD 135 Mg37
Mahmudabad IND (UPH) 81 Pa32
Mahmud Abad IR 62 Ng27
Mahmud-e 'Eraqi AFG 65 Oe28
Mahmud Jiq IR 57 Nd27
Mahnar Bazar IND (BIH) 83 Pc33
Mahneh IR 64 Nk28
Mahnešan IR 57 Nd27
Mahnomen USA (MN) 172 Fc22
Mahoba IND (UPH) 83 Ok33
Maholi IND (UPH) 81 Pa32
Mahón = Maó E 29 Le51
Mahora E 29 Kt51
Mahora IND 83 Pa34
Mahou RMM 137 Kh39
Mahoua TCH 139 Lk40
Mahrauni IND (UPH) 83 Ok33
Mahrès TN 126 Lf28
Mahri PK 65 Od32
Mahru Mosque IR 59 Ne29
Mahur IND (ASM) 86 Pg33
Mahura UA 43 Md42
Mahur Island PNG 116 Sg47
Mahuta WAN 138 Lc40
Mahuva IND (GUJ) 82 Of35
Mahwa IND (RJT) 80 Oj32
Maials E 29 La49
Maiama PNG 115 Sd49
Maiauatá BR (PA) 195 Hf46
Maibo TCH 140 Lk41
Măicănești RO 45 Mh45
Maicao CO 192 Gd40
Mai Chau VN 87 Qc35
Maîche F 25 Lg43
Maici BR (AM) 198 Gj49
Maidanshar = Kowt-e Ashrow AFG 65 Oe28
Maidenhead GB 21 Ku39
Maiden Island KIR 11 Ca10
Maiden, Mount AUS 104 Rb59
Maidi RI 91 Rd45
Maidstone CDN (SK) 169 Ef19
Maidstone GB 21 La39
Maiduguri WAN 139 Lg40
Maidukuru IND (APH) 85 Ok38
Maie RDC 144 Mf44
Maiella, P.N.della I 37 Lp48
Măieruș RO 45 Mf45
Maigatari WAN 138 Le39
Maigudo, Mount ETH 142 Mj42
Maihar IND (MPH) 83 Pa33
Maiinchi WAN 138 Ld39
Maijishan Shiku CHN 72 Qc28
Maikala Range IND 83 Pa34
Maikapshaghai KZ 67 Pc22
Maïko RDC 141 Md46
Maikonkele WAN 138 Ld41
Maïko, P.N.de la RDC 141 Md46
Maikoro TCH 140 Lj41
Mailani IND (UPH) 81 Pa31
Mailepalli IND (APH) 83 Ok37
Mailly-le-Camp F 23 Le42
Mailsi PK 65 Og31
Maimana = Meymaneh AFG 63 Oc28
Maimón DOM 186 Ge36
Main D 33 Lk41
Mainaguri IND (WBG) 86 Pe32
Mainamati BD 86 Pf34
Main Brook CDN 177 Hb20
Mainburg D 33 Lm42
Main Camp ZW 152 Md55
Main-Donau-Kanal D 33 Lm41
Maine F 22 Ku42
Maine USA 177 Ge23
Maine Maritime Museum USA 177 Gf24
Maïné-Soroa RN 133 Lg39
Maing Kwan MYA 86 Pj32
Mainit RP 90 Rc41
Mainland CDN (NF) 177 Ha21
Mainland GB 20 Kr31
Mainland GB 20 Kt30
Mainling CHN (TIB) 69 Ph31
Mainoru AUS (NT) 106 Rh53
Mainpuri IND (UPH) 81 Ok32
Main Range N.P. AUS 109 Sg59
Maintenon F 23 Lb42
Maintirano RM 157 Nc55
Mainz D 33 Lj40
Maiparu YV 193 Gk42
Maipo, Volcán RCH/RA 208 Gf63
Maipú RA (BA) 209 Hb64
Maipu RA (MD) 208 Gf62
Maipú RCH 208 Ge62
Maiquetía YV 193 Gg40
Mairi BR (BA) 201 Hk51
Mairiripotaba BR (GO) 202 Hf54
Mairwa IND (BIH) 83 Pc32
Maisandra IND (KTK) 84 Oj39
Maisan-e-Jmam IR 59 Nf29
Maisí C 186 Gc35
Maišiagala LT 39 Mf36
Maisome Island EAT 144 Mg47
Maison Carrée de Nîmes F 25 Le47
Maisonnette CDN (NB) 176 Gh22
Maisons de Champagne d'Épernay F 23 Ld41
Maitabi, Mount SOL 117 Sj49
Maitbhanga BD 86 Pf34
Maitembge RB 152 Md56
Maitioukoulou RCA 140 Lj42
Maitland AUS (NSW) 111 Sf62
Maitland AUS (SA) 110 Rj63
Maitland Range AUS 103 Rd53
Maitri ANT (IND) 7 Lc33
Maitum RP 91 Rc42
Maiurno SUD 135 Mg39
Maizhokunggar CHN (TIB) 69 Pf31
Maizuru J 79 Rh28
Maja RUS 55 Rd07
Majahual MEX (QTR) 183 Fg36
Majalengka RI 95 Qe49
Majdan UA 43 Md42
Majdanpek SCG 44 Mb46
Majenang RI 95 Qe49
Majene RI 96 Qk47
Majete Game Reserve MW 153 Mh53
Majetú BOL 206 Gh52
Majevica BIH 44 Lt46
Majgaon IND (MPH) 83 Pb34
Majhgawan IND (MPH) 83 Pa33
Majhiaon IND (JKD) 83 Pb33
Majholi IND (MPH) 83 Pa33
Maji ETH 142 Mh42
Majiahewan CHN (NHZ) 72 Qc27
Majie CHN (YUN) 87 Qb33
Majilovac SCG 44 Mb46
Majimalu EAT 146 Mh48
Maji Moto EAT 144 Mh46
Majkop RUS 49 Na23
Majli-Saj KS 63 Og25
Majors Place USA (NV) 170 Ec26
Majskij RUS (KBA) 57 Nc24
Majskij RUS 71 Re19
Majuba Hill ZA 155 Me59
Majuro Atoll MH 10 Tb09
Majz YE 60 Nb37
Maka LB 136 Ke42
Maka SN 130 Kb37
Maka SN 136 Kc39
Makabana RCB 148 Lg47
Makado ZW 152 Me56
Maka Gouye SN 136 Kc39
Makaha USA (HI) 170 Ca35
Makah Ind. Res. USA 168 Dh21
Makak CAM 139 Lf44
Makaka RCB 148 Lg47
Makalamabedi RB 151 Mb56
Makale RI 96 Qk47
Makalehi RI 91 Rc44
Makallé RA (CH) 204 Ha59
Makaloge MOC 146 Mh52
Makalondi RN 132 La39
Makalu-Barun N.P. NEP 81 Pd32
Makalu NEP/CHN 81 Pd32
Makamba BU 146 Me48
Makami EAT 147 Mj48
Makanda RCB 148 Lg47
Makanjila MW 153 Mh52
Makanshy KZ 66 Pb22
Makantaka NIC 185 Fh39
Makapak Valley ZA Me58
Makaranangang RI 96 Qk49
Makarevyči UA 41 Mf39
Makarfi WAN 138 Ld40
Makari CAM 139 Lh39
Makari GUY 194 Ha43
Makaroa NZ 113 Te68
Makarov Basin 4 Ed01
Makarovo RUS 48 Nb19
Makarska HR 35 Ls47
Makasa Z 146 Mf50
Makassar RI 96 Qk48
Makassar Strait RI 96 Qj47
Makaw MYA 86 Pj32
Makay RM 157 Nc56
Makedade TLS 97 Rc50
Makedonien GR 46 Mb50
Makekeda RDC 141 Mc44
Makekeda RDC 141 Me44
Makemo Atoll F 11 Cb11
Makeni WAL 136 Kd41
Makere EAT 146 Mf48
Maketu NZ 112 Tj64
Makgadikgadi Pans RB 151 Mc56
Makgadikgadi Pans N.P. RB 151 Mc56
Makhdumnagar IND (UPH) 83 Pb32
Makhmur IRQ 57 Nb28
Makhtal IND (APH) 82 Oj37
Makhu IND (PJB) 80 Oh30
Maki ETH 142 Mk42
Maki RI 114 Rh47
Makifeng CDN (MB) 169 Ek19
Makijivka UA 49 Mk21
Makina SOL 117 Ta50
Makindu EAK 144 Mj47
Makingeny Cave EAK 144 Mh45
Makira SOL 117 Ta51
Makiya Z 151 Md52
Makkah KSA 58 Mk35
Makkovik CDN 163 Ha08
Makkuva IND (APH) 83 Pb36
Makli Hills PK 65 Od33
Maknassy TN 126 Le28
Makó H 43 Ma44
Mako SN 136 Kd39
Makojo EAT 144 Mg46
Makokou G 148 Lg45
Makoli Z 152 Md54
Makonde EAT 146 Mh51
Makonde Plateau EAT 147 Mk51
Makongo GH 137 Kk41
Makongolosi EAT 146 Mg50
Makopong RB 154 Mb58
Makor CAM 139 Lg42
Makosa RDC 146 Me49
Makose ZW 152 Mg54
Makotipoko RCB 148 Lj46
Makou CHN (HUB) 75 Qg30
Makoua RCB 148 Lh46
Makoua TCH 140 Ma41
Makov SK 42 Lt41
Makovo MK 44 Mb49
Makowarsko PL 40 Ls37
Maków Mazowiecki PL 41 Mb38
Makrakómi GR 46 Mc52
Makran Coast Range PK 65 Ob33
Makrany BY 41 Me39
Makrigialós GR 47 Mf55
Makrinítsa GR 44 Md51
Makriráhi GR 44 Md51
Makronisi GR 47 Me53
Maksatiha RUS 48 Mh17
Maksi IND (MPH) 82 Oj34
Maksudangarh IND (MPH) 82 Oj33
Maktau EAK 144 Mk47
Makthar TN 126 Le28
Maku IR 57 Nc26
Makuende RDC 146 Me49
Makulakubu RDC 146 Mc50
Makum IND (ASM) 86 Ph32
Makumbako EAT 146 Mh50
Makumbi RDC 149 Ma48
Makumbi ZW 152 Mf54
Makunda RB 150 Ma57
Makunduchi EAT 147 Mk49
Makungo SP 145 Nb45
Makungu EAT 146 Mh50
Makunguvilo EAT 147 Mj50
Makungwe Z 146 Mf51
Makunudu Atoll MV 84 Og42
Makurazaki J 79 Rf30
Makurdi WAN 138 Le42
Makusi Island Z 151 Mc54
Makutano EAK 144 Mh44
Makutano EAK 144 Mh45
Makutano EAK 144 Mh45
Makutano EAK 144 Mj46
Makutano EAK 144 Mj47
Makuti ZW 152 Me54
Makuyeh IR 64 Ng31
Makuyuni EAT 144 Mj47
Makwate RB 152 Md57
Makwiro ZW 152 Mf54
Mâl RIM 130 Kd37
Mala PE 197 Gb52
Mala RI 97 Rf46
Malå S 16 Lk13
Mala A.L. AUS 103 Rf56
Malabang RP 91 Rc42
Malabar Coast IND 84 Og39
Malabar, Gunung RI 95 Qd49
Malabo GQ 138 Le44
Malabo RI 96 Qk47
Malabuñgan RP 94 Qj41
Malacacheta BR (MG) 203 Hj54
Malacacheta, T.I. BR 194 Gk44
Malacca IND (AAN) 88 Pg41
Malacca MAL 93 Qb44
Malacky SK 42 Lr42
Malad City USA (ID) 171 Ed24
Maladzečna BY 39 Mg36
Malá Fatra, N.P. SK 43 Lu41
Málaga CO 192 Gd42
Málaga E 27 Kq54
Malaga USA (NM) 171 Eh29
Malagan Beach Resort PNG 116 Sf47
Malagarasi EAT 146 Mf48
Malagón E 27 Kr51
Malahar RI 96 Ra50
Malahide Castle IRL 19 Ko37
Mălăiești RO 44 Mc45
Malaimbandy RM 157 Nc56
Malaita SOL 117 Ta50
Malaita ZA 155 Me58
Malaja Kuril'skaja grjada RUS 77 Sd24
Malaja Višera RUS 48 Mg16
Malakal SUD 141 Mf41
Malakand PK 63 Of28
Malakata PNG 116 Se46
Malakheti NEP 81 Pa31
Mala Kladuša BIH 35 Lq45
Malaknagiri IND (ORS) 83 Pa36
Malakula VU 118 Td54
Malakwa CDN (BC) 168 Ea20
Malakwal PK 65 Og29
Malala PNG 115 Sc48
Malala PNG 115 Sd48
Malalamai PNG 115 Sd48
Malalaua PNG 115 Sd50
Malam PNG 115 Sb50
Malambo EAT 144 Mh47
Malambo EAT 146 Mf49
Mala Mechet UA 45 Mj45
Malam Jabba Ski resort PK 63 Og28
Malammaduri WAN 138 Le39
Malampaka EAT 144 Mg47
Malampuzha IND (KER) 84 Oj40
Malanda AUS (QLD) 107 Sc54
Malandji RDC 149 Mb48
Malang RI 95 Qg49
Malanga MOC 153 Mj52
Malangas RP 91 Rb42
Malangbong RI 95 Qe49
Malangke RI 96 Ra47
Malanje ANG 148 Lj50
Malanów PL 40 Lt39
Malanville DY 138 Lb40
Malapatan RP 91 Rc43
Malar PK 65 Oc32
Malarba CAM 139 Lg42
Mälaren S 31 Lr31
Malargüe RA (MD) 208 Gf63
Malarrif IS 18 Jr26
Malartic CDN (QC) 173 Ga21
Malaryta BY 41 Me39
Malasait PNG 116 Sf48
Mala Serdoba RUS 48 Nc19
Malaspina Glacier USA 166 Ck16
Malatya TR 56 Mk26
Malaut IND (PJB) 80 Oh30
Malavalli IND (KTK) 84 Oj39
Malavi IR 59 Nd29
Mala Vyska UA 49 Mf21
Malawali MAL 94 Qj42
Malawan IND (UPH) 81 Ok32
Malawi 123 Mh11
Malawiya SUD 135 Mj38
Malax FIN 38 Mb28
Malay RP 90 Ra40
Malaybalay RP 91 Rc41
Malayer IR 57 Ne28
Malay Peninsula MAL 92 Qc43
Malaysia MAL 53 Qa09
Malazgirt TR 57 Nb26
Malbaza RN 132 Lc39
Malbebale Plain EAK 145 Mk44
Malbhanguwa NEP 81 Pa31
Malbon AUS (QLD) 107 Sa56
Malbon Vale AUS (QLD) 107 Rk56
Malbooma AUS (SA) 108 Rh61
Malbork PL 40 Lu36
Malboro CDN (AB) 168 Eb19
Malbrán RA (SE) 207 Gj60
Malbuisson F 25 Lg44
Malca Rie SP 145 Na44
Malcésine I 34 Ll45
Malchin D 32 Ln37
Malchow D 32 Ln37
Malcolm AUS (WA) 104 Ra60
Maldegem B 23 Ld39
Malden USA (MO) 175 Ff27
Maldives MV 52 Ob09
Maldives MV 53 Ob09
Maldon AUS (VIC) 111 Sc64
Maldon GB 21 La39
Maldonado EC 196 Ga45
Maldonado ROU 209 Hc63
Maldybai KZ 66 Og24
Małdyty PL 41 Lu37
Malè I 34 Ll44
Male MV 84 Og43
Male MYA 86 Pj34
Male PNG 115 Sc48
Malea, Gunung RI 93 Pk45
Malealea LS 155 Md60
Malee Downs AUS (SA) 110 Sa64
Małe Gacno PL 40 Lt37
Malegaon IND (MHT) 82 Oh35
Malegaon Jahagir IND (MHT) 82 Oj35
Malei MOC 153 Mj54
Malek SUD 141 Mf42
Malekan IR 57 Nd27
Malé Karpaty CZ 42 Ls42
Malélé RCB 148 Lg48
Malema MOC 153 Mj53
Malé Mal RN 132 Le39
Malemba-Nkulu RDC 146 Md50
Maléme GR 45 Md55
Malème-Hodar SN 130 Kc38
Malena RA (CD) 208 Gh62
Malendok Island PNG 116 Sg47
Malengwa Z 151 Mb53
Malente D 32 Ll36
Malesherbes F 23 Lc42
Malestan AFG 65 Od29
Malestroit F 22 Ks43
Maleta RUS 70 Qe20
Maletsunyane Falls LS 155 Me60
Malgobek RUS (ING) 57 Nc24
Malgrat de Mar E 29 Lc49
Malha SUD 134 Md38
Malhada BR (BA) 203 Hj53
Malhah IRQ 57 Nb28
Malhanskij hrebet RUS 70 Qe20
Malheur Nat. Wildlife Refuge USA 168 Ea24
Malhia YV 193 Gj43
Mali RDC 146 Md47
Mali RG 136 Kd39
Mali 123 Kb08
Mália GR 47 Mf55
Malibu USA (CA) 170 Ea29
Mali Đerdap SCG 44 Mb46
Maligaya RP 90 Ra38
Malihabad IND (UPH) 83 Pa32
Mali Island MYA 88 Pk39
Maliku RI 97 Rb46
Malili RI 96 Ra47
Malilla S 31 Lq33
Mali Lošinj HR 35 Lp46
Malimán de Arriba RA (SJ) 207 Gf60
Malimasindi ZW 152 Me55
Malimbong RI 96 Qk47
Malinalco MEX 182 Fa36
Malinau RI 94 Qj44
Malindang, Mount RP 91 Rb41
Malindi EAK 145 Na47
Malindi EAT 147 Mk48
Malindi Marine N.P. EAK 145 Na47
Malinga G 148 Lg47
Malingping RI 95 Qd49
Malin Head IRL 19 Kn35
Maliniec PL 40 Lt38
Malinke SN 136 Kc39
Malino RI 96 Ra46
Malino RI 96 Qk48
Malino, Gunung RI 91 Ra45
Malinska HR 35 Lp45
Malinyi EAT 147 Mj50
Malipari IND (WBG) 86 Pe32
Maliq AL 46 Ma50
Mal i Qarrishtë AL 46 Ma50
Mal i Shpatit AL 44 Ma49
Malita RP 91 Rc42
Maliya IND (GUJ) 82 Of34
Maljamar USA (NM) 174 Ej29
Maljiševo SCG 44 Ma48
Malka Mari EAK 145 Na43
Malka Mari N.P. EAK 145 Na43
Malkapur IND (APH) 82 Ok37
Malkapur IND (MHT) 82 Og37
Malkapur IND (MHT) 82 Oj35
Malkara TR 45 Mg50
Malko Tărnovo BG 45 Mj49
Mal'kovo RUS 39 Mj34
Malla IND (KTK) 82 Oj37
Mallacoota AUS (VIC) 111 Se64
Mallacoota Inlet AUS 111 Se64
Mallaig GB 20 Kp34
Mallala AUS (SA) 110 Rk63
Mallanganee AUS (NSW) 109 Sg60
Mallaoua RN 132 Le39
Mallaranny IRL 19 Kl37
Mallawi ET 129 Mf32
Mallee Cliffs N.P. AUS 111 Sb63
Mallee Highway AUS 110 Sa63
Mallén E 28 Kt49
Mälles Venosta = Mals im Vinschgau I 34 Ll44
Mallet BR (PR) 205 He58
Mallnitz A 35 Lo44
Mallorca E 29 Ld51
Mallow IRL 19 Km38
Mallwyd GB 21 Kr38
Malmal PNG 116 Sf48
Malmbäck S 31 Lp33
Malmbanan S/N 16 Lk11
Malmberget S 16 Ma12
Malmedy B 23 Lg40
Malmesbury GB 21 Ks39
Malmesbury ZA 154 Lk62
Malmköping S 31 Lr31
Malmö S 30 Lo35
Malmo USA (MN) 172 Fd22
Malmslätt S 31 Lq32
Malngin A.L. AUS 103 Re54
Malo VU 118 Td53
Maloaini SOL 117 Sh49
Maloarhangel'sk RUS 48 Mj19
Maloarhangel'sk RUS 70 Qe20
Maloca BR (PA) 194 Hc45
Maloca do Gonçalo BR (PA) 199 Hb49
Maloca Velha BR (PA) 194 Hc44
Malocu Macu BR (RR) 193 Gj44
Maloe BY 41 Me37
Maloelap Atoll MH 10 Tb09
Malojapass CH 34 Lk44
Malojaroslavec RUS 48 Mj18
Malokuril'skoe RUS 77 Sd24
Malole Z 146 Mf51
Malolo FJI 119 Tj54
Malolo Plantation Lodge PNG 115 Sc48
Malolos RP 90 Ra38
Malolotja Nature Reserve SD 155 Mf59
Malom PNG 116 Sf47
Małomice PL 40 Lq39
Malonda RDC 149 Mc50
Malone USA (FL) 175 Fh30
Malone USA (NY) 177 Gc23
Malong CHN (YUN) 87 Qb33
Malonga RDC 149 Mb51
Małopolska PL 41 Ma40
Måløy N 17 Lc15
Mal Pais - Santa Teresa CR 185 Fh41
Malpartida de Plasencia E 27 Ko51
Malpas Hut AUS (QLD) 107 Sb55
Malpaso MEX (JLC) 182 Eh35
Malpaso MEX (ZCT) 182 Ej34
Malpe Beach IND 84 Oh39
Malpica de Bergantiños E 26 Km47
Mālpils LV 39 Me33
Malpura IND (RJT) 80 Oh32
Mals im Vinschgau = Mälles Venosta I 34 Ll44
Malta I 37 Lp55
Malta LV 39 Mh34
Malta M 37 Lp55
Malta USA (MT) 169 Eg21
Malta USA (OH) 173 Fk26
Maltahöhe NAM 154 Lj58
Maltam CAM 139 Lh39
Maltatal A 35 Lo44
Maltee AUS (SA) 110 Rg62
Malton GB 21 Ku36
Malu CHN (GZG) 74 Qd35
Maluera MOC 152 Mf53
Małujowice PL 40 Ls40
Malukukukuang RI 96 Qj48
Maluku RDC 148 Lh48
Malumfashi WAN 138 Ld40
Malum Islands PNG 117 Sh47
Malunda RI 96 Qk47
Malung S 31 Lo30
Malungwishi RDC 146 Md51
Malur IND (KTK) 84 Oj39
Maluso RP 91 Ra42
Maluszyn PL 41 Lu40
Malut SUD 135 Mg40
Maluti LS 155 Me60
Maluu SOL 117 Ta50
Malvan IND (MHT) 82 Og37
Malvas PE 197 Gb50
Malvern USA (AR) 174 Fd28
Malwal SUD 141 Mf41
Malya EAT 144 Mg47
Malyj Čuraševo RUS 48 Nd18
Malyj Enisej RUS 67 Pj20
Malyj Naryn KS 66 Oj25
Malyn UA 48 Me20
Mały Płock PL 41 Mc37
Malyševo RUS 48 Na18
Mamad RP 91 Rb42
Mamãe Ana BR (PA) 199 Hb48
Mama Hatun Türbesi TR 57 Na26
Mamaia RO 45 Mj46
Mamala MOC 153 Mk53
Mamallapuram IND (TNU) 85 Pa39
Mamallapuram IND 85 Pa39
Mamallapuram Beach IND 85 Pa39
Mamana Island = Rum Cay BS 186 Gc34
Mamanguape BR (PB) 201 Jc49
Mamanuca Group FJI 119 Tj54
Mamâri SN 130 Kd38
Mamasa RI 96 Qk47
Mamasiware RI 114 Rh47
Mamba EAT 146 Mh48
Mamba LB 136 Ke42
Mamba RDC 146 Md50
Mambai BR (GO) 203 Hg53
Mambajao RP 91 Rc41
Mambal CAM 139 Lg42
Mambali EAT 146 Mg48
Mambasa RDC 141 Me45
Mambeco MOC 152 Mg57
Mamberamo RI 114 Rk47
Mamberamo Delta RI 114 Rj46
Mamberamo-Foja Mountains-Rouffaer Reserves RI 114 Rk47
Mambi RI 96 Qk47
Mambia RG 136 Kd41
Mambila Mountains CAM/WAN 139 Lf42
Mambilima Falls Z 146 Me51
Mambiri RMM 136 Kf39
Mambolo WAL 136 Kd41
Mamboré BR (PR) 204 Hd58
Mambova Z 151 Mc54
Mambova Rapids RB/NAM 151 Mc54
Mambrui EAK 145 Na47
Mamburao RP 90 Ra39
Mambusao RP 90 Rb40
Mambwe Z 146 Mf50
Mamcai RI 114 Rh46
Mamda IND (APH) 82 Ok36
Mamedkala RUS (DAG) 57 Ne24
Mamelodi ZA 155 Me58
Mamers F 22 La42
Mamfe CAM 138 Le43
Mamili N.P. NAM 151 Mb55
Mamiña RCH 206 Gf56
Maminigui CI 137 Kh42
Mamir Pawa GUY 194 Ha44
Mamisi RI 114 Rh47
Mamit IND (MZR) 86 Pg34
Mammoth Cave AUS 104 Qh63
Mammoth Cave N.P. USA 175 Fg27
Mammoth Hot Springs USA (WY) 169 Ee23
Mammoth Lakes USA (CA) 170 Ea27
Mammoth Springs USA (AR) 175 Fe27
Mamoadate, T.I. BR 197 Ge51
Mamoeiro BR (AC) 198 Gf50
Mamonas BR (MG) 203 Hj53
Mamonovo RUS 39 Lu36
Mamoré BR/BOL 198 Gh51
Mamoriá BR (AM) 198 Gg49
Mamou RG 136 Kd40
Mamoudzou F (MYT) 156 Nc52
Mampikony RM 156 Nd54
Mampodre E 26 Kp47
Mampong GH 137 Kk42
Mampongtin Range GH 137 Kk42
Mamshit IL 58 Mh30
Mamu WAN 138 Lb42
Mamudo MOC 147 Mj52
Mamue Choique RA (RN) 208 Ge66
Mamuil Malal, P. RA/RCH 208 Ge65
Mamuju RI 96 Qk47
Mamulique MEX (NL) 181 Ek32
Mamuno RB 150 Ma57
Mamure Kalesi TR 56 Mg27
Man CI 137 Kg42
Man RCA 140 Lh42
Mana F (GF) 194 Hd43
Mana Camp ZW 152 Me53
Manacapurú BR (AM) 199 Gk47
Manacor E 29 Ld51
Manadhoo MV 84 Og43
Manado RI 91 Rc45
Managua NIC 184 Fg39
Manah OM 61 Nj34
Manaíra BR (PB) 201 Ja49
Manajiv UA 43 Mf41
Manajuare CO 192 Ge43
Manakamana NEP 81 Pc31
Manakana RM 157 Nd54
Manakara RM 157 Nd57
Manak Chowk and Havelis (Jaisalmer) IND 80 Of32
Manakha YE 60 Nb38
Manalalondo RM 157 Nd55
Manali IND (HPH) 81 Oj29
Manama ZW 152 Me56
Manamadurai IND (TNU) 84 Ok41
Manambaro RM 157 Nd58
Manambolo RM 157 Nc55
Manambolosy RM 156 Ne54
Manambondro RM 157 Nd57
Manamensalo FIN 16 Md13
Manami RI 114 Rh47
Manam Island PNG 115 Sc48
Manamoc Island RP 90 Ra40
Mananara Avaratra RM 156 Ne54
Manandona RM 157 Nd56
Mananga RI 97 Rb50
Manangatang AUS (VIC) 111 Sb63
Manangoora AUS (NT) 106 Rj53
Mananjary RM 157 Ne56
Manankoro RMM 137 Kg40
Manantali RMM 136 Ke39
Manantenina RM 157 Nd58
Manantoddy IND (KER) 84 Oj40
Manantur IND (APH) 82 Ok37
Manaparai IND (TNU) 84 Ok40
Mana Pass CHN/IND 68 Ok30
Mana Pools N.P. ZW 152 Me53
Manaquiri BR (AM) 199 Gk47
Manari BR (PE) 201 Jb50
Manari PNG 115 Sd50
Manariã BR (AM) 198 Gg48
Manas CHN (XUZ) 67 Pd23
Manas PE 197 Gb51
Manasarowar = Mapam Yumco CHN 68 Pa30
Manas He CHN 67 Pc23
Manas Hu CHN 67 Pd23
Manaskent RUS (DAG) 57 Nd24
Manaslu NEP 81 Pc31
Manassas USA (VA) 177 Gb26
Manas Tiger Reserve IND 86 Pf32
Manastir Dečani SCG 44 Ma48
Manastir Đurđevi Stupovi SCG 44 Lu48
Mănăstirea RO 45 Mg46
Mănăstirea Cocoș RO 45 Mj45
Mănăstirea Cozia RO 43 Me45
Mănăstirea Hurezi RO 44 Md45
Mănăstirea Sinaia RO 45 Mf45
Mănăstirea Snagov RO 45 Mg46
Manastir Gračanica SCG 44 Mb48
Mănăstirile Basarabi RO 45 Mj46
Manastir Kalenić SCG 44 Ma47
Manastir Ljubostinja SCG 44 Mb47
Manastir Manasija SCG 44 Mb46
Manastir Mileševa SCG 44 Lu47
Manastir Ostrog SCG 44 Lu48
Manastir Ravanica SCG 44 Mb47
Manastir Savina SCG 44 Lt48
Manastir Sopoćani SCG 44 Ma47
Manastir Studenica SCG 44 Ma47
Manastir Žiča SCG 44 Ma47
Manat KZ 67 Pb21
Manatí C 179 Gb35
Manatí C 179 Ga34
Manatí USA (PR) 187 Gg36
Manatial BOL 206 Gj55
Manatuto TLS 97 Rc50
Manau PNG 115 Sd50
Man'aung MYA 86 Pg36
Manaure CO 192 Gd40
Manaus BR (AM) 199 Gk47
Manavgat TR 56 Mf27
Manavgat Şelâlesi TR 56 Mf27
Manawar IND (MPH) 82 Oh34
Manawoka RI 97 Rf48
Manay RP 91 Rd42
Manayana Rock Paintings RB 155 Mc58
Mañazo PE 197 Ge53
Manba CHN (YUN) 87 Qa34
Manbazar IND (WBG) 83 Pd34
Manbej SYR 56 Mj27
Mancha Khiri THA 89 Qb37
Mancha Real E 27 Kr53
Mancheng Hanmu Tombs CHN 73 Qh26
Manchester GB 21 Ks37
Manchester USA (CT) 177 Gd25
Manchester USA (IA) 172 Fe24
Manchester USA (KY) 178 Fj27
Manchester USA (NH) 177 Ge24
Manchester USA (TN) 175 Fh28
Manchester Center USA (VT) 177 Gd24
Manching D 33 Lm42
Manchirayal IND (APH) 83 Ok36
Manchis MAL 92 Qb44
Manchok WAN 138 Le41
Manchuria CHN 52 Ra05
Manciano I 34 Lm48
Máncora PE 196 Fk48
Mancos USA (CO) 171 Ef27
Mand PK 64 Ob32
Manda BD 86 Pe33
Manda EAT 146 Mg50
Manda EAT 146 Mh51
Manda TCH 140 Lk41
Mandabe RM 157 Nc56
Mandagadde IND (KTK) 84 Oh39
Mandaguari BR (PR) 202 He57
Mandah RI 93 Qb46
Mandai PK 65 Oe31
Manda Island EAK 145 Na47
Mandal MNG 70 Pk21
Mandal MNG 70 Qd21
Mandal N 30 Lh32
Mandalay MYA 86 Pj35
Mandalay N.W.R. USA 175 Fe31
Mandalgarh IND (RJT) 82 Oh33
Mandalgov' MNG 70 Qd23
Mandali IRQ 57 Nc29
Mandamabgwe ZW 152 Mf56
Mandan USA (ND) 172 Ek22
Mandaon RP 90 Rb39
Mandapeta IND (APH) 83 Pb37
Manda, P.N.de TCH 140 Lk41
Mandara LAR 127 Lg32
Mandara Mountains CAM/WAN 139 Lg40
Mándas I 36 Lk51
Mandasip RI 93 Pk45
Mandaue RP 90 Rb40
Mandel AFG 64 Oa29
Mandélia TCH 139 Lh40
Mandem IND (CGH) 83 Pa36
Mandera EAK 145 Na44
Mandera USA (CA) 170 Dk27
Mandeville JA 186 Gb36
Mandheera SP 143 Nc41
Mandi IND (GUJ) 82 Og35
Mandi IND (HPH) 81 Oj30
Mandiakoy RMM 131 Kj37
Mandiakur RMM 137 Kh39
Mandiana RG 136 Kf40
Mandi Bahauddin PK 65 Og29
Mandi Burewala PK 65 Og30
Mandicaba BR (PR) 202 Hd57
Mandi Dabwali IND (PJB) 80 Oh31
Mandié MOC 152 Mg54
Mandi Langwé CAM 139 Lf43
Mandimba MOC 153 Mh53
Mandioli RI 97 Rd46
Mandji = Sangala G 148 Lf46
Mandla IND (MPH) 83 Pa34
Mandlakazi MOC 155 Mg58
Mando WAN 138 Ld40
Mandoli IND (RJT) 82 Og33
Mandor RI 114 Rj46
Mandor RI 95 Qe45
Mandoro RDC 141 Me43
Mandoto RM 157 Nd55
Mandouri TG 137 La40
Măndra RO 44 Md45
Mandráki GR 47 Mh54
Mandritsara RM 156 Ne53
Mandronarivo RM 157 Nc56
Mandrosonoro RM 157 Nd56
Mandsaur IND (MPH) 82 Oh34
Mandu IND (JKD) 83 Pc34
Mandu IND 82 Oh34
Mandul RI 94 Qj44
Mandumbua ANG 151 Ma53
Mandundu Z 151 Mb54
Mandurah AUS (WA) 104 Qh62
Mandúria I 37 Ls50
Mandvi IND (GUJ) 82 Oe34
Mandwa Beach IND 82 Og36
Mandya IND (KTK) 84 Oj39
Mané BF 137 Kk39
Maneadero C 179 Fk34
Maneadero MEX (BC) 180 Eb30
Manegaon IND (MPH) 83 Ok34
Maner IND (BIH) 83 Pc33
Manèrbio I 34 Ll45
Maneromango EAT 147 Mk49
Maneron Beach RI 95 Qg49
Maneroo AUS (QLD) 109 Sb57
Manevyči UA 41 Mf39
Manfalût ET 129 Mf32
Manfeilong CHN (YUN) 87 Qa35
Manfred AUS (WA) 104 Qj59
Manfred Downs AUS (QLD) 107 Sa56
Manfredónia I 37 Lq49
Manga BF 137 Kk40
Manga BR (MG) 203 Hj53
Manga CAM 139 Lg42
Manga PNG 116 Sg48
Manga RN 133 Lg38
Mangada RDC 141 Md44
Mangada RDC 141 Me44
Manga Grande ANG 148 Lg49
Mangai EAK 145 Na46
Mangai PNG 116 Sf47
Mangai RDC 149 Lk48
Mangaïzé RN 132 La38
Mangalagiri IND (APH) 83 Pa37
Mangalia RO 45 Mj47
Mangalmé TCH 139 Lk39
Mangalore AUS (QLD) 109 Sd59
Mangalore AUS (VIC) 111 Sc64
Mangalore IND (KTK) 84 Oh39
Mangalvedha IND (MHT) 82 Oh37
Mangamaunu NZ 113 Tg67
Mangamila RM 157 Nd55
Mangango Z 151 Mc53
Manganti RI 93 Qa46
Mangaon IND (MHT) 82 Og36
Mangarwar IND (RJT) 82 Oh33
Mangawah IND (MPH) 83 Pa33
Mangaweka NZ 113 Th65
Mangaweka NZ 113 Tj65
Mangchang CHN (GZG) 74 Qd33
Mangdangshan CHN 78 Qj28
Mange PNG 115 Sd49
Mange WAL 136 Kd41
Mangen N 30 Lm31
Manggar RI 95 Qe47
Manggasi RI 114 Rj47
Manggopoh RI 93 Qa46
Mangho Pir PK 65 Od33
Manghystau shyghanaghy KZ 62 Nf23
Manghystau üstirti KZ 62 Ng24
Manglai IND (MHT) 82 Oj36
Mangindrano RM 156 Ne53
Mang'it UZ 62 Oa24
Mangkururrpa A.L. AUS 103 Re56
Manglaralto EC 196 Fk46
Manglares CO 192 Gb43
Manglar Zapoton MEX 183 Fd38
Mangnai CHN (QHI) 69 Pf27
Mangnai Zhen CHN (QHI) 69 Pf26
Mangoaka RM 156 Ne52
Mangochi MW 153 Mh53
Mango Creek BH 184 Ff37
Mango Creek BH 184 Ff37
Mangoky RM 157 Nc56
Mangole RI 97 Rc46
Mangom CAM 139 Lg42
Mangombe RDC 141 Md46
Mangonui NZ 112 Tg63
Mangoudara BF 137 Kh41
Mangral IND (GUJ) 82 Of35
Mangrove Cay BS 179 Gb33
Mangrove Cay BS 179 Ga32
Mangrul Pir IND (MHT) 82 Oj35
Mangshan CHN 73 Qg28
Mangualde P 26 Kn50
Manguchar PK 65 Od31
Mangueigne TCH 134 Ma40
Mangueira, T.I. BR 193 Gk44
Mangueirinha BR (PR) 204 Hd58
Manguel Creek AUS (WA) 102 Rb54
Mangui CHN (NMZ) 71 Rb19
Manguito C 179 Fk34
Mangum USA (OK) 174 Fa28
Mangungu RDC 148 Lj48
Mangunza Z 152 Md54
Mangut RUS 70 Qg21
Mangwe ZW 152 Mf55
Manhamade MOC 153 Mj54
Manhao CHN (YUN) 87 Qb34
Manhattan USA (KS) 174 Fb26
Manhattan USA (MT) 169 Ee23
Manhica MOC 155 Mg58
Manhuaçu BR (MG) 203 Hj56
Manhumirim BR (MG) 203 Hk56
Manhup Kale UA 49 Mg23
Mani CO 192 Gd43
Máni GR 46 Mc54
Mani RDC 149 Mc49
Mani TCH 139 Lh39
Mani WAN 138 Ld39
Mania RM 157 Nd56
Maniago I 35 Ln44
Mania-Muna RDC 149 Mb50
Maniapure YV 193 Gg42
Manicaland ZW 152 Mf55
Manicani Island RP 90 Rc40
Manicoré BR (AM) 198 Gk48
Manicouagan CDN (QC) 176 Gf20
Manifah KSA 59 Ne32
Maniganggo CHN (SCH) 69 Pk30
Manigotagan CDN (MB) 172 Fb20
Manihari IND (BIH) 83 Pd33
Manihiki Atoll NZ 11 Bb10
Manika IND (JKD) 83 Pc34
Manika RDC 151 Mc51
Manikganj BD 86 Pe34
Manikpur IND (UPH) 83 Pa33
Manila RP 90 Ra38
Manila USA (UT) 171 Ef25
Manila Bay RP 90 Ra38
Manilaid EST 39 Me32
Manildra AUS (NSW) 111 Se62
Manilla AUS (NSW) 109 Sf61
Maningrida AUS (NT) 106 Rh52
Maninjau RI 93 Qa46
Manipa RI 97 Rd47
Manipur IND 86 Pg33
Manisa TR 47 Mh52
Manises E 29 Ku51
Manistee USA (MI) 173 Fg23
Manistique USA (MI) 173 Fg23
Manitique Lake USA 173 Fh22
Manitoba CDN 163 Fa08
Manitou CDN (MB) 172 Fa21
Manitou CDN (QC) 176 Gh20
Manitou USA (OK) 174 Fa28
Manitou Lake CDN 172 Fd21
Manitoulin Island CDN 173 Fj23
Manitou Springs USA (CO) 171 Eh26
Manitouwadge CDN (ON) 173 Fh21
Manitowaning Lodge CDN 173 Fk23
Manitowish USA (WI) 172 Fe22
Manitowoc USA (WI) 173 Fg23
Manitsoq = Sukkertoppen DK 163 Hb05
Maniwaki CDN (QC) 177 Gc22
Maniwaki Ind. Res. CDN 173 Gb22
Maniwori RI 114 Rh47
Manizales CO 192 Gc43
Manja RM 157 Nc56
Manjakandriana RM 157 Nd55
Manjamba MOC 146 Mh52
Manjar Sumba IND (MHT) 82 Oh36
Manjeri IND (KER) 84 Oj40
Manjhand PK 65 Oe33
Manjira Wildlife Sanctuary IND 83 Ok36
Manjlegaon IND (MHT) 82 Oj36
Manjo CAM 138 Le43
Manjola ZW 152 Md54
Manjou CAM 139 Lg43
Mankachar IND (ASM) 86 Pe33
Mankanza RDC 140 Lk45
Mankarbo S 31 Ls30
Man Kat MYA 87 Pk35
Mankato USA (KS) 174 Fa26
Mankato USA (MN) 172 Fd23
Mankera PK 65 Of30
Mankhan MNG 70 Qa20
Mankhan Nature Reserve MNG 67 Pg22
Manki CAM 139 Lf43
Mankim CAM 139 Lg43
Mankono CI 137 Kg41
Mankpan GH 137 Kk41
Mankrangso GH 137 Kk42
Mankulam CL 85 Pa41
Manley Hot Springs USA (AK) 165 Ce13
Man Li MYA 86 Pj34
Manlleu E 29 Lc49
Manmad IND (MHT) 82 Oh35
Manna RI 93 Qb48
Manna Hill AUS (SA) 110 Rk62
Man-Namlet MYA 87 Pk34
Mannar CL 85 Ok41
Mannemkonda IND (ORS) 83 Pa36
Manners Creek AUS (NT) 108 Rj57
Mannheim D 33 Lj41
Manni CHN (TIB) 68 Pd28
Manning CDN (AB) 167 Eb17
Manning USA (ND) 169 Ej22
Manning USA (SC) 178 Fk29
Manning Prov. Park CDN 168 Dk21
Manning Range, Mount AUS 104 Qk60
Manningtree GB 21 Lb39
Mann Ranges AUS 105 Re58
Mannum AUS (SA) 110 Rk63
Mannville CDN (AB) 169 Ee19
Mano WAL 136 Kd41
Manoá Pium, T.I. BR 194 Gk44
Manogongu LB 136 Ke42
Manohardi BD 86 Pf33
Manokwari RI 114 Rh46
Manokwari RI 114 Rh47
Manole BG 45 Me48
Manolo Fortich RP 91 Rc41
Manombo Atsimo RM 157 Nb57
Manometimay RM 157 Nc56
Manompana RM 157 Ne54
Manono RDC 146 Md49
Manonwa RDC 149 Mc48
Manor IND (MHT) 82 Og36
Manorhamilton IRL 19 Km36
Manori Beach IND 82 Og36
Manosque F 25 Lf47
Manou RCA 140 Ma41
Manouane CDN (QC) 176 Gc22
Manova WAL 136 Ke41
Manp'o PRK 76 Rd25
Manpur IND (CGH) 83 Pa35
Manqabād ET 129 Mf32
Manresa E 29 Lb49
Mansa IND (PJB) 80 Oh31
Mansa Z 146 Me51
Mansabá GNB 136 Kc39
Mansa Konko WAG 136 Kc39
Mansalay RP 90 Ra39
Man Sam MYA 86 Pj34
Mansar IND (MHT) 83 Ok35
Mansehra PK 65 Og28
Mansel Island CDN 163 Fd06
Mansfeld D 32 Lm39
Mansfield AUS (VIC) 111 Sd64
Mansfield GB 21 Kt37
Mansfield USA (AR) 174 Fc28
Mansfield USA (OH) 173 Fj25
Mansfield USA (PA) 177 Gb25
Mansfield Jetty USA (TX) 181 Fb32
Mansfiled USA (LA) 174 Fd30
Mansi MYA 86 Ph33
Mansiari IND (UTT) 81 Pa30
Mansidão BR (BA) 200 Hh51
Mansilla E 28 Kr48
Mansilla E 28 Ks48
Mansilla de las Mulas E 26 Kp48
Mansinha BR (TO) 200 Hg50
Mansión CR 185 Fh40
Mansle F 24 La45
Mansôa GNB 136 Kc39
Manson Creek CDN (BC) 166 Dh18
Manso-Nkwanta GH 137 Kk42
Mansoura DZ 126 Lc27
Mansourah DZ 125 Kk28
Mansur Abad IR 64 Nk29
Mansur Abad IR 64 Ng31
Mansura Ruins PK 65 Oe33
Manta DY 137 La40
Manta EC 196 Fk46
Mantadia-Andasibe, P.N.de RM 157 Ne55
Mantalinga RI 96 Ra47
Mantalingajan, Mount RP 94 Qj41
Mantamádos GR 47 Mg51
Mantanai Besar MAL 94 Qj42
Mantare EAT 144 Mg47
Mantasoa RM 157 Nd55
Mantawa RI 96 Rb46
Manteca USA (CA) 170 Dk27
Mantecal YV 193 Gf42
Mantecal YV 193 Gh42
Mantehage RI 91 Rc45
Mantena BR (MG) 203 Hk55
Mantes-la-Jolie F 23 Lb42
Mantes-la-Ville F 23 Lb42
Manthani IND (APH) 83 Ok36
Manthiréa GR 46 Mc53
Manti USA (UT) 171 Ee26
Manticao RP 91 Rc41
Manto HN 184 Fg38
Manto PE 197 Gd52
Mantorp S 31 Lq32
Mantos Blancos RCH 207 Ge57
Mántova I 34 Ll45
Mantralayam IND (APH) 82 Oj38
Mäntsälä FIN 38 Mf30
Mänttä FIN 38 Me28
Mantua C 179 Fh34
Mantuan Downs AUS (QLD) 109 Sd58
Mantung AUS (SA) 110 Sa63
Mantup RI 95 Qg49
Mäntyharju FIN 38 Mg29
Mäntyluoto FIN 38 Mb29
Manu IND (TRP) 86 Pg34
Manú PE 197 Ge52
Manu WAN 132 Lc39
Manubepium RI 114 Rh46
Manuel MEX (TM) 182 Fa34
Manuel Antonio, P.N. CR 185 Fh41
Manuel Benavides MEX (CHH) 181 Ej31
Manuel Díaz ROU 204 Hc61
Manuel Emídio BR (PI) 200 Hj49
Manuel J.Cobo RA (BA) 209 Hb63
Manuel Ribas BR (PR) 204 He58
Manuel Tames C 186 Gc35
Manuel Urbano BR (AC) 198 Gf50
Manuel Vitorino BR (BA) 203 Hk53
Manui RI 97 Rb47
Manuk RI 97 Rf48
Manukan RP 91 Rb41
Manukau NZ 112 Th64
Manunda AUS (SA) 110 Rk62
Manunga Z 146 Me50
Manunui NZ 113 Th65
Manú, P.N. PE 197 Ge52
Manur IND (MHT) 82 Oh36
Manusela RI 97 Re47
Manusela N.P. RI 97 Re47
Manus Island PNG 116 Sd46
Manvi IND (KTK) 82 Oj38
Manville USA (WY) 171 Eh24
Manweng MYA 86 Pj34
Many USA (LA) 174 Fd30
Manyallaluk A.L. AUS 106 Rg53
Manyani EAK 145 Mk47
Manyapadu IND (APH) 82 Oj38
Manyas TR 45 Mh50
Manyberries CDN (AB) 169 Ee21
Manych Depression RUS 14 Na05
Manyelanong Game Reserve RB 155 Mc58
Manyeleti Game Reserve ZA 155 Mf58
Manyémen CAM 138 Le43
Many Farms USA (AZ) 171 Ef27
Manyikeni MOC 153 Mh57
Manyinga Z 151 Mc52
Manyo EAT 146 Mf49
Manyoni EAT 146 Mh48
Manypeaks AUS (WA) 104 Qk63
Manzai PK 65 Oe30
Manzai PK 65 Of29
Manzanares CO 192 Gc43
Manzanares E 27 Kr52
Manzanilla Beach TT 187 Gk40
Manzanillo C 179 Gb35
Manzanillo MEX (COL) 182 Eh36
Manzengele RDC 149 Lj49
Manzhouli CHN (NMZ) 71 Qj21
Manzil PK 65 Ob31
Manzini SD 155 Mf59
Manzshir Monastery MNG 70 Qd22
Manzurka RUS 70 Qd19
Mao DOM 186 Ge36
Maó E 29 Le51
Mao EAT 146 Mf50
Mao TCH 133 Lh38
Maocaojie CHN (HUN) 74 Qg31
Mao'ershan CHN (HLG) 76 Rd23
Maogong CHN (GZH) 74 Qe32
Maohutang CHN (HUB) 74 Qf30
Maojing CHN (GSU) 72 Qd27
Maokeng ZA 155 Md59
Mao Ling CHN 72 Qe28
Maoming CHN (GDG) 74 Qf35
Maope RB 152 Md57
Maopora RI 97 Rd49
Mao Xian CHN (SCH) 72 Qb30
Mapagoro EAT 146 Mg50
Mapai MOC 152 Mf57
Mapamoiwa PNG 116 Sf50
Mapam Yumco CHN 68 Pa30
Mapanda RDC 149 Mc50
Mapane RI 96 Ra46
Mapangu RDC 149 Ma48
Mapanza Z 152 Md54
Mapastepec MEX (CHP) 183 Fd38
Mapat RI 94 Qj44
Mapati RCB 148 Lg47
Mapé RCA 140 Mb43
Mapelane Nature Reserve ZA 155 Mg60
Maphisa ZW 152 Me56
Mapi RI 114 Rk49
Mapili RI 96 Qk47
Mapinhane MOC 153 Mh57
Mapire YV 193 Gh42
Mapiri BOL 206 Gf53
Mapiripán CO 192 Gd44
Maple Creek CDN (SK) 169 Ef21
Maple Ridge CDN (BC) 168 Dj21
Maplesville USA (AL) 175 Fg29
Mapleton USA (IA) 172 Fc24
Mapoon AUS (QLD) 107 Sa52
Mapoon A.L. AUS 107 Sb51
Mapor RI 93 Qc45
Mapor Beach RI 93 Qc45
Mapuera BR 194 Hb46
Mapulanguene MOC 155 Mg58
Mapunga Z 151 Md52
Mapungubwe ZA 152 Me57
Mapungubwe (Vhembe-Dongola) N.P. ZA 152 Me57
Mapusa IND (GOA) 82 Og38
Maputi RI 91 Qk45
Maputo MOC 155 Mg58
Maqên CHN (QHI) 72 Qa28
Maqna KSA 58 Mh31
Maqrat YE 61 Nf38
Maqteïr RIM 130 Ke35
Maqu CHN (GSU) 72 Qb29
Maquecha MOC 152 Mg56
Maqueda E 27 Kq50
Maquela do Zombo ANG 148 Lh49
Maqueze MOC 155 Mg58
Maquinchao RA (RN) 208 Gf66
Maquinista Levet RA (MD) 208 Gg62
Maquoketa USA (IA) 172 Fe24
Mara GUY 194 Hb42
Mara IND (MPH) 83 Pb34
Mara ZA 152 Me57
Maraã BR (AM) 198 Gh46
Maraa Urubaxi, T.I. BR 198 Gh46
Marabá BR (PA) 200 Hf48
Marabadiassa CI 137 Kh41
Marabahan RI 95 Qh47
Marabidiyah IRQ 57 Nb29
Marabitanas BR (AM) 193 Gg45
Marabout Moulay Hassan DZ 132 Lc33
Marabouts TN 126 Ld29
Maracá BR (AP) 195 He44
Maracaçumé BR (MA) 195 Hh47
Maracaí BR (SP) 202 He57
Maracaibo YV 192 Ge40
Maracaju BR (MS) 202 Hc56
Maracanã BR (MA) 195 Hj47
Maracanã BR (PA) 195 Hg46
Maracanã BR 199 Ha49
Maracanaú BR (CE) 201 Ja47
Maracás BR (BA) 201 Hk52
Maracas Beach TT 187 Gk40
Maracay YV 193 Gg40
Maracoa CO 193 Gf44
Maradah LAR 127 Lk31
Maradankadawala CL 85 Pa41
Maradi RN 132 Ld39
Maradun WAN 138 Ld39
Marafa EAK 145 Mk47
Marafa Depression (Hell's Kitchen) EAK 145 Mk47
Maragheh IR 57 Nd27
Maragogi BR (AL) 201 Jc50
Maragogipe BR (BA) 201 Ja52
Marah KSA 59 Nc33
Marahoue, P.N.de la CI 137 Kg42
Marais Poitevin F 24 Kt44
Marais Salants F 22 Ks43
Marais Vernier F 22 La41
Maraiwatsede, T.I. BR 200 He51
Marajai, T.I. BR 198 Gh47
Maraka RN 132 Ld39
Marakabei LS 155 Me60
Marakele N.P. ZA 155 Md58
Marakesa RDC 141 Md45
Marakhayy YE 61 Nf38
Marakkanam IND (TNU) 85 Ok39
Maraku WAN 138 Le40
Maralal EAK 144 Mj45
Maralal Nature Sanctuary EAK 144 Mj45
Maraldy KZ 67 Pc21
Marale HN 184 Fg38
Marali RCA 140 Lk42
Maralinga AUS (SA) 105 Rf61
Maralinga Tjarutja A.L. AUS 105 Rf60
Maramag RP 91 Rc42
Maramasike SOL 117 Ta50
Marambio ANT (RA) 6 Ha31
Maran MAL 92 Qb44
Marana USA (AZ) 171 Ee29
Maranalgo AUS (WA) 104 Qj60
Marand IR 57 Nc26
Marandala CI 137 Kh41
Marandet RN 132 Ld37
Maranello I 34 Ll46
Marang MAL 92 Qb43
Marango AUS (QLD) 109 Sd59
Maranguape BR (CE) 201 Ja47

Maranhão BR (AM) 199 Hb47
Maranhão BR 191 Hb10
Maranhão BR 202 Hf53
Maranhoto BR (AM) 198 Gj47
Marañón PE 196 Gc48
Marans F 24 Ku44
Maranura PE 197 Gd52
Marapanim BR (PA) 195 Hg46
Marapi BR 194 Hb45
Mara Rosa BR (GO) 200 Hf52
Marasende RI 96 Qk48
Mărăşeşti RO 49 Md23
Mărașu RO 45 Mh46
Marat UZ 63 Oc24
Marataízes BR (ES) 203 Hk56
Maratea I 37 Lq50
Marathon AUS (QLD) 107 Sb56
Marathon CDN (ON) 173 Fg21
Marathon USA (FL) 179 Fk33
Marathon USA (TX) 181 Ej30
Marathónas GR 45 Md52
Maratua RI 91 Qk44
Maraú BR (BA) 203 Ja53
Marau BR (RS) 204 Hd60
Maraudeur F (GF) 194 Hd44
Maravatío de Ocampo MEX (MHC) 182 Ek36
Maravilha BR (AM) 199 Gk47
Maravilha BR (SC) 204 Hd59
Maravilhas BR (MG) 203 Hh55
Maravilla BOL 198 Gg51
Marawah LAR 127 Ma29
Marawaka PNG 115 Sc49
Marawi RP 91 Rc41
Marawi SUD 135 Mf36
Maraxo Patá BR (PA) 194 Hb45
Marayes RA (SJ) 208 Gg61
Marayoun RL 56 Mh29
Mar'ayt YE 61 Nf37
Marazion GB 21 Kp40
Marbach D 33 Lk42
Marbella E 27 Kq54
Marble Bar AUS (WA) 102 Qk56
Marble Bar Road AUS 102 Ra56
Marble Canyon USA (AZ) 171 Ee27
Marble Hall ZA 155 Me58
Marble Hill USA (MO) 175 Ff27
Marble Point ANT (USA) 7 Tb34
Marburg D 32 Lj40
Marcabelí EC 196 Ga47
Marcala HN 184 Fg38
Marcali H 42 Ls44
Marcaltő H 42 Ls43
Marčana HR 35 Lo46
Marcapata PE 197 Ge52
Marcapomacocha PE 197 Gb51
Marcelândia BR (MT) 199 Hc51
Marcelino BR (AM) 193 Gg45
Marcelino BR (AM) 198 Gg46
Marcell USA (MN) 172 Fd22
Marcelo BR (PA) 195 He47
March GB 21 La38
Marchagee AUS (WA) 104 Qj61
Marche I 35 Lo47
Marche-en-Famenne B 23 Lf40
Marchena E 27 Kp53
Marchenoir F 24 Lb43
Marchinbar Island AUS 106 Rj51
Marciac F 24 La47
Marcigny F 25 Le44
Marcilla RP 90 Ra39
Marcillac-la-Croisille F 24 Lc45
Marcinkonys LT 39 Me36
Marcinkowice PL 41 Ma41
Marcionílio Sousa BR (BA) 201 Hk52
Marck F 23 Lb40
Marco USA (FL) 179 Fk33
Marco de Canaveses P 26 Km49
Marconi N.H.S. CDN 176 Ha22
Marco Rondon BR (RO) 206 Gk52
Marcos Juárez RA (CD) 209 Gj62
Marcos Parente BR (PI) 200 Hj49
Marcoux USA (MN) 172 Fb22
Marcus Baker, Mount USA (AK) 165 Cg15
Mard Abad IR 57 Nf28
Mardan PK 65 Og28
Mar de Ajó RA (BA) 209 Hb64
Mar de Espanha BR (MG) 203 Hj56
Mar del Plata RA (BA) 209 Hb65
Mardie AUS (WA) 102 Qh56
Mardie Island AUS 102 Qh56
Mardin TR 57 Na27
Mardin Dağları TR 57 Na27
Maré F (NCL) 118 Te56
Mare RI 96 Ra48
Marea del Portillo C 179 Gb36
Mare aux Crocodiles de Dounkou BF 137 Kj39
Mare aux Crocodiles de Sabou BF 137 Kj39
Marechal Cândido Rondon BR (PR) 204 Hc58
Marechal Deodoro BR (AL) 201 Jc50
Maree AUS (SA) 108 Rk60
Mareeba AUS (QLD) 107 Sc54
Mareeq SP 145 Nd44
Maremma I 34 Lm48
Maréna RMM 130 Ke38
Marenge RDC 146 Me48
Marengo USA (IA) 172 Fd25
Marengo Cave USA 175 Fg26
Marennes F 24 Kt45
Marerano RM 157 Nc56
Mareth TN 126 Lf29
Mareuil-sur-Lay F 24 Kt44
Marevo RUS 48 Mg17
Marfa M 37 Lp55
Marfa USA (TX) 181 Eh30
Margao IND (GOA) 82 Og38
Margaree Forks CDN (NS) 176 Gk22
Margaret AUS (QLD) 108 Sb59
Margareteville USA (NY) 177 Gc24
Margaret, Mount AUS 102 Qj57
Margaret River AUS (WA) 104 Qh62
Margarida BR (MS) 202 Hb56
Margarima PNG 115 Sb49
Margaríti GR 46 Ma51
Margaritove RUS 49 Mk22
Margasari RI 95 Qh47
Margate GB 21 Lb39
Margate ZA 155 Mf61
Mărgău RO 43 Mc44
Margecany SK 43 Mb42
Margherita IND (ASM) 86 Ph32
Margherita di Savóia I 37 Lr49
Marghita RO 43 Mc43
Margiana TM 62 Oa26
Marg'ilon UZ 63 Of25
Margone I 34 Lh45
Margonin PL 40 Ls38
Margosatubig RP 91 Rb42
Marguerite CDN (BC) 168 Dj19
Margyang CHN (TIB) 68 Pe31
Marhamat UZ 63 Og25
Marhanec' UA 49 Mh22
Marhoum DZ 125 Kk28
Mari BR (AM) 198 Gh49
Mari PNG 115 Sa50
Mari SYR 57 Na28
Maria BR (PA) 195 Hf46
Maria MOC 153 Mj54
Maria PE 196 Gb49
Maria Aurora RP 90 Ra38
María Elena RCH 207 Gf57
María Eugenia RA (SF) 207 Gk61
Mariager DK 30 Lk34
Mariahan IND (UPH) 83 Pb33
María Ignacia RA (BA) 209 Ha64
Maria Island AUS 106 Rh53
Maria Island N.P. AUS 111 Se67
Mariakani EAK 145 Mk47
Maria Laach D 33 Lh40
Mariala N.P. AUS 109 Sc59
Marialva P 26 Kn50
Maria, Mount GB 210 Ha71
Marian AUS (QLD) 109 Se56
Mariana BOL 206 Gj55
Mariana BR (MG) 203 Hj56
Mariana Islands 100 Sa08
Mariana Trench 100 Sa08
Mariani IND (ASM) 86 Ph32
Marianna USA (AR) 175 Fe28
Marianna USA (FL) 175 Fh30
Mariannelund S 31 Lq33
Mariano I.Loza RA (CR) 204 Ha60
Marianópolis BR (MA) 200 Hh48
Mariánské Lázně CZ 42 Ln41
Mariarano RM 156 Nd53
Maria Saal A 35 Lp44
Maria Teresa ANG 148 Lh50
María Teresa RA (SF) 209 Gk63
Mariazell A 35 Lq43
Ma'rib YE 60 Nc38
Maribo DK 30 Lm36
Maribor SLO 42 Lq44
Maribou Mountains CDN (AB) 167 Eb16
Maricá BR (RJ) 205 Hj57
Maricaban Island RP 90 Ra39
Marical Caceres PE 197 Gc52
Maricao USA (PR) 187 Gg36
Maridi SUD 141 Me43
Marie Byrd Land ANT 6 Ed34
Mariefred S 31 Ls31
Marie-Galante F (GL) 187 Gk38
Mariehamn = Maarianhamina FIN 38 Lu30
Mariel C 179 Fj34
Mari-El RUS 48 Ne17
Marie Louise SY 145 Ng49
Marielyst DK 30 Lm36
Marienberg D 33 Lo40
Mariental NAM 154 Lj58
Mariés GR 45 Me50
Mariestad S 31 Lo32
Marieta YV 193 Gg43
Marietta USA (GA) 175 Fh29
Marietta USA (OH) 175 Fk26
Mariga WAN 138 Lc40
Marigat EAK 144 Mh45
Marignane F 25 Lf47
Marigot F (GL) 187 Gj36
Marigot RH 186 Gd36
Marigot WD 187 Gk38
Marihatag RP 91 Rd41
Marija Bistrica HR 35 Lr44
Marijampolė LT 39 Md36
Marikal IND (APH) 82 Oj37
Marikina RP 90 Ra38
Marília BR (SP) 202 Hf57
Marimba ANG 148 Lj50
Marín E 26 Km48
Marina di Belvedere I 37 Lq51
Marina di Carrara I 34 Ll46
Marina di Cetraro I 37 Lq51
Marina di Grosseto I 34 Ll48
Marina di Léuca I 37 Lt51
Marina di Pisa I 34 Ll47
Marina di Ragusa I 37 Lp54
Marina di Ravenna I 34 Ln46
Marina Plains AUS (QLD) 107 Sb53
Mariñas E 26 Kn47
Marinduque Island RP 90 Ra39
Marine de Sisco F 34 Lk48
Marineland USA (FL) 178 Fk31
Marineland of Florida USA 178 Fk31
Marinella I 36 Ln53
Marineo I 36 Lo53
Mariner Glacier 7 Tb33
Marinette USA (WI) 173 Fg23
Maringá BR (PR) 202 He57
Maringa RDC 140 Ma45
Maringué MOC 153 Mh54
Maringues F 25 Ld45
Marinha Grande P 27 Km51
Marinho de Fernando de Noronha, P.N. BR 201 Jd47
Marinho dos Abrolhos, P.N. BR 203 Ja55
Marinka BG 45 Mh48
Marino de Punta Francés-Punta Pedernales, P.N. C 179 Fj35
Marino de Vallarta, P.N. MEX 182 Eh35
Marino Golfo de Chiriquí, P.N. PA 185 Fj41
Marino Isla Bastimentos, P.N. PA 185 Fk41
Marino Las Baulas, P.N. CR 184 Fh40
Marion USA (AL) 175 Fg29
Marion USA (AR) 175 Fe28
Marion USA (IA) 172 Fe24
Marion USA (IL) 175 Ff27
Marion USA (IN) 173 Fh25
Marion USA (KS) 174 Fb26
Marion USA (KY) 175 Ff27
Marion USA (NC) 178 Fk28
Marion USA (OH) 173 Fj25
Marion USA (SC) 178 Ga28
Marion USA (VA) 178 Fk27
Marion Downs AUS (QLD) 108 Rk57
Maripasoula F (GF) 194 Hd44
Maripipi Island RP 90 Rc40
Mariposa USA (CA) 170 Ea27
Mariposa Monarca MEX 182 Ek36
Mariquita CO 192 Gc43
Marisa RI 91 Ra45
Mariscala ROU 209 Hc63
Mariscal José Félix Estigarribia PY 207 Gk56
Mariscos GCA 184 Ff38
Marita Downs AUS (QLD) 109 Sb57
Maritime Alps F 25 Lg46
Maritime Museum (Geraldton) AUS 104 Qh60
Mariupol' UA 49 Mj22
Mariusa, P.N. YV 193 Gj41
Marivan IR 57 Nd28
Mariveles RP 90 Ra38
Mariveles Reef 94 Qg42
Märjamaa EST 38 Me32
Marka SP 145 Nc45
Markabougou RMM 137 Kg39
Markabygd N 16 Lf14
Markakasa IND (MHT) 83 Pa35
Markakol Nature Reserve KZ 67 Pc21
Markala RMM 137 Kg39
Markapur IND (APH) 83 Ok38
Markaryd S 31 Lo34
Marken ZA 152 Me57
Markermeer NL 23 Lf38
Market Drayton GB 21 Ks38
Market Harborough GB 21 Ku38
Market Rasen GB 21 Ku37
Market Weighton GB 21 Ku37
Markham CDN (ON) 173 Ga24
Markham, Mount 7 Tb35
Markhun PK 80 Oh27
Marki PL 41 Mb38
Markik IND (APH) 82 Ok37
Markit CHN (XUZ) 66 Oj26
Markivka UA 48 Mk21
Markkleeberg D 32 Ln39
Markópoulo GR 45 Md53
Markounda RCA 140 Lj42
Markovo BG 45 Mh47
Markoy BF 131 Kk38
Marks USA (MS) 175 Fe28
Marksewo PL 41 Mb37
Marksville USA (LA) 175 Fe30
Marktheidenfeld D 33 Lk41
Markt Indersdorf D 33 Lm42
Marktoberdorf D 33 Ll43
Marktredwitz D 33 Ln40
Mark Twain Birthplace S.H.S USA 174 Fd26
Mark Twain Boyhood Home & Museum USA 175 Fe26
Mark Twain National Forest USA 175 Fe27
Mark Twain N.W.R. USA 175 Fe26
Mark Twain N.W.R. USA 175 Fe25
Mark Twain S.P. USA 175 Fe26
Markundi SUD 134 Mb40
Markwassie ZA 155 Md59
Marl D 32 Lh39
Marla AUS (SA) 108 Rg59
Marlborough AUS (QLD) 109 Se57
Marlborough GB 21 Kt39
Marlborough GUY 194 Ha42
Marlborough Sounds NZ 113 Th66
Marle F 23 Ld41
Marlin USA (TX) 174 Fb30
Marlinton USA (WV) 175 Fk26
Marl Island PNG 115 Sc46
Marlo AUS (VIC) 111 Se64
Marloth Nature Reserve ZA 154 Ma62
Marlow GB 21 Ku39
Marlow USA (OK) 174 Fb28
Marma S 31 Ls30
Marmande F 24 La46
Marmara TR 45 Mh50
Marmara Adası TR 45 Mh50
Marmaraereglisi TR 45 Mh50
Marmara Gölü TR 47 Mj52
Marmaris TR 47 Mj54
Mármaro GR 47 Mg52
Mar Menor E 29 Ku53
Mármol MEX (SL) 180 Eg34
Marmolada I 34 Lm44
Marmot Island USA 164 Ce16
Marmul OM 61 Nh36
Marnay F 25 Lf43
Marne D 32 Lk37
Marneuli GE 57 Nc25
Marniu IND (ARP) 86 Ph32
Maro TCH 140 Lk41
Maroa YV 193 Gg44
Maroantsetra RM 156 Ne53
Marobi Raghza PK 65 Oe29
Marod IND (CGH) 83 Pa35
Maroda IND (CGH) 83 Pa36
Marofandilia RM 157 Nc56
Maroharatra RM 157 Nd56
Marojejy, P.N.de RM 156 Ne53
Marol 81 Oj28
Marolambo RM 157 Ne56
Maromandia RM 156 Ne53
Maromandia RM 156 Nf53
Maromokotro RM 156 Ne53
Marondera ZW 152 Mf55
Maronga AUS (QLD) 109 Se59
Marongora ZW 152 Me54
Maroni F (GF) 194 Hc43
Maroochydore AUS (QLD) 109 Sg59
Maroona AUS (VIC) 111 Sb64
Maroonah AUS (WA) 102 Qh57
Maropaika RM 157 Nd57
Maros RI 96 Ra48
Maroseranana RM 157 Ne55
Marotandrano RM 156 Ne54
Marotolana RM 156 Ne53
Marotta I 35 Lo47
Maroua CAM 139 Lh40
Marova BR (AM) 198 Gj46
Marovac SCG 44 Mb48
Marovato RM 156 Ne52
Marovato RM 156 Ne53
Marovato RM 157 Nc58
Marovoay RM 156 Nd54
Marowo RI 96 Ra46
Marqadeh Gharbiyeh SYR 57 Na28
Marqua AUS (NT) 108 Rj57
Marquard ZA 155 Md60
Marquelia MEX (GUR) 182 Fa37
Marquesas Islands 11 Cb10
Marquesas Keys USA 179 Fj33
Marquette USA (MI) 173 Fg22
Marquez USA (TX) 174 Fb30
Marquise F 23 Lb40
Marquq SUD 141 Mf41
Marra A.L. AUS 106 Rh53
Marracua MOC 153 Mj54
Marracuene MOC 155 Mg58
Marradi I 34 Lm46
Marradong AUS (WA) 104 Qj62
Marrak KSA 60 Na37
Marrakech MA 125 Kf30
Marrakush MA 125 Kf30
Marrawah AUS (TAS) 111 Sc66
Marrecão BR (AM) 198 Gg49
Marrecas, T.I. BR 204 He58
Marrero USA (LA) 175 Fe31
Marromeu MOC 153 Mh55
Marron AUS (WA) 104 Qh58
Marrupa MOC 147 Mj52
Marsa Alam ET 129 Mh33
Marsa-Ben-Mehidi DZ 125 Kj28
Marsabit EAK 144 Mj44
Marsabit National Reserve EAK 144 Mk44
Marsa Darur SUD 135 Mj36
Marsa Delwein SUD 129 Mj35
Marsala I 36 Ln53
Marsa Matruh ET 128 Md30
Marsa Mubârak ET 129 Mh33
Marsa Salak SUD 135 Mj35
Marsa Shin'ab SUD 129 Mj35
Marsassoum SN 136 Kc39
Maršavicy RUS 39 Mj33
Mars Bay BS 179 Gb34
Marsberg D 32 Lj39
Marsciano I 34 Ln48
Marsden AUS (NSW) 111 Sd62
Marseille F 25 Lf47
Marseille-en-Beauvaisis F 23 Lb41
Marsella CO 192 Gc43
Marsella PE 196 Gc47
Marsga al Burayqah LAR 127 Lk30
Marshall LB 136 Ke42
Marshall USA (AK) 164 Bj15
Marshall USA (AR) 174 Fd28
Marshall USA (MI) 173 Fh24
Marshall USA (MN) 172 Fc23
Marshall USA (MO) 174 Fd26
Marshall USA (NC) 178 Fj28
Marshall USA (TX) 174 Fc29
Marshall Islands 100 Ta08
Marshall Islands 101 Ta08
Marshalltown USA (IA) 172 Fd24
Marshfield USA (MO) 174 Fd27
Marshfield USA (WI) 172 Fe23
Marsh Harbour BS 179 Gb32
Mars Hill USA (ME) 176 Gg22
Marsh Island USA 175 Fe31
Mársico Nuovo I 37 Lq50
Marsoui CDN (QC) 176 Gg21
Märsta S 31 Ls31
Marstal DK 30 Ll36
Marstrand S 30 Lm33
Martaban MYA 88 Pj37
Martap CAM 139 Lg42
Martapura RI 93 Qc48
Martapura RI 95 Qh47
Marte WAN 139 Lg39
Martelange B 23 Lf41
Marten River CDN (ON) 173 Ga22
Martensøya N 16 Ma05
Martfű H 43 Ma43
Mártha GR 47 Mf55
Martha's Vineyard USA 177 Ge25
Martigné-Ferchaud F 22 Kt43
Martigny CH 34 Lh44
Martigues F 25 Lf47
Martil MA 125 Kh28
Martilla FIN 38 Mc30
Martin SK 43 Lt41
Martin USA (SD) 172 Ek24
Martin USA (TN) 175 Ff27
Martina Franca I 37 Ls50
Martinborough NZ 113 Th66
Martinésia BR (MG) 202 Hf55
Martínez de la Torre MEX (VC) 182 Fb35
Martinho Campos BR (MG) 203 Hh55
Martinique F 187 Gk38
Martinique Channel 187 Gk38
Martinópole BR (CE) 201 Hk47
Martinópolis BR (SP) 202 He57
Martinsburg USA (WV) 177 Ga26
Martinšćica HR 35 Lp46
Martin's Drift RB 152 Md57
Martinsicuro I 35 Lo48
Martinsville USA (IN) 175 Fg26
Martinsville USA (VA) 178 Ga27
Martins Well AUS (SA) 108 Rk61
Martna EST 38 Md32
Marton NZ 113 Th66
Martorell E 29 Lb49
Martos E 27 Kr53
Martti FIN 16 Me12
Martuni ARM 57 Nc25
Maru IND (AAN) 88 Pg41
Maru RI 97 Rf49
Maru WAN 138 Ld39
Maruanum BR (AP) 195 He45
Marudá BR (PA) 195 Hg46
Marudi MAL 94 Qh43
Maruf AFG 65 Od30
Marulan AUS (NSW) 111 Se63
Marum, Mount VU 118 Te54
Marungu EAT 146 Mf48
Marungua EAK 144 Mj46
Maru'ura SOL 117 Ta50
Marvanthe Beach IND 84 Oh39
Marvão P 27 Kn51
Marv Dasht IR 64 Ng31
Marve Beach IND 82 Og36
Marvejols F 25 Ld46
Marvell USA (AR) 175 Fe28
Marvik N 30 Lg31
Marvine, Mount USA 171 Ee26
Marvo Lagoon SOL 117 Sk50
Marvyn USA (AL) 175 Fh29
Marwah AFG 64 Ob28
Marwan KSA 60 Nd34
Marwayne CDN (AB) 169 Ee19
Marwick Head GB 20 Kr31
Mary TM 62 Oa27
Maryal Bai SUD 141 Md41
Mary Anne Group AUS 102 Qh56
Mary Anne Passage AUS 102 Qh56
Maryborough AUS (QLD) 109 Sg58
Maryborough AUS (VIC) 111 Sb64
Marydale ZA 154 Mb60
Maryhill USA (WA) 168 Dk23
Mary Kathleen uranium deposit AUS (QLD) 107 Rk56
Maryland USA 177 Gb26
Mary Moffat's Museum ZA 154 Mb60
Maryport GB 20 Kr36
Marystown CDN (NF) 177 Hc22
Marysville USA (CA) 170 Dk26
Marysville USA (KS) 174 Fb26
Marysville USA (OH) 173 Fj25
Maryvale AUS (NT) 108 Rh58
Maryvale AUS (QLD) 107 Sc55
Maryville USA (TN) 178 Fj28
Marzad MNG 70 Qb23
Marzagão BR (GO) 202 Hf54
Marzan Abad IR 57 Nf27
Marzuq LAR 127 Lg33
Masagua GCA 184 Fe38
Masa guara HN 184 Fg38
Masahunga EAT 144 Mg47
Masai-Mbia RDC 148 Lj47
Masai Steppe EAT 147 Mj48
Masaka EAU 144 Mf46
Masaki EAT 147 Mk49
Masalembo besar RI 95 Qh48
Masalembo kecil RI 95 Qh48
Masalima RI 96 Qj48
Masalli AZ 57 Ne26
Masamba RI 96 Ra47
Masan ROK 79 Re28
Masanga RDC 149 Mb46
Masanjor IND (JKD) 83 Pd33
Masapi RI 96 Ra46
Masapun RI 97 Rd49
Masara EAK 144 Mh46
Masasi EAT 147 Mk51
Masaurhi IND (BIH) 83 Pc33
Masawa RI 96 Qk47
Masaya NIC 184 Fg40
Masaya, P.N., Volcán NIC 184 Fg39
Masbate RP 90 Rb39
Masbate RP 90 Rb39
Mascara DZ 125 La28
Mascarene Basin 122 Nb11
Mascarene Islands 157 Nh56
Mascarene Plain 122 Nb12
Mascarene Plateau 9 Nb10
Mascareños MEX (VC) 182 Fb35
Masconi RA (BA) 209 Gk63
Mascota MEX (JLC) 182 Eh35
Mas de las Matas E 29 Ku50
Masegoso de Tajuña E 29 Ks50
Masela RI 97 Re50
Masenberg A 35 Lq43
Maseru LS 155 Md60
Mashabih KSA 58 Mj33
Mašhad IR 62 Oa27
Mashala RDC 149 Mb48
Mashan CHN (GZG) 74 Qe34
Mashar SUD 141 Md41
Mashatu Game Reserve RB 152 Me57
Mashava ZW 152 Mf56
Mashhad IR 62 Nk27
Mashhad IR 62 Oa27
Mashi CHN (HUN) 74 Qf31
Mashi ETH 142 Mh42
Mashike J 77 Sa24
Mashki Chah PK 64 Ob31
Mashonaland East ZW 152 Mf55
Mashonaland Central ZW 152 Mf54
Mashonaland West ZW 152 Me54
Mashra' ar-Raqq SUD 141 Me41
Masia RDC 148 Lj47
Masiaca MEX (SO) 180 Ef32
Masiaka WAL 136 Kd41
Masian RI 114 Rh49
Masigo EAT 146 Mf49
Masi-Manimba RDC 149 Lj48
Masimbu RI 96 Qk46
Masin RI 96 Rb48
Masindi EAU 144 Mf45
Masindi Port EAU 144 Mg45
Masinga Reservoir EAK 144 Mj46
Masingbi WAL 136 Ke41
Masinloc RP 90 Qk38
Masirah OM 61 Nk35
Masirah Channel OM 61 Nk35
Masiri IR 59 Nf30
Masis ARM 57 Nc25
Masisea PE 197 Gc50
Masisi RDC 141 Me46
Masisi ZA 152 Mf57
Masjed-e-Abolfazl IR 64 Nk31
Masjed Negar AFG 65 Oc28
Masjed Soleyman IR 59 Ne30
Masjid Basar RI 92 Pk44
Masjid-e-Jame IR 57 Nc26
Masjid-e-Jame IR 59 Nf29
Masjid-i-Jami (Herat) AFG 64 Ob28
Masjid Zahir MAL 92 Qa42
Maskall BH 184 Ff37
Maskall BH 184 Ff37
Maskana Minaret SYR 56 Mk28
Maski IND (KTK) 82 Oj38
Masku FIN 38 Mc30
Masmak Fort KSA 59 Nd33
Masoala, P.N.d' RM 156 Nf53
Masoarivo RM 157 Nc55
Masokut RI 93 Pk46
Masomeloka RM 157 Ne56
Mason USA (MI) 173 Fh24
Mason USA (TX) 174 Fa30
Mason City USA (IA) 172 Fd24
Masoni RI 97 Rc46
Maspalomas E 124 Kc32
Masparro YV 192 Ge41
Masqat OM 61 Nk34
Masrakh IND (BIH) 83 Pc32
Massa I 34 Ll46
Massaango ANG 148 Lj50
Massachusetts USA 177 Gd24
Massachusetts Bay USA 177 Ge24
Massacre Canyon Mon. USA 174 Ek25
Massada IL 58 Mh30
Massafra I 37 Ls50
Massaguet TCH 139 Lh39
Massakory TCH 139 Lh39
Massala CI 137 Kg42
Massala G 148 Lf47
Massalassef TCH 139 Lj40
Massama WAN 138 Ld39
Massa Maríttima I 34 Ll47
Massamba MOC 152 Mg53
Massambará BR (RS) 204 Hb60
Massangam CAM 139 Lf43
Massango ANG 148 Lh50
Massangena MOC 152 Mg56
Massangulo MOC 153 Mh52
Massano MOC 153 Mh53
Massantola RMM 137 Kg39
Massapê BR (CE) 201 Hk47
Massaranduba BR (SC) 205 Hf59
Massat F 24 Lb48
Massau ANG 148 Lj49
Massawa ER 142 Mk38
Massena USA (NY) 177 Gc23
Massenya TCH 139 Lj40
Masset CDN (BC) 166 Dd18
Masseube F 24 La47
Massey CDN (ON) 173 Fj22
Massiac F 25 Ld45
Massibi ANG 151 Mb51
Massif Central F 25 Ld45
Massif d'Abo TCH 133 Lh35
Massif d' Atafi RN 133 Lh34
Massif de Dahra DZ 126 La27
Massif de l' Adamaoua CAM 139 Lh42
Massif de l'Adrar DZ 132 Ld33
Massif de l'Adrar RIM 130 Ke35
Massif de l' Aurès DZ 126 Ld28
Massif de la Vanoise F 25 Lg45
Massif de l'Esterel F 25 Lg47
Massif de l' Ouarsenis DZ 126 La28
Massif des Bongo RCA 140 Mb41
Massif des Maures F 25 Lg47
Massif de Taghouaji RN 132 Le37
Massif de Tchingou F (NCL) 118 Tc56
Massif de Termit RN 133 Lf37
Massif du Humboldt F (NCL) 118 Td56
Massif du Kapka TCH 134 Ma38
Massif du Manengouba CAM 138 Le43
Massif du Sud ou de la Hotte RH 186 Gc36
Massif du Tamqué RG 136 Kd39
Massif du Yadé RCA 140 Lh42
Massif Tabulaire F 194 Hd44
Massigui RMM 137 Kg40
Massillon USA (OH) 173 Fk25
Massin RP 90 Rb40
Massina RMM 131 Kh38
Massina RMM 131 Kh38
Massinga MOC 153 Mh57
Massingir MOC 152 Mg57
Massosse ANG 150 Lj53
Mastabah KSA 58 Mk35
Masterton NZ 113 Th66
Mastic Beach USA (NY) 177 Gd25
Mastic Point BS 179 Gb33
Masthiári GR 47 Mh54
Mastuj PK 63 Og27
Mastung PK 65 Od31
Masturah KSA 58 Mk34
Masty BY 41 Me37
Masuda J 79 Rf28
Masud Palace AFG 65 Oe29
Masugnsbyn S 16 Mb12
Masuguru EAT 147 Mk51
Masuika RDC 149 Mb49
Mašuki BY 41 Mg38
Masuleh IR 57 Ne27
Masulipatnam IND (APH) 83 Pa37
Masurai, Gunung RI 93 Qa47
Masuria PL 41 Ma37
Masvingo ZW 152 Mf56
Masvingo ZW 152 Mf56
Maswa Game Reserve EAT 144 Mh47
Mata RDC 149 Ma49
Matabaie RDC 149 Mb49
Matabeleland North ZW 152 Md55
Matabeleland South ZW 152 Me56
Matabele Plain Z 151 Mb54
Mata Bia, Gunung TLS 97 Rd50
Matabis ZW 152 Mf56
Mataca MOC 147 Mj52
Matachewan CDN (ON) 173 Fk22
Matacú BOL 206 Gj54
Mata de Palma YV 192 Ge42
Mata de São João BR (BA) 201 Ja52
Matadi RDC 148 Lg48
Mata do Buçaco P 26 Km50
Matador USA (TX) 174 Ek28
Mataga ZW 152 Mf56
Matagalpa NIC 184 Fh39
Matagami CDN (QC) 173 Gb21
Matagorda USA (TX) 181 Fc31
Matagorda USA (TX) 181 Fb31
Matagorda Island USA (TX) 181 Fb31
Matagorda Peninsula USA (TX) 181 Fc31
Matagorda S.P. USA 181 Fc31
Mata Grande BR (AL) 201 Jb50
Mataguá C 179 Fk34
Matai KZ 66 Ok23
Matak RI 92 Qd44
Matakana Island NZ 112 Tj64
Matakaoa Point NZ 112 Tk64
Matakawa NZ 112 Th64
Matakohe NZ 112 Th64
Matala ANG 150 Lh53
Mátala GR 47 Me56
Matalam RP 91 Rc42
Mata Lama EAK 145 Mk44
Matalaque PE 197 Ge54
Matale CL 85 Pa42
Matam SN 130 Kd38
Matamagallanes RA (CB) 210 Gf68
Matamala de Almazán E 28 Ks49
Matamata BR (AM) 198 Gg48
Mata Mata ZA 154 Ma58
Matambo EAT 147 Mj49
Matamey RN 132 Le39
Matamoros MEX (COH) 181 Ej33
Matamoros MEX (TM) 181 Fb33
Mat'an KSA 60 Nb37
Matanana EAT 146 Mh50
Matanao RP 91 Rc42
Ma'tan as Sarah LAR 128 Ma35
Ma'tan Bishrah LAR 128 Mb34
Matanda Z 146 Me51
Matandu EAT 147 Mj50
Matane CDN (QC) 176 Gg21
Mata Negra YV 193 Gj41
Matanga RI 97 Rf46
Matanga RM 157 Nd57
Matanhi PK 65 Of29
Mataniko Falls SOL 117 Ta50
Matankari RN 132 Lc39
Matanuska Glacier USA 165 Cg15
Matanzas C 179 Fk34
Matanzas YV 193 Gj41
Matão BR (SP) 202 Hf56
Mataoleo RI 97 Rb48
Matapédia CDN (QC) 176 Gg22
Matara CL 85 Pa43
Matara ER 142 Mk38
Matará RA (SE) 207 Gj60
Mataraca BR (PB) 201 Jc49
Mataral BOL 206 Gh55
Mataram RI 96 Qj50
Mataranka AUS (NT) 106 Rg53
Mata Redonda MEX (VC) 182 Fb36
Mataró E 29 Lc49
Mata Roma BR (MA) 201 Hj47
Matarombeo Mountains RI 96 Ra47
Matassi EAT 147 Mj49
Matatiele ZA 155 Me61
Mataupa PNG 116 Sf50
Matausu RI 96 Ra48
Mata-Uta F (WF) 101 Ba11
Mataveni CO 193 Gg43
Matawai NZ 113 Tj65
Matây ET 129 Mf31
Matayaya DOM 186 Ge36
Matching Green GB 21 La39
Matechai ANG 150 Ma51
Mated IND (APH) 83 Ok37
Mategua BOL 206 Gj52
Matehuala MEX (SLP) 182 Ek34
Mateiros BR (TO) 200 Hg51
Matélica I 35 Lo47
Matelot TT 187 Gk40
Matema EAT 146 Mh50
Matema MOC 152 Mg53
Matera I 37 Lr50
Matéri DY 137 La40
Mátészalka H 43 Mc43
Matete RDC 141 Md45
Matetsi ZW 151 Mc55
Mateur TN 126 Le27
Matewar RI 114 Rk46
Matha F 24 Ku45
Mathahaw Pt. CDN 168 Dg21
Matheniko Game Reserve EAU 144 Mh44
Matheson CDN (ON) 173 Fk21
Mathews Range EAK 144 Mj45
Mathilde RA (SF) 209 Gk61
Mathis USA (TX) 181 Fb31
Mathiston USA (MS) 175 Ff29
Mathoura AUS (NSW) 111 Sc63
Mathráki GR 46 Lu51
Mathura IND (UPH) 81 Oj32
Mati RP 91 Rd42
Matiakoali BF 137 La39
Matiari PK 65 Oe33
Matías Cardoso BR (MG) 203 Hj53
Matías Olímpio BR (PI) 201 Hj47
Matías Romero MEX (OAX) 183 Fc37
Matibane MOC 153 Na53
Matienzo ANT (RA) 6 Ha32
Matima RB 151 Mc56
Matina CR 185 Fj40
Matinha BR (MA) 195 Hh47
Matinhos BR (PR) 205 Hf58
Matiši LV 39 Mf33
Matisi Shiku CHN 69 Pk26
Matjiesfontein ZA 154 Ma62
Matkasel'kja RUS 38 Ml29
Matkuli IND (MPH) 83 Ok34
Matlapaneng RB 151 Mb55
Matli PK 65 Oe33
Matlock GB 21 Kt37
Matmata RIM 130 Kd36
Matmata TN 126 Le29
Matna SUD 135 Mh39
Matnog RP 90 Rc39
Matobo Hills ZW 152 Me56
Matobo N.P. (Rhodes Matopos N.P.) ZW 152 Me56
Matões BR (MA) 201 Hj48
Mato Grosso BR 191 Ha11
Mato Grosso do Sul BR 191 Ha11
Matola MOC 155 Mg58
Matombo EAT 146 Mh50
Matondo MOC 153 Mh55
Matongo EAT 146 Mh48
Matope MW 153 Mh53
Matopos ZW 152 Me56
Matosinhos P 26 Km49
Matou CHN (JGX) 75 Qh31
Matoury F (GF) 195 Hd43
Mato Verde BR (MG) 203 Hj53
Mátra H 43 Lu43
Matraca CO 193 Gf44
Mátraháza H 43 Lu43
Matras Beach RI 95 Qd46
Matrei A 35 Ln44
Matroosberg ZA 154 Lk62
Matrouha TN 126 Ld29
Matru WAL 136 Kd42
Matrubah LAR 128 Mb29
Matsai ZW 152 Mf56
Matsanga RCB 148 Lg46
Matsari CAM 139 Lg43
Matsieng Footprints RB 155 Mc58
Matsoandakana RM 156 Ne53
Matsue J 79 Rg28
Matsu Lietao RC 75 Ra32
Matsumae J 77 Sa25
Matsumoto J 79 Rj27
Matsu Temple RC 75 Ra34
Matsuyama J 79 Rg29
Matsuzaka J 79 Rj28
Mattamuskeet N.W.R. USA 178 Gb28
Mattawa CDN (ON) 173 Ga22
Matterhorn CH/I 34 Lh45
Matterhorn USA 170 Ec25
Mattersburg A 35 Lr43
Matthews USA (NC) 178 Fk28
Matthews Ridge GUY 194 Gk42
Matthew Town BS 186 Gd35
Mattice CDN (ON) 173 Fj21
Mattighofen A 42 Lo42
Matto J 79 Rj27
Mattoon USA (IL) 175 Ff26
Matu MAL 94 Qf44
Matua RI 95 Qf47
Matucana PE 197 Gb51
Matukar PNG 115 Sc48
Matuku FJI 119 Tk55
Matumbo Z 146 Mg51
Matundu RDC 141 Mb43
Matupá BR (MT) 199 Hc51
Matupi MYA 86 Pg35
Matupika NZ 113 Tg66
Ma'tuq SUD 135 Mg38
Maturín YV 193 Gj41
Matusadona N.P. ZW 152 Me54
Matutuang RI 91 Rc43
Matveev Kurgan RUS 49 Mk22
Maty-Centre RCB 148 Lh47
Matyli BY 41 Me37
Mau IND (MPH) 83 Ok32
Mau IND (MPH) 83 Pa34
Mau IND (UPH) 83 Pa33
Mauá BR (SP) 205 Hg57
Maua EAK 144 Mj45
Maúa MOC 153 Mj52
Mauban RP 90 Ra38
Maubeuge F 23 Ld40
Maubin MYA 88 Ph37
Maubisse TLS 97 Rc50
Maubourguet F 24 La47
Maud USA (TX) 174 Fc29
Maudaha IND (UPH) 83 Pa33
Maude AUS (NSW) 111 Sc63
Maudheimvidda 6 Kc33
Maué ANG 150 Lk54
Maués BR (AM) 199 Hb47
Maugris RIM 130 Kc36
Mauhar IND (UPH) 83 Pa32
Maui USA 170 Cb35
Mauk RI 95 Qd49
Maulamyaing MYA 88 Pj37
Mauléon F 24 Ku44
Mauléon-Licharre F 24 Ku47
Maulipader IND (CGH) 83 Pa36
Maullín RCH 208 Gd66
Maumee USA (OH) 173 Fj25
Maumelle USA (AR) 175 Fd28
Maumere RI 96 Rb50
Maun RB 151 Mb55
Mauna Kea USA 170 Cc36
Maunaloa USA (HI) 170 Cb35
Mauna Loa USA 170 Cc36
Maunath Bhanjan IND (UPH) 83 Pb33
Maunda MOC 147 Mk51
Maun Game Sanctuary RB 151 Mb55
Maungdaw MYA 86 Pg35
Maungmagan Islands MYA 88 Pj38
Maungu EAK 145 Mk47
Maupin USA (OR) 168 Dk23
Maura N 30 Lm30
Mau Ranipur IND (UPH) 83 Ok33
Maurawan IND (UPH) 83 Pa32
Maure-de-Bretagne F 22 Kt43
Maurelle Is. Wilderness USA 166 Dd18
Mauriac F 25 Lc45
Mauriceville USA (TX) 174 Fd30
Mauricie, P.N. de la CDN 176 Gd22
Mauritania 123 Ka08
Mauriti BR (CE) 201 Ja49
Mauritius MS 157 Nj56
Mauritius 123 Nb11
Mauritshuis NL 23 Le38
Mauron F 22 Ks42
Maurs F 24 Lc46
Maury Mts. USA 168 Dk23
Mauterndorf A 35 Lo43
Mauthausen A 42 Lp42
Mauvezin F 24 La47
Mauyama WAN 138 Lb39
Mauzé-sur-le-Mignon F 24 Ku44
Mavengue ANG 150 Lk54
Mavericks USA (CA) 170 Dj27
Mavila PE 206 Gf51
Mavinga ANG 151 Ma53
Mavita MOC 152 Mg55
Mavréli GR 46 Mb51
Mavromáta GR 46 Mb51
Mavroúda GR 45 Md50
Mavrovi Anovi MK 44 Ma49
Mavrovo Nacionalni Park MK 44 Ma49
Mavrovoúni GR 46 Mc51
Mavua Z 151 Mb53
Mávue MOC 152 Mg56
Mavume MOC 152 Mh57
Mawa RDC 141 Md44
Mawa RDC 141 Me44
Mawab RP 91 Rc42
Mawa-Geti RDC 141 Md44
Mawa-Geti RDC 141 Me44
Mawan PNG 115 Sc48
Mawana IND (UPH) 81 Oj31
Mawang CHN (CGQ) 74 Qe31
Mawanga RDC 149 Lj49
Mawangdui Hanmu CHN 75 Qg31
Mawasangka RI 96 Rb48
Mawat IRQ 57 Nc28
Mawayela MOC 152 Mh58
Mawdin MYA 88 Ph38
Mawefan RI 114 Rh47
Mawhun MYA 86 Pj33
Mawkyrwat IND (MGA) 86 Pf33
Mawlu MYA 86 Pj33
Mawqaq KSA 58 Na32
Mawson ANT (AUS) 7 Oa32
Mawson Coast 7 Oa32
Mawson Glacier 7 Sd34
Max USA (ND) 172 Ek22
Maxaas SP 145 Nd43
Maxacali, T.I. BR 203 Hk54
Maxcanú MEX (YT) 183 Fe35
Maxixeni RO 45 Mh45
Máxiño Gómez C 179 Fk34
Maxixe MOC 153 Mh57
Maxwelton AUS (QLD) 107 Sb56
May USA (OK) 174 Fa27
Maya RI 95 Qe46
Maya SUD 135 Mg39
Mayabander IND (AAN) 88 Pg39
Mayaguana Island BS 186 Gd34
Mayagüez USA (PR) 187 Gg36
Mayahi RN 132 Ld39
Mayala RDC 149 Lj48
Mayalama RCB 148 Lg48
Mayama RCB 148 Lh47
Mayamba RDC 148 Lj48
Mayamey IR 62 Nh27
Maya Mts. BH 184 Ff37
Mayang CHN (HUN) 74 Qe32
Mayankwa Z 151 Mb53
Mayannup AUS (WA) 104 Qj62
Mayapán MEX 183 Ff35
Mayarí C 186 Gc35
Mayarí Arriba C 186 Gc35
Mayaro Beach TT 187 Gk40
Maybell USA (CO) 171 Ef25
Maybole GB 20 Kq35
Maych'ew ETH 142 Mk39
Maydena AUS (TAS) 111 Sd67
Maydh SP 143 Nd40
Maydh SP 143 Nd40
May Downs AUS (QLD) 109 Se57
Mayen D 33 Lh40
Mayenne F 22 Ku42
Mayersville USA (MS) 175 Fe29
Mayerthorpe CDN (AB) 169 Ec19
Mayfa'ah YE 60 Nd38
Mayfair CDN (SK) 169 Eg19
Mayfield USA (KY) 175 Ff27
Mayhill USA (NM) 171 Eh29
Mayiladuthurai IND (TNU) 85 Ok40
Mayingzi CHN (HLG) 76 Rc23
Maymont CDN (SK) 169 Eg19
May Myo = Pyin U Lwin MYA 86 Pj34
Maynardville USA (TN) 178 Fj27
Maynas PE 196 Ge47
Mayneside AUS (QLD) 108 Sb57
Mayni IND (MHT) 82 Oh37
Maynooth IRL 19 Ko37
Mayo CDN (YT) 165 Dc14
Mayo THA 89 Qa42
Mayo USA (FL) 178 Fj30
Mayo ZW 152 Mg54
Mayo Belwa WAN 139 Lg41
Mayobozi EAT 146 Mf48
Mayo Butale WAN 139 Lg41
Mayo Chehu WAN 139 Lf41
Mayo Darle CAM 139 Lf42
Mayo Djoi CAM 139 Lh41
Mayo Faran WAN 139 Lg41
Mayo Jarandi WAN 139 Lf42
Mayoko RCB 148 Lg47
Mayombe RCB 148 Lg48
Mayo Ndaga WAN 139 Lf42
Mayo Oulo CAM 139 Lg41
Mayor Buratovich RA (BA) 209 Gj65
Mayorga E 26 Kp48
Mayor Island NZ 112 Tj64
Mayor Villafañe RA (FO) 204 Ha59
Mayototo WAL 136 Ke41
Mayotte F (MYT) 156 Nc52
Mayotte F 156 Nc52
Mayotte F 156 Nc52
Mayoyao RP 90 Ra37
May Pen JA 186 Gb37
Mayraira Point RP 90 Ra36
Mayrhofen A 34 Lm43
May River PNG 115 Sa48
Maysville USA (KY) 175 Fj26
Maysville USA (MO) 172 Fc25
Maytiguid Island RP 90 Qk40
Mayu RI 91 Rd45
Mayuka Z 146 Mf51
Mayumba G 148 Lf47
Mayumba RDC 146 Me49
Mayumba, P.N.de G 148 Lf47
Mayum La CHN 68 Pb30
Mayville USA (ND) 172 Fb22
Maywood USA (NE) 174 Ek25
Maza WAN 139 Lg40
Mazabuka Z 152 Md53
Mazagão BR (AP) 195 He46
Mazagão Velho BR (AP) 195 He46
Mazagón E 27 Ko53
Mazama USA (WA) 168 Dk21
Mazamari PE 197 Gc51
Mazamba MOC 153 Mh55
Mazamet F 24 Lc47
Mazamitla MEX (JLC) 182 Ej36
Mazán PE 196 Gd47
Mazar CHN (XUZ) 68 Oj27
Mazar JOR 58 Mh30
Mazara del Vallo I 36 Ln53
Mazar-e Adschaeb AFG 63 Od27
Mazar-e Sharif AFG 63 Od27
Mazargão BR (MT) 202 Hc53
Mazarredo RA (SC) 210 Gg69
Mazarrón E 29 Kt53
Mazartag CHN (XUZ) 66 Pa26
Mazar Tag CHN 66 Ok26
Mazarwala CHN (XUZ) 68 Oj27
Mazatán MEX (SO) 180 Ee31
Maza tenango GCA 184 Fe38
Mazatlán MEX (SL) 180 Eg34
Mažeikiai LT 39 Mc34
Mazéla CI 137 Kg40
Mazeppa Bay ZA 155 Me62
Mazeras EAK 145 Mk47
Mazıdağı TR 57 Na27
Mazières-en-Gâtine F 24 Ku44
Mazilmāja LV 39 Mb34
Mazirbe LV 39 Mc33
Mazocahui MEX (SO) 180 Ee31
Mazoco MOC 147 Mh51
Mazocruz PE 206 Gf54
Mazombe EAT 147 Mh49
Mazomeno RDC 146 Md48
Mazomora EAT 147 Mk49
Mazong Shan CHN 67 Pj25
Mazoula DZ 126 Ld31
Mazowe ZW 152 Mf54
Mazowsze PL 41 Ma38
Mazrub SUD 134 Me39
Mazsalaca LV 39 Mf33
Mazua MOC 153 Na52
Mazunga ZW 152 Me56
Mazur Miao CHN 75 Qk33
Mazyr BY 48 Me19
Mazza RA (BA) 209 Gj64
Mazzarino I 37 Lp53
Mba CAM 139 Lf42
Mbabane SD 155 Mf59
Mbacha WAN 138 Le42
Mbadjé Akpa RCA 140 Ma42
Mbagne RIM 130 Kd37
Mbahiakro CI 137 Kh42
Mbaïki RCA 140 Lj44
Mbakaou CAM 139 Lg42
Mbako RCA 140 Lh43
Mbala Z 146 Mf50
Mbalabala ZW 152 Me56
Mbalam CAM 139 Lg44
Mbalambala EAK 145 Mk46
Mbale EAU 144 Mh45
Mbali RCA 140 Lj42
Mbali-Iboma RDC 149 Lj47
Mbalizi EAT 146 Mg50
Mbalmayo CAM 139 Lf44
Mbama CAM 139 Lg44
Mbama RCB 148 Lh46
Mbamba Bay EAT 146 Mh51
Mbambanakira SOL 117 Sk50
Mbam Minkom CAM 139 Lf44
Mbandaka RDC 140 Lk45
Mbandjok CAM 139 Lf43
Mbandza RCB 140 Lh45
Mbandza-Ndounga RCB 148 Lh48
Mbane SN 130 Kc37
Mbang CAM 139 Lh44
Mbanga CAM 138 Le43
Mbangala EAT 147 Mj50
Mbanika Island SOL 117 Sk50
M'banza Congo ANG 148 Lh49
M'banza Kongo ANG 148 Lh49
Mbanza-Ngungu RDC 148 Lh48
Mbar SN 130 Kc38
Mbarangandu EAT 147 Mj51
Mbarara EAU 144 Mf46
Mbargué CAM 139 Lg43
Mbarizunga Game Reserve SUD 141 Me43
Mbaswana ZA 155 Mg59
Mbata RCA 140 Lk44
Mbate EAT 147 Mk50
Mbati Z 146 Mf51
Mbatto CI 137 Kh42
Mbatuna SOL 117 Sk50
M'bau MOC 147 Na51
Mbaya RCB 148 Lg47
Mbé CAM 139 Lg42
Mbé RCB 148 Lh47
Mbechokó = Rea CDN 167 Ec14
Mbede EAT 146 Mf49
Mbéloba RCA 140 Ma43
Mbéna RCB 148 Lf48
Mbengué CI 137 Kh40
Mbengwi CAM 138 Lf42
Mbéni COM 156 Nb51
Mberengwa ZW 152 Me56
Mbesuma Ranch Z 146 Mg51
Mbet CAM 139 Lg43
Mbéti = Alayo RCA 140 Mb43
Mbéwe CAM 139 Lg42
Mbeya EAT 146 Mg50
Mbeya Z 146 Mg51
Mbeya, Mount EAT 146 Mg50
Mbiama WAN 138 Ld43
Mbié RCB 148 Lh46
Mbigou G 148 Lf46
Mbinda RCB 148 Lg47
Mbinga EAT 146 Mh51
Mbini GQ 138 Le45
Mbita EAK 144 Mg46
Mbitao CAM 139 Lh42
Mbitom CAM 139 Lg43
Mbiyi RCA 140 Mb42
Mbizi ZW 152 Mf56
Mbizi Mountains EAT 146 Mf50
Mbo CAM 138 Lf42
Mbo RCA 140 Lk41
Mbobo MW 146 Mg52
Mboké CAM 139 Lg43
Mboki RCA 141 Mc43
Mbokonimbeti Island SOL 117 Sk50
Mbomo RCB 140 Lh45
Mbomou RCA 141 Mb43
Mbon RCB 148 Lh47
Mboné RG 136 Ke40
Mbonge CAM 138 Le43
Mboroma Z 152 Me53
Mboro Ndeundekat SN 130 Kb38
Mbouda CAM 138 Lf43
Mboula CAM 139 Lg42
Mboula RCA 140 Lj43
Mbouma CAM 139 Lg44
Mbouna RMM 131 Kj37
Mboune SN 130 Kd38
Mboungou G 148 Lf47
Mbour SN 130 Kb38
Mbout RIM 130 Kd37
Mbozi EAT 146 Mg50
Mbrés RCA 140 Lk42
Mbuba EAT 146 Mf48
Mbudi RDC 148 Lj48
Mbugani EAT 147 Mj49
Mbuji-Mayi RDC 149 Mb49
Mbuli RDC 149 Lk46
Mbulu EAT 144 Mh47
Mburucuyá RA (CR) 204 Ha60
Mburucuyá, P.N. RA 204 Ha59
Mbut EAT 147 Mk50
Mbutu EAT 146 Mg48
Mbuvu EAK 145 Mk46
Mbuyapey PY 204 Hb59
Mbuyuni EAT 147 Mj49
Mbwamji EAT 147 Mk49
Mbwewe EAT 147 Mk49
McAdam N.P. PNG 115 Sd49
McAlester USA (OK) 174 Fc28
Mc Allen USA (TX) 181 Fa32
McArthur USA (OH) 175 Fj26
McArthur Lake CDN 167 Eg15
McBee USA (SC) 178 Fk28
McBride CDN (BC) 168 Dk19
McCall USA (ID) 168 Eb23
Mc Callum CDN (NF) 177 Hb22
McCamey USA (TX) 181 Ej30
McCammon USA (ID) 169 Ed24
McCarthy USA (AK) 165 Cj15
McCauley Island CDN 166 De19
McClellan Ck. Nat. Grassland USA 174 Ek28
McClellanville USA (SC) 178 Ga29
McClintock Channel CDN 162 Ed04
McClintock, Mount 7 Sd34
McClintock Range AUS 103 Rd55
McClure Strait CDN 162 Ea04
Mc Clusky USA (ND) 172 Ek22
McComb USA (MS) 175 Fe30
McConkey Hill AUS 104 Ra58
McConnell Range CDN 167 Dj13
McConnelsburg USA (PA) 177 Ga26
McCook USA (NE) 174 Ek25
McCreary CDN (MB) 172 Fa20
McDermitt USA (OR) 168 Eb24
Mc Donald 9 Ob15
McDonald Observatory USA 181 Eh30
McDonough USA (GA) 175 Fh29
McDouall Peak AUS (SA) 108 Rh60
McDowell Lake CDN 172 Fd19
McDowell River CDN 172 Fd19
Mcensk RUS 48 Mj19
McFaddin N.W.R. USA 174 Fc31
McGee CDN (SK) 169 Ef20
McGill USA (NV) 170 Ec26
McGraw Brook CDN (NB) 176 Gg22
Mc Gregor USA (MN) 172 Fd22
McGregor USA (ND) 169 Ej21
McGregor Range AUS 108 Sb59
McGuire, Mount USA 168 Ec23
Mcherrah DZ 125 Kh32
Mchinga EAT 147 Mk50
Mchinji MW 146 Mg52
M'Chouneche DZ 126 Ld28
Mchungu EAT 147 Mk49
McIllwrath Range AUS 107 Sb52
McIntosh USA (SD) 172 Ek23
McKenzie USA (TN) 175 Ff27
McKenzie Bridge USA (OR) 168 Dj23
McKinlay AUS (QLD) 108 Sa56
McKinley, Mount USA (AK) 165 Ce14
McKinleyville USA (CA) 168 Dh25
McKinney USA (TX) 174 Fb29
McKinney Mtn. USA 181 Ej31
McKittrick USA (CA) 170 Ea28
McLaren Vale AUS (SA) 110 Rk63
McLaughlin USA (SD) 172 Ek23
McLean's Town BS 179 Gb32
McLeod Bay CDN 167 Ee14
McLeod Lake CDN (BC) 166 Dj18
McLeod River CDN 168 Eb19

McLoughlin, Mount ◻ USA 168 Dj24
Mc Minnville ◻ USA (OR) 168 Dj23
McMinnville ◻ USA (TN) 175 Fh28
Mc Murdo ◻ ANT (USA) 7 Tb34
McMurdo Sound ▣ 7 Ta34
McMurray ◻ USA (WA) 168 Dj21
McNary ◻ USA (TX) 171 Eh30
McNeal ◻ USA (AZ) 171 Ee30
McPherson ◻ USA (KS) 174 Fb26
McRae ◻ USA (GA) 178 Fj29
McTavish ◻ CDN (MB) 172 Fb21
Mdandu ◻ EAT 146 Mh50
Mdantsane ◻ ZA 155 Md62
Mdiq ◻ MA 27 Kj45
M'Doukal ◻ DZ 126 Lc28
Mdr ◻ BY 41 Mg37
M'drac ◻ VN 89 Qe39
Mdsagaweyn ◻ SP 145 Nd44
Meacham ◻ CDN (ON) 173 Fh21
Mé Adéo ◻ F (NCL) 118 Tc56
Meade ◻ USA (KS) 174 Ez27
Meade Peak ◻ USA 169 Ee24
Meadji ◻ CI 137 Kg43
Meador Lake ◻ CDN (SK) 169 Ef18
Meadow ◻ AUS 104 Qh59
Meadowbank ◻ AUS (QLD) 107 Sc55
Meadow Creek ◻ CDN (BC) 168 Eb20
Meadow Lake Prov. Park ◻ CDN 169 Ef18
Meadowlands Racetrack ◻ USA (NJ) 177 Gc25
Meadville ◻ USA (MS) 175 Fe30
Meadville ◻ USA (PA) 173 Fk25
Meakan-dake ◻ J 77 Sb24
Meander River ◻ CDN (AB) 167 Eb16
Meane Baba Mausoleum ◻ TM 62 Nk27
Meath Park ◻ CDN (SK) 169 Eh19
Meaux ◻ F 23 Lc42
Mebo, Gunung ◻ RI 114 Rg46
Mebridege ◻ ANG 148 Lh49
Mebsi ◻ RI (BIH) 83 Pc32
Mecanhelas ◻ MOC 153 Mh53
Mecca ◻ KSA 58 Mk35
Mechang ◻ MAL 92 Qe43
Mechara ◻ ETH 142 Na41
Mechcheri ◻ IND (TNU) 84 Oj40
Mechelen ◻ B 23 Le39
Méchéria ◻ DZ 125 Kh29
Mechra-Benâbbou ◻ MA 125 Kg29
Mechra-Ben-Ksiri ◻ MA 125 Kh28
Mechra-Hassi-Boumédienne ◻ DZ 125 Kj30
Mechroha ◻ DZ 126 Lc27
Mecidiye ◻ TR 45 Mg50
Mecito ◻ MOC 153 Mj54
Mecitözü ◻ TR 56 Mh25
Mečka ◻ BG 45 Mf47
Meckering ◻ AUS (WA) 104 Qj61
Mecklenburg I ◻ USA 178 Fk28
Mecklenburgische Seenplatte ◻ D 32 Ln37
Mecklenburg-Vorpommern ◻ D 32 Ln37
Meconta ◻ MOC 153 Mk53
Mecúburi ◻ MOC 153 Mk53
Mecula ◻ MOC 147 Na52
Medak ◻ ◻ IND (APH) 82 Ok36
Medak Church ◻ IND 82 Ok36
Medak Fort ◻ IND 82 Ok37
Medan ◻ RI 92 Pk44
Medang ◻ RI 93 Qa44
Médanos ◻ RA (BA) 209 Gj65
Médanos de Coro, P.N. ◻ YV 193 Gf40
Medaramella ◻ IND (APH) 83 Ok38
Medart ◻ USA (FL) 175 Fh30
Medawachchiya ◻ CL 85 Pa41
Medd Allah ◻ RMM 131 Kh38
Mede ◻ I 34 Lj45
Medeba ◻ DZ 126 Ld27
Medeiros ◻ BR (MG) 203 Hg53
Medeiros Neto ◻ BR (BA) 203 Hk54
Medellín ◻ CO 192 Gc42
Medeltidsbveckan ◻ S 31 Lt33
Medembilk ◻ NL 23 Lf38
Medenine ◻ TN 126 Lf29
Medenyči ◻ UA 43 Md41
Meder ◻ ER 142 Na38
Méderdra ◻ RIM 130 Kc37
Medeu ◻ KZ 66 Oj24
Medford ◻ S 31 Lp32
Medford ◻ USA (OR) 168 Dj24
Medford ◻ USA (WI) 172 Fd23
Medgidia ◻ RO 45 Mj46
Medgyesegyháza ◻ H 43 Mb44
Medhane Alem ◻ ETH 142 Mk43
Medi ◻ SUD 144 Mf43
Media Luna ◻ BA (SL) 208 Gg63
Medianeira ◻ BR (PR) 204 Hc58
Mediaş ◻ RO 43 Me44
Medical Springs ◻ USA (OR) 168 Ea23
Medicina ◻ I 34 Lm46
Medicine Bow ◻ USA (WY) 171 Eg25
Medicine Bow Mts. ◻ USA 171 Eg25
Medicine Hat ◻ CDN (AB) 169 Ee20
Medicine Lake ◻ USA (MT) 169 Eh21
Medicine Lodge ◻ USA (KS) 174 Fa27
Medijana ◻ SCG 44 Mb48
Medina ◻ BR (MG) 203 Hk54
Medina ◻ KSA 58 Mk33
Medina ◻ USA (ND) 172 Fa22
Medina ◻ USA (NY) 173 Ga24
Medina ◻ USA (OH) 173 Fk25
Medinaceli ◻ E 29 Ks49
Medina del Campo ◻ E 26 Kq49
Medina de Pomar ◻ E 28 Kr48
Medina de Ríoseco ◻ E 26 Kp49
Medina Sidonia ◻ E 27 Kp54
Médina-Yorofoula ◻ SN 136 Kc39
Medinet el'Ameriya el Guedida ◻ ET 129 Me30
Medinet el-Faijûm ◻ ET 129 Mf31
Medinet Sahara ◻ ET 129 Mg34
Medininkai ◻ LT 39 Mf36
Medio Rio Negro I, T.I. ◻ BR 198 Gf46
Médiouna ◻ MA 125 Kg29
Mediterranean Sea ◻ 14 La06
Medje ◻ RDC 141 Md44
Medje ◻ RDC 141 Me44
Medjedel ◻ DZ 126 Lb28
Medjedel ◻ DZ 126 Lb28
Medley ◻ CDN (AB) 169 Ee19
Medley ◻ CDN 126 Le27
Medoğorje ◻ BIH 35 Ls46
Meduin ◻ RI 93 Qb45
Meduljin ◻ HR 35 Lo46
Medve ◻ MNE 45 Mf48
Médvedjia ◻ SCG 44 Lu48
Médvedjak ◻ SCG 44 Mb46

Medvenka ◻ RUS 48 Mj20
Medyka ◻ PL 41 Mc41
Medze ◻ LV 39 Ma34
Medžhid tabija ◻ BG 45 Mh46
Medzilaborce ◻ SK 43 Mb41
Meedo ◻ AUS (WA) 104 Qh58
Meekatharra ◻ AUS (WA) 104 Qj59
Meeker ◻ USA (CO) 171 Eg25
Meeladeen ◻ SP 143 Ne40
Meeline ◻ AUS (WA) 104 Qk60
Meemu Atoll ◻ MV 84 Og41
Meenakshi Temple ◻ IND 84 Oj41
Meerane ◻ D 32 Ln40
Meersburg ◻ D 33 Lk43
Meerut ◻ IND (UPH) 81 Oj31
Meeta ◻ CDN 146 Hc43
Mega ◻ ETH 145 Mk44
Mega ◻ IND (ARP) 86 Ph31
Mega ◻ RI 97 Rf46
Mega Escarpment ◻ ETH 144 Mk43
Megáli Panagía ◻ GR 45 Md50
Megáli Stérna ◻ GR 44 Mc49
Mégalithes (Bouar) ◻ RCA 140 Lh43
Mégalithes de Cauria ◻ F 36 Lj49
Megálithic Temples ◻ M 37 Ls55
Megáli Vríssi ◻ GR 44 Mc49
Megalohóri ◻ GR 46 Md53
Mégalo Horio ◻ GR 47 Mh54
Megalópoli ◻ GR 46 Mc53
Megalópoli ◻ GR 46 Mc53
Megáno ◻ RI 97 Rf46
Meganissi ◻ GR 46 Ma52
Mégara ◻ GR 45 Md52
Megasini ◻ IND 83 Pd35
Méga Spíleo ◻ GR 46 Mc52
Meguda ◻ SUD 135 Mf36
Megerčil ◻ MNE 45 Mf48
Megégve ◻ F 25 Lg45
Meghálaya ◻ IND 86 Pf33
Meghrí ◻ ARM 57 Nd28
Mégue ◻ BF 137 Kk39
Méhaignée ◻ DZ 125 La31
Méhana ◻ RN 131 La38
Mehar ◻ PK 65 Od32
Méharry, Mount ◻ AUS 102 Qk57
Méhdavul ◻ IND (UPH) 83 Pb32
Mehadia ◻ RO 43 Mc45
Mehdi Šahr ◻ IR 62 Ng28
Mehelata ◻ RI 97 Re46
Meherpur ◻ BD 86 Pe34
Mehikoorma ◻ EST 39 Mf32
Mehkar ◻ IND (MHT) 82 Oj35
Mehrabpur ◻ PK 65 Od31
Mehran ◻ IR 59 Nd29
Mehran ◻ IR 64 Nh32
Mehrangarh Fort ◻ IND 80 Og32
Mehravan ◻ IND (UPH) 83 Pb33
Mehrgarh ◻ PK 65 Od31
Mehria ◻ DZ 33 Lg41
Mehriz ◻ IR 64 Nh30
Mehur Jhuk ◻ PK 65 Oe28
Méhun-sur-Yèvre ◻ F 25 Lc43
Méia Meia ◻ EAT 147 Mh48
Meicheng ◻ CHN (ZJG) 75 Qk31
Meidougou ◻ CAM 139 Lh42
Meigama ◻ CAM 139 Lh42
Meigu ◻ CHN (SCH) 74 Qb31
Meihekou ◻ CHN (JLN) 76 Rc24
Meiktila ◻ MYA 86 Ph35
Meilen ◻ CH 34 Lk43
Meiners ◻ D 32 Lj38
Meinerzhagen ◻ D 33 Lh40
Meiningen ◻ D 32 Ll40
Meishan ◻ CHN (AHU) 73 Qh30
Meishan ◻ CHN (SCH) 74 Qb30
Meishan Shuiku ◻ CHN 73 Qh30
Meißen ◻ D 32 Lo39
Meißner ◻ D 32 Ll40
Meitan ◻ CHN (GZH) 74 Qd32
Meitingen ◻ D 33 Ll42
Meixian ◻ CHN (SAA) 72 Qd28
Meiyu ◻ CHN (JLN) 71 Ra23
Meiyu ◻ CHN 87 Qa32
Meizhou ◻ CHN (GDG) 75 Qj33
Meizhou Dao ◻ CHN Qk33
Meja Reserve, Gunung ◻ RI 114 Sb61
Mena Murtee ◻ AUS (NSW) 108 Sb61
Menangina ◻ AUS (WA) 104 Ra60
Mena Park ◻ AUS (QLD) 109 Sc58
Menanandra ◻ RM 157 Nc58
Menarbuu ◻ SN 130 Kc37
Menawashei ◻ SUD 134 Mc39
Menchia ◻ TN 126 Le29
Menčul ◻ UA 43 Md42
Mendala ◻ RI 93 Qc47
Mendam ◻ PNG 115 So49
Mendawai ◻ RI 95 Qg46
Mende ◻ F 25 Ld44
Mende ◻ RDC 149 Mc47
Mende ◻ D 32 Ln39
Mendeleevskoe ◻ RUS 48 Nc19
Mendenhall Glacier ◻ USA (AK) 166 Dc16
Méndez ◻ EC 196 Ga47
Méndez ◻ MEX (TM) 181 Fa33
Mendi ◻ ETH 142 Mh41
Mendi ◻ PNG 115 Sb49
Mendiay ◻ BF 137 Kk39
Mendocino Fracture Zone ◻ 11 Ca05
Mendol ◻ RI 93 Qb45
Mendooran ◻ AUS (NSW) 109 Se61
Mendoza ◻ RA (MZ) 208 Gf62

Moqor ◻ AFG 65 Od29
Moquegua ◻ PE 197 Ge54
Moquehuá ◻ RA (BA) 209 Ha63
Mór ◻ H 42 Lt43
Mora ◻ CAM 139 Lh40
Mora ◻ E 27 Km52
Mora ◻ S 17 Lh15
Mora ◻ USA (NM) 171 Eh28
Mora ◻ USA (MN) 172 Fd23
Morača klisura ◻ SCG 44 Lu48
Moradabad ◻ IND (UPH) 81 Ok31
Morada Nova ◻ BR (CE) 201 Ja48
Morada Nova de Minas ◻ BR (MG) 203 Hh55
Mora de Rubielos ◻ E 29 Ha63
Moradlu ◻ IR 57 Ne26
Morado, Cerro ◻ RM 157 Ng64
Morafenobe ◻ RM 157 Nd54
Morag ◻ PL 41 Lu37
Morahalom ◻ H 43 Lu44
Moral ◻ RI 114 Rh49
Moraine St. Park ◻ USA 173 Ga25
Morais de Almeida ◻ BR (PA) Ga25
Morakowo ◻ SCG 44 Lu48
Morakowo ◻ PL 40 Ls38
Móra la Nova ◻ E 29 La49
Moral de Calatrava ◻ E 27 Kr52
Moraleja ◻ E 27 Ko50
Moralitta ◻ RM 157 Ne58
Moramanga ◻ RM 157 Ne55
Moramo Bay ◻ RI 96 Rb48
Moramo Waterfall ◻ RI 96 Rb48
Moran ◻ USA (KS) 174 Fc27
Morangas ◻ RM (MS) 202 Hd55
Moran Junction ◻ USA (WY) 169 Ee24
Morant Cays ◻ JA 186 Gb57
Morar ◻ IND (MPH) 83 Ok32
Morarano Chrome ◻ RM 157 Ne54
Morăreşti ◻ RO 43 Me45
Moratalla ◻ E 29 Kt52
Moratuwa ◻ CL 85 Ok42
Morava ◻ CZ 42 Ls41
Moraviţa ◻ RO 44 Mb45
Morávka ◻ CZ 42 Ls41
Moravská Třebová ◻ CZ 42 Lr41
Moravské Lieskové ◻ SK 42 Ls42
Moravský Beroun ◻ CZ 42 Ls41
Moravský kras ◻ CZ 42 Lr41
Moravský Krumlov ◻ CZ 42 Lr41
Morawhanna ◻ GUY 193 Gk41
Morawica ◻ PL 41 Ma40
Moray Downs ◻ AUS (QLD) 109 Sd56
Moray Firth ◻ GB 20 Kr33
Morbach ◻ D 33 Lh41
Morbanipari, Mount ◻ PNG 115 Sb48
Morbarakeh ◻ IR 59 Nf29
Mörbylånga ◻ S 31 Lr34
Morcego ◻ BR (AM) 198 Gj47
Morcenx ◻ F 24 Ku46
Morchek Khort ◻ IR 59 Ng27
Morcillo ◻ MEX (DGO) 181 Eh33
Morcone ◻ I 37 Lp49
Mordaga ◻ CHN (NMZ) 71 Ra20
Mordelles ◻ F 22 Kt42
Mordogan ◻ TR 47 Mg52
Mordovo ◻ RUS 48 Na19
Mordvinia ◻ RUS 48 Nb18
Mordy ◻ PL 41 Mc38
Morecambe ◻ GB 21 Ks36
Morecambe Bay ◻ GB 21 Ks36
Moreda ◻ E 27 Kr53
Morée ◻ F 22 Lb43
Morehead ◻ PNG 115 Sa50
Morehead ◻ USA (NC)
Morehead City ◻ USA (NC)
Moreilândia ◻ BR (PE) 201 Ja49
Morelia ◻ CDN (PE) 176 Gj22
Morelia ◻ CO 192 Gc45
Morelia ◻ CO 196 Gd46
Morelia ◻ ◻ ◻ MEX (MHC) 182 Ek36
Morella ◻ E 29 La49
Morella ◻ AUS (QLD) 109 Sb57
Morelos ◻ E 29 Ku50
Morelos ◻ MEX (COH) 181 Ek31
Morelos ◻ MEX (SO) 180 Ee31
Morelos ◻ MEX 182 Fa36
Moremi Game Reserve ◻ RB 151 Mb55
Moremi Gorge ◻ RB 152 Md57
Morena ◻ IND (MPH) 83 Oj32
Moreni ◻ RO 45 Mf46
Moresby Island ◻ CDN 166 Dg19
Moreton ◻ AUS (QLD) 107 Sb52
Moreton-in-Marsh ◻ GB 21 Kt39
Moreton Island ◻ AUS 109 Sg59
Moreton Island N.P. ◻ AUS 109 Sg59
Moret-sur-Loing ◻ F 23 Lc42
Moreuil ◻ F 23 Lc41
Morez ◻ F 25 Lg44
Morfou = Güzelyurt ◻ CY 56 Mg28
Morgan ◻ AUS (SA) 110 Rk63
Morgan ◻ USA (UT) 171 Ee25
Morgan City ◻ USA (LA) 175 Fe31
Morganfield ◻ USA (KY) 175 Fg27
Morgan Hill ◻ USA (CA) 170 Dk27
Morganito ◻ YV 193 Gg42
Morganton ◻ USA (NC) 178 Fk28
Morgantown ◻ USA (KY) 175 Fg27
Morgantown ◻ USA (WV) 177 Ga26
Morgan Vale ◻ AUS (SA) 110 Sa62
Morgenzon ◻ ZA 155 Me59
Morges ◻ CH 34 Lg44
Morginis ◻ CH 34 Lg44
Morgongåva ◻ S 31 Lr31
Morghab ◻ RO 43 Md44
Morgram ◻ IND (WBG) 86 Pe33
Morgun-Tajga ◻ RUS 67 Pf20
Morhange ◻ F 23 Lg42
Mori ◻ CHN (XUZ) 67 Pf24
Mori ◻ J 77 Sa24
Moriah, Mount ◻ USA 171 Ec26
Morianal-Plage ◻ F 34 Lk48
Moriarty ◻ USA (NM) 171 Eg28
Morib ◻ MAL 92 Qa44
Moribaya ◻ RG 136 Kf41
Morib Beach ◻ MAL 92 Qa44
Moricetown ◻ CDN (BC) 166 Dg18
Morichal Viejo ◻ CO 192 Ge44
Morigbadougou ◻ CI 136 Kg42
Morija ◻ LS 152 Md60
Morijim ◻ IND 82 Og33
Morin Dawa ◻ CHN (NMZ) 71 Rc21
Morinville ◻ CDN (AB) 169 Ed19
Morioka ◻ J 77 Sa26
Morire ◻ MOC 153 Mh54
Moriskog ◻ S 16 Mb12
Morlaàs ◻ F 24 Ku47
Morlaix ◻ F 22 Kr42

Morley ◻ CDN (AB) 169 Ec20
Mörlunda ◻ S 31 Lq33
Morne-à-l'eau ◻ F (GL) 187 Gk37
Morne Seychellois N.P. ◻ ◻ SY 145 Nh48
Morne Trois Pitons N.P. ◻ ◻ ◻ WD 187 Gk38
Morney ◻ AUS (QLD) 108 Sa58
Mornington ◻ RDC 149 Mc50
Mornington Abyssal Plain ◻ 190 Fa15
Mornington Island ◻ AUS (QLD) 107 Rk54
Mornington Islands A. L. Trust ◻ AUS (QLD) 107 Rk54
Moro ◻ PE 197 Ga50
Moro ◻ PK 65 Od32
Moro ◻ PNG 115 Sd49
Morobe ◻ SUD 144 Mf48
Morococa ◻ I 37 Lo48
Morócne ◻ UA 41 Mf39
Morococala ◻ BOL 206 Gh55
Morocoy ◻ MEX (QTR) 183 Ff36
Morodougou ◻ RG 136 Kf40
Moro Gulf ◻ RP 91 Rb42
Moroleni ◻ RI 114 Rh49
Morombe ◻ RM 157 Nc56
Moromaha ◻ RI 114 Rh49
Morombe ◻ ◻ ◻ RM 157 Nb56
Mórón ◻ C 179 Ga54
Morón ◻ MEX (TM) 182 Fb34
Morón ◻ MNG 70 Qa21
Morón ◻ RA (BA) 209 Ha63
Morona ◻ EC 196 Ga47
Morondava ◻ ◻ ◻ RM 157 Nc56
Mórón de Almazán ◻ E 28 Ks49
Morón de la Frontera ◻ E 27 Kp53
Moroni ◻ ◻ COM 156 Nb51
Moronou ◻ CI 137 Kh42
Morotai ◻ RI 91 Re44
Moroto ◻ EAU 144 Mh44
Moroto, Mount ◻ EAU 144 Mh44
Morouba ◻ RCA 140 Lk41
Morowali Reserve ◻ RI 96 Ra46
Morozovsk ◻ RUS 49 Na21
Morpará ◻ BR (BA) 201 Hj51
Morpeth ◻ GB 21 Kt36
Morphettville Racecourse ◻ AUS (SA) 110 Rk63
Morrelros ◻ BR (PR) 205 Hf58
Morrilton ◻ USA (AR) 174 Fd28
Morrinhos ◻ BR (GO) 202 Hf54
Morris ◻ CDN 172 Fb21
Morris ◻ USA (MN) 172 Fc23
Morristown ◻ USA (TN) 178 Fj27
Morristown ◻ USA (TN) 178 Fj27
Morrito ◻ NIC 185 Fh40
Morro ◻ BR (BA) 201 Hk52
Morro Agudo ◻ BR (SP) 202 Hf56
Morro Bay ◻ USA (CA) 170 Dk28
Morro Branco ◻ BR (PI) 200 Hh50
Morro Branco, T.I. ◻ BR 200 Hg48
Morro Cabeça no Tempo ◻ BR (PI) 200 Hj50
Morro Chico ◻ RCH 210 Ge72
Morrocoy, P.N. ◻ YV 193 Gf40
Morro da Igreja ◻ BR 205 Hf60
Morro de São Paulo = Ilha de Tinharé ◻ BR 201 Ja52
Morro do Chapéu ◻ BR (BA) 201 Hk51
Morro do Padre ◻ BR 203 Hg54
Morro Jable ◻ E 124 Kc31
Morropón ◻ PE 196 Ga48
Morro Redondo ◻ BR (MA) 195 Hh47
Morro Uruçuí ◻ BR (PI) 200 Hg49
Morrow ◻ USA (LA) 175 Fe30
Mörrum ◻ S 31 Lp34
Mouchard Passage ◻ BS 186 Mh27
Moudjéria ◻ ◻ ◻ RIM 130 Kd37
Moudon ◻ CH 34 Lg44
Moudros ◻ GR 47 Mf51
Mouganou ◻ G 148 Lg46
Mougins ◻ F 25 Lg44
Mougna ◻ RMM 137 Kh39
Mouhijärvi ◻ FIN 38 Md29
Mouila ◻ G 148 Lf46
Moukoro aral ◻ KZ 62 Nf23
Moukalaba-Doudou, P.N. de ◻ G 148 Lf47
Moukoundou ◻ G 148 Lf47
Moul ◻ RN 133 Lg38
Moulamein ◻ AUS (NSW) 111 Sc63
Moulay Bouâzza ◻ MA 125 Kg29
Moulay-Bousselham ◻ MA 125 Kg28
Moulay-Idriss ◻ MA 125 Kh28
Mould Bay ◻ CDN 162 Dd03
Mouléngui Binza ◻ G 148 Lf47
Moulhoulé ◻ DJI 143 Nb39
Mouli Gbangba ◻ RCB 140 Lj44
Moulins ◻ F 25 Ld44
Moulmein = Maulamyaing ◻ MYA 88 Pj37
Moulmeingyun ◻ MYA 88 Ph37
Moulton ◻ F 25 Lf29
Moulton ◻ USA (TX) 174 Fb31
Moultrie ◻ USA (GA) 178 Fj30
Mounana ◻ G 148 Lg46
Mound City ◻ USA (KS) 174 Fc26
Mound City ◻ USA (SD) 172 Fa23
Moundou ◻ TCH 140 Lj41
Moundville ◻ USA (AL) 175 Fg29
Moundville Archaeological Park ◻ USA 175 Fg29
Moungoundou-Sud ◻ RCB 148 Lg45
Moung Russei ◻ K 89 Qb39
Mount Abbot ◻ AUS 107 Sd56
Mount Aborlan ◻ RP 91 Qk41
Mount Abu ◻ IND (RJT) 82 Og33
Mount Abu = Guru Shikhar ◻ IND 82 Og33
Mount Abu Wildlife Sanctuary ◻ IND 82 Og33
Mount Adams ◻ USA 168 Dk22
Mount Airy ◻ USA (NC)
Mount Ajax ◻ NZ 113 Tg67
Mount Albert Edward ◻ PNG 115 Sd50
Mount Alfred ◻ AUS (QLD) 109 Sc59
Mount Alma ◻ AUS (QLD) 109 Sf58
Mount Amara ◻ ETH 142 Mj43
Mount Amara ◻ AUS (WA) 103 Rd55
Mount Amungwiwa ◻ PNG 115 Sd49
Mount Anglem ◻ NZ 113 Td69
Mount Anne ◻ AUS 111 Sd67
Mount Aoraki ◻ NZ 113 Tf67
Mount Arkell ◻ CDN 166 Dc15
Mount Arlington Heights ◻ CDN (NF) 177 Hd22

Mosjøen ◻ N 16 Lg13
Moskenesøya ◻ N 16 Lg12
Moskva ◻ ◻ ◻ RUS 48 Mj18
Moskva ◻ ◻ ◻ ◻ ◻ RUS 48 Mj18
Moslavačka Podravska ◻ HR 35 Ls45
Mosnes ◻ RB 152 Md57
Mosoka ◻ USA 169 Mc58
Mosonmagyaróvár ◻ H 42 Ls43
Mosopa ◻ RB 152 Mc58
Mosqueiro ◻ BR (PA) 195 Hf46
Mosquera ◻ CO 192 Ga44
Mosquera ◻ CO 196 Ga46
Mosquitia ◻ HN 185 Fh38
Mosquito ◻ BR (TO) 200 Hg49
Mosquito ◻ PY 207 Ha57
Mosquito River ◻ USA 165 Cj13
Mossaka ◻ RCB 148 Lj45
Moss Bluff ◻ USA (LA) 174 Mb63
Mossendjo ◻ RCB 148 Lg47
Mossel Bay ◻ ◻ ◻ ZA 154 Mb63
Mossel Bay ◻ ZA 154 Mb63
Moss Hill ◻ USA (TX) 174 Fc30
Moss Landing ◻ USA (CA) 170 Dk27
Mossman ◻ AUS (QLD) 107 Sc54
Mossoró ◻ BR (RN) 201 Jb48
Mossurif ◻ MOC 153 Nb53
Moss Vale ◻ AUS (NSW) 111 Sf63
Mostaganem ◻ DZ 125 La28
Mostar ◻ ◻ ◻ BIH 35 Ls47
Mostardas ◻ BR (RS) 204 He61
Mosteiro da Batalha ◻ ◻ P 27 Km51
Mosteiro de Alcobaça ◻ ◻ P 27 Kl51
Mosteiro dos Jerónimos ◻ ◻ P 27 Ki52
Mosteiros ◻ CV 136 Jh38
Mosteiros ◻ ◻ BG 45 Mf47
Móstoles ◻ E 27 Kr51
Mosty ◻ PL 41 Md39
Mostys'ka ◻ UA 43 Md41
Mota del Cuervo ◻ E 29 Ks51
Mota del Marqués ◻ E 26 Kp49
Mota Guasanos ◻ RA (SJ) 208 Gf61
Motaba ◻ RI 96 Rb48
Motala ◻ BY 41 Mf38
Motala ◻ S 31 Lq32
Mota Lava ◻ VU 118 Td52
Moteros ◻ RA (CD) 209 Gk61
Moth ◻ IND (UPH) 83 Ok33
Motherwell ◻ GB 20 Kq35
Motihari ◻ IND (BIH) 83 Pc32
Motilla del Palancar ◻ E 29 Kt51
Motinala ◻ IND (MPH) 83 Pa34
Motihabaneng ◻ RB 152 Me56
Motloutse Ruins RB ◻ RB 152 Me57
Motobu ◻ J 79 Rd32
Motoke ◻ RB 154 Mb58
Motozintla de Mendoza ◻ MEX (CHP) 183 Fd38
Motril ◻ E 27 Kr54
Motru ◻ RO 44 Mc46
Mott ◻ USA (ND) 169 Ej22
Mottgudlam ◻ IND (CGH) 83 Pb35
Motueka ◻ NZ 113 Tg66
Motuhora Island ◻ NZ 112 Tj64
Motul ◻ MEX (YT) 183 Ff35
Motu One ◻ F (PYF) 10 Ca11
Motupe ◻ PE 196 Ga49
Motupena Point ◻ PNG 117 Sh49
Motygino ◻ RUS 54 Pe07
Mouahani ◻ COM 156 Nb52
Moučačd? ◻ BY 41 Mf37
Mouchoirbank ◻ 186 Gb55
Mouchard Passage ◻ USA 164 Cb17
Mount Chigmagak ◻ USA 164 Cb17
Mount Chilalo ◻ ETH 142 Mk44
Mount Clara ◻ NZ 113 Tg67
Mount Clark ◻ CDN 167 Dh13
Mount Clemens ◻ USA 173 Fj24
Mount Columbia ◻ CDN 168 Eb19
Mount Connor ◻ AUS 103 Rd53
Mount Cook ◻ AUS 104 Qk62
Mount Cook ◻ AUS 106 Ck15
Mount Cook ◻ NZ 113 Tf67
Mount Cook = Mount Aoraki ◻ NZ 113 Tf67
Mount Coolon ◻ AUS (QLD) 109 Sd56
Mount Cornish ◻ AUS 103 Rd56
Mount Crysdale ◻ CDN 166 Dj17
Mount Currie Ind. Res. ◻ CDN 168 Dg20
Mount Dalrymple ◻ AUS 109 Se56
Mount Dana ◻ USA 164 Bk18
Mount Darwin ◻ ZW 152 Mf54
Mount Davis ◻ USA 176 Ga26
Mount Deering ◻ AUS 103 Re58
Mount Denison ◻ AUS (NT) 103 Rg57
Mount Desert Island ◻ USA 177 Ge24
Mount Djebobo ◻ GH/TG
Mount Dockrell ◻ AUS (QLD) 103 Rd55
Mount Dora ◻ USA (FL) 178 Fk31
Mount Douglas ◻ AUS (QLD) 109 Sd56
Mount Douglas ◻ USA (AK) 164 Cd16
Mount Downton ◻ CDN 166 Dh19
Mount Draper ◻ USA (AK) 165 Dd16
Mount Dremsel ◻ PNG 116 Sd47
Mount Ebenezer Roadhouse ◻ AUS (NT) 103 Rg58
Mount Edith ◻ AUS 102 Ra56
Mount Edith ◻ AUS 103 Rc54
Mount Eduni ◻ CDN 166 Df13
Mount Edward ◻ AUS 103 Rf57
Mount Edward ◻ AUS 103 Rf57
Mount Edziza Prov. Park ◻ ◻ CDN 166 De17
Mount Elbert ◻ USA (CO) 171 Eg26
Mount Elgon N.P. ◻ ◻ EAU/EAK 144 Mh45
Mount Ellen ◻ USA 171 Ee26
Mount Elliott ◻ AUS 107 Sd55
Mount Elsie ◻ USA (ID) 168 Ec22
Mount Elvire ◻ AUS 102 Qj56
Mount Enterprise ◻ USA (TX) 174 Fc30
Mount Erebus ◻ 7 Tc34
Mount Essendon ◻ AUS 104 Ra58
Mount Etna Caves N.P. ◻ ◻ AUS 109 Sf57
Mount Everest ◻ ◻ ◻ NEP/CHN 81 Pd31
Mount Fairweather ◻ CDN 165 Da16
Mount Farnham ◻ CDN 168 Eb20
Mount Farquharson ◻ AUS 106 Rf54

Mount Field N.P. ◻ ◻ ◻ AUS 111 Sd67
Mount Fletcher ◻ ZA 155 Me61
Mount Frakes ◻ 6 Ea34
Mount Frankland N.P. ◻ AUS 104 Qj63
Mount Fraser ◻ AUS (WA) 104 Ra56
Mount Frederick A.L. ◻ AUS 103 Re55
Mount Frederick No2 A.L. ◻ AUS 103 Re56
Mount Freeling ◻ AUS (SA) 108 Rk60
Mount Frere ◻ ZA 155 Me61
Mount Fridtjof Nansen ◻ 6 Bd36
Mount Gambier ◻ AUS (SA) 110 Sa64
Mount Garnet ◻ AUS (QLD) 107 Sc54
Mount Gede-Pangrango N.P. ◻ ◻ RI 95 Qd43
Mount Gelia ◻ AUS (WA) 105 Rb60
Mount Markham ◻ 7 Tc35
Mount Spokane S.P. ◻ USA 168 Ea22
Mount Geureudong ◻ RI 92 Pj43
Mount Gilruth ◻ AUS 106 Rg52
Mount Goura ◻ WAN 138 Le40
Mount Godwin Austen ◻ PK 81 Oj38
Mount Gordon ◻ AUS 104 Ra62
Mount Gordon ◻ AUS 104 Qj58
Mount Guraghe ◻ ETH 142 Mj44
Mount Hack ◻ AUS 108 Rk61
Mount Hagen ◻ PNG 115 Sc48
Mount Hagen Show ◻ PNG 115 Sc48
Mount Hale ◻ AUS (WA) 104 Qk57
Mount Hale ◻ AUS (WA) 104 Qh58
Mount Hanang ◻ EAT 146 Mh48
Mount Hann ◻ AUS 103 Rc53
Mount Harper ◻ AUS (AK) 165 Cj13
Mount Harris ◻ AUS 103 Re58
Mount Hart ◻ AUS 103 Rc54
Mount Hayes ◻ USA (AK) 165 Cg14
Mount Hebron ◻ USA (CA) 168 Dk25
Mount Hermon ◻ RL 56 Mh29
Mount Hickman ◻ CDN 166 De17
Mount Hinkley ◻ AUS 105 Rb59
Mount Hollister ◻ AUS 102 Qg57
Mount Hood ◻ USA 168 Dk23
Mount Hope ◻ AUS (NSW) 111 Sc62
Mount Hope ◻ AUS (SA) 110 Rh63
Mount Hopeless ◻ AUS (SA) 108 Rk60
Mount House ◻ AUS (WA) 103 Rc54
Mount Howe ◻ 6 Ca36
Mount Howitt ◻ AUS 108 Sb59
Mount Howship ◻ AUS 106 Rb58
Mount Hubbard ◻ CDN 166 Da15
Mount Hutt ◻ NZ 113 Tf67
Mount Hutton ◻ AUS (QLD)
Mount Huxley ◻ NZ 113 Te68
Mount Huxley ◻ AUS 166 Ck15
Mount Ida ◻ AUS (WA) 104 Ra60
Mount Ida ◻ USA (AR) 174 Fd29
Mount Illbillee ◻ AUS 105 Rg59
Mount Ive ◻ AUS (SA) 110 Rj62
Mount Jackson ◻ 6 Gd33
Mount Jackson ◻ AUS 104 Qk61
Mount Jacques Cartier ◻ CDN 176 Gh21
Mount James A.L. ◻ AUS 104 Qj58
Mount Jefferson ◻ USA 168 Dk23
Mount Jefferson ◻ USA 170 Ec26
Mount Joffre ◻ CDN 168 Ec20
Mount Joyce ◻ 7 Sd34
Mount Junction ◻ AUS 103 Rd56
Mount Kadam ◻ EAU 144 Mh45
Mount Kagora ◻ WAN 138 Le41
Mount Kaichui ◻ AUS 157 Ta50
Mount Kaimanawa ◻ NZ 109 Sf61
Mount Kalourat ◻ AUS 109 Sf61
Mount Karimui ◻ PNG 115 Sc49
Mount Karissimbi ◻ PNG 115 Sc49
Mount Katma ◻ EAU 164 Cc16
Mount Kaye ◻ AUS 111 Sd67
Mount Keith ◻ AUS (WA)
Mount Kenya ◻ NZ 113 Tg66
Mount Kenya ◻ ◻ ◻ EAK 144 Mj46
Mount Kenya N.P. ◻ ◻ EAK 144 Mj46
Mount Kilal ◻ EAK 144 Mj44
Mount Kimball ◻ USA (AK) 165 Cj14
Mount Kirkpatrick ◻ 7 Tb35
Mount Klotz ◻ CDN (YT) 165 Da13
Mount Kosciuszko ◻ AUS 111 Se64
Mount Kuniwigasi ◻ PNG 115 Sa48
Mount Labo ◻ RP 90 Rb39
Mount Lacy ◻ AUS 103 Rc54
Mount Lambell ◻ AUS 106 Rg53
Mount Lamington ◻ AUS
Mount Larcom ◻ AUS (QLD) 109 Sf57
Mount Lawrence Wells ◻ AUS 104 Ra59
Mount Lebanon RL 56 Mh29 ◻ ◻ 178 Fk27
Mount Leichhardt ◻ AUS 103 Rg56
Mount Leinster ◻ IRL 19 Ko37
Mount Leisler ◻ AUS 103 Re57
Mount Lesueur ◻ AUS (WA)
Mount Lewis ◻ AUS (NSW)
Mount Liebig ◻ AUS 103 Rf57
Mount Lister ◻ 7 Ta34
Mount Lofty Ranges ◻ AUS 110 Rk63
Mount Longdon ◻ NZ 113 Tg67
Mount Longenot N.P. ◻ ◻ EAK 177 Ha21
Mount Luke ◻ AUS 104 Qj59
Mount Lulworth ◻ AUS 104 Qh59
Mount Lyall ◻ NZ 113 Td69
Mount Lyndhurst ◻ AUS (SA) 108 Rk61

Mount Ma'an ◻ CHN 87 Pk33
Mount Macdonald ◻ AUS 104 Te54
Mount Madley ◻ AUS 103 Rb58
Mount Magnet ◻ AUS (WA) 104 Qk62
Mount Mago ◻ ETH 144 Mj43
Mount Maiden ◻ AUS 104 Rb59
Mount Maiguodo ◻ ETH 142 Mj42
Mount Maitabi ◻ SOL 117 Sd34
Mount Malindang ◻ RP 91 Rb41
Mount Mandara Range ◻ AUS 104 Qk60
Mount Mantalingajan ◻ RP 94 Qj41
Mount Marcus Baker ◻ USA (AK) 165 Cg14
Mount Margaret ◻ AUS (WA) 105 Rb60
Mount Maria ◻ GB 210 Ha71
Mount Markham ◻ 7 Tc35
Mount Marum ◻ VU 118 Te54
Mount Marvine ◻ USA 171 Ee26
Mount Maugeanui ◻ NZ 112 Tj64
Mount Mbeya ◻ EAT 146 Mg50
Mount McClintock ◻ 7 Sd34
Mount McGuire ◻ USA (ID) 168 Ec23
Mount McKinley ◻ USA (AK) 165 Ce14
Mount McLoughlin ◻ USA
Mount Meharry ◻ AUS 102 Qk57
Mount Mellick ◻ IRL 19 Kn37
Mount Mengam ◻ PNG 115 Sb48
Mount Menzies ◻ 7 Oa33
Mount Meru ◻ EAT 144 Mj47
Mount Michael ◻ PNG 115 Sc49
Mount Miller ◻ USA 166 Cj15
Mount Milton ◻ 7 Tb35
Mount Minto ◻ 7 Tc33
Mount Misery ◻ NZ 113 Tf67
Mount Mitchell ◻ USA 178 Fj28
Mount Molloy ◻ AUS (QLD) 107 Sc54
Mount Mooros ◻ LS 155 Me61
Mount Morbanipari ◻ PNG 115 Sb48
Mount Morgan ◻ AUS (QLD) 109 Sf57
Mount Moriah ◻ USA 171 Ec26
Mount Moroto ◻ EAU 144 Mh44
Mount Morris ◻ AUS 105 Rf59
Mount Moses ◻ AUS 170 Eb25
Mount Mulgrave ◻ AUS (QLD) 107 Sb54
Mount Mulligan ◻ AUS (QLD) 107 Sc54
Mount Mulya ◻ AUS (NSW)
Mount Murchison ◻ NZ 113 Tf67
Mount Mye ◻ CDN 166 Dd14
Mount Nasi ◻ EAT 146 Mj49
Mount Nebo ◻ JOR 58 Mh30
Mount Nicholson ◻ AUS 103 Rc54
Mount Norman ◻ AUS 105 Rf59
Mount Northampton ◻ 7 Tb33
Mount Nott ◻ AUS 110 Rb62
Mount Okora ◻ WAN 138 Ld42
Mount Olga ◻ AUS 105 Rf59
Mount Olive ◻ USA (NC) 178 Ga28
Mount Olympus ◻ USA 168 Dj22
Mount Opémiska ◻ CDN 176 Gc20
Mount Oratia ◻ AUS 164 Bk16
Mount Ord ◻ AUS 103 Rc54
Mount Ossa ◻ AUS (TAS) 111 Sd66
Mount Padbury ◻ AUS 104 Ra58
Mount Palgrave ◻ AUS 102 Qk57
Mount Panshan ◻ CHN 73 Qj25
Mount Parker ◻ AUS 103 Rc54
Mount Patterson ◻ CDN 165 Dc13
Mount Patullo ◻ CDN 166 Df17
Mount Pearl ◻ CDN (NF) 177 Hd22
Mount Penot ◻ VU 118 Td54
Mount Perry ◻ AUS (QLD) 109 Sf59
Mount Petras ◻ 6 Da34
Mount Peuetsagoe ◻ RI 92 Ph43
Mount Peulik ◻ USA 164 Cb17
Mount Pfizner ◻ AUS 108 Sa60
Mount Pinapan ◻ RI 93 Qk49
Mount Pinatubo ◻ RP 90 Ra38
Mount Pleasant ◻ AUS 111 Sb66
Mount Pleasant ◻ USA (MI) 173 Fh24
Mount Pleasant ◻ USA (SC)
Mount Pleasant ◻ USA (TX)
Mount Plummer ◻ USA 164 Ca15
Mount Popa ◻ MYA 86 Ph35
Mount Popomanaseu ◻ SOL 117 Ta50
Mount Pulog ◻ RP 90 Ra37
Mount Pye ◻ NZ 113 Te69
Mount Queen Bess ◻ CDN 168 Dh20
Mount Ragang ◻ RP 91 Rc42
Mount Rainier N.P. ◻ ◻ USA 168 Dk22
Mount Ramelau ◻ TLS 97 Rc50
Mount Ranal ◻ RI 94 Qe43
Mount Ratz ◻ CDN 166 Dd17
Mount Rebecca ◻ AUS (WA) 104 Qh58
Mount Remarkable ◻ AUS 111 Se64
Mount Remarkable ◻ AUS 110 Rk62
Mount Remarkable N.P. ◻ ◻ AUS 110 Rk63
Mount Revelstoke N.P. ◻ ◻ CDN 168 Eb20
Mount Robe ◻ AUS 108 Sa61
Mount Robinson ◻ AUS 102 Qk57
Mount Robson ◻ CDN 168 Ea19
Mount Robson Prov. Park ◻ ◻ CDN 168 Ea19
Mount Rogers ◻ USA 178 Fk27
Mount Roosevelt ◻ CDN 166 De16
Mount Roraima ◻ GUY/YV 193 Gj43
Mount Ruapehu ◻ NZ 113 Th65
Mount Rungwe ◻ EAT 146 Mh50
Mount Ruogao ◻ ◻ ◻ CHN 72 Qe27
Mount Rushmore Nat. Memorial ◻ USA 169 Ej24
Mount Russell ◻ USA (AK) 165 Ce14
Mount Ryan ◻ AUS 111 Sd67
Mount Sage N.P. ◻ ◻ GB 187 Gk38
Mount Saint Helens Nat. Volcanic Mon. ◻ USA 168 Dj22
Mount Salisbury ◻ USA (AK)
Mount Sandiman ◻ AUS (WA)

Mount Sandiman ◻ AUS 104 Qh58
Mount Macdonald ◻ AUS 104 Te54
Mount Sanford ◻ USA (AK) 165 Ch14
Mount Sankanbiaiwa ◻ WAL 136 Ke41
Mount Sarari ◻ SOL 117 Sk50
Mount Saunders ◻ 7 Tb36
Mount Seelig ◻ 6 Ed35
Mount Selinda ◻ ZW 152 Mg56
Mount Selous ◻ CDN 166 Dd14
Mount Sembuang ◻ RI 92 Pj43
Mount Shasta ◻ USA 168 Dj25
Mount Sicapoo ◻ RP 90 Ra37
Mount Sidley ◻ 6 Dc34
Mount Siple ◻ 6 Cc33
Mount Sir James MacBrien ◻ CDN 166 Dg14
Mount Skinner ◻ AUS (NT)
Mount Somers ◻ NZ 113 Tf67
Mount Spokane S.P. ◻ USA 168 Ea22
Mount Stanley ◻ EAU/RDC 144 Me45
Mount Steele ◻ CDN 166 Ck15
Mount Sterling ◻ USA (IL) 175 Fe26
Mount Sterling ◻ USA (OH) 173 Fj26
Mount Sterling ◻ USA (OH) 173 Fj26
Mount Stevens ◻ NZ 113 Tg66
Mount Stewart ◻ AUS 103 Re57
Mount Stewart ◻ CDN 165 Da14
Mount Stewart ◻ CDN 176 Gh21
Mount Stinear ◻ 7 Ob33
Mount Strong ◻ PNG 115 Sd49
Mount Stuart ◻ AUS (WA)
Mount Sturgeon ◻ AUS (QLD) 107 Sc56
Mount Suckling ◻ PNG 116 Se50
Mount Sulen ◻ PNG 115 Sb47
Mount Sullivan ◻ AUS 106 Rf55
Mount Surprise ◻ AUS (QLD) 107 Sc55
Mount Tabletop ◻ AUS 109 Sd57
Mount Takahe ◻ 6 Eb34
Mount Taknan ◻ PNG 117 Sh49
Mount Taranaki ◻ NZ 113 Th65
Mount Tawani ◻ VU 118 Te54
Mount Thuillier ◻ IND 88 Pg42
Mount Tipton ◻ USA 170 Ec28
Mount Tip Tree ◻ AUS (QLD)
Mount Tobin ◻ USA 170 Eb25
Mount Tom White ◻ USA 165 Cj15
Mount Tops ◻ AUS 108 Rg56
Mount Trumbull ◻ USA 171 Ed27
Mount Tutoko ◻ NZ 113 Te68
Mount Ulbarnep ◻ PNG 115 Sb47
Mount Unbunmarco ◻ AUS 105 Sa57
Mount Vanguni ◻ SOL 117 Sj50
Mount Vernon ◻ AUS (WA) 104 Qk58
Mount Vernon ◻ USA (AL) 175 Ff30
Mount Vernon ◻ USA (IL) 175 Ff26
Mount Vernon ◻ USA (KY) 175 Fj27
Mount Vernon ◻ USA (MO) 174 Fd27
Mount Vernon ◻ USA (OH) 173 Fj25
Mount Vernon ◻ USA (OR) 168 Ea23
Mount Vernon ◻ USA (WA) 168 Dj21
Mount Victor ◻ 7 Mc33
Mount Victoria ◻ AUS 107 Sd55
Mount Victoria ◻ PNG 115 Sd50
Mount Victory ◻ PNG 116 Se50
Mount Waddington ◻ CDN 168 Dh20
Mount Walton ◻ AUS 104 Qk61
Mount Warning ◻ AUS 109 Sg60
Mount Washington ◻ USA (KY) 175 Fh26
Mount Wechecha ◻ ETH 142 Mk41
Mount Wedge ◻ AUS 110 Rg62
Mount Wells ◻ AUS 103 Rd54
Mount Wharton ◻ AUS 7 Ta35
Mount Whitney ◻ USA 170 Ea27
Mount Wilhelm ◻ PNG 115 Sc48
Mount Will ◻ CDN 166 Df17
Mount Willoughby ◻ AUS 108 Rh59
Mount William ◻ AUS 111 Sb64
Mount William N.P. ◻ ◻ AUS 111 Se66
Mount Willoughby ◻ AUS 108 Rh59
Mount Wilson ◻ CDN 166 Df14
Mount Windsor ◻ AUS (QLD)
Mount Wittenoom ◻ AUS (WA) 104 Qh59
Mount Wood ◻ AUS 169 Ee23
Mount Woodroffe ◻ AUS 105 Rf59
Mount Yawatoutou ◻ GH/TG 141 Mk41
Mount Yoma ◻ THA 87 Pb36
Mowie World ◻ AUS 109 Sg59
Mount Zeil ◻ AUS 103 Rg57

Mouzarak ◻ TCH 133 Lh39
Mouzon ◻ F 23 Lf41
Movie World ◻ AUS 109 Sg59
Movila Miresii ◻ RO 45 Mh45
Moviliţa ◻ RO 45 Mg44
Mowanjum A.L. ◻ AUS (WA) 102 Rb54
Mowjun A.L. ◻ AUS 102 Rb54
Moxey ◻ GUY 194 Ha43
Moya ◻ COM 156 Nc52
Moyale ◻ EAK 145 Mk44
Moyale ◻ ETH 145 Mk44
Moyen Atlas ◻ MA 125 Kh29
Moyen Sido ◻ RCA 140 Lk41
Moyenne Sido ◻ RCA 140 Lk41
Mo Yindu ◻ PE 196 Gb49
Mo'ynoq ◻ UZ 62 Nk24
Moyo ◻ EAU 144 Mf44
Moyo ◻ RI 96 Qj50
Moyobamba ◻ PE 196 Gb49
Moyowaosi Game Reserve ◻ EAT 146 Mf48
Moyto ◻ TCH 139 Lj39
Moyu ◻ CHN (XUZ) 68 Oc37
Moyuela ◻ E 29 Ku49
Mozáceni ◻ RO 45 Mf46
Mozaffar Abad-e Kur Gol ◻ IR 57 Nf28
Možajsk ◻ RUS 48 Mj18
Mozambique ◻ 123 Mb11
Mozambique Basin ◻ 122 Mb12
Mozambique Channel ◻ 122 Nb12
Mozambique Plateau ◻ 122 Mb11
Mozambique Ridge ◻ 122 Mb13
Mozdok ◻ RUS (SOA) 57 Nc24
Mozie ◻ IR 62 Od27
Mozie ◻ 36 Ln53
Mozirje ◻ SLO 42 Lp44
Mozogo-Gokoro, P.N.de ◻ ◻ CAM 139 Lg40
Mozuli ◻ RUS 39 Mg34
Mpagwe ◻ GH 137 Kk41
Mpaka ◻ SD 137 Kk41
Mpala ◻ RDC 146 Me49
Mpanda ◻ EAT 146 Mf49
Mpandaamatenga ◻ RB 151 Mc55
Mparo ◻ EAT 147 Mj49
Mpanta ◻ Z 146 Mf51
Mpasa ◻ EAT 147 Mj49
Mpatoba ◻ GH 137 Kj42
Mpesoba ◻ RMM 137 Kh39
Mpé ◻ RCB 148 Lh47
Mphoengs ◻ ZW 152 Md56
Mphwayungu ◻ EAT 146 Mh49
Mpika ◻ Z 146 Mf51
Mpili ◻ Z 152 Md53
Mpomgwe ◻ Z 146 Me52
Mponela ◻ MW 146 Mg52
Mporokoso ◻ Z 146 Mf50
Mpouya ◻ RCB 148 Lj47
Mpraeso ◻ GH 137 Kk42
Mpulungu ◻ Z 146 Mf50
Mpumalanga ◻ ZA 155 Mf59
Mpumalanga ◻ ZA 152 Md60
Mpwapwa ◻ EAT 147 Mj49
Mpwapwa ◻ RDC 149 Lx48
Mqabba ◻ M 37 Lp54
Mrakovo ◻ RUS 48 Nf20
Mrauk-U ◻ MYA 86 Pg35
Mrirt ◻ MA 125 Kh29
Mrkonjić Grad ◻ ◻ BIH 35 Ls46
Mrkopalj ◻ HR 35 Lp45
Mrobunyg = Mrauk-U ◻ MYA 86 Pg35
Mrzeżyno ◻ PL 40 Lg36
M'Saken ◻ TN 126 Lf28
Msak Mallat ◻ LAR 133 Lf33
Msalalo ◻ EAT 146 Mh48
Mšanec ◻ UA 43 Md41
Msanga ◻ EAT 147 Mk49
Mšanzi ◻ EAT 146 Mg50
Mscislav ◻ BY 48 Mf19
Menénlazё ◻ EAT 147 Mj51
Msekelé ◻ CAM 138 Lg43
Msesia ◻ EAT 146 Me49
M'Sied ◻ MA 124 Ke31
Mšila ◻ DZ 126 Lc28
M'simbati ◻ EAT 147 Na51
Msoro ◻ Z 146 Mf52
Msowero ◻ EAT 147 Mk49
Msta ◻ RUS 48 Mg17
Mstar ◻ EAT 147 Mk49
Mszana ◻ PL 41 Lu40
Mszczonów ◻ PL 41 Ma39
Mt Abrassenin ◻ RCA/SUD 141 Mc41
Mtakataka ◻ MW 153 Mg52
Mtama ◻ EAT 147 Mk51
Mtambi ◻ EAT 146 Mh50
Mtendere ◻ Z 146 Mf52
Mtito Andei ◻ EAK 144 Mj47
Mt. Kelly ◻ USA 165 Dj11
Mtonga ◻ EAT 146 Mh47
Mts du Fazao ◻ TG 137 La41
Mts Karé ◻ RCA 140 Lj41
Mtsketha ◻ GE 57 Nc24
Mtsou ◻ RCB 148 Lh47
Mtubatuba ◻ ZA 155 Mf60
Mtukula ◻ EAT 147 Mj51
Mtwango ◻ EAT 146 Mh50
Mtwara ◻ EAT 147 Na51
Mua ◻ EAT 147 Mk50

Muang Phu Khoun ◻ LAO 87 Qb36
Muang Samsip ◻ THA 89 Qc38
Muang Singh Historical Park ◻ ◻ THA 87 Pk38
Muang Sui ◻ LAO 87 Qb36
Muang Xai ◻ LAO 87 Qa35
Muang Xon ◻ LAO 87 Qb35
Muanda ◻ MOC 153 Mh55
Muar ◻ MAL 93 Qb44
Muarabeliti ◻ RI 93 Qb46
Muarabinuangeun ◻ RI 94 Qd47
Muaraenim ◻ RI 93 Qb46
Muarahiu ◻ RI 95 Qh48
Muarakaman ◻ RI 95 Qh46
Muarakling ◻ RI 93 Qb47
Muara Koman ◻ RI 95 Qh46
Muarakuwis ◻ RI 93 Qb46
Muarangangan ◻ RI 95 Qj46
Muarapangean ◻ RI 94 Qj47
Muarapantai ◻ RI 93 Qa46
Muararupit ◻ RI 93 Qb46
Muarasabio ◻ RI 93 Qb46
Muarasiberut ◻ RI 93 Pk46
Muarasigeo ◻ RI 93 Pk46
Muarakabaluan ◻ RI 93 Pk46
Muarasaimatalu ◻ RI 93 Pk46
Muarasiberut ◻ RI 93 Pk46
Muaratalang ◻ RI 93 Qb47
Muaratembesi ◻ RI 93 Qa46
Muarateweh ◻ RI 95 Qh46
Muarawahau ◻ RI 94 Qj47
Muari ◻ RI 97 Rd46
Muatua ◻ MOC 153 Mk53
Mubambe ◻ RDC 146 Md51
Mubanzi ◻ RDC 146 Lk48
Mubende ◻ EAU 144 Mf45
Mubi ◻ WAN 139 Lg40
Mubo ◻ CHN (GSU) 72 Qd27
Muborak ◻ UZ 63 Oc26
Mubrani ◻ RI 114 Rg46
Mubur ◻ RI 93 Qd44
Mucajaí ◻ BR (RR) 193 Gk44
Mucajaí ◻ BR 193 Gk44
Mucambi ◻ Z 151 Mc52
Mucari ◻ ANG 151 Mg56
Muchea ◻ AUS (WA) 104 Qh61
Mucheve ◻ MOC 152 Mf56
Muchinga Mountains ◻ Z 146 Mf52
Muchińwa ◻ Z 146 Md51
Muchówka ◻ PL 41 Ma41
Muck ◻ GB 20 Ko34
Muckadilla ◻ AUS (QLD) 109 Se59
Mučkapskij ◻ RUS 48 Nb20
Muckross ◻ IRL 19 Kl38
Mucojo ◻ MOC 147 Na52
Mucondo ◻ ANG 150 Lh54
Mucorea ◻ ANG 151 Ma51
Mucubela ◻ MOC 153 Mj54
Mucuchíes ◻ YV 192 Ge41
Mucugê ◻ BR (BA) 201 Hk52
Mucumba ◻ MOC 152 Mf56
Mucumbura ◻ ZW 152 Mf54
Mucupia ◻ MOC 153 Mj54
Mucurí ◻ BR 203 Ja54
Mucurici ◻ BR (ES) 203 Hk55
Mucuripl ◻ BR (MA) 200 Hh47
Mucussueje ◻ ANG 151 Ma51
Mudabidri ◻ IND 84 Oh39
Mudan ◻ CHN (HLG)
Mudanthurai Tiger Sanctuary ◻ IND 84 Oj41
Mudanya ◻ TR 45 Mj50
Mud Butte ◻ USA (SD) 169 Ej23
Mudanjiang ◻ CHN (HLG) 76 Rd23
Muddebihal ◻ IND 84 Oj37
Muddus n.p. ◻ ◻ S 16 Ma12
Muddy Gap ◻ USA (WY) 171 Eg24
Mudgal ◻ IND (KTK) 82 Oj37
Mudgee ◻ AUS (NSW) 111 Se62
Mudgod ◻ IND (KTK) 82 Oh38
Mudhol ◻ IND (KTK) 82 Oh38
Mudi ◻ OM 61 Nj34
Mudijad Falls ◻ ANG 150 Lh54
Mudjuga ravnina ◻ AZ 57 Ne26
Mudon ◻ MYA 88 Pj37
Mudug ◻ SP 145 Nb43
Muecate ◻ MOC 153 Mk53
Mueda ◻ MOC 147 Mk51
Mueller Range ◻ AUS 103 Rd55
Muembe ◻ MOC 146 Mh52
Muende ◻ MOC 153 Mh54
Muftah ◻ SUD 135 Mg35
Mufulira ◻ Z 146 Me52
Mufu Shan ◻ CHN 75 Qh31
Mugango = Legoba ◻ EAT 146 Mh48
Mugango ◻ CHN (YUN) 87 Qc34
Mugegenda ◻ EAT 146 Mg46
Mugeba ◻ MOC 153 Mj54
Mügeln ◻ D 32 Lo39
Muger ◻ ETH 142 Mk41
Muggia ◻ I 35 Lo45
Mughal Sarai ◻ IND (UPH) 83 Pb33
Mughayra ◻ KSA 58 Mj31
Mughaynah ◻ IRQ 57 Na29
Mughshin ◻ OM 61 Nh34
Mugia = Muxia ◻ E 26 Kl47
Mugila ◻ RDC 146 Me49
Mugla ◻ TR 47 Mh53
Mugoa ◻ EAU/RWA 141 Me46
Muhala ◻ RDC 146 Md50
Muhanga ◻ RWA 146 Me47
Muheza ◻ EAT 147 Mk48
Muhi ◻ EAT 147 Mk50
Mühldorf ◻ D 33 Ln42
Mühlhausen ◻ D 32 Ll39
Mühlig-Hofmann-fjella ◻ 7 La33
Muhola ◻ FIN 38 Me28
Muhos ◻ FIN 38 Me26
Muhu ◻ EST 38 Md32

Nikopol' – Nylstroom

Nikopol' UA 49 Mh22
Nikópoli GR 46 Ma51
Nikópoli GR 46 Ma51
Nikopolis ad Istrum BG 45 Mf47
Niksar TR 56 Mj25
Nikshar IR 64 Oa32
Nikšić SCG 44 Lt48
Nikumaroro KIR 10 Ba10
Nilanga IND (MHT) 82 Oj36
Nilaveli Beach CL 85 Pa41
Nile ET 122 Mb07
Nile SUD 135 Mg36
Nile Delta ET 129 Mf30
Niles USA (MI) 173 Fg25
Nilgiri IND (ORS) 83 Pd35
Nilgiri Mtn. Railway IND (KTK) 84 Oj40
Nili AFG 65 Od29
Nilka CHN (XUZ) 66 Pb24
Nillpass AFG 65 Od28
Nilphamari BD 86 Pe33
Nilt 80 Oh27
Nimach IND (MPH) 82 Oj33
Nimbahera IND (RJT) 82 Oh33
Nimbin AUS (NSW) 109 Sg60
Nimbotong RI 115 Sa47
Nîmes F 25 Le47
Nimjat RIM 130 Kc37
Nim Ka Khera IND (RJT) 82 Oh33
Nimmitabel AUS (NSW) 111 Se64
Nimrud IRQ 57 Nb27
Nimule SUD 144 Mg44
Nimule N.P. SUD 144 Mg44
Nin HR 35 Lq46
Nina NAM 154 Lk57
Ninda ANG 151 Ma53
Nindigully AUS (QLD) 109 Se60
Nine Degree Channel IND 84 Og41
Ninette CDN (MB) 172 Fa21
Ninette NAM 150 Lk57
Ninetyeast Ridge 9 Pa12
Ninety Mile Beach AUS 111 Sd65
Ninety Mile Beach NZ 112 Tg63
Ningaloo AUS (WA) 102 Qg57
Ningaloo Reef Marine Park AUS 102 Qg57
Ning'an CHN (HLG) 76 Re23
Ningari RMM 131 Kj38
Ningau Island PNG 116 Se48
Ningbo CHN (ZJG) 75 Ra31
Ningcheng CHN (NMZ) 73 Qk25
Ningde CHN (FJN) 75 Qk32
Ningdu CHN (JGX) 75 Qh32
Ningeehak USA (AK) 164 Be14
Ningera PNG 115 Sa47
Ningerum PNG 115 Sa48
Ningguo CHN (AHU) 78 Qk30
Ninghai CHN (ZJG) 75 Ra31
Ninghe CHN (TJN) 73 Qj26
Ninghua CHN (FJN) 75 Qj32
Ningi WAN 138 Le40
Ningjing Shan CHN 69 Pj30
Ningming CHN (GZG) 74 Qd34
Ningnan CHN (SCH) 87 Qb32
Ningqiang CHN (SAA) 72 Qd29
Ningshan CHN (SAA) 72 Qe29
Ningwu CHN (SAX) 72 Qg26
Ningxia Huizu Zizhiqu CHN 72 Qd27
Ning Xian CHN (GSU) 72 Qd28
Ningxiang CHN (HUN) 74 Qg31
Ningyuan CHN (HUN) 74 Qf33
Ninh Binh VN 87 Qc35
Ninh Hoa VN 89 Qe39
Ninh Son VN 89 Qe40
Ninia RI 114 Rk48
Ninigo Group PNG 115 Sc46
Ninilchik USA (AK) 164 Ce15
Ninive IRQ 57 Nb27
Ninjin CHN (SDG) 73 Qj27
Ninohe J 77 Sa25
Ninole USA (HI) 170 Cc36
Niños Héroes MEX (SL) 180 Ef32
Ninotsminda GE 57 Nb25
Ninove B 23 Le40
Nioaque BR (MS) 202 Hc56
Nioaque, T.I. BR 202 Hc56
Niobrara USA (NE) 172 Fa24
Niobrara USA 172 Ek24
Niodior SN 136 Kb39
Niofoin CI 137 Kg41
Nioka RDC 144 Mf44
Nioka RDC 149 Mb49
Nioki RDC 149 Lj47
Niokolo-Koba SN 136 Kd39
Niokolo-Koba, P.N.du SN 136 Kd39
Niono RMM 131 Kh38
Nioro du Rip SN 136 Kc39
Nioro du Sahel RMM 130 Kf38
Niort F 24 Ku44
Niou BF 137 Kk39
Nioût RIM 131 Kg37
Nipa PNG 115 Sb49
Nipahpanjang RI 93 Qc46
Nipani IND (KTK) 82 Oh37
Nipawin CDN (SK) 169 Eh19
Nipawin Prov. Park CDN 169 Eh19
Nipepe MOC 153 Mj52
Niphad IND (MHT) 82 Oh35
Nipigon CDN (ON) 173 Ff21
Nipigon Bay CDN 173 Ff21
Nipiodi MOC 153 Mj54
Nipomo USA (CA) 170 Dk28
Nippur IRQ 59 Nc29
Niquelândia BR (GO) 202 Hf53
Niquero C 179 Gb35
Nir IR 57 Nd26
Nira IND (MHT) 82 Oh36
Nirgua YV 193 Gf40
Nirmal IND (APH) 82 Ok36
Nirwana Beach RI 96 Rb48
Niš SCG 44 Mb47
Nisa P 27 Kn51
Nisa TM 62 Nk27
Nisab KSA 59 Nc31
Nisab YE 60 Nd38
Nisai RI 96 Qk50
Niscemi I 37 Lp53
Niseko Shakotan Otaru-kaigan Q.N.P. J 77 Sa24
Nish AFG 65 Oc29
Nishi CHN (HUN) 74 Qf31
Nishi-Chugokusanchi Q.N.P. J 79 Rg28
Nishino-jima J 79 Rg27
Nishi-no-Omote J 79 Rf30
Nishi-Okoppe J 77 Sb23
Nishi-Sonogi-hanto J 79 Re29
Nishon UZ 63 Oc26
Nisiá Petalií GR 47 Me53
Nísio Strofádhes GR 46 Ma53
Niška Banja SCG 44 Mc47
Nisko PL 41 Mc40
Nisporeni MD 49 Me22
Nissan Island PNG 117 Sh48
Nissedal N 30 Lj31
Nisséko BF 137 Kj40
Nissi EST 38 Me31
Nissí Ioanínon GR 46 Ma51
Níssiros GR 47 Mh54
Nissum Fjord DK 30 Lj34
Nisut Plateau CDN 166 De15
Nita'a KSA 59 Ne32
Nita Downs AUS (WA) 102 Ra55
Nītaure LV 39 Mf33
Nitchequon CDN (QC) 176 Ge19
Niterói BR (RJ) 205 Hj57
Nitinat CDN (BC) 168 Dh21
Niti Pass CHN/IND 68 Ok30
Nitmiluk N.P. AUS 106 Rg53
Nitra SK 42 Lt42
Nitrianske Pravno SK 43 Lt42
Nitriansky hrad SK 42 Lt42
Nittambuwa CL 85 Pa42
Nittedal N 30 Ll30
Nittenau D 33 Ln41
Nittur IND (KTK) 84 Oj39
Niuchang CHN (GZH) 87 Qc33
Niuchang CHN (YUN) 87 Qc34
Niue NZ 100 Bb11
Niumi N.P. WAG 136 Kb39
Niutao TUV 10 Tb10
Niut, Gunung RI 94 Qe45
Niutoushan CHN (AHU) 78 Qk30
Niuzhuang CHN (LNG) 76 Rb25
Nivala FIN 16 Mc14
Nivano PK 64 Ob32
Nivelles B 23 Le40
Nivenskoe RUS 39 Ma36
Nivernais F 25 Ld43
Niwai IND (RJT) 80 Oh32
Niwas IND (MPH) 83 Pa34
Nixi CHN (YUN) 87 Pk32
Nixon USA (NV) 170 Ea26
Nixon USA (TX) 181 Fb31
Niya = Minfeng CHN (XUZ) 68 Pb27
Nizamabad IND (APH) 82 Ok36
Nizamabad Temple IND 82 Ok36
Nizamghat IND (ARP) 86 Ph31
Nizampatam IND (APH) 83 Pa38
Nizi RDC 144 Mf45
Nizina Wielkopolska PL 40 Lq39
Nizip TR 56 Mj27
Nízke Tatry SK 43 Lu42
Nízke Tatry, N.P. SK 43 Lu42
Nižná Boca SK 43 Lu42
Nižnaja Lomov RUS 48 Nb19
Nižnevartovsk RUS 54 Od06
Nižnij Casučej RUS 71 Qh20
Nižnij Novgorod RUS 48 Nb17
Nižnij Pjandž TJ 63 Oe27
Nižnij Tagil RUS 54 Nd07
Nižnjaja Tunguska RUS 54 Pc05
Nizwa OM 61 Nj34
Nižyn UA 48 Mf20
Nizza Monferrato I 34 Lj46
Nizzana IL 58 Mh30
Njagan' RUS 54 Ob06
Njaiama- Sewafe WAL 136 Ke41
Nja Kunda WAG 136 Kc39
Njangwo EAT 147 Mk51
Njasvíž BY 41 Mg37
Njinjo EAT 147 Mk50
Njivice HR 35 Lp45
Njojane RB 154 Ma57
Njombe EAT 146 Mh50
Njoro EAK 144 Mh46
Njupeskär S 17 Lg15
Njurba RUS 55 Qd06
Njutånger S 17 Lj15
Nkalagu WAN 138 Ld42
Nkambe CAM 138 Lf42
Nkan G 148 Le45
Nkawie GH 137 Kk42
Nkayi RCB 148 Lg48
Nkayi ZW 152 Me55
Nkhaïlé RIM 131 Kg37
Nkhamenya MW 146 Mg52
Nkhata Bay MW 146 Mh51
Nkhotakota MW 146 Mh52
Nkhotakota Game Reserve MW 146 Mg52
Nko RCB 148 Lh47
Nkoambang CAM 139 Lg43
Nkolabona G 139 Lf45
Nkole Z 146 Mf51
Nkolmengboua G 139 Lf44
Nkolmetet CAM 139 Lf44
Nkome EAT 144 Mf47
Nkomfap WAN 138 Le42
Nkondwe EAT 146 Mf48
Nkongjok CAM 138 Lf43
Nkongsamba CAM 138 Le43
Nkon Ngok CAM 139 Lf43
Nkoranza GH 137 Kk42
Nkoteng CAM 139 Lg43
Nkoué RCB 148 Lh47
Nkourala RMM 137 Kg40
Nkula Falls MW 153 Mh53
Nkundi EAT 146 Mf49
Nkungulu MW 153 Mh53
Nkurenkuru NAM 150 Lk54
Nkwalini ZA 155 Mf60
Nkwanta GH 137 Kj43
Nkwanta GH 137 La41
Nnewi WAN 138 Ld42
No.24 Well AUS (WA) 103 Rb57
No.35 Well AUS (WA) 103 Rc57
Noailles F 23 Lc41
Noakhali BD 86 Pf34
Noanama CO 192 Gb43
Noatak USA (AK) 165 Bj12
Noatak National Preserve USA (AK) 165 Bk11
Nobadeer (Nantucket) USA 177 Gf25
Nobeoka J 79 Rf29
Nobéré BF 137 Kk40
Nobles Nob Mine AUS 106 Rh55
Nobokwe ZA 155 Md61
Nobol EC 196 Fk46
Noboribetsu J 77 Sa24
Nobres BR (MT) 202 Hb53
Nochi-katsuura J 79 Rh29
Noci I 37 Ls50
Nockatunga AUS (QLD) 108 Sb59
Nockberge, N.P. A 35 Lo44
Nocoleche AUS (NSW) 109 Sc60
Nocona USA (TX) 174 Fb29
Noda J 77 Sa25
Nodeland N 30 Lh32
Nödinge-Nol S 30 Ln33
Nodwengu ZA 155 Mf60
Noel CDN (NS) 176 Gj23
Noel Kempff, P.N. BOL 206 Ha53
Noenieput ZA 154 Ma59
Noépé TG 137 La42
Noetinger RA (CD) 209 Gj62
Nœux-les-Mines F 23 Lc40
Nogales E 27 Ko52
Nogales MEX (SO) 180 Ee30
Nogales MEX (VC) 182 Fb36
Nogales USA (AZ) 171 Ee30
Nogal Valley SP 143 Nd41
Nogamut USA (AK) 164 Cb15
Nogarejas E 26 Ko48
Nogata J 79 Rf29
Nogent F 25 Lf42
Nogent-le-Roi F 23 Lb42
Nogent-le-Rotrou F 22 La42
Nogent-sur-Seine F 23 Ld42
Noginsk RUS 48 Mk18
Nogoya RA (ER) 204 Ha62
Noguera E 29 Kt50
Nohalal MEX (YT) 183 Ff36
Nohar IND (RJT) 80 Oh31
Nohbec MEX (QTR) 183 Ff36
Noheji J 77 Sa25
Nohfelden D 33 Lh41
Noia E 26 Km48
Noirétable F 25 Ld45
Noirmoutier F 24 Ks44
Noirmoutier-en-l'Île F 24 Ks44
Nojack CDN (AB) 169 Ec19
Nojima-saki J 79 Rk28
Nokaneng RB 151 Mb55
Nokha IND (RJT) 80 Og32
Nokhra IND (RJT) 80 Og32
Nokia FIN 38 Md29
Nokju IR 64 Oa32
Nok Kundi PK 64 Ob31
Nokomis CDN (SK) 169 Eh20
Nokou TCH 133 Lh38
Nokuku VU 118 Td53
Nola I 37 Lp50
Nola RCA 140 Lj44
Nola USA (AR) 174 Fd28
Nolay F 25 Le44
Nolhivaranfaru MV 84 Og42
Noli EAT 147 Mk51
Noll ZA 154 Mb62
Nólsoy DK 18 Ko29
Nom CHN (XUZ) 67 Ph24
Noma misaki J 79 Rf30
Nomane PNG 115 Sc49
Nombre de Dios MEX (DGO) 181 Eh34
Nome USA (AK) 164 Bh13
Nomeny F 23 Lg42
Nomgon MNG 70 Qc21
Nomhon CHN (QHI) 69 Pj27
Nomitsís GR 46 Mc54
Nomrog Nature Reserve MNG 71 Qk22
Nomtsas NAM 154 Lj58
Nonacho Lake CDN 167 Ef15
Nonancourt F 23 Lb42
Nonántola I 34 Lm46
Non Champa THA 89 Qb37
Nondalton USA (AK) 164 Cc15
Nondo Z 146 Mf50
Nong'an CHN (JLN) 76 Rc23
Nong Bua THA 88 Qa38
Nong Bua Daeng THA 89 Qa37
Nong Bua Khok THA 89 Qa38
Nong Bua Lam Phu THA 89 Qb37
Nong Bua Rahaeo THA 89 Qa38
Nongchang CHN (SAA) 72 Qe27
Nong Chang THA 88 Pk38
Nong Haet LAO 87 Qb36
Nong Han THA 89 Qb37
Nong Khae THA 88 Qa38
Nong Khai THA 87 Qb37
Nongoma ZA 155 Mf59
Nongowa RG 136 Ke41
Nong Phai THA 88 Qa38
Nong Phok THA 89 Qc37
Nong Phu THA 89 Qc38
Nongqai Fort ZA 155 Mf60
Nong Rua THA 89 Qb37
Nongsa Beach RI 93 Qc45
Nongstoin IND (MGA) 86 Pf33
Nong Yai THA 89 Qa39
Nonning AUS (SA) 110 Rj62
Nonoai BR (RS) 204 Hd59
Nonoava MEX (CHH) 180 Eg32
Nonogasta RA (LR) 207 Gg60
Non Thai THA 89 Qb38
Nontron F 24 La45
Nonza F 34 Lk48
Nooleeye SP 145 Nd43
Noonaman AUS (NT) 106 Rf52
Noondoonia AUS (WA) 105 Rb62
Noonkabah AUS (WA) 103 Rc55
Noonkanbah A.L. AUS 103 Rc55
Noonu Atoll MV 84 Og43
Noorder Dierenpark NL 23 Lg38
Noordoewer NAM 154 Lj60
Noordoostpolder NL 23 Lf38
Noordwijk aan Zee NL 23 Le38
Noormarkku FIN 38 Mb29
Noorvik USA (AK) 165 Bk12
Nootka Island CDN 168 Dg21
Nooyeah Downs AUS (QLD) 108 Sb60
Nopiloa MEX 183 Fb36
Nopoming Prov. Park CDN 172 Fc20
Nóqui ANG 148 Lg48
Nora I 36 Lk52
Nora S 31 Lq31
Norah ER 142 Mk37
Noralee CDN (BC) 166 Dg19
Noralup AUS (WA) 104 Qj63
Norassoba RG 136 Kf40
Norberg S 31 Lq30
Norberto de la Riestra RA (BA) 209 Ha63
Nórcia I 35 Lo48
Nordagutu N 30 Lk31
Nordaustlandet N 16 Ma06
Nordaust-Svalbard naturreservat N 16 Ma06
Nordborg DK 30 Lk35
Nordby DK 30 Lj35
Nordby DK 30 Ll35
Nordðoyar DK 18 Ko28
Nordegg CDN (AB) 168 Eb19
Norden D 32 Lh37
Nordenham D 32 Lj37
Nordens Ark N 30 Lm32
Nordenskiøld Land N 16 Lh07
Norderney D 32 Lh37
Norderstedt D 32 Ll37
Nordeste ANG 149 Ma49
Nordfold N 16 Lh12
Nordhausen D 32 Ll39
Nordholz D 32 Lj37
Nordhorn D 32 Lh38
Nordkjosbotn N 16 Lk11
Nördlingen D 33 Ll42
Nordmaling S 16 Lk14
Nordman USA (ID) 168 Eb21
Nordmark S 31 Lp31
Nordmøre N 16 Ld14
Nord-Ostsee-Kanal D 32 Lk36
Nordøyane N 16 Ld14
Nord-Pas-de-Calais F 23 Lb40
Nordrhein-Westfalen D 32 Lh39
Nordvest-Spitsbergen n.p. N 16 Lg05
Norembega CDN (ON) 173 Fk21
Noresund N 30 Lk30
Norfolk USA (NE) 172 Fb24
Norfolk USA (VA) 178 Gb27
Norfolk Broads GB 21 Lb38
Norfolk Island AUS 100 Ta12
Norfolk Island AUS 100 Ta12
Norfolk Ridge 100 Ta12
Norheimsund N 30 Lg30
Noriega USA (CA) 170 Dj27
Noril'sk RUS 54 Pb05
Noring, Gunung MAL 92 Qa43
Normal USA (IL) 175 Ff25
Norman USA (OK) 174 Fb28
Normanby Island PNG 116 Sf51
Normandia BR (RR) 194 Ha44
Normandie F 22 Kt42
Normandin CDN (QC) 176 Gd21
Normandy USA (TX) 181 Ek31
Normangee USA (TX) 174 Fb30
Norman's Cay BS 179 Gb33
Normanton AUS (QLD) 107 Sa54
Normanville AUS (SA) 110 Rk63
Norman Wells CDN 162 Dc05
Normétal CDN (QC) 173 Ga21
Norotshama River Resort NAM 154 Lj60
Norquay CDN (SK) 169 Ej20
Norquinco RA (RN) 208 Ge66
Norråker S 16 Lh13
Norra Kvills n.p. S 31 Lq33
Norra Midsjöbanken 31 Ls34
Norranside AUS (QLD) 108 Sa57
Nørre Aaby DK 30 Lk35
Nørre Alslev DK 30 Lm36
Nørre Nebel DK 30 Lj35
Nørre Vorupør DK 30 Lj34
Norrhult S 31 Lq33
Norris USA (MT) 169 Ee23
Norris Point CDN (NF) 177 Ha21
Norrköping S 31 Lr32
Norrsundet S 31 Ls30
Norrtälje S 31 Lt31
Nors DK 30 Lj33
Norseman AUS (WA) 104 Ra62
Norsholm S 31 Lq32
Norsjö S 16 Lk13
Norsk RUS 71 Re19
Norsk oljemuseum N 30 Lf31
Norsup VU 118 Td54
Norte, Cerro RA 210 Gd70
Nortelândia BR (MT) 202 Hb53
North Adams USA (MA) 177 Gd24
Northallerton GB 21 Kt36
Northam AUS (WA) 104 Qj61
Northam AUS (WA) 104 Qj61
North America 160 Eb04
Northampton GB 21 Ku38
Northampton USA (MA) 177 Gd24
Northampton, Mount 7 Tb33
North Andaman IND 88 Pg39
North Arm GB (GBF) 210 Ha72
North Australia Basin 9 Qb11
North Avoca Back Reef AUS 111 Sf62
North Balabac Strait RP 94 Qj41
North Banda Basin RI 97 Rc47
North Bannister AUS (WA) 104 Qj62
North Battleford CDN (SK) 169 Ef19
North Bay CDN (ON) 173 Ga22
North Bend USA (OR) 168 Dh24
North Bend USA (WA) 168 Dk22
North Berwick GB 20 Ks34
North Bimini BS 179 Ga33
North Branch USA (MN) 172 Fd23
North Bruny Island AUS 111 Sd67
North Caicos GB 186 Ge35
North Cape N 14 Ma02
North Cape NZ 112 Tg63
North Cape May USA (NJ) 177 Gc26
North Carolina USA 178 Fk27
North Carolina USA 178 Fk27
North Carolina Aquarium at Ft. Fisher USA 178 Gb29
North Carolina Aquarium at Pine Knoll Shores USA 178 Gb28
North Carolina Aquarium at Roanoke Island USA 178 Gc28
North Cascades N.P. USA 168 Dk21
North Cay CO 185 Fk38
North Channel GB 20 Kp35
North Charleston USA (SC) 178 Ga29
North China Plain CHN 73 Qh28
Northcliffe AUS (WA) 104 Qj63
North Cove USA (WA) 168 Dh22
North Dakota USA 172 Ej22
North Downs GB 21 La39
North East RB 152 Md56
Northeast Cape USA 164 Bf14
Northeast Coast National Scenic Area RC 75 Ra33
North East Islands AUS 106 Rj52
Northeast Pacific Basin 10 Sb05
Northeast Point BS 186 Gc33
Northeast Point BS 186 Gd34
Northeast Point BS 186 Gd35
Northeast Point CDN 177 Hc20
Northeast Point USA 164 Bf17
Northeast Providence Channel BS 179 Gb33
Northeim D 32 Lk39
Northern Cape ZA 154 Lk60
Northern Cay BH 184 Fg37
Northern Cheyenne Ind. Res. USA 169 Eg23
Northern Hot Springs Park CHN 74 Qd31
Northern Indian Lake CDN 163 Fa07
Northern Ireland GB 19 Kn36
Northern Lau Group FJI 119 Ua54
Northern Mariana Islands USA 101 Sa08
Northern Sporades GR 47 Me51
Northern Territory AUS 101 Rb12
Northfield USA (MN) 172 Fd23
North Fiji Basin 100 Tb11
North Foreland GB 21 Lb39
North Fork USA (NV) 170 Ec25
North Fork Kuskokwim River USA 165 Cd14
North Frisian Islands D 32 Lj36
North Goulburn Island AUS 106 Rg51
Northhaam ZA 155 Md58
Northhampton AUS (WA) 104 Qh60
North Head AUS (QLD) 107 Sb55
North Head CDN (NB) 176 Gg23
North Head NZ 112 Th64
Northhome USA (MN) 172 Fc22
North Horr EAK 144 Mj44
North Island AUS 104 Qg60
North Island AUS 106 Rj53
North Island NZ 112 Tj64
North Kessock GB 20 Kq33
North Komelik USA (AZ) 171 Ee29
North Korea PRK 53 Ra05
North Lake Grace AUS (WA) 104 Qk62
North Lakhimpur IND (ASM) 86 Ph32
North Land RUS 54 Pb03
North Las Vegas USA (NV) 170 Ec27
Northleach GB 21 Kt39
North Little Rock USA (AR) 175 Fd28
North Luangwa N.P. Z 146 Mg51
North Luconia Shoals 94 Qg43
North Male Atoll MV 84 Og43
North Mankato USA (MN) 172 Fc23
North Miladhunmadulu Atoll = Shaviyani Atoll MV 84 Og42
North Nilandhoo Atoll = Faafu Atoll MV 84 Og44
North Ossetia RUS 57 Nc24
North Pen. CDN 172 Ff20
North Peron Island AUS 103 Re52
North Platte USA (NE) 172 Ek25
North Platte USA 171 Ej25
North Point CDN 176 Gj22
North Point WAN 138 Lc43
North Pole 5 La01
Northport USA (AL) 175 Fg29
Northport USA (MI) 173 Fh23
Northport USA (WA) 168 Eb21
North Portal CDN (SK) 169 Ej21
North Rim USA (AZ) 171 Ed27
North Ronaldsay GB 20 Ks31
North Salmara IND (ASM) 86 Pf32
North Saskatchewan River CDN 169 Ef19
North Sea 14 La04
North Sentinel Island IND 88 Pg40
North Siberian Lowland RUS 54 Pb04
North Star AUS (NSW) 109 Sf60
North Stradbroke Island AUS 109 Sg59
North Taranaki Bight NZ 113 Th65
North Thiladhunmathee Atoll = Haa-Alifu Atoll MV 84 Og42
North Tonawanda USA (NY) 173 Ga24
North Trap NZ 113 Td69
North Ubian Island RP 91 Ra42
North Uist GB 20 Kn33
Northumberland Islands AUS 109 Se56
Northumberland N.P. GB 20 Ks35
North Vancouver CDN (BC) 168 Dj21
North Vernon USA (IN) 175 Fh26
Northville USA (SD) 172 Fa23
North Walsham GB 21 Lb38
North West ZA 154 Mb59
Northwest Australian Basin 9 Qa11
North West Basin AUS 104 Qh57
Northwest Bay CDN (ON) 172 Fd21
North West Cape AUS 102 Qh56
Northwest Cape USA (AK) 164 Be14
Northwest Cay BS 186 Gd35
North West Coastal Highway AUS (WA) 104 Qh59
North West Highlands GB 20 Kq33
Northwest Pacific Basin 10 Sb05
Northwest Point BS 186 Gd35
Northwest Providence Channel BS 179 Ga32
North West River CDN 163 Gd08
Northwest Territories CDN 162 Dc06
North Windham USA (ME) 177 Ge24
Northwood USA (ND) 172 Fb22
North York Moors N.P. GB 21 Ku36
Norton USA (KS) 174 Fa26
Norton USA (VA) 178 Fj27
Norton ZW 152 Mf54
Norton Shores USA (MI) 173 Fg24
Norton Sound USA 164 Bh14
Nortonville USA (ND) 172 Fa22
Nortorf D 32 Lk36
Nort-sur-Erdre F 22 Kt43
Norwalk USA (CT) 177 Gd25
Norwalk USA (OH) 173 Fj25
Norway USA (ME) 177 Ge23
Norway 15 La03
Norway House CDN (MB) 163 Fa08
Norwegian Basin 14 Kb03
Norwegian Bay CDN 163 Fb03
Norwegian Sea 14 Kb02
Norwegian Trench 30 Lf32
Norwich GB 21 Lb38
Norwich USA (CT) 177 Gd25
Norwich USA (NY) 177 Gc24
Norwood USA (CO) 171 Ef26
Nosappu-misaki J 77 Sc24
Nosara CR 184 Fh41
Noshiro J 77 Sa25
Nosiarina RM 156 Nf53
Nosibe RM 156 Ne52
Nosivka UA 48 Mf20
nos Kaliakra BG 45 Mj47
Nosliku RI 91 Rd45
Nosovo RUS 39 Mh33
Nosrat Abad IR 64 Nk31
Nossa Senhora Aparecida BR 205 Hh57
Nossa Senhora da Conceiçào ANG 148 Lg50
Nossa Senhora da Glória BR (SE) 201 Jb51
Nossa Senhora das Dores BR (SE) 201 Jb51
Nossa Senhora da Victoria ANG 148 Lh50
Nossa Senhora do Socorro BR (SE) 201 Jb51
Nossebro S 30 Ln32
Nössemark S 30 Lm31
Nossen D 32 Lo39
Nossob NAM 150 Lj57
Nossob Camp ruskamp ZA 154 Ma58
Nossombougou RMM 137 Kg39
Nosy Antsoheribory RM 156 Nc53
Nosy Barren RM 157 Nb55
Nosy Be RM 156 Ne52
Nosy Berafia RM 156 Nd53
Nosy Faly RM 156 Ne52
Nosy Komba RM 156 Ne52
Nosy Lava RM 156 Nd53
Nosy Mitsio RM 156 Ne52
Nosy Radama RM 156 Nd53
Nosy Sainte-Marie RM 157 Ne54
Nosy Vao RM 157 Nb54
Nosy Varika RM 157 Ne56
Noszolop H 42 Ls43
Nothaburi THA 88 Qa39
Nótia Pindos GR 46 Mb51
Notintsila ZA 155 Me61
Nótio Stenó Kerkíras GR 46 Ma51
Nötö FIN 38 Mb31
Noto I 37 Lq54
Notocote MOC 153 Mk54
Notodden N 30 Lk31
Noto Gouye Diama SN 130 Kb38
Noto-hanto J 77 Rj27
Noto-jima J 77 Rj27
Noto–kongo Coast J 77 Rj27
Notre-Dame F 23 Lc42
Notre Dame Bay CDN 177 Hc21
Notre-Dame-de-Haut F 25 Lg43
Notre-Dame-de-la-Garde F 25 Lf47
Notre Dame de la Paix CI 137 Kh42
Notre-Dame de l'Épine F 23 Le41
Notre-Dame de Rouen F 23 Lb41
Notre-Dame de Saint-Omer F 23 Lc40
Notre-Damedu-Nord CDN (QC) 173 Ga22
Notre Dame Junction CDN (NF) 177 Hc21
Notre-Dame-la-Grande de Poitiers F 24 La44
Notsé TG 137 La42
Nøtterøy N 30 Ll31
Notting AUS (WA) 104 Qk62
Nottingham GB 21 Kt38
Nottingham Downs AUS (QLD) 109 Sb56
Nottingham Road ZA 155 Me60
Nott, Mount AUS 110 Rh62
Nottoway USA (VA) 178 Ga27
Nottoway Plantation USA 175 Fe30
Notu CI 137 Kg41
Nouabalé-Ndoki, P.N.de RCB 140 Lj44
Nouâdhibou RIM 130 Kb35
Nouakchott RIM 130 Kb36
Nouâmghâr RIM 130 Kb36
Nouméa F (NCL) 118 Td57
Noumoukiédougou BF 137 Kh41
Nouna BF 137 Kj39
Noupoort ZA 155 Mc61
Nourlangie Rock AUS 106 Rg52
Nouvelle CDN (QC) 176 Gg21
Nouzad AFG 65 Oc29
Növa EST 38 Md31
Nova Alvorada do Sul BR (MS) 202 Hc56
Nova Andradina BR (MS) 202 Hd57
Nova Apuá BR (AM) 198 Gh50
Nova Aurora BR (GO) 202 Hf55
Nova Borova UA 49 Me20
Nova Brasilândia BR (MT) 202 Hc53
Nova Brasilândia BR (RO) 198 Gj51
Nová Bystřice CZ 42 Lq41
Nova Caipemba ANG 148 Lh49
Nova Canaã do Norte BR (MT) 199 Hc51
Novačene BG 44 Md48
Novaci MK 44 Mb49
Novaci RO 44 Md45
Nova Coimbra MOC 146 Mh52
Nova Crnja SCG 44 Ma45
Nova Cruz BR (RN) 201 Jc49
Nova Esperança ANG 148 Lh49
Nova Esperança BR (PR) 202 Hd57
Nova Freeixo = Cuamba MOC 153 Mj53
Nova Friburgo BR (RJ) 205 Hj57
Nova Gaia ANG 149 Lj51
Nova Golega MOC 152 Mg56
Nova Gorica SLO 42 Lo45
Nova Gradiška HR 35 Ls45
Nova Granada BR (SP) 202 Hf56
Nova Iguaçu BR (RJ) 205 Hj57
Nova Independência BR (SP) 202 He56
Novaja Derevnja RUS 39 Mb36
Novaja Pahost BY 39 Mh35
Novaja Ruda BY 41 Me37
Nova Jerusalém BR 201 Jb50
Nova Jorque BR (MA) 200 Hh49
Nova Kachovka UA 49 Mg22
Nova Laranjeiras BR (PR) 204 Hd58
Novalja HR 35 Lp46
Nova Londrina BR (PR) 202 Hd57
Novalukoml' BY 48 Me18
Nova Luzitânia BR (SP) 202 He56
Nova Mambone MOC 153 Mh56
Nova Nabúri MOC 153 Mk54
Nova Odesa UA 49 Mf22
Nova Olímpia BR (PR) 202 Hd57
Nova Olinda BR (PA) 199 Hc47
Nova Olinda do Norte BR (AM) 199 Ha47
Nova Paraíso BR (RR) 194 Gk45
Nova Petrópolis BR (RS) 204 He60
Nova Prata BR (RS) 204 He60
Novara I 34 Lj45
Nova Roma BR (GO) 200 Hg52
Nova Ruda UA 41 Mf39
Nova Russas BR (CE) 201 Hk48
Nova Santarém MOC 153 Mh52
Nova Scotia CDN 163 Gd10
Nova Scotia Mus. of Industry CDN 176 Gj23
Nova Serrana BR (MG) 203 Hh55
Nova Sofala MOC 153 Mh56
Nova Soure BR (BA) 201 Ja51
Novato USA (CA) 170 Dj26
Nova Topola BIH 35 Ls45
Nova Ušycja UA 49 Md21
Nova Varoš SCG 44 Lu47
Nova Venêcia BR (ES) 203 Hk55
Nova Viçosa BR (BA) 203 Ja54
Nova Vida BR (AM) 198 Gf48
Nova Viseu MOC 147 Mj52
Nova Vodolaha UA 48 Mh21
Nova Xavantina BR (MT) 202 Hd53
Novaya Zemlya RUS 14 Nb02
Nova Zagora BG 45 Mg48
Nove BG 45 Mf47
Nove de Janeiro, T.I. BR 198 Gj49
Nové Hrady CZ 42 Lp42
Novellara I 34 Ll46
Nové Město nad Metují CZ 42 Lr40
Nové Město na Moravě CZ 42 Lr41
Nové Zámky SK 42 Lt43
Novgorod RUS 48 Mf16
Novgorodka RUS 39 Mj33
Novhorodka UA 49 Mg21
Novhorod-Sivers'kyj UA 48 Mg20
Novi Bečej SCG 44 Ma45
Novi Bilokorovyči UA 48 Me20
Novi Grad BIH 44 Lt45
Novigrad HR 35 Lo45
Novigrad-Podravski HR 35 Lr44
Novi Iskăr BG 44 Md48
Novi Kneževac SCG 44 Ma44
Novikovo RUS 77 Sb22
Novi Lígure I 34 Lj46
Novion-Porcien F 23 Le41
Novi Pazar BG 45 Mh47
Novi Pazar SCG 44 Ma47
Novi Sad SCG 44 Lu45
Novi Sanžary UA 49 Mh21
Novi Strilyšča UA 43 Me41
Nóvita CO 192 Gb43
Novi Vinodolski HR 35 Lp45
Novo Acordo BR (PA) 199 Hd47
Novo Acordo BR (TO) 200 Hg50
Novo Acre BR (BA) 201 Hk52
Novo Airão BR (AM) 199 Gk47
Novo Alegre BR (GO) 200 Hg52
Novoanninskij RUS 48 Nb20
Novo archanhel's'k UA 49 Mf21
Novo Areal BR (AM) 198 Gh49
Novo Aripuanã BR (AM) 199 Gk48
Novoazovs'k UA 49 Mk22
Novobod TJ 63 Of26
Novočeboksarsk RUS 48 Nd17
Novočerkassk RUS 49 Na22
Novo Cruzeiro BR (MG) 203 Hj54
Novočuguevka RUS 77 Rg23
Novodewitschij monastyr RUS 48 Mj18
Novofedorivka UA 49 Mg22
Novo Hamburgo BR (RS) 204 He60
Novo Horizonte BR (SP) 202 Hf56
Novohrad-Volyns'kyj UA 49 Md20
Novo Jardim BR (TO) 200 Hg51
Novokačalinsk RUS 76 Rf23
Novokievskij Uval RUS 71 Re20
Novokuzneck RUS 54 Pb08
Novolazarevskaja ANT (RUS) 7 Lc33
Novo Lino BR (AL) 201 Jc50
Novo Mesto SLO 42 Lq45
Novomičurinsk RUS 48 Mk18
Novomihajlovskij RUS 49 Mk23
Novomoskovsk RUS 48 Mk18
Novomoskovs'k UA 49 Mh21
Novo Mundo BR (GO) 200 He52
Novomykolajivka UA 49 Mg22
Novomykolajivka UA 49 Mh22
Novomyrhorod UA 49 Mf21
Novonikolaevskij RUS 48 Nb20
Novooleksijivka UA 49 Mh22
Novo Oriente BR (AM) 198 Gf50
Novo Oriente BR (CE) 201 Hk48
Novo Oriente de Minas BR (MG) 203 Hk54
Novo Paraná BR (MT) 199 Hb51
Novopavlovsk RUS 57 Nb24
Novo Pensamento BR (AM) 198 Gj46
Novopokrovka RUS 77 Rh23
Novopokrovka UA 49 Mh21
Novopokrovskaja RUS 49 Na23
Novopskov UA 48 Mk21
Novorossijsk RUS 49 Mj23
Novoržev RUS 48 Me17
Novošahtinsk RUS 49 Mk22
Novo São Joaquim BR (MT) 202 Hd53
Novo Sarandi BR (PR) 204 Hd58
Novoselci BG 45 Mh48
Novosel'e RUS 39 Mj32
Novoselec BG 45 Mg48
Novoselivs'ke UA 49 Mg23
Novo Selo BG 44 Mc48
Novo Selo BG 45 Mf47
Novo Selo BIH 35 Ls45
Novosibirsk RUS 54 Pa08
Novosibirskoe vodohranilišče RUS 54 Pa08
Novosokol'niki RUS 48 Mf17
Novotroick RUS 54 Nd08
Novotroickoe RUS (YAO) 76 Rf21
Novotroickoe RUS 48 Nc18
Novotroickoe RUS 71 Rd20
Novotrojic'ke UA 49 Mh22
Novoukrajinka UA 49 Mf21
Novovolyns'k UA 41 Me40
Novovoskresenovka RUS 71 Rd19
Novska HR 35 Lr45
Nový Bor CZ 42 Lp40
Novycja UA 43 Me42
Novy Dvor BY 41 Me37
Novy Dvor BY 41 Me38
Novyi Oskol RUS 48 Mj20
Novyj Buh UA 49 Mg22
Nový Jičín CZ 42 Ls41
Novyj Jaryčiv UA 43 Me41
Novyj Port RUS 54 Oc05
Novyj Rozdil UA 43 Me41
Novyj Urengoj RUS 54 Od05
Nowa Brzeźnica PL 41 Lu39
Nowa Cerekwia PL 40 Ls40
Nowa Dęba PL 41 Mb40
Nowa Karczma PL 40 Lt36
Nowa Nowa AUS (VIC) 111 Se64
Nowa Ruda PL 40 Lr40
Nowa Słupia PL 41 Mb40
Nowa Sól PL 40 Lq39
Nowata USA (OK) 174 Fc27
Nowa Wieś PL 41 Mb37
Nowa Wieś Ełcka PL 41 Mc37
Nowa Wieś Lęborska PL 40 Ls36
Nowbaran IR 57 Ne28
Nowe Miasteczko PL 40 Lq39
Nowe Miasto PL 41 Ma38
Nowe Miasto nad Pilicą PL 41 Ma39
Nowendoc AUS (NSW) 109 Sf61
Nowe Warpno PL 40 Lp37
Now Gonbad IR 64 Ng29
Nowgong IND (MPH) 83 Ok33
Nowinka PL 41 Mc37
Nowitna National Wildlife Refuge USA 165 Cd13
Nowogard PL 40 Lq37
Nowogród PL 41 Mb37
Nowogród Bobrzański PL 40 Lq39
Nowo Miasto nad Wartą PL 40 Ls38
Nowosiółki PL 41 Md40
Nowra AUS (NSW) 111 Sf63
Nowrangapur IND (ORS) 83 Pb36
Now Shar IR 57 Nf27
Nowshera PK 65 Of29
Nowsud IR 57 Nd28
Nowy Duninów PL 41 Lu38
Nowy Dwór PL 40 Lq39
Nowy Dwór Gdański PL 41 Lu36
Nowy Dwór Mazowiecki PL 41 Ma38
Nowy Korczyn PL 41 Ma40
Nowy Sącz PL 41 Ma41
Nowy Staw PL 40 Lt36
Nowy Targ PL 41 Ma41
Nowy Tomyśl PL 40 Lr38
Nowy Wiśnicz PL 41 Ma41
Nowy Żmigród PL 41 Mb41
Noxon USA (MT) 168 Ec22
Noxubee N.W.R. USA 175 Ff29
Noyant F 24 La43
Noyers F 25 Le43
Noyes Island USA 166 Dc18
Noyon F 23 Lc41
Nozay F 22 Kt43
Nrusinghanath Temple IND 83 Pc35
Nsadzu = Cassacatiza MOC 152 Mg53
Nsalu Caves Z 146 Mf52
Nsama Z 146 Me50
Nsanje MW 153 Mh54
Nsawam GH 137 Kk43
Nsawkaw GH 137 Kj42
Nsefu Z 146 Mf52
Nselema MW 153 Mh53
Nsem CAM 139 Lg43
Nsiza ZW 152 Me55
Nsog GQ 139 Lf45
Nsoko SD 155 Mf59
Nsombo Z 146 Me51
Nsongezi EAU 144 Mf46
Nsontin RDC 149 Lk47
Nsopzup MYA 86 Pj33
Nsukka WAN 138 Ld42
Nsumbu N.P. Z 146 Mf50
Nswatugi and Pomongwe Caves ZW 152 Me56
Ntadembele RDC 148 Lj47
Ntambu Z 151 Mc52
Ntatrat RIM 130 Kc37
Ntcheu MW 153 Mh53
Ntchisi MW 146 Mg52
Ntemwa Z 152 Md53
Ntibane ZA 155 Me61
Ntiona TCH 133 Lh38
Ntlonyane ZA 155 Me62
Ntokou RCB 140 Lh45
Ntokou RCB 140 Lj45
Ntoroko EAU 144 Mf45
Ntsou RCB 148 Lh46
Ntui CAM 139 Lf43
Ntungamo EAU 144 Mf46
Ntusi EAU 144 Mf45
Ntwetwe Pan RB 151 Mc56
Nuakata Island PNG 116 Sf51
Nuangan RI 91 Rc45
Nubeena AUS (TAS) 111 Sd67
Nubia SUD 122 Mb08
Nubian Desert SUD 135 Mg35
Nubieber USA (CA) 170 Dk25
Nuboai RI 114 Rj47
Nucet RO 43 Mc44
Nucla USA (CO) 171 Ef26
Nüden MNG 70 Qf24
Nudo Allincapac PE 197 Ge52
Nudo Ausandate PE 197 Ge52
Nudo Chicllaraza PE 197 Gc52
Nudo de Sunipani PE 197 Ge53
Nudol' RUS 48 Mj17
Nudyže UA 41 Me39
Nueltin Lake CDN 163 Fa06
Nuenen NL 23 Lf39
Nuestra Señora de Loreto RA 204 Hc59
Nuestra Señora del Rosario de Caá-Catí RA (CR) 204 Hb59
Nueva Alejandria PE 196 Gd48
Nueva Armenia HN 184 Fg38
Nueva Asunción PY 206 Gk56
Nueva California RA (MD) 208 Gf62
Nueva Concepción ES 184 Ff38
Nueva Constitución RA (SL) 208 Gg63
Nueva Esperanza RA (SE) 207 Gh59
Nueva Esperanza RA (SE) 207 Gj59
Nueva Florida YV 193 Gf41
Nueva Fortuna YV 193 Gj42
Nueva Galia RA (SL) 208 Gh63
Nueva Germania PY 202 Hb57
Nueva Gerona C 179 Fj35
Nueva Guinea NIC 185 Fh40
Nueva Helvecia ROU 209 Hb63
Nueva Imperial RCH 208 Gd65
Nueva Italia RA (SF) 207 Gk60
Nueva Italia de Ruiz MEX (MHC) 182 Ek36
Nueva Lubeka RA (CB) 210 Ge68
Nueva Ocotepeque HN 184 Ff38
Nueva Palmira ROU 204 Ha62
Nueva Patria MEX (DGO) 181 Eh33
Nueva Pompeya RA (CH) 207 Gk58
Nueva Rocafuerte EC 196 Gc46
Nueva Rosita MEX (COH) 181 Ek32
Nueva San Salvador ES 184 Ff39
Nueva Villa de Padilla MEX (TM) 181 Fa33
Nuevitas C 179 Gb35
Nuevo Berlin BOL 206 Gh52
Nuevo Berlín ROU 204 Ha62
Nuevo Campechito MEX (TB) 183 Fd36
Nuevo Casas Grandes MEX (CHH) 180 Eg30
Nuevo Coahuila MEX (CAM) 183 Fe37
Nuevo Esperanza PE 196 Gc46
Nuevo Ideal MEX (DGO) 181 Eh33
Nuevo Laredo MEX (TM) 181 Fa32
Nuevo León MEX (BC) 180 Ec29
Nuevo Leon MEX 181 Fa33
Nuevo Milagro MEX (COH) 181 Ej31
Nuevo Mundo CO 192 Ge43
Nuevo Palomas MEX (CHH) 180 Eg31
Nuevo Porvenir MEX (CHH) 181 Eh31
Nuevo Progrese PE 197 Gb50
Nuevo Progreso MEX (TM) 182 Fb34
Nuevo Torino RA (SF) 209 Gk61
Nufăru RO 45 Mj45
Nugget Point NZ 113 Te69
Nugtat bulgis al Habgilgiyah LAR 126 Lf29
Nuguaçu BR (BA) 201 Hk51
Nugur IND (CGH) 83 Pa36
Nuguria Island PNG 117 Sh47
Nuguria Islands PNG 117 Sh47
Nuhaka NZ 113 Tj65
Nuijamaa FIN 38 Mj30
Nuiqsut USA (AK) 165 Ce10
Nui Son Tra VN 89 Qe37
Núi Than VN 89 Qe38
Nuits-Saint-Georges F 25 Le43
Nukhayla SUD 134 Md36
Nukini, T.I. BR 196 Gd49
Nuku PNG 115 Sb47
Nuku'alofa TO 101 Ba11
Nukuhu PNG 116 Se48
Nukumanu Atoll = Tasman Islands PNG 117 Sk48
Nukus UZ 62 Nk24
Nulato USA (AK) 165 Ca13
Nulavik USA (AK) 165 Cb10
Nulbear AUS (QLD) 109 Sd59
Nules E 29 Ku51
Nullabor AUS (SA) 105 Rf61
Nullagine AUS (WA) 102 Ra56
Nullarbor N.P. AUS 105 Rf61
Nullarbor Plain AUS 105 Rd61
Nullarbor Regional Reserve AUS 105 Re61
Nullawa AUS (NSW) 109 Sd60
Nulli ZW 152 Mf57
Num NEP 81 Pd32
Num RI 114 Rh46
Numagalong AUS (NT) 103 Rg56
Numaligarh IND (ASM) 86 Pg32
Numan WAN 139 Lg41
Numata J 77 Sa24
Numata J 77 Rk27
Numazu J 79 Rk28
Numbulwar AUS (NT) 106 Rh53
Numedalen N 30 Lj30
Nummela FIN 38 Me30
Nummi FIN 38 Md30
Nummijärvi FIN 38 Mc28
Numurkah AUS (VIC) 111 Sc64
Nunavut CDN 162 Eb06
Nundroo AUS (SA) 105 Rg61
Nuneaton GB 21 Kt38
Nungarin AUS (WA) 104 Qk61
Nungba IND (MNP) 86 Pg33
Nungo MOC 147 Mj52
Nungwaia PNG 115 Sb49
Nungwe EAT 144 Mg47
Nunhat IND (JKD) 83 Pd33
Nunivak Island USA 164 Bg15
Nuñoa PE 197 Ge53
Nunputuo Si CHN 75 Qk33
Nunspeet NL 23 Lf38
Nunukan Timur RI 94 Qj43
Núoro I 36 Lk50
Núpsstaður IS 18 Kc27
Nur IR 62 Nf27
Nur Abad IR 57 Nd28
Nur Abad IR 57 Nf28
Nur Abad IR 59 Nf30
Nuraghe Santa Barbara I 36 Lj50
Nuraghe Santa Cristina I 36 Lj50
Nuraghe Sant'Antine I 36 Lj50
Nuraghe Santa Sabina I 36 Lj50
Nuratan N.P. UZ 63 Oe25
Nürburgring D 33 Lg40
Nurdağı TR 56 Mj27
Nur Dağları TR 56 Mj27
Nurei SUD 134 Mb39
Nurek TJ 63 Oe26
Nurek Dam TJ 63 Oe26
Nurestan AFG 63 Of28
Nur Gama PK 65 Od31
Nurhak TR 56 Mj27
Nuri MEX (SO) 180 Ef31
Nurina AUS (WA) 105 Rd61
Nuri Necropolis SUD 135 Mf36
Nurioopta AUS (SA) 110 Rk63
Nurkaat RI 97 Rf49
Nurla 81 Oj28
Nurmes FIN 16 Me14
Nurmijärvi FIN 38 Me30
Nurmo FIN 38 Mc28
Nurmo FIN 38 Md28
Nürnberg D 33 Lm41
Nurobod UZ 63 Od26
Nurota UZ 63 Oc25
Nurota tizmasi UZ 63 Od25
Nurpur PK 65 Of30
Nürtingen D 33 Lk42
Nusa Dua RI 95 Qh50
Nusa Penida RI 95 Qh50
Nusawulan RI 114 Rg48
Nusaybin TR 57 Na27
Nuşfalau RO 43 Mc43
Nush Abad IR 57 Nf28
Nushagak Peninsula USA 164 Ca16
Nushki PK 65 Oc31
Nustal SYR 57 Mk27
Nutt USA (NM) 171 Eg29
Nuttal PK 65 Oe31
Nutwood Downs AUS (NT) 106 Rh53
Nuu EAK 145 Mk46
Nuuk = Godthåb DK 163 Hb06
Nuuksion kansallispuisto FIN 38 Me30
Nuwakot NEP 81 Pc32
Nuwara Eliya CL 85 Pa42
Nuwefontain NAM 154 Lk60
Nuweh RI 114 Rk49
Nuweiba ET 129 Mh31
Nuwerus ZA 154 Lk61
Nuweveldberge ZA 154 Ma62
Nuy ZA 154 Lk62
Nuzvid IND (APH) 83 Pa37
Nwanedi Game Reserve ZA 152 Mf57
Nwanetsi ZA 155 Mf58
Nwoya EAU 144 Mf44
Nxai Pan RB 151 Mc55
Nxai Pan N.P. RB 151 Mc55
Nyabessan CAM 138 Lf44
Nyabing AUS (WA) 104 Qk62
Nyagassola RG 136 Kf39
Nyahanga EAT 144 Mg47
Nyahururu EAK 144 Mj45
Nyainqêntanglha Feng CHN 69 Pf30
Nyainqêntanglha Shan CHN 68 Pe31
Nyainrong CHN (TIB) 69 Pg29
Nyakahra EAT 144 Mf47
Nyakanazi EAT 144 Mf47
Nyakitasi EAT 147 Mk50
Nyala SUD 134 Mc39
Ny Ålesund N 16 Lf06
Nyali G 148 Lf47
Nyalikungu EAT 144 Mg47
Nyama Z 152 Me53
Nyamandhlovu ZW 152 Me55
Nyamapanda ZW 152 Mg54
Nyamassila TG 137 La42
Nyamayeropa ZW 152 Mg54
Nyamgalika EAT 146 Mf48
Nyamirembe EAT 144 Mf47
Nyamlell SUD 141 Md41
Nyamok CAM 139 Lf43
Nyamtumbo EAT 147 Mj51
Nyamuswa EAT 144 Mh46
Nyanga G 148 Lf47
Nyanga RCB 148 Lf47
Nyanga ZW 152 Mg55
Nyangana NAM 151 Ma55
Nyanga N.P. ZW 152 Mg55
Nyang'olo EAT 147 Mh49
Nyantwiga EAT 144 Mf47
Nyanza RWA 146 Me47
Nyanza-Lac BU 146 Me48
Nyarananda EAT 146 Me48
Nyaru EAK 144 Mh45
Nyarweyo EAU 144 Mf45
Nyasa RDC 146 Md48
Nyassar CAM 139 Lh42
Nyaungkhashe MYA 88 Pj37
Nyaunglebin MYA 88 Pj37
Nyaungshwe MYA 86 Pj35
Nyaung-U MYA 86 Ph35
Nyazura ZW 152 Mg55
Nybergsund N 17 Lf15
Nyborg DK 30 Ll35
Nybro S 31 Lq34
Nyékládháza H 43 Ma43
Nyengedi EAT 147 Mk51
Nyergesújfalu H 42 Lt43
Nyeri EAK 144 Mj46
Nyeri EAU/SUD 144 Mf44
Nyero Rockpaintings EAU 144 Mg45
Ny-Friesland N 16 Lj06
Nyhammar S 31 Lp30
Nyibiam WAN 138 Le41
Nýidalur IS 18 Kb26
Nyiel SUD 141 Mf42
Nyika ZW 152 Mf55
Nyika N.P. Z/MW 146 Mg51
Nyika Plateau MW 146 Mg51
Nyikine SN 136 Kb39
Nyima CHN (TIB) 68 Pd30
Nyimba Z 152 Mf53
Nyiminiama RMM 131 Kj38
Nyingchi CHN (TIB) 69 Ph31
Nyírábrány H 43 Mc43
Nyíradony H 43 Mb43
Nyiragongo RDC 141 Me46
Nyírbátor H 43 Mc43
Nyírbéltek H 43 Mc43
Nyíregyháza H 43 Mb43
Nyiri Desert EAK 144 Mj47
Nyírmada H 43 Mc42
Nyírtelek H 43 Mb43
Nyiru Range EAK 144 Mj44
Nykøbing F DK 30 Lm36
Nykøbing M DK 30 Lj34
Nykøbing S DK 30 Lm35
Nyköping S 31 Lr32
Nykroppa S 31 Lp31
Nykvarn S 31 Ls31
Nylstroom ZA 155 Me58

Osterburken – Pantalica

Osterburken D 33 Lk41
Österbybruk S 31 Ls30
Österbymo S 31 Lq33
Österforse S 16 Lj14
Östergarnsholm S 31 Lt33
Öster-Götland S 31 Lq32
Osterhofen D 33 Lo42
Osterholz-Scharmbeck D 32 Lj37
Øster Hurup DK 30 Ll34
Østerlars DK 31 Lp35
Osterode D 32 Ll39
Östersund S 16 Lh14
Östersundom = Itäsalmi FIN 38 Mf30
Östervåla S 31 Ls30
Ostfrieisische Inseln D 32 Lh37
Ostfriesland D 32 Lh37
Östhammar S 31 Lt30
Óstia Antica I 36 Ln49
Östmark S 30 Ln30
Ostrava CZ 42 Lt41
Ostren i madhë AL 44 Ma49
Ostrica BG 45 Mh48
Ostritz D 32 Lp40
Ostróda PL 41 Lu37
Ostrogožsk RUS 48 Mk20
Ostroh UA 49 Md20
Ostrołęka PL 41 Mb37
Ostrov CZ 42 Ln40
Ostrov RO 45 Mh46
Ostrov RO 45 Mj46
Ostrov RUS 39 Mj33
ostrov Ajon RUS 55 Tb04
ostrov Arga-Muora-Sise RUS 55 Ra04
ostrova Sergeja Kirova RUS 54 Pb03
ostrov Belyj RUS 54 Oc04
ostrov Bol'ševik RUS 55 Qa03
ostrov Bol'šoj Begičev RUS 55 Qd04
ostrov Bol'šoj Berezovyj RUS 38 Mj30
ostrov Bol'šoj Ljahovskij RUS 55 Sa04
ostrov Bol'soj Tjuters RUS 38 Mh31
ostrov Čečen RUS 57 Nd23
ostrov Chortycja UA 49 Mh22
ostrov Gogland RUS 38 Mg30
ostrov Greèm-Bell RUS 54 Oa02
Ostrov Iturup RUS 77 Sd23
ostrov Karaginskij RUS 55 Ta07
ostrov Kolgujev RUS 54 Nb05
ostrov Komsomolec RUS 54 Pc02
ostrov Kotel'nyj RUS 55 Rd03
ostrov Kotlin RUS 38 Mk30
ostrov Malyj RUS 38 Mj30
ostrov Malyj Tjuters RUS 38 Mg31
Ostrov Moneron RUS 77 Sa22
ostrov Moščnyj RUS 38 Mh31
ostrov Novaja Sibir' RUS 55 Sb03
ostrov Ogurchinskiy TM 62 Ng26
ostrov Oktjabr'skoj Revoljucii RUS 54 Pc03
ostrov Ol'hon RUS 70 Qd19
ostrov Onekotan RUS 55 Sc09
ostrov Paramušir RUS 55 Sd08
ostrov Rasšua RUS 55 Sc09
ostrov Rudol'fa RUS 54 Nd02
ostrov Seskar RUS 38 Mj30
ostrov Šiaškotan RUS 55 Sc09
ostrov Simušir RUS 55 Sc09
ostrov Tjullenij RUS 57 Nd23
ostrov Urup RUS 55 Sc09
ostrov Vajgač RUS 54 Oa04
ostrov Valaam RUS 38 Ml29
ostrov Vasil'evskij RUS 38 Ml31
ostrov Zapadnyj Berezovyj RUS 38 Mj30
Ostrowice PL 40 Lq37
Ostrowiec Świętokrzyski PL 41 Mb40
Ostrowieczno PL 40 Ls39
Ostrowite PL 40 Lt38
Ostrów Lubelski PL 41 Mc39
Ostrów Mazowiecka PL 41 Mb38
Ostrów Wielkopolski PL 40 Ls39
Ostrožac BIH 35 Lq46
Ostrzeszów PL 40 Ls39
Ostuni I 37 Ls50
Ostuta MEX (OAX) 183 Fc37
Osumi-hanto J 79 Rf30
Osumi Islands J 79 Rf30
Osumi Strait J 79 Rf30
Osuna E 27 Kp53
Osun-Osogbo Sacred grove WAN Lc42
Oswego USA (KS) 174 Fc27
Oswego USA (NY) 177 Gb24
Oswestry GB 21 Kr38
Oświęcim PL 41 Lu40
Osypenko UA 49 Mj22
Otacílio Costa BR (SC) 205 He59
Otago Peninsula NZ 113 Tf68
Otaki-Maori Racecourse NZ 113 Th66
Otakwa RI 114 Rj48
O'tamurot UZ 63 Oc24
Otar KZ 66 Oh24
Otaru J 77 Sa24
Otavalo EC 196 Ga45
Otavi NAM 150 Lg55
Otavi NAM 150 Lj55
Otchinjau ANG 150 Lg54
O.T.Downs AUS (NT) 106 Rh54
Otegen Batyr KZ 66 Oj24
Oțelu Roșu RO 44 Mc45
Otepää EST 39 Mg32
Otepää körgustik EST 39 Mg32
Oterkpalu GH 137 Kk42
Oteștii de Jos RO 45 Me46
Otgon Tenger Uul MNG 67 Pj22
Otgon Tenger Uul Nature Reserve MNG 67 Pj22
Othello USA (WA) 168 Ea22
Othoni GR 46 Lu51
Oti GH 137 La41
Otištić HR 35 Lr47
Otjihungwa NAM 150 Lg54
Otjijandjasemo Hot Spring NAM 150 Lg54
Otjikondo NAM 150 Lh55
Otjimbingwe NAM 150 Lj57
Otjinene NAM 150 Lk56
Otjisemba NAM 150 Lj56
Otjitanda NAM 150 Lg54
Otjitunduwa NAM 150 Lh55
Otjiwarongo NAM 150 Lj56
Otjosondu NAM 150 Lj56
Otjozondjupa NAM 150 Lj55
Otlukbeli Dağları TR 57 Mk25
Otmek KS 66 Og24
Otnes N 17 Lf15
Otoca PE 197 Gc53
Otočac HR 35 Lq46
Otog Qi CHN (NMZ) 72 Qd26
Otoineppu J 77 Sb23
Otok HR 35 Lr47
Otok HR 35 Lt45
Otongo MEX (HDG) 182 Fa35
Otong Qian Qi CHN (NMZ) 72 Qd26
Otorohanga NZ 112 Th65
Otorowo PL 40 Lr38
Otoyo J 79 Rg29
Otra N 30 Lh31
Otranto I 37 Lt50
Otrokovice CZ 42 Ls41
Ötscher A 35 Lq43
Otsu J 79 Rh28
Otsuki J 79 Rk28
Otta N 17 Le15
Ottapalam IND (KER) 84 Oj40
Ottawa CDN (ON) 177 Gc23
Ottawa USA (IL) 173 Ff25
Ottawa USA (KS) 174 Fc26
Ottawa USA (OH) 173 Fh25
Ottawa Islands CDN 163 Fd07
Ottenby S 31 Lr34
Ottenstein Stausee A 42 Lq42
Otter CDN (QC) 176 Gj21
Otter USA (MT) 169 Eg23
Otterbäcken S 31 Lp32
Otterburn GB 20 Ks35
Otter Creek USA (FL) 178 Fj31
Otter Island USA 164 Be17
Otterndorf D 32 Lj37
Otter Pt. USA 164 Bj18
Otter Rapids CDN (ON) 173 Fk20
Ottertail USA (MN) 172 Fc22
Otterup DK 30 Ll35
Ottobrunn D 33 Lm42
Ottosdal ZA 155 Md59
Ottoshoop ZA 155 Md58
Ottumwa USA (IA) 172 Fd25
Otu CAM 138 Le43
Otukpa WAN 138 Ld42
Otumpa RA (SE) 207 Gj59
Otupe PE 196 Ga49
Oturkpo WAN 138 Le42
Otuzco PE 196 Ga49
Otway N.P. AUS 111 Sb65
Otwock PL 41 Mb38
Otynja UA 43 Me42
Ötztaler Alpen A 34 Ll44
Ouachita USA (AR) 174 Fd29
Ouachita Mts. USA 174 Fc28
Ouaco F (NCL) 118 Tc56
Ouadâne RIM 130 Ke35
Ouadda RCA 140 Mb41
Ouâd Nâga RIM 130 Kc37
Ouagadou RMM 131 Kg38
Ouagadougou BF 137 Kk39
Ouahabou BF 137 Kj40
Ouahigouya BF 137 Kj39
Ouahiré CI 137 Kg40
Ouakam SN 130 Kb38
Ouaké DY 138 La41
Oualâta RIM 131 Kg37
Oualidia MA 124 Kf29
Oualla RG 136 Ke40
Ouallam RN 132 Lb38
Ouallen DZ 132 La33
Ouanazein TCH 133 Lj37
Ouanda Djallé RCA 140 Mb41
Ouandago RCA 140 Lk42
Ouandja RCA 140 Mb41
Ouandja RCA 140 Mb41
Ouando RCA 141 Mc43
Ouango RCA 140 Mb43
Ouango-Fitini CI 137 Kh41
Ouangolodougou CI 137 Kh41
Ouani RMM 131 Kk37
Ouaninou CI 136 Kg41
Ouanzerbé RN 131 La38
Ouarak SN 130 Kb38
Ouarâne RIM 130 Kf35
Ouargay BF 137 La40
Ouargla DZ 126 Lc30
Ouaritoufoulout RMM 132 Lb37
Ouarkay BF 137 Kj39
Ouarkla CAM 139 Lh41
Ouarzazate MA 125 Kg30
Ouassa Bamvélé CAM 139 Lg43
Ouatagouna RMM 131 La38
Ouatcha RN 132 Le39
Ouatér Galafondo RCA 140 Lk43
Oubangui RCB/RDC 140 Lj45
Ouchi CHN (HUB) 74 Qg31
Oudabunna AUS (WA) 104 Qj60
Ouddorp NL 23 Ld39
Oudeïka RMM 131 Kk37
Oudenaarde B 23 Ld40
Oude Pekela NL 23 Lh37
Oudjilla CAM 139 Lh40
Oudna TN 126 Lf27
Oudref TN 126 Le29
Oudtshoorn ZA 154 Mb62
Oued Djaret DZ 126 Lb32
Oued Drâa MA 125 Kh30
Oued el Abiod RIM 130 Kd37
Oued el Hajâr RMM 131 Kj36
Oued Guir DZ 125 Kj30
Oued Harket Besbes DZ 126 Lc28
Oued Mimoun DZ 125 Kk28
Oued Moulouya MA 125 Kj28
Oued Rhiou DZ 125 La28
Oued Saoura DZ 125 Kk31
Oued Tadant DZ 132 Ld34
Oued Tafassasset DZ 132 Le34
Oued Tamanrasset DZ 132 Lc34
Oued Tekouiat DZ 132 Lb34
Oued Tichkantine DZ 132 Lc35
Oued Tlelat DZ 125 Kk28
Oued-Zem MA 125 Kg29
Oued Zenati DZ 126 Ld27
Ouégoa F (NCL) 118 Tc56
Ouéla RN 132 Lb38
Ouélé CI 137 Kg40
Ouéléssébougou RMM 137 Kg40
Ouéllé CI 137 Kh42
Ouenkoro RMM 137 Kj39
Ouenza DZ 126 Le28
Oué Oué DY 138 Lb41
Ouessa BF 137 Kj40
Ouessant F 22 Kp42
Ouessé DY 138 Lb41
Ouezzane MA 125 Kh28
Oufrane DZ 125 La31
Ougarou BF 137 La39
Ougarta DZ 125 Kj31
Oughterard IRL 19 Kl37
Ouidah DY 138 Lb42
Ouidi RN 133 Lg38
Ouimet Canyon CDN 172 Ff21
Ouinardene RMM 131 Kk37
Ouinhi DY 138 Lb42
Ouistreham F 22 Ku41
Oujâf RIM 131 Kg37
Oujda MA 125 Kk28
Oujeft RIM 130 Kd35
Oukaïmeden MA 125 Kg30
Oukraal ZA 154 Lk63
Oulad-Teïma MA 124 Kf30
Oulainen FIN 16 Mc13
Oulangan kansallispuisto FIN 16 Me12
Ould Lammas Fair GB 19 Ko35
Ould Yenjé RIM 130 Ke38
Ouled Allenda DZ 126 Ld29
Ouled -Djellal DZ 126 Lc28
Ouli CAM 139 Lh43
Oulmes MA 125 Kh29
Oulnina Hill AUS 110 Rk62
Oulu FIN 16 Mc13
Oulujärvi FIN 16 Md13
Oumache DZ 126 Lc28
Oum-Chalouba TCH 134 Ma38
Oumcheggag DARS 124 Kd32
Oum Djerane DZ 125 La28
Oumé CI 137 Kh42
Oum el Achar DZ 124 Kf31
Oum el Assel DZ 125 Kg31
Oum-el-Bouaghi DZ 126 Ld28
Oum-Hadjer TCH 133 Lk39
Oumm el Khezz RIM 130 Ke37
Ounantiékaha CI 137 Kh41
Ounara MA 124 Kf30
Oundle GB 21 Ku38
Oungre CDN (SK) 169 Ej21
Ounianga Kébir TCH 134 Ma36
Ounianga Sérir TCH 134 Ma36
Ountivou TG 137 La42
Ouo RMM 131 Kj38
Ouogo RCA 140 Lj42
Ourafane RN 132 Le38
Ouragahio CI 137 Kh42
Oura-Ndia RMM 131 Kh38
Ouranoúpoli GR 45 Me50
Ouray USA (CO) 171 Eg27
Ouray USA (UT) 171 Ef25
Oureï RIM 131 Kg37
Ouré-Kaba RG 136 Ke40
Ourém BR (PA) 195 Hg46
Ourense = Orense E 26 Kn48
Ouricuri BR (PE) 201 Hk49
Ourikéla RMM 137 Kh39
Ourilândia BR (PA) 200 He49
Ourinhos BR (SP) 202 Hf57
Ourini TCH 134 Mb37
Ourique P 27 Km53
Our Lady of Health (Velangani) IND 85 Ok40
Ourlal DZ 126 Lc28
Ouro Amat SN 130 Kd38
Ouro Branco BR (MG) 203 Hj56
Ouro Fino BR (MG) 203 Hg57
Ourolândia BR (BA) 201 Hk51
Ouro-Modi RMM 131 Kh38
Ouro Preto BR (MG) 203 Hj56
Ouro Preto d'Oeste BR (RO) 198 Gj51
Ouro Sawabé RN 132 La39
Ouro Sogui SN 130 Kd38
Oursi BF 131 Kk38
Ourtzarh MA 125 Kh28
Ou-sanmyaku J 77 Sa26
Oussoubidiagna RMM 130 Ke38
Oussouye SN 136 Kb39
Outad-Oulad-El-Haj MA 125 Kj29
Outamba-Kilimi N.P. WAL 136 Kd41
Outeïd Arkâs RMM 131 Kh37
Outeniekwaberge ZA 154 Mb62
Outeniqua Choo-Tjoe ZA 154 Mb63
Outer Dowsing 21 Lb37
Outer Hebrides GB 20 Kn33
Outer Pool ZA 154 Mb63
Outer Sister Island AUS 111 Sd65
Outfene RIM 131 Kf37
Outing USA (MN) 172 Fd22
Outjo NAM 150 Lj56
Outlook CDN (SK) 169 Eg20
Outokumpu FIN 38 Mk28
Oûtoûl DZ 132 Lc34
Outram NZ 113 Tf68
Out Skerries GB 20 Ku30
Ouvéa F (NCL) 118 Td56
Ou wa-brug ZA 155 Mc60
Ouyen AUS (VIC) 110 Sb63
Ouzouer-sur-Loire F 25 Lc43
Ovacik TR 56 Mh26
Ovacık TR 57 Na25
Ovada EAT 146 Mh48
Ovada I 34 Lj46
Ovaeymiri TR 47 Mh53
Ovakışla TR 57 Nb26
Ovala G 148 Lf46
Ovalau FJI 119 Tk54
Ovalle RCH 208 Ge61
Ovambo NAM 150 Lj55
Ovamboland NAM 150 Lh55
Ovan G 148 Lg45
Ovana, Cerro YV 193 Gg43
Ovando USA (MT) 169 Ed22
Ovar P 26 Km50
Ovari Paravarnattam IND (TNU) 84 Oj41
Ovau Island SOL 117 Sj49
Ovča SCG 44 Ma46
Ovejas CO 192 Gc41
Ovejas, Cerro de las RA 208 Gh62
Oveng CAM 139 Lg44
Overath D 32 Lh40
Overflowing River CDN (MB) 169 Ek19
Overflow N.W.R. USA 175 Fe29
Øvergård N 16 Lk11
Överhörnäs S 38 Lt27
Överkalix S 16 Mb12
Overlander House AUS (WA) 104 Qh59
Overland Park USA (KS) 174 Fc26
Överlida S 30 Ln33
Övermark = Ylimarkku FIN 38 Mb28
Overpelt B 23 Lf39
Overseas Highway USA 179 Fk33
Overton USA (NV) 170 Ec27
Övertorneå S 16 Mb12
Överum S 31 Lr33
Ovidiopol' UA 49 Mf22
Ovidiu RO 45 Mj46
Oviedo DOM 186 Ge37
Oviedo E 26 Kp47
Oviniščenskaja vozvyšennost' RUS 48 Mj16
Oviston Nature Reserve ZA 155 Mc61
Övögdij MNG 67 Pj21
Ovoot MNG 71 Qg23
Övörkhangay MNG 70 Qa22
Øvre Anárjohka n.p. N 16 Mc11
Øvre Årdal N 17 Ld15
Øvre Dividal n.p. N 16 Lk11
Øvre Pasvik n.p. N 16 Me11
Øvre Rendal N 17 Lf15
Övre Soppero S 16 Ma11
Ovruč UA 48 Me20
Owabi W.S. GH 137 Kk42
Owaka NZ 113 Te69
Owando RCB 148 Lh46
Owase J 79 Rj28
Owatonna USA (MN) 172 Fd23
Owbeh AFG 64 Ob28
Owena WAN 138 Lc42
Owende G 148 Le45
Owen Falls Dam EAU 144 Mg45
Owen River NZ 113 Tg66
Owensboro USA (KY) 175 Fg27
Owen Shoal 94 Qf41
Owen Sound CDN (ON) 173 Fk23
Owen Stanley Range PNG 115 Sd50
Owensville USA (MO) 175 Fe26
Owenton USA (KY) 175 Fh26
Owerri WAN 138 Ld43
Owińska PL 40 Lr38
Owkal AFG 64 Oa29
Owl Creek Indian Mounds USA 175 Ff28
Owl River CDN 167 Ee18
Owo WAN 138 Lc42
Owode WAN 138 Lb42
Owosso USA (MI) 173 Fh24
Owutu WAN 138 Ld43
Owyhee USA (NV) 168 Eb25
Owyhee Ridge USA 168 Eb24
Oxapampa PE 197 Gc51
Öxarfjörður IS 18 Kd24
Oxbow CDN (SK) 169 Ej21
Oxbow LS 155 Me60
Oxbow USA (OR) 168 Eb23
Oxelösund S 31 Ls32
Oxenhope AUS (QLD) 109 Sc56
Oxers Lookout AUS 102 Qk57
Oxford CDN (NS) 176 Gj23
Oxford GB 21 Kt39
Oxford NZ 113 Tg67
Oxford USA (MS) 175 Ff28
Oxford USA (NC) 178 Ga27
Oxiá GR 46 Mb52
Oxie S 30 Lo35
Oxkintoc MEX 183 Ff35
Oxkutzcab MEX (YT) 183 Ff35
Oxley Wild Rivers N.P. AUS 109 Sg61
Oxnard USA (CA) 170 Ea28
Oxtotitlán MEX 182 Fa37
Oxunboboyev UZ 63 Og25
Oya MAL 94 Qf44
Oyabi RCB 148 Lh46
Oya-Kannon J 77 Rk27
Oyama CDN (BC) 168 Ea20
Oyama J 77 Rk27
Oyan G 148 Lf46
Oyem G 139 Lf45
Oyen CDN (AB) 169 Ee20
Oyé Yeska TCH 133 Lk36
Oygon MNG 67 Pj21
Oyo RCB 148 Lh46
Oyo SUD 129 Mj35
Oyo WAN 138 Lb42
Oyón PE 197 Gb51
Oyonnax F 25 Lf44
Oyoqquduq UZ 63 Oc25
Oyou Bezzé Denga RN 133 Lg37
Øyrlandsodden N 16 Lj07
Oysha RDC 141 Me45
Øyslebø N 30 Lh32
Oystercliff NAM 154 Lh58
Oyster Island MYA 86 Pg36
Oysterville USA (WA) 168 Dh22
Oyten D 32 Lk37
Ozalj HR 35 Lq45
Özalp TR 57 Nb26
Ozamiz RP 91 Rb41
Ozark USA (AL) 175 Fh30
Ozark USA (AR) 174 Fd28
Ozark USA (MO) 174 Fd27
Ozark Natl. Scenic Riverways USA 175 Fe27
Ozark Plateau USA 174 Fd27
Ożarów PL 41 Mb40
Özbaşı TR 47 Mh53
Ózd H 43 Ma42
Ožďany SK 43 Lu42
Ożenna PL 41 Mb41
ozera Tunajča RUS 77 Sb22
Ozerci UA 41 Mf39
Ožerel'e RUS 48 Mk18
Ozerki RUS 48 Nd17
Ozerna UA 43 Mf41
ozero Barun-Torej RUS 71 Qh20
ozero Bol'šaja Itarga RUS 70 Qf19
ozero Bol'šoe Eravnoe RUS 70 Qf19
ozero Čany RUS 54 Od08
ozero Gusinoe RUS 70 Qd20
ozero Hanskoe RUS 49 Mk22
ozero Hindiktig-Hol' RUS 67 Pe20
ozero Il'men' RUS 48 Mf16
ozero Imandra RUS 16 Mg11
ozero Jalpuh UA 45 Mj45
ozero Kahul UA 45 Mj45
ozero Katlabuch UA 45 Mj45
ozero Kunašir RUS 77 Sd23
ozero Nero RUS 48 Mk17
ozero Šakšinskoe RUS 70 Qg19
ozero Samro RUS 38 Mj32
ozero Šikotan RUS 77 Sd24
ozero Svitjaz'ke UA 41 Md39
Ozero Tajmyr RUS 55 Qa04
ozero Tere-Hol' RUS 67 Ph20
ozero Tere-Hol' RUS 67 Pj20
ozero Zelenyj RUS 77 Sd24
ozero Zorkul' AFG/TJ 63 Og27
ozero Zun-Torej RUS 71 Qh20
Ozersk RUS 39 Mc36
Ozerskij RUS 77 Sb22
Ozery RUS 48 Mk18
Ozhiski Lake CDN 172 Ff19
Ozhukara IND (TNU) 85 Ok39
Ožidaevo RUS 77 Sb22
Ozieri I 36 Lk50
Ozimek PL 40 Lt40
Ozona USA (TX) 174 Ek30
Ozondati NAM 150 Lh56
Ozondjache NAM 150 Lj56
Ozori G 148 Le46
Ozorków PL 41 Lu39
Ozoro WAN 138 Ld43
Ozu J 79 Rg29
Ozuluama MEX (VC) 182 Fb35
Ozumba MEX (MEX) 182 Fa36
Ozurgeti GE 57 Nb25

P

Pâ BF 137 Kj40
Paamiut = Frederikshåb DK 163 Hb06
Pa-an MYA 88 Pj37
Paanayarvi N.P. RUS 16 Mf12
Paanto RI 96 Ra46
Paar D 33 Lm42
Paardeberg ZA 155 Mc60
Paarl ZA 154 Lk62
Pabal-ri PRK 76 Re25
Pabbay GB 20 Kn33
Pabel IND (MHT) 82 Oh36
Pabellón de Arteaga MEX (AGS) 182 Ej34
Pabianice PL 41 Lu39
Pabidnan IR 64 Nj30
Pablo USA (MT) 168 Ec22
Pabna BD 86 Pe33
Pa Bon THA 88 Qa42
Pabradė LT 39 Mf36
Pacáas-Novos, T.I. BR 198 Gh51
Pacaembu BR (SP) 202 He56
Pacaipampa PE 196 Ga48
Pacajus BR (CE) 201 Ja48
Pacapausa PE 197 Gd53
Pacaraos PE 197 Gb51
Pacasmayo PE 196 Ga49
Pacatuba BR (CE) 201 Ja47
Paccha EC 196 Ga47
Pacchani PE 206 Gf52
Pace USA (FL) 175 Fg30
Pačelma RUS 48 Nb19
Pachacámac PE 197 Gb52
Pachacámac PE 197 Gb52
Pachaconas PE 197 Gd53
Pachala SUD 142 Mh42
Pachino I 37 Lq54
Pachmarhi IND (MPH) 83 Ok34
Pachmarhi Hill Resort IND 83 Ok34
Pacho CO 192 Gc43
Pachor IND (MPH) 82 Oj34
Pachora IND (MHT) 82 Oh35
Pachperwa IND (UPH) 83 Pb32
Pachuca MEX (HDG) 182 Fa35
Pacific Grove USA (CA) 170 Dk27
Pacific Ocean 10 Ta06
Pacific Ranges CDN 168 Dg20
Pacific Rim N.P. CDN 168 Dh21
Pacijan Island RP 90 Rc40
Pacitan RI 95 Qf50
Păciul lui Soare RO 45 Mh46
Packsaddle AUS (NSW) 108 Sa61
Packsattel A 35 Lp43
Paço do Lumiar BR (MA) 195 Hh47
Pacov CZ 42 Lp41
Pacoval BR (PA) 199 Hc47
Pacuária da Barra do Longa ANG 148 Lg51
Pacuativa CO 192 Ge45
Pacy-sur-Eure F 23 Lb41
Paczków PL 40 Lr40
Padaelo RI 96 Ra48
Pa Daet THA 87 Pk36
Padag PK 65 Oc31
Padako CI 137 Kh43
Padampur IND (ORS) 83 Pb35
Padang RI 93 Qa46
Padang RI 93 Qb45
Padanganget RI 93 Qb48
Padang Besar MAL 92 Qa42
Padang Endau MAL 92 Qb44
Padangguci RI 93 Qb48
Padangpanjang RI 93 Qa46
Padangsidempuan RI 93 Pk45
Padangtikar RI 95 Qe46
Padarosk BY 41 Me38
Padasjoki FIN 38 Mf29
Padawiya CL 85 Pa41
Padcaya BOL 207 Gh56
Padcoyo BOL 206 Gh56
Paddington AUS (NSW) 111 Sc62
PadeaBesar RI 97 Rb47
Padej SCG 44 Ma45
Padeniya CL 85 Pa42
Paderborn D 32 Lj39
Paderu IND (APH) 83 Pb36
Padiankayudad RI 93 Qa46
Padibe EAU 144 Mg44
Padilla BOL 206 Gh55
Padina RO 45 Mh46
Padise EST 38 Me31
Padjelanta n.p. S 16 Lj12
Padmanabhapuram IND 84 Oj41
Padnagarh IND (ORS) 83 Pb35
Pádova I 34 Lm45
Padrauna IND (UPH) 83 Pc32
Padre Bernardo BR (GO) 203 Hf53
Padre Burgos RP 90 Rc40
Padre Island USA 181 Fb32
Padre Island National Seashore USA 181 Fb32
Padre Paraíso BR (MG) 203 Hk54
Padre, T.I. BR 199 Ha47
Padre Vieira BR (CE) 201 Hk47
Padrón E 26 Km48
Padstow GB 21 Kq40
Padsville BY 39 Mh35
Padthaway AUS (SA) 110 Sa64
Paducah USA (KY) 175 Ff27
Paducah USA (TX) 174 Ek29
Padul E 27 Kr53
Padum 81 Oj29
Padwa IND (ORS) 83 Pb36
Paekdu San CHN/PRK 76 Re25
Paeroa NZ 112 Th64
Paestum I 37 Lp50
Pafos CY 56 Mg28
Pafuri ZA 152 Mf57
Pafuri Gate ZA 152 Mf57
Pag HR 35 Lq46
Pag HR 35 Lq46
Pagadenbaru RI 95 Qd49
Pagadian RP 91 Rb42
Pagai Selatan RI 93 Qa47
Pagai Utara RI 93 Qa47
Pagancillo RA (LR) 207 Gf60
Paganzo RA (LR) 207 Gg61
Pagaralam RI 93 Qb48
Pagas Divisas BR (AP) 199 Hd46
Pagatan RI 95 Qh47
Pagawyun MYA 88 Pk38
Page USA (AZ) 171 Ee27
Page USA (OK) 174 Fc28
Pagėgiai LT 39 Mb35
Pageland USA (SC) 178 Fk28
Pagelažiai LT 39 Me35
Pagergunung RI 93 Qc47
Pagimana RI 96 Rb46
Paglugaban Island RP 90 Qk40
Pagny-sur-Mosur F 23 Lg42
Pagodas (Monywa) MYA 86 Ph34
Pagodas (Pakokku) MYA 86 Ph35
Pago Pago USA 101 Ba11
Pagosa Springs USA (CO) 171 Eg27
Pagou BF 137 La39
Pagsanjan RP 90 Ra38
Paguilou G 148 Le46
Paguyaman RI 91 Rb45
Pagwa River CDN (ON) 173 Fh20
Pagwi PNG 115 Sb48
Pahala USA (HI) 170 Cc36
Pahalgam 80 Oh28
Pahari IND (MPH) 83 Ok34
Paharikhera IND (MPH) 83 Pa33
Paharpur BD 86 Pe33
Paharpur PK 65 Of29
Pahaska Tepee USA (WY) 169 Ee23
Pahepa RI 91 Rc44
Pahiatua NZ 113 Th66
Pa Hin Ngam N.P. THA 88 Qa38
Páhnes GR 47 Me55
Pahoa USA (HI) 170 Cc36
Pahokee USA (FL) 179 Fk32
Pahraničny BY 41 Md37
Pahrump USA (NV) 170 Ec27
Pahsien Cave RC 75 Ra34
Pahur IND (MHT) 82 Oh35
Pahute Peak USA 170 Ea25
Pai THA 87 Pk36
Paia USA (HI) 170 Cb35
Paiçandu BR (PR) 202 Hd57
Paide EST 38 Mf32
Paignton GB 21 Kr40
Paihia NZ 112 Th63
Paijan PE 196 Ga49
Päijänne FIN 38 Mf29
Päijänteen kansallispuisto FIN 38 Mf29
Paiko WAN 138 Ld41
Pail PK 65 Og29
Pailin K 89 Qb39
Paillaco RCH 208 Gd66
Pailón BOL 206 Gj54
Pailou CHN (HBI) 73 Qj25
Paimbœuf F 24 Ks43
Paimio FIN 38 Mc30
Paimpol F 22 Kr42
Paim Vilho BR (RS) 204 He59
Painan RI 93 Qa46
Pain de Sucre RM 156 Ne52
Paine RCH 208 Ge62
Paine Grande, Cerro RCH 210 Gd71
Painel BR (SC) 205 He59
Painesville USA (OH) 173 Fk25
Pains BR (MG) 203 Hh56
Painted Churches CY 56 Mg28
Painted Desert USA 171 Ee28
Painted Desert USA 171 Ef28
Paint Rock USA (TX) 174 Fa30
Paintsville USA (KY) 178 Fj27
Paipa CO 192 Gd43
Paipote RCH 207 Ge59
Pai River Rafting THA 87 Pk36
Paisagem Cultural de Sintra P 27 Kl52
Paisha RC 75 Qk34
Paisley GB 20 Kq35
Paisley USA (OR) 168 Dk24
País Vasco E 28 Ks48
Païta F (NCL) 118 Td57
Paita PE 196 Fk48
Paithan IND (MHT) 82 Oh36
Paiton RI 95 Qg49
Păiușeni RO 43 Mc44
Pajal GCA 184 Ff38
Pajala S 16 Mb12
Paján EC 196 Fk46
Pajaplta GCA 183 Fd38
Pajarito CO 192 Gd43
Paje EAT 147 Mk49
Paje RB 152 Md57
Pajęczno PL 40 Lt39
Pajón MEX 183 Fd38
Pajonal, Cerro RCH 207 Gf56
Pajule EAU 144 Mg44
Páka H 42 Lr44
Pakabong PNG 116 Sg47
Pakala IND (APH) 85 Ok39
Pakaraima Mountains GUY 194 Gk43
Pakashkan Lake CDN 172 Fe21
Pakaur IND (WBG) 83 Pd33
Pakbeng LAO 87 Qa36
Pak Charang THA 89 Qb38
Pak Chom THA 89 Qb37
Pak Chong THA 88 Qa38
Pa Kham THA 89 Qb38
Paki WAN 138 Le40
Pakima RDC 149 Mc47
Pakistan PK 53 Oa07
Pak Kading LAO 87 Qc36
Pakkat RI 93 Pk44
Pak Kkat THA 87 Qb36
Paklenica, N.P. HR 35 Lq46
Pak Mong LAO 87 Qb35
Pakokku MYA 86 Ph35
Pakouabo CI 137 Kh42
Pak Ou Caves LAO 87 Qb35
Pakowki Lake CDN 169 Ee21
Pakpattan PK 65 Og30
Pak Phayun THA 88 Qa42
Pakrac HR 35 Ls45
Pakruojis LT 39 Md35
Paks H 43 Lt44
Paksan LAO 87 Qb36
Pakse LAO 89 Qc38
Paksong LAO 89 Qd38
Pak Tha LAO 87 Qa35
Pak Tho THA 88 Pk39
Pak Thong Chai THA 89 Qb38
Paku RI 93 Qa46
Pakuanaji RI 93 Qc48
Pakuli RI 96 Qk46
Pakwach EAU 144 Mf44
Pakwash Prov. Park CDN 172 Fd20
Pak Xeng LAO 87 Qb35
Pala TCH 140 Lh41
Palabaka RCB 148 Lh46
Palabeck EAU 144 Mg44
Palačany BY 39 Mg36
Palace of Abbasi ET 129 Mf30
Palace on Wheels IND 80 Oh32
Palacio de la Granja de San Ildefonso E 27 Kq50
Palacios BOL 206 Gg52
Palacios HN 184 Fh38
Palacios RA (SF) 207 Gk61
Palacios USA (TX) 181 Fb31
Pałac Krasiczyn PL 41 Mc41
Pałac Nieborow PL 41 Ma38
Pałac Rogalin PL 40 Lr38
Pałac Walicki PL 41 Ma39
Palafrugell E 29 Ld49
Palagonía I 37 Lp53
Palagruža HR 35 Lr48
Palaichori CY 56 Mg28
Palais des Ducs F 25 Lf43
Palais des Papes F 25 Le47
Palais des Rois de Majorque F 25 Lc48
Palaiseau F 23 Lc42
Palaiyam IND (TNU) 84 Ok40
Palakkad IND (KER) 84 Oj40
Palakollu IND (APH) 83 Pb37
Palala LB 136 Kf42
Palala ZA 155 Me58
Palamakoloi RB 154 Mb57
Palamás GR 46 Mc51
Palamau = Daltonganj IND (JKD) 83 Pc33
Palamau N.P. IND 83 Pc34
Palamea RI 97 Rd46
Palamós E 29 Ld49
Palana AUS (TAS) 111 Sd65
Palana IND (RJT) 80 Og32
Palanan RP 90 Rb37
Palanan Bay RP 90 Rb37
Palanan Point RP 90 Rb37
Palanas RP 90 Rb39
Palanga LT 39 Mb35
Palangkaraya RI 95 Qg47
Palani IND (TNU) 84 Oj40
Palani Hills IND 84 Oj40
Palanok UA 43 Mc42
Palanpur IND (GUJ) 82 Og33
Palanro RI 96 Ra48
Palantak PK 65 Oc32
Palapag RP 90 Rc39
Palapye RB 152 Md57
Palárikovo SK 42 Lt42
Palasa RI 91 Ra45
Palasamudram IND (APH) 84 Oj39
Palas de Rei E 26 Kn48
Palashbari BD 86 Pe33
Palaspal IND (ORS) 83 Pc35
Palatae RI 96 Ra48
Palatka KS 66 Ok24
Palatka USA (FL) 178 Fk31
Palatna SCG 44 Mb47
Palattsy KZ 67 Pb21
Palau I 36 Lk49
Palau MEX (COH) 181 Ek32
Palau 101 Rb09
Palau de la Música Catalana E 29 Lc49
Palau Güell E 29 Lc49
Palaui Island RP 90 Rb36
Palau Islands PAL 90 Rg42
Palauk MYA 88 Pk39
Palaw MYA 88 Pk39
Palawan RP 91 Qk41
Palawan Passage RP 94 Qj41
Palawan Trough 94 Qh42
Palayankottai IND (TNU) 84 Oj41
Palazzina di Caccia di Stupinigi I 34 Lh46
Palazzo Ducale di Mántova I 34 Ll45
Palazzo Ducale d'Urbino I 34 Ln47
Palazzolo Acréide I 37 Lp53
Palazzolo sull'Oglio I 34 Lk45
Palazzo Madama I 34 Lh45
Palazzo Reale di Caserta I 37 Lp49
Palca PE 197 Gc51
Palca PE 197 Ge53
Palca PE 206 Gf54
Palca RCH 206 Gf55
Palcamayo PE 197 Gc51
Paldiski EST 38 Me31
Pale BIH 44 Lt47
Paleh RUS 48 Na17
Palékastro GR 47 Mg55
Paleleh RI 91 Ra45
Paleleh Mountains RI 91 Ra45
Palembang RI 93 Qc47
Palena I 37 Lp49
Palencia E 26 Kq49
Palenque MEX (CHP) 183 Fe37
Palenque MEX 183 Fd37
Palenque PA 185 Ga41
Paleo Frourio GR 46 Lu51
Paleohóra GR 45 Md55
Paleohóri GR 46 Mb51
Paleokastrítsa GR 46 Lu51
Paleópoli GR 45 Mf50
Paleópoli GR 47 Me53
Palermo CO 192 Gc44
Palermo I 36 Lo52
Palesse BY 41 Md39
Palesse BY 41 Mf38
Palestina CO 192 Gb43
Palestina EC 196 Ga46
Palestine USA (TX) 174 Fc30
Palestrina I 36 Ln49
Paletwa MYA 86 Pg35
Palè MYA 86 Ph35
Palgarup AUS (WA) 104 Qj63
Palghar IND (MHT) 82 Og36
Palghat = Palakkad IND (KER) 84 Oj40
Palgrave, Mount AUS 102 Qh57
Palhana IND (UPH) 83 Pa33
Pálháza H 43 Mb42
Palheta BR (AM) 198 Gh47
Palhoça BR (SC) 205 Hf59
Pali IND (CGH) 83 Pb34
Pali IND (MPH) 83 Pa34
Pali IND (RJT) 82 Og33
Palia IND (UPH) 81 Pa31
Pali-Aike, P.N. RCH 210 Gf72
Palian THA 88 Pk42
Palianawa IND (GUJ) 82 Of34
Paliat RI 95 Qh49
Paligrad MK 44 Mb49
Palikir FSM 101 Sb09
Palimbang RP 91 Rc42
Palin H 42 Lr44
Palindi RI 96 Ra51
Palinuro I 37 Lq50
Paliochori GR 47 Me54
Palio di Siena I 34 Lm47
Palioúri GR 45 Md51
Paliouriá GR 46 Mb51
Páliros GR 46 Mc54
Palisades Res. USA 169 Ee24
Palitana IND (GUJ) 82 Of35
Paliūniškis LT 39 Me35
Palizada MEX (CAM) 183 Fd36
Paljavaam RUS 55 Tc05
Pälkäene FIN 38 Me29
Palk Bay CL 85 Ok41
Palkino RUS 39 Mj33
Palkonda IND (APH) 83 Pb36
Palk Strait IND/CY 85 Ok41
Pal Lahara IND (ORS) 83 Pc35
Pallamadu CL 85 Pa41
Pallasca PE 197 Gb50
Pallas-Ounastunturi kansallispuisto FIN 16 Mb11
Pallipatu IND (APH) 85 Ok39
Pallisa EAU 144 Mg45
Pallu IND (RJT) 80 Oh31
Palma MOC 147 Na51
Palma Del Río E 27 Kp53
Palma de Mallorca E 29 Lc51
Palma di Montechiaro I 36 Lo53
Palmales EC 196 Fk47
Palmaner IND (APH) 85 Ok39
Palmanova I 35 Lo45
Palmar EC 196 Fk46
Palmarejo YV 192 Ge40
Palmares BR (PE) 201 Jc50
Palmar Grande BOL 207 Gj56
Palmarin SN 136 Kb39
Palmarito YV 192 Ge42
Palmarito de Cauto C 186 Gc35
Palmas BR (PR) 204 He59
Palmas BR (RS) 204 Hd61
Palmas de Cocalán, P.N. RCH 208 Ge63
Palmas de Monte Alto BR (BA) 203 Hj53
Palmas do Tocantins BR (TO) 200 Hf51
Palma Sola MEX (VC) 182 Fb36
Palma Sola RA (PJ) 207 Gh57
Palma Soriano C 179 Gb35
Palmas, T.I. BR 204 Hd59
Palma Sur CR 185 Fj41
Palm Bay USA (FL) 179 Fk32
Palm Beach USA (FL) 179 Fk32
Palm Cove AUS (QLD) 107 Sc54
Palmdale USA (CA) 170 Ea28
Palmdale USA (FL) 179 Fk32
Palmeira BR (PR) 205 He58
Palmeira CV 136 Jj37
Palmeira das Missões BR (RS) 204 Hd59
Palmeira d'Oeste BR (SP) 202 He56
Palmeira dos Indios BR (AL) 201 Jb50
Palmeirais BR (PI) 201 Hj49
Palmeirândia BR (MA) 195 Hh47
Palmeirante BR (TO) 200 Hg49
Palmeiras BR (BA) 201 Hk52
Palmeiras BR (MS) 202 Hc56
Palmeiras de Goiás BR (GO) 202 Hf54
Palmeiras do Javari BR (AM) 196 Gd48
Palmeirópolis BR (TO) 200 Hf52
Palmela P 27 Km52
Palmer USA (AK) 165 Cf15
Palmeral de Elche E 29 Ku52
Palmeral d'Elx E 29 Ku52
Palmer Land 6 Gc33
Palmer Station ANT (USA) 6 Gd31
Palmerston NZ 113 Tf68
Palmerston Atoll NZ 11 Bb11
Palmerston North NZ 113 Th66
Palmerville AUS (QLD) 107 Sc53
Palmgrove N.P. AUS (QLD) 109 Se58
Palm Harbor USA (FL) 179 Fj31
Palmi I 37 Lq52
Palmillas MEX (TM) 182 Fa34
Palmira CO 192 Gb44
Palmira EC 196 Ga47
Palmira RA (MD) 208 Gf62
Palm Islands AUS (QLD) 107 Sd55
Palmiste RH 186 Gd35
Palmital BR (PR) 204 Hd58
Palmital BR (SP) 202 He57
Palmitas ROU 204 Hb62
Palmópolis BR (MG) 203 Hk54
Palmse EST 38 Mf31
Palm Springs USA (CA) 170 Eb29
Palm Valley AUS (NT) 103 Rg58
Palm Valley USA (FL) 178 Fk30
Palmwag NAM 150 Lg55
Palmyra SYR 56 Mk28
Palmyra Atoll USA 11 Bb09
Palo RP 90 Rc40
Palo Alto USA (CA) 170 Dj27
Palo Blanco RA (CA) 207 Gg59
Palo Duro Canyon USA 174 Ek28
Palo Duro Canyon S.P. USA 174 Ek28
Paloeloeimenepeu BR/SME 194 Hc44
Paloemeu SME 194 Hc44
Palo Grande PA 185 Fj41
Paloh MAL 92 Qb44
Paloich SUD 135 Mg40
Paloje IND (MHT) 82 Og36
Palojoensuu FIN 16 Mb11
Palokastër AL 46 Ma50
Palolo RI 96 Ra46
Palomares MEX (OAX) 183 Fc37
Palomas E 27 Ko52
Palomas MEX (SLP) 182 Fa34
Palomas Viejo MEX (CHH) 180 Eg30
Palomeras E 27 Kr51
Palometas BOL 206 Gj54
Palomino CO 192 Gd40
Palompon RP 90 Rc40
Paloncha IND (APH) 83 Pa37
Palo Pinto USA (TX) 174 Fa29
Palopo RI 96 Ra47
Palora EC 196 Gb46
Palos C 179 Fk34
Palo Santo RA (FO) 204 Ha58
Palos Blancos BOL 207 Gj56
Palotina BR (PR) 204 Hd58
Palouse USA (WA) 168 Eb22
Palo Verde, P.N. CR 185 Fh40
Palpa PE 197 Gc53
Palpalá RA (PJ) 207 Gh58
Palparara AUS (QLD) 108 Sa58
Palpite C 179 Fk34
Pålsboda S 31 Lq31
Păltiniș RO 44 Mc45
Păltiniș RO 44 Md45
Palu RI 96 Qk46
Palu RI 96 Ra50
Palu TR 57 Mk26
Palung N.P. RI 95 Qf46
Palwal IND (HYA) 81 Oj31
Pama BF 137 La40
Pama RCA 140 Ma43
Pamalap RG 136 Kd41
Pamangkat RI 94 Qe45
Pamanukan RI 95 Qd49
Pamatata RI 96 Ra48
Pamban Island IND 85 Ok41
Pambarra MOC 153 Mh56
Pambeguwa WAN 138 Le40
Pambuka ZW 152 Me56
Pambula Beach AUS 111 Sf64
Pamdai RI 114 Rj47
Pamekasan RI 95 Qg49
Pameungpeuk RI 95 Qd49
Pamgarh IND (CGH) 83 Pb35
Pamiers F 24 Lb47
Pamir AFG/TJ 63 Og27
Pamir TJ 63 Of26
Pamoni YV 193 Gh44
Pampa USA (TX) 174 Ek28
Pampa Apeleg RA 210 Ge68
Pampa Aullagas BOL 206 Gg55
Pampa Cerro Morro RA 210 Gg69
Pampachiri PE 197 Gd53
Pampa de Agnía RA (CB) 210 Gf67
Pampa de Chalía RA 210 Ge68
Pampa de Chunchang PE 197 Gb53
Pampa de Cortaderas PE 197 Gd53
Pampa de Huayuri PE 197 Gc53
Pampa del Agua Amarga RA 208 Gf65
Pampa de las 3 Hermanas RA 210 Gg69
Pampa de las Salinas RA 208 Gg61
Pampa de la Varita RA 208 Gg63
Pampa de la Yoya PE 197 Ge54
Pampa del Castillo RA (CB) 210 Gf68
Pampa del Castillo RA 210 Gf68
Pampa del Diamante RA 208 Gf63
Pampa del Indio RA (CH) 204 Ha59
Pampa del Infierno RA (CH) 207 Gk59
Pampa de los Guanacos RA (SE) 207 Gk59
Pampa del Salado RA 208 Gg62
Pampa del Setenta RA 210 Gf69
Pampa del Tamarugal RCH 206 Gf56
Pampa de Talagapa RA 208 Gf67
Pampa El Toro PE 196 Fk47
Pampa Hermosa PE 196 Gc49
Pampa Húmeda RA 209 Gk64
Pampanua RI 96 Ra48
Pampa Pelada RA 210 Gg68
Pampas PE 197 Gb50
Pampas PE 197 Gc52
Pampas RA 208 Gh64
Pampa Salamanca RA 210 Gg68
Pampas de Sacramento PE 196 Gc49
Pampa Seca RA 208 Gh63
Pampa Verde RA (CH) 207 Gk59
Pampa Verdún RA 210 Ge69
Pampilhosa da Serra P 27 Kn50
Pamplemousses MS 157 Nj56
Pampliega E 28 Kr48
Pamplona CO 192 Gd42
Pamplona E 28 Kt48
Pamplona RP 90 Ra36
Pampoenpoort ZA 154 Mb61
Pamporovo = Koloro, V. BG 45 Me49
Pamucak TR 47 Mh53
Pamukkale TR 47 Mk53
Pamuru IND (APH) 85 Ok38
Pamūšis LT 39 Md34
Pana G 148 Lg46
Pana USA (IL) 175 Ff26
Panaba MEX (YT) 183 Ff35
Panabo RP 91 Rc42
Panaca USA (NV) 170 Ec27
Pañacocha EC 196 Gb46
Panaeati Island PNG 116 Sg51
Panagía GR 46 Mb51
Panagía Halkeon GR 44 Md50
Panagía Parigorítissa GR 46 Ma51
Panagjurište BG 45 Me48
Panaij IND (GOA) 82 Og38
Panaikkudi IND (TNU) 84 Oj41
Panaitan RI 93 Qc49
Panajachel GCA 184 Fe38
Panamá PA 185 Ga41
Panama 185 Fk41
Panama Canal PA 185 Ga41
Panama City USA (FL) 175 Fh30
Panama City Beach USA (FL) 175 Fh30
Panambi BR (RS) 204 Hd60
Panambí RA (MI) 204 Hc59
Panamericana (Arizona) USA 171 Ed29
Panamericana (British Columbia) CDN 169 Ee22
Panamericana (California) USA 170 Dj26
Panamericana (Coahuila) MEX 181 Ek33
Panamericana (El Salvador) ES 184 Ff39
Panamericana (Montana) USA 169 Ee22
Panamericana (Nicaragua) NIC 184 Fh39
Panamericana (Oaxaca) MEX 182 Fb37
Panamericana (Oregon) USA 168 Dj23
Panamericana (Panamá) PA 185 Fk41
Panamericana (San Luis Potosí) MEX 182 Fa34
Panamericana (Sonora) MEX 180 Ef32
Panamint Range USA 170 Eb27
Panamint Springs USA (CA) 170 Eb27
Pan'an CHN (ZJG) 75 Ra31
Panao PE 197 Gc50
Panaon Island RP 90 Rc41
Panar MAL 94 Qh43
Panare THA 89 Qa42
Panareh-Chalai Beach THA 89 Qa42
Panarik RI 94 Qe44
Panatinane Island PNG 116 Sg51
Panawina Island PNG 116 Sg51
Panay RP 90 Ra40
Panban AUS (NSW) 111 Sb62
Pancake Rocks and Blowholes NZ 113 Tf67
Pančarevo BG 44 Md48
Pancas BR (ES) 203 Hk55
Pančevo SCG 44 Ma46
Panchgani IND (MHT) 82 Og37
Panchgani Hill Resort IND 82 Og37
Panchori IND (RJT) 80 Og32
Pancho Villa MEX (CHH) 180 Ef30
Pâncota RO 43 Mb44
Pançudo BR (AP) 195 He46
Pancuma RI 96 Ra46
Pancungapang, Gunung RI 94 Qh45
Panda MOC 153 Mh58
Pandambili EAT 147 Mj49
Pandan RP 90 Rc38
Pandan RP 90 Rb40
Pandanan Island RP 94 Qj41
Pandan Beach RI 93 Pk45
Pandane MOC 153 Mh58
Pandanus AUS (QLD) 107 Sc55
Pandaria IND (CGH) 83 Pa34
Pan de Azúcar, Cerro RA 210 Gf70
Pan de Azúcar RCH 207 Ge59
Pan de Azúcar ROU 209 Hc63
Pan de Azúcar, P.N. RCH 207 Ge59
Pandegelang RI 95 Qd49
Pandėlys LT 39 Mf34
Pandhana IND (MPH) 82 Oj35
Pandharkawada IND (MHT) 82 Ok36
Pandharpur IND (MHT) 82 Oh37
Pandhurna IND (MPH) 83 Ok35
Pandi CO 192 Gc43
Pandie Pandie AUS (SA) 108 Rk59
Pandiri RI 96 Ra46
Pandivere kõrgustik EST 38 Mg31
Pando ROU 209 Hc63
Pandogari WAN 138 Ld40
Pandora CR 185 Fj41
Pandrup DK 30 Lk33
Pandu IND (ASM) 86 Pf32
Pandu RDC 140 Lk43
Pandzhikent TJ 63 Od26
Panelas BR (MT) 199 Gk50
Panelas BR (PE) 201 Jb50
Panem IND (APH) 82 Ok38
Panemunė LT 39 Mb35
Paneri IND (ASM) 86 Pf32
Panes E 26 Kq47
Panetólio GR 46 Mb52
Panevėžys LT 39 Me35
Pang 81 Oj29
Panga RDC 141 Md45
Pangala RCB 148 Lh47
Pangandaran RI 95 Qe49
Pangani EAT 147 Mk48
Pangantocan RP 91 Rc42
Panganuran RP 91 Rb42
Panga pank EST 39 Mc32
Pangeo RI 91 Re44
Panggoe SOL 117 Sj49
Pangi RDC 146 Md47
Pangia PNG 115 Sc49
Pangkajene RI 96 Qk47
Pangkajene RI 96 Ra48
Pangkalanbrandan RI 92 Pk44
Pangkalanbun RI 95 Qf47
Pangkalandurian RI 93 Qb46
Pangkalanpanduk RI 93 Qb45
Pangkalansusu RI 92 Pk43
Pang Kalom LAO 87 Qa35
Pangkalpinang RI 95 Qd47
Pangkor MAL 92 Qa43
Pangkyehtu MYA 86 Pj35
Pang La THA 87 Pk36
Panglao Beach RP 90 Rb41
Panglao Island RP 90 Rb41
Panglong MYA 86 Pj35
Pangnirtung CDN 163 Gc05
Pango PNG 116 Sg47
Pangoa PNG 115 Sa49
Pango Aluquem ANG 148 Lh50
Pangonda RCA 140 Ma42
Pangquangou Z.B. CHN 72 Qf27
Pangrango, Gunung RI 95 Qd49
Pang Sida N.P. THA 89 Qb38
Pangu CHN (HLG) 71 Rb19
Panguipulli RCH 208 Gd65
Panguitch USA (UT) 171 Ed27
Panguma WAL 136 Ke41
Pangururan RI 93 Pk44
Pangutaran Group RP 91 Ra42
Pangutaran Island RP 91 Ra42
Panhala IND 82 Oh37
Panhandle USA 175 Fh30
Paničkovo BG 45 Mf49
Panihati IND (WBG) 86 Pe34
Panikhar 81 Oj28
Panipat IND (HYA) 80 Oj31
Paniqui RP 90 Ra38
Panitan RP 90 Rb40
Panitian RP 91 Qk41
Panjab AFG 65 Od28
Panjabungan Tonga RI 93 Pk45
Panjakent TJ 63 Od26
Panjang RI 93 Qc48
Panjang RI 94 Qe44
Panjang RI 97 Rf48
Panjgur PK 65 Oc32
Panji RI 93 Pj44
Panjin CHN (LNG) 76 Rb25
Panjpai PK 65 Od31
Panjshir-Valley AFG 63 Oe28
Panka BHT 86 Pf32
Pankshin WAN 138 Le41
Pankulam CL 85 Pa41
Panlong CHN (SCH) 74 Qd30
P'anmunjom ROK 78 Rd27
Panna IND (MPH) 83 Pa33
Panna N.P. IND 83 Pa33
Pannawonica AUS (WA) 102 Qj56
Panngi VU 118 Te53
Panniar IND (MPH) 80 Oj32
Pannonhalma H 42 Ls43
Panopah RI 95 Qf46
Panorama BR (SP) 202 He56
Pánormos GR 47 Mg53
Panrutti IND (TNU) 85 Ok40
Panshan, Mount CHN 73 Qj25
Panshanu Pass WAN 138 Le41
Panshi CHN (JLN) 76 Rd24
Panskura IND (WBG) 83 Pd34
Pantai RI 95 Qj47
Pantai koka RI 96 Rb50
Pantai Remis MAL 92 Qa43
Pantalam IND (KER) 84 Oj41
Pantalica I 37 Lq53

Pantanal – Perfume Pagoda

Pantanal BR 199 Hb49
Pantanal de Nabileque BR 202 Hb56
Pantanal do Río Negro BR 202 Hb55
Pantanal do São Lourenço BR 202 Hb54
Pantanal do Taquarí BR 202 Hb55
Pantanal Matogrossense BR 202 Hb54
Pantanal Matogrossense, P.N.do BR 202 Hb54
Pântano do Sul BR (SC) 205 Hf59
Pântano Grande BR (RS) 204 Hd61
Pantar RI 97 Rc50
Pantekra RI 92 Pj43
Pantelleria I 36 Lm54
Pantemakassar TLS 97 Rc50
Pantha MYA 86 Ph34
Panther Huk NAM 154 Lh59
Panther Swamp N.W.R. USA 175 Fe29
Panti RI 93 Qa45
Panticeu RO 43 Md43
Panticpaeum UA 49 Mj23
Pantijan A.L. AUS 103 Rc54
Pantoja PE 196 Gc46
Pantoloan RI 96 Qk46
Pantu MAL 94 Qf45
Pantukan RP 91 Rc42
Pantzarané CI 137 Kj41
Panu RDC 149 Lk47
Panwari IND (UPH) 83 Ok33
Panxi CHN (YUN) 87 Qb33
Panxian CHN (GZH) 87 Qc33
Panyam WAN 138 Le41
Panzhihua CHN (SCH) 87 Qa32
Panzi RDC 149 Lj49
Paoay RP 90 Ra36
Páola I 37 Lr51
Paoli USA (IN) 175 Fg26
Paomaping CHN (YUN) 87 Qa32
Paonia USA (CO) 171 Eg26
Paonta Sahib IND (HPH) 81 Oj30
Paopao Island PNG 117 Sh47
Paoua RCA 140 Lj42
Paouignan DY 138 Lb42
Pápa H 42 Ls43
Papagaio BR (MA) 200 Hh48
Papagaios BR (MG) 203 Hh55
Papago Ind. Res. USA 171 Ed29
Papaikou USA (HI) 170 Cc36
Papakura NZ 112 Th64
Papallacta Pass BR 198 Gf46
Papalutla MEX (GUR) 182 Fa36
Papanasam Beach IND 84 Oj41
Papanduva BR (SC) 205 He59
Papantla MEX (VC) 182 Fb35
Paparoa N.P. NZ 113 Tf67
Paparoa Range NZ 113 Tf67
Papa Stour GB 20 Kt30
Papa Westray GB 20 Ks31
Papayato RI 91 Ra45
Pape LV 39 Mb34
Papeete F (PYF) 11 Cb11
Papela RI 97 Rb51
Papenburg D 32 Lh37
Papera BR (AM) 198 Gh46
Papernja BY 39 Mh36
Papey IS 18 Kf26
Paphos CY 56 Mg28
Papilė LT 39 Mc34
Papillion USA (NE) 172 Fb25
Papilys LT 39 Mf34
Papiniseri IND (KER) 84 Oh40
Papollo NIC 184 Fg40
Paposo PE 207 Ge58
Pappadahandi IND (ORS) 83 Pb36
Paprenda IND (UPH) 83 Pa33
Papua New Guinea 101 Sa10
Papuk HR 35 Ls45
Papulankutja AUS (WA) 105 Re58
Papun MYA 86 Pj36
Papunya AUS (NT) 103 Rf57
Papuri CO 193 Gf45
Papurí YV 192 Ge40
Paqiu SUD 141 Mf42
Paquera CR 185 Fh41
Paquiçamba BR (PA) 200 He47
Paquiçamba, T.I. BR 200 He47
Paquisha EC 196 Ga47
Par IND (ARP) 86 Pg32
Pará BR 191 Ha10
Pará BR 195 Hf46
Para RI 91 Rc44
Parabubure, T.I. BR 202 Hd53
Paraburdoo AUS (WA) 102 Qj57
Paracale RP 90 Rb38
Paracanã, T.I. BR 200 He48
Paračany BY 41 Mf37
Paracas PE 197 Gb52
Paracatu BR (MG) 203 Hg54
Parachilna AUS (SA) 108 Rk61
Parachinar PK 65 Of29
Paracho MEX (MHC) 182 Ej36
Paraćin SCG 44 Mb47
Paracuhuba, T.I. BR 199 Ha47
Paracuru BR (CE) 201 Ja47
Parada BR (PA) 195 He47
Paradela P 26 Kn49
Para de Minas BR (MG) 203 Hh55
Paradip IND (ORS) 83 Pd35
Paradise USA (CA) 170 Dk26
Paradise Island BS 179 Gb33
Paradise Valley USA (NV) 170 Eb25
Paradísi GR 47 Mj54
Paradísia GR 46 Mc53
Paradji RG 136 Kd40
Parado RI 96 Qk50
Paradonparp Beach THA 88 Pk40
Paragominas BR (PA) 200 Hg47
Paragoula USA (AR) 175 Fe27
Paraguaçu Paulista BR (SP) 202 He57
Paraguaí BR 202 Hb56
Paraguaipoa YV 192 Ge40
Paraguarí PY 204 Hb58
Paraguay PY 204 Hb58
Paraguay 191 Ha12
Paraíba BR 191 Ja10
Paraíba BR 201 Jc49
Paraíba do Sul BR (RJ) 205 Hj57
Paraíba do Sul BR 203 Hk56
Paraibano BR (MA) 200 Hj49
Parainen = Pargas FIN 38 Mc30
Paraiso BR (AM) 199 Ha49
Paraíso BR (MS) 202 Hd55
Paraíso CR 184 Fh40
Paraíso MEX (TB) 183 Fd36
Paraíso do Leste BR (MT) 202 Hc54
Paraíso do Norte BR (PR) 202 Hd57
Paraíso do Tocantins BR (TO) 200 Hf51
Paraisópolis BR (MG) 205 Hh57
Paraitepui YV 193 Gk43
Paraiyanalankulam CL 85 Pa41
Parajuru BR (CE) 201 Jb48
Parakan RI 95 Qf49
Parakou DY 138 Lb41
Parakylia AUS (SA) 108 Rj61
Paralía GR 46 Mc52
Paralía Porovítsis GR 46 Mc52
Paralkote IND (CGH) 83 Pa36
Parama Island PNG 115 Sb50
Paramakudi IND (TNU) 84 Ok41
Paramaribo SME 194 Hc43
Paramatti IND (TNU) 84 Oj40
Parambu BR (CE) 201 Hk49
Paramillo CO 192 Gc42
Paramillo, P.N. CO 192 Gb42
Paramirim BR (BA) 201 Hj52
Paramithiá GR 46 Ma51
Páramo Frontino CO 192 Gb42
Paramonga PE 197 Gb51
Páramos del Angel EC 196 Gb45
Páramos El Batallón y La Negra, P.N. YV 192 Ge41
Paramoti BR (CE) 201 Ja48
Paran RI 95 Qh47
Paranã BR (TO) 200 Hg52
Paraná BR 191 Ha12
Paranã BR 200 Hg52
Paraná BR 202 He56
Paraná RA (ER) 209 Gk61
Paraná do Boa Boa, T.I. BR 198 Gg46
Paraná do Parica, T.I. BR 198 Gg46
Paranaguá BR (PR) 205 Hf58
Paranaíba BR (MS) 202 He55
Paranaíba BR 202 He55
Paranaiguara BR (GO) 202 He55
Paranaita BR (MT) 199 Hb50
Paraná Juca BR (AM) 193 Gf45
Paranal PE 207 Ge58
Paranal Observatory RCH 207 Ge58
Paranam SME 194 Hc43
Paranapanema BR (SP) 205 Hf57
Paranapanema BR 202 He57
Paranapebas BR (PA) 200 Hf49
Paranatinga BR (MT) 202 Hc53
Paranavaí BR (PR) 202 Hd57
Parandak IR 57 Nf28
Paranésti GR 45 Me49
Parang RI 97 Rf47
Parang RP 91 Ra43
Parang RP 91 Rc42
Paranga EAU 144 Mg44
Parangtritis RI 95 Qf50
Paranhos BR (MS) 202 Hc57
Paranthan CL 85 Pa41
Parantij IND (GUJ) 82 Og34
Paraopeba BR (MG) 203 Hh55
Paraparaumu NZ 113 Th66
Parapuã BR (SP) 202 He56
Parasgaon IND (CGH) 83 Pa36
Parasi NEP 81 Pb32
Parasia IND (MPH) 83 Ok34
Parasunanpur IND (KTK) 84 Oj38
Paratebueno CO 192 Gd43
Parateca BR (BA) 200 Hj52
Parati BR (RJ) 205 Hh57
Paratinga BR (BA) 201 Hj52
Paratoo AUS (SA) 110 Rk62
Paratwada IND (MHT) 82 Oj35
Părău RO 45 Mf45
Paraúna BR (GO) 202 He54
Paraw Bibi Shrine TM 62 Nj26
Paray-le-Monial F 25 Le44
Parazinho BR (RN) 201 Jc48
Parbatsar IND (RJT) 80 Oh32
Parbé BF 137 Kk39
Parbhani IND (MHT) 82 Oj36
Parc de la Gatineau CDN 177 Gb23
Parc de la Jacques-Cartier CDN 176 Ge22
Parc de la Lékédi G 148 Lg46
Parc des Grands-Jardins CDN 176 Ge22
Parc d'Ivoloina RM 157 Ne55
Parc Güell E 29 Lc49
Parchim D 32 Lm37
Parc marin de Muanda RDC 148 Lg48
Parc national de la Guadeloupe F 187 Gk37
Parc National de l'Île-Bonaventure-et-du-Rocher-Percé CDN 176 Gh21
Parc National du Mont Tremblant CDN 176 Gc22
Parc Natural del Montseny E 29 Lc49
Parc Natural de Montserrat E 29 Lb49
Parc Naturel de Brière F 22 Ks43
Parc Naturel Hautes Fagnes-Eifel B 23 Lg40
Parc Naturel National de Port-Cros F 25 Lg47
Parc Naturel Régional d'Armorique F 22 Kq42
Parc Naturel Régional de Camargue F 25 Le47
Parco PE 197 Gc51
Parcoy PE 196 Gb49
Parc Prov. Baldwin CDN 176 Gg21
Parc Prov. de Forestville CDN 176 Gf21
Parc Provinciala de la Rivière Bleue F (NCL) 118 Td57
Parc Régional des Volcans d'Auvergne F 25 Lc45
Parczew PL 41 Mc39
Parding CHN (TIB) 68 Pe29
Pardo BR 202 Hd56
Pardubice CZ 42 Lq40
Pare BY 41 Mg39
Pare RI 95 Qg49
Parečča BY 41 Me37
Parecis BR (MT) 202 Hb53
Parecis BR 202 Hb52
Paredes de Nava E 26 Kq48
Pareditas RA (MD) 208 Gf62
Paredón MEX (CHP) 183 Fd37
Paredón MEX (COH) 181 Ek33
Parelhas BR (RN) 201 Jb49
Parenda IND (MHT) 82 Oh36
Parent CDN (QC) 176 Gc22
Parentis-en-Born F 24 Kt46
Parepare RI 96 Qk47
Paresido Rio Formoso, T.I. BR 202 Ha53
Paresi, T.I. BR 206 Ha53
Párga GR 46 Ma51
Pargarutan RI 93 Pk45
Pargas = Parainen FIN 38 Mc30
Pargi IND (APH) 82 Oj37
Pargnyongdo PRK 78 Rc27
Pargolovo RUS 38 Ml30
Pargua RCH 208 Gd66
Parguaza YV 193 Gg42
Parhar TJ 63 Oe27
Paria BOL 206 Gg54
Pariacoto PE 197 Gb50
Pariaguán YV 193 Gh41
Pariaman RI 93 Qa46
Paricatuba BR (AM) 198 Gk48
Paricutín, P.N. MEX 182 Ej36
Parigi RI 96 Ra46
Parika GUY 194 Ha42
Parikkala FIN 38 Mk29
Parilla AUS (SA) 110 Sa63
Parima-Tapirapecó, P.N. YV 193 Gh44
Parinacota RCH 206 Gf55
Parinacota, Volcán RCH 206 Gf55
Parinari PE 196 Gc48
Paring RI 95 Qh46
Paringa AUS (SA) 110 Sa63
Parintins BR (AM) 199 Hb47
Paripiranga BR (BA) 201 Jb51
Paris F 23 Lc42
Paris USA (AR) 174 Fd28
Paris USA (ID) 171 Ee24
Paris USA (IL) 175 Fg26
Paris USA (MO) 174 Fd26
Paris USA (TN) 175 Ff27
Paris USA (TX) 174 Fc29
Parishan Lake IR 59 Nf31
Paris USA (KY) 175 Fh26
Parit MAL 92 Qa43
Parit RI 93 Qa45
Paritsungaiburung RI 93 Qb46
Paritsungainyirih RI 93 Qb45
Parituluh RI 93 Qb46
Park IR 64 Oa33
Parkal IND (APH) 83 Ok36
Parkano FIN 38 Md28
Park City USA (KS) 174 Fb27
Parkent UZ 63 Oe25
Parker USA (AZ) 170 Ec28
Parker Island MYA 88 Pk40
Parker, Mount AUS 103 Re54
Parkersburg USA (WV) 175 Fk26
Parkers Prairie USA (MN) 172 Fc22
Parkes AUS (NSW) 111 Se62
Park Falls USA (WI) 172 Fe23
Park Hill USA (MO) 175 Fe27
Park Krajobrazowy Beskidu Śląskiego PL 41 Lt41
Park Krajobrazowy Bory Stobrawskie PL 40 Ls40
Park Krajobrazowy Dolina Baryczy PL 40 Ls39
Park Krajobrazowy Lasy Janowskie PL 41 Mc40
Park Krajobrazowy Mierzeja Wiślana PL 41 Lu36
Park Krajobrazowy Orlich Gniazd PL 41 Lu40
Park Krajobrazowy Pogórza Przemyskiego PL 41 Mc41
Parkman CDN (SK) 172 Ek21
Parkman USA (WY) 169 Eg23
Park Mużakowski PL 40 Lp39
Park Range USA 171 Eg25
Park Rapids USA (MN) 172 Fc22
Park River USA (ND) 172 Fb21
Parkston USA (SD) 172 Fb24
Parksville CDN (BC) 168 Dh21
Parlabian RI 93 Pk45
Parlakimidi IND (APH) 83 Pc36
Parlange Plantation USA 175 Fe30
Parli IND (MHT) 82 Oj36
Parma I 34 Ll46
Parmana YV 193 Gh42
Parnaguá BR (PI) 200 Hh51
Parnaíba BR (PI) 201 Hk47
Parnaíba BR 201 Hj47
Parnamirim BR (PE) 201 Ja50
Parnamirim BR (RN) 201 Jc48
Parnarama BR (MA) 201 Hj48
Parnassós GR 46 Mc52
Parnassos N.P. GR 46 Mc52
Parnassus NZ 113 Tg67
Parndana AUS (SA) 110 Rj63
Párnitha N.P. GR 45 Md52
Pärnjõe EST 38 Me32
Pärnu EST 38 Me32
Pärnu EST 39 Me32
Pärnu-Jaagupi EST 38 Me32
Pärnu laht EST 39 Me32
Paro BHT 86 Pe32
Paroa NZ 112 Tj64
Paro Dzong BHT 86 Pe32
Parola IND (MHT) 82 Oh35
Paroma, Cerro BOL/RCH 206 Gf56
Paroo AUS (WA) 104 Qj59
Paropean RI 96 Qk47
Páros GR 47 Mf53
Páros GR 47 Mf53
Parotáni BOL 206 Gg54
Parowan USA (UT) 171 Ed27
Parque Arqueológico Vale do Côa P 26 Kn49
Parque Arqueológico San Agustín CO 192 Gb45
Parque Arqueológico Tierradentro CO 192 Gb44
Parque de los Menhires RA 207 Gh59
Parque do Aripuanã BR 199 Ha51
Parque do Tumucumaque BR 194 Hc45
Parque General de Division Omar Torrijos - El Cope PA 185 Fk41
Parque Indígena Araguaia BR 200 He51
Parque Indígena do Xingu BR 199 Hd51
Parque Indígena Yanomami BR 193 Gj45
Parque Int. del Rio Bravo MEX 181 Eh31
Parque Internacional La Amistad CR/PA 185 Fj41
Parque Luro RA 208 Gh64
Parque Nacional Arrecifes de Xcalak MEX (QTR) 183 Fg36
Parque Nacional Sierra de San Pedro Mártir MEX 180 Ec30
Parque Natural Cabo de Gata E 27 Ks54
Parque Natural da Arrabida P 27 Kl52
Parque Natural da Ria Formosa P 27 Kn54
Parque Natural da Serra da Estrela P 26 Kn50
Parque Natural da Serra de São Mamede P 27 Kn51
Parque Natural das Serras Aire e Candeeiros P 27 Km51
Parque Natural de Albufera E 29 Ku51
Parque Natural de las Dunas de Corralejo E 124 Kc31
Parque Natural del Desierto Central MEX 180 Ec31
Parque Natural de Monfragüe E 27 Ko51
Parque Natural de Montesinho P 26 Kn49
Parque Natural de Sintra-Cascais P 27 Kl52
Parque Natural do Alvão P 26 Kn49
Parque Natural do Douro Internacional P 26 Ko49
Parque Natural do Sudoeste Alentejano e Costa Vicentina P 27 Km53
Parque Natural do Tejo Internacional P 27 Kn51
Parque Natural do Vale do Guadiana P 27 Kn53
Parque Natural Los Novillos MEX 181 Ek31
Parque Natural Presa de la Amistad MEX 181 Ek31
Parque Natural Río Celestún MEX 183 Fe35
Parque Natural Río Lagartos MEX 183 Fg35
Parque Natural San Felipe MEX 183 Ff35
Parque Natural Sierra de la Laguna MEX 180 Ef34
Parque Natural Sierra del Carmen MEX 181 Ek31
Parque Provincial Ischigualasto RA 207 Gg61
Parque Salus ROU 209 Hc63
Parra E 27 Kr51
Parrakie AUS (SA) 110 Sa63
Parral RCH 208 Ge64
Parramore Island USA 177 Gc27
Parras de la Fuente MEX (COH) 181 Ej33
Parres = Arriondas E 26 Kp47
Parrita CR 185 Fh41
Parrsboro CDN (NS) 176 Gh23
Parry I. Ind. Res. CDN 173 Fk23
Parry Islands CDN 162 Ea03
Parry Sound CDN (ON) 173 Fk23
Pars Abad IR 57 Nd26
Parsberg D 33 Lm41
Parsons USA (KS) 174 Fc27
Parson's Pond CDN (NF) 177 Hb20
Parsons Range AUS 106 Rh52
Parsora IND (ORS) 83 Pc35
Partago DY 138 La41
Partanna I 36 Ln53
Parthenay F 24 Ku44
Partibanur IND (TNU) 84 Ok41
Partille S 30 Ln33
Partinicio I 36 Lo53
Partizansk RUS 77 Rg24
Partizánske SK 42 Lt42
Partur IND (MHT) 82 Oj36
Paru AUS (NT) 106 Rf51
Paru BR 199 Hd46
Paruna AUS (SA) 110 Sa63
Parur IND (KER) 84 Oj40
Paruraj IND (BIH) 83 Pc32
Paruro PE 197 Ge52
Parvareh IR 64 Nj29
Parvatipuram IND (APH) 83 Pb36
Pärvomaj BG 45 Mf48
Paryang CHN (TIB) 68 Pb30
Paryčy BY 48 Me19
Påryd S 31 Lq34
Parys ZA 155 Md59
Pasaband AFG 65 Oc29
Pasada Conaf RCH 210 Gd71
Pasadena CDN (NF) 177 Hb21
Pasadena USA (CA) 170 Ea28
Pasadena USA (TX) 174 Fc31
Pasagshak S.R.S. USA 164 Cd17
Pasaje EC 196 Ga47
Pasamayo PE 197 Gb51
Pasamayo PE 197 Gb51
Pasanauri GE 57 Nc24
Pasangkayu RI 96 Qk46
Pasapuat RI 93 Qa47
Pasarbantal RI 93 Qa47
Pasarbaru RI 93 Qa46
Pasarbembah RI 93 Qb47
Pasargadae IR 64 Ng30
Pasarkambang RI 93 Qa46
Pasar Maga RI 93 Pk45
Pasarmatango RI 93 Pk45
Pasarseluma RI 93 Qb48
Pasarsibuhuan RI 93 Pk45
Pasawng MYA 86 Pj36
Pasayten W.A. USA 168 Dk21
Pascagoula USA (MS) 175 Ff30
Pasco USA (WA) 168 Ea22
Pasewalk D 32 Lp37
Pasi RI 96 Ra49
Pasiene LV 39 Mj34
Pasinler TR 57 Na25
Pasirganting RI 93 Qa47
Pasir Mas MAL 92 Qb42
Pasirpengaraian RI 93 Qa45
Pasir Puteh MAL 92 Qb43
Paskalevo BG 45 Mh47
Påskallavik S 31 Lr33
Paškovskij RUS 49 Mk23
Paskuh IR 64 Oa32
Pasłęk PL 41 Lu36
Pašman HR 35 Lq47
Pašman HR 35 Lq47
Pasman RA (BA) 209 Gj64
Pasni PK 65 Ob33
Paso Argentino RA 208 Gf62
Paso Cardenal A.Samoré RA/RCH 208 Ge66
Paso Caruachi YV 193 Gj41
Paso de Caballo YV 193 Gg41
Paso de Indios RA (CB) 210 Gf67
Paso de Jama RA/RCH 207 Gg57
Paso de la Cruz RA (SA) 207 Gh58
Paso del Agua Negro RA 207 Gf61
Paso de la Laguna RA (ER) 204 Ha61
Paso de la Patria PY 204 Ha59
Paso de los Algarrobos RA (LP) 208 Gg64
Paso de los Indios RA (NE) 208 Gf65
Paso de los Libres RA (CR) 204 Hb60
Paso de los Toros ROU 204 Hb62
Paso de los Vientos C 186 Gd35
Paso del Planchón RA/RCH 208 Ge63
Paso del Sapo RA (CB) 208 Gf67
Paso de Pino Hachado RA/RCH 208 Ge65
Paso de Vacas MEX (GUR) 182 Ek36
Paso Flores RA (RN) 208 Ge66
Paso Hondo MEX (CHP) 183 Fd38
Paso Maipo RA/RCH 208 Gf63
Paso Maule o Pehuenche RA/RCH 208 Ge64
Paso Real C 179 Fj34
Paso Real CR 185 Fj41
Paso Robles USA (CA) 170 Dk28
Paso Rodolfo Roballos RA 210 Ge69
Paso Sico RA/RCH 207 Gg57
Paso Socompa RA/RCH 207 Gf58
Pasqua CDN (SK) 169 Eh20
Pasquales MEX 182 Ej36
Pasquia Hills CDN 169 Ej19
Pasrur PK 65 Oh29
Passage de la Déroute F 22 Kt41
Passagem Franca BR (MA) 200 Hj49
Passa Tempo BR (MG) 203 Hh56
Passau D 33 Lo42
Passaya RG 136 Ke40
Passe d'Amogjâr RIM 130 Kd35
Passe de Djoûk RIM 130 Ke37
Passe de Korizo TCH 133 Lh34
Passe de Salvador RN 133 Lg34
Passe du Vent RH 186 Gd36
Passekudah Beach CL 85 Pa42
Passi RP 90 Rb40
Passi SN 136 Kb39
Passira BR (PE) 201 Jc49
Pass Island CDN (NF) 177 Hb22
Passo dello Spluga = Splügenpass I/CH 34 Lk44
Passo del San Bernardino CH 34 Lk44
Passo del Tonale I 34 Ll44
Passo di Résia = Reschenpass I 34 Ll44
Passo Fundo BR (RS) 204 Hd60
Passos BR (MG) 203 Hg56
Pastavy BY 39 Mg35
Pasteur RA (BA) 209 Gj63
Pasto CO 192 Gb45
Pastos Bons BR (MA) 200 Hh49
Pasto Ventura RA (CA) 207 Gg59
Pastrana E 29 Ks50
Pasu 80 Oh27
Pasual RP 90 Ra37
Pasul Bratocea RO 45 Mf45
Pasul Mestecăniș RO 43 Mf43
Pasul Șetref RO 43 Me43
Pasul Valișoara RO 43 Mc44
Pasuruan RI 95 Qg49
Pasvalys LT 39 Me34
Pásztó H 43 Lu43
Pata BOL 206 Gf53
Pata CO 196 Ge46
Pata RCA 140 Ma41
Pata SN 136 Kc39
Patacamaya BOL 206 Gg54
Patag N.P. RP 90 Rb40
Patagonia RA 210 Ge71
Patagonian Shelf 210 Gh70
Pata-Idié CI 137 Kg43
Pata Island RP 91 Ra43
Patamba RDC 149 Lk47
Patamundai IND (ORS) 83 Pd35
Patan IND (GUJ) 82 Og34
Patan IND (MHT) 82 Og37
Patan NEP 81 Pc32
Patani WAN 138 Ld43
Patarbar IND (JKD) 83 Pc34
Pătârlagele RO 45 Mg45
Patas IND (MHT) 82 Oh36
Patchewollock AUS (VIC) 110 Sb63
Patea NZ 113 Th65
Pategi WAN 138 Lc41
Paté Island EAK 145 Na47
Patemba RDC 149 Mb48
Patensie ZA 155 Mc62
Paternò I 37 Lp53
Paternoster ZA 154 Lj62
Pateros USA (WA) 168 Ea21
Paterson USA (NJ) 177 Gc25
Paterson USA (WA) 168 Ea23
Paterson ZA 155 Mc62
Paterson Inlet NZ 113 Te69
Paterson Range AUS 102 Rb56
Patewa IND (CGH) 83 Pb35
Pathalgaon IND (CGH) 83 Pb34
Pathalipam IND (ASM) 86 Ph32
Pathankot IND (PJB) 80 Oh29
Pathapkandi IND (ASM) 86 Pg33
Patharghata BD 86 Pe34
Patharkot NEP 83 Pc32
Pathé MEX (MEX) 182 Fa36
Pathiu THA 88 Pk40
Pathri IND (MHT) 82 Oj36
Pathrud IND (MHT) 82 Oh36
Pathum Thani THA 88 Qa38
Pati RI 95 Qf49
Pati RI 97 Rd50
Patia BD 86 Pg34
Patia = El Bordo CO 192 Gb44
Patiala IND (PJB) 80 Oj30
Patience F (GF) 194 Hd44
Patiko EAU 144 Mg44
Patikul RP 91 Ra42
Patillos RCH 206 Ge56
Patio Chiquito CO 192 Ge43
Patiram IND (WBG) 86 Pe33
Patiriti GR 45 Md51
Patiška MK 44 Mb49
Pativilca PE 197 Gb51
Patkan IR 64 Nj31
Patlong LS 155 Me61
Pátmos GR 47 Mg53
Patna IND (BIH) 83 Pc33
Patnanongan Island RP 90 Rb38
Patna Sahib IND 83 Pc33
Patnongan RP 90 Rb40
Patnos TR 57 Nb26
Pato Branco BR (PR) 204 Hd59
Patoles MEX 180 Eg34
Patomskoe nagor'e RUS 55 Qc07
Patong THA 88 Pk42
Patongo EAU 144 Mg44
Patos BR (PB) 201 Jb49
Patos de Minas BR (MG) 203 Hg55
Patos do Piauí BR (PI) 201 Hk49
Patquia RA (LR) 207 Gg61
Pátra GR 46 Mb52
Patratu IND (JKD) 83 Pc34
Patreksfjörður IS 18 Jr25
Patricia CDN (AB) 169 Ee20
Patricia USA (TX) 174 Ej29
Patrickswell IRL 19 Km38
Patrimônio BR (MG) 202 Hf55
Patrocínio BR (MG) 203 Hg55
Patroputtu IND (ORS) 83 Pb36
Patsul IND (MHT) 82 Oj35
Pattadakal IND 82 Oh38
Pattalasang RI 96 Ra48
Pattambi IND (KER) 84 Oj40
Pattani THA 89 Qa42
Pattaya THA 88 Qa39
Patten USA (MA) 176 Gf22
Patterson USA (GA) 178 Fj30
Patterson, Mount CDN 165 Dc13
Patti I 37 Lp52
Pattoki PK 65 Og30
Pattukkottai IND (TNU) 85 Ok40
Patu BR (RN) 201 Jb49
Patuakhali BD 86 Pf34
Patuanak CDN (SK) 167 Eg18
Pătulele RO 44 Mc46
Patullo, Mount CDN 166 Df17
Patur IND (MHT) 82 Oj35
Pátzcuaro MEX (MHC) 182 Ek36
Pau F 24 Ku47
Pau-A-Pique BR (BA) 201 Hk50
Paúba BR 205 Hg58
Pau Brasil, P.N.do BR 203 Hg53
Pau Brasil, T.I. BR 203 Hk55
Paucarbamba PE 197 Gc52
Paucartambo PE 197 Ge52
Paú dos Ferros BR (RN) 201 Ja49
Pauh RI 93 Qb47
Pauillac F 24 Ku45
Pauk MYA 86 Ph35
Paukkaung MYA 86 Ph36
Paulatuk CDN 162 Dd05
Paul B. Johnson S.P. USA 175 Ff30
Paul Bunyan Center USA 172 Fc22
Paulhaguet F 25 Ld45
Paúliani GR 46 Mc52
Paulina USA (OR) 168 Ea23
Paulina Peak USA 168 Dk24
Paulino Neves BR (MA) 201 Hj47
Paulista BR (PE) 201 Jc49
Paulistana BR (PI) 201 Hk50
Paulo Afonso BR (BA) 201 Ja50
Paulo de Faria BR (SP) 202 Hf55
Paulo Ramos BR (MA) 200 Hh48
Paulpietersburg ZA 155 Mf59
Paul Roux ZA 155 Md60
Paul Sauer Bridge ZA 154 Mb63
Pauls Valley USA (OK) 174 Fb28
Paumari do Cuniua, T.I. BR 198 Gh49
Paumari do Lago Manissua, T.I. BR 198 Gh48
Paumari do lago Maraha, T.I. BR 198 Gh49
Paumari do Lago Parica, T.I. BR 198 Gh48
Paumari do Rio Ituxi, T.I. BR 198 Gh49
Paungbyin MYA 86 Ph33
Paungdawthi MYA 88 Pj37
Paungde MYA 86 Ph36
Paunini BR (AM) 198 Gg49
Paup PNG 115 Sb49
Pausa PE 197 Gd53
Pau Seco BR (BA) 203 Ja53
Paute EC 196 Ga47
Pavagada IND (KTK) 84 Oj38
Pavagadh IND (GUJ) 82 Og34
Pavant Range USA 171 Ed26
Pavão BR (MG) 203 Hk54
Paveh IR 57 Nd28
Pavel Banja BG 45 Mf48
Pavia I 34 Lk45
Pavia P 27 Km52
Pavilion CDN (BC) 168 Dk20
Pavilly F 23 La41
Pāvilosta LV 39 Mb34
Pavino Polje SCG 44 Lu47
Pavlikeni BG 45 Mf47
Pavlivka UA 41 Me40
Pavlodar KZ 54 Od08
Pavlof Is. USA 164 Bk18
Pavlof Vol. USA 164 Bk18
Pavlohrad UA 49 Mh21
Pavlovo RUS 48 Nb18
Pavlovsk RUS 48 Mf16
Pavlovsk RUS 48 Na20
Pavlovskaja RUS 49 Mk22
Pavlovskij Posad RUS 48 Mk18
Pavlovskoe RUS 48 Na17
Pavlyš UA 49 Mg21
Pavullo nel Frignano I 34 Ll46
Pavuvu Island SOL 117 Sk50
Pawa RDC 141 Md44
Pawa RDC 141 Me44
Pawaia PNG 115 Sc49
Pawapuri IND 83 Pc33
Pawayan IND (UPH) 81 Pa31
Pawé CAM 139 Lf43
Pawhuska USA (OK) 174 Fb27
Pawłów PL 41 Md39
Pawnee Bill Mus. USA 174 Fb27
Pawnee Ind. Village USA 174 Fb26
Pawnee Nat. Grassland USA 171 Eh25
Pawnee Rock S.M. USA 174 Fa26
Pawtucket USA (RI) 177 Ge25
Pawu A.L. AUS 103 Rg56
Pawut MYA 88 Pk39
Pawut MYA 88 Pk39
Paxí GR 46 Ma51
Paxson USA (AK) 165 Ch14
Paxtakor UZ 63 Od25
Paxtaobod UZ 63 Oe25
Payagyi MYA 88 Pj37
Payaheislam RI 91 Rd45
Payakumbuh RI 93 Qa46
Payang, Gunung RI 94 Qh45
Payar SN 130 Kc38
Payerne CH 34 Lg44
Payette USA (ID) 168 Eb23
Paymogo E 27 Kn53
Paynes Find AUS (WA) 104 Qj60
Paysandú ROU 204 Ha62
Pays d'Auge F 22 Ku41
Pays de la Loire F 22 Kt43
Pays Dogon RMM 131 Kj38
Pays Jebala MA 125 Kh28
Payson USA (AZ) 171 Ee28
Payson USA (UT) 171 Ee25
Payún, Cerro RA 208 Gf64
Payung RI 95 Qd47
Payyanur IND (KER) 84 Oh39
Paz BR (PR) 204 Hd58
Pazar TR 57 Na25
Pazarbası Burnu TR 56 Mf25
Pazarcık TR 56 Mj27
Pazardžik BG 45 Me48
Pazarić BIH 44 Lt47
Pazarköy TR 47 Mh51
Pazarlar TR 47 Mk51
Paz de Ariporo CO 192 Ge43
Paz del Rio CO 192 Gd42
Pazha PK 65 Oe31
Pazin HR 35 Lo45
Pazña BOL 206 Gg55
Pčelarovo BG 45 Mf49
Pčelnik BG 45 Mh47
Pe MYA 88 Pk39
Peace Memorial Hiroshima J 79 Rg28
Peace Point CDN (AB) 167 Ed16
Peace River CDN (AB) 167 Eb17
Peace River CDN (AB) 167 Ed16
Peach Springs USA (AZ) 171 Ed28
Peach Tree USA (AL) 175 Fg30
Peachtree City USA (GA) 175 Fh29
Peak Charles N.P. AUS 104 Ra62
Peak District N.P. GB 21 Kt37
Peak Hill AUS (NSW) 111 Se62
Peak Hill AUS (WA) 104 Qk58
Peal de Becerro E 27 Kr53
Peale, Mount USA 171 Ef26
Pearce USA (AZ) 171 Ef30
Pea Ridge N.M.P. USA 174 Fc27
Pearisburg USA (VA) 178 Fk27
Pearl City USA (HI) 170 Cb35
Pearl Harbor USA 170 Ca35
Pearl Island MV 84 Og43
Pearl Island NZ 113 Td69
Pearl Mosque PK 65 Of31
Pearl River CHN 74 Qf34
Pearl S. Buck Mus. USA 175 Fk26
Pearsall USA (TX) 181 Fa31
Pearson USA (GA) 178 Fj30
Pearson Island AUS 110 Rh62
Pearson Reef 94 Qg41
Pearston ZA 155 Mc62
Peary Channel CDN 162 Ed03
Peary Land DK 163 Jb02
Peawanuck CDN (ON) 163 Fc07
Pebane MOC 153 Mk54
Pebas PE 196 Ge47
Pebbly Beach AUS 111 Sf63
Peć SCG 44 Ma48
Peçanha BR (MG) 203 Hj55
Pecan Island USA (LA) 175 Fd31
Pécel H 43 Lu43
Pečenjevce SCG 44 Mb47
Pečerskaja lavra UA 49 Mf20
Pechea RO 45 Mh45
Pecica RO 43 Mb44
Pećka Patrijaršija SCG 44 Ma48
Pečki RUS 39 Mh33
Pečora RUS 54 Nc05
Pečora RUS 54 Nd05
Pečorskoe more RUS 54 Nb04
Pečory RUS 39 Mh33
Pecos USA (TX) 181 Ej30
Pecos USA 171 Eh28
Pecos N.H.P. USA 171 Eh28
Pecos Plains USA 171 Eh29
Pécs H 42 Lt44
Pedana IND (APH) 83 Pa37
Pedasi PA 185 Fk42
Pedaso I 35 Lo47
Pedda Alavalapadu IND (APH) 85 Ok38
Pedda Arikatla IND (APH) 85 Ok38
Peddaballe IND (APH) 85 Ok39
Peddapalli IND (APH) 83 Ok36
Peddie ZA 155 Md62
Pedernales DOM 186 Ge36
Pedernales EC 196 Fk45
Pedernales RCH 207 Gf59
Pedernales YV 193 Gj41
Pederneiras BR (SP) 202 Hf57
Pedestal Rocks USA 174 Fd28
Pediwang RI 91 Rd45
Pedra Azul BR (MG) 203 Hk53
Pedra Azul BR 203 Hk56
Pedra Badejo CV 136 Jj38
Pedra Branca BR (CE) 201 Ja48
Pedra de Lume CV 136 Jj37
Pedra do Feitiço ANG 148 Lg48
Pedrafita do Cebreiro E 26 Kn47
Pedralba E 29 Ku51
Pedra Preta BR (MT) 202 Hc54
Pedras de Fogo BR (PB) 201 Jc49
Pedras de Maria da Cruz BR (MG) 203 Hh53
Pedras Negras ANG 148 Lh50
Pedras Negras BR (RO) 206 Gj52
Pedras Salgadas P 26 Kn49
Pedras Tinhosas STP 138 Ld45
Pedraza de la Sierra E 26 Kr49
Pedregal YV 192 Ge40
Pedregosa CO 192 Gd42
Pedregulho BR (SP) 203 Hg56
Pedreiras BR (MA) 200 Hh48
Pedreiras BR (PA) 199 Hc48
Pedrero, Cerro el RA 210 Ge68
Pedriceña MEX (DGO) 181 Ej33
Pedro Afonso BR (TO) 200 Hf50
Pedro Avelino BR (RN) 201 Jb48
Pedrobank 186 Ga37
Pedro Betancourt C 179 Fk34
Pedro Canário BR (ES) 203 Ja55
Pedro Carbo EC 196 Fk46
Pedro Cays JA 186 Gb37
Pedro de Valdivia RCH 207 Gf57
Pedro Gomes BR (MS) 202 Hc55
Pedro II BR (PI) 201 Hk48
Pedro Juan Caballero PY 202 Hc57
Pedro Luro RA (BA) 209 Gj65
Pedro Muñoz E 29 Ks51
Pedro Vaz CV 136 Jj38
Peebinga AUS (SA) 110 Sa63
Peebles GB 20 Kr35
Peel GB 21 Kq36
Peel Sound CDN 163 Fa04
Peene D 32 Lo37
Peerless CDN (SK) 169 Ef18
Peerless USA (MT) 169 Eh21
Peers CDN (AB) 168 Ec19
Peerto Iradier GQ 138 Le45
Péfkos GR 46 Ma50
Pegasus Bay NZ 113 Tg67
Pegatan RI 95 Qg47
Peggys Cove CDN (NS) 176 Gj23
Pegnitz D 33 Lm41
Pegnitz D 33 Lm41
Pego E 29 Ku52
Pegu MYA 88 Pj37
Peguis Ind. Res. CDN 172 Fa20
Pegunungan Border RI 115 Sa47
Pegunungan Fakfak RI 114 Rg47
Pegunungan Foja RI 114 Rk47
Pegunungan Gauttier RI 114 Rk47
Pegunungan Hose MAL 94 Qg44
Pegunungan Jayawijaya RI 114 Rk48
Pegunungan Kumafa RI 114 Rg47
Pegunungan Maoke RI 114 Rj48
Pegunungan Tamrau RI 114 Rg46
Pegunungan Tiyo RI 114 Rh48
Pegunungan Van Rees RI 114 Rj47
Pegunungan Wondiwoi RI 114 Rh47
Pehlivanköy TR 45 Mg49
Péhonko DY 138 La40
Pehuajó RA (BA) 209 Gk63
Pehuén-Co RA (BA) 209 Gk65
Peigan Ind. Res. CDN 169 Ed21
Peili SUD 141 Md42
Peine D 32 Ll38
Peineta, Cerro RA 210 Gd71
Peintures rupestres (Fada) TCH 134 Ma37
Peiting D 33 Ll43
Peitz D 32 Lp39
Peixe BR (TO) 200 Hf52
Pei Xian CHN (JGS) 78 Qj28
Peixoto de Azevedo BR (MT) 199 Hc51
Pejantan RI 95 Qd45
Pekabata RI 96 Qk47
Pekalongan RI 95 Qe49
Pekan MAL 92 Qb44
Pekanbaru RI 93 Qa45
Pekan Jabi MAL 92 Qb44
Pekin RI 94 Qj44
Pekin USA (IL) 175 Ff25
Pekin USA (ND) 172 Fa22
Peking CHN 73 Qj26
Pekinga DY 138 Lb39
Peking Man = Zhoukoudian CHN 73 Qh26
Péla RG 136 Kf42
Pelabuhan Ratu RI 95 Qd49
Pelabun Kelang MAL 92 Qa44
Pelaihari RI 95 Qh47
Pelapis RI 95 Qe46
Pelau Island SOL 117 Sk48
Pelawan RI 93 Qb47
Pélébina DY 138 La41
Pelechua CO 192 Gd40
Pelechuco BOL 206 Gf53
Pelegonia MK 44 Mb49
Pelejo PE 196 Gc49
Pelekech EAK 144 Mh44
Peleliu PAL 90 Rh42
Peleng RI 97 Rb46
Pelenge RDC 149 Mb47
Pèlerinage des Gitans F 25 Le47
Peletá GR 46 Mc53
Pélézi CI 137 Kg42
Pelham AUS (QLD) 107 Sb55
Pelhřimov CZ 42 Lq41
Pelican USA (AK) 166 Db17
Pelican Mtns. CDN 167 Ec18
Pelican Rapids CDN (MB) 169 Ek19
Pelican Rapids USA (MN) 172 Fb22
Pelileo EC 196 Ga46
Pelion USA (SC) 178 Fk29
Pelister, N.P. MK 44 Mb49
Pelješac HR 35 Ls48
Pelkosenniemi FIN 16 Md12
Pélla GR 46 Mc50
Pella JOR 56 Mh29
Pelland USA (MN) 172 Fd21
Pellegrini RA (BA) 209 Gj64
Pellinge = Pellinki FIN 38 Mf30
Pellinki = Pellinge FIN 38 Mf30
Pello FIN 16 Mc12
Pellworm D 32 Lj36
Pelly Mountains CDN 166 Dd15
Pelly Plateau CDN 166 De14
Pelokang RI 96 Qk49
Peloponnesus GR 46 Mb53
Pelotas BR (RS) 204 Hd61
Pelotas BR 205 He60
Pelplin PL 40 Lt37
Pelsart Island AUS 104 Qg60
Pelsor USA (AR) 174 Fd28
Pélussin F 25 Le45
Pem PNG 116 Se50
Pemalang RI 95 Qe49
Pemanggil MAL 92 Qc44
Pematangkaras RI 93 Qc47
Pematang Purba RI 93 Pk44
Pematang Siantar RI 93 Pk44
Pemba MOC 147 Na52
Pemba Z 152 Md54
Pemba Channel EAT 147 Mk48
Pemba Island EAT 147 Mk48
Pemberton AUS (WA) 104 Qj63
Pemberton CDN (BC) 168 Dj20
Pembroke AUS (QLD) 109 Se59
Pembroke CDN (ON) 177 Gb23
Pembroke GB 21 Kq39
Pembroke USA (GA) 178 Fk29
Pembroke Dock GB 21 Kq39
Pembrokeshire Coast N.P. GB 21 Kp39
Pembuanghulu RI 95 Qg47
Pemuco RCH 208 Gd64
Pen IND (MHT) 82 Og36
Peña Blanca PE 196 Gd47
Peña Blanca RCH 207 Ge59
Peñacerrada E 28 Ks48
Peñafiel E 26 Kq49
Penafiel P 26 Km49
Peñaflor RCH 208 Ge62
Penajam RI 95 Qj46
Penal Colony PA 185 Fk42
Peñalén E 29 Ks50
Penalva BR (MA) 200 Hh47
Penamacor P 27 Kn50
Penambulai RI 114 Rh49
Peña Mira E 26 Ko49
Penampang MAL 94 Qj43
Penang MAL 92 Qa43
Penápolis BR (SP) 202 He56
Peña Prieta E 26 Kq48
Peñaranda de Bracamonte E 26 Kp50
Peñaranda de Duero E 26 Kr49
Penaron RI 92 Pj43
Peñarroya-Pueblonuevo E 27 Kp52
Penarth GB 21 Kr39
Peñas de San Pedro E 27 Ks52
Peñas Negras YV 193 Gh42
Peña Ubiña E 26 Kp48
Peñausende E 26 Kp49
Pench N.P. IND 83 Ok35
Pendanga BR (BA) 200 Hj50
Pendé RCA 140 Lj42
Pendembu WAL 136 Kd41
Pendembu WAL 136 Ke41
Pendências BR (RN) 201 Jb48
Pendeng RI 92 Pj43
Pender Bay A.L. AUS 102 Rb54
Pendjari, P.N.de la DY 137 La40
Pendleton USA (OR) 168 Ea23
Pendolo RI 96 Ra47
Pendopo RI 93 Qb47
Pendra Road IND (CGH) 83 Pa34
Pendurti IND (APH) 83 Pb37
Penebangan RI 95 Qe46
Peneda-Gerês, P.N.da P 26 Km49
Penedo BR (AL) 201 Jb51
Penedo BR (AM) 196 Ge49
Pene-Katamba RDC 149 Mc46
Pene-Mende RDC 146 Me48
Peneri Tacaquiri, T.I. BR 198 Gg49
Pénéssoulou DY 138 La41
Pengalengan RI 95 Qd49
Peng'an CHN (SCH) 74 Qd30
Penganak RI 93 Qc46
Pengchia Yü RC 75 Rb33
Penge RDC 141 Md44
Penge RDC 141 Me44
Penge RDC 149 Mc48
Penge ZA 155 Mf58
Penghu Islands RC 75 Qk34
Pengkou CHN (FJN) 75 Qj33
Penglai CHN (HAN) 75 Qf36
Penglai CHN (SDG) 73 Ra27
Penglai Ge CHN 73 Ra27
Penglaizhen CHN (SCH) 74 Qc30
Pengshan CHN (SCH) 74 Qb30
Pengshui CHN (CGQ) 74 Qe31
Penguin AUS (TAS) 111 Sd66
Penguin Island CDN 177 Hb22
Pengxi CHN (SCH) 74 Qc30
Pengze CHN (JGX) 75 Qj31
Pengzhou CHN (SCH) 74 Qb30
Penhalonga ZW 152 Mg55
Péni BF 137 Kh40
Peniche P 27 Kl51
Penicuik GB 20 Kr35
Penida RI 95 Qh49
Peninjai RI 93 Qa46
Península Brunswick RCH 210 Ge72
Península de Araya YV 193 Gj40
Península de Azuero PA 185 Ga41
Península de la Guajira CO 192 Ge39
Península de Nicoya CR 184 Fh41
Península de Osa CR 185 Fj41
Península de Paracas PE 197 Gb52
Península de Paraguaná YV 192 Ge39
Península de Paría YV 193 Gj40
Península de Paría, P.N. YV 193 Gj40
Península de Taitao RCH 210 Gc69
Peninsula de Zapata C 179 Fk34
Península dos Tigres ANG 150 Lf54
Península Dumas RCH 210 Gf73
Península Ferrol PE 197 Ga50
Península Hardy RCH 210 Gf73
Península Mitre RA 210 Gh73
Península Muñoz Gamero RCH 210 Gd72
Peninsula Quevado MEX 180 Eg33
Península San Martín RCH 210 Gc70
Península Siscuelan RCH 210 Gd69
Península Skiring RCH 210 Gc68
Península Sta. Elena CR 184 Fg40
Península Staines RCH 210 Gd71
Península Tres Montes RCH 210 Gc69
Península Valdés RA 209 Gj67
Península Valiente PA 185 Fk41
Península Wharton RCH 210 Gc70
Península Wilcock RCH 210 Gd71
Péninsule de Gaspésie CDN 176 Gh21
Péninsule d'Ungava CDN 163 Gb06
Peñíscola E 29 La50
Penisola Salentina I 37 Ls50
Pénjamo MEX (GJT) 182 Ek35
Penjawan RI 94 Qg45
Penjwin IRQ 57 Nc28
Penkun D 32 Lp37
Penmarc'h F 22 Kq43
Penna Ahobilam IND 84 Oj38
Pennagaram IND (TNU) 84 Oj39
Pennant CDN (SK) 169 Ef20
Penne I 35 Lo48
Penne-d'Agenais F 24 La46
Pennell Coast 7 Tb33
Penneshaw AUS (SA) 110 Rj63
Penn Hills USA (PA) 173 Ga25
Pennines GB 14 Kb05
Pennsylvania USA 177 Ga25
Pennsylvania USA 177 Ga25
Penny CDN (BC) 166 Dk19
Penn Yan USA (NY) 177 Gb24
Pennyroyal Plateau USA 175 Fh27
Penny Strait CDN 163 Fa03
Peno RUS 48 Mg17
Penobscot Bay USA 177 Gf23
Penobscot River USA 176 Gf23
Penola AUS (SA) 110 Sa64
Peñón Blanco MEX (DGO) 181 Eh33
Penong AUS (SA) 108 Rg61
Penonomé PA 185 Fk41
Penot, Mount VU 118 Td54
Penrhyn Atoll NZ 11 Ca10
Penrith AUS (NSW) 111 Sf62
Penrith GB 21 Ks36
Penryn GB 21 Kp40
Pensa BF 137 Kk39
Pensacola USA (FL) 175 Fg30
Pensacola Mountains 6 Hb35
Penshurst AUS (VIC) 110 Sb64
Penshurst CR 185 Fj41
Pensiangan MAL 94 Qj43
Penta IND (CGH) 83 Pa36
Pentakota IND (APH) 83 Pb37
Pentálofos GR 46 Mb50
Pentápoli GR 45 Md49
Pentecost Downs AUS (WA) 103 Rd54
Pentecostes BR (CE) 201 Ja47
Pentecost Island VU 118 Te53
Penteleu RO 45 Mg45
Penticton CDN (BC) 168 Ea21
Penticton Ind. Res. CDN 168 Ea21
Pentland AUS (QLD) 107 Sc56
Pentland Hills GB 20 Kr35
Peñuelas MEX (AGS) 182 Ej35
Penukonda IND (APH) 84 Oj38
Penwegon MYA 86 Pj36
Penyal d'Ifac E 29 La52
Penza RUS 48 Nc19
Penzance GB 21 Kp40
Penzberg D 33 Lm43
Penzele RDC 149 Lk46
Penžinskaja guba RUS 55 Ta06
Penzlin D 32 Lo37
Peoria USA (AZ) 171 Ed29
Peoria USA (IL) 175 Ff25
Pepa RDC 146 Me49
Pepeekeo USA (HI) 170 Cc36
Pepel WAL 136 Kd41
Pepple Island GB 210 Ha71
Peqin AL 44 Lu49
Peque CO 192 Gc42
Pequizal, T.I. BR 206 Ha53
Perabumulih RI 93 Qc47
Perälä FIN 38 Mb28
Peraleda del Zaucejo E 27 Kp52
Perales del Alfambra E 29 Ku50
Pérama GR 46 Ma51
Pérama GR 46 Ma51
Perambalur IND (TNU) 85 Ok40
Perämeren kansallispuisto FIN 16 Mc13
Peramiho EAT 146 Mh51
Peranka FIN 16 Me13
Peranzanes E 26 Ko48
Peräseinäjoki FIN 38 Md28
Perbulan RI 93 Pk44
Percé CDN (QC) 176 Gh21
Percival Lakes AUS 103 Rc56
Percy Islands AUS 109 Sf56
Percy Quin S.P. USA 175 Fe30
Perdagangan RI 92 Pk44
Perdala IND (KER) 84 Oh39
Perďamajski BY 41 Mf37
Perdasdefogu I 36 Lk51
Perdekop ZA 155 Me59
Perdigão P 27 Kn51
Perdizes BR (MG) 203 Hg55
Perdões BR (MG) 203 Hh56
Perečyn UA 43 Mc42
Perehins'ke UA 43 Me42
Pereira CO 192 Gc43
Pereira Barreto BR (SP) 202 He56
Pereirinha BR (PA) 199 Hb50
Pereiro BR (CE) 201 Ja49
Perejaslav-Chmel'nyc'kyj UA 49 Mf20
Perejaslavka RUS 77 Rh22
Perelešinskij RUS 48 Na20
Pere Marquette S.P. USA 175 Fe26
Perembahan RI 93 Qc47
Peremyšljany UA 43 Me41
Perenjori AUS (WA) 104 Qj60
Péréré DY 138 Lb41
Pereščepyne UA 49 Mh21
Pereslavl'-Zalesskij RUS 48 Mk17
Pereslavsky N.P. RUS 48 Mk17
Perespa UA 41 Mf40
Peret AUS (QLD) 107 Sa52
Pereval Akbajtal TJ 63 Og26
Pereval Anzob TJ 63 Oe26
pereval Čyjyrčyk KS 63 Og25
pereval Durbet Daba MNG/RUS 67 Pe21
Pereval Harami RUS 57 Nd24
Pereval Kajtezek TJ 63 Og27
Pereval Krestovyi GE 57 Nc24
pereval Kyzyl-Art TJ/KS 63 Og26
Pereval Mamisonski RUS/GE 57 Nb24
Perevalovo RUS 39 Mb36
pereval Taldyk KS 63 Og26
pereval Vyškivs'kyj UA 43 Md42
Perevoz RUS 48 Nc18
Perez RA (SF) 209 Gk62
Perez USA (CA) 168 Dk25
PérezRosales , P.N. RCH 208 Gd66
Perfume Pagoda = Huong Pagoda VN 87 Qc35

Pregarten – Qijiang

Pregarten A 42 Lp42
Pregolja RUS 39 Mb36
Pregonero YV 192 Ge41
Prehistoric Footprints LS 155 Me60
Prehistoric Mounds CDN 172 Ek21
Preikestolen N 30 Lg31
Preiļi LV 39 Mg34
Prejmer RO 45 Mf45
Prejmer RO 45 Mf45
Prékété DY 138 La41
Preko HR 35 Lq46
Prek Thmei K 89 Qc40
Prek Vatt K 89 Qc40
Prelog HR 35 Lr44
Premer AUS (NSW) 109 Se61
Prémery F 25 Ld43
Premier Downs AUS (WA) 105 Rc61
Premio CDN (QC) 176 Gh20
Premnitz D 32 Ln38
Premuda HR 35 Lp46
Prend Town LB 136 Kf43
Prenn Falls VN 89 Qe40
Prenti Downs AUS (WA) 105 Rb59
Prentiss USA (MS) 175 Ff30
Prenzlau D 32 Lo37
Preobraženski manastir BG 45 Mf47
Preparis Island MYA 88 Pg38
Přerov CZ 42 Ls41
Presa de Guadelupe MEX (SLP) 182 Ek34
Presa de la Angostura MEX 183 Fd37
Presa Falcón MEX 181 Fa32
Presa J. López Portillo MEX 180 Eg33
Presa M. Alemán MEX 182 Fb36
Presa Nezahualcýotl MEX 183 Fd37
Presa Nova Ponte BR 203 Hg55
Presa P. Elias Calles MEX 180 Ef31
Presa V. Carranza MEX 181 Ek32
Prescott USA (AR) 174 Fd29
Prescott USA (AZ) 171 Ed28
Prescott USA (WA) 168 Ea22
Preševo SCG 44 Mb48
Presidencia de la Plaza RA (CH) 204 Ha59
Presidencia Roque Sáenz Peña RA (CH) 207 Gk59
Presidente Dutra BR (MA) 200 Hh48
Presidente Eduardo Frei ANT (RCH) 6 Ha30
Presidente Epitácio BR (SP) 202 He56
Presidente Figueiredo BR (AM) 199 Gk47
Presidente Getúlio BR (SC) 205 Hf59
PresidenteJânio Quadros BR (BA) 203 Hk53
Presidente Juscelino BR (MA) 195 Hh47
Presidente Juscelino BR (MG) 203 Hh55
Presidente Kennedy BR (TO) 200 Hf50
Presidente Médici BR (RO) 198 Gk51
Presidente Olegário BR (MG) 203 Hg55
Presidente Prudente BR (SP) 202 He57
Presidente Vargas BR (MA) 200 Hh47
Presidente Venceslau BR (SP) 202 He56
Presidio USA (TX) 181 Eh31
Presjaka SCG 44 Lt48
Prešov SK 43 Mb42
Préspa N.P. GR 46 Mb50
Presque Isle USA (ME) 176 Gg22
Presque Isle S.P. USA 173 Fk24
Presqu'île de Crozon F 22 Kq42
Presqu'île de Quiberon F 22 Kr43
Presqu'île du Cotentin F 22 Kt41
Presqu'ile Prov. Park CDN 177 Gb23
Pressac F 24 La44
Pressath D 33 Lm41
Prestatyn GB 21 Kr37
Prestbakki IS 18 Jt25
Prestbakki IS 18 Kb27
Prestfoss N 30 Lk30
Přeštice CZ 42 Lo41
Preston GB 21 Ks37
Preston USA (GA) 175 Fh30
Preston USA (ID) 171 Ee24
Preston USA (MN) 172 Fd24
Preston USA (MO) 174 Fd27
Preston USA (MS) 175 Ff29
Preston USA (NV) 170 Ec26
Prestonburg USA (KY) 178 Fj27
Prestwick GB 20 Kq35
Presumida MEX (QTR) 183 Ff36
Pretoria ZA 155 Me58
Pretzsch D 32 Ln39
Prevelly AUS 104 Qh62
Prevelly Park AUS 104 Qh63
Préveza GR 46 Ma52
Prey Khmer K 89 Qc39
Prey Veng K 89 Qc40
Priangarskoe plato RUS 54 Pd07
Priargunsk RUS 71 Qk20
Pribilof Islands USA 164 Bf17
Priboj BIH 44 Lt46
Priboj SCG 44 Lu47
Priboj SCG 44 Mc48
Pribojska Goleša SCG 44 Lu47
Příbor CZ 42 Lt41
Príbovce SK 43 Lt41
Příbram CZ 42 Lp41
Přibyslav CZ 42 Lq41
Price USA (UT) 171 Ee26
Price Island CDN 166 Df19
Prichard USA (AL) 175 Ff30
Priddis CDN (AB) 169 Ec20
Priego E 29 Ks50
Priego de Córdoba E 27 Kq53
Priekulė LT 39 Mb35
Priekule LV 39 Mb34
Prienai LT 39 Md36
Priene TR 47 Mh53
Prieska ZA 154 Mb60
Prieto, Cerro PE 196 Fk48
Prieuré de Merlande F 24 La45
Prievidza SK 43 Lt42
Prigi RI 95 Qf50
Prigor RO 44 Mc46
Þríhyrningsfjallgarður IS 18 Ke25
Prijedor BIH 35 Lr46
Prijepolje SCG 44 Lu47
Priko CI 137 Kj42
Prilenskoe plato RUS 55 Ra06
Prilep BG 45 Mg48
Prilep MK 44 Mb49
Prilike SCG 44 Ma47
Primate CDN (SK) 169 Ef19
Primavera BR (PA) 195 Hg46
Primavera do Leste BR (MT) 202 Hc53
Přimda CZ 42 Ln41
Primeira Cruz BR (MA) 195 Hj47
Prime Seal Island AUS (TAS) 111 Sd66
Primorsk RUS 38 Mj30
Primorsk RUS 39 Lu36
Primorski Dolac HR 35 Lr47
Primorskij hrebet RUS 70 Qc19
Primorsko BG 45 Mh48
Primorsko-Ahtarsk RUS 49 Mk22
Primošten HR 35 Lq47
Prince Albert CDN (SK) 169 Eh19
Prince Albert ZA 154 Mb62
Prince Albert Mountains 7 Sd34
Prince Albert N.P. CDN 169 Eg18
Prince Albert Peninsula CDN 162 Ea04
Prince Albert Road ZA 154 Ma62
Prince Albert Sound CDN 162 Ea04
Prince Alexander Mountains PNG 115 Sb47
Prince Charles Island CDN 163 Ga05
Prince Edward Island CDN 176 Gj22
Prince Edward Island CDN 176 Gj22
Prince Edward Island N.P. CDN 176 Gj22
Prince Edward Islands 9 Na14
Prince George CDN (BC) 166 Dj19
Prince of Wales Island AUS 107 Sb51
Prince of Wales Island CDN 163 Fa04
Prince of Wales Islands USA 166 Dd18
Prince of Wales Strait CDN 162 Ea04
Prince Olav Mountains 6 Ba36
Prince Patrick Island CDN 162 Dd03
Prince Regent Inlet CDN 163 Fb04
Prince Regent Nature Reserve AUS (WA) 103 Rc53
Prince Rupert CDN (BC) 166 De18
Princesa Isabel BR (PB) 201 Ja49
Princes Highway AUS 110 Rk64
Princess Alexandra N.P. GB 186 Ge35
Princess Charlotte Bay AUS 107 Sb53
Princess Elizabeth Land 7 Od33
Princess Island CDN 166 Df19
Prince's Town GH 137 Kj43
Prince's Town TT 187 Gk40
Princeton CDN (BC) 168 Dk21
Princeton USA (IL) 173 Ff25
Princeton USA (IN) 175 Fg26
Princeton USA (KY) 175 Fg27
Princeton USA (MN) 172 Fd23
Princeton USA (MO) 174 Fd25
Princeton USA (NJ) 177 Gc25
Princeton USA (OR) 168 Ea24
Princeton USA (WV) 178 Fk27
Princetown AUS (VIC) 111 Sb65
Princeville USA (HI) 170 Ca34
Prince William Sound USA 165 Cg15
Príncipe STP 138 Ld45
Príncipe da Beira BR (RO) 206 Gh52
Prineville USA (OR) 168 Dk23
Pringamosa CO 192 Gc43
Pringle Bay ZA 154 Lk63
Pringsewu RI 93 Qc48
Prínos GR 46 Mb51
Prinsesse Ragnhild kyst 7 Mb33
Prins Karls Forland N 16 Lf06
Priólithos GR 46 Mc53
Priolo Gargallo I 37 Lq53
Priozersk RUS 38 Ml29
Pripjat' BY 41 Mg38
Pripjat' BY 48 Me19
Pripyatsky N.P. BY 48 Md20
Prisoje BIH 35 Ls47
Priština SCG 44 Mb48
Pritzwalk D 32 Ln37
Privas F 25 Le46
Priverno I 36 Lo49
Privlaka HR 35 Lq46
Privolžsk RUS 48 Na17
Prizren SCG 44 Ma48
Prizzi I 36 Lo53
Prjadčino RUS 71 Rd20
Prjamicyno RUS 48 Mh20
Prnjavor BIH 35 Ls46
Probijnivka UA 43 Me43
Probolinggo RI 95 Qg49
Proddatur IND (APH) 85 Ok38
Professor Salvador Mazza BOL 207 Gj57
Progreso EC 196 Fk47
Progreso MEX (HDG) 182 Fa35
Progreso MEX (YT) 183 Ff35
Progreso PE 197 Gd53
Progreso ROU 209 Hb63
Progress ANT (RUS) 7 Od32
Progresso BR (AC) 196 Gd50
Prohladnyj RUS (KBA) 57 Nc24
Prokletije SCG/AL 44 Lu48
Prokop'evsk RUS 54 Pb08
Prokuplje SCG 44 Mb47
Proletarij RUS 48 Mf16
proliv Karskie Vorota RUS 54 Nd04
proliv Longa RUS 55 Td04
proliv Vil'kickogo RUS 55 Qa03
Prome MYA 86 Ph36
Promissão BR (MS) 202 Hc55
Promissão BR (SP) 202 Hf56
Promontorio del Circeo I 36 Lo49
Promontório del Gargano I 37 Lr49
Pronin RUS 48 Nb21
Prophet's Mosque KSA 58 Mk33
Propriá BR (SE) 201 Jb51
Propriano F 36 Lj49
Prorer Wiek D 32 Lo36
Prorva KZ 62 Ng23
Prosek AL 44 Lu49
Proserpine AUS (QLD) 107 Se56
Prospect AUS (QLD) 107 Sb55
Prospect Hill USA (NC) 178 Ga27
Prosperança BR (AM) 198 Gk46
Prosperidad RP 91 Rc41
Prossotsáni GR 45 Md49
Prostějov CZ 42 Ls41
Proston AUS (QLD) 109 Sf59
Proszowice PL 41 Ma40
Protem ZA 154 Ma63
Protivín CZ 42 Lp41
Proussós GR 46 Mb52
Provadija BG 45 Mh47
Provence F 25 Lf47
Provence-Alpes-Côte d'Azur F 25 Lf46
Providence USA (RI) 177 Ge25
Providence Island SY 156 Nf50
Providenciales Island GB 186 Gd35
Providenija RUS 55 Ub06
Provincetown USA (MA) 177 Ge24
Provins F 23 Ld42
Provištip MK 44 Mc48
Provo USA (UT) 171 Ee25
Provost CDN (AB) 169 Ee19
Prozor = Rama BIH 35 Ls47
Prrenjas AL 44 Ma49
Pruchnik PL 41 Mc41
Prudentópolis BR (PR) 205 He58
Prudhoe Bay USA (AK) 165 Cf10
Prudhoe Island AUS 109 Se56
Prudnik PL 40 Ls40
Prüm D 33 Lg40
Prunete F 34 Lk48
Prungle AUS (NSW) 111 Sb63
Pruské SK 42 Lt41
Pruszcz Gdański PL 40 Lt36
Pruszków PL 41 Ma38
Pružany BY 41 Me38
Pryazovs'ka vysočyna UA 49 Mj22
Pryazovs'ke UA 49 Mh22
Pryčornomors'ka nyzovyna UA 49 Me23
Prylęk PL 41 Mb40
Pryluky UA 48 Mg20
Prymors'k UA 49 Mj22
Pryor USA (MT) 169 Ef23
Pryor USA (OK) 174 Fc27
Pryp'jat' UA 41 Mf39
Przasnysz PL 41 Ma37
Przechlewo PL 40 Ls37
Przechyba PL 41 Ma41
Przedbórz PL 41 Lu39
Przemyśl PL 41 Mc41
Prževal'sk pristany KS 66 Ok24
Przeworsk PL 41 Mc40
Przewóz PL 40 Lp39
Przybiernów PL 40 Lp37
Przyborowice PL 41 Ma38
Przyłęki PL 40 Ls37
Przystawy PL 40 Lr36
Przysucha PL 41 Ma39
Przytoczno PL 41 Mc39
Przytuty PL 41 Mc37
Psahná GR 45 Md52
Psará GR 47 Mf52
Psará GR 47 Mf52
Psarádes GR 46 Mb50
Psári GR 46 Mc53
Psérimos GR 47 Mh54
Pskov RUS 39 Mj33
Pszczyna PL 41 Lt41
Pszów PL 40 Lt40
Ptolemaída GR 46 Mb50
Ptolemais LAR 127 Ma29
Ptuj SLO 42 Lq44
Ptujska Gora SLO 42 Lq44
Puah RI 96 Rb46
Pu'an CHN (GZH) 87 Qc33
Puán RA (BA) 209 Gj64
Puang THA 87 Pk37
Puas PNG 116 Sf47
Puaucho RCH 208 Gd66
Pubei CHN (GZG) 74 Qe34
Pubnico CDN (NS) 177 Gh24
Pucallpa PE 197 Gc50
Pucara PE 196 Ga48
Pucara PE 197 Ge53
Pucaurco PE 196 Gc47
Pucauro PE 196 Ge47
Pučež RUS 48 Nb17
Pucheng CHN (FJN) 75 Qk32
Pucheng CHN (SAA) 72 Qe28
Puchini BOL 206 Gg54
Puch'on ROK 78 Rd27
Púchov SK 42 Lt41
Puchuncaví RCH 208 Ge62
Pucioasa RO 45 Mf45
Pučišća HR 35 Lr47
Puck PL 40 Lt36
Puckett USA (MS) 175 Ff29
Puçol E 29 Ku51
Pucón RCH 208 Ge65
Púcuro PA 185 Gb41
Pudahuel RCH 208 Ge62
Puddukkottai IND (TNU) 84 Ok41
Pudi RI 95 Qj47
Pudimadaka IND (APH) 83 Pb37
Pudimoe ZA 155 Mc59
Pudingbesar RI 93 Qc47
Pudu Chattram IND (TNU) 84 Oj40
Puduchcheri = Pondicherry IND (PND) 85 Ok40
Pudukkottai IND (TNU) 85 Ok40
Puduvayal IND (TNU) 85 Pa39
Pue RI 115 Sa47
Puebla MEX (PUE) 182 Fa36
Puebla MEX 182 Fa36
Puebla de Alcocer E 27 Kp52
Puebla de Don Fadrique E 27 Ks53
Puebla de Don Rodrigo E 27 Kq51
Puebla de Guzmán E 27 Kn53
Puebla de Lillo E 26 Kp48
Puebla de Sanabria E 26 Ko48
Puebla de Trives E 26 Kn48
Pueblito MEX (CHH) 181 Eh31
Pueblo USA (CO) 171 Eh26
Pueblo Arrúa RA (ER) 204 Ha61
Pueblo Bello CO 192 Gd40
Pueblo Italiano RA (CD) 209 Gj62
Pueblo Nuevo CO 192 Gc41
Pueblo Nuevo CO 193 Gf44
Pueblo Nuevo YV 193 Gf40
Pueblo Pintado USA (NM) 171 Eg27
Pueblos Blancos E 27 Kp53
Pueblos Blancos (Granada-Masaya) NIC 184 Fh40
Puebloviejo EC 196 Ga46
Pueblo Viejo HN 184 Fg38
Pueblo Viejo MEX (OAX) 183 Fc37
Puelche RCH 208 Gd66
Puelches RA (LP) 208 Gh65
Puelén RA (LP) 208 Gg64
Puéllaro EC 196 Ga45
Puente Alto RCH 208 Ge62
Puente Azero BOL 206 Gh55
Puente del Inca PE 197 Ge53
Puente del Inca RA (MD) 208 Gf62
Puente-Genil E 27 Kq53
Puente la Reina E 28 Kt48
Puente la Reina de Jaca E 28 Ku48
Puentelarrá E 28 Kr48
Puente Sucre BOL 206 Gh55
Pu'er CHN (YUN) 87 Qa34
Puert Amador YV 193 Gj41
Puertecillo RCH 208 Gd63
Puertecitos MEX (BC) 180 Ec30
Puerto Acosta BOL 206 Gf53
Puerto Aisén RCH 210 Gd68
Puerto Alcatraz MEX (BCS) 180 Ee33
Puerto Alegre RA (LR) 207 Gg60
Puerto Alegria CO 196 Gc46
Puerto America PE 196 Gb48
Puerto Ángel MEX (OAX) 183 Fb38
Puerto Argentina CO 196 Gc45
Puerto Arista MEX (CHP) 183 Fd38
Puerto Armuelles PA 185 Fj41
Puerto Arquia CO 192 Gb42
Puerto Arturo CO 192 Gd44
Puerto Arturo PE 196 Gd46
Puerto Arturo RCH 210 Gf73
Puerto Asis CO 196 Gb45
Puerto Ayacucho YV 193 Gg43
Puerto Ayora EC 197 Fe46
Puerto Banegas BOL 206 Gj54
Puerto Baquerizo Moreno EC 197 Ff46
Puerto Barbery BOL 198 Gg51
Puerto Barrios GCA 184 Ff38
Puerto Belén CO 196 Gd47
Puerto Bélgica CO 192 Gc45
Puerto Belgrano RA (BA) 209 Gj65
Puerto Bermejo RA (CH) 204 Ha59
Puerto Bermudez PE 197 Gc51
Puerto Berrío CO 192 Gc42
Puerto Bolívar CO 192 Ge39
Puerto Boy CO 196 Gc45
Puerto Boyacá CO 192 Gc43
Puerto Buena Vista PY 202 Hb57
Puerto Busch BOL 202 Hb56
Puerto Caballo ES 184 Ff39
Puerto Cabello YV 193 Gg40
Puerto Cabello del Caura YV 193 Gh42
Puerto Cabezas NIC 185 Fj38
Puerto Caimán CO 196 Ge46
Puerto Caituma GUY 194 Ha42
Puerto Calvimontes BOL 206 Gh53
Puerto Canoa BOL 206 Gg53
Puerto Carabuco BOL 206 Gf53
Puerto Cárdenas PE 196 Gc46
Puerto Cárdenas RCH 210 Gd67
Puerto Carreño CO 193 Gg42
Puerto Castilla HN 184 Fh37
Puerto Catatumbo YV 192 Gd41
Puerto Cate MEX (CHP) 183 Fd37
Puerto Chale MEX (BCS) 180 Ee33
Puerto Chama YV 192 Ge41
Puerto Chicama PE 196 Ga49
Puerto Cisnes RCH 210 Gd68
Puerto Coig RA (SC) 210 Gf71
Puerto Colombia CO 196 Gc46
Puerto Colón CO 196 Gb45
Puerto Cortés HN 184 Fg38
Puerto Coyote CR 185 Fh41
Puerto Cumarebo YV 193 Gf40
Puerto Cutuco ES 184 Fg39
Puerto de Cayo EC 196 Fk46
Puerto de Fora BR (MT) 202 Hc54
Puerto de Ibañeta E 28 Kt47
Puerto de la Cruz E 124 Kb31
Puerto de la Mora E 27 Kr53
Puerto de las Palomas E 27 Ks53
Puerto de Leitariegos E 26 Ko48
Puerto del Gallo MEX (GUR) 182 Ek37
Puerto de los Ángeles, P.N. MEX 181 Eh34
Puerto del Rosario E 124 Kd31
Puerto de Maranchón E 29 Ks49
Puerto de Menga E 27 Kq50
Puerto de Monrepós E 28 Ku48
Puerto de Niefla E 27 Kq52
Puerto de Perales E 27 Ko50
Puerto de Piqueras E 28 Ks48
Puerto de San Just E 29 Ku50
Puerto de San Vicente E 27 Kp51
Puerto Deseado RA (SC) 210 Gh69
Puerto de Singra E 29 Kt50
Puerto de Tiscar E 27 Ks53
Puerto de Tórdiga E 29 Ks51
Puerto de Villarroya E 29 Ku50
Puerto Díaz NIC 184 Fh40
Puerto Díaz PE 196 Gb48
Puerto Eden RCH 210 Gc70
Puerto El Carmen de Putumayo EC 196 Gc45
Puerto Ele CO 192 Ge42
Puerto Escondido CO 192 Gb41
Puerto Escondido MEX (BCS) 180 Ee33
Puerto Escondido MEX (OAX) 182 Fb38
Puerto Esperanza C 179 Fj34
Puerto Estrella CO 192 Ge39
Puerto Etén PE 196 Ga49
Puerto Flamenco RCH 207 Ge59
Puerto Flores EC 197 Fe46
Puerto Francisco de Orellana = Coca EC 196 Gb46
Puerto Fuy RCH 208 Ge65
Puerto Gaitan CO 192 Gd43
Puerto Galera RP 90 Ra39
Puerto Galilea PE 196 Gb47
Puerto Gonzáles CR 185 Fj41
Puerto Grande EC 196 Fk47
Puerto Gumilla YV 193 Gg42
Puerto Gutierrez CO 192 Gc43
Puerto Haberton RA (TF) 210 Gg73
Puerto Heath BOL 206 Gf52
Puerto Humbria CO 192 Gb45
Puerto Iguazú RA (MI) 204 Hc58
Puerto Inca EC 196 Ga47
Puerto Inca PE 197 Gc50
Puerto Indio PA 185 Ga42
Puerto Indio PY 204 Hc58
Puerto Ingeniero Ibañez RCH 210 Gd69
Puerto Inirida CO 193 Gg44
Puerto Jiménez CR 185 Fj41
Puerto Juárez MEX (QTR) 183 Fg35
Puerto la Cruz YV 193 Gh40
Puerto la Victoria PY 202 Hb57
Puerto Leguizano CO 196 Gc46
Puerto Leitón BOL 206 Gk52
Puerto Lempira HN 185 Fj38
Puerto Libertad MEX (SO) 180 Ed31
Puerto Limón CO 192 Gb45
Puerto Limón CR 185 Fj41
Puerto-llano E 27 Kq52
Puerto Lobos MEX (SO) 180 Ed30
Puerto Lobos RA (CB) 208 Gh67
Puerto López CO 192 Gd43
Puerto Lopez CO 192 Ge40
Puerto López EC 196 Fk46
Puerto Lumbreras E 29 Kt53
Puerto Madero MEX (CHP) 183 Fd38
Puerto Madryn RA (CB) 208 Gh67
Puerto Maldonado PE 206 Gf52
Puerto Miranda YV 193 Gg42
Puerto Montt RCH 208 Gd66
Puerto Morazán NIC 184 Fg39
Puerto Morelos MEX (QTR) 183 Fg35
Puerto Napo EC 196 Gb46
Puerto Nare CO 192 Gc42
Puerto Nare CO 192 Ge45
Puerto Nariño CO 193 Gg43
Puerto Natales RCH 210 Gd71
Puerto Ninfas RA (CB) 208 Gh67
Puerto Obaldia PA 185 Gb41
Puerto Octay RCH 208 Gd66
Puerto Olaya CO 192 Gc42
Puerto Ordaz YV 193 Gj41
Puerto Ospina CO 196 Gc45
Puerto Pachitea PE 197 Gc50
Puerto Padre C 179 Gb35
Puerto Páez YV 193 Gg42
Puerto Pardo PE 196 Gb47
Puerto Patiño BOL 206 Gh54
Puerto Peñasco MEX (SO) 180 Ed30
Puerto Piedra RCH 210 Gd67
Puerto Piña PA 185 Ga42
Puerto Pinasco PY 202 Hb57
Puerto Pipa PE 196 Ge47
Puerto Pirámide RA (CB) 208 Gh67
Puerto Píritu YV 193 Gh40
Puerto Pizarro CO 192 Gb43
Puerto Pizarro CO 196 Gd46
Puerto Plata DOM 186 Ge36
Puerto Porfia CO 192 Gd43
Puerto Portillo PE 197 Gd50
Puerto Prado PE 197 Gc51
Puerto Princesa RP 91 Qk41
Puerto Pupuña CO 196 Ge47
Puerto Quetzal GCA 184 Fe39
Puerto Quijarro BOL 202 Hb55
Puerto Real E 27 Ko54
Puerto Real MEX (CAM) 183 Fe36
Puerto Rey E 27 Kp51
Puerto Rico BOL 198 Gg51
Puerto Rico PE 197 Gc51
Puerto Rico RA (MI) 204 Hc59
Puerto Rico RCH 208 Gd66
Puerto Rico USA 187 Gg36
Puerto Rico USA 187 Gg37
Puerto Rico Trench 187 Gg36
Puerto Rondón CO 192 Ge42
Puerto Rubio BOL 206 Gj52
Puerto Saavedra RCH 208 Gd65
Puerto San Carlos PE 197 Ge52
Puerto Sandino NIC 184 Fg39
Puerto San José GCA 184 Fe39
Puerto San Julián RA (SC) 210 Gg70
Puerto San Martín PE 197 Gb52
Puerto Santa Catarina MEX (BC) 180 Ec31
Puerto Santa Cruz RA (SC) 210 Gf70
Puerto Santander CO 192 Gd41
Puerto Saucedo BOL 206 Gj52
Puerto Siles BOL 206 Gh52
Puerto Silvania CO 192 Ge45
Puerto Suárez BOL 202 Hb55
Puerto Tastil RA (SA) 207 Gh58
Puerto Tejada CO 192 Gb44
Puerto Tirol RA (CH) 204 Ha59
Puerto Toro RCH 210 Gg73
Puerto Triana CO 192 Gc42
Puerto Tumaco CO 196 Gd47
Puerto Turumbán GUY 194 Gk42
Puerto Valencia CO 193 Gf44
Puerto Vallarta MEX (JLC) 182 Eh35
Puerto Varas RCH 208 Gd66
Puerto Venustiano Carranza MEX (BC) 180 Ec31
Puerto Venustiano Carranza MEX (BCS) 180 Ec32
Puerto Victoria PE 197 Gc50
Puerto Viejo CR 185 Fh40
Puerto Viejo CR 185 Fj41
Puerto Viejo RCH 207 Ge59
Puerto Villamil EC 197 Fe46
Puerto Visser RA (CB) 210 Gg68
Puerto Wilches CO 192 Gd42
Puerto Williams RCH 210 Gg73
Puerto Yungay RCH 210 Gd69
Pugal IND (RJT) 80 Og31
Puge CHN (SCH) 87 Qb32
Puger RI 95 Qg50
Puget-Ville F 25 Lg47
Púglia I 37 Lr50
Pugul RI 93 Qc46
Pugung Archaeological Site RI 93 Qc48
Pugwash CDN (NS) 176 Gj23
Pühajärv EST 39 Mg32
Puhos FIN 38 Mk28
Pühtitsa EST 38 Mh31
Pui RO 44 Md45
Puiatu EST 39 Mf32
Puig SUD 141 Me41
Puigcerdà E 28 Lb48
Puig Major E 29 Lc51
Puigmal E 28 Lc48
Puig Pedrós E 28 Lb48
Puig-reig E 29 Lb49
Puiseaux F 23 Lc42
Pujehun WAL 136 Ke42
Pujiang CHN (ZJG) 75 Qk31
Pujon RI 95 Qh46
Pujonryong Sanmaek PRK 76 Re25
Pukalaidun FIN 38 Md29
Puk'ansan N.P. ROK 78 Rd27
Pukaskwa N. P. CDN 173 Fh21
Pukatja AUS (SA) 105 Rg59
Pukavik S 31 Lp34
Pukaviksbukten S 31 Lp34
Pukchong PRK 76 Re25
Pukë AL 44 Lu48
Pukota Z 146 Me52
Puksuback PRK 76 Rd25
Pula HR 35 Lo46
Pula I 36 Lk51
Pula Amfiteatar HR 35 Lo46
Pulai RI 91 Qk45
Pulaj AL 44 Lu49
Pulandian CHN (LNG) 73 Ra26
Pulanduta Point RP 90 Rb40
Pulangpisau RI 95 Qh47
Pulanpanggung RI 93 Qb48
Pulap Atoll FSM 10 Sa09
Pular, Cerro RCH 207 Gf58
Pularumpi AUS (NT) 106 Rf51
Pulasi RI 96 Ra49
Pulaski USA (NY) 177 Gb24
Pulaski USA (TN) 175 Fg28
Pulaski USA (VA) 178 Fk27
Pulau Banding MAL 92 Qa43
Pulau Baun Wildlife Reserve RI 114 Rh49
Pulau Betong MAL 92 Qa43
Pulau Bruit MAL 94 Qf44
Pulauduku RI 93 Qb48
Pulau Supiori Reserve RI 114 Rh46
Pulau Tiga N.P. MAL 94 Qh43
Puławy PL 41 Mb39
Pulga IND (HPH) 81 Oj29
Pulgaon IND (MHT) 82 Ok35
Pulhapanzak HN 184 Ff38
Pulicat IND (TNU) 85 Pa39
Pulivendla IND (APH) 85 Ok38
Pulkkila FIN 16 Mc13
Pullampet IND (APH) 85 Ok38
Pullman USA (WA) 168 Eb22
Pullo PE 197 Gd53
Pulmoddai CL 85 Pa41
Pulo Anna Island PAL 90 Rf43
Pulo Buda MYA 88 Pk40
Pulpí E 29 Kt53
Pulsano I 37 Ls50
Pulsnitz D 32 Lo39
Pułtusk PL 41 Mb38
Pulu CHN (XUZ) 68 Pa27
Pülümür TR 57 Mk26
Puluo CHN (GZG) 74 Qe33
Pulwama 80 Oh29
Pumalín, P.N. RCH 208 Gd67
Pumpėnai LT 39 Me35
Puná EC 196 Ga47
Puna de Atacama RA/RCH 207 Gg58
Punakaiki NZ 113 Tf67
Punakha BHT 86 Pe32
Punalur IND (KER) 84 Oj41
Punata BOL 206 Gh54
Puncak Jaya RI 114 Rj48
Puncak Mandala RI 115 Sa48
Puncak Yamin RI 115 Rk48
Punch 80 Oh29
Punchh IND (UPH) 83 Ok33
Punda Hamlets PNG 115 Sa47
Punda Maria ZA 152 Mf57
Pundanhar MOC 147 Na51
Pune IND (MHT) 82 Og36
Pungalina AUS (NT) 106 Rj54
Pungan UZ 63 Of25
Punganuru IND (APH) 85 Ok39
Pungatini EAT 147 Mk50
Pungki RI 92 Pj43
Pungo Andongo ANG 148 Lh50
Punia RDC 141 Md46
Puning CHN (GDG) 75 Qj34
Punitaqui RCH 208 Ge61
Punjab IND 80 Oh30
Punjur IND (KTK) 84 Oj40
Punkaharju FIN 38 Mk29
Punkaharju FIN 38 Mk29
Punkin Center USA (CO) 174 Ej26
Puno PE 197 Ge53
Punta Abreojos MEX (BCS) 180 Ed32
Punta Aguja PE 196 Ga48
Punta Ala I 34 Ll48
Punta Albermarle EC 197 Fe45
Punta Alcalde RCH 207 Ge60
Punta Alegre C 179 Ga34
Punta Alice I 37 Ls51
Punta Allen MEX (QTR) 183 Fg36
Punta Almina MA 27 Kp46
Punta Alta EC 196 Fk46
Punta Alta RA (BA) 209 Gk65
Punta Anegada PA 185 Fk42
Punta Angamos RCH 207 Ge57
Punta Arenas RCH 207 Ge56
Punta Arenas RCH 210 Ge72
Punta Baja MEX 180 Ec31
Punta Ballena EC 196 Fk46
Punta Bandera RA (SC) 210 Gd71
Punta Baz MEX 183 Fe35
Punta Brava EC 196 Fk46
Punta Buenos Aires RA 208 Gh67
Punta Burica CR/PA 185 Fj42
Punta Burros MEX 182 Eh35
Punta Bustamante RA 210 Gf71
Punta Cachos RCH 207 Ge59
Punta Cambu BR 195 He44
Punta Cana DOM 187 Gf36
Punta Canoas CO 192 Gc40
Punta Caprara o dello Scorno I 36 Lj49
Punta Caribana CO 192 Gb41
Punta Castilla NIC 185 Fj40
Punta Castro RA 210 Gh67
Punta Catalina RCH 210 Gf72
Punta Caxinas HN 184 Fg37
Punta Celarain MEX 183 Fg35
Punta Chame PA 185 Ga41
Punta Chérrepe PE 196 Ga49
Punta Chilca PE 197 Gb52
Punta Clara RA 210 Gh67
Punta Coco CO 192 Gc44
Punta Coles PE 197 Ge54
Punta Cosigüina NIC 184 Fg39
Punta Cristo PA 185 Fk42
Punta Cristóbal EC 197 Fe46
Punta Culebras PE 197 Ga50
Punta da Pescada BR 195 He44
Punta de Arenas RA 210 Gf72
Punta de Balasto RA (CA) 207 Gg59
Punta de Bombon PE 197 Ge54
Punta de Capdepera E 29 Ld51
Punta degli Infreschi I 37 Lq51
Punta de Guañape PE 197 Ga50
Punta de la Estaca de Bares E 26 Kn47
Punta del Agua RA (MD) 208 Gf63
Punta de la Parata F 36 Lj49
Punta del Este C 179 Fj35
Punta del Este ROU 209 Hc63
Punta Delgada RA (CB) 210 Gh67
Punta Delgada RCH 210 Gf72
Punta della Penna I 37 Lp48
Punta de los Llanos RA (LR) 207 Gg61
Punta de los Lobos RCH 208 Gd63
Punta de Mita MEX (NYT) 182 Eh35
Punta de Perlas NIC 185 Fj39
Punta de Piedras YV 193 Gh40
Punta de Quemados C 186 Gc35
Punta de San Bernardo CO 192 Gb41
Punta de Santarém BR 195 Hf45
Punta Desengaño RA 210 Gg70
Punta de Vacas RA (MD) 208 Gf62
Punta di li Francesi I 36 Lk49
Punta do Costa BR 195 He43
Punta dos Reyes RCH 207 Ge58
Punta Dungenes RA 210 Gf72
Punta Estrella MEX (BC) 180 Ec30
Punta Eugenia MEX (BCS) 180 Ec32
Punta Europa GQ 138 Le44
Punta Galera EC 196 Fk45
Punta Gallinas CO 192 Ge39
Punta Gap RCH 210 Gf72
Punta Garachiné PA 185 Ga41
Punta Gorda BH 184 Ff37
Punta Gorda MEX 180 Ef34
Punta Gorda NIC 185 Fj38
Punta Gorda RCH 206 Ge55
Punta Gorda USA (FL) 179 Fj32
Punta Grande RCH 207 Ge58
Punta Gruesa, Cerro RA 210 Ge71
Punta Gualaguala RCH 207 Ge57
Punta Guascama CO 192 Ga44
Punta Hereda PE 196 Fk48
Punta Herrero MEX (QTR) 183 Fg36
Punta Hornillos PE 197 Gd54
Punta Izopo HN 184 Fg38
Punta Japerica BR 195 Hg46
Punta Kazer RCH 210 Gg73
Punta Križa HR 35 Lp46
Punta la Mármora I 36 Lk50
Punta León RA 208 Gh67
Punta Licosa I 37 Lp50
Punta Lobos RA 209 Gk65
Punta Lobos RCH 206 Ge56
Punta Magdalena CO 192 Gb44
Punta Mala CR 185 Fj41
Punta Mala PA 185 Ga42
Punta Malabrigo PE 196 Ga49
Punta Manglares CO 192 Gb43
Punta Maraguay YV 192 Ge40
Punta Mariato PA 185 Fk42
Punta Marqués RA 210 Gg69
Punta Marroquí o de Tarifa E 27 Kp55
Punta Marzo CO 192 Gb42
Punta Medanosa RA 210 Gh70
Punta Mono NIC 185 Fj40
Punta Montes RA 210 Gf71
Punta Morro RCH 207 Ge59
Punta Navarino RCH 210 Gg73
Punta Negra BH 184 Ff37
Punta Ninfas RA 208 Gh67
Punta Norte RA (CB) 210 Gh67
Punta Norte del Cabo San Antonio RA 209 Hb64
Punta Oscura GQ 138 Le44
Punta Pajaros MEX 183 Fg36
Punta Palazzu F 34 Lj48
Punta Palenque DOM 186 Ge36
Punta Pariñas PE 196 Fk48
Punta Patache RCH 206 Ge56
Punta Patuca HN 185 Fh38
Punta Pedernales EC 196 Ga45
Punta Peñas YV 193 Gk40
Punta Pichalo RCH 206 Ge55
Punta Piedras RA 209 Hb63
Punta Pozos RA 210 Gh69
Punta Prieta MEX (BC) 180 Ec31
Punta Quiroga RA 208 Gh67
Punta Ráisi I 36 Lo52
Punta Rasa RA 209 Gj66
Punta Remedios ES 184 Ff39
Puntarenas CR 185 Fh41
Punta Reyes CO 192 Gb44
Punta Roca CO 192 Gc40
Punta Roca 184 Ff39
Punta Roja RA 210 Gh68
Punta Sabaneta YV 194 Gk41
Punta Sal HN 184 Fg38
Punta Salinas PE 197 Gb51
Punta San Juan PE 197 Gc53
Punta San Pedro RCH 207 Ge58
Punta Santa Elena EC 196 Ga47
Punta Santiago GQ 138 Le44
Punta Santiago USA 187 Gh37
Punta Serpeddi I 36 Lk51
Punta Sierra RA 208 Gh66
Punta Solano CO 192 Gb42
Punta Stilo I 37 Lr52
Punta Sur CO 185 Fk39
Punta Tetas RCH 207 Ge57
Punta Tinaja PE 197 Gd54
Punta Tombo RA 210 Gh68
Punta Tombo RA 210 Gh68
Punta Tucacas YV 193 Gf40
Punta Umbría E 27 Ko53
Punta Verde EC 196 Ga45
Punta Verde RA 209 Gk65
Punta Verde YV 193 Gh45
Punta Yalkubul MEX 183 Ff35
Punta Zamora PE 197 Ga50
Puntianau RI 93 Qb46
Punto Alegre BR (PA) 195 He46
Punto Colnet MEX (BC) 180 Eb30
Punto da Barca BR (PA) 195 Hf46
Punto delle Contessa I 37 Lt50
Punto Fijo YV 192 Ge40
Punto Penne I 37 Ls50
Punxsutaweny USA (PA) 173 Ga25
Puolanka FIN 16 Md13
Puponga NZ 113 Tg66
Pupri IND (BIH) 83 Pc32
Puqi CHN (HUB) 75 Qg31
Puquina PE 197 Ge54
Puquio PE 197 Gc53
Pura IND (MPH) 82 Oj33
Pura RI 94 Qh45
Puracé, P.N. CO 192 Gb44
Puracé, Volcán CO 192 Gb44
Pura Luhur Ulu Watu RI 95 Qh50
Puranpur IND (UPH) 81 Pa31
Puraquê Ponta BR (AM) 193 Gf45
Purasa IND (RJT) 82 Of33
Purbolinggo RI 95 Qe49
Purcell USA (OK) 174 Fb28
Purcell Mtns. CDN 168 Eb20
Purcell Wilderness Conservancy CDN 168 Eb20
Purchena E 27 Ks53
Purdoški RUS 48 Nb18
Purdy Islands PNG 116 Sd47
Pureba Conservation Park AUS 110 Rh62
Purén RCH 208 Gd65
Purgatorio YV 193 Gk42
Puri ANG 148 Lh49
Puri IND (ORS) 83 Pc36
Puri Beach IND 83 Pc36
Purificasion CO 192 Gc44
Purikari neem EST 38 Mf31
Purmamarca RA (PJ) 207 Gh57
Purmerend NL 23 Lf38
Purna IND (MHT) 82 Oj36
Purnia IND (BIH) 83 Pd33
Purnululu N.P. AUS 103 Re54
Purple Downs AUS (SA) 108 Rj61
Purranque RCH 208 Gd66
Purros NAM 150 Lg55
Pursat K 89 Qb39
Purtse EST 38 Mh31
Puruándiro MEX (MHC) 182 Ek35
Puruey YV 193 Gh42
Purukcahu RI 95 Qh46
Purulia IND (WBG) 83 Pd34
Purun RI 93 Qc47
Purunakatak IND (ORS) 83 Pc35
Purureche YV 192 Ge40
Purus BR 198 Gk48
Purutu Island PNG 115 Sb50
Purwakarta RI 95 Qd49
Purwantoro RI 95 Qf49
Purwodadi RI 95 Qf49
Purwodadi RI 95 Qf49
Purwokerto RI 95 Qe49
Purworejo RI 95 Qf49
Puryong PRK 76 Re24
Purzell Mount USA (AK) 165 Cb12
Pusa MAL 94 Qf45
Pusad IND (MHT) 82 Oj36
Pusaga GH 137 Kk41
Pusan ROK 79 Re28
Pusat Gayo Range RI 92 Pj43
Pusesavli IND (MHT) 82 Oh37
Pushkar IND (RJT) 80 Oh32
Puškinskie Gory RUS 39 Mj33
Püspöki Palota H 42 Lr43
Püspökladány H 43 Mb43
Pustoška RUS 48 Me17
Pustunich MEX 183 Fe36
Puszcza Darżlubska PL 40 Lt36
Puszcza Koszalińska PL 40 Lr36
Puszcza Notecka PL 40 Lq38
Puszcza Słupska PL 40 Ls36
Putaendo RCH 208 Ge62
Putai RC 75 Ra34
Putao MYA 86 Pj32
Putao Gou CHN 67 Pe24
Putbus D 32 Lo36
Puthein MYA 88 Ph37
Putia RI 97 Rd47
Putian CHN (FJN) 75 Qk33
Putignano I 37 Ls50
Putina PE 206 Gf53
Putlitz D 32 Ln37
Putna RO 43 Mf43
Putončany RUS 54 Pc06
Putre RCH 206 Gf55
Putsonderwater ZA 154 Ma60
Puttalam CL 85 Ok41
Puttaparthi IND (APH) 84 Oj38
Putten NL 23 Lf38
Puttgarden D 32 Lm36
Putthaisong THA 89 Qb38
Puttur IND (APH) 85 Ok39
Puttur IND (KTK) 84 Oh39
Putty AUS (NSW) 111 Sf62
Putuk WAN 139 Lf41
Putukehn LB 136 Kf43
Putumayo CO/PE 196 Gd46
Putussibau RI 94 Qg45
Putyvl' UA 48 Mg20
Puuhonua o Honaunau N.H.S. USA 170 Cc36
Puukirkko FIN 38 Mf28
Puukohola Heiau N.H.S. USA 170 Cc36
Puumala FIN 38 Mj29
Puurijärven-Isonsuon kansallispuisto FIN 38 Mc29
Puurmani EST 38 Mg32
Puu Ulaula USA 170 Cb35
Puuwai USA (HI) 170 Bk35
Pu Xian CHN (SAX) 72 Qf27
Puyang CHN (HNN) 73 Qh28
Puyango Petrfied Forest EC 196 Fk47
Puyca PE 197 Gd53
Puy de Dome F 25 Lc45
Puy de Sancy F 25 Lc45
Puyehue , P.N. RCH 208 Gd66
Puyehué, Volcán RCH 208 Gd66
Puy l'Evêque F 24 Lb46
Puyo EC 196 Gb46
Puysegur Point NZ 113 Td69
Puyuhuapi RCH 210 Gd68
Puzači RUS 48 Mj20
Puzino RUS (YAO) 76 Rf22
Pwalagu GH 137 Kk40
Pweto RDC 146 Me50
Pwllheli GB 21 Kq38
Pyanangazu MYA 86 Pj35
Pyapon MYA 88 Ph37
Pyawbwe MYA 86 Pj35
Pyechin MYA 86 Pg36
Pye Is. USA (AK) 164 Ce16
Pye, Mount NZ 113 Te69
Pyhä-Hakin kansallispuisto FIN 28 Mf28
Pyhäntä FIN 16 Md13
Pyhäranta FIN 38 Mb30
Pyhäselkä FIN 38 Mk28
Pyhätunturin kansallispuisto FIN 16 Md12
Pyhtää = Pyttis FIN 38 Mg30
Pyingaing MYA 86 Ph34
Pyinmana MYA 86 Pj36
Pyin U Lwin MYA 86 Pj34
Pyinzi MYA 86 Ph35
Þykkvibær IS 18 Ju27
Pyla-sur-Mer F 24 Kt46
Pylkönmäki FIN 38 Me28
Pynjany UA 43 Md41
Pyonggang PRK 78 Rd26
Pyongsan PRK 78 Rd26
P'yongsong PRK 76 Rc26
P'yongt'aek ROK 78 Rd27
Pyongyang PRK 78 Rc26
Pyongyang PRK 78 Rc26
Pyramiden N 16 Lj06
Pyramid Lake Ind. Res. USA 170 Ea25
Pyramid of El Lâhûn ET 129 Mf31
Pyramid of Meidum ET 129 Mf31
Pyramids of Abusîr ET 129 Mf31
Pyramids of Dahshûr ET 129 Mf31
Pyramids of Gîsa ET 129 Mf31
Pyrénées F/E 24 Kt47
Pyrénées, P.N.des F 24 Ku48
Þyrill IS 18 Jt26
Pyrjatyn UA 48 Mg20
Pyrzyce PL 40 Lp37
Pyskowice PL 40 Lt40
Pytalovo RUS 39 Mh33
Pyttis = Pyhtää FIN 38 Mg30
Pyu MYA 86 Pj36
Pyzdry PL 40 Ls38

Q

Qaanaaq = Thule DK 163 Gc03
Qab CHN (NMZ) 72 Qd26
Qabane LS 155 Me60
Qabr Hud YE 60 Ne37
Qadam SUD 134 Me39
Qader Abad IR 64 Ng30
Qades AFG 64 Ob28
Qadimah KSA 58 Mk34
Qadir Purran PK 65 Of30
Qadisha RL 56 Mh28
Qadub YE 61 Ng39
Qaem Shahr IR 62 Ng27
Qa'en IR 64 Nk29
Qafa OM 61 Ng37
Qaf'e Logorajt AL 46 Lu50
Qaf'e Shtyllës AL 44 Ma49
Qafëzez AL 46 Ma50
Qaftat OM 61 Ng37
Qagan Nur CHN (NMZ) 71 Qh24
Qagan Nur CHN (NMZ) 72 Qe26
Qagan Tahoi CHN (QHI) 69 Ph28
Qagcaka CHN (TIB) 68 Pa29
Qahar You Qianqi CHN (NMZ) 73 Qg25
Qahar Youyi Houqi CHN (NMZ) 73 Qg25
Qahar You Zhongqi CHN (NMZ) 72 Qg25
Qahavand IR 57 Ne28
Qaidam Pendi CHN 69 Pg26
Qaisariye Basar IR 64 Nh32
Qala'at al-Marqab SYR 56 Mh28
Qalaat al-Rahba SYR 56 Mk28
Qala'at Ibn Maan SYR 56 Mk28
Qala'at Ja'abar SYR 56 Mk28
Qala'at Najm SYR 56 Mk27
Qala'at Salah ad-Din SYR 56 Mj28
Qala'at Samaan SYR 56 Mj27
Qala'at Samaan SYR 56 Mj27
Qala Duhtar IR 64 Ng31
Qala'en Nahl SUD 135 Mh39
Qalamat Abu Shafrah KSA 61 Ng35
Qalamat Al-Qurayni KSA 61 Ng35
Qalamat ar-Rakabah KSA 61 Ng35
Qalamat ash Sharawrah KSA 60 Nd37
Qalamat Faris KSA 60 Ne35
Qalamat Khawr al-Juhaysh KSA 60 Ne35
Qalamat Nadqar KSA 61 Nf34
Qalanah YE 61 Nf38
Qalansiyah YE 61 Ng39
Qalat AFG 65 Od29
Qalat Airif KSA 58 Na32
Qal'at al-Bahrain BRN 59 Nf32
Qalat al Hafira KSA 58 Mk33
Qal'at at Bishah KSA 60 Nb35
Qalat az Zubaidiyah KSA 58 Mk33
Qal'atov UZ 62 Oa25
Qal'at Salih IRQ 59 Nd30
Qal'at Sukkar IRQ 59 Nc30
Qal'at Zumurrud KSA 58 Mk32
Qal'eh-ye Now AFG 64 Ob28
Qal'eh-ye Panjeh AFG 63 Og27
Qalhat OM 61 Nk34
Qalti al Adusa SUD 134 Md37
Qalti al Khudaira SUD 134 Md37
Qalti Immaseri SUD 134 Mc38
Qamashi UZ 63 Od26
Qamchiyan IR 57 Nd28
Qamdo CHN (TIB) 69 Pj30
Qaminis LAR 127 Ma30
Qamishle SYR 57 Na27
Qana SYR 56 Mj29
Qanawt OM 61 Nh37
Qandala SP 143 Ne40
Qanliko'l UZ 62 Nk24
Qansaxdheere SP 145 Nb44
Qarabattaq adası AZ 57 Nf25
Qarah KSA 58 Na31
Qarah Bagh AFG 64 Oa28
Qarah Bagh AFG 65 Oe29
Qara Kilisa IR 57 Nc26
Qarat al Harah LAR 127 Lh32
Qarat as Sab'ah LAR 127 Lj32
Qarat Khalaf Allah LAR 127 Lj32
Qardho SP 143 Ne41
Qareh Aqai IR 57 Nd27
Qareh Bolagh IR 57 Ne27
Qareh Makher IR 62 Nh27
Qareh Tappeh IR 57 Ne27
Qare Ziya' Eddin IR 57 Nc26
Qarhan CHN (QHI) 69 Ph27
Qarkilik = Ruoqiang CHN (XUZ) 69 Pe26
Qarloq IR 62 Nj27
Qarokul TJ 63 Og26
Qarqan = Qiemo CHN (XUZ) 68 Pc26
Qarqin AFG 63 Oc27
Qars-e-Shirin IR 57 Nc28
Qarshi UZ 63 Oc26
Qarshi choli UZ 63 Oc26
Qartaba RL 56 Mh28
Qaryat Abu Nujaym LAR 127 Lh30
Qaryat Abu Qurays LAR 127 Lh30
Qaryat al Fa'idiyah LAR 127 Ma29
Qaryat al Faw KSA 60 Nc36
Qaryat al Ulya KSA 59 Nd32
Qaryat az Zuwaytinah LAR 127 Ma30
Qaryat Jarrufah LAR 127 Lk30
Qaryat Shumaykh LAR 127 Lg30
Qasam YE 60 Ne37
Qasem Abad IR 64 Oa32
Qasnik IR 57 Nc26
Qasr al-Hair al-Gharbi SYR 56 Mk28
Qasr al-Hair ash-Sharqi SYR 56 Mk28
Qasr Al-Hallabat JOR 56 Mj29
Qasr al-Imara KSA 60 Nc37
Qasr al Jady LAR 128 Mc30
Qasr al-Kharana JOR 58 Mj30
Qasr al Kharrubah LAR 127 Ma29
Qasr Al Libya LAR 127 Ma29
Qasr al-Mushatta JOR 58 Mj30
Qasr al Qarn LAR 128 Mc30
Qasr 'Amij IRQ 57 Na29
Qasr Amra JOR 58 Mj30
Qasr ash Shaqqah LAR 128 Mc30
Qasr el Farafra ET 128 Me32
Qasr-e-Qand IR 64 Oa32
Qasr et-Tuba JOR 58 Mj30
Qasr Himam KSA 60 Nc35
Qasr Ibn Wardan SYR 56 Mj28
Qasr Ibrim ET 129 Mf34
Qasr Khulayf LAR 127 Lg32
Qasr Larocu LAR 127 Lg32
Qasr Marid KSA 58 Mk31
Qasr Qârûn ET 129 Mf31
Qasr Shaqrah IRQ 59 Nd30
Qasr Umm el Dabadîb ET 129 Mf33
Qa'tabah YE 60 Nc39
Qatar Q 59 Nf33
Qatar Khinjak IR 64 Oa31
Qatarkuhi Pasi Alaj TJ 63 Og26
Qatarkuhi Sariqul TJ/CHN 63 Og26
Qatliš IR 62 Nj27
Qatruyeh IR 64 Nh31
Qattara Depression ET 128 Md31
Qâw el Kabîr ET 129 Mf32
Qax AZ 57 Nd25
Qaysûm ET 129 Mg32
Qayyarah IRQ 57 Nb28
Qazax AZ 57 Nc25
Qazi Ahmad PK 65 Oe32
Qazi Deh AFG 63 Of27
Qazimemmed AZ 57 Ne25
Qazvin IR 57 Ne27
Qebele AZ 57 Nd25
Qena ET 129 Mg32
Qeqertarsuaq = Godhavn DK 163 Hb05
Qerri SUD 135 Mg37
Qeshm IR 64 Nj32
Qetura IL 58 Mh31
Qeydar IR 57 Ne27
Qeysar AFG 63 Oc28
Qezel Bulaq AFG 64 Oa28
Qian'an CHN (JLN) 76 Rc23
Qianfo Dong CHN 69 Pk26
Qianfoshan CHN 73 Qj27
Qianfo Yan CHN 72 Qc29
Qian Gorlos Mongolzu Zizhixian CHN (JLN) 76 Rc23
Qianheshangyuan CHN (SAA) 72 Qe27
Qianjiang CHN (CGQ) 74 Qe31
Qianjiang CHN (HUB) 75 Qg30
Qianjin CHN (HLG) 76 Rg22
Qian Ling CHN 72 Qe28
Qianning CHN (SCH) 69 Qa30
Qianshan CHN (AHU) 78 Qj30
Qianshan CHN 76 Rb25
Qiansuo CHN (ZJG) 75 Ra31
Qianwei CHN (SCH) 74 Qb31
Qianxi CHN (GZH) 74 Qd32
Qian Xian CHN (SAA) 72 Qe28
Qianyang CHN (HUN) 74 Qf32
Qianyang CHN (SAA) 72 Qd28
Qiaochuan CHN (GSU) 72 Qd27
Qiaohou CHN (YUN) 87 Pk32
Qiaojia CHN (YUN) 87 Qb32
Qiaomaidi CHN (YUN) 87 Qb32
Qiaotou CHN (ZJG) 75 Ra32
Qiaowan CHN (GSU) 67 Pj25
Qiaozhen CHN (SAA) 72 Qe27
Qibah KSA 59 Nc32
Qichun CHN (HUB) 75 Qh30
Qiclou CHN (QHI) 69 Ph28
Qidong CHN (HUN) 74 Qg32
Qidong CHN (JGS) 78 Ra30
Qiemo CHN (XUZ) 68 Pc26
Qijiang CHN (CGQ) 74 Qd31

Qijiaojing CHN (XUZ) 67 Pf24
Qila Abdullah CHN PK 65 Od30
Qila Ladgasht PK 64 Ob32
Qilaodu Shan CHN 73 Qc25
Qila Saifullah PK 65 Oc30
Qilian CHN (QHI) 72 Qa26
Qilian Shan CHN 69 Pk26
Qilwah KSA 60 Na36
Qimen CHN (AHU) 75 Qj31
Qin'an CHN (GSU) 72 Qc28
Qincheng Shan CHN 74 Qd30
Qing'an CHN (HLG) 76 Rd22
Qingchengzi CHN (LNG) 76 Rb25
Qingdao CHN 73 Ra27
Qingdong Ling CHN 73 Qj25
Qinggang CHN (HLG) 76 Rd22
Qinghai CHN 53 Pb06
Qinghai Hu CHN 72 Qa27
Qinghai Nanshan CHN 69 Pk27
Qinghe CHN (HBI) 73 Qh27
Qinghe CHN (XUZ) 67 Pf23
Qinghemen CHN (LNG) 76 Ra25
Qingjian CHN (SAA) 72 Qf27
Qingling Mosque CHN 75 Qk33
Qinglong CHN (GZH) 87 Qc33
Qinglong CHN (HBI) 73 Qk25
Qinglong Monastery CHN 74 Qe32
Qingping CHN (SHG) 78 Ra30
Qingshan CHN (AHU) 73 Qk30
Qingshan CHN (HLG) 71 Rd21
Qingshizui CHN (QHI) 72 Qa26
Qingshui CHN (GSU) 69 Pk26
Qingshuihe CHN (NMZ) 72 Qf26
Qingshuihe CHN (QHI) 69 Pj29
Qingtang CHN (GHG) 75 Qg33
Qingtian CHN (ZJG) 75 Ra31
Qingtongxia CHN (NHZ) 72 Qd27
Qing Xiling CHN (HBI) 73 Qh26
Qingyang CHN (SAX) 72 Qg27
Qingyang CHN (AHU) 73 Qg30
Qingyang CHN (GZH) 72 Qd28
Qingyuan CHN (GDG) 75 Qg33
Qingyuan CHN (LNG) 76 Rc24
Qingyuan CHN (ZJG) 75 Qk32
Qingyuanshan CHN 75 Qk33
Qingzang CHN 75 Qh32
Qingzhen Gaoyuan CHN 68 Pb29
Qingzhou CHN (GZH) 74 Qd32
Qinhe CHN 72 Qd27
Qinzhou CHN (SDG) 73 Qj27
Qinhuangdao CHN (HBI) 73 Qk26
Qin Ling CHN 72 Qd29
Qintang CHN (GZG) 74 Qe34
Qinxian CHN (SAX) 73 Qg27
Qinyang CHN (HNN) 73 Qg28
Qinzhou CHN (GXG) 74 Qd30
Qionglai CHN (SCH) 74 Qb30
Qionglai Shan CHN 74 Qb30
Qiongzhong CHN (HAN) 75 Qe36
Qiqian CHN (NMZ) 71 Ra19
Qiqihar CHN (HLG) 71 Rb22
Qir IR 64 Ng31
Qira CHN (XUZ) 68 Pa27
Qirkan Nature Reserve AZ 57 Ne26
Qisha CHN (GHG) 72 Qe35
Qishn YE 61 Nf38
Qishran KSA 60 Mk35
Qishu CHN (QHI) 72 Qe30
Qitai CHN (XUZ) 67 Pe24
Qitaihe CHN (HLG) 76 Rf23
Qitian Ling CHN (FJN) 75 Qj33
Qiubei CHN (YUN) 87 Qc33
Qiu Cheng, Tomb of = Imperial Tombs of the Ming and Qing Dynasties CHN (JGS) 78 Qe29
Qiujin CHN (JGX) 75 Qh31
Qiuxihe CHN (SCH) 74 Qc31
Qixia CHN (SDG) 73 Ra27
Qi Xing Gong Yuan CHN 74 Qf31
Qi Xing Yan CHN 74 Qf33
Qiyang CHN (HUN) 74 Qf32
Qi Yun Ta CHN 73 Qg28
Qizhou CHN (HUB) 75 Qh30
Qizhou Liedao CHN 75 Qd35
Qizilcha UZ 63 Od25
Qiziltepa UZ 63 Od25
Qizil Qalasi AZ 57 Ne25
Qobustan AZ 57 Ne25
Qojur IR 57 Nd27
Qolaman IR 64 Nj28
Qoltag CHN 67 Pe24
Qom IR 57 Nf28
Qo'ng'ro'ton UZ 63 Od27
Qonggyai CHN (TIB) 69 Pf31
Qo'ng'irot UZ 62 Nk24
Qongkol CHN (XUZ) 67 Pd25
Qo'qon UZ 63 Oe25
Qorabovur Qirlari UZ 62 Nj24
Qorabota botig'i UZ 63 Oc25
Qorako'l UZ 63 Oc26
Qorao'zak UZ 62 Oa24
Qoraqalpog'iston UZ 62 Nj23
Qoratepa UZ 63 Od26
Qorovulbozor UZ 63 Oc26
Qorveh IR 57 Nd28
Qoryooley ESP 145 Nc45
Qosheh IR 64 Ng28
Qo'shrabot UZ 63 Od25
Qosmeliyon AZ 57 Ne26
Qotb Abad IR 64 Nf30
Qotb Abad IR 64 Ng32
Qotur IR 57 Nc26
Qoubaiyat RL 56 Mj28
Qowryah AFG 65 Oc30
Qozoqdaryo UZ 62 Nk24
Quachas Nek ZA 155 Me61
Quafmolla AL 44 Lu49
Quadé-e-Azam Residency PK 76 Ob30
Quairading AUS (WA) 104 Qj59
Quakenbrück D 32 Lh38
Qualia RMM 136 Kc49
Qualicum Beach CDN 168 Dh21
Qumarlêb CHN (QHI) 69 Pk28
Quambatook AUS (VIC) 111 Sb63
Quambone AUS (NSW) 109 Sd61

Quarré-les-Tombes F 25 Le43
Quarteira P 27 Km53
Quartu Sant' Elena I 36 Lk51
Quartz Mt. S. P. USA 174 Fa28
Quartzsite USA (AZ) 170 Ec29
Quba AZ 57 Ne25
Qubadli AZ 57 Nd26
Quchan IR 62 Nk27
Quday SYR 56 Mk28
Queanbeyan AUS (NSW) 111 Se63
Québec CDN (QC) 176 Ge22
Quebec CDN 163 Ha07
Quebó GNB 136 Kc40
Quebra-Canela BR (AM) 198 Gg49
Quebracho ROU 204 Hb61
Quebrada de Humahuaca RA 207 Gh57
Quebrada de Jaspe YV 193 Gk43
Quebrada de la Flecha RA 207 Gg58
Quebrada de las Conchas RA 207 Gh58
Quebrada del Condorito, P.N. RA 208 Gh61
Quebrada de los Cuervos ROU 204 Hc62
Quedas do Calandula BR 148 Lj50
Quedas do Iguaçu BR (PR) 204 Hd58
Quedas do Monte Negro ANG 148 Lj50
Quedas do Ruacaná ANG 148 Lh50
Quedlinburg D 32 Lm39
Queen Alexandra Range 7 Td35
Queen Bess, Mount CDN 168 Dh21
Queen Charlotte City CDN (BC) 166 Dd19
Queen Charlotte Islands CDN 162 Db08
Queen Charlotte Is. Mus. CDN 166 De19
Queen Charlotte Sound CDN 166 Dd20
Queen Charlotte Strait CDN 168 Df20
Queen Elizabeth Islands CDN 162 Ec02
Queen Elizabeth N.P. EAU 7 Sb35
Queen Elizabeth Range 7 Sb35
Queen Mary Land 7 Pc33
Queen Maud Gulf CDN
Queen Maud Mountains 6 Cc36
Queenscliff AUS (VIC) 111 Sc65
Queensland AUS 101 Sa12
Queenstown ZA 155 Md61
Queenstown AUS (TAS) 111 Sc67
Queen Victoria Rock AUS (WA) 104 Ra51
Queen Victoria Spring Nature Reserve AUS 105 Rb61
Quergou CHN (XUZ) 67 Pd24
Queimada Nova BR (PI) 201 Hk50
Queimadas BR (BA) 201 Ja51
Queimadas BR (PB) 201 Ja49
Queimadas, T.I. BR 205 Hh48
Queimados BR (RJ) 205 Hj57
Quelelé ANG 149 Lk50
Quélimane MOC 153 Mj54
Quellon RCH 210 Gd67
Quellouno PE 197 Gd52
Quelo AL 148 Lg49
Quemado USA (NM) 171 Ef28
Quemchi RCH 208 Gd67
Quemú-Quemú RA (LP) 209 Gj64
Que Phong VN 87 Qc36
Quepos CR 185 Fh41
Quequén RA (BA) 209 Ha65
Querarí CO 193 Gf45
Querência do Norte BR (PR) 202 Hd57
Querétaro MEX (QRT) 182 Ek35
Querétaro MEX 182 Ek35
Querfurt D 32 Lm38
Querobabí MEX (SO) 180 Ee30
Queromba PE 197 Gd52
Quesada E 27 Kr53
Queshan CHN (HNN) 73 Qh29
Quesnel CDN (BC) 168 Dj19
Quesnel Mus. CDN 168 Dj19
Que Son VN 89 Qe38
Quesso RCB 142 Lj45
Questembert F 22 Ks43
Quezaltenango GCA 184 Fe38
Quezon RP 90 Rb38
Quezon RP 91 Qk41
Quezon RP 91 Rc42
Quezon CHN (SDG) 78 Qj28
Quiabaya BOL 206 Gf53
Quiaca, Cerro RA 210 Ge67
Quibala ANG 148 Lh50
Quibala ANG 150 Lh51
Quibaxe ANG 148 Lh50
Quibdó CO 192 Gb43
Quiberon F 22 Kr43
Quiçama, P.N.da ANG 148 Lg50
Quiçaura, Cerro RA 210

Quilmes RA (BA) 209 Ha63
Quilombo BR (SC) 204 Hd59
Quilon = Kollam (KER) 84 Oj41
Quilpie AUS (QLD) 109 Sc59
Quilpué RCH 208 Ge62
Quilua MOC 153 Mk54
Quimantag CHN 69 Pf27
Quimbala ANG 148 Lh48
Quimbango ANG 192 Gc43
Quimbele ANG 148 Lj49
Quimili RA (SE) 207 Gj59
Quimondo ANG 148 Lh49
Quimper F 22 Kq43
Quimperlé F 22 Kr43
Quinabucasan Point RP 90 Rb38
Quinalow AUS (QLD) 109 Sf59
Quinapondan RP 90 Rc40
Quincemil PE 197 Ge52
Quincy USA (CA) 170 Dk26
Quincy USA (FL) 175 Fh29
Quincy USA (IL) 175 Fe26
Quincy USA (MA) 177 Ge24
Quincy Hills USA 175 Fe26
Quincy USA (NV) 170 Ec27
Quindanning AUS (WA) 104 Qj62
Quinhagak USA (AK) 164 Bk16
Quinhámel GNB 136 Kc40
Quinhon VN 89 Qe39
Quiniluban Group RP 90 Ra40
Quiniluban Island RP 90 Ra40
Quinkan and Regional Cultural Centre (Laura) AUS 107 Sc53
Quinn RA (BS) 204 Hd62
Quintana de Castillo E 26 Ko48
Quintana del Puente E 26 Kq48
Quintanar del Rey E 29 Kt51
Quintana Roo MEX 185 Ff37
Quintana Roo MEX 208 Ge62
Quintin F 22 Ks42
Quinto E 29 Ku49
Quinzala ANG 148 Lg49
Quionga ANG 153 Na51
Quiongua EAU 148 Lh50
Quiotepec MEX 182 Fb37
Quipapá BR (PE) 201 Jb50
Quipeio ANG 150 Lh53
Quipungo ANG 150 Lh53
Quiriego MEX (SO) 180 Ef32
Quirigua GCA 184 Ff38
Quirihue RCH 208 Gd64
Quirima ANG 150 Lk51
Quirindi AUS (NSW) 109 Sf61
Quiriquire YV 193 Gj41
Quiriza BOL 207 Gh56
Quiroga E 26 Kn48
Quiroga RA (BA) 209 Gk63
Quiroga MEX (MCH) 182 Ek36
Quiros YV 192 Ge40
Quiruvilca PE 196 Ga48
Quisiro YV 192 Ge40
Quissamã BR 203 Hk57
Quissico MOC 147 Na52
Quitapa ANG 149 Lk51
Quiteve ANG 150 Lh54
Quitexe ANG 148 Lh49
Quitman USA (MS) 175 Ff29
Quitman USA (TX) 174 Fc29
Quivicán CDN 178 Fk34
Quixeramobim BR (CE) 201 Ja48
Quixeré BR (CE) 201 Jb48
Quizenga ANG 148 Lh50
Quoin Island AUS 103 Re53
Quoich USA (UT) 171 Ed27
Quorn AUS (SA) 110 Rk62
Quruq Tagh CHN 67 Pd25
Qurveh AFG 65 Oc30
Quryn-Buratski (UPH) 83 Pd33
Qusar AZ 57 Ne25
Qusay'ir ET 128 Md23
Quss Abu Sa'id ET 128 Md32
Qutang CHN 74 Qf30
Qutubminar IND 80 Oj31
Quweirah JOR 58 Mh31
Quwu Shan CHN 72 Qc27
Qu Xian CHN 75 Qg31
Quxu CHN (TIB) 68 Pf31
Quzhou CHN (HBI) 73 Qh28
Quzhou CHN (ZJG) 75 Qk31
Qyrqqyz-Qala UZ 62 Oa25

R

Raa Atoll MV 84 Og43
Raab A 35 Lq43
Raahe FIN 16 Mc13
Rääkkylä FIN 38 Me28
Raas I MV 84 Og43
Raasay GB 20 Ko33
Raas Binna SP 143 Nf40
Raas Caluula SP 143 Nf40
Raas Caseyr SP 143 Ng40
Raas Gabbac SP 143 Nf41
Raas Illig SP 143 Ng42
Raas Khansiir SP 143 Nd40
Raas Macber SP 143 Nf41
Raas Surud SP 143 Ne40
Raas Xaafuun SP 143 Ng41
Raasiku EST 39 Me30
Raatama, T.I. BR 205 Hj49
Rab HR 35 Lp46
Rabaale SP 143 Ne41
Rabaçal P 27 Km50
Rabah NGR 138 Lc39
Rabak SUD 135 Mg39
Rabastens F 24 Lb47
Rabat M 37 Lp55
Rabat PNG 116 Se51
Rabat M 125 Kg29
Rabaul PNG 116 Sg48
Rabbit Flat AUS (NT) 103 Rf56
Rabda SP 145 Nb43
Rabi FJI 97 Rf46
Rabigh KSA 60 Mj36
Rabka-Zdroj PL 41 Lu41
Rabnita MD 49 Me22
Rabodao RI 95 Rd45
Rabo da Onça BR (AM) 198 Gh46
Rabor IR 64 Nj31
Rabt Sbayta DARS 124 Kc33
Rabyanah LAR 128 Ma35
Rabyanah LAR 128 Mb39
Raca SCG 44 Ma47
Racale I 36 Lo53
Racalmuto I 36 Lo53
Raccon Cay BS 179 Gb34
Raccuja I 34 Lm46
Raceland USA (LA) 175 Fe31
Rachal USA (TX) 181 Fa32
Rachaya RL 56 Mh29
Rach Gia VN 92 Qd40
Rachiv UA 43 Me42
Rachoqba I 81 Oj29
Raciąż PL 41 Ma38
Racibórz PL 40 Lt40
Racičy BY 41 Md37
Racine USA (WI) 173 Fg24
Răciu RO 43 Me44
Rackla Range CDN 165 Dd13
Radauti RO 49 Me42
Radcliff USA (KY) 175 Fh27
Rădăškovičy BY 39 Mh36
Radebeul D 32 Lo39
Radebul D 32 Lo39
Radechiv UA 41 Me40
Radom USA (VA) 178 Fe27
Radom PL 41 Mb40
Radomir BG 44 Md48
Radomko PL 41 Lu39
Radomsko PL 41 Ma39
Radomyśl Wielki PL 41 Mb40
Radovan BG 44 Mc46
Radoviš MK 44 Md49
Radovljica SLO 42 Lp44
Radstadt A 35 Lp43
Radstock, Cape AUS (SA) 110 Rg62
Radville CDN (SK) 169 Eh21
Radymno PL 41 Mc40
Radzanów PL 41 Ma38
Radzyń Chełmiński PL 40 Lt37
Radzyń Podlaski PL 41 Mc39
Rae-Bareli IND (UPH) 83 Pa32
Raeford USA (NC) 178 Ga28
Raeside AUS 105 Ra59
Rafaela RA (SF) 209 Gk61
Rafael Freyre CU 179 Gb35
Raffadali I 36 Ln53
Raffia-Vica CU 44 Mc49
Raffingora ZW 152 Me55
Raffin Kada WAN 138 Le42
Rafha KSA 59 Nb31
Rafiganj IND (BIH) 83 Pc33
Rafina GR 45 Me52
Rafsanjan IR 64 Nh30
Raft Mountains USA 171 Ed25
Raftópoulo GR 46 Mb51
Raga SUD 141 Mc41
Ragaciems LV 39 Mc34
Ragang, Mount RP 91 Rc42
Ragay PHL 96 Ra50
Ragged Island Range BS 186 Ga34
Ragged Islands BS 179 Gb35
Raghogur IND (MPH) 82 Oj34
Raglan NZ 112 Th64
Ragley USA (LA) 174 Fd30
Rago n.p. N 16 Lj12
Ragusa I 37 Lp54
Rahad al-Bardi SUD 134 Mb40
Rahad Game Reserve SUD 135 Mh39
Rahama WAN 138 Ld40
Rahatgarh IND (MPH) 83 Ok34
Rahden D 32 Lj38
Raheste EST 39 Md32
Rahimahad IND (WBG) 86 Pe32
Rahim ki Bazar PK 65 Oe33
Rahimyar Khan PK 65 Of31
Rahole National Reserve EAK 145 Mk45
Rahua DZ 125 La28
Rahui N 16 Lj12
Raiatea F 11 Da11
Raichur IND (KTK) 82 Oj36
Raiganj IND (WBG) 86 Pe33
Raigarh IND (GUJ) 82 Of34
Raigarh IND (CGH) 83 Pc34
Raigród PL 41 Mc37
Raika IR 64 Nh31
Raikot IND (PJB) 80 Oh30
Railroad Valley USA 170 Ec26
Railway Mus. P. CHN 76 Rb24
Raimbault CDN (QC)
Rainbow Bridge Nat. Mon. USA 171 Ee27
Rainbow City USA (AL) 175 Fh29

Rainbow Warrior Wreck Diving NZ 112 Th63
Rainier N.P., Mount USA 168 Dk22
Rainis RI 91 Rd43
Rainsville USA (AL) 175 Fh28
Rainy River CDN 172 Fc21
Raippaluoto FIN 38 Mb27
Raippo FIN 38 Mj30
Raipur IND (CGH) 83 Pa35
Raipur IND (RJT) 82 Oj33
Raipura IND (MPH) 83 Ok34
Rairangpur IND (ORS) 83 Pd34
Raisdorf D 32 Ll36
Raisen IND (MPH) 82 Oj34
Raisinghnagar IND (RJT) 80 Og31
Raisio FIN 38 Mb29
Raisoto Praskalo BG 45 Me48
Raith CDN (ON) 172 Fd21
Raja-ji N.P. IND 81 Oj30
Raja-Joeseppi FIN 16 Me11
Rajakhera IND (RJT) 81 Ok32
Rajampet IND (APH) 85 Ok38
Rajanpur PK 65 Of31
Rajapalaiyam IND (TNU) 84 Oj40
Rajapur IND (MHT) 82 Og37
Rajapur IND (UPH) 83 Pa33
Rajasthan IND 80 Og32
Rajauli IND (BIH) 83 Pc33
Rajbari BD 86 Pe34
Rajec-Jestřebí CZ 42 Lr41
Rajec Poduchowny PL 41 Mb39
Raj Gangpur IND (ORS) 83 Pc34
Rajgarh IND (RJT) 80 Oh31
Rajgarh IND (RJT) 80 Oj33
Rajgarh IND (BIH) 83 Pc33
Rajgród PL 41 Mc37
Rajik PRK 76 Rf24
Rajin PRK 76 Rf24
Rajkot IND (GUJ) 82 Of34
Rajmahal IND (JKD) 83 Pd33
Rajmahal Hills IND 83 Pd33
Raj Nandgaon IND (CGH) 83 Pa34
Rajoda IND (ORS) 83 Pb36
Rajpipla IND (GUJ) 82 Og35
Rajpur IND (WBG) 86 Pe34
Rajpur IND (MPH) 82 Oj35
Rajpura IND (PJB) 80 Oh30
Rajsamand IND (RJT) 82 Og33
Rajshahi BD 86 Pe33
Raka IND (TIB) 68 Pc31
Rakaca H 43 Ma42
Rakaia NZ 113 Tf66
Rakan, Ra's QA 59 Nf33
Rakaposhi PK 80 Oh27
Rakata IR 91 Qd49
Rakav BY 39 Mh37
Rakhine MYA 86 Pg35
Rakhiv UA 43 Me42
Rakhni PK 65 Oe30
Rakit RI 95 Qe48
Rakitnoe RUS 77 Rh23
Rakkestad N 30 Lm31
Rákóczi H 43 Mb42
Rakops RB 152 Mb56
Rako Raayo SP 143 Ne41
Ranaghat IND (WBG) 86 Pe34
Ranai RI 94 Qe44
Ranau MAL 94 Qj43
Ranas y Toluquilla MEX 182 Fa35

Ramlat ar-Rabkha OM 61 Nh35
Ramlat Dahm YE 60 Nc37
Ramlat Ghafah OM 61 Nh35
Ramlat Umm al-Hait OM 61 Ng36
Ramlat Zallaf LAR 127 Lg32
Ramlu ER/ETH 142 Na39
Ramnagar IND (MPH) 83 Pa33
Ramnagar IND (UTT) 81 Ok31
Râmnicu Sărât RO 45 Mh45
Râmnicu Vâlcea RO 43 Me45
Ramo ETH 142 Na42
Ramon RP 90 Ra37
Ramona USA (CA) 170 Ec29
Ramón Castilla PE 198 Gf48
Ramón Corona MEX (DGO) 181 Ej33
Ramos BR (PA) 199 Hd46
Ramos Island RP 94 Qj41
Ramotswa RB 155 Mc58
Rampa ANG 148 Lj50
Rampart USA (AK) 165 Ce13
Rampur IND (HPH) 81 Oj32
Rampur IND (GUJ) 82 Og34
Rampur IND (UPH) 81 Ok31
Rampur IND (MPH) 83 Ok34
Rampur IND (UPH) 81 Oj31
Rampura IND (MPH) 82 Oj33
Rampur Hat IND (WBG) 83 Pd33
Ramree IND (MHT) 82 Og36
Ramree = Rambre MYA 86 Pg36
Ramree Island = Rambré MYA 86 Pg36
Ram UAE 61 Nj33
Ram Saneshigat IND (UPH) 83 Pa32
Ramsar IR 57 Nf27
Ramsele S 16 Lj14
Ramsey GB 21 Kr36
Ramsey Island GB 21 Kp39
Ramsgate GB 21 Lb39
Ramu RI 94 Qe44
Ramu, Mount RI 94 Qe43
Ranakpur IND 82 Og33
Rapa LAR 127 Lf29
Rapallo I 34 Lk46
Rapa-Nui RCH 197 Gc54
Rapa Nui, P.N. RCH 197 Gc54
Rapar IND (GUJ) 82 Of34
Rapel, Lago RCH 208 Ge62
Rapid Bay AUS (SA) 110 Rk63
Rapid City USA (SD) 169 Ej24
Rapid River USA (MI) 173 Fg23
Räpina EST 39 Mf32
Rapla EST 38 Me31
Rappenlochschlucht A 34 Lk43
Rapperswil CH 34 Lj43
Rappottenstein A 42 Lq42
Rapu Rapu Island RP 90 Rb40
Raqqa SYR 56 Mk28
Raragala Island AUS 106 Rj51
Rara N.P. NEP 81 Pb33
Rarotonga NZ 10 Bb12
Rås Abu 'Aii KSA 59 Ne32
Rås Abu Gallum Reserve ET 129 Mh31
Rås Abu Madd KSA 58 Mj33
Rås Abu Rasas OM 61 Nk35
Rås Abu Sawmah ET 129 Mh32
Rås Abu Shagara SUD 135 Mj35
Râs al Kalb KSA 59 Ne31
Râs al-Khaimah UAE 61 Nh33
Râs al Mish'ab KSA 59 Ne31
Ra's al Qasab KSA 59 Nf32
Râs an Naqab JOR 58 Mh31
Ras Banas ET 129 Mh33
Ra's Bir DJI 142 Nb39
Rasawil IR 64 Nh47
Râs Dashen ETH 142 Na39
Rasdhoo Atoll MV 84 Og43
Ras-e Barkan IR 59 Ne30
Râs-e Hadd OM 61 Nk35
Ras-e Madani IR 64 Nk33
Ras-e Nay Band IR 64 Ng32
Rasender Roland D 32 Ln36
Ras-e Senas IR 64 Nh32
Ra's Fartak YE 61 Nf38
Rås Gârib ET 129 Mg31
Râs Hatibah KSA 60 Mj36
Rashshah YE 60 Nc38
Rasht IR 57 Ne27
Rasid SUD 135 Mh39
Rasipuram IND (TNU) 84 Oj39
Raška SCG 44 Ma47
Râs Karkuma KSA 58 Mh33
Râs Kasar KSA 135 Mk36
Râs Kebdana MA 125 Kj28
Râs Lanuf LAR 127 Lk30
Rasmadh KSA 58 Mk33
Râs Markhazn OM 61 Nh36
Râs Muhammad ET 129 Mh32
Râs Muhammad N.P. ET 129 Mh32
Raso, Ilha do CV 136 Jf37
Rason SUD 135 Mh40
Rasovo BG 44 Mc47
Rasra IND (UPH) 83 Pb32
Rasskazovo RUS 48 Na18

Ranotsara Avaratra RM 157 Nd57
Ranquil del Norte RA (NE) 208 Gf64
Rantabe RM 157 Ne57
Rantau RM 156 Ne53
Rantauprapat RI 93 Pk45
Rantaupanjang RI 95 Qh47
Rantekombola RI 96 Ra46
Ranong THA 88 Pk40
Ranongga SOL 117 Sj50
Ranot THA 88 Qa42
Ranpur IND (ORS) 83 Pc35
Ranua FIN 16 Md12
Ranwas IND (RJT) 82 Og33
Ranyah KSA 60 Na36
Raohe CHN (HLG) 76 Rg22
Raoli IND (MPH) 81 Oj32
Raon-l'Étape F 23 Lg42
Raoping CHN (GDG) 75 Qj34
Raoul Island NZ 10 Ba12
Rapale MOC 153 Mk53
Rapar IND (GUJ) 82 Of34
Rapid River USA (AK) 165 Cf14
Rasht IR 57 Ne27
Rason SUD 135 Mh40
Rasovo BG 44 Mc47
Ras Tannurah KSA 59 Nf32
Rasu, Monte I 36 Lk50
Ratangarh IND (RJT) 80 Oh31
Ratangarh IND (MPH) 82 Oj34
Ratchaburi THA 88 Pk38
Ratchathani IND (UPH) 83 Ok33
Rathdrum IRL 19 Kp38
Rathenow D 32 Ln38
Rathlin Island GB 19 Ko36
Rathnew IRL 19 Kp38
Ratia IND (HYA) 80 Oh31
Ratnagiri IND (MHT) 82 Og37
Ratnapura CL 85 Pa42
Ratodero PK 65 Oe32
Raton USA (NM) 171 Ej27
Rattaphum THA 88 Qa42
Rättvik S 17 Lh15
Rau RI 91 Re44
Rauch RA (BA) 209 Ha64
Raudhatain KZ 59 Nd31
Raukumara Range NZ 112 Tj65
Raul Soares BR (MG) 203 Hj56
Rauma FIN 38 Ma29
Raung, Gunung RI 95 Qh50
Raungwepna PNG 116 Sf48
Raurkela IND (ORS) 83 Pc34
Råsa Sadulu RO 43 Me45
Råsa Terme I 42 Lp45
Råttvik S 17 Lh15
Råsu RI 91 Re44
Ravanusa I 36 Ln53
Ravar IR 64 Nj30
Ravena USA (NY) 177 Gd24
Ravenna I 34 Ll46
Ravensburg D 34 Lk43
Ravensthorpe AUS (WA) 104 Ra62
Ravenswood AUS (QLD) 107 Sd56
Ravne na Koroškem SLO 42 Lp44
Ravnina TM 62 Ob27
Rawa MAL 92 Qa44
Rawah IRQ 56 Na29
Rawalpindi PK 65 Og29
Rawāndūz IRQ 57 Nc27
Rawannawi KIR 10 Ba10
Rawa Mazowiecka PL 41 Ma39
Rawene NZ 112 Tg63
Rawicz PL 40 Ls39
Rawil G 34 Lh44
Rawlinna AUS (WA) 105 Rc61
Rawlins USA (WY) 171 Eg25
Rawson RA (CB) 210 Gh67
Rawson RA (BA) 209 Gk63
Rayachoti IND (APH) 85 Ok38
Rayagada IND (ORS) 83 Pb36
Raya, Gunung RI 95 Qf47
Raydah YE 60 Nb38
Rayleigh CDN (BC) 168 Dj20
Raymond USA (WA) 168 Dj22
Raymondville USA (TX) 181 Fb32
Raymore CDN (SK) 169 Eh20
Rayón MEX (SLP) 182 Fa35
Rayón MEX (SON) 180 Ee31
Rayong THA 88 Qa39
Raywick USA (KY) 175 Fh27
Raz, Pointe du F 22 Kp42

Réalmont F 24 Lc47
Ream N.P. = Preah Sihanouk National Park K 89 Qb40
Reao Atoll 11 Da11
Rebaa DZ 126 La34
Rebecca, Mount AUS (WA) 104 Qh59
Rebiana Sand Sea LAR 128 Ma33
Rebild Bakker, Nationalpark DK 30 Lk34
Rebola GQ 138 Le44
Rebouças BR (PR) 205 He58
Rebun-to J 77 Sa23
Recanati I 35 Lo47
Recea RO 43 Me45
Recea RO 43 Me45
Recherche, Archipel of the AUS 104 Ra62
Recht B 23 Lg40
Recife BR (PE) 201 Jc50
Recife da Silva BR 195 Hh46
Recife Manuel Luís BR 195 Hh46
Recife de l' Astrolabe F (NCL) 118 Tc55
Récifs d'Entrecasteaux F (NCL) 118 Tb55
Récifs et Îles Chesterfield F (PYF) 10 Sb12
Recklinghausen D 32 Lh39
Reclining Buddha CHN 87 Pk33
Recoaro Terme I 34 Lm45
Reconquista RA (SF) 204 Ha59
Recontre East CDN (NF) 177 Hc22
Recreio São Felix, T.I. BR 199 Ha47
Recuay PE 197 Gb50
Recz PL 40 Lq37
Reda PL 41 Lu36
Redang MAL 92 Qa43
Redange-sur-Attert L 23 Lf41
Redbank USA (NJ) 111 Sb64
Red Basin CHN 74 Qc30
Red Bay CDN 177 Hb20
Red Bay AUS (AL) 175 Ff28
Red Bay N.H.P. CDN 177 Hb20
Red Bays BS 179 Ga34
Redbird USA (WY) 169 Eh24
Redcar GB 21 Kt36
Redcliffe USA (QLD) 109 Sg59
Red Cliff Ind. Res. USA 172 Fe22
Red Cloud USA (NE) 174 Fa25
Red Deer CDN (AB) 169 Ed19
Red Deer Valley Badlands CDN 169 Ed20
Reddersburg ZA 155 Md60
Redding USA (CA) 170 Dj25
Redditch GB 21 Kt38
Redenção BR (CE) 201 Ja48
Redenção BR (PA) 200 He50
Redenção do Gurguéia BR (PI) 200 Hh50
Redentora BR (RS) 204 Hd59
Redeyef TN 126 La29
Redfield USA (SD) 169 Fa23
Redford USA (QLD) 109 Sd58
Red Fort (Delhi) IND 81 Oj31
Red Fort IND KWT 59 Nd31
Redhakhol IND (ORS) 83 Pc35
Red Hill AUS (NM) 171 Ff28
Red Hill AUS (NM) 171 Ff28
Red Hill = Pu'u Ula'ula USA 170 Cb35
Red Hill P. Henry Nat. Mem. USA 178 Ga27
Red Hills USA 174 Fa27
Red Hills S.P. USA 175 Fg26
Red Lake CDN (ON) 172 Fc20
Red Lake Ind. Res. USA 172 Fb22
Red Lake Road CDN (ON) 172 Fc20
Redlands USA (CA) 170 Eb28
Red Lion USA (PA) 177 Gb26
Red Lodge USA (MT) 169 Ef23
Red Mercury Island NZ 112 Th64
Redon F 22 Ks43
Redonda AG 187 Gj37
Redondela E 26 Km48
Redondo USA (AK) 175 Fe27
Redoubt Flatters USA 165 Cd15
Red River CDN 166 Df16
Red River USA (KY) 178 Fj27
Red River VN 87 Qc38
Red River Delta VN 87 Qd38
Red River Gorge USA 178 Fj27
Redruth GB 21 Kq40
Red Sea 52 Mb07
Red Top USA (CO) 172 Ek21
Red Water USA (MS) 175 Fe29
Red Wing USA (MN) 172 Fc23
Redwater CDN (AB) 169 Ed18
Redwood City USA (CA)
Redwood Falls USA (MN) 172 Fc23
Redwood N.P. USA 168 Dj25
Redwood Valley USA (CA) 170 Dj27
Redziköw PL 40 Ls36
Reed Bingham S.P. USA
Reed City USA (MI) 173 Fh24
Reeder USA (ND) 169 Ej22
Reedley USA (CA) 170 Ea27
Reedsburg USA (WI) 172 Fe24
Reedsport USA (OR) 168 Dh24
Redkino RUS 48 Mj17
Redon F 22 Ks43
Reftele S 31 Lp34
Refahiye TR 57 Mk26
Reforma MEX (CPS) 183 Fe37
Reforma MEX (CPS) 183 Ff36
Református Nagytemplom H 43 Mb43
Református templom H 43 Mc43

Rocanville ☐ CDN (SK) 172 Ek20
Rocca Redonda ▲ EC 197 Fe45
Roça Tapirapé ☐ BR (PA) 200 He50
Roccadáspide ☐ I 37 Lq50
Rocca Imperiale ☐ I 37 Lr50
Roccamena ☐ I 36 Lc43
Roccaraso ☐ I 34 Lm47
Roccastrada ☐ I 34 Lm47
Roccella Ionica ☐ I 37 Lr52
Rocha ☐ ROU 209 Hc63
Rochdale ☐ GB 21 Ks37
Roche Cabrit ☐ F (GF) 194 Hd43
Rochechouart ☐ F 24 La45
Rochedo ☐ BR (MS) 202 Hc55
Rochefort ☐ B 23 Lf40
Rochefort ☐ F 24 Ku45
Rochelle ☐ USA (IL) 173 Ff25
Rocher Ako'akas ▲ CAM 139 Lf44
Rocher Corneille ▲ F 25 Ld46
Rocher d'Ihandza ▲ CAM 139 Lg44
Rocher du Mézessé ▲ CAM 139 Lg44
Rocher River ☐ CDN 167 Ed15
Rochesservière ☐ F 24 Ku44
Rochester ☐ GB 21 La39
Rochester ☐ USA (MN) 173 Fg25
Rochester ☐ USA (NH) 177 Ge24
Rochester ☐ USA (NY) 177 Gb24
Roche Tado ☐ F (GF) 194 Hd43
Rochlitz ☐ D 32 Ln39
Rockall Plateau ▣ 14 Ka04
Rockall Trough ▣ 14 Ka04
Rock Creek ☐ CDN (BC) 168 Ea21
Rock Creek ☐ USA (YT) 165 Da13
Rockdale ☐ USA 175 Fg28
Rockdale ☐ USA (TX) 174 Fb29
Rockefeller Plateau ▣ 6 Da34
Rock Engravings ◉ NAM 154 Lk59
Rock Engravings ◉ ZA 155 Mc59
Rock Falls ☐ USA (IL) 173 Ff25
Rockford ☐ USA (AL) 175 Fg29
Rockford ☐ USA (IL) 173 Ff24
Rock Fort Temple (Trichy) ◉ IND 84 Ok40
Rockglen ☐ CDN (SK) 169 Eh21
Rockhampton ☐ AUS (QLD) 109 Sf57
Rockhampton Downs ☐ AUS (NT) 106 Rh55
Rock Hill ☐ USA (SC) 178 Fk28
Rockingham ☐ AUS (WA) 104 Qh62
Rockingham ☐ USA (NC) 178 Ga28
Rockingham Bay ▣ AUS (QLD) 107 Sd55
Rocklake ☐ USA (ND) 172 Fa21
Rockland ☐ CDN (QC) 177 Gc22
Rockland ☐ USA (MA) 177 Gf23
Rock 'n' Roll Hall of Fame (Cleveland) ◉ USA 173 Fk25
Rock Paintings ◉ LS 155 Me61
Rock Paintings ◉ RB 136 Mc58
Rock Paintings ◉ ZA 154 Ma61
Rock Port ☐ USA (MO) 174 Fc25
Rockport ☐ USA (TX) 181 Fb31
Rockport ☐ USA (WA) 168 Dk21
Rock Rapids ☐ USA (IA) 172 Fb24
Rock River ☐ USA (WY) 171 Eh25
Rock Sound ▣ BS 179 Gb33
Rock Springs ☐ USA (MT) 169 Eg22
Rocksprings ☐ USA (TX) 181 Ek31
Rock Springs ☐ USA (WY) 171 Ef25
Rockstone ☐ GUY 194 Ha42
Rockville ☐ USA (IN) 175 Fg26
Rockville ☐ USA (MD) 177 Gb26
Rockwood ☐ USA (MI) 173 Fj24
Rockwood ☐ USA (TN) 175 Fh28
Rocky Boy Ind. Res. ☒ USA 169 Ef21
Rocky Ford ☐ USA (CO) 174 Ej26
Rocky Gully ☐ AUS (WA) 104 Qj63
Rocky Island ▲ ET 129 Mj34
Rocky Mount ☐ USA (NC) 178 Ga28
Rocky Mount ☐ USA (VA) 178 Ga27
Rocky Mountain House ☐ CDN (AB) 169 Ec19
Rocky Mountain N.P. ☒ USA 171 Eh25
Rocky Mountains ☒ CDN/USA 160 Db04
Rocky Mountains Forest Reserve ☒ CDN 169 Ec19
Rocky Mtn. House N.H.S. ☒ CDN 169 Ec19
Rocky Mtns. Forest Reserve ☒ CDN 168 Eb19
Rocky Point ▲ USA (AK) 164 Bj13
Rocov ☐ CZ 42 Lo40
Rocroi ☐ F 23 Le41
Roda Velha ☐ BR (BA) 200 Hh52
Rødberg ☐ N 30 Lj30
Rødbyhavn ☐ DK 30 Ll35
Roddickton ☐ CDN 177 Hb20
Rødekro ☐ DK 30 Lk35
Rødel ☐ GB 20 Ko33
Roden ☐ NL (GLD) 32 Lg38
Rodeo ☐ RA (SJ) 207 Gf61
Rodeo ☐ USA (NM) 171 Ef30
Rodi Garganico ☐ I 37 Lq49
Rodina Mat ☒ UA 49 Mf20
Roding ☐ D 33 Ln41
Rodna ☐ RO 43 Me43
Rodna, P.N. ☒ RO 43 Me43
Rodniki ☐ RUS 48 Na17
Rodolivos ☐ GR 45 Md50
Ródos ☐ GR 47 Mj54
Ródos ☐ GR 47 Mj54
Rodovia Perimetral Norte ☒ BR 194 Hb45
Rødvig ☐ DK 30 Lm35
Roebourne ☐ AUS (WA) 102 Qj56
Roebuck Plains ☐ AUS (WA) 102 Rb54
Roedtan ☐ ZA 155 Me58
Roela ☐ EST 38 Mg31
Roermond ☐ NL 32 Lg39
Roeselare ☐ B 23 Ld40
Roesevetplek ☒ SME 194 Hc44
Roeşti ☐ RO 44 Me46
Roetgen ☐ D 32 Lg40
Rofia ☐ WAN 138 Lc40
Rogač ☐ HR 35 Lq47
Rogaçeviça ☐ RUS 48 Mk20
Rogačica ☐ SCG 44 Lu46
Rogaguado ☐ BOL 206 Gh54
Rogaliński Park Krajobrazowy ☒ PL 40 Lr38
Rogaška Slatina ☐ SLO 42 Lq44
Rogatica ☐ BIH 44 Lu47
Rogers ☐ USA (AR) 174 Fc27
Rogers City ☐ USA (MI) 173 Fj23
Rogers Pass ☐ CDN (BC) 168 Ea20
Rogersville ☐ CDN 176 Gh22
Roggeveen Basin ▣ 190 Fa12
Roggeveldberge ▲ ZA 154 Ma62
Rogliano ☐ I 37 Lr51
Rogo ☐ WAN 138 Ld40

Rogone ☐ MOC 153 Mj53
Rogovo ☐ RUS 39 Mj33
Rogów ☐ PL 40 Ls38
Rogoz ☐ LT 39 Mk38
Rogoźniczka ☐ PL 41 Mc38
Rogożno ☐ PL 40 Lr38
Rohan ☐ F 22 Ks42
Rohini ☐ IND (RJT) 82 Og32
Rohatyn ☐ UA 43 Me41
Rohilcha ☐ SK 42 Ls42
Rohri ☐ PK 65 Oe32
Rohru ☐ IND (HPH) 81 Oj30
Rohtak ☐ IND (HYA) 80 Oj31
Rohtas Fort ◉ PK 65 Og29
Rohukneeme ☐ EST 38 Me31
Roi ☐ TH 89 Qb37
Roja ☐ LV 39 Mc33
Rojão ☐ P 26 Km51
Rojas ☐ RA (BA) 209 Gk63
Röjdåfors ☐ S 30 Ll30
Roka ☒ EAK 145 Mk47
Rokan ☐ RI 93 Qa45
Rokeby ☐ AUS (QLD) 107 Sb52
Rokicimy ☐ PL 41 Lu39
Rokiskis ☐ LT 39 Mf35
Rokkaido ☐ J 77 Sa25
Rokom ☐ SUD 144 Mf43
Rokoroko ☐ RI 97 Re48
Rokuan kansallispuisto ☒ FIN 16 Md13
Rokycany ☐ CZ 42 Lo41
Rokytne ☐ UA 48 Md20
Roland ☐ CDN (MB) 172 Fb21
Roland ☐ USA (NC) 174 Fb28
Roland in Bremen ◉ D 32 Lj37
Roldana ☐ N 30 Lg31
Rolde ☐ NL 23 Lg38
Rolfstorp ☐ S 30 Lk32
Rolim de Moura ☐ BR (RO) 198 Gk51
Rolla ☐ USA (ND) 172 Fa21
Rolla ☐ USA (OK) 174 Fa28
Rolleston ☐ AUS (QLD) 109 Se58
Rolleville ☐ BS 186 Gc34
Rolling Fork ☐ USA (MS) 175 Fe29
Rolling Hills ☐ CDN (AB) 175 Fe29
Rollingstone ☐ AUS (QLD) 107 Sd55
Rollo ☐ BF 137 Kk39
Roma ☐ AUS (QLD) 109 Se59
Roma ☐ I 36 Ln49
Roma ☐ LS 155 Md61
Roma ☐ S 31 Lt33
Roma ☐ USA (TX) 181 Fa32
Romaine ☐ CDN (QC) 176 Gk20
Román ☐ BG 45 Me47
Román ☐ RO 49 Md22
Roman Baths ◉ F 25 Ke39
Romanche Gap ▣ 8 Ka09
Romang ☐ RA 97 Rd49
Romania ◉ RI 97 Re49
Romania ◉ RO 15 Ma05
Romanovka ☐ RUS (BUR) 70 Qg19
Romanshorn ☐ CH 34 Lk43
Romans-sur-Isère ☐ F 25 Lf45
Romantische Straße ☒ D 33 Ll41
Romanzof Mountains ▲ USA (AK) 165 Ch11
Romaria ☐ BR (MG) 203 Hg55
Romblon ☐ RP 90 Rb39
Romblon Island ▲ RP 90 Rb39
Romblon Strait ▣ RP 90 Rb39
Rome ▲ I 34 Lq44
Rome ☐ USA (GA) 175 Fh28
Rome ☐ USA (NY) 177 Gc24
Romilly-sur-Seine ☐ F 23 Ld42
Romitan ☐ UZ 63 Oc26
Romont ☐ CH 34 Lh44
Romny ☐ UA (WV) 177 Ga26
Romny ☐ RUS 71 Re20
Rome ☐ DK 30 Lj35
Rømo ☐ DK 30 Lj35
Romodan ☐ UA 49 Mg20
Romorantin-Lanthenay ☐ F 25 Lb43
Rømø Sommerland ☒ DK 30 Lj35
Romsdalen ☒ N 17 Ld14
Rómulo Calzada ☐ MEX (TB) 183 Ff37
Ronan ☐ USA (MT) 168 Ec22
Roncador ☐ BR (PR) 204 Hd58
Roncador Reef ▲ SOL 117 Sk49
Ronchamp ☐ F 25 Lg43
Roncliglione ☐ I 36 Ln48
Ronda ☐ E 27 Kp54
Ronda Alta ☐ BR (RS) 204 Hd59
Ronde ☒ N 17 Le15
Rondane n.p. ☒ N 17 Ld15
Rondâne ▲ RO 44 Nk28
Ronça ☐ RO 44 Mc44
Ronda de Seçaş ☐ RO 44 Md44
Ronçi ☐ RO 44 Mc44
Roncole ☐ CZ 42 Ln41
Rosignano Marittimo ☐ I 34 Ll47
Rosignol ☐ GUY 194 Hb42
Rosiori de Vede ☐ RO 45 Me46
Roskilde ☐ DK 30 Lm35
Roskilde Rockfestival ◉ DK 30 Lm35
Roslagens ☐ ZA 155 Mc61
Roslavl' ☐ RUS 48 Mg19
Rosenvaal ☐ ZA 155 Md61
Rosson Point ▲ IRL 19 Kn51
Rossan Point ▲ IRL 19 Kl51
Rossano ☐ I 37 Lr51
Ross Bay Jtn. ☐ CDN (NF) ...
Ross-Bethio ☐ SN 130 Kd37
Ross Ice Shelf ☒ ANT 6 Bd35
Rössing ☐ NAM 154 Lh57
Rosskinne Daun Sam ☒ K 89 Qd39
Rosslare Harbour ☒ IRL 19 Ko38
Rosslau ☐ D 32 Ln39
Ross-on-Wye ☐ GB 21 Ks39
Rossosz ☐ PL 41 Mc39
Rossosh' ☐ RUS 48 Na20
Rossowood ☐ CDN (YT) 166 Dd15
Ross Sea ▣ ANT 6 Bd34
Rossville ☐ USA (AR) 174 Fd29
Rossville ☐ AUS (QLD) 107 Sc53
Rosswood Plantation ◉ USA 175 Fe30

Røst ▲ N 16 Lg12
Rostaq ☐ AFG 63 Oe29
Röstånga ☐ S 31 Ll34
Rosthern ☐ CDN (SK) 169 Eg19
Roshkala ☐ TJ 63 Od27
Rostock ☐ D 32 Ln36
Rostov ☐ RUS 48 Mk17
Rostov-na-Donu ☐ RUS 48 Mk22
Rostrenen ☐ F 22 Kr42
Røsvik ☐ N 16 Lh17
Roswell ☐ USA (GA) 175 Fh28
Roswell ☐ USA (NM) 171 Eh29
Rota ☐ E 27 Ko54
Rot am See ☐ D 33 Ll41
Rotenburg ☐ D 32 Lk39
Rotenburg (Wümme) ☐ D 32 Lk37
Roth ☐ D 33 Lm41
Rothenburg (Tauber) ☒ D 33 Ll41
Rothera ▲ ANT (UK) 6 Gc32
Rothes ☐ GB 20 Kr33
Rothesay ☐ GB 20 Kp35
Rothschild's ☒ USA (WY) 172 Fj23
Roti ☐ RI 97 Rb51
Roti ☐ RI 97 Rb51
Rotifunk ☐ WAL 136 Kd41
Rotorua ☒ NZ 112 Tj65
Rotorua ☐ NZ 112 Tj65
Rotsskildery ☐ ZA (AG) 175 Fb28
Rotsskildery ☐ RB 155 Mc58
Rott ☐ D 33 Lj42
Rotten ☐ CH 34 Lj44
Rottenburg ☐ D 33 Lj42
Rottenburg ☐ D 33 Ln42
Rotterdam ☐ NL 23 Le39
Rottne ☐ S 31 Lp33
Rottneros ☐ S 30 Lo31
Rottnest Island ▲ AUS 104 Qh61
Rottumerplaat ▲ NL 23 Lg37
Rottweil ☐ D 33 Lj42
Rotuma ▲ FJI 119 Tg51
Rötz ☐ D 33 Ln41
Rouaillet Bank 89 Qc41
Roubaix ☐ F 23 Ld40
Roudnice nad Labe ☐ CZ 42 Lp40
Rouen ☐ F 23 Lb41
Rougemont ☐ F 25 Lg43
Rough Rock ☐ USA (AZ) 171 Ef27
Rouilla ☐ TN 126 Le28
Rouillac ☐ F 24 Ku45
Roulans ☐ F 25 Lg43
Round Mountain ☐ AUS 109 Sg61
Round Mountain ☐ USA (AZ) 174 Ed27
Route 62 ☒ ZA 154 Lk62
Route 66 ☒ USA 171 Ef28
Route 66 (Missouri) ☒ USA 174 Fd27
Route 66 Mus. ◉ USA 174 Fa28
Route 66 (New Mexico) ☒ USA 171 Eh28
Route 66 (New Mexico) ☒ USA 171 Eh26
Route 66 S.P. ☒ USA 175 Fe26
Route des Crêtes ☒ F 25 Lg43
Route des Kasbahs ☒ MA 125 Kg30
Route Napoléon ☒ F 25 Lg47
Route transsaharienne ☒ DZ/RN 132 Lc35
Rouyn-Noranda ☐ CDN 173 Ga21
Rova d'Antongona ◉ RM 157 Nd55
Rovaniemi ☐ FIN 16 Mc12
Rovato ☐ I 34 Ll45
Roven'ki ☐ RUS 48 Mk21
Roven'ki ☐ UA (AR) 174 Fa28
Rovereto ☐ I 34 Lm45
Röversagen ☐ D 32 Ln36
Reverud ☐ N 30 Lm31
Rovigo ☐ I 34 Lm45
Rovinj ☐ HR 35 Lo45
Rovine di Roselle ☒ I 34 Lm48
Rovno ☒ UA 48 Me20
Rovuma ☒ MOC 145 Na50
Rowena ☐ AUS (NSW) 109 Se60
Rowley Shoals ▲ AUS 102 Qk54
Rowy ☐ PL 40 Lr36
Roxas ☐ RP 90 Ra37
Roxas ☐ RP 90 Ra38
Roxas ☐ RP 90 Ra39
Roxas ☐ RP 90 Rb40
Roxboro ☐ USA (NC) 178 Ga27
Roxborough Downs ☐ AUS (QLD) 108 Rk57
Roxby Downs ☐ AUS (SA) 108 Rj61
Roy ☐ USA (MT) 169 Ef22
Roy ☐ USA (NM) 171 Ej26
Roy ☐ USA (UT) 171 Ed25
Royal Bardia N.P. ☒ NEP 81 Pa31
Royal Botanic Gardens ☒ GB 21 Ku38
Royal Canal ☒ IRL 19 Kn37
Royal Chitwan N.P. ☒ NEP 81 Pb31
Royal City ☐ USA (WA) 168 Ea22
Royal Citadel (Polonnaruwa) ◉ CL 85 Pa42
Royal Exhibition Building and Carlton Gardens ◉ AUS 111 Sd64
Royal Gorge ☒ USA 174 Eh26
Royal Manas N.P. ☒ BHT 86 Pf32
Royal N.P. ☒ AUS 111 Sf63
Royal Natal N.P. ☒ ZA 155 Me60
Royal Palace ◉ K 89 Qb39
Royal Palm Beach ☐ USA (FL) 179 Fk32
Royal Pavilion ◉ GB 21 Ku40
Royal Randwick ☐ AUS (NSW) 111 Sf63
Royal Sukla Phanta N.P. ☒ NEP 81 Pa31
Royal Tombs ◉ SYN 89 Qd37
Royal Tunbridge Wells ☐ GB 21 La39
Roye ☐ F 23 Lc41
Roy Hill ☐ AUS (WA) 102 Qk57
Royston ☐ GB 21 Ku38
Roza ☐ BG 45 Mg48
Rozaj ☐ SCG 44 Ma48
Rozay-en-Brie ☐ F 23 Lc42
Rozdie'lna ☐ UA 49 Mf22
Roždestveno ☐ RUS 71 Rc20
Roždil'na ☐ UA 49 Mg23
Rožen ☐ BG 45 Me48
Rozengo ☐ RI 97 Re48
Roženovci manastir ◉ SCG 44 Md49
Rozivka ☐ UA 49 Mj22
Rožmitál pod Třemšínem ☐ CZ 42 Lo41
Rožňava ☐ SK 43 Ma42

Rožnov pod Radhoštěm ☐ CZ 42 Lt41
Rozogi ☐ PL 41 Mb37
Rozprza ☐ PL 41 Lu39
Roztoczański P.N. ☒ PL 41 Md40
Roztoky ☐ CZ 42 Lp40
Rozvadov ☐ CZ 42 Ln41
Rt Kamenjak ▲ HR 35 Lo46
Rt Ploča ▲ HR 35 Lq47
Ruacana ☐ NAM 150 Lh54
Ruacana Falls ☒ NAM 150 Lh54
Ruahine Range ▲ NZ 113 Tj66
Ruang ▲ RI 91 Rc44
Ruapuke Island ▲ NZ 113 Te69
Ruatoria ☐ NZ 112 Tk64
Ruba ☐ BY 48 Mf18
Rubafu ☐ EAT 144 Mf46
Rubcovsk ☐ RUS 54 Pa08
Rubeho Mountains ▲ EAT 147 Mj49
Rubengera ☐ RWA 146 Me47
Rubeshibe ☐ J 77 Sb24
Rubi ☐ RDC 141 Mc44
Rubiataba ☐ BR (GO) 202 Hf53
Rubino ☒ CI 137 Kh43
Rubio ☐ YV 192 Gd42
Rubondo ▲ EAT 144 Mf42
Rubuga ☐ EAT 146 Mg46
Ruby ☐ USA (AK) 165 Cc13
Ruby ☐ USA (WA) 168 Ea21
Ruby Mts. Scenic Area ☒ USA 170 Ec25
Ruby Range ▲ CDN 166 Da15
Rucar ☐ RO 45 Mf45
Rucheng ☐ CHN (HUN) 75 Qg38
Ruciane-Nida ☐ PL 41 Mb37
Rud ☐ IR 64 Oa28
Rudall ☐ AUS (SA) 110 Rj62
Rudall River N.P. ☒ AUS 102 Rb57
Ruda Śląska ☐ PL 41 Lt40
Rudauja ☐ SUD 145 Mf38
Rudbar ☐ AFG 64 Ob30
Rüdersdorf ☐ D 32 Lo38
Rudolstadt ☐ D 32 Lm40
Rudog ☐ CHN (JGS) 78 Pd28
Rudolstadt ☐ D 32 Lm40
Rud Sar ☐ IR 57 Ng27
Rue ☐ F 23 Lb40
Rueda ☐ E 26 Kq49
Ruen ☐ BG 45 Mh48
Ruente Nacional ☒ CO 192 Gd43
Rufa'a ☐ SUD 135 Mg38
Ruffec ☐ F 24 La44
Rufino ☐ RA (SF) 209 Gj63
Rufisque ☐ SN 130 Kc38
Rufunsa ☐ Z 152 Me53
Rugaji ☐ LV 39 Mg33
Rugao ☐ CHN (JGS) 78 Ra28
Rugby ☐ GB 21 Kt38
Rugeley ☐ GB 21 Kt38
Rügen ▲ D 32 Lo36
Ruhengeri ☐ RWA 141 Me46
Ruhland ☐ D 32 Lo39
Ruhner Berg ▲ D 32 Lm37
Ruhnu saar ▲ EST 39 Mc33
Rui'an ☐ CHN (ZJG) 75 Ra32
Ruichang ☐ CHN (JGX) 75 Qh31
Ruichang ☐ CHN (JGX) 72 Qf38
Ruidera ☐ E 27 Ks52
Ruidoso ☐ USA (NM) 171 Eh30
Ruijin ☐ CHN (JGX) 75 Qh33
Ruili ☐ CHN (YUN) 86 Pj33
Ruines d'Alucus ◉ SYN 89 Qd37
Ruines de Loropéni ◉ BF 137 Kj40
Ruines d'Empúries ◉ E 24 Lc48
Ruines de Ouara ◉ TCH 134 Ma38
Ruins of Aksum ◉ ETH 142 Mk38
Ruins of Fort Craig ◉ USA 171 Eg29
Ruins of Windsor ◉ USA 175 Fe30
Ruiru ☐ EAK 144 Mh46
Ruitersbos ☐ ZA 154 Mb62
Ruiz ☐ MEX (SL) 180 Eh33
Rüjiena ☐ LV 39 Me33
Rukanga ☐ EAK 145 Mk47
Rukhi ☐ EAT 144 Mf47
Rukungiri ☐ EAU 144 Mf46
Rukwa ☒ EAT 146 Mg49
Rum ▲ GB 20 Ko34
Ruma ☐ SCG 44 Lu45
Ruma N.P. ☒ EAK 144 Mf47
Rumaku ◉ YV 193 Gh41
Rumbek ☐ SUD 141 Mf42
Rumburk ☐ CZ 42 Lp40
Rum Cay ▲ BS 186 Gc34

Rumeila ☐ SUD 135 Mh39
Ryn ☐ PL 41 Mb37
Rumford ☐ USA (ME) 177 Ge23
Rumia ☐ PL 40 Lt36
Rumilly ☐ F 25 Lf45
Rumoi ☐ J 77 Sb24
Rumphi ☒ MW 146 Mg51
Rumpi Hills ▲ CAM 138 Le43
Rumšiškės ☐ LT 39 Md36
 Runan ☐ CHN (HNN) 73 Qe29
Runcorn ☐ GB 21 Ks37
Ruộn ☐ THA 89 Qa41
Runde ☒ ZW 152 Mf56
Runde ▲ EAT 147 Mj50
Rundeng ☐ RI 93 Pk45
Rungwa ☐ EAT 146 Mh49
Rungwa ☐ EAT 146 Mf49
Rungwa Game Reserve ☒ EAT 146 Mh49
Runkel ☐ D 32 Lj40
Runnumun ☐ N 30 Lt31
Runnumun ☐ S 31 Ls32
Runzewe ☐ EAT 144 Mf47
Ruokojärvi ☐ FIN 16 Mc12
Ruokolahti ☐ FIN 38 Mf29
Ruoqiang ☐ CHN (XUZ) 69 Pe26
Ruovesi ☐ FIN 38 Me28
Rupanyup ☐ AUS (VIC) 111 Sb64
Rupea ☐ RO 45 Mf44
Rupert ☐ USA (ID) 168 Ed24
Rupert ☐ USA (WV) 178 Fk27
Rupea ☐ RO 45 Mf44
Rupia ☐ EAT 147 Mj50
Rupia ☐ EAT 147 Mj50
Ruppert Coast ☒ 6 Cd34
Rupununi ☒ GUY 194 Ha44
Rurópolis Presidente Médici ☐ BR (PA) 199 Hc48
Rurrenabaque ☐ BOL 206 Gg53
Rurutu ▲ F 152 Mg55
Rusaile ☐ USA (MT) 169 Eh23
Rušani ☐ TJ 63 Oe27
Ruse ☐ BG 45 Mf47
Rusenski Lom, N.P. ☒ BG 45 Mg47
Rusera ☐ IND (BIH) 83 Pd33
Rushan ☐ CHN (SDG) 73 Qk27
Rushden ☐ GB 21 Ku38
Rushinga ☒ ZW 152 Mg54
Rushnugi ☐ EAT 147 Mj50
Rushville ☐ USA (NE) 172 Ek24
Ruskeala ☐ RUS 38 Mh29
Rusko ☐ THA 89 Qa42
Rusksele ☐ S 16 Lk25
Russas ☐ BR (CE) 201 Jb48
Russell ☐ CDN (MB) 172 Ek20
Russell Islands ▲ SOL 117 Sk50
Russell, Mount ▲ USA (AK) 165 Ce14
Russell Springs ☐ USA (KS) 174 Ek26
Russellville ☐ USA (AL) 175 Fg28
Russia ☒ RUS 53 Oa03
Russkaja ☐ ANT (RUS) 6 Ca34
Russkij ☐ UA (KY) 175 Fg27
Rust ▲ A 35 Lr43
Rust de Winter ☐ ZA 155 Me58
Rust de Winter Nature Reserve ☒ ZA 155 Me58
Rustavi ☒ GE 57 Nc25
Rustenburg ☐ ZA 155 Md58
Rustenburg Nature Reserve ☒ ZA 155 Md58
Ruston ☐ USA (LA) 175 Fd29
Rusumu Falls ☒ EAT 144 Mf47
Ruszów ☐ PL 40 Lq39
Rute ☐ E 27 Kq53
Ruteng ☐ RI 96 Ra50
Rutenga ☐ ZW 152 Mf56
Rutete ☐ EAT 146 Mf49
Rüthen ☐ D 32 Lj39
Rutherfordton ☐ USA (NC) 178 Fj28
Ruthin ☐ GB 21 Kr37
Rutigliano ☐ I 37 Lr49
Rutka-Tartak ☐ PL 41 Mc36
Rutland ☐ USA (ND) 172 Fb22
Rutland Plains ☐ AUS (QLD) 107 Sa53
Rutog ☐ CHN (TIB) 83 Pb30
Rutshuru ☐ RDC 141 Me46
Rutul ☐ RUS 57 Nd25
Ruurlo ☐ NL 23 Lg38
Ruvo di Púglia ☐ I 37 Lr49
Ruvubu, P.N.de la ☒ BU 144 Mf46
Ruvuma ☒ EAT/MOC 147 Mj51
Ruwa ☒ ZW 152 Mf55
Ruwais ☐ UAE 61 Ng33
Ruwenzori Mountains N.P. ☒ EAU 141 Me46
Ruyigi ☐ BU 146 Mf47
Ruzayevka ☐ RUS 48 Nc18
Ruzhany ☐ BY 41 Me38
Ružindol ☐ SK 43 Lr42
Ruziyah ☐ RUS 48 Mk19
Ružomberok ☐ SK 43 Lu41
Rwanda ☒ RWA 146 Me47
Rwindi ☐ RDC 141 Me46
Ry ☐ DK 30 Lk34
Ryan ☐ USA (OK) 174 Fb29
Ryan, Mount ▲ USA (AK) 165 Cf13
Ryazan ☒ RUS 48 Mk19
Ryazhsk ☐ RUS 48 Na19
Rybinsk ☐ RUS 48 Mk16
Rybinsk Reservoir ▣ RUS 48 Mk16
Rybnik ☐ PL 40 Lt40
Rybno ☐ PL 40 Lt39
Rybno ☐ PL 41 Mb38
Rychnovo ☐ PL 41 Ma38
Rychnov ☐ CZ 42 Lq41
Rychwal ☐ PL 40 Lt38
Rychnowy ☐ PL 40 Ls36
Ryczywół ☐ PL 40 Lr38
Ryde ☐ GB 21 Kt40
Rydaholm ☐ S 31 Lp34
Rydberg Peninsula ☒ 6 Ga33
Rydet ☐ S 30 Lk32
Rydultowy ☐ PL 41 Lt40
Rydzyna ☐ PL 40 Lr39
Rye ☐ GB 21 La40
Ryegate ☐ USA (MT) 169 Ef22
Ryki ☐ PL 41 Mb39
Rykene ☐ N 30 Lj32
Rykė Yseyzeme ☐ LT 39 Me36
Rylsk ☐ RUS 48 Mh20
Ryman ☐ PL 40 Lq37
Rymanów ☐ PL 41 Mb41
Rymanów-Zdrój ☐ PL 41 Mb41
Rýmařov ☐ CZ 42 Ls41

Sa ☐ PNG 115 Sc48
Sa ▲ CAM 139 Lf43
Sa'a ☒ SOL 117 Ta50
Saacow = Jilib ☐ SP 145 Nd45
Saalfeld ☐ D 32 Lm40
Saalfelden am Steinernen Meer ☐ A 35 Ln43
Saar ☒ D 33 Lg41
Saarbrücken ☐ D 33 Lg41
Saarburg ☐ D 33 Lg41
Saare ▲ EST 39 Mc33
Saarijärvi ☐ FIN 38 Me28
Saarland ☒ D 33 Lg41
Saarlouis ☐ D 33 Lg41
Saarschleife ◉ D 34 Lh41
Saas Fee ☐ CH 34 Lh44
Saatli ☒ AZ 57 Ne26
Sabadell ☐ E 29 Lc49
Sabah ☐ MAL 94 Qf44
Sabak ☐ MAL 93 Qa44
Sabalana ▲ RI 96 Qk49
Sabalang ▲ RI 94 Qj44
Sabalgarh ☐ IND (MPH) 82 Oj32
Sabaluka Game Reserve ☒ SUD 135 Mg38
Saba Marine Park ☒ NL (NA) 187 Gj37
Sabana ☐ C 186 Ga35
Sabana de Cardona ☐ YV 193 Gh42
Sabana de la Mar ☐ DOM 186 Gf36
Sabana Grande ☒ YV 192 Gg41
Sabanalarga ☐ CO 192 Gc40
Sabanalarga ☐ CO 192 Gd41
Sábanas Páramo ▲ CO 192 Gd43
Sabancuy ☐ MEX (CAM) 183 Fe36
Sabaneta ☐ DOM 186 Ge36
Sabaneta ☐ YV 192 Gd41
Sabang ☐ RI 93 Ph43
Sabang ☐ RP 90 Qk40
Sabará ☐ BR (MG) 203 Hj55
Sabaudia ☐ I 36 Lo49
Sabaya ☐ BOL 206 Gf55
Sabbioneta ◉ I 34 Ll45
Sabderat ☐ ER 142 Mj38
Sabha ☒ LAR 127 Lh32
Sabha ☐ SUD 135 Mf37
Sabidana ▲ SUD 135 Mh37
Sabie ☐ MOC 155 Mf58
Sabi Game Reserve ☒ ZW 152 Mf56
Sabile ☐ LV 39 Mc33
Sabinas ☐ MEX (COH) 181 Ek32
Sabinas Hidalgo ☐ MEX (NL) 181 Ek32
Sabine Peninsula ▲ CDN 162 Eb03
Sabine Pass ☐ USA (TX) 174 Fd31
Sabinosa ☐ E 128 Kc33
Sabinov ☐ SK 43 Mb41
Sabirabad ☒ AZ 57 Ne25
Sabkhat ad Dabbiyah ▣ KSA 59 Ne32
Sabkhat Hawaza ▣ KSA 59 Nd32
Sabkhat Matti ▣ UAE 61 Ng33
Sabkhat Mujazzam ▣ LAR 126 Lf30
Sablayan ☐ RP 90 Ra40
Sablayan ☐ RP 90 Ra40
Sable Island ▲ CDN 176 Gk23
Sable Island Bank ▣ 176 Gk24
Sablé-sur-Sarthe ☐ F 23 Ku43
Sabo Boat ☐ THA 88 Pk41
Sabodala ☐ SN 136 Kd39
Saboeiro ☐ BR (CE) 201 Ja49
Sabor ☒ P 26 Kn49
Sabou ☐ BF 137 Kj39
Sabres ☐ F 24 Ku46
Sabrina Coast ☒ 7 Rd32
Sabtang ▲ RP 90 Ra36
Sabya ☐ KSA 60 Na37
Sabzevar ☐ IR 62 Nj28
Sabzevaran ☐ IR 64 Nj31

Saca Cabra ☐ BOL 206 Gg54
Sacacama ☐ ANG 151 Ma52
Sacado do Humaitá ☐ BR (AM) 198 Gf49
Sacaca ☐ BOL 206 Gf55
Sacandica ☐ ANG 151 Ma52
Sacanana ☐ CO 192 Gd42
Sacambunge ☐ ANG 149 Mb51
Sacandica ☐ ANG 149 Ma54
Sac and Fox Ind. Res. ☒ USA 172 Fd24
Scandío ☐ ANG 148 Lh48
Sacanta ☐ RA (CD) 209 Gj61
Sacapulas ☐ GCA 184 Fe38
Sacco Uein ☐ SP 145 Nb45
Sacecorbo ☐ E 29 Ks50
Sacedón ☐ E 29 Ks50
Sácele ☐ RO 45 Mf45
Sácele ☐ RO 45 Mj46
Sáceni ☐ RO 45 Me46
Sachang ☐ CHN (GZH) 74 Qd32
Sachayoj ☐ RA (SE) 207 Gk59
Sachida ☐ IND (UPH) 81 Ok31
Sachojere ☐ BOL 206 Gh53
Sachsen ☒ D 32 Lo39
Sachsen-Anhalt ☒ D 32 Ln39
Sachsenring ◉ D 32 Ln40
Sachs Harbour ☐ CDN 162 Dd04
Säckesing ☐ D 32 Lj40
Sada ☐ E 26 Km47
Sadani ☐ EAT 147 Mk48
Sadao ☐ THA 88 Pk42
Sadah ☒ YE 60 Nb37
Sâdât City ☒ ET 129 Mf30
Sadovoe ☐ RUS 49 Nc22
Saddle Mount ▲ USA 169 Ed24
Saddle Peak ▲ IND 88 Pg35
Saddle Peaks ▲ VU 118 Tg56
Saddleworth ☐ AUS 110 Rk62
Sadeh ☐ KSA 60 Na37
Sadiman Crater Hill (Leakey's Landscape) ◉ EAT 144 Mh47
Sadimen ☐ RI 91 Rb50
Sadiola ☐ RMM 136 Ke39
Sadiqabad ☐ PK 64 Oa31
Sadiya ☐ IND (ASM) 86 Ph32
Sadievskoe ☐ RM 156 Nc52
Sadko ▲ NEP/CHN 81 Pd31
Sado ☒ P 26 Km53
Sado-jima ▲ J 77 Rk26
Sadolonga ☒ RA 90 Md22
Sadová ▲ IND 84 Oj40
Sado Yahiko Q.N.P. ☒ J 77 Rk27
Sadri ☐ IND (RJT) 82 Og33
Saga ▲ RI 114 Rg47
Saga ☐ CHN (TIB) 68 Pc31
Saga ☐ J 77 Rf29
Sagae ☐ J 77 Sa27
Sagaing ☐ MYA 86 Ph34
Sagak ▲ USA (AK) 165 Cf11
Sagamihara ☐ J 79 Rk28
Sagan ▲ SUD 141 Mf42
Saganoseki ☐ J 79 Rg29
Sagar ☐ IND (KTK) 84 Oj38
Sagar ☐ IND (MPH) 83 Ok33
Sagard ☐ D 32 Lo36
Saghar Mts. ▲ AFG 63 Oe28
Sagil ▲ NEP 81 Pd31
Saginaw ☐ USA (MI) 173 Fj24
Saginaw Bay ▣ USA 173 Fj24
Sagiz ☒ KZ 62 Ng22
Sagleg Bay ▣ CDN 163 Gd07
Sagne ▲ RIM 130 Kd38

Saint-Benoît-du-Sault – San Felipe de Jesús

Saint-Benoît-du-Sault **F** 24 Lb44
Saint Bernard **F** (GF) 194 Hd43
Saint-Bertrand-de-Comminges **F** 24 La47
Saint-Bonnet **F** 25 Lg46
Saint Brendan's **CDN** (NF) 177 Hd21
Saint-Brévin-les-Pins **F** 24 Ks43
Saint-Brice-en-Cógles **F** 22 Kt42
Saint Bride's **CDN** (NF) 177 Hc22
Saint Bride's Bay **GB** 21 Kp39
Saint-Brieuc **F** 22 Ks42
Saint Brieux **CDN** (SK) 169 Eh19
Saint-Bruno **CDN** (QC) 176 Ge21
Saint-Calais **F** 22 La43
Saint-CaSaint-le-Guildo **F** 22 Ks42
Saint Catharines **CDN** (ON) 173 Ga24
Saint Catherine's Point **GB** 21 Kt40
Saint-Céré **F** 24 Lb46
Saint-Chamond **F** 25 Le45
Saint Charles **USA** (AR) 175 Fe28
Saint Charles **USA** (MD) 177 Gb26
Saint Charles **USA** (MO) 175 Fe26
Saint-Chély-d'Apcher **F** 25 Ld46
Saint-Chinian **F** 25 Lc47
Saint-Claud **F** 24 La45
Saint-Claude **F** 25 Lf44
Saint Clears **GB** 21 Kq39
Saint Cloud **USA** (FL) 178 Fk31
Saint Cloud **USA** (MN) 172 Fc23
Saint Croix **CDN** (NB) 176 Gg23
Saint Croix **USA** 187 Gh37
Saint Croix N.S.R. **USA** 172 Fd23
Saint David's **GB** 21 Kp39
Saint David's Head **GB** 21 Kp39
Saint-Denis **F** (RE) 157 Nh56
Saint-Denis **F** 23 Lc42
Saint-Dié-des-Vosges **F** 25 Lg42
Saint-Dizier **F** 23 Le42
Saint-Doulchard **F** 25 Lc43
Sainte-Agathe des Monts **CDN** 176 Gc22
Sainte-Annade-Beaupré **CDN** (QC) 176 Ge22
Sainte Anne **CDN** (MB) 172 Fb21
Sainte-Anne **F** (GL) 187 Gk37
Sainte-Annedes-Monts **CDN** (QC) 176 Gg21
Sainte-Anne-du-Lac **CDN** (QC) 176 Gc22
Sainte-Énimie **F** 25 Ld46
Sainte-Eulalie **CDN** (QC) 176 Gd22
Sainte-Foy-la-Grande **F** 24 La46
Saint-Egrève **F** 25 Lf45
Sainte-Hedwidge **CDN** (QC) 176 Gd21
Sainte-Hermine **F** 24 Kt44
Sainte-Justine **CDN** (QC) 176 Ge22
Saint Elias Mountains **CDN** 166 Da15
Saint-Élie **F** (GF) 194 Hd43
Sainte-Livrade-sur-Lot **F** 24 La46
Saint-Eloy-les-Mines **F** 25 Lc44
Sainte-Madeleine de Vézelay **F** 25 Lc43
Sainte-Marie **CDN** (QC) 176 Ge22
Sainte-Marie **F** (MT) 187 Gk38
Sainte-Maure de-Touraine **F** 24 La43
Sainte-Maxime **F** 25 Lg47
Sainte-Menehould **F** 23 Le41
Sainte-Mère-Église **F** 22 Kt41
Saint-Émilion **F** 24 Ku46
Sainte-Monique **CDN** (QC) 176 Ge21
Sainte-Rose **F** (GL) 187 Gk37
Sainte-Rosede Poularies **CDN** (QC) 173 Ga21
Sainte Rose du Lac **CDN** (MB) 172 Fa20
Sainte-Rosedu-Nord **CDN** (QC) 176 Ge21
Saintes **F** 24 Ku45
Sainte-Savine **F** 23 Le42
Sainte-Sévère-sur-Indre **F** 25 Lc44
Saintes-Maries-de-la-Mer **F** 25 Le47
Sainte-Suzanne **F** 22 Ku42
Saint-Étienne **F** 25 Le45
Saint-Étienne-de-Saint-Geoirs **F** 25 Lf45
Saint-Étienne-du-Rouvray **F** 23 Lb41
Saint-Etienne-en-Dévoluy **F** 25 Lf46
Saint-Etienne-les-Orgues **F** 25 Lf46
Saint-Fabien **CDN** (QC) 176 Gf21
Saint-Fabiende-Panet **CDN** (QC) 176 Ge22
Saint-Fargeau **F** 25 Ld43
Saint-Félicien **CDN** (QC) 176 Gd21
Saint Fergus **GB** 20 Kt33
Saint-Florent **F** 34 Lk48
Saint-Florentin **F** 23 Ld42
Saint-Florent-sur-Cher **F** 25 Lc44
Saint Floris, P.N.de **RCA** 140 Ma41
Saint-Flour **F** 25 Ld45
Saint-Fort-sur-Gironde **F** 24 Ku45
Saint Francis **USA** (KS) 174 Ek26
Saint Francis Bay **ZA** 155 Mc63
Saint Francis Islands **AUS** 110 Rg62
Saint Francisville **USA** (LA) 175 Fe30
Saint Francois Mountains **USA** 175 Fe27
Saint-Gabriel **CDN** (QC) 176 Gd22
Saint-Gaudens **F** 24 La47
Saint Gaudens N.H.S. **USA** 177 Gd24
Saint-Gaultier **F** 24 Lb44
Saint-Geniez-d'Olt **F** 25 Lc46
Saint-Genix-sur-Guiers **F** 25 Lf45
Saint George **AUS** (QLD) 109 Se60
Saint George **CDN** (NB) 176 Gg23
Saint George **USA** (GA) 178 Fj30
Saint George **USA** (SC) 178 Fk29
Saint George **USA** (UT) 171 Ed27
Saint George, Cape **PNG** 116 Sg48
Saint George Island **USA** 164 Bf17
Saint George Island S.P. **USA** 175 Fh31
Saint George's **CDN** (NF) 177 Ha21
Saint-Georges **CDN** (QC) 176 Ge22
Saint Georges **F** (GF) 195 He44
Saint George's **WG** 187 Gk39
Saint George's Bay (NFL) **CDN** 177 Ha21
Saint George's Bay (NS) **CDN** 176 Gk23
Saint George's Castle **GH** 137 Kk43
Saint George's Channel **IND** 88 Pg42
Saint George's Channel **PNG** 116 Sg48
Saint George's Channel 19 Ko39
Saint-Georges-de-Didonne **F** 24 Ku45
Saint-Germain-du-Bois **F** 25 Lf44
Saint-Germain-en-Laye **F** 23 Lc42
Saint-Germain-Laval **F** 25 Le45
Saint-Gervais-d'Auvergne **F** 25 Lc44
Saint-Gervais-les-Bains **F** 25 Lg45
Saint-Gildas-des-Bois **F** 22 Ks43
Saint-Gilles **F** 25 Le47
Saint-Gilles-Croix-de-Vie **F** 24 Kt44
Saint-Girons **F** 24 Lb48
Saint-Girons-en-Marensin **F** 24 Kt47
Saint Govan's Head **GB** 21 Kq39
Saint Gregory, Mount **CDN** 177 Ha21
Saint-Guénolé **F** 22 Kq43
Saint-Guilhem-le-Désert **F** 25 Ld47
Saint Helena **GB** 123 Kb11
Saint Helena **GB** 123 Kb11
Saint Helena **GB** 123 Kb11
Saint Helena **GB** 123 Kb11
Saint Helena Bay **ZA** 154 Lk62
Saint Helens **AUS** (TAS) 111 Se66
Saint Helens **GB** 21 Ks37
Saint Helens **USA** (OR) 168 Dj23
Saint Helens Nat. Volcanic Mon., Mount **USA** 168 Dj22
Saint Helens Point **AUS** 111 Se66
Saint Helier **GB** 22 Ks41
Sainthia **IND** (WBG) 83 Pd34
Saint-Hilaire-du-Harcouët **F** 22 Kt42
Saint-Hilaire/Lange, P.N.de **BR** 205 Hf58
Saint-Hilaire-le-Grand de Poitiers **F** 24 La44
Saint-Hippolyte **F** 25 Lg43
Saint-Hippolyte-du-Fort **F** 25 Ld47
Saint-Honoré-les-Bains **F** 25 Ld44
Saint-Hubert **B** 23 Lf40
Saint-Hyacinthe **CDN** (QC) 177 Gd23
Saint Ignace **USA** (MI) 173 Fh23
Saint-Ignace-des-Saints **CDN** (QC) 176 Gd22
Saint Ignace Island **CDN** 173 Fg21
Saint-Imier **CH** 34 Lg43
Saint Ives **GB** 21 Kp40
Saint Ives **GB** 21 Ku38
Saint-James **F** 22 Kt42
Saint James **USA** (MN) 172 Fc24
Saint-Jean-Brévelay **F** 22 Ks43
Saint-Jean-d'Angely **F** 24 Ku45
Saint-Jeande-Dieu **CDN** (QC) 176 Gf21
Saint-Jean-de-Luz **F** 24 Kt47
Saint-Jean-de-Maurienne **F** 25 Lg45
Saint-Jean-de-Monts **F** 24 Ks44
Saint-Jean-Pied-de-Port **F** 24 Kt47
Saint-Jean-Port-Joli **CDN** (QC) 176 Ge22
Saint-Jean-Poutge **F** 24 La47
Saint-Jean-surRichelieu **CDN** (QC) 177 Gd23
Saint John **CDN** (NB) 176 Gg23
Saint John **GB** 187 Gh36
Saint John **USA** (KS) 174 Fa27
Saint John Bay **CDN** 177 Hb20
Saint John Island **CDN** 177 Hb21
Saint John's **AG** 187 Gk37
Saint John's **CDN** (NF) 177 Hd22
Saint Johns **USA** (AZ) 171 Ef28
Saint Johns **USA** (MI) 173 Fh24
Saint Johnsbury **USA** (VT) 177 Gd23
Saint John's Island **ET** 129 Mj34
Saint John's Town of Dalry **GB** 20 Kq35
Saint Jorge de Limpopo **MOC** 152 Mg57
Saint Joseph **F** (NCL) 118 Td56
Saint-Joseph **F** (RE) 157 Nh56
Saint Joseph **SY** 145 Ng48
Saint Joseph **USA** (MN) 172 Fc23
Saint Joseph **USA** (MO) 174 Fc26
Saint Joseph's **CDN** (NF) 177 Hd22
Saint Jovite **CDN** (QC) 176 Gc22
Saint-Julien-en-Genevois **F** 25 Lg44
Saint-Junien **F** 24 La45
Saint-JuSaint-en-Chaussée **F** 23 Lc41
Saint-Just-en-Chevalet **F** 25 Ld45
Saint-Justin **F** 24 Ku47
Saint-Just-Saint-Rambert **F** 25 Le45
Saint Kilda **GB** 20 Km33
Saint Kitts and Nevis 187 Gj37
Saint-Lary-Soulan **F** 24 La48
Saint-Laurent-de-la-Cabrerisse **F** 24 Lc47
Saint-Laurent- de-la-Salanque **F** 25 Lc48
Saint Laurent du Maroni **F** (GF) 194 Hc43
Saint-Laurent-en-Grandvaux **F** 25 Lf44
Saint Lawrence **AUS** (QLD) 109 Se57
Saint Lawrence Island **USA** 164 Be14
Saint Lawrence River **CDN** 176 Gf21
Saint Lazare **CDN** (MB) 172 Ek20
Saint-Léonard **CDN** (NB) 176 Gg22
Saint-Léonard-de-Noblat **F** 24 Lb45
Saint Leu **F** (RE) 157 Nh56
Saint-Lô **F** 22 Kt41
Saint Louis **CDN** (SK) 169 Eh19
Saint-Louis **F** (GL) 187 Gk38
Saint-Louis **F** (RE) 157 Nh56
Saint Louis **SN** 130 Kb37
Saint Louis **USA** (MO) 175 Fe26
Saint-Loup-sur-Semouse **F** 25 Lg43
Saint Lucia **WL** 187 Gk38
Saint Lucia **ZA** 155 Mg60
Saint Lucia 187 Gk39
Saint Lucia Channel 187 Gk38
Saint Magnus Bay **GB** 20 Kt30
Saint-Maixent-l'École **F** 24 Ku44
Saint-Malo **F** 22 Ks42
Saint-Marc **RH** 186 Gd36
Saint-Marcellin **F** 25 Lf45
Saint Margaret Bay **CDN** 177 Hb20
Saint Maries **USA** (ID) 168 Eb22
Saint Marks **USA** (FL) 175 Fh30
Saint Marks **ZA** 155 Md62
Saint-Mars-la-Jaille **F** 22 Kt43
Saint-Martin **F** (GL) 187 Gj36
Saint-Martin-de-Ré **F** 24 Kt44
Saint-Martin-du-Canigou **F** 24 Lc48
Saint Martins **CDN** (NB) 176 Gh23
Saint-Martin-Vésubie **F** 25 Lh46
Saint Mary **USA** (MT) 169 Ed21
Saint Marys **AUS** (TAS) 111 Se66
Saint Mary's **GB** 21 Ko41
Saint Marys **USA** (GA) 178 Fk30
Saint Marys **USA** (PA) 173 Ga25
Saint Marys **USA** (WV) 175 Fk26
Saint Mary's **Z** 151 Md52
Saint Mary's Bay **CDN** 177 Hd22
Saint Marys Peak **AUS** 108 Rk61
Saint-Mathieu **F** 24 La45
Saint Matthew Island **USA** 164 Bd15
Saint Matthews **USA** (SC) 178 Fk29
Saint Matthias Group **PNG** 116 Se46
Saint-Maximin-la-Sainte-Baume **F** 25 Lf47
Saint-Médard-en-Jalles **F** 24 Ku46
Saint-Méen-le-Grand **F** 22 Ks42
Saint Michael **USA** (AK) 164 Bj14
Saint Michaels **USA** (AZ) 171 Ef28
Saint Michael's Mount **GB** 21 Kp40
Saint-Michel **F** 23 Le41
SaintMichel de l'Attalaye **RH** 186 Gd36
Saint-Michel-des-Saint **CDN** (QC) 176 Gd22
Saint-Mihiel **F** 23 Lf42
Saint Mungo **GB** 20 Kq35
Saint-Nazaire **F** 24 Ks43
Saint Neots **GB** 21 Ku38
Saint-Nicolas- de-Port **F** 23 Lg42
Saint-Omer **F** 23 Lc40
Saintonge **F** 24 Ku45
Saint-Pamphile **CDN** (QC) 176 Gf22
Saint-Pascal **CDN** (QC) 176 Gf22
Saint Paul **CDN** (AB) 169 Ee18
Saint-Paul **F** (RE) 157 Nh56
Saint Paul **USA** (AK) 164 Be17
Saint Paul **USA** (MN) 172 Fd23
Saint Paul **USA** (NE) 172 Fa25
Saint Paul 9 Ob13
Saint-Paul-de-Fenouillet **F** 24 Lc48
Saint-Paulien **F** 25 Ld45
Saint Paul Island **CDN** 176 Gk22
Saint Paul Island **USA** 164 Be17
Saint-Paul-lès-Dax **F** 24 Kt47
Saint Paul's Cathedral **RP** 90 Ra38
Saint Paul's Subterranean N.P. **RP** 90 Qk40
Saint-Péray **F** 25 Le46
Saint-Père-en-Retz **F** 24 Ks43
Saint Peter **CDN** (NS) 176 Gk23
Saint Peter **USA** (MN) 172 Fd23
Saint Peter Island **AUS** 110 Rg62
Saint Peter-Port **GB** 22 Ks41
Saint Peters **CDN** (PE) 176 Gj22
Saint Petersburg **RUS** 38 Ml31
Saint Petersburg **USA** (FL) 179 Fj32
Saint-Philbert-de-Grand-Lieu **F** 24 Kt43
Saint-Philémon **CDN** (QC) 176 Ge22
Saint-Philippe **F** (RE) 157 Nh56
Saint-Pierre **F** (CT) 177 Hb22
Saint-Pierre **F** (MT) 187 Gk38
Saint-Pierre **F** (RE) 157 Nh56
Saint-Pierre **F** 25 Lc47
Saint-Pierre **F** 177 Hb22
Saint Pierre **SY** 156 Nf50
Saint Pierre and Miquelon **F** 177 Hb22
Saint-Pierre-de-Chignac **F** 24 La45
Saint-Pierre-d'Oléron **F** 24 Kt45
Saint-Pierre-Jolys **CDN** (MB) 172 Fb21
Saint-Pierre-le-Moûtier **F** 25 Ld44
Saint-Pierre-sur-Dives **F** 22 Ku41
Saint-Pol-de-Léon **F** 22 Kr42
Saint-Pol-sur-Mer **F** 23 Lc39
Saint-Pol-sur-Ternoise **F** 23 Lc40
Saint-Pons-de-Thomières **F** 25 Lc47
Saint-Pourçain-sur-Sioule **F** 25 Ld44
Saint-Priest **F** 25 Le45
Saint-Privat **F** 24 Lc45
Saint-Quay-Portrieux **F** 22 Ks42
Saint-Quentin **CDN** (NB) 176 Gg22
Saint-Quentin **F** 23 Ld41
Saint-Raphaël **F** 25 Lg47
Saint-Raymond **CDN** (QC) 176 Ge22
Saint-Rémy-de-Provence **F** 25 Le47
Saint-Renan **F** 22 Kq42
Saint-Saëns **F** 23 Lb41
Saint-Saulge **F** 25 Ld43
Saint-Sauveur-en-Puisaye **F** 25 Ld43
Saint-Sauveur-le-Vicomte **F** 22 Kt41
Saint-Sauveur-sur-Tinée **F** 25 Lh46
Saint-Savin **F** 24 La44
Saint-Seine-l'Abbaye **F** 25 Le43
Saint-Sernin **F** 24 Lb47
Saint-Sever **F** 24 Ku47
Saint Shotts **CDN** (NF) 177 Hd22
Saint-Siméon **CDN** (QC) 176 Gf22
Saint Simons Island **USA** (GA) 178 Fk30
Saint Stephen **CDN** (NB) 176 Gg23
Saint-Sulpice **F** 24 Lb47
Saint François **SY** 145 Ng49
Saint-Thégonnec **F** 22 Kr42
Saint Thomas **CDN** (ON) 173 Fk24
Saint Thomas **USA** 187 Gh36
Saint-Tite **CDN** (QC) 176 Gd22
Saint-Tropez **F** 25 Lg47
Saint Urbain **CDN** (QC) 176 Ge22
Saint-Ursanne **CH** 34 Lh43
Saint-VaaSaint-la-Hougue **F** 22 Kt41
Saint-Valéry-en-Caux **F** 22 La41
Saint-Valery-sur-Somme **F** 23 Lb40
Saint-Vallier **F** 25 Le45
Saint Victor's Petroglyphs Prov. H.S. **CDN** 169 Eh21
Saint Vincent **I** 34 Lh45
Saint Vincent **WV** 187 Gk39
Saint Vincent and the Grenadines 187 Gk39
Saint Vincent N.W.R. **USA** 175 Fh31
Saint Vincent Passage 187 Gk39
Saint-Vith **B** 23 Lg40
Saint Walburg **CDN** (SK) 169 Ef19
Saint Xavier **USA** (MT) 169 Eg23
Saint-Yorre **F** 25 Ld44
Saint-Yrieix-la-Perche **F** 24 Lb45
Saint-Zénon **CDN** (QC) 176 Gd22
Sainyabuli **LAO** 87 Qa36
Sainyinan-Daji **WAN** 138 Lc39
Saiotesh **KZ** 62 Ng23
Saïoua **CI** 137 Kg42
Saipal **NEP** 81 Pa31
Saipan **USA** 100 Sa08
Saipina **BOL** 206 Gh55
Sai Ree Beach **THA** 88 Pk40
Saisombun **LAO** 87 Qb36
Saissac **F** 24 Lc47
Sai Thong N.P. **THA** 88 Qa38
Saito **J** 79 Rf29
Saiwa Swamp N.P. **EAK** 144 Mh45
Saiyala **SUD** 135 Mg37
Saiyid **PK** 65 Og29
Sai Yok **THA** 88 Pk38
Sai Yok Noi Waterfall **THA** 88 Pk38
Sai Yok N.P. **THA** 88 Pk38
Sajam **RI** 114 Rg46
Sajama, Nevado **BOL** 206 Gf55
Sajama, P.N. **BOL** 206 Gf55
Sajano-Šušenskoe vodohranilišče **RUS** 54 Pc08
Sajir **KSA** 59 Nc33
Sajkaš **SCG** 44 Ma45
Šajmak **TJ** 63 Oh27
Sajósvámos **H** 43 Ma42
Saka **ETH** 142 Mj41
Saka **LV** 39 Mb34
Saka **MA** 125 Kj28
Sakabinda **RDC** 151 Mc51
Sakaeo **THA** 89 Qb39
Sakai **GH** 137 Kj40
Sakai **J** 79 Rh28
Sakaide **J** 79 Rg28
Sakaiminato **J** 79 Rg28
Sakai N.P. **J** 79 Re29
Sakakah **KSA** 58 Na30
Sakakemang **RI** 93 Qb47
Sakala kõrgustik **EST** 39 Mf32
Sakania **RDC** 146 Me52
Sakar **TM** 63 Ob26
Sakaraha **RM** 157 Nc57
Sakar Dağı **TR** 47 Mh51
Sakar Island **PNG** 116 Se48
Sakartvelo = Georgia **GE** 57 Nb25
Sakarya = Adapazarı **TR** 56 Mf25
Sakarya **TR** 56 Mf25
Sakassou **CI** 137 Kh42
Sakata **J** 77 Rk26
Sakbayeme **CAM** 138 Lf43
Saké **RDC** 141 Me46
Sakété **DY** 138 Lb42
Saketi **RI** 95 Qd49
Sakha **RUS** 55 Qc05
Sakhalin **RUS** 55 Sa08
Sakhi Gopal **IND** (ORS) 83 Pc36
Sakhon Nakhon **THA** 89 Qc37
Saki **WAN** 138 Lb41
Šakiai **LT** 39 Md36
Sakiet Eddaïr **TN** 126 Lf28
Sakiet Sidi Youssef **TN** 126 Le27
Säkilahti **FIN** 38 Mk29
Sakiramke **RI** 115 Sa50
Sakju **PRK** 76 Rc25
Sakkara **ET** 129 Mf31
Sakke **IND** (MPH) 83 Pa34
Sak Lek **THA** 88 Qa37
Sakleshpur **IND** (KTK) 84 Oh39
Sakoamadinika **RM** 157 Ne54
Sakone **SN** 136 Kb39
Sakony **RUS** 48 Nb18
Sakrand **PK** 65 Oe32
Sakré Déléb **TCH** 140 Lk41
Sakri **IND** (BIH) 83 Pd32
Sakri **IND** (MHT) 82 Oh35
Sakrivier **ZA** 154 Ma61
Sakskøbing **DK** 30 Lm36
Saku **J** 77 Rk27
Saky **UA** 49 Mg23
Sakya Monastery **CHN** 68 Pe31
Säkylä **FIN** 38 Mc29
Sala **EAK** 145 Mk47
Sala **S** 31 Lr31
Šaľa **SK** 42 Ls42
Salaberry-deValleyfield **CDN** (QC) 177 Gc23
Salacgrīva **LV** 39 Me33
Sala Consilina **I** 37 Lq50
Saladas **RA** (CR) 204 Ha60
Saladero M.Cabal **RA** (SF) 209 Gk61
Saladillo **RA** (BA) 209 Ha63
Salado **RA** 207 Gj59
Saladougou **RG** 136 Kf40
Salaga **GH** 137 Kk41
Salagle **SP** 145 Nb45
Salahly **SP** 143 Nc41
Salaiman Range **PK** 65 Oe31
Salajwe **RB** 155 Mc57
Salakas **LT** 39 Mg35
Salal **TCH** 133 Lj38
Salala **LB** 136 Ke42
Salala **SUD** 129 Mj35
Salalah **OM** 61 Nh37
Salama **EAK** 144 Mj46
Salamá **GCA** 184 Fe38
Salamá **HN** 184 Fg38
Salamajärven kansallispuisto **FIN** 38 Me27
Salamanca **E** 26 Kp50
Salamanca **MEX** (GJT) 182 Ek35
Salamanca **PA** 185 Ga41
Salamanca **RCH** 208 Ge61
Salamanca **USA** (NY) 173 Ga24
Salamanga **MOC** 155 Mg59
Salamaua **PNG** 115 Sd49
Salamey **IR** 64 Nk28
Salamina **CO** 192 Gc40
Salamina **CO** 192 Gc43
Salamina **GR** 45 Md53
Salamína **GR** 45 Md53
Salamiyyeh **SYR** 56 Mj28
Salamo **PNG** 116 Sf50
Salang-Tunnel **AFG** 63 Oe28
Salantai **LT** 39 Mb34
Salar de Aguilar **RCH** 207 Gf58
Salar de Antofalla **RA** 207 Gg58
Salar de Arizaro **RA** 207 Gg58
Salar de Atacama **RCH** 207 Gf57
Salar de Cauchari **RA** 207 Gg57
Salar de Chiguana **BOL** 207 Gg56
Salar de Coipasa **BOL** 206 Gf55
Salar de Empexa **BOL** 206 Gf56
Salar de la Mina **RA** 207 Gg59
Salar del Hombre Muerto **RA** 207 Gg58
Salar de Llamara **RCH** 207 Gf56
Salar de Pajonales **RCH** 207 Gf58
Salar de Pedernales **RCH** 207 Gf59
Salar de Pintados **RCH** 206 Gf56
Salar de Pipanaco **RA** 207 Gg60
Salar de Pocitos **RA** (SA) 207 Gg58
Salar de Uyuni **BOL** 206 Gg56
Salar Pocitos **RA** 207 Gg58
Salar Punta Negra **RCH** 207 Gf58
Salas **E** 26 Ko47
Salas **PE** 196 Ga49
Salas de los Infantes **E** 28 Kr48
Salasil **KSA** 59 Ne32
Salaspils **LV** 39 Me34
Salatiga **RI** 95 Qf49
Sălătrucu **RO** 43 Me45
Salavan **LAO** 89 Qd38
Salavat **IR** 57 Nd26
Salavat **RUS** 54 Nd08
Salavat Abad **IR** 57 Nd28
Sala Vichey **K** 89 Qc39
Salawati **RI** 97 Rf46
Salawin N.P. **THA** 87 Pj36
Sala-y-Gomez-Fracture Zone 190 Fa12
Salayie **LB** 136 Kf42
Salazar **RA** (BA) 209 Gj64
Salbris **F** 25 Lc43
Salcabamba **PE** 197 Gc52
Salcantay, Nevado **PE** 197 Gd52
Salcedo **EC** 196 Ga46
Salcia **RO** 44 Mc46
Salcia **RO** 44 Mc46
Salcia **RO** 45 Me47
Salcia **RO** 45 Me47
Šalčininkai **LT** 39 Mf36
Saldaña **CO** 192 Gc44
Saldaña **E** 26 Kq48
Saldanha **ZA** 154 Lj62
Saldanhabaai **ZA** 154 Lj62
Saldanha Bay **ZA** 154 Lj62
Saldé **SN** 130 Kd37
Saldungaray **RA** (BA) 209 Gk65
Saldus **LV** 39 Mc34
Sale **AUS** (VIC) 111 Sd65
Salé **MA** 125 Kg28
Sale **MYA** 86 Ph35
Salebhatta **IND** (ORS) 83 Pb35
Saleé **RIM** 130 Kf36
Saleh Abad **IR** 57 Ne28
Salehan **AFG** 64 Oa30
Salem **IND** (TNU) 84 Ok40
Salem **USA** (IN) 175 Fg26
Salem **USA** (MO) 175 Fe27
Salem **USA** (NJ) 177 Gc26
Salem **USA** (OR) 168 Dj23
Salem **USA** (SD) 172 Fb24
Salem **USA** (VA) 178 Fk27
Salem **ZA** 155 Md62
Salémata **SN** 136 Kd39
Salemi **I** 36 Ln53
Salem Plateau **USA** 175 Fe27
Sälenfjällen **S** 17 Lg15
Salerno **I** 37 Lp50
Salers **F** 25 Lc45
Sales **BR** (SP) 202 Hf56
Salesópolis **BR** (SP) 205 Hg57
Salewara **IND** (CGH) 83 Pa35
Saleye **CI** 137 Kj41
Salgado **BR** (SE) 201 Jb51
S'Algar **E** 29 Le51
Salgótarján **H** 43 Lu42
Sälgrund **FIN** 38 Mb28
Salgueiro **BR** (PE) 201 Ja50
Salher **IND** 82 Og35
Sali **DZ** 125 Kk32
Sali **HR** 35 Lq47
Šali **RUS** (CHE) 57 Nc24
Salibabu **RI** 91 Rd44
Salibabu **RI** 91 Rd44
Salida **USA** (CO) 171 Eh26
Saliente Alto **E** 27 Ks53
Saligbé **TG** 137 La42
Salihler **TR** 47 Mg51
Salihli **TR** 47 Mj52
Salihorsk **BY** 48 Md19
Salikene **WAG** 136 Kc39
Salikénie **SN** 136 Kc39
Salima **MOC** 147 Mj52
Salima **MW** 153 Mh52
Salima **SUD** 129 Me35
Salimgarh **IND** (RJT) 82 Oh34
Salimi **IND** (ORS) 83 Pb36
Salin **MYA** 86 Ph35
Salina **USA** (KS) 174 Fb26
Salina **USA** (UT) 171 Ee26
Salina Cruz **MEX** (OAX) 183 Fc37
Salina Point **BS** 186 Gc34
Salinas **BR** (MG) 203 Hj54
Salinas **EC** 196 Fk47
Salinas **MEX** (CHH) 180 Eg32
Salinas **MEX** (VC) 183 Fc36
Salinas **PE** 196 Fk49
Salinas **USA** (CA) 170 Dk27
Salinas de Garci Mendoza **BOL** 206 Gg55
Salinas de Hidalgo **MEX** (SLP) 182 Ek34
Salinas Peak **USA** 171 Eg29
Salinas Pueblo Missions Nat. Mon. **USA** 171 Eg28
Salinau **RI** 95 Qj47
Saline Royale **F** 25 Lf43
Salinópolis **BR** (PA) 195 Hg46
Salins-les-Bains **F** 25 Lf44
Salira Indah Beach **RI** 95 Qd48
Salisbury **CDN** (NB) 176 Gh22
Salisbury **GB** 21 Kt39
Salisbury **USA** (MD) 177 Gc26
Salisbury **USA** (NC) 178 Fk28
Salisbury Plain **GB** 21 Kt39
Salispuedas **MEX** 180 Eb30
Săliște **RO** 44 Md45
Salistral **YV** 193 Gh41
Salitral **PE** 196 Ga48
Salitre **BR** (CE) 201 Hk49
Salitre **EC** 196 Ga46
Salitrillo **MEX** (PUE) 182 Fb36
Salka **WAN** 138 Lc40
Šalkar **KZ** 54 Nd09
Salkhad **SYR** 56 Mj29
Sallanches **F** 25 Lg45
Sallent **E** 29 Lb49
Salling **DK** 30 Lj34
Salliqueló **RA** (BA) 209 Gj64
Sallisaw **USA** (OK) 174 Fc28
Sallisbury Island **AUS** 105 Rb63
Sallom **SUD** 135 Mj36
Sallum **ET** 128 Mc30
Salmana **ET** 129 Mg30
Salmas **IR** 57 Nc26
Salme **EST** 39 Mc32
Salmenkylä **FIN** 38 Me28
Salmerón **E** 29 Ks50
Salmiya **KWT** 59 Ne31
Salmo **CDN** (BC) 168 Eb21
Salmon **USA** (ID) 168 Ed23
Salmon Arm **CDN** (BC) 168 Ea20
Salmon Fork **USA/CDN** (AK/YT) 165 Ck12
Salmon Gums **AUS** (WA) 105 Ra62
Salmon River Mountains **USA** 168 Ec23
Salmossi **BF** 131 Kk38
Salo **FIN** 38 Md30
Salò **I** 34 Ll45
Salo **RCA** 140 Lj44
Salon **IND** (UPH) 83 Pa32
Salon-de-Provence **F** 25 Lf47
Salonga Nord, P.N.de la **RDC** 149 Ma46
Salonga Sud, P.N.de la **RDC** 149 Ma47
Salonica **GR** 46 Mc50
Salonta **RO** 43 Mb44
Salpausselkä **FIN** 38 Mf29
Sal Rei **CV** 136 Jj37
Salsacate **RA** (CD) 208 Gh61
Salsbruket **N** 16 Lf13
Salses-le-Château **F** 25 Lc48
Salsomaggiore Terme **I** 34 Lk46
Salta **RA** (SA) 207 Gh58
Salta **RA** 207 Gg58
Saltaire **GB** 21 Kt37
Saltash **GB** 21 Kq40
Saltburn-by-the-Sea **GB** 21 Ku36
Salt Cay **GB** 186 Ge35
Saltcoats **CDN** (SK) 169 Ej20
Salt Desert **IR** 64 Ng28
Saltee Islands **IRL** 19 Ko38
Saltery Bay **CDN** (BC) 168 Dh21
Saltfjellet-Svartisen n.p. **N** 16 Lh12
Saltholm **DK** 30 Ln35
Saltillo **MEX** (COH) 181 Ek33
Salt Lake City **USA** (UT) 171 Ee25
Salto **BR** (SP) 205 Hg57
Salto **I** 36 Ln48
Salto **MEX** (SL) 180 Eg33
Salto **RA** (BA) 209 Gk63
Salto **ROU** 204 Hb61
Salto Angel **YV** 193 Gj42
Salto da Divisa **BR** (MG) 203 Ja54
Salto de Agua **MEX** (CHP) 183 Fd37
Salto de Cavalo **ANG** 148 Lh50
Salto de Eqipantla **MEX** 183 Fc36
Salto de Las Rosas **RA** (MD) 208 Gf63
Salto del Guaíra **PY** 204 Hc58
Salto del Laja **RCH** 208 Gd64
Salto de Pirapora **BR** (SP) 205 Hg57
Salto do Jacuí **BR** (RS) 204 Hd60
Salto Hacha **YV** 193 Gj42
Salton Sea **USA** 170 Ec29
Salt Plains N.W.R. **USA** 174 Fa27
Salt Range **PK** 65 Og29
Salt River Canyon **USA** 171 Ee29
Salt Springs **USA** (FL) 178 Fk31
Saltstraumen **N** 16 Lh12
Saltvik **FIN** 38 Ma30
Saltwater Hot Springs **RC** 75 Ra34
Salua **RI** 96 Qk46
Saluda **USA** (SC) 178 Fk29
SalueBesar **RI** 97 Rb46
Salue Kecil **RI** 97 Rb47
Salug **RP** 91 Rb41
Salugan **RI** 91 Ra45
Salumbar **IND** (RJT) 82 Oh33
Salumpaga **RI** 91 Ra45
Salur **IND** (APH) 83 Pb36
Saluzzo **I** 34 Lh46
Salvador **BR** (BA) 201 Ja52
Salvaterra **BR** (PA) 195 Hf46
Salvatierra **MEX** (GJT) 182 Ek35
Salvatierra-Agurain **E** 28 Ks48
Salvatierra de los Barros **E** 27 Ko52
Salween 87 Pk36
Salyan **AZ** 57 Ne26
Salyersville **USA** (KY) 178 Fj27
Šalyhyne **UA** 48 Mh20
Salza **A** 35 Lq43
Salzach **A** 35 Ln43
Salzach **D** 33 Ln42
Salzbergwerk **A** 35 Lo43
Salzburg **A** 35 Lo43
Salzgitter **D** 32 Ll38
Salzkotten **D** 32 Lj39
Salzwedel **D** 32 Lm38
Sam **G** 148 Lf45
Sam **IND** (RJT) 80 Of32
Sama **PE** 197 Ge54
Samachique **MEX** (CHH) 180 Eg32
Samachvalavičy **BY** 39 Mh37
Samad **OM** 61 Nk34
Samad Abag **IR** 64 Nk29
Samagaltaj **RUS** (TUV) 67 Ph20
Sama Grande **PE** 197 Ge54
Samah **KSA** 59 Nc31
Samail **OM** 61 Nj34
Samaipata **BOL** 206 Gj55
Samakhial **IND** (GUJ) 82 Of34
Samako **RI** 96 Rb46
Samakona **CI** 137 Kg41
Samakoulou **RMM** 136 Kf39
Samakro **CI** 137 Kj43
Samal **RP** 91 Rc42
Samalayuca **MEX** (CHH) 180 Eg30
Samales Group **RP** 91 Ra43
Samal Island **RP** 91 Rc42
Samalkot **IND** (APH) 83 Pb37
Samâlût **ET** 129 Mf31
Samama **RI** 91 Qk44
Saman **PNG** 116 Sh51
Samaná **DOM** 186 Gf36
Samana Cay **BS** 186 Gd34
Samanco **PE** 197 Ga50
Samanda **IND** (MGA) 86 Pf33
Samandağ **TR** 56 Mh27
Samangan = Aybak **AFG** 63 Oe27
Samanlı Dağları **TR** 45 Mk50
Samar **RP** 90 Rc40
Sámara **CR** 184 Fh41
Samarga **RUS** 77 Rk22
Samari **PNG** 115 Sb50
Samaria N.P. **GR** 47 Me55
Samariapo **YV** 193 Gg43
Samarína **GR** 46 Mb50
Samarinda **RI** 95 Qj46
Samarkand **UZ** 63 Od26
Samarqand **UZ** 63 Od26
Samarra **IRQ** 57 Nb28
Samarskoye **KZ** 67 Pb21
Samaru **WAN** 138 Ld40
Samaruma **IND** (CGH) 83 Pb34
Samastipur **IND** (BIH) 83 Pc33
Samasuma Island **PNG** 115 Sc46
Samate **RI** 97 Rf46
Samatiguila **CI** 137 Kg41
Samatwa **EAT** 147 Mj48
Samaúma **BR** (AM) 198 Gj46
Şamaxi **AZ** 57 Ne25
Samba **BF** 137 Kj39
Samba **RCA** 140 Lj43
Samba **RDC** 140 Ma45
Samba **RDC** 146 Md48
Samba 80 Oh29
Samba Caju **ANG** 148 Lh50
Sambaïlo **RG** 136 Kd39
Sambalgou **BF** 137 La39
Sambaliung Mountains **RI** 94 Qj45
Sambalpur **IND** (ORS) 83 Pb35
Sambas **RI** 94 Qe45
Sâmbăta **RO** 43 Mc44
Sambau **RI** 93 Qc46
Sambava **RM** 156 Nf53
Sambhal **IND** (UPH) 81 Ok31
Sambhar **IND** (RJT) 80 Oh32
Sambialgou **BF** 137 La39
Sambir **UA** 43 Md41
Sambo **ANG** 150 Lj52
Samboja **RI** 95 Qj46
Samborondón **EC** 196 Ga46
Sâmbra Oilor **RO** 43 Md43
Sambro **CDN** (NS) 176 Gj23
Sambuca di Sicília **I** 36 Lo53
Samburu **EAK** 145 Mk47
Samburu National Reserve **EAK** 144 Mj45
Sambusu **NAM** 150 Lk54
Sambwa **EAT** 147 Mj48
Samch'ok **ROK** 79 Re27
Samch'onp'o **ROK** 79 Re28
Samding Monastery **CHN** 68 Pf31
Same **EAT** 147 Mj48
Samé **RMM** 130 Ke38
Samen **IR** 57 Ne28
Samer **F** 23 Lb40
Samford **AUS** (QLD) 109 Sg59
Samfya **Z** 146 Me51
Samhah **YE** 61 Ng39
Samharam **OM** 61 Nh37
Sämi **EST** 38 Mg31
Sámi **GR** 46 Ma52
Sami **IND** (GUJ) 82 Of34
Sami **PK** 65 Ob32
Sămica **BG** 45 Me49
Samirah **KSA** 58 Nb32
Samitah **KSA** 60 Nb37
Samjiyon **PRK** 76 Re25
Samka **MYA** 86 Pj35
Šamkir **AZ** 57 Nc25
Samlaut W.S. **K** 89 Qb39
Şamlı **TR** 47 Mh51
Sammallahdenmäki **FIN** 38 Mb29
Samnapur **IND** (MPH) 83 Pa34
Sam Ngao **THA** 88 Pk37
Samnu **LAR** 127 Lh32
Samo **PNG** 116 Sg47
Samoa **ANG** 149 Ma50
Samoa 101 Ba11
Samoa Islands **WS/USA** 100 Ba11
Samobor **HR** 35 Lq45
Samoeng **THA** 87 Pk36
Samoëns **F** 25 Lg44
Samohaji = Vasco da Gama **IND** (GOA) 82 Og38
Samokov **BG** 44 Md48
Samolva **RUS** 39 Mh32
Samorogouan **BF** 137 Kh40
Sámos **GR** 47 Mg53
Sámos **GR** 47 Mg53
Samos **SCG** 44 Ma45
Samosir **RI** 93 Pk44
Samostan Stična **SLO** 42 Lp45
Samothrake **GR** 45 Mf50
Samothráki **GR** 45 Mf50
Samothráki **GR** 45 Mf50
Samoyé **RG** 136 Kf42
Sampa **GH** 137 Kj42
Sampaga **RI** 96 Qk47
Sampaka **RI** 91 Rb45
Sampanahan **RI** 95 Qj47
Sampang **RI** 95 Qg49
Sampano **RI** 96 Ra47
Sampelga **BF** 137 La39
Samphamit Falls **K/LAO** 89 Qc38
Sampit **RI** 95 Qg47
Sampun **PNG** 116 Sg48
Sampwe **RDC** 146 Md50
Samrala **IND** (PJB) 80 Oj30
Samraong **K** 89 Qb38
Samreboi **GH** 137 Kj43
Samro **RUS** 38 Mj32
Samsang **CHN** (TIB) 68 Pb30
Samsø **DK** 30 Ll35
Samson **USA** (AL) 175 Fh30
Sam Son **VN** 87 Qc36
Samsong Temple **PRK** 78 Rc26
Samson Ind. Res. **CDN** 169 Ed19
Samsu **TR** 57 Nb26
Samsun **TR** 56 Mj25
Samtens **D** 32 Lo36
Samthar **IND** (UPH) 83 Ok33
Samtredia **GE** 57 Nb24
Samucumbi **ANG** 150 Lk52
Samuda **RI** 95 Qg47
Samuhú **RA** (CH) 207 Gk59
Samulondo **RDC** 149 Mb50
Samundri **PK** 65 Og30
Samur **AFG** 64 Oa30
Samurai Houses **J** 77 Sa26
Samut Prakan **THA** 88 Qa39
Samut Sakhon **THA** 88 Qa39
Samut Songkhram **THA** 88 Qa39
Samye Monastery **CHN** 69 Pf31
San **RMM** 137 Kh39
San'a **YE** 60 Nc38
Sanaa **YE** 60 Nc38
Sanaba **BF** 137 Kj39
Sanabria **CO** 192 Gb44
Sanadinovo **BG** 45 Me47
SANAE IV **ANT** (SA) 6 Kd33
Sanaga **CAM** 138 Lf44
San Agustín **YV** 193 Gg42
San Agustín de Valle Fértil **RA** (SJ) 208 Gg61
Sanak **USA** (AK) 164 Bj18
Sanak Island **USA** 164 Bj18
Sanak Islands **USA** 164 Bj18
San Alberto **PY** 204 Hc58
San Alejandro **PE** 197 Gc50
Sanam Abu Dom **SUD** 135 Mf36
Sanamxai **LAO** 89 Qd38
Sanana **RI** 97 Rd47
Sanana **RI** 97 Rd47
Sanand **IND** (GUJ) 82 Og34
Sanandağ **IR** 57 Nd28
Sanando **RMM** 137 Kg39
Sânandrei **RO** 44 Mb45
San Andrés **C** 179 Gb35
San Andrés **CO** 185 Fk39
San Andrés **CO** 185 Fk39
San Andrés **E** 124 Kb31
San Andrés **GCA** 183 Ff37
San Andres **RP** 90 Rb39
San Andres **RP** 90 Rc39
San Andrés de Giles **RA** (BA) 209 Ha63
San Andrés Tuxtla **MEX** (VC) 183 Fc36
Sananduva **BR** (RS) 204 He59
San Angelo **USA** (TX) 174 Ek30
Sanankoroba **RMM** 137 Kg39
San Antón **PE** 197 Ge53
San Antonio **BH** 184 Ff37
San Antonio **C** 179 Ga35
San Antonio **CO** 192 Ga45
San Antonio **MEX** (BCS) 180 Ef34
San Antonio **MEX** (CHH) 180 Eg30
San Antonio **MEX** (TM) 181 Fa33
San Antonio **RA** (CA) 207 Gh60
San Antonio **RA** (SL) 208 Gg62
San Antonio **RCH** 208 Ge62
San Antonio **USA** (NM) 171 Eg29
San Antonio **USA** (TX) 181 Fa31
San Antonio **YV** 193 Gg44
San Antonio **YV** 193 Gj42
San Antonio de Areco **RA** (BA) 209 Ha63
San Antonio de Caparo **YV** 192 Ge42
San Antonio de Esquilache **PE** 197 Ge54
San Antonio de Getucha **CO** 192 Gc45
San Antonio del Mar **MEX** (BC) 180 Eb30
San Antonio de los Cobres **RA** (SA) 207 Gg58
San Antonio del Parapetí **BOL** 206 Gj55
San Antonio del Sur **C** 186 Gc35
San Antonio de Táchira **YV** 192 Gd42
San Antonio de Tamanaco **YV** 193 Gg41
San Antonio Mts. **USA** 171 Eh29
San Antonio Oeste **RA** (RN) 208 Gh66
San Antonio Rayon **MEX** (TM) 182 Fa34
Sanarate **GCA** 184 Fe38
Sanare **YV** 193 Gf40
Sanaré **YV** 193 Gf41
Sanaroa Island **PNG** 116 Sf50
Sanary-sur-Mer **F** 25 Lf47
Sanasombun **LAO** 89 Qc38
San Augustin **CO** 192 Gb44
San Augustín **MEX** (BC) 180 Ec31
San Augustin **RP** 90 Rb39
San Augustine **USA** (TX) 174 Fc30
Sanaw **OM** 61 Nj34
Sanaw **YE** 61 Nf37
Sanawad **IND** (MPH) 82 Oj34
San Bartolo **BOL** 206 Gg53
San Bartolo **MEX** (SLP) 182 Ek34
San Bartolo **PA** 185 Fk41
San Bartolo **PE** 197 Gb52
San Bartolomé de la Torre **E** 27 Kn53
San Bartolomé de Tirajana **E** 124 Kc32
San Bartolomeo in Galdo **I** 37 Lq49
San Bautista **ROU** 209 Hc63
Sanbei Yangshan **CHN** (NMZ) 72 Qd26
San Benedetto del Tronto **I** 35 Lo48
San Benedetto Po **I** 34 Ll45
San Benito **NIC** 184 Fg39
San Benito **USA** (TX) 181 Fb32
San Benito Abad **CO** 192 Gc41
San Benito Mtn. **USA** 170 Dk27
San Bernado **RA** (BA) 209 Gk64
San Bernardino **USA** (CA) 170 Eb28
San Bernardino de Milpillas Chico **MEX** (DGO) 181 Eh34
San Bernard N.W.R. **USA** 181 Fc31
San Bernardo **MEX** (DGO) 181 Eh32
San Bernardo **MEX** (SO) 180 Ef32
San Bernardo **RA** (CH) 207 Gk59
San Bernardo del Viento **CO** 192 Gc41
San Blas **MEX** (COH) 181 Ek32
San Blas **MEX** (NYT) 182 Eh35
San Blas **MEX** (SL) 180 Ef32
San Borja **BOL** 206 Gg53
San Borjitas **MEX** 180 Ed32
San Buenaventura **MEX** (COH) 181 Ek32
Sanca **CDN** (BC) 168 Eb21
Sancak **TR** 57 Na26
San Carlos **CR** 185 Fh40
San Carlos **GQ** 138 Le44
San Carlos **MEX** (BC) 180 Ec31
San Carlos **MEX** (BCS) 180 Ed33
San Carlos **MEX** (COH) 181 Ek31
San Carlos **MEX** (SO) 180 Ee32
San Carlos **NIC** 185 Fh40
San Carlos **PA** 185 Ga41
San Carlos **PY** 202 Hb57
San Carlos **RA** (CR) 204 Hc59
San Carlos **RA** (MD) 208 Gf62
San Carlos **RA** (SA) 207 Gh58
San Carlos **RCH** 208 Ge64
San Carlos **ROU** 209 Hc63
San Carlos **RP** 90 Ra38
San Carlos **RP** 90 Rb40
San Carlos **USA** (AZ) 171 Ee29
San Carlos **YV** 193 Gf41
San Carlos de Bariloche **RA** (RN) 208 Ge66
San Carlos de Bolívar **RA** (BA) 209 Gk64
San Carlos de Guaroa **CO** 192 Gd44
San Carlos del Zulia **YV** 192 Ge41
San Carlos de Río Negro **YV** 193 Gg45
San Carlos Ind. Res. **USA** 171 Ee29
San Carlos Park **USA** (FL) 179 Fk32
San Cataldo **I** 36 Lo53
San Cataldo **I** 37 Lt50
San Cayetano **CO** 192 Gc43
San Cayetano **RA** (BA) 209 Ha65
Sancerre **F** 25 Lc43
Sancha **CHN** (GZG) 74 Qe33
Sancha **CHN** (SAX) 72 Qf26
Sanchahe **CHN** (JLN) 76 Rc23
Sanchakou **CHN** (XUZ) 66 Ok26
Sánchez **DOM** 186 Gf36
Sanchez, Cerro **RA** 210 Gf71
Sanchi **IND** (MPH) 82 Oj34
Sanchi **IND** 82 Oj34
Sanchidrián **E** 26 Kq50
Sanchor **IND** (RJT) 82 Of33
San Christobal **DOM** 186 Ge36
San Christoval Range **CDN** 166 De19
San Cirilo, Cerro **PE** 196 Ga49
San Ciro de Acosta **MEX** (SLP) 182 Fa35
San Clemente **E** 29 Ks51
San Clemente **RCH** 208 Ge63
San Clemente = Cerro San Valentín **RCH** 210 Gd69
San Clemente **USA** (CA) 170 Eb29
San Clemente del Tuyú **RA** (BA) 209 Hb64
San Clemente Island **USA** 170 Ea29
Sanclerlândia **BR** (GO) 202 He54
Sancoins **F** 25 Lc44
Sancos **PE** 197 Gd53
San Cosme y Damián **PY** 204 Hb59
San Cristóbal **BOL** 206 Gg56
San Cristobal **RA** (SF) 207 Gk61
San Cristóbal **RCH** 207 Gf57
San Cristóbal **YV** 192 Gd42
San Cristóbal de Entreviñas **E** 26 Kp48
San Cristóbal de la Barranca **MEX** (JLC) 182 Ej35
San Cristóbal de las Casas **MEX** (CHP) 183 Fd37
Sancti Spiritu **RA** (SF) 209 Gj63
Sancti-Spíritus **C** 179 Ga35
Sancti-Spíritus **E** 26 Ko50
Sanctuaire de Mont Iboundji **G** 148 Lf46
Sančursk **RUS** 48 Nd17
Sand **N** 30 Lg31
Sand **N** 30 Lm30
Sanda **FIN** 38 Ma30
Sandai **RI** 95 Qf46
Sandakan **MAL** 91 Qk43
Sandal **EAK** 144 Mh45
Sandama **RMM** 136 Kf39
Sandan **K** 89 Qd39
Sandando **ANG** 151 Ma51
Sandane **N** 17 Ld15
San Daniele di Friuli **I** 35 Lo44
Sandanski **BG** 44 Md49
Sandaré **RMM** 130 Ke38
Sanday **GB** 20 Ks31
Sandbach **GB** 21 Ks37
Sandbanks Prov. Park **CDN** 177 Gb23
Sandberg **ZA** 154 Lk62
Sand Dunes (Tottori) **J** 79 Rh28
Sande **D** 32 Lj37
Sandefjord **N** 30 Ll31
Sandégué **CI** 137 Kj42
Sandema **GH** 137 Kk40
Sanderao **IND** (RJT) 82 Og33
Sandercock Nunataks 7 Nc32
Sanderk **IR** 64 Nj32
Sanders **USA** (AZ) 171 Ef28
Sanderson **USA** (TX) 181 Ej30
Sandersville **USA** (GA) 178 Fj29
Sandfire Flat **AUS** (WA) 102 Ra55
Sandgerði **IS** 18 Js26
Sandhammeren **S** 31 Lp35
Sand Hill **BH** 184 Ff37
Sandhill **USA** (MS) 175 Ff29
Sand Hills **GUY** 194 Ha42
Sand Hills **USA** 172 Ek24
Sandi **SUD** 135 Mg37
Sandia **PE** 206 Gf53
San Diego **USA** (CA) 170 Eb29
San Diego **USA** (TX) 181 Fa32
San Diego de Alcalá **MEX** (CHH) 181 Eh31
San Diego de Cabrutica **YV** 193 Gh41
San Diego de la Unión **MEX** (GJT) 182 Ek35
Sandıklı **TR** 56 Mf26
Sandila **IND** (UPH) 83 Pa32
Sandilands Prov. Forest **CDN** 172 Fb21
Sandiman, Mount **AUS** 104 Qh58
Sanding **RI** 93 Qa47
Sandino **C** 179 Fh34
Sand in Taufers = Campo Túres **I** 34 Lm44
San Dionisio **RP** 75 Ra36
Sandl **A** 42 Lq42
Sandnes **N** 30 Lf32
Sandnessjøen **N** 16 Lg12
Sando **MOC** 153 Mh54
Sandoa **RDC** 149 Mb50
Sandoméri **GR** 46 Mb53
Sandomierz **PL** 41 Mb40
Sandön **FIN** 38 Mb27
San Donà di Piave **I** 35 Ln45
Sandougou **CI** 137 Kh42
Sandovo **RUS** 48 Mj16
Sandoway **MYA** 86 Ph36
Sandoy **DK** 18 Ko29
Sandøysund **N** 30 Ll31
Sandpit **CDN** (BC) 166 De19
Sand Point **USA** (AK) 164 Bk18
Sandpoint **USA** (ID) 168 Eb21
Sandrakatsy **RM** 156 Ne54
Sandrandahy **RM** 157 Nd56
Sandray **GB** 20 Kn34
Sandringham **AUS** (QLD) 108 Rk58
Šandrivka **UA** 49 Mh21
Sand Springs **USA** (MT) 169 Eg22
Sand Springs **USA** (OK) 174 Fb27
Sandstad **N** 16 Le14
Sandstone **AUS** (WA) 104 Qj59
Sandur **IND** (KTK) 84 Oj38
Sandusky **USA** (MI) 173 Fj24
Sandusky **USA** (OH) 173 Fj25
Sandu Suizu **CHN** (GZH) 74 Qd32
Sandveld Nature Reserve **ZA** 155 Mc59
Sandverhaar **NAM** 154 Lj59
Sandvik **S** 31 Lr33
Sandvika **N** 16 Lg13
Sandviken **S** 31 Lr30
Sandvikvåg **N** 30 Lf31
Sandwich **GB** 21 Lb39
Sandwich **USA** (IL) 173 Ff25
Sandwich Bay **NAM** 154 Lh57
Sandwich Harbour **NAM** 154 Lh57
Sandwip Island **BD** 86 Pf34
Sandy **GB** 21 Ku38
Sandy **USA** (UT) 171 Ee25
Sandy Bar **CDN** 172 Fb19
Sandy Bay **NZ** 112 Th63
Sandy Bay Ind. Res. **CDN** 172 Fa20
Sandy Bight **AUS** 105 Rb62
Sandy Cape **AUS** (TAS) 111 Sc66
Sandy Cape **AUS** 109 Sg58
Sandy Cove **CDN** 177 Hb20
Sandy Desert **PK** 65 Ob31
Sandy Hills **USA** 174 Fc29
Sandykachi **TM** 62 Ob27
Sandy Lake **CDN** (AB) 167 Ed18
Sandy Lake **CDN** (ON) 163 Fb08
Sandy Lake **CDN** 177 Hb21
Sandy Point **BS** 179 Gb32
Sandy Point **GB** 186 Gd35
Sandy Point **IND** 88 Pg40
Sandy's Beach **USA** (HI) 170 Cb35
Sané **RMM** 131 Kk37
San Estanislao **CO** 192 Gc40
San Estanislao **PY** 204 Hb58
San Estebán **HN** 184 Fh38
San Esteban de Gormaz **E** 26 Kr49
San Evaristo **MEX** (BCS) 180 Ee33
San Faustino **MEX** (BC) 180 Eb29
San Felipe **CO** 192 Gc40
San Felipe **CO** 193 Gg45
San Felipe **MEX** (BC) 180 Ec30
San Felipe **MEX** (GJT) 182 Ek35
San Felipe **RCH** 208 Ge62
San Felipe **YV** 193 Gf40
San Felipe de Jesús **MEX** (CHH) 180 Eg32

San Felipe de Vichayal ⊡ PE 196 Fk48
San Felipe Jalapa de Díaz ⊡ MEX (OAX) 182 Fb36
San Felipe Nuevo Mercurio ⊡ MEX (ZCT) 181 Ej33
San Félix ⊡ RCH 207 Ge60
San Félix ⊡ ROU 204 Ha62
San Félix ⊡ YV 192 Ge40
San Ferdinando di Púglia ⊡ I 37 Lq49
San Fermín ⊡ MEX (DGO) 181 Eh32
Sanfermino ⊡ E 28 Kt48
San Fernando ⊡ E 27 Ko54
San Fernando ⊡ MEX (TM) 181 Fa33
San Fernando ⊡ RCH 208 Ge63
San Fernando ⊡ RP 90 Ra37
San Fernando ⊡ RP 90 Ra38
San Fernando ⊡ TT 187 Gk40
San Fernando de Apure ⊡ YV 193 Gg42
San Fernando de Atabapo ⊡ YV 193 Gg43
San Fernando del Valle de Catamarca ⊡ RA (CA) 207 Gh60
Sänfjällets n.p. ⊡ S 17 Lg14
Sanford ⊡ CDN (MB) 172 Fb21
Sanford ⊡ USA (FL) 178 Fk31
Sanford ⊡ USA (ME) 177 Ge24
Sanford ⊡ USA (NC) 178 Ga28
Sanford, Mount ⊡ USA (AK) 165 Ch14
San Francesco d'Arezzo ⊡ I 34 Lm47
San Francisco ⊡ BOL 206 Gh53
San Francisco ⊡ BOL 206 Gh54
San Francisco ⊡ MEX (CHH) 181 Eh32
San Francisco ⊡ RA 185 Fk41
San Francisco ⊡ PE 197 Gd52
San Francisco ⊡ RCH (CD) 207 Gj61
San Francisco ⊡ YV 193 Gk43
San Francisco de Becerra ⊡ HN 184 Ff38
San Francisco de Bellocq ⊡ RA (BA) 209 Gk65
San Francisco de Borja ⊡ MEX (CHH) 180 Eg32
San Francisco de la Paz ⊡ HN 184 Fg38
San Francisco del Chañar ⊡ RA (CD) 207 Gj60
San Francisco del Laishi ⊡ RA (FO) 204 Ha59
San Francisco del Monte de Oro ⊡ RA (SL) 208 Gg62
San Francisco del Rincón ⊡ MEX (GJT) 182 Ek35
San Francisco de Mostazal ⊡ RCH 208 Ge62
San Francisco Gotera ⊡ ES 184 Ff39
San Francisco (BC) ⊡ MEX 180 Ed31
San Fratello ⊡ I 37 Lp52
Sang ⊡ GH 137 Kk41
Sanga ⊡ BF 137 La40
Sanga = Makaloge ⊡ MOC 146 Mh52
Sanga ⊡ RMM 131 Kj38
San Gabriel ⊡ EC 196 Gb45
San Gabriel Mts. ⊡ USA 170 Ea28
Sangala ⊡ G 148 Lf46
San Galgano ⊡ I 34 Lm47
Sangali ⊡ IND (APH) 85 Ok38
San Gallan ⊡ PE 197 Gb52
Sangam (Allahabad) ⊡ IND 83 Pa33
Sangameshwar ⊡ IND (MHT) 82 Og37
Sangamner ⊡ IND (MHT) 82 Oh36
Sangan ⊡ IR 84 Oa29
Sanganeb Atoll Marine N.P. ⊡ SUD 135 Mj36
Sangar ⊡ IR 57 Ne27
Sangar ⊡ RUS 55 Rb06
Sangarafa ⊡ RIM 130 Kd37
Sangardo ⊡ RG 136 Ke41
Sangareddi ⊡ IND (APH) 82 Og37
Sangarhi ⊡ IND (MHT) 83 Pa35
Sangasanga ⊡ RI 95 Qj46
Sangaste ⊡ EST 39 Mg33
Sangatanga ⊡ G 148 Le46
San Gavino Monreale ⊡ I 36 Lj51
Sangay, P.N. ⊡ EC 196 Gb46
Sangay, Volcán ⊡ EC 196 Ga47
Sangazi ⊡ TR 56 Me25
Sangbé ⊡ CAM 139 Lg42
Sangdo ⊡ AFG 64 Ob28
Sangcharak = Tokzar ⊡ AFG 63 Oc28
Sang Chom ⊡ THA 87 Qb36
Sange ⊡ RDC 146 Me49
Sangeang ⊡ RI 96 Qk50
San Genaro Norte ⊡ RA (SF) 209 Gk62
Sangejo = Sanxenxo ⊡ E 26 Km48
Sângeorgiu de Pădure ⊡ RO 43 Me44
Sângeorz-Bãi ⊡ RO 43 Me43
Sângerei ⊡ MD 49 Me22
Sangerfield ⊡ USA (NY) 177 Gc24
San Gergorio ⊡ RA (SF) 209 Gj63
Sangha ⊡ D 32 Lm39
San Germán ⊡ USA (PR) 187 Gg36
Sângeru ⊡ RO 45 Mg45
Sanggau ⊡ RI 95 Qf45
Sanghar ⊡ PK 65 Oe32
Sangihe ⊡ RI 91 Rc44
San Gil ⊡ CO 192 Gd42
San Gimignano ⊡ I 34 Lm47
Sangin ⊡ AFG 65 Oc29
San Giovanni ⊡ I 34 Lm47
San Giovanni di Sinis ⊡ I 36 Lj51
San Giovanni in Fiore ⊡ I 37 Lr51
San Giovanni in Persiceto ⊡ I 34 Lm46
San Giovanni Rotondo ⊡ I 37 Lq48
San Giovanni Valdarno ⊡ I 34 Lm47
San Giuliano Terme ⊡ I 34 Ll47
San Giusto di Trieste ⊡ I 35 Lo45
Sangiyn Dalay ⊡ MNG 72 Qg24
Sangiyn Dalay ⊡ MNG 70 Qc22
Sangkhla Buri ⊡ THA 88 Pk38
Sangkulirang ⊡ RI 95 Qj45
Sangngen Andet ⊡ K 89 Qd39
Sanglang ⊡ CHN (GZH) 74 Qd33
Sangli ⊡ IND (MHT) 82 Oh37
Sanglia Dol ⊡ RI 97 Rf49
Sangmélima ⊡ CAM 139 Lg42
Sango ⊡ ZW 152 Mf56
Sangod ⊡ IND (RJT) 82 Oj33
Sangola ⊡ IND (MHT) 82 Oh37
Sangolquí ⊡ EC 196 Ga46
Sangoshe ⊡ RB 151 Mb55
Sangpang Bum ⊡ MYA 86 Ph32
Sangre de Christo Mts. ⊡ USA 171 Ek27
Sangre de Cristo Mts. ⊡ USA 171 Ej27

San Gregorio ⊡ PE 197 Gd50
San Gregorio Carrio ⊡ ROU 204 Hb62
San Gregorio de Polanco ⊡ ROU 204 Hc62
Sangre Grande ⊡ TT 187 Gk40
Sangrampur ⊡ IND (PJB) 80 Oh30
Sangrur ⊡ IND (PJB) 80 Oh30
Sangsang ⊡ CHN (TIB) 68 Pd31
Sangsit ⊡ RI 95 Qh50
Sangüesa ⊡ E 28 Kt48
Sangüeya ⊡ RG 136 Ke40
Sanguiana ⊡ RG 136 Ke40
San Guillermo, P.N. ⊡ RA 207 Gf60
Sanguily ⊡ C 179 Ga35
Sangyai ⊡ CHN (HUN) 74 Qf31
Sanhe ⊡ CHN (GZH) 74 Qd32
Sanhe ⊡ CHN (NMZ) 71 Ra20
Sanhuizhen ⊡ CHN (SCH) 74 Qd30
Sani ⊡ RIM 130 Kf37
Sanibel ⊡ USA (FL) 179 Fj32
Sanibel Island ⊡ USA (FL) 179 Fj32
San Ignacio ⊡ BH 184 Ff37
San Ignacio ⊡ CR 185 Fh41
San Ignacio ⊡ MEX (BCS) 180 Ed32
San Ignacio ⊡ MEX (NL) 181 Fa32
San Ignacio ⊡ MEX (SL) 180 Eg33
San Ignacio ⊡ MEX (SLP) 182 Ek34
San Ignacio ⊡ PE 196 Ga48
San Ignacio de Moxos ⊡ BOL 206 Gh53
San Ignacio de Velasco ⊡ BOL 206 Gk54
San Ignacio Guazú ⊡ PY 204 Hb59
San Ignacio Mini ⊡ RA (MI) 204 Hc59
San Ignacio Mini ⊡ RA 204 Hc59
San Ignacio Río Muerto ⊡ MEX (SO) 180 Ed32
San'in-kaigan N.P. ⊡ J 79 Rh28
Sanipah ⊡ RI 95 Qj47
San Pass ⊡ LS/ZA 155 Me60
San Isidro ⊡ NIC 184 Fg39
San Isidro ⊡ RA (BA) 209 Ha63
San Isidro ⊡ RP 90 Rc39
San Isidro ⊡ RP 91 Rd42
San Isidro de El General ⊡ CR 185 Fj41
San Isidro del Curuguaty ⊡ PY 204 Hc58
Sanitz ⊡ D 32 Ln36
Saniyat al Daffah ⊡ LAR 128 Mc30
San Jacinto ⊡ PE 196 Fk47
San Jacinto ⊡ RP 90 Rb39
San Jaime de la Frontera ⊡ RA (ER) 204 Ha61
San Javier ⊡ BOL 206 Gh53
San Javier ⊡ E 29 Ku53
San Javier ⊡ MEX (BCS) 180 Ee33
San Javier ⊡ RA (MI) 204 Hc59
San Javier ⊡ RA 204 Ha61
San Javier ⊡ RCH 208 Ge63
San Javier ⊡ ROU 204 Ha62
Sanjay Gandhi N.P. ⊡ IND 82 Og36
San Jerónimo ⊡ MEX (VC) 182 Fb35
San Jerónimo ⊡ MEX (ZCT) 181 Ej33
Sanjia ⊡ CHN (GDG) 75 Qf35
Sanjiang ⊡ CHN (GZG) 74 Qe33
Sanjiangkou ⊡ CHN (YUN) 87 Qa32
San Joaquin ⊡ BOL 206 Gh52
San Joaquin, Cerro ⊡ EC 197 Ff46
San Joaquín ⊡ MEX (QRT) 182 Fa35
San Joaquin ⊡ RP 90 Rb40
San Joaquin Valley ⊡ USA 170 Ea27
San Jorge ⊡ CO 193 Gf42
San Jorge ⊡ NIC 184 Fh40
San Jorge ⊡ ROU 209 Gk61
San Jorge Island ⊡ SOL 117 Se50
San José ⊡ CO 192 Gh54
San José ⊡ CR 185 Fh41
San José ⊡ PY 204 Hb58
San José ⊡ RA (MI) 204 Hc59
San José ⊡ RP 90 Ra39
San José ⊡ RP 90 Ra38
San José ⊡ RP 90 Ra37
San José ⊡ USA (CA) 170 Dk27
San José de Buenavista ⊡ RP 90 Ra40
San José de Buja ⊡ YV 193 Gj41
San José de Chimbo ⊡ EC 196 Ga46
San José de Chiquitos ⊡ BOL 206 Gk54
San José de Comondú ⊡ MEX (BCS) 180 Ee32
San José de Feliciano ⊡ RA (ER) 204 Ha61
San José de Gracia ⊡ MEX (BCS) 180 Ed32
San José de Guaribe ⊡ YV 193 Gh41
San José de Jáchal ⊡ RA (SJ) 207 Gf61
San José de la Costa ⊡ YV 193 Gh41
San José de la Dormida ⊡ RA (CD) 207 Gj61
San José de la Esquina ⊡ RA (SF) 209 Gk62
San José de La Mariquina ⊡ RCH 208 Gd65
San José de la Piedra ⊡ RA (BC) 180 Ec31
San José de las Lajas ⊡ C 179 Fj34
San José de las Palomas ⊡ MEX (BC) 180 Ec31
San José de las Salinas ⊡ RA (CD) 207 Gh60
San José del Bocay ⊡ NIC 184 Fh39
San José del Cabo ⊡ MEX (BCS) 180 Ef34
San José del Guaviare ⊡ CO 192 Gd44
San José del Monte ⊡ RP 90 Ra38
San José del Morro ⊡ RA (SL) 208 Gh62
San José de los Molinos ⊡ PE 197 Gc52
San José de Lourdes ⊡ PE 196 Ga48
San José del Palmar ⊡ CO 192 Gb43
San José del Progreso ⊡ MEX (OAX) 182 Fb37

San José de Maipo ⊡ RCH 208 Ge62
San José de Mayo ⊡ ROU 209 Hb63
San José de Moradillas ⊡ MEX (SO) 180 Ee31
San José de Ocoa ⊡ DOM 186 Ge36
San José de Pimas ⊡ MEX (SO) 180 Ee31
San José de Quero ⊡ PE 197 Gc52
San José de Tiznados ⊡ YV 193 Gg41
San José Island ⊡ USA 181 Fb32
San José, Volcán ⊡ RA/RCH 208 Gf62
San Juán ⊡ CR/NIC 185 Fh40
San Juan ⊡ DOM 186 Ge36
San Juan ⊡ PE 197 Gc52
San Juan ⊡ RA (SJ) 208 Gf61
San Juan ⊡ RA 207 Gd61
San Juan ⊡ RP 90 Ra39
San Juan ⊡ RIM 130 Kf37
San Juan ⊡ USA (PR)
San Juan ⊡ YV 192 Gd40
San Juan Bautista ⊡ PY 204 Hb59
San Juan Bautista ⊡ RCH
San Juan de Arama ⊡ CO 192 Gd44
San Juan de Flores ⊡ HN 184 Fg38
San Juan de Guadalupe ⊡ MEX (DGO) 181 Ej33
San Juan del César ⊡ CO 192 Gd40
San Juán de Limay ⊡ NIC 184 Fg39
San Juán de los Cayos ⊡ YV 193 Gf40
San Juan de los Lagos ⊡ MEX (JLC) 182 Ej35
San Juán de los Lagos ⊡ MEX (JLC) 182 Ej35
San Juán de los Morros ⊡ YV 193 Gg41
San Juan del Río ⊡ MEX (DGO) 181 Eh33
San Juan del Rio ⊡ MEX (QRT) 182 Fa35
San Juan del Rio ⊡ MEX (SO) 180 Ef30
San Juan del Sur ⊡ NIC 184 Fh40
San Juan de Manapiare ⊡ YV 193 Gg43
San Juán de Payara ⊡ YV 193 Gg42
San Juán de Urabá ⊡ CO 192 Gb41
San Juan de Yanac ⊡ PE 197 Gc52
San Juan Evangelista ⊡ MEX (VC) 183 Fc37
San Juanico ⊡ MEX (BCS) 180 Ed32
San Juanito ⊡ MEX (CHH)
San Juán Ixcaquixtla ⊡ MEX (PUE) 182 Fb37
San Juan Mts. ⊡ USA 171 Eg27
San Juan Nepomuceno ⊡ CO 192 Gc41
San Juan Nepomuceno ⊡ PY 204 Hc59
San Juan y Martinez ⊡ C 179 Fj34
San Justo ⊡ RA (BA) 209 Ha63
San Justo ⊡ RA (SF) 207 Gk61
Sankadiokro ⊡ CI 137 Kj42
Sankanbiaiwa, Mount ⊡ WAL
Sankarayinarkovil ⊡ IND (TNU) 84 Oj41
Sankaridrog ⊡ IND (TNU) 84 Oj40
Sankeshwar ⊡ IND (KTK) 82 Oh37
Sankha ⊡ THA 89 Qd38
Sankosh ⊡ BHT 86 Pf32
Sankra ⊡ IND (RJT) 80 Of32
Sankt André ⊡ A 35 Lr44
Sankt Anna ⊡ S 31 Lr32
Sankt Annen in Annaberg-Buchholz ⊡ D 33 Ln40
Sankt Anton ⊡ A 34 Ll43
Sankt Brigitta ⊡ FIN 16 Mb14
Sankt Efrasinnia monastyr ⊡ BY 48 Me18
Sankt Elisabeth in Marburg ⊡
Sankt Florian ⊡ A 42 Lp42
Sankt Gallen ⊡ CH 34 Lk43
Sankt Georgen ⊡ D 33 Lj42
Sankt Georg in Wiener Neustadt ⊡ A 35 Lr43
Sankt Gilgen ⊡ S 35 Lo43
Sankt Goar ⊡ D 33 Lh40
Sankt Gotthard ⊡ CH 34 Lj44
Sankt Ingbert ⊡ D 33 Lj41
Sankt Jakob ⊡ A 34 Ln44
Sankt Johann ⊡ A 34 Ln43
Sankt Johann ⊡ A 35 Lo43
Sankt Leon-Rot ⊡ D 33 Lj41
Sankt Martin ⊡ CH 34 Lk44
Sankt Margrethen ⊡ CH 34 Lk43
Sankt Michael ⊡ A BY 48 Md19
Sankt Michaelisdonn ⊡ D 32 Lk36
Sankt-Peterburg ⊡ RUS 38 Mi31
Sankt Peter-Ording ⊡ D 32 Lj36
Sankt Pölten ⊡ A 42 Lq42
Sankt Sophia ⊡ BY 48 Me18
Sankt Ulrich = Ortisei ⊡ I 34 Lm44
Sankt Valentin ⊡ A 42 Lp42
Sankt Veit an der Glan ⊡ A 35 Lp44
Sankt Vika ⊡ S 31 Ls32
Sankt Wendel ⊡ D 33 Lh41
Sankuru ⊡ RDC 149 Mb47
San Leo ⊡ I 34 Ln47
San Leonardo de Yagüe ⊡ E 26 Kr49
Sanlitian ⊡ CHN (HUB) 75 Qh30
Şanlıurfa ⊡ TR 56 Mk27
San Lorenzo ⊡ BOL 206 Ha54
San Lorenzo ⊡ EC 196 Ga45
San Lorenzo ⊡ MEX (JLC) 182 Fb35
San Lorenzo ⊡ PE 198 Gf51
San Lorenzo ⊡ PY 204 Hb58
San Lorenzo ⊡ RA (SF) 209 Gk62
San Lorenzo, Cerro ⊡ RA 196 Ga49
San Lorenzo de Calatrava ⊡ E 27 Kr50
San Lorenzo de El Escorial ⊡ E 27 Kq50
San Lorenzo de la Parrilla ⊡ E 29 Ks51
San Lorenzo Tenochtitlan ⊡ MEX 183 Fc37
San Lourdes ⊡ BOL 198 Gf51
Sanlúcar de Barrameda ⊡ E 27 Ko54
Sanlúcar de Guadiana ⊡ E 26 Km54
San Lucas ⊡ BOL 206 Gh56
San Lucas ⊡ MEX (BCS)

San Lucas ⊡ USA (CA) 170 Dk27
San Lucas de Abajo ⊡ (ZCT) 181 Ej33
San Lúcido ⊡ I 37 Lr51
San Luis ⊡ C 186 Gc35
San Luis ⊡ GCA 183 Ff37
San Luis ⊡ MEX (SO) 180 Ee31
San Luis ⊡ PE 197 Gd50
San Luis ⊡ RA (SL) 208 Gg62
San Luis ⊡ RCH 207 Gf59
San Luis ⊡ USA (AZ) 170 Eb28
San Luis ⊡ USA (CO) 171 Eh27
San Luis ⊡ YV 193 Gf40
San Luis al Medio ⊡ ROU 204 Hd62
San Luis de la Loma ⊡ MEX (GUR) 182 Ek37
San Luis de la Paz ⊡ MEX (GJT) 182 Ek35
San Luis del Cordero ⊡ MEX (DGO) 181 Ej33
San Luis de Montagnes Belos ⊡ BR (GO) 202 He54
San Luis de Palmar ⊡ RA (CR) 204 Ha59
San Luis de Shuaro ⊡ PE 197 Gc51
San Luis Gonzaga ⊡ MEX (BCS) 180 Ee33
San Luis Obispo ⊡ USA (CA) 170 Dk28
San Luis Potosí ⊡ MEX (SLP) 182 Ek34
San Luis Potosí ⊡ MEX 182 Ek34
San Luis Río Colorado ⊡ MEX (SO) 180 Ec29
San Luis Valley ⊡ USA 171 Eh27
Sanluri ⊡ I 36 Lj51
San Manuel ⊡ USA (AZ) 171 Ee29
San Marco ⊡ RP 90 Rb40
San Marco ⊡ I 34 Ln45
San Marco ⊡ MEX (TB) 183 Fe37
San Marco in Lámis ⊡ I 37 Lq49
San Marcos ⊡ BR (PA) 195 Hh46
San Marcos ⊡ CO 192 Gc41
San Marcos ⊡ MEX (GUR) 182 Fa37
San Marcos ⊡ MEX (GUR)
San Marcos ⊡ PE 196 Ga49
San Marcos ⊡ RP 90 Rb37
San Marino ⊡ RSM 34 Ln47
San Marino ⊡ RSM 34 Ln47
San Marino ⊡ AUS (SA) 108 Rh60
San Marino ⊡ RP 90 Rb37
San Martin ⊡ BOL 206 Gh52
San Martin ⊡ RA (CA) 207 Gh60
San Martín ⊡ RA (MD) 208 Gf62
San Martín ⊡ ANT (RA) 6 Hb31
San Martín 2 ⊡ RA (FO) 204 Ha58
San Martín de Frómista ⊡ E 26 Kq48
San Martín de los Andes ⊡ RA (NE) 208 Ge66
San Martin del Pimpollar ⊡ E 27 Kp50
San Martin de Montalbán ⊡ E 27 Kq51
San Martin de Valdeiglesias ⊡ E 27 Kq50
San Martino di Castrozza ⊡ I 34 Ln44
San Martín Texmelucan ⊡ MEX (PUE) 182 Fa36
San Mateo ⊡ CR 185 Fh41
San Mateo ⊡ EC 196 Fk46
San Mateo ⊡ USA (CA) 170 Dk27
San Mateo ⊡ USA (NM) 171 Eg28
San Mateo ⊡ YV 193 Gh41
San Mateo Ixtatán ⊡ GCA 184 Fe38
San Matias ⊡ BOL 206 Ha54
Sanmaur ⊡ CDN (QC) 176 Gd22
Sanmaxia ⊡ CHN (ZG) 75 Ra31
Sanmenxia ⊡ CHN (HNN) 72 Qf28
San Miguel ⊡ BOL 206 Gk54
San Miguel ⊡ CO 196 Gb45
San Miguel ⊡ CO 196 Ga45
San Miguel ⊡ CO/EC 196 Gb45
San Miguel ⊡ ES 184 Ff39
San Miguel ⊡ MEX (COH) 181 Ej31
San Miguel ⊡ PA 185 Ga41
San Miguel ⊡ PE 196 Ga49
San Miguel ⊡ PE 197 Gd52
San Miguel ⊡ RA (BA) 209 Ha63
San Miguel ⊡ RA (CR) 204 Ha59
San Miguel ⊡ RP 90 Ra38
San Miguel ⊡ RP 90 Rd41
San Miguel ⊡ USA (AZ) 171 Ee30
San Miguel ⊡ USA (CA) 170 Dk28
San Miguel de Allende ⊡ MEX (GJT) 182 Ek35
San Miguel de Azapa ⊡ RCH 206 Gf56
San Miguel de Baga ⊡ C 179 Gb35
San Miguel de Huachi ⊡ BOL 206 Gg53
San Miguel del Cantil ⊡ MEX (DGO) 180 Eg33
San Miguel del Monte ⊡ RA (BA) 209 Ha63
San Miguel de Salinas ⊡ E 29 Ku53
San Miguel de Temoaya ⊡ MEX (DGO) 181 Eh34
San Miguel de Tucumán ⊡ RA (TU) 207 Gh59
San Miguel do Araguaia ⊡ BR (GO) 200 He52
San Miguelito ⊡ HN 184 Ff38
San Miguelito ⊡ NIC 185 Fh40
San Miguel Palmas ⊡ MEX (QRT) 182 Fa35
San Miguel Suchixtepec ⊡ MEX (OAX) 183 Fb37
Sânmihaiu de Câmpie ⊡ RO 43 Me44
San Miniato ⊡ I 34 Ll47
Sanna ⊡ IND (MHT) 82 Og35
San Narciso ⊡ RP 90 Ra38
San Nicandro Gargánico ⊡ I 37 Lq49
San Nicolás ⊡ MEX (SO) 180 Ef31
San Nicolás de la Joya ⊡ MEX (CHH) 180 Eg32
San Nicolás de los Arrócos ⊡ RA (BA) 209 Gk62
San Nicolás de la Garza ⊡ MEX (NL) 181 Ek33
San Nicolas Island ⊡ USA 170 Ea29
Sânnicolau Mare ⊡ RO 43 Ma44
Sänniidukh ⊡ ZA 155 Mc59
Sanniquellie ⊡ LB 136 Kf42
Sano ⊡ J 79 Rk28
Sannohe ⊡ J 77 Sb26
Sannār ⊡ SUD 135 Mh39
Sanok ⊡ PL 41 Mc41
San Onofre ⊡ CO 192 Gc41
San Onofre ⊡ USA (CA) 170 Eb29

Šánovo ⊡ BG 45 Mf48
Sanoyie ⊡ LB 136 Kt42
San Pablo ⊡ CO 192 Gd42
San Pablo ⊡ CO 192 Gb45
San Pablo ⊡ EC 196 Ga46
San Pablo ⊡ PE 196 Ga49
San Pablo ⊡ RP 90 Ra38
San Pablo ⊡ YV 193 Gg42
San Pablo de Huacareta ⊡ BOL 206 Gj56
San Pablo de Lípez ⊡ BOL 207 Gg56
San Paolo fuori le Mura ⊡ I 36 Ln49
San Pascual ⊡ RP 90 Rb39
San Pedro ⊡ BH 184 Ff37
San Pédro ⊡ CI 137 Kg43
San Pedro ⊡ CI 137 Kg43
San Pedro ⊡ E 27 Ks52
San Pedro ⊡ MEX (BC) 180 Ee33
San Pedro ⊡ MEX (MI) 204 Hc59
San Pedro ⊡ RP 90 Rb36
San Pedro ⊡ RCH 208 Gd64
San Pedro ⊡ RCH 207 Gj58
San Pedro ⊡ (SE) 207 Gd59
San Pedro ⊡ YV 193 Gg43
San Pedro Amuzgos ⊡ MEX (OAX) 182 Fa37
San Pedro de Atacama ⊡ RCH 207 Gg57
San Pedro de Buena Vista ⊡ BOL 206 Gh55
San Pedro de Cachi ⊡ PE 197 Gc52
San Pedro de Colalao ⊡ RA (TU) 207 Gh59
San Pedro de Coris ⊡ PE 197 Gc52
San Pedro de la Roca Castle = El Morro ⊡ C 186 Gc35
San Pedro de las Colonias ⊡ MEX (COH) 181 Ej33
San Pedro de la Soledad ⊡ MEX (BCS) 180 Ee34
San Pedro de Lloc ⊡ PE 196 Ga49
San Pedro del Norte ⊡ NIC 185 Fh39
San Pedro del Paraná ⊡ PY 204 Hb59
San Pedro del Pinatar ⊡ E 29 Ku53
San Pedro de Quemez ⊡ BOL 206 Gf56
San Pedro de Ycuamandiyú ⊡ PY 204 Hb58
San Pedro d.M. ⊡ DOM 186 Gf36
San Pedro Juchatengo ⊡ MEX (OAX) 182 Fb37
San Pedro Norte ⊡ RA (CD) 207 Gh61
San Pedro Sula ⊡ HN 184 Ff38
San Pedro Tapanatepec ⊡ MEX (OAX) 183 Fb37
San Pedro Totolapan ⊡ MEX (OAX) 182 Fb37
San Pedro, Volcán ⊡ RCH
San Pellegrino Terme ⊡ I 34 Lk45
Sanpoku ⊡ J 77 Rk26
San Policarpio ⊡ RP 90 Rc39
Sanquhar ⊡ GB 20 Kr35
Sanquianga, P.N. ⊡ CO 192 Ga44
San Quintin ⊡ MEX (BC) 180 Ec30
San Quintin ⊡ MEX (CHP) 183 Fe37
San Quírico d'Orcia ⊡ I 34 Lm47
San Rafael ⊡ BOL 206 Gk53
San Rafael ⊡ BOL 206 Gh54
San Rafael ⊡ CR 185 Fh40
San Rafael ⊡ USA (CA) 170 Dk27
San Rafael ⊡ CO 193 Gd45
San Rafael ⊡ CO 192 Gc41
San Rafael ⊡ RA (MD) 208 Gf63
San Rafael ⊡ USA (NM) 171 Ed27
San Rafael de Atamaica ⊡ YV 193 Gg42
San Rafael de Canagua ⊡ YV 192 Ge41
San Rafael de Imataca ⊡ YV 193 Gk42
San Rafael Desert ⊡ USA 171 Ee26
San Rafael Glacier ⊡ RCH 210 Gd69
San Rafael Knob ⊡ USA 171 Ee26
San Ramón ⊡ BOL 206 Gh52
San Ramón ⊡ BOL 206 Gj53
San Ramón ⊡ C 179 Gb35
San Ramón ⊡ PE 197 Gc51
San Ramón ⊡ YV 193 Gk42
San Ramón de la Nueva Orán ⊡ RA (SA) 207 Gh57
San Remigio ⊡ RP 90 Qk38
San Remo ⊡ AUS (VIC) 111 Sc65
San Remo ⊡ I 34 Lh47
San Rolando ⊡ MEX (TM) 182 Fa34
San Roque ⊡ E 27 Kp54
San Roque ⊡ RA (CR) 204 Ha60
San Roque ⊡ RP 90 Rc39
Sans Souci, Citadelle/ ⊡ RH 186 Gd36
San Saba ⊡ USA (TX) 174 Fa30
Sansalé ⊡ RG 136 Kc40
San Salvador ⊡ BS 186 Gd33
San Salvador ⊡ ES 184 Ff39
San Salvador ⊡ PE 196 Ga47
San Salvador ⊡ RA (ER) 204 Ha61
San Salvador de Jujuy ⊡ RA (PJ) 207 Gh58
San Salvador El Seco ⊡ MEX (PUE) 182 Fb36
San Sandingo ⊡ RMM 137 Kh39
Sansanné-Mango ⊡ TG 137 La40
Sansarpur ⊡ IND (UPH) 81 Pa31
San Sebastián = Donostia ⊡ E 28 Ks47
San Sebastián ⊡ MEX (JLC) 182 Eh35
San Sebastián ⊡ RA (TF) 210 Gf72
San Sebastián de la Gomera ⊡ E 124 Kb31
San Sebastián de los Reyes ⊡ E 27 Kr50
San Sebastián Zinacatepec ⊡ MEX (PUE) 182 Fb36
Sansepolcro ⊡ I 34 Ln47
San Severino Marche ⊡ I 34 Ln47
San Severo ⊡ I 37 Lq49
Sansha ⊡ CHN (FJN) 75 Ra32
Sansha ⊡ CHN (GDG) 75 Qg34
San Silvestre ⊡ BOL 206 Gf51
San Silvestre ⊡ YV 192 Ge41
Sanski Most ⊡ BIH 35 Lr46
Sanso ⊡ RMM 137 Kg40
San Stéfano di Camastra ⊡ I 37 Lp52
Sansui ⊡ CHN (GZH) 74 Qe32
Sansundi ⊡ RI 114 Rh46

Sansu-ri ⊡ PRK 76 Rd25
Santa ⊡ PE 197 Ga50
Santa ⊡ USA (ID) 168 Eb22
Santa Albertina ⊡ BR (SP) 202 He55
Santa Amália ⊡ BOL 206 Gh52
Santa Ana ⊡ BOL 206 Gk54
Santa Ana ⊡ CO 192 Gc41
Santa Ana ⊡ EC 207 Gh56
Santa Ana ⊡ PE 197 Gd50
Santa Ana ⊡ YV 193 Gg42
Santa Ana Island ⊡ SOL 117 Tb51
Santa Anita ⊡ MEX (BCS) 180 Ef34
Santa Anita Park ⊡ USA (CA) 170 Ea28
Santa Anna ⊡ USA (TX) 174 Fa30
Santa Bárbara ⊡ BR (AM)
Santa Bárbara ⊡ CO 192 Gc43
Santa Bárbara ⊡ HN 184 Ff38
Santa Bárbara ⊡ MEX (CHH) 180 Eh32
Santa Bárbara ⊡ RCH 208 Gd64
Santa Bárbara ⊡ YV 192 Ge42
Santa Bárbara ⊡ YV 193 Gg44
Santa Bárbara ⊡ CO 192 Gc41
Santa Barbara Channel ⊡ USA 170 Ea28
Santa Bárbara de Casa ⊡ E 27 Kn53
Santa Bárbara d'Oeste ⊡ BR (SP) 203 Hg57
Santa Barbara Island ⊡ USA 170 Ea29
Santa Birgitta Kapell ⊡ S 31 Lr34
Santa Brígida ⊡ BR (BA) 201 Ja50
Santa Catalina ⊡ CO 192 Gc40
Santa Catalina ⊡ PA 185 Fk42
Santa Catalina ⊡ PE 196 Ga49
Santa Catalina ⊡ PY 207 Gg56
Santa Catalina ⊡ (SE) 207 Gd60
Santa Catalina ⊡ RP 91 Rb41
Santa Catalina ⊡ YV 193 Gf42
Santa Catalina Island ⊡ USA 170 Ea29
Santa Catarina ⊡ BR 191 Hb12
Santa Catarina ⊡ BR (BC)
Santa Catarina ⊡ MEX (NL) 181 Ek33
Santa Cecilia ⊡ CR 184 Fh40
Santa Cesárea Terme ⊡ I 37 Lt50
Santa Clara ⊡ BR (AP) 195 He46
Santa Clara ⊡ BR (PA) 199 Hd47
Santa Clara ⊡ BR (PA) 199 Hd47
Santa Clara ⊡ C 179 Ga34
Santa Clara ⊡ ROU 209 Hb63
Santa Clara ⊡ USA (UT) 171 Ed27
Santa Clara ⊡ YV 193 Gh41
Santa Clara-Velha ⊡ P 27 Km53
Santa de Olimar ⊡ ROU 204 Hc62
Santa Clara do Ingai ⊡ BR (RS) 204 Hd60
Santa Clara Ind. Res. ⊡ USA 171 Eg28
Santa Clotilde ⊡ PE 196 Gd47
Santa Coloma de Queralt ⊡ E 29 Lb49
Santa Comba ⊡ E 26 Km47
Santa Croce Camarina ⊡ I 37 Lp54
Santa Cruz ⊡ BOL 206 Gj53
Santa Cruz ⊡ BR (ES) 203 Hk55
Santa Cruz ⊡ BR (PA) 199 Hd47
Santa Cruz ⊡ BR (PB) 201 Jb49
Santa Cruz ⊡ BR (RN) 201 Jb49
Santa Cruz ⊡ CHN 134 Ll44
Santa Cruz ⊡ CO 192 Gc43
Santa Cruz ⊡ CV 136 Jj37
Santa Cruz ⊡ MEX (NYT)
Santa Cruz ⊡ RA (CA) 207 Gg59
Santa Cruz ⊡ RP 91 Rc42
Santa Cruz ⊡ RA (CR) 204 Ha60
Santa Cruz ⊡ YV 192 Ge42
Santa Cruz ⊡ YV 193 Gk42
Santa Cruz Cabrália ⊡ BR (BA) 203 Ja54
Santa Cruz das Palmeiras ⊡ BR 203 Hg56
Santa Cruz de Bucaral ⊡ YV 193 Gf40
Santa Cruz de Campezo ⊡ E 28 Ks48
Santa Cruz de la Palma ⊡ E 124 Kb31
Santa Cruz de la Sierra ⊡ BOL 206 Gj54
Santa Cruz del Norte ⊡ C 179 Fk34
Santa Cruz del Quiché ⊡ GCA 184 Fe38
Santa Cruz del Sur ⊡ C 179 Ga35
Santa Cruz de Mompox ⊡ CO 192 Gc41
Santa Cruz de Mudela ⊡ E 27 Kr52
Santa Cruz de Tenerife ⊡ E 124 Kb31
Santa Cruz do Arari ⊡ BR (PA) 195 Hf46
Santa Cruz do Rio Pardo ⊡ BR (SP) 202 Hf57
Santa Cruz do Sul ⊡ BR (RS) 204 Hd60
Santa Cruz do Oeste ⊡ BR (PR) 204 Hd58
Santa Cruz do Suaçuí ⊡ BR (MG) 203 Hj55
Santa Cruz Island ⊡ USA 170 Ea29
Santa Cruz Islands ⊡ SOL 118 Tb50
Santa Cruz Verapaz ⊡ GCA 184 Fe38
Santadi ⊡ I 36 Lj51

Santa Elena ⊡ RA (ER) 204 Ha61
Santa Elena, Cerro ⊡ RA 210 Gh68
Santa Elena ⊡ YV 193 Gj41
Santa Eleodora ⊡ RA (BA) 209 Gj63
Santa Eufemia ⊡ E 27 Kq52
Santa Eugenia ⊡ E 26 Km48
Santa Eulalia ⊡ E 29 Kt50
Santa Eulalia ⊡ MEX (COH) 181 Ek31
Santa Eulària des Riu ⊡ E 29 Lc52
Santa Fé ⊡ BR (AM) 196 Gd48
Santa Fé ⊡ BR (AM) 198 Gf50
Santa Fe ⊡ RP 90 Rb36
Santa Fe ⊡ C 179 Fj34
Santa Fé ⊡ RA (SF) 209 Gk61
Santa Fé de Antioquia ⊡ CO 192 Gc42
Santa Fe de Minas ⊡ BR (MG) 203 Hh54
Santa Fé do Sul ⊡ BR (SP) 202 He56
Santa Filomena ⊡ BR (PE) 201 Hk50
Santa Filomena ⊡ BR (PI) 201 Hh50
Santa Fé de la Antioquia ⊡ CO 192 Gc42
Sant'Ágata di Militello ⊡ I 37 Lp52
Santa Helena ⊡ BR (AC) 197 Ge50
Santa Helena ⊡ BR (MA) 195 Hh47
Santa Helena ⊡ BR (PR) 204 Hc58
Santa Helena de Cusima ⊡ CO 192 Ge43
Santa Helena de Goiás ⊡ BR (GO) 202 He54
Santa Inês ⊡ BR (BA) 201 Ja52
Santa Inês ⊡ CO 192 Gd45
Santa Inés ⊡ MEX (SLP) 182 Ek34
Santa Isabel ⊡ BR (AM) 197 Ge48
Santa Isabel ⊡ NIC 184 Fh40
Santa Isabel ⊡ PA 185 Ga41
Santa Isabel ⊡ PE 196 Gd48
Santa Isabel ⊡ SOL 117 Tk49
Santa Isabel do Araguaia ⊡ BR (PA) 200 Hf49
Santa Isabel do Rio Negro ⊡ BR (AM) 198 Ha48
Santa Isabella ⊡ RA (LP) 208 Gh64
Santa Juana ⊡ RCH 208 Gd64
Santa Juana ⊡ YV 193 Gg42
Santa Júlia ⊡ BR (AM) 199 Hg49
Santa Juliana ⊡ BR (MG) 203 Hg55
Santa Lucía ⊡ C 179 Fh34
Santa Lucía ⊡ C 179 Gb35
Santa Lucía ⊡ EC 196 Ga46
Santa Lucía ⊡ ROU 209 Hb63
Santa Lucia ⊡ YV 193 Gf41
Santa Lucía ⊡ YV 193 Gh41
Santa Lucia Bank ⊡ USA 170 Dk28
Santa Lucia Range ⊡ USA 170 Dk28
Santaluz ⊡ BR (BA) 201 Ja51
Santa Luzia ⊡ BR (PI) 200 Hh50
Santa Luzia ⊡ BR (MA) 200 Hf48
Santa Luzia ⊡ BR (MG) 203 Hj55
Santa Luzia ⊡ BR (RS) 204 Hc62
Santa Luzia ⊡ BR (PB) 201 Jb49
Santa Luzia de Paru ⊡ BR (PA)
Santa Magdalena ⊡ RA (CD) 208 Gj63
Santa Margherita ⊡ I 36 Lj52
Santa María ⊡ ANG 150 Lg52
Santa María ⊡ BR (AM) 198 Gh48
Santa María ⊡ BR (AM) 199 Ha48
Santa María ⊡ BR (BA) 195 He46
Santa María ⊡ BR (BA) 201 Ja51
Santa María ⊡ BR (RR) 198 Ha47
Santa María ⊡ CV 136 Jj37
Santa María ⊡ MEX (JLC)
Santa María ⊡ MEX (NYT) 182 Ek35
Santa María ⊡ MEX (NYT)
Santa María ⊡ MEX (CAM) 183 Fe36
Santa María ⊡ MEX (QTR)
Santa María ⊡ RA (CA) 207 Gg59
Santa María ⊡ RP 91 Rc42
Santa María ⊡ RA (LR) 207 Gf61
Santa María ⊡ ROU 209 Hc63
Santa María ⊡ RP 90 Ra37
Santa María ⊡ RP 90 Ra42
Santa María ⊡ YV 192 Ge41
Santa María Asunción Tlaxiaco ⊡ MEX (OAX) 182 Fb37
Santa María Ayoquezco ⊡ MEX (OAX) 182 Fb37
Santa María Cápua Vétere ⊡ I 37 Lp49
Santa María da Boa Vista ⊡ BR (PE) 201 Ja50
Santa María da Vitória ⊡ BR (BA) 200 Hh52
Santa María de Ipire ⊡ YV 193 Gh41
Santa María de Jetibá ⊡ BR (ES) 203 Hk56
Santa María de la Peña ⊡ E 28 Ku48
Santa María del Azogue ⊡ E 26 Km53
Santa María del Camí ⊡ E 29 Lc51
Santa María delle Grazie ⊡ I 34 Lk45
Santa María del Oro ⊡ MEX (DGO) 181 Eh33
Santa María del Oro ⊡ MEX (NYT) 182 Eh35
Santa María de Nanay ⊡ PE 196 Gd47
Santa María de Nieva ⊡ PE 196 Ga48
Santa María de Socorro ⊡ PE 197 Gc52
Santa María del Río ⊡ MEX (SLP) 182 Ek34
Santa María del Regno ⊡ I 36 Lj50
Santa María del Páramo ⊡ E 26 Kp48
Santa María Ecatepec ⊡ MEX (OAX) 182 Fb37
Santa María Huatulco ⊡ MEX (OAX) 182 Fb38
Santa María Huazolotitlán ⊡ MEX (OAX) 182 Fb37

Santa María Island ⊡ VU
Santa María la Real de Nieva ⊡ E 27 Kq49
Santa Marinella ⊡ I 36 Lm48
Santa Mário do Pará ⊡ BR (PA) 195 Hg46
Santa Marta ⊡ ANG 150 Lg52
Santa Marta ⊡ CO 192 Gc40
Santa Marta ⊡ E 27 Ko52
Santa Martha ⊡ MEX (BCS) 180 Ed33
Santa Mónica ⊡ MEX (MEX) 182 Fa36
Santa Mónica ⊡ MEX (COH) 181 Ek31
Santa Monica ⊡ USA (CA) 170 Ea28
Santan ⊡ RI 94 Qj46
Santana ⊡ BR (AM) 198 Gj46
Santana ⊡ BR (AM) 198 Gg50
Santana ⊡ BR (AP) 195 He45
Santana ⊡ BR (AP) 195 He46
Santana ⊡ BR (BA) 200 Hh52
Santana ⊡ BR (AM) 200 Hj48
Santana ⊡ CO 192 Gc44
Santana ⊡ CO 192 Gd42
Santana da Boa Vista ⊡ BR (RS) 204 Hd61
Santana de Pirapama ⊡ BR (MG) 203 Hh55
Santana do Acaraú ⊡ BR (CE) 201 Hk47
Santana do Araguaia ⊡ BR (PA) 200 He50
Santana do Cariri ⊡ BR (CE) 201 Ja49
Santana do Ipanema ⊡ BR (AL) 201 Jb50
Santana do Livramento ⊡ BR (RS) 204 Hc62
Santana do Livramento ⊡ BR 151 Mb55
Santana, T.I. ⊡ BR 202 Hc53
Santana do Matos ⊡ BR (RN) 201 Jb49
Santana do Sugçuí ⊡ BR (MG) 203 Hj55
Santana do Tocantins ⊡ BR 200 Hg51
Santana dos Montes ⊡ BR (MG) 203 Hj56
Santa Nova ⊡ BR (PA) 195 Hg46
Santaquin ⊡ USA (UT) 171 Ee26
Santarcángelo di Romagna ⊡ I 34 Ln46
Santarém ⊡ BR (PA) 199 Hd47
Santarém ⊡ P 27 Km51
Santarém ⊡ BR (PA) 195 Hf47
Santaren Channel ⊡ BS 179 Ga34
Santa Rita ⊡ BR (AM) 198 Gf47
Santa Rita ⊡ BR (AM) 198 Gf47
Santa Rita ⊡ BR (BA) 201 Jc49
Santa Rita ⊡ CO 193 Gf43
Santa Rita ⊡ CO 193 Gf43
Santa Rita ⊡ HN 184 Fg38
Santa Rita ⊡ USA 180 Ed33
Santa Rita ⊡ YV 192 Gd40
Santa Rita de Araguaia ⊡ BR (GO) 202 Hd54
Santa Rita do Araguaia ⊡ BR (MS)
Santa Rita de Cássia ⊡ BR (BA) 200 Hj51
Santa Rita de Catuna ⊡ RA (LR) 207 Gg61
Santa Rita do Araguaia ⊡ BR (GO) 202 Hd54
Santa Rita do Pardo ⊡ BR (MS) 202 Hd56
Santa Rita do Passa Quatro ⊡ BR (SP) 203 Hg56
Santa Rita do Sapucaí ⊡ BR (MG) 203 Hh57
Santa Rosa ⊡ BOL 206 Gg53
Santa Rosa ⊡ BOL 206 Gj53
Santa Rosa ⊡ BR (BA) 195 He46
Santa Rosa ⊡ BR (RR) 193 Gk44
Santa Rosa ⊡ BR (RS) 204 Hc59
Santa Rosa ⊡ CO 192 Gd42
Santa Rosa ⊡ CO 196 Gc45
Santa Rosa ⊡ USA (CA) 170 Dj26
Santa Rosa ⊡ USA (NM) 171 Eh28
Santa Rosa ⊡ PE 197 Gc52
Santa Rosa ⊡ PE 197 Gd52
Santa Rosa ⊡ RA (CR) 204 Ha60
Santa Rosa ⊡ YV 192 Ge41
Santa Rosa ⊡ YV 193 Gk42
Santa Rosa Beach ⊡ USA (FL) 175 Fg30
Santa Rosa de Abuná ⊡ BOL 198 Gg51
Santa Rosa de Amonadona ⊡ YV 193 Gg45
Santa Rosa de Copán ⊡ HN 184 Ff38
Santa Rosa de las Misiones ⊡ PY 204 Hb59
Santa Rosa de Conlara ⊡ RA (SL) 208 Gh62
Santa Rosa de Leales ⊡ RA (TU) 207 Gh59
Santa Rosa de Lima ⊡ ES 184 Ff39
Santa Rosa del Monday ⊡ PY 204 Hc58
Santa Rosa del Río Primera ⊡ RA (CD) 207 Gj61
Santa Rosa de Mbutuy ⊡ PY 204 Hb58
Santa Rosa de Ocopa ⊡ PE 197 Gc51
Santa Rosa Island ⊡ USA 170 Dk29
Santa Rosalía ⊡ MEX (BCS) 180 Ed32
Santa Rosalía ⊡ YV 193 Gh42
Santa Rosa, P.N. ⊡ CR 184 Fh40

Šantarskie ostrova ⊡ RUS 55 Rd07
Santa Severa ⊡ F 34 Lk48
Santa Sylvina ⊡ RA (CH) 207 Gk59
Santa Teresa ⊡ (NYT) 181 Eh34
Santa Teresa ⊡ MEX (TM) 181 Fa33
Santa Teresa ⊡ MEX (TM) 181 Fb33
Santa Teresa ⊡ PE 196 Gd48
Santa Teresa di Riva ⊡ I 37 Lq53
Santa Teresa de Goiás ⊡ BR (GO) 200 Hf52
Santa Teresa do Tocantins ⊡ BR (TO) 200 Hg51
Santa Teresa Gallura ⊡ I 36 Lk49
Santa Teresinha, P.N. ⊡ ROU 204 Hd62
Santa Teresinha de Goiás ⊡ BR (GO) 202 Hf53
Santa Teresita ⊡ RA (BA) 209 Hb64
Santa Terezinha ⊡ BR (MT) 200 He51
Santa Terezinha ⊡ BR (SC) 205 He59
Santa Theresa ⊡ AUS (NT) 108 Rh58
Santa Victoria ⊡ RA (SA) 207 Gh57
Santa Victória ⊡ BR (MG) 202 He55
Santa Vitória do Palmar ⊡ BR (RS) 204 Hd62
San-Ta-Wani Safari Camp ⊡ RB 151 Mb55
Sant Carles de la Ràpita ⊡ E 29 Lb51
Sant Carles de Peralta ⊡ E 29 Lc51
Sant Celoni ⊡ E 29 Lc48
Sant Bennur ⊡ IND (KTK)
Santee Ind. Res. ⊡ USA 172 Fb24
Sant'Angelo dei Lombardi ⊡ I 37 Lq50
Sant'Elia a Pianisi ⊡ I 37 Lp49
Santemarahalli ⊡ IND (KTK) 84 Oj40
San Teodoro ⊡ I 36 Lk50
Santérano in Colle ⊡ I 37 Lr50
Santerno ⊡ I 34 Lm46
Santestéban ⊡ E 28 Kt47
Sant'Antônio di Santadi ⊡ I
Santanyí ⊡ E 29 Ld51
Sant'Eufémia Lamézia ⊡ I 37 Lr52
Sant Feliu de Guíxols ⊡ E 29 Ld49
Sant Francesc de Formentera ⊡ E 29 Lb52
Santhe ⊡ MW 146 Mg52
Santhià ⊡ I 34 Lj46
Santiago ⊡ BR (AM) 198 Hc60
Santiago ⊡ BR (PA) 185 Fh41
Santiago ⊡ EC 196 Ga47
Santiago ⊡ GCA 184 Fd48
Santiago ⊡ MEX (NL) 181 Ek33
Santiago ⊡ PA 185 Fk41
Santiago ⊡ RCH 208 Ge62
Santiago ⊡ RP 90 Ra37
Santiago Astata ⊡ MEX (OAX) 183 Fc38
Santiago Choapan ⊡ MEX (OAX) 183 Fc37
Santiago de Alcántara ⊡ E 27 Kn51
Santiago de Anchucaya ⊡ PE 197 Gb52
Santiago de Andamarca ⊡ BOL 206 Gg55
Santiago de Cao ⊡ PE 196 Ga49
Santiago de Chiquitos ⊡ BOL 206 Ha55
Santiago de Chocorvos ⊡ PE 197 Gc52
Santiago de Chuco ⊡ PE 197 Gb50
Santiago de Compostela ⊡ E 26 Km48
Santiago de Cotagaita ⊡ BOL 206 Gh56
Santiago de Cuba ⊡ C 186 Gc35
Santiago de Huari ⊡ BOL 206 Gg55
Santiago de las Vegas ⊡ C 179 Fj34
Santiago del Estero ⊡ RA 207 Gh59
Santiago del Estero ⊡ RA
Santiago de los Caballeros ⊡ MEX (SL) 180 Eg33
Santiago de los Caballeros ⊡ DOM 186 Ge36
Santiago del Teide ⊡ E 124 Kb31
Santiago de Machaca ⊡ BOL 206 Gf54
Santiago de Pacaguaras ⊡ BOL 206 Gg52
Santiago do Cacém ⊡ P 27 Km52
Santiago Ixcuintla ⊡ MEX (NYT) 182 Eh35
Santiago, James = Isla San Salvador ⊡ EC 197 Fe46
Santiago Juxtlahuaca ⊡ MEX (OAX) 182 Fb37
Santiago Mts. ⊡ USA 181 Ej31
Santiago Papasquiaro ⊡ MEX (DGO) 181 Eh33
Santiago Pinotepa Nacional ⊡ MEX (OAX) 182 Fa37
Santiago Tuxtla ⊡ MEX (VC) 183 Fc36
Santiago ⊡ MEX (ZCT) 182 Ej34
Santibáñez de la Sierra ⊡ E 27 Kp50
San Tiburcio ⊡ MEX (ZCT) 181 Ek33
Santigi ⊡ RMM 137 Kg39
Santillana del Mar ⊡ E 26 Kq47
San Timoteo ⊡ YV 192 Ge41
Santipur ⊡ IND (CGH) 83 Pa34
Säntis ⊡ CH 34 Lk43
Santíssima Trinità di Saccárgia ⊡ I 36 Lj50
Sant Suk ⊡ THA 87 Qa36
San Joan d'Alacant ⊡ E 29 Ku52
Sant Llorenç de Morunys ⊡ E 28 Lb48
San Mateu ⊡ E 29 La50
Santo Anastácio ⊡ BR (SP) 202 He56
Santo André ⊡ ANG 150 Lh52
Santo André ⊡ BR (PA) 195 Hf46
Santo André ⊡ BR (SP) 203 Hg57
Santo Angelo ⊡ BR (RS) 204 Hc60
San Antonio ⊡ BR (AM) 199 Hc49
Santo Antônio ⊡ BR (AM) 199 Ha49
Santo Antônio ⊡ BR (BA) 201
Santo Antônio ⊡ BR (AM) 194 Hb46
Santo Antônio ⊡ BR (RN) 201 Jc49

Slieve Bloom Mountains ▲ IRL 19 Kn37
Slieve League ▲ IRL 19 Km36
Sligachan ▣ GB 20 Ko33
Sligo ▣ IRL 19 Km36
Sligo Bay ▣ IRL 19 Km36
Slim ▣ DZ 126 Lb28
Slisenvaara ▣ RUS 38 Mk29
Slite ▣ S 31 Lt33
Slivata ▣ BG 44 Md47
Sliven ▣ BG 45 Mg48
Slivnica ▣ BG 44 Md48
Slivo Pole ▣ RUS 70 Qb20
Sliwice ▣ PL 40 Lt37
Sljudjanka ▣ RUS 70 Qb20
Slobozia ▣ LV 39 Mh34
Sloboda ▣ CO 192 Gc43
Slobozia Mare ▣ MD 45 Mj45
Slocan ▣ CDN (BC) 168 Eb21
Słomniki ▣ PL 41 Ma40
Slonim ▣ BY 41 Mf37
Slough ▣ GB 21 La37
Slovakia ▣ SK 43 Lu42
Slovenia ▣ SLO 42 Lp45
Slovenj Gradec ▣ SLO 42 Lq44
Slovenska Bistrica ▣ SLO 42 Lq44
Slovenská Ľupča ▣ SK 43 Lu42
Slovenský raj N.P. ▣ SK 43 Ma42
Slov'jans'k ▣ UA 49 Mj21
Stowiński P.N. ▣ PL 40 Ls36
Stubice ▣ PL 40 Lp38
Sluck ▣ BY 48 Md19
Słupca ▣ PL 40 Ls38
Stupca ▣ PL 40 Ls38
Stupia ▣ PL 41 Mb40
Stupno ▣ PL 41 Lu38
Stupsk ▣ PL 40 Ls36
Slurry ▣ ZA 155 Mc58
Slussfors ▣ S 16 Lj12
Slyne Head ▲ IRL 19 Kk37
Smáland ▲ S 31 Lq33
Smålandsstenar ▣ S 31 Lo33
Smalininkai ▣ LT 39 Mc35
Smaljanica ▣ BY 41 Me18
Smaljavičy ▣ BY 48 Me18
Small Malaita = Maramasike ▲ SOL 117 Ta50
Smallwood Reservoir ▣ CDN 163 Gd08
Smara ▣ DARS 124 Ke32
Smårdioasa ▣ RO 45 Mf47
Smarhon' ▣ BY 39 Mg36
Šmarje pri Jelšah ▣ SLO 42 Lq44
Smeaton ▣ CDN (SK) 169 Eh19
Smeberg ▣ S 30 Lm32
Smedby ▣ S 31 Lr34
Smederevo ▣ SCG 44 Ma46
Smedjebacken ▣ S 31 Lq30
Smethport ▣ USA (PA) 173 Ga25
Smidovič ▣ RUS (YAO) 76 Rg21
Šmierdnica ▣ PL 40 Lp37
Smigiel ▣ PL 40 Lr38
Smilec ▣ BG 45 Me48
Smiley ▣ CDN (SK) 169 Ef20
Smiltene ▣ LV 39 Mf33
Smith ▣ CDN (AB) 167 Ed18
Smith Bay ▣ USA (AK) 165 Cc10
Smith Center ▣ USA (KS) 174 Fa26
Smithers ▣ CDN (BC) 166 Dg18
Smith Ferry ▣ USA (ID) 168 Eb23
Smithfield ▣ USA (NC) 178 Ga28
Smithfield ▣ ZA 155 Md61
Smith Group, Sir J. ▣ AUS 107 Se56
Smith Island ▣ IND 88 Pg39
Smith Island ▣ USA (VA) 173 Gb26
Smith Point ▣ AUS 106 Rg51
Smith River ▣ CDN (BC) 166 Dg16
Smith's Knoll ▣ 21 Lc38
Smithton ▣ AUS (TAS) 111 Sc66
Smithtown ▣ AUS (NSW) 109 Sg61
Smithville ▣ USA (TN) 175 Fh28
Smithville ▣ USA (WV) 175 Fh26
Smithville House ▣ AUS (NSW) 108 Sa61
Smjadovo ▣ BG 45 Mh47
Smjörfjöll ▲ IS 18 Kf25
Smogulec ▣ PL 40 Lr38
Smoljovo ▣ RUS 39 Mj33
Smolnik ▣ PL 41 Mc41
Smolsko ▣ BG 44 Md48
Smooth Rock Falls ▣ CDN (ON) 173 Fk21
Smoże ▣ UA 43 Md42
Smygehamn ▣ S 31 Lo35
Smygehuk ▣ S 31 Lo35
Smyha ▣ UA 41 Mf40
Smyley Island ▲ 6 Fc33
Smyrna ▣ USA (DE) 177 Gc26
Smyrna ▣ USA (GA) 175 Fh29
Snabai ▣ RI 114 Rh46
Snæfell ▲ IS 23 Kq36
Snæfell ▲ IS 18 Ke26
Snæfellsnes ▲ IS 18 Jz26
Snækollur ▲ IS 18 Ka26
Snake and Manjang Caverns ▣ ROK 78 Rd29
Snake Indian River ▣ CDN 168 Ea19
Snake Island ▲ AUS 111 Sd65
Snake River ▣ CDN (YT) 165 Dd13
Snake River ▣ USA 168 Eb23
Snake River Canyon ▣ USA 168 Ed24
Snaran Jogizai ▣ PK 65 Oe30
Snare Lakes ▣ CDN 167 Ec13
Snåsa ▣ N 16 Lg12
Snedsted ▣ DK 30 Lj34
Sneek ▣ NL 23 Le37
Sneekermeer ▣ NL 23 Lf37
Sneem ▣ IRL 19 Kl39
Sneeuberg ▲ ZA 155 Mc61
Snežnaja ▣ RUS 70 Qc20
Sniebal ▣ PL (MZR) 86 Pg34
Śnieżka ▲ PL 40 Lq40
Śnieżnik Kłodzki ▲ PL 40 Lr40
Snina ▣ SK 43 Mc42
Snjatyn ▣ UA 43 Mf42
Snježna Marija ▣ HR 35 Lr45
Snøhetta ▲ N 16 Lg31
Snøhøtten ▲ N 30 Lg31
Snoqualmie Pass ▣ USA (WA) 168 Dk22
Snøtoppen ▲ N 16 Lk05
Snov ▣ UA 48 Mg19
Snoul W.S. ▣ K 89 Qd39
Snowdon ▲ GB 21 Kq37
Snowdonia N.P. ▣ GB 21 Kr38
Snowdrift ▣ CDN 167 Ee14
Snowflake ▣ USA (AZ) 171 Ee28
Snow Hill ▣ USA (MD) 177 Gc26

Snow Lake ▣ CDN (MB) 169 Ek18
Snow Lake ▣ USA (AR) 175 Fe28
Snow Mount ▲ USA 170 Dj26
Snowshoe Peak ▲ USA 168 Ec21
Snowtown ▣ AUS (SA) 110 Rk62
Snowville ▣ USA (UT) 171 Ed25
Snowy Mountains ▲ AUS 111 Se64
Snowy River N. ▣ AUS 111 Se64
Snug Corner ▣ BS 186 Ga34
Snyder ▣ USA (TX) 174 Ek29
So ▣ BF 131 Kh38
Soacha ▣ CO 192 Gc43
Soalala ▣ RM 157 Nc55
Soalara ▣ RM 157 Nb57
Soaloka ▣ RM 157 Nc55
Soamanonga ▣ RM 157 Nc57
Soanierana-Ivongo ▣ RM 157 Nd56
Soanindrariny ▣ RM 157 Nd55
Soap Lake ▣ USA (WA) 168 Ea22
Soaserana ▣ RM 157 Nc56
Soata ▣ CO 192 Gd42
Soave ▣ I 34 Lm45
Soavina ▣ RM 157 Nd56
Soavina ▣ RM 157 Ne56
Soavinandriana ▣ RM 157 Nd55
Soba ▣ WAN 138 Le40
Sobaek Sanmaek ▲ ROK 78 Rd28
Sobeekasan N.P. ▣ ROK 78 Re27
Sobat ▣ SUD 141 Mg41
Sobernheim ▣ D 32 Lh41
Sobibór ▣ PL 41 Md39
Sobinka ▣ RUS 48 Na18
Sobolevo ▣ RUS 48 Na18
Sobótka ▣ PL 41 Mb40
Sobradinho ▣ BR (BA) 201 Hk50
Sobradinho ▣ BR (DF) 203 Hg53
Sobradinho ▣ BR (RS) 204 Hd60
Sobral ▣ BR (CE) 201 Hk47
Sobral ▣ BR (PB) 201 Ja50
Sobral ▣ BR (SA) 34 Mc42
Søby ▣ DK 30 Ll36
Socaire ▣ RCH 207 Gg42
Socastee ▣ USA (SC) 178 Ga29
Socavão ▣ BR (PR) 205 Hf58
Sochaczew ▣ PL 41 Ma38
Sochinsky nacional'nyj park ▣ RUS 49 Mk23
Soči ▣ RUS 49 Mk24
Society Hill ▣ USA (SC) 178 Ga28
Socodor ▣ RO 43 Ma44
Socompa ▣ PE 207 Gf58
Socompa, Volcán ▲ RCH/RA 207 Gf58
Socorro ▣ BR (PR) 204 He58
Socorro ▣ BR (SP) 203 Hg57
Socorro ▣ CO 192 Gd42
Socorro ▣ RP 90 Rc41
Socorro ▣ USA (NM) 171 Eg28
Socotra ▣ CO 192 Gd42
Socotra ▣ PE 196 Ga49
Socotra ▣ YE 61 Nh39
Soc Trang ▣ VN 89 Qe41
Socuéllamos ▣ E 29 Ks51
Soda Creek ▣ CDN (BC) 168 Dj19
Sodankylä ▣ FIN 16 Md12
Sodankylä ▣ FIN 16 Md12
Soda Springs ▣ USA (ID) 169 Ee24
Söderarm ▣ S 31 Lu31
Söderåsens n.p. ▣ S 30 Lo35
Söderbärke ▣ S 31 Lq30
Söderfors ▣ S 31 Ls30
Söderhamn ▣ S 17 Lj15
Södermanland ▣ S 31 Lr31
Södertälje ▣ S 31 Ls31
Södertörn ▣ S 31 Ls31
Sodi ▣ RI 96 Qk46
Sodo ▣ SUD 134 Mk08
Sodium ▣ ZA 154 Mb61
Sodo'evsk ▣ RUS 71 Qh21
Sodus ▣ USA 71 Ga24
Soe ▣ RI 97 Rc50
Soekmekaar ▣ ZA 152 Me57
Soeng San ▣ THA 89 Qb38
Soesdyke ▣ GUY 194 Ha42
Soe ▣ D 32 Lj39
Soetdoring Nature Reserve ▣ ZA 155 Md60
Sofádes ▣ GR 46 Mc51
Sofara ▣ RMM 131 Kh38
Sofija ▣ BG 44 Md48
Sofija ▲ BG 44 Md48
Sofiivka ▣ UA 49 Mg21
Sofijski sobor ▣ RUS 48 Mf16
Sofijsky sobor ▣ UA 48 Mf01
Sof Omar Caves ▣ ETH 142 Na42
Sofporog ▣ RUS 16 Mf13
Sogakofe ▣ GH 137 La42
Sogamoso ▣ CO 192 Gd43
Sögel ▣ D 32 Lh38
Sogeri ▣ PNG 115 Sd57
Sogi Xian ▣ CHN (TIB) 69 Pg30
Sohåg ▣ ET 129 Mf32
Sohar ▣ OM 61 Nj33
Sohela ▣ IND (ORS) 83 Pb35
Sohey ▣ IR 64 Nd29
Sohna ▣ IND (HYA) 80 Oj32
Sohren ▣ D 32 Lh41
Soignies ▣ B 23 Le40
Soila ▣ IND (RJT) 80 Og32
Şoimi ▣ RO 43 Mc44
Soin ▣ BF 137 Kj39
Soira ▲ ER 142 Mk39
Soisalo ▣ FIN 38 Md30
Soissons ▣ F 23 Ld41
Soja ▣ J 79 Rg28
Sojat ▣ IND (RJT) 82 Og33
Sojod ▣ RI 91 Ra45
Sojotin Point ▣ RP 90 Rb41
Sojat' (RUS) ▣ 6 Ob33
sor Arys ▣ KZ 63 Oa23
sor Aschkol ▣ KZ 63 Oa23
Sokal ▣ UA 43 Md40
Sokaraja ▣ RI 95 Qe49
Sokelo ▣ RDC 149 Mc50
Sokhumi ▣ GE 57 Na24
Soko ▣ GE 57 Na24
Sokhumi ▣ GE 30 Lc30
Soko Banja ▣ SCG 44 Mb47
Sokol ▣ RUS 48 Na17
Sokółka ▣ PL 41 Md37

Sokollu Camii ▣ TR 45 Mh49
Sokolo ▣ RMM 131 Kg38
Sokolov ▣ CZ 42 Ln40
Sokołów Małopolski ▣ PL 41 Mc38
Sokołów Podlaski ▣ PL 41 Mc38
Sokolski manastir ▣ BG 45 Mf48
Sokoły ▣ PL 41 Mc38
Sokorbey ▣ RN 132 Lb39
Sokoto ▣ WAN 132 Ld39
Sokoto ▣ WAN 138 Ld40
Sokoukama ▣ TG 136 Kf41
Sokoura ▣ RMM 137 Kj39
Soksok ▣ RN 132 Ld38
Sola ▣ C 179 Gb35
Sola ▣ N 30 Lf32
Sola ▣ VU 118 Td52
Sola de Vega ▣ MEX (OAX) 182 Fb57
Solahpet ▣ IND (KTK) 82 Oj37
Solai ▣ IND (HPH) 81 Oj30
Solana ▣ PL 45 Lr46
Solana del Pino ▣ E 27 Kp52
Solander Island ▲ NZ 113 Td69
Solânea ▣ BR (PB) 201 Jc49
Solano de Mateus ▣ BR (PI) 201 Hk50
Solano ▣ YV 193 Gg45
Solares ▣ E 29 Kr47
Solat ▣ RI 91 Rd45
Solberg ▣ S 16 Lj14
Sol'cy ▣ RUS 48 Mf16
Soldado Monge ▣ EC 196 Gb47
Sol de Julio ▣ RA (SE) 207 Gj60
Sol de Mañana ▣ BOL 207 Gh57
Soldänu ▣ RO 45 Mg47
Soldotna ▣ USA (AK) 164 Ce15
Soledad ▣ CO 192 Gc40
Soledad ▣ USA (CA) 170 Dk27
Soledad ▣ YV 193 Gj41
Soledad de Doblado ▣ MEX (VC) 182 Fb56
Soledade ▣ BR (PB) 201 Jb49
Soledade ▣ BR (RS) 204 Hd60
Soledade ▣ BR (SA) 34 Mc42
Soledade de G. Sánchez ▣ MEX (SLP) 182 Ek34
Solenzara ▣ F 36 La49
Sole Pit ▣ 21 Lc37
Solh Abad ▣ IR 64 Nj28
Soli ▣ RN 132 Ld38
Solihull ▣ GB 21 Kt38
Solikamsk ▣ RUS 54 Nd07
Solimbo = Amazon ▣ BR 198 Gj47
Solingen ▣ D 32 Lh39
Solis de Matajojo ▣ ROU 209 Hc63
Sollefteå ▣ S 16 Lj14
Sollebrunn ▣ S 30 Ln32
Soller ▣ E 29 Lc51
Sollgada ▣ N 31 Ls31
Sollichau ▣ D 32 Ln39
Solnce ▣ C 42 Lr40
Solncev ▣ RUS 48 Mj20
Solnečnogorsk ▣ RUS 48 Mj17
Solnice ▣ CZ 42 Lr40
Soloma ▣ GCA 184 Fe38
Solomon Islands ▣ 101 Ta10
Solomon Islands ▣ 117 Sj48
Solomon Sea ▣ PNG 116 Sf49
Solomon's Wall ▣ RB 152 Md49
Solon ▣ CHN (NMZ) 71 Ra22
solonchakovyye vpadiny Unguz ▣ TM 62 Nk26
Solonópole ▣ BR (CE) 201 Ja48
Solor ▣ RI 97 Rb50
Solothurn ▣ CH 34 Lh43
Solotvyn ▣ UA 43 Me42
Solotvyna ▣ UA 43 Md43
Sòltan Abad ▣ IR 62 Ng25
Sòltan Bagh ▣ AFG 65 Oe29
Soltaniyeh ▣ IR 57 Ne27
Soltau ▣ D 32 Lk38
Şoltoi-lapály ▣ H 43 Lu44
Soltvadkert ▣ H 43 Lu44
Solvang ▣ USA (CA) 170 Dk28
Solvarbo ▣ S 31 Lq30
Sölvesborg ▣ S 31 Lq34
Solway Firth ▣ GB 20 Kr36
Soly ▣ BY 39 Mg36
Solymar ▣ ROU 209 Hc63
Sol y Nieve ▣ E 27 Kr53
Soma ▣ IND (RJT) 82 Og33
Soma ▣ TR 47 Mh51
Somabhula ▣ ZW 152 Me55
Somadougou ▣ RMM 131 Kh38
Somaén ▣ E 29 Ks49
Somalia ▣ 123 Na09
Somali Basin ▣ 9 Nb09
Somali Plateau ▣ ETH 142 Na41
Somalomo ▣ CAM 139 Lg44
Somavaram ▣ IND (APH) 83 Pb37
Somba ▣ RI 96 Qk47
Sómbak'e = Yellowknife ▣ CDN 167 Ec14
Sombo ▣ ANG 149 Ma50
Sombor ▣ SCG 44 Lu45
Sombrerete ▣ MEX (ZCT) 182 Ej34
Sombrero ▣ KNA 187 Gj36
Sombrero ▣ RCH 210 Gf72
Sombrio ▣ BR (SC) 205 Hf60
Somcuta Mare ▣ RO 43 Md43
Someo ▣ RO 43 Md43
Somero ▣ FIN 38 Md30
Somers ▣ USA (VIC) 111 Sd65
Somerset ▣ AUS (QLD) 107 Sb51
Somerset ▣ AUS (TAS) 111 Sd65
Somerset ▣ USA (MD) 172 Fa21
Somerset ▣ USA (PA) 177 Ga26
Somerset East ▣ ZA 155 Mc62
Somerset Island ▣ CDN 163 Fb04
Somerset Oos ▣ ZA 155 Mc62
Somerset West ▣ ZA 154 Lk63
Somerton ▣ AUS (NSW) 109 Sf61
Somerton ▣ USA (AZ) 171 Ec29
Somers Point ▣ USA 173 Gc26
Sømidal ▣ RI 96 Qk47
Somino ▣ RUS 48 Mj16
Sömmerda ▣ D 32 Lm39
Sommesous ▣ F 23 Le42
Somogy ▣ H 42 Ls44

Somonino ▣ PL 40 Lt36
Somosomo ▣ FJI 119 Ua54
Somotillo ▣ NIC 184 Fg39
Sompeta ▣ IND (APH) 83 Pc36
Somport ▣ E 28 Ks49
Sompolno ▣ PL 40 Lt38
Somra ▣ MYA 86 Ph33
Soná ▣ PA 185 Fk41
Sonaco ▣ GNB 136 Kc39
Sonagiri ▣ IND 83 Ok33
Sonai-Rupa N.P. ▣ IND 86 Pg32
Sonamukhi ▣ IND 86 Pe33
Sonamukhi ▣ IND (WBG) 83 Pd34
Sonapur ▣ IND (ORS) 83 Pb35
Sonari ▣ IND (ASM) 86 Ph32
Sonargaon ▣ IND (ASM) 86 Ph32
Songbo ▣ PL 40 Lt36
Songong ▣ PRK 78 Rf24
Sonch'on ▣ PRK 76 Rc26
Soncillo ▣ E 28 Kr48
Sonda ▣ PK 65 Oe33
Sonda ▣ IND 30 Lk32
Sondeled ▣ N 30 Lk32
Sønderborg ▣ DK 30 Lk36
Sønder Nissum ▣ DK 30 Lj34
Sønder Omme ▣ DK 30 Lj35
Søndershausen ▣ D 32 Ll39
Søndervig ▣ DK 30 Lj35
Sonepat ▣ IND (HYA) 80 Oj31
Song ▣ WAN 138 Lg40
Songa ▣ RI 97 Rd46
Songa ▣ MOC 149 Mg53
Songa ▣ RI 97 Rd46
Songbai ▣ CHN (HUB) 75 Qh30
Songda ▣ VN 87 Qb35
Songea ▣ EAT 146 Mh51
Songgwangsa Temple ▣ ROK 78 Rd28
Song Hong ▣ VN 87 Qc34
Songma Hu ▣ CHN 76 Rd24
Songjiang ▣ CHN (SHG) 78 Ra30
Songjiang ▣ CHN (JLN)
Song Khwae ▣ THA 87 Qa36
Song-Köl ▣ KS 66 Oh25
Songkhla ▣ THA 89 Qb43
Songköl ▣ CHN (JLN)
Song Ling ▣ CHN 73 Qk25
Song Luy ▣ VN 89 Qe40
Songming ▣ CHN (YUN) 87
Songnim ▣ PRK 78 Rc26
Songpan ▣ CHN 72 Qc29
Songo ▣ EAT 146 Mh51
Songo ▣ ANG 148 Lh50
Songo ▣ SUD 141 Mc41
Songo-Iolo ▣ RDC 148 Lh48
Songo Mnara ▣ EAT 147 Na50
Song Phinong ▣ THA 88 Qa38
Songsha ▣ CHN (TIB) 68 Pa30
Songshan ▣ CHN 73 Qg28
Songshan Z.B. ▣ CHN 73 Qh25
Songtao ▣ CHN (GZH) 74 Qd31
Songxi ▣ CHN (FJN) 75 Qk32
Song Xian ▣ CHN (HNN) 72 Qg28
Songyang ▣ CHN (ZJG) 75 Qk31
Songyu ▣ ROK 79 Re27
Songyuan ▣ CHN (JLN) 76 Rc23
Song Youl ▣ CHN (SCH) 72 Qb29
Songzi ▣ CHN (GZH) 83 Pd34
Son Hiep ▣ VN 89 Qe40
Son Hoa ▣ VN 89 Qe40
Sonid Youqi ▣ CHN (NMZ) 70 Qg24
Sonid Zuoqi ▣ CHN (NMZ) 71 Qg24
Sonjo ▣ EAT 144 Mf47
Sonkovo ▣ RUS 48 Mj17
Sonkwale Mountains ▣ WAN 138 Le42
Son La ▣ VN 87 Qb35
Son Mbong ▣ CAM 138 Lf44
Sonmiani ▣ PK 65 Od32
Sonneberg ▣ D 32 Lm40
Sonobe ▣ J 79 Rj28
Sonoita ▣ USA (AZ) 171 Ee30
Sonoma Range ▣ USA 170 Eb25
Sonora ▣ BR (MS) 202 Hc56
Sonora ▣ MEX 180 Ee31
Sonora ▣ USA (CA) 170 Dk27
Sonora ▣ USA (TX) 174 Ek30
Sonoran Desert ▣ USA 170 Ec29
Sonoran State ▣ MEX 170 Ed29
Sonoyta ▣ MEX (SO) 180 Ed30
Sonozo ▣ CI 137 Kg41
Sonpur ▣ IND (GUJ) 82 Of35
Sonqor ▣ IR 57 Ne27
Sonsón ▣ CO 192 Gc43
Sonsonate ▣ ES 184 Fe39
Sonsorol Islands ▣ PAL 90 Rg43
Sonstraal ▣ ZA 154 Mb59
Sonta ▣ RDC 146 Me51
Sonthofen ▣ D 33 Ll43
Sontra ▣ D 32 Lk39
Sonwabile ▣ ANG 148 Lh48
Sooke ▣ CDN (BC) 168 Dk22
Sooretama, R. Bio. ▣ BR 203 Hk55
Soûr ▣ RL 60 Mh29
Soos ▣ CHN (ZJG) 75 Qk31
Sopelana ▣ E 28 Kr47
Soperton ▣ USA (GA) 178 Fj29
Sophie ▣ F (GF) 194 Hd43
Son Huai ▣ THA 87 Pk36
Sopianae ▣ H 42 Ls44
Soplin ▣ PE 196 Gd47
Soppero ▣ S 16 Lk11
Sop Prap ▣ THA 88 Pk37
Sopron ▣ H 42 Lr43
Sopot ▣ BG 45 Me48
Sopot ▣ PL 40 Lt36
Sopron ▣ H 42 Lr43
Soputan, Gunung ▣ RI 95 Rb45
Sopztrán ▣ GCA 184 Fe37
Sora ▣ I 36 Lo49
Sorab ▣ IND (KTK) 84 Oh38
Soraisan ▣ PK 65 Oe33
Soraker ▣ S 16 Lj14
Sora Mboum ▣ CAM 139 Lh42

Sør-Gutvika ▣ N 16 Lf13
Soria ▣ E 28 Ks49
Soriano ▣ ROU 204 Ha62
sor Kajdak ▣ KZ 62 Ng23
Serkappøya ▣ N 16 Li77
Sorkh Ab ▣ AFG 64 Ob29
Soná ▣ PA 185 Fk41
Sơn La ▣ N 30 Lg32
Sornac ▣ F 25 Lc45
Soro ▣ DK 30 Ln35
Soro ▣ IND (ORS) 83 Pd35
Soro ▣ PK 65 Od30
Sorobango ▣ CI 137 Kj41
Soroca ▣ MD 49 Me21
Sorocaba ▣ BR (SP) 205 Hg57
sor Oli Kultyk ▣ KZ 62 Ng23
Sorombéo ▣ CAM 139 Lh41
Sorondieri ▣ RI 114 Rh46
Sorong ▣ RI 97 Rf46
Soroti ▣ EAU 144 Mg45
Sorrento ▣ CDN (BC) 168 Ea20
Sorrento ▣ I 37 Lp50
Sorriso ▣ BR (MT) 202 Hc52
Sorsakoski ▣ FIN 38 Md30
Sorsan Grasslands ▣ IND 82 Oj33
Sorsele ▣ S 16 Lj13
Sorso ▣ I 36 Lj50
Sorsogon ▣ RP 90 Rc39
Sortavala ▣ RUS 38 Mf31
Sort ▣ E 28 Lb48
Sortavala ▣ RUS 38 Mf31
Sortland ▣ N 16 Lh11
Sorumsand ▣ N 30 Ln31
Sørvagur ▣ N 16 Lj12
Sørvágr ▣ DK 18 Kn28
Sosan ▣ ROK 78 Rd27
Sösdala ▣ S 31 Lo34
Sos del Rey Católico ▣ E 28 Kt48
Sosedka ▣ RUS 48 Nb19
Sosneado, Cerro ▲ RA 208 Gf63
Sosnenskij ▣ RUS 48 Mj19
Sosnova ▣ UA 49 Mg20
Sosnovka ▣ RUS 48 Na19
Sosnovo ▣ RUS 38 Mf30
Sosnovo-Ozërskoe ▣ RUS (BUR) 70 Qf19
Sosnovyj Bor ▣ RUS 38 Mk31
Sosnowica ▣ PL 41 Md39
Sosnowiec ▣ PL 41 Mb40
Sosopol ▣ IND (CGH) 83 Pa36
Sosua ▣ DOM 186 Ge36
Sossob ▣ RMM 131 Kh38
Sossusvlei ▣ NAM 154 Lh58
Sossusvlei Lodge ▣ NAM 154 Lh58
Sossusvlei Pan ▣ NAM 154 Lh58
Šoštanj ▣ SLO 42 Lq44
Šostka ▣ UA 48 Mg20
Sosúa ▣ DOM 186 Ge36
Sosyčne ▣ UA 41 Me39
Sotara, Volcán ▲ CO 192 Gb44
Soteapan ▣ MEX (VC) 183 Fc36
Soto del Barco ▣ E 26 Ko47
Sotogrande ▣ E 27 Ko54
Soto La Marina ▣ MEX (TM) 182 Fa34
Sotomayor ▣ CO 192 Gb45
Sotouboua ▣ TG 137 La41
Sotra ▣ N 30 Lf31
Sottunga ▣ FIN 38 Ma30
Sottunga ▣ FIN 38 Ma30
Souanké ▣ RCB 139 Lh44
Souássi ▣ TN 126 Lf29
Soubakanièdougou ▣ BF 137 Kk40
Soubré ▣ CI 137 Kg42
Soúda ▣ GR 47 Me53
Soudan ▣ AUS (NT) 106 Rj56
Soudougui ▣ BF 137 La40
Souf ▣ DZ 126 Le29
Souffelweyersheim ▣ F 23 Lh42
Soufli ▣ GR 45 Mg49
Soufrière ▣ WL 187 Gk39
Soufrière ▣ DZ 126 La28
Souhault ▣ F 23 Le42
Souillac ▣ F 24 Lb46
Souillac ▣ MS 157 Nj56
Souilly ▣ F 23 Lf41
Souk-Ahras ▣ DZ 126 Ld27
Souk-el-Arba-Beni-Hassan ▣ MA 125 Kg28
Souk-el-Arba-du-Rharb ▣ MA 125 Kg28
Souk-Jemâa-de-Oulad-Abbou ▣ MA 125 Kg28
Soul ▣ ROK 78 Rd27
Soulabali ▣ SN 136 Kc39
Soûr ▣ RL 60 Mh29
Soûl ▣ ROK 78 Rd27
Soulac-sur-Mer ▣ F 24 Kt45
Souliou ▣ GR 46 Ma51
Souloupéo ▣ BF 146 Ma51
Sound of Barra ▣ IRL 20 Kn33
Sound of Harris ▣ GB 20 Kn33
Sound of Monach ▣ GB 20 Kn33
Sound of Mull ▣ GB 20 Kp34
Sound of Sleat ▣ GB 20 Kp33
Sounds of Starlight Theatre ▣ AUS 108 Rg55
Soungrougrou ▣ SN 136 Kc39
Source Bleu de Meski ▣ MA 125 Kh30
Source chaude de Déssikou ▣ RCA 140 Lk42
Source chaude de Soborom ▣ TCH 133 Lj35
Source du Nil ▣ BU 146 Me47
Sour-el-Ghozlane ▣ DZ 126 Ld27
Souris ▣ CDN (PE) 176 Gj22
Souroukoudinga ▣ BF 137 Kh39
Souroutouna ▣ BF 131 Kj39
Sous ▣ MA 124 Ke30
Sousa ▣ BR (PB) 201 Ja49
Souss-Massa, P.N. ▣ MA 124 Ke30
Sous ▣ MA 124 Ke30
Sousceyrac ▣ F 27 Kn52
Sous Mboum ▣ CAM 139 Lh42
Soustons ▣ F 24 Kt47
Souterraine, La ▣ F 24 Lb44
Souto Soares ▣ BR (BA)
South America ▣ 8 Gb11
South Andaman ▣ IND 88 Ph40
South Australia ▣ AUS 101 Rb13
South Australian Basin ▣ 100 Ra14
South-Baltic Sea ▣ (MS) 175 Ff28

South Banggi Strait ▣ MAL 94 Qj42
Southbank ▣ CDN (BC) 166 Dh18
South Bay ▣ CDN (ON) 172 Fd20
South Bay ▣ USA (FL) 179 Fk32
South Baymouth ▣ CDN (ON) 173 Fj23
South Bend ▣ USA (IN) 173 Fg25
South Bimini ▣ BS 179 Ga33
South Boston ▣ USA (VA) 178 Ga27
South Branch ▣ CDN (NF) 177 Ha22
Southbridge ▣ NZ 113 Tg67
South Brook ▣ CDN (NF) 177 Hb21
South Brookfield ▣ CDN (NS) 176 Gh23
South Bruny N.P. ▣ AUS 111 Sd67
South Carolina ▣ USA 178 Fk28
South Carolina ▣ USA 178 Fk28
South Cay ▣ CO 185 Fk38
South Channel ▣ RP 90 Ra38
South China Basin ▣ 10 Qb08
South China Sea ▣ 10 Qb08
South Dakota ▣ USA 172 Ek23
South Downs ▣ GB 21 Ku40
South East ▣ RB 155 Mc58
South East Aru Marine Reserve ▣ RI 114 Rh49
Southeast Cape ▣ USA 164 Bf14
Southeast Forests N.P. ▣ AUS 111 Se64
Southeast Indian Ridge ▣ 100 Oa14
South East Pacific Basin ▣ 190 Fa14
South East Point ▣ AUS 111 Sd65
South East Point ▣ BS 186 Gd35
Southend-on-Sea ▣ GB 21 La39
Spain ▣ 15 Kb06
Southern Alps ▣ NZ 113 Td68
Southern Altay Gold Nature Reserve ▣ CHN 67 Pj24
Southern Central Reserve A.L. ▣ AUS 105 Rc59
Southern Cross ▣ AUS (WA) 104 Qk61
Southern Indian Lake ▣ CDN 163 Fa07
Southern Laos Cruise ▣ LAO/K 89 Qc38
Southern N.P. ▣ SUD 141 Me42
Southern Pines ▣ USA (NC) 178 Ga28
Southern Sporades ▣ GR 47 Mf52
Southern Uplands ▣ GB 20 Kq35
Southey ▣ CDN (SK) 169 Eh20
South Fiji Basin ▣ 100 Tb12
South Foreland ▣ GB 21 Lb39
South Fork ▣ USA 171 Ef26
Spas-Klepiki ▣ RUS 48 Na18
South Francisco de Macoris ▣ DOM 186 Ge36
South Galway ▣ AUS (QLD) 108 Sb58
South Georgia ▣ 192 Ja15
South Georgia ▣ USA 191 Ja15
South Goulburn Island ▣ AUS 106 Rg51
South Gulf Saint Ann's ▣ CDN (NS) 176 Gk22
South Harbour ▣ CDN (NS) 176 Gk22
South Hatia Island ▣ BD 86 Pf34
South Haven ▣ USA (MI) 173 Fg24
South Hill ▣ USA (VA) 178 Ga27
South Honshu Ridge ▣ 10 Rb06
South Horr ▣ EAK 144 Mj45
South Island ▣ AUS 109 Sf56
South Island ▣ EAK 144 Mj44
South Island N.P. ▣ EAK 144 Mj44
South Junction ▣ CDN 172 Fc21
South Kinangop ▣ EAK 144 Mj46
South Korea ▣ ROK 53 Ra06
South Lake Tahoe ▣ USA (NV) 170 Ea26
South Luangwa N.P. ▣ Z 146 Mf52
South Luconia Shoals ▣ 94 Qg43
South Male Atoll ▣ MV 84 Og44
South Maldhunmadulu Atoll = Noonu Atoll ▣ MV 84 Og43
South Molton ▣ GB 21 Kr39
South Nahanni River ▣ CDN 166 Dh15
South Nilandhoo Atoll = Dhaalu Atoll ▣ MV 84 Og44
South Orkney Islands ▣ 190 Hb14
South Orkney Islands ▣ GB 191 Hb15
South Ossetia ▣ GE 57 Nc24
South Padre Island ▣ USA (TX) 181 Fb32
South Pass City ▣ USA (WY) 171 Ef24
South Platte River ▣ USA 171 Ef25
South Porcupine ▣ CDN (ON) 173 Fk21
Southport ▣ AUS (QLD) 109 Sg59
Southport ▣ GB 21 Kr37
Southport ▣ USA (NC) 178 Ga29
South Prince of Wales Wilderness ▣ USA 166 Dd18
South Pt. ▣ BS 186 Gc34
South Ronaldsay ▣ GB 20 Ks32
South Salmara ▣ IND (ASM) 86 Pf32
South Sandwich Islands ▣ 190 Jb15
South Sandwich Islands ▣ GB 191 Jb15
South Sandwich Trench ▣ 190 Jb15
South Saskatchewan River ▣ CDN 169 Ed20
South Scotia Ridge ▣ 6 Hb31
South Shetland Islands ▣ ANT 6 Ha31
South Shields ▣ GB 20 Kt36
South Sioux City ▣ USA (IA) 172 Fb25
South Solomon Trench ▣ 117 Ta51
Southtown ▣ USA 154 Lh59
South Stradbroke Island ▣ AUS 109 Sg59
South Taranaki Bight ▣ NZ 113 Th66
South Tasman Rise ▣ 100 Sa14
South Thiladhummathee Atoll = Haa-Dhaalu Atoll ▣ MV 84 Og43

South Tucson ▣ USA (AZ) 171 Ee29
South Uist ▣ GB 20 Kn33
South West Cape ▣ AUS 111 Sc67
Southwest Cape ▣ NZ 113 Td69
Southwest Indian Ridge ▣ 9 Na14
Southwest N.P. ▣ AUS 111 Sd67
Southwest Pacific Basin ▣ 11 Cb13
Southwest Point ▣ BS 179 Gb33
Southwest Point ▣ BS 186 Gc34
South West Rocks ▣ AUS (NSW) 109 Sg61
Southwold ▣ GB 21 Lb38
South Yandaminta ▣ AUS (NSW) 108 Sa60
South Zeal ▣ GB 21 Kr40
Soutpansberg ▣ ZA 152 Me57
Souvigny ▣ F 25 Ld44
Sovata ▣ RO 43 Mf44
Soverato ▣ I 37 Lr52
Sovereign Hill ▣ AUS (VIC) 111 Sb64
Sovetsk ▣ RUS 39 Mb36
Sovetsk ▣ RUS 48 Nb18
Sovetskaja ▣ ANT (RUS) 7 Pb34
Sovetskaja ▣ RUS 48 Na17
Sovetskij ▣ RUS 38 Mj30
Sovetskoe ▣ RUS (KBA) 57 Nb24
Sowa Pan ▣ RB 151 Mc56
Sowczyce ▣ PL 40 Lt40
Soweto ▣ ZA 155 Md59
Sowsa ▣ EAK 144 Mh45
Sowma'eh Sara ▣ IR 57 Ne27
Soyalo ▣ MEX (CHP) 183 Fd37
Soya-misaki ▣ J 77 Sb23
Soyet ▣ IND (MPH) 82 Oj34
Soyo ▣ ANG 148 Lg49
Soyopa ▣ MEX (SO) 180 Ee32
Sozu ▣ J 77 Rj27
Sozopol ▣ BG 45 Mh48
Spa ▣ B 23 Lf40
Spaaland ▣ ZA 155 Md62
Spalding ▣ GB 21 Ku38
Spalding ▣ USA (ID) 168 Eb23
Spándou Polikí ▣ CZ 42 Lo41
Spaniard's Bay ▣ CDN (NF) 177 Hd22
Spanish Fork ▣ USA 171 Ee25
Spanish Head ▣ GB 21 Kq36
Spanish Town ▣ JA 186 Gb37
Spanwerk ▣ ZA 155 Md58
Sparta ▣ USA (NC) 178 Fk27
Sparta ▣ USA (TN) 175 Fh28
Sparta ▣ USA (WI) 172 Fe24
Spartanburg ▣ USA (SC) 178 Fk28
Spárti ▣ GR 46 Mc53
Spas-Demensk ▣ RUS 48 Mh18
Spasovo ▣ BG 45 Mj47
Spassk-Dal'nij ▣ RUS 76 Rg23
Spassk-Rjazanskij ▣ RUS 48 Mk17
Spatsizi Plateau ▣ CDN 166 Df17
Spatsizi Plateau Wilderness Prov. Park ▣ CDN 166 Df17
Spaun Bridge ▣ GB 20 Kq34
Spearfish ▣ USA (SD) 169 Ej23
Speculator ▣ USA (NY) 177 Gc24
Speedwell Island ▣ GB 210 Ha72
Speightstown ▣ BDS 187 Ha39
Spelle ▣ D 32 Lh38
Spencer ▣ USA (IA) 172 Fc24
Spencer ▣ USA (IN) 175 Fg26
Spencer ▣ USA (NE) 172 Fa24
Spencer ▣ USA (NZ) 113 Te67
Spencer Bay ▣ NAM 154 Lf60
Spencer Bridge ▣ CDN (BC) 168 Dk20
Spencer Gulf ▣ AUS 110 Rj63
Spennymoor ▣ GB 20 Kt36
Speos of Horemheb ▣ ET 129 Mg33
Spercheiós ▣ GR 46 Mc51
Spessart ▣ D 33 Lk41
Spétses ▣ GR 46 Md53
Spétses ▣ GR 45 Md53
Spey ▣ GB 20 Kr33
Speyer ▣ D 33 Lj41
Speyside Beach ▣ TT 187 Gk40
Spezand ▣ PK 65 Od30
Spezzano Albanese ▣ I 37 Lr51
Spezzano della Sila ▣ I 37 Lr51
Spiddle ▣ IRL 19 Kl37
Spiekeroog ▣ D 32 Lh37
Spielcasino Baden-Baden ▣ D 33 Lj42
Spigelino ▣ MEX (SO)
Spilimbergo ▣ I 35 Ln44
Spiinan ▣ IR 57 Nb26
Spilsby ▣ GB 21 La37
Spin Boldak ▣ AFG 65 Oc29
Spiro ▣ I 34 Lj43
Spirit Lake Ind. Res. ▣ USA 172 Fa22
Spirit Lake ▣ USA (IA) 172 Fc24
Spirit River ▣ CDN (AB) 167 Ea18
Spišská Belá ▣ SK 43 Ma41
Spišská Nová Ves ▣ SK 43 Ma42
Spišský hrad ▣ SK 43 Ma42
Spišský Štvrtok ▣ SK 43 Ma42
Spitalfields ▣ NAM 150 Lh56
Spittal an der Drau ▣ A 35 Lo44
Spitz ▣ A 42 Lq42
Spitzkoppe ▣ NAM 150 Lh56
Spitzkoppe Rock Paintings ▣ NAM 150 Lh56
Split ▣ HR 35 Lr47
Splügen ▣ CH 34 Lk44
Spoffard ▣ USA (TX) 181 Ek31
Spoggies ▣ AUS 104 Qh57
Spogi ▣ LV 39 Mg34
Spokane ▣ USA (WA) 168 Eb22
Spokane House ▣ USA 168 Eb22
Spokane Ind. Res. ▣ USA 168 Eb22
Špola ▣ UA 49 Mf21
Spoleto ▣ I 36 Ln48
Spondin ▣ CDN (AB) 169 Ee20
Spooner ▣ USA (WI) 172 Fe23
Spornoe ▣ RUS 54 Sb07
Spotorno ▣ I 34 Lj46
Spotted House ▣ USA (WY)
Spragge ▣ CDN (ON) 173 Fh22
Sprague ▣ USA (WA) 168 Eb22
Spratly Islands ▣ 94 Qh40
Spray ▣ USA (OR) 168 Ea23

Spree ▣ D 32 Lp39
Spreewald ▣ D 32 Lp39
Spremberg ▣ D 32 Lp39
Sprengisandur ▣ IS 18 Kb26
Spring ▣ RO 44 Md45
Stalker Castle ▣ GB 20 Kp34
Stäkliökés ▣ LT 39 Me36
Stalbe ▣ LV 39 Mf33
Stakišskés ▣ LT 39 Me36
Stäkliäien ▣ S 31 Lp31
Staller Sattel ▣ I/A 34 Ln44
Staloluokta ▣ S 16 Lj12
Staloluokta fjällstation ▣ S 16 Lj12
Stalowa Wola ▣ PL 41 Mc40
Stambolijski ▣ BG 45 Me48
Stamford ▣ AUS (QLD) 109 Sb56
Stamford ▣ GB 21 Ku38
Stamford ▣ USA (CT) 177 Gd25
Stamford ▣ USA (TX) 174 Fa29
Stamford Bridge ▣ GB 21 Ku37
Stampriet ▣ NAM 154 Lj58
Stamsund ▣ N 16 Lg11
Standard ▣ CDN (AB) 178 Fk29
Standerton ▣ ZA 155 Me59
Standing Rock Ind. Res. ▣ USA 172 Ek23
Standing Stone S.P. ▣ USA 175 Fh27
Standish ▣ USA (MI) 173 Fj24
Stanford ▣ USA (KY) 175 Fh27
Stanford ▣ USA (MT) 169 Ee22
Stånga ▣ S 31 Lt33
Stanhope ▣ GB 21 Ks36
Staniard Creek ▣ BS 179 Gb33
Stanica Bagaevskaja ▣ RUS 49 Na22
Staniel Cay Beach ▣ BS 186 Gb34
Staniší ▣ SCG 44 Lu45
Staňkov ▣ CZ 42 Lo41
Stanley ▣ AUS (TAS) 111 Sc66
Stanley ▣ GB (GBF) 210 Hb71
Stanley ▣ USA (ND) 169 Ej21
Stanley Mission ▣ CDN (SK) 167 Eh18
Stanley, Mount ▣ EAU/RDC 144 Md45
Stanley Reservoir ▣ IND 84 Oj40
Stanmore ▣ ZW 152 Me56
Stannum ▣ AUS (NSW) 109 Sf60
Stanovoy Nar'ye'a ▣ RUS 55 Qc07
Stanovoy Khrebet ▣ RUS 55 Ra07
Stans ▣ CH 34 Lj44
Stansmore Range ▣ AUS 104 Rb57
Stansmore Range ▣ AUS 103 Rd56
Stanthorpe ▣ AUS (QLD) 109 Sf60
Stanton Bank ▣ GB 20 Kn34
Stanwell ▣ AUS (QLD) 109 Sf57
Stanwell Park ▣ AUS (NSW) 111 Sf63
Stanycno-Luhans'ke ▣ UA 48 Mk21
Stapleford ▣ ZW 152 Mg55
Stapleton ▣ USA (MN) 172 Fc22
Stapleton ▣ USA (NE) 172 Ek25
Staporków ▣ PL 41 Ma39
Stara ▣ PL 41 Lu39
Starachowice ▣ PL 41 Mb39
Stara Kiszewa ▣ PL 40 Lt37
Stara Moravica ▣ SCG 44 Lu45
Stara Novalja ▣ HR 35 Lp46
Stara Pazova ▣ SCG 44 Ma46
Stara Reka ▣ BG 45 Mg48
Stara Vyživka ▣ UA 41 Me38
Stara Zagora ▣ BG 45 Mf48
Starbuck Island ▣ KIR 11 Ca10
Star City ▣ USA (AR) 175 Fe29
Stare Dolistovo ▣ PL 41 Mc37
Stare Jezewo ▣ PL 41 Mc37
Stare Kiełbonki ▣ PL 41 Mb37
Stare Stracze ▣ PL 40 Lr38
Stargard Szczeciński ▣ PL 40 Lq37
Starica ▣ RUS 48 Mh17
Starică ▣ RUS 48 Mh17
Staring ▣ RI 96 Ra47
Staritsa ▣ RUS 48 Mh17
Starkville ▣ USA (MS) 175 Ff29
Starkweather ▣ USA (ND) 172 Fa21
Starnberg ▣ D 33 Lm42
Starnberger See ▣ D 33 Lm43
Starobil's'k ▣ UA 48 Mk21
Starodub ▣ BY 48 Mg19
Starodub ▣ RUS 48 Mg19
Starodubcevo ▣ PL 41 Lu37
Starogard Gdański ▣ PL 40 Lt37
Starominskaya ▣ RUS 49 Mk22
Staro Nagoričane ▣ MK 44 Mb48
Staro Petrovo Selo ▣ HR 35 Ls45
Staroselskaja ▣ RUS 71 Qj19
Starosel ▣ BG 45 Mf48
Staro Selo ▣ BG 45 Mg47
Starotitarovskaja ▣ RUS 49 Mj23
Starozilovo ▣ RUS 48 Na18
Start Point ▣ GB 21 Kr40
Staryy Krym ▣ UA 49 Mj23
Stary Dzierzgoń ▣ PL 41 Lu37
Staryy Oskol ▣ RUS 48 Mj20
Staryja Darohi ▣ BY 48 Me19
Staryj Sambir ▣ UA 43 Mc41
Staryj Smokovec ▣ SK 43 Ma41
Staßfurt ▣ D 32 Lm39
Staszów ▣ PL 41 Mb40
State College ▣ USA (PA) 177 Gb25
State Line ▣ USA (MS) 175 Ff30
State Mosque ▣ MAL 92 Qa44
Statesboro ▣ USA (GA) 178 Fj30
Statesville ▣ USA (NC) 178 Fk28
Stathelle ▣ N 31 Lk31
Station de capture d'Epulu ▣ RDC 144 Mc45
Statue of Liberty ▣ USA 177 Gd25
Stäucheni ▣ MD 49 Me22
Staunton River S.P. ▣ USA 178 Ga27
Staunton ▣ USA (VA) 177 Ga26
Stavanger ▣ N 30 Lf32
Stavelot ▣ B 23 Lf40
Stavern ▣ N 30 Lk32
Stavky ▣ UA 41 Me38
Stavne ▣ UA 43 Mc42
Stavón ▣ GR 45 Me48
Stavropol ▣ RUS 57 Nb23
Stavroúpoli ▣ GR 45 Me49
Stavsiö ▣ S 31 Ls31
Stawiszyn ▣ PL 40 Lt39
Steamboat ▣ CDN (QC) 176 Gf27
Ste-CharlesGranier ▣ CDN 176 Gf27
Steamboat ▣ USA (OR) 168 Dj24
Steamboat Springs ▣ USA (CO) 171 Eg25
Stębark ▣ PL 40 Ma37
Stebbins ▣ USA (AK) 164 Bj14
Steele ▣ USA (ND) 172 Ek22
Steele ▣ USA (MO) 175 Ff27
Steele, Mount ▣ CDN 166 Ck15
Steelpoort ▣ ZA 152 Me58
Steelville ▣ USA (MO) 175 Fe27
Steenbergen ▣ NL 23 Le39
Steenstrup Gletscher ▣ DK 163 Hb03
Steen River ▣ CDN (AB) 167 Eb17
Steenvoorde ▣ B 23 Lc40

Steenwijk ☐ NL 23 Lg38
Steep Point ▲ AUS 104 Qg59
Steese Highway ▦ USA (AK) 165 Cf13
Stefan Karadža ☐ BG 45 Md47
Stefansson Island ☐ CDN 162 Ec04
Steffen, Cerro ▲ RA/RCH 210 Gg68
Stefflburg ☐ CH 34 Lh44
Stege ☐ DK 30 Ln34
Stegna ☐ PL 40 Lo36
Stei ☐ RO 43 Mc44
Steigen ☐ N 16 Lh12
Steillopsbrog ☐ ZA 152 Me57
Steilrand ☐ ZA 155 Mf59
Steilrandberge ▲ NAM 150 Lg54
Stein ☐ D 33 Lm41
Steinach ☐ D 33 Lm41
Steinach ☐ D 33 Lm40
Stein am Rhein ☐ CH 34 Lj43
Steinau ☐ D 33 Lm41
Steinbach ☐ CDN (MB) 172 Fb21
Steine ☐ N 16 Lh11
Steinfeld ☐ D 32 Lj38
Steinfeld ☐ NAM 154 Lj58
Steinfurt ☐ D 32 Lh36
Steinhagen ☐ D 32 Ln36
Steinhatchee ☐ USA (FL) 178 Fj31
Steinhausen ☐ NAM 150 Lk56
Steinheim ☐ D 32 Lk39
Steinhuder Meer ☐ D 32 Lk39
Steinkjer ☐ N 16 Ll14
Steinkopf ☐ ZA 154 Lj60
Steinsdalsfossen ▦ N 30 Lg30
Steins Ghost Town ☐ USA (AZ) 171 Ef29
Steinstaðabyggð ☐ IS 18 Ka25
Stekenjokvägen ▦ S 16 Lh13
Steki ☐ LV 39 Mg34
Stella ☐ ZA 155 Mc59
Stella Maris ☐ BS 186 Gc34
Stellarton ☐ CDN (NS) 176 Gj23
Stellenbosch ☐ ZA 154 Lk62
Stelling van Amsterdam ☐ ▦ NL 23 Lg38
Stelmužė ☐ LT 39 Mg35
Stélvio, P.N.delle = Stilfser Joch, N.P. ☐ ▦ I 34 Ll44
Stená Foúrkas ☐ ▦ GR 46 Mc52
Stendal ☐ D 32 Lm38
Stende ☐ LV 39 Mc33
Stenhouse ☐ AUS (SA) 110 Rk63
Stenó Andikithira ☐ GR 46 Md55
Stenó Kafiréa ☐ GR 47 Me52
Stenó Kéas ☐ GR 47 Me53
Stenó Kímolou Sífnou ☐ GR 47 Me54
Stenó Kithíra ☐ GR 45 Md54
Stenó Koufonísi ☐ GR 47 Mg56
Stenón Kíthnou ☐ GR 47 Me53
Stenó Pétsai ☐ GR 45 Md53
Stenó Poíegou Folégandrou ☐ GR 47 Me54
Stenó Serífou ☐ GR 47 Me53
Stenó Sífnou ☐ GR 47 Me53
Stènovice ☐ CZ 42 Lo41
Stensnhuvuste n.p. ☐ ▦ S 31 Lg35
Stenstorp ☐ S 31 Lo32
Stenungsund ☐ S 30 Lm32
Stepan' ☐ UA 41 Mg39
Stepanakert = Xankendi ☐ AZ 57 Nd26
Stepanavan ☐ ARM 57 Nc25
Stepancí ☐ MK 44 Md49
Stephanie Wildlife Reserve ☐ ETH 144 Mj43
Stephenville ☐ CDN (NF) 177 Ha21
Stephenville ☐ USA (TX) 174 Fa29
Stephenville Crossing ☐ CDN (NF) 177 Ha21
Štĕpivka ☐ UA 48 Mh20
Štĕpnica ☐ PL 40 Lg37
Stepovac ☐ SCG 44 Ma46
Stepp Rock ☐ CDN (MB) 172 Fa20
Sterdyń-Osada ☐ PL 41 Ma40
Sterkfontein ☐ ZA 155 Md59
Sterkfontein Dam Nature Reserve ☐ ZA 155 Me60
Sterkspruit ☐ ZA 155 Md61
Sterkstroom ☐ ZA 155 Md61
Sterling ☐ USA (CO) 174 Ej25
Sterling ☐ ZA 154 Ma61
Sterling City ☐ USA (TX) 174 Ek30
Sterling Highway ▦ USA (AK) 164 Cd16
Sterling Hts. ☐ USA (MI) 173 Fj24
Sterling Landing ☐ USA (AK) 165 Cc14
Sterlitamak ☐ RUS 54 Nd08
Sternberg ☐ D 32 Lm37
Šternberk ☐ CZ 42 Ls41
Stérnes ☐ GR 47 Me55
Steroh ☐ YE 61 Np39
Sterzing = Vipiteno ☐ I 34 Lm44
Stettin Lagoon ☐ D/PL 40 Lp37
Stettler ☐ CDN (AB) 169 Ed19
Steubenville ☐ USA (OH) 173 Fk25
Stevenage ☐ GB 21 Ks39
Stevens, Mount ▲ NZ 113 Tg66
Stevens Peak ▲ AUS 105 Rf58
Stevens Pass ▦ USA (WI) 172 Ff23
Stevens Village ☐ USA (AK) 165 Cf12
Stevensville ☐ USA (MT) 168 Ec22
Stevns Klint ☐ DK 30 Ln35
Stewart ☐ CDN (BC) 166 Dd15
Stewart Crossing ☐ CDN (YT) 165 Db14
Stewart Island ☐ NZ 113 Te69
Stewart Island ▲ SOL 117 Tb50
Stewart, Mount ▲ AUS (QLD) 107 Sc56
Stewart, Mount ▲ CDN 165 Da14
Stewart Plateau ☐ CDN 165 Dc14
Stewarts Point ☐ USA (CA) 170 Dj26
Stewart Valley ☐ CDN (SK) 169 Eg20
Steyerberg ☐ D 32 Lk38
Steynsburg ☐ ZA 155 Mc61
Steynsrus ☐ ZA 155 Md59
Steyr ☐ A 42 Lp42
Steytlerville ☐ ZA 155 Mc62
Stężyca ☐ PL 40 Ls37
Stiegler's Gorge ▲ EAT 147 Mk49
Stift Admont ☐ A 42 Lp43
Stift Göttweig ☐ A 42 Lq42
Stift Klosterneuburg ☐ A 42 Lr42
Stift Kremsmünster ☐ A 42 Lp42
Stift Melk ☐ A 42 Lq42
Stift Sankt Paul ☐ A 35 Lp44
Stift Seckau ☐ A 35 Lp43
Stiftskirche Innichen ☐ I 34 Ln44
Stift Zwettl ☐ A 42 Lq42
Stiges ☐ E 27 Lb49
Stigler ☐ USA (OK) 174 Fc28
Stigliano ☐ I 37 Lr50
Stigtomta ☐ S 31 Lg32
Stikine Plateau ☐ CDN 166 De16
Stikine Ranges ☐ CDN 166 De16
Stile ☐ DZ 126 Lc23
Stiles ☐ USA (TX) 174 Ek30
Stilfontein ☐ ZA 155 Md59

Stilfser Joch, N.P. = Stélvio, P.N.delle ☐ ▦ I 34 Ll44
Stilída ☐ GR 46 Mc52
Stillwater ☐ USA (NV) 170 Ea26
Stillwater ☐ USA (OK) 174 Fb28
Stilo ☐ I 37 Lr52
Stilwell ☐ USA (OK) 174 Fc28
Štímlje ☐ SCG 44 Mb49
Stînapari ☐ RO 44 Mb46
Stinear, Mount ▲ 7 Ob33
Stinnett ☐ USA (TX) 174 Ek28
Stip ☐ MK 44 Md49
Stira ☐ GR 47 Me52
Stirling ☐ AUS (NT) 108 Rg56
Stirling ☐ AUS (QLD) 107 Sa54
Stirling ☐ GB 20 Kr34
Stirling ▲ AUS (QLD) 107 Sa54
Stirling North ☐ AUS (SA) 110 Rj62
Stirling Range N.P. ☐ ▦ AUS 104 Qk63
Stíttary ☐ CZ 42 Lq42
Stittar ☐ SK 43 Mf42
Stjordal ☐ N 16 Ll14
Saint Joseph ☐ WD 187 Gk38
Stob ☐ BG 44 Md48
Stobi ☐ MK 44 Md49
Stockach ☐ D 33 Lk43
Stockaryd ☐ S 31 Lp33
Stockbridge ☐ GB 21 Kt39
Stockbridge Ind. Res. ☐ USA 111 Sc63
Stockdale ☐ USA (TX) 181 Fb31
Stockerau ☐ A 42 Lr42
Stockholm ⊛ S 31 Ls31
Stockman's Hall of Fame ☐ AUS (QLD) 109 Sc57
Stockport ☐ GB 21 Ks37
Stockport ☐ USA 152 Md57
Stockton ☐ AUS (QLD) 109 Sc56
Stockton ☐ USA (CA) 170 Dk27
Stockton ☐ USA (KS) 174 Fa26
Stockton-on-Tees ☐ GB 21 Kt36
Stockton Plateau ☐ USA 181 Ej31
Stockton S.P. ☐ ▦ USA 174 Fd27
Stoczek Łukowski ☐ PL 41 Mb39
Stod ☐ CZ 42 Lo41
Stöde ☐ S 17 Lj14
Stödi ☐ N 16 Lh12
Stöðvarfjörður ☐ IS 18 Kg26
Stoffberg ☐ ZA 155 Me58
Stoholm ☐ DK 30 Lk34
Stoke-on-Trent ☐ GB 21 Ks37
Stokes N.P. ☐ ▦ AUS 104 Ra62
Stokes Point ▲ AUS 111 Sb66
Stokkseyri ☐ IS 18 Jt27
Stokksnes ☐ IS 18 Kf26
Stokkvägen ☐ N 16 Lg12
Stolbarneso ☐ N 16 Lh11
Stolberg ☐ D 32 Lh40
Stólin ☐ BY 48 Mf20
Stolkertsijver ☐ SME 194 Hc43
Stollberg ☐ D 32 Ln40
Stömio ☐ GR 46 Mc51
Stolin ☐ BY 48 Mf20
Stone ☐ GB 21 Ks38
Stone Circles ☐ WAG 136 Kc39
Stone Forest ☐ CHN 87 Qb33
Stoneham ☐ USA (CO) 174 Ej25
Stonehaven ☐ GB 20 Ks34
Stonehenge ☐ AUS (QLD) 108 Sb58
Stonehenge ☐ ▦ GB 21 Kt39
Stone Mtn. Park ☐ USA 178 Fh29
Stone Mtn. Prov. Park ☐ ▦ CDN 166 Dh16
Stone Rondavel ☐ NAM 154 Lk59
Stonewall ☐ CDN (MB) 172 Fb20
Stone-walled ruins ☐ RB 152 Md57
Stöng ☐ IS 18 Ka26
Stonglandet ☐ N 16 Lj11
Stonhoekoe ☐ SME 194 Hc44
Stony Creek Ind. Res. ☐ CDN 166 Dh19
Stony Ind. Res. ☐ CDN 168 Ec20
Stony Plain ☐ CDN (AB) 169 Ed19
Stony Rapids ☐ CDN (SK) 169 Eh16
Stony Rapids ☐ CDN 162 Ed07
Stopnica ☐ PL 41 Ma40
Stör ☐ D 32 Lk37
Stora Aakö ☐ S 31 Lq33
Stóra Dímun ☐ DK 18 Ko29
Stora Sjöfallets n.p. ☐ ▦ S 16 Lg12
Storby ☐ FIN 31 Ls31
Stordalen ☐ N 17 Lf14
Storebæltsbro ☐ DK 30 Ll35
Store mosse n.p. ☐ ▦ S 31 Lp33
Stören ☐ N 16 Ll14
Storfjorden ☐ N 16 Lk07
Storforsen ☐ S 16 Ma13
Storjord ☐ N 16 Lj12
Storjorda ☐ N 16 Lj12
Storkerson Peninsula ☐ CDN 162 Ec04
Storkow ☐ D 32 Lo38
Stormberg ☐ ZA 155 Md61
Stormberg ▲ ZA 155 Md61
Storm Lake ☐ USA (IA) 172 Fc24
Stornoway ☐ GB 20 Kn33
Storöya ☐ N 16 Me05
Storøya ☐ N 16 Lk07
Storøjorden ☐ N 16 Lk07
Storsjön ☐ S 31 Lr31
Storsjön ☐ S 31 Lq30
Storsudret ☐ S 31 Ls33
Storuman ☐ S 16 Lj13
Storvorde ☐ DK 30 Ll34
Storvreta ☐ S 31 Lr31
Story ☐ USA (AR) 174 Fd28
Story City ☐ USA (WY) 169 Eg24
Stosti ☐ USA (IA) 172 Fd24
Stoughton ☐ CDN (SK) 169 Ej21
Stour ☐ GB 21 Kt39
Stourhead ☐ GB 21 Ks39
Stovbcy ☐ BY 41 Mg37
Stovbcy ☐ BY 41 Mg37
Stowe ☐ DK 30 Lk34
Stowiecino ☐ PL 40 Ls36
Stowmarket ☐ GB 21 La38
Stow-on-the-Wold ☐ GB 21 Kt39
Strabane ☐ GB 19 Kn36
Stradella ☐ I 34 Lk45
Straelen ☐ D 32 Lg39
Strahan ☐ AUS (TAS) 111 Sc67
Strait of Belle Isle ☐ CDN 163 Ha08
Strait of Canso ☐ CDN 176 Gk23
Strait of Dover ☐ 23 Lb40
Strait of Gibraltar ☐ 27 Kp55
Strait of Hormuz ☐ 62 Nj32
Strait of Jubal ☐ ET 129 Mg32
Strait of Magellan ☐ 210 Ge72
Strait of Malacca ☐ MAL/RI 92 Pk43
Strait of Messina ☐ I 37 Lq52
Strait of Otranto ☐ 37 Lt50
Straits of Florida ☐ 179 Fk33
Strakonice ☐ CZ 42 Lo41
Straldža ☐ BG 45 Mf48
Stralki ☐ BY 39 Mj35
Stralsund ☐ D 32 Lo36
Strambino ☐ I 34 Lh45
Strāmture ☐ RO 43 Me43
Stranda ☐ N 17 Ld14
Strandakirkja ☐ IS 18 Jt27
Strandby ☐ DK 30 Ll33
Strande ☐ N 30 Lg30
Strandfontein ☐ ZA 154 Lk61
Strandir ☐ IS 18 Ju24
Strandvägen ☐ HR 35 Mk18
Stranford ☐ GB 19 Ko36

Strängnäs ☐ S 31 Ls31
Strängsjö ☐ S 31 Lr32
Stranraer ☐ GB 19 Kq36
Strasbourg ☐ F 23 Lh42
Strasburg ☐ D 32 Lo37
Strašeni ☐ MD 49 Me22
Stratford ☐ NZ 113 Tf65
Stratford ☐ USA (TX) 174 Ej27
Stratford-upon-Avon ☐ GB 21 Kt38
Strathalbyn ☐ AUS (SA) 110 Rk63
Strathbogie ☐ AUS (QLD) 107 Sa54
Strathburn ☐ AUS (QLD) 107 Sb55
Strathcona Prov. Park ☐ CDN 168 Dh21
Strathfillan ☐ GB (QLD) 108 Sb57
Strathgordon ☐ AUS (QLD) 107 Sb53
Strathgordon ☐ AUS (TAS) 111 Sd67
Strathhaven ☐ AUS (QLD) 107 Sb53
Strathmay ☐ AUS (QLD) 107 Sb53
Strathmerton ☐ AUS (VIC) 111 Sc63
Strathmore ☐ AUS (QLD) 107 Sa54
Strathmore ☐ AUS (QLD) 107 Sd56
Strathmore ☐ CDN (AB) 169 Ed20
Strathroy ☐ AUS (QLD) 109 Sc56
Stratford ☐ CDN (ON) 173 Fk24
Stratinska ☐ BIH 35 Lr46
Stratinska ☐ BIH 35 Lr46
Stratonikeia ☐ TR 47 Mj53
Strátos ☐ GR 46 Mb52
Stratton ☐ GB 21 Kq40
Stratton ☐ USA (ME) 177 Ge23
Straubing ☐ D 33 Ln42
Straumnes ▲ IS 18 Jr25
Strausberg ☐ D 32 Lo38
Strawberry Mountain ▲ USA 168 Dk23
Streaky Bay ☐ AUS (SA) 110 Rh62
Streaky Bay ☐ AUS 110 Rh62
Streator ☐ USA (IL) 173 Ff25
Streetsville ☐ SK 43 Lt41
Strehaia ☐ RO 44 Md46
Strekov ☐ SK 42 Ls43
Strelčá ☐ BG 45 Me48
Strešer ☐ SCG 44 Mb48
Strevell ☐ USA (ID) 171 Ed24
Streymoy ☐ DK 18 Kn28
Strezovce ☐ SCG 44 Mc48
Stříbro ☐ CZ 42 Lo41
Strilky ☐ UA 43 Mc41
Strimonikó ☐ GR 44 Md49
Strmica ☐ HR 35 Lr46
Stroeder ☐ RA 209 Gj66
Strofiliá ☐ GR 46 Mc52
Strogonoit Point ☐ USA 164 Ca17
Strokkur ☐ IS 18 Ka26
Strómboli ▲ I 37 Lq52
Stromeferry ☐ GB 20 Kp33
Stromiec ☐ PL 41 Mb39
Strommnes ☐ GB 20 Kr32
Strömsbruk ☐ S 31 Lr31
Strömstad ☐ S 30 Lm32
Strömsund ☐ S 16 Lh14
Stronsay ☐ GB 20 Ks32
Strontian ☐ GB 20 Kp34
Stropkov ☐ SK 43 Mb41
Strošinci ☐ SCG 44 Lu46
Stroud ☐ AUS (NSW) 111 Sf62
Stroud ☐ GB 21 Ks39
Struan ☐ CDN (OK) 174 Fb28
Struan ☐ CDN (SK) 169 Eg19
Struer ☐ DK 30 Lk34
Struga ☐ MK 44 Mb49
Strugi-Krasnye ☐ RUS 38 Mk32
Strusshamn ☐ N 30 Lf31
Struthers ☐ MK 44 Md49
Struve Geodetic Arc ☐ ▦ BY 41 Me37
Struve Geodetic Arc ☐ ▦ EST 39 Mg32
Struve Geodetic Arc ☐ ▦ FIN 38 Mg30
Struve Geodetic Arc ☐ ▦ LT 39 Mf36
Struve Geodetic Arc ☐ ▦ LV 39 Mf36
Struve Geodetic Arc ☐ ▦ N 16 Mb11
Struve Geodetic Arc ☐ ▦ S 16 Mb12
Struve Geodetic Arc ☐ ▦ UA 49 Md21
Stryj ☐ UA 43 Md41
Stryker ☐ USA (MT) 168 Ec21
Stryn ☐ N 17 Ld15
Strzegom ☐ PL 40 Lr40
Strzegowo-Osada ☐ PL 41 Ma38
Strzelce Krajeńskie ☐ PL 40 Lq38
Strzelce Opolskie ☐ PL 40 Lt40
Strzelecki National Park ☐ ▦ AUS (TAS) 111 Sc66
Strzelecki Regional Reserve ☐ ▦ AUS 108 Rk60
Strzelecki River ☐ AUS 108 Sa60
Strzelin ☐ PL 40 Ls40
Strzelno ☐ PL 40 Lt38
Stuart ☐ USA (FL) 179 Fk32
Stuart ☐ USA (IA) 178 Fk27
Stuart Bluff Range ▲ AUS 103 Rg57
Stuartburn ☐ CDN (MB) 172 Fb21
Stuart Highway (Northern Territory) ▦ AUS 106 Rg53
Stuart Highway (South Australia) ▦ AUS (SA) 108 Rh59
Stuart Lake ☐ CDN (AK) 164 Bj14
Stuart Range ▲ AUS 108 Rh60
Stuart Rocks ☐ USA (FL)
Stubbekøbing ☐ DK 30 Ln35
Studabekárbrú ☐ IS 18 Ka24
Stubaier Alpen ▲ A 34 Lm43
Stubbekøbing ☐ DK 30 Ln35
Stubbenkammer ☐ D 32 Lo36
Stubičke Toplice ☐ HR 35 Lq45
Stublina ☐ SCG 44 Mb46
Studénka ☐ CZ 42 Ls41
Studina ☐ RO 45 Me47
Study Butte ☐ USA (TX) 181 Ej31
Stugun ☐ S 16 Lh14
Stuhr ☐ D 32 Lk37
Stuibenfall ☐ A 34 Lm43
Stule ☐ CDN (BC) 166 Dg19
Stung Treng ☐ K 89 Qc39
Stupava ☐ SK 42 Lr42
Stupnik ☐ HR 35 Lq45
Sturg Treng ☐ K 89 Qc39

Sturgeon Bay ☐ USA (WI) 173 Fg23
Sturgeon Falls ☐ CDN (ON) 173 Ga22
Sturgeon L. Ind. Res. ☐ CDN 167 Eb18
Sturgeon River ☐ CDN 169 Eg19
Sturgis ☐ USA (MI) 173 Fg25
Sturgis ☐ USA (SD) 169 Ej23
Šturlić ☐ BIH 35 Lq45
Šturovo ☐ SK 43 Lt43
Sturt Creek ☐ AUS (WA) 103 Re55
Sturt Highway (New South Wales) ▦ AUS 111 Sd62
Sturt N.P. ☐ ▦ AUS 108 Sa60
Stutterheim ☐ ZA 155 Md62
Stuttgart ⊛ D 33 Lk42
Stuttgart ☐ USA (AR) 175 Fe28
Sturmansfontein Corbelled House ☐ ZA 154 Ma61
Sturmanfontein Karbeelde huise ☐ ZA 154 Ma61
Stuyahok ☐ USA (AK) 164 Bk14
Stykkishólmur ☐ IS 18 Js25
Sual ☐ TLS 97 Rc50
Suaín ☐ BIH 35 Lq45
Suakhevi ☐ GE 57 Nb25
Suakin ☐ SUD 135 Mj36
Suakin Archipelago ☐ SUD 135 Mk36
Suakoko ☐ LB 136 Kf42
Suam ☐ EAK 144 Mh45
Suan ☐ RDC 149 Mf49
Suan Phung ☐ THA 88 Pk39
Suápi ☐ BOL 206 Gg53
Suaqui Grande ☐ MEX (SO) 180 Ef31
Suardi ☐ RA (ER) 135 Mk37
Suardi ☐ RA 207 Gk61
Suarmar ☐ IND (CGH) 83 Pb35
Sua-Sua ☐ VY 193 Gf42
Suata ☐ IND (MPH) 83 Ok34
Suay Rieng ☐ K 89 Qc40
Subah ☐ RI 95 Qe49
Subanburung ☐ IND 93 Qd47
Subang ☐ RI 93 Qb47
Subansiri ☐ IND (ORS) 83 Pb35
Subashi ☐ CHN 66 Pb25
Subasi ☐ TR 56 Me25
Subay ☐ SYR 56 Mf34
Subcarpatii Buzāului ☐ RO 45 Mg45
Subei ☐ CHN (GSU) 69 Ph26
Subei Besar ▲ RI 94 Qe44
Subei ☐ RP 90 Ra38
Subi Kecil ▲ RI 94 Qe44
Sublette ☐ USA (KS) 174 Ek27
Sublette ☐ USA (KS) 174 Ek27
Subotica ☐ SCG 44 Lu44
Subrahmanya ☐ IND (KTK) 84 Oh39
Subtenierte Point ▲ RA (FO) 207 Gk58
Subugo ▲ EAK 144 Mh47
Subway Caves ☐ USA (CA) 170 Dk25
Sucating ☐ BR (CE) 201 Jb48
Suceava ☐ RO 49 Md22
Sucesso ☐ BR (CE) 201 Hk48
Sucha Beskidzka ☐ PL 41 Lu41
Sucha ☐ CHN (GSU) 83 Qa38
Súchil ☐ MEX (DGO) 182 Ej34
Suchorze ☐ PL 40 Ls36
Suciu de Sus ☐ RO 43 Me43
Sucker River ☐ CDN (SK) 167 Eh18
Suckling, Mount ▲ PNG 116 Se60
Sucre ⊛ BOL 206 Gh55
Sucre ☐ CO 192 Gc41
Sucre ☐ EC 196 Fk46
Sucúa ☐ EC 196 Ga47
Sucuba, T.I. ☐ BR 193 Gk44
Sucúa ☐ RO 45 Mg45
Sucupira do Norte ☐ BR (MA) 200 Hh49
Sucuru ☐ HR 35 Ls47
Sucuruju ☐ BR (AP) 195 Hf45
Sudak ☐ UA 49 Mh23
Sudan ☐ 123 Ma08
Sudbury ☐ CDN (ON) 173 Fk22
Sudbury ☐ GB 21 Kt38
Sudbury ☐ SUD 141 Mf41
Sūdest Island ☐ PNG 116 Sg61
Sudislavl' ☐ RUS 48 Na18
Sudogda ☐ RUS 48 Na18
Sudova Vyšnja ☐ UA 43 Md41
Sudoreyri ☐ IS 18 Jr24
Sudova ☐ SUD 141 Me43
Sueca ☐ E 27 Kt51
Suemez Island ▲ USA 166 Dd18
Sueno's Stone ☐ GB 20 Kr33
Suez ☐ ET 129 Mg31
Sufayrah ☐ KSA 60 Nb34
Sufetula ☐ TN 126 Le28
Suffield ☐ CDN (AB) 169 Ee20
Suffolk ☐ USA (VA) 178 Gb27
Sufuh ☐ IR 57 Nc26
Sug al Khamis ☐ LAR 127 Lg29
Sugarloaf Mtn. ▲ USA 164 Cb16
Sugihwaras ☐ RI 93 Qb48
Sugoj ☐ RUS 55 Sd06
Sugun ☐ WAN 138 Lf41
Suha ☐ RUS 149 Mf49
Suhaic ☐ BR (XUZ) 66 Oj26
Suhait ☐ CHN (NMZ) 72 Qc26
Suhbaatar ▲ RI 96 Qk50
Suhindol ☐ BG 45 Me48
Sühl ☐ D 33 Ll40
Suhlendorf ☐ D 32 Ll38
Suho Polje ☐ BIH 35 Lt46
Suhopolje ☐ HR 35 Ls45
Suhostrel ☐ RO 44 Md49
Suhum ☐ GH 138 Kk42
Sui ☐ PNG 115 Sb50
Suia-Miçu ☐ BR 199 Hd51
Suibará ☐ RI 95 Qd47
Suichang ☐ CHN (ZJG) 75 Qk41
Suichuan ☐ CHN (JGX) 75 Qh32
Suida ☐ RI 95 Qe47
Suifenhe ☐ CHN (HLG) 76 Rf23
Suihua ☐ CHN (HLG) 76 Rd22
Suileng ☐ CHN (HLG) 76 Rd22
Suilion ☐ CHN 74 Qf32
Suiluan ☐ CHN (IGS) 78 Qj37
Suin ☐ CHN (HNN) 73 Qg29
Suines ☐ CHN 74 Qf34
Suining ☐ CHN (SCH) 74 Qd30
Suinula ☐ FIN 38 Md29
Suir ☐ IRL 19 Km38
Suita ☐ J 79 Rj28
Suixi ☐ CHN (GDG) 74 Qf35
Sui Xian ☐ CHN (HUB) 74 Qg30
Suiyang ☐ CHN (GZH) 74 Qd32
Suizhong ☐ CHN (LNG) 76 Ra25
Suizhou ☐ CHN (HUB) 74 Qg30

Suj ☐ PK 65 Oe33
Sujangarh ☐ IND (RJT) 80 Oh32
Sujawal ☐ PK 65 Oc33
Sukadana ☐ RI 95 Qd49
Sukadana ☐ RI 93 Qa46
Sukagawa ☐ J 77 Sa27
Sukajadi ☐ RI 93 Pk44
Suk Ahad ☐ KSA 60 Nb34
Sukamade ☐ RI 95 Qg50
Sukamara ☐ RI 95 Qd47
Sukamenang ☐ RI 93 Qb47
Sukanagara ☐ RI 93 Qb47
Sukaraja ☐ RI 95 Qd47
Sukaraja ☐ RI 95 Qd47
Sukarame ☐ RI 93 Qc47
Sukau ☐ MAL 91 Qk43
Sükhbaatar ☐ MNG 70 Qg20
Sukhothai ☐ THA 88 Pk37
Sukhothai Historical Park ☐ ▦ THA 88 Pk37
Sumasas ☐ LT 39 Mf36
Sukhumi ☐ GE 57 Nb24
Sukkur ☐ PK 65 Oe32
Sukkwan Island ▲ USA 166 Dd18
Sumi ☐ CHN (TIB) 68 Pa28
Sukna ☐ SYR 56 Mk28
Sukorejo ☐ RI 95 Qe49
Sükösd ☐ H 43 Lu44
Sukpay ☐ RUS 76 Rg22
Sukses ☐ NAM 150 Lj56
Sukumo ☐ J 79 Rh29
Sukur Cultural Landscape ☐ ▦ WAN 139 Lg40
Sulagiri ☐ IND (TNU) 84 Oj39
Sulaiyimah ☐ KSA 60 Ne35
Sulawesi ☐ RI 96 Ra10
Sulawesi ☐ RI 96 Ra10
Sulaymaniyah ☐ IRQ 57 Nc28
Sulaymiyah ☐ KSA 60 Ne35
Suleça ☐ PL 40 Lq38
Sulejów ☐ PL 41 Lu39
Sulejówek ☐ PL 41 Mb38
Sulem, Mount ▲ PNG 115 Sd47
Sule Skerry ▲ GB 20 Kq31
Sule ☐ IND (ORS) 83 Pb35
Sulia ☐ RDC 141 Md46
Suliki ☐ RI 93 Qa46
Sulima ☐ WAL 136 Ke42
Sulina ☐ RO 45 Mk45
Sulingen ☐ D 32 Lj38
Suliszewo ☐ PL 40 Lq38
Sulitjelma ▲ N 16 Lj12
Sulkava ☐ FIN 38 Mg29
Sulkita ☐ KS 63 Oe26
Sullana ☐ PE 196 Fj48
Sullivan ☐ USA (IL) 175 Fg26
Sullivan ☐ USA (MO) 175 Fe26
Sullivan Bay ☐ CDN (BC) 168 Dg20
Sullivan, Mount ▲ AUS 106 Rf54
Sullom Voe ☐ GB 20 Kt30
Sully-sur-Loire ☐ F 25 Lc43
Sulmierzyce ☐ PL 40 Ls39
Sulmona ☐ I 37 Lo48
Sulok ☐ BR 159 Sk50
Sulphur ☐ USA (LA) 175 Fd30
Sulphur ☐ USA (OK) 174 Fb28
Sulphur Springs ☐ USA (TX) 174 Fc29
Sultan ☐ CDN (ON) 173 Fj22
Sultan ☐ LAR 127 Ma30
Sultanabad ☐ RI 93 Qc47
Sultan Dağları ▲ TR 56 Mf26
Sultan Hamud ☐ EAK 144 Mj47
Sultanhanı ☐ TR 56 Mg26
Sultanhanı ▲ RI 95 Qd46
Sultanhanı Caravanserai ☐ TR 56 Mg26
Sultan Kudarat ☐ RP 91 Rc42
Sultanlyazbiy-kalasy ☐ TM 63 Oc26
Sultan Iskandar ☐ IND (UPH) 83 Pb32
Sultan's Palace ☐ BRU 94 Qh43
Sultan's Palace ☐ MAL 92 Qa43
Sultan's Palace ☐ RI 95 Qf46
Sultan's Palace (Say'un) ☐ YE 60 Ne38
Sultepec ☐ MEX (MEX) 182 Fa36
Sulu ☐ CDN 149 Mc48
Suluan Island ▲ RP 90 Rc40
Sulu Archipelago ☐ RP 91 Ra43
Sulu Basin ☐ RP 91 Rae42
Suluk ☐ ETH 142 Mk41
Suluk ☐ ETH 142 Mk41
Sulutah ☐ LAR 127 Ma29
Suluq ☐ LAR 127 Ma30
Sulu Sea ☐ RP 91 Qk41
Suluova ☐ TR 56 Mj25
Sulya ☐ IND (KTK) 84 Oh39
Sulzbach-Rosenberg ☐ D 33 Lm41
Sumaco ☐ EC 196 Gb46
Sumaco, Volcán ▲ EC 196 Ga46
Sumadija ☐ SCG 44 Mb46
Sumampa ☐ RA (SE) 207 Gj60
Sumana ☐ RA 207 Gj60
Suman Khayrkhan ▲ MNG 67 Qa23
Sumapaz, P.N. ☐ ▦ CO 192 Gc43
Sumar ☐ IR 57 Nc29
Sumara ☐ YE 60 Nc38
Sumaré ☐ BR (SP) 203 Hg57
Sumatera ☐ RI 92 Pk44
Sumatra ☐ USA (MT) 169 Ef22
Sumatra ☐ RI 92 Ph49
Sumaúma ☐ BR (AM) 198 Gk49
Sumaúma ☐ BR (AM) 198 Ha49
Šumava ☐ CZ 42 Lo41
Sumba ☐ DK 18 Kn28
Sumba ☐ RI 96 Qk50
Sumbawa ☐ RI 96 Qk50
Sumbawa Besar ☐ RI 96 Qj50
Sumbawanga ☐ EAT 146 Mh49
Sumbe ☐ ANG 148 Lg50
Sumbing ▲ RI 95 Qe49
Sumbu ☐ KZ 66 Pa24
Sumbul ☐ RDC 148 Lg48
Sumburgh ☐ GB 20 Kt31
Sumburgh Head ☐ GB 20 Kt31
Sumby ☐ WAL 136 Ke42
Sumedang ☐ RI 93 Qc49
Sumé ☐ BR (PB) 201 Jb49
Sume ☐ Z 149 Mh50
Sumedang ☐ RI 93 Qc49
Sumeih ☐ SUD 142 Mc39
Sumen ☐ BG 45 Mg48
Sumenep ☐ RI 95 Qf49
Sumgait = Sumgayit ☐ AZ 57 Nf25
Sumgayit ☐ AZ 57 Nf25
Sumiswald ☐ CH 34 Lh44
Sumiyoshi ☐ J 79 Rj28
Šumjačskoje Plato, N.P. ☐ ▦ BG
Summel ☐ IRQ 57 Nc28
Summer Lake ☐ USA (OR) 168 Dk24
Summerberg ☐ NAM 154 Lk58
Summerland ☐ CDN (BC) 168 Ea21
Summer Palace ☐ ▦ CHN 73 Qj26
Summerside ☐ CDN (PE) 176 Gj22

Summerstrand ☐ ZA 155 Mc63
Summersville ☐ USA (WV) 175 Fk26
Summerton ☐ USA (SC) 178 Fk29
Summerville ☐ USA (GA) 178 Fk29
Summerville ☐ USA (SD) 172 Fb23
Summit Lake ☐ CDN (BC) 166 Dh16
Summit Lake ☐ CDN (BC) 166 Dj18
Summit Lake Ind. Res. ☐ CDN 170 Ea25
Sumpango ☐ J 79 Rh28
Šumperk ☐ CZ 42 Lr41
Sumprabum ☐ MYA 86 Pj33
Sumqayit ☐ AZ 57 Ne25
Šumskas ☐ LT 39 Mf36
Sumter ☐ USA (SC) 178 Fk29
Sumuna ☐ PNG 116 Sf47
Sumur ☐ RI 93 Qc49
Sumurbungkar ☐ RI 95 Qd49
Sumxi ☐ CHN (TIB) 68 Pa28
Suná ☐ IND (GUJ) 82 Og35
Sunagawa ☐ J 77 Sa24
Sunah ☐ YE 60 Nb38
Sunakhalla ☐ IND (ORS) 83 Pc35
Sunam ☐ IND (PJB) 80 Oh30
Sunan ☐ CHN (GSU) 69 Ph26
Sunan ☐ PRK 78 Rc26
Sunbay Beach ☐ USA 187 Gb36
Sunbeam ☐ USA (ID) 168 Ec23
Sunbury ☐ USA (VIC) 111 Sc64
Sunbury ☐ USA (OH) 178 Gb27
Suncho Corral ☐ RA (SE) 207 Gj59
Sunch'ŏn ☐ PRK 76 Rc26
Sunch'ŏn ☐ ROK 78 Rd28
Sundance ☐ USA (WY) 169 Eh23
Sundarbans ▲ IND/BD 86 Pe34
Sundarbans National Park ☐ ▦ IND 86 Pe34
Sundarnagar ☐ IND (HPH) 81 Oj30
Sunda Shelf ☐ RI 95 Qd45
Sunda Strait ☐ RI 95 Qc49
Sundargarh ☐ IND (ORS) 83 Pc34
Sundborn ☐ S 31 Lq30
Sundby ☐ DK 30 Lj34
Sunde ☐ N 30 Lf31
Sunden ☐ S 31 Lq32
Sündiken Dağları ▲ TR 56 Mf26
Sundre ☐ CDN (AB) 169 Ec20
Sundown N.P. ☐ AUS 109 Sf60
Sundsvall ☐ S 17 Lj14
Sungai ☐ RI 95 Qd45
Sungaibaru ☐ RI 95 Qd47
Sungaibelida ☐ RI 95 Qc47
Sungaibengkali ☐ RI 93 Qc47
Sungaibliul ☐ RI 93 Qa46
Sungai Buloh ☐ RI 94 Qc46
Sungaibuntu ☐ RI 95 Qd47
Sungaidareh ☐ RI 93 Qa46
Sungaiguntung ☐ RI 93 Qa46
Sungai Kolok ☐ THA 88 Qa40
Sungaiisat ☐ RI 95 Qd46
Sungaipenuh ☐ RI 93 Qa47
Sungaipierak ☐ RI 93 Qa46
Sungai Petani ☐ MAL 92 Qa43
Sungaisalak ☐ RI 93 Qa46
Sungai Siput ☐ MAL 92 Qa43
Sungaitapang ☐ RI 95 Qd47
Sungbo's Eredo ☐ WAN 138 Lc42
Sungguminasa ☐ RI 96 Ra48
Sungikal ☐ SUD 135 Mf38
Sungkup ☐ RI 95 Qd47
Sung Men ☐ THA 87 Qa36
Sung Noen ☐ THA 89 Qb38
Sungo ☐ MOC 152 Mg54
Sungsang ☐ RI 93 Qc47
Sungurlare ☐ BG 45 Mg48
Sungurlu ☐ TR 56 Mh25
Suni ☐ SUD 134 Mc39
Sunizona ☐ USA (AZ) 171 Ef30
Sun Kosi Reservoir ☐ NEP 83 Pd32
Sun Kosi River Rafting ☐ ▦ NEP 83 Pd32
Šunjska Stijena = Šula ☐ SCG 44 Lu47
Sun Lake ☐ RC 75 Ra34
Sunndal ▲ N 30 Lg30
Sunndalsøra ☐ N 17 Le14
Sunne ☐ S 31 Lo31
Sunnersberg ☐ S 31 Lo31
Sunnmøre ▲ N 17 Lc14
Sunnyside ☐ USA (NV) 170 Ec26
Sunuk Island ▲ USA 164 Cb17
Sun Prairie ☐ USA (WI) 172 Ff24
Sunrise Park Ski Resort ☐ USA (AZ) 171 Ef29
Sunset Beach ☐ USA 187 Gc36
Sunset Country ☐ AUS 110 Sa63
Sunset Crater Nat. Mon. ☐ USA 171 Ee28
Sunshine Coast ☐ AUS 109 Sg59
Suntaii ☐ WAN 138 Lf42
Suntazī ☐ LV 39 Me34
Sun Temple (Konark) ☐ ▦ IND 83 Pd36
Suntsar ☐ PK 64 Oa33
Suntu ☐ ETH 142 Mj41
Sun Nuraxi ☐ I 36 Lj51
Sunwapta Falls ☐ CDN (AB) 168 Ea20
Sunwi Do ▲ PRK 78 Rc27
Sunwu ☐ CHN (HLG) 71 Rd21
Sunyani ☐ GH 137 Kk42
Suoi Rut ☐ VN 87 Qd34
Sur-Yat-sen ☐ CHN 78 Qk29
Suol Island ▲ RP 90 Rc40
Suoming ☐ USA
Suolahti ☐ FIN 38 Me28
Suomenniemi ☐ FIN 38 Mh29
Suomenselkä ☐ FIN 38 Md28
Suomusjärvi ☐ FIN 38 Md30
Suomussalmi ☐ FIN 16 Me13
Suonenjoki ☐ FIN 38 Mf28
Suoyarvi ☐ RUS 48 Na17
Supaul ☐ IND (BIH) 83 Pd32
Supaul ☐ IND (MHT) 82 Oh36
Supeqrgaui, P.N. ☐ ▦ BR
Superior ☐ USA (AZ) 171 Ee29
Superior ☐ USA (NE) 174 Fa25
Superior ☐ USA (WI) 172 Fd22
Supia ☐ CO 192 Gb43
Supino ☐ I 37 Lo49
Supiori ▲ RI 114 Rh46

Tabon Caves ☒ RP 91 Qk41
Tabong ☒ MYA 86 Pj32
Tábor ☒ CZ 42 Lp41
Tabora ☒ EAT 146 Mg48
Tabora ☒ EAT 147 Mf51
Tabou ☒ BF 137 Vf40
Tabou ☒ CI 137 Kg43
Tabrinkout ☒ RIM 130 Kc36
Tabriz ☒ IR 57 Nd26
Tabriz ☒ IR 57 Nd27
Tabuaeran ☒ KIR 11 Ca09
Tabuan ☒ RI 93 Qc48
Tabubil ☒ PNG 115 Sa48
Tabudarat ☒ RI 93 Qd47
Tabuenca ☒ E 28 Kt49
Tabuk ☒ KSA 58 Mj31
Tabuk Fort ☒ KSA 58 Mj31
Tabuleiro do Norte ☒ BR (CE) 201 Ja48
Tabur ☒ SUD 134 Mb40
Tabwemasana ☒ VU 118 Td53
Tāby ☒ S 31 Lt31
Taça ☒ E 124 La32
Tacabamba ☒ PE 196 Ga49
Tacajó ☒ C 186 Gc35
Tacalaya ☒ PE 197 Ge54
Tacamá, Volcán ☒ GCA/MEX (MHC) 182 Ek34
Tacamá, Volcán ☒ GCA/MEX 183 Ef38
Tacaratu ☒ BR (PE) 201 Ja50
Tacarigua ☒ YV 193 Gg40
Tachakou ☒ CHN (XUZ) 67 Pc23
Tachang ☒ CHN (BO) 166 Dr18
Tachiké ☒ MYA 87 Pk35
Tachiumet ☒ LAR 126 Lf32
Tachov ☒ CZ 42 Ln41
Tach Thu ☒ VN 89 Qd40
Tacipi ☒ RI 96 Ra48
Tacloban ☒ RP 90 Rc42
Tacna ☒ PE 206 Ge55
Tacoma ☒ USA (WA) 168 Dj22
Tacora, Volcán ☒ RCH 206 Gf54
Taco Pozo ☒ RA (CH) 207 Gj58
Tacora ☒ RCH 206 Gf54
Tacuana ☒ MOC 153 Mj54
Tacuarembó ☒ ROU 204 Hc61
Tacuati ☒ PY 202 Hd57
Tacugama Chimpanzee Sanctuary ☒ WAL 136 Kd41
Taculi ☒ TZ 152 Md53
Tacurong ☒ RP 91 Rc42
Tacuru ☒ BR (MS) 202 Hc57
Tad ☒ PK 65 Ob33
Tada ☒ IND 85 Ok39
Tada ☒ CI 137 Ta51
Tadalt ☒ MA 124 Kt31
Tadânet Keyna ☒ RMM 131 Kj36
Tadarimana, T.I. ☒ BR 202 Hc54
Taddert ☒ MA 124 Kg33
Tadepallegudem ☒ IND (APH) 83 Pa37
Tadientour ☒ DZ 126 Le32
Tadine ☒ F (NCL) 118 Td56
Tadjemout ☒ DZ 126 Lb29
Tadjemout ☒ DZ 126 Lb33
Tadjoura ☒ DJI 143 Nb40
Tadjrouna ☒ DZ 126 Lb29
Tado ☒ IND (ARP) 86 Pg32
Tadoba-Andhari N.P. ☒ IND 83 Ok35
Tadohae Haesang N.P. ☒ ROK 78 Rd28
Tadoussac ☒ CDN (QC) 176 Gf21
Tadpatri ☒ IND (APH) 85 Ok38
Tadubi ☒ IND (MNP) 86 Ph33
Taduno ☒ RI 97 Rd46
Taech'on ☒ ROK 78 Rd27
Taech'ongdo ☒ PRK 78 Rc27
Taedong ☒ ROK 78 Re28
Taejon ☒ ROK 78 Rd27
Taejong ☒ ROK 78 Rd29
T'aepaek ☒ ROK 78 Re27
Ta'er Si ☒ CHN 72 Qa27
Taevaskoja ☒ EST 39 Mg32
Tafalla ☒ TO 10 Ba11
Tafalla ☒ E 28 Kt48
Tafelberg ☒ SME 194 Hb44
Tafermaar ☒ RI 114 Rh49
Tafetán ☒ MEX (MHC) 182 Ek36
Tafila ☒ JOR 58 Mh30
Tafinkar ☒ RMM 132 Ld38
Tafiré ☒ CI 137 Kh41
Tafraoute ☒ MA 124 Kf31
Tafresh ☒ IR 57 Nf28
Taft ☒ IR 57 Nh28
Taft ☒ RP 90 Rc40
Taft ☒ USA (CA) 170 Ea28
Taga ☒ RMM 131 Kh38
Taga ☒ RO 43 Me44
Tagab ☒ SUD 135 Mf36
Taganrog ☒ RUS 49 Mk22
Tagarak ☒ IR 57 Ne28
Tagarare Gabout ☒ RMM 131 La38
Tagaung ☒ MYA 86 Pj34
Tagbalé ☒ RCA 140 Ma43
Tagbilaran ☒ RP 90 Rb41
Tagbuni ☒ IND (MNP) 86 Ph33
Tagg ☒ YV 193 Gg41
Tagula ☒ PNG 116 Se51
Tagum ☒ RP 91 Rc42
Tagus ☒ E/P 27 Kn51
Tah ☒ MA 124 Kd32
Tahakara ☒ LAR 133 Lh33
Tahrauli ☒ IND (MHY) 82 Oh36
Tahsis ☒ CDN (BC) 168 Dg21
Tahal ☒ E 29 La31
Tahami Dağları ☒ TR 56 Mj26
Tahhtai ☒ MYA 91 Rc44
Tahlandang ☒ RI 91 Rc44
Tahuna ☒ RI 91 Rc44
Taï ☒ CI 137 Kg43
Tai ☒ CHN (HLG) 77 Rc19
Tai'an ☒ CHN (SDG) 73 Qg37
Tai'an ☒ CHN (SDG) 73 Qg37
Taibai Shan ☒ CHN 72 Qd29
Taibaishan Z.B. ☒ CHN 72 Qd29
Taibao D. ☒ CHN 73 Qg37
Taibet ☒ DZ 126 Ld29

Taibique ☒ E 124 Ka32
Taibus Qi ☒ CHN (NMZ) 73 Qh25
Taicang ☒ CHN 73 Qg27
Taichung ☒ RC 75 Ra33
Taihang ☒ CHN 73 Qg27
Taihantesu, T.I. ☒ BR 206 Ha53
Taihape ☒ NZ 113 Th65
Taihe ☒ CHN (AHU) 73 Qg38
Taihe ☒ CHN (JGX) 75 Qj32
Taihu ☒ CHN (AHU) 73 Qg38
Tai Hu ☒ CHN 78 Ra30
Taikang ☒ CHN (HNN) 73 Qf28
Taikkyi ☒ MYA 88 Ph37
Tailai ☒ CHN (HLG) 71 Rb22
Tailem Bend ☒ AUS (SA) 110 Rk63
Tailin ☒ BR (RS) 204 Hd62
Taima ☒ RMM 137 Kg39
Taimati ☒ PA 185 Ga41
Tainan ☒ CHN (SAX) 72 Qg27
Tai ☒ RI 93 Qa45
Tainaro ☒ GR 46 Mc54
Taigu ☒ CHN (SAX) 72 Qg27
Taihang ☒ CHN 73 Qg27
Tainan ☒ RC 75 Ra34
Tainhas ☒ BR (RS) 205 Hd60
Taining ☒ CHN (FJN) 75 Qj32
Taï-l'Hermitage ☒ F 25 Le45
Taiobeiras ☒ BR (MG) 203 Hj53
Taï Island ☒ PNG 117 Sh48
Taioqua do Tocantins ☒ BR (TO) 200 Hg52
Taipai ☒ RC 75 Ra33
Taipei Financial Centre ☒ RC 75 Ra33
Taiping ☒ CHN (GZG) 74 Qd34
Taiping ☒ CHN 72 Qf34
Taiping ☒ MAL (PRK) 92 Qa44
Taipingchuan ☒ CHN (JLN) 77 Rb25
Taió ☒ BR (SC) 205 He59
Taisei ☒ J 79 Rg28
Taishan ☒ CHN (GDG) 75 Qg34
Taisha ☒ EC 196 Gd47
Taisha ☒ J 79 Rg28
Taishan ☒ CHN (ZJG) 75 Qk32
Taishun ☒ CHN 75 Ra34
Taitao, Península ☒ RCH 208 Gd69
Taitai ☒ RP 90 Ra38
Taita-Taveta ☒ EAK 145 Na46
Taitung ☒ RC 75 Ra34
Taivalkoski ☒ FIN 38 Mh30
Tai Xian ☒ CHN (JGS) 78 Ra29
Taixing ☒ CHN (JGS) 78 Ra29
Taiyang Dao ☒ CHN 76 Rd23
Taiyuan ☒ CHN (SAX) 72 Qf27
Taizhou ☒ CHN (JGS) 78 Ra29
Ta'izz ☒ YE 60 Nd39
Tajae ☒ RN 132 La38
Tajae ☒ RC 75 Ra34
Tajikistan ☒ TJ 53 Oa06
Taj Mahal (Agra) ☒ IND 80 Oj32
Tajpur ☒ IND (BIH) 83 Pc33
Tajra ☒ LAR 127 Lg29
Tajura ☒ LAR 127 Lg29
Tajsa ☒ THA 88 Pk37
Tak ☒ THA 88 Pk37
Takab ☒ IR 57 Nd27
Takaba ☒ EAK 145 Na44
Takachiho ☒ J 79 Rf29
Takahashi ☒ J 79 Rg28
Takalou ☒ TCH 139 Lk40
Takamaka, Mount ☒ SA 158 Nj50
Takamaka ☒ SY 145 Nh48
Takamatsu ☒ J 79 Rh28
Takanabe ☒ J 79 Rf29
Takan, Gunung ☒ RI 96 Qg50
Takanosu ☒ J 77 Sa25
Takapau ☒ NZ 112 Th64
Takapuna ☒ IND (ORS) 83 Pd35
Takara ☒ RCA 140 Ma41
Takara-jima ☒ J 79 Re31
Takasaki ☒ J 77 Rk27
Takatokwane ☒ RB 155 Mc57
Takaungu ☒ EAK 145 Na47
Takayama ☒ J 79 Rj27
Takefu ☒ J 79 Rj28
Take-jima ☒ J 79 Rf30
Take Jima ☒ ROK 79 Rf27
Takeo ☒ J 79 Rf29
Takeo ☒ K 89 Qc40
Takestan ☒ IR 57 Nf27
Taketa ☒ J 79 Rf29
Takhadid ☒ IRQ 59 Nc31
Takhilt ☒ RN 132 Lg38
Takhfif ☒ AFG 63 Oc30
Takhli Soleyman ☒ IR 57 Nd27
Takht-e-Bahi ☒ PK 65 Of28
Takhteh Pol ☒ AFG 65 Oc30
Takht-i-Sangin ☒ TJ 63 Oe27
Takht-i-Sulaiman ☒ PK 65 Oe30
Takiéta ☒ RN 132 La39
Takiéta ☒ RN 132 La39
Takikawa ☒ J 77 Sa24
Takla ☒ CI 137 Kj42
Takinoue ☒ J 77 Sb24
Takis ☒ PNG 116 Sf48
Takisung ☒ RI 95 Qh48
Takla Landing ☒ CDN (BC) 167 Dg19
Takla Makan Desert ☒ CHN 52 Pa06
Takla Dhokeshwar ☒ IND (MHT) 82 Oh36
Taknan, Mount ☒ PNG 117 Sh49
Takoba ☒ RCA 140 Ma42
Takobanda ☒ RCA 140 Ma42
Takolekaju Mountains ☒ RI 96 Qk46
Takoradi ☒ GH 137 Kk43
Takorka ☒ RN 132 La39
Takotna ☒ USA (AK) 165 Cb14
Takoutala ☒ SN 130 Kd38
Takpoima ☒ LB 136 Ke42
Takro Falls ☒ PNG 116 Se47
Taksin Maharat N.P. ☒ THA
Takua Pa ☒ THA 88 Pk41
Takua Thung ☒ THA 88 Pk41
Takum ☒ WAN 138 Le41
Takundi ☒ RDC 148 Lj46
Taku Plateau ☒ CDN 166 Dd16
Takurgaon ☒ BD 86 Pe34
Tala ☒ IND (MPH) 83 Pa34
Tala ☒ IND (JLC) 182 Ej35
Tala ☒ ROU 209 Hc63
Talacasto ☒ RA (SJ) 208 Gf61
Talacyn ☒ BY 48 Me18
Talagabeira ☒ RCH 208 Ge62
Talaghe ☒ IRCH 208 Ge62
Talahini-Tomora ☒ CI 137 Kj41
Talahini ☒ CI 135 Ok41
Talaimannar ☒ CL 85 Ok40
Talaimannar ☒ RIM 130 Kd36
Talaimannar ☒ RIM 130 Kd36
Talaimannar ☒ RIM 182 Fa33
Talala ☒ IND (GUJ) 82 Og35
Talali ☒ RUS 71 Rd09
Talampaya, P.N. ☒ RA

Talanga ☒ HN 184 Fg38
Talangbatu ☒ RI 93 Qc48
Talangbetutu ☒ RI 93 Qc47
Talangjauh ☒ RI 93 Qc47
Talang Rimbo ☒ RI 93 Qc47
Talang Selengku ☒ RI 93 Qc47
Talang Sipucuk ☒ RI 93 Qc47
Talao ☒ RI 93 Qa45
Talara ☒ PE 196 Fk48
Talaroo ☒ AUS (QLD) 107 Sb55
Talarrubias ☒ E 27 Kp51
Talas ☒ KS 66 Og24
Tala Ala Yol ☒ KS/KG 63 Of24
Talasea ☒ PNG 116 Sf48
Talata-Ampano ☒ RM 157 Nd56
Talata Mafara ☒ RN 138 Lc38
Talata Mafara ☒ RN 96 Rb46
Talavera ☒ RP 90 Ra38
Talavera de la Reina ☒ E 27 Kq51
Talawanta ☒ AUS (QLD) 107 Sa55
Talawdi ☒ SUD 135 Mf40
Talaya ☒ RI 93 Qd45
Talbingo ☒ AUS (NSW) 111 Se63
Talbotton ☒ USA (GA) 175 Fh29
Talbrak ☒ SYR 57 Na27
Talca ☒ RCH 208 Ge63
Talcahuano ☒ RCH 208 Gd64
Talcho ☒ RN 132 La38
Taldom ☒ RUS 48 Mj17
Taldy-Bulak ☒ KS 66 Og24
Taldykorgan ☒ KZ 66 Og23
Taldy-Kurgan ☒ KZ 66 Og23
Taleex ☒ SP 143 Ne41
Talegaon ☒ IND (MHT) 82 Ok35
Talera ☒ IND (MHT) 82 Og37
Talgar ☒ KZ 66 Of24
Talgarth ☒ GB 21 Kr39
Talghar ☒ KZ 66 Of24
Talguharani ☒ SUD 135 Mh36
Talhah ☒ KSA 60 Nb37
Talhar ☒ PK 65 Oe33
Taliabu ☒ RI 97 Rc46
Taliabu ☒ RI 97 Rc46
Talikota ☒ IND (KTK) 82 Oj37
Tali Laki Reef ☒ PNG 116 Sf51
Talimā ☒ BR (PA) 194 Hc45
Taling Chan ☒ THA 88 Qa39
Talisay ☒ RP 90 Rb42
Talisei ☒ RI 91 Rc45
Talitsa ☒ RUS 54 Oa04
Talīzhan ☒ RUS 70 Qb19
Tal'jany ☒ RUS 70 Qd19
Talkeetna ☒ USA (AK) 165 Cc14
Talkeetna Mountains ☒ USA (AK) 165 Cf14
Talking Rocks Cavern ☒ USA 174 Fd27
Talladega ☒ USA (AL) 175 Fg29
Talladega Superspeedway ☒ USA 175 Fg29
Tall Afar ☒ IRQ 57 Na27
Talladi ☒ IND (GUJ) 82 Oh35
Tallahassee ☒ USA (FL) 175 Fh30
Tallahatchie N.W.R. ☒ USA 175 Fe29
Tallangatta ☒ AUS (VIC) 111 Sd64
Tallapalem ☒ IND (APH) 83 Pb37
Tallarook ☒ F 25 Lg46
Tallaringa Conservation Park ☒ AUS 108 Rg60
Tallasee ☒ USA (AL) 175 Fh29
Tallimbāda ☒ IND (GUJ) 82 Ok35
Tallimm ☒ USA (SE) 38 Me31
Tall Kala ☒ AFG 65 Oh32
Tall Kayf ☒ IRQ 57 Na27
Talloires ☒ BF 25 Lg45
Tallopa ☒ S 16 Lk13
Tall Trees Grove ☒ USA 168 Dj25
Tallulah ☒ USA (LA) 175 Fe29
Talmakan ☒ BF 137 La40
Talmage ☒ USA (UT) 171 Ee25
Talmont-Saint-Hilaire ☒ F 24 Kt44
Tainah ☒ RUS 54 Pb05
Tai'ne ☒ UA 49 Mf21
Taloda ☒ IND (GUJ) 82 Oh35
Taloga ☒ USA (OK) 174 Fa27
Talogan ☒ AFG 63 Oe27
Taloloai Beach ☒ RI 96 Qj45
Talos Dome ☒ 7 Sd33
Taloyoak ☒ CDN 163 Fb05
Talpada ☒ IND (ORS) 83 Pd35
Talping Ling ☒ CHN 71 Ra22
Talras ☒ RN 132 Le38
Talsara ☒ IND (ORS) 83 Pc34
Talshand ☒ MNG 67 Pk23
Talsi ☒ LV 39 Mc33
Talsint ☒ MA 125 Kj29
Tal Siyah ☒ IR 64 Oa31
Taltal ☒ RCH 207 Ge58
Talu ☒ RI 93 Pk45
Taludusantan ☒ RI 95 Qd46
Talwood ☒ AUS (QLD) 109 Se60
Tama ☒ RN 132 Lc38
Tama ☒ USA (IA) 172 Fd24
Tamadam ☒ RI 114 Rg48
Tamagam-Takava ☒ RN 132 Le38
Tamala ☒ AUS (WA) 104 Qg59
Tamala ☒ RUS 48 Nb19
Tamale ☒ CO 192 Gd41
Tamale ☒ GH 137 Kk41
Tamale Port – Yapei ☒ GH 137 Kk41
Tamanaco, Cerro ☒ CO 192 Gb43
Tamanaco, Cerro ☒ CO 192 Gb43
Tamanco ☒ PE 196 Gc48
Tamandaré ☒ BR (PE) 201 Jb50
Tamandourint ☒ RMM 131 Kk36
Tamanhint ☒ LAR 127 Lg31
Tamanhos ☒ P 26 Kn50
Tamanrasset ☒ DZ 132 Le34
Tamanredjo ☒ SME 194 Hc43
Taman Safari Indonesia ☒ RI 95 Qd49
Taman Rata ☒ MAL 92 Qa43
Tamani ☒ PK 65 Oe29
Tamanalu ☒ IND (APH) 84 Ok39
Tamano ☒ J 79 Rg28
Tamanthi ☒ MYA 86 Pg33
Tamarac N.W.R. ☒ USA 172 Fc22
Tamaraguda ☒ RI 97 Rc43
Tamari ☒ IND (JKD) 83 Pd34
Tamarida ☒ YE 61 Nf40
Tamarindo ☒ CR 184 Fh40
Tamarite de Litera ☒ E 28 La49
Tamási ☒ H 42 Lt44
Tamaso ☒ CI 137 Kj42
Tamasola ☒ RIM 130 Kd36
Tamaula ☒ YV 193 Gg44
Tamazula ☒ MEX 182 Ej35
Tamazula ☒ MEX (DGO) 180 Eg33

Tamazula de Gordiano ☒ MEX (JLC) 182 Ej36
Tamazunchale ☒ MEX (SLP) 182 Fa35
Tambacounda ☒ SN 136 Kd39
Tambakera ☒ RMM 130 Ke38
Tambakrejo ☒ RI 95 Qg50
Tambangsawah ☒ RI 93 Qc47
Tambaqui ☒ BR (AM) 198 Gj48
Tambarana ☒ RI 96 Ra46
Tambarga ☒ BF 137 La40
Tambawel ☒ WAN 138 Lc39
Tambea ☒ RI 96 Ra48
Tambea ☒ SOL 117 Sk50
Tambelan Besar ☒ RI 95 Qd45
Tambellup ☒ AUS (WA) 104 Qj63
Tambero ☒ Z 152 Md54
Tamberu ☒ RI 95 Qg49
Tambillo ☒ EC 196 Ga46
Tambillo ☒ RN 132 Ld36
Tambisan al Mali ☒ RI 110 Qa32
Tambo ☒ AUS (QLD) 109 Sd58
Tambo Colorado ☒ PE 197 Gc52
Tambo Grande ☒ PE 196 Fk48
Tamboborano ☒ RM 157 Nb54
Tambon ☒ RI 96 Ra47
Tambolongang ☒ RI 96 Ra49
Tambo Pucacuro ☒ PE 196 Gc47
Tambo Quemado ☒ BOL 206 Gf55
Tambo Quemado, Port.d. ☒ BOL/RCH 206 Gf55
Tambor ☒ CR 184 Fh40
Tambores ☒ ROU 204 Hb61
Tamboril ☒ BR (CE) 201 Hk48
Tamboril ☒ BR (PI) 201 Hj49
Tamboril do Piauí ☒ BR (PI) 201 Hj50
Tamborra, Gunung ☒ RI 96 Qj50
Tambovka ☒ RUB 71 Re20
Tambrey ☒ AUS (WA) 102 Qj56
Tambu ☒ PNG 115 Sb48
Tambuk Tinggi ☒ MAL 92 Qa44
Tambunan ☒ MAL 94 Qh43
Tambung ☒ RI 96 Ra46
Tamburu ☒ CL 85 Pa41
Tamchekket ☒ RIM 130 Kd37
Tame ☒ CO 192 Gd42
Tamegroute ☒ MA 125 Kh30
Tamei ☒ IND (MNP) 86 Pg33
Tamelelt ☒ MA 125 Kg30
Tamelhat ☒ DZ 126 Ld29
Tamenglong ☒ IND (MNP) 86 Pg33
Tamesna ☒ RMM 132 Lc36
Tamesna ☒ RN/RMM 132 Lc36
Tamezret ☒ TN 126 Le29
Tamgaly Petroglyphs ☒ KZ 66 Oj23
Tamghas ☒ NEP 81 Pb31
Tamiahua ☒ MEX (VC) 182 Fb35
Tamil Nadu ☒ IND 84 Oj40
Tamir ☒ KSA 59 Nc33
Tamkuhi ☒ IND (UPH) 83 Pc32
Tam Ky ☒ VN 89 Qe38
Tamluk ☒ IND (WBG) 83 Pd34
Tammisaaren saariston kansallispuisto = Ekenäs skärgårds n.p. ☒ FIN 38 Md31
Tammisaari = Ekenäs ☒ FIN 38 Md31
Tamna dupka ☒ BG 45 Me47
Tamnava ☒ SCG 44 Lu46
Tamou ☒ RN 138 La39
Tampa ☒ ANG 150 Lg53
Tampe ☒ FIN 38 Md30
Tampere ☒ FIN 38 Md30
Tampico ☒ MEX (VC) 182 Fb34
Tampin ☒ MAL 92 Qb44
Tampioea ☒ BF 137 La40
Tamri ☒ MA 124 Ke31
Tamrau ☒ RP 90 Rb40
Tam Thanh Grottoes ☒ VN 87 Qd35
Tamu ☒ MYA 86 Pg33
Tamulyn ☒ MEX (SLP) 182 Fa35
Tamsag Bulag ☒ MNG 70 Qg22
Tamsagan ☒ BF 137 La40
Tamtay ☒ IND (UTT) 81 Pa30
Tamworth ☒ AUS (NSW) 109 Sf61
Tamworth ☒ GB 21 Kt38
Tana ☒ VU 118 Te55
Tanabe ☒ J 79 Rh29
Tanaf ☒ SN 136 Kc40
Tanafiord ☒ N 16 Me10
Tana Hayk ☒ ETH 142 Mj39
Tan-Ahenet ☒ DZ 132 Le34
Tanahjampea ☒ RI 96 Ra49
Tanahmasa ☒ RI 93 Pk46
Tanahmalalla ☒ RI 96 Ra49
Tanahmerah Indah-Lempake ☒ RI 95 Qj46
Tanai ☒ PK 65 Oe29
Tanakallu ☒ IND (APH) 84 Ok39

Tandaro ☒ EAK 144 Mj45
Tanda Urmar ☒ IND (PJB) 80 Oh30
Tandek ☒ MAL 94 Qj42
Tandi ☒ IND (HPH) 81 Oj29
Tambakera ☒ RMM 130 Ke38
Tandin ☒ MYA 86 Pg36
Tandjungsimpang ☒ RI 95 Qd46
Tandjungtuweng ☒ RI 93 Qc46
Tando Allahyar ☒ PK 65 Oe33
Tando Bago ☒ PK 65 Oe33
Tando Jam ☒ PK 65 Oe33
Tando Muhammad Khan ☒ PK 65 Oe33
Tando Zinze ☒ ANG 148 Lg48
Tanega-jima ☒ J 79 Rf30
Taneichi ☒ J 77 Sa25
Tanezrouft ☒ DZ 132 La34
Taneka ☒ Z 146 Me52
Tan Emellel ☒ DZ 126 Le30
Tanezoukat ☒ DZ/RMM 131 Kk24
Tanezzuft ☒ LAR 127 Lg31
Tanga ☒ EAT 147 Mk48
Tang ☒ RUS 70 Qf20
Tāngaberg ☒ S 30 Ln33
Tangadee ☒ AUS (WA) 104 Qk58
Tangafoss ☒ IS 18 Ka26
Tangail ☒ BD 86 Pe33
Tangalle ☒ CL 85 Pa42
Tanga Islands ☒ PNG 116 Sg47
Tangale Peak ☒ WAN 139 Lf41
Tangará ☒ CL 85 Pa43
Tangará a Serra ☒ BR (MT) 202 Hb53
Tangare ☒ BR (RN) 201 Jc49
Tangandapan ☒ RI 95 Qd47
Tangba ☒ CHN (CGQ) 74 Qc31
Tang Chenar ☒ IR 64 Nh30
Tangen ☒ N 30 Lm30
Tangent Point ☒ USA (AK) 165 Cc10
Tanggade ☒ RI 95 Qd49
Tangger ☒ RI 95 Qd49
Tangerang ☒ RI 93 Qd49
Tangermünde ☒ D 32 Lm38
Tanggu ☒ CHN (SCH) 87 Qa31
Tanggu ☒ CHN (TJN) 73 Qj26
Tanggula Shan ☒ CHN 68 Pe29
Tanggula Shankou ☒ CHN 69 Pf29
Tanghai ☒ CHN (HBI) 73 Qk26
Tanghe ☒ CHN (HNN) 73 Qg29
Tangi ☒ PK 65 Of28
Tangier ☒ MA 125 Kh28
Tangjiahe Z.B. ☒ CHN 72 Qc29
Tangjiatai ☒ CHN (GSU) 72 Qd27
Tangjiwan ☒ CHN (ZJG) 78 Qk30
Tangkak ☒ MAL 92 Qa44
Tangkiling ☒ RI 95 Qf47
Tangkoko Batuangus Dua Saudara N.R. ☒ RI 96 Rc45
Tanglan ☒ RP 90 Ra36
Tangmai ☒ CHN (TIB) 69 Ph30
Tangonmarkkung ☒ RI 95 Qd49
Tangorin ☒ AUS (QLD) 100 Sc56
Tangoutranat = Tin-Aguelhaj ☒ RMM 131 Kj37
Tang'po ☒ PRK 76 Rd26
Tangra Yumco ☒ CHN 68 Pd30
Tangra Yumco ☒ CHN 68 Pd30
Tangse ☒ RI 92 Ph43
Tangse ☒ RI 81 Qk28
Tangshan ☒ CHN (HBI) 73 Qk26
Tangsibigi ☒ BHT 86 Pf32
Tang Sorkheh ☒ IR 64 Nk32
Tangua ☒ CO 192 Gb45
Tanguelbaï ☒ EAK 144 Mj45
Tanguen-Dassouri ☒ BF 137 Kk39
Tanguiéta ☒ DY 137 La40
Tangungasmal ☒ RI 95 Qd46
Tangyan ☒ MYA 87 Pk34
Tangyuan ☒ CHN (HLG) 76 Re22
Tanhaçu ☒ BR (BA) 203 Hk53
Tanh hoa ☒ VN 89 Qd40
Tan Hiep ☒ VN 89 Qd40
Tanico ☒ RUS (BUR) 70 Qc20
Tanihebi ☒ RI 92 Ph43
Taniniga ☒ MOC 155 Mg58
Tanintharyi ☒ MYA 88 Pj39
Tanis ☒ ET 129 Mf30
Tanisagata ☒ RI 114 Rg47
Tanjay ☒ RP 90 Rb41
Tanjong Astana ☒ RM 156 Nf53
Tanjona Angontsy ☒ RM 156 Nf52
Tanjona Anorontany ☒ RM 156 Ne52
Tanjona Bejao ☒ RM 156 Ne54
Tanjona Bobaomby ☒ RM 156 Ne51
Tanjona Larrée ☒ RM 157 Ne54
Tanjona Masoala ☒ RM 156 Nf53
Tanjona Vilanandro ☒ RM 156 Nc54
Tanjona Vohimena ☒ RM 157 Ne57
Tanjore = Thanjavur ☒ IND (TNU) 85 Ok40
Tan-Tan ☒ MA 124 Ke31
Tanaooola ☒ AUS (SA) 110 Sa64
Tantoyuca ☒ MEX (VC) 182 Fa35
Tanu ☒ IND (APH) 83 Pa37
Tanuf ☒ IR 64 Nk31
Tanumah ☒ KSA 60 Nb36
Tanunda ☒ AUS (SA) 110 Rk63
Tanushimaru ☒ J 79 Rf29
Tanzania ☒ EAT 146 Mf49
Tanzaniabe ☒ RI 96 Ra46

Tanjung Kait ☒ RI 95 Qd47
Tanjung Karang ☒ MAL 92 Qa44
Tanjung Karawong ☒ RI 95 Qd48
Tanjung Keling Beach ☒ MAL 93 Qb44
Tanjung Keluang ☒ RI 95 Qe46
Tanjung Keluang ☒ RI 95 Qe46
Tanjung Kenam ☒ RI 93 Qc48
Tanjung Kidurong ☒ MAL 94 Qg44
Tanjung Kiduong ☒ RI 95 Qd46
Tanjunglabu ☒ RI 95 Qd47
Tanjung Labuanbini ☒ RI 91 Qk45
Tanjung Laru Mat ☒ RI 97 Rf49
Tanjung Layar ☒ RI 95 Qd46
Tanjung Leman ☒ MAL 92 Qc44
Tanjung Malatayur ☒ RI 95 Qf47
Tanjung Malim ☒ MAL 92 Qa44
Tanjung Mangali ☒ RI 93 Qc47
Tanjung Taq ☒ IR 64 Nj28
Tanjung Mangkalihat ☒ RI 91 Qk45
Ta Prohm ☒ K 89 Qc39
Tanjung Manundi ☒ RI 114 Rh46
Tanjung Marsimang ☒ RI 97 Rf47
Tanjung Medang ☒ RI 93 Qa45
Tanjung Momfafa ☒ RI 97 Rh46
Tanjung Nasong ☒ MAL 94 Qh43
Tanjung Ngabordamlu ☒ RI 114 Rh49
Tanjung Pacinan ☒ RI 95 Qh49
Tanjung Pandan ☒ RI 95 Qd47
Tanjung Pepisol ☒ RI 114 Rg48
Tanjung Pasir ☒ MAL 94 Qf44
Tanjung Payong ☒ MAL 94 Qg44
Tanjung Pemarung ☒ RI 95 Qj46
Tanjung Pertandangan ☒ RI 93 Qa44
Tanjung Perupuk ☒ RI 91 Qk45
Tanjung Peureulak ☒ RI 92 Pj43
Tanjung Piandang ☒ MAL 92 Qa43
Tanjung Pinang ☒ RI 93 Qc45
Tanjung Pisau ☒ MAL 94 Qj42
Tanjungpuro ☒ RI 95 Qh50
Tanjung Puting ☒ RI 95 Qf47
Tanjung Puting N.P. ☒ RI 95 Qf47
Tanjung Raja ☒ RI 93 Qc47
Tanjung Raya ☒ RI 95 Qd46
Tanjung Redeb ☒ RI 94 Qj45
Tanjung Sabra ☒ RI 114 Rg47
Tanjung Samak ☒ RI 93 Qc46
Tanjung Saribu ☒ RI 114 Rh46
Tanjung Sedari ☒ RI 95 Qd48
Tanjung Selokan ☒ RI 95 Qd47
Tanjung Sekopong ☒ RI 93 Qc48
Tanjungselor ☒ RI 94 Qj45
Tanjung Sempang Mangayau ☒ MAL 94 Qj42
Tanjung Senebui ☒ RI 93 Qa46
Tanjung Sepat ☒ MAL 92 Qa44
Tanjung Sianuk ☒ RI 95 Qd47
Tanjung Sigep ☒ RI 93 Pk46
Tanjung Sipang ☒ MAL 94 Qf45
Tanjung South ☒ MAL 94 Qj42
Tanjung Sungai ☒ MAL 94 Qj42
Tanjung Tongerai ☒ RI 114 Rg47
Tanjung Tua ☒ RI 93 Qc48
Tanjungubam ☒ RI 93 Qc45
Tanjunguban ☒ RI 93 Qc45
Tanjung Uban ☒ RI 114 Rg50
Tanjung Wamong ☒ RI 97 Rf46
Tanjung Wamonek ☒ RI 97 Rf46
Tanjung Watukebo ☒ RI 114 Rg48
Tanjung Weduar ☒ RI 114 Rg49
Tanjungsamatra ☒ RI 95 Qd48
Tanjungungai ☒ RI 95 Qf45
Tanyang ☒ MYA 87 Pk34
Tanyaivera-Karoo N.P. ☒ ZA 154 La62
Tan Ky ☒ VN 87 Qc36
Tan Ky ☒ VN 89 Qd40
Tank ☒ PK 65 Oe29
Tannay ☒ F 25 Ld43
Tānnforsen ☒ S 16 Lj14
Tannis Bugt ☒ DK 30 Lj33
Tanniyuttu ☒ CL 85 Pa41
Tannu-Ola Range ☒ RUS 54 Pc08
Tannah ☒ IND (MHT) 82 Oh37
Tannu ☒ MH 10 Ta08
Tanot ☒ IND (RJT) 80 Of32
Tanout ☒ RN 132 Lb38
Tanout-ou-Fillali ☒ MA 125 Kh29
Tanque de Piau ☒ BR (PI) 201 Hj49
Tanque Novo ☒ BR (BA) 201 Hj52
Tanquinho ☒ BR (BA) 201 Hk52
Tansaroa ☒ BF 137 La40
Tansen ☒ NEP 81 Pb32
Tansila ☒ BF 137 Kh39
Tansukoh ☒ LAR 127 Ma29
Tansy ☒ IR 57 Ne29
Tantamayo ☒ PE 197 Gb50
Tantanoola ☒ AUS (SA) 110 Sa64
Tantou ☒ RG 136 Kf41
Tanuf ☒ IR 64 Nk31
Tanumah ☒ KSA 60 Nb36

Tarokehn ☒ LB 136 Kg43
Taroko ☒ RC 75 Ra33
Taroko N.P. ☒ RC 75 Ra33
Tarom ☒ AUS (QLD) 109 Se58
Taroudannt ☒ MA 124 Kf30
Taroum ☒ RN 132 Lb38
Tarpaisezele ☒ RI 114 Rg48
Tarpon Springs ☒ USA (FL)
Tarporley ☒ GB 21 Ks37
Tarr Aike ☒ RA (SC) 210 Ge71
Tarra-Buga National Park ☒ AUS 111 Sd65
Tárraco romana ☒ ☒ E 28 Lb49
Tárrega ☒ E 29 Lb49
Tarrafal ☒ CV 136 Jh37
Tarrafal ☒ CV 136 Jh37
Tarraleah ☒ AUS (TAS) 111 Sd67
Tàrrega ☒ E 29 La49
Tärs ☒ DK 30 Lm36
Tarsa Khurd ☒ IND (MHT) 83 Ok38
Tarso Emissi ☒ TCH 133 Lk35
Tarso Lango ☒ TCH 133 Lk35
Tarso Tieroko ☒ TCH 133 Lj35
Tarso Voon ☒ TCH 133 Lj35
Tarsus ☒ TR 56 Mf27
Tartagal ☒ RA (SA) 201 Hd56
Tartagal ☒ RA (SF) 204 Ha60
Tartarugalzinho ☒ BR (AP) 195 He45
Tarte ☒ F 24 Ku47
Tärtäsbel ☒ TR 40 Mf46
Tartu ☒ EST 39 Mg32
Tarucani ☒ PE 197 Ge54
Tarume ☒ RUS 48 Mj18
Taruntang ☒ RI 91 Rc44
Tarut ☒ KSA 59 Nf32
Tarut Castle ☒ KSA 59 Nf32
Tarvagatay Nuruu ☒ MNG 70 Pk21
Tarvin ☒ GB 21 Ks37
Tarvisio ☒ I 35 Lo44
Tarzán ☒ LAR 127 Lj31
Tašanta ☒ RUS (ALT) 67 Pe21
Tašbogo ☒ KZ 63 Oa22
Táscates ☒ MEX (SL) 180 Eg32
Taschereau ☒ CDN (QC) 173 Ga21
Taseyevo ☒ RUS 54 Pb06
Taseyevo ☒ RUS 48 Mj18
Tašgon ☒ IND (MHT) 82 Oh37
Tashk ☒ IR 64 Nk31
Tashkent ☒ UZ 63 Oe25
Tashkepri ☒ TM 62 Ob25
Tash-Kumyr ☒ KS 63 Og25
Tašišu ☒ RI 96 Qk47
Tasikmalaya ☒ RI 95 Qd49
Tasker ☒ RN 133 Lf38
Task-ligan ☒ CHN 68 Pe27
Taskesken ☒ KZ 66 Pa22
Tasman Sea ☒ USA (WA) 104
Tasman Bay ☒ NZ 113 Tg66
Tasman Peninsula ☒ AUS 111 Se67
Tasman Sea ☒ 100 Sb13
Tasker ☒ RN 133 Lf38
Taskesken ☒ KZ 66 Pa22
Tasman Basin ☒ 100 Sb14
Tasman Bay ☒ NZ 113 Tg66
Tasman Head ☒ AUS (TAS) 111 Sd67
Tasman Peninsula ☒ AUS 111 Se67
Tasman Sea ☒ 100 Sb13
Tasmania ☒ AUS 101 Sa14
Tasmanian Wilderness World Heritage Area ☒ AUS (TAS) 111 Sc67
Tasman Islands ☒ PNG 116 Sk48
Tasman Mountains ☒ NZ 113 Tg66
Tasman Peninsula ☒ AUS 111 Se67
Tasman Point ☒ AUS 106 Rj53
Tasman Sea ☒ 100 Sb13
Tarso ☒ BR (AC) 196 Ga50
Tarauacá ☒ BR (AC) 196 Gc50
Tasso Fragoso ☒ BR (MA) 200 Hh50
Tasuki ☒ IR 57 Nc26
Tasuki ☒ IR 57 Nc26
Tat ☒ F 42 Lt43
Tatabánya ☒ H 42 Lt43
Ta Ta Creek ☒ CDN (BC) 168 Ec21
Tatarbunary ☒ UA 49 Mf21
Tataouine ☒ TN 126 Le30
Tatarsk ☒ RUS (BUR) 70 Qd20
Tatarbunary ☒ UA 49 Mf21
Tatarskiy Proliv ☒ RUS 55 Sa08
Tatarsk ☒ RUS (BUR) 70 Qd20
Tatatila ☒ MEX (VC) 182 Fb36
Tatarskiy Proliv ☒ RUS 55 Sa08
Tate-yama ☒ J 77 Rj27
Tateyama ☒ J 79 Rk28
Tatham ☒ AUS (NSW) 111 Se64
Tathra ☒ AUS (NSW) 111 Se64
Tati ☒ RB 152 Md56
Tatitlek ☒ USA (AK) 165 Cg15
Tatla Lake ☒ CDN (BC) 168 Dh20
Tatláui Prov. ☒ PE 197 Ge54
Tatry ☒ SK/PL 41 Lu41
Tatshenshini-Alsek Wilderness Prov. Park ☒ CDN 166 Db16
Tatta ☒ PK 65 Oe33
Tattenhall ☒ GB 21 Ks37
Tatti ☒ IND (MHT) 82 Oh37
Tatum ☒ USA (NM) 174 Ej29
Tatvan ☒ TR 57 Nb26
Taubaté ☒ BR (SP) 205 Hh57
Tauber ☒ D 33 Lk41
Tauberbischofsheim ☒ D 33 Lk41

Taucha ☒ D 32 Ln39
Taufikia ☒ SUD 141 Mf41
Taufkirchen ☒ D 33 Lm42
Taukum ☒ KZ 66 Oh23
Taulov ☒ DK 30 Lk34
Taumaranui ☒ NZ 112 Th65
Taumarunui ☒ NZ (AC) 197 Gd50
Tau Munly ☒ KZ 66 Of22
Taunay/Ipegue, T.I. ☒ BR 202 Hb56
Taung ☒ ZA 155 Mc59
Taung Skull Fossil Site ☒ ☒ ZA 155 Mc59
Taungdwin ☒ MYA 86 Ph34
Taunggyi ☒ MYA 86 Pj35
Taunggyi ☒ MYA 86 Pj35
Taungnonion ☒ MYA 86 Ph33
Taungup ☒ MYA 86 Ph36
Taunsa ☒ PK 65 Of30
Taunton ☒ GB 21 Kr39
Taunus ☒ D 33 Lj40
Taupo ☒ NZ (BP) 112 Tj64
Taupo, Lake ☒ NZ 112 Th64
Tauragė ☒ LT 39 Mc35
Tauramena ☒ CO 192 Gd43
Tauranga ☒ NZ 112 Tj64
Tauravaara ☒ FIN 17 Mf12
Taurianova ☒ I 37 Lr52
Taurisano ☒ I 37 Lt51
Tauroa Point ☒ NZ 112 Tg63
Taurus Mountains ☒ TR 56 Mf27
Taushyk ☒ KZ 62 Nf23
Tauste ☒ E 28 Kt49
Tauta ☒ PNG 115 Sc48
Tauu Islands ☒ PNG 117 Sj48
Tauz ☒ AZ 57 Nc25
Tavani ☒ CDN 163 Fd06
Tavani ☒ MNG 67 Pd21
Tavani, Mount ☒ VU 118 Te54
Tavares ☒ TN 56 Mc27
Tavas ☒ TR 56 Mc27
Taveta ☒ F 25 Lg47
Taveta ☒ EAK 147 Mk47
Tavda ☒ RUS 49 Ob07
Tavernes ☒ F 25 Lg47
Tavernes de la Valldigna ☒ E 29 Ku51
Taveta ☒ EAT 146 Mh50
Tavik ☒ S 31 Lo44
Tavira ☒ P 27 Kn53
Tavistock ☒ GB 21 Kq40
Tavoi ☒ MYA 88 Pk38
Tavoi ☒ MYA 88 Pk38
Tavsanli ☒ TR 47 Mk51
Tavua ☒ FIJ 119 Tj54
Tavunasici ☒ FIJ 119 Ua54
Tavurvur ☒ PNG 116 Sg48
Tawa ☒ IND (NT) 106 Rh54
Tawa ☒ IND (ARP) 86 Pf32
Tawang ☒ IND (ARP) 86 Pf32
Tawas Reservoir ☒ IND 83 Ok34
Tawargin ☒ IND (KTK) 82 Oj38
Tawas City ☒ USA (MI) 173 Fj23
Tawau ☒ MAL 94 Qj43
Tawilah ☒ ET 129 Mg32
Tawilah ☒ SUD 134 Mc39
Tawitawi Island ☒ RP 91 Qk43
Tawi-Tawi Island ☒ RP 90 Ra43
Tawleh ☒ RC 75 Ra34
Tawsman Islands ☒ PNG 116 Sk48
Tawurgha ☒ LAR 127 Lg29
Taxco ☒ MEX (GRO) 182 Fa36
Taxi ☒ CHN (HLG) 71 Rd21
Taxiatosh ☒ UZ 62 Nk24
Taxila ☒ PK 65 Og28
Taxinco ☒ MEX (CHP) 183 Fd38
Taxkorgan ☒ CHN (XUZ) 66 Oh27
Taxtako'pir ☒ UZ 62 Oa24
Tayabamba ☒ PE 197 Gb50
Tayabas Bay ☒ RP 90 Ra39
Tayan ☒ RI 95 Qf46
Tayandu ☒ RI 114 Rg48
Tayan Uul ☒ MNG 67 Ph23
Taylor ☒ IR 64 Oa28
Taylor ☒ USA (AK) 165 Ca14
Taylor ☒ CDN (BC) 167 Dk17
Taylor ☒ USA (AK) 165 Bh13
Taylor ☒ S 12 La17
Taylor ☒ USA (NE) 172 Fa25
Taylor ☒ USA (TX) 174 Fb30
Taylor Canyon ☒ USA (NV) 170 Eb25
Taylor Highway ☒ USA (AK) 165 Cj14
Taylor Mts. ☒ USA (AK) 164 Cb15
Taylorville ☒ USA (IL) 175 Ff26
Taymouth ☒ USA (ME)
Taymyr ☒ RUS 54 Mk32
Taymyr (Dolgan-Nenets) Autonomous District ☒ RUS 54 Po04
Taymyr Peninsula ☒ RUS 54 Pa02
Tay Ninh ☒ VN 89 Qd40
Tayoltita ☒ MEX (DGO) 180 Eh33
Tay Phuong Pagoda ☒ VN 87 Qc35
Tayrona, P.N. ☒ CO 192 Gc40
Taytay ☒ RP 90 Qk40
Tayu ☒ RI 95 Qf49
Tayuan ☒ CHN 77 Rc21
Tayu Island ☒ PNG 116 Sf48
Tayug ☒ RP 90 Ra38
Taza ☒ MA 125 Kh29
Taza, P.N.de ☒ DZ 126 Lc27
Taza monastery ☒ ARM 57 Nd26
Tazara ☒ RI 114 Rh47
Tazane ☒ RGG 136 Kf41
Tazakadt ☒ DZ 132 La34
Tazan ☒ MYA 86 Ph34
Tazin Lake ☒ CDN 167 Ee16
Tazirbu Oasis ☒ LAR 128 Ma33
Tazna, Cerro ☒ BOL 206 Gg57
Tazoult ☒ DZ 126 Lc28
Tazovskaya guba ☒ RUS 54 Od05
Tazovskiy ☒ RUS 54 Od05
Tazrouk ☒ DZ 132 Le34
Tazzarine ☒ MA 125 Kh30
Tbilisi ☒ GE 57 Nc25
Tbilisi ☒ GE 57 Nc25
T'boli ☒ RP 91 Rc42
Tchabal Gangdaba ☒ CAM 139 Lg42
Tchabal Mbabo ☒ CAM 139 Lg42
Tchabao ☒ CAM 139 Lg41
Tchamba ☒ TG 137 La41
Tchangsou ☒ TCH 140 Lh41
Tchaourou ☒ DY 138 La41
Tchazzanti ☒ DY 138 La41
Tcheferi ☒ RCB 148 Lh45
Tchetti ☒ DY 138 La41
Tchibanga ☒ G 148 Lf46
Tchin-Tabaradene ☒ RN 132 Lc38
Tchibemba ☒ ANG 150 Lh53
Tchidoudou ☒ TCH 133 Lk38
Tchikala ☒ RCB 148 Lg48
Tchilounga ☒ RCB 148 Lg46
Tchin-n-Salatine ☒ RN 132 Lc36
Tchibanga ☒ G 148 Lf46
Tchin-Tabaradene ☒ RN 132 Lc38
Tchissakata ☒ RCB 148 Lg48

Tchizalamou – Tinguipaya

Tchizalamou **RCB** 148 Lf48
Tcholliré **CAM** 139 Lh41
Tchula **USA** (MS) 175 Fe29
Tczew **PL** 40 Lt36
Tczów **PL** 41 Mb39
Teabo **MEX** (YT) 183 Ff35
Teaca **RO** 43 Me44
Teacapan **MEX** (SL) 181 Eh34
Te Anau **NZ** 113 Td68
Teano **I** 37 Lp49
Teapa **MEX** (TB) 183 Fd37
Te Araroa **NZ** 112 Tk64
Te Aroha Racecourse **NZ** 112 Tj65
Teatre-Museu Dalí **E** 28 Ld48
Teatro Amazonas (Manaus) **BR** 199 Ha47
Teatro Greco di Catánia **I** 37 Lq53
Teatro Greco di Siracusa **I** 37 Lq53
Teatro Greco di Taormina **I** 37 Lq53
Teba **E** 27 Kq54
Teba **RI** 114 Rj46
Tebak, Gunung **RI** 93 Qc48
Teban **RI** 93 Qc45
Tébarat **RN** 132 Lc38
Tebarumbayan **RI** 93 Qb48
Tebay **GB** 21 Ks36
Tébé **G** 148 Lg46
Tebedu **MAL** 94 Qf45
Teberda **RUS** (KCH) 57 Na24
Teberdinskij zapovednik **RUS** 57 Na24
Tebessa **DZ** 126 Le28
Tebesselamane **RMM** 132 Lb37
Tebingtinggi **RI** 92 Pk44
Tebingtinggi **RI** 93 Qb45
Tebingtinggi **RI** 93 Qb47
Tebito **EAU** 144 Mf44
Teboulba **TN** 126 Lf28
Tébourba **TN** 126 Le27
Téboursouk **TN** 126 Le27
Tecalitlán **MEX** (JLC) 182 Ej36
Tecamachalco **MEX** (PUE) 182 Fb36
Tecate **MEX** (BC) 180 Eb29
Tecer Dağları **TR** 56 Mj26
Techiman **GH** 137 Kk42
Techirghiol **RO** 45 Mj46
Techirimba **ANG** 150 Lh51
Techissanha **ANG** 150 Lj53
Techongolola **ANG** 148 Lj51
Tecka **RA** (CB) 210 Ge67
Tecojate **GCA** 184 Fe38
Tecolotlán **MEX** (JLC) 182 Eh35
Tecolutla **MEX** (VC) 182 Fb35
Tecomán **MEX** (COL) 182 Ej36
Tecomatlán **MEX** (PUE) 182 Fa36
Tecoriname **MEX** (SO) 180 Ef31
Tecoripa **MEX** (SO) 180 Ef31
Tecpan de Galeana **MEX** (GUR) 182 Ek37
Tecuala **MEX** (NYT) 180 Eh34
Tecuci **RO** 49 Md23
Tecumseh **USA** (MI) 173 Fj25
Tecumseh **USA** (NE) 174 Fb25
Tecumseh **USA** (OK) 174 Fb28
Ted **SP** 145 Nb43
Tedodita Sekan **MYA** 86 Pj36
Tedzhen **TM** 62 Oa27
Tedzhenstroy **TM** 62 Oa27
Teel **MNG** 70 Qa21
Teepee **CDN** (BC) 166 Dc16
Tees **GB** 21 Kt36
Tefé **BR** (AM) 198 Gh47
Tefedest **DZ** 132 Lc33
Tefeer **MA** 125 Kh28
Tefeya **WAL** 136 Ke41
Tegada **IND** (APH) 83 Pa36
Tegal **RI** 95 Qe49
Tegalbuleud **RI** 95 Qd49
Tegernsee **D** 33 Lm43
Teghra **IND** (BIH) 83 Pc33
Tegina **WAN** 138 Ld40
Tegineneng **RI** 93 Qc48
Tegua **VU** 118 Td52
Tegucigalpa **HN** 184 Fg38
Teguidda-n-Tessoumt **RN** 132 Ld37
Tehachapi Mts. **USA** 170 Ea28
Te Haroto **NZ** 113 Tj65
Teheran **IR** 57 Nf28
Téhini **CI** 137 Kj41
Tehoru **RI** 97 Re47
Tehran **IR** 57 Nf28
Tehuacán **MEX** (PUE) 182 Fb36
Teide, P.N.del **E** 124 Kb31
Teignmouth **GB** 21 Kr40
Teilta **AUS** (NSW) 108 Sa61
Teimoori Tomb **IR** 62 Nj27
Teimur **IR** 64 Oa31
Teiskot **RMM** 131 La37
Teiti **SUD** 135 Mf36
Teiuş **RO** 43 Md44
Teixeira **BR** (PB) 201 Jb49
Teixeira de Freitas **BR** (BA) 203 Ja54
Teixeiras **BR** (MG) 203 Hj56
Tejakula **RI** 95 Qh50
Teji **ETH** 142 Mk41
Tejira **RN** 132 Le38
Tejkovo **RUS** 48 Na17
Tejoruco **MEX** (GUR) 182 Fa37
Tejucupapo **BR** (PE) 201 Jc49
Tejupilco de Hidalgo **MEX** (MEX) 182 Ek36
Te Kaha **NZ** 112 Tj64
Tekamah **USA** (NE) 172 Fb25
Tékane **RIM** 130 Kc37
Tekax **MEX** (YT) 183 Ff35
Teke **TR** 45 Mk49
Tekeim **SUD** 135 Mf40
Tekeli **KZ** 66 Ok23
Tekes **CHN** (XUZ) 66 Pa24
Tekes **KZ** 66 Ok24
Tekirdağ **TR** 45 Mh50
Tekit **MEX** (YT) 183 Ff35
Tekkali **IND** (APH) 83 Pc36
Tekke **TR** 56 Mh26
Tekman **TR** 57 Na26
Teknaf **BD** 86 Pg35
Tekoa **USA** (WA) 168 Eb22
Tékro **TCH** 134 Ma36
Teku **RI** 97 Rb46
Te Kuiti **NZ** 113 Th65
Tela **HN** 184 Fg38
Telaga **RI** 92 Qc44
Telagakulon **RI** 95 Qe49
Telagapulang **RI** 95 Qg47
Télagh **DZ** 125 Kk28
Telanaipura = Jambi **RI** 93 Qb46
Télataï **RMM** 132 La37
Telavi **GE** 57 Nc25
Tel Aviv **IL** 56 Mh29
Telč **CZ** 42 Lq41
Telchac Puerto **MEX** (YT) 183 Ff35
Telciu **RO** 43 Me43
Telde **E** 124 Kc32
Tele **RI** 93 Pk44
Telefomin **PNG** 115 Sa48
Telegraph Creek **CDN** (BC) 166 De17
Telegraph Point **AUS** (NSW) 109 Sg61
Telegraph Range **CDN** 168 Dj19
Telegraph Station Ruins **AUS** 105 Re61
Teleköl kanal **KZ** 63 Od23
Telêmaco Borba **BR** (PR) 205 He58
Telemark **N** 30 Lh31
Telemzane **DZ** 126 Lc29
Telén **RA** (LP) 208 Gh64
Telerghma **DZ** 126 Ld27
Telese **I** 37 Lp49
Telfer **AUS** (WA) 102 Rb56
Telford **GB** 21 Ks38
Telfs **A** 34 Lm43
Telgte **D** 32 Lh39
Telhan Kalesi **TR** 57 Na27
Teli **RDC** 141 Md44
Teli **RDC** 141 Me44
Telica **NIC** 184 Fg39
Télimélé **RG** 136 Kd40
Telkapalli **IND** (APH) 82 Ok37
Tell Abyad **SYR** 56 Mk27
Tellamura **IND** (TRP) 86 Pf34
Tell As'samn **SYR** 56 Mk27
Tell el-Amârna **ET** 129 Mf32
Teller **USA** (AK) 164 Bg13
Tellicherry = Thalasseri **IND** (KER) 84 Oh40
Tellier **RA** (SC) 210 Gg69
Tellis **TCH** 133 Lj38
Tell Tamir **SYR** 57 Na27
Telluride **USA** (CO) 171 Eg27
Telluride Ski Area **USA** 171 Eg27
Tel'manove **UA** 49 Mk22
Telmessos **TR** 56 Me27
Telo **RI** 93 Pk46
Telok Brunei **MAL** 94 Qh43
Telok Kimanis **MAL** 94 Qh43
Telok Labuk **MAL** 94 Qj42
Telok Lahad Datu **MAL** 91 Qk43
Telok Loak **MAL** 94 Qg43
Teloloapan **MEX** (GUR) 182 Fa36
Telouèt **MA** 125 Kg30
Telpani **NEP** 81 Pa31
Telsang **IND** (KTK) 82 Oh37
Telsen **RA** (CB) 208 Gg67
Telšiai **LT** 39 Mc35
Teltele **ETH** 144 Mj43
Telten nuur **MNG** 67 Pj21
Teltow **D** 32 Lo38
Teluk Adang **RI** 95 Qj46
Teluk Airhitam **RI** 95 Qf47
Telukapanji **RI** 93 Qa44
Teluk Apar **RI** 95 Qj47
Telukbatang **RI** 95 Qe46
Telukbayur **RI** 93 Qa46
Teluk Bengkolan **RI** 95 Qe46
Teluk Berau **RI** 114 Rg47
Teluk Bintuni **RI** 114 Rg47
Telukbutun **RI** 94 Qe43
Teluk Cenderawasih **RI** 114 Rh47
Teluk Chempedak Beach **MAL** 92 Qb44
Telukdalam **RI** 93 Pj45
Teluk Datu **MAL** 94 Qf44
Teluk Gelintin **RI** 96 Rb50
Teluk Intan **MAL** 92 Qa43
Telukkabung **RI** 93 Qa46
Teluk Kaibus **RI** 97 Rf46
Teluk Kampa **RI** 93 Qc46
Teluk Kamrau **RI** 114 Rg47
Teluk Klabat **RI** 93 Qc46
Teluk Kotawaringin **RI** 95 Qf47
Teluk Kumai **RI** 95 Qf47
Teluk Lampung **RI** 93 Qc48
Teluk Langsa **RI** 92 Pk43
Teluknibung **RI** 92 Pk44
Teluk Nuri **RI** 95 Qe46
Teluk Painan **RI** 93 Qa46
Teluk Pamukan **RI** 95 Qj47
Teluk Saleh **RI** 96 Qj50
Teluk Sangkulirang **RI** 91 Qk45
Teluk Sebakor **RI** 114 Rg47
Teluk Sebangan **RI** 95 Qg47
Teluk Sebuku **RI** 94 Qj44
Teluk Sekatak **RI** 94 Qj44
Teluk Semangka **RI** 93 Qc48
Teluk Sempit **RI** 95 Qg47
Teluk Sibolga **RI** 93 Pk45
Teluk Sindeh **RI** 96 Ra50
Teluk Sukadana **RI** 95 Qe46
Teluk Telaga **RI** 93 Pj44
Teluk Triton **RI** 114 Rg47
Telukumpai **RI** 95 Qe46
Teluk Walckenaer **RI** 114 Rk47
Teluk Waromge **RI** 97 Rf46
Teluk Waropen **RI** 114 Rj47
Teluk Weda **RI** 91 Re45
Téma **GH** 137 Kk43
Temacine **DZ** 126 Ld29
Temagami **CDN** (ON) 173 Ga22
Temaju **RI** 95 Qe45
Temanggung **RI** 95 Qf49
Temax **MEX** (YT) 183 Ff35
Temba **ZA** 155 Me58
Tembagapura **RI** 114 Rj48
Tembe Elephant Reserve **ZA** 155 Mg59
Tembenči **RUS** 54 Pd05
Tembe, T.I. **BR** 195 Hf47
Tembhurni **IND** (MHT) 82 Oh37
Tembilahan **RI** 93 Qb46
Tembisa **ZA** 155 Me58
Tembladera **PE** 196 Ga49
Temblador **YV** 193 Gj41
Tembleque **E** 27 Kr51
Tembo **RDC** 149 Lj49
Tembo Aluma **ANG** 148 Lj49
Tembwe **Z** 146 Mg51
Temecula **USA** (CA) 170 Eb29
Temelon **GQ** 138 Lf45
Téméra **RMM** 131 Kk37
Temerin **SCG** 44 Lu45
Temerloh **MAL** 92 Qb44
Temiang **RI** 93 Qc45
Teminabuan **RI** 97 Rf46
Temirlan **KZ** 63 Oe24
Temirovka **KS** 66 Oj24
Temirtau **KZ** 54 Oc08
Témiscaming **CDN** (QC) 173 Ga22
Temki **TCH** 139 Lk40
Temman-gu **J** 79 Rf29
Temó **MEX** (CHP) 183 Fd37
Te-Moak Ind. Res. **USA** 170 Ec25
Temora **AUS** (NSW) 111 Sd63
Témoris **MEX** (CHH) 180 Ef32
Temósachic **MEX** (CHH) 180 Eg31
Tempe **USA** (AZ) 171 Ee29
Tempeh **RI** 95 Qg50
Tempestad **PE** 196 Gc46
Tempino **RI** 93 Qb46
Tempio di Giove Ánxur **I** 36 Lo49
Tempio di Hera Lacínia **I** 37 Ls51
Tempio Malatestiano di Rímini **I** 35 Ln46
Témpio Pausánia **I** 36 Lk50
Tempio Távole Palatine **I** 37 Lr50
Temple **USA** (TX) 174 Fb30
Temple d'Auguste et de Livie **F** 25 Le45
Templemore **IRL** 19 Kn38
Temple of Amun **ET** 129 Mg33
Temple of Hatshepsut **ET** 129 Mg33
Temple of Haven **CHN** 73 Qj25
Temple of Hibis **ET** 129 Mf33
Temple of Horus **ET** 129 Mg33
Temple of Kawa **SUD** 135 Mf36
Temple of Khnum **ET** 129 Mg33
Temple of Kôm Ombo **ET** 129 Mg33
Temple of Luxor **ET** 129 Mg33
Temple of Nadura **ET** 129 Mf33
Temple of Philae **ET** 129 Mg33
Temple of Poseidón **GR** 47 Me53
Temple of Yeha **ETH** 142 Mk38
Templer Bank 90 Qj40
Temples of Musawwarat **SUD** 135 Mg37
Temples of Naqa **SUD** 135 Mg37
Temples of Sesebi **SUD** 135 Mf35
Templin **D** 32 Lo37
Tempoal de Sánchez **MEX** (VC) 182 Fa35
Tempué **ANG** 150 Lk52
Temrjuk **RUS** 49 Mj23
Temuco **RCH** 208 Gd65
Temuka **NZ** 113 Tf68
Tena **EC** 196 Gb46
Tenabo **MEX** (CAM) 183 Fe35
Tenacatita **MEX** (JLC) 182 Eh36
Ténado **BF** 137 Kj39
Tenaha **USA** (TX) 174 Fc30
Tenakee Springs **USA** (AK) 166 Dc17
Tenala = Tenhola **FIN** 38 Md30
Tenali **IND** (APH) 83 Pa37
Tenamatua, Gunung **RI** 96 Ra46
Tenancingo de Degollado **MEX** (MEX) 182 Fa36
Tenasserim = Taninthari **MYA** 88 Pk39
Tenasserim = Taninthari **MYA** 88 Pk39
Tenasserim Island **MYA** 88 Pj39
Tenaún **RCH** 208 Gd67
Tenby **GB** 21 Kq39
Tench Island **PNG** 116 Sf46
Tendaho **ETH** 142 Na40
Ten Degree Channel **IND** 88 Pg41
Tendilla **E** 29 Ks50
Tendjedj **DZ** 132 Ld34
Tendo **J** 77 Sa26
Tendoy **USA** (ID) 168 Ed23
Tendrara **MA** 125 Kk29
Tendukheda **IND** (MPH) 83 Ok34
Téné **RMM** 137 Kh39
Ténenkou **RMM** 131 Kh38
Tenente Portela **BR** (RS) 204 Hd59
Ténentou **RMM** 137 Kg40
Tenerapa **MEX** (DGO) 181 Eh33
Ténéré **RN** 133 Lf36
Ténéré du Tafassasset **RN** 133 Lf35
Tenerife **E** 124 Kb31
Ténès **DZ** 126 La27
Tengahdai **RI** 96 Rb50
Tengchong **CHN** (YUN) 87 Pk33
Tenggarong **RI** 95 Qj46
Tengger Shamo **CHN** 72 Qc26
Tenggol **MAL** 92 Qb43
Tengkis **RI** 93 Qc46
Tengréla **BF** 137 Kh40
Tengréla **CI** 137 Kg40
Te-n-Guembo **RIM** 130 Kf37
Teng Xian **CHN** (GZG) 74 Qf34
Tengzhou **CHN** (SDG) 78 Qj28
Tenharim Igarapé Prêto, T.I. **BR** 198 Gk50
Tenharim Marmelos, T.I. **BR** 198 Gk50
Tenhola = Tenala **FIN** 38 Md30
Tenhult **S** 31 Lp33
Teni **IND** (TNU) 84 Oj40
Teniente Agripino Enciso, P.N. **PY** 206 Gk56
Teniente Luis Carvajal **ANT** (RCH) 6 Gc32
Teniente Maza **RA** (RN) 208 Gg66
Teniente Pinglo **PE** 196 Gb48
Tenille **USA** (FL) 178 Fj31
Tenindewa **AUS** (WA) 104 Qh60
Tenja **HR** 35 Lt45
Tenkasi **IND** (TNU) 84 Oj41
Tenke **RDC** 146 Md51
Tenkodogo **BF** 137 Kk40
Tenlaa **IND** (AAN) 88 Pg42
Tenmalai **IND** (KER) 84 Oj41
Ten-month Solar Calendar Park **CHN** 87 Qa33
Tennam **AUS** (QLD) 108 Sb58
Tennant Creek **AUS** (NT) 106 Rh55
Tennessee **USA** 175 Ff28
Tennessee N.W.R. **USA** 175 Ff27
Tennessee N.W.R. **USA** 175 Fg28
Tenom **MAL** 94 Qh43
Tenosique **MEX** (TB) 183 Fe37
Tenoûmer **RIM** 130 Ke34
Tensas River N.W.R. **USA** 175 Fe29
Ten Sleep **USA** (WY) 169 Eg23
Tenstrike **USA** (MN) 172 Fc22
Tentena **RI** 96 Ra46
Tenterden **GB** 21 La39
Tenterfield **AUS** (NSW) 109 Sf60
Ten Thousand Islands **USA** 179 Fk33
Tentolomatinan, Gunung **RI** 91 Rb45
Tentra **IND** (MPH) 82 Oj32
Tentyra **ET** 129 Mg32
Tenzug **GH** 137 Kk40
Teocaltiche **MEX** (JLC) 182 Ej35
Teodoro Sampaio **BR** (SP) 202 Hd57
Teofilândia **BR** (BA) 201 Ja51
Teófilo Otoni **BR** (MG) 203 Hk54
Teofipol' **UA** 49 Md21
Teolândi **BR** (BA) 201 Ja52
Teomabal Island **RP** 91 Ra42
Teos **TR** 47 Mg52
Teotihuacán **MEX** 182 Fa36
Teotilán de Flores Magón **MEX** (OAX) 182 Fb36
Teotitlán del Valle **MEX** (OAX) 183 Fb37
Teovo **MK** 44 Mb49
Tepa **GH** 137 Kj42
Tepache **MEX** (SO) 180 Ef31
Te Paki **NZ** 112 Tg63
Tepalcatepec **MEX** (MHC) 182 Ej36
Tepalcingo **MEX** (MOR) 182 Fa36
Tepatitlán de Morelos **MEX** (JLC) 182 Ej35
Tepeguajes **MEX** (TM) 182 Fb34
Tepehuanes **MEX** (DGO) 180 Eh33
Tepelenë **AL** 46 Lu50
Tepeleu **RI** 91 Re45
Tepere **MOC** 153 Mk52
Tepexi de Rodríguez **MEX** (PUE) 182 Fb36
Tepi **ETH** 142 Mh42
Tepic **MEX** (NYT) 182 Eh35
Tepich **MEX** (QTR) 183 Ff35
Teplá **CZ** 42 Ln41
Teplice **CZ** 42 Lo40
Teploe **RUS** 48 Mj19
Teploključenka **KS** 66 Ok24
Teporechi **MEX** (CHH) 180 Eg32
Tepoztlán **MEX** (MOR) 182 Fa36
Te Puke **NZ** 112 Tj64
Tequila **MEX** (JLC) 182 Ej35
Tequisquiapan **MEX** (QRT) 182 Fa35
Téra **RN** 131 La38
Teradomari **J** 77 Rk27
Teraina **KIR** 11 Ca09
Terakeka **SUD** 144 Mf43
Terälahti **FIN** 38 Md29
Téramo **I** 35 Lo48
Terán **CO** 192 Ga45
Terang **AUS** (VIC) 111 Sb65
Teranum **MAL** 92 Qa44
Te Rapa Racecourse **NZ** 112 Th64
Ter Apel **NL** 23 Lh38
Terapo **PNG** 115 Sd50
Teratyn **PL** 41 Md40
Te Raupua **NZ** 112 Tg63
Terbanggibesar **RI** 93 Qc48
Terbuny **RUS** 48 Mk19
Tercan **TR** 57 Na26
Terceira Aliança **BR** (SP) 202 He56
Terceiro Acampamento **BR** (AP) 194 Hd45
Terdal **IND** (KTK) 82 Oh37
Terebo **PNG** 115 Sb49
Terebovlja **UA** 43 Mf41
Terek **RUS** (KBA) 57 Nc24
Terekhol **IND** 82 Og38
Terekli-Mekteb **RUS** (DAG) 57 Nc23
Terekti **KZ** 67 Pc21
Terelj **MNG** 70 Qd22
Teremia Mare **RO** 44 Ma45
Terenos **BR** (MS) 202 Hc56
Terenozek **KZ** 63 Oc23
Terepaima, P.N. **YV** 193 Gf41
Teresa **RCH** 207 Gf56
Teresina **BR** (PI) 201 Hj48
Teresópolis **BR** (RJ) 205 Hj57
Terezinha de Goiás **BR** (GO) 200 Hg52
Tergnier **F** 23 Ld41
Teriang **MAL** 92 Qb44
Terjît **RIM** 130 Kd35
Terlizzi **I** 37 Lr49
Termachivka **UA** 48 Me20
Termas de Arapey **ROU** 204 Hb61
Termas de Catillo **RCH** 208 Ge64
Termas de Cauquenes **RCH** 208 Ge63
Termas de Chillán **RCH** 208 Ge64
Termas de Daymán **ROU** 204 Hb61
Termas de Falco **RCH** 208 Ge63
Termas de Gravatal **BR** 205 Hf60
Termas de Guaviyú **ROU** 204 Hb61
Termas de Pernué **RCH** 208 Ge65
Termas de Reyes **RA** 207 Gh58
Termas de Río Hondo **RA** (SE) 207 Gh59
Termas de Villavicencio **RA** (MD) 208 Gf62
Termas do Quilombo **BR** 202 Hf56
Termas El Sosneado **RA** (MD) 208 Ge63
Terme **TR** 56 Mj25
Terme di Lurísia **I** 34 Lh46
Termessé **RG** 136 Kd39
Termessos **TR** 56 Mf27
Termessos Milli Parkı **TR** 56 Mf27
Términi Imerese **I** 36 Lo53
Termit **RN** 133 Lf37
Termit-Kaoboul **RN** 133 Lf38
Térmoli **I** 37 Lp49
Ternate **RI** 91 Rd45
Ternej **RUS** 77 Rj23
Terneuzen **NL** 23 Ld39
Terni **I** 34 Ln48
Ternitz **A** 35 Lr43
Ternopil' **UA** 43 Mf41
Terntory Wildlife Park **AUS** 106 Rf52
Terowie **AUS** (SA) 110 Rk62
Terpnás **GR** 46 Mb51
Terra Alta **BR** (PA) 195 Hg46
Terrace **CDN** (BC) 166 Df18
Terrace Bay **NAM** 150 Lg55
Terrace (Long Island) **USA** 177 Ge25
Terrace Mtn. **USA** 171 Ed25
Terracina **I** 36 Lo49
Terracotta Army **CHN** 72 Qe28
Terra de Areia **BR** (RS) 205 He60
Terra Firma **ZA** 154 Mb58
Terråk **N** 16 Lg13
Terralba **I** 36 Lj51
Terra Mitica **E** 29 Ku52
Terra Nova **BR** (AC) 198 Gf50
Terra Nova **BR** (PE) 201 Ja50
Terra Nova B. **ANT** (I) 7 Tc33
Terra Nova do Norte **BR** (MT) 199 Hc51
Terra Nova N. P. **CDN** 177 Hd21
Terra Preta **BR** (AM) 199 Ha49
Terra Preta **BR** (AM) 199 Ha49
Terra Rica **BR** (PR) 202 Hd57
Terrassa **E** 29 Lc49
Terra Verhelma, T.I. **BR** 198 Gj48
Terre Adélie 7 Rd32
Terrebonne **CDN** (QC) 177 Gd23
Terre Clarie 7 Rc32
Terre Haute **USA** (IN) 175 Fg26
Terrell **USA** (TX) 174 Fb29
Terreros **MEX** (COH) 181 Ek31
Terreton **USA** (ID) 169 Ed24
Terry **USA** (MT) 169 Eh22
Terry Hie Hie **AUS** (NSW) 109 Sf60
Terschelling **NL** 23 Lf37
Tersef **TCH** 139 Lj39
Terskej Ala-Too **KS** 66 Oj24
Teruel **CO** 192 Gc44
Teruel **E** 29 Kt50
Terujak **RI** 92 Pj43
Terusan **RI** 93 Qb47
Tervakoski **FIN** 38 Me30
Tervel **BG** 45 Mh47
Tervo **FIN** 28 Mg28
Tervola **FIN** 16 Mc12
Terwood **AUS** (QLD) 107 Sb54
Tesalia **CO** 192 Gc44
Tešanj **BIH** 35 Ls46
Tešel **BG** 45 Me49
Teseny **ER** 142 Mj38
Teshikaga **J** 77 Sc24
Tešica **SCG** 44 Mb47
Teslić **BIH** 35 Ls46
Teslin **CDN** (YT) 166 Dd15
Teso Santo **E** 26 Kp49
Tessalit **RMM** 132 La35
Tessaoua **RN** 132 Ld39
Tesséroukane **RN** 132 Ld36
Tessit **RMM** 131 La38
Tessounfat **RMM** 132 La35
Testa del Gargano **I** 37 Lr49
Testour **TN** 126 Le27
Tesuque Ind. Res. **USA** 171 Eh28
Tét **H** 42 Ls43
Tetachuk Lake **CDN** 166 Dh19
Tetari, Cerro **CO/YV** 192 Gd40
Tetari **IND** (UPH) 83 Pb32
Tetbury **GB** 21 Ks39
Tete **MOC** 152 Mg54
Tête-à-la Baleine **CDN** (QC) 176 Ha20
Tetehui **PNG** 115 Sc49
Tête Jaune Cache **CDN** (BC) 168 Ea19
Te Teko **NZ** 112 Tj65
Tetela **MEX** (PUE) 182 Fb36
Tetepare **SOL** 117 Sj50
Tetere **SOL** 117 Ta51
Teterow **D** 32 Ln37
Tetetes **EC** 196 Gb45
Teteven **BG** 45 Me48
Tetijiv **UA** 49 Me21
Tétini **RG** 136 Kf41
Tetlin Junction **USA** (AK) 165 Cj14
Tetlin Lake **USA** 165 Cj14
Tetlin National Wildlife Refuge **USA** 165 Cj14
Tétouan **MA** 125 Kh28
Tetovo **BG** 45 Mg47
Tetovo **MK** 44 Ma48
Tettnang **D** 33 Lk43
Teturi **RDC** 141 Me45
Teuchern **D** 32 Ln39
Teuchira **LAR** 127 Ma29
Teulada **I** 36 Lj52
Teulada-Moraira **E** 29 La52
Teulon **CDN** (MB) 172 Fb20
Teun **RI** 97 Re49
Teunom **RI** 92 Ph43
Teuri-to **J** 77 Sa23
Teutoburger Wald **D** 32 Lj38
Teutônia **BR** (RS) 204 He60
Teutonic **AUS** (WA) 104 Ra60
Teuva **FIN** 38 Mb28
Teverya **IL** 56 Mh29
Tewah **RI** 95 Qg46
Te Wahi-pounamou **NZ** 113 Td68
Tewantin-Noosa **AUS** (QLD) 109 Sg59
Tewaukon N.W.R. **USA** 172 Fb22
Tewkesbury **GB** 21 Ks39
Têwo **CHN** (GSU) 72 Qb28
Tewure **WAN** 138 Lc41
Texada Island **CDN** 168 Dh21
Texarkana **USA** (TX) 174 Fc29
Texas **AUS** (NSW) 109 Sf60
Texas **USA** 174 Fa30
Texas Motor Speedway **USA** (TX) 174 Fb29
Texas Rangers Hall of Fame **USA** 174 Fb30
Texel **NL** 23 Le38
Teyateyaneng **LS** 155 Md60
Teywarah **AFG** 65 Oc29
Teziutlán **MEX** (PUE) 182 Fb36
Tezpur **IND** (ASM) 86 Pg32
Tezu **IND** (ARP) 86 Pj32
Tfaritiy **DARS** 124 Ke32
T.G.V. Paris-Marseille **F** 25 Le45
Thaa Atoll **MV** 84 Og44
Thaba-Bosiu **LS** 155 Md60
Thabana-Ntlenyana **LS** 155 Me60
Thaba Nchu **ZA** 155 Md60
Thaba Putsoa **LS** 155 Md60
Thabazimbi **ZA** 155 Md58
Thabeikkyin **MYA** 86 Pj34
Tha Bo **THA** 87 Qb37
Thabong **ZA** 155 Md59
Thac Bac **VN** 87 Qb34
Tha Champa **THA** 87 Qc37
Tha Chana **THA** 88 Pk41
Thach Tru **VN** 89 Qe38
Thadiq **KSA** 59 Nc33
Thadlaskein **IND** (MGA) 86 Pg33
Thagaya **MYA** 86 Pj36
Thai Binh **VN** 87 Qd35
Thai Elephant Conservation Centre **THA** 87 Pk36
Thailand **T** 53 Qa08
Thai Lu Tribe Village **THA** 87 Qa36
Thai Muang **THA** 88 Pk41
Thaing-ngin **MYA** 86 Pg34
Thai Nguyen **VN** 87 Qc35
Thaj **KSA** 59 Ne32
Thakadu **RB** 152 Md56
Thakgameng **ZA** 155 Mc59
Tha Khaek **LAO** 87 Qc37
Thal **PK** 65 Of29
Thala **TN** 126 Le28
Thalabarivat **K** 89 Qc39
Thalang **THA** 88 Pk41
Thalasseri **IND** (KER) 84 Oh40
Thale Ban N.P. **THA** 88 Qa42
Thale Sap Songkhla **THA** 88 Qa42
Thallon **AUS** (QLD) 109 Se60
Thalpan 80 Oh28
Thamad al Hadh **LAR** 127 Lj32
Thamad al Qattar **LAR** 127 Lh31
Thamad Bu Hashishah **LAR** 127 Lk32
Thamad Bu Maras **LAR** 127 Lk31
Thamad Qabr Salih **LAR** 126 Lf30
Thamaga **RB** 155 Mc58
Tha Mai **THA** 89 Qb39
Thamantha **MYA** 86 Ph34
Thamarit **OM** 61 Nh37
Thamat ash Sham **KSA** 60 Na36
Thamayapeta **IND** (APH) 83 Pb37
Thames **GB** 21 Kt39
Thames **NZ** 112 Th64
Thames Valley **GB** 21 Kt39
Tham Jang Cave **LAO** 87 Qb36
Tham Khao Luang **THA** 88 Qa39
Tha Mot **THA** 88 Qa42
Tham Phra **THA** 89 Qa37
Tham Phraya Nakhon Cave **THA** 88 Pk39
Tham Phu Kham Cave **LAO** 87 Qb36
Tham Piu Cave **LAO** 87 Qb36
Tham Than Souphanouvong **LAO** 87 Qc35
Thamud **YE** 60 Ne37
Thamun **YE** 61 Nf38
Thana **PK** 65 Ob31
Thana Kasba **IND** (RJT) 82 Oj33
Thanatpin **MYA** 88 Pj37
Thanbyuzayat **MYA** 88 Pj38
Thandla **IND** (MPH) 82 Oh34
Thane **IND** (MHT) 82 Og36
Thanesar **IND** (HYA) 80 Oj31
Thang Binh **VN** 89 Qe38
Thangool **AUS** (QLD) 109 Sf58
Thanh Hóa **VN** 87 Qc36
Than Island **MYA** 88 Pj41
Thaniyah **KSA** 60 Nb36
Thanjavur **IND** (TNU) 85 Ok40
Than Lod Noi Cave **THA** 88 Pk38
Thanlon **IND** (MNP) 86 Pg33
Thann **F** 25 Lh43
Thano Bula Khan **PK** 65 Od33
Than Uyen **VN** 87 Qb35
Thanwin Myir **MYA** 87 Pk35
Thanwin Myir 87 Pk36
Thanze **MYA** 88 Ph37
Thaon-les-Vosges **F** 25 Lg42
Tha Pla **THA** 87 Qa37
Thap Lan N.P. **THA** 89 Qb38
Thap Put **THA** 88 Pk41
Thap Sakae **THA** 88 Pk40
Tharad **IND** (GUJ) 82 Of33
Tharb **KSA** 58 Na33
Thar Desert **IND/PK** 80 Of32
Thargomindah **AUS** (QLD) 109 Sb59
Thárros **I** 36 Lj51
Tha Rua **THA** 87 Pk36
Tharwaniyyah **UAE** 61 Ng34
Tha Sae **THA** 88 Pk40
Tha Song Yang **THA** 88 Pk37
Thássos **GR** 45 Me50
Thássos **GR** 45 Me50
Tha Tako **THA** 88 Qa38
Thatcher **USA** (AZ) 171 Ef29
Thathaganyana Hill **RB** 152 Md57
Thaton **MYA** 88 Pj37
That Phanom **THA** 89 Qc37
That Sikhotabong **LAO** 87 Qc37
Thatta **PK** 65 Od33
Tha Uthen **THA** 87 Qc37
Tha Wang Pha **THA** 87 Qa36
Thayatal, N.P. **A** 42 Lq42
Thayawthadangyi **MYA** 88 Pj39
Thayer **USA** (MO) 175 Fe27
Thayetmyo **MYA** 86 Ph36
Thaygon **MYA** 88 Pj37
Thayne **USA** (WY) 169 Ee24
Thay Pagoda **VN** 87 Qc35
Thazi **MYA** 86 Pj35
The Alley **JA** 186 Gb37
The Alps **AUS** 109 Se57
The Ancient City = Muang Boran **THA** 88 Qa39
Théâtre antique d'Orange **F** 25 Le46
The Balconies **AUS** 110 Sb64
The Bayon **K** 89 Qb39
Thebes **GR** 45 Md52
The Bottom **NL** (NA) 187 Gj37
The Brothers = Lloyd Rock **BS** 186 Gc35
The Brothers = Al Ikhwan **YE** 61 Ng39
The Butt **USA** (AK) 165 Ch13
The Caves **AUS** (QLD) 109 Sf57
The Cheviot Hills **GB** 20 Ks35
The Cove Palisades S.P. **USA** 168 Dk23
The Dalles **USA** (OR) 168 Dk23
Thedford **USA** (NE) 172 Ek25
The English Company's Islands **AUS** 106 Rj51
The Entrance **AUS** (NSW) 111 Sf62
The Everglades **USA** 179 Fk32
The Fens **GB** 21 La38
The Ghan (Northern Territory) **AUS** (SA) 106 Rg54
The Ghan (Southern Australia) **AUS** (SA) 108 Rh60
The Grampians **AUS** 111 Sb64
The Greater Saint Lucia Wetland Park **ZA** 155 Mg59
The Great Wall **CHN** 73 Qj25
The Hague **NL** 23 Le38
The Haven **ZA** 155 Me62
The Hermitage (Cat Island) **BS** 186 Gc33
Theinkun **MYA** 88 Pk40
Thekerani **MW** 153 Mh54
Thekkady **IND** (KER) 84 Oj40
The Lakes N.P. **AUS** 111 Sd65
The Little Minch **GB** 20 Ko33
Theme **MYA** 86 Pj36
The Monument **AUS** (QLD) 108 Rk56
The Mumbles **GB** 21 Kq39
The Naze **GB** 21 Lb39
The Needles **GB** 21 Kt40
The Needles **USA** 171 Ef26
The New Forest **GB** 21 Kt40
Thenia **DZ** 126 Lb27
Theniet El Had **DZ** 126 Lb28
Theniet El Had, P.N.de **DZ** 126 La28
Thenzawl **IND** (MZR) 86 Pg34
Theodore **AUS** (QLD) 109 Sf58
Theodore **CDN** (SK) 169 Ej20
Theodore **USA** (AL) 175 Ff30
Theodor Roosevelt Lake **USA** 171 Ee29
The Olgas **AUS** 105 Rf58
Theológos **GR** 44 Md52
The Overland **AUS** 110 Sa64
Thepa **THA** 89 Qa42
The Pas **CDN** (MB) 169 Ek19
The Pennines **GB** 21 Kt36
The Pride of Africa 152 Md54
Thep Sa Thit **THA** 88 Qa38
Théra **GR** 47 Mf54
The Registan **UZ** 63 Od26
Theri **IND** (UTT) 81 Ok30
Thermes de Migioky **RM** 156 Ne52
Thermí **GR** 47 Mg51
Thermo **GR** 46 Mb52
Thermopolis **USA** (WY) 169 Ef24
The Rock **AUS** (NSW) 111 Sd63
Theron Mountains 6 Jc34
The Royal Orient **IND** 80 Oh32
The Sands **GUY** 194 Gk42
The Slot = New Georgia Sound **SOL** 117 Sj49
The Sound **DK** 30 Ln35
Thesprotikó **GR** 46 Ma51
Thessalon **CDN** (ON) 173 Fj22
Thessaloníki **GR** 46 Mc50
The Steppe **KZ** 54 Oa09
Thetford **GB** 21 La38
Thetford Mines **CDN** (QC) 176 Ge22
Thet ke gyin **MYA** 86 Ph34
The Twins **AUS** (SA) 108 Rh60
Theunissen **ZA** 155 Md60
The Valley **GB** 187 Gj36
Thevenard Island **AUS** 102 Qh56
The Village **USA** (OK) 174 Fb28
The Wash **GB** 21 La38
The Wedge **USA** (CA) 170 Eb29
The Witties **NIC** 185 Fj38
The Woodlands **USA** (TX) 174 Fc30
Thialf **NL** 23 Lg38
Thiba **EAK** 144 Mj46
Thiboudaux **USA** (LA) 175 Fe31
Thief River Falls **USA** (MN) 172 Fb21
Thiel Mountains 6 Fc36
Thiene **I** 34 Lm45
Thiérache **F** 23 Ld41
Thiers **F** 25 Ld45
Thiès **SN** 130 Kb38
Thiesi **I** 36 Lj50
Thika **EAK** 144 Mj46
Thillé Boubakar **SN** 130 Kc37
Thilogne **SN** 130 Kd38
Thimad al Fata'im **LAR** 127 Lk30
Thimlich Ohinga **EAK** 144 Mh46
Thimphu **BHT** 86 Pe32
Thingsai **IND** (MZR) 86 Pg34
Thio **F** (NCL) 118 Td56
Thionville **F** 23 Lg41
Thíra = Santorini **GR** 47 Mf54
Thíra **GR** 47 Mf54
Thíra **GR** 47 Mf54
Third Cataract **SUD** 134 Mf36
Thirsk **GB** 21 Kt36
Thirukkovilur **IND** (TNU) 85 Ok40
Thiruthuraipundi **IND** (TNU) 85 Ok40
Thiruvananthapuram **IND** (KER) 84 Oj41
Thisted **DK** 30 Lj34
Thistle **USA** (UT) 171 Ee26
Thistle Island **AUS** 110 Rj63
Thitani **EAK** 144 Mj46
Thíva **GR** 45 Md52
Thiviers **F** 24 La45
Thizy **F** 25 Le44
Thkov **K** 89 Qb39
Thma Pok **K** 89 Qb39
Thnal Bek **K** 89 Qc40
Thoen **THA** 88 Pk37
Thoeng **THA** 87 Qa36
Thohoyandou **ZA** 152 Mf57
Tholária **GR** 47 Mg54
Thomas Mann Haus **LT** 39 Mb35
Thomaston **USA** (GA) 175 Fh29
Thomaston Corner **CDN** (NB) 176 Gg23
Thomasville **USA** (AL) 175 Fg30
Thomasville **USA** (GA) 178 Fj30
Thomasville **USA** (NC) 178 Fk28
Thomonde **RH** 186 Ge36
Thompson **CDN** (MB) 163 Fa07
Thompson Landing **CDN** 167 Ee14
Thompson Pass **USA** 165 Ch15
Thompsons Falls **USA** (MT) 168 Ec22
Thomson **USA** (GA) 178 Fj29
Thomson River **AUS** (QLD) 109 Sb57
Thomson's Falls = Nyahururu **EAK** 144 Mj45
Thong Pha Phum **THA** 88 Pk38
Thong Sala **THA** 88 Pk41
Thongwa **MYA** 88 Pj37
Thon Hai **VN** 89 Qd37
Thon Kiang **THA** 88 Pk41
Thonon-les-Bains **F** 25 Lg44
Thoreau **USA** (NM) 171 Ef28
Thorndale **ZA** 152 Me57
Thorne **GB** 21 Ku37
Thornhill **GB** 20 Kr35
Thorntonia **AUS** (QLD) 106 Rk55
Thorshavnheiane 7 Mc33
Thorsminde **DK** 30 Lj34
Thorton Peak **AUS** (QLD) 107 Sc54
Thot Not **VN** 89 Qc40
Thouars **F** 24 Ku44
Thoubal **IND** (MNP) 86 Ph33
Thowada Goemba **BHT** 86 Pf32
Thowak **SUD** 135 Mh38
Thrace **GR/TR** 45 Mf49
Thrakikó Pélagos **GR** 45 Me50
Thrapston **GB** 21 Ku38
Thredbo Village **AUS** (NSW) 111 Se64
Three Forks **USA** (MT) 169 Ee23
Three Gorges Dam **CHN** 74 Qf30
Three Gorges of Wuyang R. **CHN** 74 Qe32
Three Hills **CDN** (AB) 169 Ed20
Three Hummrock Island **AUS** (TAS) 111 Sc66
Three Kings Islands **NZ** 112 Tg63
Three Kings Ridge 10 Ta13
Three Pagodas Pass **THA** 88 Pk38
Three Parallel Rivers of Yunnan Protected Areas **CHN** 87 Pk32
Three Rivers **AUS** (WA) 104 Qk58
Three Rivers **USA** (MI) 173 Fh25
Three Rivers **USA** (NM) 171 Eg29
Three Rivers **USA** (TX) 181 Fa31
Three Sisters **AUS** 108 Sa58
Three Sisters **AUS** 111 Sf62
Three Sisters **USA** 168 Dk23
Three Sisters **ZA** 154 Mb61
Three Sisters Islands **SOL** 117 Tb51
Three Springs **AUS** (WA) 104 Qh60
Three Way Roadhouse **AUS** (NT) 106 Rh55
Thrissur **IND** (KER) 84 Oj40
Throckmorton **USA** (TX) 174 Fa29
Throssell Range **AUS** 102 Ra57
Thrumching La N.P. **BHT** 86 Pf32
Thrushton N.P. **AUS** 109 Sd59
Thuburbo Majus **TN** 126 Le27
Thu Dau Mot **VN** 89 Qd40
Thud Point **AUS** 107 Sa52
Thueyts **F** 25 Le46
Thuillier, Mount **IND** 88 Pg42
Thuir **F** 24 Lc48
Thul **PK** 65 Oe31
Thula **YE** 60 Nb38
Thulamela **ZA** 152 Mf57
Thule = Qaanaaq **DK** 163 Gc03
Thuli **ZW** 152 Me56
Thun **CH** 34 Lh44
Thunda **AUS** (QLD) 108 Sb58
Thundelarra **AUS** (WA) 104 Qj60
Thunder Bay **CDN** (ON) 172 Ff21
Thuner See **CH** 34 Lh44
Thung Hua Chang **THA** 87 Pk36
Thung Muang **THA** 87 Qa36
Thung Nao **THA** 87 Qa36
Thung Salaeng Luang N.P. **THA** 88 Qa37
Thung Song **THA** 88 Pk41
Thung Tako **THA** 88 Pk40
Thung Wa **THA** 88 Pk42
Thung Wua Laen Beach **THA** 88 Pk40
Thung Yai **THA** 88 Pk41
Thungyai-Huai Kha Kaeng Wildlife Sanctuaries **THA** 88 Pk38
Thurayban **KSA** 60 Na36
Thüringen **D** 32 Ll40
Thüringer Wald **D** 32 Ll40
Thurles **IRL** 19 Kn38
Thurlga **AUS** (SA) 110 Rh62
Thurloo Downs **AUS** (NSW) 108 Sb60
Thursby **GB** 20 Kr36
Thursday Island **AUS** (QLD) 107 Sb51
Thurso **GB** 20 Kr32
Thury-Harcourt **F** 22 Ku42
Thusis **CH** 34 Lk44
Thyborøn **DK** 30 Lj34
Thylungra **AUS** (QLD) 108 Sb59
Thymania **AUS** (QLD) 108 Sb57
Thyolo **MW** 153 Mh54
Thysville = Mbanza-Ngungu **RDC** 148 Lh48
Tiabge **CI** 137 Kh43
Tiadiaye **SN** 130 Kb38
Tiago **BR** (PA) 194 Hb46
Tiahuanaco **BOL** 206 Gf54
Tiahuanacu **BOL** 206 Gf54
Tianbanjie **CHN** (JGX) 75 Qj31
Tianchang **CHN** (AHU) 78 Qk29
Tian Chi **CHN** 67 Pd24
Tiandeng **CHN** (GZG) 74 Qd34
Tiandong **CHN** (GZG) 74 Qd34
Tian'e **CHN** (GZG) 74 Qd33
Tianeti **GE** 57 Nc24
Tianguá **BR** (CE) 201 Hk47
Tianguel-Bori **RG** 136 Kd40
Tianjin **CHN** 73 Qj26
Tianjin Shi **CHN** 73 Qj26
Tianjun **CHN** (QHI) 69 Pk27
Tiankoura **BF** 137 Kj40
Tianlin **CHN** (GZG) 74 Qd33
Tianmen **CHN** (HUB) 75 Qg30
Tianmu Shan **CHN** 78 Qk30
Tianmushan Z.B. **CHN** 78 Qk30
Tianqiaoling **CHN** (JLN) 76 Re24
Tian-Shan' **CHN** 66 Pa24
Tianshui **CHN** (GSU) 72 Qc28
Tianshuihai 68 Ok28
Tiantai **CHN** (ZJG) 75 Ra31
Tiantaishan **CHN** 75 Ra31
Tiantong Si **CHN** 75 Ra31
Tiantoubarak **RN** 132 Ld38
Tian Ya Hai Jiao **CHN** 75 Qe36
Tianyang **CHN** (GZG) 74 Qd34
Tianyi Ge **CHN** 75 Ra31
Tianzhen **CHN** (SAX) 73 Qh25
Tianzhou Jiaotang **CHN** 73 Ra27
Tianzhu **CHN** (GSU) 72 Qb27
Tianzhu **CHN** (GZH) 74 Qe32
Tianzhushan **CHN** 78 Qj30
Tiaret **DZ** 126 La28
Tiaro **AUS** (QLD) 109 Sg58
Tiassalé **CI** 137 Kh43
Tibagi **BR** (PR) 205 He58
Tibana **CO** 192 Gd43
Ţibana **RO** 49 Md22
Tibati **CAM** 139 Lg42
Tibaú **BR** (RN) 201 Jb48
Tibau, Gunung **RI** 94 Qh45
Tibel'ti **RUS** 70 Qb20
Tiber **I** 36 Ln48
Tiberghamine **DZ** 125 La31
Tiberias **IL** 56 Mh29
Tibesti **TCH** 133 Lj35
Tibet **CHN** 53 Pa07
Tibilisi **GE** 57 Nc25
Tibiri **RN** 132 Lb39
Tibiri **RN** 132 Ld39
Tibo **BF** 131 Kj38
Tibo **RDC** 141 Md44
Tibo **RDC** 141 Me44
Tibo **RI** 96 Qk47
Tibooburra **AUS** (NSW) 108 Sb60
Tibro **S** 31 Lp32
Tibú **CO** 192 Gd41
Tiburon **RH** 186 Gc36
Tiča **BG** 45 Mg48
Tica **MOC** 153 Mh55
Ticao Island **RP** 90 Rb39
Tica Tica **BOL** 206 Gg56
Tichet **RMM** 131 La36
Tichît **RIM** 130 Kf36
Tichla **DARS** 130 Kc35
Ticho **ETH** 142 Mk42
Ticino **CH** 34 Lj44
Tickalara **AUS** (QLD) 108 Sb60
Ticonderoga **USA** (NY) 177 Gd24
Ticsani, Volcán **PE** 197 Ge54
Ticul **MEX** (YT) 183 Ff35
Tidaholm **S** 31 Lo32
Tidal River **AUS** (VIC) 111 Sd65
Tidan **S** 31 Lp32
Tidarmène **RMM** 132 Lb37
Tiddim **MYA** 86 Pg34
Tiddis **DZ** 126 Ld27
Tidi Dunes **RN** 133 Lh35
Tidjikja **RIM** 130 Ke36
Tidore **RI** 91 Rd45
Tiébissou **CI** 137 Kh42
Tiéblé **BF** 137 Kk40
Tiebl'gahl **SYR** 57 Na28
Tiéboro **TCH** 133 Lj35
Tiefa **CHN** (LNG) 76 Rb24
Tiéfala **RMM** 137 Kg40
Tiéfora **BF** 137 Kh40
Tiel **NL** 23 Lf39
Tiel **SN** 130 Kc38
Tieli **CHN** (HLG) 76 Re22
Tieling **CHN** (LNG) 76 Rb24
Tielong 68 Ok28
Tielt **B** 23 Ld40
Tiémé **CI** 137 Kg41
Tié-Ndiékro **CI** 137 Kh42
Tienen **B** 23 Le40
Téningboué **CI** 137 Kh41
Tienko **CI** 137 Kg40
Tienko **CI** 137 Kg41
Tien Yen **VN** 87 Qd35
Tiera **BF** 137 Kh40
Tiéré **RMM** 137 Kh40
Tierfontein **ZA** 155 Md60
Tierir **AUS** (QLD) 109 Se57
Tierp **S** 31 Ls30
Tierra Amarilla **RCH** 207 Ge59
Tierra Amarilla **USA** (NM) 171 Eg27
Tierra Blanca **MEX** (VC) 183 Fb36
Tierra Colorada **MEX** (GUR) 182 Fa37
Tierra de Campos **E** 26 Kp49
Tierra del Fuego **RA** 210 Gf72
Tierra del Fuego **RA** 210 Gg73
Tierra del Fuego, P.N. **RA** 210 Gg73
Tierra del Vino **E** 26 Kp49
Tierralta **CO** 192 Gb41
Tierranueva **MEX** (SLP) 182 Ek35
Tierras Blancas **RCH** 207 Ge61
Tierras de Sayago **E** 26 Ko49
Tiesa **E** 27 Kp53
Tie Siding **USA** (WY) 171 Eh25
Tie Ta **CHN** 73 Qh28
Tietê **BR** (SP) 205 Hg57
Tietê **BR** 202 He56
Tieyon **AUS** (SA) 108 Rg59
Tiffin **USA** (OH) 173 Fj25
Tiflèt **MA** 125 Kg29
Tifore **RI** 91 Rd45
Tifrirt **RIM** 130 Kd35
Tifton **USA** (GA) 178 Fj30
Tifu **RI** 97 Rd47
Tiga **F** (NCL) 118 Td56
Tiga **MAL** 94 Qh43
Tigaon **RP** 90 Rb39
Tigapulan Mountains **RI** 93 Qb46
Tigbauan **RP** 90 Rb40
Tiger **USA** (WA) 168 Eb21
Tiger Island **GUY** 194 Ha42
Tigharry **GB** 20 Kn33
Tighenif **DZ** 125 La28
Tighina **MD** 49 Me22
Tignère **CAM** 139 Lg42
Tigniré **RIM** 130 Kc36
Tignish **CDN** (PE) 176 Gh22
Tigoumatene **RMM** 131 Kh37
Tigre **PE** 196 Gc47
Tigre **RA** (BA) 209 Ha63
Tigre **YV** 193 Gj41
Tigris **IRQ** 57 Nb27
Tigrovaya Balka zapovednik **TJ** 63 Oe27
Tiguelguemine **DZ** 126 Lb32
Tiguent **RIM** 130 Kb37
Tiguentourine **DZ** 126 Le32
Tiguézéfene **RN** 132 Lb38
Tigui **TCH** 133 Lk36
Tiguili **TCH** 139 Lk40
Tigzirt **DZ** 126 Lc27
Tihamat **YE** 60 Nb37
Tihany **H** 42 Ls44
Tiholop **MEX** (YT) 183 Ff35
Tihoreck **RUS** 49 Na23
Tihosuco **MEX** (QTR) 183 Ff35
Tihvin **RUS** 48 Mg16
Tihvinskaja grjada **RUS** 48 Mh16
Tiilikkajärven kansallispuisto **FIN** 16 Me14
Tijara **IND** (RJT) 80 Oj32
Tiji **LAR** 126 Lf29
Tijuana **MEX** (BC) 180 Eb29
Tijuca, P.N.da **BR** 205 Hj57
Tijucas **BR** (SC) 205 Hf59
Tika **CDN** (QC) 176 Gh20
Tikal **GCA** 183 Ff37
Tikal **GCA** 183 Ff37
Tikal, P.N. **GCA** 183 Ff37
Tikamgarh **IND** (MPH) 83 Ok33
Tikanlik **CHN** (XUZ) 67 Pd25
Tikaré **BF** 137 Kk39
Tikarpara **IND** (ORS) 83 Pb35
Tikarpara **IND** (ORS) 83 Pc35
Tikem **TCH** 140 Lh41
Tikitiki **NZ** 112 Tk64
Tikkaballi **IND** (ORS) 83 Pc35
Tikkakoski **FIN** 38 Mf28
Tiko **CAM** 138 Le43
Tikokino **NZ** 113 Tj65
Tikopia **SOL** 118 Te52
Tikota **IND** (KTK) 82 Oh37
Tikrit **IRQ** 57 Nb28
Tiku **RI** 93 Pk46
Tikuna de Feijoal, T.I. **BR** 198 Gf48
Tikus **RI** 93 Qb47
Tila **MEX** (CHP) 183 Fd37
Tiladru **IND** (APH) 83 Pa37
Tilaj **H** 42 Ls44
Tilal an-Nuba **SUD** 135 Mf39
Tilama **RCH** 208 Ge62
Tilamuta **RI** 91 Rb45
Tilbooroo **AUS** (QLD) 109 Sc59
Tilburg **NL** 23 Lf39
Tilbury **GB** 21 La39
Tilcara **RA** (PJ) 207 Gh57
Tilcha **AUS** (SA) 108 Sa60
Til-Châtel **F** 25 Lf43
Tilda **IND** (CGH) 83 Pa35
Tildega **IND** (ORS) 83 Pb34
Tilden **USA** (TX) 181 Fa31
Tileagd **RO** 43 Mc43
Tilemsen **MA** 124 Ke31
Tilemsès **RN** 132 Lc38
Tilemsi = Lerneb **RMM** 131 Kh37
Tilemsi **RMM** 131 La36
Tilisaro **RA** (SL) 208 Gh62
Tiliviche **RCH** 206 Gf55
Tillabéri **RN** 132 La38
Tillamook **USA** (OR) 168 Dj23
Tillamook Bay **USA** 168 Dh23
Tillanchang Dwip **IND** 88 Pg41
Tillberga **S** 31 Lr31
Tillia **RN** 132 Lc37
Tillsonburg **CDN** (ON) 173 Fk24
Tiloa **RN** 132 Lb38
Tilopozo **RCH** 207 Gf57
Tílos **GR** 47 Mh54
Tilpa **AUS** (NSW) 109 Sc61
Tilrhempt **DZ** 126 Lb29
Tiltagoonah **AUS** (NSW) 109 Sc61
Tilža **LV** 39 Mh34
Tim **RUS** 48 Mj20
Tim **UZ** 63 Oc26
Tima **ET** 129 Mf32
Timahdite **MA** 125 Kh29
Timampu **RI** 96 Ra47
Timanfaya, P.N.de **E** 124 Kd31
Timanskiy Kryazh **RUS** 14 Na03
Timare **RI** 114 Rj48
Timargarha **PK** 63 Of28
Timaru **NZ** 113 Tf68
Timaševsk **RUS** 49 Mk23
Timau **EAK** 144 Mj45
Timba **CO** 192 Gb44
Timbalier Bay **USA** 175 Fe31
Timbauba **BR** (PE) 201 Jc49
Timbavati Game Reserve **ZA** 155 Mf58
Timbedgha **RIM** 131 Kf37
Timber Creek **AUS** (NT) 106 Rf53
Timber Lake **USA** (SD) 172 Ek23
Timberline Lodge Ski Area **USA** 168 Dk23
Timber Mill **AUS** (NT) 106 Rg51
Timber Mtn. **USA** 170 Ec26
Timbiras **BR** (MA) 200 Hj48
Timbó **BR** (SC) 205 Hf59
Timbo **LB** 136 Kf43
Timbo **RG** 136 Ke40
Timbó Grande **BR** (SC) 205 He59
Timboroa **EAK** 144 Mh45
Timbulun **RI** 93 Qa46
Timbunke **PNG** 115 Sb48
Timbun Mata **MAL** 91 Qk43
Timé **BF** 131 Kk38
Timellouline **DZ** 126 Le31
Timétrine **RMM** 131 Kk36
Timfristós **GR** 46 Mb52
Timgad **DZ** 126 Ld28
Timia **RN** 132 Le36
Timiaouine **DZ** 132 La35
Timika **RI** 114 Rj48
Timimoun **DZ** 125 La31
Timişoara **RO** 44 Mb45
Timissa **RMM** 137 Kh39
Timmele **S** 31 Lo33
Timmelsjoch **A/I** 34 Lm44
Timmerkpuk Mt. **USA** (AK) 165 Bj11
Timmins **CDN** (ON) 173 Fk21
Tim-Missao **DZ** 132 Lb35
Timna **YE** 60 Nc38
Timna Park **IL** 58 Mh31
Timon **BR** (MA) 201 Hj48
Timor **TLS** 97 Rc50
Timor Museum **RI** 97 Rb51
Timor Sea 97 Rd51
Timor Trough 97 Rc51
Timote **RA** (BA) 209 Gj63
Timoteo **BR** (MG) 203 Hj55
Timotes **YV** 192 Ge41
Timoudi **DZ** 125 Kk31
Timpanogos Cave Nat. Mon. **USA** 171 Ee25
Timpas **USA** (CO) 174 Ej27
Timpaus **RI** 97 Rb46
Timrå **S** 17 Lj14
Timun **RI** 93 Qb45
Timurni **IND** (MPH) 82 Oj34
Tinaco **YV** 193 Gf41
Tinaga Island **RP** 90 Rb38
Ti-n-Aguelhaj **RMM** 131 Kj37
Ti-n-Akof **BF** 131 Kk38
Tin Alkoum **DZ** 133 Lf33
Tinambac **RP** 90 Rb39
Tinambung **RI** 96 Qk47
Tinaquillo **YV** 193 Gf41
Ti-n-Azabo **RMM** 131 La37
Ti-n-Bessaïs **RIM** 131 Kf34
Ti-n-Brahim **RIM** 130 Kc36
Tin Can Bay **AUS** (QLD) 109 Sg58
Tindangou **BF** 137 La40
Tindari **I** 37 Lq52
Tindila **RG** 136 Kf40
Tindivanam **IND** (TNU) 85 Ok39
Tindouf **DZ** 124 Kf32
Tiné **SUD** 134 Mb38
Tinejdad **MA** 125 Kh30
Tineo **E** 26 Ko47
Tinerhir **MA** 125 Kh30
Ti-n-Essako **RMM** 132 Lb36
Tinfouchy **DZ** 125 Kh31
Tin Fouye **DZ** 126 Ld31
Tinfunqué, P.N. **PY** 207 Ha57
Tinga **GH** 137 Kj41
Tingal **SUD** 135 Mf40
Tinggi **MAL** 92 Qc44
Tinglayan **RP** 90 Ra37
Tinglev **DK** 30 Lk36
Tingmiarmiut Fjord **DK** 163 Hd06
Tingo Maria **PE** 197 Gb50
Tingo María, P.N. **PE** 197 Gb50
Tingong **CHN** (GZH) 74 Qe33
Tingri **CHN** (TIB) 68 Pd31
Tingsryd **S** 31 Lp34
Tingstäde **S** 31 Lt33
Tinguipaya **BOL** 206 Gh55

Troy ⚑ USA (NY) 177 Gd24
Troy ⚑ USA (OH) 173 Fh25
Troy ⚑ USA (AL) 175 Ff28
Troyes ⚑ F 23 Le42
Troyitsko monastyr ⚑ UA 48 Mf20
Troy Peak ▲ USA 170 Ec26
Troyya ⚑ J 37 Tg25
Trsa ⚑ SCG 44 Lt47
Trsat ⚑ HR 35 Lp45
Tršćo ⚑ HR 35 Lp45
Truant Island ▲ AUS 106 Rj51
Truaru, T.I. ▲ BR 193 Gk44
Trubčevsk ⚑ RUS 48 Mg19
Truch ⚑ CDN (BC) 166 Dj17
Truckee ⚑ USA (CA) 170 Dk26
Trud ⚑ BG 45 Me46
Truer Range ▲ AUS 103 Rf57
Trujillo ⚑ E 27 Kp51
Trujillo ⚑ HN 193 Fg38
Trujillo ⚑ PE 197 Ga50
Trujillo ⚑ YV 192 Ge41
Truk Islands ⚑ FSM 100 Sb09
Trulli di Alberobello ⚑ I 37 Ls50
Trumann ⚑ USA (AR) 175 Fe28
Trumbull, Mount ▲ USA 171 Ed27
Trumieje ⚑ PL 41 Lu37
Trumon ⚑ RI 93 Pj44
Trun ⚑ F 22 La42
Trundle ⚑ AUS (NSW) 111 Sf62
Trung ⚑ VN 89 Qd34
Truro ⚑ CDN (NS) 176 Gj23
Truro ⚑ GB 21 Kp40
Trusan ⚑ MAL 94 Qd43
Truskavec' ⚑ UA 43 Md41
Trus Madi, Gunung ▲ MAL 94 Qd43
Trussville ⚑ USA (AL) 175 Fg29
Trustrup ⚑ DK 30 Lk34
Truth or Consequences ⚑ USA (NM) 171 Eg29
Truva ⚑ TR 47 Mg51
Tryon ⚑ USA (NE) 172 Ek25
Tryphena ⚑ NZ 112 Th64
Tryškiai ⚑ LT 39 Mc34
Tržac ⚑ BIH 35 Lq46
Trzcianka ⚑ PL 40 Lt37
Trzcianne ⚑ PL 41 Mc37
Trzciel ⚑ PL 40 Lq38
Trzcinna ⚑ PL 40 Lq38
Trzcińsko-Zdrój ⚑ PL 40 Lp38
Trzebiatów ⚑ PL 40 Lp37
Trzebień ⚑ PL 40 Lq39
Trzebinia ⚑ PL 41 Lu40
Trzebień ⚑ PL 40 Lq39
Trzemeszno ⚑ PL 40 Ls38
Trzydnik Duży ⚑ PL 41 Mc40
Tsabit ⚑ DZ 125 Kk31
Tsadumu ⚑ IND (KTK) 84 Oh39
Tsagaan Agui Cave ⚑ MNG 70 Qa29
Tsagaan Chulunta ⚑ CHN (QHI) 69 Pg26
Tsagaandörvölj ⚑ MNG 70 Qe23
Tsagaannuur ⚑ MNG 67 Pe21
Tsagaannuur ⚑ MNG 71 Qd22
Tsagaan Olom ⚑ MNG 70 Qa23
Tsagaan-Ovoo ⚑ MNG 70 Qa23
Tsagaan Shiveet Uul Nature Reserve ⚑ MNG 67 Pf20
Tsagaan Tsavyn ▲ MNG 70 Qa22
Tsagaan ⚑ MNG 70 Qb22
Tsagerl ⚑ GE 57 Nb24
Tsama ⚑ RCB 148 Lh46
Tsamia ⚑ RN 132 Le38
Tsandi ⚑ NAM 150 Lh54
Tsangano ⚑ MW 153 Mh53
Tsant ⚑ MNG 70 Qa22
Tsanyawa ⚑ WAN 138 Ld39
Tsaobis Leopard Nature Park ⚑ NAM 150 Lh57
Tsarahonenana ⚑ RM 156 Ne53
Tsaramandroso ⚑ RM 156 Nd54
Tsaratanana ⚑ RM 156 Ne53
Tsaratanana ⚑ RM 157 Ne55
Tsaravinany ⚑ RM 157 Ne55
Tsarishoogte Pass ⚑ NAM 154 Lj58
Tsast Uul ▲ MNG 67 Pg21
Tsatsu ⚑ RB 151 Mb56
Tsau ⚑ RB 151 Mb56
Tsavdan ⚑ MNG 67 Ph21
Tsavo ⚑ EAK 145 Mk47
Tsavo East N.P. ⚑ EAK 145 Mk47
Tsavo West N.P. ⚑ EAK 144 Mk47
Tsawah ⚑ LAR 127 Lg32
Tseepantee Lake ⚑ CDN 167 Dk14
Tseikuru ⚑ EAK 144 Mk46
Tsembo ⚑ RCB 148 Lg47
Tsengel ⚑ MNG 70 Qa21
Tse-Ndia-Wei S.P., T.I. ⚑ CHN 175 Fa26
Tsepélovo ⚑ GR 46 Ma51
Tses ⚑ NAM 154 Lh58
Tseteng ⚑ RB 154 Mb57
Tsetserleg ⚑ MNG 70 Qa22
Tsévié ⚑ TG 137 La42
Tshabong ⚑ RB 154 Mb59
Tshako ⚑ RDC 149 Mb50
Tshala ⚑ RDC 149 Mb50
Tshane ⚑ RB 154 Ma58
Tshela ⚑ RDC 148 Lg48
Tshesebe ⚑ RB 152 Md56
Tshibala ⚑ RDC 149 Ma49
Tshibamba ⚑ RDC 149 Mb50
Tshibeke ⚑ RDC 146 Me47
Tshibua ⚑ RDC 149 Mb49
Tshibwika ⚑ RDC 149 Mb49
Tshidilamolomo ⚑ ZA 155 Mc58
Tshie ⚑ RDC 149 Mb50
Tshikapa ⚑ RDC 149 Mb50
Tshikula ⚑ RDC 149 Mb49
Tshilenge ⚑ RDC 149 Mb49
Tshimbalanga ⚑ RDC 149 Mb49
Tshimbulu ⚑ RDC 149 Mb49
Tshimbumbu ⚑ RDC 149 Mb49
Tshimpungu ⚑ RDC 149 Ma49
Tshinsenda ⚑ RDC 151 Md52
Tshintshanku ⚑ RDC 149 Mb49
Tshipise ⚑ ZA 152 Mf57
Tshisenge ⚑ RDC 149 Ma49
Tshisoege ⚑ RDC 149 Ma49
Tshitadi ⚑ RDC 149 Ma49
Tshitanzu ⚑ RDC 149 Ma49
Tshiturapadsi ⚑ ZW 152 Mf57
Tshob ⚑ RDC 149 Mb49
Tshokwane ⚑ ZA 155 Mf58
Tsholotsho ⚑ ZW 152 Md55
Tshootsha ⚑ RB 151 Mb59
Tshuapa ⚑ RDC 149 Mb49
Tshuau ⚑ ZW 194 Gk42
Tshwane = Pretoria ⚑ ZA 155 Me58
Tsiaki ⚑ RCB 148 Lg47
Tsialoka ⚑ RM 157 Nc58
Tsimafana ⚑ RM 157 Nc55
Tsimanampetsotsa, P.N.de ⚑ RM 157 Nd59
Tsimazava ⚑ RM 157 Nc56
Tsimpseni Ind. Res. ⚑ CDN 166 De18
Tsineng ⚑ ZA 154 Mb59
Tsingtao ⚑ CHN 73 Ra27
Tsingy de Bemaraha, P.N.des ⚑ RM 157 Nc55
Tsinjoariva ⚑ RM 156 Nd55
Tsinjomitondraka ⚑ RM 156 Nd53
Tsintsabis ⚑ NAM 150 Lj55
Tsiombe ⚑ RM 157 Nc58
Tsiroanomandidy ⚑ RM 157 Nc55
Tsitondroina ⚑ RM 157 Nd56

Tsitsikamma N.P. ⚑ ZA 154 Mb63
Tsivory ⚑ RM 157 Nd58
Tsodilo ⚑ RB 151 Ma55
Tsodilo Hills ⚑ RB 151 Ma55
Tsogni ⚑ G 148 Lf47
Tsogstsalu ⚑ J 81 Ok28
Tsolo ⚑ ZA 155 Me61
Tsomo ⚑ ZA 155 Md62
Tsonjiyn Chuluu ⚑ MNG 70 Qf23
Tsqaltubo ⚑ GE 57 Nb24
Tsu ⚑ J 79 Rj28
Tsubata ⚑ J 77 Rh27
Tsuchiura ⚑ J 77 Sa27
Tsugaru Q.N.P. ⚑ J 77 Sa25
Tsugaru Strait ⚑ J 77 Sa25
Tsujima ⚑ J 79 Rg28
Tsukumi ⚑ J 79 Rf29
Tsukuba ⚑ RDC 148 Lj47
Tsukume ⚑ NAM 151 Ma55
Tsumkwe ⚑ NAM 151 Ma55
Tsunodupalle ⚑ IND (APH) 85 Ok39
Tsuruga ⚑ J 79 Rj28
Tsurugi-san ▲ J 79 Rh29
Tsuruoka ⚑ J 77 Rk26
Tsuyama ⚑ J 79 Rg28
Tsuruoka ⚑ RB 154 Mb57
Tswalu Private Desert Reserve ⚑ ZA 154 Mb58
Tswapong Hills ⚑ RB 152 Md56
T-Tree Bay ⚑ AUS 109 Sg59
Tual ⚑ RI 91 Rd46
Tuam ⚑ IRL 19 Kn37
Tua Marine National Park = Bunaken-Manado Tua Marine National Park ⚑ RI 91 Rc45
Tuamotu Archipelago ⚑ 11 Cb11
Tuamotu Ridge ⚑ 11 Cb12
Tuanan ⚑ RI 95 Qh47
Tuan Giao ⚑ VN 87 Qb35
Tuangku ⚑ RI 93 Pj44
Tuao ⚑ RP 90 Ra37
Tuapse ⚑ RUS 49 Mk23
Tuba City ⚑ USA 171 Ee27
Tuban ⚑ RI 95 Qg44
Tubarão ⚑ BR (SC) 205 Hf60
Tubarão Latunde, T.I. ⚑ BR 206 Gk52
Tubaru ▲ KSA 58 Mk30
Tubau ⚑ MAL 94 Qg44
Tubbataha Reef National Marine Park ⚑ RP 91 Qk41
Tubbergen ⚑ NL 23 Lg38
Tubeya ⚑ RDC 149 Mb49
Tubigon ⚑ RP 90 Rb41
Tübingen ⚑ D 33 Lk42
Tubisbyanita ⚑ RI 114 Rg46
Tubize ⚑ B 23 Le40
Tübod ⚑ RP 91 Rb41
Tubod ⚑ RP 91 Rb41
Tubruq War Cemeteries ⚑ LAR 128 Md29
Tubuai Islands ⚑ 11 Ca12
Tuburan ⚑ RP 90 Ra40
Tubutama ⚑ MEX 180 Ee30
Tucano ⚑ BR (BA) 201 Ja51
Tuchan ⚑ F 24 Lc48
Tucheng ⚑ CHN (GZG) 74 Qd32
Tuchita ⚑ CDN (YT) 166 Df15
Tuchola ⚑ PL 40 Ls37
Tucholski Park Krajobrazowy ⚑ PL 40 Ls37
Tuchów ⚑ PL 41 Mb41
Tuckanarra ⚑ AUS (WA) 104 Qj59
Tucker Glacier ⚑ 7 Tb33
Tucson ⚑ USA 171 Ee29
Tucson ⚑ USA (AZ) 171 Ee29
Tucumán ⚑ RA (TM) 207 Gh58
Tucumcari ⚑ USA (NM) 174 Ej28
Tucunuaré, T.I. ⚑ BR 198 Gg49
Tucuco ⚑ YV 192 Ge45
Tucunaré ⚑ BR (AM) 198 Gh45
Tucupita ⚑ YV 193 Gj41
Tucuriba ⚑ BR (AM) 199 Ha48
Tucuruí ⚑ BR (PA) 200 Hf47
Tucu-Tucu ⚑ RA (SC) 210 Ge70
Tuczna ⚑ PL 41 Md39
Tuczno ⚑ PL 40 Lq38
Tudela ⚑ E 28 Kt48
Tudela de Duero ⚑ E 26 Kq49
Tudu ⚑ EST 38 Mg31
Tudulinna ⚑ EST 38 Mh31
Tudun Wada ⚑ WAN 138 Le40
Tuéjar ⚑ E 29 Kt51
Tuena ⚑ AUS (NSW) 111 Se63
Tufanbeyli ⚑ TR 56 Na26
Tufeni ⚑ RO 45 Me46
Tufi ⚑ PNG 116 Se50
Tufi Dive Resort ⚑ PNG 116 Se50
Tugela ⚑ ZA 155 Mf60
Tugela Ferry ⚑ ZA 155 Mf60
Tugela ⚑ ZA 155 Mf60
Tughyl ⚑ KZ 67 Pc22
Tugidak Island ⚑ USA 164 Cc17
Tugu ⚑ RP 137 Kk41
Tuguegarao ⚑ RP 90 Ra37
Tuham, Gunung ▲ RI 94 Qg45
Tui ⚑ E 26 Km48
Tuilibigeal ⚑ AUS (NSW) 111 Sd62
Tuineje ⚑ E 124 Kc31
Tuiuê ⚑ BR (AM) 198 Gj48
Tuiyik ⚑ KZ 62 Nf24
Tüja ⚑ LV 39 Me33
Tuki ⚑ ET 129 Mf30
Tuki ⚑ SOL 117 Sj49
Tukola Tolha ⚑ CHN (QHI) 69 Ph29
Tukoamera ⚑ VU 118 Te55
Tukrah ⚑ LAR 128 Ma29
Tuktoyaktuk ⚑ CDN 162 Dc05
Tukums ⚑ LV 39 Md34
Tukuna Porto Espiritual, T.I. ⚑ BR 198 Gf48
Tukuna Santo Antonio, T.I. ⚑ BR 198 Gf48
Tukuyu ⚑ EAT 146 Mg50
Tula ⚑ MEX (TM) 182 Fa34
Tula ⚑ RUS 48 Mj19
Tula de Allende ⚑ MEX (HDG) 182 Fa35
Tulak ⚑ AFG 65 Oa29
Tulamben ⚑ RDC (BC) 168 Dk21
Tulancingo ⚑ MEX (HDG) 182 Fa35
Tulare ⚑ SCG 44 Mb48
Tulare ⚑ USA (CA) 170 Ea27
Tularosa ⚑ USA (NM) 171 Eg29
Tulbagh ⚑ ZA 154 Lk62
Tulcán ⚑ EC 196 Gb45
Tulcea ⚑ RO 45 Mh45
Tul'čyn ⚑ UA 49 Me21
Tülden araldary ⚑ KZ 62 Nf23

Tulehu ⚑ RI 97 Re47
Tulga ⚑ AUS (QLD) 108 Sb57
Tulia ⚑ USA (TX) 174 Ek28
Tuli Block ⚑ RB 155 Md58
Tulja ⚑ CHN (NMZ) 71 Ra20
Tulita ⚑ CDN 167 Dh13
Tuljapur ⚑ IND (MHT) 82 Oj37
Tullah ⚑ AUS (TAS) 111 Sc66
Tullamore ⚑ AUS (NSW) 111 Sd62
Tullamore ⚑ IRL 19 Kn37
Tulle ⚑ F 24 Lb45
Tullin ⚑ A 42 Lr42
Tullos ⚑ USA (LA) 175 Fd30
Tulln ⚑ IRL 19 Ko38
Tullus ⚑ SUD 134 Mc40
Tully ⚑ AUS (QLD) 107 Sc54
Tulowice ⚑ PL 40 Ls40
Tulsa ⚑ USA (OK) 174 Fb27
Tulsipur ⚑ IND (UPH) 83 Pb32
Tulsipur ⚑ NEP 81 Pb31
Tulu ⚑ IRL 19 Kn38
Tulu Deemtu ▲ ETH 142 Mk42
Tuluksak ⚑ USA (AK) 164 Bk15
Tulul Al Ashaqif ▲ JOR 56 Mj29
Tulum ⚑ MEX (QR) 183 Fg35
Tulum ▲ RA (SJ) 207 Gf61
Tulum, Parque Nacional ⚑ MEX 183 Fg35
Tulun ⚑ RUS 68 Qa20
Tulungagung ⚑ RI 95 Qf50
Tulungselapan ⚑ RI 93 Qc45
Tulu Welel ▲ ETH 142 Mh41
Tulyčiv ⚑ UA 41 Me39
Tumaco ⚑ CO 192 Ga45
Tuman ⚑ PE 196 Ga49
Tumauini ⚑ RP 90 Ra37
Tumba ⚑ RDC 149 Md47
Tumba ⚑ S 31 Ls31
Tumbangsamba ⚑ RI 95 Qf46
Tumbangmirih ⚑ RI 95 Qf46
Tumbangtalaken ⚑ RI 95 Qg46
Tumbanlahung ⚑ RI 95 Qf46
Tumbarumba ⚑ AUS (NSW) 111 Sd63
Tumbes ⚑ PE 196 Fk47
Tumbiscatio de Ruiz ⚑ MEX (MHC) 182 Ej36
Tumbler Ridge ⚑ CDN (BC) 166 Dk18
Tumbuk ⚑ MYA 86 Pj33
Tumby Bay ⚑ AUS (SA) 110 Rj63
Tumd Youyi ⚑ CHN (NMZ) 72 Qf25
Tumd Zuoqi ⚑ CHN (NMZ) 72 Qf25
Tumen ⚑ CHN (JLN) 76 Re29
Tumeremo ⚑ YV 193 Gk42
Tumgaon ⚑ IND (CGH) 83 Pb35
Tumia, T.I. ⚑ BR 198 Gg49
Tumindao Island ⚑ RP 91 Qk43
Tumlingtar ⚑ NEP 83 Pd32
Tumong ▲ CHN (CGH) 83 Pa36
Tumsar ⚑ IND (MHT) 83 Ok35
Tumtum ⚑ RI 39 Me33
Tumu ⚑ GH 137 Kk41
Tumucumaque, P.N. do ⚑ BR 194 Hd45
Tumupasa ⚑ BOL 206 Gg53
Tumut ⚑ AUS (NSW) 111 Se63
Tuna ⚑ GH 137 Kj41
Tuna ⚑ IND (GUJ) 82 Og34
Tuna Gain ⚑ RI 114 Rg47
Tunapa, Cerro ▲ BOL 206 Gg55
Tunapuna ⚑ TT 187 Gk40
Tunari, P.N. ⚑ BOL 206 Gg54
Tunas de Zaza ⚑ C 179 Ga35
Tunayidha ⚑ SUD 135 Mh39
Tuncbilek ⚑ TR 47 Mk51
Tunceli ⚑ TR 57 Nb26
Tunchang ⚑ CHN (HAN) 75 Qf36
Tuncurry ⚑ AUS (NSW) 111 Sg62
Tundavala ⚑ ANG 150 Lg53
Tundla ⚑ IND (JKD) 83 Pd33
Tundlo ⚑ IND (UPH) 81 Ok32
Tundulu ⚑ Z 146 Mf51
Tunduma ⚑ EAT 146 Mg50
Tunduru ⚑ EAT 147 Mj51
Tungabhadra ⚑ IND 82 Oj38
Tungabhadra Reservoir ⚑ IND 82 Oj38
Tungaru ⚑ SUD 135 Mh40
Tungaztarintin ⚑ CHN (XUZ) 68 Pd27
Tungho ⚑ RC 75 Ra34
Tungkaranasam ⚑ RI 95 Qj47
Tungkočen ⚑ RUS 71 Qh19
Tungshih ⚑ RC 75 Ra33
Tungting Lake = CHN 74 Qg31
Tunguahua, Volcán ▲ EC 196 Ga46
Tungwatu ⚑ RI 114 Rh48
Tuni ⚑ IND (APH) 83 Pb37
Tunia ⚑ CO 192 Gc44
Tunja ⚑ CO 192 Gc44
Tunka La ⚑ IND 86 Pf32
Tunkas ⚑ MEX (YT) 183 Ff35
Tünkhel ⚑ MNG 70 Qd21
Tunku Abdul Rahman Park ⚑ MAL 94 Qj42
Tunnel Creek N.P. ⚑ AUS 103 Rc54
Tunnel de Tende ⚑ F/I 25 Lh46
Tunnel du Fréjus ⚑ F/I 25 Lg45
Tunnel las Raíces ⚑ RCH 208 Ge65
Tunnels ⚑ USA (HI) 170 Ca34
Tunquu ⚑ CHN (GZG) 74 Qd32
Tunstall ⚑ GB 21 Ks36
Tuntum ⚑ BR (MA) 200 Hh48
Tuntutuliak ⚑ USA (AK) 164 Bj15
Tununak ⚑ USA (AK) 164 Bh15
Tunzam ⚑ RN 132 Le38
Tunisica ⚑ BR (GZG) 74 Qd34
Tumena Lake ⚑ USA 164 Ce15
Tutaev ⚑ RUS 48 Mk17
Tutak ⚑ TR 57 Nc26
Tuticorin ⚑ IND (TNU) 84 Ok41
Tutoko Heyan ▲ CHN (QHI) 69 Pg28
Tutira ⚑ NZ 113 Tj65
Tutrakan ⚑ BG 45 Mg46
Tutshi ⚑ CDN 166 De16
Tuttle ⚑ USA (ND) 172 Fa22
Tuttlingen ⚑ D 33 Lj43
Tutube ⚑ TLS 112 Rd49
Tutume ⚑ RB 152 Md56
Tutupaca, Volcán ▲ PE 197 Ge54
Tutut ⚑ RI 93 Pj43
Tutwiler ⚑ USA (MS) 175 Fe29
Tuupovaara ⚑ FIN 38 Mj28
Tuusula ⚑ FIN 38 Mf30
Tuvalu ⚑ 101 Tb10
Tuvcua ⚑ FIJI 119 Ua54
Tuwaq ▲ KSA 59 Nb34

Tupper Lake ⚑ USA (NY) 177 Gc23
Tupran ⚑ IND (APH) 82 Ok37
Tuxtepec ⚑ CDN (SK) 169 Eh20
Tupungato, Cerro ▲ RA/RCH 208 Gf62
Tuquan ⚑ CHN (NMZ) 71 Ra23
Tuquerres ⚑ CO 192 Gb45
Tura ⚑ CHN (XUZ) 68 Pd27
Tura ⚑ IND (MGA) 86 Pf33
Tura ⚑ RUS 54 Qa06
Turabah ⚑ KSA 59 Nb31
Turabah ⚑ KSA 60 Na33
Turagua, Cerro ▲ YV 193 Gh42
Turaida ⚑ LV 39 Me33
Turaiyur ⚑ IND (TNU) 84 Ok40
Turan ⚑ KZ 63 Of24
Turayf ⚑ KSA 58 Mk30
Turbaco ⚑ CO 192 Gc40
Turbat ⚑ PK 65 Ob33
Turbeville ⚑ USA (SC) 178 Ga29
Turbiá ⚑ WAN 138 Lf39
Turbo ⚑ EAK 144 Mh45
Turco ⚑ BOL 206 Gf55
Turek ⚑ PL 40 Ls38
Tureia Atoll ⚑ 11 Da12
Tureingan Arm ⚑ USA 165 Ce15
Tureis ▲ KZ 63 Of24
Turek ⚑ PL 40 Ls38
Turégano ⚑ E 26 Kq49
Türi ⚑ EST 38 Mf31
Turiaçu ⚑ BR (MA) 195 Hh46
Turiaçu ⚑ MEX (MHC) 182 Ek36
Turjak's ⚑ UA 43 Md41
Turiani ⚑ CDN (AB) 169 Ed21
Turilari ⚑ RA (PJ) 207 Gg57
Turin ⚑ CDN (AB) 169 Ed21
Turin ⚑ I 34 Lh45
Turinsk ⚑ RUS 54 Oa07
Turiščevo ⚑ RUS 48 Mh20
Turda ⚑ RO 43 Md44
Tureev ⚑ SCG 44 Ma48
Turka ⚑ RUS (BUR) 70 Qc20
Turka ⚑ UA 43 Mc41
Turkana ⚑ EAK 144 Mh44
Türkeli ⚑ TR 47 Mk50
Turkestan ⚑ KZ 63 Oe24
Turkmenbat ⚑ TM 62 Ob26
Turkmengala ⚑ TM 62 Ng25
Turkmenistan ⚑ TM 53 Nb06
Turkmenskiy zaliv ⚑ TM 62 Ng26
Türkoğlu ⚑ TR 56 Mj27
Turks and Caicos Islands ⚑ GB 186 Ge36
Turks Island Passage ⚑ BS 186 Ge35
Turku ⚑ USA (CA) 170 Ff20
Turkwel Gorge Reservoir ⚑ EAK 144 Mh45
Turlock ⚑ USA (CA) 170 Dk27
Turmalina ⚑ BR (MG) 203 Hj54
Turmi ⚑ ETH 144 Mj43
Turnagain Arm ⚑ USA 165 Ce15
Turneffe Islands ⚑ BH 184 Fg37
Turner ⚑ USA (MT) 169 Ee21
Turner Falls Park ⚑ USA 174 Fb28
Turner Lake ⚑ CDN 167 Ef17
Turners Peninsula ⚑ WAL 136 Kd42
Turnhout ⚑ B 23 Le39
Türkiye ⚑ 167 Ef17
Türnitz ⚑ A 35 Lq43
Turnu Măgurele ⚑ RO 45 Me47
Turos ⚑ PL 41 Mb37
Turpan ⚑ CHN (XUZ) 67 Pe24
Turriabla ⚑ CR 185 Fj41
Turriff ⚑ GB 20 Ks33
Turt ⚑ MNG 70 Qa20
Tursunzoda ⚑ TJ 63 Oe26
Turt ⚑ MNG 70 Qa20
Turtle Beach ⚑ USA (FL) 178 Fk32
Turtle Beach ⚑ YE 61 Nj39
Turtleford ⚑ CDN (SK) 169 Ef19
Turtle Harbour ⚑ HN 184 Fg37
Turtle Islands Marine Park ⚑ MAL 91 Qk43
Turtle Islands ⚑ CDN 169 Ef19
Turtle Lake ⚑ USA (ND) 172 Ek22
Turuépano, P.N. ⚑ YV 193 Gj40
Turuvekere ⚑ IND (KTK) 84 Oj39
Turvânia ⚑ BR (GO) 202 Hd54
Turvelândia ⚑ BR (GO) 202 Hd54
Turvo ⚑ BR (PR) 204 He58
Turzovka ⚑ SK 42 Lt41
Tuscania ⚑ I 34 Ln48
Tuscaloosa ⚑ USA (AL) 175 Ff29
Tuscany ⚑ I 34 Ll47
Tuscola ⚑ USA (TX) 174 Fa29
Tuscumbia ⚑ USA (AL) 175 Fg28
Tusen-eyane ⚑ N 16 Ma07
Tushabugha shyghanagh ⚑ KZ 62 Nk22
Tushkadi ⚑ BD 86 Pe34
Tuskegee ⚑ USA (AL) 175 Fh29
Tusnica ⚑ BIH 35 Lq47
Tusmandu ⚑ RI 93 Pj45

Tuwwal ⚑ KSA 58 Mk34
Tuxcueca ⚑ MEX (JLC) 182 Ej35
Tuxford ⚑ CDN (SK) 169 Eh20
Tuxpam (Tuxpan) ⚑ MEX (VC) 182 Fb35
Tuxpan ⚑ MEX (NYT) 182 Eh35
Tuxpan = Tuxpam ⚑ MEX (VC) 182 Fb35
Tuxtepec ⚑ MEX (OAX) 183 Fb36
Tuxtla Gutiérrez ⚑ MEX (CHP) 183 Fd37
Tuy Duc ⚑ VN 89 Qd39
Tuborska ⚑ RUS 77 Rh23
Tubique ⚑ E 27 Kp54
Tuy Hoa ⚑ VN 89 Qe40
Tuy Phong ⚑ VN 89 Qe40
Tuysarkan ⚑ IR 57 Ne28
Tuzantán ⚑ MEX (CHP) 183 Fa36
Tuz Gölü ⚑ TR 56 Mf26
Tuz ⚑ SCG 44 Lu48
Tuz Khurmatu ⚑ IRQ 57 Nc28
Tuzla ⚑ BIH 44 Lt46
Tuzla ⚑ TR 57 Nb25
Tuzule ⚑ RDC 149 Md49
Tvåaker ⚑ S 30 Lo33
Tvärdica ⚑ BG 45 Mf48
Tvedestrand ⚑ N 30 Lj32
Tveitsund ⚑ N 30 Lj31
Tver ⚑ RUS 48 Mh17
Tving ⚑ S 31 Lq34
Tvrda ⚑ HR 35 Lt45
Tvrdava ⚑ SCG 44 Md47
Tvrdošin ⚑ SK 43 Lu41
Twardogóra ⚑ PL 40 Ls39
Tweed ⚑ CDN (ON) 173 Gb23
Tweed ⚑ GB 20 Ks35
Tweed Heads ⚑ AUS (NSW) 109 Sg60
Tweedsmuir Prov. Park ⚑ CDN 166 Dg19
Tweefontein ⚑ ZA 154 Lk62
Tweeling ⚑ ZA 155 Me60
Twee River ⚑ NAM 154 Lh58
Twee Rivieren ⚑ ZA 154 Ma59
Tweespruit ⚑ ZA 155 Md60
Twelfte ⚑ NL 23 Lg38
Twelve Apostles ⚑ AUS 111 Sb65
Twelve Foot Davis Prov. Hist. Site ⚑ CDN 167 Ea06
Twentynine Palms ⚑ USA 171 Ec28
Twin Bridges ⚑ USA (MT) 169 Ed23
Twin Falls ⚑ USA 106 Rg52
Twin Falls ⚑ CDN (BC) 168 Ec24
Twin Falls Gorge ⚑ USA 167 Eb15
Twingi ⚑ Z 146 Me51
Twin Lakes ⚑ CDN (AK) 165 Cj13
Twin Peaks ⚑ AUS (WA) 104 Qh61
Twin Ring Motegi ⚑ J 77 Sa27
Twin Wells ⚑ AUS (NSW) 110 Sa62
Twistringen ⚑ D 32 Lj38
Twizel ⚑ NZ 113 Tf68
Two Harbors ⚑ USA (MN) 172 Fc22
Two Hills ⚑ CDN (AB) 169 Ee19
Two Rivers ⚑ USA (WI) 173 Fg23
Two Rocks ⚑ AUS (WA) 104 Qh61
Twyfelfontein Rock Engraving ⚑ NAM 150 Lh56
Tychowo ⚑ PL 40 Lr37
Tychy ⚑ PL 41 Lt40
Tyczyn ⚑ PL 41 Mc41
Tyele ⚑ NAM 137 Kg39
Tymnet ⚑ S 31 Lf14
Tyoplye Klyuchi ⚑ KS 66 Oh24
Tyrell Falls ⚑ EAT 146 Mg50
Tyresta n.p. ⚑ S 31 Ls31
Tyringe ⚑ S 31 Lo34
Tyringham ⚑ AUS (NSW) 109 Sg61
Tyristrand ⚑ N 30 Lk30
Tyro ⚑ RA 33 Lg49
Tyrnavos ⚑ GR 46 Mc51
Tyrnyauz ⚑ RUS (KBA) 57 Nb24
Tyrol Basin Ski Area ⚑ USA 172 Ff24
Tyrrell Lake ⚑ CDN 167 Eh14
Tyrrhenian Sea ⚑ 14 Lo36
Tyškivka ⚑ UA 49 Mf21
Tyssedal ⚑ N 30 Lg31
Tytuvenai ⚑ LT 39 Md34
Tywyn ⚑ GB 21 Kq38
Tzaneen ⚑ ZA 152 Mf57
Tzermiádo ⚑ GR 47 Mf55
Tzintzuntzan ⚑ MEX 182 Ek36
Tziscao ⚑ MEX (CHP) 183 Fe37
Tzucacab ⚑ MEX (YT) 183 Ff35

U

Uaçá, T.I. ⚑ BR 195 He44
Uaco Cungo ⚑ ANG 150 Lh51
Uamba ⚑ AUS (QLD) 109 Sc56
Uanle Uen = Wankaawayn ⚑ SP 145 No44
Uape ⚑ MOC 153 Mk54
Uar Addol ⚑ SP 145 Na44
Uarges ⚑ EAK 144 Mj45
Uari Igarore ⚑ SP 145 Nb45
Uarini ⚑ BR (AM) 198 Gg47
Uari-Paraná, T.I. ⚑ BR 198 Gg47
Uaru ⚑ BR (AM) 193 Gj44
Uauaretê ⚑ BR (AM) 198 Ge45
Uaua ⚑ BR (BA) 201 Ja50
Uaxactún ⚑ GCA 184 Ff37
Uba ⚑ BR (MG) 203 Hh54
Ubaí ⚑ PNG 116 Sd48
'Ubaid ⚑ SUD 134 Mc39
Ubaira ⚑ BR (BA) 201 Ja52
Ubaitaba ⚑ BR (BA) 203 Ja53
Ubajara ⚑ BR (CE) 201 Hj47
Ubajara, P.N. de ⚑ BR 201 Hj48
Ubaldini ⚑ RCB/RDC 140 Lj45
Ubangi ⚑ RCB 148 Lj46
Ubaté ⚑ CO 192 Gc43
Ubaté ⚑ BR (BA) 203 Ja53
Ubauro ⚑ PK 65 Oe31
Ubay ⚑ RP 90 Rb41

Uberlândia ⚑ BR (MG) 202 Hf55
Überlingen ⚑ D 33 Lk43
Ubia, Gunung ▲ RI 114 Rj48
Ubiaja ⚑ WAN 138 Ld42
Ubiesyn ⚑ PL 41 Mc40
Ubiratā ⚑ BR (PR) 204 Hd58
Ubli ⚑ SK 43 Mc42
Ubli ⚑ SCG 44 Lt48
Ubombo ⚑ ZA 155 Mg59
Ubon Ratchathani ⚑ THA 89 Qc38
Uborka ⚑ RUS 77 Rh23
Ubrique ⚑ E 27 Kp54
Ubudiah Mosque ⚑ MAL 92 Qa43
Ubundu ⚑ RDC 149 Md47
Ucacha ⚑ RA (CD) 209 Gj62
Ucapinima ⚑ CO 193 Gf45
Ucar ⚑ AZ 57 Nd25
Ucayali ⚑ PE 196 Gc49
Ucero ⚑ E 26 Kr49
Uceš ⚑ BY 41 Mf38
Uch-Adzhi ⚑ TM 62 Ob26
Uchajovo ⚑ RUS 48 Na20
Uchalon ⚑ IRQ (WBG) 83 Pd34
Ucharonidge ⚑ AUS (NT) 106 Rh54
Uchiza ⚑ PE 197 Gb50
Uchqo'rg'on ⚑ UZ 63 Og25
Uchquduq ⚑ UZ 62 Ob24
Uchnoy ⚑ UZ 62 Nk24
Uchte ⚑ D 32 Lj38
Uckermark ⚑ D 32 Lo37
Uckfield ⚑ GB 21 La40
Ucluelet ⚑ CDN (BC) 168 Dh21
Ucross ⚑ USA (WY) 169 Eg23
Ucua ⚑ ANG 148 Lh49
Udachny ⚑ RUS 55 Qc05
Udaigiri ⚑ IND 83 Pd35
Udainagar ⚑ IND (MPH) 82 Oj34
Udaipur ⚑ IND (RAJ) 82 Og34
Udaipur ⚑ IND (TRP) 86 Pf34
Udaipura ⚑ IND (MPH) 83 Ok34
Udakatela ⚑ IND (MPH) 82 Oj34
Udala ⚑ IND (ORS) 83 Pd35
Udaquiola ⚑ RA (BA) 209 Ha64
Udayagiri Caves ⚑ IND 82 Ok35
Udayagiri ⚑ IND (ORS) 83 Pd35
Udaypur ⚑ IND 83 Ok34
Udbina ⚑ HR 35 Lq46
Uddevalla ⚑ S 30 Lm32
Uddel ⚑ NL 23 Lf38
Uddjaure ⚑ S 16 Lj13
Udgir ⚑ IND (MHT) 82 Oj36
Udhagamandalam = ... ⚑ IND 84 Oj40
Udhampur ⚑ IND (JKT) 80 Oh29
Udi ⚑ IND (UPH) 83 Ok32
Udine ⚑ I 35 Lo44
Udipi ⚑ IND (KTK) 84 Oh39
Udmurtija ⚑ RUS 48 Nh17
Udomlja ⚑ RUS 48 Mh17
Udon ⚑ IND (APH) 83 Pa36
Udon Thani ⚑ THA 89 Qb37
Udumalaippettai ⚑ IND (TNU) 84 Oj40
Udupi ⚑ IND (KTK) 84 Oh39
Udzungwa Mountains N.P. ⚑ EAT 147 Mh49
Udzungwa Range ⚑ EAT 147 Mh50
Ueckermünde ⚑ D 32 Lp37
Ueda ⚑ J 77 Rk27
Uegit = Waajid ⚑ SP 145 Nb44
Uele ⚑ RDC 140 Ma44
Uelen ⚑ RUS 55 Ub05
Uelzen ⚑ D 32 Lm37
Uereré ⚑ BR (AM) 199 Ha48
Uetersen ⚑ D 32 Lk37
Uetze ⚑ D 32 Ll38
Ufa ⚑ RUS 54 Nd07
Ufeyn ⚑ SP 143 Ne40
Uffenheim ⚑ D 33 Ll41
Ugab Rock Finger ⚑ NAM 150 Lh56
Ugale ⚑ LV 39 Mc33
Ugalla ⚑ EAT 146 Mf48
Ugalla River Game Reserve ⚑ EAT 146 Mf48
Uganda ⚑ 141 Mf45
Uganik Island ⚑ USA 164 Cd16
Ugärcin ⚑ BG 45 Me47
Ugasak Lake ⚑ USA (AK) 164 Cb17
Ugashik ⚑ USA (AK) 164 Cb16
Ugba ⚑ WAN 138 Le42
Ugbala ⚑ WAN 138 Lc42
Ugbe ⚑ WAN 138 Lc41
Ugbo ⚑ WAN 138 Ld42
Ugbadi ⚑ WAN 138 Ld42
Ugep ⚑ WAN 138 Le42
Ugga ⚑ USA 155 Mf61
Ugie ⚑ ANG 148 Lh49
Uglovoe Kopi ⚑ RUS 55 Td06
Ugra ⚑ RUS 48 Mh19
Ugtam Nature Reserve ⚑ MNG 71 Qg21
Ugun ⚑ WAN 138 Lf40
Ugüd Tepe ▲ TR 45 Mk50
Uhaymir ⚑ SUD 135 Mg38
Uhekora ⚑ EAT 146 Mg48
Uhen ⚑ WAN 138 Lc42
Uherské Hradiště ⚑ CZ 42 Ls41
Uhersky Brod ⚑ CZ 42 Ls41
Uhira ⚑ WAN 138 Ld42
Uhlenhorst ⚑ NAM 154 Lj57
Uhlig ⚑ NAM 154 Lh57
Uhniv ⚑ UA 41 Md40
Uhrichsville ⚑ USA (OH) 173 Fk25
Uig ⚑ GB (BA) 200 Hh49
Uíge ⚑ ANG 148 Lh49
Uiju ⚑ PRK 76 Rc27
Uil ⚑ KZ 62 Nf22
Uinta Mountains ⚑ USA 171 Ee25
Uiraúna ⚑ BR (PB) 201 Jb49
Uiraúna ⚑ BR (MT) 206 Ha53
Uis Mine ⚑ NAM 150 Lh56
Uisŏng ⚑ ROK 79 Re27
Uitenhage ⚑ ZA 155 Mc62
Uithoorn ⚑ NL 23 Le38
Uitkyk ⚑ NAM 154 Lj58
Ujae Atoll ⚑ MH 100 Ta09
Ujain ⚑ RP 91 Rb41

Ujdah ⚑ MA 125 Kk28
Üjelang Atoll ⚑ MH 10 Ta09
Üjezdziec Mafy ⚑ PL 40 Ls39
Ujfehérto ⚑ H 43 Mc43
Ujhani ⚑ IND (UPH) 81 Ok32
Uji ⚑ J 79 Rh28
Uji-gunto ⚑ J 79 Re30
Ujjain ⚑ IND (MPH) 82 Oh34
Ujjhani ⚑ IND 83 Ok33
Ujohbilang ⚑ RI 94 Qh45
Ujŝcie ⚑ PL 40 Lr38
Ujŝcie Warty, P.N. ⚑ PL 40 Lp38
Ujjungbalong ⚑ RI 93 Qb44
Ujungkulon N.P. ⚑ RI 93 Qc49
Ujung Pandang ⚑ RI 96 Qk48
Ukata ⚑ WAN 138 Ld40
Ukdungle ⚑ 81 Ok29
Ukenyengi ⚑ EAT 144 Mg47
Ukerewe Island ⚑ EAT 144 Mg46
uKhahlamba-Drakensberg N.P. ⚑ ZA 155 Me60
Ukhia ⚑ BD 86 Pg35
Ukhrul ⚑ IND (MNP) 86 Ph33
Ukiah ⚑ USA (CA) 170 Dj26
Ukholovo ⚑ RUS 48 Na19
Ukienicia ⚑ PL 40 Lq37
Ukku Ni Masi Island ⚑ SOL 117 Ta51
Ukkamba ⚑ IND 83 Pb36
Ukmergé ⚑ LT 39 Me35
Ukraine ⚑ 15 Ma05
Ukrainian Cultural Heritage Village ⚑ CDN 169 Ed19
Ukui ⚑ RI 93 Qa46
Uku-jima ⚑ J 79 Re30
Ukwatutu ⚑ RDC 141 Md43
Ul ⚑ TR 47 Mj53
Ulaanbaatar ⚑ MNG 70 Qd22
Ulaangom ⚑ MNG 67 Pg21
Ulaanhudag ⚑ MNG 71 Qd22
Ulaan-Ereg ⚑ MNG 70 Qb23
Ulaan-Uul ⚑ MNG 70 Qa23
Ulaanzireeg ⚑ MNG 70 Qb23
Ulakmakan ⚑ RI 93 Pk44
Ulamona ⚑ PNG 116 Sf48
Uldjaure ⚑ S 16 Lj13
Udegi ⚑ WAN 138 Ld41
Ulan Bator ⚑ MNG 70 Qd22
Ulanbel ⚑ KZ 63 Of23
Ulanhot ⚑ CHN (NMZ) 71 Ra22
Ulanlinggi ⚑ CHN (XUZ) 67 Pd24
Ulanów ⚑ PL 41 Mc40
Ulapara ⚑ BD 86 Pe33
Ulas ⚑ TR 56 Na26
Ulaya ⚑ EAT 147 Mh49
Ulbroka ⚑ LV 39 Me34
Ulcinj ⚑ SCG 44 Lu49
Ulco ⚑ ZA 155 Mc60
Ulea ⚑ E 29 Ks52
Uleåborg = Oulu ⚑ FIN 38 Mf25
Ul-el-Jimal ⚑ JOR 56 Mj29
Ulen ⚑ USA (MN) 172 Fb22
Ulety ⚑ RUS (BUR) 71 Qf20
Ulfborg ⚑ DK 30 Lj34
Ulft ⚑ NL 23 Lg38
Ulhasnagar ⚑ IND (MHT) 82 Og36
Uliastay ⚑ MNG 67 Ph22
Ulithi Atoll ⚑ FSM 91 Rc41
Uljanovsk ⚑ RUS 48 Ne19
Uljanovka ⚑ UA 49 Mf21
Ujin ⚑ ROK 79 Re27
Ulken sor ⚑ KZ 62 Ng23
Ülken Borsyky kumy ⚑ KZ 62 Nf24
Ulladulla ⚑ AUS (NSW) 111 Sf63
Ullal ⚑ IND (KTK) 84 Oh39
Ullal Beach ⚑ IND 84 Oh39
Ullared ⚑ S 30 Lo33
Ullatti ⚑ S 16 Ma11
Ulla Ulla ⚑ BOL 206 Gf53
Ullawarra ⚑ AUS (WA) 102 Qg57
Ulldecona ⚑ E 29 La50
Ullmer ⚑ IND (MHT) 82 Oh35
Ullŭng ⚑ ROK 79 Rf27
Ulŭn ⚑ RA (SJ) 208 Gf61
Ullŭng Do ⚑ ROK 79 Rg27
Ulm ⚑ USA (AR) 175 Fd28
Ulm ⚑ D 33 Lk42
Ulma ⚑ RO 45 Me46
Ulmu ⚑ RO 45 Mh46
Ulongwe ⚑ MOC 153 Mh53
Ulricehamn ⚑ S 30 Lo33
Ulsan ⚑ ROK 79 Re28
Ulsberg ⚑ N 30 Lk28
Ulsta ⚑ GB 18 La31
Ulsteinvik ⚑ N 30 Lf28
Ulster ⚑ D 32 Lk40
Ulster ⚑ IRL/GB 19 Kn36
Ultima ⚑ AUS (VIC) 111 Sb63
Ultimo ⚑ I 34 Ll44
Ulu ⚑ MYA 88 Pk40
Ulu ⚑ RI 91 Rc44
Ulu Layar ⚑ MAL 94 Qf43
Ulubey ⚑ TR 56 Na25
Ulubey ⚑ TR 47 Mj52
Uluborlu ⚑ TR 47 Mk53
Uludağ Milli Parkı ⚑ TR 47 Mk50
Uluguru Mountains ⚑ EAT 147 Mj49
Uluikalan ⚑ TR (XUZ) 68 Pd27
Ulukan ⚑ WAN 138 Le42
Ulukişla ⚑ TR 56 Mg26
Ulundi ⚑ ZA 155 Mf60
Ulungur ⚑ CHN (XUZ) 67 Pe23
Ulungur ⚑ CHN (XUZ) 67 Pe23
Ulurŭu = Ayers Rock ⚑ AUS 105 Rh58
Uluru ⚑ AUS 105 Rf58
Ulŭ ⚑ AUS (QLD) 109 Sc56
Ulva ⚑ GB 20 Ko34
Ulvåker ⚑ S 31 Lo32
Ulverston ⚑ GB 21 Kr36
Ulverstone ⚑ AUS (TAS) 111 Sd66
Ulvik ⚑ N 17 Ld15
Ulvila ⚑ FIN 38 Md29
Ulwe ⚑ RI 16 Lh11
Ulyanovsk ⚑ RUS 48 Ne19
Uma ⚑ CHN (NMZ) 71 Ra19
Uma Daro ⚑ MAL 94 Qg44
Umala ⚑ BOL 206 Gf54
Umán ⚑ MEX (YT) 183 Ff35
Uman' ⚑ UA 49 Mf21
Umanak = Uummannaq ⚑ DKN 163 Hc04
Umargam ⚑ IND (MHT) 82 Og36
Umargaon ⚑ IND (MHT) 82 Og36
Umarga ⚑ IND (MHT) 82 Oj36
Umaria ⚑ IND (MPH) 83 Pa34
Umarkot ⚑ IND (ORS) 83 Pb36

União ⚑ BR (AM) 198 Gf47
União ⚑ BR (PI) 201 Hj48
União da Vitória ⚑ BR (PR) 204 He59
União de Minas ⚑ BR (MG) 202 Hd55
União dos Palmares ⚑ BR (AL) 201 Jc50
Uniara ⚑ IND (RJT) 82 Oj33
Unica ⚑ BOL 206 Gg55
Unichowo ⚑ PL 40 Ls36
Uničov ⚑ CZ 42 Ls41
Unije ⚑ HR 35 Lp46
Unije ⚑ HR 35 Lp46
Unimak ⚑ USA (AK) 164 Bh18
Unimak Bay ⚑ USA (AK) 164 Bh18
Union ⚑ USA (MO) 175 Fe26
Union ⚑ USA (SC) 178 Fk28
Union ⚑ USA (OR) 168 Ea23
Union ⚑ WV 187 Gk39
Union Center ⚑ USA (SD) 172 Ek24
Union City ⚑ USA (PA) 173 Ga25
Union City ⚑ USA (TN) 175 Ff27
Union Creek ⚑ USA (OR) 168 Dj24
Union da Tula ⚑ MEX (JLC) 182 Eh36
Unión Hidalgo ⚑ MEX (OAX) 183 Fc37
Unión Juárez ⚑ MEX (CHP) 182 Mf54
Union Springs ⚑ USA (AL) 175 Fh29
Uniontown ⚑ USA (AL) 175 Ff29
Uniontown ⚑ USA (MO) 174 Fd25
Unionville ⚑ USA (NV) 170 Ea25
Unipołuces Ind. Res. ⚑ CDN 169 Ef19
United Arab Emirates ⚑ UAE 61 Ng34
United Kingdom ⚑ 15 Kb04
United States ⚑ USA 161 Ea06
Unity City ⚑ CDN (SK) 169 Ef19
Unity ⚑ CDN (SK) 169 Ef19
Universal City ⚑ USA (TX) 181 Fa31
Universal Studios ⚑ USA 179 Fk31
Um er-Rasas = Umm al-Rasas ⚑ JOR 58 Mh30
University Place ⚑ USA (WA) 168 Dj22
Umm an-Nar ⚑ UAE 61 Nh33
Umm az Zumul ⚑ UAE 61 Nh34
Umm Ar Rasas ⚑ JOR 58 Mh30
Umm as-Samim ⚑ OM 61 Nh35
Umm Badir ⚑ SUD 135 Me40
Umm Barbit ⚑ SUD 135 Mg40
Umm Buru ⚑ SUD 134 Mb40
Umm Dafag ⚑ SUD 134 Mb40
Umm Dam ⚑ SUD 135 Mf39
Umm Defeis ⚑ SUD 134 Md40
Umm Durman ⚑ SUD 135 Mg38
Umm Gederil ⚑ SUD 134 Md40
Umm Haraz ⚑ SUD 134 Mb40
Umm Hawsh ⚑ SUD 134 Md40
Umm Hisin ⚑ UAE 61 Ng34
Umm Inderaba ⚑ SUD 135 Mf38
Umm Kaddada ⚑ SUD 134 Md40
Umm Lajj ⚑ KSA 58 Mj33
Umm Marahik ⚑ SUD 134 Mc39
Umm Qaser ⚑ SUD 134 Mc39
Umm Quzein ⚑ SUD 134 Md40
Umm Rahaw ⚑ SUD 135 Mg37
Umm Rumeila ⚑ SUD 134 Md40
Umm Ruwaba ⚑ SUD 135 Mf39
Umm Said = Mesaieed ⚑ Q 59 Nf33
Umm Sayyala ⚑ SUD 135 Mf38
Umm Urumah al ⚑ KSA 58 Mj33
Umm Said ⚑ Q 59 Nf33
Un Phang ⚑ THA 88 Pk37
Umpire ⚑ USA (AR) 174 Fc28
Umrer ⚑ IND (MHT) 83 Ok35
Umri ⚑ IND (MPH) 82 Oj36
Umsini, Gunung ▲ RI 114 Rg46
Umsning ⚑ IND (MGA) 86 Pf33
Umtamvuna Nature Reserve ⚑ ZA 155 Mf61
Umuahia ⚑ WAN 138 Le42
Umuarama ⚑ BR (PR) 202 Hd57
Umu-Duru ⚑ WAN 138 Ld43
Umunede ⚑ WAN 138 Ld42
Umurbey ⚑ TR 46 Mg50
Umurga ⚑ LV 39 Me33
Umurlu ⚑ TR 47 Mh53
Umutina, T.I. ⚑ BR 202 Hb53
Umutu ⚑ WAN 138 Ld42
Umutwe Range ⚑ ZW 152 Mf54
Umzimkulu ⚑ ZA 155 Me61
Umzinto ⚑ ZA 155 Mf61
Un ⚑ IRQ 57 Nd29
Una ⚑ BIH 35 Lq46
Una ⚑ BR (BA) 203 Ja53
Una ⚑ HR (BA) 203 Ja53
Una ⚑ BR (MG) 203 Hj54
Una ⚑ IND (HPH) 80 Oj30
Unai ⚑ BR (MG) 202 Hf54
Unaizah ⚑ KSA 59 Nb33
Unalakleet ⚑ USA (AK) 164 Bk14
Unare ⚑ FIN 16 Mc12
Unari ⚑ FIN 16 Mc12
Unnamed Conservation Park ⚑ AUS 105 Rd60
Unnao ⚑ IND (UPH) 83 Pa32
Unnaryd ⚑ S 31 Lo34
Uno ⚑ GNB 136 Kc40
Unpongko ⚑ VU 118 Te55
Unryul ⚑ PRK 78 Rc26
Unst ⚑ GB 20 Lb31
Unstrut ⚑ D 32 Ll39
Unteres Odertal, N.P. ⚑ D 32 Lp38
Unterhaching ⚑ D 33 Lm42
Unteruckersee ⚑ D 32 Lo37
Unye ⚑ TR 56 Mj25
Unzen ⚑ J 79 Re29
Uotsuri Jima ⚑ J 79 Rb33
Uozu ⚑ J 77 Rj27
Upa ⚑ EST 39 Me32
Upata ⚑ YV 193 Gj41
Upemba, P.N.de l' ⚑ RDC 146 Md50
Upernavik ⚑ DK 163 Ha04
Upington ⚑ ZA 154 Ma60
Upolu ⚑ USA (HI) 170 Cc34
Upolu ⚑ WS 101 Tk11
Upper Canada Vill. ⚑ CDN 177 Gc23
Upper Daby A.L. ⚑ USA 106 Rf53
Upper Guinea ⚑ 122 Kb09
Upper Karoo ⚑ ZA 154 Mb62
Upper Mississippi N.W.R. ⚑ USA 172 Fe24
Upper-Normandie ⚑ F 22 La41
Upper Peninsula ⚑ USA 173 Fh22
Upper Sandusky ⚑ USA (OH) 173 Fj25
Upper Sioux Ind. Res. ⚑ USA 172 Fc23
Upper Svaneti ⚑ GE 57 Nb24
Uppingang adI ⚑ IND (KTK) 84 Oh39
Uppland ⚑ S 31 Ls31
Uppsala-Väsby ⚑ S 31 Lt31
Uppsala ⚑ S 31 Ls31
Upshi ⚑ IND 81 Oj29
Upshur ⚑ USA (WV) 169 Eh23
Uptar ⚑ RUS 55 Tc06
Uracca ⚑ BR (AM) 203 Hj53
Urad Houqi ⚑ CHN (NMZ) 72 Qd25
Urad Qianqi ⚑ CHN (NMZ) 72 Qe25
Urad Zhongqi ⚑ CHN (NMZ) 72 Qe25
Uraho ⚑ J 77 Sb24
Urakawa ⚑ J 77 Sb24
Ural ⚑ KZ 54 Nd07
Urals ⚑ RUS 109 Sf61
Urambo ⚑ EAT 146 Mg48
Urandangi ⚑ AUS (QLD) 108 Rk56
Urandi ⚑ BR (BA) 203 Hj53
Uranga ⚑ BR (AM) 199 Ha48
Uranium City ⚑ CDN (SK) 167 Eh16
Uran-Togoo Tulga Mountain Nature Reserve ⚑ MNG 70 Qb21
'Ura-Vajgoror ⚑ SAL 46 Lu50
Urawa ⚑ J 79 Rk28
Urayan ⚑ KSA 59 Nc33
Urayirah ⚑ KSA 59 Ne33
Urbana ⚑ USA (IL) 175 Ff26
Urbana ⚑ USA (OH) 173 Fj25
Urbandale ⚑ USA (IA) 172 Fc25
Urbánia ⚑ I 34 Ln47
Urbano Noris ⚑ C 179 Gb35
Urbano Santos ⚑ BR (MA) 201 Hj47
Urbino ⚑ I 34 Ln47
Urbinasopon ⚑ RI 97 Rf46
Urcos ⚑ PE 197 Ge52
Urdampilleta ⚑ RA (BA) 209 Gk63
Urdgol ⚑ MNG 67 Pg22
Urdinarrain ⚑ RA (ER) 204 Ha62
Ureca ⚑ GQ 138 La44
Urepel ⚑ F 24 Kt47
Ureparapara ⚑ VU 118 Td52

Ures · MEX (SO) 180 Ee31
Urewera N.P. · NZ 113 Tj65
Urganch · UZ 62 Oa25
Urganlı · TR 47 Mh52
Urgench = Urganch · UZ 62 Oa25
Ürgüp · TR 56 Mh26
Urgut · UZ 63 Od26
Urho · CHN (XUZ) 67 Pc22
Urho Kekkosen kansallispuisto · FIN 16 Me11
Uri · TCH 133 Lk35
Uria · RO 43 Me43
Uriah · USA (AL) 175 Fg30
Uribante · CO 192 Gd40
Uribia · CO 192 Gd40
Uribicha · BOL 206 Gj53
Urica · YV 193 Gh41
Uri Hauchab Mountains · NAM 154 Lh58
Uriman · YV 193 Gj43
Urique · MEX (CHH) 180 Eg32
Urisirinna · GUY 194 Ha42
Uriuk · RUS 70 Qd20
Uriz · UA 43 Me41
Urjala · FIN 38 Md29
Urjankanskij hrebet · RUS 71 Qk20
Urjupino · RUS 71 Qk19
Urjupinsk · RUS 48 Na20
Urk · NL 23 Lf38
Urla · TR 47 Mg50
Urlați · RO 45 Mg46
Urlingford · IRL 19 Kn38
Urmary · RUS 48 Nd18
Urnes · N 17 Ld15

Wińsko ◻ PL 40 Lr39
Winslow ◻ USA (AZ) 171 Ee28
Winston ◻ USA (NM) 171 Eg29
Winston ◻ USA (OR) 168 Dj24
Winston-Salem ◻ USA (NC) 178 Fk27
Winsum ◻ NL 23 Lg37
Winterberg ◻ D 32 Lj39
Winterberge ■ ZA 155 Md62
Winter Harbour ◻ CDN (BC) 168 Df20
Winters ◻ USA (TX) 174 Fa30
Winterset ◻ USA (IA) 172 Fc25
Winter Springs ◻ USA (FL) 178 Fk31
Winterswijk ◻ NL 23 Lg39
Winterthur ◻ CH 34 Lj43
Winterton ◻ ZA 155 Me60
Winthrop ◻ USA (ME) 177 Ge23
Winthrop ◻ USA (WA) 168 Dk21
Wintinna ◻ AUS (SA) 108 Rj59
Winton ◻ AUS (QLD) 108 Sb57
Winton ◻ NZ 113 Te69
Winton ◻ USA (NC) 178 Gb27
Winyaw ◻ MYA 88 Pj38
Wipim ◻ PNG 115 Sb50
Wipperfürth ◻ D 32 Lh39
Wirawa ◻ AUS (NSW) 109 Sd60
Wirges ◻ D 32 Lh40
Wirliyajarrayi A.L. ■ AUS 103 Rg56
Wirmaf ◻ RI 97 Rf48
Wirrabara ◻ AUS (SA) 110 Rk62
Wirrealpa ◻ AUS (SA) 108 Rk61
Wirrulla ◻ AUS (SA) 110 Rh62
Wirth Peninsula ▲ 6 Fd33
Wisbech ◻ GB 21 La38
Wiscasset ◻ USA (MA) 177 Gf24
Wisconsin ◻ USA 172 Fe23
Wisconsin Range ▲ 6 Dd36
Wisconsin Rapids ◻ USA (WI) 172 Ff23
Wisdom ◻ USA (MT) 168 Ed23
Wiseman ◻ USA (AK) 165 Cf12
Wisemans Ferry ◻ AUS (NSW) 111 Sf62
Wishart ◻ CDN (SK) 169 Eh20
Wishek ◻ USA (ND) 172 Fa22
Wisil ◻ SP 143 Ne43
Wisła ◻ PL 41 Lt41
Wiślica ◻ PL 41 Ma40
Wismar ◻ ☐ ■ D 32 Lm37
Wiśnice ◻ PL 41 Md39
Wiśniowa ◻ PL 41 Mb41
Wissembourg ◻ ■ F 23 Lh41
Wissen ◻ D 32 Lh40
Wistari Reef ■ AUS (QLD) 109 Sf57
Wisznia Mała ◻ PL 40 Ls39
Witagron ◻ SME 194 Hb43
Witaitonga ▲ RI 97 Rb48
Witbank ◻ ZA 155 Me58
Witbooisvlei ◻ NAM 154 Lk58
Witfonteinrand ▲ ZA 155 Md58
Witham ◻ GB 21 La39
Withernsea ◻ GB 21 La37
Witjira N.P. ■ AUS (SA) 108 Rh59
Witkowo ◻ PL 40 Ls38
Witkransnek ▲ ZA 155 Mc61
Witless Bay Ecological Res. ■ CDN 177 Hd22
Witney ◻ GB 21 Kt39
Witnica ◻ PL 40 Lp38
Witoszyce ◻ PL 40 Lr39
Witpütz ◻ NAM 154 Lj59
Witrivier ◻ ZA 155 Mf58
Witsand ◻ ZA 154 Ma63
Witteberge ▲ ZA 154 Ma62
Witteberge ▲ ZA 154 Mb62
Witteberge ■ ZA 155 Md60
Witteklip ◻ ZA 155 Mc62
Witten ◻ D 32 Lh39
Wittenberg ◻ USA (WI) 173 Ff23
Wittenberge ◻ D 32 Lm37
Wittenburra ◻ AUS (QLD) 109 Sc60
Wittenoom ◻ AUS (WA) 102 Qk57
Wittingen ◻ D 32 Ll38
Wittlich ◻ D 33 Lg41
Wittmund ◻ D 32 Lh37
Wittstock ◻ D 32 Ln37
Witu ◻ EAK 145 Na47
Witu ◻ PNG 116 Se48
Witu Islands ▲ PNG 116 Se48
Witvlei ◻ NAM 150 Lk57
Witwater ◻ ZA 154 Lk61
Witzenhausen ◻ D 32 Lk39
Wiżajny ◻ PL 41 Mc36
Wizna ◻ PL 41 Mc37
Władysławowo ◻ PL 40 Lt36
Wli Falls ■ GH 137 La42
Wlingi ◻ RI 95 Qg50
Włocławek ◻ PL 41 Lu38
Włodawa ◻ PL 41 Md39
Włodzimierzów ◻ PL 41 Lu39
Włoszakowice ◻ PL 40 Lr39
Włoszczowa ◻ PL 41 Lu40
Wlotzkasbaken ◻ NAM 150 Lh57
Wobulenzi ◻ EAU 144 Mg45
Woburn ◻ CDN (QC) 176 Ge23
Woburn Abbey ■ GB 21 Ku39
Woddy Point ◻ CDN (NF) 177 Ha21
Wodonga ◻ AUS (VIC) 111 Sd64
Wodzisław Śląski ◻ PL 40 Lt40
Woe ◻ GH 137 La43
Woganakai ◻ PNG 116 Sf48
Wohlen ◻ CH 34 Lj43
Woippy ◻ F 23 Lg41
Woitape ◻ PNG 115 Sd50
Woito ◻ ETH 144 Mj43
Wokam ▲ RI 114 Rh48
Wokha ◻ IND (NGL) 86 Ph32
Woking ◻ GB 21 Ku39
Wokole ◻ RI 97 Rb48
Wola Uhruska ◻ PL 41 Md39
Wolbrom ◻ PL 41 Lu40
Wołczyn ◻ PL 40 Lt39
Woldegk ◻ D 32 Lo37
Woleai Atoll ▲ FSM 10 Sa09
Wolf Bayou ◻ USA (AR) 175 Fe28
Wolf Creek ◻ USA (MT) 169 Ed22
Wolf Creek ◻ USA (OR) 168 Dj24
Wolfe Creek Meteorite Crater ■ AUS 103 Rd55
Wolfe Creek Meteorite National Park ■ AUS 103 Rd55
Wolfen ◻ D 32 Ln39
Wolfenbüttel ◻ D 32 Ll38
Wolfgangsee ■ A 35 Lo43
Wolfgangsee ■ A 35 Lo43
Wolf Point ◻ USA (MT) 169 Eh21
Wolfratshausen ◻ D 33 Lm43
Wolfsberg ◻ A 35 Lp44
Wolfsburg ◻ D 32 Ll38
Wolf, Volcán ■ EC 197 Fe45
Wolgast ◻ D 32 Lo36
Wolhusen ◻ CH 34 Lj43
Woliński P.N. ■ ■ PL 40 Lp37
Wólka ◻ PL 41 Mc39
Wólka Kraśniczyńska ◻ PL 41 Md40
Wolkefit Pass ≡ ETH 142 Mj39
Wollaston Lake ◻ CDN 162 Ed07
Wollaston Lake ≋ CDN 162 Ed07
Wollaston Peninsula ▲ CDN 162 Eb05
Wollemi N.P. ☐ ■ AUS 111 Sf62
Wollogorang ◻ AUS (NT) 106 Rj54
Wollongong ◻ AUS (NSW) 111 Sf63
Wolmaransstad ◻ ZA 155 Mc59
Wolmirstedt ◻ D 32 Lm38
Wolo ◻ RI 114 Rk47
Wologizi Range ▲ LB 136 Kf41
Wołomin ◻ PL 41 Mb38
Wolong Giant Panda Reserve ■ CHN 74 Qb30
Wołosate ◻ PL 43 Mc41
Wołów ◻ PL 40 Lr39
Wolseley ◻ CDN (SK) 169 Ej20
Wolseley ◻ ZA 154 Lk62
Wolsey ◻ USA (SD) 172 Fa23
Wolsztyn ◻ PL 40 Lr38
Wolvega ◻ NL 23 Lg38
Wolverhampton ◻ ☐ ■ GB 21 Ks38
Wolwefontein ◻ ZA 155 Mc62
Wombil Downs ◻ AUS (QLD) 109 Sd60
Womblebank ◻ AUS (QLD) 109 Se58
Wondai ◻ AUS (QLD) 109 Sf59
Wonderfontein ◻ ZA 155 Me58
Wonder Gorge ■ Z 152 Me53
Wonderwerk Caves ■ ZA 154 Mb59
Wonderwerkgrotte ■ ZA 154 Mb59
Wondinong ◻ AUS (WA) 104 Qj59
Wonegizi Mountain ▲ LB 136 Kf42
Wonegizi N.P. ■ LB 136 Kf41
Wongan Hills ◻ AUS (WA) 104 Qj61
Wonganoo ◻ AUS (WA) 104 Ra59
Wonga Wongué ◻ G 148 Le46
Wongoondy ◻ AUS (WA) 104 Qh60
Wonju ◻ ROK 78 Rd27
Wono ◻ RI 96 Qk47
Wonogiri ◻ RI 95 Qf49
Wonoka ◻ AUS (SA) 108 Rk61
Wonosari ◻ RI 95 Qf49
Wonosobo ◻ RI 95 Qe49
Wonsan ◻ PRK 76 Rd26
Wonto Koto ◻ RI 97 Rd46
Wonyulgunna Hill ▲ AUS 104 Qk58
Woodanilling ◻ AUS (WA) 104 Qj62
Woodbine ◻ USA (GA) 178 Fk30
Woodbine Race Track ■ CDN (ON) 173 Ga24
Woodbourne ◻ USA (NY) 177 Gc25
Woodbridge ◻ GB 21 Lb38
Wood Buffalo National Park ■ ■ CDN (AB) 167 Ed16
Woodburn ◻ AUS (NSW) 109 Sg60
Woodburn ◻ USA (OR) 168 Dj23
Woodenbong ◻ AUS (NSW) 109 Sg60
Woodend ◻ NZ 113 Tg67
Woodford ◻ AUS (QLD) 109 Sg59
Woodgate ◻ AUS (QLD) 109 Sg58
Woodgreen ◻ AUS (NT) 108 Rh57
Woodhall Spa ◻ GB 21 Ku37
Wood Island ◻ CDN (PE) 176 Gj23
Woodland ◻ USA (CA) 170 Dk26
Woodland ◻ USA (WA) 168 Dj23
Woodland Caribou Prov. Park ■ ■ CDN 172 Fc20
Woodland Park ◻ USA (CO) 171 Eh26
Woodlands ◻ AUS (QLD) 109 Sd59
Woodlands ◻ AUS (WA) 104 Qk58
Woodlark Island ▲ PNG 116 Sg50
Wood, Mount ▲ USA 169 Ee23
Wood Mountain ◻ CDN (SK) 169 Eg21
Woodridge ◻ CDN (MB) 172 Fb21
Woodroffe, Mount ▲ AUS 105 Rf59
Woodrow ◻ USA (AK) 165 Cf15
Woodrow ◻ USA (CO) 174 Ej26
Woodruff ◻ USA (UT) 171 Ee25
Woodruff ◻ USA (WI) 172 Ff23
Woodsfield ◻ USA (OH) 173 Fk26
Woodside ◻ AUS (VIC) 111 Sd65
Woodside Beach ■ ■ AUS 111 Sd65
Woodson ◻ USA (TX) 174 Fa29
Woods Point ◻ AUS (VIC) 111 Sd64
Woodstock ◻ AUS (QLD) 107 Sd55
Woodstock ◻ AUS (QLD) 108 Sa57
Woodstock ◻ AUS (WA) 102 Qk56
Woodstock ■ AUS 102 Qk57
Woodstock ◻ CDN (NB) 176 Gg22
Woodstock ◻ CDN (ON) 173 Fk24
Woodstock ◻ GB 21 Kt39
Woodstock ◻ USA (AL) 175 Fg29
Woodstock ◻ USA (IL) 173 Ff24
Woodsville ◻ USA (NH) 177 Gd23
Woodvale ◻ AUS (QLD) 109 Sd59
Woodville ◻ NZ 113 Th66
Woodville ◻ USA (MS) 175 Fe30
Woodville ◻ USA (TX) 174 Fc30
Woodward ◻ USA (OK) 174 Fa27
Woodworth ◻ USA (ND) 172 Fa22
Wooi ◻ RI 114 Rh46
Wooler ◻ GB 20 Ks35
Woolfield ◻ AUS (QLD) 109 Sb56
Woolgoolga ◻ ■ AUS (NSW) 109 Sg61
Woolgorong ◻ AUS (WA) 104 Qh59
Wooli ◻ AUS (NSW) 109 Sg60
Woolomombi ◻ AUS (NSW) 109 Sg61
Woomera ◻ AUS (SA) 108 Rj61
Woomerangee Hill ▲ AUS 104 Qg59
Woonsocket ◻ USA (SD) 172 Fa23
Woorabinda ◻ AUS (QLD) 109 Se58
Wooramel ◻ AUS (WA) 104 Qh58
Wooster ◻ USA (OH) 173 Fk25
Woraksan N.P. ■ ROK 78 Re27
Worb ◻ CH 34 Lh44
Worbis ◻ D 32 Ll39
Worcester ◻ GB 21 Ks38
Worcester ◻ USA (MA) 177 Ge24
Worcester ◻ ZA 154 Lk62
Worden ◻ USA (OR) 168 Dk24
Wörgl ◻ A 34 Ln43
Worin ◻ PNG 115 Sd49
Workai ▲ RI 114 Rh49
Workington ◻ GB 20 Kr36
Worksop ◻ GB 21 Kt37
Workum ◻ NL 23 Lf38
Worland ◻ USA (WY) 169 Eg23
World Park ▲ 7 Tc34
World's Largest Mineral Hot Springs ■ USA (WY) 169 Ef24
World's View ■ ZW 152 Mg55
Wörlitzer Park ☐ ■ D 32 Ln39
Worms ◻ D 33 Lj41
Worofla ◻ CI 137 Kg41
Wörth ◻ D 33 Lj41
Wörth ◻ D 33 Lk41
Worthing ◻ GB 21 Ku40
Worthington ◻ USA (MN) 172 Fc24
Worthington ◻ USA (OH) 173 Fj25
Wosi ◻ RI 97 Re46
Wosu ◻ RI 96 Ra47
Wotap ▲ RI 97 Rf49
Wotjalum Aboriginal Reserve ■ AUS 102 Rb54
Wotu ◻ RI 96 Ra47
Woumbou ◻ CAM 139 Lh43
Wounded Knee Battlefield ☒ USA 169 Ej24
Wour ◻ TCH 133 Lh35
Wowan ◻ AUS (QLD) 109 Sf57
Wowoni ▲ RI 97 Rb48
Woziwoda ◻ PL 40 Ls37
W, P.N.du- ■ ■ BF 132 Lb39
«W», P.N.du ■ ■ RN 138 Lb39
Wrabanay ◻ AFG 65 Oe29
Wrangel Island ▲ RUS 55 Ua04
Wrangell ◻ USA (AK) 166 Dd17
Wrangell Island ▲ USA 166 Dd17
Wrangell Mountains ▲ USA 165 Cj15
Wrangell - Saint Elias National Park and Preserve ■ ■ ■ USA 165 Cj15
Wray ◻ USA (CO) 174 Ej25
Wreck Bay ≋ AUS 111 Sf63
Wreck diving (Anegada) ■ GB 187 Gh36
Wreck diving (Anguilla) ■ GB 187 Gj36
Wreck diving (Antigua) ■ AG 187 Gk37
Wreck diving (Barbuda) ■ AG 187 Gk37
Wrens ◻ USA (GA) 178 Fj29
Wrentham ◻ CDN (AB) 169 Ed21
Wrexham ◻ GB 21 Ks37
Wreys Bush ◻ NZ 113 Te68
Wriezen ◻ D 32 Lp38
Wright ◻ RP 90 Rc40
Wright ◻ USA (WY) 169 Eh24
Wright Brothers Nat. Mem. ■ USA 178 Gc28
Wrightsville ◻ USA (GA) 178 Fj29
Wrightsville Beach ◻ USA (NC) 178 Gb28
Wrigley ◻ CDN 167 Dj14
Writing Rock ■ USA 169 Ej21
Wrocki ◻ PL 41 Lu37
Wrocław ◻ ■ PL 40 Ls39
Wronki ◻ PL 40 Lr38
Wrotham Park ◻ AUS (QLD) 107 Sb54
Wroxton ◻ CDN (SK) 172 Ek20
Września ◻ PL 40 Ls38
Wschowa ◻ PL 40 Lr39
Wu'an ◻ CHN (HBI) 73 Qh27
Wubin ◻ AUS (WA) 104 Qj61
Wubu ◻ CHN (SAX) 72 Qf27
Wuchang ◻ CHN (HLG) 76 Rd23
Wuchang ◻ CHN (HUB) 75 Qh30
Wuchuan ◻ CHN (GDG) 74 Qf35
Wuchuan ◻ CHN (NMZ) 72 Qf25
Wuda ◻ CHN (NMZ) 72 Qd26
Wudalianchi ◻ CHN (HLG) 71 Rd21
Wudalianchi Lake Excursion Area ■ CHN 71 Rd21
Wudang Shan ▲ CHN 72 Qf29
Wudangshan ☐ ▲ ■ CHN 72 Qf29
Wudang Zhao ▲ CHN 72 Qf25
Wudao ◻ CHN (LNG) 73 Ra26
Wudaogou ◻ CHN (HLG) 71 Rd20
Wuday'ah ◻ KSA 60 Nd37
Wudi ◻ WAN 138 Le40
Wuding ◻ CHN (YUN) 87 Qb33
Wuding He ≋ CHN 72 Qe26
Wudinna ◻ AUS (SA) 110 Rh62
Wudong Shan ▲ CHN 75 Qh32
Wudu ◻ CHN (GSU) 72 Qc29
Wudu ◻ CHN (SCH) 72 Qc30
Wufeng ◻ CHN (HUB) 74 Qf30
Wugang ◻ CHN (HUN) 74 Qf32
Wugong ◻ CHN (SAA) 72 Qe28
Wuhai ◻ CHN (NMZ) 72 Qd26
Wuhan ◉ CHN (HUB) 75 Qh30
Wuhe ◻ CHN (AHU) 78 Qj29
Wuhou Shrine ■ CHN 73 Qg29
Wuhu ◻ CHN (AHU) 78 Qk30
Wuhua ◻ CHN (GDG) 75 Qh34
Wüjang ◻ CHN (TIB) 68 Ok29
Wuji ◻ CHN (HBI) 73 Qh26
Wujiang ◻ CHN (GZH) 74 Qd32
Wu Jiang ■ CHN (GZH) 74 Qd32
Wujiang ◻ CHN (JGS) 78 Ra30
Wujiangdu ◻ CHN (GZH) 74 Qd32
Wukari ◻ WAN 138 Le42
Wulai ■ RC 75 Ra33
Wulgo ◻ WAN 139 Lh39
Wuli ◻ CHN (QHI) 69 Pg28
Wulian ◻ CHN (SDG) 78 Qk28
Wuliang Shan ▲ CHN 87 Qa34
Wu Liang, Tomb of = Imperial Tombs of the Ming and Qing Dynasties ☐ ■ CHN (JGS) 78 Qk29
Wuliaru ▲ RI 97 Rf49
Wulichuan ◻ CHN (HNN) 72 Qf29
Wuling Shan ▲ CHN 74 Qe32
Wulingshan Z.B. ■ CHN 73 Qj25
Wulingyuan ☐ ■ ■ CHN 74 Qf31
Wulong ◻ CHN (CGQ) 74 Qd31
Wum ◻ CAM 138 Lf42
Wumei Shan ▲ CHN 75 Qh31
Wuming ◻ CHN (GZG) 74 Qe34
Wümme ≋ D 32 Lk37
Wunagak ◻ SUD 141 Mg41
Wunarual ◻ SUD 141 Mf41
Wundanyi ◻ EAK 145 Mk47
Wun-dwin ◻ MYA 86 Pj35
Wunen ◻ RI 114 Rk47
Wunga ◻ AUS (WA) 103 Rd55
Wuning ◻ CHN (JGX) 75 Qh31
Wun Rog ◻ SUD 141 Me41
Wun Shwai ◻ SUD 141 Me42
Wunsiedel ◻ D 33 Ln40
Wunstorf ◻ D 32 Lk38
Wuntau ◻ SUD 135 Mg40
Wuntho ◻ MYA 86 Ph34
Wupatki Nat. Mon. ■ USA 171 Ee28
Wuping ◻ CHN (FJN) 75 Qj33
Wupo ◻ CHN (SCH) 74 Qb31
Wuppertal ◻ D 32 Lh39
Wupperthal ◻ ▲ ZA 154 Lk62
Wuqi ◻ CHN (SAA) 72 Qe27
Wuqia ◻ CHN (XUZ) 66 Oh26
Wurarga ◻ AUS (WA) 104 Qj60
Wuriyanga Mosque ■ GH 137 Kk40
Wurno ◻ WAN 132 Lc39
Wurralibi A.L. ■ AUS 106 Rj53
Würzburg ◻ D 33 Lk41
Wurzen ◻ D 32 Ln39
Wuse ◻ WAN 138 Le41
Wushan ◻ CHN (AHU) 78 Qj29
Wushan ◻ CHN (CGQ) 74 Qe30
Wushan ◻ CHN (GSU) 72 Qc28
Wushao Ling ▲ CHN 72 Qb27
Wusheng ◻ CHN (SCH) 74 Qd30
Wushi ◻ CHN (XUZ) 66 Ok25
Wushishi ◻ WAN 138 Ld41
Wushizen ◻ CHN (GZG) 74 Qe35
Wusterhausen ◻ D 32 Ln38
Wutachschlucht ■ D 33 Lj43
Wutai ◻ CHN (SAX) 73 Qg26
Wutaishan ▲ CHN 73 Qg26
Wutan ◻ CHN (HUN) 74 Qf31
Wuta Si ■ CHN 72 Qf25
Wutingqiao ■ CHN 78 Qk29
Wutongqiao ◻ CHN (SCH) 74 Qb31
Wutul ◻ AUS (QLD) 109 Sf59
Wutung ◻ PNG 115 Sa47
Wuvulu Island ▲ PNG 115 Sb46
Wuwei ◻ CHN (AHU) 78 Qj30
Wuwei ◻ CHN (GSU) 72 Qb27
Wuwu ◻ PNG 115 Sd49
Wuxi ◻ CHN (CGQ) 74 Qe30
Wuxi ◻ CHN (JGS) 78 Ra30
Wu Xia ■ CHN 74 Qf30
Wuxuan ◻ CHN (GZG) 74 Qe34
Wuxue ◻ CHN (HUB) 75 Qh31
Wuya ◻ WAN 139 Lf40
Wuyan ◻ CHN (ZJG) 75 Ra32
Wuyang ◻ CHN (HNN) 73 Qg29
Wuyi ◻ CHN (ZJG) 75 Qk31
Wuyiling ◻ CHN (HLG) 76 Re21
Wuyishan ◻ CHN (FJN) 75 Qk32
Wuyi Shan ▲ CHN 75 Qj32
Wuyishan Z.B. ☐ ■ ▲ CHN 75 Qj32
Wuyuan ◻ CHN (JGX) 75 Qj31
Wuyuan ◻ CHN (NMZ) 72 Qe25
Wuzhai ◻ CHN (SAX) 72 Qf26
Wu Zhen, Tomb of = Imperial Tombs of the Ming and Qing Dynasties ☐ ■ CHN (JGS) 78 Qk29
Wuzhi ◻ CHN (HNN) 73 Qg28
Wuzhi Shan ■ CHN 75 Qe36
Wuzhong ◻ CHN (NHZ) 72 Qd27
Wuzhou ◻ CHN (GZG) 74 Qf34
Wyalkatchem ◻ AUS (WA) 104 Qj61
Wyamdero Plain ▲ EAK 145 Mk45
Wyandotte Cave ■ USA 175 Fg26
Wyandra ◻ AUS (QLD) 109 Sc59
Wycheproof ◻ AUS (VIC) 111 Sb64
Wydgee ◻ AUS (WA) 104 Qj60
Wygoda ◻ PL 40 Lt39
Wygoda ◻ PL 41 Lu40
Wygoda ◻ PL 41 Mc37
Wyk ◻ D 32 Lj36
Wylatowo ◻ PL 40 Ls38
Wyllie's Port ◻ ZA 152 Me57
Wyloo ◻ AUS (WA) 102 Qj57
Wymiet ◻ AUS (SA) 108 Rh61
Wymondham ◻ GB 21 Lb38
Wynbring ◻ AUS (SA) 108 Rg61
Wyndham ◻ AUS (NSW) 111 Se64
Wyndham ◻ AUS (WA) 103 Re53
Wynne ◻ USA (AR) 175 Fe28
Wynyard ◻ AUS (TAS) 111 Sc66
Wynyard ◻ CDN (SK) 169 Eh20
Wyoming ◻ USA (MI) 173 Fh24
Wyoming ◻ USA 171 Ef24
Wyoming Range ▲ USA 169 Ee24
Wyperfeld N.P. ■ ■ AUS 110 Sa63
Wyralinu Hill ▲ AUS 105 Rb62
Wyrzysk ◻ PL 40 Ls37
Wyseby ◻ AUS (QLD) 109 Se58
Wysoka ◻ PL 40 Lq38
Wysokie ◻ PL 41 Mc37
Wysokie ◻ PL 41 Mc40
Wysokie Mazowieckie ◻ PL 41 Mc38
Wyszków ◻ PL 41 Mb38
Wyszogród ◻ PL 41 Ma38
Wytheville ◻ USA (VA) 178 Fk27
Wyżyna Lubelska ▲ PL 41 Mc39

X

Xaafuun ◻ SP 143 Nf40
Xàbia ◻ ■ E 29 La52
Xaçmaz ◻ AZ 57 Ne25
Xagdomba ◻ CHN (SCH) 72 Qb28
Xagquka ◻ CHN (TIB) 69 Pg30
Xaidulla ◻ CHN (XUZ) 68 Oj27
Xainza ◻ CHN (TIB) 68 Pe30
Xaitongmoin ◻ CHN (TIB) 68 Pe31
Xai-Xai ◻ ■ ▲ MOC 155 Mg58
Xakriabá, T.I. ■ BR 203 Hh53
Xalapa = Jalapa ◉ MEX (VC) 182 Fb36
Xalin ◻ SP 143 Ne41
Xa Lon Pagoda ▲ VN 89 Qc41
Xalqobod ◻ UZ 62 Nk24
Xa Mat ◻ VN 89 Qd40
Xambioia ◻ BR (TO) 200 Hf49
Xamindele ◻ ANG 148 Lg49
Xam Neua ◻ LAO 87 Qc35
Xam Tay ◻ ■ LAO 87 Qc35
Xá-Muteba ◻ ANG 149 Lj50
Xanadu Beach ■ BS 179 Ga32
Xandel ◻ ANG 148 Lj50
Xangongo ◻ ANG 150 Lh54
Xankendi ◉ AZ 57 Nd26
Xan Saray ■ AZ 57 Nd25
Xanten ◻ D 32 Lg39
Xánthi ◻ ■ GR 45 Me49
Xanthos ☐ ■ TR 56 Me27
Xanxerê ◻ BR (SC) 204 Hd59
Xapetuba ◻ BR (MG) 202 Hf55
Xapuri ◻ BR (AC) 198 Gf51
Xarar ◻ SP 143 Ne43
Xarardheere ◻ SP 145 Nd43
Xar Hure ◻ CHN (NMZ) 71 Qk23
Xarlag ◻ CHN (NMZ) 72 Qe26
Xassengue ◻ ANG 149 Lk51
Xàtiva ◻ ■ E 29 Ku52
Xayar ◻ CHN (XUZ) 66 Pb25
Xazorasp ◻ UZ 62 Oa25
Xcalak ◻ ■ ■ MEX (QTR) 183 Fg36
Xcalak, Parque Nacional Arrecifes de ≋ MEX (QTR) 183 Fg36
X-Can ◻ MEX (YT) 183 Fg35
Xcaret ◻ ■ MEX (QTR) 183 Fg35
Xe Bang Nouan N.B.C.A. ■ LAO 89 Qd38
Xebert ◻ CHN (NMZ) 71 Rb23
Xel-Ha ◻ ≋ MEX (QTR) 183 Fg35
Xenia ◻ USA (OH) 175 Fj26
Xe Pian N.B.C.A. ■ LAO 89 Qd38
Xerente, T.I. ■ BR 200 Hf50
Xert ◻ E 29 La50
Xerta ◻ E 29 La50
Xertigny ◻ F 25 Lg42
Xe Sap N.B.C.A. ■ LAO 89 Qd37
Xhami Ethem-Bey ■ AL 44 Lu49
Xhorodomo ◻ RB 151 Mc56
Xhumaga ◻ RB 151 Mc56
Xhumbo ◻ RB 151 Mc56
Xiachuan Dao ▲ CHN 75 Qg35
Xiadong ◻ CHN (GZG) 74 Qe34
Xiaguan ◻ ■ CHN (YUN) 87 Qa33
Xiahe ◻ CHN (GSU) 72 Qb28
Xiamen ◻ CHN (FJN) 75 Qk33
Xi'an ◉ ■ CHN (SAA) 72 Qe28
Xianfeng ◻ CHN (HUB) 74 Qe31
Xianfeng ◻ CHN (SAX) 72 Qf28
Xiang'an ◻ CHN (AHU) 78 Qj30
Xiangbi Shan ■ CHN 74 Qf33
Xiangcheng ◻ CHN (HNN) 73 Qg29
Xiangcheng ◻ CHN (HNN) 73 Qh29
Xiangcheng ◻ CHN (SCH) 69 Pk31
Xiangfan ◻ CHN (HUB) 73 Qg29
Xianggang ◻ CHN 75 Qh34
Xianghuang Qi ◻ CHN (NMZ) 73 Qg24
Xianghui ◻ CHN (JGS) 78 Qk28
Xiangji Temple ▲ CHN 72 Qe29
Xiangning ◻ CHN (SAX) 72 Qf28
Xiangshan ◻ CHN (ZJG) 75 Ra31
Xiangsha Wan ■ CHN 72 Qe25
Xiangtan ◻ CHN (HUN) 75 Qg32
Xiangtang ◻ CHN (JGX) 75 Qj31
Xiangtangshan Shiku ▲ CHN 73 Qh27
Xiangxiang ◻ CHN (HUN) 74 Qg32
Xiangyin ◻ CHN (HUN) 75 Qg31
Xiangyun ◻ CHN (YUN) 87 Qa33
Xianju ◻ CHN (ZJG) 75 Ra31
Xianling Tomb ☐ ■ CHN (HUB) 73 Qg30
Xianning ◻ CHN (HUB) 75 Qh31
Xiantao ◻ CHN (HUB) 75 Qg30
Xiantong Si ▲ CHN 73 Qg26
Xianxia Ling ▲ CHN 75 Qk31
Xianyang ◻ CHN (SAA) 72 Qe28
Xianyou ◻ CHN (FJN) 75 Qk33
Xianzhou ◻ CHN (GZG) 74 Qe34
Xiaochang ◻ CHN (HUB) 75 Qh30
Xiaodianzi ◻ CHN (HUB) 72 Qf29
Xiaogan ◻ CHN (HUB) 75 Qg30
Xiaoguanxi ◻ CHN (YUN) 87 Qb32
Xiaohe ◻ CHN (SAA) 72 Qe29
Xiaojiahe ◻ CHN (HLG) 76 Rg22
Xiaojin ◻ CHN (SCH) 74 Qb30
Xiaoling Tomb = Imperial Tombs of the Ming and Qing Dynasties ☐ ■ CHN (JGS) 78 Qk29
Xiaomei Guan ≡ CHN 75 Qh33
Xiaonanchuan ◻ CHN (QHI) 69 Ph28
Xiao San Xia ■ CHN 74 Qe30
Xiaoshan ◻ CHN (ZJG) 78 Ra30
Xiaoshi ◻ CHN (LNG) 76 Rc25
Xiaotian ◻ CHN (AHU) 78 Qj30
Xiaowutai Shan ▲ CHN 73 Qh25
Xiao Xian ◻ CHN (AHU) 78 Qj28
Xiaoxita ◻ CHN (HUB) 74 Qf30
Xiaoyangjie ◻ CHN (YUN) 87 Qb33
Xiapu ◻ CHN (FJN) 75 Qk32
Xiasi ◻ CHN (GZH) 74 Qd33
Xiatai ◻ CHN (XUZ) 66 Pa24
Xia Xian ◻ CHN (SAX) 72 Qf28
Xiaxiyu ◻ CHN (HBI) 73 Qg26
Xiayi ◻ CHN (HNN) 78 Qj28
Xiazha ◻ CHN (YUN) 87 Qc33
Xiazhuang ◻ CHN (HNN) 73 Qh29
Xichang ◻ CHN (GZG) 74 Qe35
Xichang ◻ CHN (SCH) 87 Qb32
Xichong ◻ CHN (SCH) 74 Qc30
Xichou ◻ CHN (YUN) 87 Qc34
Xichú ◻ MEX (GJT) 182 Ek35
Xichuan ◻ CHN (HNN) 72 Qf29
Xicoténcatl ◻ MEX (TM) 182 Fa34
Xicotepec de Juarez ◻ MEX (PUE) 182 Fb35
Xidi ☐ ■ CHN 75 Qk31
Xieng Ngeun ◻ LAO 87 Qb36
Xien Hon ◻ LAO 87 Qa36
Xiezhou Guandimiao ■ CHN 72 Qf28
Xifeng ◻ CHN (GSU) 72 Qd28
Xifeng ◻ CHN (GZH) 74 Qd32
Xifeng ◻ CHN (LNG) 76 Rc24
Xigangzi ◻ CHN (HLG) 71 Rd21
Xigaze ◻ CHN (TIB) 68 Pe31
Xiheying ◻ CHN (HBI) 73 Qh26
Xi Hu ■ CHN 78 Ra30
Xihua ◻ CHN (HNN) 73 Qh29
Xiis ◻ SP 143 Nd40
Xiji ◻ CHN (NHZ) 72 Qc28
Xi Jiang ≋ CHN 74 Qf34
Xijishui ◻ CHN (GSU) 72 Qc27
Xikou ◻ CHN (ZJG) 75 Ra31
Xikouzi ◻ CHN (NMZ) 71 Ra19
Xikrin do Rio Cateté, T.I. ■ BR 200 He49
Xilamuren Caoyuan ■ CHN 72 Qf25
Xilin ◻ CHN (GZG) 87 Qc33
Xi Ling Xia ■ CHN 74 Qf30
Xilinhot ◻ CHN (NMZ) 71 Qj24
Xilinji = Mohe ◻ CHN (HLG) 71 Rb19
Xıllı ◻ AZ 57 Ne26
Xilókastro ◻ GR 46 Mc52
Xilong-Shan Z.B. ■ CHN 72 Qb28
Xime ◻ GNB 136 Kc40
Ximeng ◻ CHN (YUN) 87 Pk34
Ximucheng ◻ CHN (LNG) 76 Rb25
Xin'anjiang Sk. ■ CHN 75 Qk31
Xin'ansuo ◻ CHN (YUN) 87 Qb34
Xinavane ◻ MOC 155 Mg58
Xin Barag Youqi ◻ CHN (NMZ) 71 Qj21
Xin Barag Zuoqi ◻ CHN (NMZ) 71 Qk21
Xinbin ◻ CHN (LNG) 76 Rc25
Xincai ◻ CHN (HNN) 73 Qh29
Xinchang ◻ CHN (GZH) 74 Qd33
Xinchang ◻ CHN (ZJG) 75 Ra31
Xincheng ◻ CHN (HBI) 73 Qh26
Xincheng Weijin Mu ■ CHN 69 Pk26
Xindeng ◻ CHN (ZJG) 75 Qk31
Xindian ◻ CHN (HLG) 76 Rd23
Xindu ◻ CHN (SCH) 74 Qc30
Xinduqiao ◻ CHN (SCH) 69 Qa30
Xinfeng ◻ CHN (JGX) 75 Qh33
Xingalool ◻ SP 143 Ne41
Xing'an ◻ CHN (GZG) 74 Qf33
Xingan ◻ CHN (JGX) 75 Qh32
Xingcheng ◻ ■ CHN (LNG) 76 Ra25
Xinge ◻ ANG 149 Lk50
Xingfeng ◻ CHN (GDG) 75 Qh33
Xingguo ◻ CHN (JGX) 75 Qh32
Xinghe ◻ CHN (NMZ) 73 Qg25
Xinghua ◻ CHN (JGS) 78 Qk29
Xinglong ◻ CHN (HAN) 75 Qf36
Xinglong ◻ CHN (HBI) 73 Qj25
Xingning ◻ CHN (GDG) 75 Qh33
Xingod ◻ SP 143 Ne42
Xingou ◻ CHN (HUB) 75 Qg30
Xingpan ◻ CHN (GZG) 74 Qe35
Xingren ◻ CHN (GZH) 87 Qc33
Xingrenbu ◻ CHN (NHZ) 72 Qc27
Xingshan ◻ CHN (HUB) 74 Qf30
Xingtai ◻ CHN (HBI) 73 Qh27
Xingtang ◻ CHN (HBI) 73 Qh26
Xingu ≋ BR 199 Hd48
Xinguara ◻ BR (PA) 200 Hf49
Xingwen ◻ CHN (SCH) 74 Qc31
Xing Xian ◻ CHN (SAX) 72 Qf26
Xingxingxia ◻ CHN (XUZ) 67 Ph25
Xingyi ◻ CHN (GZH) 87 Qc33
Xinhe ◻ CHN (XUZ) 66 Pb25
Xinhuang ◻ CHN (HUN) 74 Qe32
Xining ◉ CHN (QHI) 72 Qa27
Xiniujiao ◻ CHN (GZG) 74 Qe35
Xinji ◻ CHN (HBI) 73 Qh27
Xinjian ◻ CHN (JGX) 75 Qh31
Xinjie ◻ CHN (YUN) 87 Qc34
Xinjie ◻ CHN (YUN) 87 Qb33
Xinjin ◻ CHN (SCH) 74 Qb30
Xinlicheng ■ CHN 76 Rc24
Xinlong ◻ CHN (SCH) 69 Qa30
Xinmin ◻ CHN (LNG) 76 Rb25
Xinning ◻ CHN (HUN) 74 Qf32
Xinqing ◻ CHN (HLG) 76 Re21
Xinshizhen ◻ CHN (SCH) 74 Qb31
Xintai ◻ CHN (SDG) 78 Qj28
Xintian ◻ CHN (HUN) 74 Qg33
Xin Xian ◻ CHN (HNN) 73 Qh30
Xinxiang ◻ CHN (HNN) 73 Qg28
Xinxing ◻ CHN (GDG) 74 Qg34
Xinxing ◻ CHN (HAN) 75 Qe36
Xinxu ◻ CHN (GZG) 74 Qd34
Xinyang ◻ CHN (HNN) 73 Qh29
Xinye ◻ CHN (HNN) 73 Qg29
Xinyi ◻ CHN (GDG) 74 Qf34
Xinyi ◻ CHN (JGS) 78 Qk28
Xinying ◻ CHN (HAN) 75 Qe36
Xinyu ◻ CHN (JGX) 75 Qh32
Xinyuan ◻ CHN (XUZ) 66 Pb24
Xinzhan ◻ CHN (GZH) 74 Qd31
Xinzhan ◻ CHN (HLG) 76 Rc23
Xinzhao Shan ▲ CHN 72 Qd26
Xinzheng ◻ CHN (HNN) 73 Qg28
Xinzhou ◻ CHN (GZG) 74 Qd33
Xinzhou ◻ CHN (SAX) 73 Qg26
Xinzhu ◻ CHN (HUB) 75 Qh30
Xinzo de Limia ◻ E 26 Kn48
Xinzuotang ◻ CHN (GDG) 75 Qh34
Xiongyuecheng ◻ CHN (LNG) 76 Rb25
Xiping ◻ CHN (HNN) 72 Qf29
Xiping ◻ CHN (HNN) 73 Qh29
Xi Qiao ■ CHN 75 Qg34
Xiqu ◻ CHN (SCH) 87 Qa32
Xique-Xique ◻ BR (BA) 201 Hj51
Xirdalan ◻ AZ 57 Ne25
Xishui ◻ CHN (GZH) 74 Qd31
Xishui ◻ CHN (HUB) 75 Qh30
Xitole ◻ GNB 136 Kc40
Xi Ujimqin Qi ◻ CHN (NMZ) 71 Qj23
Xiushui ◻ CHN (JGX) 75 Qh31
Xiuwen ◻ CHN (GZH) 74 Qd32
Xiuwu ◻ CHN (HNN) 73 Qg28
Xiuyan ◻ CHN (LNG) 76 Rb25
Xiuying ◻ CHN (HAN) 75 Qf36
Xiwu ◻ CHN (QHI) 69 Pj29
Xixabangma Feng ■ CHN 68 Pc31
Xixia ◻ CHN (HNN) 72 Qf29
Xi Xian ◻ CHN (HNN) 73 Qh29
Xi Xian ◻ CHN (SAX) 72 Qf27
Xixiang ◻ CHN (SAA) 72 Qd29
Xixia Wangling ■ CHN 72 Qd26
Xixona ◻ E 29 Ku52
Xiyang ◻ CHN (SAX) 73 Qg27
Xizang Zizhiqu ◻ CHN 53 Pa07
Xmaben ◻ MEX (CAM) 183 Ff36
Xocavand ◻ AZ 57 Nd26
Xochiapa ◻ MEX (VC) 183 Fc37
Xochicalco ☐ ■ MEX 182 Fa36
Xochimilco ◻ MEX (MEX) 182 Fa36
Xochob ■ MEX 183 Ff36
Xo'jayli ◻ UZ 62 Nk24
Xom Tang ◻ VN 87 Qc35
Xovos ◻ UZ 63 Oe25
Xpujil ◻ MEX (CAM) 183 Ff36
Xpujil ■ MEX 183 Ff36
Xuan'en ◻ CHN (HUB) 74 Qe31
Xuanhan ◻ CHN (SCH) 74 Qd30
Xuanhua ◻ CHN (HBI) 73 Qh25
Xuankong Monastery ▲ CHN 73 Qg26
Xuan Loc ◻ VN 89 Qd40
Xuan Mai ◻ VN 87 Qc35
Xuanwei ◻ CHN (YUN) 87 Qc32
Xuanzhong Si ▲ CHN 72 Qg27
Xuanzhou ◻ CHN (AHU) 78 Qk30
Xuchang ◻ CHN (HNN) 73 Qg28
Xudat ◻ AZ 57 Ne25
Xu Da, Tomb of = Imperial Tombs of the Ming and Qing Dynasties ☐ ■ CHN (JGS) 78 Qk29
Xuddur ◻ SP 145 Nb43
Xudun ◻ SP 143 Nd41
Xuebao Ding ▲ CHN 72 Qb29
Xuefeng Shan ▲ CHN 74 Qf32
Xuejiadao ◻ CHN (SDG) 78 Ra28
Xueshan ▲ CHN 72 Qc27
Xugui ◻ CHN (QHI) 69 Pj28
Xultún ■ GCA 183 Ff37
Xumishan Shiku ▲ ■ CHN 72 Qc27
Xunantunich ■ BH 184 Ff37
Xundian ◻ CHN (YUN) 87 Qb33
Xungru ◻ CHN (TIB) 68 Pc31
Xunhua ◻ CHN (QHI) 72 Qb28
Xunke ◻ CHN (HLG) 76 Re21
Xunwu ◻ CHN (JGX) 75 Qh33
Xun Xian ◻ CHN (HNN) 73 Qh28
Xunyang ◻ CHN (SAA) 72 Qe29
Xunyi ◻ CHN (SAA) 72 Qe28
Xupu ◻ CHN (HUN) 74 Qf32
Xushui ◻ CHN (HBI) 73 Qh26
Xuwen ◻ CHN (GDG) 74 Qf35
Xuyi ◻ CHN (JGS) 78 Qk29
Xuyong ◻ CHN (SCH) 74 Qc31
Xuzhou ◻ CHN (JGS) 78 Qj28
Xylóskalo ◻ GR 45 Md55

Y

Yaak ◻ USA (MT) 168 Ec21
Yaamba ◻ AUS (QLD) 109 Sf57
Ya'an ◻ CHN (SCH) 74 Qb31
Yaaq Braaway ◻ SP 145 Nb45
Yaba ◻ RI 97 Rd46
Yaba-Hita-Hikosan N.P. ■ J 79 Rf29
Yabassi ◻ CAM 138 Le43
Yabayo ◻ CI 137 Kg43
Yabebyry ◻ PY 204 Hb59
Yabello ◻ ETH 144 Mk43
Yabello Sanctuary ■ ETH 144 Mk43
Yabia ◻ RDC 140 Mb44
Yablonovyy Range ▲ RUS 55 Qc08
Yabroud ◻ SYR 56 Mj29
Yabucoa ◻ USA (PR) 187 Gh36
Yabuli ◻ CHN (HLG) 76 Re23
Yabuyanos ◻ PE 196 Gd46
Yacambú, P.N. ■ ■ YV 193 Gf41
Yacaré Norte ≡ PY 207 Ha57
Yacata ▲ FJI 119 Ua54
Yachats ◻ USA (OR) 168 Dh23
Yacheng ◻ CHN (HAN) 75 Qe36
Yacimiento Río Turbio ◻ ■ RA (SC) 210 Gd71
Yacuiba ◻ BOL 207 Gj56
Yadagiri Gutta ■ IND 83 Ok37
Yadavindra Gardens ■ IND 81 Oj30
Yadgir ◻ IND (KTK) 82 Oj37
Yadibikro ◻ CI 137 Kh42
Yadkinville ◻ USA (NC) 178 Fk27
Yadmah ◻ KSA 60 Nc36
Yafase ◻ RI 115 Sa47
Yafran ◻ ■ LAR 127 Lg29
Yagaba ◻ GH 137 Kk40
Yagaji ◻ RN 132 Le38
Yagasa Cluster ▲ FJI 119 Ua55
Yago ◻ CAM 139 Lh40
Yagradagzê Shan ▲ CHN 69 Ph28
Yaguachi Nuevo ◻ EC 196 Ga47
Yaguajay ◻ C 179 Ga34
Yaguaraparo ◻ YV 193 Gj40
Yaguarón ◻ ■ PY 204 Hb58
Yaguas ◻ CO 196 Ge47
Yaha ◻ THA 89 Qa42
Yahekou ◻ CHN (HNN) 73 Qg29
Yahk ◻ CDN (BC) 168 Eb21
Yaho ◻ BF 137 Kj40
Yahualica de González Gallo ◻ MEX (JLC) 182 Ej35
Yahuma ◻ RDC 140 Mb45
Yahyalı ◻ TR 56 Mh26
Yaibrai ◻ CHN (NMZ) 72 Qb26
Yaita ◻ J 77 Rk27
Yajalón ◻ MEX (CHP) 183 Fd37
Yajiang ◻ CHN (SCH) 69 Qa30
Yaka ◻ RCA 140 Lk43
Yakana ◻ RDC 140 Mb45
Yakarra ◻ AUS (QLD) 109 Sb60
Yakassé-Attobrou ◻ CI 137 Kj42
Yakassé Mé ◻ CI 137 Kj43
Yakeshi ◻ CHN (NMZ) 71 Ra21
Yakima ◻ USA (WA) 168 Dk22
Yakima Ind. Res. ■ USA 168 Dk22
Yakkabog ◻ UZ 63 Od26
Yakmach ◻ PK 65 Ob31
Yako ◻ BF 137 Kj39
Yakoma ◻ RDC 140 Mb43
Yakote ◻ J 77 Sa26
Yaku ◻ J 79 Rf30
Yaku-jima ▲ J 79 Rf30
Yakumo ◻ J 77 Sa24
Yakushima N.P. ☐ ■ J 79 Rf30
Yakutat ◻ USA (AK) 166 Da16
Yakutia ◻ RUS 55 Qc05
Yala ◻ GH 137 Kk40
Yala ◻ THA 89 Qa42
Yalagüina ◻ NIC 184 Fg39
Yalakdere ◻ TR 45 Mk50
Yalaki ◻ RDC 140 Mb45
Yalama ◻ AZ 57 Ne25
Yala N.P. ■ ■ CL 85 Pa42
Yalape ■ PE 196 Gb49
Yalardy ◻ AUS (WA) 104 Qh59
Yalata ◻ AUS (SA) 105 Rf61
Yalata A.L. ■ AUS 105 Rf61
Yalbalgo ◻ AUS (WA) 104 Qh58
Yale ◻ CDN (BC) 168 Dk21
Yale ◻ EAK 144 Mh45
Yale ◻ USA (WA) 168 Dj22
Yaleko ◻ RDC 141 Mc45
Yalgo ◻ BF 137 Kk39
Yalgoo ◻ AUS (WA) 104 Qj60
Yalgorup N.P. ■ AUS 104 Qh62
Yali ◻ NIC 184 Fg39
Yaligimba ◻ RDC 140 Mb44
Yalıkavak ◻ TR 47 Mh53
Yalıköy ◻ TR 45 Mj49
Yalinga ◻ RCA 140 Mb42
Yallalong ◻ AUS (WA) 104 Qh59
Yalleroi ◻ AUS (QLD) 109 Sc58
Yallingup ◻ ■ ■ AUS (WA) 104 Qh62
Yallo ◻ BF 137 Kj39
Yalock ◻ AUS (NSW) 111 Sc62
Yaloké ◻ RCA 140 Lj43
Yalongwa ◻ RDC 140 Mb45
Yalova ◻ TR 45 Mk50
Yalpirakinu A.L. ■ AUS 103 Rg57
Yalsihón ◻ MEX (YT) 183 Ff35
Yalta ◻ ■ ≋ UA 48 Mh23
Yalufi ◻ RDC 141 Mc45
Yalu Jiang ≋ CHN/PRK 76 Rd25
Yalvaç ◻ TR 56 Mf26
Yamada ◻ J 77 Sa26
Yamagata ◻ J 77 Sa26
Yamaguchi ◻ J 79 Rf28
Yamakawa ◻ J 79 Rh28
Yamal Nenets Autonomous District ◻ RUS 54 Oc05
Yamal Poluostrov ▲ RUS 54 Ob04
Yamanashi ◻ J 79 Rk28
Yamara ◻ YV 193 Gg43
Yamarna ◻ AUS (WA) 105 Rb59
Yamasa ◻ DOM 186 Ge36
Yamasaki ◻ J 79 Rh28
Yamatan ◻ CHN (QHI) 69 Pk28
Yamato Rise ■ 77 Rg26
Yamatsun ◻ J 77 Sa27
Yamba ◻ AUS (NSW) 109 Sg60
Yamba ◻ BF 137 La39
Yambala ◻ RCA 140 Ma42
Yambala Koudouvélé ◻ RCA 140 Ma42
Yambarran Range ▲ AUS 106 Rf53
Yambata ◻ RDC 140 Ma44
Yamba-Yamba ◻ RDC 146 Md48
Yambéring ◻ RG 136 Kd40
Yambi ◻ G 148 Lf46
Yambio ◻ SUD 141 Me43
Yambuya ◻ RDC 141 Mc45
Yamdena ▲ RI 97 Rf49
Yamethin ◻ MYA 86 Pj35
Yamnotri ◻ IND (UTT) 81 Ok30
Yamoussoukro ● ■ ■ CI 137 Kh42
Yampa ◻ USA (CO) 171 Eg25
Yamparaez ◻ BOL 206 Gh55
Yamuna ≋ IND 83 Pa33
Yamunanagar ◻ IND (HYA) 81 Oj30
Yamzho Yumco ≋ CHN 69 Pf31
Yan ◻ MAL 92 Qa43
Yanaba Island ▲ PNG 116 Sf50
Yanac ◻ AUS (VIC) 110 Sa64
Yanac ◻ PE 197 Gb50
Yanachaga Chemillén , P.N. ■ ■ PE 197 Gc51
Yanadani ◻ J 79 Rg29
Yanahuanca ◻ PE 197 Gb51
Yanai ◻ J 79 Rg29
Yanam ◉ IND (PND) 83 Pb37
Yanam Pondicherry ◻ IND 83 Pb37
Yanan ◻ CHN (GDG) 74 Qf34
Yan'an ◻ CHN (SAA) 72 Qe27
Yanaoca ◻ PE 197 Ge53
Yanbian ◻ CHN (SCH) 87 Qa32
Yanbu al Bahr ◻ KSA 58 Mk33
Yancannia ◻ AUS (NSW) 108 Sb61
Yanchang ◻ CHN (SAA) 72 Qf27
Yancheng ◻ CHN (JGS) 78 Ra29
Yanchi ◻ CHN (NHZ) 72 Qd27
Yanco ◻ AUS (NSW) 111 Sd63
Yanco Glen ◻ AUS (NSW) 108 Sa61
Yancun ◻ CHN (GDG) 75 Qh34
Yandal ◻ AUS (WA) 104 Ra59
Yandang shan ■ CHN 75 Ra32
Yandaran ◻ AUS (QLD) 109 Sg58
Yandaxkak ◻ CHN (XUZ) 69 Pe26
Yandev ◻ WAN 138 Le42
Yandil ◻ AUS (WA) 104 Qj59
Yandina ◻ SOL 117 Sk50
Yandina Plantation Resort ■ SOL 117 Sk50
Yandja ◻ RDC 149 Lj46
Yandon ◻ MYA 88 Ph37
Yandongi ◻ RDC 140 Mb44
Yandun ◻ CHN (XUZ) 67 Ph24
Yanfolila ◻ RMM 136 Kf40
Yanga ◻ CAM 139 Lh44
Yanga ◻ TCH 140 Lk41
Yangalia ◻ RCA 140 Ma42
Yangambi ◻ RDC 141 Mc45
Yangas ◻ PE 197 Gb51
Yangasso ◻ RMM 137 Kh39
Yangbajain ◻ CHN (TIB) 69 Pf30
Yangchang ◻ CHN (YUN) 87 Qc32
Yangcheng ◻ CHN (SAX) 73 Qg28
Yangchuan ◻ CHN (GZH) 74 Qd32
Yangchun ◻ CHN (GDG) 74 Qf34
Yangcun ◻ CHN (TJN) 73 Qj26
Yangdok ◻ PRK 78 Rd26
Yangga ◻ RI 115 Sa50
Yangi Qal'eh ◻ AFG 63 Oe27
Yangiqishloq ◻ UZ 63 Od25
Yangirabot ◻ UZ 63 Oc25
Yangiyer ◻ UZ 63 Oe25
Yangiyo'l ◻ UZ 63 Oe25
Yangizang ◻ UZ 63 Od27
Yangjiang ◻ CHN (GDG) 74 Qf35
Yanglin ◻ CHN (YUN) 87 Qb33
Yangling ◻ CHN (SAA) 72 Qd28
Yangluo ◻ CHN (HUB) 75 Qh30
Yangmingshan N.P. ■ RC 75 Ra33
Yangon ● ▲ MYA 88 Pj37
Yangon ● ▲ MYA 88 Pk37
Yangpingguan ◻ CHN (SAA) 72 Qd29
Yangquan ◻ CHN (SAX) 73 Qg27
Yangquangu ◻ CHN (SAX) 72 Qf27
Yangqu Shan ▲ CHN 73 Qg27
Yangshan ◻ CHN (GDG) 75 Qg33
Yangshuo ◻ CHN (GZG) 74 Qf33
Yangtouyan ◻ CHN (YUN) 87 Qa33
Yangtze ■ CHN 74 Qe30
Yangudi Rassa N.P. ■ ETH 142 Na40
Yangxi ◻ CHN (GDG) 74 Qf35
Yangxin ◻ CHN (HUB) 75 Qh31
Yang-Yang ◻ SN 130 Kc38
Yangyuan ◻ CHN (HBI) 73 Qh25
Yangzhou ◻ ■ CHN (JGS) 78 Qk29
Yangzi'e Z.B. ■ CHN 78 Qk30
Yanhu ◻ CHN (TIB) 68 Pb29
Yanhuitlán ■ MEX 182 Fb37
Yanji ◻ CHN (JLN) 76 Re24
Yanjin ◻ CHN (YUN) 74 Qc31
Yanjing ◻ CHN (CGQ) 74 Qd31
Yankari NationalPark ■ ■ WAN 138 Lf41
Yankton ◻ USA (SD) 172 Fb24
Yankton Ind. Res. ■ USA 172 Fa24
Yanling ◻ CHN (HNN) 73 Qh28
Yanmen ◻ CHN (YUN) 87 Pk31
Yanmen G ≡ CHN 73 Qg26
Yanonge ◻ RDC 141 Mc45
Yanqi ◻ CHN (XUZ) 67 Pd24
Yanqing ◻ CHN (BJG) 73 Qh25
Yanqul ◻ OM 61 Nj34
Yanrey ◻ AUS (WA) 102 Qh57
Yanshan ◻ CHN (HBI) 73 Qj26
Yanshan ◻ CHN (YUN) 87 Qc34
Yanshou ◻ CHN (HLG) 76 Re23
Yansoribo ◻ RI 114 Rg46
Yantabulla ◻ AUS (NSW) 109 Sc60
Yantai ◻ ■ CHN (SDG) 73 Ra27
Yantou ◻ CHN (ZJG) 75 Ra31
Yantzaza ◻ EC 196 Ga47
Yanxi ◻ CHN (HUN) 74 Qf31
Yanyuan ◻ CHN (SCH) 87 Qa32
Yanzikou ◻ CHN (GZH) 87 Qc32
Yao ◻ RCA 140 Lk43
Yao ◻ TCH 139 Lj39
Yao'an ◻ CHN (YUN) 87 Qa33
Yaodian ◻ CHN (GSU) 72 Qd28
Yaodian ◻ CHN (SAA) 72 Qe27
Yaolin Dong ■ CHN 75 Qk31
Yaoundé ● ■ ■ CAM 139 Lf44
Yaowang Shan ▲ CHN 72 Qe28
Yao Xian ◻ CHN (SAA) 72 Qe28
Yapacana, P.N. ■ YV 193 Gg44
Yapei ◻ GH 137 Kk41
Yapen ■ RI 114 Rj46
Yapero ◻ RI 114 Rj48
Yapeyú ◻ RA (CR) 204 Hb60
Yap Islands ■ ■ FSM 101 Rb09
Yapuparra A.L. ■ AUS 105 Rd59
Yara ◻ C 179 Gb35
Yaraka ◻ AUS (QLD) 109 Sc58
Yaraligöz Dağı ▲ TR 56 Mh25
Yarawin ◻ AUS (NSW) 109 Sd61
Yarbasan ◻ TR 47 Mj52
Yarda ■ TCH 133 Lk36
Yardea ◻ AUS (SA) 110 Rh62
Yardımcı Burnu ▲ TR 56 Mf27
Yardimli ◻ AZ 57 Ne26
Yaré Lao ◻ SN 130 Kc37
Yaren ● NAU 101 Ta10
Yargatenga ◻ BF 137 Kk40
Yargatti ◻ IND (KTK) 82 Oh38
Yari ≋ CO 196 Gd45
Yarim ◻ YE 60 Nc38
Yaringa North ◻ AUS (WA) 104 Qh58
Yaritagua ◻ YV 193 Gf40
Yarkant ◻ ■ CHN 66 Oj26
Yarkant He ≋ CHN 68 Oj27
Yarlarweelor ◻ AUS (WA) 104 Qj58
Yarloop ◻ AUS (WA) 104 Qh62
Yarlung Zangbo Jiang ≋ CHN 68 Pf31
Yarmouth ◻ CDN (NS) 177 Gg24
Yarmouth ◻ USA (ME) 177 Ge24
Yaro Lund ◻ PK 65 Oe32
Yarra ◻ DY 138 Lb40
Yarrabubba ◻ AUS (WA) 104 Qj59
Yarraden ◻ AUS (QLD) 107 Sb53
Yarram ◻ AUS (VIC) 111 Sd65
Yarra Ranges N.P. ■ AUS (VIC) 111 Sc64
Yarrie ◻ AUS (WA) 102 Ra56
Yarronvale ◻ AUS (QLD) 109 Sc59
Yarrowitch ◻ AUS (NSW) 109 Sg61
Yarrowmere ◻ AUS (QLD) 109 Sc56
Yarrum ◻ AUS (QLD) 107 Rk54
Yarumal ◻ CO 192 Gc42
Yarvicoya, Cerro ▲ RCH 206 Gf56
Yasa ◻ RDC 149 Ma47
Yasawa ■ ≋ FJI 119 Tj54
Yasawa Group ≋ ■ ■ FJI 119 Tj54
Yashi ◻ WAN 138 Ld39
Yashikela ◻ WAN 138 Lb41
Yashiro-jima ▲ J 79 Rg29
Yasinza'i Kalay ◻ AFG 65 Oc30
Yasothon ◻ THA 89 Qc38
Yass ◻ AUS (NSW) 111 Se63
Yasuj ◻ IR 59 Nf30
Yasun Burnu ▲ TR 56 Mj25
Yasuni ◻ PE 196 Gc46
Yasuní, P.N. ■ ■ EC 196 Gc46
Yat ◻ RN 133 Lg35
Yata ◻ BOL 206 Gg52
Yatağan ◻ TR 47 Mj53
Yatako ◻ BF 131 La38
Yatang ◻ CHN (YUN) 87 Pk32
Yate ◻ F (NCL) 118 Td57
Yates Center ◻ USA (KS) 174 Fc27
Yatha ◻ MYA 86 Ph34
Yathon ◻ AUS (NSW) 111 Sc62
Yathon Nature Reserve ■ AUS 111 Sc62
Yati ◻ CO 192 Gc42
Yatolema ◻ RDC 141 Mc45
Yatsushiro ◻ J 79 Rf29
Yatsu-take ▲ J 79 Rk28
Yatta ◻ EAK 144 Mj46
Yatta Plateau ▲ EAK 144 Mj46
Yatung ◻ CHN (TIB) 68 Pe32
Yauca ◻ PE 197 Gc53
Yáuco ◻ USA (PR) 187 Gg36
Yauhannah ◻ USA (SC) 178 Ga29
Yauli ◻ PE 197 Gc52
Yaupita ◻ BOL 206 Gh56
Yauri ◻ PE 197 Ge53
Yauyos ◻ PE 197 Gc52
Yauyupe ◻ HN 184 Fg39
Yaval ◻ IND (MHT) 82 Oh35
Yavari ≋ BR/PE 196 Ge48
Yavaros ◻ MEX (SO) 180 Ef32
Yavaşlar ◻ TR 56 Me26
Yavatmal ◻ IND (MHT) 82 Ok35
Yavita ◻ YV 193 Gg44
Yaviza ◻ PA 185 Gb41
Yavuzeli ◻ TR 56 Mj27
Yawatahama ◻ J 79 Rg29
Yawatongguzlangar ◻ CHN (XUZ) 68 Pb27
Yawatoutou, Mount ▲ GH/TG 137 La42
Yawgu ◻ GH 137 La40
Yawimu ◻ RI 114 Rk49
Yawngo ◻ MYA 87 Pk34
Yaxcabá ◻ MEX (YT) 183 Ff35
Yaxchilán ■ MEX (CHP) 183 Fe37
Yayama ◻ RDC 149 Mb46
Yayvantepe ◻ TR 57 Na27
Yazd ◻ ■ IR 64 Nh30
Yazdan ◻ IR 64 Oa29
Yazhou ◻ CHN (GZH) 74 Qd33
Yazıhan ◻ TR 56 Mk26
Yazman ◻ PK 65 Of31
Yazoo City ◻ USA (MS) 175 Fe29
Ybbs ≋ A 35 Lp43
Ybbs ◻ A 42 Lq42
Ybycuí ◻ PY 204 Hb59
Ybycuí, P.N. ■ PY 204 Hb58
Ybytyruzú, P.N. ■ ■ PY 204 Hb58
Yby-Yaú ◻ PY 202 Hb57
Ydby Hede ■ DK 30 Lj34
Ye ◻ MYA 88 Pj38
Yea ◻ AUS (VIC) 111 Sc64
Yeadon ◻ GB 21 Kt37
Yebawmi ◻ MYA 86 Ph33
Yebbi-Bou ◻ TCH 133 Lk35
Yebbi Souma ◻ TCH 133 Lj35
Yebok ◻ MYA 86 Pg36
Yebya ◻ MYA 86 Ph35
Yecheng ◻ CHN (XUZ) 66 Oj27
Yecla ◻ E 29 Kt52
Yécora ◻ MEX (SO) 180 Ef31
Yedisu ◻ TR 57 Na26
Yeehaw Junction ◻ USA (FL) 179 Fk32
Yeelanna ◻ AUS (SA) 110 Rh63
Yeelirrie ◻ AUS (WA) 104 Ra59
Yegguebo ◻ RN 133 Lg36
Yeghegnadzor ◻ ARM 57 Nc26
Yégué ◻ TG 137 La41
Yegyi ◻ MYA 88 Ph37
Yeha ◻ ETH 142 Mk38
Yei ◻ SUD 144 Mf43
Yeji ◻ CHN (AHU) 73 Qh30
Yeji ◻ GH 137 Kk41
Yekaterinburg ◻ RUS 54 Oa07
Yekepa ◻ LB 136 Kf42
Yekia ◻ TCH 133 Lj37
Yek Shaba ◻ IR 57 Nd27
Yelahanga ◻ IND (KTK) 84 Oj39
Yela Island ■ PNG 117 Sh51
Yelbarsli ◻ TM 62 Oa27
Yelcho ◻ ANT (RCH) 6 Gd31
Yele ◻ WAL 136 Ke41
Yeleğen ◻ TR 47 Mj52
Yelerbon ◻ AUS (QLD) 109 Sf60
Yélimané ◻ RMM 130 Ke38
Yelkaturti ◻ IND (APH) 83 Ok36
Yell ▲ GB 20 Kt30
Yellabinna Regional Reserve ■ AUS 108 Rg61
Yellandu ◻ IND (APH) 83 Pa37
Yellapur ◻ IND (KTK) 82 Oh38
Yellareddi ◻ IND (APH) 82 Ok36
Yellowdine ◻ AUS (WA) 104 Qk61
Yellowdine Nature Reserve ■ AUS (WA) 104 Qk61
Yellow Gras ◻ CDN (SK) 169 Eh21
Yellowhead Pass ≡ CDN 168 Ea19
Yellowknife ◉ CDN 167 Ec14
Yellowknife Bay ≋ CDN 167 Ec14
Yellowknife Highway ■ CDN 167 Eb15
Yellowknife River ≋ CDN 167 Ec14
Yellow Pine ◻ USA (ID) 168 Ec23
Yellow River ≋ CHN 73 Qg28
Yellow Sea ≋ 78 Rb28
Yellowstone ≋ USA 169 Eg22
Yellowstone National Park ■ ■ USA 169 Ee23
Yellville ◻ USA (AR) 174 Fd27
Yelma ◻ AUS (WA) 104 Ra59
Yeloten ◻ TM 62 Ob27
Yelvertoft ◻ AUS (QLD) 106 Rk56
Yelwa ◻ WAN 138 Lc40
Yelwa ◻ WAN 138 Le41
Yema ◻ RDC 148 Lg48
Yema Nanshan ▲ CHN 69 Ph26
Yema Shan ▲ CHN 69 Ph26
Yemassee ◻ USA (SC) 178 Fk29
Yembo ◻ ETH 142 Mh41
Yemen ■ YE 53 Na08
Yemnu ◻ PNG 115 Sb47
Ye-myet-ni ◻ MYA 86 Ph35
Yen ◻ CAM 139 Lg44
Yenagoa ◻ WAN 138 Ld43
Yenan-gyaung ◻ MYA 86 Ph35
Yen Bai ◻ VN 87 Qc35
Yenchang ◻ CHN (TIB) 68 Pe30
Yen Chau ◻ VN 87 Qc35
Yendé Milimou ◻ RG 136 Ke41
Yendéré ◻ BF 137 Kh40
Yendi ◻ GH 137 Kk41
Yénéganou ◻ RCB 148 Lg47
Yengema ◻ WAL 136 Ke41
Yengi Kand ◻ IR 57 Nd27
Yengisar ◻ CHN (XUZ) 66 Oj26
Yengo ◻ RCB 140 Lh45
Yengo N.P. ☐ ■ AUS 111 Sf62
Yenibaşak ◻ TR 57 Na26
Yenice ◻ TR 47 Mj53
Yeniceoba ◻ TR 56 Mg26
Yeniçubuk ◻ TR 56 Mj26
Yenifoça ◻ TR 47 Mg52
Yenihisar ◻ TR 47 Mh53
Yeniköy ◻ TR 47 Mj51
Yeniköy ◻ TR 47 Mj52
Yenipazar ◻ TR 47 Mj53
Yenişehir ◻ TR 45 Mk50
Yenişehir ◻ TR 47 Mk52
Yen Ly ◻ VN 87 Qc36
Yenne ◻ F 25 Lf45
Yéno ◻ G 148 Le46
Yeno ◻ G 148 Lf46
Yeola ◻ IND (MHT) 82 Oh35
Yeo Lake ≋ AUS 105 Rc59
Yeo Lake Nature Reserve ■ AUS 105 Rc60
Yeoval ◻ AUS (NSW) 111 Se62
Yeovil ◻ GB 21 Ks40
Yepachic ◻ MEX (CHH) 180 Ef31
Yepes ◻ E 27 Kr51
Yeppoon ◻ AUS (QLD) 109 Sf57
Yeraltı şehri (Derinkuyu) ■ TR 56 Mh26
Yerba Loca ■ RCH 208 Ge62
Yercaud ◻ IND (TNU) 84 Ok40
Yeremarou ◻ DY 138 Lb41
Yerevan ● ARM 57 Nc25
Yergara ◻ IND (KTK) 82 Oj37
Yeriho ◻ IL 58 Mh30
Yerilla ◻ AUS (WA) 104 Ra60
Yerington ◻ USA (NV) 170 Ea26
Yerköprü ■ TR 56 Mg27
Yerköy ◻ TR 56 Mh26
Yermala ◻ IND (MHT) 82 Oh36
Yerupaja, Cerro ▲ PE 197 Gb51
Yerville ◻ F 22 La41
Yesagyo ◻ MYA 86 Ph35
Yesan ◻ ROK 78 Rd27
Yeshin ◻ MYA 86 Ph34
Yesilbağ ◻ TR 56 Mf27
Yeşil Camii (Bursa) ■ TR 45 Mk50
Yeşil Camii (İznik) ■ TR 45 Mk50
Yeşilhisar ◻ TR 56 Mh26
Yesilırmak ≋ TR 56 Mh25
Yeşilova ◻ TR 56 Me27
Yeşilvadi ◻ TR 45 Mk49
Yeste ◻ E 27 Ks52
Yet ◻ ETH 145 Nb43
Yetla de Juárez ◻ MEX (OAX) 182 Fb37
Yetman ◻ AUS (NSW) 109 Sf60
Ye-u ◻ MYA 86 Ph34
Yevlax ◻ AZ 57 Nd25
Ye Xian ◻ CHN (HNN) 73 Qg29
Yexianggu ■ CHN 87 Qa34
Yeyik ◻ CHN (XUZ) 68 Pb27
Yeyungou ◻ CHN (XUZ) 66 Pc25
Yhú ◻ PY 204 Hc58
Yi'an ◻ CHN (HLG) 76 Rc22
Yibin ◻ CHN (SCH) 74 Qc31
Yichang ◻ CHN (HUB) 74 Qf30
Yicheng ◻ CHN (HUB) 73 Qg30
Yicheng ◻ CHN (SAX) 72 Qf28
Yichuan ◻ CHN (HNN) 73 Qg28
Yichuan ◻ CHN (SAA) 72 Qf28
Yichun ◻ CHN (HLG) 76 Re22
Yichun ◻ CHN (JGX) 75 Qh32
Yidun ◻ CHN (SCH) 69 Pk30
Yiew ▲ RI 97 Re45
Yifag ◻ ETH 142 Mj40
Yifeng ◻ CHN (JGX) 75 Qh31
Yığılca ◻ TR 56 Mf25
Yihuang ◻ CHN (JGX) 75 Qj32
Yijun ◻ CHN (SAA) 72 Qe28
Yilan ◻ CHN (HLG) 76 Re22
Yildirim Camii ■ TR 47 Mh51
Yıldız Dağları ▲ TR 45 Mh49
Yıldızeli ◻ TR 56 Mj26
Yilehuli Shan ▲ CHN 71 Rc20
Yiliang ◻ CHN (YUN) 87 Qc32
Yiliang ◻ CHN (YUN) 87 Qb33
Yilingyan ■ CHN 74 Qe34
Yilong ◻ CHN (SCH) 74 Qd30
Yilou ◻ BF 137 Kk39
Yilui ◻ PNG 115 Sb47
Yima ◻ CHN (HNN) 72 Qf28
Yimen ◻ CHN (SAA) 72 Qd28
Yimin ◻ CHN (NMZ) 71 Qk21
Yimuhe ◻ CHN (NMZ) 71 Ra19
Yinan ◻ CHN (SDG) 78 Qk28
Yinchuan ◉ CHN (NHZ) 72 Qd26
Yindi ◻ AUS (WA) 105 Rb61
Yingcheng ◻ CHN (HUB) 75 Qg30
Yingchengzi Tomb ■ CHN 73 Ra26
Yingde ◻ CHN (GDG) 75 Qg33

Yinggehai ◻ CHN (HAN) 75 Qe36
Yingde ◻ CHN (AHU) 78 Qg29
Yingjiang ◻ CHN (YUN) 86 Pj33
Yingkou ◻ CHN (LNG) 76 Rb25
Yingkou ◻ CHN (LNG) 76 Rb25
Yingpanshan ◻ CHN (SCH) 87 Qc32
Yingshan ◻ CHN (AHU) 78 Qf29
Yingshan ◻ CHN (SCH) 74 Qd30
Yingtan ◻ CHN (JGX) 75 Qj31
Yingui ◻ CAM 138 Lf43
Ying Xian ◻ CHN (SAX) 73 Qf26
Yingxian Mu Ta ⌘ CHN 73 Qg26
Yingxiuwan ◻ CHN (SCH) 74 Qd30
Yining ◻ CHN (XUZ) 66 Pa24
Yiningarra A.L. ◻ AUS 103 Re56
Yinjiang ◻ CHN (GZH) 74 Qe32
Yinjiang ◻ CHN (GZH) 74 Qe32
Yin Shan ▲ CHN 73 Qh27
Yinxu ▲ CHN 73 Qg27
Yipinglang ◻ CHN (YUN) 87 Qa33
Yiqikal ◻ CHN (HBI) pk28
Yirba Muda ◻ ETH 142 Mk42
Yirga Chefe ◻ ETH 142 Mk42
Yirol ◻ SUD 141 Mf42
Yirol ◻ SUD 141 Mf42
Yirrkala ◻ AUS (NT) 106 Rj52
Yirshi ◻ CHN (NMZ) 71 Qj23
Yishui ◻ CHN (SDG) 78 Qa28
Yitong ◻ CHN (JLN) 76 Rc24
Yitulihe ◻ CHN (NMZ) 71 Ra20
Yiwu ◻ CHN (XUZ) 67 Pn24
Yiwu ◻ CHN (ZJG) 75 Ra31
Yiwulu Shan ▲ CHN (LNG) 76 Ra25
Yi Xian ◻ CHN (HBI) 73 Qh26
Yiyang ◻ CHN (HUN) 74 Qg31
Yiyang ◻ CHN (JGX) 75 Qj31
Yiyang ◻ CHN (SAX) 73 Qg28
Yiyu ◻ IND (ARP) 86 Ph31
Yiyuan ◻ CHN (SDG) 73 Qk27
Yizhang ◻ CHN (HUN) 75 Qg33
Yizheng ◻ CHN (JGS) 78 Qk29
Yizhou ◻ CHN (GZG) 74 Qe33
Yizhou ◻ CHN (LNG) 76 Ra25
Ylakiai ◻ LT 39 Mh34
Ylämaa ◻ FIN 38 Mj30
Yläne ◻ FIN 38 Mc28
Yliharma ◻ FIN 38 Mc27
Ylimarkku = Övermark ◻ FIN 38 Mb28
Ylistaro ◻ FIN 38 Mc28
Ylistaro ◻ FIN 38 Md28
Ylitornio ◻ FIN 16 Mb12
Ylivieska ◻ FIN 16 Mc13
Ylöjärvi ◻ FIN 38 Md29
Yoakum ◻ USA (TX) 181 Fb31
Yobbki ◻ DJI 142 Nd40
Yocalla ◻ BOL 206 Gh55
Yof ◻ SN 130 Kb38
Yofor ◻ RI 114 Rj48
Yogoum ◻ TCH 133 Lk37
Yogyakarta ◻ RI 95 Qf49
Yohaltun ◻ MEX (CAM) 183 Fe36
Yoho N.P. ◻ CDN 168 Ed20
Yohualichan ▲ MEX 182 Fb35
Yoichi ◻ J 77 Sa24
Yokadouma ◻ CAM 139 Lh44
Yoko N.P. ◻ WN 89 Qd39
Yokkaichi ◻ J 79 Rj28
Yoko ◻ CAM 139 Lg43
Yokoate-jima ◻ J 79 Re31
Yokoboué ◻ CI 137 Kh43
Yokohama ◻ J 79 Sa25
Yokohama ◻ J 79 Rk28
Yokosuka ◻ J 79 Rk28
Yola ◻ CAM 139 Lh43
Yola ◻ WAN 139 Lg41
Yolande ◻ F (GF) 194 Hd43
Yolcular ◻ TR 57 Nb26
Yoliatl ◻ MEX (ZGT) 182 Ek34
Yolombo ◻ RDC 149 Mb48
Yolosti ◻ TR 57 Na26
Yomou ◻ RG 136 Kf42
Yomuka ◻ RI 114 Rk49
Yonago ◻ J 79 Rg28
Yonezawa ◻ J 77 Sa27
Yong'an ◻ CHN (FJN) 75 Qj33
Yongcheng ◻ CHN (GSU)
72 Qa26
Yongcheng ◻ CHN (HNN)
78 Qj29
Yongcheng ◻ CHN (JGX)
Yongchuan ◻ CHN (CGQ)
74 Qc31
Yongde ◻ CHN (YUN) 87 Pk34
Yongdeng ◻ CHN (GSU) 72
Qb27
Yongding ◻ CHN (FJN) 75 Qj33
Yongdok ◻ ROK 79 Re27
Yongfeng ◻ CHN (JGX) 75 Qh32
Yongfeng ◻ CHN (JGX) 75 Qh32
Yongfu ◻ CHN (GZG) 74 Qf33
Yonghung ◻ PRK 78 Rd26
Yongjia ◻ CHN (ZJG) 75 Ra31
Yongji ◻ CHN (GSU) 72 Qa28
Yongju ◻ ROK 79 Re27
Yongkang ◻ CHN (ZJG) 75 Ra31
Yongle ◻ CHN (SAX) 73 Qf28
Yonglegong ◻ CHN 72 Qf28
Yongling Tomb ◻ CHN
76 Rb25
Yongning ◻ CHN (GZG) 74 Qe34
Yongning ◻ CHN (NMZ) 72 Qd26
Yongofondo ◻ RCA 140 Mb43
Yong Peng ◻ MAL 93 Qb44
Yongning ◻ CHN (GSU) 72 Qa28
Yongren ◻ CHN (YUN) 87 Qa32
Yongsheng ◻ CHN (YUN) 87 Qa31
Yongsheng ◻ CHN
87 Qa32
Yongxing ◻ CHN (HUN) 74 Qe31
Yongxin ◻ CHN (HUN) 75 Qh32
Yongxin ◻ CHN (JGX) 75 Qh31
Yongxin ◻ CHN (JGX) 75 Qh31
Yongzhou ◻ CHN (HUN) 74 Qf32
Yonibana ◻ WAL 136 Kd41
Yonkers ◻ USA (NY) 177 Gd25
Yopal ◻ CO 192 Gd43
Yopie Podogle ◻ LB 136 Kf42
Yopurga ◻ CHN (XUZ) 66 Oj26
Yorito ◻ HN 184 Fg34
York ◻ AUS (WA) 104 Qj61
York ◻ GB 21 Kt37
York ◻ GB (PT) 21 K37
York ◻ USA (NE) 174 Fb25
York ◻ USA (PA) 177 Gb26
York ◻ USA (SC) 178 Fk28
York, C. ▲ AUS 106 Sc54
Yorke Peninsula ◻ AUS 110 Rj63
Yorketown ◻ AUS (SA) 110 Rj63
Yorkshire ◻ USA (NY) 173 Ga24
Yorkshire Dales N.P. ◻ GB
21 Ks36
Yorkshire Wolds ▲ GB 21 Ku36
Yorkton ◻ CDN 169 Ej20
Yorkton ◻ USA (TX) 181 Fb31
Yornaning ◻ AUS (WA) 104 Qj62
Yoro ◻ HN 184 Fg38
Yoro ◻ RMM 131 Kj38
Yoroboangoula ◻ RMM 136 Kg40
Yoron ◻ J 79 Re32
Yoron-jima ◻ J 79 Re32
Yorubaland Plateau ▲ WAN
Yoshino-Kumano N.P. ◻ J
79 Rh29

Yoshino sacred site ◻ J
79 Rh28
Yosu ◻ ROK 78 Rd28
Yosua ◻ PNG 115 Sb48
Yotai-santi ◻ J 77 Sa24
Youanygarra ◻ AUS (WA) 104
Qk60
Youanmi Downs ◻ AUS (WA)
104 Qk60
Youbou ◻ ETH 143 Nc42
Youdunzi ◻ CHN (QHI) 69 Pf26
Youghal ◻ IRL 19 Km19
Youkounkoun ◻ RG 136 Kd39
You Le Yuan ◻ CHN 75 Qg31
Youllemmedene ▲ RMM
131 La37
Young ◻ AUS (NSW) 111 Se63
Young ◻ CDN (SK) 169 Eh20
Young ◻ ROU 204 Hb62
Youngerina ◻ AUS (NSW)
109 Sc60
Younghusband Peninsula ▲ AUS
110 Rk63
Youngstown ◻ CDN (AB)
169 Ee20
Youngstown ◻ USA (OH)
173 Fk25
Youngsville ◻ MA 125 Kf29
Youssoufia ◻ MA 125 Kf29
Youvarou ◻ RMM 131 Kh38
You Xian ◻ CHN (HUN) 75 Qg32
Youyang ◻ CHN (CGQ) 74 Qe31
Youyi Feng ▲ CHN 67 Pd21
Youyu ◻ CHN (SAX) 73 Qg28
Yowergabbie ◻ AUS (WA)
104 Qj60
Yo Yo Park ◻ AUS (QLD)
109 Sd59
Yozgat ◻ TR 56 Mh26
Yozgat Çamlığı Milli Parkı ◻ TR
56 Mh26
Ypacaraí, P.N. ◻ PY 204 Hb58
Ype Jhú ◻ PY 204 Hd57
Ypsilanti ◻ USA (MI) 173 Fj24
Yreka ◻ USA (CA) 170 Dj25
Yssingeaux ◻ F 25 Le45
Ystad ◻ S 31 Lo35
Ytterhogdal ◻ S 17 Lh34
Yttermalung ◻ S 31 Lo30
Yu ◻ RI 97 Re46
Yuanbao Shan ▲ CHN 74 Qe33
Yuanjiang ◻ CHN (YUN) 87 Qb34
Yuanlin ◻ CHN (HUN) 71 Ra21
Yuanlin ◻ RC 75 Ra34
Yuanling ◻ CHN (HUN) 74 Qf31
Yuanmou ◻ CHN (YUN) 87 Qa33
Yuanping ◻ CHN (SAX) 73 Qg28
Yuanqu ◻ CHN (SAX) 73 Qf29
Yuantan ◻ CHN (AHU) 78 Qj30
Yuantouzhu ◻ CHN 78 Qk29
Yuanyang ◻ CHN (YUN) 87 Qb34
Yuba ◻ USA (OK) 174 Fb29
Yuba City ◻ USA (CA) 170 Dk26
Yubari ◻ J 77 Sa24
Yubdo ◻ ETH 142 Mh41
Yubetsu ◻ J 77 Sb23
Yubetu-dake ▲ J 77 Sa24
Yucatán ◻ MEX (YT) 183 Fg35
Yucatán ◻ MEX 183 Ff35
Yucatán Basin ◻ 179 Fh35
Yucatán Channel ◻ 179 Fh34
Yucatán Peninsula ◻ MEX
Yucca House Nat. Mon. ◻ USA
171 Ef27
Yucca Valley ◻ USA (CA)
170 Eb28
Yücebağ ◻ TR 57 Na26
Yuchan ◻ RA (SE) 207 Gj59
Yuci ◻ CHN (SAX) 73 Qg27
Yucumo ◻ BOL 206 Gg53
Yudi Shan ▲ CHN 71 Rb19
Yuechi ◻ CHN (SCH) 74 Qd30
Yuelushan ▲ CHN 75 Qg31
Yuendumu A.L. ◻ AUS (NT) 103 Rf57
Yuendumu A.L. ◻ AUS (NT)
Yueqing ◻ CHN (ZJG) 75 Ra31
Yuexi ◻ CHN (AHU) 78 Qh30
Yueyang ◻ CHN (HUN) 75 Qg31
Yueyang ◻ CHN (SCH) 74 Qc30
Yueya Quan ◻ CHN 72 Qf28
Yueya Quan ◻ CHN 69 Ph26
Yufle ◻ SP 143 Nd40
Yugan ◻ CHN (JGX) 75 Qj31
Yugia ◻ CHN (QHI) 69 Ph26
Yuguk Dağı ▲ TR 56 Mg27
Yuhe ◻ CHN (AHU) 74 Qf28
Yuhuan ◻ CHN (ZJG) 75 Ra31
Yuhuan Dao ◻ CHN 75 Ra31
Yuhuang Wola ◻ PL 41 Lh39
Yukamenskoye ◻ RUS 48 Ng17
Yukansan ◻ PL 40 Lj36
Yükarı Sakarya Ovaları ◻ TR
56 Mf26
Yuki ◻ RDC 149 Lk47
Yukon Charley Rivers Nat.
Preserve ◻ USA (AK) 165 Cj13
Yukon Delta ◻ USA 164 Bj14
Yukon Delta National Wildlife
Refuge ◻ USA (AK) 165 Bh15
Yukon Flats National Wildlife
Refuge ◻ USA 165 Cg12
Yukon Plateau ◻ CDN 165 Db14
Yukon River ◻ USA 165 Cj13
Yukon Territory ◻ CDN 162 Da06
Yükseova ◻ TR 57 Nc27
Yukuhashi ◻ J 79 Rf29
Yulara ◻ AUS (NT) 105 Rf58
Yuldybayevo ◻ RUS (QLD) 109 Se59
Yulee ◻ USA (FL) 178 Fk30
Yuli ◻ CHN (XUZ) 67 Pd25
Yuli ◻ RC 75 Ra34
Yuli ◻ WAN 138 Lf41
Yulin ◻ CHN (GZG) 74 Qf34
Yulin ◻ CHN (HUN) 75 Qe33
Yulin ◻ CHN (SAA) 72 Qe28
Yulingshi Shiku ◻ CHN 67 Ph25
Yulong Xueshan ▲ CHN 87 Qa32
Yuma ◻ USA (AZ) 171 Ec29
Yuma ◻ USA (CO) 174 Ej25
Yumare ◻ YV 193 Gg40
Yumariba ◻ YV 193 Gj43
Yumbarra Conservation Park ◻
AUS 108 Rg61
Yumbe ◻ EAU 144 Mf44
Yumbel ◻ RCH 208 Gd64
Yumbi ◻ RDC 148 Lk46
Yumbo ◻ CO 192 Gb44
Yumenguan ◻ CHN (GSU) 69 Pj26
Yumenguan ◻ CHN (GSU)
67 Pg25
Yumen Guan ◻ CHN 67 Pg25
Yumen Zhen ◻ CHN (GSU)
Yuna ◻ AUS (WA) 104 Qh60
Yunak ◻ TR 56 Mf26
Yuncheng ◻ CHN (SAX) 73 Qf28
Yuncheng ◻ CHN (SDG) 78 Qj28
Yunda ◻ RCH 208 Gd64
Yundou ◻ RCH 208 Gd64
Yunfu ◻ CHN (GDG) 74 Qg34
Yungaburra ◻ AUS (QLD)
105 Sc54
Yungas ◻ BOL 206 Gg54
Yungay ◻ PE 197 Gb50
Yunguyu ◻ PE 206 Gf54
Yunjinghong ◻ CHN (YUN)
87 Qa34
Yunkai Dashan ▲ CHN 74 Qf34
Yunmeng ◻ CHN (HUB) 74 Qg30
Yunnan ◻ CHN (YUN) 87 Qa33
Yunta ◻ AUS (SA) 110 Rk61

Zaki Biam ◻ WAN 138 Le42
Zákinthos ◻ GR 46 Ma53
Zákinthos ◻ GR 46 Ma53
Zakliczyn ◻ PL 41 Ma41
Zakobjakino ◻ RUS 48 Na16
Zakopane ◻ PL 41 Lu41
Zakouma ◻ TCH 139 Lk40
Zakouma, P.N.de ◻ TCH
139 Lk40
Zakou Shankou ▲ CHN 69 Pk27
Zakroczym ◻ PL 41 Ma38
Zákros ▲ GR 47 Mg55
Zákros ◻ GR 47 Mg55
Zala ◻ ANG 148 Lh49
Zalaa ◻ MNG 70 Pk23
Zalaapáti ◻ H 42 Ls44
Zalabaska ◻ H 42 Lf44
Zalaegerszeg ◻ H 42 Lr44
Zalaegerszeg ◻ H 42 Lr44
Zalakomár ◻ H 42 Ls44
Zalamea la Real ◻ E 27 Ko53
Zalanga ◻ WAN 138 Lf40
Zalantun ◻ CHN (NMZ) 71 Rb22
Zalaszentgrót ◻ H 42 Ls44
Zalaú ◻ RO 43 Md43
Zalegošč ◻ RUS 48 Mj19
Zalesie ◻ PL 41 Mb38
Zalim ◻ KSA 60 Nb34
Zalingei ◻ SUD 134 Mb39
Zaliouan ◻ CI 137 Kg42
Zalíščyky ◻ UA 49 Me41
Zaliv Aniva ◻ RUS 77 Sa23
zaliv Proztor ◻ RUS 55 Sd06
zaliv Selideba ◻ RUS 55 Sd06
Zalizci ◻ UA 49 Md41
Zalki ◻ RUS 82 Oh37
Zalla ◻ E 26 Kq49
Zaltbommel ◻ NL 23 Lf39
Zalut ◻ CHN (GZH) 74 Qd33
Zalut ◻ CHN (YUN) 87 Qa33
Zalukka ◻ BY 41 Me37
Zalut ◻ CHN (YUN) 87 Qa33
Zama ◻ YE 60 Nd37
Zamakh ◻ YE 60 Nd37
Zamanalrykty tau ▲ KZ 62 Nh23
Zamania ◻ IND (UPH) 83 Pb33
Zamardi ◻ H 42 Ls44
Zamarte ◻ PL 40 Ls37
Zamatobgwe ◻ ZW 152 Mf55
Zamay ◻ CAM 139 Lh41
Zambelji ◻ KZ 54 Nc08
Zambesi ◻ RDC 141 Mc44
Zambezi ◻ Z 151 Mb52
Zambézi Deka ◻ ZW 152 Md55
Zambezi Escarpment ▲ Z/ZW
152 Md54
Zambezi N.P. ◻ ZW 151 Mc51
Zambezi Source ◻ Z 151 Mc51
Zambia ■ 123 Ma11
Zamboanga ◻ RP 91 Rb42
Zamboanga Peninsula ▲ RP
91 Rb42
Zambrano ◻ CO 192 Gc41
Zambrano ◻ HN 184 Fg38
Zambrów ◻ PL 41 Mc38
Zambué ◻ MOC 152 Mf53
Zamfara ◻ WAN 138 Le39
Zamiercie ◻ PL 41 Mc38
Zamilah ◻ LAR 127 Lh32
Zamin ◻ UZ 63 Oe26
Zamkova ◻ UA 49 Md20
Zamlet Amagraj ◻ DARS
124 Kc33
Zamora ◻ E 26 Kp49
Zamora ◻ EC 196 Ga47
Zamora de Hidalgo ◻ MEX
(MHC) 182 Ej36
Zamość ◻ PL 41 Md40
Zamrud-Uud ◻ MNG 70 Qb24
Zamtang ◻ CHN (SCH) 87 Qa29
Zamuro ◻ YV 193 Gg42
Zanaga ◻ RCB 148 Lg47
Zanaortaklý ◻ KZ 66 Od24
Zanang ◻ CHN (TIB) 69 Pf31
Zanaozen ◻ KZ 62 Ng24
Zanatas ◻ KZ 63 Oe24
Zangbei ◻ CHN (HBI) 73 Qh25
Zanger ◻ CHN (AHU)
Zanjon ◻ PL 40 Ld38
Zanquan ◻ CHN (GSU) 72 Qe28
Zangsu ◻ CHN (GSU) 72 Qc27
Zansang ◻ CHN (SAA) 72 Qe27

Z

Zachila ◻ MEX 182 Fb37
Zachodni ◻ TN 126 Le29
Zaamar Uul ◻ MNG 70 Qa21
Zaangarskoe plato ◻ RUS
54 Pc07
Zaankhoshuu ◻ MNG 70 Qa22
Zaanstad ◻ NL 23 Le38
Zababadani ◻ SYR 56 Mj29
Zabajkal'sk ◻ RUS 71 Qj21
Żabali ◻ SCG 44 Ma45
Zabalocce ◻ BY 48 Mf19
Zabata ◻ RCB 148 Lh47
Zabid ◻ YE 60 Nb38
Zabierzów ◻ PL 41 Lu40
Żabinka ◻ BY 41 Md38
Żąbkowice Śląskie ◻ PL 40 Lr40
Żabljak ◻ SCG 44 Lu47
Żabludów ◻ PL 41 Md38
Zabol ◻ AFG 64 Ob30
Zabol ◻ IR 64 Oa30
Zabolotów ◻ UA 49 Me41
Zabolova ◻ LV 39 Mh33
Zaboracza ◻ RO 43 Mb44
Żabórz ◻ PL 41 Ma41
Zaborski Park Krajobrazowy ◻
PL 40 Ls37
Zaboua ◻ BY 48 Mh19
Zabré ◻ BF 137 Kk40
Zabrodzie ◻ PL 41 Mb38
Zábřeh ◻ CZ 42 Lr41
Zabrze ◻ PL 40 Lt40
Zabzugu ◻ GH 137 La41
Zacapa ◻ GCA 184 Ff38
Zacapu ◻ MEX (MHC) 182 Ek36
Zacatal ◻ MEX (PUE) 182 Fb36
Zacatecas ◻ □ ◻ MEX (ZCT)
182 Ej34
Zacatecas ◻ MEX 182 Ej34
Zacatecoluca ◻ ES 184 Ff39
Zacatepec ◻ MEX (MOR)
182 Fa36
Zacatlán ◻ MEX (PUE) 182 Fb36
Zacharý ◻ USA (LA) 175 Fe30
Zachariova ◻ GR 46 Mc52
Zacoalco de Torres ◻ MEX (JLC)
182 Ej35
Zacualtipan ◻ MEX (HDG)
182 Fb35
Zadar ◻ HR 35 Lq46
Zadarski kanal ◻ HR 35 Lq46
Zadetkile Island ◻ MYA 88 Pj40
Zadetkyi Island ◻ MYA 88 Pj41
Zadgay ◻ MNG 70 Qb21
Zadonsk ◻ RUS 48 Mk19
Za'faranah ◻ ET 129 Mg31
Zafar Qand ◻ IR 64 Ng29
Zafarulla ◻ PK 65 Oh29
Zafer, C. ◻ 129 Mf28
Zafra ◻ E 27 Ko52
Zag ◻ MA 124 Kf31
Zag ◻ MNG 70 Pk22
Zaga Island ◻ AUS 107 Sb50
Zagare ◻ CI 137 Kg42
Żagarė ◻ LT 39 Md34
Zagarolo ◻ I 34 Ln49
Zaghdeb ◻ RUS 48 Mj18
Zaghouan ◻ TN 126 Lf27
Zaghouan ◻ TN 126 Lf27
Żagań ◻ PL 40 Lp39
Zagnansk ◻ PL 41 Ma40
Zagora ◻ MA 125 Kh30
Zagora ob Savi ◻ SLO 42 Lp44
Zagórz ◻ PL 41 Mc41
Zagora Mountains ▲ IR 52 Na06
Zagoulnasso ◻ CI 137 Kg40
Zagustaj ◻ RUS 70 Qf20
Zagvozd ◻ HR 35 Ls47
Zahamena, P.N.de ◻ RM
157 Ne54
Zaharo ◻ GR 46 Mb53
Zahedan ◻ IR 64 Ob31
Zahirabad ◻ IND (APH) 82 Oj37
Zahirsbord ◻ PL 41 Ma38
Zahle ◻ RL 56 Mh29
Zahn al Ibbi ◻ IRQ 59 Nh30
Zahna ◻ D 32 Ln39
Zaia ◻ RCH 208 Gd64
Zaila ◻ RDC 149 Nc50
Zailiyskiy Alatau ▲ KZ 63 Oe24
Zaimovo ◻ RUS 48 Mj18
Zai N.P. ◻ IR 57 Na28
Zaisan ◻ KZ 67 Pc22
Żair ◻ RIM 130 Kc37
Zaire ◻ ANG 148 Lf49
Zaiza ◻ ANG 148 Lf49
Zajas ◻ MK 46 Ma49
Zaječar ◻ SCG 44 Mc47
Zaka ◻ ZW 152 Mf56
Zakamensk ◻ RUS 70 Qe20
Zakhmet ◻ TM 62 Ob27
Zako ◻ IRQ 57 Nb27

Żagań ◻ PL 40 Lp39
Zararan ◻ IR 64 Nj32
Zhetisai ◻ KZ 63 Oe25
Zhicheng ◻ CHN (HUB) 74 Qf30
Zhidan ◻ CHN (SAA) 72 Qe27
Zhidoi ◻ CHN (QHI) 69 Ph29
Zhigan ◻ CHN (TIB) 68 Pb30
Zhijiang ◻ CHN (HUB) 74 Qf30
Zhijiang ◻ CHN (HUN) 74 Qf31
Zhijin ◻ CHN (GZH) 87 Qc32
Zhi Jin Cave ◻ CHN
69 Ph28
Zhijin ◻ CHN (GZH) 87 Qc32
Zhi Jin Cave ◻ CHN
Zhilmo ◻ CHN (TIB) 68 Pc31
Zhirjatino ◻ RUS 48 Mh18
Zhishan ◻ CHN (HUN) 74 Qf31
Zhiziluo ◻ CHN (YUN) 87 Pk32
Zhlobin ◻ BY 48 Mf19
Zhob ◻ PK 65 Oe30
Zhob ◻ PK 65 Oe30
Zhongba ◻ CHN (TIB) 68 Pa31
Zhongcheng ◻ CHN (YUN)
87 Pk32
Zhongdian ◻ CHN 87 Qa31
Zhongguo = China 50 Pd07
Zhonghuang ◻ CHN (GZH)
74 Qe32
Zhongjiang ◻ CHN (SCH)
Zhongning ◻ CHN (NHZ)
72 Qc27
Zhongrankou ◻ CHN (GDG)
74 Qg34
Zhongshan ◻ CHN (GZG)
75 Qg34
Zhongshan ◻ CHN (GZG)
Zhongwei ◻ CHN (NHZ) 72 Qc27
Zhongxiang ◻ CHN (HUB)
74 Qg30
Zhongxingqiao ◻ CHN (JGS)
78 Ra29
Zhongzhai ◻ CHN (ZJG) 75 Rb31
Zhongzhou ◻ CHN (CGQ)
74 Qd32
Zhoukou ◻ CHN (HNN) 73 Qh29
Zhoukoudian ◻ CHN 73 Qj26
Zhouning ◻ CHN (FJN) 75 Qk32
Zhouqu ◻ CHN (GSU) 72 Qb28
Zhouzhi ◻ CHN (SAA) 72 Qd28
Zhouzhuang ◻ CHN (JGS)
Zhoubei ◻ CHN 78 Qj29
Zhosaly ◻ KZ 62 Oc23
Zhoukoudian ◻ CHN 73 Qj26
Zhouzhuang ◻ CHN (JGS)
Zhuanghe ◻ CHN (LNG) 73 Rb26
Zhucheng ◻ CHN (SDG) 78
Qa28
Zhud ◻ EC 196 Ga47
Zhuguo ◻ CHN (GSU) Qf29
Zhuhai ◻ CHN (GDG) 75 Qg34
Zhuji ◻ CHN (ZJG) 75 Ra31
Zhumadian ◻ CHN (HNN)
73 Qg29
Zhuo Zhou ◻ CHN (HBI)
73 Qh26
Zhuozi ◻ CHN (NMZ) 73 Qg25
Zhushan ◻ CHN (HUB) 72 Qe29
Zhuxi ◻ CHN (HUB) 72 Qe29
Zhuzhou ◻ CHN (HUN) 74 Qf31
Zia Ind. Res. ◻ USA 171 Eg28
Zial ◻ PK 65 Oe30
Zibo ◻ CHN (SDG) 73 Qk27
Zichang ◻ CHN (SAA) 72 Qe27
Zibebowice ◻ PL 40 Lr40
Zidani Most ◻ SLO 42 Lq44

Żywiec ◻ PL 40 Lt41

Photo Index, Credits/Contributers

Abbreviations:
G = Getty
Bav = Bavaria
Mau = Mauritius
P = Premium
Hub = Huber
Pic = Pictor
Lo = Look

Cover: globe image © NASA
p. I: Spacecapes; PhotoDisc Vol. 34
p. II–III: World Landmarks and Travel, PhotoDisc Vol. 60
p. IV: both P
p. V – l.: P, r.: Hub/Damm
p. VI – l.: Monheim, r.: P
p. VII – l.: P, r.: ifa/Jacobs
p. VIII – l.: G/Tomlinson, r.: G/Waite
p. IX – l.: P/Petsch, r.: G/Layda
p. X – l.: DasFotoarchiv, r.: Hub/Damm
p. XI: both P
p. XII – l.: P/p.Bunka, r.: ifa
p. XIII – l.: P/NGS, r.: P/Schwabel
p. XIV – t.: P, big pict.: P/Raymer/NGS
p. 1 – b.: P/Marka
p. 12 – t.: P, big pict.: ifa/PictureFinders
p. 13 – b.: M.Schneiders
p. 50 – t.: P, big pict.: Mau/Krinninger
p. 51 – b.: G/Ehlers
p. 98 – t.: ifa/Hunter, big pict.: P
p. 99 – b.: Alamy/R.Harding
p. 120 – t.: P, big pict.: P/Marka
p. 121 – b.: Cristofori
p. 158 – t.: P/Nawrocki, big pict.: P
p. 159 – b.: Essick/Aurora
p. 188 – t.: P, big pict.: G
p. 189 – b.: G/G. Pile
p. 211: Spacecapes; PhotoDisc Vol. 34, f.l.t.r.: G, G/R. Passmore, G/A. Wolfe
p. 216 – l.t.: G/W. Eastep, l.b.: G/N. Turner
p. 217 – r.t.: G/Del Vecchio, 1: G/R. Stahl,
    2: G/D. Armand, 3: G/R. Everts, 4: G/J. Willis
p. 218 – l.t.: G/R. v. d. Hils, l.b.: G/J. Warden
p. 219 – r.t.: G, 1: G/M. Rogers, 2: G/D. Armand, 3: G/R. Klevansky,
    4: G/Y. Layama
p. 220 – l.t.: G/N. DeVore, l.b.: G/H. Schmitz
p. 221 – r.t.: G/A. Cassidy, 1: G/p. Chelsey, 2: P/R. Eastwood, 3: Bav
p. 222 – l.t.: G/R. v. d. Hils, l.b.: G/Viennaslide-Jahn
p. 223 – r.t.: G/p. Chelsey, 1: G/C. Harvey, 2:G/E. Lansner, 3: G/G. Pile,
    4: G/p. Chelsey
p. 224 – l.t.: G/A. Diesendruck, l.b.: G/A. Diesendruck
p. 225 – r.t.: G/p. Chelsey, 1: G/B. De Hogues, 2: G/J. Lamb, 3: G/B. Rieger,
    4: G/R. Evans
p. 226 – l.t.: Pic, l.b.:G/J. Cornish
p. 227 – r.t.: G/D. Hiser, 1: BAV, 2: G/J. Horner, 3: G/T. Craddock
p. 228 – l.t.: G/C. Simpson, l.b.: Mau/Coll
p. 229 – r.t.: G/C. Burki, 1: G/J.Willis, 2: G/R. Ziak, 4: G/D. Waugh, 3: G/K.Morris,
    2: G/R. Ziak, 4: G/D. Waugh
p. 230 – r.t.: G/p. Chelsey, l.b.: G/p. G.
p. 231 – r.t.: G/p. Harris, 1: G/p. Harris, 2: G/ A. Latham, 3: G/J. Horner,
    4: G/M. Busselle
p. 232 – l.t.: A. Cassidy, l.b.: G/G. Grigoriou
p. 233 – r.t.: G/D. Hiser, 1: G/G. Grigoriou, 2: G/R. Frerck, 3: G/J. Cornish,
    4: J. Strachan
p. 234 – l.t.: G/J. M. Truchet, l.b.: G/B. de Hogues
p. 235 – r.t.: G/H Kavanch, 1: PSP/Segal, 2: G/D. Hiser, 3: G/D. Nausbaum,
    4: G/p. Weinberg
p. 236 – l.t.: G/A. Cassidy, l.b.: G/H. Kavanagh
p. 237 – r.t.: Pic, 1: G/D. Sutherland, 2: G/ p. Poulides, 3: Mau/T. Müller,
    4: G/C. Haigh
p. 238 – l.t.: G/p. Chesley, l.b.: G/H. Kavanagh
p. 239 – r.t.: G/A. Wolfe, 1: BAV/K. Yamashita, 2: G/N. Giambi, 3: G/G. Jecan, 4:
    G/W. Krecichwost
p. 240 – l.t.: G/G. Chan, l.b.: G/M. Rees
p. 241 – r.t.: G/M. Busselle, 1: G/G. Allison, 2: Mau/Torino, 3: Pic., 4: G/A. Wolfe
p. 242 – l.t.: Mau/b. Kerth, l.b.: G/J. Strachan
p. 243 – r.t.: Mau/R. Mayer, 1: G/H. Molenkanp, 2: G/C. Coleman,
    3: G/N. DeVore, 4: Mau
p. 244 – l.t.: G/H. Sitton, l.b.: G/H. Sitton
p. 245 – r.t.: Mau, 1: G/G. Hellier, 2: p. Seaward, 3: G/p. Tweedie, 4: G
p. 246 – l.t.: G/J. Running, l.b.: G/R. Frerck
p. 247 – r.t.: G/R. Giles, 1: Bav, 2: G/J. Beatty, 3: G/p. Rothfeld, 4: G/H. Kurihara
p. 248 – l.t.: G/p. Harris, l.b.: G
p. 249 – r.t.: G/J. Strachan, 1: G/p. Chelsey, 2: G/H. Kavanagh, 4: G/p. Harris
p. 250 – l.t.: G/K. Graham, l.b.: G/M. Mehlig
p. 251 – r.t.: G/T. Wood, 1: G, 2: P/Z. Williams, 3: G/J. Chard, 4: G/L. Ulrich
p. 252 – l.t.: G/N. DeVore, l.b.: G
p. 253 – r.t.: Pic, 1: G/p. Grandadam, 2: G, 3: G/J. Strachan, 4: Bav
p. 254 – l.t.: G/D. Levy, l.b.: G/A. Cassidy
p. 255 – r.t.: G/D. Tarckler, 1: P, 2: G/p. Huber, 3: G/p. Chesley, 4: G/p. Tansey
p. 256 – l.t.: G/B. Krist, l.b.: Pic
p. 257 – r.t.: p. Harris, 1: G/D. Carrasco, 2: P/R. Klein, 3: Bav/Picture Finders
p. 258 – l.t.: G/A. Booher, l.b.: G/R. Everts
p. 259 – r.t.: G/D. Hiser, 1: G/p. Egan, 2: Bav/Kanus, 3: G/A. Puzey, 4: G/A. Drake
p. 260 – l.t.: Mau/SDP, l.b.: G/p. Dietrich
p. 261 – r.t.: Pic, 1: G/p. Bauduin, 2: P/A. Mackillop, 3: G/B. Baunton
p. 262 – l.t.: G/A. Cassidy, l.b.: G/J. Strachan
p. 263 – r.t.: G/A. Booher, 1: Bav/Images, 2: G/J. Lamb, 4: G/C. Ehlers
p. 264 – l.t.: G/H. Schmitz, l.b.: G
p. 265 – r.t.: Pic, 1: P/B. Hedberg, 2: G/A. Mackillop, 3: G/R. Evans, 4: G/N.
    Parfitt
p. 266 – l.t.: G/L. Resnick, l.b G/L.Dutton
p. 267 – r.t.: G/D. Armand, 1: G/p. Seaward, 2: p. Seaward, 3: G/J.Jangoux,
    4: G/R. Frerck
p. 268 – l.t.: G/A. Milliken, l.b.: G/J. Cornish
p. 269 – r.t.: G/Nick, 1: P/M. Segal, 2: P/T. Jelen, 3: G/D. Reese
p. 270 – l.t.: G/t. Benn, l.b.: G/p. Stone
p. 271 – r.t.: G/G. Pile, 1: G/t. Franken, 2: D. Paterson, 3: G/J. Strachan,
    4: Hub/Schmid
p. 272 – r.t.: G/p. Mayman, 1: PSP/p. Petsch, 2: P/Mackillop
p. 273 – top: all dpa, b.: Mau/O'Brien
p. 274 – top: all dpa, b.l.: G/Rudolf, b.r.: both dpa

© 2006 Verlag Wolfgang Kunth GmbH & Co. KG, Munich
© GeoGraphic Publishers GmbH & Co. KG, Munich
Innere Wiener Straße 13
81667 Munich
Tel.: (49) 89 45 80 20-0
Fax: (49) 89 45 80 20-21
info@geographicmedia.de
www.geographicmedia.de

© Cartography: GeoGraphic Publishers GmbH & Co. KG, Munich
Map relief: 1 : 2,25 Mio./1 : 4,5 Mio./1 : 15 Mio./1 : 36 Mio./1 : 44 Mio./ 1 : 50 Mio./ 1 : 80 Mio. MHM ® Copyright © Digital Wisdom, Inc.

© English translation: Verlag Wolfgang Kunth GmbH & Co. KG, Munich

English language distribution:
GeoCenter International Ltd
Meridian House, Churchill Way West
Basingstoke Hampshire, RG21 6YR
United Kingdom
Tel.: (44) 1256 817 987
Fax: (44) 1256 817 988
sales@geocenter.co.uk
www.insightguides.com

Editing: Calina Kunth, Wolfgang Kunth, Norbert Pautner
Texts: Heike Barnitzke, Gesa Bock, Dirk Brietzke, Michael Kaiser, Wolfgang Kunth, Michael Elser, Ursula Klocker, Norbert Pautner
Picture research: Calina Kunth, Wolfgang Kunth, Micaëla Verfürth

Coordination and editing English version: Katja Baldewein, Demetri Lowe
Proofreading English version: Alison Moffat-McLynn, Penny Phenix

Design, Layout: Um|bruch, München
Graphic: Alexandra Matheis, Dorothea Happ, Christopher Kunth, Monika Preißl, Verena Ribbentrop
Reproduction: Fotolito Varesco, Auer (Italy)

Printed in the Slovak Republic